The Council
of State
Governments

THE BOOK OF THE STATES

2019 EDITION · VOLUME 51

LEXINGTON, KENTUCKY

p 859.244.8000 | f 859.244.8001 | www.csg.org

Facebook: facebook.com/CSGovts · **Twitter:** twitter.com/CSGovts
LinkedIn: linkedin.com/company/council-of-state-governments
Issuu: issuu.com/csg.publications

**The Council
of State
Governments**

Headquarters	**Southern**
David Adkins, Executive Director/CEO	Colleen Cousineau, Director
1776 Avenue of the States	P.O. Box 98129
Lexington, KY 40511	Atlanta, GA 30359
859.244.8000 • *www.csg.org*	404.633.1866 • *www.slcatlanta.org*
Eastern	**Western**
Wendell M. Hannaford, Director	Edgar Ruiz, Director
22 Cortlandt Street, 22nd Floor	1107 9th Street, Suite 730
New York, NY 10007	Sacramento, CA 95814
212.482.2320 • *www.csg-erc.org*	916.553.4423 • *www.csgwest.org*
Midwestern	**Washington, D.C.**
Michael H. McCabe, Director	444 N. Capitol Street, NW, Suite 401
701 E. 22nd Street, Suite 110	Washington, D.C. 20001
Lombard, IL 60148	202.624.5460 • *www.csgdc.org*
630.925.1922 • *www.csgmidwest.org*	

Foreword

Dear friends,

Sources of information are everywhere and the sheer scale of it all can be rather daunting. YouTube uploads 500 hours of new content every minute, Facebook has more than 2.3 billion users and Google processes 3.8 million searches per minute. Amidst this explosion of data, The Council of State Governments works to cut through the noise and curate relevant information that can help inform and empower state officials to enact sound public policy. Since 1935, CSG has produced *The Book of the States* as a testament to our founding principles. CSG has always believed that the states are the laboratories of democracy and that state leaders perform better when they can learn from the experiences of other states.

We also know that data-driven public policy analysis allows lawmakers of all ideological persuasions to share a common language. Facts matter and CSG works hard to be a trusted, nonpartisan broker of insights and information and a reliable, trusted partner for state officials across the nation. The complexity of today's public policy challenges can easily overwhelm citizens and citizen legislators alike. State officials rely on CSG to help them know what works and to leverage that knowledge to improve their state.

Working with leaders in all three branches of state government, the CSG national public policy team pursues work focused on the priority issues of our member states. The four pillars of work are strengthening democracy; helping states achieve prosperity in the new economy; learning and sharing what works; and elevating justice for all. We convene state officials for courageous conversations about the challenges they face in enacting change and engage thought leaders and experts to provide advice and guidance to help them address those challenges. CSG is a place where people of purpose pursue their passion for public service and come together to advance the common good. We are proud of the role the states allow us to play in this important work.

This edition of *The Book of the States* is a labor of love for our team members, whose many hours of work have made it possible. I am grateful for the leadership of Audrey Francis, who has helped create 19 editions of *The Book of the States*. She would be the first to thank all our friends in the states who provide the information contained in these pages. She is supported by Kelley Arnold, chief communications officer, and our communications team members Heather Perkins and Chris Pryor. I am proud of their commitment to place in your hands an accurate and well-designed volume of useful information.

As with all CSG programs and services, we are committed to continuous improvement with this publication. We welcome your suggestions on how we can make future editions of *The Book of the States* even more useful to you. And, if for some reason the pages of this book do not contain the information you're looking for, please remember our dedicated team of public policy professionals is always just an email or phone call away.

Yours truly,

David Adkins

David Adkins
Executive Director / CEO
The Council of State Governments

The Council of State Governments is our nation's only organization serving all three branches of state government. CSG is a region-based forum that fosters the exchange of insights and ideas to help state officials shape public policy. This offers unparalleled regional, national and international opportunities to network, develop leaders, collaborate and create problem-solving partnerships.

Staff Acknowledgements

The staff wishes to thank the hundreds of individuals in the states who responded to surveys conducted by The Council of State Governments; and national organizations of state officials, federal agencies and think tank organizations who made their most recent data and information available for this volume.

The Book of the States 2019

Managing Editor.......... Audrey S. Wall

Associate Editor........... Heather M. Perkins

Copy Editors .... Shawntaye Hopkins
                             Lisa McKinney

Lead Designer .... Chris Pryor

Graphic Designers ...... Theresa Carroll
                             Stephanie Northern

Disclaimer

Table of Contents

CHAPTER FOUR

State Executive Branch

TABLES

CHAPTER FIVE
State Judicial Branch

TABLES

CHAPTER SIX
Elections

TABLES

CHAPTER SEVEN
State Finance

TABLES

CHAPTER EIGHT
State Management, Administration and Demographics

TABLES

CHAPTER NINE

Selected State Policies and Programs

TABLES

CHAPTER TEN
State Pages

TABLES

CHAPTER ONE

STATE
CONSTITUTIONS

 Additional information is available online at *www.csg.org*.

TABLE 1.1
State Constitutional Changes By Legislative, Initiative, and Commission Proposal: 2018

State	Legislative proposal			Constitutional initiative			Commission referral (f)		
	Number proposed	Number adopted	Percentage adopted	Number proposed	Number adopted	Percentage adopted	Number proposed	Number adopted	Percentage adopted
Alabama	19 (a)	18 (a)	94.7						
Arizona	1	1	100.0	2	1	50.0			
Arkansas	1	1	100.0	1	1	100.0			
California	4	3	75.0	2	0	0.0			
Colorado	6	4	66.7	3	0	0.0			
Connecticut	2	2	100.0						
Delaware	(b)	1	(b)						
Florida	3	2	66.7	2	2	100.0	7	7	100.0
Georgia	5	5	100.0						
Indiana	1	1	100.0						
Kentucky	1	1 (c)	100.0						
Louisiana	6	6	100.0						
Maryland	2	2	100.0						
Michigan				2	2	100.0			
Missouri	1	1	100.0	3	2	66.7			
Nevada	1	1	100.0	3 (d)	2 (d)	66.7			
New Hampshire	2	2	100.0						
New Mexico	2	2	100.0						
North Carolina	6	4	66.7						
North Dakota				2	2	100.0			
Ohio	1	1	100.0	1	0	0.0			
Oklahoma	4	1	25.0	1	0	0.0			
Oregon	1	1	100.0	3	0	0.0			
South Carolina	1	0	0.0						
South Dakota	3	2	66.7	1	0	0.0			
Utah	3	2	66.7						
Virginia	2	2	100.0						
West Virginia	2	2	100.0						
Wisconsin	1	0	0.0						
Totals	81	68	82.7 (e)	26	12	46.2	7	7	100.0

Source: John Dinan and The Council of State Governments.
Key:
(a) Fifteen of the Alabama amendments were local amendments voted on in the affected localities. Fourteen were approved.
(b) Delaware does not provide for submission of amendments to voters. The amendment adopted in 2018 was approved by the legislature in consecutive sessions.
(c) Although Kentucky voters approved the lone amendment on the ballot, shortly before the election a state circuit judge ruled the ballot language was inaccurate and enjoined its enactment. The state supreme court ruled the amendment is invalid because the entire text of the proposed constitutional amendment wasn't on the ballot as is required by Kentucky state law.
(d) One of the citizen-initiated amendments on the Nevada ballot approved in 2018 must be re-approved by voters in 2020, per Nevada rules for citizen-initiated amendments.
(e) Percentage excludes the Delaware amendment that was not submitted to voters.
(f) Florida is the only state that permits a commission to refer amendments directly to voters.

TABLE 1.2

Themes and Patterns in State Constitutional Amendments Enacted in 2018

Rights

Victims' Rights: Florida, Georgia, Nevada, North Carolina, and Oklahoma voters approved Marsy's Law victims' rights amendments (as did voters in Kentucky, but the state supreme court ruled the amendment is invalid because the entire text of the proposed constitutional amendment wasn't on the ballot as is required by Kentucky state law). A South Dakota amendment altered and clarified an existing Marsy's Law provision.

Abortion: Alabama and West Virginia voters approved amendments declaring their state constitutions provide no more protection for abortion rights than is guaranteed by the U.S. Constitution.

Hunting and fishing: Passage of a North Carolina hunting-and-fishing rights amendment brings to 22 the number of states with such constitutional provisions.

Privacy: New Hampshire voters approved an amendment protecting privacy of personal information, bringing to 11 the number of states with privacy provisions of some sort.

Standing to sue: A New Hampshire amendment grants taxpayers standing to sue state or local governments and without having to show a personal injury from a governmental action.

Juries: Louisiana voters approved an amendment requiring a unanimous jury verdict for felony convictions.

Slavery/involuntary servitude: A Colorado amendment removed the qualifying language "except as a punishment for crime, whereof the party shall have been duly convicted" from a provision banning slavery or involuntary servitude, so that the new provision simply states: "There shall never be in this state either slavery or involuntary servitude." This qualifying language is found in several state constitutions and tracks similar language in the 13th Amendment to the U.S. Constitution but has recently been targeted for elimination in several states.

Religious establishment: An Alabama amendment authorizes display of the Ten Commandments on public property.

Elections

Redistricting: Voters in Ohio, Colorado, Michigan, and Missouri approved amendments creating redistricting commissions or adjusting procedures for existing redistricting commissions.

Voter ID: Amendments in Arkansas and North Carolina require voters to present photo identification.

Voter access/eligibility: Florida voters approved an amendment significantly relaxing the state's felon disfranchisement rules. Maryland voters approved an amendment authorizing an election-day registration system. Michigan voters approved a wide-ranging amendment enacting automatic voter registration, among other changes in voting and elections.

Institutions

Judiciary: A Florida amendment raises the retirement age to 75 and directs judges not to defer to administrative agency interpretations of statutes or rules. A West Virginia amendment gives the legislature control over the budget for the state judiciary.

Lobbying/ethics: Amendments in New Mexico and North Dakota create ethics commissions. A Florida amendment imposes additional lobbying restrictions on public officials.

Policies

Tax limitations: An Arizona amendment prohibits any new sales tax on services. A Florida amendment requires a two-thirds legislative vote to raise taxes. A North Carolina amendment lowers the maximum allowable income tax rate from 10 to 7 percent.

Revenue lockbox: Amendments in California and Louisiana require revenue from certain taxes and fees to be spent only on transportation projects. An amendment in Maryland requires all revenue from the state lottery to be spent on education.

Budgeting: Indiana became the latest state to adopt a constitutional amendment requiring a balanced budget.

Gaming: A Florida amendment stipulates that casinos can only be authorized through a state-wide popular referendum. Another Florida amendment bans wagering on greyhound dog racing.

Marijuana: A Missouri amendment legalizes medicinal marijuana.

Source: John Dinan and The Council of State Governments.

TABLE 1.3
General Information on State Constitutions (As of January 1, 2019)

State or other jurisdiction	Number of constitutions*	Dates of adoption	Effective date of present constitution	Estimated length (number of words)**	Number of amendments Submitted to voters	Adopted
Alabama	6	1819, 1861, 1865, 1868, 1875, 1901	Nov. 28, 1901	402,852 (a)	1,280	946 (c)
Alaska	1	1956	Jan. 3, 1959	13,479	43	29
Arizona	1	1911	Feb. 14, 1912	47,306	280	156
Arkansas	5	1836, 1861, 1864, 1868, 1874	Oct. 30, 1874	59,120	208	108 (d)
California	2	1849, 1879	July 4, 1879	76,930	909	538
Colorado	1	1876	Aug. 1, 1876	84,239	355	164
Connecticut	2	1818 (f), 1965	Dec. 30, 1965	16,401	35	33
Delaware	4	1776, 1792, 1831, 1897	June 10, 1897	25,445	(e)	150
Florida	6	1839, 1861, 1865, 1868, 1886, 1968	Jan. 7, 1969	49,230	185	137
Georgia	10	1777, 1789, 1798, 1861, 1865, 1868, 1877, 1945, 1976, 1982	July 1,1983	41,684	107 (g)	83 (g)
Hawaii	1 (h)	1950	Aug. 21, 1959	21,498	140	114
Idaho	1	1889	July 3, 1890	24,626	214	126
Illinois	4	1818, 1848, 1870, 1970	July 1, 1971	16,401	22	15
Indiana	2	1816, 1851	Nov. 1, 1851	11,610	81	49
Iowa	2	1846, 1857	Sept. 3, 1857	11,089	59	54 (i)
Kansas	1	1859	Jan. 29, 1861	14,097	128	98 (i)
Kentucky	4	1792, 1799, 1850, 1891	Sept. 28, 1891	27,234	76	42
Louisiana	11	1812, 1845, 1852, 1861, 1864, 1868, 1879, 1898, 1913, 1921, 1974	Jan. 1, 1975	76,730	281	196
Maine	1	1819	March 15, 1820	16,313	206	173 (j)
Maryland	4	1776, 1851, 1864, 1867	Oct. 5, 1867	43,198	269	233 (k)
Massachusetts	1	1780	Oct. 25, 1780	45,283 (l)	148	120
Michigan	4	1835, 1850, 1908, 1963	Jan. 1, 1964	31,164	76	32
Minnesota	1	1857	May 11, 1858	12,016	218	121
Mississippi	4	1817, 1832, 1869, 1890	Nov. 1, 1890	26,229	164	126
Missouri	4	1820, 1865, 1875, 1945	March 30,1945	84,924	193	126
Montana	2	1889, 1972	July 1, 1973	12,790	58	32
Nebraska	2	1866, 1875	Oct. 12, 1875	34,934	354 (m)	230 (m)
Nevada	1	1864	Oct. 31, 1864	37,418	238	140
New Hampshire	2	1776, 1784	June 2, 1784	13,238	291 (n)	147
New Jersey	3	1776, 1844, 1947	Jan. 1, 1948	26,360	88	72
New Mexico	1	1911	Jan. 6, 1912	33,198	306 (y)	172 (x)
New York	4	1777, 1822, 1846, 1894	Jan. 1, 1895	49,360	305	229
North Carolina	3	1776, 1868, 1970	July 1, 1971	17,177	51	41
North Dakota	1	1889	Nov. 2, 1889	18,746	282	161 (o)
Ohio	2	1802, 1851	Sept. 1, 1851	63,140	294	177
Oklahoma	1	1907	Nov. 16, 1907	84,956	373 (p)	199 (p)
Oregon	1	1857	Feb. 14, 1859	49,430	505 (q)	258 (q)
Pennsylvania	5	1776, 1790, 1838, 1873, 1968 (r)	1968 (r)	26,078	39 (r)	33 (r)
Rhode Island	2	1842 (f) 1986 (s)	Dec. 4, 1986	11,407	14 (s)	12 (s)
South Carolina	7	1776, 1778, 1790, 1861, 1865, 1868, 1895	Jan. 1, 1896	27,421	690 (t)	500 (t)
South Dakota	1	1889	Nov. 2, 1889	28,840	243	122
Tennessee	3	1796, 1835, 1870	Feb. 23, 1870	13,960	66	43
Texas	5 (u)	1845, 1861, 1866, 1869, 1876	Feb. 15, 1876	92,025	676 (v)	498
Utah	1	1895	Jan. 4, 1896	20,700	178	122
Vermont	3	1777, 1786, 1793	July 9, 1793	8,565	212	54
Virginia	6	1776, 1830, 1851, 1869, 1902, 1970	July 1, 1971	22,570	60	52
Washington	1	1889	Nov. 11, 1889	32,578	181	107
West Virginia	2	1863, 1872	April 9, 1872	33,324	126	75
Wisconsin	1	1848	May 29, 1848	15,102	197	147 (i)
Wyoming	1	1889	July 10, 1890	26,349	130	101
American Samoa	2	1960, 1967	July 1, 1967	6,000	15 (y)	7 (y)
CNMI***	1	1977	Jan. 9, 1978	13,700	60 (y)	56 (w)(y)
Puerto Rico	1	1952	July 25, 1952	9,400	8 (y)	6 (y)

See footnotes at end of table

TABLE 1.3
General Information On State Constitutions (As of January 1, 2019) (continued)

Source: John Dinan and The Council of State Governments, with research assistance from Wake Forest students Bradley Harper and Alec Papovich.

*The constitutions referred to in this table include those Civil War documents customarily listed by the individual states.

**In calculating word counts, supplemental information regarding dates of adoption and other material not formally a part of the constitution are generally excluded. In some cases, word counts are taken from the total as of January 2011.

***Commonwealth of Northern Mariana Islands

Key:

(a) The Alabama constitution includes numerous local amendments that apply to only one county. An estimated 70 percent of all amendments are local. A 1982 amendment provides that after proposal by the legislature to which special procedures apply, only a local vote (with exceptions) is necessary to add them to the constitution.

(b) Computer word count.

(c) The total number of Alabama amendments includes one that is commonly overlooked.

(d) Eight of the approved amendments have been superseded and are not printed in the current edition of the constitution. The total adopted does not include five amendments proposed and adopted since statehood.

(e) Proposed amendments are not submitted to the voters in Delaware.

(f) Colonial charters with some alterations served as the first constitutions in Connecticut (1638, 1662) and in Rhode Island (1663).

(g) The Georgia constitution requires amendments to be of "general and uniform application throughout the state," thus eliminating local amendments that accounted for most of the amendments before 1982.

(h) As a kingdom and republic, Hawaii had five constitutions.

(i) The figure includes amendments approved by the voters and later nullified by the state supreme court in Iowa (three), Kansas (one), Nevada (six) and Wisconsin (two).

(j) The figure does not include one amendment approved by the voters in 1967 that is inoperative until implemented by legislation.

(k) Two sets of identical amendments were on the ballot and adopted in the 1992 Maryland election. The four amendments are counted as two in the table.

(l) The printed constitution includes many provisions that have been annulled.

(m) The 1998 and 2000 Nebraska ballots allowed the voters to vote separately on "parts" of propositions. In 1998, 10 of 18 separate propositions were adopted; in 2000, 6 of 9.

(n) The constitution of 1784 was extensively revised in 1792. Figure shows proposals and adoptions since the constitution was adopted in 1784.

(o) The figures do not include submission and approval of the constitution of 1889 itself and of Article XX; these are constitutional questions included in some counts of constitutional amendments and would add two to the figure in each column.

(p) The figures include six amendments submitted to and approved by the voters which were, by decisions of the Oklahoma or federal courts, rendered inoperative or ruled invalid, unconstitutional, or illegally submitted.

(q) One Oregon amendment on the 2000 ballot was not counted as approved because canvassing was enjoined by the courts.

(r) Certain sections of the constitution were revised by the limited convention of 1967–68. Amendments proposed and adopted are since 1968.

(s) Following approval of eight amendments and a "rewrite" of the Rhode Island Constitution in 1986, the constitution has been called the 1986 Constitution.

(t) In 1981 approximately two-thirds of the proposed and four-fifths of the adopted amendments were local. Since then the amendments have been statewide propositions.

(u) The Constitution of the Republic of Texas preceded five state constitutions.

(v) The number of proposed amendments to the Texas Constitution excludes three proposed by the legislature but not placed on the ballot.

(w) The total excludes one amendment ruled void by a federal district court.

(x) The total excludes one amendment approved by voters in November 2008 but later declared invalid on single subject grounds by the state supreme court.

(y) These totals for territorial constitutions are in some cases taken from 2011 data.

Table 1.3 | State Constitutions

70%
of Alabama's constitution

is made up of local amendments that apply to only one county.

Constitution Length by Word Count

LONGEST		SHORTEST
Alabama • 402,852		Vermont • 8,565
Texas • 92,025		Iowa • 11,089
Oklahoma • 84,956		Rhode Island • 11,407
Missouri • 84,924		Indiana • 11,610
Colorado • 84,239		Minnesota • 12,016

Amendments Submitted

HIGHEST

#1 Alabama • 1,280
#2 California • 909
#3 South Carolina • 690
#4 Texas • 676
#5 Oregon • 505

LOWEST

#1 Rhode Island • 14
#2 Illinois • 22
#3 Connecticut • 35
#4 Pennsylvania • 39
#5 Alaska • 43

Amendments Adopted

HIGHEST

#1 Alabama • 946
#2 California • 538
#3 South Carolina • 500
#4 Texas • 498
#5 Oregon • 258

LOWEST

#1 Rhode Island • 12
#2 Illinois • 15
#3 Alaska • 29
#4 Michigan • 32
#5 Montana • 32

Amendments Adopted Per Year

HIGHEST
#1 Alabama • 8.0
#2 Louisiana • 4.5
#3 South Carolina • 4.1
#4 California • 3.8
#5 Texas • 3.5

LOWEST
#1 Vermont • 0.2
#2 Tennessee • 0.3
#3 Indiana • 0.3
#4 Illinois • 0.3
#5 Kentucky • 0.3

Highest Number of Constitutions

LOUISIANA • 11

GEORGIA • 10

SOUTH CAROLINA • 7

TABLE 1.4
Constitutional Amendment Procedure: By the Legislature, Constitutional Provisions

State or other jurisdiction	Legislative vote required for proposal (a)	Consideration by two sessions required	Vote required for ratification	Limitation on the number of amendments legislature can submit at one election
Alabama	3/5	No	Majority vote on amendment	None
Alaska	2/3	No	Majority vote on amendment	None
Arizona	Majority	No	Majority vote on amendment	None
Arkansas	Majority	No	Majority vote on amendment	3
California	2/3	No	Majority vote on amendment	None
Colorado	2/3	No	55% vote on amendment (y)	(b)
Connecticut	(c)	(c)	Majority vote on amendment	None
Delaware	2/3	Yes	Not required	No referendum
Florida	3/5	No	3/5 vote on amendment (d)	None
Georgia	2/3	No	Majority vote on amendment	None
Hawaii	(e)	(e)	(f)	None
Idaho	2/3	No	Majority vote on amendment	None
Illinois	3/5	No	(g)	3 articles
Indiana	Majority	Yes	Majority vote on amendment	None
Iowa	Majority	Yes	Majority vote on amendment	None
Kansas	2/3	No	Majority vote on amendment	5
Kentucky	3/5	No	Majority vote on amendment	4
Louisiana	2/3	No	Majority vote on amendment (h)	None
Maine	2/3	No	Majority vote on amendment	None
Maryland	3/5	No	Majority vote on amendment (h)	None
Massachusetts	Majority (j)	Yes	Majority vote on amendment	None
Michigan	2/3	No	Majority vote on amendment	None
Minnesota	Majority	No	Majority vote in election	None
Mississippi	2/3 (k)	No	Majority vote on amendment	None
Missouri	Majority	No	Majority vote on amendment	None
Montana	2/3 (i)	No	Majority vote on amendment	None
Nebraska	3/5 (w)	No	Majority vote on amendment (f)	None
Nevada	Majority	Yes	Majority vote on amendment	None
New Hampshire	3/5	No	2/3 vote on amendment	None
New Jersey	(l)	(l)	Majority vote on amendment	None (m)
New Mexico	Majority (n)	No	Majority vote on amendment (n)	None
New York	Majority	Yes	Majority vote on amendment	None
North Carolina	3/5	No	Majority vote on amendment	None
North Dakota	Majority	No	Majority vote on amendment	None
Ohio	3/5	No	Majority vote on amendment	None
Oklahoma	Majority (w)	No	Majority vote on amendment	None
Oregon	(o)	No	Majority vote on amendment (x)	None
Pennsylvania	Majority (p)	Yes (p)	Majority vote on amendment	None
Rhode Island	Majority	No	Majority vote on amendment	None
South Carolina	2/3 (q)	Yes (q)	Majority vote on amendment	None
South Dakota	Majority	No	Majority vote on amendment	None
Tennessee	(r)	Yes (r)	Majority vote in election (s)	None
Texas	2/3	No	Majority vote on amendment	None
Utah	2/3	No	Majority vote on amendment	None
Vermont	(t)	Yes	Majority vote on amendment	None
Virginia	Majority	Yes	Majority vote on amendment	None
Washington	2/3	No	Majority vote on amendment	None
West Virginia	2/3	No	Majority vote on amendment	None
Wisconsin	Majority	Yes	Majority vote on amendment	None
Wyoming	2/3	No	Majority vote in election	None
American Samoa	2/3	No	Majority vote on amendment (u)	None
CNMI*	3/4	No	Majority vote on amendment	None
Puerto Rico	2/3 (v)	No	Majority vote on amendment	3

See footnotes at end of table

TABLE 1.4

Constitutional Amendment Procedure: By the Legislature, Constitutional Provisions (continued)

Source: John Dinan and The Council of State Governments.
*Commonwealth of Northern Mariana Islands
Key:

(a) In all states not otherwise noted, the figure shown in the column refers to the proportion of elected members in each house required for approval of proposed constitutional amendments.

(b) Legislature may not propose amendments to more than six articles of the constitution in the same legislative session.

(c) Three-fourths vote in each house at one session, or majority vote in each house in two sessions between which an election has intervened.

(d) Three-fifths vote on amendment, except that an amendment for "new state tax or fee" not in effect on Nov. 7, 1994 requires two-thirds of voters in the election.

(e) Two-thirds vote in each house at one session, or majority vote in each house in two sessions.

(f) In Hawaii, the majority vote on amendment must be at least 50 percent of the total votes cast at the election; or, at a special election, a majority of the votes tallied which must be at least 30 percent of the total number of registered voters. In Nebraska the majority vote on amendment must be at least 35 percent of the total votes cast at the election.

(g) Majority voting in election or three-fifths voting on amendment.

(h) In Louisiana, if five or fewer political subdivisions of the state are affected, majority in state as a whole and also in each of affected subdivisions is required. In Maryland, if an amendment affects only the City of Baltimore or only one county, majority in state as a whole and also in affected subdivision is required.

(i) Two-thirds of all members of the legislature.

(j) Majority of members elected sitting in joint session.

(k) The two-thirds must include not less than a majority elected to each house.

(l) Three-fifths of all members of each house at one session, or majority of all members of each house for two successive sessions.

(m) If a proposed amendment is not approved at the election when submitted, neither the same amendment nor one which would make substantially the same change for the constitution may be again submitted to the people before the third general election thereafter.

(n) Amendments concerning certain elective franchise and education matters require three-fourths vote of members elected and approval by three-fourths of electors voting in state and two-thirds of those voting in each county.

(o) Majority vote to amend constitution, two-thirds to revise ("revise" includes all or a part of the constitution).

(p) Emergency amendments may be passed by two-thirds vote of each house, followed by ratification by majority vote of electors in election held at least one month after legislative approval.

(q) Two-thirds of members of each house, first passage; majority of members of each house after popular ratification.

(r) Majority of members elected to both houses, first passage; two-thirds of members elected to both houses, second passage.

(s) Majority of all citizens voting for governor.

(t) Two-thirds vote in the senate and majority vote in the house on first passage; majority in both houses on second passage. As of 1974, amendments may be submitted only every four years.

(u) Within 30 days after voter approval, governor must submit amendment(s) to U.S. Secretary of the Interior for approval.

(v) If approved by two-thirds of members of each house, amendment(s) submitted to voters at special referendum; if approved by not less than three-fourths of total members of each house, referendum may be held at next general election.

(w) The legislature may, by a four-fifths vote in Nebraska or a two-thirds vote in Oklahoma, call a special election for voters to consider amendments.

(x) There is an exception for an amendment containing a super-majority voting requirement, which must be ratified by an equal supermajority.

(y) An amendment repealing, in whole or in part, any constitutional provision only requires approval by a majority on the amendment.

TABLE 1.5
Constitutional Amendment Procedure: By Initiative, Constitutional Provisions

State or other jurisdiction	Number of signatures required on initiative petition	Distribution of signatures	Referendum vote
Arizona	15% of total votes cast for all candidates for governor at last election.	None specified.	Majority vote on amendment.
Arkansas	10% of voters for governor at last election.	Must include 5% of voters for governor in each of 15 counties.	Majority vote on amendment.
California	8% of total voters for all candidates for governor at last election.	None specified.	Majority vote on amendment.
Colorado	5% of total legal votes for all candidates for secretary of state at last general election.	2% of registered voters in each of the state senate districts.	55% vote on amendment, except any amendment repealing a constitutional provision only requires a majority vote on amendment.
Florida	8% of total votes cast in the state in the last election for presidential electors.	8% of total votes cast in each of 1/2 the congressional districts.	Three-fifths vote on amendment except any amendment for "new state tax or fee" not in effect Nov. 7, 1994 requires 2/3 of voters voting in election.
Illinois (a)	8% of total votes cast for candidates for governor at last election.	None specified.	Majority voting in election or 3/5 voting on amendment.
Massachusetts (b)	3% of total votes cast for governor at preceding biennial state election (not less than 25,000 qualified voters).	No more than 1/4 from any one county.	Majority vote on amendment which must be 30% of total ballots cast at election.
Michigan	10% of total voters for all candidates at last gubernatorial election.	No more than 15% from any one congressional district. (e)	Majority vote on amendment.
Mississippi (c)	12% of total votes for all candidates for governor in last election.	No more than 20% from any one congressional district.	Majority vote on amendment and not less than 40% of total vote cast at election.
Missouri	8% of legal voters for all candidates for governor at last election.	The 8% must be in each of 2/3 of the congressional districts in the state.	Majority vote on amendment.
Montana	10% of qualified electors, the number of qualified voters to be determined by number of votes cast for governor in preceding election in each county and in the state.	The 10% to include at least 10% of qualified voters in 2/5 of the legislative districts. (d)	Majority vote on amendment.
Nebraska	10% of registered voters.	The 10% must include 5% in each of 2/5 of the counties.	Majority vote on amendment which must be at least 35% of total vote at the election.
Nevada	10% of voters who voted in entire state in last general election.	10% of voters in each of the state's congressional districts.	Majority vote on amendment in two consecutive general elections.
North Dakota	4% of population of the state.	None specified.	Majority vote on amendment.
Ohio	10% of total number of electors who voted for governor in last election.	At least 5% of qualified electors in each of 1/2 of counties in the state.	Majority vote on amendment.
Oklahoma	15% of votes cast at last general election for governor.	None specified.	Majority vote on amendment.
Oregon	8% of total votes for all candidates for governor at last election at which governor was elected for four-year term.	None specified.	Majority vote on amendment except for supermajority equal to supermajority voting requirement contained in proposed amendment.
South Dakota	10% of total votes for governor in last election.	None specified.	Majority vote on amendment.
CNMI*	50% of qualified voters of commonwealth.	In addition, 25% of qualified voters in each senatorial district.	Majority vote on amendment if legislature approved it by majority vote; if not, at least 2/3 vote in each of two senatorial districts in addition to a majority vote.

Source: John Dinan and The Council of State Governments.
Key:
(a) Initiatives can only be used to amend substantive or procedural aspects of Article IV, the Legislature Article, and cannot be used to amend any other articles.
(b) Before being submitted to the electorate for ratification, initiated measures must be approved at two sessions of a successively elected legislature by not less than one-fourth of all members elected, sitting in joint session.
(c) Before being submitted to the electorate, initiated measures are sent to the legislature, which has the option of submitting an amended or alternative measure alongside the original measure.

(d) A 2002 amendment changed this geographic distribution rule to require at least 10% of voters in 1/2 of the counties. After this amendment was held unconstitutional by a federal district court in a 2005 ruling, the state attorney general advised that the prior rule–2/5 of legislative districts–was in effect.
(e) In May 2019 the Michigan attorney general determined that this signature-distribution requirement, which was added through a 2018 statute, was unconstitutional, in an opinion likely to be challenged in state court.

TABLE 1.6
Procedures for Calling Constitutional Conventions, Constitutional Provisions

State or other jurisdiction	Provision for convention	Procedure for calling a convention by initiative	Legislative vote for submission of convention question (a)	Popular vote to authorize convention	Periodic submission of convention question required (b)	Popular vote required for ratification of convention proposals
Alabama	Yes	No	Majority	ME	No	Not specified
Alaska	Yes	No	No provision (c)(d)	(c)	10 years; 2012 (c)	Not specified (c)
Arizona	Yes	No	Majority	(e)	No	MP
Arkansas	No	No	No			
California	Yes	No	2/3	MP	No	MP
Colorado	Yes	No	2/3	MP	No	ME
Connecticut	Yes	No	2/3	MP	20 years; 2008 (f)	MP
Delaware	Yes	No	2/3	MP	No	No provision
Florida	Yes	Yes (m)	(g)	MP	No	3/5 voting on proposal
Georgia	Yes	No	(d)	No	No	MP
Hawaii	Yes	No	Not specified	MP	10 years; 2018	MP (h)
Idaho	Yes	No	2/3	MP	No	Not specified
Illinois	Yes	No	3/5	(i)	20 years; 2008	MP
Indiana	No	No	No			
Iowa	Yes	No	Majority	MP	10 years; 2010	MP
Kansas	Yes	No	2/3	MP	No	MP
Kentucky	Yes	No	Majority (j)	MP (k)	No	No provision
Louisiana	Yes	No	(d)	No	No	MP
Maine	Yes	No	(d)	No	No	No provision
Maryland	Yes	No	Majority	ME	20 years; 2010	MP
Massachusetts	No	No		No		
Michigan	Yes	No	Majority	MP	16 years; 2010	MP
Minnesota	Yes	No	2/3	ME	No	3/5 voting on
Mississippi	No	No	No			
Missouri	Yes	No	Majority	MP	20 years; 2002	Not specified (l)
Montana	Yes	Yes (m)	2/3	MP	20 years; 2010	MP
Nebraska	Yes	No	3/5	MP (o)	No	MP
Nevada	Yes	No	2/3	ME	No	No provision
New Hampshire	Yes	No	Majority	MP	10 years; 2012	2/3 voting on proposal
New Jersey	No	No	No			
New Mexico	Yes	No	2/3	MP	No	Not specified
New York	Yes	No	Majority	MP	20 years; 2017	MP
North Carolina	Yes	No	2/3	MP	No	MP
North Dakota	No	Yes (m)	No			
Ohio	Yes	No	2/3	MP	20 years; 2012	MP
Oklahoma	Yes	No	Majority	(e)	20 years; 1970	MP
Oregon	Yes	No	Majority	(e)	No	No provision
Pennsylvania	No	No	No			
Rhode Island	Yes	No	Majority	MP	10 years; 2014	MP
South Carolina	Yes	No	(d)	ME	No	No provision
South Dakota	Yes	Yes (m)	(d)	No	No	(p)
Tennessee	Yes (q)	No	Majority	MP	No	MP
Texas	No	No	No			
Utah	Yes	No	2/3	ME	No	ME
Vermont	No	No	No			
Virginia	Yes	No	(d)	No	No	MP
Washington	Yes	No	2/3	ME	No	Not specified
West Virginia	Yes	No	Majority	MP	No	Not specified
Wisconsin	Yes	No	Majority	MP	No	No provision
Wyoming	Yes	No	2/3	ME	No	Not specified
American Samoa	Yes	No	(r)	No	No	ME (s)
*CNMI	Yes	Yes (t)	Majority	2/3	10 years	MP and at least 2/3 in each of 2 senatorial districts
Puerto Rico	Yes	No	2/3	MP	No	MP

See footnotes at end of table

TABLE 1.6
Procedures for Calling Constitutional Conventions, Constitutional Provisions (continued)

Source: John Dinan and The Council of State Governments.
*Commonwealth of Northern Mariana Islands
Key:
MP–Majority voting on the proposal.
ME–Majority voting in the election.
(a) In all states not otherwise noted, the entries in this column refer to the proportion of members elected to each house required to submit to the electorate the question of calling a constitutional convention.
(b) The number listed is the interval between required submissions on the question of calling a constitutional convention; where given, the date is that of the most recent submission of the mandatory convention referendum.
(c) Unless provided otherwise by law, convention calls are to conform as nearly as possible to the act calling the 1955 convention, which provided for a legislative vote of a majority of members elected to each house and ratification by a majority vote on the proposals. The legislature may call a constitutional convention at any time.
(d) In these states, the legislature may call a convention without submitting the question to the people. The legislative vote required is two-thirds of the members elected to each house in Georgia, Louisiana, South Carolina and Virginia; two-thirds concurrent vote of both branches in Maine; three-fourths of all members of each house in South Dakota; and not specified in Alaska, but bills require majority vote of membership in each house.
(e) The law calling a convention must be approved by the people.
(f) The legislature shall submit the question 20 years after the last convention, or 20 years after the last vote on the question of calling a convention, whichever date is last.
(g) The power to call a convention is reserved to the people by petition.
(h) The majority must be 50 percent of the total votes cast at a general election or at a special election, a majority of the votes tallied which must be at least 30 percent of the total number of registered voters.
(i) Majority voting in the election, or three-fifths voting on the question.
(j) Must be approved during two legislative sessions.
(k) Majority must equal one-fourth of qualified voters at last general election.
(l) Majority of those voting on the proposal is assumed. Vote must take place at a special election held no less than 60 days and no more than 6 months after convention.
(m) In Montana, North Dakota and South Dakota, conventions can be called by initiative petition in the same manner as provided for initiated amendments, and with approval by a majority of voters. In Florida, conventions can be called by filing an initiative petition with signatures equal to 15 percent of the votes cast in the preceding presidential election and also equal to 15 percent of signatures in half of the congressional districts in the state and then obtaining a majority of the voters at the ensuing election.
(n) Two-thirds of all members of the legislature.
(o) Majority must be 35 percent of total votes cast at the election.
(p) Convention proposals are submitted to the electorate at a special election in a manner to be determined by the convention. Ratification by a majority of votes cast.
(q) Conventions may not be held more often than once in six years.
(r) Five years after effective date of constitutions, governor shall call a constitutional convention to consider changes proposed by a constitutional committee appointed by the governor. Delegates to the convention are to be elected by their county councils. A convention was held in 1972.
(s) If proposed amendments are approved by the voters, they must be submitted to the U.S. Secretary of the Interior for approval.
(t) The petition must be signed by 25 percent of the qualified voters or at least 75 percent in a senatorial district.

CHAPTER TWO

FEDERALISM AND INTERGOVERNMENTAL RELATIONS

TABLE 2.1
Summary of State Intergovernmental Expenditures: 1944–2017 (In thousands of dollars)

Fiscal year	Total	To Federal government(a)	Total	For general local government support	Education	Public welfare	Highways	Health	Miscellaneous and combined
1944	$1,842,000	...	$1,842,000	$274,000	$861,000	$368,000	$298,000	...	$41,000
1946	2,092,000	...	2,092,000	357,000	953,000	376,000	339,000	...	67,000
1948	3,283,000	...	3,283,000	428,000	1,554,000	648,000	507,000	...	146,000
1950	4,217,000	...	4,217,000	482,000	2,054,000	792,000	610,000	...	279,000
1952	5,044,000	...	5,044,000	549,000	2,523,000	976,000	728,000	...	268,000
1953	5,384,000	...	5,384,000	592,000	2,737,000	981,000	803,000	...	271,000
1954	5,679,000	...	5,679,000	600,000	2,930,000	1,004,000	871,000	...	274,000
1955	5,986,000	...	5,986,000	591,000	3,150,000	1,046,000	911,000	...	288,000
1956	6,538,000	...	6,538,000	631,000	3,541,000	1,069,000	984,000	...	313,000
1957	7,440,000	...	7,440,000	668,000	4,212,000	1,136,000	1,082,000	...	342,000
1958	8,089,000	...	8,089,000	687,000	4,598,000	1,247,000	1,167,000	...	390,000
1959	8,689,000	...	8,689,000	725,000	4,957,000	1,409,000	1,207,000	...	391,000
1960	9,443,000	...	9,443,000	806,000	5,461,000	1,483,000	1,247,000	...	446,000
1962	10,906,000	...	10,906,000	839,000	6,474,000	1,777,000	1,327,000	...	489,000
1963	11,885,000	...	11,885,000	1,012,000	6,993,000	1,919,000	1,416,000	...	545,000
1964	12,968,000	...	12,968,000	1,053,000	7,664,000	2,108,000	1,524,000	...	619,000
1965	14,174,000	...	14,174,000	1,102,000	8,351,000	2,436,000	1,630,000	...	655,000
1966	16,928,000	...	16,928,000	1,361,000	10,177,000	2,882,000	1,725,000	...	783,000
1967	19,056,000	...	19,056,000	1,585,000	11,845,000	2,897,000	1,861,000	...	868,000
1968	21,950,000	...	21,950,000	1,993,000	13,321,000	3,527,000	2,029,000	...	1,080,000
1969	24,779,000	...	24,779,000	2,135,000	14,858,000	4,402,000	2,109,000	...	1,275,000
1970	28,892,000	...	28,892,000	2,958,000	17,085,000	5,003,000	2,439,000	...	1,407,000
1971	32,640,000	...	32,640,000	3,258,000	19,292,000	5,760,000	2,507,000	...	1,823,000
1972	36,759,246	...	36,759,246	3,752,327	21,195,345	6,943,634	2,633,417	...	2,234,523
1973	40,822,135	N/A	40,822,135	4,279,646	23,315,651	7,531,738	2,953,424	...	2,741,676
1974	45,941,111	341,194	45,599,917	4,803,875	27,106,812	7,028,750	3,211,455	...	3,449,025
1975	51,978,324	974,780	51,003,544	5,129,333	31,110,237	7,136,104	3,224,861	...	4,403,009
1976	57,858,242	1,179,580	56,678,662	5,673,843	34,083,711	8,307,411	3,240,806	...	5,372,891
1977	62,459,903	1,386,237	61,073,666	6,372,543	36,964,306	8,756,717	3,631,108	...	5,348,992
1978	67,287,260	1,472,378	65,814,882	6,819,438	40,125,488	8,585,558	3,821,135	...	6,463,263
1979	75,962,980	1,493,215	74,469,765	8,224,338	46,195,698	8,675,473	4,148,573	...	7,225,683
1980	84,504,451	1,746,301	82,758,150	8,643,789	52,688,101	9,241,551	4,382,716	...	7,801,993
1981	93,179,549	1,872,980	91,306,569	9,570,248	57,257,373	11,025,445	4,751,449	...	8,702,054
1982	98,742,976	1,793,284	96,949,692	10,044,372	60,683,583	11,965,123	5,028,072	...	9,228,542
1983	100,886,902	1,764,821	99,122,081	10,364,144	63,118,351	10,919,847	5,277,447	...	9,442,292
1984	108,373,188	1,722,115	106,651,073	10,744,740	67,484,926	11,923,430	5,686,834	...	10,811,143
1985	121,571,151	1,963,468	119,607,683	12,319,623	74,936,970	12,673,123	6,019,069	...	13,658,898
1986	131,966,258	2,105,831	129,860,427	13,383,912	81,929,467	14,214,613	6,470,049	...	13,862,386
1987	141,278,672	2,455,362	138,823,310	14,245,089	88,253,298	14,753,727	6,784,699	...	14,786,497
1988	151,661,866	2,652,981	149,008,885	14,896,991	95,390,536	15,032,315	6,949,190	...	16,739,853
1989	165,415,415	2,929,622	162,485,793	15,749,681	104,601,291	16,697,915	7,376,173	...	18,060,733
1990	175,027,632	3,243,634	171,783,998	16,565,106	109,438,131	18,403,149	7,784,316	...	19,593,296
1991	186,398,234	3,464,364	182,933,870	16,977,032	116,179,860	20,903,400	8,126,477	...	20,747,101
1992	201,313,434	3,608,911	197,704,523	16,368,139	124,919,686	25,942,234	8,480,871	...	21,993,593
1993	214,094,882	3,625,051	210,469,831	17,690,986	131,179,517	31,339,777	9,298,624		20,960,927
1994	225,635,410	3,603,447	222,031,963	18,044,015	135,861,024	30,624,514	9,622,849	...	27,879,561
1995	240,978,128	3,616,831	237,361,297	18,996,435	148,160,436	30,772,525	10,481,616	...	28,926,886
1996	252,079,335	3,896,667	248,182,668	20,019,771	156,954,115	31,180,345	10,707,338	10,790,396	18,530,703
1997	264,207,209	3,839,942	260,367,267	21,808,828	164,147,715	35,754,024	11,431,270	11,772,189	15,453,241
1998	278,853,409	3,515,734	275,337,675	22,693,158	176,250,998	32,327,325	11,648,853	12,379,498	20,037,843
1999	308,734,917	3,801,667	304,933,250	25,495,396	192,416,987	35,161,151	12,075,195	13,611,228	26,173,293
2000	327,069,829	4,021,471	323,048,358	27,475,363	208,135,537	40,206,513	12,473,052	15,067,156	19,690,737
2001	350,326,546	4,290,764	346,035,782	31,693,016	222,092,587	41,926,990	12,350,136	16,518,461	21,454,592
2002	364,789,480	4,370,330	360,419,150	28,927,053	227,336,087	47,112,496	12,949,850	20,816,777	23,276,887
2003	382,781,397	4,391,095	378,390,302	30,766,480	240,788,692	49,302,737	13,337,114	20,241,742	23,953,537
2004	388,559,152	4,627,356	383,931,796	29,718,225	249,256,844	42,636,305	14,008,581	19,959,396	28,352,445
2005	405,925,287	4,620,167	401,305,120	28,320,648	263,625,820	48,370,718	14,500,232	17,515,138	28,972,564
2006	432,265,206	6,502,059	425,763,147	30,486,739	280,090,982	48,409,237	15,495,306	18,144,795	33,136,088
2007	459,742,295	4,670,648	455,071,647	31,207,955	301,062,065	56,899,141	14,881,789	20,067,198	30,953,499
2008	478,530,574	4,765,734	473,764,840	32,035,268	315,424,647	57,730,369	16,549,366	20,342,928	31,682,262
2009	490,887,391	4,894,977	485,992,414	30,421,570	324,374,036	58,741,316	16,492,780	21,019,353	34,943,359
2010	485,557,187	4,339,166	481,218,021	27,821,681	317,389,500	58,858,443	18,043,061	18,274,329	40,831,007

See footnotes at end of table

TABLE 2.1
Summary of State Intergovernmental Expenditures: 1944–2017 (In thousands of dollars) (continued)

| | | | To local governments | | | | | | |
| | | | | For specified purposes | | | | | |
Fiscal year	Total	To Federal government(a)	Total	For general local government support	Education	Public welfare	Highways	Health	Miscellaneous and combined
2011	$496,832,436	$4,295,922	$492,536,514	$27,577,126	$330,482,270	$56,678,841	$17,243,590	$18,745,863	$41,808,824
2012	481,883,230	4,157,695	477,725,535	27,289,870	317,839,562	55,913,067	17,787,581	19,350,451	39,545,004
2013	488,782,863	3,392,576	485,390,287	28,412,169	324,995,548	55,565,254	18,158,521	20,242,808	38,015,987
2014	498,710,149	3,389,399	495,320,750	30,459,571	330,140,870	54,781,687	20,992,876	19,979,130	38,966,616
2015	515,045,908	3,408,376	511,637,532	32,193,005	345,859,861	52,704,375	20,420,805	18,739,461	41,720,025
2016	532,665,290	3,388,085	529,277,205	31,189,834	360,117,773	57,049,413	19,675,932	19,529,120	41,715,133
2017	549,908,261	3,228,642	546,679,619	31,718,872	372,997,261	60,129,920	20,276,398	18,505,675	43,051,493

Source: U.S. Census Bureau, Census of Governments: Finance (years ending in "2" and "7"), and Annual Survey of State Government Finances (remaining years).
Notes:
1. Data users who create their own estimates using these data should cite only the U.S. Census Bureau as the source of the original data. Data in this table are based on information from public records and contain no confidential data. Although the data in this table come from a census of governmental units and are not subject to sampling error, the census results may contain nonsampling error. Additional information on nonsampling error, response rates, and definitions may be found within the survey methodology https://www.census.gov/programs-surveys/state/technical-documentation/methodology.html.
2. Detail may not add to total due to rounding.
Key:
...–Not available.
(a) Represents primarily state reimbursements for the supplemental security income program.

TABLE 2.2
Summary of State Intergovernmental Expenditures, By State: 2008-2017 (In thousands of dollars)

State	2017	2016	2015	2014	2013	2012	2011	2010	2009	2008
United States	$549,908,261	$532,665,290	$515,045,908	$498,710,149	$488,782,863	$481,883,230	$496,832,436	$485,557,187	$490,887,391	$478,530,574
Alabama	6,931,626	6,672,049	6,612,535	6,474,302	6,476,073	6,563,313	6,800,787	6,604,013	6,535,634	6,720,814
Alaska	1,829,640	2,038,078	2,036,112	2,059,333	2,032,061	1,897,331	1,723,023	1,655,467	1,616,689	1,487,649
Arizona	8,094,626	10,904,370	7,832,147	7,448,459	8,209,708	8,023,697	8,668,387	9,179,514	9,618,970	10,320,506
Arkansas	5,373,102	5,882,840	5,214,039	5,199,089	4,937,560	5,047,345	5,151,981	5,057,598	4,698,889	4,392,340
California	107,877,299	103,512,395	97,968,328	91,869,167	95,069,461	85,425,616	91,501,553	90,530,131	94,909,240	94,872,980
Colorado	7,604,250	7,310,747	7,151,882	6,749,839	6,291,390	6,105,130	6,334,861	6,513,704	6,403,127	5,912,545
Connecticut	9,190,177	5,438,230	5,338,357	4,899,005	4,908,546	4,614,954	4,485,808	4,846,870	4,316,376	4,193,874
Delaware	1,583,343	1,511,805	1,454,859	1,390,686	1,271,359	1,161,381	1,293,106	1,235,608	1,205,247	1,172,083
Florida	21,484,868	20,407,866	19,173,628	18,707,624	17,809,542	17,340,127	19,725,217	18,478,449	17,677,928	19,703,095
Georgia	12,325,151	11,835,632	11,088,286	10,557,747	10,361,359	10,223,211	10,600,099	10,747,620	10,816,572	10,415,395
Hawaii	328,020	134,933	267,863	255,885	220,844	194,791	207,988	177,624	159,452	137,771
Idaho	2,408,604	2,277,298	2,156,220	2,015,071	1,981,659	1,956,717	2,036,312	2,022,896	2,077,028	2,037,507
Illinois	19,192,558	18,109,138	18,558,946	18,638,884	15,549,167	15,866,914	15,711,057	15,530,746	15,034,787	14,585,898
Indiana	9,987,853	9,711,681	9,548,136	9,314,957	9,292,344	9,313,044	9,265,386	9,705,254	8,214,991	7,976,702
Iowa	5,505,683	5,470,729	5,298,032	4,963,899	4,753,646	4,804,976	5,151,627	4,528,319	4,660,802	4,142,960
Kansas	4,860,119	4,799,630	4,849,983	4,108,481	4,057,504	3,953,778	4,208,664	4,176,958	4,314,940	4,214,475
Kentucky	5,730,213	4,780,430	4,709,948	4,649,395	4,802,691	5,029,106	5,069,137	5,078,845	4,769,871	4,700,971
Louisiana	6,415,070	5,766,006	5,726,498	6,053,019	6,241,308	6,387,767	6,580,164	6,658,397	6,505,389	6,022,791
Maine	2,428,618	1,288,779	1,254,898	1,285,064	1,238,618	1,286,233	1,301,692	1,346,639	1,325,723	1,335,469
Maryland	9,631,764	9,398,276	9,158,679	8,733,983	8,641,281	8,380,215	8,124,451	8,592,779	8,654,935	8,509,003
Massachusetts	9,129,315	9,080,507	9,379,933	9,811,813	9,401,248	9,291,231	8,826,190	9,107,483	8,890,500	8,840,769
Michigan	21,279,004	20,788,310	20,487,354	19,779,302	19,249,754	19,021,267	19,878,322	19,410,018	19,656,877	19,519,271
Minnesota	13,546,867	13,143,647	12,827,108	12,620,852	12,975,915	10,833,320	11,102,449	10,427,657	11,199,230	11,188,797
Mississippi	4,527,299	5,251,972	5,138,598	4,919,968	5,053,070	5,138,081	5,253,307	5,272,442	5,156,650	5,111,703
Missouri	6,298,000	6,172,736	5,987,018	5,785,229	5,771,802	5,877,847	5,948,493	6,227,955	5,936,688	5,743,498
Montana	1,128,565	1,094,338	1,395,263	1,382,045	1,373,069	1,316,548	1,352,917	1,334,478	1,276,112	1,318,649
Nebraska	2,457,060	2,417,506	2,303,467	2,202,196	2,170,630	2,170,016	2,306,692	2,192,338	2,064,173	1,981,940
Nevada	4,772,756	4,429,481	4,336,630	4,169,439	4,214,581	4,120,103	3,905,016	3,703,574	3,864,223	3,860,236
New Hampshire	831,584	460,600	573,048	1,268,583	1,300,770	1,226,012	1,191,097	1,261,454	1,278,589	1,451,976
New Jersey	11,662,914	11,672,318	12,470,093	12,104,168	11,102,269	11,789,109	11,167,301	11,877,592	11,135,809	10,927,571
New Mexico	4,878,597	4,986,006	4,871,707	4,604,669	4,500,634	4,450,387	4,325,766	4,322,463	4,766,207	4,363,063
New York	62,034,380	61,639,619	58,063,694	58,134,561	56,236,537	57,406,012	59,697,916	54,318,363	55,107,082	52,820,634
North Carolina	13,438,382	12,858,738	12,771,155	13,172,777	13,172,640	13,514,695	13,633,379	13,429,946	13,562,079	13,152,908
North Dakota	1,978,549	2,111,716	2,555,758	2,261,886	1,632,316	1,643,402	1,300,989	1,245,686	933,974	805,351
Ohio	18,796,046	18,552,156	17,872,592	16,647,880	16,517,064	17,932,406	18,488,325	18,348,743	18,963,232	18,080,744
Oklahoma	4,446,655	4,458,922	4,342,470	4,278,505	4,213,211	4,230,427	4,477,819	4,546,446	4,506,456	4,391,706
Oregon	5,732,009	5,551,653	6,209,293	6,007,393	5,495,337	5,657,912	5,774,682	5,864,882	5,703,775	5,640,993
Pennsylvania	22,256,314	20,050,597	19,407,646	18,835,531	18,834,325	18,526,116	19,944,576	18,871,434	19,144,305	17,826,902
Rhode Island	1,277,277	1,236,874	1,226,790	1,198,256	1,170,440	1,143,486	1,074,302	1,193,600	1,002,915	1,067,849
South Carolina	6,735,297	6,393,932	5,955,882	5,581,255	5,454,008	5,312,018	5,585,665	5,369,519	5,520,979	5,719,235
South Dakota	863,182	775,059	784,855	745,993	740,104	753,622	774,778	737,190	707,862	679,868
Tennessee	7,882,887	7,617,664	7,233,618	7,221,663	7,074,682	7,181,421	7,104,790	6,664,828	6,797,935	6,516,598
Texas	30,619,865	31,763,445	29,951,157	29,191,904	27,590,295	29,860,716	29,665,803	27,461,315	29,252,364	26,089,474
Utah	3,767,592	3,511,958	3,344,201	3,266,053	3,069,082	3,029,283	3,106,230	3,027,680	3,120,527	3,050,173
Vermont	1,800,627	1,771,590	1,725,060	1,695,983	1,501,657	1,636,024	1,552,853	1,518,129	1,532,766	1,340,755
Virginia	11,927,574	12,466,977	12,584,936	11,792,595	11,255,705	11,653,818	11,489,163	10,959,394	11,894,394	11,260,089
Washington	12,690,612	11,871,289	11,017,248	10,438,534	9,777,797	9,530,116	9,346,712	9,798,444	10,043,789	9,143,766
West Virginia	2,457,100	2,385,313	2,344,701	2,413,663	2,469,535	2,618,032	2,533,582	2,382,633	2,232,558	2,131,100
Wisconsin	8,826,031	9,031,939	10,387,801	9,890,474	9,637,247	9,741,343	10,428,954	10,253,124	10,199,520	9,881,119
Wyoming	3,083,271	1,867,516	2,097,456	1,913,090	1,681,018	1,702,814	1,653,068	1,760,946	1,919,231	1,769,009

Source: U.S. Census Bureau, Census of Governments: Finance (years ending in "2" and "7"), and Annual Survey of State Government Finances (remaining years).

Notes:

1. Data users who create their own estimates using these data should cite only the U.S. Census Bureau as the source of the original data. Data in this table are based on information from public records and contain no confidential data. Although the data in this table come from a census of governmental units and are not subject to sampling error, the census results may contain nonsampling error. Additional information on nonsampling error, response rates, and definitions may be found within the survey methodology https://www.census.gov/programs-surveys/state/technical-documentation/methodology.html.

2. Includes payments to the federal government, primarily state reimbursements for the supplemental security income program. The statistics reflect state government fiscal years that end on June 30, except for four states with other ending dates: Alabama and Michigan (September 30), New York (March 31), and Texas (August 31).

3. Detail may not add to total due to rounding.

TABLE 2.3
State Intergovernmental Expenditures, By Function and By State: 2017 (In thousands of dollars)

State	Total	General local government support	Education	Public Welfare	Highways	Health	Miscellaneous and combined
United States	$549,908,261	$31,718,872	$372,997,261	$60,129,920	$20,276,398	$18,505,675	$46,280,135
Alabama	6,931,626	356,061	5,259,061	104,850	11,548	136,784	1,063,322
Alaska	1,829,640	53,754	1,130,946	157,657	710	82,638	403,935
Arizona	8,094,626	1,964,694	4,678,463	298,320	800,792	75,988	276,369
Arkansas	5,373,102	300,426	4,598,451	2	268,009	1,608	204,606
California	107,877,299	308,210	61,295,098	30,522,269	3,172,666	6,124,555	6,454,501
Colorado	7,604,250	191,196	5,126,484	995,774	559,138	120,905	610,753
Connecticut	9,190,177	593,280	7,274,962	542,356	100,674	136,025	542,880
Delaware	1,583,343	0	1,438,961	9,047	5,573	10,881	118,881
Florida	21,484,868	3,013,095	15,879,095	0	1,170,283	938	1,421,457
Georgia	12,325,151	0	10,767,580	470,476	298,540	238,015	550,540
Hawaii	328,020	255,039	141	1,364	5,599	31	65,846
Idaho	2,408,604	269,457	1,896,300	3,966	184,196	5,748	48,937
Illinois	19,192,558	3,737,897	9,890,844	2,384,818	733,425	161,289	2,284,285
Indiana	9,987,853	624,361	8,142,033	47,632	862,317	22,370	289,140
Iowa	5,505,683	323,802	3,870,881	127,163	697,955	137,443	348,439
Kansas	4,860,179	77,135	4,366,424	6,028	256,088	55,941	98,563
Kentucky	5,730,213	0	5,012,709	103,154	140,036	135,305	339,009
Louisiana	6,415,070	154,737	5,026,770	0	73,484	0	1,160,079
Maine	2,428,618	48,983	2,244,040	18,670	107,077	106	9,742
Maryland	9,631,764	151,491	6,997,707	2,954	183,299	995,661	1,300,652
Massachusetts	9,129,315	1,484,072	6,048,888	248,160	366,224	72,154	909,817
Michigan	21,279,004	1,287,619	14,191,972	3,051,931	1,542,163	152,414	1,052,905
Minnesota	13,546,867	1,679,347	9,366,127	741,188	1,025,156	112,915	622,134
Mississippi	4,527,299	967,735	2,737,066	323,034	101,670	117,411	280,383
Missouri	6,298,000	217,665	5,690,280	3,048	158,530	1,457	227,020
Montana	1,128,565	214,405	881,828	0	16,677	2,024	13,631
Nebraska	2,457,060	558,013	1,622,091	51,866	15,706	45,034	164,350
Nevada	4,772,756	1,342,547	3,089,378	175,574	89,929	25,816	49,512
New Hampshire	831,584	68,805	281,860	390,757	65,565	0	24,597
New Jersey	11,662,914	1,114,578	7,727,157	1,761,368	164,760	52,577	842,474
New Mexico	4,878,597	1,498,637	3,151,767	0	25,467	30,513	172,213
New York	62,034,380	1,224,390	32,990,231	8,630,559	1,222,966	5,803,772	12,162,462
North Carolina	13,438,382	0	11,106,423	1,406,182	259,125	198,297	468,355
North Dakota	1,978,549	380,020	1,151,708	33,536	129,285	12,840	271,160
Ohio	18,796,046	1,602,815	12,251,654	2,199,896	587,848	438,657	1,715,176
Oklahoma	4,446,655	147,983	3,532,185	36,627	395,171	175,248	159,451
Oregon	5,732,009	136,905	4,742,323	328,545	13,494	55,744	454,998
Pennsylvania	22,256,314	233,927	14,778,662	1,965,221	922,163	1,018,974	3,337,367
Rhode Island	1,277,277	65,989	1,104,921	87,221	7,726	0	11,420
South Carolina	6,735,297	1,885,177	4,218,590	102,384	120,394	57,704	351,048
South Dakota	863,182	27,792	679,734	2,069	70,163	10,307	73,117
Tennessee	7,882,887	340,501	5,593,696	943,643	240,705	91,079	673,263
Texas	30,619,865	299,147	27,292,729	864,411	215,747	333,565	1,614,266
Utah	3,767,592	0	3,618,314	19,228	46,143	27,277	56,630
Vermont	1,800,627	25,469	1,656,183	0	64,306	0	54,669
Virginia	11,927,574	659,263	7,479,979	682,811	1,246,843	547,115	1,311,563
Washington	12,690,612	135,797	10,709,343	8,301	678,683	405,981	752,507
West Virginia	2,457,100	133,169	2,018,417	28,654	12,354	59,004	205,502
Wisconsin	8,826,031	41,781	6,973,453	247,135	821,797	215,240	526,625
Wyoming	3,083,277	1,521,716	1,413,352	71	18,229	325	129,584

Source: U.S. Census Bureau, 2017 Annual Survey of State Government Finances.

Notes:

1. Data users who create their own estimates using these data should cite only the U.S. Census Bureau as the source of the original data. Data in this table are based on information from public records and contain no confidential data. Although the data in this table come from a census of governmental units and are not subject to sampling error, the census results may contain nonsampling error. Additional information on nonsampling error, response rates, and definitions may be found within the survey methodology https://www.census.gov/programs-surveys/state/technical-documentation/methodology.html.

2. Detail may not add to total due to rounding.

Table 2.3 | State Intergovernmental Expenditures

Total State Intergovernmental Expenditures *(in thousands of dollars)*

HIGHEST

HIGHEST	LOWEST
California • $107,877,299	Hawaii • $328,020
New York • $62,034,380	New Hampshire • $831,584
Texas • $30,619,865	South Dakota • $863,182
Pennsylvania • $22,256,314	Montana • $1,128,565
Florida • $21,484,868	Rhode Island • $1,277,277

Highest and Lowest Spending by Category *(in thousands of dollars)*

EDUCATION

- CA • $61,295,098
- NY • $32,990,231
- TX • $27,292,729
- FL • $15,879,095
- PA • $14,778,662
- RI • $1,104,921
- MT • $881,828
- SD • $679,734
- NH • $281,860
- HI • $141

HEALTH

- CA • $6,124,555
- NY • $5,803,772
- PA • $1,018,974
- MD • $995,661
- VA • $547,115
- HI • $31
- LA • $0
- NH • $0
- RI • $0
- VT • $0

PUBLIC WELFARE

- CA • $30,522,269
- NY • $8,630,559
- MI • $3,051,931
- IL • $2,384,818
- OH • $2,199,896
- FL • $0
- LA • $0
- MT • $0
- NM • $0
- VT • $0

HIGHWAYS

- CA • $3,172,666
- MI • $1,542,163
- VA • $1,246,843
- NY • $1,222,966
- FL • $1,170,283
- AL • $11,548
- RI • $7,726
- HI • $5,599
- DE • $5,573
- AK • $710

TABLE 2.4

State Intergovernmental Expenditures, By Type of Receiving Government and By State: 2017
(In thousands of dollars)

State	Total intergovernmental expenditure	Federal	School districts	Other local governments
United States	$549,908,261	$3,228,642	$303,084,115	$243,595,504
Alabama	6,931,626	0	5,080,209	1,851,417
Alaska	1,829,640	0	0	1,829,640
Arizona	8,094,626	0	4,635,964	3,458,662
Arkansas	5,373,102	398	4,598,451	774,253
California	107,877,299	2,886,443	57,394,804	47,596,052
Colorado	7,604,250	1,138	5,124,098	2,479,014
Connecticut	9,190,177	0	254,624	8,935,553
Delaware	1,583,343	1,026	1,417,647	164,670
Florida	21,484,868	0	15,600,139	5,884,729
Georgia	12,325,151	0	10,767,009	1,558,142
Hawaii	328,020	382	0	327,638
Idaho	2,408,604	0	1,892,300	516,304
Illinois	19,192,558	5,900	9,846,688	9,339,970
Indiana	9,987,853	2,125	8,142,033	1,843,695
Iowa	5,505,683	0	3,870,700	1,634,983
Kansas	4,860,179	62	4,366,424	493,693
Kentucky	5,730,213	0	4,912,940	817,273
Louisiana	6,415,070	0	5,015,812	1,399,258
Maine	2,428,618	0	695,652	1,732,966
Maryland	9,631,764	0	0	9,631,764
Massachusetts	9,129,315	12,328	898,065	8,218,922
Michigan	21,279,004	5,368	14,191,972	7,081,664
Minnesota	13,546,867	0	9,361,878	4,184,989
Mississippi	4,527,299	0	2,737,066	1,790,233
Missouri	6,298,000	30,909	5,690,007	577,084
Montana	1,128,565	0	881,828	246,737
Nebraska	2,457,060	51,866	1,622,091	783,103
Nevada	4,772,756	1,721	3,089,378	1,681,657
New Hampshire	831,584	0	181,246	650,338
New Jersey	11,662,914	16,500	5,682,189	5,964,225
New Mexico	4,878,597	0	3,151,767	1,726,830
New York	62,034,380	0	17,964,131	44,070,249
North Carolina	13,438,382	0	0	13,438,382
North Dakota	1,978,549	0	1,141,110	837,439
Ohio	18,796,046	4,824	12,245,707	6,545,515
Oklahoma	4,446,655	38,999	3,522,580	885,076
Oregon	5,732,009	0	4,725,694	1,006,315
Pennsylvania	22,256,314	125,138	14,223,697	7,907,479
Rhode Island	1,277,277	18,735	66,295	1,192,247
South Carolina	6,735,297	0	4,175,166	2,560,131
South Dakota	863,182	0	679,734	183,448
Tennessee	7,882,887	1,710	335,617	7,545,560
Texas	30,619,865	0	27,103,756	3,516,109
Utah	3,767,592	1	3,618,314	149,277
Vermont	1,800,627	0	1,656,183	144,444
Virginia	11,927,574	14	0	11,927,560
Washington	12,690,612	0	10,663,032	2,027,580
West Virginia	2,457,100	0	2,005,466	451,634
Wisconsin	8,826,031	0	6,441,300	2,384,731
Wyoming	3,083,277	23,055	1,413,352	1,646,870

Source: U.S. Census Bureau, 2017 Annual Survey of State Government Finances.

Notes:

1. Data users who create their own estimates using these data should cite only the U.S. Census Bureau as the source of the original data. Data in this table are based on information from public records and contain no confidential data. Although the data in this table come from a census of governmental units and are not subject to sampling error, the census results may contain nonsampling error. Additional information on nonsampling error, response rates, and definitions may be found within the survey methodology *https://www.census.gov/programs-surveys/state/technical-documentation/methodology.html*.

2. Detail may not add to total due to rounding.

TABLE 2.5
State Intergovernmental Revenue from Federal and Local Governments: 2017
(In thousands of dollars)

State	Total intergovernmental revenue	From federal government Total (a)	Education	Public welfare	Heath & hospitals	Highways
United States	$656,283,270	$638,676,307	$83,301,859	$433,289,034	$26,333,544	$44,545,062
Alabama	9,949,247	9,857,029	1,676,402	6,402,819	251,239	829,164
Alaska	3,286,785	3,278,747	335,616	1,674,966	88,709	601,521
Arizona	15,247,776	14,985,446	1,713,482	11,711,961	263,789	812,245
Arkansas	7,916,365	7,865,670	803,750	5,323,189	122,829	779,349
California	93,013,830	88,470,052	10,851,621	67,019,954	1,614,595	4,603,873
Colorado	8,463,350	8,372,473	1,442,990	4,729,231	523,406	860,391
Connecticut	7,535,049	7,517,893	703,627	5,123,663	297,173	628,934
Delaware	2,415,919	2,345,980	244,658	1,521,585	100,754	207,338
Florida	27,852,122	27,543,372	4,422,382	17,134,705	2,306,009	2,216,451
Georgia	15,183,797	15,120,402	2,864,107	7,777,641	1,964,266	1,458,144
Hawaii	2,787,412	2,779,631	538,568	1,707,788	9,031	123,916
Idaho	2,622,679	2,605,787	386,195	1,441,955	214,889	266,853
Illinois	19,736,635	19,344,203	3,274,770	12,110,664	508,125	1,588,615
Indiana	14,712,679	14,629,767	1,609,030	10,806,057	335,188	991,461
Iowa	6,245,956	6,214,180	968,499	3,851,466	160,184	650,575
Kansas	4,160,844	4,112,926	745,654	2,318,033	229,620	463,638
Kentucky	10,829,538	10,787,958	427,357	8,553,461	224,707	786,098
Louisiana	12,636,842	12,146,564	1,409,768	8,192,527	237,187	767,160
Maine	3,020,597	2,943,046	294,330	2,037,309	46,538	223,119
Maryland	13,203,944	12,800,839	1,715,199	7,149,083	2,005,582	670,941
Massachusetts	16,331,054	15,740,268	1,528,870	11,019,623	446,426	557,860
Michigan	21,350,680	21,176,260	3,330,544	13,678,460	1,464,422	817,685
Minnesota	10,939,218	10,744,596	1,358,632	7,904,337	247,158	635,085
Mississippi	8,211,496	8,096,276	893,219	5,788,318	181,458	513,796
Missouri	11,322,122	11,130,640	1,278,689	6,540,337	1,754,065	862,709
Montana	3,054,845	3,049,060	320,025	1,574,341	361,154	446,531
Nebraska	3,179,745	3,101,736	200,846	2,358,036	2,166	322,304
Nevada	5,234,577	4,998,908	603,175	3,302,967	147,144	368,632
New Hampshire	2,720,430	2,330,182	223,275	1,432,522	41,628	185,853
New Jersey	18,615,719	17,973,775	1,982,527	11,075,919	507,574	974,870
New Mexico	7,226,565	6,997,655	778,306	5,312,884	151,523	381,579
New York	60,371,092	59,141,359	4,956,277	45,100,918	1,107,593	2,270,923
North Carolina	16,412,180	16,219,950	2,593,764	10,715,303	561,655	1,203,602
North Dakota	1,825,979	1,783,503	265,363	1,026,191	12,176	300,449
Ohio	24,305,702	23,665,806	2,528,813	18,145,559	402,433	1,449,162
Oklahoma	7,280,359	7,135,308	995,571	3,708,218	1,288,677	664,160
Oregon	9,988,321	9,957,896	1,320,640	7,157,952	413,869	494,215
Pennsylvania	29,475,131	29,243,846	3,430,502	21,898,182	445,114	1,975,227
Rhode Island	2,519,225	2,463,337	304,111	1,412,115	181,597	244,214
South Carolina	9,007,621	8,347,399	1,420,394	5,146,959	290,461	854,960
South Dakota	1,567,365	1,529,633	275,238	626,554	113,444	308,597
Tennessee	11,161,689	11,084,882	1,444,310	7,463,496	312,097	846,456
Texas	44,657,763	41,962,867	7,166,987	26,476,814	1,364,517	4,349,137
Utah	4,524,182	4,521,247	911,493	2,635,624	242,038	426,819
Vermont	1,991,516	1,989,234	251,688	1,199,472	64,099	231,884
Virginia	10,699,877	9,966,484	1,939,528	5,792,520	528,519	1,136,501
Washington	14,228,084	13,764,198	2,418,557	7,805,776	1,812,513	939,040
West Virginia	5,109,431	5,023,407	543,896	3,529,436	98,189	442,121
Wisconsin	9,583,175	9,361,012	1,443,541	6,423,910	234,316	588,801
Wyoming	2,566,761	2,453,618	165,073	448,234	51,699	222,104

See footnotes at end of table

TABLE 2.5

State Intergovernmental Revenue from Federal and Local Governments: 2017

(In thousands of dollars) (continued)

| State | Total (a) | | | From local governments | |
		Education	Public welfare	Health & hospitals	Highways
United States	$17,606,963	$5,224,391	$5,201,533	$1,137,735	$2,253,388
Alabama	92,218	13,176	0	7,349	46,548
Alaska	8,038	6,515	0	0	0
Arizona	262,330	9,577	186,956	306	30,474
Arkansas	50,695	49,167	0	83	0
California	4,543,778	311,491	2,678,895	11,289	567,015
Colorado	90,877	25,290	245	29	23,911
Connecticut	17,156	1,913	0	0	0
Delaware	69,939	66,448	0	0	0
Florida	308,750	16,367	0	224,757	0
Georgia	63,395	12,224	0	0	20,082
Hawaii	7,781	0	0	0	0
Idaho	16,892	380	11,295	0	5,215
Illinois	392,432	41,340	243,988	0	89,530
Indiana	82,912	6,293	1,292	0	75,317
Iowa	31,776	192	0	4,512	17,367
Kansas	47,918	12,062	17	782	30,536
Kentucky	41,580	25,363	0	0	0
Louisiana	490,278	2,750	365,973	0	28,096
Maine	77,551	10,959	0	0	64,610
Maryland	403,105	21,420	0	181,951	31,358
Massachusetts	590,786	26,817	0	0	0
Michigan	174,420	8,689	50,362	52,070	18,377
Minnesota	194,622	13,774	94,407	0	62,953
Mississippi	115,220	3,954	0	0	82,405
Missouri	191,482	2,310	123,360	15,013	42,258
Montana	5,785	0	5,076	0	0
Nebraska	78,009	58,027	275	6	19,512
Nevada	235,669	28,079	150,321	21,107	16,988
New Hampshire	390,248	3,971	372,212	0	2,868
New Jersey	641,944	302,223	0	90,564	129,870
New Mexico	228,910	64,511	23,242	140,630	0
New York	1,229,733	312,583	5,861	35,422	10,022
North Carolina	192,230	9,254	122,926	7,716	29,243
North Dakota	42,476	1	603	3,733	26,009
Ohio	639,896	34,217	380,203	25,771	77,992
Oklahoma	145,051	1,933	520	3,007	36,310
Oregon	30,425	16,975	0	0	0
Pennsylvania	231,285	204,045	0	839	14,228
Rhode Island	55,888	0	0	0	1,660
South Carolina	660,222	101,367	308,394	6,745	182,826
South Dakota	37,732	17,361	76	8,372	11,036
Tennessee	76,807	25,079	1,928	3,796	33,503
Texas	2,694,896	2,530,910	5,933	157,757	0
Utah	2,935	2,481	0	216	0
Vermont	2,282	0	0	0	2,257
Virginia	733,393	423,186	0	70,419	219,889
Washington	463,886	227,506	0	29,025	163,778
West Virginia	86,024	3,178	0	0	0
Wisconsin	222,163	73,694	67,094	32,280	25,973
Wyoming	113,143	95,339	79	2,189	13,372

Source: U.S. Census Bureau, 2017 Annual Survey of State Government Finances.

Notes:

1. Data users who create their own estimates using these data should cite only the U.S. Census Bureau as the source of the original data. Data in this table are based on information from public records and contain no confidential data. Although the data in this table come from a census of governmental units and are not subject to sampling error, the census results may contain nonsampling error. Additional information on nonsampling error, response rates, and definitions may be found within the survey methodology *https://www.census.gov/ programs-surveys/state/technical-documentation/methodology.html*.

2. Detail may not add to total due to rounding.

Key:

(a) Total includes other types of intergovernmental revenue not shown separately in this table.

Table 2.5 | State Intergovernmental Revenue

Total intergovernmental revenue *(in thousands of dollars)*

HIGHEST

LOWEST

HIGHEST	LOWEST
California • $93,013,830	South Dakota • $1,567,365
New York • $60,371,092	North Dakota • $1,825,979
Texas • $44,657,763	Vermont • $1,991,516
Pennsylvania • $29,475,131	Delaware • $2,415,919
Florida • $27,852,122	Rhode Island • $2,519,225

Highest and Lowest Federal Spending by Category *(in thousands of dollars)*

EDUCATION

- CA • $10,851,621
- TX • $7,166,987
- NY • $4,956,277
- FL • $4,422,382
- PA • $3,430,502
- VT • $251,688
- DE • $244,658
- NH • $223,275
- NE • $200,846
- WY • $165,073

HEALTH & HOSPITALS

- FL • $2,306,009
- MD • $2,005,582
- GA • $1,964,266
- WA • $1,812,513
- MO • $1,754,065
- ME • $46,538
- NH • $41,628
- ND • $12,176
- HI • $9,031
- NE • $2,166

PUBLIC WELFARE

- CA • $67,019,954
- NY • $45,100,918
- TX • $26,476,814
- PA • $21,898,182
- OH • $18,145,559
- RI • $1,412,115
- VT • $1,199,472
- ND • $1,026,191
- SD • $626,554
- WY • $448,234

HIGHWAYS

- CA • $4,603,873
- TX • $4,349,137
- NY • $2,270,923
- FL • $2,216,451
- PA • $1,975,227
- ME • $223,119
- WY • $222,104
- DE • $207,338
- NH • $185,853
- HI • $123,916

CHAPTER THREE

STATE LEGISLATIVE BRANCH

TABLE 3.1
Names of State Legislative Bodies and Convening Places

State or other jurisdiction	Both bodies	Upper house	Lower house	Convening place
Alabama	Legislature	Senate	House of Representatives	State House
Alaska	Legislature	Senate	House of Representatives	State Capitol
Arizona	Legislature	Senate	House of Representatives	State Capitol
Arkansas	General Assembly	Senate	House of Representatives	State Capitol
California	Legislature	Senate	Assembly	State Capitol
Colorado	General Assembly	Senate	House of Representatives	State Capitol
Connecticut	General Assembly	Senate	House of Representatives	State Capitol
Delaware	General Assembly	Senate	House of Representatives	Legislative Hall
Florida	Legislature	Senate	House of Representatives	The Capitol
Georgia	General Assembly	Senate	House of Representatives	State Capitol
Hawaii	Legislature	Senate	House of Representatives	State Capitol
Idaho	Legislature	Senate	House of Representatives	State Capitol
Illinois	General Assembly	Senate	House of Representatives	State House
Indiana	General Assembly	Senate	House of Representatives	State House
Iowa	General Assembly	Senate	House of Representatives	State Capitol
Kansas	Legislature	Senate	House of Representatives	State Capitol
Kentucky	General Assembly	Senate	House of Representatives	State Capitol
Louisiana	Legislature	Senate	House of Representatives	State Capitol
Maine	Legislature	Senate	House of Representatives	State House
Maryland	General Assembly	Senate	House of Delegates	State House
Massachusetts	General Court	Senate	House of Representatives	State House
Michigan	Legislature	Senate	House of Representatives	State Capitol
Minnesota	Legislature	Senate	House of Representatives	State Capitol
Mississippi	Legislature	Senate	House of Representatives	State Capitol
Missouri	General Assembly	Senate	House of Representatives	State Capitol
Montana	Legislature	Senate	House of Representatives	State Capitol
Nebraska	Legislature	----------------------- (a) -----------------------		State Capitol
Nevada	Legislature	Senate	Assembly	Legislative Building
New Hampshire	General Court	Senate	House of Representatives	State House
New Jersey	Legislature	Senate	General Assembly	State House
New Mexico	Legislature	Senate	House of Representatives	State Capitol
New York	Legislature	Senate	Assembly	State Capitol
North Carolina	General Assembly	Senate	House of Representatives	State Legislative Building
North Dakota	Legislative Assembly	Senate	House of Representatives	State Capitol
Ohio	General Assembly	Senate	House of Representatives	State House
Oklahoma	Legislature	Senate	House of Representatives	State Capitol
Oregon	Legislative Assembly	Senate	House of Representatives	State Capitol
Pennsylvania	General Assembly	Senate	House of Representatives	Main Capitol Building
Rhode Island	General Assembly	Senate	House of Representatives	State House
South Carolina	General Assembly	Senate	House of Representatives	State House
South Dakota	Legislature	Senate	House of Representatives	State Capitol
Tennessee	General Assembly	Senate	House of Representatives	State Capitol
Texas	Legislature	Senate	House of Representatives	State Capitol
Utah	Legislature	Senate	House of Representatives	State Capitol
Vermont	General Assembly	Senate	House of Representatives	State House
Virginia	General Assembly	Senate	House of Delegates	State Capitol
Washington	Legislature	Senate	House of Representatives	State Capitol
West Virginia	Legislature	Senate	House of Delegates	State Capitol
Wisconsin	Legislature	Senate	Assembly (b)	State Capitol
Wyoming	Legislature	Senate	House of Representatives	State Capitol
Dist. of Columbia	Council of the District of Columbia	----------------------- (a) -----------------------		Council Chamber
American Samoa	Legislature	Senate	House of Representatives	Maota Fono
Guam	Legislature	----------------------- (a) -----------------------		Congress Building
CNMI*	Legislature	Senate	House of Representatives	Civic Center Building
Puerto Rico	Legislative Assembly	Senate	House of Representatives	The Capitol
U.S. Virgin Islands	Legislature	----------------------- (a) -----------------------		Capitol Building

Source: The Council of State Governments, *Directory I–Elective Officials 2018.*
*Commonwealth of Northern Mariana Islands

Key:
(a) Unicameral legislature. Except in the District of Columbia, members go by the title Senator.
(b) Members of the lower house go by the title Representative.

TABLE 3.2
Legislative Sessions: Legal Provisions

State or other jurisdiction	Year	Regular sessions Legislature convenes Month	Day	Limitation on length of session (a)
Alabama	Annual	Jan.; Mar.; Feb.	2nd Tues. (b); 1st Tues. (c); 1st Tues. (d)(e)	30 L in 105 C
Alaska	Annual	Jan.	3rd Tues. (g)	121 C; 90 Statutory (g)
Arizona	Annual	Jan.	2nd Mon.	(h)
Arkansas	Annual	Jan.	2nd Mon.; 2nd Mon.	60 C (i); 30 C (i)
California	Biennium (k)	Jan.	1st Mon. (d)	None
Colorado	Annual	Jan.	No later than 2nd Wed.	120 C
Connecticut	Annual	Jan. (odd-yrs.); Feb. (even-yrs.)	Wed. after 1st Mon.	(m)
Delaware	Biennium	Jan.	2nd Tues.	June 30
Florida	Annual	Mar.	1st Tues. after 1st Mon. (o)	60 C (i)
Georgia	Annual	Jan.	2nd Mon.	40 L
Hawaii	Annual	Jan.	3rd Wed.	60 L (i)
Idaho	Annual	Jan.	Mon. on or nearest 9th day	None
Illinois	Biennium	Jan.	2nd Wed.	None (q)
Indiana	Annual	Jan.	2nd Mon. (r)	odd–61 C or Apr. 29; even–30 C or Mar. 14
Iowa	Annual	Jan.	2nd Mon.	None (bbb)
Kansas	Annual	Jan.	2nd Mon.	odd–None; even–90 C (i)
Kentucky	Annual	Jan.	1st Tues. after 1st Mon.	even–60 L; odd–30 L (s)
Louisiana	Annual	Mar. (even-years); Apr. (odd-years)	2nd Mon. (even- and odd-years)	even–60 L in 85 C; odd–45 L in 60 C
Maine	(t)	Dec. (even-years); Jan. (subsequent even-year)	1st Wed. (quadrennial election year); Wed. after 1st Tues.	Calendar days set by statute (u)
Maryland	Annual	Jan.	2nd Wed.	90 C
Massachusetts	Biennium	Jan.	1st Wed.	(v)
Michigan	Annual	Jan.	2nd Wed.	None
Minnesota	Biennium	Jan.	1st Tues. after 1st Mon. (odd-years)	120 L
Mississippi	Annual	Jan.	Tues. after 1st Mon.	125 C (y); 90 C (y)
Missouri	Annual	Jan.	Wed. after 1st Mon.	May 30
Montana	Biennial	Jan.	1st Mon. (vv)	90 L
Nebraska	Annual	Jan.	Wed. after 1st Mon.	odd–90 L; even–60 L
Nevada	Biennial	Feb.	1st Mon.	120 C
New Hampshire	Annual	Jan.	Wed. after 1st Tues.	45 L
New Jersey	Biennium	Jan.	2nd Tues. of even year	None
New Mexico	Annual	Jan.	3rd Tues.	odd–60 C; even–30 C
New York	Annual	Jan. (dd)	Wed. after 1st Mon.	None
North Carolina	(ee)	Jan.	3rd Wed. after 2nd Mon. (odd-years)	None
North Dakota	Biennial–odd year	Jan.	First Tues. after the third day in Jan.	80 L in the biennium
Ohio	Biennium	Jan.	1st Mon. (gg)	None
Oklahoma	Annual	Feb.	1st Mon.	last Fri. in May
Oregon	Annual	Feb.	1st Mon.	(ff)
Pennsylvania	Biennium (hh)	Jan.	1st Tues.	None
Rhode Island	Annual	Jan.	1st Tues.	None
South Carolina	Biennium	Jan.	2nd Tues.	(ii)
South Dakota	Annual	Jan.	2nd Tues.	odd–40 L; even–40 L
Tennessee	Biennium (kk)	Jan.	2nd Tues.	90 L (ll)
Texas	Biennial–odd year	Jan.	2nd Tues.	140 C
Utah	Annual	Jan.	4th Mon.	45 C
Vermont	Annual (yy)	Jan.	Wed. after 1st Mon. (yy)	None
Virginia	Annual	Jan.	2nd Wed.	odd–30 C (i); even–60 C (i)
Washington	Annual	Jan.	2nd Mon.	odd–105 C; even–60 C
West Virginia	Annual	Jan	2nd Wed.	60 C (i)
Wisconsin	Biennium	Jan.	1st Mon.	None
Wyoming	Biennium	Jan. (odd-yrs.); Feb. (even-yrs.)	2nd Tues. (odd-yrs.); 2nd Mon. (even-yrs.)	odd–40 L; even–20 L; biennium–60 L
Dist. of Columbia	(oo)	Jan.	2nd day	None
American Samoa	Annual	Jan.; July	2nd Mon.; 3rd Mon.	45 L; 45 L
Guam	(pp)	Jan.	2nd Mon.	None (pp)
CNMI*	Annual	(rr)	(d)(rr)	90 L (qq)
Puerto Rico	Annual (rr)	Jan.; Aug.	2nd Mon.; 3rd Mon.	5 mo.; 4 mo.
U.S. Virgin Islands	Annual	Jan. (ss)	2nd Mon. (ss)	None

See footnotes at end of table

TABLE 3.2
Legislative Sessions: Legal Provisions (continued)

State or other jurisdiction	Special sessions Legislature may call	Legislature may determine subject	Limitation on length of session
Alabama	No	Yes (f)	12 L in 30 C
Alaska	By petition, 2/3 members, each house	Yes	30 C
Arizona	By petition, 2/3 members, each house	Yes	None
Arkansas	No	No	None (j)
California	No	No	None
Colorado	By petition, 2/3 members, each house	Yes (l)	None
Connecticut	By petition, majority, each house (n)	Yes	None
Delaware	Joint call, presiding officers, both houses	Yes	None
Florida	Joint call, presiding officers, both houses or by petition	Yes	20 C (zz)
Georgia	By petition, 3/5 members, each house	No (p)	40 L
Hawaii	By petition, 2/3 members, each house (uu)	Yes	30 L (i)
Idaho	No	No	20 C
Illinois	Joint call, presiding officers, both houses; Governor also may call	Yes	None
Indiana	No	Yes	30 L or 40 C
Iowa	By petition, 2/3 members, each house	Yes	None
Kansas	Petition to governor of 2/3 members, each house	Yes	None
Kentucky	No	No	None
Louisiana	By petition, majority, each house	Yes	30 C
Maine	Joint call, presiding officers of both houses with the consent of a majority of the members of each political party	Yes	None
Maryland	By petition, majority, each house	Yes	30 C
Massachusetts	By petition (w)	Yes	None
Michigan	No	No	None
Minnesota	No (x)	Yes	None
Mississippi	No	No	None
Missouri	By petition, 3/4 members, each house	Yes (l)	30 C (z)
Montana	By petition, majority, each house (ww)	Yes	None
Nebraska	By petition, 2/3 members, each house	Yes	None
Nevada	By petition, 2/3 members, each house	Yes (aa)	20 C (aa)
New Hampshire	By petition, (xx)	Yes	15 L (bb)
New Jersey	By petition, majority, each house (cc)	Yes	None
New Mexico	By petition, 3/5 members, each house (l)	Yes (l)	30 C
New York	By petition, 2/3 members, each house	Yes (l)	None
North Carolina	By petition, 3/5 members, each house	Yes	None
North Dakota	No	Yes	None
Ohio	Joint call, presiding officers, both houses	Yes	None
Oklahoma	By petition, 2/3 members, each house	Yes	None
Oregon	By petition, majority, each house	Yes	None
Pennsylvania	Governor may call	No	None
Rhode Island	Joint call, presiding officers, both houses	Yes	None
South Carolina	By vote, 2/3 members, each house	Yes	None
South Dakota	By petition, 2/3 members, each house	Yes (jj)	None
Tennessee	By petition, 2/3 members, each house	Yes	30 L (ll)
Texas	No	No	30 C
Utah	No	No	30 C
Vermont	No	Yes	None
Virginia	(tt)	Yes	None (mm)
Washington	By vote, 2/3 members, each house	Yes	30 C
West Virginia	By petition, 3/5 members, each house	Yes (l)	None
Wisconsin	(nn)	No	None
Wyoming	By petition, majority members, each house	Yes	20 L (aaa)
Dist. of Columbia	...	...	...
American Samoa	No	No	None
Guam	Only the governor may call	No	None (pp)
CNMI*	Upon request of presiding officers, both houses	Yes (j)	10 C
Puerto Rico	No	No	20 C
U.S. Virgin Islands	No, governor calls	No	None

See footnotes at end of table

TABLE 3.2
Legislative Sessions: Legal Provisions (continued)

Source: The Council of State Governments survey January 2019.
*Commonwealth of Northern Mariana Islands
Key:
Annual–holds legislative sessions every year.
Biennial-odd year–holds legislative sessions every other year.
Biennium–holds legislative sessions in a two-year term of activity.
C–Calendar day
L–Legislative day (in some states called a session day or workday; definition may vary slightly, however, generally refers to any day on which either house of legislature is in session).
(a) Applies to each year unless otherwise indicated.
(b) General election year (quadrennial election year).
(c) In first year after quadrennial election.
(d) Legal provision for organizational session prior to stated convening date.
Alabama–in the year after quadrennial election, second Tuesday in January for 10 C.
California–in the even-numbered general election year, first Monday in December for an organizational session, recess until the first Monday in January of the odd-numbered year.
Commonwealth of Northern Mariana Islands–in year after general election, second Monday in January.
(e) In second and third years of quadrennium.
(f) By 2/3 vote each house.
(g) Convening date is statutory. Length of session is 121 calendar days, 90 by statute.
(h) No constitutional or statutory provision; however, by legislative rule regular sessions shall be adjourned sine die no later than Saturday of the week during which the 100th day from the beginning of each regular session falls. The Speaker/President may by declaration authorize the extension of the session for a period not to exceed seven additional days. Thereafter the session can be extended only by a majority vote of the House/Senate.
(i) Session may be extended by vote of members in both houses. Arkansas–2/3 vote to extend up to 75 days; 3/4 vote to go beyond 75 days. Even-year fiscal session may be extended one-time only by a 3/4 vote, with the extension no more than 15 C days. Florida–3/5 vote, session may be extended by vote of members in each house. Hawaii–petition of 2/3 membership for maximum 15-day extension. Kansas–2/3 vote. Virginia–2/3 vote for 30 C extension. West Virginia–may be extended by the governor.
(j) After governor's business has been disposed of, members may remain in session up to 15 C days by a 2/3 vote of both houses.
(k) Regular sessions begin after general election, in December of even-numbered year. In California, in the even-numbered general election year, first Monday in December for an organizational session, recess until the first Monday in January of the odd-numbered year.
(l) Only if legislature convenes itself. In New York, special sessions may also be called by the governor. Legislature may determine subject only if it has convened itself. In New Mexico, special sessions may only be called by the governor and subjects are limited to issues included in governor's proclamation; extraordinary session may only be called by the legislature and have no limitations on subject.

(m) Odd-numbered years–not later than Wednesday after first Monday in June; even-numbered years– not later than Wednesday after first Monday in May.
(n) Adoption of a joint resolution by a majority of each house.
(o) A regular session of the legislature shall convene on the first Tuesday after the first Monday of each odd-numbered year, and on the first Tuesday after the first Monday in March, or such other date as may be fixed by law, of each even-numbered year.
(p) If three-fifths of the General Assembly certifies to governor that an emergency exists, governor must convene a special session for all purposes.
(q) Constitution encourages adjournment by May 31.
(r) Legislators may reconvene at any time after organizational meeting; however, second Monday in January is the final date by which regular session must be in process.
(s) During the odd-year session, the members convene for four days, then break until February.
(t) Regular session begins after general election in even-numbered years. Session which begins in December of general election year runs into the following year (odd-numbered); second session begins in next even-numbered year. The second session is limited to budgetary matters; legislation in the governor's call; emergency legislation; legislation referred to committee for study.
(u) Statutory adjournment for the First Regular Session (beginning in December of even-numbered years and continuing into the following odd-numbered year) is the third Wednesday of June; statutory adjournment for the Second Regular Session (beginning in January of the subsequent even-numbered year) is the third Wednesday in April. The statutes provide for up to two extensions of up to five legislative days each for each session.
(v) Legislative rules say formal business must be concluded by Nov. 15th of the 1st session in the biennium, or by July 31st of the 2nd session for the biennium.
(w) Joint rules provide for the submission of a written statement requesting special session by a specified number of members of each chamber.
(x) Special session is called by the governor.
(y) 90 C sessions every year, except the first year of a gubernatorial administration during which the legislative session runs for 125 C.
(z) 30 C if called by legislature; 60 C if called by governor.
(aa) Legislature may determine the subject if it calls itself into special session. Special sessions are limited to 20 calendar days except in cases of impeachment of state and judicial officers or expulsion of a member of the Legislature.
(bb) Limitation is on legislative pay and mileage.
(cc) Or by joint call, presiding officers, both houses.
(dd) Session officially begins on the first Wednesday following the first Monday of the new legislative term (commencing the first of the year), and lasts until the legislature completes its business and adjourns sine die. However, over the past several years, both houses have adopted the tactic of declaring a recess at the call of the leaders, in order to facilitate easy recall of the legislature to override vetoes, etc. Over time the custom has become to formally adjourn both houses just before the new session opens. This leads to the rather interesting convention that when the governor calls the legislature into session, it is considered "special" or "executive," even though the regular session is ongoing.

TABLE 3.2
Legislative Sessions: Legal Provisions (continued)

(ee) Legal provision for session in odd-numbered year; however, legislature may divide, and in practice has divided, to meet in even-numbered years as well.

(ff) The Oregon Constitution establishes a maximum of 160 calendar days for an odd-year regular session and a maximum of 35 calendar days for an even-year regular session. Each regular session may be extended in five-day increments by the affirmative vote of two-thirds of the members of each house.

(gg) Unless Monday is a legal holiday; in second year, the General Assembly convenes on the same date.

(hh) Sessions are two years and begin on the 1st Tuesday of January of the odd-numbered year. Session ends on November 30 of the even-numbered year. Each calendar year receives its own legislative number.

(ii) The regular session ends the first Thursday in June; it can be extended with a two-thirds majority vote.

(jj) Legislators must address topic for which the special session was called.

(kk) Each General Assembly convenes for a First and Second Regular Session over a two-year period.

(ll) 90 legislative days over a two-year period. During special sessions members will be paid up to 30 legislative days; further days will be without pay or per diem.

(mm) No limitation, but the convening of the new General Assembly following an election would by operation end the special session.

(nn) The Legislature may call itself into Extraordinary Session on any subject by a majority vote of the organizing committees of each house, by joint resolution, or by a petition of a majority of each house. Only the governor may call a special session.

(oo) Each Council period begins on January 2 of each odd-numbered year and ends on January 1 of the following odd-numbered year.

(pp) Legislature meets on the first Monday of each month following its initial session in January. One legislative day or one special session day may become several calendar days. Special sessions may address only one subject.

(qq) 60 L before April 1 and 30 L after July 31.

(rr) Legislature meets twice a year. During general election years, the legislature only convenes on the January session.

(ss) The legislature convenes in January on the second Monday, March, June and September, the third Wednesday.

(tt) The Constitution provides that the governor must call a special session upon "application" of 2/3 of the members of each house.

(uu) Governor may call both houses of the legislature or the Senate alone into special session. Also, upon a 2/3 affirmative vote, the Senate may call itself into special session to consider judicial nominations.

(vv) If the first Monday falls on New Years Day, the Legislature convenes on the first Wednesday.

(ww) Majority of the total Legislature; i.e., 76 members of the combined 100-member House and 50-member Senate.

(xx) Petition filed with Secretary of State signed by not less than 50 members of House (not more than 10 from the same county) and not less than eight members of the Senate.

(yy) Constitutionally the sessions are convened biennially in the odd year. Since the late 1960s a second-year adjourned session has been held. Adjourned session date is legislatively set for a date during the first 10 days of January.

(zz) Session may be extended by 3/5 vote Per s. 11.011, Florida Statutes, if 20 percent of the members of the Legislature certify in writing that conditions warrant convening a special session, the Department of State shall, within seven days after receiving the required number of certificates, poll the members. Upon affirmative vote of 3/5 of the members of both houses, the Department of State shall fix the day and hour for convening the special session.

(aaa) Twenty legislative days if Legislature calls themselves. Unlimited if governor calls special session.

(bbb) No formal limitation, but legislator per diems are limited by statute to 110 calendar days during odd-year sessions and 100 calendar days during even-year sessions.

TABLE 3.3
The Legislators: Numbers, Terms, and Party Affiliations: 2019

State or other jurisdiction	Senate						House/Assembly						Senate and House/ Assembly totals
	Democrats	Republicans	Other	Vacancies	Total	Term	Democrats	Republicans	Other	Vacancies	Total	Term	
State and territory totals	900	1,082	10	13	2,072*	...	2,596	2,828	31	27	5,502	...	7,574*
State totals	857	1,049	4	13	1,972*	...	2,580	2,779	25	27	5,411	...	7,383*
Alabama	8	27	...	...	35	4	28	77	...	...	105	4	140
Alaska	7	13	...	...	20	4	16	22	1 (k)	1	40 (k)	2	60
Arizona	13	17	...	...	30	2	29	31	...	...	60	2	90
Arkansas	9	26	...	...	35	4	24	76	...	...	100	2	135
California	28	10	...	2	40	4	60	20	...	...	80	2	120
Colorado	19	16	...	...	35	4	41	24	...	...	65	2	100
Connecticut	20	13	...	3	36	2	90	59	...	2	151	2	187
Delaware	12	9	...	...	21	4 (g)	26	15	...	...	41	2	62
Florida	17	23	...	...	40	4	46	72	...	2	120	2	160
Georgia	21	35	...	...	56	2	75	103	...	2	180	2	236
Hawaii	24	1	...	...	25	4	46	5	...	...	51	2	76
Idaho	7	28	...	...	35	2	14	56	...	...	70	2	105
Illinois	40	19	...	...	59	(a)	72	44	...	2	118	2	177
Indiana	10	40	...	...	50	4	33	67	...	...	100	2	150
Iowa	18	32	...	...	50	4	46	54	...	...	100	2	150
Kansas	11	28	1 (b)	...	40	4	40	85	...	...	125	2	165
Kentucky	9	28	...	1	38	4	39	61	...	...	100	2	138
Louisiana (r)	14	25	...	...	39	4	36	59	3 (b)	7	105	4	144
Maine	21	14	...	...	35	2	88	57	6 (c)	...	151	2	186
Maryland	32	15	...	...	47	4	99	42	...	...	141	4	188
Massachusetts	34	6	...	...	40	2	127	32	1 (q)	...	160	2	200
Michigan	16	22	...	...	38	4 (p)	52	58	...	...	110	2 (p)	148
Minnesota	32 (d)	34	...	1	67	4	75 (d)	59	...	...	134	2	201
Mississippi	19	33	...	...	52	4	47	74	...	...	122	4	174
Missouri	10	24	...	...	34	4	47	115	...	1	163	2	197
Montana	20	30	...	...	50	4	42	58	...	...	100	2	150
Nebraska	-------- Nonpartisan election --------			...	49	4	------------------ Unicameral ------------------						49
Nevada	13	8	...	...	21	4	29	13	...	...	42	2	63
New Hampshire	14	10	...	...	24	2	233	167	...	...	400	2	424
New Jersey	25	15	...	...	40	4 (f)	53	26	...	1	80	2	120
New Mexico	26	16	...	...	42	4	46	24	...	...	70	2	112
New York	40	23	...	...	63	2	106	43	1 (e)	...	150	2	213
North Carolina	21	28	...	1	50	2	55	65	...	...	120	2	170
North Dakota	10	37	...	...	47	4	15	79	...	...	94	4	141
Ohio	9	23	...	1	33	4	38	60	...	1	99	2	132
Oklahoma	9	39	...	...	48	4	24	77	...	...	101	2	149
Oregon	18	12	...	...	30	4	38	22	...	...	60	2	90
Pennsylvania	21	28	...	1	50	4	91	110	...	2	203	2	253
Rhode Island	33	5	...	...	38	2	66	8	1 (b)	...	75	2	113
South Carolina	19	26	...	1	46	4	44	79	...	1	124	2	170
South Dakota	5	30	...	...	35	2	11	59	...	...	70	2	105
Tennessee	5	26	1 (b)	1	33	4	26	73	...	...	99	2	132
Texas	12	19	...	...	31	4	67	83	...	...	150	2	181
Utah	6	23	...	...	29	4	16	59	...	...	75	2	104
Vermont	22	6	2 (r)	...	30	2	94	42	12 (r)	2	150	2	180
Virginia	19	21	...	...	40	4	48	51	...	1	100	2	140
Washington	28	20	...	1	49	4	57	41	...	...	98	2	147
West Virginia	14	20	...	...	34	4	41	59	...	...	100	2	134
Wisconsin	14	19	...	...	33 (h)	4	35	63	...	1	99 (h)	2	132
Wyoming	3	27	...	...	30	4	9	51	...	...	60	2	90
Dist. of Columbia (i)	11	0	2 (b)	...	13	4	------------------ Unicameral ------------------						13
American Samoa	------------ Nonpartisan election ------------				18 (j)	4	------------ Nonpartisan election ------------				21 (j)	2	38
Guam	10	5	...	...	15	2	------------------ Unicameral ------------------						15
CNMI**	...	7	2 (b)	...	9	4	...	15	5 (b)	...	20	2	29
Puerto Rico	7 (m)	21(n)	2 (l)	...	30 (o)	4	16 (m)	34 (n)	1 (l)	...	51 (o)	4	78
U.S. Virgin Islands	15	...	...	...	15	2	------------------ Unicameral ------------------						15

See footnotes at end of table

TABLE 3.3
The Legislators: Numbers, Terms, and Party Affiliations: 2019 (continued)

Source: The Council of State Governments, January 2019.

*Note: Senate and combined body (Senate and House/Assembly) totals include Unicameral legislatures.

**Commonwealth of Northern Mariana Islands

Key:

…–Does not apply

(a) The entire Senate comes up for election in every year ending in "2" with districts based on the latest decennial Census. Senate districts are divided into three groups. One group elects senators for terms of four years, four years and two years; the second group for terms of four years, two years and four years; the third group for terms of two years, four years, and four years.

(b) Independent.

(c) Five Independent and Common Sense Independent.

(d) Democratic-Farmer-Labor.

(e) Independence Party.

(f) All 40 Senate terms are on a ten-year cycle which is made up of a 2-year term, followed by two consecutive four-year terms, beginning after the decennial census.

(g) Some terms of 2 years occur during reapportionment.

(h) All House seats contested in even-numbered years; In the Senate 17 seats contested in gubernatorial years; 16 seats contested in presidential years.

(i) Council of the District of Columbia.

(j) Senate: senators are not elected by popular vote, but by county council chiefs. House: 21 seats; 20 are elected by popular vote and one appointed, non-voting delegate from Swains Island.

(k) Non-affiliated.

(l) Senate: 1 Independent and 1 Puerto Rican Independence Party. House: 1 Puerto Rican Independence Party.

(m) Popular Democratic Party.

(n) New Progressive Party.

(o) Constitutionally, the Senate consists of 27 seats and the House consists of 51 seats. However, extra at-large seats can be granted to the opposition to limit any party's control to 2/3.

(p) If a person is elected or appointed to fill a vacancy for more than one-half of a term, it shall be counted as one of the 2 times.

(q) Unenrolled.

(r) Senate: 2 Progressive. House: 5 Independent and 7 Progressive.

Table 3.3 | Legislative Partisan Control

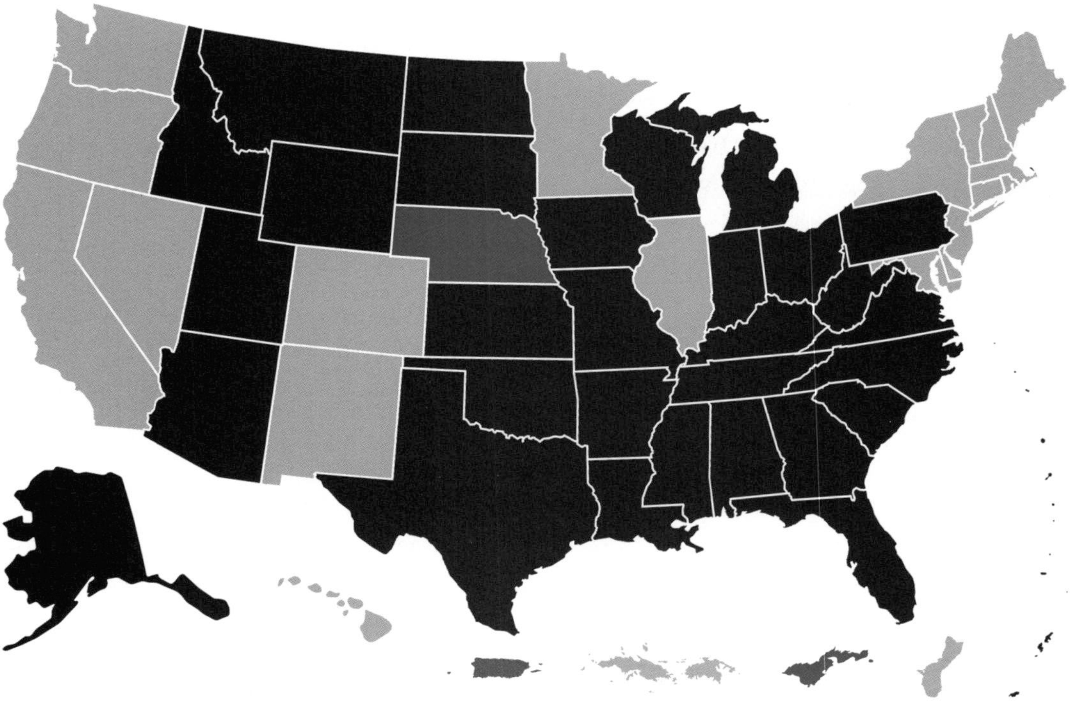

- ● Democrat (22, D.C. included)
- ● Republican (31)
- ● Split (0)
- ● Nonpartisan (2)
- ● New Progressive Party (1)

NEBRASKA IS THE ONLY STATE to have both a nonpartisan and unicameral legislature. It is also the smallest at 49 members.

Legislatures with highest percentage of Democrats

HI	RI	MA	CA	MD
92.1%	87.6%	80.5%	73.3%	69.7%

Legislatures with highest percentage of Republicans

WY	SD	ND	ID	UT
86.7%	84.7%	82.2%	80.0%	78.8%

TABLE 3.4
Membership Turnover in the Legislatures: 2018

State or other jurisdiction	Senate			House/Assembly		
	Total number of members	Number of membership changes	Percentage change of total	Total number of members	Number of membership changes	Percentage change of total
Alabama	35	13	37	105	29	28
Alaska	20	5	25	40	12	30
Arizona	30	14	47	60	25	42
Arkansas	35	8	23	100	25	25
California	40	9	23	80	8	10
Colorado	35	11	31	65	24	37
Connecticut	36	12	33	151	32	21
Delaware	21	4	19	41	12	29
Florida	40	9	23	120	44	37
Georgia	56	5	9	180	35	19
Hawaii	25	4	16	51	9	18
Idaho	35	5	14	70	21	30
Illinois	59	13	22	118	31	26
Indiana	50	5	10	100	18	18
Iowa	50	9	18	100	22	22
Kansas	40	4	10	125	30	24
Kentucky	38	2	5	100	33	33
Louisiana	39	1	3	105	3	3
Maine	35	12	34	151	54	36
Maryland	47	16	34	141	43	30
Massachusetts	40	5	13	160	25	16
Michigan	38	30	79	110	46	42
Minnesota	67	1	1	134	39	29
Mississippi	52	0	0	122	2	2
Missouri	34	10	29	163	62	38
Montana	50	10	20	100	32	32
Nebraska	49	13	27	---------------- Unicameral ----------------		
Nevada	21	7	33	42	12	29
New Hampshire	24	7	29	400	166	42
New Jersey	40	0	0	80	1	1
New Mexico	42	2	5	70	19	27
New York	63	17	27	150	19	13
North Carolina	50	14	28	120	27	23
North Dakota	47	7	15	94	12	13
Ohio	33	11	33	99	36	36
Oklahoma	48	12	25	101	47	47
Oregon	30	3	10	60	11	18
Pennsylvania	50	7	14	203	44	22
Rhode Island	38	7	18	75	15	20
South Carolina	46	1	2	124	19	15
South Dakota	35	8	23	70	25	36
Tennessee	33	4	12	99	28	28
Texas	31	6	19	150	29	19
Utah	29	7	24	75	19	25
Vermont	30	5	17	150	39	26
Virginia	40	0	0	100	2	2
Washington	49	6	12	98	22	22
West Virginia	34	5	15	100	35	35
Wisconsin	33	5	15	99	16	16
Wyoming	30	7	23	60	11	18
Dist. of Columbia	13	0	0	---------------- Unicameral ----------------		
American Samoa	18	2	11	20	8	40
Guam	15	8	53	---------------- Unicameral ----------------		
CNMI*	9	1	11	18	5	28
Puerto Rico	30	0	0	51	0	0
U.S. Virgin Islands	15	6	40	---------------- Unicameral ----------------		

Source: The Council of State Governments, January 2019.
*Commonwealth of Northern Mariana Islands

TABLE 3.5
Legislators: Qualifications for Election

State or other jurisdiction	Minimum age	U.S. citizen (years) (a)	House/Assembly State resident (years) (b)	District resident (years)	Qualified voter (years)
Alabama	21	...	3 (c)	1	★
Alaska	21	★	3	1	★
Arizona	25	★	3	1	...
Arkansas	21	★	2	1	★
California	18	3	3	1	★
Colorado	25	★	1	1	...
Connecticut	21	★	★	★	★
Delaware	24	★	3	1	...
Florida	21	...	2	...	★
Georgia	21	★	2 (c)	...	★
Hawaii	18	★	3	★	...
Idaho	21	★	1	...	...
Illinois	21	★	2	2 (d)	...
Indiana	21	★	2	1	...
Iowa	21	★	1	60 days	...
Kansas	18	★	★(c)	★	★
Kentucky	24	★	2 (c)	1	...
Louisiana	18	★	2	1	...
Maine	21	5	1	3 mo.	...
Maryland	21	...	1 (c)	6 mo. (e)	★
Massachusetts	18	...	...	1	★
Michigan	21	★	★	(f)	...
Minnesota	21	...	1	6 mo.	...
Mississippi	21	...	4 (c)	2	★
Missouri	24	★	★	1	2
Montana	18	...	1	6 mo. (g)	...
Nebraska	U	U	U	U	U
Nevada	21	★	1 (c)	30 days (h)	★
New Hampshire	18	...	2 (c)	★	...
New Jersey	21	★	2 (c)	2	...
New Mexico	21	★	★	★	...
New York	18	★	5	1 (i)	★
North Carolina	21	...	...	1	★
North Dakota	18	...	1	30 days in precinct	★
Ohio	18	★	30 days	1 (o)	...
Oklahoma	21	★	★(c)	★	★
Oregon	21	★	...	1	...
Pennsylvania	21	...	4 (c)	1	...
Rhode Island	18	★	30 days	...	★
South Carolina	21	...	...	★(j)	...
South Dakota	21	★	2	...	★
Tennessee	21	★	(c)	1	★
Texas	21	★	2	1	...
Utah	25	★	3 (c)	6 mo.	★
Vermont	...	★	2	1	★
Virginia	21	★	★	1	★
Washington	18	★	...	...	★
West Virginia	18	1	1 (c)	...	...
Wisconsin	18	★	1	★(k)	★(k)
Wyoming	21	★	★(c)	1	...
Dist. of Columbia	U	U	U	U	U
American Samoa	25	★(l)	5	1	...
Guam	U	U	U	U	U
CNMI*	21	...	3	(f)	★
Puerto Rico	25	★	2	1 (n)	...
U.S. Virgin Islands	U	U	U	U	U

See footnotes at end of table

TABLE 3.5
Legislators: Qualifications for Election (continued)

State or other jurisdiction	Minimum age	U.S. citizen (years) (a)	Senate State resident (years) (b)	District resident (years)	Qualified voter (years)
Alabama	25	...	3 (c)	1	★
Alaska	25	★	3	1	★
Arizona	25	★	3	1	...
Arkansas	25	★	2	1	★
California	18	3	3	1	★
Colorado	25	★	1	1	...
Connecticut	21	★	★	★	★
Delaware	27	★	3 (c)	1	...
Florida	21	...	2	...	★
Georgia	25	★	2 (c)	...	★
Hawaii	18	★	3	★	...
Idaho	21	★	1	...	★
Illinois	21	★	2	2 (d)	...
Indiana	25	2	2	1	...
Iowa	25	★	1	60 days	...
Kansas	18	★	★(c)	★	★
Kentucky	30	★	6 (c)	1	...
Louisiana	18	★	2	1	...
Maine	25	5	1	3 mo.	...
Maryland	25	...	1 (c)	6 mo. (e)	★
Massachusetts	18	...	5	(j)	★
Michigan	21	★	★	(f)	...
Minnesota	21	...	1	6 mo.	...
Mississippi	25	...	4 (c)	2	★
Missouri	30	★	★	1	3
Montana	18	...	1	6 mo. (g)	...
Nebraska	21	★	★(c)	1	...
Nevada	21	★	1 (c)	30 days (h)	★
New Hampshire	30	...	7 (c)	★	...
New Jersey	30	★	2 (c)	(j)	...
New Mexico	25	★	★	★	...
New York	18	★	5	1 (i)	★
North Carolina	25	...	2	1	★
North Dakota	18	...	1	30 days in precinct	★
Ohio	18	★	30 days	1 (o)	...
Oklahoma	25	★	★(c)	★	★
Oregon	21	★	★	1	...
Pennsylvania	25	...	4 (c)	1	...
Rhode Island	18	★	30 days	...	★
South Carolina	21	...	...	★(j)	...
South Dakota	21	★	2	...	★
Tennessee	30	★	3	1	★
Texas	26	★	5	1	...
Utah	25	★	3 (c)	6 mo.	★
Vermont	...	★	2	1	...
Virginia	21	★	★	1	★
Washington	18	★	...	...	★
West Virginia	25	5	5 (c)	...	...
Wisconsin	18	★	1	★(k)	★(k)
Wyoming	25	★	★(c)	1	...
Dist. of Columbia	18	...	1	★	★
American Samoa	30 (m)	★(l)	5	1	...
Guam	25	★	5	...	★
CNMI*	25	...	5	(f)	★
Puerto Rico	30	★	2	1 (n)	...
U.S. Virgin Islands	21	...	3 (c)	3	★

See footnotes at end of table

TABLE 3.5

Legislators: Qualifications for Election (continued)

Source: The Council of State Governments survey, January 2019 and state websites 2019.

*Commonwealth of Northern Mariana Islands

Note: Many state constitutions have additional provisions disqualifying persons from holding office if they are convicted of a felony, bribery, perjury or other infamous crimes.

Key:

U–Unicameral legislature; members are called senators, except in District of Columbia.

★–Formal provision; number of years not specified.

…–No formal provision.

(a) In some states candidate must be a U.S. citizen to be an elector, and must be an elector to run.

(b) In some states candidate must be a state resident to be an elector, and must be an elector to run.

(c) State citizenship requirement. In Tennessee, must be a citizen for three years.

(d) In the first election after a redistricting, a candidate may be elected from any district that contains a part of the district in which (s)he resided at the time of redistricting, and may be re-elected if a resident of the district (s)he represents for 18 months before re-election.

(e) If the district was established for less than six months, residency is length of establishment of district.

(f) Must be a qualified voter of the district; number of years not specified.

(g) Shall be a resident of the county if it contains one or more districts or if the district contains all or parts of more than one county.

(h) 30 days prior to close of filing for declaration of candidacy.

(i) After redistricting, candidate must have been a resident of the county in which the district is contained for one year immediately preceding election.

(j) At the time of filing.

(k) Twenty-eight days prior to election.

(l) Or U.S. national.

(m) Must be registered matai.

(n) The district legislator must live in the municipality he/she represents.

(o) One year unless absent from the district on the public business of the United States or Ohio.

TABLE 3.6
Senate Leadership Positions: Methods of Selection

State or other jurisdiction	President	President pro tem	Majority leader	Assistant majority leader	Majority floor leader	Assistant majority floor leader	Majority whip	Majority caucus chair
Alabama (b)	(a)	ES	(b)	...	...	...	...	...
Alaska	ES	...	EC	...	...	...	EC	EC
Arizona	ES	AP	EC	...	...	...	EC	...
Arkansas	(a)	ES	EC	...	...	...	EC	...
California	(a)	ES	EC	...	...	...	EC	EC
Colorado	ES	ES	EC	EC	...	...	EC	EC
Connecticut	(a)	ES (oo)	EC (pp)	AT (qq)	...	...	...	...
Delaware	(a)	ES	EC	...	...	...	EC	...
Florida (mm)	EC/ES	ES	AP	AL	...	...	...	...
Georgia	(a)	ES	EC	...	...	...	EC	EC
Hawaii	ES	ES (e)	EC	...	EC	...	EC	EC (f)
Idaho	(a)	ES	EC	EC	...	...	...	EC
Illinois	ES	AP	AP	AP	...	...	AP	AP
Indiana	(a)	ES	...	...	AT	AT	AT	EC
Iowa	ES	ES	EC	EC	...	...	EC	...
Kansas	ES	ES (e)	EC	EC	...	...	EC	EC
Kentucky (i)	ES	ES	...	...	EC	...	EC	EC
Louisiana	ES	ES	...	...	...	...	...	...
Maine (ll)	ES	ES	EC	EC	(j)	(j)	(k)	...
Maryland	ES	ES	AP (n)	AP (n)	(n)	(n)	AP	...
Massachusetts	EC	...	AP	AP	...	...	...	(p)
Michigan (q)	(a)	ES	EC	EC	EC	EC	EC	EC
Minnesota	ES	ES	EC	EC	...	...	AL	...
Mississippi	(a)	ES	...	...	...	...	...	...
Missouri (d)	(a)	ES	...	...	EC	EC	EC	EC
Montana	ES	ES	EC	...	EC (j)	...	EC	...
Nebraska (U)(g)	(a)	ES (r)	...	...	...	...	...	...
Nevada (s)	(a)	ES	...	...	EC	EC	EC (s)	...
New Hampshire	ES	AP	AP	...	...	...	...	...
New Jersey	ES	ES	MA	MA	MA	MA	MA	MA
New Mexico	(a)	ES	EC (t)	...	EC (t)	...	EC	EC
New York (u)	(a)	ES	(v)	AT (v)	AT (v)	...	AT	AT (v)
North Carolina	(a)	ES	EC	...	...	...	EC	EC
North Dakota	(a)	ES	EC	EC	...	...	...	EC
Ohio (w)(x)	ES (x)	ES	...	...	ES	...	ES	...
Oklahoma	(a)	ES	EC	EC	EC	EC	EC	EC
Oregon	ES	ES	EC	EC	...	...	EC	...
Pennsylvania	ES	ES	EC	EC	EC	EC	EC	EC
Rhode Island (y)	ES	ES	EC	AL	...	...	AL	...
South Carolina	(a)	ES	EC	...	...	...	...	...
South Dakota	(a)	ES	EC	EC	...	...	EC	...
Tennessee	ES	AP	EC	...	EC	EC	...	EC
Texas	(a)	ES	...	...	...	...	...	...
Utah	ES	AL (z)	EC	...	...	EC (z)	EC	...
Vermont	(a)	ES	EC	EC	EC (aa)	EC (aa)	EC (aa)	EC (aa)
Virginia	(a)	ES	EC (bb)	...	EC (bb)	...	...	EC
Washington (cc)	(a)	ES	EC	EC	EC	EC	EC	EC
West Virginia	ES	AP	AP	...	...	...	AP	...
Wisconsin	ES (dd)	ES	EC	EC	...	...	...	EC
Wyoming	ES	ES (e)	...	...	EC	...	...	...
Dist. of Columbia (U)	(ee)	(ff)	...	...	...	...	...	...
American Samoa	ES	ES	...	...	...	...	...	...
Guam (U)(gg)	ES (r)	ES (e)	EC	EC	EC	EC	EC	...
CNMI*	ES (hh)	...	(hh)	...	ES (ii)	...	...	...
Puerto Rico	ES (p)	EC	EC	EC (jj)	...	...	...	(kk)
U.S. Virgin Islands (U)	ES	...	ES	...	...	...	...	ES

See footnotes at end of table

TABLE 3.6
Senate Leadership Positions: Methods of Selection (continued)

State or other jurisdiction	Minority leader	Assistant minority leader	Minority floor leader	Assistant minority floor leader	Minority whip	Minority caucus chair
Alabama (b)	(b)	...	...	...	...	...
Alaska	EC	...	...	...	EC	EC
Arizona	EC	EC	...	...	EC	...
Arkansas	EC	...	...	...	EC	...
California	EC	...	...	...	EC	EC
Colorado	EC	EC	...	...	EC	EC
Connecticut	EC (rr)	AL (ss)	...	...	AL (c)	...
Delaware	EC	...	...	...	EC	EC
Florida (mm)	EC	EC	...	...	AL	AL
Georgia	EC	...	...	...	EC	EC
Hawaii	EC	...	EC	...	...	...
Idaho	EC	EC	...	...	...	EC
Illinois	EC	AL	...	...	AL	AL
Indiana	EC	...	EC	(h)	(h)	EC
Iowa	EC	EC	...	...	EC	...
Kansas	EC	EC	...	...	EC	EC
Kentucky (i)	...	...	EC	...	EC	...
Louisiana	...	...	...	...	...	...
Maine (ll)	EC	EC	(l)	(l)	(m)	...
Maryland	EC (o)	...	(o)	...	EC	...
Massachusetts	EC	...	...	...	...	(p)
Michigan (q)	EC	EC	EC	EC	EC	EC
Minnesota	EC	EC	...	...	EC	...
Mississippi	...	...	...	...	...	...
Missouri (d)	...	...	...	EC	EC	EC
Montana	EC	...	EC (l)	...	EC	...
Nebraska (U)(g)	...	...	...	...	...	...
Nevada (s)	...	...	EC	EC	EC	(nn)
New Hampshire	EC	...	...	...	AL	...
New Jersey	MI	MI	MI	MI	MI	MI
New Mexico	EC (t)	...	EC (t)	...	EC	EC
New York (u)	EC (v)	AL (v)	AL (v)	AL (v)	AL (v)	AL (v)
North Carolina	EC	...	...	...	EC	EC
North Dakota	EC	EC	...	...	...	EC
Ohio (w)(x)	ES (x)	ES	...	...	ES	...
Oklahoma	EC	EC	EC	EC	EC	EC
Oregon	EC	EC	...	...	EC	...
Pennsylvania	EC	EC	EC	EC	EC	EC
Rhode Island (y)	EC	AL	...	...	AL	...
South Carolina	EC	...	...	...	...	...
South Dakota	EC	EC	...	...	EC	...
Tennessee	EC	...	EC	...	...	EC
Texas	...	...	...	...	...	...
Utah	EC	...	...	EC (z)	EC	EC (z)
Vermont	EC	EC	EC (aa)	EC (aa)	EC (aa)	EC (aa)
Virginia	EC	...	EC	...	...	EC
Washington (cc)	EC	EC	EC	EC	EC	EC
West Virginia	EC	...	...	...	AL	...
Wisconsin	EC	EC	...	...	...	EC
Wyoming	...	...	EC	...	EC	EC
Dist. of Columbia (U)	...	...	...	...	...	...
American Samoa	...	...	...	...	...	...
Guam (U)(gg)	EC	EC	EC	EC	EC	...
CNMI*	EC	...	...	...	...	...
Puerto Rico	EC (p)	...	EC (jj)	...	...	(p)
U.S. Virgin Islands (U)	ES	...	...	...	...	ES

See footnotes at end of table

TABLE 3.6
Senate Leadership Positions: **Methods of Selection** (continued)

Sources: The Council of State Governments' survey, January 2019 and state websites 2019.

*Commonwealth of Northern Mariana Islands

Note: In some states, the leadership positions in the Senate are not empowered by the law or by the rules of the chamber, but rather by the party members themselves.

Key:

ES–Elected or confirmed by all members of the Senate.

EC–Elected by party caucus.

AP–Appointed by president.

AT–Appointed by president pro tempore.

AL–Appointed by party leader.

MA–Elected by majority party.

MI–Elected by minority party.

(U)–Unicameral legislative body.

…–Position does not exist or is not selected on a regular basis.

(a) Lieutenant governor is president of the Senate by virtue of the office. Idaho–(Idaho Const. art.IV, § 13, Senate Rule 1.)

(b) Majority leader elected by the members of the majority party. Minority leader elected by members of the minority party. Additional leadership positions: deputy president pro tempore–appointed by Committee on Assignments and Dean of Senate–appointed by Committee on Assignments.

(c) Evenly split–Senate Republican caucus has 3 Senate Republican Majority Whips.

(d) Additional positions of minority caucus secretary (EC) and majority caucus secretary (EC).

(e) Official title is vice president. In Guam, vice speaker.

(f) Official title is majority caucus leader.

(g) Additional positions appointed by the majority leader: Senate Finance Committee chair, vice president pro tem, Majority Program Development Committee Chair, Majority Steering Committee chair, two assistant majority leaders, various deputies and assistants. Additional positions appoint by the minority leader: Senate Finance Committee ranking member, Minority Policy Committee chair, Minority Program Development chair, three additional minority leaders, various deputies and assistants.

(h) Appointed by minority leader.

(i) In each chamber, the membership elects chief clerk; assistant clerk; enrolling clerk; sergeant-at-arms; doorkeeper; janitor; cloakroom keeper; and pages.

(j) Same position as majority leader.

(k) Same position as assistant majority leader.

(l) Same position as minority leader.

(m) Same position as assistant minority leader.

(n) Majority leader also serves as majority floor leader; deputy majority leader is official title and serves as assistant majority floor leader. There is also an assistant deputy majority leader, a majority whip, deputy majority whip, and two assistant majority whips.

(o) Minority leader also serves as the minority floor leader.

(p) President and minority floor leader are also caucus chairs. In Puerto Rico, president and minority leader. In Oregon, majority leader and minority leader.

(q) Senate Rule 1.104 provides that the president pro tempore (ES), assistant president pro tempore (ES), and the associate president pro tempore (ES) are elected by a majority of the Senate.

(r) Official title is speaker. In Guam the Speaker is elected on the Floor by majority and minority members on Inauguration Day.

(s) Co-whips elected for 2017 session.

(t) Majority leader also serves as majority floor leader. Minority leader also serves as minority floor leader.

(u) Majority, appointed by president pro tem: Assistant majority leader on conference operations, Deputy majority whip, Assistant Senate majority whip, Deputy majority leader for policy, et al. Minority, appointed by minority leader: Assistant democratic conference leader for conference operations, Vice chair of democratic conference, Deputy democratic conference whip, Assistant democratic conference whip, et al.

(v) President pro tem is also majority leader. Assistant majority leader is called deputy majority leader for legislative operations. Majority floor leader is called assistant majority leader for house operations. Majority caucus chair called Senate majority caucus chair. Minority leader is called democratic conference leader, and independent democratic conference leader (i.e. two minority conferences); voting usually falls along conference lines. Assistant minority leader is called deputy democratic conference leader and deputy independent democratic conference leader. Minority floor leader is called assistant democratic leader for floor operations. Assistant minority floor leader is called deputy democratic conference floor leader. Minority whip is called democratic conference whip, and independent democratic conference whip. Minority caucus chair is called chair of democratic conference.

(w) While the entire membership actually votes on the election of leaders, selections generally have been made by the members of each party prior to the date of this formal election.

(x) In Ohio president acts as majority leader and caucus chair; minority leader also acts as minority caucus chair; the fourth ranking minority leadership position is assistant minority whip (ES).

(y) Additional positions include deputy president pro tempore.

(z) President pro tem appointed by party leader via Legislative Rules, SR1-3-103. Official title for majority floor leader is known as the assistant majority whip; the assistant minority floor leader is known as the assistant minority whip and the minority caucus chair is known as minority caucus manager.

(aa) Majority leader serves as majority floor leader and majority caucus chair. Assistant majority leader serves as assistant majority floor leader and majority whip. Minority leader serves as minority floor leader and minority caucus chair. Assistant minority leader serves as assistant minority floor leader and minority whip.

(bb) Majority party and Minority party in Senate elects caucus officers.

(cc) Washington Senate also has the leadership position of vice-president pro tem.

(dd) Caucus nominee elected by whole membership.

(ee) Chair of the Council, which is an elected position.

(ff) Appointed by the chair; official title is chair pro tem.

(gg) Additional positions include: Parliamentarian, elected by majority caucus and Senior Senator, elected by majority caucus.

(hh) Speaker also serves as majority leader.

(ii) Official title is floor leader.

(jj) Official title is alternate floor leader.

(kk) Official title is caucus chair.

TABLE 3.6
Senate Leadership Positions: Methods of Selection (continued)

(ll) Secretary of the Senate and Assistant Secretary of the Senate, both elected by the Senate membership.

(mm) All positions other than president, president pro tempore and majority leader are party caucus designations.

(nn) Co-Minority Caucus Coordinators elected by party caucus.

(oo) Evenly split–Senate held by Democratic senator.

(pp) Evenly split–Senate Democratic caucus elects Majority Leader.

(qq) Evenly split–Senate Democratic caucus has 1 Chief Deputy President Pro Tempore, 8 Deputy Presidents Pro Tempore and 7 Deputy Majority Leaders.

(rr) Evenly split–Senate Republican caucus elects Senate Republican President Pro Tempore.

(ss) Evenly split–Senate Republican caucus has 1 Deputy Senate Republican President Pro Tempore, 3 Chief Deputy Senate Republican Majority Leaders, 3 Deputy Senate Republican Majority Leaders and 7 Assistant Senate Republican Majority Leaders.

TABLE 3.7
House/Assembly Leadership Positions: Methods of Selection

State or other jurisdiction	Speaker	Speaker pro tem	Majority leader	Assistant majority leader	Majority floor leader	Assistant majority floor leader	Majority whip	Majority caucus chair
Alabama	EH	EH	EC	...	...	...	...	...
Alaska	EH	...	EC	...	...	...	EC	EC
Arizona	EH	AS	EC	...	...	...	EC	...
Arkansas	EH	AS	EC	...	...	...	EC	...
California	EH	AS	...	...	AS	AS	AS	EC
Colorado (a)	EH	AS	EC	EC	...	...	EC	EC
Connecticut	EH	AS (b)	EC	(b)	...	AS	AS (b)	AS (b)
Delaware	EH	(hh)	EC	...	...	...	EC	...
Florida	EH	EH	AS	AS (ee)	...	...	AS (ee)	...
Georgia	EH	EH	EC	...	...	...	EC	EC
Hawaii (c)	EH	EH (d)	EC	EC	EC	EC	EC	...
Idaho	EH	...	EC	EC	...	...	...	EC
Illinois	EH	...	AS	AS (e)	...	...	...	AS (e)
Indiana	EH	AL	EC	AL	AL	AL	AL	AL
Iowa	EH	EH	EC	EC	...	...	EC	...
Kansas (f)	EH	EH	EC	EC	...	...	EC	EC
Kentucky (g)	EH	EH	...	...	EC	...	EC	EC
Louisiana	EH	EH	...	...	...	...	...	...
Maine (bb)	EH	AS (h)	EC (h)	EC (h)	(h)	(h)	(h)	...
Maryland (cc)	EH	EH (i)	AS (j)	AS (j)	(j)	AS	AS	(k)
Massachusetts	EC	...	AS	AS	...	...	...	...
Michigan (n)	EH	EH	...	...	EC	EC	EC	EC
Minnesota	EH	AS	EC	EC	...	...	EC	...
Mississippi	EH	EH	...	...	...	...	...	...
Missouri (ff)	EH	EH	...	...	EC	EC	EC	EC
Montana	EH	EH	...	...	...	...	EC	...
Nebraska				(o)				
Nevada (gg)	EH	EH	...	...	EC	EC	EC	...
New Hampshire	EH	AS (d)	AS	AS (dd)	...	...	AS	...
New Jersey	EH	EH	MA	MA	MA	MA	MA	MA
New Mexico	EH	...	EC	...	EC (m)	...	EC	EC
New York (p)	EH	AS	AS	AS	(p)	...	AS	AS (q)
North Carolina	EH	EH	EC	...	...	...	EC	EC
North Dakota	EH	...	EC	EC	...	...	...	EC
Ohio (r)	EH (k)	EH	...	...	EH	EH	EH	...
Oklahoma	EH	EH	AS	AS	AS	AS	AS	EC
Oregon	EH	EH	EC	EC	...	...	EC	...
Pennsylvania	EH	EH	EC	EC	EC	EC	EC	EC
Rhode Island	EH	EH	EC	AL	...	...	AL	...
South Carolina	EH	EH	EC	...	...	...	EC	...
South Dakota	EH	EH	EC	EC	...	...	EC	...
Tennessee	EH	EH	EC	EC	EC	...	EC	EC
Texas	EH	AS	...	...	...	...	...	...
Utah	EH	AS	EC	EC (s)	...	...	EC	...
Vermont	EH	...	EC	EC	(t)	(t)	(t)	(t)
Virginia (u)	EH	...	EC (v)	...	EC (v)	...	EC	EC
Washington	EH	EH	EC	EC	EC	EC	EC	EC
West Virginia	EH	AS	AS	AS	...	...	AS	AS
Wisconsin	EH (x)	EH (x)	EC	EC	...	...	...	EC
Wyoming	EH	EH	...	...	EC	...	EC	...
Dist. of Columbia				(o)				
American Samoa	EH	EH (d)	...	...	...	...	...	...
Guam				(o)				
CNMI*	EH (y)	...	(y)	...	EH (z)	...	...	...
Puerto Rico	EH (k)	EH (d)	EC	...	EC (aa)	...	...	...
U.S. Virgin Islands				(o)				

See footnotes at end of table

TABLE 3.7
House/Assembly Leadership Positions: Methods of Selection (continued)

State or other jurisdiction	Minority leader	Assistant minority leader	Minority floor leader	Assistant minority floor leader	Minority whip	Minority caucus chair
Alabama	EC	...	...	...	...	...
Alaska	EC	...	...	...	EC	EC
Arizona	EC	EC	...	EC	EC	...
Arkansas	EC	...	...	...	EC	...
California	EC	...	EC	EC	EC	EC
Colorado (a)	EC	EC	...	...	EC	EC
Connecticut	EC	AL (b)	...	...	AL (b)	AL (b)
Delaware	EC	...	...	...	EC	...
Florida	EC	EC (ee)	AL	...	AL (ee)	AL (ee)
Georgia	EC	...	...	...	EC	EC
Hawaii (c)	EC	EC	EC	EC	EC	...
Idaho	EC	EC	...	...	...	EC
Illinois	EC	(e)	...	...	...	AL (e)
Indiana	EC	AL	EC	AL	AL	AL
Iowa	EC	EC	...	...	...	...
Kansas (f)	EC	EC	...	...	EC	EC
Kentucky (g)	...	...	EC	...	EC	EC
Louisiana	...	...	...	...	...	...
Maine (bb)	EC (h)	EC (h)	(h)	(h)	(h)	...
Maryland (cc)	EC (l)	EC	EC (l)	EC (l)	EH	(k)
Massachusetts	EC	AL	...	...	...	...
Michigan (n)	EC	EC	EC	EC	EC	EC
Minnesota	EC	AL	...	...	...	...
Mississippi	...	...	...	...	...	...
Missouri (ff)	...	...	EC	EC	EC	EC
Montana	EC	...	...	...	EC	...
Nebraska	--- (o) ---
Nevada (gg)	...	...	EC	EC	EC	...
New Hampshire	AS	AL (dd)	...	...	...	...
New Jersey	MI	MI	MI	MI	MI	MI
New Mexico	EC	...	EC (m)	...	EC	EC
New York (p)	EH	AL	...	...	AL	AL (q)
North Carolina	EC	...	...	...	EC	EC
North Dakota	EC	EC	...	...	...	EC
Ohio (r)	EH (k)	EH	...	...	EH	...
Oklahoma	EC	...	AL	AL	AL	EC
Oregon	EC	EC	...	...	EC	...
Pennsylvania	EC	EC	EC	EC	EC	EC
Rhode Island	EC	AL	...	...	AL	...
South Carolina	EC	...	...	...	...	...
South Dakota	EC	EC	...	...	EC	...
Tennessee	EC	EC	EC	EC	EC	EC
Texas	...	...	...	...	...	...
Utah	EC	...	...	EC (s)	EC	EC (s)
Vermont	EC	EC	(t)	(t)	(t)	(t)
Virginia (u)	EC (w)	...	EC (w)	...	AL	EC
Washington	EC	EC	EC	EC	EC	EC
West Virginia	EC	...	...	...	...	...
Wisconsin	EC	EC	...	...	...	EC
Wyoming	...	...	EC	...	EC	EC
Dist. of Columbia	--- (o) ---
American Samoa	...	...	...	...	...	...
Guam	--- (o) ---
CNMI*	EC	...	...	...	...	...
Puerto Rico	EC (k)	EC	...	...	...	(k)
U.S. Virgin Islands	--- (o) ---

See footnotes at end of table

TABLE 3.7
House/Assembly Leadership Positions: Methods of Selection (continued)

Sources: The Council of State Governments' survey, January 2019 and state websites 2019.

*Commonwealth of Northern Mariana Islands

Note: In some states, the leadership positions in the House are not empowered by the law or by the rules of the chamber, but rather by the party members themselves.

Key:

EH–Elected or confirmed by all members of the House.

EC–Elected by party caucus.

AS–Appointed by speaker.

AL–Appointed by party leader.

MA–Elected by majority party.

MI–Elected by minority party.

…–Position does not exist or is not selected on a regular basis.

(a) Additional positions include deputy majority whip (EC) and assistant majority caucus chair (EC).

(b) Speaker pro tem–1 Deputy Speaker Pro Tempore, 8 Deputy Speakers and 3 Assistant Deputy Speakers. Assistant majority leader–Majority leader appoints 7 Deputy Majority Leaders; Speaker appoints 12 Assistant Minority Leaders(in consultation with Majority Leader). Majority Whip–1 Chief Majority Whip, 1 Majority Whip At-Large, 1 Deputy Majority Whip At-Large and 6 Assistant Majority Whips (in consultation with Majority Leader). Majority caucus chair–selected in consultation with Majority Leader. Assistant Minority Leader–1 Deputy Minority Leader, 3 Deputy Minority Leaders At-Large and 12 Assistant Minority Leaders. Minority Whip–1 Chief Minority Whip, 2 Senior Minority Whips and 7 Minority Whips. Minority Caucus Chair–1 Minority Caucus Chair and 1 Deputy Minority Caucus Chair.

(c) Other positions in Hawaii include speaker emeritus, majority policy leader (EC) and minority leader emeritus.

(d) Official title is deputy speaker. In Hawaii, American Samoa and Puerto Rico, vice speaker.

(e) Assistant Majority Leader, Majority Caucus Chair, Minority Caucus Chair–The two deputy majority leaders appointed by the speaker are among eight assistant majority leaders; and the two deputy Republican (minority) leaders appointed by the Republican (minority) leader are among the eight assistant leaders. (The term "Minority" is in the state Constitution, but has not been recently used by the leadership of the Republican (minority) party).

(f) Additional positions include minority agenda chair (EC) and minority policy chair (EC).

(g) In each chamber , the membership elects chief clerk; assistant chief clerk; enrolling clerk; sergeant-at-arms; doorkeeper; janitor; cloakroom keeper; and pages.

(h) Speaker pro tem each occurrence. Majority leader also serves as majority floor leader; assistant majority leader also serves as assistant majority floor leader and majority whip; minority leader also serves as minority floor leader; assistant minority leader also serves as assistant minority floor leader and minority whip.

(i) There is also a deputy speaker pro tem.

(j) Majority leader also serves as majority floor leader. Official title of assistant majority leader is deputy majority leader. There are also an assistant majority floor leader, majority whip, chief deputy majority whips, and deputy majority whips.

(k) Speaker and minority leader are also caucus chairs.

(l) Minority leader also serves as the minority floor leader. There are also a minority whip, assistant minority leader, a chief deputy minority whip, an assistant minority whip, and several deputy minority whips.

(m) Majority leader also serves as majority floor leader; minority leader also serves as minority floor leader.

(n) Other positions include: two associate speakers pro tempore (EH); majority caucus chair (EC); assistant majority whip (EC); assistant associate minority floor leader (EC); minority assistant caucus chair (EC); assistant minority whip (EC).

(o) Unicameral legislature; see entries in Table 3.6, "Senate Leadership Positions–Methods of Selection."

(p) Majority floor leader duties assumed by majority leader. Additional majority positions appointed by the speaker: deputy speaker, assistant speaker, deputy majority leader, deputy majority whip, assistant majority whip Steering Committee chair, various deputies and assistants. Minority leader voting along conference lines, the member with the second highest number of votes; minority floor leader duties are assumed by minority leader pro tem. Additional minority positions appointed by the minority leader: deputy minority leader, assistant minority leader, deputy minority whip, assistant minority whip, various deputies and assistants.

(q) Official titles: the majority caucus chair is majority conference chair; minority caucus chair is minority conference chair.

(r) While the entire membership actually votes on the election of leaders, selections generally have been made by the members of each party prior to the date of this formal election. Additional positions include assistant majority whip, the 6th ranking majority leadership position (EH) and assistant minority whip, the 4th ranking minority leadership position (EH).

(s) Assistant majority leader is known as majority assistant whip; assistant minority floor leader known as minority assistant whip; minority caucus chair known as minority caucus manager.

(t) Majority leader also serves as majority floor leader; assistant majority leader also serves as assistant majority floor leader and majority whip; minority leader also serves as minority floor leader; assistant minority leader also serves as assistant minority floor leader and minority whip.

(u) The majority caucus also has a secretary, who is appointed by the speaker; the minority caucus has 2 vice-chairs, 1 vice-chair/treasurer and an interim sergeant-at-arms.

(v) The title of majority leader is not used in Virginia; the title is majority floor leader.

(w) The title of minority leader is not used in Virginia; the title is minority floor leader.

(x) Caucus nominee elected by whole membership.

(y) Speaker also serves as majority leader.

(z) Official title is floor leader.

(aa) Official title is alternate floor leader.

(bb) Clerk of the House and Assistant Clerk of the House, both elected by the House leadership.

(cc) There is a parliamentarian for the majority appointed by the Speaker and a minority parliamentarian elected by the minority party caucus.

TABLE 3.7
House/Assembly Leadership Positions: Methods of Selection (continued)

(dd) Assistant majority leader official title is deputy majority leader. Assistant minority leader official title is deputy minority leader. Additional position is deputy majority whip (AS).

(ee) The position of assistant majority leader is known as deputy majority leader. In addition to a majority whip, deputy whips are also appointed by the speaker. The position of assistant minority leader is known as minority leader pro tem. In addition to a minority whip, deputy whips are appointed by the party leader. There is no minority caucus chair—instead there is a policy chair.

(ff) Additional positions of minority and majority caucus secretaries (EC).

(gg) Co-assistant leaders, called deputy minority floor leaders, elected for 2017 session and two minority whips elected for the 2017 session; a chief deputy majority whip and 2 assistant majority whips elected for 2017 session.

(hh) The most Senior member of the Majority Party.

TABLE 3.8
Method of Setting Legislative Compensation

State	Method
Alabama	Constitutional Amendment 57
Alaska	Compensation Commission; Alaska Stat. §24.10.100 , §24.10.101; §39.23.200 thru 39.23.260
Arizona	Compensation Commission Send to a Public Vote Arizona Revised Statutes 41-1103 and 41-1904
Arkansas	Amendment 70, Ark. Stat. Ann. §10-2-212 et seq.
California	State Constitution - Art. III, §8, which establishes a compensation commission.
Colorado	Colorado Stat. 2-2-307 (1)
Connecticut	Conn. Gen. Stat. Ann. §2-9a ; The General Assembly takes independent action pursuant to recommendations of a compensation commission.
Delaware	Del. Code Ann. Title 29, §710 et seq.; §§3301-3304; Are implemented automatically if not rejected by resolution.
Florida	Florida Statutes §11.13(1); statute provides members same percentage increase as state employees
Georgia	Ga. Code Ann. §45-7-4 and §28-1-8
Hawaii	Hawaii State Constitution Article XVI §3.5; Legislative Salary Commission recommendations take effect unless rejected by concurrent resolution
Idaho	Idaho Code 67-406a and 406b; Citizen's Committee on Legislative Compensation makes recommendations that the legislature can reduce or reject, but not increase
Illinois	25 ILCS 120-Compensation Review Act and 25 ILCS 115-General Assembly Compensation Act
Indiana	IC 2-3-1-1: An amount equal to 18% of the annual salary of a judge under IC 33-38-5-6, as adjusted under IC 33-38-5-8.1.
Iowa	Iowa Code Ann. §2.10; Iowa Code Ann. §2A.1 thru 2A.5
Kansas	Kan. Stat. Ann. §46-137a et seq.; §75-3212
Kentucky	Kentucky Rev. Stat. Ann. §6.226-229. The Kentucky committee has not met since 1995; the most recent pay raise was initiated and passed by the General Assembly.
Louisiana	La. Rev. Stat. 24:31 & 31.1
Maine	Maine Constitution Article IV, part third, §7 and 3 MRSA, §2 and 2-A. Increase in compensation is presented to the legislature as legislation; the legislature must enact and the governor must sign into law. Takes effect only for subsequent legislatures.
Maryland	Article III, §15. Commission meets before each four-year term of office and presents recommendations to the General Assembly for action. Recommendations may be reduced or rejected.
Massachusetts	Massachusetts Gen. Laws Ann. ch. 3, §§9, 10. In 1998, the voters passed a legislative referendum that, starting with the 2001 session, members will receive an automatic increase or decrease according to the median household income for the commonwealth for the following two-year period.
Michigan	Article IV §12. Compensation Commission recommends legislature by majority vote; must approve or reduce for change to be effective for the session immediately following the next general election.
Minnesota	Minn. Stat. Ann §3.099 et seq.; §15A.082; The Council submits salary recommendations to the presiding officers by May 1 in odd numbered years.
Mississippi	Miss. Code Ann. 5-1-41
Missouri	Art. III, §§16, 34; Mo. Ann. Stat. §21.140; Recommendations are adjusted by legislature or governor if necessary.
Montana	Mont. Laws 5-2-301; Tied to executive broadband pay plan.
Nebraska	Neb. Const. Art. III, §7; Neb. Rev. Stat. 50-123.01
Nevada	§218.210–§218.225
New Hampshire	Art. XV, part second
New Jersey	Article IV Sec. IV 7, 8; NJSA 52:10A-1; NJSA 52:14-15.111–114
New Mexico	Art. IV. §10 ; 2-1-8 NMSA
New York	Constitution - Art. 3, §6 ; Consolidated Laws of NY - Legislative Law, Section 5.
North Carolina	N.C.G.S. 120-3
North Dakota	NDCC 54-03-10 and 54-03-20
Ohio	Art. II, §31; Ohio Rev. Code Ann. title 1 ch. 101.27 thru 101.272
Oklahoma	Okla. Stat. Ann. title 74, §291 et seq.; Art V, §21; Title 74, §291.2 et seq.; Legislative Compensation Board
Oregon	Or. Rev. Stat. §171.072
Pennsylvania	Pa. Cons. Stat. Ann. 46 PS §5; 65 PS §366.1 et seq.; Legislators receive annual cost of living increase that is tied to the Consumer Price Index.
Rhode Island	Art. VI, §3
South Carolina	S.C. Code Ann. 2-3-20 and the annual General Appropriations Act
South Dakota	Art. III, §6 and Art. XXI, §2; S.D. Codified Laws Ann. §20402 et seq.
Tennessee	Art. II, §23; Tenn. Code Ann. §3-1-106 et seq.
Texas	Art. III, §24; In 1991, a constitutional amendment was approved by voters to allow Ethics Commission to recommend the salaries of members. Any recommendations must be approved by voters to be effective. The provision has yet to be used.
Utah	Art. VI, §9; Utah Code Ann. §36-2-2, et seq.
Vermont	Vt. Stat. Ann. title 32, §1051 and §1052
Virginia	Art. IV, §5; Va. Code Ann. §30-19.11 thru §30-19.14
Washington	Article II §§23 and 43.03.060, Washington Rev. Code Ann. §43.03.028. The salary commission sets salaries of the legislature and other state officials based on market study and input from citizens.
West Virginia	Art. 6, §33; W. Va. Code §4-2A-1 et seq.; Submits by resolution and must be concurred by at least four members of the commission. The Legislature must enact the resolution into law and may reduce, but shall not increase, any item established in such resolution.
Wisconsin	Wisconsin Statutes §§20.923 and 230.12, created by Chapter 90, Laws of 1973, and amended by 1983 Wisconsin Acts 27 and 33. Generally, compensation is determined as part of the state compensation plan for non-represented employees and is approved by vote of the joint committee on employment relations.
Wyoming	Wyo. Stat. §28-5-101 thru §28-5-105

Source: National Conference of State Legislatures 2016.

TABLE 3.9
Legislative Compensation and Living Expense Allowances During Sessions, 2019

State	Salaries Regular sessions Per diem salary	Salaries Regular sessions Limit on days	Salaries Annual salary	Mileage cents per mile	Session per diem rate
Alabama	...	...	$48,123	58/mile	Up to $100/d depending on length of trip.
Alaska	...	...	$50,400	58/mile.	$322/d.
Arizona	...	...	$24,000	58/mile.	$35/day for the first 120 days of the regular session and for special sessions and $10/day thereafter. Members residing outside Maricopa County receive an additional $25/day for the first 120 days of the regular session and for special sessions and an additional $10/day thereafter. Set by statute.
Arkansas	...	...	$41,394	58/mile.	Current per diem rate for legislators who live more than 50 miles from the Capitol in Little Rock is $149. Members who live within 50 miles of the Capitol are eligible to receive a reduced per diem (meals and incidentals, no lodging) of $55. Per diem rates are based on amounts published by the federal General Services Administration.
California	...	...	$110,459	53/mile.	$201/d for each day in session.
Colorado	...	...	$40,242 for members whose tems commmence Jan. 2019; $30,000 for members whose term began prior to Jan. 2019	52/mile.	Up to $171 for members who live more than 50 miles from the capitol; $45/d for members who live 50 or fewer miles from the capitol. Set by the legislature.
Connecticut	...	...	$28,000	58/mile.	No per diem is paid.
Delaware	...	...	$46,291	40/mile.	No per diem is paid.
Florida	...	...	$29,697	44.5/mile.	$163/d based on the number of days in Tallahassee (V).
Georgia	...	...	$17,342	58/mile. Tied to federal rate.	$173/d (U). Set by the Legislative Services Committee.
Hawaii	...	...	$62,604	(a)	$225/d throughout session for members who do not reside on the island of Oahu; $10/d for members living on Oahu during the mandatory five-day recess only.
Idaho	...	...	$17,879	58/mile. One roundtrip per week.	$139/d for members whose primary residence is over 50 miles from the statehouse; $55/d for members whose primary residence is less than 50 miles from the statehouse. (U)
Illinois	...	...	$65,836	39/mile	$111/session day.
Indiana	...	...	$26,490	58/mile. Tied to federal rate.	$181/d (U).
Iowa	...	...	$25,000	39/mile.	$169/d; $126.75/d for Polk County legislators (U).
Kansas	$88.66/d (C)	...	...	58/mile.	$149/d. Tied to federal rate.
Kentucky	$188.22/d	...	...	58/mile.	$163.90/d.
Louisiana	...	...	"$16,800 Senate; $22,800 House"	58/mile.	$161/d (U). Tied to federal rate.
Maine	...	...	$10,131	44/mile.	$38/d lodging (or mileage and tolls up to $38/d in lieu of housing). $32/d meals. Set by statute.
Maryland	...	...	$50,330	58/mile.	$47/d meals. $109/d lodging.
Massachusetts	...	...	$66,257	(b)	No per diem is paid.
Michigan	...	...	$71,685	58/mile. One roundtrip per week.	$10,800/y expense allowance for session and interim (V). Set by the compensation commission.
Minnesota	...	...	$45,000	58/mile. One roundtrip per week.	$86/d for senators; $66/d for representatives.
Mississippi	...	...	$23,500	58/mile.	$149/day (U). Tied to federal rate.
Missouri	...	...	$35,915	37.5/mile.	$119/d
Montana	$92.46 (L)	...	...	58/mile. Tied to federal rate.	$120.11/d
Nebraska	...	...	$12,000	58/mile. Tied to federal rate.	$149/d for members residing 50 miles or more from the capitol; $55/d for members residing within 50 miles.
Nevada	$150.71/d for members elected in 2016; $159.89/d for members elected in 2018	Up to 60 days.	...	(c)	$149/d.
New Hampshire	...	...	$200/2-y term.	(d)	No per diem is paid.
New Jersey	...	...	$49,000	None	No per diem is paid.
New Mexico	...	...	...	58/mile. Tied to federal rate.	$161/d (Jan 15 - Feb. 28), $184/d (Mar. 1 - Mar. 16)
New York	...	...	$110,000	58/mile. Tied to federal rate.	$174/d (including overnight) or $61/d (no overnight).

See footnotes at end of table

TABLE 3.9

Legislative Compensation and Living Expense Allowances During Sessions, 2019 (continued)

State	Salaries Regular sessions Per diem salary	Salaries Regular sessions Limit on days	Annual salary	Mileage cents per mile	Session per diem rate
North Carolina	...	...	$13,951	29/mile. One roundtrip per week.	$104/d (U). Set by statute.
North Dakota		...	$495/month	54/mile. One roundtrip per week. Tied to federal rate.	$177/d.
Ohio	...	...	$63,007	52/mile. (e)	No per diem is paid.
Oklahoma	...	...	$35,021	58/mile. Tied to federal rate.	$156/d (U). Tied to federal rate.
Oregon	...	...	$31,200	58/mile.	$149/d.
Pennsylvania	...	...	$88,610	58/mile. Tied to federal rate.	$177/d. Tied to federal rate.
Rhode Island	...	...	$15,959	54.5/mile.	No per diem is paid.
South Carolina	...	...	$10,400	58/mile. One trip per week.	$170/d. Tied to federal rate.
South Dakota			$11,379	(f)	$149/d (L) (U).
Tennessee	...	...	$24,316	47/mile.	$240/d for members residing greater than 50 miles from capitol; $61/d for members residing 50 miles or less.
Texas	...	...	$7,200	58/mile. $1.26/ mile for single, twin and turbo engine airplanes. Set by general appropriations bill.	$221/d. Set by ethics commission.
Utah	$285/d (C)	...	...	54/mile.	Up to $100 plus tax/d for members that live more than 100 miles round trip from the capitol.
Vermont	...	...	$733.04/w during session.	58/mile. Tied to federal rate.	$126/d lodging (including overnight) or $66/d (no overnight).
Virginia	...	...	$18,000/y Senate; $17,640/y House.	58/mile.	$213/d.
Washington	...	...	$48,731/y; increases to $52,766/y eff. 7/1/2019.	58/mile.	$120/d.
West Virginia	...	...	$20,000	48.5/mile.	$131/d (U). Set by compensation commission.
Wisconsin	...	...	$52,999	51/mile. One roundtrip per week.	"Senate - $115/d Assembly - up to $162/d (including overnight) or up to $81/d (no overnight). Dane County members are authorized up to to $81/d. The maximum number of days per year that per diem can be claimed is 153 days. "
Wyoming	$150/d	...	...	58/mile.	$109/d (V). Set by legislature.

Source: National Conference of State Legislatures, 2019.
Key:
C–Calendar day
L–Legislative day
(U)–Unvouchered
(V)–Vouchered
…–Not applicable
(a) Hawaii. Members may claim a mileage reimbursement for reasonable and necessary use of a personal automobile in the conduct of official legislative business and discharge of duties when meeting certain criteria.
(b) Massachussetts. Legislators are no longer reimbursed for mileage. Instead legislators receive an office expense stiped of $16,248 for legislators that live 50 miles or less from the state house and $21,664 for members who live more than 50 miles– this stipend can be used for travel expenses.

(c) Nevada. Travel allowance is $10,000 for a regular session - can be used for travel to and from the capital or elsewhere within the State on legislative business and $1,200 for a special session. Additional travel allowance is $5,000 for a regular session.
(d) New Hampshire. Round trip home to and from the State House at either a) 38/mile for the first 45 miles and 19/mile thereafter, or b) reimbursed for round trip mileage at the federal rate; or when on other business, members may be reimbursed for actual expenses and mileage will be paid at the federal rate.
(e) Ohio. One roundtrip per wk from home to the state House for legislators outside Franklin County only.
(f) South Dakota. One trip is paid at 5/mile and the remaining are paid at 42/mile.

TABLE 3.10

Legislative Compensation: Other Payments and Benefits

State	Legislator's compensation for office supplies, district offices and staffing	Insurance benefits				
		Health	Dental	Vision	Disability insurance	Life insurance benefits
Alabama	None	S.A.	S.A.	S.A.	None	None
Alaska	$20,000/y Senators. $12,000/y Representatives for postage, stationery and other legislative expenses. Staffing allowance determined by rules and presiding officers, depending on time of year.	S.A.	S.A.	S.A.	S.A.	S.A.
Arizona	None	S.A., S.P.P.	S.A., O.P.	S.A., O.P.	S.P.P.	S.P.P.
Arkansas	Up to $3,600/y additional reimbursement for committee chairs, vice chairs and standing subcommittee chairs.	S.A.	S.A.	S.A.	S.A.	S.A.
California	Senate member expenses are paid directly and maintained by the Senate Rules Committee. Assembly member expenses are paid directly and maintained by the Assembly Rules Committee.	S.A., S.P.P.	(a)	(a)	Senators are covered by a long-term disability insurance policy; Assembly members do not have disability insurance coverage.	Senators are eligible for up to $250,000 term coverage: members pay 10% of the age-based premium plus the taxable value on coverage above $50,000. $250,000 term policy for the Assembly: members pay the taxable value on coverage above $50,000.
Colorado	None	S.A., S.P.P.– Amount differs according to plan selected	S.A., S.P.P.– Amount differs according to plan selected	(b)	None	S.A. State pays full amount for $50,000 policy. Additional is optional at legislator's expense.
Connecticut	$5,500 senators. $4,500 representatives.	S.P.P.	S.P.P.	Some health insurance plans include discounts on eyewear.	S.A., O.P.	S.A., O.P.
Delaware	None	S.A.	S.A.	S.A.	S.A.	S.A.
Florida	$44,452/y Senate district office expenses. $39,534/y House district office expenses.	S.A.	S.A.	S.A., O.P.	S.P.	S.A. State pays for $25,000 coverage.
Georgia	None	S.A.	S.A.	S.A.	S.A.	S.A.
Hawaii	Members receive $13,804/y for legislative related expenses, including office supplies, postage, official travel etc.	S.A. (e)	S.A. (c)	S.A. (c)	None	S.A., S.P.
Idaho	$2,500/y for unvouchered constituent expense.	S.A., S.P.P.	S.A., S.P.P.	S.A., S.P.P.	S.A., S.P.P.	S.A., S.P.P.
Illinois	$69,409/y for office expenses, including district offices and staffing.	S.A.	S.A.	S.A.	S.A.	S.A.
Indiana	None	S.A.	S.A.	S.A.	S.A.	S.A.
Iowa	$300/m district constituency postage, travel, telephone and other expenses.	S.A.	S.A.	S.A.	S.A.	S.A
Kansas	$7,083/y. Staffing allowances vary for leadership.	S.A.	S.A.	S.A.	S.A.	S.A.
Kentucky	$1,789/y district expenses during interim.	S.A.	S.A.	S.A.	None	S.A.
Louisiana	$2,000/m supplemental allowance for vouchered office expenses, rent and travel mileage in district. Newly elected members receive $2,000 for office furniture allowance and $500 upon each re-election Staff allowance based on promotional grade, beginning at $27,300/y.	S.A., S.P.P.	S.A.–legislator pays 100%.	S.A.–legislator pays 100%.	O.P.–legislator pays 100%	O.P.–legislator pays 100%
Maine	None. However, supplies for staff offices are provided and paid for out of general legislative account.	S.A.–State pays up to 100% of legislator coverage and 50% of dependent coverage.	S.A., S.P.	O.P.	None	O.P.

See footnotes at end of table

TABLE 3.10
Legislative Compensation: Other Payments and Benefits (continued)

State	Legislator's compensation for office supplies, district offices and staffing	Insurance benefits				
		Health	Dental	Vision	Disability insurance	Life insurance benefits
Maryland	Senate–$45,165/y plus one institutionally compensated legislative aide. House–$54,732/y.	S.A.	S.A.	S.A.	S.A.	S.A.
Massachusetts	$16,248/y office stipend for legislators who live 50 miles or less from the statehouse; $21,664/y for members who live more than 50 miles from the statehouse.	S.A.	S.A.	S.A.	S.A.	S.A.
Michigan	Senate–No response House–$104,000/y office allowance per maj. member. $101,000/y office allowance per min. member.	No response			No response	No response
Minnesota	$2,112/y postage allotment. No allowance for district offices.	S.A.	S.A.	None	S.A.	S.A.
Mississippi	None	S.A.	O.P.	O.P.	O.P.	S.A., S.P.P.–State pays 50% and legislator pays 50%.
Missouri	$94,464/y for staff salaries. $24,100/y for mailings, travel, supplies and other office expenses.	S.A.	S.A.	S.A.	S.A.	S.A.
Montana	$1,500/y for constituent services.	S.A.	S.A.	S.A.	None	S.A.
Nebraska	None	O.P.	S.A., O.P.	S.A., O.P.	S.A., O.P.	S.A., O.P.
Nevada	None	S.A., O.P.	S.A., O.P.	S.A., O.P.	None	S.A., O.P.
New Hampshire	None	S.A., O.P.	S.A., O.P.	S.A., O.P.	None	None
New Jersey	$135,000/y district office personnel. State provides stationery for each legislator and 10,000 postage stamps.	S.A. (d)	S.A. (d)	S.A. (d)	Permanent disability available if enrolled in pension plan.	Members enrolled in the pension plan–up to three times annual salary. Members enrolled in defined contribution plan–one and a half times annual salary. Members not covered by either plan–no death benefit.
New Mexico	None	S.A., O.P.	S.A., O.P.	S.A., O.P.	None	S.A., O.P.
New York	No response	No response	No response	No response	No response	No response
North Carolina	$2,275 per biennium for office expenses. No staffing allowance.	S.A.	S.A.	S.A.	S.A., O.P.	S.A.
North Dakota	None	S.A., S.P.	S.A.–premium paid by legislator.	S.A.–premium paid by legislator.	None	S.A. State pays for $7,000 term life policy.
Ohio	None	S.A.	S.A.	S.A.	S.A.	S.A.
Oklahoma	$2,000/y for office supplies and expense.	S.A.		S.A.		S.A.
Oregon	$65,939 per biennium for interim expenses. $56,008 session staffing. $4,880 for session services and supplies.	S.A., S.P.P.	S.A., S.P.P.	S.A., S.P.P.	S.A., O.P.	S.A., O.P.
Pennsylvania	$20,000 per fiscal year for office expenses. Staffing is determined by leadership.	(e)	(e)	(e)	None	S.A.
Rhode Island	None	S.A.	S.A.	S.A.	None	None
South Carolina	$1,000/m each member district expenses.	S.A.	S.A.	S.A.	None	S.A.
South Dakota	None	None	None	None	S.P.–accidental death/dismemberment ins. only.	None
Tennessee	$1,000/m expenses in district.	S.A.	S.A.	S.A.	None	S.A. State pays first $35,000 of the basic life insurance; remainder paid by legislator.
Texas	No response	No response	No response	No response	No response	No response
Utah	None	S.A., S.P.P.	S.A., S.P.P.	S.A.	S.A., S.P.	S.A., S.P.–State pays full premium for $25,000 basic term life coverage.
Vermont	No response	No response	No response	No response	No response	No response

See footnotes at end of table

TABLE 3.10

Legislative Compensation: **Other Payments and Benefits** (continued)

State	Legislator's compensation for office supplies, district offices and staffing	Insurance benefits				
		Health	Dental	Vision	Disability insurance	Life insurance benefits
Virginia	Leaders: $78,668/y staffing allowance. $1,750/m office expense allowance. Legislators: $57,783/y staffing allowance. $1,250/m office expense allowance.	S.A., S.P.P.	S.A.	S.A., O.P.	None	S.A., S.P.–The state pays for basic group life insurance. Optional Life Insurance (up to 4x salary) available at legislator's expense.
Washington	$9,000/y for legislative expenses, for which the legislator has not been otherwise entitled to reimbursement. No staffing allowance.	S.A.	S.A.	Included in health coverage.	S.A., S.P.P.	S.A., S.P.P.
West Virginia	None	O.P.	O.P.	O.P.	None	S.A., O.P.
Wisconsin	Senate: $223,650 per biennium staffing allowance. $55,955 per biennium office expenses. Assembly: $20,000 per biennium session office expenses.	S.A.	S.A.	S.A.	S.A.	S.A.
Wyoming	$750/quarter through constituent service allowance.	None	None	None	None	None

Source: National Conference of State Legislatures, 2019.
Key:
(U)–Unvouchered.
(V)–Vouchered.
d–day.
m–month.
w–week.
y–year.
O.P.–Optional at legislator's expense.
S.A.–Same as state employees.
S.P.–State pays full amount.
S.P.P.–State pays portion and legislator pays portion.

(a) California: State pays for basic plan; enhanced coverage is available at an additional cost to member.
(b) Colorado: Vision is part of health coverage without extra cost.
(c) Hawaii: Several plans are available with differing employee contribution rates and copayments.
(d) New Jersey: Members appointed or elected after 5/21/10 must pay full cost of coverage.
(e) Pennsylvania: Legislators pay 1% of salary toward medical/hospital, dental, vision and prescription benefits.

TABLE 3.11
Additional Compensation for Senate Leaders

State	Presiding officer	Majority leader	Minority leader	Other leaders and committee chairs
Alabama	Lt. gov. holds this position.	None	None	None
Alaska	$500/y	None	None	None
Arizona	(a)	(a)	(a)	None
Arkansas	Lt. gov. holds this position.	None	None	$5,600/y pres. pro tem.
California	Lt. gov. holds this position.	None	None	None
Colorado	(b)	(b)	(b)	(b)
Connecticut	Lt. gov. holds this position.	$8,835/y	$8,835/y	Leaders: $10,689/y pres. pro tem. $6,446/y each for dep. maj. ldrs, dep. min. ldrs. $4,241/y each for asst. maj. ldrs., asst. min. ldrs., maj. whips, min. whips. Committee chairs: $4,241/y.
Delaware	Lt. gov. holds this position.	$12,376/y	$12,376/y	Leaders: $19,983/y pres. pro tem. $7,794/y each for maj. whips, min. whips. Committee chairs: $11,459/y each for joint fin. Chair and vice chair. $4,578/y each for capital improvement chair and vice chair.
Florida	$11,484/year	None	None	None
Georgia	Lt. gov. holds this position.	$200/m	$200/m	Leaders: $400/m pres. pro tem. $100 floor leaders. Committee chairs: None.
Hawaii	$7,500/y	None	None	None
Idaho	$5,000/y	$2,000	$2,000	None
Illinois	$27,477/y	$20,649/y	$27,477/y	Leaders: $20,649/y each for asst. maj. ldrs., asst. min. ldrs., maj. caucus chairs, min. caucus chairs. Committee chairs: $10,327/y.
Indiana	Lt. gov. holds this position.	$5,500/y for maj. flr. leader	$6,000/y min. flr. leader	Leaders: $7,000/y pres. pro tem. $5,500/y maj. caucus chair. $4,000/y for majority whip. $2,000/y minority whip. Committee Chairs: $1,000/y for each chair.
Iowa	$12,500/y	$12,500/y	$12,500/y	Leaders: $2,000/y pres. pro tem. Committee chairs: None.
Kansas	$14,039/y	$12,665/y	$12,665/y	Leaders: $7,165/y each for vice pres., asst. maj. ldrs, asst. min. ldrs. Committee chairs: $11,290/y w&m chair.
Kentucky	$47.35/d	$37.40/d	$37.40/d	Leaders: $28.66/d each for maj. caucus chairs, min. caucus chairs, maj. caucus whips, min. caucus whips. Committee chairs: $18.71/d.
Louisiana	$15,200/y	None	None	Leaders: $7,700/y pres. pro tem. Committee chairs: $15,200/y joint budget chair.
Maine	50% of base salary/y	25% of base salary/y	12.5% of base salary/y	None
Maryland	$15,041/y	None	None	None
Massachusetts	$86,656/y	$64,992/y	$64,992/y	Leaders: $54,160/y for pres. pro tem, $37,912/y for asst. maj. ldrs and asst. min. ldrs. Committee leaders: $70,408/y w&m chair. $32,496/y division chairs. $16,248/y for all other chairs. $5,633/y vice chairs.
Michigan	Lt. gov. holds this position.	$23,400/y	$19,800/y	Leaders: $10,800/y for maj. flr. ldr., $9,000/y for min. flr. ldr. Committee chairs: $6,300/y for app. cmte. chairs.
Minnesota	$3,600/y	$18,000/y	$18,000/y	Leaders: $3,600/y deputy ldrs. Committee chairs: $3,600/y fin. chair and tax chair.
Mississippi	$5,000/m	None	None	$1,250/m pres. pro tem
Missouri	Lt. gov. holds this position.	$1,500	$1,500	Leaders: $2,500 for pres. pro tem.
Montana	$5/d during session	None	None	None
Nebraska	Lt. gov. holds this position.	None	None	None
Nevada	Lt. gov. holds this position.	None	None	None
New Hampshire	$50/2-y term	None	None	None
New Jersey	$16,333	None	None	None
New Mexico	Lt. gov. holds this position.	None	None	None
New York	No Response	No Response	No Response	No Response
North Carolina	Lt. gov. holds this position.	$3,097/y	$3,097/y	Leaders: $24,200/year pres. pro tem. $7,788/year deputy pres. pro tem.
North Dakota	Lt. gov. holds this position.	$15/d during legislative sessions.	$15/d during legislative sessions.	Leaders: $10/d during session asst. ldrs. Committee chairs: $10/d all standing cmtes.

See footnotes at end of table

TABLE 3.11
Additional Compensation for Senate Leaders (continued)

State	Presiding officer	Majority leader	Minority leader	Other leaders and committee chairs
Ohio	$35,207/y	None	$26,605/y	Leaders: $26,605/y pres. pro tem. $21,403/y asst. pres. pro tem. $16,209 maj. whip. $18,808/y asst. min ldr. $11,013/y min whip. $2,909/y asst. min. whip. Committee chairs: $13,500/y fin. chair. $9,000/y each for fin. ranking min. member, fin. cmte standing subcmte chair, all other standing cmte chairs. $7,500/y fin. vice chair. $6,750/y each for ranking min. member fin. standing subcmte, vice chairs, ranking min. members, standing subcmte chairs. $3,250/y standing subcmte ranking min. members.
Oklahoma	No Response	No Response	No Response	No Response
Oregon	$2,600/month	None	None	None
Pennsylvania	Lt. gov. holds this position.	$39,745/year	$39,745/year	Leaders: $49,716/y pres. pro tem. $30,186/y maj. whips, min. whips. $12,430/y each for maj. caucus secretaries, min. caucus secretaries, maj. policy chairs, min. policy chairs, maj. caucus admin., min. caucus admin. Committee chairs: $30,186/y each for maj. app. chair, min. app. chair. $18,832/y each for maj. caucus chair, min. caucus chair.
Rhode Island	$15,959/y	None	None	None
South Carolina	Lt. gov. holds this position	None	None	Leaders: $11,000/y pres. pro tem. Committee Chairs: $600/y
South Dakota	Lt. gov. holds this position.	None	None	None
Tennessee	None	None	None	None
Texas	No Response	No Response	No Response	No Response
Utah	$5,000/y	$4,000/y	$4,000/y	Leaders: $3,000/y each for maj. whips, min. whips, asst. maj. whips, asst. min. whips. Committee leaders: $3,000/y app. chair.
Vermont	Lt. gov. holds this position.	None	None	Leaders: $482.50 bi-weekly pres. pro tem.
Virginia	None	None	None	None
Washington	Lt. gov. holds this position	$9,259/y	$4,629/y	None
West Virginia	$150/d during session.	$50/d during session	$50/d during session	Leaders: $150/d (up to 30 days) for a maximum of six add'l persons named by presiding officer. Committee chairs: $150.00/d (up to 30 days) fin. & judiciary chairs.
Wisconsin	None	None	None	None
Wyoming	$3/day	None	None	None

Source: National Conference of State Legislatures, 2019.
Key:
d–day
m–month
w–week
y–year

app.– Appropriations
w&m–Ways and means
Lt. gov.–lieutenant governor who is not a member of the Senate.
(a) Arizona. Generally approved for additional interim per diem.
(b) Colorado. All leaders receive $99/d salary during interim when in attendance at committee or leadership matters.

TABLE 3.12
Additional Compensation for House/Assembly Leaders

State	Presiding officer	Majority leader	Minority leader	Other leaders and committee chairs
Alabama	$18,000/y	None	None	None
Alaska	$500/y	None	None	None
Arizona	(a)	(a)	(a)	(a)
Arkansas	$5,883/y	None	None	None
California	$16,567/y	$8,284/y	$16,567/y	Leaders: $8.284/y second ranking min. ldr. Committee chairs: None.
Colorado	(b)	(b)	(b)	(b)
Connecticut	$10,689/y	$8,835/y	$8,835/y	Leaders: $6,446/y each for dep. spkr., dep. maj. ldrs., min. ldrs., asst. maj. ldrs., asst. min. ldrs. $4,241/y each for maj. whips, min. whips. Committee chairs: $4,241/y
Delaware	$19,893/y	$12,376/y	$12,376/y	Leaders: $7,794/y each for maj. whips, min. whips. Committee chairs: $11,459/y each for joint fin. Chair and vice chair. $4,578/y each for capital improvement chair and vice chair.
Florida	$11,484/y	None	None	None
Georgia	$6,811/m	$200/m	$200/m	Leaders: $400/m for spkr. pro tem. $100/m for gov.'s floor ldr. $100/m for asst. floor ldr. Committee chairs: None.
Hawaii	$7,500/y	None	None	None
Idaho	$5,000/y	$2,000	$2,000	None
Illinois	$27,477/y	$23,230/y	$27,277/y	Leaders: $19,791/y each for dep. maj. ldrs., dep. min. ldrs. $18,067/y each for asst. maj. ldrs., asst. min. ldrs and maj. conference chair. Committee chairs: $10,327/y each for chairs.
Indiana	No Response	No Response	No Response	No Response
Iowa	$12,500/y	$12,500/y	$12,500/y	Leaders: $2,000/y spkr. pro tem. Committee chairs: None.
Kansas	$14,039/y	$12,665/y	$12,665/y	Leaders: $7,165/y each for spkr. pro tem, asst. maj. ldrs., asst. min. ldrs. Committee chairs: $11,290/y app. chair.
Kentucky	$47.35/d	$37.40/d	$37.40/d	Leaders: $28.66/d each for maj. caucus chairs & whips, min. caucus chairs & whips. Committee chairs: $18.71/d.
Louisiana	$15,200/y	None	None	Leaders: $13,700/y spkr. pro tem.
Maine	50% of base salary	25% of base salary	12.5% of base salary	None
Maryland	$15,041/y	None	None	None
Massachusetts	$86,656/y	$64,992/y	$64,992/y	Leaders: $54,160/y for spkr. pro tem, $37,912/y for asst. maj. ldrs and asst. min. ldrs. Committee leaders: $70,408/y w&m chair. $32,496/y division chairs. $16,248/y for all other chairs. $5,633/y vice chairs.
Michigan	$24,300/y	None	$19,800/y	Leaders: $10,800/y for maj. floor ldr., $9,000/y for min. flr. ldr., $4,962/y for spkr. pro tem. Committee chairs: $6,300/y for app. cmte. chairs.
Minnesota	$18,000/y	$18,000/y	$18,000/y	None
Mississippi	No Response	No Response	No Response	No Response
Missouri	$2,500/y	$1,500/y	$1,500/y	None
Montana	$5/d during session	None	None	None
Nebraska	N/A–Unicameral legislature			
Nevada	$2/d during session	None	None	None.
New Hampshire	$50/2-y term.	None	None	None
New Jersey	$16,333	None	None	None
New Mexico	None	None	None	None
New York	No Response	No Response	No Response	No Response
North Carolina	$24,200/y	$3,097/y	$3,097/y	Leaders: $7,788/y spkr. pro tem.
North Dakota	$15/d during session	$15/d during session	$15/d during session	Leaders: $10/d for asst. ldrs. during session. Committee chairs: $10/d for all standing cmtes.
Ohio	$35,207/y	$21,403/y maj. flr. ldr.	$26,605/y	Leaders: $26,605/y spkr. pro tem. $16,209/y asst. maj. floor ldr. $11,013/y maj. whip. $5,815/y asst. maj. whip. $18,808/y asst. min. floor ldr. $11,013 min. whip. $2,909/y asst. min. whip. Committee chairs: $13,500/y fin. chair. $9,000/y each for fin. ranking min. member, fin. cmte standing subcmte chair, all other standing cmte chairs. $7,500/y fin. vice chair. $6,750/y each for ranking min. member fin. standing subcmte, vice chairs, ranking min. members, standing subcmte chairs. $3,250/y standing subcmte ranking min. members.
Oklahoma	$16,354/y	$11,276/y	$11,276/y	Committee chairs: $11,276/y each for app. chair, budget chair.
Oregon	$2,600/m	None	None	None
Pennsylvania	No Response	No Response	No Response	No Response
Rhode Island	$15,959/y	None	None	None
South Carolina	$11,000/y	None	None	Leaders: $3,600/y spkr. pro tem. Committee Chairs: $650/y
South Dakota	None	None	None	None

See footnotes at end of table

TABLE 3.12

Additional Compensation for House/Assembly Leaders (continued)

State	Presiding officer	Majority leader	Minority leader	Other leaders and committee chairs
Tennessee	$48,632/y	None	None	None
Texas	No Response	No Response	No Response	No Response
Utah	$5,000/y	$4,000/y	$4,000/y	Leaders: $3,000/y each for whips, asst. whips, minority caucus leaders and executive app. chair.
Vermont	$482.50 bi-weekly.	None	None	None
Virginia	$18,681/y	None	None	None
Washington	$9,259/y; $8,000/y eff. 7/1/2019.	None	$4,629/y; $4,000/y eff. 7/1/2019.	None
West Virginia	$150/d during session.	$50/d during session	$50/d during session	Leaders: $150/d (up to 30 days) for a maximum of six add'l persons named by presiding officer. Committee chairs: $150.00/d (up to 30 days) fin. & judiciary chairs.
Wisconsin	$25/m	None	None	None
Wyoming	$3/d	None	None	None

Source: National Conference of State Legislatures, 2019.
Key:
d–day.
m–month.
w–week.
y–year.

app.–Appropriations
w&m–Ways and means
(a) Arizona. Generally approved for additional interim per diem.
(b) Colorado. All leaders receive $99/d salary during interim when in attendance at committee or leadership matters.

TABLE 3.13
State Legislative Retirement Benefits

State	Participation	Requirements for regular retirement	Employee contribution rate	Benefit formula
Alabama	None available.			
Alaska	Optional	Four tiers. Varies depending upon tier. Detailed information set forth in Public Employees' Retirement System (PERS) plan comparison chart.	Four tiers. Varies depending upon tier. Detailed information set forth in Public Employees' Retirement System (PERS) plan comparison chart.	Four tiers. Varies depending upon tier. Detailed information set forth in Public Employees' Retirement System (PERS) plan comparison chart.
Arizona	Mandatory	No requirements, same as other federal qualified defined contribution plans.	Employee: 8%; Employer: 6%	2016 information: 4% x years of credited service x highest 3 yr. average in the past 10 years The benefit is capped at 80% of FAS. An elected official may purchase service credit in the plan for service earned in a non-elected position by buying it at an actuarially determined amount. AZ SB 1609 of 2011–For those elected to office after 1/1/2012: 3% x years of credited service x highest 5 yr. average in the past 10 years The benefit is capped at 75% of FAS.
Arkansas	Mandatory for those legislators first elected in 2003 or after. Optional for those elected before 2003.	Age 65 with 10 years of service; 55/12; any age with 28 years of service; any age if serving in the General Assembly on 7/1/79; any age if in elected office on 7/1/79 with 17½ years of service. As a regular employee, 65/5 or any age/28 years. Members of the contributory plan established in 2005 must have a minimum of 10 years legislative service if they have only legislative state employment.	Members pay 5%, state pays 15.32%	(Years of service) x (Final Average Compensation–high 3 years) x (Multiplier–2.00 for contributory members; 1.75 for service rendered prior to 7/1/07 and 1.72 for service after 7/1/07 for non-contributory members) = Retirement Annual Benefit
California	Legislators elected after 1990 are not eligible for retirement benefits for legislative service.			
Colorado	Mandatory	PERA: age 65 with 5 years of service; age 55 with 35 years of service; when age + service equals 85 or more (min. age of 55). State Defined Contribution Plan (DCP): no age requirement and immediate vesting.	Employee: 8% (inc. to 10% by 7/1/21)	PERA: 2.5% x FAS x years of service, capped at 100% of FAS. DCP benefit depends upon contributions and investment return.
Connecticut	Mandatory	Age 60 with 25 years credited service; age 62 with 10-25 years credited service; age 62 with 5 years actual state service. If elected after 2011–age 63 with 25 years of vesting service or age 65 with 10-25 years of vesting service. Reduced benefit available with earlier retirement ages.	Employee 2%	(1.33% x average annual salary) + (5% x average salary over "breakpoint") x credited service up to 35 years; 2003–$36,400; 2004–$38,600; 2005–$40,900; 2006–$43,400; 2007–$46,000; 2008–$48,800; 2009–$51,700. After 2009–increase breakpoint by 6% per year rounded to nearest $100.
Delaware	Mandatory. DE HB 81 of 2011–Mandatory for those elected after January 1, 2012.	Elected before 2012–Age 60 with 5 years of credited service; or 55 with 10 years of service. Elected after 2012–65 with 10 years of service; or 60 with 20 years of service. Vesting at 10 years.	Elected before 2012–3% of annual compensation in excess of $6,000. Elected after 2012–5% of annual compensation in excess of $6,000.	2% x FAS x years of service before 1997 + 1.85% times FAS times years of service from 1997 on. FAS = average of highest 3 years.
Florida	Optional.	DB Plan: Six to eight years to vest depending on the start date of service: Retirement at age 62 with at least 6 service years or 30 years of service regardless of age; or, Retirement at age 65 with at least 8 service years or 33 years of service regardless of age. DC Plan: One year to vest, retirement at any age.	Legislator contribution is 3%; employer contribution is 56.75%	DB plan–3% x years of creditable service x average final compensation (average of highest 5 years). DC plan–dependent upon investment experience.
Georgia	Optional.	Vested after 8 years. Age 62 with 8 years of service; age 60 with reduction for early retirement.	Employee: 3.75% + $7/m.	$36/month for each year of service.
Hawaii	Optional	Age 60 and 10 years service for normal retirement.	9.8% of monthly base salary.	3% x years of service x average final compensation.

See footnotes at end of table

TABLE 3.13
State Legislative Retirement Benefits (continued)

State	Participation	Requirements for regular retirement	Employee contribution rate	Benefit formula
Idaho	Mandatory; same plan as public employees (PERSI) except legislators are automatically vested.	Age 65 with 5 years of service; reduced benefit at age 55 with 5 years of service.	7.16% paid by member, 11.94% paid by employer.	Average monthly salary for highest 42 consecutive months x 2% x months of credited service.
Illinois	Optional; not the same as the State Employees' Retirement System. Only state senators, representatives and statewide elected officials have the option to participate.	Tier 1–age 55 with 8 years of service or age 62 with 4 years of service. Tier 2–age 67 with 8 years of service or age 62 with 8 years of service reduced ½ of 1% for each month.	11.5% of salary (includes contributions for retirement annuity and survivors annuity) or 9.5% of salary as contributions for just retirement annuity (no survivor annuity).	First 4 yrs x 3.0% = 12%; next 2 yrs x 3.5% = 7.0%; next 2 yrs x 4.0% = 8.0%; next 4 yrs x 4.5% = 18.0%; next 8 yrs x 5.0% = 40.0%
Indiana	Mandatory	Age 65 with 10 years of service; age 60 with at least 15 years of service or at least age 55 and years of service plus age equal at least 85. Reduced benefits available for those age 55 with at least 10 years of service.	5% paid by legislator, 7% paid by state contribution.	DB plan–monthly benefit: Lesser of (a) $40 x years of General Assembly service completed before 11/8/89; or (b) 1/12 of the average of the three highest consecutive years of General Assembly service salary. DC plan–numerous options for withdrawing accumulations in accord with IRS regulations. Loans are available. A participant in both plans may receive a benefit from both plans.
Iowa	Optional. Same as state employees plan (IPERS).	Age 65; age 62 with 20 years of service; Rule of 88; age 55 with reduced benefits.	6.29% paid by legislator, 9.44% paid by state.	2% x FAS. x years of service for first 30 years, + 1% x FAS x years in excess of 30 but no more than 5 in excess of 30. FAS is average of 3 highest years taken at June 2012, or average of 5 highest years.
Kansas	Legislators may elect to join the state retirement program unless they have already retired from state employment. Those individuals receive an 8% of income deposit by the state into a deferred compensation plan.	2016 info–Age 65; age 62 with 5 years of service, or when age plus years of service equals 85.	6% of the annualized salary.	2016 information–3 highest years x 1.75% x years of service ÷ 12= monthly benefit.
Kentucky	Optional. Those who opt out are covered by the state employees' plan. Legislators who were first elected prior to 1/1/2014 are eligible for the DB plan. Legislators first elected after 1/1/14 are eligible for the hybrid plan.	DB Plan: Vesting after 5 years of legislative service of 8 years of state governmental service. Age 65 for normal retirement benefits. Hybrid Plan: Age 65 with 5 years of active service credit or age 57 with 30 years of service.	DB Plan: Members electing to participate in the plan prior to 9/1/2008 contribute 5% of creditable compensation. Members electing to participate in the plan on or after 9/1/2008 contribute 6% of creditable compensation. Hybrid Plan: Members contribute 6% of creditable compensation, employer contributes 4%.	DB Plan: Final compensation x service credit rate x years of service. Final compensation is calculated as the average of the member's three highest years of legislative creditable compensation. Hybrid Plan: Multiple options available. Primary option is to receive monthly allowance payable for life by having accumulated account balance annuitized.
Louisiana	Not available			
Maine	Mandatory	Age 60 if 10 years of service on 7/1/93; age 62 if less than 10 years of service on 7/1/93. Reduced benefit available for earlier retirement.	7.65% legislators; employer contribution is actuarially determined.	2% of average final compensation (the average of the 3 high salary years) x years of service.
Maryland	Mandatory	Age 60 with 8 years; age 50 with 8+ years creditable service for early reduced retirement.	7% of annual salary.	2016 info: 3% of legislative salary for each year of service up to 22 years 3 months. Benefits are recalculated when legislative salaries are changed.
Massachusetts	Mandatory unless they are already receiving a pension from the Massachusetts State Employee Retirement System.	Vesting after 10 years. Eligible to retire at age 55 or 60 after 10 years of service depending on their hire date, eligible to retire at any age after 20 years of service.	9%, although some legislators are grandfathered at lower rates.	Age factor x years of creditable service x FAS. FAS = average of highest 60 or 36 months depending on when service began.
Michigan	Optional. Same as state employee retirement plan.	Age 55 with 5 years or when age plus years of service equal 70. Employee contributions are immediately vested. Employer contributions are vested as follows: Zero after one year; 50% after two years; 75% after three years; 100% after four years.	For legislators elected before 3/31/97–7–10% for (DB) plan. Elected after 3/31/97–(DC) plan, the state contributes 4% of salary. Members may contribute up to 3% of salary. The state will match the member's contribution in addition to the state 4% contribution.	Vesting for contributions to 401(k)– 2 years of service vested 50%; 3 years vested 75% and 4 years vested 100%.

See footnotes at end of table

TABLE 3.13
State Legislative Retirement Benefits (continued)

State	Participation	Requirements for regular retirement	Employee contribution rate	Benefit formula
Minnesota	Mandatory. Legislators elected since 1997 participate in a mandatory retirement plan called the Unclassified Plan; it is a defined contribution 401 (a) plan. Legislators elected prior to 1997 participate in the Legislators Plan which was closed to new members at that time; it is a defined benefit pension plan. All members may choose to participate in the Minnesota deferred compensation plan 457 (b).	Legislators Retirement Plan (LRP) before 7/1/97–62 years with 6 years of service and fully vested. LRP members do not have Social Security coverage. Defined Contribution Plan (DCP) since 1997–age 55 and immediate vesting. DCP members have Social Security coverage.	LRP–9%. DCP–5.75% (inc. to 6% 7/1/19) from member, 6% (inc. to 6.25% 7/1/19) from state.	LRP–2.5% x high 5 year average salary x years of service. DCP benefits depend upon contributions and investment return.
Mississippi	Mandatory	Age 60 with 4 or more years of service, or 25 years of service.	Regular–15.75% state, 9.00% member. Supplemental Legislative Retirement Plan–7.40% state, 3.00% member.	Legislators who qualify for regular state retirement benefits also automatically qualify for the legislators' supplemental benefits. Regular–2% x average compensation x years of service up to and including 25 years of service + 2.5% x average compensation x service in excess of 25 years. Average compensation is calculated using the highest 4 years of compensation. Supplement–1% x average compensation x years of legislative service through 25 years + 1.25% x average compensation x years of service in excess of 25.
Missouri	Mandatory. The retirement plan for Legislators is calculated differently from the plan for other state employees.	For those hired on or before 12/31/2010 –vesting at 6 years of service. Age 55; service in three full biennial assemblies (6 years) or Rule of 80. For those entering system after 1/1/2011 –vesting at 6 years of service. Age 62; service in three full biennial assemblies (6 years) or the Rule of 90 with a minimum age of 55.	For those hired on or before 12/31/2010–non-contributory. For those entering system after 1/1/2011–contribution of 4% of salary.	For those hired on or before 12/31/2010 –monthly pay divided by 24 x years of creditable service, capped at 100% of salary. Benefit is adjusted by the percentage increase in pay for an active legislator. For those entering system after 1/1/2011 –no change.
Montana	Optional. Same as state employees retirement plan.	Members hired before 7/1/11– Age 60 with at least 5 years service; age 65 regardless of years of service; or 30 years of service regardless of age. After 7/1/11–vesting at 5 years. Age 65 with 5 years service, or age 70 and in active service.	7.9% employee and 8.67% employer for DB and DC plan.	2016 info: DB plan–Membership Service Factor (see below) x years of Service Credit x HAC. More than 5 years and less than 10 years of membership service–1.5% Less than 30 years of membership service–1.7857% 30 years or more of membership service–2%
Nebraska	None available			
Nevada	Mandatory, but a legislator, within 30 days after he/she is first elected or appointed, may elect not to participate; a decision to terminate participation in the plan cannot be reversed. The legislators' retirement system is separate from the state employee retirement plan.	Must have at least 10 years of service, be age 60, and no longer be a legislator in order to retire without benefit reduction. A legislator who is no longer serving, has at least 10 years of service, but is under the age of 60 can elect to wait to receive his/her benefit until the age of 60 or begin receiving a reduced benefit prior to the age of 60.	15% of session salary.	Number of years (not to exceed 30) x $25 = monthly allowance.
New Hampshire	None available			
New Jersey	Mandatory	Age 60; no minimum service requirement.	7.5%	3% x FAS x years of service. FAS = higher of three highest years or three final years. Benefit is capped at 2/3 of FAS. Other formulas apply if a legislator also has other service covered by the Public Employee Retirement System.
New Mexico	Optional	Age 65 with 5 years of service or at any age with 10 years of legislative service.	$600 per year.	11% of the per diem rate in effect on the first day of the calendar year that the legislator retires x 60 and further multiplied by credited service as a legislator.

See footnotes at end of table

TABLE 3.13

State Legislative Retirement Benefits (continued)

State	Participation	Requirements for regular retirement	Employee contribution rate	Benefit formula
New York	Detailed information set forth in Your Retirement Plan: Legislative and Executive Plan, published by New York State Office of the State Comptroller.	Detailed information set forth in Your Retirement Plan: Legislative and Executive Plan, published by New York State Office of the State Comptroller.	Detailed information set forth in Your Retirement Plan: Legislative and Executive Plan, published by New York State Office of the State Comptroller.	Detailed information set forth in Your Retirement Plan: Legislative and Executive Plan, published by New York State Office of the State Comptroller.
North Carolina	Mandatory	Age 65 with 5 years of service; reduced benefit available at earlier ages.	7%.	Highest annual compensation x 4.02% x years of creditable service.
North Dakota	None available.			
Ohio	Optional. OPERS offers three plans for retirement–the traditional plan (a defined benefit plan); the member directed plan (a defined contribution plan); and the combined plan.	Varies depending upon plan. Detailed information set forth in Legislative Benefits, Privileges, and Restrictions of Office.	Varies depending upon plan. Detailed information set forth in Legislative Benefits, Privileges, and Restrictions of Office.	Varies depending upon plan. Detailed information set forth in Legislative Benefits, Privileges, and Restrictions of Office.
Oklahoma	Mandatory. Same as state employees retirement plan.	Vesting at 8 years. If member joined plan before 11/1/11: Age 62 with 6 years of service. If member joined plan after 11/1/11: Age 65 with 6 years of service. Early retirement with reduced benefits at age 55 or 60 with 10 years of service.	3.5% of total compensation.	2% FAS x total years of service. FAS = average of 3 or 5, depending on when member joined plan, highest years of last 10.
Oregon	Optional	OPSRP for general service members is age 65, or age 58 with 30 years of retirement credit. Tier 2–60 years or 30 years of retirement credit. Tier 1–58 or 30 years of retirement credit.	OPRSP DC component–employees contribute 6% of salary. DB component–non-contributory. 457 plans–members may contribute amounts to limits set by IRS.	OPRSP individual account component, or DC component–at retirement, employees may receive the IAP as a lump-sum payment or in equal installments over a 5, 10, 15 or 20-year period. DB component–benefit calculation is 1.5 percent x final average salary x years of service.
Pennsylvania	Optional. Same as state employee retirement plan.	Vesting at 10 years. Retirement age is 55 with 3 years of credited service or according to the Rule of 92 with a minimum of 35 years of service.	7.5% or 8.25% depending on plan.	Annual accrual rate x final average salary x credited years of service. FAS = average of 3 final years of service.
Rhode Island	None available.			
South Carolina	Optional (but not available to anyone first elected to the General Assembly after November 2012). Legislators elected after 2012 have the option of participating in the state employee retirement plan.	2016 information: Age 60 with 8 years of service. 30 years of service regardless of age. Act 278, Laws of 2012–SCRS: vesting at 8 years; retirement benefits at age 65 with 8 years of service or in accord with the Rule of 90. Reduced benefits are available at age 60 with 8 years of service. ORP: immediate vesting in employer contributions.	2016 information: 10% 11% as of January 1, 2013. Act 278, Laws of 2012–SCRS: 7% as of July 1, 2012, rising to 8% on July 1, 2014. ORP: 7% + 5% employer contribution, immediately vested.	2016 information: 4.82% x earnable compensation x years of service. "Earnable compensation" means 40 x the daily rate of remuneration, plus $12,000, of a member of the General Assembly, as from time to time in effect. Act 278, Laws of 2012–SCRS: 2.25% x years of service x final average compensation, which is the average of the member's 5 highest years of earned compensation. ORP: upon retirement a member may annuitize the balance in the account or take a lump sum or partial distribution. Federal provisions apply.
South Dakota	None available.			
Tennessee	Optional. Same as state employees retirement plan.	Hybrid plan–Vesting at 5 years, age 60 or any combination of age and service to equal 80. Legacy plan–Vesting at 4 years, age 55.	State contributes 4% toward defined benefit, 5% into 401K Member contributes 5% toward defined benefit, 2% into 401K. Legacy Plan–19.66% for original members.	Hybrid plan–$57.28 x years of service. Legacy plan–$89.72 x years of service.
Texas	Optional	Age 60 with 8 years of service; or age 50 with 12 years of service.	9.5%	2.3% x district judge's salary x length of service, with the monthly benefit capped at the level of a district judge's salary, and adjusted when such salaries are increased. Various annuity options are available. In September 2018, a district judge's salary was set at $140,000 a year.

See footnotes at end of table

TABLE 3.13
State Legislative Retirement Benefits (continued)

State	Participation	Requirements for regular retirement	Employee contribution rate	Benefit formula
Utah	Optional	Age 62 with 10 years and an actuarial reduction; age 65 with 4 years of service for full benefits.	Non-contributory. For the DC plan, employer will contribute 10% of compensation, which will vest after four years of service. Employees may, but are not required, to contribute.	$30.40/month (as of July 2018) x years of service; adjusted semi-annually according to consumer price index up to a maximum increase of 2%. An additional $3.50/month for each year of service is payable to elected and appointed legislators who were members of this plan before March 1, 2000.
Vermont	None available. Deferred compensation plan available.			
Virginia	Mandatory. Eligibility for various plans based on membership date. Same as state employees plan.	Plan 1–Age 50 with 30 years of service (unreduced); age 55 with 5 years of service; age 50 with 10 years (reduced). Plan 2–When age and service = 90; or normal Social Security retirement age with 5 years of service (unreduced); age 60 with 5 years of service (reduced). Hybrid plan–When age and service = 90; or normal Social Security retirement age with 5 years of service (unreduced); age 60 with 5 years of service (reduced).	Plan 1–members who qualify do not make an employee contribution. Plan 2–5% of creditable compensation. Hybrid plan–mandatory and voluntary contributions to defined benefit and defined contribution components.	Plan 1–1.7% of average final compensation x years of service (average over highest 36 consecutive months). Plan 2–1.65% of average final compensation x years of service (average over highest 60 consecutive months). Hybrid plan–1.65% of average final compensation x years of service (average over highest 60 consecutive months).
Washington	Optional. If before an election the legislator belonged to a state public retirement plan, he or she may continue in that plan by making contributions. Otherwise, new legislators may join PERS Plan 2 or Plan 3.	Plan 2–age 65 with 5 years of service credit. Plan 3–age 65 with 10 years of service credit for the DB side of the plan; immediate benefits (subject to federal restrictions) on the DC side of the plan. The member may choose various options for investment of contributions to the DC plan.	Plan 2–employee contribution of 7.41% for 2019. Plan 3–no required member contribution for the DB component. The member may contribute from 5% to 15% of salary to the DC component.	Plan 2–2% x years of service credit x average final compensation. Plan 3–DB is 1% x service credit years x average final compensation. DC benefit depends upon the value of accumulations.
West Virginia	Optional	Age 55, if years of service + age equal 80.	Before 10/1/87–7%. After 10/1/87–5%.	2% x final average salary x years of service. Final average salary is based on 3 highest years out of last 10 years.
Wisconsin	Mandatory. Same as state employees retirement plan.	Age 62 for members who began employment before 1/1/17; Age 65 for members who began employment on or after 1/1/17. Age 55 with reduced benefits.	2019 contribution rate is 6.6% of monthly gross salary to their state pension The employer matches this for a total contribution of 13.2%.	Final average monthly earnings x creditable service x formula multiplier x age reduction factor (if any) = monthly amount. Final average monthly earnings is calculated by adding the highest earnings for three calendar years and dividing this total by the creditable service earned during these years and then dividing by 12.
Wyoming	Optional–Deferred 457 Plan.		$20 minimum monthly contribution is required to participate.	

Source: National Conference of State Legislatures, 2019.
Key:
COLA–Cost of living adjustment.
CPI–Consumer price index.
DB–Defined Benefit.
DC–Defined Contribution.

FAS–Final average salary.
None available–No retirement benefit provided.
OPERS–Ohio Public Employee's Retirement System.
OPSRP–Oregon Public Employee's Retirement System.
PERA–Public Employee Retirement Association.
PERS–Public Employee's Retirement System.

TABLE 3.14
Bill Pre-Filing, Reference and Carryover

State or other jurisdiction	Pre-filing of bills allowed (b)	Bills referred to committee by:		Bill referral restricted by rule (a)		Bill carryover allowed (c)
		Senate	House/Assembly	Senate	House/Assembly	
Alabama	★(d)	(e)(f)	Speaker (f)	L, M	L, M	...
Alaska	★	President	Speaker	L, M	L, M	★
Arizona	★	President	Speaker	L	L	...
Arkansas	★	President (g)	Speaker	L	L	...
California	★(h)	Rules Cmte.	Rules Cmte.	L	L	★(h)
Colorado	★	President	Speaker	(i)	(i)	...
Connecticut	★	Pres. Pro Tempore	Speaker	M	M	...
Delaware	★	Pres. Pro Tempore	Speaker	L	L	★
Florida	★	President	Speaker	M	...	...
Georgia	★	President (f)	Speaker	...	...	★
Hawaii	(j)	(j)	Speaker	...	...	★
Idaho	...	President (e)	Speaker (e)	(qq)	(qq)	...
Illinois	★	Cmte. on Assignments	Rules Cmte.	(k)	(k)	★
Indiana	★(l)	Pres. Pro Tempore	Speaker	(m)	...	...
Iowa	★	President	Speaker	M	M	★
Kansas	★	President	Speaker	L(n)	L(n)	★
Kentucky	★	Cmte. on Cmtes.	Cmte. on Cmtes.	L, M	L, M	...
Louisiana	★	President (o)	Speaker (o)	L	L	...
Maine	★	Secy. of Senate	Clerk of House	(p)	(p)	★(rr)
Maryland	★	President (q)	Speaker (q)	L	L	...
Massachusetts	★	Clerk	Clerk	M	M	★
Michigan	...	Majority Ldr.	Speaker	(uu)	(uu)	★
Minnesota	★(r)	President	Speaker	L, M	L, M	★(r)
Mississippi	★	President (e)	Speaker	L	L	...
Missouri	★	Pres. Pro Tempore	Speaker	L	L	...
Montana	★	President	Speaker	L(tt)	L(tt)	...
Nebraska	★	Reference Cmte. (s)	U	L	U	★(t)
Nevada	★	President (u)	Speaker (u)	L(v)	...	...
New Hampshire	★	President	Speaker	M	M	★(ss)
New Jersey	★	President	Speaker	L, M	L, M	★
New Mexico	★	(w)	Speaker	L	L, M	...
New York	★	President pro tem in consultation with Independent democratic conference leader	Speaker	L, M	L, M	★
North Carolina	...	Rules Chair	Speaker	M	M	★
North Dakota	★	Majority Leader	Speaker	L	L	...
Ohio	★(y)	Reference Cmte.	Rules & Reference Cmte.	L(z)	L, M(aa)	★(bb)
Oklahoma	★	Majority Leader	Speaker	L	L	★(cc)
Oregon	★	President	Speaker	(dd)	(ee)	...
Pennsylvania	(x)	President Pro Tempore	Chief Clerk	M	M	...
Rhode Island	★	President	Speaker	M	M	★
South Carolina	★	President	Speaker	M	M	★(ff)
South Dakota	★	President Pro Tempore	Speaker	L	L	...
Tennessee	★	Speaker	Speaker	L, M	L, M	★(gg)
Texas	★	President	Speaker	L	L	...
Utah	★	President	Speaker	L	L	...
Vermont	(hh)	President	Speaker	L, M	L, M	★
Virginia	★	Clerk	Clerk (ii)	L, M(jj)	(kk)	★(ll)
Washington	★	(mm)	Speaker	L	L	★
West Virginia (nn)	★	President	Speaker	L, M	L, M	...
Wisconsin	...	President	Speaker	L, M	L, M	★(oo)
Wyoming	★	President	Speaker	L(vv)	L(vv)	...
American Samoa	...	...	...	...	...	...
Guam	★	Committee on Calendar Chairs	U	L, M(pp)	U	★
CNMI*	★	President	Speaker	L	L	...
Puerto Rico	...	President	Secretary	M	M	...
U.S. Virgin Islands	...	Senate President in Pro-Forma meeting	U	L	U	★

See footnotes at end of table

TABLE 3.14
Bill Pre-Filing, Reference and Carryover (continued)

Source: The Council of State Governments' survey, January 2019 and update from state websites 2019.

*Commonwealth of Northern Mariana Islands

Key:

★–Yes

…–No

L–Rules generally require all bills be referred to the appropriate committee of jurisdiction.

M–Rules require specific types of bills be referred to specific committees (e.g., appropriations, local bills).

U–Unicameral legislature.

(a) Legislative rules specify all or certain bills go to committees of jurisdiction.

(b) Unless otherwise indicated by footnote, bills may be introduced prior to convening each session of the legislature. In this column only: ★–pre-filing is allowed in both chambers (or in the case of Nebraska, in the unicameral legislature); …–pre-filing is not allowed in either chamber.

(c) Bills carry over from the first year of the legislature to the second (does not apply in Alabama, Arkansas, Montana, Nevada, North Dakota, Oregon and Texas, where legislatures meet biennially). Bills generally do not carry over after an intervening legislative election.

(d) Except between the end of the last regular session of the legislature in any quadrennium and the organizational session following the general election and for special sessions.

(e) Lieutenant governor is the president of the Senate. Senate Rule 14. House Rule 43.

(f) Senate bills referred by president with concurrence of president pro tem. House bills referred by president pro tem with concurrence of president, if no concurrence, referred by majority leader for assignment.

(g) Senate chief counsel makes recommendations to the presiding officer.

(h) Bills may be drafted prior to session, but may not be introduced until the first day of session. Bills introduced in the first year of the regular session and passed by the house of origin on or before the January 31st constitutional deadline in the second year are carryover bills.

(i) In either house, state law requires any bill which affects the sentencing of criminal offenders and which would result in a net increase of imprisonment in state correctional facilities must be assigned to the appropriations committee of the house in which it was introduced. In the Senate, a bill must be referred to the Appropriations Committee if it contains an appropriation from the state treasury or the increase of any salary. Each bill which provides that any state revenue be devoted to any purpose other than that to which it is devoted under existing law must be referred to the Finance Committee.

(j) Prefiling allowed in the House by rule, seven calendar days before the commencement of the regular session, in even-numbered years. Senate allows prefiling of bills as determined on a year-to-year basis. Senate bills are referred to committee by the members of the majority leadership appointed by the President.

(k) In even-numbered years, the Committee on Assignments (Senate) or Rules Committee (House) is to refer to substantive committees only appropriation bills implementing the budget, and bills deemed by the Committee on Assignments (Senate) or Rules Committee (House) to be of an emergency nature or of substantial importance to the operation of government.

(l) Only in the Senate.

(m) At the discretion of President Pro Tempore.

(n) Appropriation bills are the only "specific type" mentioned in the rules to be referred to either House Appropriation Cmte. or Senate Ways and Means.

(o) Subject to approval or disapproval. Louisiana–majority members present.

(p) Maine Joint Rule 308 sections 1,2,3, "All bills and resolves must be referred to committee, except that this provision may be suspended by a majority vote in each chamber."

(q) The President and Speaker may refer bills to any of the standing committees or the Rules Committees, but usually bills are referred according to subject matter.

(r) Pre-filing of bills allowed prior to the convening of the 2nd year of the biennium. Bill carryover allowed if in second year of a two-year session.

(s) The Nebraska Legislature's Executive Board serves as the Reference Committee.

(t) Bills are carried over from the 90-day session beginning in the odd-numbered year to the 60-day session, which begins in even-numbered year. Bills that have not passed by the last day of the 60-day session are all indefinitely postponed by motion on the last day of the session. The odd-numbered year shall be carried forward to the even-numbered year.

(u) In the Senate any member may make a motion for referral, but committee referrals are under the control of the Majority Floor Leader. In the House any member may make a motion for referral, and a chart is used to guide bill referrals based on statutory authority of committee, but committee referrals are under the control of the Majority Floor Leader.

(v) Rules do not require specific types of bills be referred to specific committees.

(w) Sponsor subject to approval of the body.

(x) Only in the Senate.

(y) Senate Rule 33: Between the general election and the time for the next convening session, a holdover member or member-elect may file bills for introduction in the next session with the Clerk's office. Those bills shall be treated as if they were bills introduced on the first day of the session. House Rule 61(d): Bills introduced prior to the convening of the session shall be treated as if they were bills introduced on the first day of the session. Between the general election and the time for the next convening session, a member-elect may file bills for introduction in the next session with the Clerk's office. The Clerk shall number such bills consecutively, in the order in which they are filed, beginning with the number "1".

TABLE 3.14
Bill Pre-Filing, Reference and Carryover (continued)

(z) Rule 35. (Bills, Second Consideration and Committee on Reference, Public Hearing.) On the second reading of a bill, the Committee on Reference shall, if no motion or order be made to the contrary, refer the bill to the proper standing committee in regular order. Further, no bill shall be reported for a third reading and passage unless the same shall have been considered at a meeting of the committee to which the same has been referred. All Senate bills and resolutions referred by the Committee on Reference on or before the first day of April in an even-numbered year shall be scheduled by the chairperson of the committee to which the same has been referred for a minimum of one public hearing.

(aa) House Rule 37: (a) All House bills and resolutions introduced on or before the fifteenth day of May in an even-numbered year, and in compliance with the rules of the House, shall be referred to a standing, select, or special committee or standing subcommittee, and shall be scheduled by the chairman of the committee for a minimum of one public hearing. (b) The sponsor of a bill or resolution shall appear at least once before the committee that is considering the bill or resolution unless excused by the chairman of the committee or the Speaker. It is not in order for the committee to report the bill or resolution unless its sponsor has appeared or has been excused from appearing before the committee. Rule 65. (Bills carrying appropriations.) All bills carrying an appropriation shall be referred to the Finance Committee for consideration and report before being considered the third time.

(bb) Bills carry over between the first and second year of each regular annual session, but not to the next biennial 2-year General Assembly.

(cc) A legislature consists of two years. Bills from the first session can carry over to the second session only.

(dd) The President can refer bills to any standing or special committee and may also attach subsequent referrals to other committees following action by the first committee.

(ee) Rules specify bills shall be referred by the Speaker to any standing or special committee and may also attach subsequent referrals to other committees following action by the first committee.

(ff) Allowed during the first year of the two year session.

(gg) Bills and resolutions introduced in the First Regular Session may carry over to the Second Regular Session (odd-numbered year to even-numbered year) only.

(hh) Bills are drafted prior to session but released starting first day of session.

(ii) Under the direction of the speaker.

(jj) Jurisdiction of the committees by subject matter is listed in the Rules.

(kk) The House Rules establish jurisdictional committees. The Speaker refers legislation to those committees as he deems appropriate.

(ll) Even-numbered year session to odd-numbered year session.

(mm) By the floor leader.

(nn) Prefiling allowed only in the house in even-numbered years.

(oo) From odd-year to even-year, but not between biennial sessions.

(pp) Substantive resolutions referred to sponsor for public hearing.

(qq) Bills may be referred by the President to an appropriate standing committee (Senate Rule 14). In the House the " Speaker shall refer the instrument to a standing committee or shall order the instrument for a second reading."(House Rule 43).

(rr) Allowed between session in a biennium, not to subsequent legislatures.

(ss) Referred bills may be held in committee and acted on during second year session.

(tt) President and Speaker have broad discretion.

(uu) Senate Rule 3.203
a) The Senate Majority Leader shall refer all bills, joint resolutions and alternative measures to a standing committee no later than one (1) Senate legislative day after being submitted to the Secretary of the Senate. The presiding officer shall announce the reference of all bills, joint resolutions and alternative measures ...
c) The Senate Majority Leader may change the original referral of a bill, resolution or alternative measure by oral notice to the Senate or written communication submitted to the Secretary of the Senate before the end of session on the next Senate legislative day following the day of the original referral. Notices of the written communication shall be announced by the Secretary of the Senate during session and both oral and written notifications shall be printed in the Journal. House Rule 41: (4) The Speaker shall refer all bills and joint resolutions to a standing committee no later than one House legislative day after being submitted to the Clerk. (5) The Speaker may change the original referral of a bill or resolution by written communication submitted to the Clerk before the end of session on the next House legislative day following the day of the original referral. Notice of the referral shall be announced by the Clerk and printed in the Journal.

(vv) Bills containing an appropriation are rereferred to the Appropriations Committee.

TABLE 3.15
Time Limits on Bill Introduction

State or other jurisdiction	Time limit on introduction of bills	Procedures for granting exception to time limits
Alabama	House: no limit. Senate: 24th legislative day of regular session (a).	House: N.A. Senate: Unanimous vote to suspend rules.
Alaska	35th C day of 2nd regular session.	Introduction by committee or by suspension of operation of limiting rule.
Arizona	House: 29th day of regular session; 10th day of special session. Senate: 22nd day of regular session; 10th day of special session.	House: Permission of rules committee. Senate: Permission of rules committee.
Arkansas	55th day of regular session (50th day for appropriations bills). Retirement and health care legislation affecting licensures shall be introduced during the first 15 days.	2/3 vote of membership of each house for appropriations bills and all others except retirement and health care legislation affecting licensures which require 3/4 vote of the membership of each house.
California	Deadlines established by the Joint Rules Committee adopted in each session.	Approval of Rules Committee and 3/4 vote of membership.
Colorado	House: 22nd C day of regular session. Senate: 17th C day of regular session.	Committees on delayed bills may extend deadline.
Connecticut	10 days into session in odd-numbered years, 3 days into session in even-numbered years (b).	2/3 vote of members present.
Delaware	House: no limit. Senate: no limit.	
Florida	House: noon of the first day of regular session (h). Senate: noon first day of regular session (h).	House: No exception as such; if needed, one would be granted by waiving the rule by 2/3 vote on the floor. Senate: Existence of an emergency reasonably compelling consideration notwithstanding the deadline.
Georgia	Only for specific types of bills	
Hawaii	Actual dates established during session.	Majority vote of membership.
Idaho	House: 20th day of session for personal bills; 36th day of session for all committees; beyond that only privileged cmtes. Senate: 12th day of session for personal bills; 36th day of session for all committees; beyond that only privileged cmtes.	House: speaker may designate any standing committee to serve as a privileged committee temporarily. House Rule 24. Senate: President may refer bill to privileged committee. Senate Rule 14.
Illinois	House: determined by speaker. Senate: determined by senate president.	House: the speaker may set deadlines for any action on any category of legislative measure, including deadlines for introduction of bills. Senate: At any time, the president may set alternative deadlines for any legislative action with written notice filed with the secretary.
Indiana	House: Mid-January. Senate: Date specific–set in Rules, different for long and short session. Mid-January	House: 2/3 vote. Senate: If date falls on weekend/Holiday–extended to next day. Sine die deadline set by statute, does not change.
Iowa	House: Drafting request received by Friday of 5th week of 1st regular session; or by Friday of 2nd week of 2nd regular session. Senate: Drafting request received by Friday of 5th week of 1st regular session; or by Friday of 2nd week of 2nd regular session.	House: Constitutional majority. Senate: Constitutional majority.
Kansas	Actual dates established in the Joint Rules of the House and Senate every two years when the joint rules are adopted.	Resolution adopted by majority of members of either house may make specific exceptions to deadlines.
Kentucky	House: No introductions during the last 14 L days of odd-year session, during last 22 L days of even-year session. Senate: No introductions during the last 14 L days of odd-year session, during last 20 L days of even-year session.	None.
Louisiana	House: 10th C day of odd-year sessions and 23rd C day of even-year sessions. Senate: 10th C day of odd-year sessions and 23rd C day of even-year sessions.	None.
Maine	House: Cloture dates established by the Legislative Council. Senate: Cloture dates established by the Legislative Council.	House: Bills filed after cloture date must be approved by a majority of the Legislative Council. Senate: Appeals heard by Legislative Council. Six votes required to allow introduction of legislation.
Maryland	House and Senate: No introductions during the last 35 days of regular session, unless 2/3 of the elected members of a chamber vote yes. Additional limitations involve committee action. Senate bills introduced after the 24th calendar day must be referred to the Senate Rules Committee and also Senate bills introduced after the 10th calendar day on behalf of the administration, i.e. the governor, must be referred to the Senate Rules Committee. House bills introduced during the last 59 calendar days (after the 31st day) are referred to the House Rules Committee. The Senate Rules and House Rules contain further provisions concerning the requirements for forcing legislation out of these committees.	House: 2/3 vote of elected members of each house.
Massachusetts	1st Wednesday in December even-numbered years, 1st Wednesday in November odd-numbered years.	2/3 vote of members present and voting.
Michigan	No limit.	
Minnesota	No limit.	

See footnotes at end of table

TABLE 3.15
Time Limits on Bill Introduction (continued)

State or other jurisdiction	Time limit on introduction of bills	Procedures for granting exception to time limits
Mississippi	14th C day in 90 day session; 49th C day in 125 day session (e).	2/3 vote of members present and voting.
Missouri	House: 60th L day of regular session. Senate: March 1.	Majority vote of elected members each house; governor's request for consideration of bill by special message.
Montana	Introduction of bills & resolutions: 10th L day if requested prior to convening or 2 days after receipt of finished bill draft after session convenes, whichever is earlier. Requests for general bills & resolutions: 12th L day; revenue bills: 17th L day; committee bills & resolutions: 36th L day; appropriations bills: 45th L day; interim study resolutions: 60th L day; committee revenue bills and bills proposing referenda: 62nd L day; committee bills implementing provision of a general appropriation act: 67th L day; resolutions confirming governor appointees or bill amending/repealing administrative rule: no deadline.	2/3 vote of members.
Nebraska	10th L day of any session (f).	3/5 vote of elected membership.
Nevada	Actual dates established at start of session.	Waiver granted by majority leader of the Senate and speaker of the Assembly acting jointly.
New Hampshire	Determined by rules.	2/3 vote of members present.
New Jersey	No limit.	
New Mexico	House: 15 days in short session/even years, 30 days in long session/odd years. Senate: 15 days in short session/even years, 30 days in long session/odd years.	None. Statutory limit for legislators; governor not limited and can send bill with message.
New York	Assembly: for unlimited introduction of bills, the final day is the last Tuesday in May of the 2nd year of the legislative term. Senate: Determined by the Majority Conference leaders, but no earlier than 1st Tuesday in March; except introduction by agencies is March 1, for all other program bills it is 1st Tuesday in April.	Assembly: By unanimous consent, by introduction by Rules Cmte., by message from the Senate, consent of the Speaker, or by members elected at special election who take office after the first Tuesday in May. Senate: Introduction by Rules Committee after 2nd Friday in June, or by message from the Assembly.
North Carolina	Actual dates established during session.	Senate: 2/3 vote of membership present and voting shall be required.
North Dakota	House: 8th L day. Senate: 13th L day.	2/3 vote of the floor or by approval of Delayed Bills Committee.
Ohio	No limit.	
Oklahoma	Time limit set in rules.	2/3 vote of membership.
Oregon	House: Set by House rules for odd-numbered year sessions. It was the 17th calendar day in 2015. All measures must be presession filed for even-year session. Senate: Set by Senate rules for odd-numbered year sessions. It was the 23rd calendar day in 2015. All measures must be presession filed for even-year session.	House: Bills approved by the Rules Committee; appropriation or fiscal measures sponsored by the Cmte. on Ways and Means; other committee bills approved by the Speaker; member priority requests (limited to 5 measures for odd-year session, none for even-year session). Senate: Measures approved by the Senate President: appropriations or fiscal measures sponsored by the Cmte. On Ways and Means.
Pennsylvania	No limit.	
Rhode Island	Second week of February for Public Bills.	Sponsor must give one legislative day's notice.
South Carolina	House: Prior to April 15 of the 2nd yr. of a two-yr. legislative session; May 1 for bills first introduced in Senate. Rule 5.12. Senate: May 1 of regular session for bills originating in House. Rule 47.	House and Senate: 2/3 vote of members present and voting.
South Dakota	Individual bills: 40-day session: 15th L day; 35-day session: 10th L day. Committee bills: 40-day session: 16th L day; 35-day session: 11th L day. If a session calendar is adopted for a period of 36 days to 39 days, the legislative deadlines for the 35-day session shall be increased by the number of days by which the length of the session calendar exceeds 35 days.	2/3 approval of members-elect.
Tennessee	General bills, 10th L day of regular session (g).	Unanimous approval by Delayed Bills Committee.
Texas	60th C day of regular session, except for local bills, emergency appropriations and all emergency matters submitted by the governor in a special message to the legislature.	4/5 vote of members present and voting.
Utah	12:00 p.m. on 11th day of session.	Motion for request must be approved by a constitutional majority vote.
Vermont	House: 1st session–last day of February; 2nd session–last day of January. Senate: 1st session–70-day limit; 2nd session–25 C days before start of session.	Approval by Rules Committee.
Virginia	Set by joint procedural resolution adopted at the beginning of the session (usually the second Friday of the session is the last day to introduce legislation that does not have any earlier deadline).	As provided in the joint procedural resolution (usually unanimous consent or at written request of the governor).
Washington	Until 10 days before the end of session unless 2/3 vote of elected members of each house.	2/3 vote of elected members of each house.
West Virginia	House: 42nd C day. Senate: 41st C day.	2/3 vote of members present.

See footnotes at end of table

TABLE 3.15
Time Limits on Bill Introduction (continued)

State or other jurisdiction	Time limit on introduction of bills	Procedures for granting exception to time limits
Wisconsin	No limit.	
Wyoming	House and Senate: 15th L day of session in odd-numbered years. 5th L day in even-numbered years.	House: 2/3 vote of elected members. Senate: 2/3 vote of elected members. (During Budget Session need unanimous consent)
American Samoa	House: After the 25th L day of the fourth Regular Session. Senate: After the 15th L day.	
Guam	Public hearing on bill must be held no more than 120 days after date of bill introduction.	
CNMI*	No limit.	
Puerto Rico	1st session–within first 125 days; 2nd session–within first 60 days.	None.
U.S. Virgin Islands	No limit.	

Source: The Council of State Governments' survey, January 2019 and updates from state websites 2019.
*Commonwealth of Mariana Islands
Key:
C–Calendar
L–Legislative
(a) Not applicable to local bills, advertised or otherwise.
(b) Specific dates set in Joint Rules.
(c) Not applicable to appropriations bills.
(d) Not applicable to local bills and joint resolutions.
(e) Except Appropriation and Revenue bills (51st/86th C day) and Local & Private bills (83rd/118th C day).
(f) Except appropriations bills and bills introduced at the request of the governor, bills can be introduced during the first 10 legislative days of the session. Appropriation bills and bills introduced at the request of the governor can be introduced at any time during the session.

(g) Local bills have no cutoff.
(h) House: For Member-filed bills, noon of the first day of regular session. House Rule 5.2 sets a time limit for the introduction of bills, but this applies to Member-filed bills only. Proposed committee bills, local bills (dependent on completion of 30-day public notice period), and committee substitutes (treated by House Rules as new bills) are routinely filed after the first day of Session. Senate: Not applicable to appropriations bills, concurrent resolutions regarding certain subjects, local bills (which have no deadline), claim bills (deadline is August 1 of the year preceding consideration or within 62 days of a Senator's election), committee bills, trust fund bills, and public records exemptions linked to timely filed bills.

TABLE 3.16
Enacting Legislation: Veto, Veto Override and Effective Date

State or other jurisdiction	Governor may item veto appropriation bills		Days allowed governor to consider bill (a)		
			During session	After session	
	Amount	Other (b)	Bill becomes law unless vetoed	Bill becomes law unless vetoed	Bill dies unless signed
Alabama	★(e)	...	6 (f)	10A	
Alaska	★	...	15	20P	
Arizona	★	★	5	10A	
Arkansas	★	...	5	20A	
California	★(i)	...	12 (j)	30A	
Colorado	★	(l)	10P (ggg)	30A (m)	
Connecticut	★	...	5	15P	(o)
Delaware	★	...	10P	10P	30A
Florida	...	★	7 (ddd)	15P (m)	
Georgia	★	★	6	40A	
Hawaii (q)	★(r)	...	10 (s)	45A (s)(p)	10P (p)
Idaho	★	★	5	10P	
Illinois	★	...	60 (m)	60P (m)	
Indiana	...	...	7	7P	
Iowa	★	★	3		30A
Kansas	★	★	10 (m)		10P
Kentucky	★	...	10	90A	
Louisiana (q)	★	★	10 (m)	20P (m)	
Maine	★	...	10		(v)
Maryland	★(w)	★	6 (x)	30P (y)	(z)
Massachusetts	★	★	10	10P	10A
Michigan	★	★	14 (m)		14P
Minnesota	★	(i)	3P	14A, 3P	3A, 14P
Mississippi	★	...	5	15P (dd)	
Missouri	★	...	15	45A	
Montana (q)	★	★	10 (m)	25A (m)	
Nebraska	★	...	5	5A, 5P	(ff)
Nevada	...	...	5 (gg)	10A (gg)	
New Hampshire	...	...	5	5P	
New Jersey	★	...	45		
New Mexico	★	★	3 (hh)		20A
New York	★	...	10 (ii)	(ii)	30A
North Carolina	...	...	10	30A	
North Dakota	★	...	3	15A	
Ohio	★	★	10	10P	10A
Oklahoma	★	...	5 (mm)		15A (mm)
Oregon	★	...	5	30A (s)	
Pennsylvania	★	★	10	30A	
Rhode Island	...	...	6	10P (oo)	(oo)
South Carolina	★	...	5	(qq)	
South Dakota	★	...	5 (rr)	15P (rr)	
Tennessee	★	...	10	(ss)	
Texas	★	★(iii)	10	20A	
Utah	★	...	10P	20A	
Vermont	...	...	5	5A	(fff)
Virginia	★	★(tt)	7 (m)	30A (uu)	
Washington	★	★	5	20A	
West Virginia	...	(i)	5	15A (xx)	
Wisconsin	★	★(eee)	6	6P	
Wyoming	★	★	3	15A	
American Samoa	★	...	10		30A
Guam	★	★	10	10P	30P (zz)
CNMI*	★	★	40 (m)(aaa)		
Puerto Rico	★	...	10		30P
U.S. Virgin Islands	★(ccc)	★(ccc)	10	10P	30A

See footnotes at end of table

TABLE 3.16
Enacting Legislation: Veto, Veto Override and Effective Date (continued)

State or other jurisdiction	Votes required in each house to pass bills or items over veto (c)	Effective date of enacted legislation (d)
Alabama	Majority of elected body	Date signed by governor, unless otherwise specified.
Alaska	2/3 elected (g)	90 days after enactment or the specified effective date.
Arizona	2/3 elected (h)	90 days after adjournment
Arkansas	Majority elected	91st day after adjournment
California	2/3 elected (hhh)	(k)
Colorado	2/3 elected	90 days after adjournment (n)
Connecticut	2/3 elected	Oct. 1, unless otherwise specified.
Delaware	3/5 elected	Immediately or enactment clause
Florida	2/3 members present in each house	60 days after adjournment sine die or on specified date.
Georgia	2/3 elected	Unless other date specified, July 1 for generals, date signed by governor for locals.
Hawaii (q)	2/3 elected	Immediately or on the prospective date stated in the legislation.
Idaho	2/3 present	July 1
Illinois	3/5 elected (g)	Usually Jan. 1 of next year (t)
Indiana	Majority elected	(u)
Iowa	2/3 elected	July 1, unless otherwise specified. Effective date for bills which become law on or after July 1, 45 days after approval, unless otherwise specified.
Kansas	2/3 membership	Upon publication or specified date after publication
Kentucky	Majority elected	90 days after adjournment sine die. Unless the bill contains an emergency clause or special effective date.
Louisiana (q)	2/3 elected	Aug. 1
Maine	2/3 elected	90 days after adjournment unless enacted as an emergency.
Maryland	3/5 elected (aa)	June 1 (bb)
Massachusetts	2/3 present	90 days after enactment
Michigan	2/3 elected and serving	Immediate effect if vote of 2/3 elected and serving. 90 days after adjournment, if immediate effect not given.
Minnesota	2/3 elected–90 House; 45 Senate	Aug. 1 (cc)
Mississippi	2/3 elected	July 1 unless specified otherwise.
Missouri	2/3 elected	Aug. 28 (ee)
Montana (q)	2/3 present	Oct. 1 (cc)
Nebraska	3/5 elected	90 days following adjournment sine die. Unless bill contains an emergency clause.
Nevada	2/3 elected	Oct. 1, unless measure stipulates a different date.
New Hampshire	2/3 present	60 days after enactment, unless otherwise noted.
New Jersey	2/3 elected	Dates usually specified
New Mexico	2/3 present	90 days after adjournment unless other date specified. General appropriations acts or emergency clauses passed by 2/3 present take effect immediately.
New York	2/3 present	20 days after enactment unless otherwise prescribed in the bill.
North Carolina	3/5 elected	60 days after adjournment
North Dakota	2/3 elected	(jj)
Ohio	3/5 elected (kk)	91st day after filing with secretary of state. (ll)
Oklahoma	2/3 elected	90 days after adjournment unless specified in the bill.
Oregon	2/3 present	Jan. 1st of following year. (nn)
Pennsylvania	2/3 majority	60 days after signed by governor
Rhode Island	3/5 present	Immediately (pp)
South Carolina	2/3 vote of the members present and voting	Date of signature
South Dakota	2/3 elected	July 1
Tennessee	Constitutional majority	40 days after enactment unless otherwise specified
Texas	2/3 present	90 days after adjournment unless otherwise specified
Utah	2/3 elected	60 days after adjournment of the session at which it passed.
Vermont	2/3 present	July 1 unless otherwise specified.
Virginia	2/3 present (vv)	July 1 (ww)
Washington	2/3 present	90 days after adjournment
West Virginia	Majority elected	90 days after enactment
Wisconsin	2/3 present	Day after publication date unless otherwise specified
Wyoming	2/3 elected	Specified in act
American Samoa	2/3 elected	60 days after adjournment (yy)
Guam	10 votes to override	Immediately (bbb)
CNMI*	2/3 elected	Upon signing by the governor.
Puerto Rico	2/3 elected	Specified in act
U.S. Virgin Islands	2/3 elected	Immediately

See footnotes at end of table

TABLE 3.16
Enacting Legislation: Veto, Veto Override and Effective Date (continued)

Source: The Council of State Governments' survey, January 2019 and state websites 2019.

*Commonwealth of Northern Mariana Islands

Key:

★–Yes

…–No

A–Days after adjournment of legislature.

P–Days after presentation to governor.

(a) Sundays excluded, unless otherwise indicated.

(b) Includes language in appropriations bill.

(c) Bill returned to house of origin with governor's objections.

(d) Effective date may be established by the law itself or may be otherwise changed by vote of the legislature. Special or emergency acts are usually effective immediately.

(e) The governor may line item distinct items or item veto amounts in appropriation bills, if returned prior to final adjournment.

(f) Except bills presented within five days of final adjournment, Sundays are included.

(g) Different number of votes required for revenue and appropriations bills. Alaska–3/4 elected. Illinois–Only the usual majority of members elected is required to restore a reduced item.

(h) Several specific requirements of 3/4 majority.

(i) Line item veto.

(j) For a bill to become law during session, if 12th day falls on a Saturday, Sunday, or holiday, the period is extended to the next day that is not a Saturday, Sunday, or holiday.

(k) For legislation enacted in regular sessions: January 1 of the following year. Urgency legislation: immediately upon chaptering by Secretary of State. Legislation enacted in special session: 91st day after adjournment of the special session at which the bill was passed.

(l) The governor may not line-item veto any portion of any bill (including appropriation clauses in bills) other than line items in the Long Appropriations Bill. The governor may line-item veto individual lines in the Long Appropriations Bill. In those instances, the governor must line-item veto the entire amount of any item; an item is an indivisible sum of money dedicated to a single purpose.

(m) Sundays included.

(n) An act takes effect on the date stated in the act, or if no date is stated in the act, then upon signature of the governor. If no safety clause on a bill, the bill takes effect 90 days after sine die if no referendum petition has been filed. The state constitution allows for a 90-day period following adjournment when petitions may be filed for bills that do not contain a safety clause.

(o) Bill enacted if not signed/vetoed within time frames.

(p) The governor must notify the legislature 10 days before the 45th day of his intent to veto a measure on that day. The legislature may convene at or before noon on the 45th day after adjournment to consider the vetoed measures. If the legislature fails to reconvene, the bill does not become law. If the legislature reconvenes, it may pass the measure over the governor's veto or it may amend the law to meet the governor's objections. If the law is amended, the governor must sign the bill within 10 days after it is presented to him in order for it to become law.

(q) Constitution withholds right to veto constitutional amendments proposed by the legislature.

(r) Governor can also reduce amounts in appropriations bills. In Hawaii, governor can reduce items in executive appropriations measures, but cannot reduce or item veto amounts appropriated for the judicial or legislative branches.

(s) Except Sundays and legal holidays. In Hawaii, except Saturdays, Sundays, holidays and any days in which the legislature is in recess prior to its adjournment. In Oregon, if the governor does not sign the bill within 30 days after adjournment, it becomes law without the governor's signature, Saturdays and Sundays are excluded.

(t) Effective date for bills which become law on or after July 1: A bill passed after May 31 cannot take effect before June 1 of the following year unless it states an earlier effective date and is approved by 3/5 of the members elected to each house.

(u) Varies with date of the veto.

(v) "If the bill or resolution shall not be returned by the governor within 10 days (Sundays excepted) after it shall have been presented to the governor, it shall have the same force and effect as if the governor had signed it unless the Legislature by their adjournment prevent its return, in which case it shall have such force and effect, unless returned within 3 days after the next meeting of the same Legislature which enacted the bill or resolution; if there is no such next meeting of the Legislature which enacted the bill or resolution, the bill or resolution shall not be a law." (excerpted from Article IV, Part Third, Section 2 of the Constitution of Maine).

(w) The governor cannot veto the budget bill but may exercise a total veto or item veto on a supplementary appropriations bill. In practice this means the governor may strike items in the annual general capital loan bill. Occasionally the governor will also veto a bond bill or a portion of a bond bill.

(x) If a bill is presented to the governor in the first 83 days of session, the governor has only six days (not including Sunday) to act before the bill automatically becomes law.

(y) All bills passed at regular or special sessions must be presented to the governor no later than 20 days after adjournment. The governor has a limited time to sign or veto a bill after it is presented. If the governor does not act within that time, the bill becomes law automatically; there is no pocket veto. The time limit depends on when the presentment is made. Any bill presented in the last 7 days of the 90-day session or after adjournment must be acted on within 30 days after presentment. Bills vetoed after adjournment are returned to the legislature for reconsideration at the next meeting of the same General Assembly.

(z) The governor has a limited time to sign or veto a bill after it is presented. If the governor does not act within that time, the bill becomes law automatically; there is no pocket veto. The time limit depends on when the presentment is made.

(aa) Vetoed bills are returned to the house of origin immediately after that house has organized at the next regular or special session. When a new General Assembly is elected and sworn in, bills vetoed from the previous session are not returned. These vetoed bills are not subject to any further legislative action.

TABLE 3.16
Enacting Legislation: Veto, Veto Override and Effective Date (continued)

(bb) Unless otherwise provided, June 1 is the effective date for bond bills, July 1 for budget, tax and revenue bills. By custom October 1 is the usual effective date for other legislation. If the bill is an emergency measure, it may take effect immediately upon approval by the governor or at a specified date prior to June 1. For vetoed legislation, 30 days after the veto is overridden or on the date specified in the bill, whichever is later. An emergency bill passed over the governor's veto takes effect immediately.

(cc) Different date for fiscal legislation. Minnesota–July 1. Montana–Appropriations effective July 1 unless otherwise specified in bill; revenue bills effected July 1 unless otherwise specified in bill, often next Jan. 1.

(dd) Bills vetoed after adjournment are returned to the legislature for reconsideration. Mississippi–returned within three days after the beginning of the next session.

(ee) If bill has an emergency clause, it becomes effective upon governor's signature. If a bill is neither signed nor vetoed by a governor, it becomes law.

(ff) Bills are carried over from the 90-day session beginning in the odd-numbered year to the 60-day session, which begins in even-numbered years. Bills that have not passed by the last day of the 60-day session are all indefinitely postponed by motion on the last day of the session.

(gg) The day of delivery and Sundays are not counted for purposes of calculating these periods.

(hh) Except bills presented to the governor in the last three days of session, for which the governor has 20 days from adjournment.

(ii) If the legislature adjourns during the governor's consideration of a 10-day bill, the bill shall not become law without the governor's approval.

(jj) August 1 after filing with the secretary of state. Appropriations and tax bills July 1 after filing with secretary of state, or date set in legislation by Legislative Assembly, or by date established by emergency clause in a bill that passes each house by a vote of two-thirds of the members-elect of each house.

(kk) The exception covers such matters as emergency measures and court bills that originally required a 2/3 majority for passage. In those cases, the same extraordinary majority vote is required to override a veto.

(ll) Emergency, current appropriation, and tax legislation effective immediately. The General Assembly may also enact an uncodified section of law specifying a desired effective date that is after the constitutionally established effective date.

(mm) During session the governor has 5 days (except Sunday) to sign or veto a bill or it becomes law automatically. After Session a bill becomes a pocket veto if not signed 15 days after sine die.

(nn) Unless emergency declared or date specific in text of measure, which must be at least 90 days after adjournment sine die unless emergency is declared. Emergency cannot be declared in bills regulating taxation or exemption.

(oo) Bills become effective without signature if not signed or vetoed.

(pp) Date signed, date received by Secretary of State if effective without signature, date that veto is overridden, or other specified date.

(qq) Two days after the next meeting.

(rr) During a session, a bill becomes law if a governor signs it or does not act on it within five days, not including Saturdays, Sundays or holidays. If the legislature has adjourned or recessed or is within five days of a recess or an adjournment, the governor has 15 days to act on the bill. If he does not act, the bill becomes law.

(ss) Adjournment of the legislature is irrelevant; the governor has 10 days to act on a bill after it is presented to him or it becomes law without his signature.

(tt) If part of the item.

(uu) The governor has thirty days after adjournment of the legislature to act on any bills. The Constitution of Virginia provides that: "If the governor does not act on any bill, it shall become law without his signature."

(vv) Must include majority of elected members.

(ww) Unless a different date is stated in the bill. Special sessions–first day of fourth month after adjournment.

(xx) Five days for supplemental appropriation bills.

(yy) Laws required to be approved only by the governor. An act required to be approved by the U.S. Secretary of the Interior only after it is vetoed by the governor and so approved takes effect 40 days after it is returned to the governor by the secretary.

(zz) After Legislature adjourns sine die at end of two-year term.

(aaa) Twenty days for appropriations bills.

(bbb) U.S. Congress may annul.

(ccc) May item veto language or amounts in a bill that contains two or more appropriations.

(ddd) The governor has seven days, Sundays included, to act on presented bills while the Legislature is in session. If the Legislature adjourns sine die during the seven-day period or takes a recess of more than 30 days, the governor has 15 consecutive days from the date of presentation to act on the bill(s).

(eee) Governor may partially veto words or numbers in the case of appropriation bills.

(fff) Three days subsequent to presentation following adjournment in even-numbered years.

(ggg) Ten calendar days after receipt of bill. When the Governor receives bills within the last 10 days of session, the Governor has 30 days to act on the bills.

(hhh) Per Joint Rule 58.5, the Legislature may consider a Governor's veto for only 60 legislative days or until adjournment sine die of the session in which the bill subject to the veto was passed by the Legislature, whichever period is shorter.

(iii) The governor has also vetoed budget riders.

TABLE 3.17

Legislative Appropriations Process: Budget Documents and Bills

State or other jurisdiction	Legal source of deadline		Budget document submission					Budget bill introduction		
				Submission date relative to convening						
	Constitutional	Statutory	Prior to session	Within one week	Within two weeks	Within one month	Over one month	Same time as budget document	Another time	Not until cmte. review of budget document
Alabama	★	★	(a)	★	...	...	...	★	...	...
Alaska	★	★	...	(a)	...	...	...	★	...	...
Arizona	...	★	★	...	...	...	...	...	...	★
Arkansas	...	★	★	...	...	...	...	...	...	★
California	★	...	...	...	...	(a)	...	★(b)	...	...
Colorado	...	★	★(a)	...	...	...	...	...	76th day by rule	...
Connecticut	...	★	...	...	...	(a)	...	★	...	...
Delaware	...	...	...	...	...	...	...	...	...	★
Florida	★	★	★	...	...	...	...	...	...	★
Georgia	★	...	...	(a)	...	...	...	★	...	...
Hawaii	...	★	30 days	...	...	...	...	...	★	...
Idaho	...	★	...	...	...	...	★(a)	...	...	★
Illinois	...	★	...	...	...	...	★(a)	...	★(c)	...
Indiana	...	★	...	...	...	...	...	...	★	...
Iowa	...	★	...	...	...	(a)	...	...	...	★(d)
Kansas	...	★	...	...	★(e)	...	...	...	★	...
Kentucky	★	...	...	...	(a)	...	...	★	...	...
Louisiana	...	★	(f)	(f)	...	...	...	(g)	...	...
Maine	...	★	...	(a)	...	...	...	★	...	...
Maryland	★	...	...	★(e)	...	...	...	★(h)	...	...
Massachusetts	...	★	...	...	...	★	...	★	...	...
Michigan	...	★	...	...	...	★	...	★	...	...
Minnesota	...	★	...	...	...	(a)	...	...	...	★
Mississippi	...	★	★	...	...	...	...	...	★	...
Missouri	★	...	...	...	...	★	...	...	...	★
Montana	...	★	★	...	...	...	...	...	★	...
Nebraska	...	★	★	...	...	★	...	★(i)	...	...
Nevada	★	...	(a)	...	...	...	...	...	...	★
New Hampshire	...	★	...	...	...	...	(a)	...	★	...
New Jersey	...	★	...	...	...	...	...	...	...	★
New Mexico	...	★	★	...	...	(a)	...	...	★	...
New York	★	...	(a)	...	★(a)	...	...	...	★(j)	...
North Carolina	...	...	...	...	...	...	...	★	...	...
North Dakota	...	★	(k)	...	...	...	...	...	★(k)	...
Ohio	...	★	...	...	...	★(d)(e)	...	★(x)	...	...
Oklahoma	★	★	...	★	...	...	...	...	★	...
Oregon	...	★	★	...	...	...	★(l)	★(m)	...	★
Pennsylvania	★	...	...	...	...	...	★	...	...	★
Rhode Island	...	★	...	...	...	...	★	...	★	...
South Carolina	...	★	...	★	...	...	...	...	...	★
South Dakota	...	★	...	...	...	...	★(o)	...	★(p)	...
Tennessee	...	★	...	...	★(a)(e)	★(a)(e)	...	★	...	...
Texas	...	★	...	(n)	...	...	...	★(q)	...	...
Utah	...	★(t)	(a)	...	...	...	...	...	...	★
Vermont	...	★	(s)	...	...	...	...	...	...	★
Virginia	...	★	Dec. 20	...	...	...	...	★	...	...
Washington	★(t)	...	(u)	...	...	...	...	★	...	...
West Virginia	★	...	...	★	...	...	...	★	...	...
Wisconsin	...	★	...	...	...	★(v)	...	★	...	...
Wyoming	...	★	Dec. 1	...	...	...	...	...	...	★
American Samoa	...	★	★	...	...	...	...	★	...	...
Guam	...	★	...	...	...	★(w)	...	★	...	...
CNMI*	★	★	April 1	...	...	...	...	...	★	★
Puerto Rico	...	★	...	...	...	★	...	...	...	★
U.S. Virgin Islands	...	★	May 30	...	...	...	...	...	★	...

See footnotes at end of table

TABLE 3.17
Legislative Appropriations Process: Budget Documents and Bills (continued)

Sources: The Council of State Governments' survey, January 2019 and state websites, 2019.

*Commonwealth of Northern Mariana Islands

Key:

★–Yes

…–No

(a) Specific time limitations:
Alabama–within first five days of session;
Alaska–December 15, 4th legislative day;
California–January 10;
Connecticut–not later than the first session day following the third day in February, in each odd-numbered year;
Colorado–presented by November 1 to the Joint Budget Committee;
Georgia–first five days of session;
Idaho–September 1 (I.C. § 67-3502);
Illinois–Third Wednesday in February;
Iowa–no later than February 1;
Kentucky–10th legislative day;
Maine–The Governor shall transmit the budget document to the Legislature not later than the Friday following the first Monday in January of the first regular legislative session. … A Governor-elect elected to a first term of office shall transmit the budget document to the Legislature not later than the Friday following the first Monday in February of the first regular legislative session (Maine Revised Statutes, Title 5, Chapter 149, Section 1666);
Minnesota–by the 4th Tuesday in January each odd-numbered year;
Nevada–no later than 14 days before commencement of regular session;
New Hampshire–by February 15;
New Mexico–by January 10 in an odd year, January 5 in an even year. Legislative Finance Cmte. must submit budget no later than first week of session;
New York–The legislative budget must be submitted to the governor no later than December 1. The executive budget must be submitted by the governor to the legislature by the 2nd Tuesday following the opening of session (or February 1 for the first session following a gubernatorial election);
Tennessee–on or before February 1 for sitting governor;
Utah–Must submit to the legislature by the calendared floor time on the first day of the annual session.

(b) Budget and Budget Bill are annual–to be submitted within the first 10 days of each calendar year.

(c) Deadlines for introducing bills in general are set by Senate president and House speaker.

(d) Executive budget bill is introduced and used as a working tool for committee.

(e) Later for first session of a new governor; Kansas–21 days; Maryland–10 days after; New Jersey–February 15; Ohio–by March 15; Tennessee–March 1.

(f) The governor shall submit his executive budget to the Joint Legislative Committee on the budget no later than 45 days prior to each regular session; except that in the first year of each term, the executive budget shall be submitted no later than 30 days prior to the regular session. Copies shall be made available to the entire legislature on the first day of each regular session.

(g) Bills appropriating monies for the general operating budget and ancillary appropriations, bills appropriating funds for the expenses of the legislature and the judiciary must be submitted to the legislature for introduction no later than 45 days prior to each regular session, except that in the first year of each term, such appropriation bills shall be submitted no later than 30 days prior to the regular session.

(h) Appropriations bill other than the budget bill (supplementary) may be introduced at any time. They must provide their own tax source and may not be enacted until the budget bill is enacted.

(i) Governor's budget bill is introduced and serves as a working document for the Appropriations Committee. The governor must submit the budget proposal by January 15 of each odd-numbered year. (Neb.Rev.Stat. sec.81-125). The statute extends this deadline to February 1 for a governor who is in his first year of office.

(j) Submission of the governor's budget bills to the legislature occurs with submission of the executive budget.

(k) Legislative Council's Budget Section hears the executive budget recommendations during legislature's December organizational session. Budget bill introduction one week after governor's budget message.

(l) By December 1st of even-numbered year unless new governor is elected; if new governor is elected, then February 1st of odd-numbered year.

(m) Legislature often introduces other budget bills during legislative session that are not part of the governor's recommended budget.

(n) The Legislative Budget Board is required to submit a copy of the budget of estimated appropriations to the governor and members of the legislature not later than the fifth day after session convenes. The board is required to submit a copy of the general appropriations bill not later than the seventh day after session convenes.

(o) It is usually over a month. The budget must be delivered to the Legislature not later than the first Tuesday after the first Monday in December.

(p) It must be introduced no later than the 16th legislative day.

(q) State law does not specify a special deadline for filing the General Appropriations Act, but it is generally filed soon after the Legislative Budget Board submits the budget document.

(r) Legislative rules require budget bills to be introduced by the 43rd day of the session.

(s) Third Tuesday each year.

(t) And Rules.

(u) For fiscal period other than biennium, 20 days prior to first day of session.

(v) Last Tuesday in January. A later submission date may be requested by the governor.

(w) Usually January before end of current fiscal year.

(x) Bill may actually be officially introduced a few days later; it is usually not immediately introduced upon the presentation of the governor's budget.

TABLE 3.18
Fiscal Notes: Content and Distribution

State or other jurisdiction	Content						Distribution						
							Legislators						Executive budget staff
										Appropriations committee			
	Intent or purpose of bill	Cost involved	Projected future cost	Proposed source of revenue	Fiscal impact on local govt.	Other	All	Available on request	Bill sponsor	Members	Chair only	Fiscal staff	Executive budget staff
Alabama	★	★	...	★	★	★(a)	★	★	★	★	...	★	★
Alaska	...	★	★	★	...	...	★	★	★	...	...	★	★
Arizona	★	★	★	★	★	★	★	★	★	★	...	★	★
Arkansas (b)	...	★	★	...	★	★	★	...	...	...	...	...	...
California	★	★	★	★	★	...	★	...	...	...	...	★	★
Colorado	★	★	★	★	★	...	★	...	...	...	...	...	...
Connecticut	★	★	★	★	★	...	(c)	...	...	...	...	...	...
Delaware	★	★	★	★	★(m)	...	★	...	...	...	...	...	...
Florida	★	★	★	★	★	...	★	...	...	...	...	★	...
Georgia	...	★	★	...	★	...	★	★	...	...	...	...	...
Hawaii	...	...	...	...	...	★(hh)	...	...	...	...	...	...	...
Idaho	★	★	★	★	★	(ll)	★	...	...	...	...	(e)	(e)
Illinois	...	★	★	★	★	...	★(f)	★	★	...	...	...	...
Indiana	★	★	★	★	★	...	★	...	...	...	...	★	★
Iowa	★	★	★	★	★	...	(g)						
Kansas	★	★	★	★	★	...	★	★	★	...	★	★	★
Kentucky	★	★	★	★	★	★	...	★	★	★	...	★	...
Louisiana	...	★	★	...	...	...	★	★	...	...	★(h)	...	...
Maine	...	★	★	★	★	...	...	★(i)	★	...	...	★	★
Maryland	★	★	★	★	★	★(j)	...	...	★(k)	...	...	...	...
Massachusetts	...	★(l)	★	...	...	★	★	...	...	...	★	...	...
Michigan	★	★	★	★	★	★(m)	★(n)	...	...	...	...	...	...
Minnesota	★	★	★	★	★	...	...	...	★	...	★	★	★
Mississippi	...	★	★	★	...	...	...	...	★(o)	...	...	...	...
Missouri	★	★	★	★	★	...	...	★	...	...	...	★	★
Montana	...	★	★	...	★	★(p)	★	...	...	...	...	★	★
Nebraska	...	★	★	★	★	...	★	★	...	...	...	★	★
Nevada	...	★	★	★	★	...	★(kk)	...	...	...	...	...	...
New Hampshire (ii)	★	★	...	★	★	...	...	★	...	★	...	★	★
New Jersey	...	★	...	★	★	...	★	...	...	...	...	★	...
New Mexico	★	★	★	★	★	...	★	...	...	★	...	(q)	(q)
New York	★	★	★	...	★	★(r)	...	★	★	★	...	★	...
North Carolina	...	★	★	...	★	★	(s)	...	...	...	...	...	...
North Dakota	...	...	★	★	★	★(t)	(u)	★	...	...	...	★	★
Ohio	★	★	★	★	★	...	(v)	★	★	...	...	★	...
Oklahoma	★	★	★	★	...	...	...	★	...	★	★	...	...
Oregon	★	★	★	★	★	...	★	...	...	...	...	★	★
Pennsylvania	...	★	★	★	...	...	...	...	...	★	...	★	...
Rhode Island	★	★	★	★	★	...	...	★	...	★	...	★	★
South Carolina	★	★	★	★	★	...	...	★	...	(w)	...	★	★
South Dakota	...	★	★	★	★	...	...	★	...	...	...	...	...
Tennessee	★	★	★	...	★	...	★	★	★	...	...	...	...
Texas	...	★	★	★	★	★(x)	★	★	★	(jj)	...	...	...
Utah	...	★	★	★	★	★(y)	★	★	★	...	...	★	★
Vermont	(z)						...	★	...	...	★	...	...
Virginia	★	★	★	★	★	★(aa)	(bb)	...	★	...	★	★(cc)	...
Washington	...	★	★	★	★	★(dd)	★	★	★	★	★	...	...
West Virginia	...	★	★	★	★	...	...	...	...	★	...	...	...
Wisconsin	...	★	★	★	★	...	(ee)	...	...	...	...	(ee)	...
Wyoming	...	★	★	★	...	...	★	...	...	...	...	...	...
Guam	...	★	...	...	★	★(ff)	★	...	...	★	★	★	...
CNMI*	★	★	★	★	★	★	...	...	...	...	★	★	★
Puerto Rico	(gg)												
U.S. Virgin Islands	★	★	...	★	...	...	★	...	...	...	...	...	...

See footnotes at end of table

TABLE 3.18
Fiscal Notes: Content and Distribution (continued)

Source: The Council of State Governments' survey, January 2019.
*Commonwealth of Northern Mariana Islands
Note: A fiscal note is a summary of the fiscal effects of a bill on government revenues, expenditures and liabilities.
Key:
★– Yes
...–No
(a) Fiscal notes included on final passage calendar.
(b) Only retirement, corrections, revenue, tax and local government bills require fiscal notes. During the past session, fiscal notes were provided for education.
(c) The fiscal notes are printed with the bills favorably reported by the committees.
(d) Statement of purpose.
(e) Attached to bill, so available to both fiscal and executive budget staff. Joint Rule 18.
(f) A summary of each fiscal note is attached to the summary of its bill in the printed Legislative Synopsis and Digest, and on the General Assembly's Web site. Fiscal notes are prepared for the sponsor and attached to the bill on file with the House Clerk or Senate Secretary.
(g) Fiscal notes are available to everyone.
(h) Prepared by the Legislative Fiscal Office when a state agency is involved and prepared by Legislative Auditor's office when a local board or commission is involved; copies sent to House and Senate staff offices respectively.
(i) Distributed to members of the committee of reference; also available on the Legislature's Web site.
(j) A fiscal note is now known as a fiscal and policy note to better reflect the contents. Fiscal and policy notes also identify any mandate on local government and include analyses of the economic impact on small businesses.
(k) In practice fiscal and policy notes are prepared on all bills and resolutions prior to a public hearing on the bills/resolutions. After initial hard copy distribution to sponsor and committee, the note is released to member computer system and thereafter to the legislative Web site.
(l) Fiscal notes are prepared only if cost exceeds $100,000 or matter has not been acted upon by the Joint Committee on Ways and Means.
(m) In regards to Impact on Local Government, Fee Impact Statements are written.
(n) At present, fiscal information is part of the bill analysis on the legislative Web site.
(o) And committee to which bill referred.
(p) Mechanical defects in bill.
(q) Fiscal impact statements prepared by Legislative Finance Committee staff are available on the legislature's Web site.
(r) Fiscal notes are required for retirement bills, bills enacting or amending tax expenditures, and all bills increasing or decreasing state revenues, or affecting appropriation or expenditure of state monies.
(s) Fiscal notes are posted on the Internet and available to all members.
(t) Notes required only if impact is $5,000 or more. Bills impacting workforce safety and insurance benefits or premiums have actuarial statements as do bills proposing changes in state and local retirement systems.

(u) Fiscal notes are available online to anyone from the legislative branch Web site.
(v) Fiscal notes are prepared for bills before being voted on in any standing committee or floor session. Fiscal notes for all introduced bills are posted on the Web. They are also distributed to the committees in which the bills are heard.
(w) Fiscal impact statements on proposed legislation are prepared by the Revenue and Fiscal Affairs Office and sent to the House or Senate standing committee that requested the impact. All fiscal impacts are posted on the Revenue and Fiscal Affairs website.
(x) Some bills may also require the preparation of one or more of the following fiscal impact statements: an actuarial impact statement, a criminal justice policy impact statement, an equalized education funding impact statement, a higher education impact statement, an open government impact statement, an impact statement regarding the economic effect of tax changes, a tax/fee equity note, or a water development policy impact statement.
(y) Fiscal notes are to include cost and revenue estimates on all bills that anticipate direct impact on state government, local government, residents, and businesses.
(z) Fiscal notes are not mandatory and their content will vary.
(aa) Technical amendments, if needed. Fiscal notes do not provide statements or interpretations of legislative intent for legal purposes. A summary of the stated objective, effect, and impact may be included.
(bb) Fiscal impact statements are widely available because they are also posted on the Internet shortly after they are distributed. The Joint Legislative Audit Review Commission (JLARC) also prepares a review of the fiscal impact statement if requested by a standing committee chair. The review statement is also available on the Internet.
(cc) Legislative budget directors.
(dd) Impact on private sector.
(ee) The fiscal estimate is printed as an appendix to the bill; anyone that has a copy of the bill has a copy of the fiscal estimate.
(ff) Fiscal impact on local economy.
(gg) The Legislature of Puerto Rico does not prepare fiscal notes, but upon request the economics unit could prepare one. The Department of Treasury has the duty to analyze and prepare fiscal notes.
(hh) Hawaii does not require the submission of fiscal notes.
(ii) Whenever possible, fiscal notes appear at end of introduced version of bill.
(jj) After a bill has been set for hearing, the Legislative Budget Board distributes the fiscal note to the committee clerk and the sponsor of the bill. In the House, the fiscal note must be attached to the affected bill before a public hearing on the bill may be held, and Senate practice is for a copy of the fiscal note to be provided to the committee members before a final vote on a bill in committee is taken. If the bill is reported from committee, the fiscal note is attached to the bill as part of the committee report when it is printed and distributed to the legislators. Fiscal notes are publicly available online for bills that have been voted out of committee.
(kk) Fiscal notes are posted on the Legislature's website.
(ll) Joint Rule 18.

TABLE 3.19

Bill and Resolution Introductions and Enactments: 2018 Regular Sessions

State	Duration of session**	Introductions		Enactments/adoptions		Measures vetoed by governor (a)(b)	Length of session
		Bills	Resolutions*	Bills	Resolutions*		
Alabama	Jan. 9 – Mar. 29, 2018	922	682	311	485	0	30L
Alaska (c)	Jan. 17 – May 17, 2017; Jan. 16 – May 13, 2018	376	141	26	58	0	90C
Arizona	Jan. 8 – May 4, 2018	1,206	94	346	17	23	N/A
Arkansas	Feb. 12 – Mar. 13, 2018	263	30	260	0	0	30C
California (c)	Dec. 5, 2016 – Sept. 15, 2017; Jan. 3 – Aug. 31, 2018	4,775	786	1,875	673	319	N/A
Colorado	Jan. 10 – May 9, 2018	721	54	420	1	9	120C
Connecticut (e)	Feb. 7 – May 9, 2018	1,135	267	213	0	7	65C
Delaware (c)	Jan. 10 – Jun. 30, 2017; Jan. 9 – Jun. 30, 2018	746	262	435	18	1	N/A
Florida	Jan. 9 – Mar. 11, 2018	2,988	140	185	55	2	60C
Georgia (c)	Jan. 9 – Mar. 30, 2017; Jan. 8 – Mar. 29, 2018	1,573	2,989	542	2,584	30	N/A
Hawaii	Jan. 17 – May 3, 2018	2,260	815	220	178	8	60L
Idaho	Jan. 8 – Mar. 28, 2018	561	78	355	51	2	80C
Illinois (c)	Jan. 24 – May 31, 2017; Jan. 8 – May 31, 2018	9,649	3,808	1,450	3,465	N/A	N/A
Indiana	Jan. 2 – Mar. 16, 2018	886	287	210	215	0	30L
Iowa (c)	Jan. 9 – Apr. 28, 2017; Jan. 8 – May 5, 2018	2,094	153	345	1	1	N/A
Kansas	Jan. 8 – Apr. 7, 2018	573	100	118	68	10 (a)	91C
Kentucky	Jan. 2 – Apr. 14, 2018	873	701	185	503	13 (a)(b)	60L
Louisiana	Mar. 12 – May 18, 2018	1,465	749	720	697	6	60L
Maine (c)	Dec. 7, 2016 – July 3, 2017; Jan. 3 – Jun. 19, 2018	1,924	79	541	N/A	57 (b)	N/A
Maryland	Jan. 10 – Apr. 9, 2018	3,101	26	852	0	37	90C
Massachusetts (c)	Jan. 4 – Dec. 31, 2017; Jan. 3 – Dec. 31, 2018	7,723	0	605	0	3	N/A
Michigan (c)	Jan. 11 – Dec. 28, 2017; Jan. 10 – Dec. 31, 2018	3,879	834	955	626	64 (a)(b)	N/A
Minnesota	Feb. 20 – May 21, 2018	3,493	0	100	0	16	90C
Mississippi	Jan. 2 – Mar. 28, 2018	2,789	272	329	220	4	90C
Missouri	Jan. 3 – May 18, 2018	2,066	225	112	21	1	N/A
Montana				---- No regular session in 2018 ----			
Nebraska (U) (c)	Jan. 4 – May 23, 2017; Jan. 3 – Apr. 18, 2018	1,184	496	325	235	N/A	N/A
Nevada				---- No regular session in 2018 ----			
New Hampshire	Jan. 3 – Jun. 30, 2018	1,085	12	382	3	6(b)	N/A
New Jersey (d)	Jan. 9, 2018 – Jan. 8, 2019; Jan. 9, 2019	8,380	988	206	76	N/A	(d)
New Mexico	Jan. 16 – Feb. 15, 2018	687	35	80	4	36 (a)(f)	30C
New York	Jan. 4, 2017 – Jan. 2, 2018; Jan. 3 – Jun. 30, 2018	20,050	N/A	1,027	N/A	N/A	365C
North Carolina	Jan. 11 – Jun. 30, 2017; Jan. 10 – Jul. 4, 2018	1,951	N/A	425	N/A	N/A	N/A
North Dakota				---- No regular session in 2018 ----			
Ohio	Jan. 2 – Dec. 31, 2017; Jan. 2 – Dec. 31, 2018	1,144	1,521	117	1,440	N/A	N/A
Oklahoma (c)	Feb. 6 – May 26, 2017; Feb. 5 – May 3, 2018	4,330	242	715	76	34	N/A
Oregon	Feb. 5 – Mar. 3, 2018	233	25	122	19	1	N/A
Pennsylvania (c)	Jan. 3 – June 30, 2017; Jan. 2 – Nov. 30, 2018	3,954	1,670	277	1,450	8	N/A

See footnotes at end of table

TABLE 3.19

Bill and Resolution Introductions and Enactments: 2018 Regular Sessions (continued)

State	Duration of session**	Introductions		Enactments/adoptions		Measures vetoed by governor (a)(b)	Length of session
		Bills	Resolutions*	Bills	Resolutions*		
Rhode Island	Jan. 2 - Jun. 25, 2018	1,936	446	505	353	5	N/A
South Carolina (c)	Jan. 10 - May 11, 2017; Jan. 9 - May 10, 2018	1,796	1,949	256	1,509	4	N/A
South Dakota	Jan. 9 - Mar. 26, 2018	535	50	282	3	3	40L
Tennessee (c)	Jan. 10 - May 10, 2017; Jan. 9 - Apr. 27, 2018	5,577	2,895	2,255	2,674	N/A	N/A
Texas	No regular session in 2018						
Utah	Jan. 22 - Mar. 8, 2018	731	86	469	28	3 (b)	45C
Vermont (c)	Jan. 4 - May 18, 2017; Jan. 3 - May 13, 2018	1,224	548	242	478	13	N/A
Virginia	Jan. 10 - Mar. 10, 2018	2,606	1,116	854	953	20 (b)	60C
Washington (c)	Jan. 9 - Apr. 23, 2017; Jan. 8 - Mar. 8, 2018	3,646	268	676	18	9 (a)	N/A
West Virginia	Jan. 10 - Mar. 10, 2018	1,778	315	249	131	11	60C
Wisconsin (c)	Jan. 3 - Dec. 31, 2017; Jan. 16 - Mar. 22, 2018	1,960	276	348	84	N/A	N/A
Wyoming	Feb. 12 - Mar. 15, 2018	315	49	15	4	1	N/A

Source: The Council of State Governments' survey of state websites and *legiscan.com*, March 2019.

*Includes Joint and Concurrent resolutions.

**Actual adjournment dates are listed regardless of constitutional or statutory limitations. For more information on provisions, see Table 3.2, "Legislative Sessions: Legal Provisions."

Key:

C–Calendar day.

L–Legislative day (in some states, called a session or workday; definition may vary slightly; however, it generally refers to any day on which either chamber of the legislature is in session).

U–Unicameral legislature.

N/A–Not available.

(a) Line item or partial vetoes: Kansas–10; Kentucky–3; Michigan–2; New Mexico–5; Washington–8.

(b) Number of vetoes overridden: Kentucky–5; Maine–33; Michigan–1; New Hampshire–2; Utah–2; Virginia–1.

(c) Information reported for a full 2-year session.

(d) Information for the 2018-2019 two-year session as of March 4, 2019.

(e) 1. There is some redundancy in the numbers because committee bills are based on proposed bills, which are introduced by individual legislators at the beginning of the session. 2. Governor's Bills are introduced on behalf of the Governor by legislative leaders of the Governor's party. They reflect initiatives of the Governor, and not necessarily those of the introducing legislators.

(f) Number includes 21 pocket vetoes.

TABLE 3.20

Bill and Resolution Introductions and Enactments: 2018 Special Sessions

State	Duration of session**	Introductions Bills	Introductions Resolutions*	Enactments/adoptions Bills	Enactments/adoptions Resolutions*	Measures vetoed by governor	Length of session
Alabama	---------- No special session in 2018 ----------						
Alaska	---------- No special session in 2018 ----------						
Arizona	Jan. 25, 2018	2	0	1	0	0	1L
Arkansas	Mar. 13 - 15, 2018	18	4	15	1	0	N/A
California	---------- No special session in 2018 ----------						
Colorado	---------- No special session in 2018 ----------						
Connecticut	---------- No special session in 2018 ----------						
Delaware	---------- No special session in 2018 ----------						
Florida	---------- No special session in 2018 ----------						
Georgia	Nov. 13 - 17, 2018	5	35	3	33	0	N/A
Hawaii	Jul. 10, 2018; Oct. 25, 2018	0; 0	1; 0	0; 0	1; 0	0; 0	1L; 1L
Idaho	---------- No special session in 2018 ----------						
Illinois	---------- No special session in 2018 ----------						
Indiana	May 14, 2018	5	1	5	1	0	1L
Iowa	---------- No special session in 2018 ----------						
Kansas	---------- No special session in 2018 ----------						
Kentucky	Dec. 17 - 18, 2018	2	5	0	4	0	2C
Louisiana	Feb. 19 - Mar. 5, 2018; May 22 - Jun. 4, 2018; Jun. 18 - Jun. 24, 2018	38; 57; 14	33; 113; 115	2; 12; 2	29; 106; 56	0; 1; 0	N/A
Maine	Jun. 19 - Sept. 13, 2018	---------- No information available ----------						
Maryland	---------- No special session in 2018 ----------						
Massachusetts	---------- No special session in 2018 ----------						
Michigan	---------- No special session in 2018 ----------						
Minnesota	---------- No special session in 2018 ----------						
Mississippi	Aug. 23 - 29, 2018	5	26	3	15	0	N/A
Missouri	Sept. 10 - 19, 2018	4	5	2	1	0	N/A
Montana	---------- No special session in 2018 ----------						
Nebraska (U)	---------- No special session in 2018 ----------						
Nevada	---------- No special session in 2018 ----------						
New Hampshire	---------- No special session in 2018 ----------						
New Jersey	---------- No special session in 2018 ----------						
New Mexico	---------- No special session in 2018 ----------						
New York	---------- No special session in 2018 ----------						
North Carolina	Jul. 24 - Aug. 4, 2018; Aug. 24 - 27, 2018; Oct. 2 - 15, 2018	12; 8; 9	0; 0; 0	5; 5; 7	0; 0; 0	0; 0; 0	N/A
North Dakota	---------- No special session in 2018 ----------						
Ohio	---------- No special session in 2018 ----------						
Oklahoma	Dec. 18, 2017 - Apr. 19, 2018 (a)	56	2	18	0	0	N/A
Oregon	May 21, 2018	1	1	1	1	0	1C
Pennsylvania	---------- No special session in 2018 ----------						
Rhode Island	---------- No special session in 2018 ----------						
South Carolina	---------- No special session in 2018 ----------						
South Dakota	Sept. 12, 2018	3	0	3	0	0	1C
Tennessee	---------- No special session in 2018 ----------						
Texas	---------- No special session in 2018 ----------						
Utah	Jul. 18, 2018; Dec. 3, 2018	9; 3	0; 0	9; 3	0; 0	0; 0	1C; 1C
Vermont	May 23 - Jun. 29, 2018	24	23	10	22	1	N/A
Virginia	Apr. 11 - May 30, 2018; Aug. 30 - Nov. 30, 2018	2; 3	214; 14	2; 0	204; 11	0; 0	N/A
Washington	---------- No special session in 2018 ----------						
West Virginia	May 20 - 21, 2018; Jun. 26 - Oct. 15, 2018	17; 2	4; 12	8; 0	4; 8	0; 0	N/A
Wisconsin	Jan. 18 - Feb. 27, 2018; Mar. 15 - 29, 2018	20; 6	0; 0	9; 0	0; 0	0; 0	N/A
Wyoming	---------- No special session in 2018 ----------						

See footnotes at end of table

TABLE 3.20
Bill and Resolution Introductions and Enactments: 2018 Special Sessions (continued)

Source: The Council of State Governments' survey of state legislative websites and *legiscan.com*, Feb. 2019.

*Includes Joint and Concurrent resolutions.

**Actual adjournment dates are listed regardless of constitutional or statutory limitations. For more information on provisions, see Table 3.2, "Legislative Sessions: Legal Provisions."

Key:
N/A–Not available.
C–Calendar day.
L–Legislative day (in some states, called a session or workday; definition may vary slightly; however, it generally refers to any day on which either chamber of the legislature is in session).
U–Unicameral legislature.
(a) The special session ran concurrent with the 2018 regular session.

TABLE 3.21
Staff for Individual Legislators

State or other jurisdiction	Senate Capitol Personal	Senate Capitol Shared	Senate District	House/Assembly Capitol Personal	House/Assembly Capitol Shared	House/Assembly District
Alabama	YR	YR/2	(a)	YR	YR/10	(a)
Alaska (b)	YR/SO	...	YR	YR/SO	...	YR
Arizona	YR (c)	...	...	...	YR (c)	...
Arkansas	...	YR	...	...	YR (d)	...
California	YR	...	YR	YR	...	YR
Colorado	SO (e)	YR (e)	...	YR (e)	YR (e)	...
Connecticut (f)	YR/36	...	...	...	YR/38	...
Delaware	-- (g) --					
Florida	YR (h)	...	YR (h)	YR (h)	...	YR (h)
Georgia	...	YR/3, SO/68	...	...	YR/25, SO/113	...
Hawaii (nn)	YR/2	...	...	YR/1	...	...
Idaho	...	SO, YR (i)	...	...	SO, YR (i)	...
Illinois	YR (j)	YR (j)	YR (j)	YR (j)	YR (j)	YR (j)
Indiana	...	YR/2 (k)	...	...	YR	...
Iowa	SO/1 (oo)	...	(oo)	SO/1 (oo)	...	(oo)
Kansas	SO/1	...	...	(l)	SO/3	...
Kentucky	...	YR (m)	...	...	YR (m)	...
Louisiana	(n)	YR (o)	YR (n)	(n)	YR (o)	YR (n)
Maine	YR, SO (p)	YR/27, SO/7	YR	...	YR (q)	...
Maryland	YR, SO (r)	...	YR (r)	YR (r)	SO (r)	YR (r)
Massachusetts	YR	...	...	YR	...	...
Michigan	YR (s)	...	...	YR/2 (s)	...	...
Minnesota	YR (t)	Varies	...	YR/3	Varies	...
Mississippi	...	YR	...	...	YR	...
Missouri	YR	YR	...	YR	YR	...
Montana	...	SO	...	...	SO	...
Nebraska	YR (u)	...	...	-- Unicameral		
Nevada	SO (pp)	YR	...	SO (pp)	YR	...
New Hampshire	...	YR	...	...	YR	...
New Jersey	YR (h)	...	YR (h)	YR (h)	...	YR (h)
New Mexico	SO/1	...	...	...	SO/2	...
New York	YR (w)	...	YR (w)	YR (w)	...	YR (w)
North Carolina	YR (x)	YR	...	YR (x)	YR	...
North Dakota	...	SO (v)	...	...	SO (v)	...
Ohio	YR/2 (y)	...	(z)	YR/1 (aa)	...	(z)
Oklahoma	YR/1 (bb)	YR (bb)	...	YR (bb)	YR/1 (bb)	...
Oregon	YR (cc)	YR	YR (dd)	YR (cc)	YR	YR (dd)
Pennsylvania	YR	...	YR	YR	...	YR
Rhode Island	...	YR (ee)	...	...	YR (ee)	...
South Carolina	...	YR/2	...	YR/4	...	...
South Dakota	(ff)	(ff)	...	(ff)	(ff)	...
Tennessee	YR/1	...	...	(gg)	YR/1	...
Texas	(hh)	...	(hh)	(hh)	...	(hh)
Utah	SO (ii)	YR /5-8 (ii)	...	SO (ii)	...	...
Vermont	YR/1 (jj)	...	...	YR/1 (jj)	...	...
Virginia	SO/1 (kk)	...	(kk)	SO (kk)	SO/2	(kk)
Washington	YR/1	...	IO/1	YR/1	...	YR/1
West Virginia	SO	...	...	...	SO/17	...
Wisconsin	(ll)	...	(ll)	(ll)	...	...
Wyoming	...	...	...	...	...	...
American Samoa	...	...	...	...	...	...
Guam	...	...	...	-- Unicameral		
CNMI*	YR (mm)	(mm)	...	YR (mm)	(mm)	(ll)
Puerto Rico	YR (mm)	...	...	YR (mm)	...	...
U.S. Virgin Islands	YR (mm)	...	...	-- Unicameral		

See footnotes at end of table

TABLE 3.21
Staff for Individual Legislators (continued)

Source: The Council of State Governments' survey, March 2019.
*Commonwealth of Northern Mariana Islands
Note: For entries under column heading "Shared," figures after
slash indicate approximate number of legislators per staff person,
where available.
Key:
…–Staff not provided for individual legislators.
YR–Year-round.
SO–Session only.
IO–Interim only.
(a) Six counties have local delegation offices with shared staff.
(b) The number of staff per legislator varies depending on their
position.
(c) Representatives share a secretary with another legislator; however,
House leadership and committee chairs usually have their own secretarial staff. All legislators share professional research staff.
(d) The legislators share 21 staff people; 4.76 legislators per staff
person.
(e) Senate: Personal–Each Senator is granted 570 aide hours and
may employ up to two aides each fiscal year, with each aide working a maximum of 40 hours each week. Shared–18 session-only
employees are employed by the Senate: 2 each by the majority
and the minority and 14 by the non-partisan staff. 17 year-round
employees are employed by the Senate: 8 by the majority, 5 by
the minority, and 4 by the non-partisan staff. There are also 4 session-only employees in the bill room who are jointly managed by
the Colorado Senate and House. House: Personal–Each Representative is allowed to hire up to 2 paid Legislative Aides who share a
limit of 790 hours per fiscal year. Representatives may have an
unlimited number of unpaid interns and volunteers. Shared–65
House legislators share 17 full time staff. 6 majority caucus staff, 5
minority caucus staff, 6 non-partisan staff. 65 Representatives
share 28 session only staff: 3 majority caucus staff, 2 minority caucus staff, 23 non-partisan staff.
(f) The numbers are for staff assigned to specific legislators. There is
additional staff working in the leadership offices that also support
the rank and file members.
(g) Staffers are a combination of full time, part time, shared, personal, etc. and their assignments change throughout the year.
(h) Personal and district staff are the same. In Florida, district
employees may travel to the capitol for sessions (two district
employees in the Senate and one district employee in the House).
(i) In the Senate, Idaho has one year-round full-time (Chief of Staff)
and two part-time (Secretary of the Senate and Minority Chief of
Staff) year-round employees, with 53 additional employees during the session (January–March). The House has two full-time
(Assistant to the Speaker and Chief Fiscal Officer) and for the January–March Legislative Session 29 full-time staff.
(j) Each senator has one secretary and two House members share a
secretary. Partisan staffers also help legislators with many issues
as well as staffing committees. Most senators and representatives
have one or two district office employees, paid from a separate
allowance for that purpose.
(k) Leadership has one legislative assistant. During session, college
interns are hired to provide additional staff–one for every two
members. Leadership has one intern.

(l) One clerical staff person for three individual House members is
the norm. Chairpersons are provided their own individual clerical
staff person.
(m) The General Assembly is provided professional and clerical staff
services by a centralized, non-partisan staff, with the exception of
House and Senate leadership which employs partisan staff. No
district staff provided.
(n) Each legislator may hire as many assistants as desired, but pay
from public funds ranges from $2,000 to $3,000 per month per
legislator. Assistant(s) generally work in the district office but may
also work at the capitol during the session.
(o) The six caucuses are assigned one full-time position each (poten-
tially 24 legislators per one staff person).
(p) President's office: six year round; Majority office: 7 year round, 1
session only; Secretary's office: nine year round, five session only.
(q) The 151 House members do not have individual staff. There are
21 people who work year round in the two partisan offices, 12 of
whom are legislative aides who primarily work directly with legislators. Speaker's office: 8 year round. Clerk's office: 12 year round,
1 part-time, 10 session-only.
(r) Senators have one year round administrative aide and one session only secretary. Delegates have one part-time year round
administrative aide and a shared session only secretary. Legislators may increase staff and also hire student interns if their district
office funds are used.
(s) Senate–majority, 2–6 staff per legislator; minority, 2–3 staff per
legislator. House–2 staff per legislator.
(t) One to two staff persons per legislator.
(u) Two to five staff persons per legislator.
(v) Secretarial staff; in North Dakota, leadership only.
(w) Varies depending upon allowance allocated to each member.
Members have considerable independence in hiring personal and
committee staffs. Legislative employees can be annual, session, or
temporary.
(x) Part time during interim.
(y) Some leadership offices have more.
(z) Some legislators maintain district offices at their own expense.
(aa) Some offices have more.
(bb) Senate: Pro Tem–6 staff persons; Senate minority leader–1
staff person. House: year round one to five, majority party only;
minority party one staff person per legislator. Committee, fiscal
and legal staffs are available to legislators on a year round.
(cc) Two staff persons per legislator during session.
(dd) Senate–Equivalent of one full-time staff. House–1 during
interim.
(ee) The General Assembly has a total of 280 full time positions,
267 full-time shared staff and additional 13 full-time positions for
the House.
(ff) The non-partisan Legislative Research Council serves all members of both houses year round. Committee secretaries and
legislative interns and pages provide support during the sessions.
(gg) Several House members have year-round personal staff. It
depends on seniority, duties (such as committee chairs), and committee assignments.
(hh) Staff numbers vary depending on the legislator. Each legislator

TABLE 3.21
Staff for Individual Legislators (continued)

is allotted and office budget and has independence in using that budget for hiring staff.

(ii) Most legislators are assigned one student intern during session who is temporarily employed by OLRGC. Some legislators provide their own personal intern (volunteer or financial arrangements are made between them). Senate shared staff: 5-8. In the fall of 2014, the Senate hired four full-time constituent services staff to take care of administrative matters and constituent inquiries year round. Three were hired for 24 majority members, one for five minority members.

(jj) No personal staff except one administrative assistant for the Speaker and one for the Senate Pro Tempore.

(kk) Senate–One administrative assistant (secretary) provided to the members during the session by the Clerk's offices. Members also receive a set dollar allowance to hire additional legislative assistants who may serve year round at the capitol and in the district. House–Members also receive a set dollar allowance to hire additional legislative assistants who may serve year round at the capitol and in the district.

(ll) Staffing levels vary according to majority/minority status and leadership or committee responsibilities. Members may assign staff to work in the district office.

(mm) Individual staffing and staff pool arrangements are at the discretion of the individual legislator.

(nn) Each senator has the authority to hire at least two full-time, year-round staff. Each representative has the authority to hire at least one full-time, year-round staff. Depending on leadership or committee chair assignment, additional staff positions may be authorized.

(oo) One clerk provided in capitol. District/Caucus–11 staff persons for Republicans and 9 staff persons for Democrats.

(pp) Senate–Majority Leader, 3 staff; Minority Leader, 2 staff; Other Senators 1 staff per legislator. Secretarial staff. House–1 staff per legislator. Secretarial staff; Leadership positions are assigned additional staff.

TABLE 3.22
Staff for Legislative Standing Committees

State or other jurisdiction	Committee staff assistance				Source of staff services**							
	Senate		House/Assembly		Joint central agency (a)		Chamber agency (b)		Caucus or leadership		Committee or committee chair	
	Prof.	Cler.	Prof.	Cler.	Prof.	Cler.	Prof.	Cler.	Prof.	Cler.	Prof.	Cler.
Alabama	•	★	•	★	B	...	...	B	...	...	...	...
Alaska	★	★	★	★	B	B	...	...	...	...	B	B
Arizona	★	★	★	★	B	B	B	B	B	B	B	B
Arkansas	★	★	★	★	B	B	B	B	...	...	...	...
California	★	★	★	★	B	B	B	B	B	B	B	B
Colorado	★	...	★	...	B	...	B	B	B	B (c)	...	...
Connecticut (t)	★	★	★	★	B	...	...	...	B	B	...	B
Delaware	...	★	...	★	B	...	B	...	B	...	...	B
Florida	★	★	★	★	B	B	B	B	B	B	B	B
Georgia	•	★	•	★	B	B	B	B	B	B	B	...
Hawaii	★	★	★	★	B	B	B	B	B	B	B	B
Idaho	...	★	...	★	B (d)	B (d)	B	B	...	B	...	...
Illinois	★	★	★	★	...	...	B	B	B	B	...	...
Indiana	★	...	...	...	...	...	S	...	S	...	...	...
Iowa	★	★	★	★	B	...	B (f)	B	B	...	...	B
Kansas	★	★	★	★	B	B (g)	B	B	B	B	B	B
Kentucky	★	★	★	★	B	B	...	...	B (h)	B (h)	...	...
Louisiana	★(i)	★	★(i)	★	B	B	B	B	B	B	B (j)	B (j)
Maine	★(k)	★(k)	★(k)	★(k)	B	B	B	B	B	B	...	B
Maryland	★(l)	★(l)	★(l)	★(l)	B	B	...	...	...	...	...	...
Massachusetts	★	★	★	★	...	...	...	...	...	...	...	...
Michigan	★	★	★	★	B	...	B	B	B	S	...	...
Minnesota	★	★	★	★	...	...	B	H	S	B	B	B
Mississippi	•	★	•	★	...	...	B	B	...	...	B	B
Missouri	★	...	★	...	B	...	B	...	S	S	B	...
Montana	★	★	★	★	B	...	...	B	...	...	...	...
Nebraska	★	★	U	U	(m)	...	(m)	...	(m)	...	S	S
Nevada	★	★	★	★	B	...	...	B	...	...	...	...
New Hampshire	★	★	★	★	B	B	B	B	...	S	...	S
New Jersey	★	★	★	★	B	B	B	B	...	...	...	...
New Mexico	★	★	★	★	...	...	B	B	...	...	...	...
New York	★	★	★	★	...	...	B	B	B	B	B	B
North Carolina	★	★(n)	★	★(n)	B	...	...	...	...	...	...	B (n)
North Dakota	...	★	...	★	B	B	...	...	...	B	...	...
Ohio	★	★	★	★	B	...	...	...	B	...	B	B
Oklahoma	★	★	★	★	...	...	B	B	S	...	B	B
Oregon	★	★	★	★	B	B	B	B	B	B	B	B
Pennsylvania	★	★	★	★	B	B	B	B	B	B	B	B
Rhode Island	•	★	•	★	B	B	B	...	...	...	B	...
South Carolina	★	★	★	★	B	B	B	B	B	B	B	B
South Dakota	★	★	★	★	B	...	...	(l)	...	(l)	...	(l)
Tennessee	★	★	★	★	B	...	...	...	...	...	...	B
Texas	★	★	★	★	B	B	B	B	...	...	B	B
Utah	★	★(r)	★	★(r)	B	B	...	B	B (s)	B	...	...
Vermont	★	•	★	•	B	B	...	...	...	...	...	...
Virginia	★	★	★	★	B	...	B	B	...	...	(o)	(o)
Washington	★	★	★	★	...	...	B	B	B	B	B	B
West Virginia	★	★	★	★	B	B	B	B	B	B	B	B
Wisconsin	★	★	★	★	B	...	...	...	...	...	(p)	B
Wyoming	...	★	...	★	B	...	...	B	...	...	...	...
American Samoa	•	★	•	★	B	B	B	B	...	...	B	...
Guam	★	★	U	U	...	...	S	S	...	...	...	...
CNMI*	★	★	★	★	B (q)	B (q)	B (q)	B (q)	B (q)	B (q)	B (q)	B (q)
Puerto Rico	★	★	★	★	B (q)	B (q)	B (q)	B (q)	B (q)	B (q)	B (q)	B (q)
U.S. Virgin Islands	★	★	U	U	S (q)	S (q)	S (q)	S (q)	S (q)	S (q)	S (q)	S (q)

See footnotes at end of table

TABLE 3.22
Staff for Legislative Standing Committees (continued)

Source: The Council of State Governments' survey, March 2019.
*Commonwealth of Northern Mariana Islands
**Multiple entries reflect a combination of organizations and location of services.
Key:
★–All committees
●–Some committees
…–Services not provided
B–Both chambers
H–House
S–Senate
U–Unicameral
(a) Includes legislative council or service agency or central management agency.
(b) Includes chamber management agency, office of clerk or secretary and House or Senate research office.
(c) Senate–there is secretarial staff for both majority and minority offices for the Senate in the Capitol. Most of the clerical work is done by caucus staff. House–the clerical and secretarial staff for the House is more centralized and is supervised by the Clerk of the House.
(d) Professional staff and clerical support is provided via the Legislative Services Office, a non-partisan office serving all members of the House and Senate on a year-round basis. There are currently 65 employees working in the Legislative Services Office. Leadership in each party hire their respective support staff.
(e) Leadership in each party hire their respective support staff.
(f) The Senate secretary and House clerk maintain supervision of committee clerks.
(g) Senators and House chairpersons select their secretaries and notify the central administrative services agency; all administrative employee matters handled by the agency.

(h) Leadership employs partisan staff to provide professional and clerical services. However, all members, including leadership are also served by the centralized, non-partisan staff.
(i) House Appropriations and Senate Finance Committees have Legislative Fiscal Office staff at their hearings.
(j) Staff are assigned to each committee but work under the direction of the chair.
(k) Standing committees are joint House and Senate committees.
(l) The clerical support comes from employees who are hired to work only during the legislative sessions. They are employees of either the House or the Senate, and are not part of the central agency.
(m) Professional services are not provided, except that the staff of the Legislative Fiscal Office serves the Appropriations Committee. Individual senators are responsible for the process of hiring their own staff.
(n) Member's personal secretary serves as a clerk to the committee or subcommittee that the member chairs.
(o) The House Appropriations Committee and the Senate Finance Committees have their own staff. The staff members work under the direction of the chair.
(p) Standing committees are staffed by subject specialist from the Joint Legislative Council.
(q) In general, the legislative service agency provides legal and staff assistance for legislative meetings and provides associated materials. Individual legislators hire personal or committee staff as their budgets provide and at their own discretion.
(r) Clerical staff not assigned to Rules Cmtes.
(s) Refers only to Chief Deputy of the Senate and Chief of Staff in the House.
(t) Committees are joint Senate and House. Professional nonpartisan staff serves committees, individual legislators and legislature as a whole, regardless of chamber or party.

TABLE 3.23
Standing Committees: Appointment and Number

State or other jurisdiction	Committee members appointed by:		Committee chairpersons appointed by:		Number of standing committees during regular 2019 session		Number of joint committees during 2019 session
	Senate	House/Assembly	Senate	House/Assembly	Senate	House/Assembly	
Alabama	(v)	S	(v)	S	20	33	0
Alaska	CC	CC	CC	CC	10	10	3
Arizona	P	S	P	S	13	18	1
Arkansas	(a)	(b)	(a)	S	12	13	7
California	CR	S	CR	S	22	32	8
Colorado	MjL	S	MjL	S	10	11	8
Connecticut	PT (y)	S	PT (y)	S	(c)	(c)	26 (c)
Delaware	PT	S	PT	S	17	23	4
Florida	P	S	P	S	18	9	4
Georgia	CC	S	CC	S	29	37	0
Hawaii	P	S	P	(d)	16	18	0
Idaho	PT (f)	S	PT	S	10	15	5
Illinois	P, MnL (w)	S, MnL (w)	P, MnL (w)	S, MnL (w)	27	40	0
Indiana	PT	S	PT	S	21	21	1
Iowa	MjL, MnL	S (x)	MjL	S	16	19	0
Kansas	(g)	(g)	P	S	15	28	12
Kentucky	CC	CC	CC	CC	15	19	0
Louisiana	P	S (h)	P	S	17	16	0
Maine	P	S	P	S	5	6	18
Maryland	P	S	P	S	6	7	19
Massachusetts	P	S	P	S	11	11	29
Michigan	MjL	S	MjL	S	20	22	3
Minnesota	CR	S	S	S	21	10	2
Mississippi	P	S	P	S	39	47	0
Missouri	PT (j)	S	PT	S	22	28	13
Montana	CC	S	CC	S	17	16	0
Nebraska	CC	U	E	U	14	U	0
Nevada	MjL (e)	S	MjL	S	10	10	0
New Hampshire	P (k)	S (k)	P (k)	S (k)	12	24	0
New Jersey	CC	CC	CC	CC	16	25	7
New Mexico	CC	S	CC	S	9 (l)	14 (l)	0
New York	PT	S	PT	S	41	37	0
North Carolina	PT	S	PT	S	18	34	0
North Dakota	CC	CC	CC	CC	12	12	0
Ohio	P (m)	S (m)	P (m)	S (m)	14	20	5
Oklahoma	PT (e)	S	PT	S	14	22	0
Oregon	P	S	P	S	13	13	11
Pennsylvania	PT	S	PT	S	22	28	0
Rhode Island	P	S	P	S	10	13	2
South Carolina	(n)	S	(o)	E	15	13	4
South Dakota	PT	S	PT	S	14	14	2
Tennessee	S	S	S	S	9	14	4
Texas	P	S (p)	P	S	16	34	0
Utah	P	S	P	S	12	15	7
Vermont	CC	S	CC	S	13	15	16
Virginia	E	S	(q)	S	11	14	0
Washington	CC	CC	CC (r)	CC (s)	15	20	12
West Virginia	P	S	P	S	19	20	0
Wisconsin	MjL	S	MjL	S	19	47	10
Wyoming	P	S	P	S	...	...	12
Dist. of Columbia	(t)	U	(t)	U	13	U	0
American Samoa	P	S	E	S	N/A	N/A	N/A
Guam	(u)	U	(u)	U	11	U	0
CNMI*	P	S	P	S	7	11	0
Puerto Rico	P	S	P	S	25	35	8
U.S. Virgin Islands	E	U	E	U	11	U	0

See footnotes at end of table

TABLE 3.23
Standing Committees: Appointment and Number (continued)

Source: The Council of State Governments' survey, April 2019.
*Commonwealth of Northern Mariana Islands
Key:
CC–Committee on Committees
CR–Committee on Rules
E–Election
MjL–Majority Leader
MnL–Minority Leader
P–President
PT–President pro tempore
S–Speaker
U–Unicameral Legislature
…–None reported
N/A–Not available
(a) Selection process based on seniority.
(b) Members of the standing committees shall be selected by House District Caucuses with each caucus selecting five members for each "A" standing committee and five members for each "B" standing committee.
(c) Substantive standing committees are joint committees. There are also three joint statutory committees.
(d) By resolution with members of majority party designating the chair, vice-chairs and majority party members of committees, and members of minority party designating minority party members.
(e) Minority Leader selects minority members.
(f) "The following standing committees shall be appointed by the leadership under the direction of the President Pro Tempore, by and with the advice and consent of the Senate … provided that the President Pro Tempore shall appoint a majority of each committee and the chairman of each committee from the membership of the political party having a majority in the Senate. …" (Senate Rule 19).
(g) Committee on Organization, Calendar and Rules.
(h) Speaker appoints only 12 of the 19 members of the Committee on Appropriations.
(i) There are currently 16 Joint Standing Committees, two Joint Select Committees, and a joint Government Oversight Committee.

(j) Senate minority committee members chosen by minority caucus, but appointed by president pro tempore.
(k) Senate president and House speaker consult with minority leaders.
(l) Senate: includes eight substantive committees and one procedural committee. House: includes 12 substantive committees and two procedural committees.
(m) The minority leader may recommend for consideration minority party members for each committee.
(n) Appointment based on seniority (Senate Rule 19D).
(o) Appointed by seniority which is determined by tenure within the committee rather than tenure within the Senate. Also, chair is based on the majority party within the committee (Senate Rule 19E).
(p) For each standing substantive committee of the House, except for the appropriations committee, a maximum of one-half of the membership, exclusive of chair and vice-chair, is determined by seniority; the remaining membership of the committee is determined by the speaker.
(q) In the Virginia Senate, the chair is the committee member from the majority party who has the most seniority.
(r) Recommended by the Committee on Committees, approved by the president, then confirmed by the Senate.
(s) Recommended by the Committee on Committees, then confirmed by the House.
(t) Chair of the Council.
(u) Members are appointed by the Chairperson; Chairperson is elected during majority caucus prior to inauguration.
(v) Committee on Assignments.
(w) Senate: President and Minority Leader appoint committee members including chairperson and minority spokesperson. House: Speaker appoints chairperson and majority members; Minority Leader appoints minority members.
(x) Speaker confers with Minority Leader regarding minority member appointments.
(y) The Senate is evenly-split. For each committee–President Pro Tempore appoints Senate Democratic chair and members, and Senate Republican President Pro Tempore appoints Senate Republican chair and members.

TABLE 3.24
Rules Adoption and Standing Committees: Procedure

State or other jurisdiction	Constitution permits each legislative body to determine its own rules	Committee meetings open to public*		Specific, advance notice provisions for committee meetings or hearings	Voting/roll call provisions to report a bill to floor
		Senate	House/ Assembly		
Alabama	★	★	★	Senate: four hours, if possible. House: twenty-four hours, except Rules & Local Legislations Committee. Exceptions after 27th legislative day and special sessions.	Senate: final vote on a bill, except a local bill, is recorded. House: recorded vote if requested by member of committee and sustained by one additional committee member.
Alaska	...	★	★	For meetings, by 4:00 p.m. on the preceding Thurs.; for first hearings on bills, 5 days.	Roll call vote on any measure taken upon request by any member of either house.
Arizona	★	★	★	Senate: written agenda for each regular and special meeting containing all bills, memorials and resolutions to be considered shall be distributed to each member of the committee and to the Secretary of the Senate at least five days prior to the committee meeting. House: the committee chair shall prepare an agenda and distribute copies to committee members, the Information Desk and the Chief Clerk's Office by 4 p.m. each Wednesday for all standing committees meeting on Monday of the following week and 4 p.m. each Thursday for all standing committees meeting on any day except Monday of the following week.	Senate and House: roll call vote.
Arkansas	★	★	★	Senate: 2 days (anytime with 2/3 vote of the committee). House: 18 hours (2 hours with 2/3 vote of the committee).	Senate: roll call votes are recorded. House: report of committee recommendation signed by committee chair.
California	★	★	★	Senate: advance notice provisions exist and are published in the agendas of each house. House: public notice is published in the agendas of each house. For bill hearings, the first committee of reference has a four-day notice and the second committee of reference has a two-day notice. Informational hearings have a four-day notice. No public notice is required for resolutions or special session bills.	Senate and House: roll call.
Colorado	★	★	★	Senate: final action on a measure is prohibited unless notice is posted one calendar day prior to its consideration. The prohibition does not apply if the action receives a majority vote of the committee. House: meeting publicly announced while the House is in actual session as much in advance as possible.	Senate and House: final action by recorded roll call vote.
Connecticut	★	★(e)	★(e)	Senate and House: one day notice for meetings, five days notice for hearings.	Senate and House: roll call required.
Delaware	★	★	★	Senate: agenda released one day before meetings. House: agenda for meetings released four days before meetings.	Senate and House: results of all committee reports are recorded.
Florida	★	★	★	Senate: during session–3 weekdays for first 40 days, 4 hours thereafter. House: two days for first 45 days, 1 day thereafter.	Senate and House: vote on final passage is recorded.
Georgia	★	★	★	Senate: a list of committee meetings shall be posted by 10:00 a.m. the preceding Friday. House: none.	Senate and House: bills can be voted out by voice vote or roll call.
Hawaii	★	★(a)	★(a)	Senate: 72 hours before 1st referral committee meetings, 48 hours before subsequent referral committee. House: 48 hours.	Senate and House: A quorum of committee members must be present before voting.
Idaho	★	★(a)	★(a)	Senate: yes, for committee meetings to be held in executive session. (Senate Rule 20). House: yes, for committee meetings to be held in executive session. (House Rule 57). "The chair of each standing or select committee shall lay on the Clerk's desk, to be read previous to adjournment, notice of the time and place of meeting of such committee." (House Rule 55).	Senate: bills can be voted out by voice vote or roll call. (Senate Rule 39). House: bills can be voted out by voice vote or roll call. (House Rule 36).
Illinois	★	★(b)	★(b)	Senate and House: 6 days.	Senate and House: votes on all legislative measures acted upon are recorded.
Indiana	★	★	★	Senate: 48 hours. House: prior to adjournment of the meeting day next preceding the meeting or announced during session.	Senate: committee reports–do pass; do pass amended, reported out without recommendation. House: majority of quorum; vote can be by roll call or consent.

See footnotes at end of table

TABLE 3.24
Rules Adoption and Standing Committees: Procedure (continued)

State or other jurisdiction	Constitution permits each legislative body to determine its own rules	Committee meetings open to public*		Specific, advance notice provisions for committee meetings or hearings	Voting/roll call provisions to report a bill to floor
		Senate	House/ Assembly		
Iowa	★	★	★	Senate and House: yes, but can be suspended.	Senate: final action by roll call. House: committee reports include roll call on final disposition.
Kansas	★	★	★	Senate and House: none.	Senate: vote recorded upon request of member. House: total for and against actions recorded.
Kentucky	★	★	★	Senate and House: none.	Senate and House: each member's vote recorded on each bill.
Louisiana	★	★(a)	★(a)	Senate: no later than 1:00 p.m. the preceding day. House: no later than 4:00 p.m. the preceding day.	Senate and House: any motion to report an instrument is decided by a roll call vote.
Maine	★	★	★	Senate and House: must be advertised two weekends in advance.	Senate and House: recorded vote is required to report a bill out of committee.
Maryland	★	★	★	Senate and House: none. General directive in the Senate and House rules to the Department of Legislative Services to compile a list of the meetings and to arrange for distribution which in practice is done on a regular basis.	Senate and House: the final vote on any bill is recorded.
Massachusetts	★	★	★	Senate and House: 48 hours for public hearings.	Senate: voice vote or recorded roll call vote at the request of 2 committee members. House: recorded vote upon request by a member.
Michigan	★	★	★	Senate and House: notice shall be published in the journal in advance of a hearing. Notice of a special meeting shall be posted at least 18 hours before a meeting. Special provisions for conference committees.	Senate: committee reports include the vote of each member on any bill. House: the daily journal reports the roll call on all motions to report bills.
Minnesota	★	★	★	Senate and House: 3 days.	Senate and House not needed.
Mississippi	★	★	★	Senate and House: none	Senate and House: bills are reported out by voice vote or recorded.
Missouri	★	★	★	Senate and House: 24 hours	Senate and House: bills are reported out by a recorded roll call vote.
Montana	★	★	★	Senate and House: 3 legislative days or as circumstances require.	Senate and House: every vote of each member is recorded and made public.
Nebraska	★	★	U	Seven calendar days notice before hearing a bill.	In executive session, majority of the committee must vote in favor of the motion made.
Nevada	★	★	★	Senate and House: by rule–"adequate notice" shall be provided. Senate: This rule may be suspended for emergencies by a two-thirds vote of appointed committee members. House: This rule may be suspended for emergencies by a majority vote of appointed committee members. In the Assembly this rule does not apply to committee meetings held on the floor during recess or conference committee meetings.	Senate and House: recorded vote is taken upon final committee action on bills.
New Hampshire	★	★	★	Senate: 4 days. House: no less than 4 days.	Senate and House: committees report bills out by recorded roll call votes.
New Jersey	★	★	★	Senate and House: 5 days.	Senate and House: the chair reports the vote of each member present on a motion to report a bill.
New Mexico	★	★	★	Senate and House: none.	Senate and House: vote on the final report of the committee taken by yeas and nays. Roll call vote upon request.
New York	★	★(a)	★(a)	Senate: 1 week for meetings; Rules require that notice be given for public hearings, but the Rules are silent as to how long. House: 1 week for hearings, Thursday of prior week for meetings.	Senate and House: majority vote required.
North Carolina	(c)	★	★	Senate and House: none. If public hearing, five calendar days.	Senate: majority vote required. House: roll call vote taken on any question when requested by member and sustained by one-fifth of members present.
North Dakota	★	★	★	Senate and House: printed and online hearing schedules, electronic signage, floor announcements, rss feeds, handheld device application.	Senate and House: recorded roll call vote of the committee members on each bill or resolution referred out of the committee and, in the case of divided reports, on each report.

See footnotes at end of table

TABLE 3.24
Rules Adoption and Standing Committees: Procedure (continued)

State or other jurisdiction	Constitution permits each legislative body to determine its own rules	Committee meetings open to public*		Specific, advance notice provisions for committee meetings or hearings	Voting/roll call provisions to report a bill to floor
		Senate	House/ Assembly		
Ohio	★	★	★	Senate: Rule 21 Each committee shall meet upon the call of its chairperson, and in case of the chairperson's absence, or refusal to call the committee together, a meeting may be called by a majority of the members of the committee. At least two days preceding the day bills or joint resolutions to propose a constitutional amendment are to be given a first hearing, the Clerk shall post in the Clerk's office the schedule of such bills and joint resolutions in each standing committee or subcommittee with the exception of the standing Committee on Rules and Reference. In a case of necessity, the notice of hearing may be given in a shorter period than two days by such reasonable method as shall be prescribed by the Committee on Rules. Where applicable, the rules of the Senate apply to the committee proceedings of the Senate. In addition, all where applicable, the rules of the Senate apply to the committee proceedings of the Senate. In addition, all committee meetings shall be governed by section 101.15 of the Revised Code. On any occasion when a majority or more of the members of a standing committee, select committee, or subcommittee of a standing or select committee of the Senate meet together for a prearranged discussion of the public business of the committee or subcommittee, the meeting shall be open to the public unless closed in accordance with Ohio Constitution, Article II, Section 13. House: Rule 36(a) The chair of a standing committee, subcommittee, select committee, or joint committee shall give due notice of a meeting of the committee, subcommittee, select committee, or joint committee not later than twenty-four hours before the meeting, in accordance with section 101.15 of the Revised Code, and shall attempt to give that notice not later than five days before the meeting. The notice shall identify the committee; identify the chair; state the date, time, and place at which the meeting will be held; and set forth an agenda showing each bill, resolution, or other matter that will be considered at the meeting. (b) It is not in order for a committee to meet at a date, time, or place, or to consider any bill, resolution, or other matter at a meeting, other than as stated in the notice of the meeting, unless otherwise ordered by the House or the committee. If, however, an emergency requires consideration of a matter at a meeting, and the matter has not been stated in the notice of the meeting, the chair may revise or supplement the notice at any time before or during the meeting to include the matter and the matter may then be considered as the emergency requires.	Senate: Rule 24 The affirmative votes of a majority of all members of a committee shall be necessary to report or to postpone further consideration of bills or resolutions. Every member present shall vote, unless excused by the chair. At discretion of chair the roll call may be continued for a vote by any member who was present at the prior meeting, but no later than 10:00 a.m. of next calendar day. House: Rule 40 (b) The affirmative votes of a majority of all members constituting a committee shall be necessary to report a bill or resolution out of committee, and a record of every vote shall be kept by the committee. The affirmative vote of a majority of all the members constituting the committee shall be necessary to agree to any motion to recommend for passage or to postpone indefinitely further consideration of bills or resolutions, and a record of such vote shall be kept by the committee. Every member present shall vote unless excused by the committee. Rule 41(a) No proxy vote shall be valid. Nor shall any member vote except while sitting in committee in actual session, unless the member shall have first been present and recorded as such immediately before or during actual session before the vote is taken, and by motion the roll call on a motion to recommend a bill or resolution for passage is continued for a vote by any member who is temporarily absent from the meeting until the adjournment thereof, which shall be not later than 12:00 o'clock noon one day following the committee meeting. It is not in order for a member to vote on an amendment unless the member is actually present when the amendment is voted upon. (b) Three consecutive absences from regular committee meetings shall operate to suspend a member from such committee, unless excused by the chair of said committee.
Oklahoma	★	★	★	Senate: 48 hours notice. House: 3 days notice.	Senate and House: roll call vote.
Oregon	★	★	★	Senate: at least 48 hrs. notice except at the end of session when President invokes 1 hr. notice when adjournment sine die is imminent. House: First public hearing on a measure must have at least 72 hours notice, all other meetings at least 48 hours notice except in case of emergency.	Senate and House: affirmative roll call vote of majority of members of committee and recorded in committee minutes.
Pennsylvania	★	★	★	Senate and House: written notice to members containing date, time, place and agenda.	Senate and House: a majority vote of committee members.
Rhode Island	★	★	★	Senate and House: notice required.	Senate and House: majority vote of the members present.
South Carolina	★	★	★	Senate and House: 24 hours.	Senate and House: favorable report out of committee (majority of committee members voting in favor).
South Dakota	★	★	★	Senate and House: at least one legislative day must intervene between the date of posting and the date of consideration in both houses.	Senate and House: a majority vote of the members-elect taken by roll call is needed for final disposition on a bill. This applies to both houses.
Tennessee	★	★	★	Senate: 6 days; House: 72 hours.	Senate and House: majority referral to Calendar and Rules Committee, majority of Calendar and Rules Committee referral to floor.

See footnotes at end of table

TABLE 3.24
Rules Adoption and Standing Committees: Procedure (continued)

State or other jurisdiction	Constitution permits each legislative body to determine its own rules	Committee meetings open to public*		Specific, advance notice provisions for committee meetings or hearings	Voting/roll call provisions to report a bill to floor
		Senate	House/ Assembly		
Texas	★	★	★	Senate: 24 hours; House: the House requires five calendar days notice before a public hearing at which testimony will be taken, and two hours notice or an announcement from the floor before a formal meeting (testimony cannot be taken at a formal meeting). 24 hour advance notice is required for a public hearing during special session.	Senate: bills are reported by recorded roll call vote. House: committee reports include the record vote by which the report was adopted, including the vote of each member.
Utah	★	★	★	Senate and House: not less than 24 hours public notice.	Senate and House: voice vote accepting the recommendation of the committee.
Vermont	★	★	★	Senate and House: none.	Senate and House: vote is recorded for each committee member for every bill considered.
Virginia	★	★(a)	★(a)	Senate and House: none.	Senate: recorded vote, except resolutions that do not have a specific vote requirement under the Rules. In these cases, a voice vote is sufficient. House: vote of each member is taken and recorded for each measure.
Washington	★	★	★	Senate and House: 5 days.	Senate: bills reported from a committee carry a majority report which must be signed by a majority of the committee. House: every vote to report a bill out of committee is by yeas and nays; the names of the members voting are recorded in the report.
West Virginia	★	★	★	Senate and House: none.	Senate and House: majority of committee members voting.
Wisconsin	★	★	★	Senate and House: Monday noon of the preceding week.	Senate: number of ayes and noes, and members absent or not voting are reported. House: number of ayes and noes are recorded.
Wyoming	★	★	★	Senate and House: by 3:00 p.m. of previous day	Senate and House: bills are reported out by recorded roll call vote.
American Samoa	★	★(d)	★(d)	Senate and House: at least 3 calendar days in advance.	Senate and House: there are four methods of ascertaining the decision upon any matter: by raising of hands; by secret ballot, when authorized by law; by rising; and by call of the members and recorded by the Clerk of the vote of each.
Guam	★	★	U	Five days prior to public hearings.	Majority vote of committee members.
CNMI**	★	★	★	Senate: 3 days. House: 1 day.	Senate and House: majority.
Puerto Rico	★	★	★	Senate: must be notified every Thurs., one week in advance. House: 24 hours advance notice, no later than 4:00 p.m. previous day.	Senate: bills reported from a committee carry a majority vote. House: bills reported from a committee carry a majority vote by referendum or in an ordinary meeting.
U.S. Virgin Islands	★	★	U	Seven calendar days.	Bills must be reported to floor by Rules Committee.

Source: The Council of State Governments' survey, March 2019.
**Commonwealth of Northern Mariana Islands
Key:
*–Notice of committee meetings may also be subject to state open meetings laws; in some cases, listed times may be subject to suspension or enforceable only to the extent "feasible" or "whenever possible."
★–Yes
U–Unicameral.
(a) "Each house when assembled shall ... determine its own rules of proceeding. ..." (Idaho Const. art. III, § 9). "The business of each house, and of the committee of the whole shall be transacted openly and not in secret session." (Idaho Const. art. III, § 12). "All meetings of any standing, special or select committee of either house of the legislature of the state of Idaho shall be open to the

public at all times, except in extraordinary circumstances as provided specifically in the rules of procedure in either house, and any person may attend any meeting of a standing, special or select committee, but may participate in the committee only with the approval of the committee itself." (I.C. § 74-207; see also House Rule 57 and Senate Rule 20).
(b) A session of a house or one of its committees can be closed to the public if two-thirds of the members elected to that house determine that the public interest so requires. A meeting of a joint committee or commission can be closed if two-thirds of the members of both houses so vote.
(c) Not referenced specifically, but each body publishes rules.
(d) Unless privileged information is being discussed with counsel or the security of the territory is involved.
(e) Committees are joint.

TABLE 3.25
Legislative Review of Administrative Regulations: Structures and Procedures

State or other jurisdiction	Type of reviewing committee	Rules reviewed	Time limits in review process
Alabama	Joint bipartisan, standing committee	P	If not approved or disapproved within 45 days of filing, rule is approved. If disapproved by committee, disapproval may be appealed to the lieutenant governor.
Alaska	Joint bipartisan, standing committee and Legislative Affairs Agency review of proposed regulations.	P, E	...
Arizona	Joint bipartisan	P, E	...
Arkansas	Joint bipartisan	P, E (f)	...
California	Standing committee	P, E	The Legislature may study and make recommendations regarding existing or proposed regulations. Comprehensive regulation review conducted by independent executive branch agency.
Colorado	Joint bipartisan	E	Rules continue unless the annual legislative Rule Reviews Bill discontinues a rule. The Rule Reviews Bill is effective upon the governor's signature, however, the governor needs to sign the Rule Review Bill on or before midnight on May 15 or all of the rules and amendments to rules adopted during the year before will automatically expire pursuant to statute.
Connecticut	Joint bipartisan, standing committee	P	Submittal of proposed regulation shall be on the first Tuesday of month; after first submittal committee has 65 days after date of submission to review/take action on revised regulation. Second submittal: 35 days for committee to review /take action on revised regulation.
Delaware	Joint bipartisan, standing committee	P, E (e)	...
Florida	Joint bipartisan	P, E	...
Georgia	Standing committee	P	The agency notifies the Legislative Counsel 30 days prior to the effective dates of proposed rules.
Hawaii	Legislative agency	P, E	The legislative reference bureau assists agencies to comply with a uniform format of style. This does not affect the status of rules.
Idaho	Germane joint subcommittees	P, E	There is no set time limit for rules review other than by the end of session. Typically they review rules during the first 3-4 weeks of session. Proposed rules: Reviewed pursuant to I.C. § 67-454. Existing rules: "The legislature may review any administrative rule to ensure it is consistent with the legislative intent of the statute that the rule was written to interpret, prescribe, implement or enforce. After that review, the legislature may approve or reject, in whole or in part, any rule as provided by law." (Idaho Const. art. III, § 29).
Illinois	Joint bipartisan	P, E	An agency proposing non-emergency regulations must allow 45 days for public comment. At least five days after any public hearing on the proposal, the agency must give notice of the proposal to the Joint Committee on Administrative Rules, and allow it 45 days to approve or object to the proposed regulations.
Indiana	------------------------------- No formal rule review is performed by both legislative and executive branches. -------------------------------		
Iowa	Joint bipartisan	P, E	...
Kansas	Joint bipartisan	P	Agencies must give 60-day notice to the public and the Joint Committee of their intent to adopt or amend specific rules and regulations, a copy of which must be provided to the committee. Within the 60-day comment period, the Joint Committee must review and comment, if it feels necessary, on the proposals. Final rules and regulations which differ in subject matter or in any material respect from the rules and regulations originally proposed or which are not a logical outgrowth of the rules and regulations originally proposed must be resubmitted to the Joint Committee as part of new rulemaking.
Kentucky	Joint bipartisan statutory committee	P, E	45 days.
Louisiana (a)	Standing committee	P	All proposed rules and fees are submitted to designated standing committees of the legislature. If a rule or fee is unacceptable, the committee sends a written report to the governor. The governor has 10 days to disapprove the committee report. If both Senate and House committees fail to find the rule unacceptable, or if the governor disapproves the action of a committee within 10 days, the agency may adopt the rule change. If the committees of both houses fail to find a fee unacceptable, it can be adopted. Committee action on proposed rules must be taken within 5 to 30 days after the agency reports to the committee on its public hearing (if any) and whether it is making changes on proposed rules.
Maine	Joint bipartisan, standing committee	P (d)	One legislative session.
Maryland	Joint bipartisan	P, E	Proposed regulations are submitted for review at least 15 days before publication. Publication triggers 45-day review period which may be extended by the committee, but if agreement cannot be reached, the governor may instruct the agency to modify or withdraw the regulation, or may approve its adoption.
Massachusetts (a)	Public hearing by agency	P	In Massachusetts, the General Court (Legislature) may by statute authorize an administrative agency to promulgate regulations. The promulgation of such regulations are then governed by Chapter 30A of the Massachusetts General Laws. Chapter 30A requires 21 day notice to the public of a public hearing on a proposed regulation. After public hearing the proposed regulation is filed with the state secretary who approves it if it is in conformity with Chapter 30A. The state secretary maintains a register entitled "Massachusetts Register" and the regulation does not become effective until published in the register. The agency may promulgate amendments to the regulations following the same process.

See footnotes at end of table

TABLE 3.25

Legislative Review of Administrative Regulations: Structures and Procedures (continued)

State or other jurisdiction	Type of reviewing committee	Rules reviewed	Time limits in review process
Michigan	Joint bipartisan	P	Joint Committee on Administrative Rules (JCAR) has 15 session days in which to consider the rule. JCAR may waive the remaining session days, object to the rule, propose that the rule be changed, or decide to enact the subject of the rule into law. (1) If JCAR does not object or waives the remaining session days, the rule goes into effect. (2) If JCAR objects, a member of the JCAR shall introduce bills in both houses to rescind the rule, repeal the authorizing statute, or stay the effective date for up to one year. If the legislation does not pass within 15 session days, the agency may file the rule. (3) If the JCAR proposes the rule be changed, the agency has 30 days to change the rule and resubmit or decide to not change the rule. If the agency agrees to change the proposed rule, it withdraws the rule and resubmits it. If the agency does not agree to change the proposed rule, it notifies the JCAR which again has 15 session days to consider the rule. (4) If the JCAR decides to enact the subject of the rule into law, the JCAR chair or alternate chair shall introduce legislation in both houses to do so and the agency may not file the rule for 270 days after the introduction of the legislation. The JCAR can also meet between legislative sessions and suspend rules promulgated during the interim between sessions.
Minnesota	Joint bipartisan, standing committee	P, E	Minnesota Statute Sec. 3.842, subd. 4a
Mississippi	No formal rule review is performed by both legislative and executive branches.		
Missouri	Joint bipartisan, statutory 536.037 RSMo.	P, E	The committee must disapprove a final order of rulemaking within 30 days upon receipt or the order of rulemaking is deemed approved.
Montana	Germane joint bipartisan committees	P	Prior to adoption.
Nebraska	Standing committee	P	If an agency proposes to repeal, adopt or amend a rule or regulation, it is required to provide the Executive Board Chair with the proposal at least 30 days prior to the public hearing, as required by law. The Executive Board Chair shall provide to the appropriate standing committee of the legislature, the agency proposal for comment.
Nevada	Ongoing statutory committee (Legislative Commission)	P	Proposed regulations are either reviewed at the Legislative Commission's next regularly scheduled meeting (if the regulation is received more than 10 working days before the meeting), or they are referred to the Commission's Subcommittee to Review Regulations. If there is no objection to the regulation, then the Commission will "promptly" file the approved regulation with the Secretary of State. If the Commission or its subcommittee objects to a regulation, then the Commission will "promptly" return the regulation to the agency for revision. Within 60 days of receiving the written notice of objection to the regulation, the agency must revise the regulation and return it to the Legislative Counsel. If the Commission or its subcommittee objects to the revised regulation, the agency shall continue to revise and resubmit it to the Commission or subcommittee within 30 days after receiving the written notice of objection to the revised regulation.
New Hampshire	Joint bipartisan	P	Under APA, for regular rulemaking, the joint committee of administrative rules has 45 days to review a final proposed rule from an agency. Otherwise the rule is automatically approved. If JLCAR makes a preliminary or revised objection, the agency has 45 days to respond, and JLCAR has another 50 days to decide to vote to sponsor a joint resolution, which suspends the adoption process. JLCAR may also, or instead, make a final objection, which shifts the burden of proof in court to the agency. There is no time limit on making a final objection. If no JLCAR action in the 50 days to vote to sponsor a joint resolution, the agency may adopt the rule.
New Jersey	Joint bipartisan	...	...
New Mexico	---------------- No formal review is performed by legislature. Periodic review and report to legislative finance committee is required of certain agencies. ----------------		
New York	Joint bipartisan commission	P, E	...
North Carolina	Rules Review Commission; Public membership appointed by legislature	P, E	The Rules Review Commission must review a permanent rule submitted to it on or before the 20th of the month by the last day of the next month. The commission must review a permanent rule submitted to it after the 20th of the month by the last day of the second subsequent month.
North Dakota	Interim committee	E	The Administrative Rules Committee meets in each calendar quarter to consider rules filed in previous 90 days.
Ohio	Joint bipartisan	P, E (c)	The committee's jurisdiction is 65 days from date of original filing plus an additional 30 days from date of re-filing. Rules filed with no changes, pursuant to the five-year review, are under a 90-day jurisdiction.
Oklahoma	Standing committee (b)	P, E	The legislature has 30 legislative days to review proposed rules. The legislature reviews all agency rules submitted prior to April 1st. Any rules submitted after April 1st are to be reviewed the next legislative session.
Oregon	Office of Legislative Counsel	E	Agencies must copy Legislative Counsel within 10 days of rule adoption.
Pennsylvania	Joint bipartisan, standing committee	P	Time limits decided by the president pro tempore and speaker of the House.
Rhode Island	---------------- No formal rule review is performed by both legislative and executive branches. ----------------		
South Carolina	Standing committee. Submitted by General Assembly for approval	P	General Assembly has 120 days to approve or disapprove. If not disapproved by joint resolution before 120 days, regulation is automatically approved. It can be approved during 120-day review period by joint resolution.
South Dakota	Joint bipartisan	P	Rules must be adopted within 75 days of the commencement of the public hearing; emergency rules must be adopted within 30 days of the date of the publication of the notice of intent. Many other deadlines exist; see SDCL 1-26-4 for further details.

See footnotes at end of table

TABLE 3.25

Legislative Review of Administrative Regulations: Structures and Procedures (continued)

State or other jurisdiction	Type of reviewing committee	Rules reviewed	Time limits in review process
Tennessee	Joint bipartisan	P	All permanent rules take effect 90 days after filing with the secretary of state. Emergency rules take effect upon filing with the secretary of state and may be effective for not longer than 180 days.
Texas	Standing committee	P, E	No time limit.
Utah	Created by statute (63G-3-501).	P, E	Except as provided in Subsection (2)(b), every agency rule that is in effect on February 28 of any calendar year expires May 1 of that year unless it has been reauthorized by the legislature. (UCA 63G-3-502)
Vermont	Joint bipartisan	P	The Joint Legislative Committee on Rules must review a proposed rule within 30 days of submission to the committee.
Virginia	Joint bipartisan, standing committee	P	Standing committees and the Joint Commission on Administrative Rules may object to a proposed or final adopted rule before it becomes effective. This delays the process for 21 days and the agency must respond to the objection. In addition or as an alternative, standing committees and the Commission may suspend the effective date of all or a part of a final regulation until the end of the next regular session, with the concurrence of the Governor.
Washington	Joint bipartisan	P, E	If the committee determines that a proposed rule does not comply with legislative intent, it notifies the agency, which must schedule a public hearing within 30 days of notification. The agency notifies the committee of its action within seven days after the hearing. If a hearing is not held or the agency does not amend the rule, the objection may be filed in the state register and referenced in the state code. The committee's powers, other than publication of its objections, are advisory.
West Virginia	Joint bipartisan	P, E	…
Wisconsin	Joint bipartisan	P, E	The standing committee in each house has 30 days to conduct its review for a proposed rule. If either objects the Joint Committee for the Review of Administrative Rules has 30 days to introduce legislation in each house overturning the rules. After 40 days the bills are placed on the calendar. If either bill passes, the rules are overturned. If they fail to pass, the rules go into effect. As an alternative, JCRAR may make an indefinite objection and the agency may not promulgate the rule unless a bill authorizing the promulgation is enacted.
Wyoming	Joint bipartisan	P, E	An agency shall submit copies of adopted, amended or repealed rules to the legislative service office for review within ten days after the date of the agency's final action adopting, amending or repealing those rules. The legislature makes its recommendations to the governor who within 15 days after receiving any recommendation, shall either order that the rule be amended or rescinded in accordance with the recommendation or file in writing his objections to the recommendation.
American Samoa	Standing committee	E	…
Guam	Standing committee	P	45 calendar days
Puerto Rico	------------------------- No formal rule review is performed by both legislative and executive branches. -------------------------		
U.S. Virgin Islands	------------------------- No formal rule review is performed by both legislative and executive branches. -------------------------		

Source: The Council of State Governments' survey, March 2019.
Key:
P–Proposed rules
E–Existing rules
…–No formal time limits
(a) Review of rules is performed by both legislative and executive branches.
(b) House has a standing committee to which all rules are generally sent for review. In the Senate rules are sent to standing committee which deals with that specific agency.
(c) The Committee reviews proposed new, amended, and rescinded rules. The Committee participates in a five-year review of every existing rule.

(d) Major substantive Rules (as designated by the Legislature) are subject to legislative review and approval; Routine Technical Rules are not subject to any formal legislative review and approval process.
(e) The chair of a standing committee can call a hearing to review the rule during the interim. The Joint Legislative Oversight Committee can order a review of an agency's rules during regular session.
(f) Amendment 92 to the Arkansas Constitution, which passed in 2014, and laws enacted by Act 1258 of 2015 provided the General Assembly with the power of review and approval of all administrative rules and regulations.

TABLE 3.26
Legislative Review of Administrative Rules/Regulations: Powers

| State or other jurisdiction | Reviewing committee's powers | | | Legislative powers: |
	Advisory powers only (a)	No objection constitutes approval of proposed rule	Committee may suspend rule	Method of legislative veto of rules
Alabama	...	★	★	If not approved or disapproved within 45 days of filing, rule is approved. If disapproved by committee, disapproval may be appealed to the lieutenant governor. If the lieutenant governor doesn't approve rule, it is disapproved. If lieutenant governor approves rule, rule is suspended until final adjournment, next regular session. Rule takes effect upon that final adjournment unless committee's approval is sustained by legislature. The committee may approve a rule.
Alaska	★	...	(b)	Constitution and Statute
Arizona	★	N.A.	N.A.	N.A.
Arkansas	(gg)	★	...	A motion may be made in the Legislative Council or its Administrative Rules and Regulations Subcommittee to not approve the rule. If such a motion is made, the legislator making the motion must state the basis for not approving the rule. The only two valid reasons for not approving the rule are that it is inconsistent with state or federal law or inconsistent with legislative intent.
California	★(cc)	...	...	Statute
Colorado	...	★	...	Rules that the General Assembly has determined should not be continued are listed as exceptions to the continuation.
Connecticut	...	★	...	Statute CGS 4-170 (d) and 4-171; (c)
Delaware	★(ff)	...	...	N.A.
Florida	★(ee)	...	...	Statute
Georgia	...	★	...	Resolution (d)
Hawaii	★	...	...	...
Idaho	(ii)	★	(jj)	Concurrent resolution. All rules are terminated one year after adoption unless the legislature reauthorizes the rule.
Illinois	...	(e)	★(f)	(f)
Indiana	...	...	...	(g)
Iowa	...	...	(h)	By constitutional majority vote of each house, by joint resolution, with approval of governor not required.
Kansas	★	...	...	Statute
Kentucky	(x)	(y)	(z)	Enacting legislation to void. (z)
Louisiana	...	★	(i)	Concurrent resolution to suspend, amend or repeal adopted rules or fees. Proposed rules and emergency rules exist (i).
Maine	★(aa)	★(bb)	...	(j)
Maryland	★(k)	...	...	...
Massachusetts	...	...	...	The legislature may pass a bill which would supersede a regulation if signed into law by the governor.
Michigan	...	...	(l)	Joint Committee on Administrative Rules (JCAR) has 15 session days in which to consider the rule. JCAR may waive the remaining session days, object to the rule, propose that the rule be changed, or decide to enact the subject of the rule into law. (1) If JCAR does not object or waives the remaining session days, the rule goes into effect. (2) If JCAR objects, a member of the JCAR shall introduce bills in both houses to rescind the rule, repeal the authorizing statute, or stay the effective date for up to one year. If the legislation does not pass within 15 session days, the agency may file the rule. (3) If the JCAR proposes the rule be changed, the agency has 30 days to change the rule and resubmit or decide to not change the rule. If the agency agrees to change the proposed rule, it withdraws the rule and resubmits it. If the agency does not agree to change the proposed rule, it notifies the JCAR which again has 15 session days to consider the rule. (4) If the JCAR decides to enact the subject of the rule into law, the JCAR chair or alternate chair shall introduce legislation in both houses to do so and the agency may not file the rule for 270 days after the introduction of the legislation. The JCAR can also meet between legislative sessions and suspend rules promulgated during the interim between sessions.
Minnesota	★	...	...	(m)
Mississippi			(n)	
Missouri	...	★	★	Concurrent resolution passed by both houses of the General Assembly.
Montana	...	...	★(o)	Statute
Nebraska	★	★	...	...

See footnotes at end of table

TABLE 3.26
Legislative Review of Administrative Rules/Regulations: Powers (continued)

State or other jurisdiction	Reviewing committee's powers			Legislative powers:
	Advisory powers only (a)	No objection constitutes approval of proposed rule	Committee may suspend rule	Method of legislative veto of rules
Nevada	N.A.	★	★	Proposed regulations are either reviewed at the Legislative Commission's next regularly scheduled meeting (if the regulation is received more than 10 working days before the meeting), or they are referred to the Commission's Subcommittee to Review Regulations. If there is no objection to the regulation, then the Commission will "promptly" file the approved regulation with the Secretary of State. If the Commission or its subcommittee objects to a regulation, then the Commission will "promptly" return the regulation to the agency for revision. Within 60 days of receiving the written notice of objection to the regulation, the agency must revise the regulation and return it to the Legislative Counsel. If the Commission or its subcommittee objects to the revised regulation, the agency shall continue to revise and resubmit it to the Commission or subcommittee within 30 days after receiving the written notice of objection to the revised regulation.
New Hampshire	★	(q)	...	(r)
New Jersey	★	...	...	(s)
New Mexico	N.A.	N.A.	N.A.	No formal mechanism exists for legislative review of administrative rules.
New York	(hh)	...	...	There is no legislative veto of administrative rules outside of bill process in New York.
North Carolina	★	★	★	...
North Dakota	...	★(t)	...	...
Ohio	★	...	...	Concurrent resolution. Committee recommends to the General Assembly that a rule be invalidated. The General Assembly invalidates a rule through adoption of concurrent resolution.
Oklahoma	★(p)	★(p)	★(p)	The legislature may disapprove (veto) proposed rules by concurrent or joint resolution. A concurrent resolution does not require the governor's signature. Existing rules may be disapproved by joint resolution. A committee may not disapprove; only the full legislature may do so. Failure of the legislature to disapprove constitutes approval. Pursuant to HB 2055 enacted in 2013, legislature shall adopt omnibus resolution approving all proposed permanent rules except those listed in resolution which are to be disapproved.
Oregon	★	★	(dd)	By passing statute that overrides terms of rule.
Pennsylvania	...	★	★	Upon vote of General Assembly
Rhode Island	...............................(n)...............................			
South Carolina	...	★	...	...
South Dakota	...	★	★	The Interim Rules Review Committee may, by statute, suspend rules that have not become effective yet by an affirmative vote of the majority of the committee.
Tennessee	...	...	★	The Government Operations committee of either house may stay a permanent rule for up to 60 days, and may request an agency to repeal, amend or withdraw. In accordance with statutorily-imposed termination dates, all permanent rules filed in one calendar year expire on June 30 of the subsequent year unless the general assembly enacts legislation to extend the rules to a date certain or indefinitely.
Texas	★	...	...	N.A.
Utah	★	...	...	All rules must be reauthorized by the legislature annually. This is done by omnibus legislation, which also provides for the sunsetting of specific rules listed in the bill.
Vermont	...............................(u)...............................			Statute
Virginia	...	...	(v)	The General Assembly must pass a bill enacted into law to directly negate the administrative rule.
Washington	★	★	★	N.A.
West Virginia	★	...	...	(w)
Wisconsin	...	★	★	The standing committee in each house has 30 days to conduct its review for a proposed rule. If either objects the Joint Committee for the Review of Administrative Rules has 30 days to introduce legislation in each house overturning the rules. After 40 days the bills are placed on the calendar. If either bill passes, the rules are overturned. If they fail to pass, the rules go into effect. As an alternative, JCRAR may make an indefinite objection and the agency may not promulgate the rule unless a bill authorizing the promulgation is enacted.
Wyoming	★	★	...	Action must be taken by legislative order adopted by both houses before the end of the next succeeding legislative session to nullify a rule.
American Samoa				The enacting clause of all bills shall be: Be it by the Legislature of American Samoa, and no law shall be except by bill. Bills may originate in either house, and may be amended or rejected by the other. The Governor may submit proposed legislation to the Legislature for consideration by it. He may designate any such proposed legislation as urgent, if he so considers it.
Guam	N.A.	N.A.	N.A.	Legislation to disapprove rules and regulations.
CNMI*	★	★	★	
U.S. Virgin Islands	...............................(n)...............................			

See footnotes at end of table

TABLE 3.26

Legislative Review of Administrative Rules/Regulations: Powers (continued)

Source: The Council of State Governments' survey, March 2019.
*Commonwealth of Northern Mariana Islands
Key:
★–Yes
...–No
N.A.–Not applicable
(a) This column is defined by those legislatures or legislative committees that can only recommend changes to rules but have no power to enforce a change.
(b) Authorized, although constitutionally questionable.
(c) Disapproval of proposed regulations may be sustained, or reversed by action of the General Assembly in the ensuing session. The General Assembly may by resolution sustain or reverse a vote of disapproval.
(d) The reviewing committee must introduce a resolution to override a rule within the first 30 days of the next regular session of the General Assembly. If the resolution passes by less than a two-thirds majority of either house, the governor has final authority to affirm or veto the resolution.
(e) The Administrative Procedure Act is not clear on this point, but implies that the Joint Committee should either object or issue a statement of no objections.
(f) Joint Committee on Administrative Rules can send objections to issuing agency. If it does, the agency has 90 days from then to withdraw, change, or refuse to change the proposed regulations. If the Joint Committee determines that proposed regulations would seriously threaten the public good, it can block their adoption. Within 180 days the Joint Cmte., or both houses of the General Assembly, can "unblock" those regulations; if that does not happen, the regulations are dead.
(g) None–except by passing statute.
(h) Committee may delay or suspend object to rules, and has authority to approve emergency filed rules.
(i) If the committee determines that a proposed rule is unacceptable, it submits a report to the governor who then has 10 days to accept or reject the report. If the governor rejects the report, the rule change may be adopted by the agency. If the governor accepts the report, the agency may not adopt the rule. Emergency rules become effective upon adoption or up to 60 days after adoption as provided in the rule, but a standing committee or governor may void the rule by finding it unacceptable within 2 to 61 days after adoption and reporting such finding to agency within four days.
(j) No veto allowed. If Legislature wishes to stop a rule from being adopted, it must enact appropriate legislation prohibiting the agency from adopting the rule.
(k) Except for emergency regulations which require committee approval for adoption.
(l) Committee can suspend rules during interim.
(m) The Legislative Commission to Review Administrative Rules (LCRAR) ceased operating, effective July 1, 1996. The Legislative Coordinating Commission (LCC) may review a proposed or adopted rule. Contact the LCC for more information. See Minn. Stat. 3.842, subd. 4a.
(n) No formal mechanism for legislative review of administrative rules. In Virginia, legislative review is optional.

(o) A rule disapproved by the reviewing committee is reinstated at the end of the next session if a joint resolution in the legislature fails to sustain committee action.
(p) Pursuant to HB 2055 enacted in 2013, the legislature shall adopt omnibus resolution approving all proposed permanent rules except those listed in resolution which are to be disapproved. Full legislature may suspend rules.
(q) Failure to object or approve within 45 days of agency filing of final proposal constitutes approval.
(r) The legislature may permanently block rules through legislation. The vote to sponsor a joint resolution suspends the adoption of a proposed rule for a limited time so that the full legislature may act on the resolution, which would then be subject to governor's veto and override.
(s) Article V, Section IV, par. 6 of the NJ Constitution, as amended in 1992, says the legislature may review any rule or regulation to determine whether the rule or regulation is (s) Article V, Section IV, par. 6 of the NJ Constitution, as amended in 1992, says the legislature may review any rule or regulation to determine whether the rule or regulation is consistent with legislative intent. The legislature transmits its objections to existing or proposed rules or regulations to the governor and relevant agency via concurrent resolutions. The legislature may invalidate or prohibit an existing or proposed rule from taking effect by a majority vote of the authorized membership of each house, in compliance with constitutional provisions.
(t) Unless formal objections are made or the rule is declared void, rules are considered approved.
(u) JLCAR may recommend that an agency amend or withdraw a proposal. A vote opposing rule does not prohibit its adoption but assigns the burden of proof in any legal challenge to the agency.
(v) Standing committees and The Joint Commission on Administrative Rules may suspend the effective date of all or a part of a final regulation until the end of the next regular legislative session with the concurrence of the governor.
(w) State agencies have no power to promulgate rules without first submitting proposed rules to the legislature which must enact a statute authorizing the agency to promulgate the rule. If the legislature during a regular session disapproves all or part of any legislative rule, the agency may not issue the rule nor take action to implement all or part of the rule unless authorized to do so. However, the agency may resubmit the same or a similar proposed rule to the committee.
(x) The promulgating agency's proposed language may be amended upon agreement of the committee and the promulgating agency.
(y) The committee does not approve or disapprove administrative regulations. It reviews them and can propose amendments that will be made, if the promulgating agency agrees to the amendment.
(z) The committee may make a finding of deficiency. If that happens, a letter is sent to the Governor requesting the Governor's determination whether the administrative regulation should be withdrawn, withdrawn and amended, or put into effect notwithstanding the finding of deficiency. The finding itself does not stop the rule from going into effect. If the Governor determines that the administrative regulation should go into effect notwithstanding the finding of deficiency, the General Assembly will usually address that issue

TABLE 3.26
Legislative Review of Administrative Rules/Regulations: Powers (continued)

in its next regular session, either by its own finding that the administrative regulation found deficient is null, void, and unenforceable,
or by amending the authorizing statute to restrict the need for the
administrative regulation.

(aa) Committee makes recommendations on Major Substantive Rules,
but approval or disapproval is by the full Legislature (the instrument
used is a resolve).

(bb) Under very specific circumstances the answer is yes with respect
to Major Substantive Rules: if the rules are submitted in accordance
with the timelines established by law, and the Legislature fails to
act on them, the rules may be adopted as if the Legislature approved
them.

(cc) Executive branch agency has more than advisory power.

(dd) Negative rule determinations are made public and remain on
website until rule is modified to comply with statutory authority,
statute is modified to establish validity of rule or court case upholds
validity of rule.

(ee) Joint Administrative Procedures Committee, with approval of
the president and speaker, may seek judicial review of validity or
invalidity of rules.

(ff) A standing committee can recommend a special session to consider committee's recommendations.

(gg) Amendment 92 to the Arkansas Constitution, which passed in
2014, and laws enacted by Act 1258 of 2015 provided the General
Assembly with the power of review and approval of all administrative rules and regulations.

(hh) Commission may hold hearings, subpoena witnesses, administer oaths, take testimony, and compel the production of books,
papers, documents and other evidence.

(ii) Germane joint subcommittees can submit a report of objection
to a rule to the germane standing committee and the Legislature.
The Legislature as a whole has the final say in the rejection of rules
when voting on the concurrent resolution of the rejection.

(jj) Final rules previously approved by the Legislature, can still be
rejected in a subsequent session.

TABLE 3.27
Summary of Sunset Legislation

State or other jurisdiction	Scope	Preliminary evaluation conducted by	Other legislative review	Other oversight mechanisms in law	Phase-out period	Life of each agency (in years)	Other provisions
Alabama	C	Dept. of Examiners of Public Accounts	Standing Cmtes.	Perf. audit	No later than Oct. 1 of the year following the regular session or a time as may be specified in the Sunset bill.	(Usually 4)	Schedules of licensing boards and other enumerated agencies are repealed according to specified time tables.
Alaska	C	Budget & Audit Cmte.	...	...	1/y	...	...
Arizona	C	Legislative staff	Joint Cmte.	...	6/m	10	...
Arkansas	D	...	...	...	...	...	...
California	S	Jt. Legis. Sunset Review Cmte. (a)	...	Perf. eval.	...	Established by the Legislature	...
Colorado	R	Dept. of Regulatory Agencies	Legis. Cmtes. of Reference	Bills need adoption by the legislature.	1/y	Up to 15	State law provides certain criteria that are used to determine whether a public need exists for an entity or function to continue and that its regulation is the least restrictive regulation consistent with the public interest.
Connecticut	D (b)	Committee of cognizance of program/ entity being reviewed.	...	per CGS 2c-21: unless otherwise provided, a provision of law creating board/commission/ other body on or after Jan. 4, 1995, with primary purpose of issuing report, is deemed repealed 120 days after the date of required submission of such report	...	...	...
Delaware	C	Agencies under review submit reports to Joint Legislative Oversight Cmte. based on criteria for review and set forth in statute. Cmte. staff conducts separate review.	...	Perf. audit	Dec. 31 of next succeeding calendar year	4	Yearly sunset review schedules must include at least four agencies.
Florida	S (f)	...	...	...	...	...	...
Georgia	R	Dept. of Audits	Standing Cmtes.	Perf. audit	...	...	A performance audit of each regulatory agency must be conducted upon the request of the Senate or House standing committee to which an agency has been assigned for oversight and review. (d)
Hawaii	R	Legis. Auditor	Standing Cmtes.	Perf. eval.	None	Established by the legislature	Schedules various professional and vocational licensing programs for repeal. Proposed new regulatory measures must be referred to the Auditor for sunrise analysis.
Idaho	S (e)	...	...	...	...	...	...
Illinois	R,S	Governor's Office of Mgmt. and Budget	Cmte. charged with re-enacting law	(g)	...	Usually 10	...
Indiana	...	...	...	...	...	...	...
Iowa	--- No program ---						
Kansas	(h)	...	...	...	...	...	...
Kentucky	R	Administrative Regulation Review Subcommittee	Joint committee with subject matter jurisdiction.	Perf. Eval.	...	...	...

See footnotes at end of table

TABLE 3.27
Summary of Sunset Legislation (continued)

State or other jurisdiction	Scope	Preliminary evaluation conducted by	Other legislative review	Other oversight mechanisms in law	Phase-out period	Life of each agency (in years)	Other provisions
Louisiana	C	Standing cmtes. of the two houses with subject matter jurisdiction.	...	Perf. eval.	1/y	Up to 6	Act provides for termination of a department and all offices in a department. Also permits committees to select particular agencies or offices for more extensive evaluation. Provides for review by Jt. Legis. Cmte. on Budget of programs that were not funded during the prior fiscal year for possible repeal.
Maine	S (w)	Joint standing cmte. of jurisdiction.	Office of Program Evaluation & Government Accountability	...	...	Generally 10 years	...
Maryland	R	Dept. of Legislative Services	Standing Cmtes.	Perf. eval.	...	Varies (usually 10)	...
Massachusetts	-- No program --						
Michigan	(e)	...	...	...	...	...	...
Minnesota	S (e)	...	...	...	...	...	...
Mississippi	(i)	...	...	...	...	...	...
Missouri	R	Oversight Division of Cmte. on Legislative Research	...	...	...	6, not to exceed total of 12	Can be extended.
Montana	(e)	...	...	...	...	...	...
Nebraska	D (e) (j)	...	...	...	...	...	...
Nevada	C (e) (c)	Sunset Subcommittee	Legislative Commission, Full Legislature	...	...	...	...
New Hampshire	(k)	...	...	...	...	...	...
New Jersey	(e)	...	...	...	...	...	...
New Mexico	S	Legis. Finance Cmte.	...	Public hearing before termination	1/y	Varies	...
New York	(e)	...	...	...	...	...	...
North Carolina	(l)	...	...	...	...	...	...
North Dakota	-- No program --						
Ohio	C (m)	Sunset Review Cmte.	...	Perf. eval.	(n)	6	...
Oklahoma	S, D	Stndng cmtes. with jurisdiction over sunset bills (Senate) Jt. Cmtes. With jurisdiction over sunset bills (House)	Appropriations and Budget Cmte.	...	1/y	6	...
Oregon	D (o)	...	(o)	(o)	...	...	...
Pennsylvania	R	Leadership Cmte.	...	...	...	Varies	...
Rhode Island	(p)	...	No	...	...	...	...
South Carolina	(q)	...	...	Perf. Eval.	1/y	...	...
South Dakota	(r)	...	...	...	...	...	...
Tennessee	C	Office of the Comptroller	Government Operations Committees	...	1/y	Up to 6 years	...
Texas	S	Sunset Advisory Commission staff	...	...	1/y	12	...
Utah	S	Interim cmtes., then Legislative Mngmt. Cmte.	Standing cmtes. as amendments may be made to bill	...	(v)	(v)	...

See footnotes at end of table

TABLE 3.27
Summary of Sunset Legislation (continued)

State or other jurisdiction	Scope	Preliminary evaluation conducted by	Other legislative review	Other oversight mechanisms in law	Phase-out period	Life of each agency (in years)	Other provisions
Vermont	(s)	Legis. Council staff	Senate and House Government Operations Cmtes.	...	...	...	...
Virginia	S (e)	...	...	...	...	...	Sunset provisions vary in length. The only standard sunset required by law is on bills that create a new advisory board or commission in the executive branch of government. The legislation introduced for these boards and commissions must contain a sunset provision to expire the entity after three years.
Washington	D	...	...	Perf. Eval.	1/y	...	...
West Virginia	S	Jt. Cmte. on Govt. Operations	Performance Evaluation and Research Division	Perf. audit	1/y	6	Jt. Cmte. on Govt. Operations composed of five House members, five Senate members and five citizens appointed by governor. Agencies may be reviewed more frequently.
Wisconsin	(e)	...	...	...	...	...	...
Wyoming	D (t)	Program evaluation staff who work for Management Audit Cmte.	...	Perf. eval. (u)	...	...	...
CNMI*			No	Perf. Eval.	1/y		

See footnotes at end of table

TABLE 3.27
Summary of Sunset Legislation (continued)

Source: The Council of State Governments' survey, April 2019.
*Commonwealth of Mariana Islands
Key:
C–Comprehensive–requires all statutory agencies to be subject to a
 sunset review once per review cycle.
R–Regulatory–review focus is on regulatory and licensing agencies
 and bureaus.
S–Selective–selective implementation and reviews are concentrated
 on entities such as occupational licensing and administrative agencies such as highway, health and education departments.
D–Discretionary–sunset review board has the ability to select which
 entities will face review.
d–day
m–month
y–year
…– No provision
(a) Jt. Legis. Sunset Review Cmte.–Review by the Jt. Legislative Sunset
 Review Cmte. of professional and vocational licensing boards, pursuant to Government Code 9147.7. Sunset clauses are included in
 other selected programs and legislation.
(b) No longer comprehensive–in 2016, funding for Legislative Program Review and Investigations Committee and staff eliminated; in
 2017, provisions of law requiring decennial review of certain pro-
 grams/entities repealed.
(c) The 2011 Nevada Legislature created the Sunset Subcommittee of
 the Legislative Commission with the enactment of Senate Bill 251
 (Chapter 480, Statutes of Nevada). The Subcommittee is to conduct
 reviews of all boards and commissions not provided for in the
 Nevada Constitution or created by Executive Order of the Governor,
 and is charged with determining whether those entities should be
 terminated, modified, consolidated, or continued. The Subcommittee must review each entity no less often than once every ten years.
 After making it's initial recommendations no later than June 30,
 2012, the Subcommittee must submit all subsequent recommendations to the Legislative Commission on or before June 30 of each
 even-numbered year. The Legislative Commission may accept or
 reject the recommendations in whole or part and may then request
 that legislation be drafted for consideration by the full Legislature.
(d) The automatic sunsetting of an agency every six years was eliminated in 1992. The legislature must pass a bill in order to sunset a
 specific agency.
(e) While they have not enacted sunset legislation in the same sense
 as the other states with detailed information in this table, the legislatures in Idaho, Michigan, Minnesota, Montana, Nebraska, Nevada,
 New Jersey, New York, Virginia and Wisconsin have included sunset
 clauses in selected programs or legislation.
(f) Comprehensive agency sunset review and repeal was repealed in
 2011. Florida does have Open Government Sunset Review of public
 records and meetings exemptions with a 5-year review period.

(g) Governor is to read GOMB report and make recommendations to
 the General Assembly every even-numbered year.
(h) Sunset legislation terminated July 1992. Legislative oversight of
 designated state agencies, consisting of audit, review and evaluation, continues.
(i) Sunset Act terminated December 31, 1984. House and Senate
 Rules are available at *billstatus.ls.state.ms.us.* New Rules were
 adopted in January 2012.
(j) Sunset legislation is discretionary, meaning that senators are free
 to offer sunset legislation or attach termination dates to legislative
 proposals. There is no formal sunset commission. Nebraska. Revised
 Statutes section 50-1303 directs the Legislature's Government, Military and Veteran's Committee to conduct an evaluation of any board,
 commission, or similar state entity. The review must include, among
 other things, a recommendation as to whether the board, commission, or entity should be terminated, continued or modified.
(k) New Hampshire's Sunset Committee was repealed July 1, 1986.
(l) North Carolina's sunset law terminated on July 30, 1981. Successor
 vehicle, the Legislative Committee on Agency Review, operated until
 June 30, 1983.
(m) There are statutory exceptions.
(n) Authority for latest review (SB 171 of the 129th General Assembly)
 expires December 31, 2016.
(o) Sunset legislation was repealed in 1993. No general law sunsetting rules or agencies. Oversight mechanisms, including auditing,
 reporting or performance measures, are discretionary but may be
 included in specific bills as determined by legislature.
(p) No standing sunset statutes or procedures at this time.
(q) Law repealed by 1998 Act 419, Part II, Sect. 35E.
(r) South Dakota suspended sunset legislation in 1979. A later law
 directing the Executive Board of the Legislative Research Council to
 establish one or more interim committees each year to review state
 agencies was repealed in 2012.
(s) Sunsets are at the legislature's discretion. Their structure will vary
 on an individual basis.
(t) Wyoming repealed sunset legislation in 1988.
(u) The program evaluation process evolved out of the sunset process,
 but Wyoming currently does not have a scheduled sunset of programs.
(v) Default is ten years, although years may be decreased by legislative
 decisions.
(w) Sometimes programs or agencies are subject to sunset provisions;
 this is entirely ad hoc as the Legislature determines appropriate. There
 is a general law, however, called State Government Evaluation Law that
 provides for regular reviews of agencies and boards by committee of
 jurisdiction; the committees can recommend termination (sunset)
 but, again, this is ad hoc.

CHAPTER FOUR

STATE EXECUTIVE BRANCH

TABLE 4.1
The Governors, 2019

State or other jurisdiction	Name and party	Length of regular term in years	Date of first service	Present term ends	Number of previous terms	Term limits	Joint election of governor & lieutenant governor (a)	Official who succeeds governor	Birthdate	Birthplace
Alabama	Kay Ivey (R)	4	4/2017 (c)	1/2023	(c)	2-4	No	LG	10/15/44	AL
Alaska	Mike Dunleavy (R)	4	12/2018	12/2022	...	2-4	Yes	LG	5/5/61	PA
Arizona	Doug Ducey (R)	4	1/2015	1/2023	1	2-4	(b)	SS	4/9/64	OH
Arkansas	Asa Hutchinson (R)	4	1/2015	1/2023	1	2A	No	LG	12/3/50	AR
California	Gavin Christopher Newsom (D)	4	1/2019	1/2023	...	2A	No	LG	10/10/67	CA
Colorado	Jared Schutz Polis (D)	4	1/2011	1/2019	1	2-4	Yes	LG	5/12/75	CO
Connecticut	Ned Lamont (D)	4	1/2019	1/2023	...	...	Yes	LG	1/3/54	DC
Delaware	John Carney Jr. (D)	4	1/2017	1/2021	...	2A	No	LG	5/20/56	DE
Florida	Ronald Dion DeSantis (R)	4	1/2019	1/2023	1	2-4	Yes	LG	9/14/78	FL
Georgia	Brian P. Kemp (R)	4	1/2019	1/2023	...	2-4	No	LG	11/2/63	GA
Hawaii	David Ige (D)	4	12/2014	12/2018	1	2-4	Yes	LG	6/26/38	NY
Idaho	Brad Little (R)	4	1/2019	1/2023	2	...	No	LG	2/15/54	ID
Illinois	Bruce Rauner (R)	4	1/2015	1/2023	1	...	Yes	LG	12/16/48	IL
Indiana	Eric Holcomb (R)	4	1/2017	1/2021	...	2-12	Yes	LG	5/2/68	IN
Iowa	Kim Reynolds (R)	4	5/2017 (d)	1/2023	1 (d)	...	Yes	LG	8/4/59	IA
Kansas	Laura Kelly (D)	4	1/2019	1/2023	...	2-4	Yes	LG	1/24/50	NY
Kentucky	Matt Bevin (R)	4	12/2015	12/2019	...	2-4	Yes	LG	1/9/67	NH
Louisiana	John Bel Edwards (D)	4	1/2016	1/2020	...	2-4	No	LG	9/16/66	LA
Maine	Janet Trafton Mills (D)	4	1/2019	1/2023	...	2-4	(b)	PS	12/30/47	ME
Maryland	Larry Hogan (R)	4	1/2015	1/2023	1	2-4	Yes	LG	5/25/56	DC
Massachusetts	Charlie Baker (R)	4	1/2015	1/2023	1	...	Yes	LG	11/13/56	NY
Michigan	Gretchen Esther Whitmer (D)	4	1/2019	1/2023	...	2A	Yes	LG	8/23/71	MI
Minnesota	Timothy James Walz (DFL)	4	1/2019	1/2023	...	...	Yes	LG	4/6/64	NE
Mississippi	Phil Bryant (R)	4	1/2012	1/2020	1	2A	Yes	LG	12/9/54	MS
Missouri	Mark Parson (R)	4	6/2018 (e)	1/2021	...	2A	No	LG	9/17/55	MO
Montana	Steve Bullock (D)	4	1/2013	1/2021	1	2-16	Yes	LG	4/11/66	MT
Nebraska	Pete Ricketts (R)	4	1/2015	1/2023	1	2-4	Yes	LG	8/19/64	NE
Nevada	Steve Sisolak (D)	4	1/2019	1/2023	...	2A	No	LG	12/26/53	WI
New Hampshire	Chris Sununu (R)	2	1/2017	1/2023	1	...	(b)	PS	11/5/74	NH
New Jersey	Phil Murphy (D)	4	1/2018	1/2022	...	2-4	Yes	LG	8/16/57	MA
New Mexico	Michelle Lujan Grisham (D)	4	1/2019	1/2023	...	2-4	Yes	LG	10/24/59	NM
New York	Andrew Cuomo (D)	4	1/2011	1/2023	2	...	Yes	LG	12/6/57	NY
North Carolina	Roy Cooper (D)	4	1/2017	1/2021	...	2-4	No	LG	6/13/57	NC
North Dakota	Doug Burgum (R)	4	12/2016	12/2020	...	...	Yes	LG	8/1/56	ND
Ohio	Mike DeWine (R)	4	1/2019	1/2023	...	2-4	Yes	LG	1/5/47	OH
Oklahoma	Kevin Stitt (R)	4	1/2019	1/2023	...	2-4	No	LG	12/28/72	OK
Oregon	Kate Brown (D)	4	2/2015 (f)	1/2023	1 (f)	2-12	(b)	SS	3/5/47	WA
Pennsylvania	Tom Wolf (D)	4	1/2015	1/2023	1	2-4	Yes	LG	11/17/48	PA
Rhode Island	Gina Raimondo (D)	4	1/2015	1/2023	1	2-4	No	LG	5/17/71	RI
South Carolina	Henry McMaster (R)	4	1/2017 (g)	1/2023	1(g)	2-4	No	LG	5/27/47	SC
South Dakota	Kristi Noem (R)	4	1/2019	1/2023	...	2-4	Yes	LG	11/30/71	SD
Tennessee	Bill Lee (R)	4	1/2019	1/2023	...	2-4	No	SpS (h)	10/9/59	TN
Texas	Greg Abbott (R)	4	1/2015	1/2023	1	...	No	LG	11/13/57	TX
Utah	Gary Herbert (R)	4	8/2009 (i)	1/2021	3	...	Yes	LG	5/7/47	UT
Vermont	Phil Scott (R)	2	1/2011	1/2021	4	...	No	LG	8/4/58	VT
Virginia	Ralph Northam (D)	4	1/2018	1/2022	...	1-4	No	LG	9/13/59	VA
Washington	Jay Inslee (D)	4	1/2013	1/2021	1	...	No	LG	2/9/51	WA
West Virginia	Jim Justice (R) (j)	4	1/2017	1/2021	...	2-4	(b)	PS (h)	4/27/51	WV
Wisconsin	Anthony Steven Evers (D)	4	1/2019	1/2023	...	...	Yes	LG	11/5/51	WI
Wyoming	Matt Mead (R)	4	1/2011	1/2019	1	2-16	(b)	SS	3/11/62	WY
American Samoa	Lolo Matalasi Moliga (I)	4	1/2013	1/2021	1	2-4	Yes	LG	1949	AS
Guam	Lourdes Leon Guerrero (D)	4	1/2019	1/2023	...	2-4	Yes	LG	11/8/50	Guam
CNMI*	Ralph Deleon Guerrero Torres (R)	4	12/28 (k)	1/2023	1 (k)	2-4	Yes	LG	8/6/79	CNMI
Puerto Rico	Wanda Vázquez Garced (PNP) (l)	4	8/2019 (l)	1/2021 (l)	...	...	(b)	SS (l)	7/9/60	PR
U.S. Virgin Islands	Albert Bryan (D)	4	1/2019	1/2023	...	2-4	Yes	LG	2/21/68	USVI

See footnotes at end of table

TABLE 4.1

The Governors, 2019 (continued)

Source: The Council of State Governments, June 2019.

Key:

*Commonwealth of the Northern Mariana Islands

C–Covenant

D–Democrat

DFL–Democratic-Farmer-Labor Party

I–Independent

PDP–Popular Democratic Party

PNP– New Progressive Party

R–Republican

LG–Lieutenant Governor

SS–Secretary of State

PS–President of the Senate

SpS–Speaker of the Senate

…–Not applicable

2A–Two terms, absolute.

2-4–Two terms, re-eligible after four yrs.

2-12–Two terms, eligible for eight out of 12 yrs.

2-16–Two terms, eligible for eight out of 16 yrs.

1-4–One term, re-eligible after four years.

N/A–Not available

(a) The following also choose candidates for governor and lieutenant governor through a joint nomination process: Florida, Kansas, Maryland, Minnesota, Montana, North Dakota, Ohio, Utah, American Samoa, Guam, No. Mariana Islands and U.S. Virgin Islands.

(b) No lieutenant governor.

(c) Kay Ivey (R) took office on April 10, 2017, following the resignation of former governor Robert Bentley. Ivey then ran and was elected to a full term in the 2018 general election.

(d) Lt. Gov. Kim Reynolds was sworn in as governor on May 24, 2017 when Gov. Branstad accepted the U.S. Ambassadorship to China. She then ran and won a full term in office in the 2018 general election.

(e) Lt. Gov. Mark Parson was sworn in as governor in June 2018 after Eric Greitens resigned.

(f) Oregon Secretary of State Kate Brown became governor on February 18, 2015, following Gov. John Kitzhaber's resignation. Brown won a November 2016 special gubernatorial election to officially fill the position for the final two years of Gov. Kitzhaber's term. She was elected for a full term in the 2018 general election.

(g) Gov. McMaster was sworn in on January 24, 2017 after Gov. Nikki Haley resigned to become the United State ambassador to the United Nations. He was elected to a full term in the Nov. 2018 general election.

(h) Official bears the additional title of " lieutenant governor."

(i) Lt. Gov. Gary Herbert was sworn in as Governor on August 10, 2009 after Gov. Huntsman resigned to accept President Obama's appointment as ambassador to China. Utah law states that a replacement governor elevated in a term's first year will face a special election at the next regularly scheduled general election, November 2010, instead of serving the remainder of the term. Gov. Herbert was re-elected to serve full terms in Nov. 2012 and again in Nov. 2016.

(j) Gov. Jim Justice switched parties in August 2017.

(k) Torres became governor on Dec. 28, 2015 after Gov. Inos passed away. He was elected to a full term in November 2018.

(l) Justice Secretary Wanda Vázquez Garced took the oath of office on Aug. 7, 2019 becoming Puerto Rico's third governor within a week.

TABLE 4.2
The Governors: Qualifications for Office

State or other jurisdiction	Minimum age	State citizen (years)	U.S. citizen (years) (a)	State resident (years) (b)	Qualified voter (years)
Alabama	30	7	10	7	★
Alaska	30	★	7	7	★
Arizona	25	5	10	5	★
Arkansas	30	★	★	7	★
California	18	...	5	5	★
Colorado	30	...	★	2	...
Connecticut	30	6 months	★	★	★
Delaware	30	...	12	6	...
Florida	30	★	★	7	7
Georgia	30	...	15	6	...
Hawaii	30	...	5	5	★
Idaho	30	2	★	2	★
Illinois	25	★	★	3	★
Indiana	30	...	5	5	★
Iowa	30	2	★	2	★
Kansas	...	...	...	...	...
Kentucky	30	6	...	6	...
Louisiana	25	5	5	5	★
Maine	30	...	15	5	...
Maryland	30	...	(c)	5	5
Massachusetts	...	...	...	7	★
Michigan	30	...	★	★	4
Minnesota	25	...	★	1	★
Mississippi	30	★	20	5	★
Missouri	30	...	15	10	...
Montana	25	★	★	2	★
Nebraska	30	5	★	5	...
Nevada	25	2	...	2	★
New Hampshire	30	...	...	7	...
New Jersey	30	...	20	7	...
New Mexico	30	...	★	5	★
New York	30	...	★	5	...
North Carolina	30	...	5	2	★
North Dakota	30	...	★	5	★
Ohio	18	...	★	★	★
Oklahoma	31	...	10	10	(d)
Oregon	30	...	★	3	★
Pennsylvania	30	★	★	7	★
Rhode Island	18	30 days	30 days	30 days	30 days
South Carolina	30	5	★	5	...
South Dakota	21	★	★	★	★
Tennessee	30	7	★	...	...
Texas	30	...	★	5	...
Utah	30	5	3	5	★
Vermont	18	...	★	4	★
Virginia	30	★	★	5	1
Washington	18	...	★	★	★
West Virginia	30	5	★	★	★
Wisconsin	18	★	★	★	★
Wyoming	30	★	★	5	★
American Samoa	35	...	★	5	...
Guam	30	...	5	5	★
CNMI*	35	...	★	10	★
Puerto Rico	35	5	5	5	...
U.S. Virgin Islands	30	...	5	5	★

Source: The Council of State Governments' survey of governors' offices, March 2019.

*Commonwealth of the Northern Mariana Islands

Key:
★–Formal provision; number of years not specified.
...–No formal provision.
(a) In some states you must be a U.S. citizen to be an elector, and must be an elector to run.
(b) In some states you must be a state resident to be an elector, and must be an elector to run.

(c) *Crosse v. Board of Supervisors of Elections* 243 Md. 555, 221A.2d431 (1966)–opinion rendered indicated that U.S. citizenship was, by necessity, a requirement for office.
(d) In order to file as a candidate for nomination by a political party to any state or county office, a person must have been a registered voter of that party for the six-month period preceding the first day of the filing perod (26 O.S.§. 5-105A-A).

TABLE 4.3

The Governors: Compensation, Staff, Travel and Residence

State or other jurisdiction	Salary	Governor's office staff (a)	Access to state transportation			Receives travel allowance	Reimbursed for travel expenses	Official residence
			Automobile	Airplane	Helicopter			
Alabama	120,395	37	★	★	★	...	★(b)	★
Alaska	145,000	82	★	★	...	...	★(b)	★
Arizona	95,000	26 (f)	★	★	...	...	★(b)	...
Arkansas	148,134	60	★	★	★	...	★	★
California	201,680	88	★	...	...	...	(d)	★
Colorado	90,000	50	★	★	...	★	★	★
Connecticut	150,000 (c)	27	★	...	...	...	...	(e)
Delaware	171,000	28	★	...	...	...	...	★
Florida	130,273	276 (f)	★	★(j)	...	(b)	(b)	★
Georgia	175,000	56 (f)	★	★	★	...	...	★
Hawaii	158,700	51	★	...	...	★	★	★
Idaho	138,302	17	★	★	...	...	★	...(e)
Illinois	177,412 (c)	91	★	...	...	...	...	★
Indiana	121,331	34	★	★	★	★(b)	★(b)	★
Iowa	130,000	18	★	...	...	...	★	★
Kansas	99,636	24	★	★	★	...	★	★
Kentucky	148,781	45	★	★	★	...	★(b)	★
Louisiana	130,000	93 (f)	★	★	★	...	★	★
Maine	70,000	21	★	★	...	★	★	★
Maryland	170,000	85 (f)	★	★	★	(b)	(b)	★
Massachusetts	185,000	approx. 60	★	...	★	★(b)	★(b)	...(e)
Michigan	159,300	75	★	★	★	(b)	(b)	★
Minnesota	127,629	37	★	★	★	...	★	★
Mississippi	122,160	29	★	★(k)	...	...	★	★
Missouri	133,821	21	★	★	...	(b)	(d)	★
Montana	115,505	58 (f)	★	★	★	...	★	★
Nebraska	105,000	9	★	★	...	★	★	★
Nevada	149,573(c)	18 (f)	★	★	...	(b)	★(b)	★
New Hampshire	134,581	18	★	...	...	(b)	(d)	(e)
New Jersey	175,000	128	★	...	★	★	★(b)	★
New Mexico	110,000	33	★	★	★	...	★	★
New York	200,000	180	★	★	★	...	★	★
North Carolina	144,349	59	★	★	...	★	★	★
North Dakota	129,096 (c)	18	★	★	...	...	★	★
Ohio	153,650	58	★	★	★	(b)	(d)	(e)
Oklahoma	147,000	34	★	★	...	...(b)	★(b)	★
Oregon	98,600	65 (f)	★	...	...	★(b)	★(b)	★
Pennsylvania	194,850	68	★	★	...	...	★(b)	★
Rhode Island	145,755	39	★	...	★	...	★(b)	...
South Carolina	106,078	16	★	★	...	...	★	★
South Dakota	113,961	18.75	★	★	...	...	★	★
Tennessee	194,112	37	★	★	★	★(b)	(d)	★
Texas	153,750	277	★	★	★	...	★	★
Utah	150,000	23	★	★	★	...	★	★
Vermont	178,274	14	★	★	...	...	...	...
Virginia	175,000	36	★	★	★	...	★	★
Washington	183,072	36	★	★	...	(b)	(d)	★
West Virginia	150,000	56	★	★	★	(b)	...	★
Wisconsin	152,756	34	★	★	...	...	(d)	★
Wyoming	105,000	18	★	★	...	...	★(b)	★
American Samoa	90,000	23	★	...	...	(b)	...	★
Guam	130,000	42	★	...	...	$218/day	...	★
CNMI*	70,000	16	★	...	...	(b)	...	★
Puerto Rico	70,000	28	★	(g)	(g)	...	★	★
U.S. Virgin Islands	150,000	84	★	...	...	...	★	★

See footnotes at end of table

TABLE 4.3
The Governors: Compensation, Staff, Travel and Residence (continued)

Source: The Council of State Governments survey of governors'
offices, September 2017.
* Commonwealth of Northern Mariana Islands
Key:
★–Yes
...–No
N.A.–Not available.
(a) Definitions of "governor's office staff" vary across the states–from
general office support to staffing for various operations within the
executive office.
(b) Travel expenses.
Alabama–According to state policy.
Alaska–$60/day per diem plus actual lodging expenses.
American Samoa–$105,000. Amount includes travel allowance for
entire staff.
Arizona–Receives up to $64/day for meals based on location;
receives per diem for lodging out of state; default $41/day for
meals and $93/day lodging in state.
Florida–The Executive Office of the Governor allocates an annual budget for the governor's travel expenses. Gov. Scott is not reimbursed
for personally incurred travel expenses. The Executive Office of the
Governor pays the governor's travel expenses directly (hotel accom-
modations, meals, etc.) out of funds allocated for travel.
Guam–The amount varies based on destination but averages $218/
per day.
Indiana–Statute allows $12,000 but due to budget cuts the amount
has been reduced to $9,800 and reimbursed for actual expenses
for travel/lodging.
Kentucky–Mileage at same rate as other state officials.
Maryland–Travel allowance included in office budget.
Massachusetts–As necessary.
Michigan–The Governor is provided a $54,000 annual expense allow-
ance, as determined by the State Officers Compensation Commission
in 2010. "Expense allowance" is for normal, reimbursable personal
expenses such as food, lodging, and travel costs incurred by an individual in carrying out the responsibilities of state office.
Missouri–Amount includes travel allowance for entire staff. Amount
not available.
Nevada–Amount includes travel allowance for entire staff. The following figures include travel expenses for governor and staff,
$28,982 in state; $12,767 out of state. Reimbursed for travel
expenses per GSA/Conus rate.
New Hampshire–Travel allowance included in office budget.
New Jersey–Reimbursement may be provided for necessary expenses.
Northern Mariana Islands–Travel allowance included in office budget.
Governor has a "contingency account" that can be used for travel
expenses and expenses in other departments or other projects.
Ohio–Set administratively.
Oklahoma–Reimbursed for actual and necessary expenses.
Oregon–$1,000 a month for expenses, not specific to travel. Reim-
bursed for actual travel expenses.
Pennsylvania–Reimbursed for reasonable expenses.
Rhode Island–The majority of travel expenses are not reimbursed
since the State has centralized direct pay agreements with the var-

ious airlines / hotels for approved travel for state employees. If
necessary, the governor is subject to the same per diem allowance
for personal meals as other state employees, which is a maximum
of $35 per day.
Tennessee–Travel allowance included in office budget.
Washington–Travel allowance included in office budget.
West Virginia–Included in general expense account.
Wyoming–Actual lodging and transportation/federal M&IE rates.
(c) Governor's salary:
Connecticut–Governor Ned Lamont will forego his salary of $150,000.
Illinois–Governor Pritzker will not take his salary of $177,412.
Nevada–Governor Sisolak pledged to donate his salary to K-12
schools all four years of his term.
North Dakota–Governor Doug Burgum has declined his salary of
$129,096.
(d) Information not provided.
(e) Governor's residence: Many governors are choosing to live in
their own residences even when an official residence is provided .
Connecticut–Provided by the Department of Administrative Services.
Idaho–A housing stipend of $54,608 annually is provided.
Massachusetts–Does not have an official governor's residence but
allows a $65,000 housing alowance.
New Hampshire–The current governor does not occupy the official
residence.
Ohio–The governor chooses not to live in the state provided housing.
(f) Governor's staff:
Arizona–There are 26 members of the governor's executive staff,
not including administrative staff.
Florida–There are 276 full-time employees. Those are broken into the
following areas: Executive Direction and Support Services–124 posi-
tions; Systems Development and Design–48 positions; Office of
Policy and Budget–104 positions.
Georgia–Full-time employees–56 and 2 part-time employees.
Louisiana–Full-time employees–93, part-time (non-student)–21,
students–25.
Maryland–Full-time employees–85 and 1 part-time employee.
Montana–Including 16 employees in the Office of Budget and Program Planning.
Nevada–Currently 18. Maximum permitted is 23.
Oregon–Of this total, 45 are true Governor's staff and 20 are on
loan for agency staff.
Vermont–Voluntary 5 percent salary reduction.
(g) The Governor's office pays for access to an airplane or helicopter
with a corporate credit card and requests a refund of those expenses
with the corresponding documentation to the Dept. of Treasury.
(h) Provided for security reasons as determined by the state police.
(i) When not in use by other state agencies.
(j) Gov. Scott does not utilize a state-owned airplane, but instead
uses his personal aircraft.
(k) Only for official business.

TABLE 4.4
The Governors: Powers

State or other jurisdiction	Budget making power		Item veto power				Legislative votes required to override governor's veto	Authorization for reorganization through executive order (a)
	Full responsibility	Shares responsibility	Governor has line item veto power	Governor has line item veto power on appropriations amounts	Governor has line item veto power on appropriations language	Governor has no item veto power		
Alabama	★(b)	...	★	★	★	...	Majority elected	...
Alaska	★	...	★	★	...	...	Three-fourths	★
Arizona	★(b)	...	★	...	...	...	Two-thirds elected	...
Arkansas	...	★	★	...	★	...	Majority elected	★
California	★(b)	...	★	★	★	...	Two-thirds elected	★(c)
Colorado	...	★	★	★	★	...	Two-thirds elected	★
Connecticut	...	★	★	★	...	...	Two-thirds elected	★(d)
Delaware	★(b)	...	★	...	...	...	Three-fifths elected	★
Florida	...	★	★	★	...	...	Two-thirds elected	★
Georgia	★	...	★	...	...	...	Two-thirds elected	★
Hawaii	...	★	★	★	...	...	Two-thirds elected	★
Idaho	...	★	★	★	★	...	Two-thirds elected	...
Illinois	...	★	★	★	...	...	Three-fifths elected	★
Indiana	★	...	...	...	...	★	Majority elected	★
Iowa	...	★	★	★	★	...	Two-thirds elected	★
Kansas	★	...	★	...	...	...	Two-thirds elected	★
Kentucky	★(b)	...	★	★	★	...	Majority elected	★
Louisiana	...	★	★	★	★	...	Two-thirds elected	★(e)
Maine	...	★	★	★	...	...	Majority elected	★
Maryland	★	...	★	★	...	...	Majority elected	★
Massachusetts	★	...	★	★	★	...	Two-thirds elected	★(c)
Michigan	★(f)	...	★	★	★	...	Two-thirds elected	★
Minnesota	...	★	★	★	★	...	Two-thirds elected	★(g)
Mississippi	...	★(h)	★	★	★	...	Two-thirds elected	★
Missouri	★(b)	...	★	★	★	...	Two-thirds elected	★
Montana	★	...	★	★	★	...	Two-thirds elected	★(i)
Nebraska	...	★	★	★	...	...	Three-fifths elected	...
Nevada	★	...	...	...	...	★	Two-thirds elected	★(j)
New Hampshire	★(b)	...	...	...	...	★	Two-thirds elected	...
New Jersey	★(b)	...	★	★	★	...	Two-thirds elected	★ (k)
New Mexico	★	...	★	★	★	...	Two-thirds elected	...
New York	...	★	★	★	★	...	Two-thirds elected	...
North Carolina	...	★	...	...	...	★	Three-fifths elected	★(l)
North Dakota	★	...	★	...	...	...	Two-thirds elected	★
Ohio	★	...	★	★	★	...	Three-fifths elected	...
Oklahoma	...	★	★	★	...	...	Two-thirds elected	★(m)
Oregon	...	★	★	★	...	...	Two-thirds elected	★
Pennsylvania	★	...	★	...	★	...	Two-thirds elected	...
Rhode Island	...	★	...	...	...	★	Three-fifths elected	★
South Carolina	...	★	★	★	...	...	Two-thirds elected	...
South Dakota	★	...	★	★	...	...	Two-thirds elected	★
Tennessee	...	★	★	★	...	...	Two-thirds elected	★
Texas	...	★	★	★	...	...	Two-thirds elected	...
Utah	...	★	★	...	...	...	Two-thirds elected	★
Vermont	★	...	...	...	...	★	Two-thirds elected	★
Virginia	★	...	★	...	...	...	Two-thirds elected	★(n)
Washington	★	...	★	★	★	...	Two-thirds elected	...
West Virginia	★	...	★	★	★	...	Majority elected	...
Wisconsin	★(b)	...	★	★	★	...	Two-thirds elected	...
Wyoming	...	★	★	★	★	...	Two-thirds elected	...
American Samoa	...	★	...	...	...	...	...	★
Guam	★	...	★	★	...	...	Two-thirds elected	★
CNMI*	...	★	★	★	★	...	Two-thirds elected	★
Puerto Rico	...	★	★	★	★	...	Two-thirds elected	★(o)
U.S. Virgin Islands	★	...	★	★	★	★	Two-thirds elected	★

See footnotes at end of table

TABLE 4.4
The Governors: Powers (continued)

Source: The Council of State Governments' survey of governors' offices, March 2019.

*Commonwealth of the Northern Mariana Islands

Key:

★ –Yes; provision for.

…–No; not applicable.

(a) For additional information on executive orders, see Table 4.5.

(b) Full responsibility to propose; legislature adopts or revises and governor signs or vetoes.

(c) Authorization for reorganization provided for in state constitution.

(d) Governor cannot create a budgeted agency but may "direct such action by the several budgeted agencies as will, in his judgment, effect efficiency and economy in the conduct of the affairs of the state government."

(e) Only for agencies and offices within the Governor's Office.

(f) Governor has sole authority to propose annual budget. No money may be paid out of state treasury except in pursuance of appropriations made by law and passed by the legislature.

(g) Statute provides for reorganization by the Commissioner of Administration with the approval of the governor.

(h) Governor has the responsibility of presenting a balanced budget. The budget is based on revenue estimated by the Governor's office and the Legislative Budget Committee.

(i) The office of the governor shall continuously study and evaluate the organizational structure, management practices, and functions of the executive branch and of each agency. The governor shall, by executive order or other means within the authority granted to him, take action to improve the manageability of the executive branch.

(j) Only as to commissions, boards and councils.

(k) Executive reorganization plans can be disapproved by majority vote in both houses of the legislature.

(l) Executive Order must be approved by the legislature if changes affect existing law.

(m) The governor has the authority, through state statute , to enact executive orders that: create agencies, boards and commissions; and reassigns agencies, boards and commissions to different cabinet secretaries. However, in order for the continued operation of any agency created by executive order the state legislature must approve legislation that allows the agency to continue to operate, if not, the agency cannot continue operation beyond sine die adjournment of the legislature for the session.

(n) The governor submits a reorganization plan to the General Assembly which must approve the plan by a vote of a majority of the membership in each house.

(o) Only if it is not prohibited by law.

TABLE 4.5
Gubernatorial Executive Orders: Authorization, Provisions, Procedures

State or other jurisdiction	Authorization for executive orders	Civil defense disasters, public emergencies	Energy emergencies and conservation	Other emergencies	Executive branch reorganization plans and agency creation	Create advisory, coordinating, study or investigative committees/commissions	Respond to federal programs and requirements	State personnel administration	Other administration	Filing and publication procedures	Subject to administrative procedure act	Subject to legislative review
		Provisions								Procedures		
Alabama	S, I, Case Law	★	★	★	...	★	...	...	...	★	...	★
Alaska	C	...	...	...	★	...	...	...	...	★	...	★
Arizona	I	★(a)	★(a)	★(a)	★(a)	★(a)	★(a)	★(a)	★(a)	★(b)	...	...
Arkansas	I, Common Law	★	★	★	★	★	...	...	...	...	...	...
California	I(c)	★	★	★	★	★	★	★	★	...	...	...
Colorado	C	★	★	★	★	★	★	★	★	★	★	★
Connecticut	C, S	★	★	★	...	★	...	★	★	(b)	...	...
Delaware	C	★	★	★	...	★	★	★	...	★	...	...
Florida	C, S	★	★	★	★	★	★	★	...	...	★	...
Georgia	S, I(d)	★	★	★	★	★	★	★	...	★	...	...
Hawaii	C, S, Common Practice	★	★	★	★	★	★	★	...	★	★	★
Idaho	S	★	★	★	★	★	...	★	...	★	...	...
Illinois	C, S	★	★	★	★	★	★	★	★	★	★	★
Indiana	C, S, Case Law	★	★	...	★	★	★	★	...	★	...	...
Iowa	(e)	★	★	★	★	★	★	★	(f)	★	★	★
Kansas	C, S	★	★	★	★	★	...	★	★	★	...	(g)
Kentucky	C, S	★	★	★(h)	★	★	★	★	★(i)(j)(k)	★(b)	★	★
Louisiana	C, S(l)	★	★	★	★	★	★	★	★	★	...	...
Maine	I	★	★	★	★	★	★	★	...	...	...	...
Maryland	C, S	★	★	★	★	★	★	★	★(m)	★	★	★(n)
Massachusetts	C, S	★	★	★	★	★	★	★	★	★	...	...
Michigan	C	★	★	★	...	★	★	...	...	★(o)	...	...
Minnesota	S	★	★	★	★	★	★	...	(p)(q)	★(b)	★	★(n)
Mississippi	C, S	★	★	★	★	★	★	...	...	(r)	(r)	...
Missouri	C, S, Common Law	★	...	★	★	★	★	★	★	★(n)	...	★(n)(s)
Montana	S, I, Common Law	★	★	★	★	★	★	★	★	★	...	...
Nebraska	C, S	★	★	★	...	★	...	...	...	★	...	...
Nevada	S, I	★	★	★	★	★	★	★	★	★(t)	...	...
New Hampshire	S	★	★(a)	★	...	★	★	...	★(j)	★	...	...
New Jersey	C, S, I	★	★	★	...	★	★	...	★(u)	★	...	...
New Mexico	C, S	★	★	★	★	★	★	★	★	★	...	...
New York	C, S	★	★	★	...	★	...	...	...	★	...	...
North Carolina	C, S	★	★	★	...	★	★	...	★	★	...	★(v)
North Dakota	S, I	★	★	★	...	...	...	...	(k)(p)(u)(w)(x)(y)	...	...	...
Ohio	C, S, I(z)	★	★	★	★	★	★	★	(aa)	★	...	...
Oklahoma	C	★	★	★	(bb)	★	★	★	...	★	...	...
Oregon	I	★	★	★	...	★	★	★	...	...	...	...
Pennsylvania	C, S	★	...	★(m)(cc)(dd)(ee)	...	★	★	...	★(dd)(ee)	★(b)(cc)	...	...
Rhode Island	S, I, Case Law	★	★	★	★	★	★	★	...	★(b)	...	...
South Carolina	S	★	★	★	...	★	★	...	★	★	...	...
South Dakota	C	★	★	★	★	★	★	★	★	★	...	...
Tennessee	C, S	★	★	★	★	★	★	★	★	★(b)	...	...
Texas	C, S, I	★	★	★	...	★	★	★	★	...	...	...
Utah	S, I	★	★	★	★	★	★	★	...	...	...	...
Vermont	S, I	★	★	...	★(ff)	★	★	...	...	...	...	★(gg)
Virginia	C, S	★	★	★	★	★	★	...	...	...	...	★(hh)
Washington	S	★	...	...	...	...	...	...	...	...	...	...
West Virginia	C, S	★	★	...	...	★	★	...	(ii)	...	...	...
Wisconsin	C, S	★	★	★	★	★	★	...	(jj)	★	...	...
Wyoming	(kk)	...	...	...	...	...	...	...	...	...	...	...
American Samoa	C, S	★	★	★	★	★	★	★	★	★(ll)	★(ll)	...
Guam	C	★	★	...	(mm)	★	★	★	★	★	...	...
CNMI*	C	★	...	★	...	...	...	...	...	★	...	...
Puerto Rico	C, S, I, Case Law	★	★	★	★	★	★	★	★	(nn)	...	...
U.S. Virgin Islands	S	★	★	★	★	★	★	★	★	...	...	...

See footnotes at end of table

TABLE 4.5
Gubernatorial Executive Orders: Authorization, Provisions, Procedures (continued)

Source: The Council of State Governments survey of governors' offices, April 2019.

*Commonwealth of the Northern Mariana Islands

Key:

C–Constitutional
S–Statutory
I–Implied
★ –Formal provision.
… –No formal provision.

(a) Broad interpretation of gubernatorial authority. In Arizona, the governor is authorized to make executive orders in all of these areas and situations so long as there is not a conflicting statute in place.

(b) Executive orders must be filed with secretary of state or other designated officer.

(c) Authorization implied from constitution and statute as recognized by 63 ops. Cal. Atty. Gen. 583.

(d) Implied from Constitution.

(e) Constitution, statute, implied, case law, common law.

(f) Executive clemency.

(g) Only for EROs. When an ERO is submitted the legislature has 30 days to veto the ERO or it becomes law.

(h) To give immediate effect to state regulation in emergencies.

(i) To control administration of state contracts and procedures.

(j) To impound or freeze certain state matching funds.

(k) To reduce state expenditures in revenue shortfall.

(l) Inherent.

(m) To control procedures for dealing with public.

(n) Reorganization plans and agency creation.

(o) Executive reorganizations not effective if rejected by both houses of legislature within 60 calendar days. Executive orders reducing appropriations not effective unless approved by appropriations committees of both houses of legislature.

(p) To assign duties to lieutenant governor, issue writ of special election.

(q) Filing.

(r) Governor is exempt from the Administrative Procedures Act and filing and administrative procedures Miss. Code Ann. § 25-43-102 (1972).

(s) Reorganization plans and agency creation and for meeting federal program requirements. To administer and govern the armed forces of the state.

(t) In addition to filing and publication procedures - Executive Orders are countersigned by and filed with the Secretary of State and published.

(u) To administer and govern the armed forces of the state.

(v) Must submit to the Secretary of State who must compile, index and publish Executive Orders. Copies must also be sent to President of the Senate, Speaker of House and Principal Clerk of each chamber.

(w) To suspend certain officials and/or other civil actions.

(x) To designate game and wildlife areas or other public areas.

(y) Appointive powers.

(z) Executive authority implied by constitution except for emergencies which are established by statute.

(aa) General power to issue executive orders to execute the authority of the Governor as provided in the Constitution and state statute.

(bb) The governor has the authority, through state statute , to enact executive orders that: create agencies, boards and commissions; and reassigns agencies, boards and commissions to different cabinet secretaries. However, in order for the continued operation of any agency created by executive order the state legislature must approve legislation that allows the agency to continue to operate, if not, the agency cannot continue operation beyond sine die adjournment of the legislature for the session.

(dd) For fire emergencies.

(ee) To transfer funds in an emergency.

(ff) Subject to legislative approval when inconsistent with statute.

(gg) Only if reorganization order filed with the legislature.

(hh) Some statutes set forward requirements for executive orders, but few established procedures.

(ii) Expansion of governor's existing state of emergency power to now create a state of prepardness. The governor has the authority to issue an executive order for a state of preardness in advance of an anticipated event affecting public safety (as of March 8, 2014). During the first special session in 2016 the legislature gave the governor the power, in the event a budget bill has not been enacted by June 30 of any year, to, by executive order, direct scheduled payments of principal and interest due on bonds or notes of the state or its agencies, boards, or commissions.

(jj) The governor has power to direct the Department of Administration to conduct investigations of any executive or administrative agency in order to determine feasibility of consolidating , creating or rearranging agencies for the purpose of affecting the elimination of unnecessary state functions, avoiding duplication, reducing the cost of administration and increasing efficiency. Wis. Stat. 16.004(3)(a). The governor has power to coordinate services of personnel across state agencies. Wis. Stat. 14.03.

(kk) No specific authorization granted, general authority only.

(ll) If executive order fits definition of rule.

(mm) Can reorganize, but not create.

(nn) Executive Orders are filed in the Department of State.

TABLE 4.6
State Cabinet Systems

State or other jurisdiction	Authorization for cabinet system				Criteria for membership			Number of members in cabinet (including governor)	Frequency of cabinet meetings	Open cabinet meetings
	State statute	State constitution	Governor created	Tradition in state	Appointed to specific office (a)	Elected to specified office (a)	Gubernatorial appointment regardless of office			
Alabama	★	★	★	★	★	...	...	23	Quarterly	...
Alaska	★	★	...	...	★	...	★	17	Gov.'s discretion	★
Arizona	...	...	★	...	★	...	★	37	Quarterly	...
Arkansas	...	...	★	...	★	...	...	40	Quarterly	...
California	...	★	★	...	★	...	★	11	Every two weeks	...
Colorado	...	★	★	...	★	...	★	21	Bi-monthly	...
Connecticut	★(k)	...	...	...	...	...	★	29	Gov.'s discretion	...
Delaware	★	...	...	...	★	...	★	17	Gov.'s discretion	...
Florida	★	★	...	...	...	★	...	4	Appox. 1-2 per month	★
Georgia					(d)					
Hawaii	★	★	...	★	★	...	★	43	Bi-monthly	...
Idaho	★	★	...	...	...	...	★	39	Gov.'s discretion	...
Illinois (o)	★	...	★	...	...	...	★	65	Gov.'s discretion	(b)
Indiana	...	...	★	...	...	...	★	16	Bi-monthly	...
Iowa	★	★	★	★	★	...	...	30	Monthly	...
Kansas	...	★	...	...	...	...	★	15	Bi-weekly	...
Kentucky	...	★	★	...	★	...	★	13	Quarterly	...
Louisiana	★	...	★	★	★	...	...	16	Monthly	...
Maine	...	...	★	...	...	...	★	16	Monthly	...
Maryland	★	...	...	...	★	...	...	25	Every other week	...
Massachusetts	...	★	...	...	★	...	...	11	Weekly	...
Michigan	★	★	★	...	★	★	(e)	22	Gov.'s discretion	...
Minnesota	...	...	★	...	★	...	...	25	Quarterly	...
Mississippi					(d)					
Missouri	★	...	...	★	★	...	...	17	Gov.'s discretion	...
Montana	★	★	...	...	★	...	...	19	Monthly	★
Nebraska	...	...	★	★	★	...	★	30	Monthly	...
Nevada			(d)					21	At call of the governor	...
New Hampshire					(d)					
New Jersey	★	★	...	...	★	...	...	24	Gov.'s discretion	...
New Mexico	★	★	...	★	★	...	...	31	Gov.'s discretion	...
New York	...	...	★	...	...	...	★	75	Gov.'s discretion	...
North Carolina (f)	...	...	★	...	...	...	★	11	Weekly	(n)
North Dakota	...	...	★	...	...	...	★	17	Monthly	★
Ohio	...	...	★	...	★	...	...	27	Gov.'s discretion	...
Oklahoma	...	★	...	...	...	...	★	16 (h)	Monthly	...
Oregon					(d)					
Pennsylvania	★	★	★	...	★(i)	...	★	27	Gov.'s discretion	★(m)
Rhode Island	...	...	★	★	...	...	★(l)	22	Gov.'s discretion	★(m)
South Carolina	★	★	...	...	★(i)	...	...	18	Monthly	★
South Dakota	★	★	...	...	★	...	...	20	Monthly	...
Tennessee	★	...	...	...	★	...	...	31	Monthly	...
Texas					(d)					
Utah	...	★	★	...	★	...	★	24	Monthly, weekly during legislative session	...
Vermont	★	★	...	...	★	...	...	12	Gov.'s discretion	...
Virginia	...	...	★	★(j)	★	...	★	16	Weekly	...
Washington	...	...	★	...	★	...	...	25	Monthly	...
West Virginia	...	...	★	★	★	...	...	17	Weekly	...
Wisconsin	★	★	...	...	★	...	...	17	Gov.'s discretion	★
Wyoming	...	...	★	...	...	...	★	44	Quarterly	...
American Samoa	★	★	...	...	★	...	★	16	Gov.'s discretion	★
Guam	...	...	★	...	★	...	...	55	Bi-monthly	...
CNMI*	...	★	...	...	★	...	...	17	Gov.'s discretion	★
Puerto Rico	★	★	...	...	...	...	★	10 (c)	Every 6 weeks	...
U.S. Virgin Islands	★	...	...	...	★	...	...	21	Monthly	★

See footnotes at end of table

TABLE 4.6
State Cabinet Systems (continued)

Sources: The Council of State Governments survey of governors'
offices, September 2017.
*Commonwealth of the Northern Mariana Islands
Key:
★ –Yes
…–No
N/A–Not available
(a) Individual is a member by virtue of election or appointment to a
cabinet-level position.
(b) Certain cabinet meetings are open to the public and media.
(c) The Constitutional Cabinet has 10 members including the
governor. There are other members of the Cabinet provided by
statute.
(d) No formal cabinet system. In Nevada, the cabinet is traditionally
comprised of Directors, Chairpersons and leaders of Nevada's top
agencies, departments, institutions and the National Guard, in
addition to the Lt. Governor.
(e) Membership determined by governor. Some officers formally
designated as cabinet member by executive order.
(f) The Governor's cabinet consists of 10 department heads who
have responsibility for the majority of the executive branch.
They are appointed by the governor and report to the governor.

The Council of State exists as a separate body and is composed
independently elected statewide officials who oversee certain
areas of the executive branch. While the Council of State is
provided for in the Constitution and state statutes, the cabinet is
created by the governor.
(g) Frequency of meetings may fluctuate with Governor's schedule.
(h) State statute allows for 15 cabinet members. With the Governor
included there are 16 members.
(i) With the consent of the senate.
(j) While there is no specific state statute that establishes the
cabinet system, the state code makes repeated references to
cabinet secretaries and sets forth the duties of each secretary and
the agencies assigned to the secretary.
(k) Governor's cabinet is specified in statute, but no longer in use.
Governor directs department heads through commissioners'
meetings and subject matter groups called clusters.
(l) At the discretion of the governor.
(m) Varies by meeting.
(n) Council of State, but not cabinet meetings, are open to the
public.
(o) Agency directors are provided by statute. Governor may create
and appoint other cabinet-level positions.

TABLE 4.7
The Governors: Provisions and Procedures for Transition

State or other jurisdiction	Legislation pertaining to gubernatorial transition	Appropriation available to gov-elect	Provision for:					
			Gov-elect's participation in state budget for coming fiscal year	Gov-elect to hire staff to assist during transition	State personnel to be made available to assist gov-elect	Office space in buildings to be made available to gov-elect	Acquainting gov-elect staff with office procedures and routing office functions	Transfer of information (files, records, etc.)
Alabama	...	...	★	•	•	•	•	•
Alaska	•	•	...	•	•	•	•	★
Arizona	...	...	★	...	•	•	•	•
Arkansas	•	10,000	...	...	...	...	...	...
California	★	450,000	★	★	★	★	★	•
Colorado	★	10,000	★	★	★	★	•	★
Connecticut	★	★	★	★	★	★	★	★
Delaware	★	15,000	•	★	•	•	•	•
Florida	★	(b)	•	★	•	•	•	•
Georgia	★	50,000	•	★	★	★	•	★
Hawaii	★	50,000	★	★	•	★	•	•
Idaho	★	15,000	★	★	★	★	★	★
Illinois	★	...	...	•	...	★	★	★
Indiana	★	40,000	...	...	...	★	★	★
Iowa	•	100,000	★	•	•	•	•	★
Kansas	★	150,000 (c)	★	★	★	★	★	★
Kentucky	★	220,000	★	★	★	★	★	★
Louisiana	★	• 65,000	★	★	...	★	...	•
Maine	•	5,000	★	•	•	•	•	•
Maryland	★	•	...	★	★	★	★	•
Massachusetts	•	•	•	...	•	•	•	•
Michigan	•	$1.5 million • (v)	...	•	•	•	•	•
Minnesota	★	(e)	★	★	★	★	•	★
Mississippi	•	★(f)	★	★	★	★	★	★
Missouri	★	100,000	★	★	•	★	•	• (g)
Montana	★	★	★	★	★	★	★	★
Nebraska	★	85,288	★	...	★	★	★	★
Nevada	★	Reasonable amount	★	★	...	★	...	★
New Hampshire	★	75,000	★	★	★	★	★	...
New Jersey	★	★(j)	•	★	★	★	•	★
New Mexico	★	(k)	★	★	★	★	★	★
New York	...	...	...	...	★	★	★	★
North Carolina	★	★(l)	...	★	•	★	★	★
North Dakota	•	10,000	(m)	(n)	•	...	•	★
Ohio	★	Unspecified (o)	•	★	•	•	•	•
Oklahoma	•	•	★	•	•	★	•	•
Oregon	★	★	★	★	★	★	★	★
Pennsylvania	★	...	...	•	•	•	•	...
Rhode Island	★	(u)	•	★	★	•	•	•
South Carolina	...	•	•	•	•	•	•	•
South Dakota	★	...	...	...	...	...	...	•(u)
Tennessee	★	★	•	★	★	★	•	•(u)
Texas	•	•	•	•	•	•	•	•
Utah	★	★(p)	★	★	★	★	★	★
Vermont	•	★(q)	★	...	★	...	...	...
Virginia	★	★(h)	★	★	★	★	★	★
Washington	★	★	•	★	•	★	•	•
West Virginia	...	•	...	•	...	•	•	•
Wisconsin	★	Unspecified	★	★	★	★	★	★
Wyoming	•	...	•	•	•	•	•	•
American Samoa	...	Unspecified	★(i)	★	•	•	★	•
Guam	★	(t)	...	...	★	•	★	...
CNMI*	★	Unspecified	•	★	★	★	★	★
Puerto Rico	★	...	★	★	★	★	★	★
U.S. Virgin Islands	★	100,000	...	★	★	★	★	★

See footnotes at end of table

TABLE 4.7
The Governors: Provisions and Procedures for Transition (continued)

Sources: The Council of State Governments' survey of governors' offices, March 2019.

* Commonwealth of the Northern Mariana Islands

Key:

…–No provisions or procedures.

★–Formal provisions or procedures.

●–No formal provisions, occurs informally.

N.A.–Not applicable.

(a) Varies.

(b) Section 14.057, Florida Statute provides: Governor-elect; establishment of operating fund.– (1) There is established an operating fund for the use of the Governor-elect during the period dating from the certification of his or her election by the Elections Canvassing Commission to his or her inauguration as Governor. The Governor-elect during this period may allocate the fund to travel, expenses, his or her salary, and the salaries of the Governor-elect's staff as he or she determines. Such staff may include, but not be limited to, a chief administrative assistant, a legal adviser, a fiscal expert, and a public relations and information adviser. The salary of the Governor-elect and each member of the Governor-elect's staff during this period shall be determined by the Governor-elect, except that the total expenditures chargeable to the state under this section, including salaries, shall not exceed the amount appropriated to the operating fund. The Executive Office of the Governor shall supply to the Governor-elect suitable forms to provide for the expenditure of the fund and suitable forms to provide for the reporting of all expenditures therefrom. The Chief Financial Officer shall release moneys from this fund upon the request of the Governor-elect properly filed.

(c) Transition funds are used by both the incoming and outgoing administrations.

(d) Amount to be determined.

(e) 1.5% of amount appropriated for the fiscal year to the Governor's office.

(f) Miss. Code Ann.§ 7-1-101 provides as follows: the governor's office of general services shall provide a governor-elect with office space and office equipment for the period between the election and inauguration. A special appropriation to the governor's office of general services is hereby authorized to defray the expenses of providing necessary staff employees and for the operation of the office of governor-elect during the period between the election and inauguration. The department of finance and administration shall make available to a governor-elect and his designated representatives information on the following: (a) all information and reports used in the preparation of the budget report; and (b) all information and reports on projected income and revenue estimates for the state.

(g) Activity is traditional and routine, although there is no specific statutory provision.

(h) Determined every 4 years.

(i) Can submit reprogramming or supplemental appropriation measure for current fiscal year.

(j) No specific amount - necessary services and facilities.

(k) Legislature required to make appropriation; no dollar amount stated in legislation.

(l) Governor receives $80,000 and lieutenant governor receives $10,000.

(m) Responsible for submitting budget for coming biennium.

(n) Governor usually hires several incoming key staff during transition.

(o) Determined in budget.

(p) Appropriated by legislature at the time of transition.

(q) Governor-elect entitled to 70% of Governor's salary.

(t) Appropriations given upon the request of governor-elect.

(u) The governor's transition team was authorized $130,000 for transition costs during the 2014 - 2015 transition. Approximately $120,000 was spent.

(v) Typically the appropriation is included in the budget but may fluctuate in size.

(u) Subject to records retention and archival requirements.

TABLE 4.8
Impeachment Provisions in the States

State or other jurisdiction	Governor and other state executive and judicial officers subject to impeachment	Legislative body which holds power of impeachment	Vote required for impeachment	Legislative body which conducts impeachment trial	Chief justice presides at impeachment trial (a)	Vote required for conviction	Official who serves as acting governor if governor impeached (b)	Legislature may call special session for impeachment
Alabama	★	H	maj. mbrs.	S	★	2/3 mbrs. present	LG	★
Alaska	★	S	2/3 mbrs.	H	(c)	2/3 mbrs.	LG	★
Arizona	★(d)	H	maj. mbrs.	S	★(e)	2/3 mbrs.	SS	★
Arkansas	★	H	maj. mbrs.	S	★	2/3 mbrs.	LG	...
California	★	H	...	S	...	2/3 mbrs.	LG	...
Colorado	★	H	maj. mbrs.	S	★	2/3 mbrs.	LG	...
Connecticut	★	H	maj. mbrs.	S	★(f)	2/3 mbrs. must be present	LG	★
Delaware	★	H	2/3 mbrs.	S	★	2/3 mbrs.	LG	...
Florida	★	H	2/3 mbrs.	S	★(g)	2/3 mbrs. present (h)	LG (i)	★
Georgia	★	H	...	S	★(e)	2/3 mbrs.	...	★(j)
Hawaii	★	H	2/3 mbrs.	S	...	2/3 mbrs.	LG	★
Idaho	★	H	2/3 mbrs.(k)	S	★	2/3 mbrs.	LG	...
Illinois	★	H	2/3 mbrs.	S	★	2/3 mbrs.	LG	...
Indiana	★(l)	H	2/3 mbrs.	S	...	2/3 mbrs.	LG	...
Iowa	★	H	maj. mbrs.	S	...	majority of elected mbrs.	LG	★
Kansas	★	H	(m)	S	...	2/3 mbrs.	LG	...
Kentucky	★	H	...	S	★	2/3 mbrs. present	LG	...
Louisiana	★	H	(n)	S	...	(n)	LG	★
Maine	★	H	maj. mbrs.	S	...	2/3 mbrs. present	PS	★
Maryland	★	H	maj. mbrs.	S	...	2/3 mbrs.	LG	...
Massachusetts	★	H	maj. mbrs.	S	...	...	LG	★
Michigan	★	H	maj. mbrs.	S	★	2/3 mbrs.	LG	...
Minnesota	★	H	maj. mbrs.	S	...	2/3 mbrs. present	LG	...
Mississippi	★	H	maj. mbrs.	S	★(r)	2/3 mbrs. present (s)	LG	(u)
Missouri	★	H	...	(t)	(t)	(t)	LG	...
Montana	★	H	2/3 mbrs.	S	★	2/3 mbrs.	LG	★
Nebraska	★	S (v)	maj. mbrs.	(w)	(w)	(w)	LG	...
Nevada	★(d)	H	maj. mbrs.	S	★	2/3 mbrs.	LG	...
New Hampshire	★	H	...	S	★	...	PS	★
New Jersey	★	H	maj. mbrs.	S	★	2/3 mbrs.	LG	★(aa)
New Mexico	★	H	maj. mbrs.	S	★(p)	2/3 mbrs.	LG	★
New York	★	H	maj. mbrs.	S	★	2/3 mbrs. present	LG	★
North Carolina	★	H	2/3 mbrs.	S	★(x)	2/3 mbrs. present	LG	★
North Dakota	★(d)	H	maj. mbrs.	S	★	2/3 mbrs.	LG	...
Ohio	★	H	maj. mbrs.	S	...	2/3 mbrs. present	LG	★
Oklahoma	★	S	maj. mbrs.	H & S	★	2/3 mbrs. present	LG	★
Oregon				(y)				
Pennsylvania	★	H	...	S	...	2/3 maj. mbrs.	LG	★
Rhode Island	★	H	2/3 maj. mbrs.	S	★	2/3 maj. mbrs.	LG	★
South Carolina	★	H	2/3 mbrs.	S	★	2/3 mbrs.	LG	...
South Dakota	★	H	maj. mbrs.	S	★	2/3 mbrs.	LG	★
Tennessee	★	H	maj. mbrs.	S	★	2/3 mbrs. (z)	PS	★
Texas	★	H (o)	maj. mbrs.	S	...	2/3 mbrs. present	LG	...
Utah	★	H	2/3 mbrs.	S	★(f)	2/3 mbrs.	LG	★
Vermont	★	H	2/3 mbrs.	S	...	2/3 mbrs.	LG	...
Virginia	★	H	maj. mbrs. present	S	...	2/3 mbrs. present	LG	★(bb)
Washington	★(d)	H	maj. mbrs.	S	★	2/3 mbrs.	LG	...
West Virginia	★	H	maj. mbrs.	S	★	2/3 mbrs.	PS	★
Wisconsin	★	H	maj. mbrs.	S	...	2/3 mbrs.	LG	...
Wyoming	★	H	maj. mbrs.	S	★	2/3 mbrs.	SS	★
Dist. of Columbia				(p)				
American Samoa	(q)	H	2/3 mbrs.	S	★	2/3 mbrs.	...	...
Guam				(p)				
CNMI*	★	H	2/3 mbrs.	S	...	2/3 mbrs.	LG	...
Puerto Rico	★	H	2/3 mbrs.	S	★	3/4 mbrs.	SS	★
U.S. Virgin Islands				(p)				

See footnotes at end of table

TABLE 4.8
Impeachment Provisions in the States (continued)

Sources: The Council of State Governments survey of governors' offices, March 2019.
* Commonwealth of the Northern Mariana Islands
Key:
★–Yes; provision for.
...–Not specified, or no provision for.
H–House or Assembly (lower chamber).
S–Senate.
LG–Lieutenant Governor
PS–President or Speaker of the Senate
SS–Secretary of state.
(a) Presiding justice of state court of last resort. In many states, provision indicates that chief justice presides only on occasion of impeachment of governor.
(b) For provisions on official next in line of succession if governor is convicted and removed from office, refer to Chapter 4, "The Governors."
(c) An appointed Supreme Court justice presides.
(d) With exception of certain judicial officers. In Arizona and Washington–justices of courts not of record. In Nevada–justices of the peace. In North Dakota–county judges, justices of the peace, and police magistrates.
(e) Should the Chief Justice be on trial, or otherwise disqualified, the Senate shall elect a judge of the Supreme Court to preside.
(f) Only if Governor is on trial.
(g) Except in a trial of the chief justice, in which case the governor shall preside.
(h) An officer impeached by the house of representatives shall be disqualified from performing any official duties until acquitted by the senate, and, unless impeached, the governor may by appointment fill the office until completion of the trial.
(i) Governor may appoint someone to serve until the impeachment procedures are final.
(j) Special sessions of the General Assembly shall be limited to a period of 40 days unless extended by 3/5 vote of each house and approved by the Governor or unless at the expiration of such period an impeachment trial of some officer of state government is pending, in which event the House shall adjourn and the Senate shall remain in session until such trial is completed.

(k) No person shall be convicted without the concurrence of two-thirds of there senators elected. When the governor is impeached, the chief justice shall preside.
(l) Judges not included.
(m) No statute, simple majority is the assumption.
(n) Concurrence of 2/3 of the elected senators.
(o) House votes on articles of impeachment; Senate presides over impeachment trial to remove official.
(p) Removal of elected officials by recall procedure only.
(q) Governor, lieutenant governor.
(r) When the governor is tried; if Chief Justice is unable to preside, the next longest serving justice shall preside.
(s) No person shall be convicted without concurrence of 2/3 of all senators present. Miss Const. 1890 Art. IV § 52.
(t) All impeachments are tried before the state Supreme Court, except that the governor or a member of the Supreme Court is tried by a special commission of seven eminent jurists to be elected by the Senate. A vote of 5/7 of the court of special commission is necessary to convict.
(u) It is implied but not addressed directly in Miss Const. 1890 Art. IV §§ 49-53.
(v) Unicameral legislature; members use the title "senator."
(w) Court of impeachment is composed of chief justice and supreme court. A vote of 2/3 present of the court is necessary to convict.
(x) Chief Justice presides if it is the Governor or Lieutenant Governor; otherwise , the President of the Senate presides.
(y) No provision for impeachment. Public officers may be tried for incompetence, corruption, malfeasance, or delinquency in office in same manner as criminal offenses.
(z) Vote of 2/3 of members sworn to try the officer impeached.
(aa) In the event of simultaneous vacancies in both the offices of Governor and Lieutenant Governor resulting from any cause, the President of the Sensate shall become Governor until a new Governor or Lieutenant Governor is elected and qualifies.
(bb) Two-thirds of both houses may call a special session for any purpose. The Senate may try impeachments in recess; the House may not impeach unless in session.

TABLE 4.9

Constitutional and Statutory Provisions for Number of Consecutive Terms of Elected State Officials
(All terms are four years unless otherwise noted)

State or other jurisdiction	Governor	Lt. Governor	Secretary of state	Attorney general	Treasurer	Auditor	Comptroller	Education	Agriculture	Labor	Insurance
Alabama	2 C	2 C	2 C	2 C	2 C	2 C	...	2 C	2 C	...	...
Alaska	2 C	2	(a)	...	(b)	...	...	...	...	...	...
Arizona	2 C	(c)	2	2	2	...	...	2	...	...	...
Arkansas	2 T	2 T	2 T	2 T	2 T	2 T	...	...	...	...	...
California	2 T	2 T	2 T	2 T	2 T	...	2 T	2 T	...	...	2 T
Colorado	2 C	2 C	2 C	2 C	2 C	...	...	...	...	...	...
Connecticut	N	N	N	N	N	...	N	...	...	...	...
Delaware	2 T	2 T	...	N	N	N	...	...	...	...	N
Florida	2 C	2 C	N	2 C	2 C (d)	...	2 C (d)	N	2 C	...	2 C (d)
Georgia	2 C	N	N	N	...	...	...	N	N	N	N
Hawaii	2 C	2 C	(a)	...	...	...	...	...	...	...	...
Idaho	N	N	N	N	N	...	N	N	...	...	...
Illinois	N	N	N	N	N	...	N	...	...	...	...
Indiana	2 (e)	2C	2 (e)	...	2 (e)	2 (e)	(f)	...	...	...	...
Iowa	N	N	N	N	N	N	...	...	N	...	...
Kansas	2 C	2 C	N	N	N	...	...	...	...	...	N
Kentucky	2 C	2 C	2 C	2 C	2 C	2 C	...	...	2 C	2 C	...
Louisiana	2 C	N	N	N	N	...	...	N	N	...	N
Maine	2 C	(g)	...	...	...	...	...	...	...	...	...
Maryland	2 C	N	...	N	...	...	N	...	...	...	...
Massachusetts	N	N	N	N	N	N	...	...	...	...	...
Michigan	2 T	2 T	2 T	2 T	...	...	...	...	...	...	...
Minnesota	N	N	N	N	...	N	...	...	...	...	(h)
Mississippi	2 T	2 T	N	N	N	N	...	...	...	...	...
Missouri	2 T	N	N	N	2 T	N	...	...	...	...	...
Montana	2 (i)	2 (i)	2 (i)	2 (i)	...	2 (i)	...	2 (i)	...	...	...
Nebraska	2 C	2 C	N	N	2 C	N	...	...	...	...	...
Nevada	2 T	2 T	2 T	2 T	2 T	...	2 T	...	...	...	...
New Hampshire	N (j)	...	...	...	...	...	...	...	...	...	...
New Jersey	2 C	2 C	...	...	...	...	...	...	...	...	...
New Mexico	2 C	2 C	2 C	2 C	2 C	2 C	...	...	...	...	...
New York	N	N	...	N	...	N (k)	N	...	...	...	...
North Carolina	2 C	2 C	N	N	N	N	...	N	N	N	N
North Dakota	N	N	N	N	N	N	...	N	N	N	N
Ohio	2 C	2 C	2 C	2 C	2 C	2 C	...	...	...	...	...
Oklahoma	2 (l)	N	...	N	N	N	...	N	...	N	N
Oregon	2 (e)	(m)	2 (e)	N	2 (e)	...	...	...	...	...	...
Pennsylvania	2 C	2 C	...	2 C	2 C (n)	2 C	...	...	...	...	...
Rhode Island	2 C	2 C	2 C	2 C	2 C	...	...	...	...	...	...
South Carolina	2 C	2 C	N	N	N	...	N	N	N	...	...
South Dakota	2 C	2 C	2 C	2 C	2 C	2 C	...	2 C	...	...	...
Tennessee	2 C	(f)	...	(o)	...	...	...	...	...	...	...
Texas	N	N	...	N	(k)	...	N	...	N	...	...
Utah	N	N	(a)	N	N	N	...	...	...	...	...
Vermont	N (j)	N (j)	N (j)	N (j)	N (j)	N (j)	...	...	...	...	...
Virginia	1 C	N	...	N	...	...	...	...	...	...	...
Washington	N	N	N	N	N	N	...	N	...	...	...
West Virginia	2 C	N (g)	N	N	N	...	N	...	N	...	...
Wisconsin	N	N	N	N	N	...	...	N	...	...	...
Wyoming	2 (i)	(m)	N	...	N	N	...	N	...	...	...
Dist. of Columbia	N (p)	...	...	...	...	...	...	...	...	...	...
American Samoa	2 C	2 C	(a)	...	...	...	(q)	...	...	...	...
Guam	2 C	2 C	(a)	2 C	...	2 C	(r)	...	...	...	...
CNMI*	2 T	2 T	...	...	...	2 T	(q)	...	...	...	(h)
Puerto Rico	N	(m)	...	...	...	...	...	...	...	...	...
U.S. Virgin Islands	2 C	2 C	(k)	...	(c)	...	(c)	...	...	...	(a)

See footnotes at end of table

TABLE 4.9

Constitutional and Statutory Provisions for Number of Consecutive Terms of Elected State Officials (All terms are four years unless otherwise noted) (continued)

Source: The Council of State Governments, April 2019.

*Commonwealth of Northern Mariana Islands

Note: All terms last four years unless otherwise noted. Footnotes specify if a position's functions are performed by an official under a different title.

Key:

N–No provision specifying number of terms allowed.

C–Consecutive Terms

T–Total Terms

…–Position is appointed or elected by governmental entity (not chosen by the electorate).

(a) Lieutenant Governor performs this function.

(b) Deputy Commissioner of Department of Revenue performs function.

(c) Finance Administrator performs function.

(d) Chief Financial Officer performs this function as of January 2003.

(e) Eligible for eight years out of any period of 12 years.

(f) State auditor performs this function.

(g) President or speaker of the Senate is next in line of succession to the governorship. In Tennessee and West Virginia, speaker of the Senate has the statutory title " lieutenant governor."

(h) Commerce administrator performs this function.

(i) Eligible for eight out of 16 years.

(j) Two-year term.

(k) Comptroller performs this function.

(l) Limited to 8 years per office during a lifetime.

(m) Secretary of state is next in line to the governorship.

(n) Treasurer must wait four years before being eligible for the office of auditor general.

(o) Term is eight years; attorney general is appointed by the state Supreme Court.

(p) Mayor.

(q) State treasurer performs this function.

(r) General services administrator performs function.

TABLE 4.10
Selected State Administrative Officials: Methods of Selection

State or other jurisdiction	Governor	Lieutenant governor (a-1)	Secretary of state (a-2)	Attorney general (a-3)	Treasurer (a-4)	Adjutant general (a-5)	Admin. (a-6)	Agriculture (a-7)	Auditor (a-8)	Banking (a-9)
Alabama	CE	CE	CE	CE	CE	G	G	SE	CE	GS
Alaska	CE	CE	(a-1)	GB	AG	GB	GB	AG	L	AG
Arizona	CE	(a-2)	CE	CE	CE	GS	GS	GS	L	GS
Arkansas	CE	CE	CE	CE	CE	G	G	BG	CE	GS
California	CE	CE	CE	CE	CE	GS	N.O.	G	GB	GS
Colorado	CE	CE	CE	CE	CE	GS	GS	GS	L	A
Connecticut	CE	CE	CE	CE	CE	G	GE	GE	(b)	GE
Delaware	CE	CE	GS	CE	CE	GS	(c)	GS	CE	GS
Florida	CE	CE	GS	CE	CE	GS	GS	CE	L	CE
Georgia	CE	CE	CE	CE	B	G	G	CE	CL	G
Hawaii	CE	CE	N.O.	GS	GS	GS	(b)	GS	CL	AG
Idaho	CE	CE	CE	CE	CE	GS	GS	GS	N.O.	(a-24)
Illinois	CE	CE	CE	CE	CE	GS	GS	GS	CL	GS
Indiana	CE	CE	CE	SE	CE	G	G	LG	CE	G
Iowa	CE	CE	CE	CE	CE	GS	GS	CE	CE	GS
Kansas	CE	CE	CE	CE	CE	GS	GS	GS	N.O.	GS
Kentucky	CE	CE	CE	CE	CE	G	N.O.	CE	CE	G
Louisiana	CE	CE	CE	CE	CE	GS	GS	CE	GS	GS
Maine	CE	N.O.	CL	CL	CL	GLS	GLS	GLS	L	GLS
Maryland	CE	CE	GS	CE	CL	G	(a-16)	GS	N/A	AG
Massachusetts	CE	CE	CE	CE	CE	G	G	CG	CE	G
Michigan	CE	CE	CE	CE	GS	GS	GS	GS	CL	GS
Minnesota	CE	CE	CE	CE	(a-24)	GS	GS	GS	CE	A
Mississippi	CE	CE	CE	CE	CE	GE	GS	SE	CE	GS
Missouri	CE	CE	CE	CE	CE	GS	GS	GS	CE	GS
Montana	CE	CE	CE	CE	GS	GS	GS	GS	CE	A
Nebraska	CE	CE	CE	CE	CE	GS	GS	GS	CE	GS
Nevada	CE	CE	CE	CE	CE	G	G	BG	N.O.	A
New Hampshire	CE	(e)	CL	GC	CL	GC	GC	GC	...	GC
New Jersey	CE	CE	(a-1)	GS	GS	GS	N.O.	BG	(g)	GS
New Mexico	CE	CE	CE	CE	CE	G	(a-26)	A	CE	N/A
New York	CE	CE	GS	CE	GS	G	G	GS	CE	GS
North Carolina	CE	CE	CE	CE	CE	A	G	CE	CE	G
North Dakota	CE	CE	CE	CE	CE	G	N.O.	CE	CE	GS
Ohio	CE	CE	CE	CE	CE	G	GS	GS	CE	A
Oklahoma	CE	CE	GS	CE	CE	GS	GS	GS	CE	GS
Oregon	CE	(a-2)	CE	SE	CE	G	GS	GS	SS	N.O.
Pennsylvania	CE	CE	GS	CE	CE	GS	G	GS	CE	GS
Rhode Island	SE	SE	CE	SE	SE	GS	GS	GS	LS	GS
South Carolina	CE	CE	CE	CE	CE	CE	B	CE	B	A
South Dakota	CE	CE	CE	CE	CE	GS	GS	GS	L	AB
Tennessee	CE	CL(e)	CL	CT	CL	G	G	G	(a-14)	G
Texas	CE	CE	G	CE	(a-14)	G	A	SE	L	B
Utah	CE	CE	(a-1)	CE	CE	GS	GS	GS	CE	GS
Vermont	CE	CE	CE	SE	CE	SL	GS	GS	CE	GS
Virginia	CE	CE	GB	CE	GB	GB	GB	GB	SL	B
Washington	CE	CE	CE	CE	CE	G	GS	GS	CE	GS
West Virginia	CE	(e)	CE	CE	CE	GS	GS	CE	CE	GS
Wisconsin	CE	CE	CE	CE	CE	G	GS	GS	LS	GS
Wyoming	CE	(a-2)	CE	GS	CE	G	GS	GS	CE	AG
American Samoa	CE	CE	(a-1)	GB	GB	N/A	GB	GB	N/A	N/A
Guam*	CE	CE	...	CE	CS	GS	GS	GS	CE	GS
CNMI*	CE	CE	...	GS	CS	...	G	...	GB	C
Puerto Rico	CE	...	GS	GS	GS	GS	...	GS	GS	GS
U.S. Virgin Islands	SE	SE	(a-1)	GS	GS	GS	GS	GS	GS	LG

See footnotes at end of table

TABLE 4.10
Selected State Administrative Officials: Methods of Selection (continued)

State or other jurisdiction	Budget (a-10)	Civil rights (a-11)	Commerce (a-12)	Community affairs (a-13)	Comptroller (a-14)	Consumer affairs (a-15)	Corrections (a-16)	Economic development (a-17)	Education (a-18)	Election admin. (a-19)
Alabama	CS	N.O.	G	G	CS	CS	G	(a-12)	B	CS
Alaska	G	GB	GB	(a-12)	AG	(a-12)	GB	(a-12)	BG	LG
Arizona	G	G	B	N/A	A	A	GS	B	CE	(a-2)
Arkansas	AG	N.O.	N.O.	N/A	AG	N.O.	B	GS	BG	B
California	(a-24)	N.O.	N.O.	GS	CE	G	GS	N.O.	CE	G
Colorado	G	A	N.O.	A	A	AT	GS	G	AB	CS
Connecticut	CS	B	GE	GE	CE	GE	GE	GE	GE	CS
Delaware	GS	CG	(a-2)	N.O.	CG	AT	GS	N.O.	GS	GS
Florida	G	A	N/A	A	CE	A	GS	GS	B	A
Georgia	G	G	B	B	N.O.	G	GD	GB	CE	SS
Hawaii	GS	B	GS	N.O.	GS	A	GS	GS	B	B
Idaho	GS	B	GS	N.O.	CE	(a-3)	B	(a-12)	CE	(a-2)
Illinois	G	GS	GS	(a-12)	CE	(a-3)	GS	(a-12)	B	B
Indiana	G	G	G	G	(a-8)	AT	G	G	CE	(b)
Iowa	GS	GS	N.O.	A	N.O.	AT	GS	GS	GS	SS
Kansas	G	B	GS	C	C	AT	GS	C	B	CE
Kentucky	G	B	G	G	CG	AT	G	GC	B	B
Louisiana	CS	B	GS	G	GS	A	GS	GS	BG	A
Maine	A	B	(a-17)	(a-17)	A	GLS	GLS	GLS	GLS	SS
Maryland	GS	G	GS	N.O.	CE	A	GS	GS	B	B
Massachusetts	C	G	G	G	G	G	CG	G	B	CE
Michigan	GS	B	GS	N.O.	CS	N.O.	GS	N/A	B	(b)
Minnesota	(a-24)	GS	GS	(a-17)	(a-24)	A	GS	GS	GS	(a-2)
Mississippi	(a-6)	N.O.	SE	A	(a-6)	A	GS	GS	BS	A
Missouri	AGS	B	GS	A	A	CE	GS	GS	B	SS
Montana	G	CP	GS	CP	CP	CP	GS	G	CE	SS
Nebraska	A	B	GS	A	A	CE	GS	GS	B	A
Nevada	(a-6)	G	G	N.O.	CE	A	G	G	G	(b)
New Hampshire	GC	CS	GC	N.O.	AGC	AGC	GC	AGC	B	CL
New Jersey	GS	A	(a-17)	GS	GS	A	GS	G	GS	A
New Mexico	G	N/A	(a-17)	N/A	N/A	AT	GS	GS	GS	CE
New York	G	GS	GS	GS	CE	GS	GS	GS	B	(b)
North Carolina	(a-24)	A	G	A	G	N/A	G	A	CE	G
North Dakota	A	G	G	N.O.	A	AT	G	(i)	CE	SS
Ohio	GS	B	GS	A	GS	A	GS	GS	B	CE
Oklahoma	A	B	GS	N.O.	A	B	B	GS	CE	L
Oregon	A	A	GS	G	N.O.	GS	GS	GS	SE	A
Pennsylvania	G	B	G	G	G	AT	GS	GS	GS	AG
Rhode Island	A	B	GS	N.O.	A	SE	GS	GS (j)	B	B
South Carolina	A	B	GS	N.O.	CE	B	GS	GS	CE	B
South Dakota	CP	CP	(a-44)	(a-48)	(a-40)	AT	GS	GS	GS	SS
Tennessee	A	G	G	G	SL	A	G	G	G	A
Texas	G	B	G	G	CE	(i)	B	G	B	(b)
Utah	G	A	GS	AB	AG	GS	GS	GS	B	LG
Vermont	CG	AT	GS	CG	CG	AT	CG	CG	GS	CE
Virginia	GB	AT	GB	GB	GB	A	GB	B	GB	GB
Washington	N.O.	I	GS	N.O.	G	N.O.	GS	N.O.	CE	N.O.
West Virginia	G	GS	GS	B	(a-8)	(a-3)	GS	(a-13)	B	(a-2)
Wisconsin	A	A	N.O.	N.O.	CS	A	GS	CS	CE	B
Wyoming	AG	(a-37)	GS	N.O.	(a-8)	SS	GS	(a-12)	CE	A
American Samoa	GB	N/A	GB	(a-12)	(a-4)	(a-3)	A	(a-12)	GB	G
Guam	GS	...	GS	...	CS	CS	GS	B	B	GS
CNMI*	G	A	GS	GS	C	GS	C	C	B	B
Puerto Rico	G	N/A	GS	N/A	GB	GS	GS	GS	GS	N/A
U.S. Virgin Islands	GS	GS	GS	GS	(a-24)	GS	GS	GS	GS	B

See footnotes at end of table

TABLE 4.10
Selected State Administrative Officials: Methods of Selection (continued)

State or other jurisdiction	Emergency management (a-20)	Employment services (a-21)	Energy (a-22)	Environmental protection (a-23)	Finance (a-24)	Fish & wildlife (a-25)	General services (a-26)	Health (a-27)	Higher education (a-28)	Highways (a-29)
Alabama	G	CS	CS	B	G	CS	CS	B	B	G
Alaska	AG	AG	(k)	GB	AG	GB	AG	GB	B	AG
Arizona	G	A	N/A	GS	(a-14)	B	A	GS	B	A
Arkansas	GS	G	N.O.	BG/BS	G	B	GS	BG	BG	BS
California	GS	GS	G	GS	G	G	GS	GS (b)	B	(a-49)
Colorado	A	A	G	A	A	A	A	GS	GS	GS
Connecticut	GE	GE	GE	GE	GE	(b)	GE	GE	BG	GE
Delaware	CG	CG	CG	(a-35)	GS	CG	CG	CG	B	(a-49)
Florida	G	GS	A	GS	CE	B	GS	GS	B	GOC
Georgia	G	A	CE	BG	G	A	A	GD	B	A
Hawaii	A	CS	CS	CS	(b)	CS	GS	GS	B	CS
Idaho	A	GS	AGS	GS	GS	B	N.O.	GS	B	(a-49)
Illinois	GS	GS	(a-42)	GS	(a-10)	(a-35)	(a-6)	GS	B	(a-49)
Indiana	G	G	LG	G	G	A	(a-6)	G	G	(a-49)
Iowa	GS	GS	GS	A	A	A	A	GS	N.O.	A
Kansas	(b)	GS	B	C	N/A	CS	GS	GS	B	GS
Kentucky	AG	AG	AG	G	G	G	N.O.	CG	B	CG
Louisiana	GS	A	CS	GS	GS	GS	GS	GS	B	GS
Maine	A	(a-32)	(a-38)	GLS	(a-6)	GLS	A	GLS	N/A	(a-49)
Maryland	AG	A	G	GS	GS	GS	(a-6)	GS	G	AG
Massachusetts	G	CG	CG	CG	G	CG	G	CG	BC	G
Michigan	GS	CS	CS	GS	(a-10)	(b)	N.O.	GS	N.O.	(a-49)
Minnesota	GS	N.O.	A	GS	GS	A	(a-6)	GS	B	GS
Mississippi	GS	GS	A	GS	(a-6)	GS	N.O.	BS	BS	B
Missouri	A	A	G	A	AGS	(b)	A	GS	B	B
Montana	CP	CP	CP	GS	CP	GS	CP	GS	CP	(a-49)
Nebraska	A	A	GS	GS	(b)	A	A	GS	B	GS
Nevada	A	A	G	A	(a-14)	GD	N.O.	(b)	B	(a-49)
New Hampshire	G	GC	G	GC	(a-6)	BGS	GC	AGC	B	(a-49)
New Jersey	GS	A	A	GS	GS	B	(b)	GS	B	A
New Mexico	GS	(a-32)	GS	GS	GS	A	GS	GS	GS	A
New York	GS	GS	B	GS	CE	GS	G	GS	B	GS
North Carolina	G	G	A	G	G	G	G	G	B	A
North Dakota	A	G	G	A	A	G	G	G	B	(a-49)
Ohio	AG	GS	GS	GS	A(b)	A	A	GS	B	GS
Oklahoma	GS	B	GS	B	GS	B	GS	B	B	B
Oregon	AG	GS	G	B	(a-4)	B	(a-6)	A	B	A
Pennsylvania	G	AG	AG	GS	G	(b)	GS	GS	AG	AG
Rhode Island	G	GS	A	GS	GS	GS	GS	GS	B (b)	GS
South Carolina	A	B	A	(b)	B	B	A	GS	B	B
South Dakota	A	A	(a-42)	(a-35)	GS	GS	(a-6)	GS	B	A
Tennessee	A	G	A	G	G	B	G	G	B	(a-49)
Texas	A	B	N.O.	B	(a-14)	B	B	BG	B	(a-49)
Utah	A	GS	G	GS	AG	A	A	GS	N.O.	(a-49)
Vermont	AG	GS	GS	CG	CG	CG	CG	CG	N.O.	CG
Virginia	GB	GB	A	GB	GB	B	GB	GB	B	GB
Washington	N.O.	GS	N.O.	GS	N.O.	GD	N.O.	G	N.O.	N.O.
West Virginia	GS	GS	GS	GS	CS	CS	CS	GS	B	GS
Wisconsin	A	A	A	A	A	A	GS	GS	N/A	(a-49)
Wyoming	G	GS	G	GS	N.O.	GD	AG	GS	GB	GS
American Samoa	G	A	GB	GB	(a-4)	GB	G	GB	(a-18)	(a-49)
Guam	GS	GS	G	GS	GS	GS	CS	GS	B	GS
CNMI*	G	C	C	G	GS	C	GS	GS	B	C
Puerto Rico	N/A	GS	N/A	N/A	G	N/A	GS	GS	N/A	GS
U.S. Virgin Islands	GS	GS	GS	GS	GS	GS	GS	GS	GS	GS

See footnotes at end of table

TABLE 4.10

Selected State Administrative Officials: Methods of Selection (continued)

State or other jurisdiction	Information systems (a-30)	Insurance (a-31)	Labor (a-32)	Licensing (a-33)	Mental health & developmental disabilities (a-34)	Natural resources (a-35)	Parks & recreation (a-36)	Personnel (a-37)	Planning (a-38)	Post audit (a-39)
Alabama	CS	G	G	N.O.	G	G	CS	B	(a-12)	LS
Alaska	AG	AG	GB	AG	B	GB	AG	AG	N.O.	(a-8)
Arizona	A	GS	BS	N.O.	B	GS	GS	A	(a-10)	N.O.
Arkansas	GS	GS	GS	N.O.	A	G	GS	AG	N.O.	L
California	G	CE	AG	G	(b)	GS	GS	GS	N.O.	N.O.
Colorado	G	BA	GS	A	A	GS	A	A	G	(a-8)
Connecticut	A	GE	GE	CS	(b)	CS	CS	CS	A	(a-8)
Delaware	GS	CE	GS	CG	(b)	GS	CG	GS	CG	(a-8)
Florida	GS	GOC	GS	A	N/A	GS	A	A	A	CE
Georgia	GD	CE	CE	SS	B	GB	A	A	(a-10)	(a-8)
Hawaii	A	AG	GS	CS	G	GS	CS	GS	CS	CS
Idaho	(a-6)	GS	GS	GS	N.O.	B	B	GS	N.O.	(a-14)
Illinois	(a-6)	GS	GS	(a-9)	(a-45)	GS	(a-35)	(a-6)	N.O.	(a-8)
Indiana	G	G	G	G	A	G	A	G	N.O.	G
Iowa	GS	GS	GS	N.O.	A	GS	A	A	N.O.	N.O.
Kansas	G	SE	GS	B	C	GS	CS	C	N.O.	L
Kentucky	G	G	G	N.O.	CG	G	CG	G	G	CE
Louisiana	A	CE	GS	N.O.	GS	GS	LGS	B	CS	CL
Maine	A	GLS	GLS	A	(a-45)	GLS	(a-35)	A	N/A	N/A
Maryland	A	GS	GS	A	(b)	GS	A	A	GS	A
Massachusetts	CG	G	C	G	(b)	CG	CG	CG	G	CE
Michigan	GS	(a-9)	GS	(a-32)	CS	GS	CS	CS	N.O.	CL
Minnesota	GS	A	GS	A	GS	GS	A	(a-24)	N/A	(a-8)
Mississippi	BS	SE	N.O.	N.O.	B	GS	GS	B	A	CE
Missouri	A	GS	GS	A	BS	GS	A	G	AGS	CE
Montana	A	CE	GS	CP	CP	GS	CP	CP	G	L
Nebraska	GS	GS	GS	A	GS	GS	B	A	GS	CE
Nevada	G	A	A	N.O.	(b)	G	A	GS	N.O.	N.O.
New Hampshire	GC	GC	GC	GC	AGC	GC	AGC	AGC	...	(a-14)
New Jersey	A	GS	GS	N.O.	A(b)	A	A	GS	A	N.O.
New Mexico	GS	G	GS	G	N.O.	GS	N/A	GD	N/A	(a-8)
New York	G	GS	GS	(b)	GS	GS	GS	GS	GS	CE
North Carolina	G	CE	CE	N.O.	A	G	A	G	N/A	(a-8)
North Dakota	G	CE	G	N.O.	A	N.O.	G	A	N.O.	A
Ohio	G	GS	A	N.O.	GS(b)	GS	A	A	GS	CE
Oklahoma	A	CE	CE	N.O.	B	(a-48)	(a-48)	GS	N.O.	N.O.
Oregon	A	GS	SE	N.O.	A	N.O.	B	A	N.O.	SS
Pennsylvania	G	GS	GS	AG	G	GS	A	G	G	(a-8)
Rhode Island	A	GS	GS	(i)	GS	GS	GS	A	A	N.O.
South Carolina	A	GS	GS	GS	(b)	B	GS	A	AB	B
South Dakota	GS	A	GS	N.O.	GS	GS	A	GS	N.O.	(a-8)
Tennessee	A	G	G	A	G	G	A	G	A	SL
Texas	B	G	B	B	B	B	B	N.O.	G	L
Utah	GS	GS	GS	AG	A	GS	AB	GS	G	(a-8)
Vermont	CG	GS	GS	SS	CG	GS	CG	CG	N.O.	(a-8)
Virginia	B	B	GB	GB	GB	GB	GB	GB	(a-10)	(a-8)
Washington	GS	SE	GS	GS	N.O.	CE	I	N.O.	N.O.	N.O.
West Virginia	G	GS	GS	N.O.	(a-27)	(a-25)	(a-25)	C	(a-17)	LS
Wisconsin	A	GS	GS	GS	A	GS	A	A	N.O.	LS
Wyoming	GS	GS	AG	CS	(b)	G	GS	AG	G	AG
American Samoa	(a-49)	G	N/A	N/A	(a-45)	AG	GB	A	(a-12)	G
Guam	GS	GS	GS	GS	GS	GS	GS	GS	GS	CE
CNMI*	C	CS	C	B	C	GS	C	GS	G	GS
Puerto Rico	N/A	N/A	GS	N/A	N/A	GS	GS	GS	GS	N/A
U.S. Virgin Islands	G	SE	GS	GS	GS	GS	GS	GS	GS	L

See footnotes at end of table

TABLE 4.10
Selected State Administrative Officials: Methods of Selection (continued)

State or other jurisdiction	Pre-audit (a-40)	Public library development (a-41)	Public utility regulation (a-42)	Purchasing (a-43)	Revenue (a-44)	Social services (a-45)	Solid waste mgmt. (a-46)	State police (a-47)	Tourism (a-48)	Transportation (a-49)	Welfare (a-50)
Alabama	(a-14)	B	SE	CS	G	B	CS	G	G	(a-29)	(a-45)
Alaska	N.O.	AG	GB	AG	GB	GB	AG	GB	AG	GB	AG
Arizona	(a-14)	SS	B	A	GS	GS	A	GS	GS	GS	(a-45)
Arkansas	N/A	B	GS	AG	AG	GS	BG/BS	BG	AG	BS	GS
California	(a-14)	N.O.	GS	(a-26)	BS	GS	G	GS	N.O.	GS	(a-45)
Colorado	(a-14)	BA	CS	CS	GS	GS	CS	A	CS	GS	GS
Connecticut	CE	B	GB	CS	GE	GE	CS	GE	A	GE	GE
Delaware	(a-8)	CG	CG	(a-26)	CG	(b)	B	CG	CG	GS	CG
Florida	CE	A	B	A	GOC	GS	A	GOC	N.O.	GS	A
Georgia	(a-8)	AB	CE	A	GS	GD	A	G	A	GB	A
Hawaii	CS	B	GS	GS	GS	GS	CS	N.O.	B	GS	CS
Idaho	(a-14)	B	GS	(a-6)	GS	(a-27)	N.O.	GS	GS	B	A
Illinois	(a-14)	SS	GS	(a-6)	GS	GS	(a-23)	GS	(a-12)	GS	GS
Indiana	CE	G	G	A	G	G	A	G	LG	G	(a-45)
Iowa	A	B	GS	A	GS	GS	A	GS	A	GS	A
Kansas	CS	GS	B	C	GS	GS	C	GS	C	GS	C
Kentucky	N.O.	G	G	G	G	G	AG	G	G	G	(a-45)
Louisiana	A	BGS	BS	A	GS	GS	GS	GS	LGS	GS	GS
Maine	(a-14)	B	G	CS	A	GLS	CS	A/GLS	(a-17)	GLS	(a-45)
Maryland	A	A	GS	A	A	GS	A	GS	A	GS	(a-45)
Massachusetts	CE	B	CG	CG	CG	CG	CG	CG	G	G	CG
Michigan	N.O.	N.O.	GS	CS	CS	GS	CS	GS	N.O.	GS	GS
Minnesota	(a-8)	N/A	(b)	A	GS	(a-34)	(a-23)	A	A	GS	(a-34)
Mississippi	CE	B	GS	A	GS	GS	A	GS	A	B	GS
Missouri	A	B	GS	A	GS	GS	A	GS	A	B	A
Montana	(a-39)	CP	CE	CP	GS	GS	GS	CP	CP	GS	GS
Nebraska	A	B	B	A	GS	GS	A	GS	B	GS	GS
Nevada	N.O.	(b)	G	A	G	G	(a-23)	G	GD	B	(b)
New Hampshire	(a-14)	AGC	GC	CS	GC	GC	AGC	AGC	AGC	GC	AGC
New Jersey	N.O.	N.O.	GS	GS	A	(b)	A	GS	A	GS	A
New Mexico	N/A	N/A	G	N/A	GS	N/A	N/A	GS	GS	GS	N/A
New York	CE	B	GS	G	GS	GS	GS	GS	GS	GS	GS
North Carolina	(a-8)	A	G	A	G	A	A	G	A	G	A
North Dakota	N.O.	N.O.	CE	A	CE	G	A	G	G	G	G
Ohio	GS	B	BG	A	GS	(b)	A	GS	LG	GS	GS
Oklahoma	(a-14)	B	(b)	A	GS	GS	A	A	B	B	GS
Oregon	(a-10)	B	GS	A	GS	GS	N.O.	GS	N.O.	GS	(a-45)
Pennsylvania	(a-4)	G	GS	AG	GS	GS	AG	GS	A	GS	GS
Rhode Island	(a-14)	A	GS	A	GS	GS (b)	(h)	G	(a-17)	GS	GS
South Carolina	(a-14)	B	B	A	GS	GS	BS	B	GS	GS	(a-45)
South Dakota	CE	A	CE	A	GS	GS	A	A	GS	GS	(a-45)
Tennessee	A	A	SE	A	G	A	A	G	G	G	G
Texas	(a-14)	A	B	A	(a-14)	(i)	N.O.	B	A	B	BG
Utah	AG	A	A	A	A	GS	A	A	A	GS	GS
Vermont	(a-24)	CG	BGS	CG	CG	GS	CG	GS	CG	GS	CG
Virginia	(a-14)	B	(b)	A	GB	GB	GB	GB	G	GB	GB
Washington	N.O.	N.O.	GS	N.O.	GS	GS	N.O.	GS	N.O.	GS	N.O.
West Virginia	(a-8)	B	GS	CS	GS	(a-27)	B	GS	GS	(a-29)	(a-27)
Wisconsin	LS	A	GS	A	GS	GS	A	A	GS	GS	A
Wyoming	(a-8)	AG	G	CS	GS	(a-27)	AG	AG	AG	(a-29)	(a-45)
American Samoa	(a-4)	(a-18)	N/A	A	(a-4)	GB	GB	GB	(a-12)	(a-29)	N/A
Guam	GS	(i)	GS	GS	GS	GS	GS	GS	B	...	GS
CNMI*	G	B	B	C	C	C	A	GS	GB	CS	A
Puerto Rico	N/A	N/A	GS	GS	GS	N/A	N/A	GS	GS	GS	N/A
U.S. Virgin Islands	GS	GS	G	GS	GS	G	GS	GS	GS	GS	GS

See footnotes at end of table

TABLE 4.10
Selected State Administrative Officials: Methods of Selection (continued)

Source: The Council of State Governments' survey of state personnel agencies and state websites, June 2019.
*Commonwealth of Northern Mariana Islands
Key:
N/A–Not available.
N.O.–No specific chief administrative official or agency in charge of function.
CE–Constitutional, elected by public.
CL–Constitutional, elected by legislature.
SE–Statutory, elected by public.
SL–Statutory, elected by legislature.
L–Selected by legislature or one of its organs.
CT–Constitutional, elected by state court of last resort.
CP–Competitive process.

Appointed by:	Approved by:
G–Governor	
GS–Governor	Senate (in Nebraska, unicameral legislature)
GB–Governor	Both houses
GE–Governor	Either house
GC–Governor	Council
GD–Governor	Departmental board
GLS–Governor	Appropriate legislative committee & Senate
GOC–Governor & Council or cabinet	
LG–Lieutenant Governor	
LGS–Lieutenant Governor	Senate (in Nebraska, unicameral legislature)
AT–Attorney General	
ATS–Attorney General	Senate (in Nebraska, unicameral legislature)
SS–Secretary of State	
C–Cabinet Secretary	
CG–Cabinet Secretary	Governor
A–Agency head	
AB–Agency head	Board
AG–Agency head	Governor
AGC–Agency head	Governor & Council
AGS–Agency head	Senate (in Nebraska, unicameral legislature)
ALS–Agency head	Appropriate legislative committee
ASH–Agency head	Senate president & House speaker
B–Board or commission	
BG–Board	Governor
BGS–Board	Governor & Senate
BS–Board or commission	Senate (in Nebraska, unicameral legislature)
BA–Board or commission	Agency head
CS–Civil Service	
LS–Legislative Committee	Senate (in Nebraska, unicameral legislature)

(a) Chief administrative official or agency in charge of function:
(a-1) Lieutenant governor.
(a-2) Secretary of state.
(a-3) Attorney general.
(a-4) Treasurer.
(a-5) Adjutant general.
(a-6) Administration.
(a-7) Agriculture.
(a-8) Auditor.
(a-9) Banking.
(a-10) Budget.
(a-11) Civil rights.
(a-12) Commerce.
(a-13) Community affairs.
(a-14) Comptroller.
(a-15) Consumer affairs.
(a-16) Corrections.
(a-17) Economic development.
(a-18) Education (chief state school officer).
(a-19) Election administration.
(a-20) Emergency management.
(a-21) Employment Services.
(a-22) Energy.
(a-23) Environmental protection.
(a-24) Finance.
(a-25) Fish and wildlife.
(a-26) General services.
(a-27) Health.
(a-28) Higher education.
(a-29) Highways.
(a-30) Information systems.
(a-31) Insurance.
(a-32) Labor.
(a-33) Licensing.
(a-34) Mental Health & Developmental Disabilities.
(a-35) Natural resources.
(a-36) Parks and recreation.
(a-37) Personnel.
(a-38) Planning.
(a-39) Post audit.
(a-40) Pre-audit.
(a-41) Public library development.
(a-42) Public utility regulation.
(a-43) Purchasing.
(a-44) Revenue.
(a-45) Social services.
(a-46) Solid waste management.
(a-47) State police.
(a-48) Tourism.
(a-49) Transportation.
(a-50) Welfare.
(b)
California–Health–Responsibilities shared between Director of Health Care Services, Jennifer Kent, and Director of Public Health, Karen L. Smith, both (GS).
California–Mental Health and Developmental Disabilities–Responsibilities shared between Director of State Hospitals, vacant, (GS) and Director of Developmental Services, Nancy A. Bargmann, (GS).

TABLE 4.10
Selected State Administrative Officials: Methods of Selection (continued)

Connecticut–Auditors–Responsibilities shared between Robert J. Kane and John C. Geragosian. Positions are filled by the legislature.

Connecticut–Fish and Wildlife–Responsibilities shared between Director of Wildlife, Richard Jacobson, (CS), Director of Inland and Marine Fisheries, Peter Aarrestad, (CS).

Connecticut–Mental Health and Developmental Disabilities–Responsibilities shared between Commissioner of Mental Health, Miriam Delphin-Rittmon, (GE) and Commissioner, Dept. of Developmental Services, Jordan Scheff, (GE).

Delaware–Mental Health and Developmental Disabilities–Responsibilities shared between Director, Division of Substance Abuse and Mental Health (CG); and Director, Division of Developmental Disabilities Services, same department (CG).

Delaware–Social Services–Responsibilities shared between Secretary of Health and Social Services (GS); and Acting Secretary, Department of Services of Children, Youth and their Families (GS).

Hawaii–Administration–the functions are divided among the Director of Budget and Finance, Director of Human Resources Development, and the Comptroller.

Hawaii–Finance–Responsibilities shared between Director of Budget and Finance, Roderick K. Becker, (GS) and the Comptroller, Curt Otaguru, (GS).

Indiana–Election Administration–Responsibilities shared between Co-Directors, Brad King and Angela Nussmeyer.

Kansas–Emergency management–Responsibilities shared between Adjutant General (GS) and Deputy Director (C).

Maryland–Mental Health and Developmental Disabilities–Responsibilities shared between Executive Director, Mental Hygiene Administration (A); and Secretary, Department of Disabilities (A).

Massachusetts–Mental Health and Developmental Disabilities–Responsibilities shared between Commissioner, Department of Developmental Disabilities (CG); and Commissioner, Department of Mental Health, Executive Office of Human Services (CG).

Michigan–Election Administration–Responsibilities shared between Secretary of State, (CE); and Director, Sally Williams, Bureau of Elections (CS).

Michigan–Fish and Wildlife–Responsibilities shared between Director, Chief of Fisheries, Jim Dexter, (CS) and Chief of Wildlife, Russ Mason, (CS).

Minnesota–Human/Social Services, Mental Health and Developmental Disabilities and Welfare are under the Commissioner of Human Services (GS).

Minnesota–Public Utility Regulation–Responsibilities shared between the five Public Utility Commissioners (G).

Missouri–Fish and Wildlife–Responsibilities shared between Administrator, Division of Fisheries, Department of Conservation; Administrator, Division of Wildlife, same department (AB).

Nebraska–Finance–Responsibilities shared between State Tax Commissioner, Department of Revenue (GS); Administrator, Budget Division (A) and the Auditor of Public Accounts (CE).

Nevada–Election Administration–Responsibilities shared between Secretary of State (CE), Deputy Secretary of State (SS), Chief Deputy, Secretary of State (A).

Nevada–Health–Responsibilities shared between Director of Health and Human Services (G) and Division Administrator, Health (AG).

Nevada–Mental Health and Developmental Disabilities–Responsibilities shared between Director of Health and Human Services (G) and Division Administrator, MHDS (G).

Nevada–Public Library–Responsibilities shared between Director, Dept. of Tourism and Cultural Affairs (G) and Division Administrator of Library and Archives (A).

Nevada–Welfare–Responsibilities shared between Director of Health and Human Services (G) and Division Administrator, Welfare and Support Services (AG).

New Jersey–General Services–Responsibilities shared between Director, Division of Purchase and Property, Dept. of Treasury (GS), and Director, Division of Property Management and Construction, Dept. of the Treasury (A).

New Jersey–Mental Health and Developmental Disabilities–Responsibilities shared between Director, Division of Mental Health Services, Dept. of Human Services (A) and Director, Division of Developmental Disabilities, Dept. of Human Services (A).

New Jersey–Commissioner, Dept. of Human Services (GS) and Commissioner Dept. of Children and Families (GS).

New York–Responsibilities shared between Board of Election members. Two co-chairs and two commissioners. (B)

New York–Licensing–Responsibilities shared between Secretary of State (GS) and Commissioner of State Education Department (B).

Ohio–Finance–Responsibilities shared between Assistant Director, Office of Budget and Management (A) and Deputy Director same office (A).

Ohio–Mental Health and Developmental Disabilities–Responsibilities shared between Director, Dept. of Developmental Disabilities (GS) and Director, Department of Mental Health and Addiction Services. (GS).

Ohio–Social Services–Responsibilities shared between Director, OH Dept. of Job and Family Services (GS), Superintendent of Public Instruction, Dept. of Education (B), Executive Director of Opportunities for Ohioans with Disabilities (B), Director of Dept. of Aging (GS).

Oklahoma–Public Utility Regulation–Responsibilities shared between General Administrator Public Utility Division, Corporation Commission (B); and 3 Commissioners, Corporation Commission (SE).

Pennsylvania–Shared between Executive Director (Fish) (B) and Executive Director (Game) (B).

Rhode Island–Higher Education–This employee serves in a dual role as Commissioner of Higher Education and as the President of the Community College of Rhode Island.

Rhode Island–Social Services–This position is filled by two employees, one, Stephen Costantino, is the Commissioner, Office of Health and Human Services; Sandra Powell serves as the Director of Human Services and reports to the Commissioner, Office of Health and Human Services.

South Carolina–Environmental Protection–Responsibilities shared between two Directors, one selected by (BS) and the other by (B).

South Carolina–Health and Human Services (GS) and Director of Health & Environmental Control (GS).

South Carolina–Mental Health and Developmental Disabilities–Responsibilities shared between Director of Disabilities and Special Needs (B) and Director of Mental Health (B).

Texas–Election Administration–Responsibilities shared between

TABLE 4.10
Selected State Administrative Officials: Methods of Selection (continued)

Secretary of State (G); and Division Director of Elections, Elections Division, Secretary of State (A).

Virginia–Public Utility Regulation–No single position. Functions are shared between Energy Regulation and Utility and Railroad Safety, all (B).

Wyoming–Mental Health and Developmental Disabilities–Responsibilities shared between Director, State Hospital (AG) and Director, Life Resource Center, (AG).

(c) Department abolished July 1, 2005; responsibilities transferred to office of Management and Budget, General Services and Department of State.

(d) Appointed by the House and approved by the Senate.

(e) In Maine, New Hampshire, Tennessee and West Virginia, the Presidents (or Speakers) of the Senate are next in line of succession to the Governorship. In Tennessee and West Virginia, the Speaker of the Senate bears the statutory title of Lieutenant Governor.

(f) The Governor has assigned the role of Secretary of State (GS) to the Lieutenant Governor, with no additional salary.

(g) The New Jersey State constitution states: "The State Auditor shall be appointed by the Senate and General Assembly in joint meeting for a term of five years and until his successor shall be appointed and qualify." So it is a Constitutional Officer, but is appointed, not elected by the legislature.

(h) Solid waste is managed by the Rhode Island Resource Recovery Corporation (RIRRC). Although not a department of the state government, RIRRC is a public corporation and a component of the State of Rhode Island for financial reporting purposes. To be financially self-sufficient, the agency earns revenue through the sale of recyclable products, methane gas royalties and fees for it services.

(i) Method not specified.

(j) The Rhode Island Economic Development Corporation is a quasi-public agency.

(k) The authority is a public corporation of the state and a body corporate and politic constituting a political subdivision within the Department of Commerce, Community, and Economic Development, but with separate and independent legal existence.

TABLE 4.11
Selected State Administrative Officials: Annual Salaries

State or other jurisdiction	Governor	Lieutenant governor (a-1)	Secretary of state (a-2)	Attorney general (a-3)	Treasurer (a-4)	Adjutant general (a-5)	Admin. (a-6)	Agriculture (a-7)	Auditor (a-8)	Banking (a-9)
Alabama	$120,395	$60,830	$85,248	$168,002	$85,248	$91,014	N/A	$84,655	$85,248	$157,380
Alaska	145,000	115,000	(a-1)	141,156	159,001	141,156	141,156	110,304	158,757	122,988
Arizona	95,000	(a-2)	70,000	90,000	70,000	146,000	N/A	132,000	141,986	130,000
Arkansas	148,134	43,584	94,554	136,578	89,300	179,892	157,182	122,953	89,300	152,859
California	201,680	151,260	151,260	175,182	161,342	190,101	N.O.	209,944	209,944	191,109
Colorado	90,000	93,360	93,260	107,676	93,360	163,644	158,556	155,004	183,312	118,956
Connecticut	150,000 (d)	110,000	119,625	119,625	119,625	165,000	175,000	140,000	(c)	149,625
Delaware	171,000	81,239	131,011	148,893	116,582	125,126	(c)	122,333	111,667	114,595
Florida	130,273	124,851	141,000	128,972	(a-24)	170,352	141,000	128,972	140,004	(a-24)
Georgia	175,000	91,609	123,637	139,169	165,000	160,000	153,000	121,557	152,160	148,358
Hawaii	158,700	154,812	N.O.	154,812	154,812	222,441	(c)	147,444	147,444	119,664
Idaho	138,302	42,909	105,771	124,000	104,207	145,121	95,201	130,936	N.O.	(a-24)
Illinois	177,412 (d)	135,669	156,541	156,541	135,669	115,613	142,339	133,273	157,212	135,081
Indiana	121,331	95,162	82,640	99,418	82,640	139,869	142,041	148,000	82,640	126,072
Iowa	130,000	103,212	103,212	123,669	103,212	175,106	142,938	103,212	103,212	117,832
Kansas	99,636	54,000	86,003	98,901	86,003	106,392	120,000	110,000	N/A	120,000
Kentucky	148,781	126,485	126,485	126,485	126,485	137,000	N.O.	126,485	126,485	128,553
Louisiana	130,000	117,303	115,000	115,000	115,000	200,262	237,500	115,000	132,620	145,000
Maine	70,000	(e)	104,104	105,914	79,518	139,734	139,734	139,734	111,134	115,274
Maryland	170,000	141,500	99,500	141,500	141,500	144,052 (b)	146,743 (b)	143,488 (b)	N.O.	101,463 (b)
Massachusetts	185,000	122,058	136,402	136,402	133,277	171,392	161,522	136,000	140,607	130,000
Michigan	159,300	111,510	112,410	112,410	174,204	180,269	(a-10)	165,000	176,636	165,000
Minnesota	127,629	82,959	95,722	121,248	(a-24)	184,579	144,991	144,991	108,485	126,491
Mississippi	122,160	60,000	90,000	108,960	90,000	141,105	150,000	90,000	90,000	156,900
Missouri	133,821	86,484	107,746	116,437	107,746	111,116	129,509	125,381	107,746	116,150
Montana	115,505	86,990	95,695	137,008	(a-6)	122,621	111,895	110,787	92,236	110,787
Nebraska	105,000	75,000	85,000	95,000	85,000	111,236	160,001	116,727	85,000	107,338
Nevada	149,573 (d)	63,648	102,898	141,086	102,898	118,200	128,998	118,200	N.O.	98,880
New Hampshire	134,581	(e)	105,930	128,260	105,930	105,930	117,913	100,171	N.O.	105,929
New Jersey	175,000	141,000	(a-1)	140,000	141,000	141,000	N.O.	141,000	144,629	141,000
New Mexico	110,000	85,000	85,000	95,000	85,000	202,552	128,000	79.788	85,000	90,000
New York	200,000	151,500	120,800	151,500	N/A	120,800	183,040	120,800	151,500	127,000
North Carolina	144,349	127,561	127,561	127,561	127,561	107,490	145,218	127,561	127,561	127,561
North Dakota	129,096 (d)	103,221	105,770	157,009	99,881	200,160	N.O.	108,656	105,770	140,004
Ohio	153,650	176,426	113,506	113,506	113,506	140,005	1,550,002	140,005	113,506	125,299
Oklahoma	147,000	114,713	140,000	132,825	114,713	184,568	110,750	126,508	114,713	196,721
Oregon	98,600	(a-2)	77,000	82,220	72,000	185,508	204,058	152,652	136,488	N.O.
Pennsylvania	194,850	163,672	140,291	162,115	162,115	140,291	155,874	140,291	162,115	140,291
Rhode Island (g)	145,755	122,740	122,740	132,521	122,740	141,259	136,510	(a-23)	159,248	135,000
South Carolina	106,078	46,545	92,007	92,007	92,007	92,007	201,297	92,007	147,052	135,273
South Dakota	113,961	(h)	89,700	112,096	89,700	119,675	102,811	118,000	89,700	109,313
Tennessee	194,112	72,948 (e)	209,520	188,952	209,520	161,904	209,520	161,904	(a-14)	161,904
Texas	153,750	7,200	197,415	153,750	(a-14)	178,196	N.O.	137,500	181,128	242,925
Utah	150,000	135,000	(a-1)	104,405	104,405	131,997	140,004	125,008	104,405	130,000
Vermont	178,274	70,470	113,042	131,019	109,449	121,056	136,448	136,448	109,449	118,726
Virginia	175,000	36,321	172,000	150,000	172,430	139,614	172,000	165,000	178,950	175,100
Washington	183,072	103,937	124,108	162,599	144,679	184,568	168,792	161,268	124,108	140,724
West Virginia	150,000	20,000 (e)	95,000	95,000	95,000	125,000	95,000	95,000	95,000	75,000
Wisconsin	152,756	80,684	72,551	148,242	72,551	135,512	152,755	130,000	132,142	135,013
Wyoming	105,000	(a-2)	92,000	175,000	92,000	142,816	112,012	124,378	92,000	107,184
Guam	130,000	85,000	N.O.	105,286	52,492	68,152	88,915	60,850	100,000	88,915
CNMI*	70,000	65,000	N.O.	80,000	40,800 (b)	N.O.	54,000	40,800 (b)	80,000	40,800 (b)
Puerto Rico	70,000	N.O.	125,000	N/A	N/A	N/A	N/A	N/A	N/A	N/A
U.S. Virgin Islands	150,000	75,000	(a-1)	76,500	76,500	85,000	76,500	76,500	76,500	75,000

See footnotes at end of table

TABLE 4.11
Selected State Administrative Officials: Annual Salaries (continued)

State or other jurisdiction	Budget (a-10)	Civil rights (a-11)	Commerce (a-12)	Community affairs (a-13)	Comptroller (a-14)	Consumer affairs (a-15)	Corrections (a-16)	Economic development (a-17)	Education (a-18)	Election admin. (a-19)
Alabama	$177,266	N.O.	$162,232	$164,419	$138,305	$72,686	$71,712	(a-12)	$250,000	$72,686
Alaska	195,000	110,304	141,156	(a-12)	137,664	(a-12)	141,156	(a-12)	141,156	145,008
Arizona	130,000	145,000	250,000	N/A	140,000	133,729	185,000	(a-12)	85,000	142,518
Arkansas	136,309	N.O.	N.O.	N/A	142,470	N.O.	155,052	149,861	235,823	71,171
California	(a-24)	N.O.	N.O.	158,738	161,342	191,109	265,920	N.O.	175,182	149,244
Colorado	173,616	126,960	N.O.	155,000	147,672	158,712	170,004	155,000	262,656	139,260
Connecticut	161,922	136,269	11,146	(a-12)	119,625	142,800	167,500	(a-12)	192,500	116,537
Delaware	151,088	81,950	(a-2)	N.O	151,088	125,102	151,088	(c)	164,055	91,173
Florida	145,000	99,500	N/A	110,000	128,972	100,000	160,000	141,000	276,000	97,250
Georgia	175,615	105,202	132,600	164,800	N/A	124,836	160,000	169,500	123,270	97,850
Hawaii	154,812	113,616	147,444	N.O.	147,444	118,776	147,444	147,444	240,000	119,664
Idaho	122,990	67,787	130,000	N.O.	104,207	(a-3)	139,984	(a-12)	104,207	(a-2)
Illinois	150,000	115,613	142,339	(a-12)	135,669	(a-3)	150,228	(a-12)	225,000	130,008
Indiana	137,700	115,400	(a-17)	122,400	(a-8)	105,500	154,400	195,850	98,418	(c)
Iowa	141,960	87,000	N.O.	98,592	N.O	128,890	142,500	154,300	140,000	106,309
Kansas	130,000	76,476	125,000	N.O.	115,000	95,000	135,000	72,050	175,000	(a-2)
Kentucky	137,000	126,200	137,000	115,000	108,286	86,940	115,000	250,000	200,000	73,500
Louisiana	148,865	86,715	237,500	162,198	(a-6)	108,139	136,719	237,500	275,000	112,195
Maine	104,645	95,098	(a-17)	(a-17)	118,934	130,811	139,734	139,734	139,734	110,219
Maryland	174,417 (b)	114,865 (b)	172,021 (b)	N.O	141,500	134,749 (b)	159,072 (b)	172,021 (b)	153,532 (b)	130,059 (b)
Massachusetts	134,589	137,382	161,522	145,000	176,624	145,000	150,000	161,522	161,522	136,402
Michigan	165,000	159,800	(a-32)	N.O.	150,420	N.O.	175,000	N/A	216,240	(c)
Minnesota	(a-24)	144,991	144,991	(a-17)	(a-24)	128,036	150,002	150,002	1,500,002	(a-2)
Mississippi	(a-6)	N.O.	90,000	130,000	(a-6)	108,960	132,761	183,000	300,000	80,000
Missouri	118,473	83,761	129,526	108,004	99,668	116,437	125,381	129,526	193,464	62,712
Montana	122,412	85,451	110,781	74,940	115,495	79,524	111,904	105,857	107,127	88,880
Nebraska	164,303	79,170	134,172	101,653	140,000	95,000	188,957	143,998	227,390	97,562
Nevada	(a-6)	88,651	128,998	N.O.	102,898	75,111	128,998	N/A	128,998	(c)
New Hampshire	105,930	80,971	114,554	N.O.	106,575	100,171	117,913	87,423	114,553	(a-2)
New Jersey	132,000	120,000	(a-17)	141,000	141,000	136,000	141,000	225,000	141,000	125,000
New Mexico	92,032	N.O.	128,000	N.O.	120,359	91,398	N/A	(a-12)	128,000	85,000
New York	199,547	109,800	120,800	120,800	151,500	127,000	136,000	1 (d)	250,000	(i)
North Carolina	(a-24)	N/A	152,944	N.O.	158,501	N/A	N/A	N/A	127,561	107,590
North Dakota	(a-24)	(a-12)	208,000	N.O.	N.O.	141,384	150,000	126,504	120,410	53,640
Ohio	177,008	117,104	150,010	155,002	177,008	109,990	155,002	155,002	189,571	113,506
Oklahoma	110,000	N.O.	141,000	N.O.	120,000	132,833	185,000	N.O.	124,373	117,885
Oregon	157,884	112,428	168,276	156,773	N.O.	185,508	185,104	(a-13)	157,581	150,336
Pennsylvania	168,490	144,157	135,179	135,179	154,015	145,976	155,879	148,085	155,879	84,930
Rhode Island (g)	185,739	86,342	205,706	N/A	140,645	(a-3)	145,644	185,000 (j)	212,106	145,993
South Carolina	123,730	115,000	175,980	N/A	92,007	115,836	168,043	(a-12)	92,007	103,264
South Dakota	75,656	51,072	(a-44)	(a-48)	(a-40)	61,138	124,462	138,823	123,864	74,427
Tennessee	163,248	116,964	(a-17)	(a-17)	209,520	82,236	161,904	169,392	200,004	144,612
Texas	205,000	123,769	N.O.	180,084	153,750	155,224	266,500	164,701	220,375	(c)
Utah	158,995	98,176	144,997	70,554	(a-24)	(a-12)	131,997	145,995	230,069	83,200
Vermont	127,088	107,806	136,177	109,907	127,088	107,806	121,056	112,756	136,448	109,449
Virginia	172,699	97,850	172,000	137,296	172,567	115,682	184,051	350,200	235,000	111,000
Washington	N.O.	120,432	168,792	N.O.	N.O.	(a-3)	181,440	(a-12)	134,212	(a-2)
West Virginia	93,000	55,000	95,000	81,548	(a-8)	(a-3)	90,504	(a-13)	230,000	(a-2)
Wisconsin	130,000	107,016	N.O.	N.O.	108,243	103,625	150,009	N.O.	127,047	122,013
Wyoming	134,358	(a-37)	142,943	N.O.	(a-8)	134,260	148,628	(a-12)	92,000	98,133
Guam	88,915	N.O.	88,915	N.O.	83,400	55,341	67,150	82,025	82,025	61,939
CNMI*	54,000	49,000	52,000	52,000	40,800 (b)	52,000	40,800 (b)	45,000	80,000	53,000
Puerto Rico	N/A	N/A	N/A	N/A	N/A	N/A	N/A	N/A	N/A	N/A
U.S. Virgin Islands	76,500	60,000	76,500	(c)	76,500	76,500	76,500	85,000	76,500	135,000

See footnotes at end of table

TABLE 4.11
Selected State Administrative Officials: Annual Salaries (continued)

State or other jurisdiction	Emergency management (a-20)	Employment services (a-21)	Energy (a-22)	Environmental protection (a-23)	Finance (a-24)	Fish & wildlife (a-25)	General services (a-26)	Health (a-27)	Higher education (a-28)	Highways (a-29)
Alabama	$124,200	$88,543	$97,766	$152,618	$177,266	$113,479	$97,766	$282,446	$206,184	$169,000
Alaska	114,420	124,452	160,000	141,156	142,140	141,156	(a-43)	141,156	325,000	133,620
Arizona	112,500	135,000	N/A	175,000	(a-14)	160,000	120,000	205,505	120,000	145,000
Arkansas	110,272	151,913	N.O.	137,094	(a-6)	135,383	138,918	221,976	170,437	218,998
California	209,944	192,325	158,573	209,944	209,944	189,091	191,109	(c)	311,928	(a-49)
Colorado	158,424	133,848	155,000	162,864	139,368	153,216	117,420	207,778	155,000	160,920
Connecticut	183,340	157,000	139,050	139,050	209,439	(c)	175,000	190,000	335,000	190,749
Delaware	93,583	99,014	99,108	(a-35)	151,088	101,525	116,355	174,040	113,602	(a-49)
Florida	141,000	141,000	91,960	150,000	128,972	140,737	141,000	N/A	200,000	150,000
Georgia	105,000	108,150	116,452	170,000	155,400	135,000	162,761	175,000	500,500	124,409
Hawaii	128,268	106,572(b)	106,572(b)	N/A	(c)	106,572 (b)	(a-14)	147,444	395,004	106,572 (b)
Idaho	122,532	126,152	86,174	115,960	106,890	136,572	N.O.	157,185	126,048	(a-49)
Illinois	128,920	142,339	(a-42)	133,273	(a-10)	(a-35)	(a-6)	150,228	200,004	(a-49)
Indiana	133,110	168,500	81,159	134,415	159,878	88,997	(a-6)	175,000	192,560	(a-49)
Iowa	112,070	135,000	(a-17)	134,472	140,629	102,690	118,019	135,387	N.O.	163,634
Kansas	(c)	113,400	85,010	105,019	115,000	84,000	114,000	190,000	200,000	(a-49)
Kentucky	84,349	90,000	137,000	105,000	137,000	140,000	N.O.	157,500	275,000	120,000
Louisiana	130,000	102,149	113,464	137,197	(a-6)	123,614	(a-6)	236,001	350,000	176,900
Maine	91,270	(a-32)	(a-38)	139,734	(a-6)	139,734	115,586	170,477	N/A	(a-49)
Maryland	150,000 (b)	161,975 (b)	138,631 (b)	104,235 (b)	174,417 (b)	116,185 (b)	(a-6)	170,997 (b)	157,558 (b)	160,742
Massachusetts	143,000	161,522	135,000	139,050	161,522	129,000	158,000	140,000	220,763	153,536
Michigan	(a-47)	143,517	N/A	165,000	(a-10)	(c)	N.O.	175,000	N.O.	(a-49)
Minnesota	154,992	N.O.	140,000	150,002	154,992	137,599	(a-6)	150,002	390,000	154,992
Mississippi	120,000	135,315	90,000	129,347	(a-6)	147,216	N.O.	215,000	300,000	157,000
Missouri	101,458	108,004	103,020	111,100	118,473	(c)	99,668	143,420	176,750	179,256
Montana	95,100	105,820	131,427	111,895	115,495	111,904	102,515	111,895	320,122	(a-49)
Nebraska	88,549	134,172	152,249	152,249	(c)	117,260	160,001	153,772	187,180	151,840
Nevada	118,200	128,998	107,973	125,021	(a-14)	118,200	N.O.	(c)	N/A	(a-49)
New Hampshire	105,930	105,930	80,971	114,554	(a-10)	100,171	(a-6)	100,171	79,664	(a-49)
New Jersey	132,300	N/A	100,000	141,000	133,507	105,783	(c)	141,000	141,000	123,500
New Mexico	128,000	128,000	128,000	128,000	110,000	115,003	128,000	128,000	128,000	128,000
New York	136,000	127,000	120,800	136,000	151,500	136,000	136,000	136,000	250,000	136,000
North Carolina	109,068	122,815	104,000	145,129	195,352	141,382	N/A	192,560	775,000	164,511
North Dakota	98,916	187,500	208,000	136,116	170,000	128,136	170,000	170,004	372,000	(a-49)
Ohio	116,106	169,998	155,002	152,006	(c)	107,557	100,922	230,006	190,008	155,002
Oklahoma	135,000	115,110	140,000	136,913	170,000	140,000	110,750	189,000	412,031	(a-49)
Oregon	129,936	168,276	145,476	152,652	(a-4)	152,652	(c)	185,508	186,084	184,724
Pennsylvania	142,964	135,003	140,187	155,879	168,490	(c)	148,085	155,879	142,553	148,128
Rhode Island (g)	136,489	135,000	140,513	135,000	(a-44)	(a-23)	(a-6)	134,975	265,000 (c)	(a-49)
South Carolina	102,155	161,507	113,609	(c)	180,189	135,072	136,874	(c)	166,280	162,313
South Dakota	89,904	67,902	(a-42)	(a-35)	119,675	124,462	(a-6)	128,598	378,813	109,791
Tennessee	127,932	161,904	165,000	168,708	209,520	168,708	161,904	176,880	179,904	161,904
Texas	198,164	182,500	N.O.	211,415	(a-14)	200,643	177,982	242,353	212,135	(a-49)
Utah	98,945	147,992	124,176	140,004	139,672	114,004	104,000	202,425	N.O.	(a-49)
Vermont	81,660	121,056	118,726	118,726	127,088	101,920	121,056	148,262	N.O.	118,227
Virginia	148,860	161,679	99,419	190,188	175,980	N/A	167,214	225,000	199,479	212,661
Washington	N.O.	168,792	N.O.	168,792	(a-14)	168,300	(a-6)	168,792	N.O.	N.O
West Virginia	80,000	75,000	82,404	95,000	75,902	75,000	82,668	150,000	289,388	120,000
Wisconsin	109,075	114,130	92,477	113,027	130,000	113,027	(a-7)	150,010	525,000	(a-49)
Wyoming	100,147	142,000	100,000	130,577	N.O.	148,593	116,552	180,000	165,000	156,000
Guam	68,152	73,020	55,303	60,850	88,915	60,850	60,528	74,096	195,000	88,915
CNMI*	45,000	40,800 (b)	45,000	58,000	54,000	40,800 (b)	54,000	80,000	80,000	40,800 (b)
Puerto Rico	N/A	N/A	N/A	N/A	N/A	N/A	N/A	N/A	N/A	N/A
U.S. Virgin Islands	71,250	76,500	69,350	76,500	76,500	76,500	76,500	76,500	76,500	65,000

See footnotes at end of table

TABLE 4.11
Selected State Administrative Officials: Annual Salaries (continued)

State or other jurisdiction	Information systems (a-30)	Insurance (a-31)	Labor (a-32)	Licensing (a-33)	Mental health & developmental disabilities (a-34)	Natural resources (a-35)	Parks & recreation (a-36)	Personnel (a-37)	Planning (a-38)	Post audit (a-39)
Alabama	$177,266	$164,419	$139,859	N.O.	$152,618	$141,000	$100,198	$168,622	(a-12)	$241,695
Alaska	137,976	131,112	141,156	124,452	106,452	141,156	110,304	137,664	N.O.	(a-8)
Arizona	180,000	120,000	150,000	N.O.	120,058	175,000	175,000	130,000	(a-10)	N.O.
Arkansas	152,859	137,094	134,068	N.O.	134,406 (b)	116,160	134,405	125,665	N.O.	189,293
California	191,109	161,342	209,944	180,086	(c)	209,944	180,086	191,109	N.O.	N.O.
Colorado	165,000	159,996	170,000	145,704	153,996	170,004	161,952	N/A	160,584	(a-8)
Connecticut	176,960	175,000	157,000	118,362	(c)	151,223	155,767	140,000	150,000	(a-8)
Delaware	164,055	111,667	122,333	109,098	(c)	131,011	101,525	131,011	98,093	(a-8)
Florida	130,000	134,158	141,000	71,400	N/A	150,000	114,000	111,000	100,000	(a-24)
Georgia	160,000	120,394	122,786	89,309	175,000	175,000	119,882	140,000	(a-10)	(a-8)
Hawaii	200,004	122,052	147,444	101,508 (b)	131,952	147,444	106,572 (b)	147,444	106,572	106,572 (b)
Idaho	(a-6)	102,273	(a-21)	83,116	N.O.	129,771	91,561	99,548	N.O.	(a-14)
Illinois	(a-6)	135,081	124,090	(a-9)	(a-45)	133,273	(a-35)	(a-6)	N.O.	(a-8)
Indiana	131,402	115,895	115,895	110,376	119,195	125,700	92,302	114,400	N.O.	125,044
Iowa	140,400	128,890	112,070	N.O	128,066	128,890	(a-25)	127,317	N.O.	N.O.
Kansas	185,000	86,003	113,400	63,000	69,000	111,490	111,490	95,000	N.O.	115,296
Kentucky	375,000	103,000	137,000	N.O.	116,500	105,000	116,802	137,000	137,000	126,485
Louisiana	150,000	115,000	137,000	N.O.	130,000	129,210	117,300	145,704	124,946	N/A
Maine	130,811	115,274	139,734	139,734	(a-45)	139,734	(a-35)	118,934	N/A	N/A
Maryland	167,433 (b)	157,386 (b)	161,975 (b)	105,000 (b)	(b)(c)	159,312 (b)	116,053 (b)	141,365 (b)	135.048 (b)	73,361 (b)
Massachusetts	(a-44)	130,000	119,060	115,000	(c)	161,522	130,000	158,000	161,522	(a-8)
Michigan	165,000	(a-9)	165,000	(a-32)	289,193	165,000	135,907	181,927	N.O.	(a-8)
Minnesota	150,002	N/A	144,991	N.O.	154,992	154,992	137,599	(a-24)	N/A	(a-8)
Mississippi	173,209	90,000	N.O.	N.O.	170,180	129,347	147,216	145,000	86,407	(a-8)
Missouri	161,600	125,380	129,280	113,322	142,521	125,381	111,100	110,000	118,473	107,746
Montana	128,482	95,695	111,895	103,008	105,636	111,895	97,818	107,373	105,857	118,037
Nebraska	195,821	130,307	134,172	81,321	141,718	151,919	149,751	160,001	144,352	85,000
Nevada	118,200	118,200	98,880	N.O.	(c)	128,998	108,540	108,540	N.O.	N.O.
New Hampshire	117,913	105,930	105,930	105,930	105,930	114,554	91,965	88,933	N.O.	(a-14)
New Jersey	140,000	130,000	141,000	N.O.	(c)	125,000	110,000	141,000	95,000	N.O.
New Mexico	128,000	116,280	128,000	128,000	N.O.	128,000	91,799	128,000	77,721	85,000
New York	170,000	127,000	127,000	(c)	(c)	136,000	127,000	120,800	1 (d)	151,500
North Carolina	184,206	127,561	127,561	N.O.	N/A	152,944	120,597	142,100	N/A	(a-8)
North Dakota	190,000	105,770	208,000	N.O.	114,000	N.O.	112,000	120,000	N.O.	120,000
Ohio	144,997	150,571	N/A	(k)	(c)	169,998	114,816	119,662	155,002	(a-8)
Oklahoma	160,750	126,713	105,053	N.O.	173,318	126,508	141,000	110,750	N.O.	N.O.
Oregon	211,440	129,936	77,000	N.O.	136,488	N.O.	152,652	157,884	N.O.	(a-8)
Pennsylvania	150,006	140,291	155,879	119,433	148,128	148,085	140,715	146,211	148,069	(a-8)
Rhode Island (g)	205,706	(a-9)	(a-21)	(l)	135,000	(a-23)	(a-23)	146,994	102,860	N/A
South Carolina	173,400	143,420	127,950	127,950	(c)	135,072	132,806	136,290	N/A	109,976
South Dakota	129,268	99,619	112,805	N.O.	113,692	119,675	92,212	119,675	N.O.	(a-8)
Tennessee	207,420	161,904	161,904	125,364	161,904	168,708	119,676	161,904	N.O.	(a-14)
Texas	184,792	202,383	182,500	179,375	227,000	211,415	200,643	N.O.	205,000	(a-8)
Utah	131,996	125,008	130,000	119,850	112,736	140,004	113,235	125,590	(a-10)	(a-8)
Vermont	136,448	118,726	121,056	95,097	120,827	136,448	105,476	121,056	N.O.	(a-8)
Virginia	189,263	170,000	139,647	N/A	212,661	172,000	151,577	158,738	(a-10)	(a-8)
Washington	182,076	126,555	168,792	168,792	(a-45)	138,225	156,258	(a-14)	(a-14)	N.O.
West Virginia	127,500	92,500	70,000	N.O.	(a-27)	(a-25)	(a-25)	70,000	(a-17)	105,664
Wisconsin	126,901	130,000	140,005	130,000	133,474	147,000	113,027	N/A	N.O.	(a-8)
Wyoming	153,300	122,900	96,804	69,783	(c)	123,257	108,433	94,351	175,000	100,000
Guam	88,915	88,915	73,020	88,915	75,208	60,850	60,850	88,915	88,915	100,000
CNMI*	45,000	40,800 (b)	45,000	45,360	40,800 (b)	52,000	40,800 (b)	60,000	45,000	80,000
Puerto Rico	N/A	N/A	N/A	N/A	N/A	N/A	N/A	N/A	N/A	N/A
U.S. Virgin Islands	71,250	75,000	76,500	76,500	70,000	76,500	76,500	76,500	76,500	55,000

See footnotes at end of table

TABLE 4.11
Selected State Administrative Officials: Annual Salaries (continued)

State or other jurisdiction	Pre-audit (a-40)	Public library development (a-41)	Public utility regulation (a-42)	Purchasing (a-43)	Revenue (a-44)	Social services (a-45)	Solid waste mgmt. (a-46)	State police (a-47)	Tourism (a-48)	Transportation (a-49)	Welfare (a-50)
Alabama	(a-14)	$95,000	$103,490	$95,359	$164,419	$140,000	$105,403	$149,000	$91,014	(a-29)	(a-45)
Alaska	N.O.	137,664	133,332	120,144	141,156	(a-27)	110,304	141,156	122,988	141,156	142,140
Arizona	(a-14)	73,000	154,320	95,176	175,000	215,250	121,992	197,000	175,000	150,000	(a-45)
Arkansas	N/A	114,158	137,094	125,665	142,470	282,800	137,094	152,859	111,136	(a-29)	(a-45)
California	(a-14)	N.O.	158,573	(a-26)	205,816	244,274	180,086	274,300	N.O.	197,947	(a-45)
Colorado	(a-14)	145,500	140,928	121,248	166,812	N/A	150,000	94,932	126,708	170,000	171,444
Connecticut	(a-14)	150,797	N/A	149,423	190,400	190,400	144,021	183,340	155,000	190,750	190,400
Delaware	(a-8)	86,572	109,733	(a-26)	127,980	(c)	184,000	172,157	66,000	141,572	118,255
Florida	(a-24)	83,000	131,036	110,000	150,000	140,000	113,000	140,100	N.O.	141,000	N/A
Georgia	(a-8)	N/A	116,452	143,595	158,000	166,860	112,931	170,000	132,600	250,000	137,940
Hawaii	106,572 (b)	120,000	128,280	120,864	147,444	147,444	N/A	N.O.	270,000	147,444	101,508(b)
Idaho	(a-14)	96,636	95,899	(a-6)	88,908	(a-27)	N.O.	117,707	(a-12)	184,849	125,195
Illinois	(a-14)	102,252	130,008	(a-6)	142,339	150,228	(a-23)	132,566	(a-12)	150,228	142,339
Indiana	82,640	113,622	127,500	96,900	139,256	190,550	101,999	147,070	112,200	171,600	(a-45)
Iowa	111,259	117,832	128,890	110,302	154,300	154,300	(a-23)	110,240	102,066	147,014	128,066
Kansas	80,460	85,000	N/A	88,000	125,000	105,000	86,965	110,000	84,000	110,000	N.O.
Kentucky	N.O.	82,500	110,000	86,205	117,265	120,750	90,000	125,000	113,558	137,000	(a-45)
Louisiana	126,880	113,506	137,000	122,554	250,000	129,995	102,000	177,436	117,000	176,900	110,411
Maine	(a-14)	104,104	135,179	N/A	130,811	170,477	85,301	136,781	(a-17)	139,734	(a-45)
Maryland	114,752 (b)	123,236 (b)	165,565	(b)	132,569 (b)	167,488 (b)	140,489 (b)	167,661 (b)	113,763 (b)	174,419 (b)	(a-45)
Massachusetts	(a-8)	121,142	129,000	158,000	N/A	140,000	139,050	251,922	121,800	161,522	150,000
Michigan	N.O.	N.O.	140,000	150,420	134,077	175,000	130,082	165,000	N.O.	165,000	175,000
Minnesota	(a-8)	N/A	(c)	132,859	154,992	154,992	150,002	137,599	137,599	154,992	(a-34)
Mississippi	(a-8)	94,000	120,745	75,501	134,935	130,000	88,184	138,116	120,000	157,000	130,000
Missouri	99,668	80,808	109,847	99,668	129,526	143,420	78,864	N/A	80,800	179,256	101,772
Montana	(a-39)	102,335	108,282	91,855	111,895	(a-27)	93,400	110,620	89,473	111,895	(a-27)
Nebraska	140,000	109,051	137,025	120,001	163,781	220,001	100,630	152,249	104,449	151,840	220,001
Nevada	N.O.	(c)	125,021	98,880	128,998	128,998	(a-23)	128,998	118,200	128,998	(c)
New Hampshire	(a-14)	91,965	111,687	75,410	117,913	121,896	100,171	105,930	91,965	117,913	100,171
New Jersey	N.O.	N.O.	125,301	130,000	128,000	(c)	108,128	132,300	92,490	141,000	127,200
New Mexico	92,032	N/A	90,000	101,001	128,000	128,000	91,480	128,000	128,000	128,000	128,000
New York	151,500	250,000	127,000	136,000	N/A	136,000	136,000	136,000	1 (d)	136,000	136,000
North Carolina	(a-8)	110,704	141,947	N/A	145,218	138,290	108,605	125,260	82,066	195,352	N/A
North Dakota	N/A	N/A	108,656	103,272	114,791	182,004	84,000	125,004	126,864	170,000	182,004
Ohio	(a-10)	110,552	N/A	107,952	155,002	(c)	98,218	155,002	107,910	155,002	169,998
Oklahoma	(a-14)	96,000	(c)	105,750	162,500	185,000	112,806	136,471	141,000	150,000	185,000
Oregon	(a-10)	138,504	160,285	123,828	168,276	185,508	N.O.	168,276	N.O.	185,103	(a-45)
Pennsylvania	(a-4)	142,553	150,585	140,715	148,085	155,879	140,187	154,248	140,715	155,879	155,879
Rhode Island (g)	(a-14)	113,146	117,412	125,874	130,100	(c)	(m)	148,937	(a-17)	135,000	(a-45)
South Carolina	(a-14)	108,207	169,820	124,773	174,966	168,043	146,618	162,313	132,806	187,200	(a-45)
South Dakota	76,694	84,513	104,611	62,897	113,692	124,462	N/A	109,791	112,676	124,462	(a-45)
Tennessee	163,248	139,944	164,688	162,408	163,800	161,904	137,760	161,904	161,904	161,904	161,904
Texas	(a-14)	143,500	159,782	168,000	(a-14)	220,000	N.O.	232,969	164,701	299,812	275,000
Utah	(a-24)	117,520	101,836	(a-26)	84,032	131,081	122,928	121,534	123,905	163,425	(a-45)
Vermont	127,088	98,176	150,737	121,056	121,056	136,448	118,726	136,448	99,195	136,448	121,056
Virginia	(a-14)	153,585	(c)	135,000	164,651	209,000	190,188	184,705	183,890	212,661	209,000
Washington	(a-4)	(a-2)	142,596	N.O.	168,792	190,392	N.O.	192,888	N.O.	194,136	(a-45)
West Virginia	(a-8)	72,000	90,000	90,160	95,000	(a-27)	82,364	85,000	87,160	92,160	(a-27)
Wisconsin	(a-8)	126,006	128,502	103,646	144,997	135,013	113,027	115,794	130,000	145,018	119,018
Wyoming	(a-8)	105,600	121,692	84,960	126,994	(a-27)	115,620	124,152	139,000	(a-29)	(a-45)
Guam	88,915	55,303	1,200	88,915	88,915	74,096	88,915	74,096	88,591	N.O.	74,096
CNMI*	54,000	45,000	80,000	40,800 (b)	45,000	40,800 (b)	54,000	54,000	70,000	40,800 (b)	52,000
Puerto Rico	N/A	N/A	N/A	N/A	N/A	N/A	N/A	N/A	108,000	N/A	N/A
U.S. Virgin Islands	76,500	53,350	54,500	76,500	76,500	76,500	76,500	76,500	76,500	65,000	76,500

See footnotes at end of table

TABLE 4.11

Selected State Administrative Officials: Annual Salaries (continued)

Source: The Council of State Governments' survey of state personnel agencies and state websites, May 2019.

*Commonwealth of Northern Mariana Islands

Key:

N/A–Not available.

N.O.–No specific chief administrative official or agency in charge of function.

(a) Chief administrative official or agency in charge of function:
(a-1) Lieutenant governor.
(a-2) Secretary of state.
(a-3) Attorney general.
(a-4) Treasurer.
(a-5) Adjutant general.
(a-6) Administration.
(a-7) Agriculture.
(a-8) Auditor.
(a-9) Banking.
(a-10) Budget.
(a-11) Civil rights.
(a-12) Commerce.
(a-13) Community affairs.
(a-14) Comptroller.
(a-15) Consumer affairs.
(a-16) Corrections.
(a-17) Economic development.
(a-18) Education (chief state school officer).
(a-19) Election administration.
(a-20) Emergency administration.
(a-21) Employment Services.
(a-22) Energy.
(a-23) Environmental protection.
(a-24) Finance.
(a-25) Fish and wildlife.
(a-26) General services.
(a-27) Health.
(a-28) Higher education.
(a-29) Highways.
(a-30) Information systems.
(a-31) Insurance.
(a-32) Labor.
(a-33) Licensing.
(a-34) Mental Health.
(a-35) Natural resources.
(a-36) Parks and recreation.
(a-37) Personnel.
(a-38) Planning.
(a-39) Post audit.
(a-40) Pre-audit.
(a-41) Public library development.
(a-42) Public utility regulation.
(a-43) Purchasing.
(a-44) Revenue.
(a-45) Social services.
(a-46) Solid waste management.
(a-47) State police.
(a-48) Tourism.
(a-49) Transportation.
(a-50) Welfare.
(b) Salary ranges, top figure in ranges follow:
Arkansas: Mental Health and Developmental Disabilities, $167,000.
Hawaii: Employment Services, $177,408; Energy, $177,408; Fish and Wildlife, $177,408; Highway, $177,408; Licensing, $168,936; Parks and Recreation, $177,408; Planning, $177,408; Post-Audit, $177,408; Pre-Audit, $177,408; Welfare, $168,936.
Maryland: For these positions the salary in the chart is the actual salary and the following are the salary ranges: Adjutant General, $114,874–$153,532; Administration, $114,874–$153,532; Agriculture, $114,874–$153,532; Banking, $73,612–$118,197; Budget, $133,069–$177,977; Civil Rights, $92,333–$123,236; Commerce, $133,069–$177,977; Consumer Affairs, $83,836–$134,749; Corrections, $133,069–$177,977; Economic Development, $133,069–$177,977; Elections Administration, $99,275–$132,569; Emergency Management, $114,784–$153,532; Workforce Development, $123,618–$165,281; Energy, $99,275–$132,569; Environmental Protection, $123,618–$165,281; Finance, $133,069–177,977; Fish and Wildlife, $92,333–$123,236; Health, $133,069–$177,977; Higher Education, $123,618–$165,281; Information Services, $133,069–$177,977; Insurance, $133,069–$177,977; Labor, $123,618–$165,281; Licensing, $92,333–$123,236; Mental Health shared duties, $154,064–$254,576 (vacant at press time) and $114,874–$153,532 (actual, $140,526); Natural Resources, $123,618–$165,281; Parks and Recreation, $78,596–$126,186; Personnel, $106,773–$142,646; Planning, $114,874–$153,532; Post-Audit, $53,193–$85,401; Pre-Audit, $99,275–$132,569; Public Library, $92,333–$123,236; Public Utility Regulation, $153,027–$256,866, Purchasing, $85,902–114,600 (vacant at press time); Revenue, $99,275–$132,569; Social Services, $133,069–$177,977; Solid Waste Management, $106,773–$142,646; State Police, $133,069–$177,977; Tourism, $106,773–$142,646; Transportation, $133,069–$177,977; Welfare, $92,333–$123,236.
Northern Mariana Islands: $49,266 top of range applies to the following positions: Treasurer, Banking, Comptroller, Corrections, Employment Services, Fish and Wildlife, Highways, Insurance, Mental Health and Retardation, Parks and Recreation, Purchasing, Social/Human Services, Transportation.
(c) Responsibilities shared between:
California–Health–Responsibilities shared between Director Jennifer Kent of Health Care Services, $207,850 and Director Karen L. Smith, Department of Public Health, $266,329.
California–Mental health & developmental disabilities–Responsibilities shared between Director of State Hospitals, $207,844 and Director Nancy A. Baumann of Developmental Services, $207,850.
Connecticut–Auditor–Responsibilities shared between John C. Geragosian, $178,590 and Robert J. Kane, $150,263.
Connecticut–Fish and Wildlife–Responsibilities shared between Chief Richard Jacobson of Wildlife, $151,223 and Director Peter Aarrestad of Inland and Marine Fisheries, $128,962.
Connecticut–Mental Health & Developmental Disabilities–Responsibilities shared between Commissioner Miriam Delphin-Rittmon

TABLE 4.11
Selected State Administrative Officials: Annual Salaries (continued)

Mental Health: $160,000 and Commissioner Jordan Scheff, Dept. of Developmental Services: $168,000.

Delaware–The Dept. of Administration was abolished in 2005. Responsibilities are now shared between the Office of Management and Budget, General Services and Dept. of State.

Delaware–The Delaware Economic Development Office was abolished in FY 2019; most responsibilities assigned to a new public-private partnership.

Delaware–Mental Health–Responsibilities shared between Director, Division of Substance Abuse and Mental Health, Department of Health and Social Services, $147,376 and Director, Division of Developmental Disabilities Service, same department, $118,150.

Delaware–Social Services–Function split between two cabinet positions: Secretary, Dept. of Health and Social Services: $151,088 and Secretary, Dept. of Svcs. for Children, Youth and their Families, $136,240.

Hawaii–Administration–There is no single agency for Administration. The functions are divided among the Director of Budget and Finance, Director of Human Resources Development and the Comptroller.

Hawaii–Finance–Responsibilities shared between Director Roderick K. Becker of Budget and Finance, $154,812 and Comptroller Curt T. Otaguro, $147,444.

Indiana–Elections Administration–Responsibilities shared between Co-Directors Brad King, $79,129 and Angela Nussmeyer, $78,555.

Kansas–Emergency Management–Responsibilities shared between Adjutant General, $106,392 and deputy director, $75,608.

Maryland–Mental Health–Responsibilities shared between Executive Director of Mental Hygiene Administration, salary range $154,064–$254,576 (position vacant at press time) and Secretary, Dept. of Disabilities ,$140,525, salary range $114,874–$153,532.

Massachusetts–Mental Health–Responsibilities shared between Commissioners Joan Mikula, $157,982 and Elin M. Howe, $153,511.

Michigan–Elections Administration–Responsibilities shared between Secretary of State, $112,410 and Director of Elections, $136,058.

Michigan–Fish and Wildlife–Responsibilities shared between Chief of Fisheries, Jim Dexter, $136,058 and Chief of Wildlife, James Russ Mason, $132,874.

Minnesota–Public Utility Regulation–Responsibilities shared between four commissioners with salaries of $140,000 for each.

Missouri–Fish and Wildlife–Responsibilities shared between Administrator, Division of Fisheries, Department of Conservation, position vacant; Administrator, Division of Wildlife, same department, $86,724.

Nebraska–Finance–Responsibilities shared between, Auditor of Public Accounts, Charlie Janssen–$85,000; Director of Administration, Gerry Oligmueller–$164,303 and State Tax Commissioner, Tony Fulton–$163,781.

Nevada–Elections Administration–Responsibilities shared between Secretary of State, $102,898; Deputy Secretary of State for Elections, $108,540 and Chief Deputy, Secretary of State, $118,200.

Nevada–Health–Responsibilities shared between Richard Whitley, Director, Health and Human Services, $128,998 and Cody Phinney, Division Administrator, DPBH, $125,021.

Nevada–Mental Health–Responsibilities shared between Director,

Health and Human Services, $128,998 and Division Administrator, $125,021.

Nevada–Public Library Development–Responsibilities shared between Director, Department of Tourism and Cultural Affairs, $118,200 and Division Administrator, Library and Archives, $98,880.

Nevada–Welfare–Responsibilities shared between Richard Whitley, Director, Health and Human Services, $128,998 and Steve Fisher, Division Administrator, Welfare and Support Services, $118,200.

New Jersey–General Services–Responsibilities shared between Jignasa Desai Director, Division of Purchase and Property, Dept. of the Treasury, $130,000 and Steven Sutkin, Director, Division of Property Management and Construction, Dept. of the Treasury, $130,000.

New Jersey–Mental Health–Responsibilities shared between Assistant Commissioner Lynn Kovich, Division of Mental Health Services, Dept. of Human Services, $128,000 and position of Assistant Commissioner Elizabeth Shea, Division of Developmental Disabilities, Dept. of Human Services, $128,000.

New Jersey–Social Services–Responsibilities shared between Jennifer Velez, Commissioner, Department of Human Services, $141,000 and Allison Blake, Commissioner, Department of Children and Families, $141,000.

New York–Licensing–Responsibilities shared between Commissioner, State Education Department, $250,000; Secretary of State, Department of State, $120,800.

New York–Mental Health–Responsibilities shared between Commissioner of Office for People with Developmental Disabilities, $136,000 and Commissioner of Office of Mental Health, $136,000.

Ohio–Finance–Responsibilities shared between, Assistant Director of Budget and Management,$153,005 and Deputy Director, Office of Budget and Management, $119,538.

Ohio–Mental Health–Responsibilities shared between Director of Dept. of Developmental Disabilities, $150,010 and Director, Dept. of Mental Health and Addiction Services, $165,006.

Ohio–Social Services–Responsibilities shared between Director, Dept. of Job and Family Services, $169,998; Superintendent of Public Instruction Dept. of Education, $189,571; Executive Director Opportunities for Ohioans with Disabilities, $130,000 and Director of Dept. of Aging, $137,072.

Oklahoma–Public Utility Regulation–Responsibilities shared between three Commissioners, Commissioner Bob Anthony, $114,713, Commissioner Dana Murphy, $116,713 and Commissioner Jimmie Hiett, $116,713 and Timothy Rhodes, Director of Administration Div., $142,000.

Pennsylvania–Fish and Wildlife–Responsibilities shared between Executive Director (Fish), $144,157 and Executive Director (Game), $132,010.

Rhode Island–Higher Education–Serves a dual role as Commissioner of Higher Education and as the President of the Community College of Rhode Island.

Rhode Island–Social Services–Responsibilities shared between Commissioner, Office of Health and Human Services,$141,828 and Director of the Dept. of Human Services, $135,000, and reports to the Commissioner, Office of Health and Human Services.

South Carolina–Environmental Protection–Responsibilities shared

TABLE 4.11

Selected State Administrative Officials: Annual Salaries (continued)

between Acting Director David Wilson, $146,618 (BS) and Director Alvin Taylor $135,072 (B).

South Carolina–Health–Responsibilities shared between Director of Health and Human Services Joshua Baker, $168,043 and Director of Health and Environmental Control David Wilson, $146,618.

South Carolina–Mental Health–Responsibilities shared between Interim Director for Disabilities and Special Needs, Patrick Maley, $106,000 and Director of Mental Health, John Magill $214,901.

Texas–Elections Administration–Responsibilities shared between Secretary of State, $197,415; and Division Director, $132,600.

U.S. Virgin Islands–Community Affairs–Responsibilities for St. Thomas, $74,400; St. Croix, $76,500; St. John, $74,400.

Virginia–Public Utility Regulation–Functions shared between William F. "Bill" Stephens; Energy Regulation, $175,100; Utility and Railroad Safety, Stephen C. Bradley, $164,181.

Wyoming–Mental Health–Responsibilities shared between State Hospital, Heather Babbitt, $116,527 and Life Resource Center, William Rein, $150,000.

(d) These individuals have voluntarily taken no salary or a reduced salary:

Connecticut–Governor Ned Lamont will forego his salary of $150,000.

Illinois–Governor Pritzker will not take his salary of $177,412.

Nevada–Governor Sisolak pledged to donate his salary to K-12 schools all four years of his term.

New York–Howard A. Zemsky–takes $1 of his salary of $120,800. He is the chair and Commissioner of Empire State Development, which oversees Commerce, Economic Development, Planning and Tourism.

North Dakota–Governor Doug Burgum has declined his salary of $129,096.

(e) In Maine, New Hampshire, Tennessee and West Virginia, the presidents (or speakers) of the Senate are next in line of succession to the governorship. In Tennessee and West Virginia, the speaker of the Senate bears the statutory title of lieutenant governor.

(g) A number of the employees receive a stipend for their length of service to the State (known as a longevity payment). This amount can vary significantly among employees and, depending on state turnover, can show dramatic changes in actual salaries from year to year.

(h) $68,680 part-time.

(i) The statutory salary for each of the four members of the Board of Elections is $25,000, including the two co-chairs, Douglas A. Kellner and Peter S. Kosinski.

(j) The Rhode Island Economic Development Corporation is a quasi-public agency. The salary shown is for the previous director.

(k) Numerous licensing boards, too many to list.

(l) Varies by department.

(m) Solid waste is managed by the Rhode Island Resource Recovery Corporation (RIRRC). Although not a department of the state government, RIRRC is a public corporation and a component of the State of Rhode Island for financial reporting purposes. To be financially self-sufficient, the agency earns revenue through the sale of recyclable products, methane gas royalties and fees for it services.

TABLE 4.12
The Lieutenant Governors, 2019

State or other jurisdiction	Name and party	Method of selection	Length of regular term in years	Date of first service	Present term ends	Number of previous terms	Joint election of governor and lieutenant governor (a)
Alabama	Will Ainsworth (R)	CE	4	1/2019	1/2023	...	No
Alaska	Kevin Meyer (R)	CE	4	12/2018	12/2022	...	Yes
Arizona	------(b)------						
Arkansas	Tim Griffin (R)	CE	4	1/2015	1/2023	...	No
California	Eleni Kounalakis (D)	CE	4	1/2019	1/2023	...	No
Colorado	Dianne Primavera (D)	CE	4	1/2019	1/2023	...	Yes
Connecticut	Susan Bysiewicz (D)	CE	4	1/2019	1/2023	...	Yes
Delaware	Bethany Hall-Long (D)	CE	4	1/2017	1/2021	...	No
Florida	Jeanette Núñez (R)	CE	4	1/2019	1/2023	...	Yes
Georgia	Geoff Duncan (R)	CE	4	1/2019	1/2023	...	No
Hawaii	Joshua B. Green (D)	CE	4	1/2019	1/2023	...	Yes
Idaho	Janice McGeachin (R)	CE	4	1/2019	1/2023	...	No
Illinois	Juliana Stratton (D)	CE	4	1/2019	1/2023	...	Yes
Indiana	Suzanne Crouch (R)	CE	4	1/2017	1/2021	...	Yes
Iowa	Adam Gregg (R)	CE	4	5/2017 (c)	1/2023	...	Yes
Kansas	Lynn Rogers (D)	CE	4	1/2019	1/2023	...	Yes
Kentucky	Jenean Hampton (R)	CE	4	12/2015	12/2019	...	Yes
Louisiana	Billy Nungesser (R)	CE	4	1/2016	1/2020	...	No
Maine	------(b)------						
Maryland	Boyd Rutherford (R)	CE	4	1/2015	1/2023	1	Yes
Massachusetts	Karyn Polito (R)	CE	4	1/2015	1/2023	1	Yes
Michigan	Garlin Gilchrist II (D)	CE	4	1/2019	1/2023	...	Yes
Minnesota	Peggy Flanagan (DFL)	CE	4	1/2019	1/2023	...	Yes
Mississippi	Tate Reeves (R)	CE	4	1/2012	1/2020	1	No
Missouri	Mike Kehoe (R) (q)	CE	4	(d)	(d)	...	No
Montana	Mike Cooney (D)	CE	4	1/2017	1/2021	...	Yes
Nebraska	Mike Foley (R)	CE	4	1/2015	1/2023	1	Yes
Nevada	Kate Marshall (D)	CE	4	1/2019	1/2023	...	No
New Hampshire	------(b)------						
New Jersey	Sheila Oliver (D)	CE	4	1/2018	1/2022	1	Yes
New Mexico	Henry "Howie" C. Morales (D)	CE	4	1/2019	1/2023	...	Yes
New York	Kathy Hochul (D)	CE	4	1/2015	1/2023	1	Yes
North Carolina	Dan Forest (R)	CE	4	1/2013	1/2021	1	No
North Dakota	Brent Sanford (R)	CE	4	12/2017	12/2020	...	Yes
Ohio	John Husted (R)	SE	4	1/2019	1/2023	...	Yes
Oklahoma	Matt Pinnell (R)	CE	4	1/2019	1/2023	...	No
Oregon	------(b)------						
Pennsylvania	John Fetterman (D)	CE	4	1/2019	1/2023	...	Yes
Rhode Island	Dan McKee (D)	SE	4	1/2015	1/2023	1	No
South Carolina	Pamela Evette (R)	CE	4	1/2019	1/2023	...	No
South Dakota	Larry Rhoden (R)	CE	4	1/2019	1/2023	...	Yes
Tennessee	Randy McNally (R)	(f)	2	1/2019	1/2021	1	No
Texas	Dan Patrick (R)	CE	4	1/2015	1/2023	1	No
Utah	Spencer J. Cox (R)	CE	4	10/2013 (e)	1/2021	1	Yes
Vermont	David Zuckerman (D)	CE	2	1/2017	1/2021	1	No
Virginia	Justin Fairfax (D)	CE	4	1/2018	1/2022	...	No
Washington	Cyrus Habib (D)	CE	4	1/2017	1/2021	...	No
West Virginia	Mitch Carmichael (R)	(g)	2	1/2017	1/2021	1	No
Wisconsin	Mandela Barnes (D)	CE	4	1/2019	1/2023	...	Yes (h)
Wyoming	------(b)------						
American Samoa	Lemanu Peleti Mauga (D)	CE	4	1/2013	1/2021	...	Yes
Guam	Josh Tenorio (D)	CE	4	1/2019	1/2013	...	Yes
CNMI*	Arnold Palacios (R)	CE	4	1/2019	1/2023	...	Yes
Puerto Rico	------(b)------						
U.S. Virgin Islands	Tregenza Roach (I)	SE	SE	1/2019	1/2023	...	Yes

See footnotes at end of table

TABLE 4.12
The Lieutenant Governors, 2019 (continued)

Source: The Council of State Governments, Jan. 2019.
*Commonwealth of the Northern Mariana Islands
Key:
…–Not applicable.
C–Covenant
CE–Constitutional, elected by public.
D–Democrat
DFL–Democratic-Farmer-Labor Party
I–Independent
LG–Lieutenant Governor
PDP–Popular Democratic Party
R–Republican
SE–Statutorily elected.
(a) The following also choose candidates for governor and
lieutenant governor through a joint nomination process: Florida,
Kansas, Maryland, Minnesota, Montana, North Dakota, Ohio, Utah,
American Samoa, Guam, No. Mariana Islands, and U.S. Virgin
Islands. For additional information see The National Lieutenant
Governors Association website at *http://www.nlga.us.*
(b) No lieutenant governor.
(c) Gov. Kim Reynolds appointed Adam Gregg, the state's public
defender, as lieutenant governor when she ascended to the office
upon Terry Branstad's resignation. She and Gregg ran for and were
elected to a full term in the 2018 general election.
(d) Mike Parson became Governor upon the resignation of Eric
Greitens. There is no provision for filling this office. The President

Pro Tem of the Missouri Senate is next in line to become governor,
followed by Speaker of the House, and Secretary of State. On
June 18, 2018, Governor Mike Parson appointed Mike Kehoe
(R), as Lieutenant Governor. The appointment comes with legal
uncertainty, as the Constitution of Missouri states that
the governor can fill all vacancies "other than in the offices of
lieutenant governor, state senator or representative … ." However,
Parson stated that he believed that the Constitution gave him
authority to name Kehoe as lieutenant governor."
(e) Spencer J. Cox was appointed to the office of lieutenant
governor in Oct. 2013 after Lt. Gov. Greg Bell resigned to return to
the private sector.
(f) In Tennessee, the president of the senate and the lieutenant
governor are one in the same. The legislature provided in statute
the title of lieutenant governor upon the senate president. The
senate president serves two-year terms, elected by the Senate on
the first day of the first session of each two year legislative term.
(g) In West Virginia, the president of the senate and the lieutenant
governor are one in the same. The legislature provided in statute
the title of lieutenant governor upon the senate president. The
senate president serves two-year terms, elected by the Senate on
the first day of the first session of each two year legislative term.
(h) The governor and lt. governor are elected on a joint ticket at the
November general election. However, they run on separate party
primary ballots in the August primary election.

TABLE 4.13
Lieutenant Governors: Qualifications and Terms

State or other jurisdiction	Minimum age	State citizen (years)	U.S. citizen (years) (a)	State resident (years) (b)	Qualified voter (years)	Length of term (years)	Maximum consecutive terms allowed
Alabama	30	7	10	7	…	4	2
Alaska	30	7	7	7	★	4	2
Arizona				(c)			
Arkansas	30	7	★	7	…	4	2
California	18	★	★	5	★	4	2
Colorado	30	…	★	2	…	4	2
Connecticut	30	★	★	★	★	4	…
Delaware	30	★	12	6	★	4	…
Florida	30	★	★	7	★	4	2
Georgia	30	10	★	15	★	4	…
Hawaii	30	5	★	5	★	4	2
Idaho	30	…	★	2	…	4	…
Illinois	25	…	★	3	…	4	…
Indiana	30	★	★	★	★	4	2
Iowa	30	…	2	2	…	4	…
Kansas	…	…	…	…	…	4	2
Kentucky	30	6	★	★	★	4	2
Louisiana	25	5	5	5	…	4	…
Maine				(c)			
Maryland	30	★	★	★	★	4	…
Massachusetts	…	★	★	★	★	4	…
Michigan	30	★	★	4	4	4	2 (d)
Minnesota	25	…	★	1	…	4	…
Mississippi	30	…	20	5	★	4	2
Missouri	30	10	15	10	…	4	…
Montana	25	2	★	2	…	4	2 (e)
Nebraska	30	5	★	5	★	4	2
Nevada	25	2	★	2	★	4	2
New Hampshire				(c)			
New Jersey	30	…	20	7	…	4	2
New Mexico	30	★	★	5	★	4	2
New York	30	★	★	5	★	4	…
North Carolina	30	…	5	2	…	4	2
North Dakota	30	5	…	…	…	4	…
Ohio	18	…	★	★	★	4	2
Oklahoma	31	10	★	★	★	4	…
Oregon				(c)			
Pennsylvania	30	★	★	7	★	4	2
Rhode Island	18	★	★	★	★	4	2
South Carolina	30	5	5	5	★	4	2
South Dakota	21	2	★	2	★	4	2
Tennessee (f)	30	★	★	3	1	2	…
Texas	30	…	★	5	…	4	…
Utah	30	★	★	★	★	4	…
Vermont	18	4	★	4	★	2	…
Virginia	30	…	★	5	5	4	…
Washington	18	★	★	★	★	4	…
West Virginia (g)	25	5	…	5	★	2	…
Wisconsin	18	★	★	★	★	4	…
Wyoming				(c)			
American Samoa	35	(h)	★	5	★	4	2
Guam	30	…	5	5	★	4	2
CNMI*	35	★	★	★	★	4	2
Puerto Rico				(c)			
U.S. Virgin Islands	30	…	5	5	5	4	2

See footnotes at end of table

TABLE 4.13
Lieutenant Governors: Qualifications and Terms (continued)

Source: The Council of State Government's survey of state government websites, March 2019.

*Commonwealth of the Northern Mariana Islands

Note: This table includes constitutional and statutory qualifications.

Key:

★ –Formal provision; number of years not specified.

… –No formal provision.

(a) In some states you must be a U.S. citizen to be an elector, and must be an elector to run.

(b) In some states you must be a state resident to be an elector, and must be an elector to run.

(c) No lieutenant governor.

(d) In 1993 a constitutional limit of two lifetime terms in the office was enacted.

(e) Eligible for eight out of 16 years.

(f) In Tennessee, the speaker of the senate, elected from Senate membership, has statutory title of "lieutenant governor."

(g) In West Virginia, the president of the senate and the lieutenant governor are one in the same. The legislature provided in statute the title of lieutenant governor upon the senate president. The senate president serves two-year terms, elected by the Senate on the first day of the first session of each two year legislative term.

(h) Must be a U.S. national.

TABLE 4.14
Lieutenant Governors: Powers and Duties

State or other jurisdiction	Presides over Senate	Appoints committees	Breaks roll-call ties	Assigns bills	Authority for governor to assign duties	Member of governor's cabinet or advisory body	Serves as acting governor when governor out of state	Other duties (a)
Alabama	★	...	★	★	...	...	★(b)	...
Alaska	...	...	...	...	★	★	...	(c)
Arizona	--(d)--							
Arkansas	★	...	★	...	...	...	...	(c)
California	★(r)	...	★	...	★	...	★	(c)
Colorado	...	...	...	...	★	★	★	(c)
Connecticut	★	...	★	...	★	...	★	(c)
Delaware	★	...	★	...	...	...	...	(c)
Florida	...	...	...	...	★	...	...	...
Georgia	★	★	...	★	★	★	...	(c)
Hawaii	...	...	...	...	★	...	★	(c)
Idaho	★	...	★	...	★	...	★	...
Illinois	...	...	...	...	★	★	...	(c)
Indiana	★	...	★	...	...	...	...	(c)
Iowa	...	(e)	...	...	★	(f)	(g)	...
Kansas	...	...	...	...	...	★	...	...
Kentucky	...	...	...	...	★	...	(h)	(c)
Louisiana	...	...	...	...	★	★	★	(c)
Maine	--(i)--							
Maryland	...	...	...	...	★	★	...	...
Massachusetts	...	★	...	...	★	★	★	(c)
Michigan	★	...	★	...	★	★	★(j)	(c)
Minnesota	...	...	...	...	★	...	★	(c)
Mississippi	★	★	★	★	...	...	★	(c)
Missouri	★	...	★	...	★	...	★	(c)
Montana	...	...	...	...	★	★	(q)	...
Nebraska	★(k)	...	★	...	...	★	★	...
Nevada	★	...	★(l)	...	...	★	★	...
New Hampshire	--(i)--							
New Jersey	...	...	...	...	★	★	★	(c)
New Mexico	★	...	★	...	...	★	★	...
New York	★	...	★(m)	...	★	★	★	...
North Carolina	★	...	★	...	★	...	★	(c)
North Dakota	★	...	...	...	...	★	...	...
Ohio	...	...	...	...	★	★	...	...
Oklahoma	★(n)	...	★	...	...	...	★	(c)
Oregon	--(d)--							
Pennsylvania	★	...	★	...	...	...	...	(c)
Rhode Island	...	★	...	★	★	...	★	(c)
South Carolina	★	★	★	★	...	★	★	(c)
South Dakota	★	...	★	...	★	★	★	(c)
Tennessee	★	★	★	★	...	...	...	...
Texas	★	★	★	★	...	...	★	...
Utah	...	...	...	...	...	★	...	(c)
Vermont	★	★(o)	★	★(o)	...	★	★	...
Virginia	★	...	★	...	...	★	...	...
Washington	★	★	★	...	...	...	★	...
West Virginia	★	★	...	★	...	...	...	(c)
Wisconsin	...	...	...	...	★	★	★	...
Wyoming	--(d)--							
American Samoa	...	...	...	...	...	...	★	...
Guam	(k)	...	...	...	★	★	★	...
CNMI*	...	...	...	...	...	★	★	(c)
Puerto Rico	--(d)--							
U.S. Virgin Islands	...	...	...	...	★(f)	★	★	...

See footnotes at end of table

TABLE 4.14
Lieutenant Governors: Powers and Duties (continued)

Sources: The Council of State Governments' survey of state government websites, March 2019.
*Commonwealth of Northern Mariana Islands
Key:
★–Provision for responsibility.
…–No provision for responsibility.
(a) Lieutenant governors may obtain duties through gubernatorial appointment, statute, the Constitution, direct democracy action, or personal initiative. Hence, an exhaustive list of duties is not maintained, but this chart provides examples which are not all inclusive.
(b) The lieutenant governor performs the duties of the governor in the event of the governor's death, impeachment, disability, or absence from the state for more than 20 days.
(c) Alaska–The lieutenant governor bears these additional responsibilities: Alaska Historical Commission Chair; Alaska Workforce Investment Board; supervise the Division of Elections; supervise the certification process for citizen ballot initiative and referenda; provide constituent care and communications; lend support to governor's legislative and administrative initiatives; sign and file regulations; publish the Alaska Administrative Code and the Online Public Notice System; commission notaries public; regulate commercial and advertising use of State Seal, and the National Lieutenant Governors' Association; Arctic Winter Games.
Arkansas–Lieutenant Governor Tim Griffin gets to appoint a member to two commissions: the Judicial Discipline and Disability Commission and the Ethics Commission.
California–Lieutenant governor is an ex-officio regent, University of California Board of Regents; ex-officio regent, California State University Board of Trustees; chair, California Commission for Economic Development; member and current chair, California State Lands Commission (chair rotates annually between Lt. Governor and State Controller); member, California Ocean Protection Council (membership rotates with chair of State Lands Commission); and ex-officio commissioner of the California Coastal Commission (membership rotates with chair of State Lands Commission).
Colorado–Additional responsibilities include: chair of the Colorado Commission of Indian Affairs (by statute); may be appointed by the governor to concurrently serve as the head of a department (by statute).
Connecticut–The lieutenant governor is a member of the Finance Advisory Committee, the Commission on Intergovernmental Cooperation and the Corporation of Yale University.
Delaware–Serves as president of the Board of Pardons.
Georgia–The lieutenant governor, by statute, is responsible for board, commission and committee appointments. In addition the lieutenant governor appoints conference committees, rules on germaneness, and must sign all acts of the General Assembly. Also statutorily serves on the Georgia State Financing and Investment Commission, One Georgia Board and the Georgia Aviation Authority.
Hawaii–Also serves as Secretary of State.
Illinois–The lt. governor serves on or chairs several bodies according to statute and executive order including the: Illinois River Coordinating Council, Mississippi River Coordinating Council, Wabash and Ohio River Coordinating Council, Military Economic Development

Committee, Governor's Rural Affairs Council, Illinois Farmers Market Task Force, Illinois Local Food, Farms, & Jobs Council, Commission to End Hunger, Illinois Main Street, Housing Task Force, Commission to Eliminate Poverty, ISBE/ROE Service Evaluation Committee, Charitable Trust Stabilization Committee, Opioid Overdose Prevention & Intervention Task Force, Local Government Consolidation & Unfunded Mandates Task Force, and Illinois School Funding Reform Commission.
Indiana–Serves as Secretary of Agriculture and Rural Development. Oversees six state agencies: Department of Agriculture, Office of Community and Rural Affairs, Office of Defense Development, Office of Tourism Development, Indiana Small Business Development Center and the Indiana Housing and Community Development Authority.
Louisiana–Serves as commissioner of the Department of Culture, Recreation & Tourism.
Kentucky–In addition to the duties set forth by the Kentucky Constitution, state law also gives the lieutenant governor the responsibility to act as chair, or serve as a member, on various boards and commissions. Some of these include: the State Property and Buildings Commission, Kentucky Turnpike Authority and Board of the Kentucky Housing Corporation. The governor also has the power to give the lieutenant governor other specific job duties.
Massachusetts–The lieutenant governor is a member of, and presides over, the Governor's Council, an elected body of 8 members which approves all judicial nominations.
Michigan–The lieutenant governor serves as a member of the State Administrative Board; and represents the governor and the state at selected local, state, and national meetings. In addition the governor may delegate additional responsibilities.
Minnesota–Serves as the Chair of the Capitol Area Architectural and Planning Board Committee.
Mississippi–The lieutenant governor also appoints chairs of standing committees, appoints conferees to committees and is a member of the Legislative Budget Committee, chair of this committee every other year.
Missouri–The lieutenant governor is the only statewide elected official that is part of both the executive and legislative branches of state government. Under the constitution, the lieutenant governor is ex officio president of the Missouri Senate. The lieutenant governor is elected independently from the governor, and each can be members of different political parties. Upon the governor's death, conviction, impeachment, resignation, absence from the state or other disabilities, the lieutenant governor shall act as governor. By law, the lieutenant governor is a member of the Board of Public Buildings, Board of Fund Commissioners, Missouri Development Finance Board, Missouri Community Service Commission, Missouri State Capitol Commission, Missouri Housing Development Commission and the Tourism Commission. The lieutenant governor is an advisor to the Department of Elementary and Secondary Education on early childhood education and the Parents-as-Teachers program. The lieutenant governor is the state's official advocate for senior citizens, and serves on the Special Health, Psychological, and Social Needs of Minority Older Individuals Commission.
New Jersey–The Lieutenant Governor will serve as the head of a

TABLE 4.14
Lieutenant Governors: Powers and Duties (continued)

principal department or other executive or administrative agency or delegate duties of the office of governor or both.

North Carolina–Serves as a voting member on the State Board of Education. Serves on the State Board of Economic Development. Serves on the State Community College Board. Serves as Chairman of the Energy Policy Council. Serves on the Military Affairs Commission. Serves as Chair of the eLearning Commission.

Oklahoma–Lieutenant Governor also serves on 10 boards and commissions: Tourism and Recreation Commission, Indian Cultural and Educational Authority, State Board of Equalization, School Land Commission, the Oklahoma Capitol Improvement Authority, the Oklahoma Archives and Records Commission, the Oklahoma Film and Music Advisory Commission, CompSource Oklahoma Board of Managers, the Commissioners of the Land Office, and the Oklahoma Linked Deposit Review Board.

Pennsylvania–Chairs the Board of Pardons (Constitutional); chairs the Pa. Emergency Management Council (appointed by Gov.); chairs the Pa. Military Community Enhancement Commission (member by statute, elected chair by members); chairs Local Government Advisory Commission (statute).

Rhode Island–Serves as Chair of a number of advisory councils including issues related to emergency management, long term care and small business. Each year submits a legislative package to the General Assembly.

South Carolina–The lieutenant governor heads the State Office on Aging; appoints members and chairs the South Carolina Affordable Housing Commission.

South Dakota–The lieutenant governor also serves as the Chair of the Workers Compensation Advisory Commission and as a member of the Constitutional Revision Commission.

Utah–The lieutenant governor serves as chief election officer (statutory); chair of the Lieutenant Governor's Commission on Volunteers (statutory); chair of the Lieutenant Governor's Commission on Civic and Character Education (statutory); chair of the Utah Capitol Preservation Board (statutory).

West Virginia–The President of the Senate and the Lieutenant Governor are one in the same. The legislature provided in statute the title of Lieutenant Governor upon the Senate President. The West Virginia Constitution requires that, in case of the death, conviction or impeachment, failure to qualify, resignation, or other disability of the governor, the President of the Senate shall act as governor until the vacancy is filled, or the disability removed.

Northern Mariana Islands–The Lieutenant Governor is charged with overseeing administrative functions.

(d) No lieutenant governor; secretary of state is next in line of succession to governorship.

(e) Appoints all standing committees. Iowa–appoints some special committees.

(f) Presides over cabinet meetings in absence of governor.

(g) Only in emergency situations.

(h) The Kentucky Constitution specifically gives the lieutenant governor the power to act as governor, in the event the governor is unable to fulfill the duties of office.

(i) No lieutenant governor; senate president or speaker is next in line of succession to governorship.

(j) As defined in the state constitution, the lieutenant governor performs gubernatorial functions in the governor's absence. In the event of a vacancy in the office of governor, the lieutenant governor is first in line to succeed to the position.

(k) Unicameral legislative body. In Guam, that body elects own presiding officer.

(l) Except on final passage of bills and joint resolutions.

(m) With respect to procedural matters, not legislation.

(n) May preside over the Senate when desired.

(o) Appoints committees with the Pres. Pro Tem and one Senator on Committee on Committees. Committee on Committees assigns bills.

(p) In the event of a vacancy in the office of Governor resulting from the death, resignation or removal of a Governor in office, or the death of a Governor-elect, or from any other cause the Lieutenant Governor shall become Governor, until a new Governor is elected and qualifies.

(q) Only when asked or after 45 days of absence.

(r) Only upon the invitation from the Senate.

Table 4.14 | Gubernatorial Succession

If Something Happens to the Governor, Who Fills the Office?

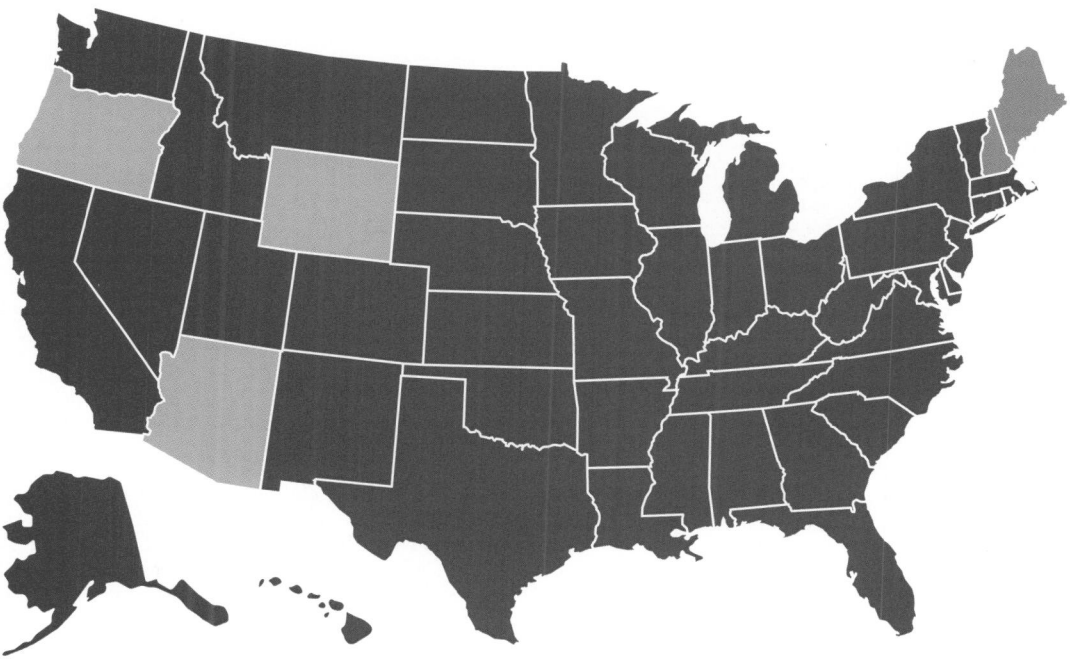

THE
Secretary of State
fills the office in 3 states.

Arizona
Oregon
Wyoming

These states have no lieutenant governor

THE
Lieutenant Governor
fills the office in 45 states.

Alabama	Kentucky	North Dakota
Alaska	Louisiana	Ohio
Arkansas	Maryland	Oklahoma
California	Massachusetts	Pennsylvania
Colorado	Michigan	Rhode Island
Connecticut	Minnesota	South Carolina
Delaware	Mississippi	South Dakota
Florida	Missouri	Tennessee
Georgia	Montana	Texas
Hawaii	Nebraska	Utah
Idaho	Nevada	Vermont
Illinois	New Jersey	Virginia
Indiana	New Mexico	Washington
Iowa	New York	West Virginia
Kansas	North Carolina	Wisconsin

THE
Senate President
fills the office in 2 states.

Maine
New Hampshire

These states have no lieutenant governor

TABLE 4.15
The Secretaries of State, 2019

State or other jurisdiction	Name and party	Method of Selection	Length of regular term in years	Date of first service	Present term ends	Number of previous terms	Maximum consecutive terms allowed by constitution
Alabama	John Merrill (R)	E	4	1/2015	1/2023	1	2
Alaska	---(a)---						
Arizona	Katie Hobbs (D)	E	4	1/2019	1/2023	0	2
Arkansas	John Thurston (R)	E	4	1/2019	1/2023	0	2
California	Alex Padilla (D)	E	4	1/2015	1/2023	1	2
Colorado	Jena Griswold (D)	E	4	1/2019	1/2023	0	2
Connecticut	Denise Merrill (D)	E	4	1/2011	1/2023	2	...
Delaware	Jeffrey Bullock (D)	A (b)	4	1/2009	...	0	...
Florida	Laurel Lee (R)	A	4	2/2019	...	0	2
Georgia	Brad Raffensperger (R)	E	4	1/2019	1/2023	0	...
Hawaii	---(a)---						
Idaho	Lawerence Denney (R)	E	4	1/2015	1/2023	1	...
Illinois	Jesse White (D)	E	4	1/1999	1/2023	5	...
Indiana	Connie Lawson (R)	E	4	3/2012 (h)	1/2023	2	2
Iowa	Paul Pate (R)	E	4	12/2014	12/2022	1	...
Kansas	Scott Schwab (R)	E	4	1/2019	1/2023	0	...
Kentucky	Alison Lundergan Grimes (D)	E	4	12/2011	12/2019	1	2
Louisiana	Kyle Ardoin (R)	E	4	5/2018 (c)	1/2020	...	...
Maine	Matt Dunlap (D)	L	2	1/2005 (d)	1/2021	(d)	5 (e)
Maryland	John Wobensmith (R)	A	...	1/2015	...	...	...
Massachusetts	William Francis Galvin (D)	E	4	1/1995	1/2023	6	...
Michigan	Jocelyn Benson (D)	E	4	1/2019	1/2023	0	2
Minnesota	Steve Simon (DFL)	E	4	1/2015	1/2023	1	...
Mississippi	C. Delbert Hosemann Jr.(R)	E	4	1/2008	1/2020	2	...
Missouri	Jay Ashcroft (R)	E	4	1/2017	1/2021	0	...
Montana	Corey Stapleton (R)	E	4	1/2017	1/2021	0	(f)
Nebraska	Robert Evnen (R)	E	4	1/2019	1/2023	0	...
Nevada	Barbara Cegavske (R)	E	4	1/2015	1/2023	1	2
New Hampshire	William Gardner (D)	L	2	12/1976	12/2020	21	...
New Jersey	Tahesha Way (D)	A	...	1/2018	...	0	...
New Mexico	Maggie Toulouse Oliver (D)	E	4	12/2016 (g)	12/2022	(g)	2
New York	Rossanna Rosado D)	A	...	6/2016	...	0	...
North Carolina	Elaine Marshall (D)	E	4	1/1997	1/2021	5	...
North Dakota	Alvin A. Jaeger (R)	E	4	1/1993	12/2022	6	...
Ohio	Frank LaRose (R)	E	4	1/2019	1/2023	0	2
Oklahoma	Michael Rogers (R)	A	4	1/2019	1/2023	0	...
Oregon	Bev Clarno (R)	E	4	4/2019 (l)	1/2021	0	2
Pennsylvania	Kathy Boockvar (D) (acting)	A	...	1/2019 (i)	...	0	...
Rhode Island	Nellie Gorbea (D)	E	4	1/2015	1/2023	1	2
South Carolina	Mark Hammond (R)	E	4	1/2003	1/2023	4	...
South Dakota	Steve Barnett (R)	E	4	1/2019	1/2023	0	2
Tennessee	Tre Hargett (R)	L	4	1/2009	1/2021	2	...
Texas	Vacant	A	...	...	...	0	...
Utah	---(a)---						
Vermont	Jim Condos (D)	E	2	1/2011	1/2021	4	...
Virginia	Kelly Thomasson (D)	A	...	4/2016	...	0	...
Washington	Kim Wyman (R)	E	4	1/2013	1/2021	1	...
West Virginia	Andrew "Mac" Warner (R)	E	4	1/2017	1/2021	0	...
Wisconsin	Douglas LaFollette (D)	E	4	1/1974 (j)	1/2023	11 (j)	...
Wyoming	Ed Buchanan (R)	E	4	3/2018 (k)	1/2023	(k)	...
American Samoa	---(a)---						
Guam	---(a)---						
CNMI*	---(a)---						
Puerto Rico	(m)	A	...	(m)	...	...	...
U.S. Virgin Islands	---(a)---						

See footnotes at end of table

TABLE 4.15
The Secretaries of State, 2019 (continued)

Source: The Council of State Governments, June 2019.
*Commonwealth of Northern Mariana Islands
Key:
E–Elected by voters
A–Appointed by governor
L–Elected by legislature
...–No provision for
(a) No secretary of state; lieutenant govenor performs functions of this office.
(b) Appointed by the governor and confirmed by the Senate.
(c) Ardoin became acting secretary on May 2018. He replaced Tom Schedler.
(d) Secretary Matthew Dunlap previously served as secretary of state from 2005 to 2010. He was elected by the Legislature to serve again in January 2013 and re-elected in January 2015, 2017 and 2019.
(e) Statutory term limit of four consecutive two-year terms.
(f) Eligible for eight out of 16 years.

(g) Secretary Oliver was elected in November 2016 to fill the remaining two years of an unexpired term and was re-elected to her first full term in November 2018.
(h) Lawson was appointed in 2012 to serve out an unexpired term. She was then elected in 2014 and 2018.
(i) Secretary Boockvar was named acting secretary upon the resignation of Robert Torres in January 2019.
(j) LaFollette was first elected in 1974 and served a four-year term. He was elected again in 1982 and has been re-elected since. The present term ends in 2019.
(k) Edward Buchanan was appointed March 5, 2018 to fill Ed Murray's term and was elected to his first full term in November 2018.
(l) Secretary Clarno was appointed in April 2019 by Gov. Kate Brown to fill the unexpired term of Dennis Richardson, who died in February 2019.
(m) Luis Rivera Marín, the territory's secretary of state, resigned in July 2019.

TABLE 4.16
Secretaries of State: Qualifications for Office

State or other jurisdiction	Minimum age	U.S. citizen (years) (a)	State resident (years) (b)	Qualified voter (years)	Method of selection to office
Alabama	25	7	5	★	E
Alaska			(c)		
Arizona	25	10	5	★	E
Arkansas	18	★	★	★	E
California	18	★	★	★	E
Colorado	25	★	2	...	E
Connecticut	18	★	★	★	E
Delaware	...	...	...	...	A
Florida			(d)		A
Georgia	25	10	4	★	E
Hawaii			(c)		
Idaho	25	★	2	★	E
Illinois	25	★	3	...	E
Indiana	...	★	★	★	E
Iowa	18	★	★		E
Kansas	...	...	...	...	E
Kentucky	30	★	2	★	E
Louisiana	25	5	5	★	E
Maine	...	...	...	...	(e)
Maryland	...	...	...	...	A
Massachusetts	18	★	5	★	E
Michigan	18	★	★	★	E
Minnesota	21	★	30 days	★	E
Mississippi	25	★	5	★	E
Missouri	...	★	1	...	E
Montana	25	★	2	★	E
Nebraska	★	★	★	★	E
Nevada	25	2	2	...	E
New Hampshire	18	...	...	...	(e)
New Jersey	18	★	★	★	A
New Mexico	30	★	5	★	E
New York	18	★	★	...	A
North Carolina	21	★	★	★	E
North Dakota	25	★	5	5	E
Ohio	18	★	★	★	E
Oklahoma	31	★	★	10	A
Oregon	18	★	★	★	E
Pennsylvania	...	...	...	...	A
Rhode Island	18	★	30 days	★	E
South Carolina	...	★	★	★	E
South Dakota	...	...	...	...	E
Tennessee	...	...	...	...	(e)
Texas	18	★	...		A
Utah			(c)		
Vermont	18	★	★	★	E
Virginia	...	...	...	...	A
Washington	18	★	★	★	E
West Virginia	...	★	★	★	E
Wisconsin	18	★	★	★	E
Wyoming	25	★	1	★	E
American Samoa			(c)		
Guam			(c)		
CNMI*			(c)		
Puerto Rico	...	5	5	...	A
U.S. Virgin Islands			(c)		

See footnotes at end of table

TABLE 4.16
Secretaries of State: Qualifications for Office (continued)

Source: The Council of State Governments survey of secretaries of
state offices, 2019.
*Commonwealth of Northern Mariana Islands
Key:
★–Formal provision; number of years not specified.
…–No formal provision.
A–Appointed by governor.
E–Elected by voters.
(a) In some states you must be a U.S. citizen to be an elector, and
must be an elector to run.

(b) In some states you must be a state resident to be an elector, and
must be an elector to run.
(c) No secretary of state.
(d) As of January 1, 2003, the office of Secretary of State shall be an
appointed position (appointed by the governor). It will no longer
be a cabinet position, but an agency head and the Department of
State shall be an agency under the governor's office.
(e) Chosen by joint ballot of state senators and representatives. In
Maine and New Hampshire, every two years. In Tennessee, every
four years.

TABLE 4.17
Secretaries of State: Election and Registration Duties

State or other jurisdiction	Election								Registration				
	Chief election officer	Determines ballot eligibility of political parties	Receives initiative and/or referendum petition	Files certificate of nomination or election	Supplies election ballots or materials to local officials	Files candidates' expense papers	Files other campaign reports	Conducts voter education programs	Registers charitable organizations	Registers corporations (a)	Processes and/or commissions notaries public	Registers securities	Registers trade names/ marks
Alabama	★	★	...	★	★	★	★	★	★	★	★	...	★
Alaska (b)	★	★	★	★	★	...	...	★	...	★	...	...	...
Arizona (aa)	★	★	★	★	...	★	★	★	...	★	...	...	★
Arkansas	★	★	★	★	...	★	★	★	...	★	★	...	★
California	★(c)	★	...	★	★	★	★	★	(d)	★	★	...	★
Colorado	★	★	...	★	★	...	★	★	★	★	★	...	★
Connecticut	★	★	...	★	★	...	...	★	★	★	★	...	★
Delaware (g)	...	...	...	(e)	...	...	(f)	...	★	★	★	...	★
Florida (v)	★	★	★	★	...	★	★	...	...	★	★	...	★
Georgia	★	★	...	★	★	...	...	★	★	...	★	★	★
Hawaii (b)	...	...	★	...	...	...	...	★	...	★	★	...	★
Idaho	★	★	★	★	★	★	★	★	...	★	★	...	★
Illinois	...	...	★	(h)	...	...	...	...	...	★	★	★	★
Indiana (i)	★	★	...	★	★	★	★	★	★	★	★	★	★
Iowa	★	★	...	★	...	...	...	★	★	★	★	...	★
Kansas	★	★	...	★	★	★	...	★	★	★	★	...	★
Kentucky	★	★	...	★	...	...	...	★	...	★	★	...	★
Louisiana	★	...	...	★	★	...	...	★	★	★	★	...	★
Maine	★	★	★	★	★	...	...	★	(y)	★	★	...	★
Maryland	...	★	★	★	...	...	...	...	★	...	★	...	★
Massachusetts	★	★	★	★	★	(f)	(f)	★	...	★	★	★	★
Michigan	★	★	★	★	...	★	★	★	...	...	★	...	...
Minnesota (z)	★	★	...	★	★	...	...	★	...	★	★	...	★
Mississippi	★	★	★	★	...	★	★	★	★	★	★	★	★
Missouri (bb)	★	★	★	★	★	...	...	★	★	★	★	★	★
Montana	★	★	★	★	...	...	...	★	★	★	★	...	★
Nebraska	★	★	★	★	★	...	...	★	★	★	★	...	★
Nevada (j)	★	★	★	★	★	★	★	★	★	★	★	★	★
New Hampshire	★	★	...	★	★	★	★	...	★	★	★	★	★
New Jersey	★	★	★	★	★	★	★	★	...	★	★	...	★
New Mexico	★	★	...	★	★	★	★	★	...	★	★	...	★
New York	...	...	...	...	...	...	...	...	...	★	★	...	★
North Carolina (k)	...	...	...	...	...	...	...	...	★	★	★	★	★
North Dakota	★	★	★	★	★	★	★	★	★	★	★	...	★
Ohio (l)	★	★	★	★(m)	★	★	★	★	★	★	★	★	★
Oklahoma	...	...	★	...	...	...	...	...	★	★(n)	★	...	★
Oregon	★	★	★	★	★	★	★	★	★	★	★	...	★
Pennsylvania	★	★	...	★	...	...	★	★	★	★	★	...	★
Rhode Island (o)	★	★	...	★	★	...	...	★	...	★	★	...	★
South Carolina	...	...	...	...	...	...	...	...	★	★(p)	★	...	★
South Dakota	★	★	★	★	...	★	★	★	★	★	★	...	★
Tennessee (q)	★	★	★	★	★	...	...	★	★	★	★	...	★
Texas	★	★	...	★	★	...	...	★	...	★	★	...	★
Utah (b)	★	★	★	★	★	★	★	★	...	...	...	...	...
Vermont (r)	★	...	...	★	★	★	★	★	...	★	★	...	★
Virginia (x)	...	...	...	...	...	...	...	...	★	...	★	...	...
Washington (w)	★	...	★	★	...	...	...	★	★	★	...	★	★
West Virginia	★	★	...	★	...	★	★	★	★	★	★	...	★
Wisconsin (s)	...	...	...	...	...	...	...	...	...	...	...	...	...
Wyoming	★	★	★	★	(t)	★	★	★	★	★	★	★	★
American Samoa (b)	...	...	...	★	...	★	★	★	★	★	★	...	...
Guam (b)	...	...	...	...	...	...	...	...	...	...	...	...	...
Puerto Rico	...	...	...	...	...	...	...	...	★	★	★	★	★
U.S. Virgin Islands (b)	...	...	...	...	...	...	...	...	★	★(u)	★	...	★

See footnotes at end of table

TABLE 4.17
Secretaries of State: Election and Registration Duties (continued)

Source: The Council of State Governments' survey of secretaries of state offices, 2019.

Key:

★–Responsible for activity.

…–Not responsible for activity.

(a) Unless otherwise indicated, office registers domestic, foreign and non-profit corporations.

(b) No secretary of state. Duties indicated are performed by lieutenant governor. In Hawaii, election related responsibilities have been transferred to an independent Chief Election Officer. In U. S. Virgin Islands election duties are performed by Supervisor of Elections.

(c) Other election duties include: tallying votes from all 58 counties, testing and certifying voting systems for use by local elections officials, maintaining statewide voter registration database, publishing state Voter Information Guide/State Ballot Pamphlet and qualifying statewide ballot initiatives and referenda.

(d) This office does not register charitable trusts, but does register charitable organizations as nonprofit corporations; also limited partnerships, limited liability corporations, and domestic partners, Advanced Health care Directives, and administers the Safe at Home mail forwarding program.

(e) Files certificates of election for publication purposes only; does not file certificates of nomination.

(f) Federal candidates only.

(g) Registration duties include alternative business entities such as LLCs and partnerships.

(h) Office issues document, but does not receive it.

(i) Additional election duties include: statewide voter registration system administrator. Additional registration duties include securities enforcement and auto dealer registration and enforcement.

(j) Additional registration duties include: issues annual State Business License, registers domestic partnerships, registers advanced directives for health care, registers guardianship nominations. Charitable organizations soliciting tax deductible charitable contributions must file a charitable solicitation registration statements or claim of exemption before soliciting charitable contributions in Nevada.

(k) Other election duties: administers the Electoral College. Other registration duties: Maintains secure online registry of advance health care directives.

(l) Supplies poll worker training materials to county boards of elections: certifies official form of the ballot to county board of elections.

(m) Issues certificate of nomination or election to all statewide candidates and U.S. Representatives.

(n) Certifies U.S. Congressional election results to Washington D.C. Also registers limited partnerships, limited liability companies and limited liability partnerships.

(o) Additional registration duties include: Non-resident landlord appointment of agent for service and Uniform Commercial Code.

(p) Also registers the Cable Franchise Authority.

(q) Appoints the Coordinator of Elections who performs the election duties indicated above, and also prepares the elections manual and elections handbook for use by state officials. Also registers athlete agents, as well as individuals and entities seeking exemption from Tennessee's workers' compensation requirements.

(r) Additional registration duties include: registers temporary officiants for civil marriages.

(s) Additional registration duties include: Issues authentications and apostilles.

(t) Materials not ballots.

(u) Both domestic and foreign profit; but only domestic non-profit.

(v) Additional registration duties include: registers fictitious names and other types of business entities.

(w) Additional registration duties include: registers domestic partnerships and registers international student exchange programs.

(x) Additional registration duties include: registering organizations' mottos; registering logos and insignias; authentications.

(y) Registers nonprofit entities.

(z) Additional registration duties include: registers LLCs, limited partnerships.

(aa) Additional registration duties include partnerships, telephonic seller, advance directives and uniform commercial code.

(bb) Also administers the Safe at Home address confidentiality/mail forwarding program; issues authentications and apostilles.

TABLE 4.18
Secretaries of State: Custodial, Publication and Legislative Duties

State or other jurisdiction	Custodial				Publication					Legislative			
	Archives state records and regulations	Files state agency rules and regulations	Administers uniform commercial code provisions	Files other corporate documents	State manual or directory	Session laws	State constitution	Statutes	Administrative rules and regulations	Opens legislative sessions (a)	Enrolls or engrosses bills	Retains copies of bills	Registers lobbyists
Alabama	...	...	★	★	...	★	★	★	...	...	★	★	...
Alaska (b)	...	★	...	...	...	★	...	...	★	★	...	★	...
Arizona (w)	★	★	★	...	...	...	...	...	★	...	...	★	★
Arkansas (c)	★	★	★	★	...	★	...	...	★	...	...	★	★
California	★	★	★	★	★	...	★	...	...	...	(d)	...	★
Colorado	...	★	★	★	...	...	★	...	★	...	...	★	★
Connecticut	★(e)	★	★	★	★	...	...	...	★	S	...	★	★
Delaware (x)	★	★	★	★	...	...	...	...	★	...	...	★	★
Florida (u)	★	★	★	★	...	★	★	★	★	...	...	...	...
Georgia	★	★	...	...	★	...	...	...	★	...	...	...	...
Hawaii (b)	...	...	...	...	...	★	...	★	...	...	...	★	...
Idaho	...	...	★	★	...	...	★	★	...	...	...	★	★
Illinois	★	★	★	★	★	★	★	...	★	H	★	★	★
Indiana	(n)	...	★	★	...	...	...	...	...	H	...	(n)	...
Iowa (y)	★	...	★	★	...	★	★	...	...	...	★	★	...
Kansas (s)	...	★	★	★	★	★	...	(o)	★	★	...	★	★
Kentucky	★	...	★	★	...	★	...	...	...	...	★	★	...
Louisiana	★	...	★	★	...	...	★	...	★	...	★	★	(f)
Maine	★	★	★	★	...	...	★	...	★	...	★	★	...
Maryland	...	★	...	...	...	★	...	...	...	...	★	★	...
Massachusetts	★	★	★	★	★	★	★	★	★	...	★	★	★
Michigan	★	★	★	...	...	★	★	★	★	...	...	...	★
Minnesota	★	★	★	★	★	...	...	...	...	H	...	★	...
Mississippi	★	★	★	★	★	★	★	★	★	H	...	(p)	★
Missouri	★(h)	★	★	★	★	...	...	...	...	H	...	★	...
Montana	★	★	★	★	...	...	★	...	★	H	★	★	...
Nebraska	★	★	★	★	...	...	...	...	★	...	...	★	...
Nevada	★	★	★	★	...	...	...	...	★	...	...	★	...
New Hampshire	★	...	★	★	★	...	★	...	...	...	★	★	★
New Jersey	★	...	...	...	...	...	★	...	...	...	...	★	...
New Mexico (z)	...	...	★	★	...	★	★	★	...	H	...	★	...
New York	...	★	★	...	★	...	★	...	★	...	...	★	...
North Carolina (t)	★	★	★	...	★	...	...	...	...	...	★	★	★
North Dakota	...	...	★	★	...	...	...	...	...	...	...	★	★
Ohio (i)	★	★	★	★	★	★	★	...	...	...	...	★	...
Oklahoma (j)	...	★	...	★	...	...	...	...	★	...	...	★	...
Oregon	★	★	★	★	★	...	★	...	★	...	...	★	...
Pennsylvania	...	...	★	★	...	...	...	...	...	...	★	★	...
Rhode Island (k)	★	★	★	★	★	...	★	...	...	...	...	★	★
South Carolina	...	...	★	★	...	...	...	...	...	...	...	★	...
South Dakota	★	★	★	★	★	★	...	★	★	H	...	★	★
Tennessee	★(q)	★	★	★	★(l)	★	...	★	★	...	...	...	...
Texas	...	★	★	★	...	★	...	...	★	H	...	★	...
Utah (b)	...	...	...	...	...	...	...	...	...	...	...	★	★
Vermont (m)	★	★	★	★	★	★	★	...	★	H	...	★	★
Virginia (g)	...	...	...	...	★	...	...	...	...	...	...	...	...
Washington (v)	★	...	...	★	...	...	★	...	...	...	★	★	...
West Virginia	★	★	★	★	...	...	...	...	★	...	...	★	...
Wisconsin	★	...	...	...	...	...	...	...	...	...	...	...	...
Wyoming	★	★	★	★	★	...	★	...	...	H	...	★	★
American Samoa (b)	...	★	...	★	...	★	★	...	★	...	...	...	...
Guam (b)	...	...	...	...	...	...	...	★	...	...	...	...	...
Puerto Rico	...	★	★	★	...	★	★	★	★	...	...	...	...
U.S. Virgin Islands (b)	...	★	★	★	...	...	...	...	...	...	★	★	...

See footnotes at end of table

TABLE 4.18
Secretaries of State: Custodial, Publication and Legislative Duties (continued)

Sources: The Council of State Governments' survey of secretaries of state offices, 2019.

Key:

★–Responsible for activity.

…–Not responsible for activity.

(a) In this column only: ★–Both houses; H–House; S–Senate.

(b) No secretary of state. Duties indicated are performed by lieutenant governor.

(c) Additional custodial duties for the Arkansas Secretary of State include serving as the caretaker for the Arkansas State Capitol Building and Grounds, including all custodial duties, HVAC system, building maintenance, historic preservation and conducting tours.

(d) Office does not enroll or engross bills but does chapter bills that are signed into law and retains final chaptered copies.

(e) The secretary of state is keeper of public records, but the state archives is a department of the Connecticut State Library.

(f) Only registers political pollsters.

(g) Other custodial duties include: restoration of civil rights; liaison to Virginia Indians; gubernatorial appointments. Other publication duties include: state organization charts. Other registration duties include: Pardons; Service of Process.

(h) Also responsible for the State Library.

(i) Additional publication duties include: elections statistics, official roster of federal, state, and county officers and official roster of township and municipal officers. Additional legislative duties include: Distributing laws to specified state and local government agencies.

(j) Other custodial duties include: Effective Financing Statements identifying farm products that are subject to a security interest, UCC and mortgage documents pertaining to transmitting utilities and also railroads and files open meeting notices.

(k) Additional duties include administering oaths of office to general officers and legislators.

(l) The Division of Publications of the Office of the Secretary of State also publishes the following: The Tennessee Blue Book, Board and Commission vacancies, and Executive Orders and Proclamations.

(m) Additional custodial duties include: records management, and certifying vital records.

(n) The Secretary of State's office receives and authenticates Bills and Enrolled Acts, but does not keep or maintain them. Post-session legislative materials are maintained by the Indiana Public Records Commission.

(o) Responsible for distribution only.

(p) Chapters and indexes all signed bill and chamber and concurrent resolutions.

(q) The Division of Records Management of the Office of the Secretary of State assists state agencies in the appropriate utilization, disposition, retention and destruction of state records.

(s) Additionally, the secretary of state publishes the Kansas Register and opens legislative reorganization meetings.

(t) Other publication duties include: Publishes state board and commission meeting notices online. Other legislative duties include: The Secretary of State is responsible for the certification of election results before legislators take the oath of office at the opening of each session of the General Assembly.

(u) Files other types of business entity and cable franchise documents, records federal tax liens and judgement liens and issues Apostilles

(v) Legislative duties also include: chapters bills.

(w) The secretary of state works hand-in-hand with the business community. The office is tasked with recording the partnerships of those who do business in Arizona and they register trademarks and issue certificates of registration. They also register telemarketers and veterans' charitable organizations. Improving the quality of life for Arizonans has been a priority of the office. The Arizona State Library, Archives and Public Records provides Arizonans access to information about their government, their state and their world. The information available from the State Library empowers citizens to become informed citizens. The Address Confidentiality Program allows victims of domestic violence, sexual abuse or stalking to keep their residential addresses confidential by giving them a substitute address.

(x) Other publication duties include constitutional amendments.

(y) Began administering a Safe at Home address confidentiality program for victims of domestic abuse, sexual assault and other violent crimes. Approves voluntary non-urbanized annexations and files all annexations of territory by Iowa cities.

(z) Files Agency Code of Conduct; Administers Confidential Address Program Publish State Roster of Elected Officials; State Blue Book.

TABLE 4.19
The Attorneys General, 2019

State or other jurisdiction	Name and party	Method of selection	Length of regular term in years	Date of first service	Present term ends	Number of previous terms	Maximum consecutive terms allowed
Alabama	Steve Marshall (R)	E	4	2/2017 (h)	1/2023	1 (h)	2
Alaska	Kevin Clarkson (R)	A	…	1/2019	…	0	…
Arizona	Mark Brnovich (R)	E	4	1/2015	1/2023	1	2
Arkansas	Leslie Rutledge (R)	E	4	1/2015	1/2023	1	2
California	Xavier Becerra (D)	E	4	1/2017 (l)	1/2023	(l)	2
Colorado	Phil Weiser (D)	E	4	1/2019	1/2023	0	2
Connecticut	William Tong (D)	E	4	1/2019	1/2023	…	★
Delaware	Kathleen Jennings (D)	E	4	1/2019	1/2023	0	★
Florida	Ashley Moody (R)	E	4	1/2019	1/2023	…	2
Georgia	Christopher Carr (R)	E	4	10/2016 (j)	1/2023	1 (j)	★
Hawaii	Clare Connors (D)	A	4 (a)	1/2019	1/2023	0	…
Idaho	Lawrence Wasden (R)	E	4	1/2003	1/2023	4	★
Illinois	Kwame Raoul (D)	E	4	1/2019	1/2023	0	★
Indiana	Curtis Hill (R)	E	4	1/2017	1/2021	0	★
Iowa	Tom Miller (D)	E	4	1/1979 (b)	1/2023	9 (b)	★
Kansas	Derek Schmidt (R)	E	4	1/2011	1/2023	2	★
Kentucky	Andy Beshear (D)	E	4	12/2016	12/2020	0	2
Louisiana	Jeff Landry (R)	E	4	1/2016	1/2020	0	★
Maine	Aaron Frey (D)	L (c)	2	1/2019	1/2021	0	4
Maryland	Brian Frosh (D)	E	4	1/2015	1/2023	1	★
Massachusetts	Maura Healey (D)	E	4	1/2015	1/2023	1	…
Michigan	Dana Nessel (D)	E	4	1/2019	1/2023	0	2
Minnesota	Keith Ellison (DFL)	E	4	1/2019	1/2023	0	★
Mississippi	Jim Hood (D)	E	4	1/2004	1/2020	3	★
Missouri	Eric Schmitt (R)	E	4	1/2019 (d)	1/2021	0	★
Montana	Tim Fox (R)	E	4	1/2013	1/2021	1	2
Nebraska	Doug Peterson (R)	E	4	1/2015	1/2023	1	★
Nevada	Aaron Ford (D)	E	4	1/2019	1/2023	0	2
New Hampshire	Gordon MacDonald (R)	A	4	4/2017	1/2021	0	…
New Jersey	Gubir Grewal (D)	A	4	1/2018	1/2022	0	…
New Mexico	Hector Balderas (D)	E	4	1/2015	1/2023	1	2 (f)
New York	Letitia James (D)	E	4	1/2019	1/2023	0	★
North Carolina	Josh Stein (D)	E	4	1/2017	1/2021	0	★
North Dakota	Wayne Stenehjem (R)	E	4 (g)	1/2001	12/2022	4 (g)	★
Ohio	David Yost (R)	E	4	1/2019	1/2023	0	2
Oklahoma	Mike Hunter (R)	E	4	2/2017 (e)	1/2023	0	★
Oregon	Ellen F. Rosenblum (D)	E	4	6/2012 (i)	1/2021	1	★
Pennsylvania	Josh Shapiro (D)	E	4	1/2017	1/2021	0	2
Rhode Island	Peter Neronha (D)	E	4	1/2019	1/2023	0	2
South Carolina	Alan Wilson (R)	E	4	1/2011	1/2023	2	★
South Dakota	Jason Ravnsborg (R)	E	4	1/2019	1/2023	0	2 (f)
Tennessee	Herbert Slatery (R)	(k)	8	10/2014	8/2022	0	…
Texas	Ken Paxton (R)	E	4	1/2015	1/2023	1	★
Utah	Sean Reyes (R)	E	4	12/2013	1/2021	1	★
Vermont	TJ Donovan	E	2	1/2017	1/2021	1	★
Virginia	Mark Herring (D)	E	4	1/2014	1/2022	1	(m)
Washington	Bob Ferguson (D)	E	4	1/2013	1/2021	1	★
West Virginia	Patrick Morrisey (R)	E	4	1/2013	1/2021	1	★
Wisconsin	Josh Kaul (D)	E	4	1/2019	1/2023	0	★
Wyoming	Bridget Hill (R)	A	…	1/2019	…	0	…
Dist. of Columbia	Karl Racine (D)	A	…	1/2015	1/2023	1	…
American Samoa	Talauega Eleasalo V. Ale (D)	A	4	1/2014	…	…	…
Guam	Leevin Camacho (I)	E	4	1/2019	1/2023	0	…
CNMI*	Edward Manibusan (I)	A	4	11/2015	…	0	…
Puerto Rico	Wanda Vázquez Garced	A	4	1/2017	…	0	…
U.S. Virgin Islands	Denise George-Counts	A	4	4/2019	…	0	…

See footnotes at end of table

TABLE 4.19
The Attorneys General, 2019 (continued)

Sources: The Council of State Governments, June 2019.
*Commonwealth of Northern Mariana Islands
Key:

★ –No provision specifying number of terms allowed.
… –No formal provision, position is appointed or elected by governmental entity (not chosen by the electorate).
A–Appointed by the governor.
E–Elected by the voters.
L–Elected by the legislature.
N.A.–Not available.
(a) Term runs concurrently with the governor.
(b) Attorney General Miller was elected in 1978, 1982, 1986, 1994, 1998, 2002, 2006, 2010 and 2014.
(c) Chosen biennially by joint ballot of state senators and representatives.
(d) Eric Schmitt was appointed in January 2019 to fill the unexpired term of Joshua Hawley, who was elected the U.S. Senate in November 2018.
(e) Mike Hunter was appointed in Feb. 2017 after Scott Pruitt left to serve as administrator of the U.S. Environmental Protection Agency.

(f) After two consecutive terms, must wait four years and/or one full term before being eligible again.
(g) The term of the office of the elected official is four years, except that in 2004 the attorney general was elected for a term of two years.
(h) Steve Marshall was appointed on Feb. 10, 2017 to fill the unexpired term of Luther Strange. Strange was elected to the U.S. Senate in Nov. 2016.
(i) Rosenblum was appointed by Gov. Kitzhaber on June 29, 2012 to fill the term left vacant when AG John Kroger resigned to become President of Reed College. She was elected in Nov. 2012 to a full term.
(j) Christopher Carr was appointed in October 2016 to fill the unexpired term of Sam Olens. Olens resigned to become president of Kennesaw State University.
(k) Appointed by judges of state Supreme Court.
(l) Attorney General Bercerra was appointed in January 2017 to fill the unexpired term of Kamala Harris and elected to his first full term in November 2018.
(m) Provision specifying individual may hold office for an unlimited number of terms.
(n) Must be confirmed by the Senate.

TABLE 4.20
Attorneys General: Qualifications for Office

State or other jurisdiction	Minimum age	U.S. citizen (years) (a)	State resident (years) (b)	Qualified voter (years)	Licensed attorney (years)	Membership in the state bar (years)	Method of selection to office
Alabama	25	7	5	★	...	...	E
Alaska	18	★	...	...	★	★	A
Arizona	25	10	5	★	5	...	E
Arkansas	...	...	★	★	...	...	E
California	18	★	★	★	★	5	E
Colorado	27	★	2	★	★	...	E
Connecticut	18	★	★	★	10	10	E
Delaware	...	...	...	...	...	...	E
Florida	30	★	7	★	★	5	E
Georgia	25	10	4	★	7	7	E
Hawaii	...	1	1	...	★	(d)	A
Idaho	30	★	2	...	★	★	E
Illinois	25	★	3	★	★	★	E
Indiana	...	2	2	★	5	...	E
Iowa	18	★	★	...	...	...	E
Kansas	...	...	...	...	...	...	E
Kentucky	30	...	2 (e)	...	8	2	E
Louisiana	25	★	5	★	★	★	E
Maine	...	...	...	...	★	★	(f)
Maryland	...	★(g)	★	★	★	10	E
Massachusetts	18	...	5	★	...	★	E
Michigan	18	★	★	...	★	★	E
Minnesota	21	★	30 days	★	...	...	E
Mississippi	26	★	5	★	5	★	E
Missouri	...	★	1	...	...	...	E
Montana	25	★	2	...	5	★	E
Nebraska	...	...	★	...	...	...	E
Nevada	25	★	2	★	...	...	E
New Hampshire	...	★	★	...	★	★	A (h)
New Jersey	18	...	★	...	...	...	A
New Mexico	30	★	5	★	★	...	E
New York	30	★	5	...	(i)	...	E
North Carolina	21	★	★	★	★	(i)	E
North Dakota	25	★	5	★	★	★	E
Ohio	18	★	★	★	...	...	E
Oklahoma	31	★	★	10	...	...	E
Oregon	18	★	★	★	...	...	E
Pennsylvania	30	★	...	...	★	...	E
Rhode Island	18	...	...	...	★	★	E
South Carolina	...	★	30 days	★	...	...	E
South Dakota	18	★	★	★	(i)	(i)	E
Tennessee	...	...	...	...	...	...	(j)
Texas	...	★	1	...	(i)	(i)	E
Utah	25	★	5 (e)	★	★	★	E
Vermont	18	★	★	★	...	...	E
Virginia	30	★	1 (k)	★	...	5 (k)	E
Washington	18	★	★	★	★	★	E
West Virginia	25	...	5	★	...	...	E
Wisconsin	...	★	★	...	...	...	E
Wyoming	...	★	★	★	4	4	A (l)
Dist. of Columbia	...	...	★	...	★	★	A
American Samoa	...	...	(c)	...	(i)	(i)	A
Guam	...	...	...	...	...	...	A
CNMI*	...	...	3	...	5	...	A
Puerto Rico	...	★	...	...	★	★	A
U.S. Virgin Islands	...	...	★	★	★	★	A

See footnotes at end of table

TABLE 4.20
Attorneys General: Qualifications for Office (continued)

Sources: The Council of State Governments' survey of attorneys general, state constitutions and statutes, 2019.

*Commonwealth of Northern Mariana Islands

Key:

★ –Formal provision; number of years not specified.

… –No formal provision.

A–Appointed by governor.

E–Elected by voters.

(a) In some states you must be a U.S. citizen to be an elector, and must be an elector to run.

(b) In some states you must be a state resident to be an elector, and must be an elector to run.

(c) No statute specifically requires this, but the State Bar Act can be interpreted as making this a qualification.

(d) No period specified, all licensed attorneys are members of the state bar.

(e) State citizenship requirement.

(f) Chosen biennially by joint ballot of state senators and representatives.

(g) *Crosse v. Board of Supervisors of Elections* 243 Md. 555, 221A.2d431 (1966)–opinion rendered indicated that U.S. citizenship was, by necessity, a requirement for office.

(h) Appointed by the governor and confirmed by the governor and the executive council.

(i) Implied.

(j) Appointed by state supreme court.

(k) Same as qualifications of a judge of a court of record.

(l) Must be confirmed by the Senate.

TABLE 4.21
Attorneys General: Prosecutorial and Advisory Duties

State or other jurisdiction	Authority in local prosecutions: Authority to initiate local prosecutions	May intervene in local prosecutions	May assist local prosecutor	May supersede local prosecutor	Issues advisory opinions (a): To state executive officials	To legislators	To local prosecutors	On the constitutionality of bills or ordinances	Reviews legislation (b): Prior to passage	Before signing
Alabama	A	A,D	A,D	A	★	★	★	...	★	...
Alaska	(c)	(c)	(c)	(c)	★	★	...	★	★	★
Arizona	A,D,F	A,D	A,D,F	D,F	★	★	★	★(x)	(u)	(u)
Arkansas	D	...	D		★	★	★	★	...	...
California	A,B,C,D,E,F	A,B,C,D,E,F	A,B,C,D,E,F	A,B,C,D,E,F,G	★	★	★	★	(v)	(v)
Colorado	A, F	A	D,F	A	★	★	★	★	★	★
Connecticut	...	...	...	...	★	(d)	...	★	(e)	(e)
Delaware	A(f)	(f)	(f)	(f)	★	★	...	★	(g)	(g)
Florida	F	...	D		★	★	★	...	...	...
Georgia	B,D,F,G	...	A,D	...	★	★	★	...	...	...
Hawaii	A,B,C,D,E	A,B,C,D,E	A,B,C,D,E	A,B,C,D,E	★	★	...	★(h)	★	★
Idaho	B,D,F	D,F	D	...	★	★	★	★	★	★
Illinois	D,F	D,G	D	G	★	★	★	...	(i)	(i)
Indiana	F	...	D	...	★	★	★	★	...	...
Iowa	D,F	D,F	D,F	D,E,F	★	★	★	...	(j)	(j)
Kansas	B,C,D,F	B,C,D,F,G	D	B,C,D,F,G	★	★	★	...	...	...
Kentucky	D,F,G	B,D,G	D	B	★	★	★	★	...	...
Louisiana	D,E,G	D,E,G	D,E,G	E,G	★	★	★	...	★	★
Maine	A	A	A	A	★	★	★	...	...	...
Maryland	B,F	D	D	...	★	★	★	★	★	★
Massachusetts	A	A	A,D	A	★	★(k)	★	★	(l)	(l)
Michigan	A	A	A	A	★	★	★	★	...	...
Minnesota	B,D,F	B,D,G	A,B,D,G	B	★	★(k)	★	...		(l)
Mississippi	A,D,F	D,F	A,D,F	D,F	★	★	★	...	...	...
Missouri	B,F,G	F	B,F	G	★	★	★	...	(l)	(l)
Montana	D	E	D,E	E	★	★(m)	★	...	...	...
Nebraska	A,D	A,D	A,D,E,F	...	★	★	★	★	...	...
Nevada	A,B,D,E,F	A,B,D,E,F	A,B,D,E,F	A,B,D,E,F	★	...	★	★	...	...
New Hampshire	A,E (y)	A,E (y)	A,D,E	A,E	★	★	★	...	(n)	(n)
New Jersey	A,B,C,D	A,B,C,D	A,B,C,D	A,B,C,D	★	★	★	★	★	★
New Mexico	B,D,E,F	D,E,F	A,B,D,E,F	D,E,F,G	★	★	★	★	★	★
New York	B,F	B,D,F	D	B	★	★(k)	★	★	★	★
North Carolina	...	D	D	...	★	★	★	★	★	...
North Dakota	D,E,F,G	A,D,E,G	A,D,E,F,G	A,D,E,G	★	★	★	...	...	...
Ohio	D, F	D	D	F	★	(m)	★	...	...	...
Oklahoma	A,B,C,D,E,F,G	A,B,C,D,E,F,G	A,B,C,D,E,F,G	A,B,C,D,E,F,G	★	★	★	★	★	★
Oregon	B,D,F	B,D	B,D	B	★	★	★	...	...	★
Pennsylvania	A,D,F	D,F,G	D,F	G	★	...	...	...	...	...
Rhode Island	A	A	A	A	★	★	...	...	...	...
South Carolina	A,D,E,F	A,B,C,D,E,F	A,D,E	A,E	★	(q)	★	★	★(w)	★(w)
South Dakota	A,B,D,E,F (p)	D,G	A,B,D,E	D,F	★	★	★	★	★	...
Tennessee	D,F,G	D,G	D,F	F,G	★	★	★	★	...	...
Texas	F	...	D	...	(z)	(z)	(z)	(z)	...	...
Utah	A,B,D,E,F,G	E,G	D,E	E	★	★(q)	★	★	★(l)	★(l)
Vermont	A	A	A	G	★	★	★	★	★	★
Virginia	B,F	B,D,F	B,D,F	B	★	★	★	★	★	★
Washington	B,D,G	B,D,G	B,D,G	B,D,G	★	★	★	...	(o)	(o)
West Virginia	(r)	...	...	...	★	★	★	★	...	...
Wisconsin	B,C,D,F	B,C,D	D	B	★	★	★	★	(e)	(e)
Wyoming	B,D,F	B,D	B,D	G	★	★	★	★(h)	★	★
Dist. of Columbia	F	D	D	F	★	★	(s)	...	★	★
American Samoa	A(t)	(t)	(t)	(t)	★	...	(t)	(e)	(l)	(l)
Guam	A	A	A	A	★	★	★	★	(l)	B
CNMI*	A(t)	(t)	(t)	(t)	★	★	...	★	...	...
Puerto Rico	A	(t)	(t)	(t)	★	★	...	...	★	★
U.S. Virgin Islands	A(t)	(t)	(t)	(t)	★	...	...	★	★	★

See footnotes at end of table

TABLE 4.21
Attorneys General: Prosecutorial and Advisory Duties (continued)

Sources: The Council of State Governments' survey of attorneys general, state constitutions and statutes, 2019.
*Commonwealth of Northern Mariana Islands
Key:
A–On own initiative.
B–On request of governor.
C–On request of legislature.
D–On request of local prosecutor.
E–When in state's interest.
F–Under certain statutes for specific crimes.
G–On authorization of court or other body.
★–Has authority in area.
...–Does not have authority in area.
(a) Also issues advisory opinions to: Alabama–Designated heads of state departments, agencies, boards, and commissions; local public officials; and political subdivisions. Hawaii–Judges/judiciary as requested. Kansas–to counsel for local units of government. Montana–county and city attorneys, city commissioners. Wisconsin–corporation counsel.
(b) Also reviews legislation: Alabama–when requested by the governor. Alaska–after passage. Arizona–at the request of the legislature. Kansas–upon request of Legislator, no formal authority.
(c) The attorney general functions as the local prosecutor.
(d) To legislative leadership.
(e) Informally reviews bills or does so upon request.
(f) The attorney general functions as the local prosecutor.
(g) Discretion to informally review upon request of legislative or executive branch, but reviews are not legal advice or formal action.
(h) Bills, not ordinances.
(i) Review and track legislation that relates to the Office of Attorney General and the office mission.
(j) No requirements for review.
(k) To legislature as a whole not individual legislators.
(l) Only when requested by governor or legislature.
(m) To either the House of Representatives or the Senate, when so requested by resolution or passed by membership; To law directors of townships that have adopted limited self-government under R.C. Chapter 504.

(n) Provides information when requested by the Legislature. Testifies for or against bills on the Attorney General's own initiative.
(o) May review legislation at request of clients or legislature.
(p) Certain statutes provide for concurrent jurisdiction with local prosecutors.
(q) Only when requested by legislature.
(r) Can be involved in local at request of local prosecutors. If requested by local authority, can participate in criminal prosecutions.
(s) The office of attorney general prosecutes local crimes to an extent. The office's Legal Counsel Division may issue legal advice to the office's prosecutorial arm. Otherwise, the office does not usually advise the OUSA, the district's other local prosecutor.
(t) The attorney general functions as the local prosecutor.
(u) Reviews enacted legislation only when there is a compelling need.
(v) May review legislation at any time but does not have a de jure role in approval of bills as to form or constitutionality; California has a separate Legislative Counsel to advise the legislature on bills.
(w) Has concurrent jurisdiction with states' attorneys. Only when requested by governor or legislature.
(x) At the request of one or more members of the legislature, the attorney general shall investigate any ordinance, regulation, order or other official action adopted or taken by the governing body of a county, city or town that the member alleges violates state law or the Constitution of Arizona.
(y) Attorney general has statewide prosecutorial authority in any court. No request or order is required for the AG to initiate a prosecution. The Attorney General has authority to intervene, no request or order is required, but does not do so except in an extreme circumstance.
(z) The attorney general's office may issue an opinion on a question affecting the public interest or concerning the official duties of the requesting person. The opinion is a written interpretation of existing law. Authorized requestors are: the governor, head of a department of state government, the head or board or a penal institution, the head or board of an eleemosynary institution, the head of a state board, a regent or trustee of a state educational institution, a committee of a house of the Texas Legislature, a county auditor authorized by law, the chair of the governing board of a river authority and a district or county attorney.

Table 4.21 | Duties of Attorneys General

The length of a regular term for most attorneys general is FOUR YEARS.

In Vermont and Maine, the term is only two years.

In Tennessee, the length is eight years.

Iowa Attorney General Tom Miller is the longest continuously serving state attorney general.

He has been in office since 1995. He also served from 1979-1991.

The average time in office for the current group of attorneys general is

3.9 YEARS.

IN 6 STATES,
attorneys general are appointed rather than elected.

Alaska, Hawaii, New Hampshire, New Jersey, Tennessee and Wyoming

IN TENNESSEE, the Supreme Court is responsible for the appointment as opposed to the governor.

IN MAINE, the attorney general is elected by the Legislature.

Top 5 Salaries for Current Attorneys General

Tennessee **$188,952**

California **$175,182**

Wyoming **$175,000**

Alabama **$168,002**

Washington **$162,599**

Average **$126,687**

In seven states, you have to be at least 30 years old to serve as attorney general (Florida, Idaho, Kentucky, New Mexico, New York, Pennsylvania, Virginia). In Oklahoma, you must be at least 31.

20% of attorneys general currently in office are women.

In 31 states and territories, the attorney general is required to be a licensed attorney.

TABLE 4.22

Attorneys General: Consumer Protection Activities, Subpoena Powers and Antitrust Duties

State or other jurisdiction	May commence civil proceedings	May commence criminal proceedings	Represents the state before regulatory agencies (a)	Administers consumer protection programs	Handles consumer complaints	Subpoena powers (b)	Antitrust duties
Alabama	★	★	★	★	★	●	A,B,C
Alaska	★	...	★	★	★	★	A,B,C,D
Arizona	★	★	...	★	★	★	A,B,C,D
Arkansas	★	...	★	★	★	●	A,B
California	★	★	★	★	★	★	A,B,C,D
Colorado	★	★	★	★	★	●	A,C,D
Connecticut	★	(d)	★	★	★	●	A,B,D
Delaware	★	★	★	★	★	★	A,B,D
Florida	★	...	...	★	★	★	A,B,D
Georgia	★	★	★	★	★	●	...
Hawaii	★	★	★	...	★	★	A,B,C,D
Idaho	★	...	★	★	★	★	A,B,D
Illinois	★	...	★	★	★	●	A,B,C
Indiana	★	...	★	★	★	★	A,B
Iowa	★	★	★	★	★	★	B,C
Kansas	★	★	...	★	★	★	A,B,D
Kentucky	★	★	★	★	★	★	A,B,C,D
Louisiana	★	...	★	★	★	(n)	A,B,D
Maine	★	★	★	★	★	★	A,B,C
Maryland	★	★(e)	★	★	★	★	B,C,D
Massachusetts	★	★	★	★	★	★	A,B,C,D
Michigan	★	★	★	★	★	★	A,B,C,D
Minnesota	★	...	★	★	★	★	A,B,C,D
Mississippi	★	...	...	★	★	★	A,B,C,D
Missouri	★	★	★	★	★	★	A,B,C,D
Montana	★	★	...	★	★	...	A,B
Nebraska	★	★	★	★	★	★	A,B,C,D
Nevada	★	★	★	★	★	●	A,B,C,D
New Hampshire	★	★	★	★	★	★	A,B,C
New Jersey	★	★	★	★	★	★	A,B,C,D
New Mexico	★	★	★	★	★	★	A,B,C (g)
New York	★	★	★	★	★	★	A,B,C,D
North Carolina	★	★(f)	★	★	★	★	A,B,C,D
North Dakota	★	...	...	★	...	★	A,B,C
Ohio (c)	★	...	...	★	★	★	A,B,C,D
Oklahoma	★	★	★	★	★	★	A,B,C,D
Oregon	★	★(f)	★	★	★	●	A,B,C,D
Pennsylvania	★	★	★	★	★	★	A,B
Rhode Island	★	★	...	★	★	★	A,B,C
South Carolina	★(a)	★(h)	★	...	(i)	●	A,B,C,D
South Dakota	★	★	★	★	★	★	A,B,C
Tennessee	★	(e)(f)	(f)	★	...	★	A,B,C,D
Texas	★	...	★	★	★	●	A,B,D
Utah	★(j)	★	★(j)	...	★(k)	●	A (l),B,C,D (l)
Vermont	★	★	★	★	★	★	A,B,C
Virginia	★	(f)	★	★(k)	★(k)	●	A,B,C,D
Washington	★	...	★	★	★	★	A,B,D
West Virginia	★	...	★	★	★	★	A,B,D
Wisconsin	★	★	★	★	★	●	A,B,C (g)
Wyoming	★	...	★	★	★	●	A,B
Dist. of Columbia	★	★(m)	★	★	★	★	A,B,C,D
American Samoa	★	★	★	★	★	...	...
Guam	★	★	★	★	★	●	A,B,C,D
CNMI*	★	★	★	★	★	★	A,B
Puerto Rico	★	★	...	...	...	★	A,B,C,D
U.S. Virgin Islands	★	★	★	★	★	●	A

See footnotes at end of table

TABLE 4.22

Attorneys General: Consumer Protection Activities, Subpoena Powers and Antitrust Duties (continued)

Sources: The Council of State Governments' survey of attorneys general, state constitutions and statutes, March 2019.

*Commonwealth of the Northern Mariana Islands

Key:

A–Has parens patriae authority to commence suits on behalf of consumers in state antitrust damage actions in state courts.

B–May initiate damage actions on behalf of state in state courts.

C–May commence criminal proceedings.

D–May represent cities, counties and other governmental entities in recovering civil damages under federal or state law.

★ –Has authority in area.

…–Does not have authority in area.

(a) May represent state on behalf of: the "people" of the state; an agency of the state; or the state before a federal regulatory agency.

(b) In this column only: ★ broad powers and ● limited powers.

(c) Also provides service to consumers through the Identity Theft Unit, administration of Ohio's Title Defect Rescission Fund, and the registration of non-charitable telephone solicitors.

(d) In certain cases only.

(e) May commence criminal proceedings with local district attorney.

(f) To a limited extent.

(g) May represent other governmental entities in recovering civil damages under federal or state law.

(h) When permitted to intervene.

(i) On a limited basis because the state has a separate consumer affairs department.

(j) Attorney general has exclusive authority.

(k) Attorney general handles legal matters only with no administrative handling of complaints.

(l) Opinion only, since there are no controlling precedents.

(m) In antitrust, not criminal proceedings.

(n) The office can issue Civil Investigative Demands, but would go to court in order to get a subpoena.

TABLE 4.23
Attorneys General: Duties to Administrative Agencies and Other Responsibilities

State or other jurisdiction	Serves as counsel for state	Appears for state in criminal appeals	Duties to administrative agencies					Prepares or reviews legal documents	Represents the public before the agency	Involved in rule-making	Reviews rules for legality
			Issues official advice	Interprets statutes or regulations	Conducts litigation:						
					On behalf of agency	Against agency					
Alabama	A,B,C (a)	★(a)	★	★	★	★	(b)	(b)	★	★
Alaska	A,B,C	★	★	★	★	★	★	★	★	★
Arizona	A,B,C	★	★	★	★	...	★	...	★	★
Arkansas	A,B,C	★	★	★	★	★	★	★	...	...
California	A,B,C	★	★	★	★	...	★	...	★	★
Colorado	A,B,C	★	★	★	★	★	★	★	★	★
Connecticut	A,B,C	(b)	★	★	★	★	★	★	★	★
Delaware	A,B,C	★(d)	★	★	★	★	★	★	★	★
Florida	A,B,C	★	★	★	★	...	★	...	...	...
Georgia	A,B,C	★	★	★	★	...	★	...	...	★
Hawaii	A,B,C	★	★	★	★	★	★	★	★	★
Idaho	A,B,C	★	★	★	★	★	★	★	★	★
Illinois	A,B,C	★	...	★	★	...	★	...	...	...
Indiana	A,B,C	★	★	★	★	...	★	...	★	★
Iowa	A,B,C	★	★	★	★	★	★	★	★	★
Kansas	A,B,C	★	★	★	★	★	★	...	★	★
Kentucky	A,B,C	★	★	★	★	...	...	★	...	...
Louisiana	A,B,C	★(m)	★	★	★	...	★	★	★	★
Maine	A,B,C	★	★	★	★	...	★	...	...	★
Maryland	A,B,C	★	★	★	★	(b)	★	★	★	★
Massachusetts	A,B,C	(b)(c)(d)	★	★	★	★	★	★	★	★
Michigan	A,B,C	★	★	★	★	★	★	★	★	★
Minnesota	A,B,C	(c)(d)	★	★	(a)	★	★	★	★	★
Mississippi	A,B,C	...	★	★	★	...	★	...	...	...
Missouri	A,B,C	★	★	★	★	...	★	...	★	...
Montana (f)	A,B,C	★	★	★	★	...	★	...	...	...
Nebraska	A,B,C	★	★	★	★	★	★	...	...	★
Nevada	A,B,C	★	★	★	★	...	★	...	★	★
New Hampshire	A,B,C	★	★	★	★	...	★	(l)	★	...
New Jersey	A,B,C	★	★	★	★	...	★	...	★	★
New Mexico	A,B,C	★	★	★	★	★	★	★	★	★
New York	A,B,C	(b)	...	★	★	(b)	★	(b)	...	...
North Carolina	A,B,C	★	...	★	★	★	★	(b)	★	★
North Dakota	A,B,C	★	★	★	★	★	★	...	★	★
Ohio	A,B,C	...	★	...	★	...	★	...	...	...
Oklahoma	A,B,C	★	★	★	★	★	★	★	★	★
Oregon	A,B	★	★	★	★	...	★	...	★	★
Pennsylvania	A,B	...	...	...	★	...	★	...	...	★
Rhode Island	A,B,C	★	★	★	★	★	★	...	...	...
South Carolina	A,B,C	★(d)	(a)	★	★	(b)	★	...	★	★
South Dakota	A,B,C	★	★	★	★	★	★	...	...	...
Tennessee	A,B,C	★	★	★	★	...	★	(e)	(e)	★
Texas (g)	A,B	★(k)	★	★	★	...	★	...	★	...
Utah	A,B,C	★(a)	★	★	★	★	★	(b)	★	★
Vermont	A,B,C	★	★	★	★	★	★	★	★	★
Virginia	A,B,C	★	★	★	★	★	★	★	★	★
Washington	A,B,C	★(i)	★	★	★	★	★	★	★	★
West Virginia	A,B,C	★	★	★	★	★	★	...	(j)	(j)
Wisconsin	A,B,C	★	★	★	★	(b)	(b)	(b)	(b)	(b)
Wyoming	A,B,C	★	★	★	★	★	★	...	★	★
Dist. of Columbia	A,B	★(h)	★	★	★	...	★	...	★	★
American Samoa	A,B,C	★(a)	★	★	★	...	★	...	★	★
Guam	A,B,C	★	★	★	(d)	★	★	(b)	★	★
CNMI*	A,B,C	★	★	★	★	★	★	...	★	★
Puerto Rico	A,B,C	★	★	★	★	...	★	...	★	★
U.S. Virgin Islands	A,B	★	★	★	★	★	★	★	...	★

See footnotes at end of table

TABLE 4.23

Attorneys General: Duties to Administrative Agencies and Other Responsibilities (continued)

Sources: The Council of State Governments' survey of attorneys general, state constitutions and statutes, March 2019.

*Commonwealth of Northern Mariana Islands

Key:

A–Defend state law when challenged on federal constitutional grounds.

B–Conduct litigation on behalf of state in federal and other states' courts.

C–Prosecute actions against another state in U.S. Supreme Court.

★–Has authority in area.

…–Does not have authority in area.

(a) Attorney general has exclusive jurisdiction.

(b) In certain cases only to prepare or review legal documents and represent the public before the agency.

(c) When assisting local prosecutor in the appeal.

(d) Can appear on own discretion.

(e) Consumer Advocate Division represents the public in utility rate making hearings and rule making proceedings.

(f) Most state agencies are represented by agency counsel who do not answer to the attorney general. The attorney general does provide representation for agencies in conflict situations and where the agency requires additional or specialized assistance.

(g) Other administrative duties include representing one state agency before another state agency.

(h) However, OUSA handles felony cases and most major misdemeanors.

(i) Limited to certain collateral challenges to state criminal convictions.

(j) On request of agency. Office acts as legal counsel to any state agency on request and that can include reviewing legislation and drafting rules and regulations.

(k) Regarding criminal appeals, the Office of Attorney General handles federal habeas corpus appeals only.

(l) The Attorney General serves as counsel for the public before 1 administrative body, but otherwise does not represent the public before agencies.

(m) May appear for the state in criminal appeals either as the actual prosecutor in the case or through the solicitor general if the state has a broader interest.

TABLE 4.24
The Treasurers and Other Chief Financial Officers: 2019

State or other jurisdiction	Name and party	Method of selection	Length of regular term in years	Date of first service	Present term ends	Maximum consecutive terms allowed by constitution
Alabama	John McMillan (R)	E	4	1/2019	1/2023	2
Alaska	Pamela Leary	A	Governor's Discretion	1/2014	...	...
Arizona	Kimberly Yee (R)	E	4	1/2019	1/2023	2
Arkansas	Dennis Milligan (R)	A	4	1/2015	1/2023	2
California	Fiona Ma (D)	E	4	1/2019	1/2023	2
Colorado	Dave Young (D)	E	4	1/2019	1/2023	2
Connecticut	Shawn Wooden (D)	E	4	1/2019	1/2023	★
Delaware	Colleen Davis (D)	E	4	1/2019	1/2023	★
Florida (a)	Jimmy Patronis (R) (b)	E	4	6//2017 (b)	1/2023	2
Georgia	Steve McCoy	A	Pleasure of the Board	11/2011	...	...
Hawaii (c)	Roderick Becker	A	Governor's Discretion	2019	...	...
Idaho	Julie Ellsworth (R)	E	4	1/2019	1/2023	★
Illinois	Mike Frerichs (D)	E	4	1/2015	1/2023	★
Indiana	Kelly Mitchell (R)	E	4	11/2014	1/2023	(d)
Iowa	Michael L. Fitzgerald (D)	E	4	1/1983	1/2023	★
Kansas	Jacob LaTurner (R)	E	4	4/2017	1/2023	★
Kentucky	Alison Ball (R)	E	4	1/2016	1/2020	2
Louisiana	John Michael Schroder Sr. (e)	E	4	11/2017 (e)	12/2019	★
Maine	Henry Beck	L	2	1/2019	1/2021	4
Maryland	Nancy K. Kopp (D)	L	4	2/2002	1/2023	★
Massachusetts	Deb Goldberg (D)	E	4	1/2015	1/2023	★
Michigan	Rachael Eubanks	A	Governor's Discretion	2019	...	...
Minnesota (f)	Myron Frans	A	Governor's Discretion	1/2015	...	...
Mississippi	Lynn Fitch (R)	E	4	1/2012	1/2020	★
Missouri	Scott Fitzpatrick (R)	E	4	1/2019	1/2023	2
Montana	Gene Walborn	A	Governor's Discretion	5/2018	...	...
Nebraska	John Murante (R)	E	4	1/2019	1/2023	2
Nevada	Zach Conine (D)	E	4	1/2019	1/2023	2
New Hampshire	William Dwyer	L	2	12/2014	1/2021	★
New Jersey	Elizabeth Muoio	A	Governor's Discretion	1/2018	...	...
New Mexico	Tim Eichenberg (D)	E	4	1/2015	1/2023	2
New York	Christopher Curtis	A	Governor's Discretion	8/2016	...	...
North Carolina	Dale Folwell (R)	E	4	1/2017	1/2021	★
North Dakota	Kelly L. Schmidt (R)	E	4	1/2005	1/2021	★
Ohio	Robert Sprague (R)	E	4	1/2019	1/2023	2
Oklahoma	Randy McDaniel (R)	E	4	1/2019	1/2023	★
Oregon	Tobias Read (D)	E	4	1/2017	1/2021	2
Pennsylvania	Joseph Torsella (D)	E	4	1/2017	1/2021	2
Rhode Island	Seth Magaziner (D)	E	4	1/2015	1/2023	2
South Carolina	Curtis Loftis (R)	E	4	1/2011	1/2023	★
South Dakota	Josh Haeder (R)	E	4	1/2019	1/2023	2
Tennessee	David H. Lillard Jr.	L	2	1/2009	1/2021	...
Texas (g)	Glenn Hegar (R)	E	4	1/2015	1/2023	★
Utah	David Damschen (R)	E	4	12/2015	12//2019	★
Vermont	Elizabeth Pearce (D)	E	2	1/2011	1/2021	★
Virginia	Manju Ganeriwala	A	Governor's Discretion	1/2009	....	...
Washington	Duane Davidson (R)	E	4	1/2017	1/2021	★
West Virginia	John D. Perdue (D)	E	4	1/1997	1/2021	★
Wisconsin	Sarah Godlewski (D)	E	4	1/2019	1/2023	★
Wyoming	Curt Meier (R)	E	4	1/2019	1/2023	★
American Samoa	Ueli Tonumaipea	A	4	N/A	...	...
Dist. of Columbia	Bruno Fernandes	A	Pleasure of CFO	8/2018	N/A	...
Guam	Rosita Fejeran	CS	...	N/A	...	...
CNMI*	Mark Rabauliman	A	4	N/A	N/A	...
Puerto Rico	Raul Maldonado	A	4	1/2017	N/A	...
U.S. Virgin Islands	Kirk Callwood Sr.	A	4	1/2019	N/A	...

See footnotes at end of table

TABLE 4.24

The Treasurers and Other Chief Financial Officers: 2019 (continued)

Source: The Council of State Governments, April 2019.
*Commonwealth of Northern Mariana Islands
Key:
★–No provision specifying number of terms allowed.
…–No formal provision, position is appointed or elected by governmental entity (not chosen by the electorate).
A–Appointed by the governor. (In the District of Columbia, the Treasurer is appointed by the Chief Financial Officer. In Georgia, position is appointed by the State Depository Board.)
E–Elected by the voters.
L–Elected by the legislature.
CS–Civil Service
N/A–Not available

(a) The official title of the office of state treasurer is Chief Financial Officer.
(b) Gov. Rick Scott appointed Patronis after Jeff Atwater's resignation.
(c) The Director of Finance performs this function.
(d) Eligible for eight out of any period of twelve years.
(e) John Michael Schroder Sr. won the special election to fill John Kennedy's term after he was elected to the U.S. Senate.
(f) The Commissioner of Management and Budget performs this function.
(g) The Comptroller of Public Accounts performs this function.

TABLE 4.25
Treasurers: Qualifications for Office

State	Minimum age	U.S. citizen (years)	State resident (years)	Qualified voter (years)
Alabama	25	7	5	...
Alaska	...	...	...	...
Arizona	25	10	5	★
Arkansas	18	★	★	★
California	18	★	★	★
Colorado	25	★	2	...
Connecticut	18	★	★	★
Delaware	18	...	...	...
Florida	30	★	7	★
Georgia	...	...	...	...
Hawaii	...	★	1	...
Idaho	25	★	2	...
Illinois	25	★	3	...
Indiana	...	★	★	★
Iowa	18	...	★	★
Kansas	...	...	...	...
Kentucky	30	2	2	★
Louisiana	25	5	5	★
Maine	...	★	★	...
Maryland	...	...	...	...
Massachusetts	...	5	5	...
Michigan	...	...	...	...
Minnesota	...	...	...	...
Mississippi	25	★	5	...
Missouri	30	15	10	★
Montana	...	...	...	...
Nebraska	...	★	★	★
Nevada	25	2	2	★
New Hampshire	...	...	...	...
New Jersey	...	...	★	...
New Mexico	30	★	5	★
New York	30	★	5	...
North Carolina	21	★	1	★
North Dakota	25	★	5	★
Ohio	18	★	★	★
Oklahoma	31	★	10	★
Oregon	31	★	10	★
Pennsylvania	...	...	...	...
Rhode Island	18	★	★	★
South Carolina	18	★	★	★
South Dakota	...	...	...	...
Tennessee	...	...	...	...
Texas	18	★	★	...
Utah	25	★	5	★
Vermont	...	★	★	...
Virginia	...	...	...	...
Washington	18	★	...	★
West Virginia	18	★	5	★
Wisconsin	18	★	★	★
Wyoming	25	★	★	★
Dist. of Columbia	...	★	...	...

Source: The Council of State Governments' survey of state treasurers
offices, April 2019.
Key:
★–Formal provision; number of years not specified.
...–No formal provision.
(a) 5 years immediately preceding the date of qualification for
office.

TABLE 4.26
Responsibilities of the Treasurer's Office

State or other jurisdiction	Cash management	Banking services	Investment of retirement funds	Investment of trust funds	Deferred compensation	Management of bonded debt	Bond issuance	Debt service	Arbitrage	Unclaimed property	Archives for disbursement of documents	College savings	Collateral programs	Local government investment pool	Other
Alabama	★	★	...	...	...	★	...	★	...	★	...	★	★	...	...
Alaska	★	★	★	★	...	...	★	★	★	★	...	...	...	...	...
Arizona	★	★	...	★	...	...	...	...	...	...	...	...	...	★	...
Arkansas	★	★	★	...	...	...	...	...	...	...	...	★	...	★	...
California	★	★	...	★	...	★	★	★	★	...	...	★	★	★	...
Colorado	★	★	...	...	...	...	★	★	...	★	...	...	...	...	...
Connecticut	★	★	★	★	...	★	★	★	★	★	...	★	...	★	(a)
Delaware	★	★	★	★	★	★	★	★	...	...	...	★	...	...	(b)
Florida	★	★	...	★	★	...	...	...	...	★	...	...	★	...	(c)
Georgia	★	★	...	★	...	...	...	★	...	...	...	...	★	★	(d)
Hawaii	★	★	★	★	...	...	★	★	...	★	...	★	...	...	...
Idaho	★	★	...	...	...	...	★	...	...	★	...	★	...	★	...
Illinois	★	★	...	★	...	...	...	★	★	★	...	★	...	★	...
Indiana	★	★	★	★	...	★	...	...	...	...	★	★	...	★	(n)
Iowa	★	★	★	...	...	★	★	★	...	★	...	★	...	★	...
Kansas	★	★	...	...	...	...	...	...	...	★	...	★	...	...	(e)
Kentucky	★	★	...	...	...	...	...	...	...	★	★	...	...	...	...
Louisiana	★	★	...	★	...	★	★	★	★	★	...	...	★	...	...
Maine	★	★	...	★	...	★	★	★	★	★	...	★	...	...	(f)
Maryland	★	★	...	...	...	★	★	★	★	...	...	...	★	★	...
Massachusetts	★	★	★	★	★	...	★	★	★	★	...	★	...	...	...
Michigan	★	★	★	★	...	★	★	★	★	★	...	★	...	...	...
Minnesota	★	★	...	...	...	...	★	★	...	...	...	...	...	...	...
Mississippi	★	★	...	★	...	★	★	★	★	★	...	★	★	★	...
Missouri	★	★	...	★	...	...	...	...	★	★	...	★	...	...	(g)
Montana	★	★	...	...	...	★	★	★	★	...	...	...	...	...	(o)
Nebraska	★	★	...	...	...	...	...	...	...	★	...	★	...	...	(h)
Nevada	★	★	...	★	...	★	★	★	...	★	...	★	★	★	(m)
New Hampshire	★	★	...	★	...	★	★	★	★	★	...	★	...	...	...
New Jersey	★	★	★	★	★	★	★	★	★	★	...	...	...	★	...
New Mexico	★	★	...	...	...	★	...	★	...	...	★	...	...	★	...
New York	★	★	★	★	...	...	...	...	...	...	...	...	★	...	...
North Carolina	★	★	★	★	...	★	★	★	★	★	...	★	...	★	...
North Dakota	★	...	...	...	...	...	...	...	...	...	...	...	...	...	(i)
Ohio	★	★	...	★	...	★	★	★	★	...	...	...	★	★	...
Oklahoma	★	★	...	★	...	...	...	★	...	★	...	★	★	...	...
Oregon	★	★	★	★	★	★	★	★	★	...	...	★	★	★	...
Pennsylvania	★	★	...	...	...	★	★	★	★	★	...	★	...	★	...
Rhode Island	★	★	★	★	...	★	★	★	★	★	...	★	...	★	...
South Carolina	★	★	★	★	...	★	★	★	★	★	...	★	...	★	...
South Dakota	★	★	★	★	...	...	...	...	...	★	...	...	...	...	...
Tennessee	★	★	...	...	★	...	...	...	...	★	...	★	★	★	...
Texas	★	★	...	★	...	...	...	...	...	★	...	★	★	★	(j)
Utah	★	★	...	...	...	★	★	★	★	★	...	...	...	★	...
Vermont	★	★	★	★	★	★	★	★	★	★	...	...	...	...	...
Virginia	★	★	...	★	...	★	★	★	★	★	...	...	★	★	(k)
Washington	★	★	...	★	...	★	★	★	★	★	...	...	...	...	...
West Virginia	★	★	...	★	★	...	...	★	...	★	...	★	★	★	...
Wisconsin	...	...	...	...	...	...	...	...	...	★	...	...	...	★	...
Wyoming	★	★	...	★	...	★	★	★	★	★	...	...	★	★	(n)
Dist. of Columbia	★	★	★	★	★	★	★	★	★	★	...	★	★	...	...

See footnotes at end of table

TABLE 4.26
Responsibilities of the Treasurer's Office (continued)

Source: The Council of State Governments' survey of state treasurers offices, March 2019.

Key:

★ –Responsible for activity.

… –Not responsible for activity.

(a) Second Injury Fund.

(b) General Fund account reconcilement.

(c) State Accounting Disbursement, Fire Marshall, Insurance and Banking Consumer Services, Insurance Rehabilitation.

(d) Merchant Card Services.

(e) Municipal bond servicing.

(f) Municipal Revenue Sharing.

(g) Investment of all State funds and ABLE program.

(h) Nebraska Child Support Payment Center, Long-Term Care Savings Plan.

(i) The treasurer serves on the State Investment Board, the Teachers Fund for Retirement Board, the Board of University and School Lands, the State Historical Society, and the State Board of Equalization. Other duties include: tax collections and distributions, financial literacy, and the office provides analysis, data and education of various tax distributions and state laws to legislators, other state agencies, officials and employees of local political subdivision and the general public. North Dakota has a state-owned bank which provides banking services for the state.

(j) Tax Administration/Collection/Estimating.

(k) Risk Management.

(l) Several other legislatively designated programs.

(m) Education Savings Accounts.

(n) The treasurer serves as the trustee of the Indiana State Police Pension Trust.

(o) Social Security Section 218 agreements; merchant card (Procard) services.

TABLE 4.27
State Auditors: 2019

State or other jurisdiction	State Agency	Agency head	Title	Legal basis for office	Method of selection	Term of office	U.S. citizen	State resident	Maximum consecutive terms allowed
Alabama	Department of Examiners of Public Accounts	Rachel Riddle	Chief Examiner	S	LC	7 yrs.	★	...	None
Alaska	Division of Legislative Audit	Kris Curtis	Legislative Auditor	C, S	L	(a)	...	...	None
Arizona	Office of the Auditor General	Lindsey Perry	Auditor General	S	LC	5 yrs.	...	...	None
Arkansas	Division of Legislative Audit	Roger A. Norman	Legislative Auditor	S	LC	Indefinite	★	★	None
California	Bureau of State Audits	Elaine M. Howle	State Auditor	S	G	4 yrs.	★		None
Colorado	Office of the State Auditor	Dianne E. Ray	State Auditor	C, S	LC	5 yrs.	...	...	None
Connecticut	Office of the Auditors of Public Accounts	John C. Geragosian and Robert Kane	State Auditors	S	L	4 yrs.	...	...	None
Delaware	Office of the Auditor of Accounts	Kathleen McGuiness	Auditor of Accounts	C, S	E	4 yrs.	★	★	None
Florida	Office of the Auditor General	Sherrill F. Norman	Auditor General	C, S	L	(a)	...	...	None
Georgia	Department of Audits and Accounts	Greg S. Griffin	State Auditor	S	L	Indefinite	...	...	None
Hawaii	Office of the Auditor	Les Kondo	State Auditor	C	L	8 yrs.	...	★	None
Idaho	Legislative Services Office– Legislative Audits	April J. Renfro	Division Manager	S	LC	(b)	...	...	None
Illinois	Office of the Auditor General	Frank Mautino	Auditor General	C, S	L	10 yrs.	...	...	None
Indiana	State Board of Accounts	Paul D. Joyce	State Examiner	S	GLC	4 yrs.	...	...	None
Iowa	Office of the Auditor of State	Rob Sand	Auditor of State	C, S	E	4 yrs.	★	★	None
Kansas	Legislative Division of Post Audit	Justin Stowe	Interim Legislative Post Auditor	S	LC	(b)	...	...	None
Kentucky	Office of the Auditor of Public Accounts	Mike Harmon	Auditor of Public Accounts	C, S	E	4 yrs.	★	★	2
Louisiana	Office of the Legislative Auditor	Daryl G. Purpera	Legislative Auditor	C, S	L	(a)	...	★	None
Maine	Department of Audit	Pola A. Buckley	State Auditor	S	L	4 yrs.	...	...	2
Maryland	Office of Legislative Audits	Gregory A. Hook	Legislative Auditor	S	ED	Indefinite	...	...	None
Massachusetts	Office of the Auditor of the Commonwealth	Suzanne M. Bump	Auditor of the Commonwealth	C, S	E	4 yrs.	★	★	None
Michigan	Office of the Auditor General	Doug Ringler	Auditor General	C	L	8 yrs.	...	★	None
Minnesota	Office of the Legislative Auditor	James R. Nobles	Legislative Auditor	S	LC	6 yrs. (a)	...	...	None
Mississippi	Office of the State Auditor	Julie Blaha	State Auditor	C	E	4 yrs.	★	★	None
Missouri	Office of the State Auditor	Shad White	State Auditor	C	E	4 yrs.	★	★	None
Montana	Office of the State Auditor	Nicole Galloway	State Auditor	C, S	E	4 yrs.	★	★	None
Nebraska	Legislative Audit Division	Angus Maciver	Legislative Auditor	C, S	LC	2 yrs.	...	...	None
	Office of the Auditor of Public Accounts	Charlie Janssen	Auditor of Public Accounts	C	E	4 yrs.	★	★	None
Nevada	Legislative Counsel Bureau, Audit Division	Rocky Cooper	Legislative Auditor	S	LC	Indefinite	...	...	None
New Hampshire	Office of the Legislative Budget Assistant	Michael W. Kane	Legislative Budget Assistant	S	LC	2 yrs. (b)	...	...	None
New Jersey	Office of the State Auditor	Stephen M. Eells	State Auditor	C, S	L	5 yr. term and until successor is appointed	★	★	None
	Office of the State Comptroller	Philip Degnan	State Comptroller	S	G	6 yrs.	...	★	2
New Mexico	Office of the State Auditor	Brian S. Colon	State Auditor	C, S	E	4 yrs.	★	★	2
New York	Office of the State Comptroller, State Audit Bureau	Thomas P. DiNapoli	State Comptroller	C, S	E	4 yrs.	★	★	None
North Carolina	Office of the State Auditor	Beth A. Wood	State Auditor	C	E	4 yrs.	★	★	None
North Dakota	Office of the State Auditor	Joshua Gallion	State Auditor	C, S	E	Indefinite	...	★	None
Ohio	Office of the Auditor of State	Keith Faber	Auditor of State	C, S	E	4 yrs.	...	...	2
Oklahoma	Office of the State Auditor and Inspector	Cindy Byrd	State Auditor and Inspector	C, S	E	4 yrs.	★	★	None
Oregon	Division of Audits	Kip Memmott	Director	C, S	SS	Indefinite	...	...	None
Pennsylvania	Department of the Auditor General	Eugene DePasquale	Auditor General	C, S	E	4 yrs.	...	...	2
Rhode Island	Office of the Auditor General	Dennis E. Hoyle	Auditor General	S	LC	(b)	...	...	None
South Carolina	Legislative Audit Council	Earle Powell	Director	S	LC	4 yrs.	...	...	None
	Office of the State Auditor	George Kennedy	State Auditor	S	SB	Indefinite (c)	...	...	None
South Dakota	Department of Legislative Audit	Martin L. Guindon	Auditor General	S	L	8 yrs. (a)	...	...	None

See footnotes at end of table

TABLE 4.27
State Auditors: 2019 (continued)

State or other jurisdiction	State Agency	Agency head	Title	Legal basis for office	Method of selection	Term of office	U.S. citizen	State resident	Maximum consecutive terms allowed
Tennessee	Comptroller of the Treasury, Dept. of Audit	Justin P. Wilson	Comptroller of the Treasury	C, S	L	2 yrs.	...	...	None
Texas	Office of the State Auditor	Lisa Collier	State Auditor	S	LC	(b)	...	...	None
Utah	Office of the State Auditor	John Dougall	State Auditor	C, S	E	4 yrs.	★	★	None
Vermont	Office of the State Auditor	Douglas R. Hoffer	State Auditor	C, S	E	2 yrs.	...	★	None
Virginia	Office of the Auditor of Public Accounts	Martha S. Mavredes	Auditor of Public Accounts	C, S	L	4 yrs.	...	...	None
Washington	Office of the State Auditor	Pat McCarthy	State Auditor	C, S	E	4 yrs.	★	★	None
West Virginia	Legislative Auditor's Office	Aaron Allred	Legislative Auditor	S	L	(a)	...	...	None
Wisconsin	Legislative Audit Bureau	Joe Chrisman	State Auditor	S	LC	Indefinite (b)	...	...	None
Wyoming	Department of Audit	Jeffrey C. Vogel	Director	S	GC	6 yrs.	...	★	None
Dist. Of Columbia	Office of the D.C. Auditor	Kathleen Patterson	District of Columbia Auditor						
American Samoa	AS Territorial Auditor Office	Liua Fatuesi	Territorial Auditor						
Guam	Office of the Public Auditor	Benjamin Cruz	Public Auditor	S	E	4 yrs.	★	★	None
CNMI*	Office of the Public Auditor	Michael Pai	Public Auditor	C,S,	GL	6 yrs.	N.A.	N.A.	2
Puerto Rico	Office of the Comptroller	Yesmin M. Valdivieso-Galib	Comptroller	C,S,	GL	10 yrs.	★	★	1
U.S. Virgin Islands	Office of the Inspector General	Steven van Beverhoudt	Inspector General						

Source: Auditing in the States: A Summary, 2018 edition, The National Association of State Auditors, Comptrollers and Treasurers.
*Commonwealth of Northern Mariana Islands
Key:
★–Provision for.
…–No provision for.
E–Elected by the public.
L–Appointed by the legislature.
G–Appointed by the governor.
SS–Appointed by the secretary of state.
LC–selected by legislative committee, commission or council.
ED–appointed by the executive director of legislative services.

GC–Appointed by governor, secretary of state and treasurer.
GL–Appointed by the governor and confirmed by both chambers of the legislature.
GLC–Appointed by the governor and confirmed by legislative council.
SB–Appointed by state budget and control board.
C–Constitutional.
S–Statutory.
N.A.–Not applicable.
(a) Serves at the pleasure of the legislature.
(b) Serves at the pleasure of a legislative committee.
(c) The term is indefinite, but the state auditor serves at the pleasure of the five-member board.

TABLE 4.28

State Auditors: Audit of Basic Financial Statements and Single Audit

State or other jurisdiction	Auditing of basic financial statements				Conducting the single audit			
	State audit agency conducts audit (100%)	State audit agency is primary auditor— % of total governmental, business type, fiduciary and component unit expenditures contracted to CPA firms	CPA firm(s) conducts audit (100%)	Selection of auditor if part/all of financial audit is contracted out	State audit agency conducts audit (100%)	State audit agency conducts part/ CPA firm conducts part— % conducted by CPA firm	CPA firm(s) conducts audit (100%)	Selection of auditor if part/all of single audit is contracted out
Alabama	...	N/A	...	Individual departments/agencies	...	★ ~0.4%	...	Individual departments/agencies
Alaska	...	★ —We summarize outside audit coverage by percent of assets and percent of revenue. Governmental activities: 89% assets/59% revenues; business type activities: 77% assets/66% of revenues; aggregate discretely presented component units: 91% assets/90% revenues	...	Most of the outside audited entities are governmental corporations and the University. The outside entities select their own auditors. However, there are a few that require the legislative auditor approve the outside auditor.	...	★ ~70%	...	State corporations select their own auditor, Department of Administration, Division of Finance selected contractor to audit Department of Health and Social Services FY 15 major federal programs.
Arizona	...	★ —governmental (50.8%), business type activities (14.9%), fiduciary (99.6%), component unit (100%)	...	The audited agency selects the auditor with help from the Auditor General's Office.	...	★ ~79.67%	...	The audited agncy selects the auditor with help from the Auditor General's Office.
Arkansas	...	★ —7; 7.68%	...	State agency	...	★ ~4.59%	...	The individual agency receiving a private audit selects the auditor.
California	★	...	...		...	...	★	The state auditor selects the contract auditor.
Colorado	...	★	...	State auditor	...	★ ~47%	...	State auditor
Connecticut	...	★ —governmental (0%), business type activities (<1%), fiduciary (0%), component unit (100%)	...		★	...	...	
Delaware	...		★	Office of Auditor of Accounts	...	...	★	Office of Auditor of Accounts
Florida	...	★ —governmental (0.2%), business type activities (1.3%), component unit (4.4%)	...	The agencies or entities being audited.	★	...	...	
Georgia	...	★ —governmental (4% of total assets/deferred outflows of resources), business type activities (3% total assets/deferred outflows of resources); aggregate discretely presented component units (86% of total assets/ deferred outflows of resources and 87% of total revenues/additions); governmental fund - general obligation bond fund projects (100% of total assets,deferred outflows of resources and 100% of total revenues/ additions; aggregate remaining fund information (88% of total assets/deferred outflows of resources and 48% of total revenues/additions)	...	The entity being audited selects the CPA firm through a bid process. The cost of audits performed by CPAs are paid by the audited entity.	★	...	...	
Hawaii	...		★	Office of the Auditor	...	...	★	Office of the Auditor
Idaho	...	★ —governmental (3.6%), business type activities (82.2%), fiduciary (100%), component unit (99%)	...	The entity going out for contract.	★	...	...	

See footnotes at end of table

TABLE 4.28

State Auditors: Audit of Basic Financial Statements and Single Audit (continued)

State or other jurisdiction	Auditing of basic financial statements				Conducting the single audit			
	State audit agency conducts audit (100%)	State audit agency is primary auditor—% of total governmental, business type, fiduciary and component unit expenditures contracted to CPA firms	CPA firm(s) conducts audit (100%)	Selection of auditor if part/all of financial audit is contracted out	State audit agency conducts audit (100%)	State audit agency conducts part/CPA firm conducts part—% conducted by CPA firm	CPA firm(s) conducts audit (100%)	Selection of auditor if part/all of single audit is contracted out
Illinois	★	...	...		...	...	★	Office of the Auditor General
Indiana	...	★ -2% (public employee's retirement system and component units are contracted to CPA firms)	...	The governing body of the component unit.	★	...	...	...
Iowa	...	★	...	Office of Auditor of State	★	...	...	
Kansas	...	...	★	Contract Audit Committee	...	...	★	Contract Audit Committee
Kentucky	...	★ -governmental activities (1.57%), business type activities (26.12%), component units (90.88%)	...	The Office of the Auditor of Public Accounts has the right of first refusal for all agencies and component units of the state. We decline some agencies/component units and allow the agency to contract with a CPA firm.	★	...	...	...
Louisiana	...	★ -governmental (.03%), business type activities (6.65%), fiduciary (65.55%), aggregate discretely component unit (14.1%) - Note: fiduciary funds are included in aggregate remaining funds	...	Legislative auditor	★	Single audits of some agencies are performed by CPA firms. The SEFA amounts in these stand-alone reports are not included in the SEFA in LA's Single Audit report.	...	
Maine	★	...	...	State Comptroller's Office	...	...	★	State Comptroller's Office
Maryland	...	...	★	Office of the State Comptroller	...	...	★	Office of the State Comptroller
Massachusetts	...	...	★		...	...	★	
Michigan	...	★ -14%	...	14 component units (10 state universities and four others) and one enterprise fund select their own auditor. All other contract auditors are selected by the auditor general.		★ -5%	...	One component unit selects their own and the auditor general selects the rest.
Minnesota								
Legislative Auditor	...	★ -business type activities (67.6%), component units (98.2%)	...	Each BTA and CU selects their own auditor		★ -7.3% (student financial assistance cluster)	...	The Minnesota State Colleges and Universities selects its own auditor.
State Auditor	...	Not involved in the state's financial audit	...	Proposals are submitted to the Office of the State Auditor and are selected by representatives of the office with comments by the agencies being audited and Department of Finance and Administration considered.		...	...	Not involved in state's single audit.
Mississippi	...	★ -governmental (6-19%), business type activities (100%), fiduciary (100%), component units (100%)	...			★ -10%	...	The auditor is selected by the Office of the State Auditor with input from the state agencies and the Department of Finance and Administration.
Missouri	...	★ -31.7%	...	Generally, the entity being audited selects the auditor.	...	★	...	The auditor is selected by the entity being audited.
Montana	★	...	...		★			...
Nebraska	★	...	...		★			...

See footnotes at end of table

TABLE 4.28

State Auditors: Audit of Basic Financial Statements and Single Audit (continued)

State or other jurisdiction	Auditing of basic financial statements				Conducting the single audit			
	State audit agency conducts audit (100%)	State audit agency is primary auditor—% of total governmental, business type, fiduciary and component unit expenditures contracted to CPA firms	CPA firm(s) conducts audit (100%)	Selection of auditor if part/all of financial audit is contracted out	State audit agency conducts audit (100%)	State audit agency conducts part/ CPA firm conducts part—% conducted by CPA firm	CPA firm(s) conducts audit (100%)	Selection of auditor if part/all of single audit is contracted out
Nevada	...	...	★	Audit Subcommittee of the Legislative Commission	...	...	★	Audit Subcommittee of the Legislative Commission
New Hampshire	...	★~80%	...	Legislative budget assistant	...	...	★	Legislative budget assistant
New Jersey								
State Auditor	...	★—governmental activities (4%), business type activities (47%), fiduciary (99%), component units (100%)	...	Department of the Treasury, Judiciary, individual component units.	...	...	★	Department of the Treasury, Office of Management and Budget
State Comptroller	...	...	...		...	...	...	
New Mexico	...	★—Financial statement audits are prepared at a department level. The department level financial statements are used to compile the statewide CAFR. The Office of the State Auditor has a limited staff of auditors who conduct audits of agencies. Therefore, most of these engagements are performed by Independent Public Accountants.	...	Agencies that are contracting with Independent Public Accountants select an auditor from a list of audit firms approved on an annual basis by the Office of the State Auditor.	...	★—OSA has a limited staff of auditors who conduct audits of agencies. Therefore, most of these engagements are performed by Independent Public Accountants.	...	Single audits are done at the department level, not statewide. Agencies that contract with Independent Public Accountants select an auditor from a list of audit firms approved on an annual basis by the OSA.
New York	...	...	★	Office of the State Comptroller	...	...	★	Office of the State Comptroller and Governor's Division of the Budget
North Carolina	★	...	...		★	...	...	
North Dakota	...	★—governmental (26%), business type (83%), fiduciary & component unit (100%)	...	The state auditor selects the auditor.	...	★~10% contracted to CPA firms	...	The state auditor selects the auditor.
Ohio	...	★	...	Auditor of state makes selection with input from component units and other state officials.	★	...	...	
Oklahoma	...	★—governmental (6.75%), fiduciary (100%), component unit (100%); combined (40.82%)	...		...	★—outside audited major programs to total audited major programs (2.08%)	...	It varies depending on statutory requirements.
Oregon	...	★—fiduciary (95%), component unit (100%)	...	Division of Audits, via RFP process	★	...	...	
Pennsylvania	...	★—governmental (14%), business type (5%), fiduciary & component unit (100%)	...	Governor's Office of the Budget (audited entity)	...	★~15% major program expenditure coverage	...	Governor's Office of the Budget
Rhode Island	N/A	N/A	N/A	N/A	N/A	N/A	N/A	N/A
South Carolina								
Legislative Audit Council	...	Our office does not have anything to do with financial audits in our state. The office of the state auditor is responsible for all financial audits, including contracting out.	...		...	...	...	
State Auditor	...	★—governmental (60%), business type (80%), component units (100%)	...	Office of the State Auditor	...	★—single audit is a joint opinion issues by our office and a CPA firm	...	Office of the State Auditor

See footnotes at end of table

TABLE 4.28
State Auditors: Audit of Basic Financial Statements and Single Audit (continued)

State or other jurisdiction	Auditing of basic financial statements				Conducting the single audit			
	State audit agency conducts audit (100%)	State audit agency is primary auditor—% of total governmental, business type, fiduciary and component unit expenditures contracted to CPA firms	CPA firm(s) conducts audit (100%)	Selection of auditor if part/all of financial audit is contracted out	State audit agency conducts audit (100%)	State audit agency conducts part/CPA firm conducts part—% conducted by CPA firm	CPA firm(s) conducts audit (100%)	Selection of auditor if part/all of single audit is contracted out
South Dakota	...	★–business type (11.1%), fiduciary (100%), discretely presented component units (55.7%); remaining fund information (89.1%)	...	The audited entity with approval of Department of Legislative Audit	...	★–it depends of the year. A few grants are audited by CPA firms for agencies that have contracted audit services. Department of Legislative Audit audits the majority of grants.	...	Auditor is selected by the state agency, but the auditor and the final report must be approved by the Department of Legislative Audit.
Tennessee	★	...	...		★		...	
Texas	...	★–19.2%	...	The state entity receiving the audit	...	★–CPA firm is the primary auditor for the federal compliance portion of the single audit providing 66% coverage. Our office covers the remaining.	...	Texas State Auditor's Office
Utah	...	★–governmental (0.34%), business type (20.61%), fiduciary (19.86%), component unit (42.25%)	...	State auditor or an assigned director over contracting	...	★–15.9%	...	State auditor or an assigned director over contracting
Vermont	...	...	★	Auditor of Accounts	...	...	★	Auditor of accounts
Virginia	...	★–We audit all of the primary government, but do not audit some component units representing 30% of assets and deferred outflows, 24% of net position, and 8% of revenues of the aggregated discretely presented component unit.	...	Most of the outsourced component units select their own auditor; however, we do handle the bidding process for a few of these entities.	★			
Washington	...	★–18%	...	We have allowed agencies to select their auditor.	★		...	
West Virginia Performance Evaluation Research Division	...	...	★		...	...	★	Office of the Legislative Auditor
Post Audit Division	...	...	★	West Virginia Department of Administration's Financial Accounting and Reporting System (FARS) conducts the annual financial audit (CAFR).	...	...	★	Single audit performed by Ernst & Young
Wisconsin	★	...	...		★		...	
Wyoming	...	...	★	Department of Audit	...	...	★	Department of Audit
Guam	...	...	★	The public auditor in conjunction with the audited agencies.	...	...	★	The public auditor in conjunction with the audited agencies.
Puerto Rico	...	...	★	The CEO of each agency	...	...	★	The CEO of each agency

Sources: Auditing in the States: A Summary, 2018 edition. The National Association of State Auditors, Comptrollers and Treasurers.

Key:
★–Provision for responsibility.   ...–No provision for responsibility.   N/A–Did not respond.

TABLE 4.29
State Auditors: Audits of Local Governments

State or other jurisdiction	Audits local governments	Types of local governments audited			
		Cities, towns & villages	Counties	Non-profit organizations/ for-profits receiving state/ federal awards	School districts
Alabama	★	...	★(100%)	...	★(100% county school districts)
Alaska	...	...	...	...	...
Arizona	★	...	★(57%)	...	...
Arkansas	★	★(92.4%)	★(100%)	...	★(82.13%)
California	★	★	★	★	★
Colorado	...	...	...	...	...
Connecticut	...	★	...	...	...
Delaware	...	...	...	...	...
Florida	★	...	...	...	★(100%)
Georgia	★	...	...	...	★(approx. 85%)
Hawaii	...	...	...	...	...
Idaho	...	...	...	...	...
Illinois	★	...	...	...	...
Indiana	★	★(99%)	★(99%)	...	★(99%)
Iowa	★	★(10%)	★(40%)	...	★(1%)
Kansas	...	...	...	...	...
Kentucky	★	...	★(approx. 60%)	...	...
Louisiana	...	...	...	...	...
Maine	...	...	...	...	...
Maryland	...	...	...	...	...
Massachusetts	★	★	★	★	★
Michigan	...	...	...	...	...
Minnesota					
Legislative Auditor	...	...	...	...	...
State Auditor	★	★(0.4%)	★(70%)	...	...
Mississippi	★	...	★(37%)	...	...
Missouri	★	...	★(78%)	...	★
Montana	...	...	...	...	...
Nebraska	★	★(1%)	★(18%)	★(<1%)	★(<1%)
Nevada	...	...	...	...	...
New Hampshire	...	...	...	...	...
New Jersey					
State Auditor	★	...	...	...	★(<5% a year)
State Comptroller	★	★	★	★	★
New Mexico	★	...	...	...	...
New York	★	★(100%)	★(100%)	★(100%)	★(100%)
North Carolina	...	...	...	...	...
North Dakota	★	★(a)	★(62%)	...	★(a)
Ohio	★	★cities (38%); townships (53%); villages (62%)	★(74%)	...	★(60%)
Oklahoma	★	★(a)	★(100%)	★(a)	★(a)
Oregon	...	...	...	...	...
Pennsylvania	★	★	★	★	★(100%)
Rhode Island	N/A	N/A	N/A	N/A	N/A
South Carolina					
Legislative Audit Council	...	...	...	...	...
State Auditor	...	...	...	...	...
South Dakota	★	★a few, varies year to year	★(100%)	...	★a few, varies year to year
Tennessee	★	...	★(95%)	...	...
Texas	...	...	...	...	...
Utah	...	...	...	...	...
Vermont	...	...	...	...	...
Virginia	...	...	...	...	...
Washington	★	★(100%)	★(100%)	...	★(100%)
West Virginia					
Performance Evaluation Research Division	...	...	...	...	...
Post Audit Division	...	...	...	...	...
Wisconsin	...	...	...	...	...
Wyoming	★	★(2%)	...	...	★(20%)
Guam	★	★	...	★	★
Puerto Rico	★	★(100%)	...	...	★(100%)

See footnotes at end of table

TABLE 4.29

State Auditors: Audits of Local Governments (continued)

State or other jurisdiction	Types of local governments audited (con't.) Other	Audit standards used	GAAP required for local government financial statements
Alabama	...	GAAS, GAGAS	★
Alaska	...	...	...
Arizona	Community College Districts (92%)	GAAS, GAGAS, Uniform Guidance	★
Arkansas	Prosecuting attorney judicial districts (100%)	GAAS, GAGAS; very small local governments may have a financial and compliance report in lieu of a full audit report.	No, regulatory basis per Arkansas Code.
California	Any publicly-created entity.	GAGAS	...
Colorado	...	...	...
Connecticut	...	GAGAS	★
Delaware	...	...	...
Florida	Cities, towns, etc., as directed by the Legislative Auditing Committee, through citizen petition, or the auditor general's discretion	GAAS, GAGAS	★
Georgia	...	GAGAS	★
Hawaii	...	...	...
Idaho	...	...	...
Illinois	As directed by the General Assembly	GAAS, GAGAS	By statute, GAAP is to be followed to the extent possible. Some smaller units of local government report on a cash basis.
Indiana	Audits all public libraries, townships, special taxing districts, state universities, and 10% of public hospitals.	GAAS, GAGAS (c)	No, regulatory basis.
Iowa	Intergovernmental entities organized under Chapter 28E of the Code of Iowa, landfills, community colleges, area education agencies, merged area schools, hospitals	GAAS, GAGAS	GAAP is required for counties, schools, hospitals, community colleges, area education agencies and merged area schools; cash basis is used for cities, landfills and entitites organized under Chapter 28E of the Code of Iowa.
Kansas	...	...	...
Kentucky	Clerk fee–100%; sheriff fee–100%; sheriff tax settlements–100%	GAAS, GAGAS	No. Regulatory basis for 115/120 counties; 5 of 120 counties follow GAAP.
Louisiana	The audit and other attest engagements of local governments in Louisiana are performed by CPA firms. These firms and engagements are approved by the legislative auditor.	GAGAS (d)	★ Louisiana local governments that may issue debt are required by LRS 24:514 to prepare their financial statements in accordance with GAAP.
Maine	...	GAAS, GAGAS	★
Maryland	...	GAAS	★
Massachusetts	Counties, cities, towns and school districts are audited by request. Nonprofit organizations are audited as vendors receiving state funds.	GAAS, GAGAS	★
Michigan	...	GAAS (e)	★
Minnesota Legislative Auditor	...	...	...
State Auditor	Regional development commissions–10%	GAGAS	Most entities are required to prepare financial statements in accordance with GAAP. Very small entities report on a non-GAAP basis. Entities use both a cash basis and regulatory basis.
Mississippi	...	GAAS, GAGAS	Some counties prepare GAAP financial statements and some prepare OCBOA (cash/modified cash) financial statements.
Missouri	Other political subdivisions such as cities and special districts upon petition by a subdivision's voters. Also, performace audits of transportation development districts and community improvement districts under separate statutory authority.	GAGAS	No. Some local governments use cash basis.
Montana	...	GAAS, GAGAS	★
Nebraska	...	GAAS, GAGAS	No, cash basis
Nevada	...	...	...
New Hampshire	...	...	...
New Jersey State Auditor	There are 590 school districts in the state. The office is statutorily required to audit any district with a negative fund balance. Also audits others based on a risk assessment. Acutal school district audits–3 to 4 per year.	GAGAS	School districts and public authorities follow GAAP; cities and counties follow OCBOA (modified cash basis) as required by Department of Community Affairs, Division of Local Government Services.
State Comptroller	...	GAGAS	...

See footnotes at end of table

TABLE 4.29
State Auditors: Audits of Local Governments (continued)

State or other jurisdiction	Types of local governments audited (con't.) Other	Audit standards used	GAAP required for local government financial statements
New Mexico	The Office of the State Auditor has a limited staff of auditors who conduct audits of agencies, therefore, most of these engagements are performed by Independent Public Accountants.	GAAS, GAGAS	★(f)
New York	...	GAGAS	★ The city of New York is required by law to prepare GAAP financial statements. School districts and Boards of Cooperative Education Services (BOCES) are required by the State Education Department to prepare GAAP financial statements. All other local governments are encouraged to do so, but are not required.
North Carolina	...	...	...
North Dakota	...	GAGAS	No. Counties are required to prepare financial statements. Other local governments are not required to prepare their own financial statements. Cash/modified cash is used.
Ohio	Community schools–31%	GAAS, GAGAS	Ohio Administrative Code 117-2-03 requires counties, cities and school districts, including educational service centers and community schools, and government insurance pools organized pursuant to section 9.833 or 2744.081 of the Ohio Revised Code to file annual financial reports prepared using GAAP. Other local governments follow OCBOA and regulatory basis.
Oklahoma	District attorneys–100%; emergency medical service districts–100%	GAAS, GAGAS (g)	No. Counties may choose GAAP or regulatory basis.
Oregon	...	GAAS, GAGAS	Cities and counties are required to follow GAAP, but other local government entities may not. They use cash/modified cash basis.
Pennsylvania	Audits of cities, towns, villages, and counties are only if part of the entity and not an audit of the complete entity. Examples are audits of pension plans that receive state funds and county offices that receive state funds or collect funds for the state with the audit limited to the state funds. All nonprofit volunteer firefighters' relief associations are audited, but other nonprofit or for-profit entities may receive state funds that we do not audit.	GAGAS (h)	No. Conducts primarily compliance audits related to state funding. Any financial audits are conducted by other auditors. For some engagements of counties and municipal government, conducts attestation examinations of statements prepared on a regulatory basis. Other audits of local governments are conducted as performance audits with the primary focus on compliance.
Rhode Island	N/A	N/A	N/A
South Carolina Legislative Audit Council State Auditor	... ...	... ...	... ...
South Dakota	...	GAGAS	No. Not required of any local governments, but school districts all prepare GAAP statements. Local governments (other than school districts) generally use modified cash basis.
Tennessee	...	GAGAS	★
Texas	...	GAAS, GAGAS	★
Utah	...	GAAS, GAGAS	★
Vermont	...	(i)	No. Towns that do not use GAAP ususally use cash basis.
Virginia	...	GAAS, GAGAS (j)	★
Washington	94%	GAAS, GAGAS	Local governments generally have a choice to report on either a regulatory cash basis of GAAP, although certain governments are required by regulatory or granting agencies to report GAAP. Also, school districts may report on regulatory modified-accrual basis, regulatory cash basis or GAAP.
West Virginia Performance Evaluation Research Division Post Audit Division	... We do not conduct audits of Volunteer Fire Departments that receive state grant funds. Typically, the amount of these annual grants is less than $50,000, and we can only audit the use of these state funds.	... GAGAS	... ...
Wisconsin	...	...	...
Wyoming	Audits not for financial purpose; schools done on about a 5-year cycle; town under 4,000 population done randomly approximately 2% per year.	GAGAS	★ Smaller entities can use cash basis.
Guam	...	GAAS, GAGAS	No. Cash/modified cash is used.
Puerto Rico	...	GAAS (b)	★

See footnotes at end of table

TABLE 4.29
State Auditors: **Audits of Local Governments** (continued)

Sources: Auditing in the States: A Summary, 2018 edition. The National Association of State Auditors, Comptrollers and Treasurers and state constitutions and statutes.

Key:

★–Yes

…–No

N/A–Did not respond

GAAP–Generally Accepted Accounting Principles

GAAS–Generally Accepted Auditing Standards

GAGAS–Generally Accepted Government Auditing Standards

SAS–Statement on Auditing Standards

(a) Unknown. In Oklahoma, special investigative audits only.

(b) For audits started before June 30, 2016, the Office of the Comptroller had its own set of auditing standards. After July 1, 2016, all audits are performed under GAGAS.

(c) GAGAS is the standard for single audits only.

(d) The engagement contracts for CPA firms performing audits of local governments in Louisiana are approved by the legislative auditor. These contracts require all local government audits to comply with GAGAS.

(e) If a single audit is required, the audit must be in accordance with GAGAS.

(f) Very small local governments may be eligible for an agreed-upon procedures engagement in lieu of a full audit. The determination is made based on cash basis annual revenue. Use cash basis.

(g) Special investigative audits do not follow standards.

(h) Most, but not all, local government audits are conducted in accordance with GAGAS.

(i) Some towns have elected auditors and others hire external auditors (CPA firms). For those towns that hire external auditors, GAGAS is utilized.

(j) Localities are also required to follow the Auditor of Public Accounts Specifications for Audits, which include additional audit procedures specifically related to compliance with state laws and regulations.

TABLE 4.30
State Comptrollers, 2019

State	Agency or office	Name	Title	Legal basis for office	Method of selection	Approval or confirmation, if necessary	Length of term	Elected comptrollers maximum consecutive terms	Civil service or merit system employee
Alabama	Office of the State Comptroller	Kathleen Baxter	State Comptroller	S	(c)	AG	(b)	...	★
Alaska	Division of Finance	Dan BeBartolo	Acting Division Director	S	(d)	AG	(a)	...	★
Arizona	General Accounting Office	D. Clark Partridge	State Comptroller	S	(d)	AG	(b)	...	...
Arkansas	Dept. of Finance and Administration	Larry Walther	Chief Fiscal Officer, Director	S	G	...	(a)	...	...
	Office of the State Auditor	Andrea Lea	State Auditor						
California	Office of the State Controller	Betty Yee (D)	State Controller	C	E	...	4 yrs.	2 terms	...
	Department of Finance	Todd Jerue	Chief Operating Officer						
Colorado	Department of Personnel and Administration	Bob Jaros	State Controller	S	(d)	AG	(o)	...	★
Connecticut	Office of the Comptroller	Kevin P. Lembo (D)	Comptroller	C	E	...	4 yrs.	unlimited	...
Delaware	Dept. of Finance	Jane Cole	Director, Division of Accounting	S	G	AL	(a)	...	...
Florida	Dept. of Financial Services	Jimmy Patronis	Chief Financial Officer	C,S	E	...	4 yrs.	2 terms	...
Georgia	State Accounting Office	Alan Skelton	State Accounting Officer	S	G	...	(a)	...	...
Hawaii	Dept. of Accounting and General Services	Curt Otaguro	State Comptroller	S	G	AS	4 yrs.	...	...
Idaho	Office of State Controller	Brandon Woolf	State Controller	C	E	...	4 yrs.	2 terms	...
Illinois	Office of the State Comptroller	Susana Mendoza (D)	State Comptroller	C	E	...	4 yrs.	unlimited	...
Indiana	Office of the Auditor of State	Tera Klutz	Auditor of State	C	E	...	4 yrs.	2 terms	...
Iowa	State Accounting Enterprise	Jay Cleveland	Chief Operating Officer	S	(d)	...	(i)	...	...
Kansas	Office of the Chief Financial Officer	Vacant	Chief Financial Officer	S	(d)	...	(b)	...	...
Kentucky	Office of the Controller	Edgar C. Ross	Controller	S	(f)	AG	(i)	...	...
Louisiana	Office of Statewide Reporting and Accounting Policy	Jay Dardenne	Commissioner of Administration	S	G	...	(a)	...	...
Maine	Office of the State Controller	Douglas Cotnoir	State Controller	S	(f)	AG	(i)	...	...
Maryland	Office of the Comptroller of the Treasury	Peter Franchot (D)	State Comptroller	C	E	...	4 yrs.	unlimited	...
Massachusetts	Office of the Comptroller	Andrew Maylor	Comptroller	S	G	...	4 yrs	...	...
Michigan	Office of Financial Management	Michael J. Moody	Director	S	SBD	SBD	(k)	...	★
Minnesota	Department of Finance	Myron Frans	Commissioner	S	G	AS	(a)	...	★
Mississippi	Department of Finance and Administration	Lisa Dunn	Director, Office of Fiscal Management	C,S	G	...	(a)	...	...
Missouri	Division of Accounting	Stacy Neal	Director of Accounting	S	(d)	...	(i)	...	...
Montana	State Accounting Division	Cheryl Grey	Administrator	S	(m)	...	(b)	...	★
Nebraska	Accounting Division	Jason Jackson	Interim Accounting Administrator	S	(d)	...	(b)	...	...
Nevada	Office of the State Controller	Catherine Byrne (D)	State Controller	C, S	E	...	4 yrs.	2 terms	...
New Hampshire	Department of Administration	Dana Call	State Comptroller	S	G	...	4 yrs.	...	...
New Jersey	Office of Management and Budget	David Ridolfino	State Comptroller	S	G	AS	(a)	...	...
New Mexico	Department of Finance and Administration, Financial Control Division	Ronald Spilman	State Controller	S	G	...	(a)	...	★
New York	Office of the State Comptroller	Thomas P. DiNapoli	State Comptroller	C,S	E	...	4 yrs.	unlimited	...
North Carolina	Office of the State Controller	Linda Combs	State Controller	S	G	GA	7 yrs.	...	...
North Dakota	Office of Management and Budget	Joe Morrisette	Director	S	G	...	(a)	unlimited	...
Ohio	Office of Budget and Management	Kim Murnieks	Director	S	G	...	(a)	...	...
Oklahoma	Office of State Finance	Lynne Bajema	State Comptroller	S	(g)	...	(h)	...	...
Oregon	Chief Financial Office	Robert Hamilton	Manager, Statewide Accounting and Reporting	S	(d)	...	(i)	...	...
Pennsylvania	Office of the Budget/ Comptroller Operations	Anna Maria Kiehl	Chief Accounting Officer	S	SBD	AG	(a)	...	...
Rhode Island	Office of Accounts and Control	Peter Keenan	State Controller	S	(d)	...	(b)	...	★

See footnotes at end of table

TABLE 4.30
State Comptrollers, 2019 (continued)

State	Agency or office	Name	Title	Legal basis for office	Method of selection	Approval or confirmation, if necessary	Length of term	Elected comptrollers maximum consecutive terms	Civil service or merit system employee
South Carolina	Office of the Comptroller General	Richard Eckstrom (R)	Comptroller General	C,S	E	...	4 yrs.	unlimited	...
South Dakota	Office of the State Auditor	Richard Sattgast (R)	State Auditor	C	E		4 yrs.	2 terms	...
	Bureau of Financial Management	Liza Clark	Commissioner	S	(n)	...	(a)		...
Tennessee	Division of Accounts	Mike Corricelli	Chief of Accounts	S	(f)	...	(b)	...	...
Texas	Office of the Comptroller of Public Accounts	Glenn Hegar (R)	Comptroller of Public Accounts	C,S	E	...	4 yrs.	unlimited	...
Utah	Division of Finance	John C. Reidhead	Director	S	(d)	AG	(i)	...	...
Vermont	Department of Finance and Management	Adam Greshen	Commissioner	S	(d)	AG,AS	(i)	...	...
Virginia	Department of Accounts	David A. Von Moll	State Comptroller	S	G	...	4 yrs.		...
Washington	Office of Financial Management	David Schumacher	Director	C	G	...	...	...	...
West Virginia	Office of the State Auditor	John McCuskey (R)	State Auditor	C	E	...	4 yrs.	unlimited	...
	Finance Division, Office of the State Comptroller	Dave Mullins	Acting Finance Director	S	(d)	AG	(a)(i)	...	...
Wisconsin	State Controller's Office	Jeffrey Anderson	State Controller	S	CS	...	(b)	...	★
Wyoming	Office of the State Auditor	Kristi Racines (R)	State Auditor	C	E	...	4 yrs.	2 terms	...

Sources: *Comptrollers: Technical Activities and Functions, 2018 edition*, National Association of State Auditors, Comptrollers and Treasurers and The Council of State Governments, April 2019.

Key:
★ –Yes, provision for.
... –No provision for.
C–Constitutional
S–Statutory
N.A.–Not applicable.
E–Elected by the public.
G–Appointed by the Governor.
CS–Civil Service.
AG–Approved by the governor.
AS–Approved/confirmed by the Senate.
AL–Approved by the Legislature.
SBD–Approved by State Budget Director.
GA–Confirmed by the General Assembly.
SDB–Confirmed by State Depository Board.
(a) Serves at the pleasure of the governor. In South Dakota, also serves at the pleasure of the CFO.
(b) Indefinite.

(c) State merit system appointment; selected and recommended by state finance director.
(d) Appointed by the head of the department of administration or administrative services.
(e) Appointed by the head of finance. department or agency.
(f) Appointed by the head of financial and administrative services.
(g) Appointed by the director of management & enterprise services.
(h) Serves at the pleasure of the head of the director of management & enterprise services.
(i) Serves at the pleasure of the head of the financial and administrative services or administration.
(j) Appointed by the governor for a term coterminous with the governor.
(k) Two-year renewable contractual term; classified executive service.
(l) As of July 1, 2005, the responsibility for accounting and financial reporting in Georgia was transferred to the newly-created State Accounting Office.
(m) Hired through a selection process.
(n) Hired by the chief financial officer.
(o) One year contract similar to other division director.

TABLE 4.31
State Comptrollers: Qualifications for Office

State	Minimum age	U.S. citizen (years)	State resident (years)	Education years or degree	Professional experience and years	Professional certification and years	Other qualifications
Alabama	...	★	...	(n)	★, 10 yrs.	(a)	...
Alaska	...	...	...	...	...	...	...
Arizona	...	...	...	...	...	...	...
Arkansas	30	...	...	...	...	...	...
California	...	...	...	...	...	...	...
Colorado	...	...	...	...	...	...	...
Connecticut	...	...	...	...	...	...	...
Delaware	...	...	...	...	...	...	...
Florida	30	...	★, 7 yrs.	...	...	...	...
Georgia	...	...	...	...	...	...	...
Hawaii	...	...	30 days	...	...	...	...
Idaho	25	(b)	★, 2 yrs.	...	...	...	...
Illinois	25	★	★, 3 yrs.	...	...	...	...
Indiana	...	...	...	...	...	...	...
Iowa	...	...	...	...	...	...	...
Kansas	...	...	...	...	...	...	...
Kentucky	...	...	...	(c)	...	...	...
Louisiana	...	...	...	...	...	...	...
Maine	...	...	...	...	...	...	...
Maryland	...	...	...	...	...	...	...
Massachusetts	...	...	...	★(d)	...	...	...
Michigan	...	...	...	★, B.S.	★, 2 yrs.	...	...
Minnesota	...	...	...	...	...	...	...
Mississippi	...	...	...	...	...	...	(e)
Missouri	...	...	...	...	...	...	...
Montana	...	...	...	★(f)	★, 10 yrs.	★, CPA	...
Nebraska	...	...	...	★(g)	★, 3 yrs.	★, CPA	...
Nevada	25	★	★, 2 yrs.	...	...	...	...
New Hampshire	...	...	...	...	...	...	...
New Jersey	...	...	...	...	...	...	...
New Mexico	...	★	...	...	...	...	...
New York	30	★	★(h)	...	...	...	...
North Carolina	...	...	...	★(i)	★	...	★(i)
North Dakota	...	...	...	...	...	...	...
Ohio	...	...	...	...	...	...	...
Oklahoma	...	★	...	...	...	...	...
Oregon	...	...	...	...	...	...	...
Pennsylvania	21	...	...	★(j)	★, 10 yrs.	★, CPA	...
Rhode Island	...	★	...	★(k)	...	★, CPA	...
South Carolina	18	...	...	...	...	...	...
South Dakota	...	★	...	...	...	...	...
Tennessee	...	...	...	...	...	...	...
Texas	...	★(b)	...	...	...	...	...
Utah	...	★	...	★(l)	★, 6 yrs.	★, CPA	...
Vermont	...	...	...	...	...	...	...
Virginia	...	...	...	...	...	...	...
Washington	...	★, Whole life	...	...	...	...	...
West Virginia– Office of State Auditor	25	★	...	...	...	...	...
Division of Finance, Office of State Comptroller	...	★	...	★(m)	★, 4 yrs.	...	...
Wisconsin	...	...	...	★(j)	...	★, CPA	...
Wyoming	25	★	...	...	...	...	...

See footnotes at end of table

TABLE 4.31
State Comptrollers: Qualifications for Office (continued)

Sources: Comptrollers: Technical Activities and Functions, 2018 edition, National Association of State Auditors, Comptrollers and Treasurers and The Council of State Governments, April 2019.

Key:
★–Formal provision.
…–No formal provision.
N.A.–Not applicable.
(a) One of the following CPA, CIA, CPM, CGFM or CGFO.
(b) Years not specified.
(c) In part the statute reads "the state controller shall be a person qualified by education and experience for the position and held in high esteem in the accounting community."
(d) Advanced degree in accounting, auditing, financial management, business administration or public administration (M.G.L.C. 7A, S.1)
(e) The executive director (a) shall be a certified public accountant; or (b) shall possess a master's degree in busioness, public administration or a related field; or (c) shall have at least 10 yrs. experience in management in the private or public sector and a minimum of 5 yrs. experience in high level management with a documented record of management.
(f) Bachelor's degree in accounting.
(g) Four-year degree with a concentration in accounting.
(h) Five preceding elections.
(i) Qualified by education and experience for the office.
(j) Bachelor's degree.
(k) Master's degree in accounting or business administration.
(l) Accounting or related college degree.
(m) College education with a major in business or public administration.
(n) Bachelor's degree with a major in accounting and a master's degree in accounting, business administration or public administration, both of which must be from an accredited college or university that is a member of one of the six regional accreditation associations in the United States.

TABLE 4.32
State Comptrollers: Duties, Responsibilities and Functions

State	Disbursements	Payroll	Tax reporting	Pre-audit	Post-audit	Operating the financial management system	Financial reporting	Debt management
Alabama	★	★	★	★	...	★	★	...
Alaska	★	★	★	...	...	★	★	...
Arizona	★	★	★	...	★	★	★	★
Arkansas	...	★	★	...	...	★	★	...
California	★	★	★	★	★	...	★	...
Colorado	★	★	★	★	...	★	★	...
Connecticut	★	★	★	★	★	★	★	...
Delaware	★	...	...	★	★	★	★	★
Florida	★	★	★	★	★	★	★	★
Georgia	...	...	...	...	...	★	★	...
Hawaii	★	★	...	★	★	★	★	...
Idaho	★	★	...	★	...	★	★	...
Illinois	★	★	★	★	★	★	★	...
Indiana	★	★	★	★	...	★	★	...
Iowa	★	★	★	★	★	★	★	...
Kansas	★	★	★	★	...	★	★	...
Kentucky	★	...	...	★	...	★	★	★
Louisiana	★	★	...	...	...	★	★	...
Maine	★	★	★	★	★	★	★	...
Maryland	★	★	★	★	★	★	★	...
Massachusetts	★	★	★	★	★	★	★	★
Michigan	...	★	★	...	...	★	...	...
Minnesota	★	★	...	...	...	★	★	★
Mississippi	★	★	...	★	★	★	★	...
Missouri	★	★	★	★	★	★	★	★
Montana	★	...	...	...	...	★	★	...
Nebraska	★	★	★	★	★	★	★	★
Nevada	★	...	★	...	...	★	★	...
New Hampshire	★	★	★	★	★	★	★	...
New Jersey	★	★	★	...	...	★	★	...
New Mexico	★	★	★	★	★	★	★	...
New York	★	★	★	★	★	★	★	★
North Carolina	★	★	...	...	...	★	★	...
North Dakota	★	★	★	...	...	★	★	...
Ohio	★	...	★	★	★	★	★	★
Oklahoma	★	★	★	★	★	★	★	...
Oregon	★	★	★	...	...	★	★	...
Pennsylvania	...	★	★	★	★	★	★	...
Rhode Island	★	★	...	★	★	★	★	...
South Carolina	★	★	...	★	...	★	★	...
South Dakota	★	★	★	★	...	...	...	...
Tennessee	★	★	...	★	★	...	★	...
Texas	★	★	★	★	★	★	★	...
Utah	★	★	...	...	★	★	★	★
Vermont	★	...	...	...	...	★	★	...
Virginia	★	★	...	★	★	★	★	...
Washington	...	...	...	...	...	...	★	...
West Virginia	★	★	★	★	★	...	★	...
Wisconsin	★	★	...	★	★	★	★	...
Wyoming	★	★	...	...	...	★	★	...

See footnotes at end of table

TABLE 4.32

State Comptrollers: Duties, Responsibilities and Functions (continued)

State	Investment management	Internal control oversight	Transparency	Quality assurance	Enterprise resource planning system responsibility	Data warehouse	Other
Alabama	...	CMIA	...	★	...	★	...
Alaska	...	...	...	★	...	★	(a)
Arizona	...	CMIA	★	★	...	★	...
Arkansas	...	...	...	★	...	★	...
California	...	★	★	★	...	...	(b)
Colorado	...	...	★	★	★	★	(c)
Connecticut	...	...	★	★	...	★	(d)
Delaware	...	...	★	★	★	...	(e)
Florida	★	★	★	★	...	★	(f)
Georgia	...	...	★	...	...	...	(g)
Hawaii	...	...	★	...	...	...	(h)
Idaho	...	...	...	★	...	★	(i)
Illinois	...	...	...	★	★	...	...
Indiana	...	...	...	★	...	★	(j)
Iowa	...	...	...	...	...	★	(k)
Kansas	...	...	★	★	...	...	(l)
Kentucky	★	★	★	★	...	★	(m)
Louisiana	...	...	...	★	...	★	(n)
Maine	...	...	★	★	★	★	(o)
Maryland	...	...	...	★	★	★	(p)
Massachusetts	...	...	★	★	★	★	(q)
Michigan	...	...	...	★	...	...	...
Minnesota	...	★	★	★	...	★	(r)
Mississippi	...	...	★	★	★	★	...
Missouri	...	...	★	★	...	...	(s)
Montana	...	★	...	...	...	...	(t)
Nebraska	...	...	★	★	★	...	(u)
Nevada	...	...	...	★	...	★	(v)
New Hampshire	...	...	...	★	...	...	(w)
New Jersey	...	★	...	...	...	...	(x)
New Mexico	...	★	★	...	★	...	(y)
New York	★	★	★	★	...	...	...
North Carolina	...	★	★	★	★	...	...
North Dakota	...	...	...	★	...	★	(z)
Ohio	...	...	★	★	★	...	(aa)
Oklahoma	...	...	...	★	★	...	(ab)
Oregon	...	...	...	★	★	★	(ac)
Pennsylvania	...	...	★	★	★	★(ad)	(ae)
Rhode Island	...	...	...	★	...	...	...
South Carolina	...	...	★	★	★	★	(af)
South Dakota	...	...	★	...	...	...	(ag)
Tennessee	...	...	...	★	★	...	(ah)
Texas	★	★	...	★	...	★	(ai)
Utah	...	...	★	★	★	★	(aj)
Vermont	...	...	★	...	...	...	(ak)
Virginia	...	...	★	★	★	...	...
Washington	...	...	...	...	...	...	(al)
West Virginia	...	...	...	...	...	...	(am)
Wisconsin	...	★	★	★	★	...	(an)
Wyoming	...	...	...	...	★(ao)	★(ao)	(ap)

See footnotes at end of table

TABLE 4.32

State Comptrollers: Duties, Responsibilities and Functions (continued)

Source: State Comptrollers: Technical Activities and Functions, 2018 edition, National Association of State Auditors, Comptrollers and Treasurers.

Key:

★ –Formal provision.

… –No formal provision.

CMIA –Cash Management Improvement Act of 1990

(a) Enterprise travel office and one-card program. Performs accounting for the Department of Revnue debt manager, but does not actually manage the debt program.

(b) Unclaimed property.

(c) Financial system operations; central collection services, purchasing and contracts.

(d) Also responsible for providing health insurance and other benefits to state employees and retirees; administer State Employee Retirement System and other retirement systems, and pays retiree pensions.

(e) Payroll compliance (not processing).

(f) State treasury–deposit security and funds management, risk management, and unclaimed property.

(g) Payroll shared services, state travel office and a/p shared services.

(h) Archives, records management, risk management, land survey, public works, office leasing, central services–repairs, custodial, district offices–school repairs and maintenance, motor pool and parking.

(i) Data center.

(j) Distributions to local governments. Administers the state's deferred compensation plan, Hoosier Start.

(k) Income offsets, CMIA and SWCAP, 1099 MISC and 1095 reporting.

(l) Municipals statewide, audit of agencies - new audit plan, internal control/systems monitoring. Tax reporting includes payroll tax withholding and remittance.

(m) State risk pools (fire and auto).

(n) Planning and budgeting, and facility planning and control (capital outlay).

(o) Risk management/self-insurance.

(p) Tax collection, tax compliance, field enforcement and revenue estimates.

(q) Risk management.

(r) Budget, human resources, cash management and management consulting.

(s) State Social Security administrator; general revenue cash flow monitoring/projections.

(t) Statewide procurement and contract services, local government audit and financial report review, and Social Security administration.

(u) Tax reporting limited to payroll and 1099; financial reporting includes SWCAP and single audit; P-card and federal letter of credit delayed draw administration.

(v) Tax reporting limited to 1099 reporting.

(w) Financial reporting includes SWCAP and single audit; financial management system is operated in conjunction with separate Division of Financial Data Management.

(x) Grant accounting and cash accouting.

(y) Systems functions are shared with the Deparment of Information Technology.

(z) Purchasing card program administration.

(aa) Budget, accounting and shared services, internal audit and 1099 reporting.

(ab) P-card administration (with state procurement) and state travel office.

(ac) Purchase card program administration. Statewide accounts receivable management.

(ad) The comptroller maintains reporting hierarchies for the CAFR in the data warehouse.

(ae) Employee travel planning and reimbursement, policy/planning, payable service center, contract review and internal audits.

(af) P-card administration (with state procurement) and state employee unemployment insurance program.

(ag) Bureau of Finance and Management also performs numerous comptroller functions.

(ah) Policy development, technical accounting training, CMIA and certain banking relationships.

(ai) The comptroller's office serves virtually every citizen in the state. As Texas' chief tax collector, accountant, revenue estimator, treasurer and purchasing managet, the agency is reponsible for writing the check and keeping the books for the multi-billon dollar business of state government.

(aj) Loan servicing, debt collection, debt service, statewide accounting policies, CMIA, P-card administration, 1099 reporting. Shares system responsibilities with the Department of Technology Services.

(ak) Developing statewide budget, statewide accounting policies, SWCAP, SMIA, CAFR, single audit, train users in uses of statewide accounting system and 1099 reporting.

(al) Developing statewide budget, setting statewide admin. policies and procedures, HR policies/Labor Relations Office, and forecasting statewide population.

(am) Statewide accounting policies, SWCAP, Single Audit, and 1099 reporting.

(an) State treasury, SEFA report, Local Government Investement Pool, CAFR, Central Federal Draw, CMIA, 1099-Misc reporting, E-Payments.

(ao) Quailty Assurance in the Office of State Auditor is for training on the state's uniform accounting system. Also, the data warehouse is for the state's uniform accounting system, which inlcudes payroll data as well as financial data.

(ap) SEFA, TIN matching, 1099 reporting.

CHAPTER FIVE
STATE JUDICIAL BRANCH

TABLE 5.1
State Courts of Last Resort

State or other jurisdiction	Name of court	Justices chosen (a)		No. of judges (b)	Term (in years) (c)	Chief justice	
		At large	By district			Method of selection	Term of office for chief justice
Alabama	S.C.	★		9	6	Partisan election	6 years
Alaska	S.C.	★		5	10	By court	3 years
Arizona	S.C.	★		7	6	By court	5 years
Arkansas	S.C.	★		7	8	Non-partisan popular election	8 years
California	S.C.	★		7	12	Gubernatorial appointment with consent of Commission on Judicial Appointments	12 years
Colorado	S.C.	★		7	10	By court	10 years
Connecticut	S.C.	★		7	8	Gubernatorial appointment with consent of the legislature	8 years
Delaware	S.C.	★		5	12	Gubernatorial appointment from judicial nominating commission with consent of the legislature	12 years
Florida	S.C.	★(d)	★(d)	7	6	By court	2 years
Georgia	S.C.	★		9	6	By court	6 years
Hawaii	S.C.	★		5	10	Gubernatorial appointment from judicial nominating commission with consent of the senate	10 years
Idaho	S.C.	★		5	6	By court	4 years
Illinois	S.C.	★(e)	★(e)	7	10	By court	3 years
Indiana	S.C.	★		5	10	Judicial nominating commission	5 years
Iowa	S.C.	★		7	8	By court	8 years
Kansas	S.C.	★		7	6	By seniority of service	Duration of service
Kentucky	S.C.		★	7	8	By court	4 years
Louisiana	S.C.		★	7	10	By seniority of service	Duration of service
Maine	S.J.C.	★		7	7	Appointed by governor with consent of the legislature	7 years
Maryland	C.A.		★	7	10	Appointed by governor	To age 70
Massachusetts	S.J.C.	★		7	To age 70	Gubernatorial appointment with approval of elected executive council	To age 70
Michigan	S.C.	★		7	8	By court	2 years
Minnesota	S.C.	★		7	6	Non-partisan popular election	6 years
Mississippi	S.C.		★(g)	9	8	By seniority of service	Duration of service
Missouri	S.C.	★		7	12	By court	2 years
Montana	S.C.	★		7	8	Non-partisan popular election	8 years
Nebraska	S.C.	★(h)	★(h)	7	6	Gubernatorial appointment from judicial nominating commission	Duration of service
Nevada	S.C.	★		7	6	Rotation by seniority	(i)
New Hampshire	S.C.	★		5	To age 70	Gubernatorial appointment with approval of elected executive council	To age 70
New Jersey	S.C.	★		5	(j)	Gubernatorial appointment with consent of the senate	7 years, plus tenure, to age 70
New Mexico	S.C.	★		5	8	By court	2 years
New York	C.A.	★		7	14	Gubernatorial appointment from judicial nominating commission with consent of the senate	14 years
North Carolina	S.C.	★		7	8	Partisan popular election	8 years
North Dakota	S.C.	★		5	10	By Supreme and District Court judges	5 years
Ohio	S.C.	★		7	6	Popular election (k)	6 years
Oklahoma	S.C.		★	9	6	By court	2 years
	C.C.A.		★	5	6	By court	2 years
Oregon	S.C.	★		7	6	By court	6 years
Pennsylvania	S.C.	★		7	10	Seniority	Duration of service
Rhode Island	S.C.	★		5	Life	Gubernatorial appointment from judicial nominating commission with consent of the legislature	Hold office during good behavior
South Carolina	S.C.	★		5	10	Legislative appointment	10 years
South Dakota	S.C.	★(l)	★(l)	5	8	By court	4 years
Tennessee	S.C.	★		5	8	By court	4 years / 2 years (m)
Texas	S.C.	★		9	6	Partisan election	6 years
	C.C.A.	★		9	6	Partisan election	6 years
Utah	S.C.	★		5	10	By court	4 years
Vermont	S.C.	★		5	6	Gubernatorial appointment from judicial nominating commission with consent of the legislature	6 years
Virginia	S.C.	★		7	12	By court	4 years
Washington	S.C.	★		9	6	By court	4 years
West Virginia	S.C.A.	★		5	12	By court	4 years
Wisconsin	S.C.	★		7	10	By court	2 years
Wyoming	S.C.	★		5	8	By court	4 years
Dist. of Columbia	C.A.	★		9	15	Judicial Nominating Commission appointment	4 years
Puerto Rico	S.C.	★		9	To age 70	Gubernatorial appointment with consent of the legislature	To age 70

See footnotes at end of table

TABLE 5.1
State Courts of Last Resort (continued)

Sources: National Center for State Courts. January 1, 2019.
Key:

★–Yes
S.C.–Supreme Court
S.C.A.–Supreme Court of Appeals
S.J.C.–Supreme Judicial Court
C.A.–Court of Appeals
C.C.A.–Court of Criminal Appeals
(a) See Table 5.6, entitled, "Selection and Retention of Appellate Court Judges," for more detail.
(b) Number includes chief justice.
(c) The initial term may be shorter. See Table 5.6, entitled, "Selection and Retention of Appellate Court Judges," for more detail.
(d) Elected statewide, but each of 5 regional appellate districts entitled to at least 1 justice.
(e) Three justices chosen from First District (Cook County), rest from other Districts.

(g) Three justices chosen from each of three districts.
(h) Chief justice chosen statewide; associate judges chosen by district.
(i) The senior justice in commission is the Chief Justice, and in case the commissions of two or more of the justices bear the same date, the justices shall determine by lot who is the Chief Justice.
(j) All judges are subject to gubernatorial reappointment and consent by the Senate after an initial seven-year term; thereafter, they may serve until mandatory retirement at age 70.
(k) Party affiliation is not included on the ballot in the general election, but candidates are chosen through partisan primary nominations.
(l) Initially chosen by district; retention determined statewide.
(m) 4 years for initial term; 2 years for additional terms.

Table 5.1 | State Courts of Last Resort

Number of Judges

9 JUDGES

 AL, GA, MS, OK, TX, WA, D.C., PR

7 JUDGES

AZ, AR, CA, CO, CT, FL, IL, IA, KS, KY, LA, ME, MD, MA, MI, MN, MO, MT, NE, NV, NY, NC, OH, OR, PA, VA, WI

5 JUDGES

AK, DE, HI, ID, IN, NH, NJ, NM, ND, RI, SC, SD, TN, UT, VT, WV, WY

Term of Office for Judges

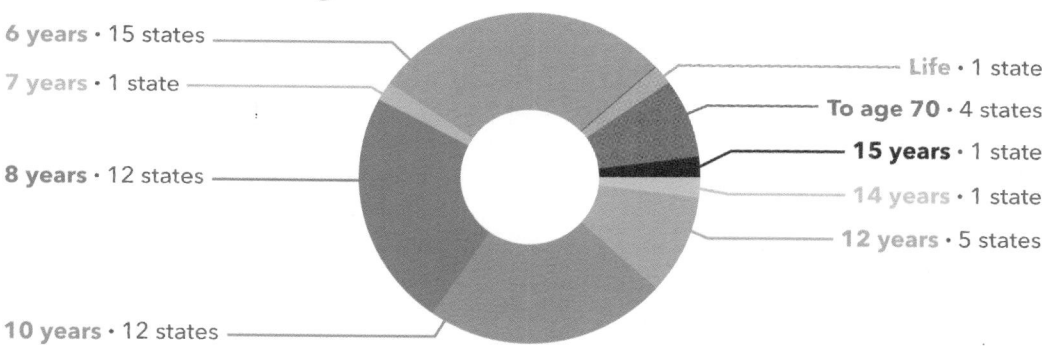

6 years · 15 states
7 years · 1 state
8 years · 12 states
10 years · 12 states

Life · 1 state
To age 70 · 4 states
15 years · 1 state
14 years · 1 state
12 years · 5 states

Term of Office for Chief Justices

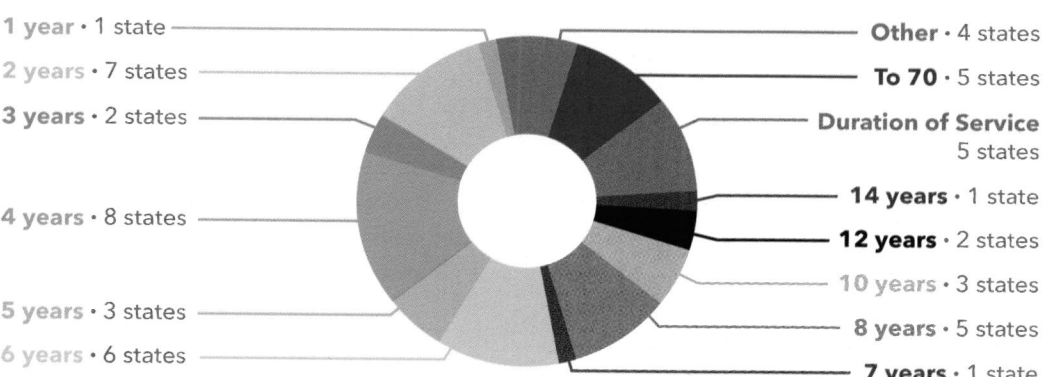

1 year · 1 state
2 years · 7 states
3 years · 2 states
4 years · 8 states
5 years · 3 states
6 years · 6 states

Other · 4 states
To 70 · 5 states
Duration of Service 5 states
14 years · 1 state
12 years · 2 states
10 years · 3 states
8 years · 5 states
7 years · 1 state

TABLE 5.2
State Intermediate Appellate Courts and General Trial Courts: Number of Judges and Terms

State or other jurisdiction	Intermediate appellate court			General trial court		
	Name of court	2019 No. of judges	Term (years)	Name of court	2019 No. of judges	Term (years)
Alabama	Court of Criminal Appeals Court of Civil Appeals	5 5	6 6	Circuit Court	144	6
Alaska	Court of Appeals	3	8	Superior Court	42	6
Arizona	Court of Appeals	22	6	Superior Court Tax Court	180 1	4 4 (a)
Arkansas	Court of Appeals	12	8	Circuit Court	121	6
California	Courts of Appeal	99	12	Superior Court	1,680	6
Colorado	Court of Appeals	22	8	District Court Denver Juvenile Court Denver Probate Court	177 (b) 3 1	6 6 6
Connecticut	Appellate Court	9	8	Superior Court	163	8
Delaware	...	...	...	Superior Court Court of Chancery	21 5	12 12
Florida	District Courts of Appeals	64	6	Circuit Court	599	6
Georgia	Court of Appeals	15	6	Superior Court	213	4
Hawaii	Intermediate Court of Appeals	6	10	Circuit Court	30	10
Idaho	Court of Appeals	4	6	District Court	45	4
Illinois	Appellate Court	54	10	Circuit Court	934 (c)	6
Indiana	Court of Appeals Tax Court	15 1	10 10	Superior Court, Probate Court and Circuit Court	317	6
Iowa	Court of Appeals	9	6	District Court	337 (d)	6
Kansas	Court of Appeals	14	4	District Court	245 (e)	4
Kentucky	Court of Appeals	14	8	Circuit Court Family Court	95 52	8 8
Louisiana	Courts of Appeal	53	10	District Court Juvenile & Family Court	218 18	6 6
Maine	...	...	...	Superior Court District Court	17 36	7 7
Maryland	Court of Special Appeals	15	10	Circuit Court	162	15
Massachusetts	Appeals Court	25	To age 70	Superior Court	77	To age 70
Michigan	Court of Appeals	27	6	Circuit Court Court of Claims	214 4	6 6
Minnesota	Court of Appeals	19	6	District Court	290	6
Mississippi	Court of Appeals	10	8	Circuit Court	57	4
Missouri	Court of Appeals	32	12	Circuit Court	346 (f)	6 (g)
Montana	...	...	...	District Court Water Court Workers' Compensation Court	46 (h) 5 1	6 4 6
Nebraska	Court of Appeals	6	6	District Court	55	6
Nevada	Court of Appeals	3	6	District Court	82	6
New Hampshire	...	...	...	Superior Court	22	To age 70
New Jersey	Appellate Division of Superior Court	33	(i)	Superior Court	386	(i)
New Mexico	Court of Appeals	10	8	District Court	94	6
New York	Appellate Division of Supreme Court Appellate Terms of Supreme Court	53 11	5 (j) Duration of term	Supreme Court County Court	269 122	14 10
North Carolina	Court of Appeals	15	8	Superior Court	104 (k)	8 (l)
North Dakota	Temporary Court of Appeals	3	1 (m)	District Court	51	6
Ohio	Courts of Appeals	69	6	Court of Common Pleas	449	6
Oklahoma	Court of Civil Appeals	12	6	District Court	241 (n)	4 (o)
Oregon	Court of Appeals	13	6	Circuit Court Tax Court	172 1	6 6
Pennsylvania	Superior Court	23	10	Court of Common Pleas	449 (p)	10
Rhode Island	...	...	...	Superior Court	25 (q)	Life
South Carolina	Court of Appeals	9	6	Circuit Court	58	6
South Dakota	...	...	...	Circuit Court	43	8
Tennessee	Court of Appeals Court of Criminal Appeals	12 12	8 8	Chancery Court Circuit Court Criminal Court Probate Court	83 35 33 2	8 8 8 8
Texas	Courts of Appeals	80	6	District Court	465	4

See footnotes at end of table

TABLE 5.2

State Intermediate Appellate Courts and General Trial Courts: Number of Judges and Terms (continued)

State or other jurisdiction	Intermediate appellate court			General trial court		
	Name of court	2019 No. of judges	Term (years)	Name of court	2019 No. of judges	Term (years)
Utah	Court of Appeals	7	6	District Court	72	6
Vermont	…	…	…	Superior Court	34	6
Virginia	Court of Appeals	11	8	Circuit Court	157	8
Washington	Courts of Appeal	22	6	Superior Court	192	4
West Virginia	…	…	…	Circuit Court	70	8
Wisconsin	Court of Appeals	16	6	Circuit Court	249	6
Wyoming	…	…	…	District Court	23	6
Dist. of Columbia	…	…	…	Superior Court	62	15
Puerto Rico	Court of Appeals	39	16	Court of First Instance	338 (r)	12 (s)

Sources: National Center for State Courts, May 2019.
Key:
…–Court does not exist in jurisdiction or not applicable.
(a) Unless rotated to a different court by the presiding judge.
(b) Judges also serve Water Court.
(c) 514 Circuit Court Judges and 378 Associate Judges.
(d) 146 of these are part-time judicial magistrates.
(e) Includes both district judges and district magistrate judges.
(f) The number of Circuit Court judges includes associate judges.
(g) Associate Circuit judges serve a term of four years.
(h) Three of those judges serve the Water Court.
(i) Followed by tenure. All judges are subject to gubernatorial reappointment and consent by the Senate after an initial seven-year term; thereafter, they may serve until mandatory retirement at age 70.

(j) Or duration.
(k) The number of Superior Court judges includes special judges.
(l) Special judges serve a term of four years.
(m) Assignments are for a specified time, not to exceed one year or the completion of one or more cases on the docket of the supreme court.
(n) The number of District Court judges includes associate judges and special judges.
(o) District and associate judges serve four year terms; special judges serve at pleasure.
(p) Includes both active and senior judges.
(q) The number of judges includes magistrates.
(r) The number of Court of First Instance judges includes Municipal Division judges.
(s) Municipal judges serve a term of eight years.

TABLE 5.3
Qualifications of Judges of State Appellate Courts and General Trial Courts

State or other jurisdiction	Residency requirement				Minimum age		Legal Credentials	
	State		Local					
	A	T	A	T	A	T	A	T
Alabama	1 yr.	1 yr.	...	1 yr.	...	18	10 years state bar	5 years state bar
Alaska	5 yrs.	5 yrs.	...	...	...	...	8 years practice	5 years practice
Arizona	5/10 yrs. (a)	5 yrs.	(b)	1 yr.	30	30	(c)	(d)
Arkansas	...	...	★	...	...	...	8 years practice	6 years licensed in state
California	★	...	...	...	...	...	10 years state bar	10 years state bar
Colorado	★	★	...	★	...	...	5 years state bar	5 years state bar
Connecticut	★	★	...	...	...	...	Licensed attorney	Member of the bar
Delaware	★	★	...	★	...	...	"Learned in law"	"Learned in law"
Florida	★	★	★(f)	★(g)	...	...	10 years state bar	5 years state bar
Georgia	★	3 yrs.	...	must reside within court circuit	...	30		7 years state bar
Hawaii	★	★	...	...	...	30	10 years state bar	10 years state bar
Idaho	2 yrs.	1 yr.	...	...	30	...	10 years state bar	10 years state bar
Illinois	★	★	★	★	...	...	Licensed attorney	Law degree
Indiana	★	1 yr.	...	★	...	...	10 years state bar (h)	Licensed attorney
Iowa	★	★	...	★	...	...	Licensed attorney	Admitted to state bar
Kansas	...	5 yrs.	...	...	30	30	"10 years active and continuous practice (i)"	5 year state bar
Kentucky	2 yrs.	2 yrs.	2 yrs.	2 yrs.	...	...	"8 years state bar and licensed attorney"	8 years state bar
Louisiana	1 yrs.	1 yrs.	1 yrs.	1 yrs.	...	...	10 years state bar	8 years state bar
Maine	...	...	...	...	...	...	"Learned in law"	1 year state bar
Maryland	5 yrs.	5 yrs.	6 mos.	6 mos.	30	30	State bar member	State bar member
Massachusetts	...	...	...	...	...	...	...	State bar member
Michigan	★	★	...	...	...	...	"State bar member and 5 years practice"	State bar member
Minnesota	30 days	30 days	...	30 days	...	...	Licensed attorney	Licensed attorney
Mississippi	5 yrs.	5 yrs.	★(j)	...	30	26	5 years state bar	5 years practice
Missouri	9 yrs. (k)	3 yrs. (k)	...	1 yr. (k)	30	30	State bar member	State bar member
Montana	2 yrs.	2 yrs.	...	...	30	30	5 years state bar	5 years state bar
Nebraska	3 yrs.	★	★	★	30	30	5 years practice	5 years practice
Nevada	2 yrs.	2 yrs.	...	...	25	25	State bar member (l)	"2 years state bar member and 10 years practice"
New Hampshire	...	...	...	...	...	...	10 years practice	State bar member
New Jersey	★	(m)	...	(m)	...	...	"Admitted to practice in state for at least 10 years"	10 years practice of law
New Mexico	3 yrs.	3 yrs.	...	★	35	35	10 years practice	6 years active practice
New York	★	★	...	...	...	18	10 years state bar	10 years state bar
North Carolina	...	★	...	(n)	...	...	State bar member	State bar member
North Dakota	★	★	...	★	...	...	License to practice law	State bar member
Ohio	★	★	...	★	...	...	6 years practice	6 years practice
Oklahoma	★	(o)	1 yr.	★	30	...	5 years state bar	(p)
Oregon	3 yrs.	3 yrs.	...	1 yr.	...	...	State bar member	State bar member
Pennsylvania	1 yr.	★	...	1 yr.	...	21	State bar member	State bar member
Rhode Island	...	...	...	...	21	...	License to practice law	State bar member
South Carolina	5 yrs.	5 yrs.	...	(q)	32	32	8 years state bar	8 years state bar
South Dakota	★	★	★	★	...	...	State bar member	State bar member
Tennessee	5 yrs.	5 yrs.	★(r)	1 yr.	35/30 (s)	30	License to practice law	License to practice law
Texas	★	...	...	2 yrs.	35	25	(t)	(u)
Utah	5 yrs.	3 yrs.	...	★	30	25	State bar member	State bar member
Vermont	...	...	...	...	...	...	5 years state bar	5 years state bar
Virginia	...	★	...	...	...	...	5 years state bar	5 years state bar
Washington	1 yr.	1 yr.	1 yr.	1 yr.	...	...	State bar member	State bar member
West Virginia	5 yrs.	★	...	★	30	30	10 years state bar	5 years state bar
Wisconsin	28 days	28 days	28 days	28 days	...	18	5 years state bar	5 years state bar
Wyoming	3 yrs.	2 yrs.	...	...	30	28	9 years practice	Law degree
Dist. of Columbia	N.A.	N.A.	90 days	90 days	...	...	5 years practice	5 years state bar (v)
Puerto Rico	5 yrs.	...	...	...	...	...	10 years practice	7 years state bar

See footnotes at end of table

TABLE 5.3
Qualifications of Judges of State Appellate Courts and General Trial Courts (continued)

Source: National Center for State Courts, May 2019.

Key:

A–Judges of courts of last resort and intermediate appellate courts.

T–Judges of general trial courts.

★–Provision; length of time not specified.

...–No specific provision.

N.A.–Not applicable.

(a) For court of appeals, five years.

(b) No local residency requirement stated for Supreme Court. Local residency of 3 years required for Court of Appeals.

(c) Supreme Court–ten years state bar, Court of Appeals–five years state bar.

(d) Admitted to the practice of law in Arizona for five years.

(e) Court of Appeals minimum age is 30.

(f) The candidate must be a resident of the district at the time of the original appointment.

(g) Circuit court judge must reside within the territorial jurisdiction of the court.

(h) In the Supreme Court and the Court of Appeals, five years service as a general jurisdiction judge may be substituted.

(i) Relevant legal experience, such as being a member of a law faculty or sitting as a judge, may qualify under the 10 year requirement.

(j) Must reside within the district.

(k) At the appellate level must have been a state voter for nine years. At the general trial court level must have been a state voter for three years and resident of the circuit for 1 year.

(l) Minimum of two years state bar member and at least 15 years of legal practice.

(m) Restricted Superior court judgeships require residence within the particular county of assignment at time of appointment and reappointment.

(n) Resident judges of the Superior Court are required to have local residency, but special judges are not.

(o) District and associate judges must be state residents for six months if elected, and associate judges must be county residents.

(p) District Court: judges must be a state bar member for four years or a judge of court record. Associate judges must be a state bar member for two years or a judge of a court of record.

(q) Circuit judges must be county electors and residents of the circuit.

(r) Supreme Court: One justice from each of three divisions and two seats at large; no more than two may be from any grand division. Court of Appeals and Court of Criminal Appeals: Must reside in the grand division served.

(s) 35 for Supreme Court, 30 for Court of Appeals & Court of Criminal Appeals.

(t) Ten years practicing law or a lawyer and judge of a court of record at least 10 years.

(u) District Court: judges must have been a practicing lawyer or a judge of a court in this state, or both combined, for four years.

(v) Superior Court: Judge must also be an active member of the unified District of Columbia bar and have been engaged, during the five years immediately preceding the judicial nomination, in the active practice of law as an attorney in the District, been on the faculty of a law school in the District, or been employed by either the by the United States or District of Columbia government.

TABLE 5.4

Compensation of Judges of Appellate Courts and General Trial Courts

State or other jurisdiction	Court of last resort	Appellate courts Chief Justice salaries	Associate Justice salaries	Intermediate appellate court	Judges salaries	General trial courts	Salary
Alabama	Supreme Court	$181,127	$172,716	Court of Criminal Appeals	$184,244	Circuit courts	$138,991
Alaska	Supreme Court	205,776	205,176	Court of Appeals	193,836	Superior courts	189,720
Arizona	Supreme Court	164,836	159,685	Court of Appeals	154,534	Superior courts	149,383
Arkansas	Supreme Court	183,600	174,925	Court of Appeals	169,672	Chancery courts	168,096
California	Supreme Court	256,059	253,189	Court of Appeals	237,365	Superior court	207,424
Colorado	Supreme Court	181,219	182,671	Court of Appeals	175,434	District courts	168,202
Connecticut	Supreme Court	200,599	185,610	Appellate Court	174,323	Superior courts	167,634
Delaware	Supreme Court	204,148	196,245	...	...	Superior courts	184,444
Florida	Supreme Court	178,420	220,600	District Court of Appeals	169,554	Circuit courts	160,688
Georgia	Supreme Court	175,600	175,600	Court of Appeals	174,500	Superior courts	173,714
Hawaii	Supreme Court	231,468	227,664	Intermediate Court	210,780	Circuit courts	205,080
Idaho	Supreme Court	149,700	151,400	Court of Appeals	141,400	District courts	135,400
Illinois	Supreme Court	229,345	234,391	Court of Appeals	220,605	Circuit courts	202,433
Indiana	Supreme Court	173,599	177,244	Court of Appeals	172,296	Circuit courts	147,164
Iowa	Supreme Court	183,001	174,808	Court of Appeals	158,420	District courts	147,494
Kansas	Supreme Court	142,793	142,089	Court of Appeals	137,502	District courts	125,499
Kentucky	Supreme Court	140,508	138,890	Court of Appeals	133,299	Circuit courts	127,733
Louisiana	Supreme Court	177,703	170,325	Court of Appeals	159,347	District courts	153,143
Maine	Supreme Judicial Court	154,981	138,070	...	...	Superior courts	129,397
Maryland	Court of Appeals	195,433	181,433	Court of Special Appeals	168,633	Circuit courts	159,433
Massachusetts	Supreme Judicial Court	199,989	200,984	Appellate Court	190,087	Superior courts	184,694
Michigan	Supreme Court	164,610	164,610	Court of Appeals	160,695	Circuit courts	146,721
Minnesota	Supreme Court	190,699	177,697	Court of Appeals	167,438	District courts	157,179
Mississippi	Supreme Court	159,000	152,250	Court of Appeals	144,827	Chancery courts	136,000
Missouri	Supreme Court	181,677	176,157	Court of Appeals	161,038	Circuit courts	151,840
Montana	Supreme Court	145,621	144,061	...	...	District courts	132,558
Nebraska	Supreme Court	173,694	176,299	Court of Appeals	167,484	District courts	163,077
Nevada	Supreme Court	170,000	170,000	Court of Appeals	165,000	District courts	160,000
New Hampshire	Supreme Court	167,271	175,837	...	...	Superior courts	164,911
New Jersey	Supreme Court	192,795	201,842	Appellate division of	191,534	Superior courts	181,000
New Mexico	Supreme Court	133,174	139,819	Court of Appeals	132,838	District courts	126,187
New York	Court of Appeals	222,500	230,200	Appellate divisions of	219,200	Supreme courts	208,000
North Carolina	Supreme Court	150,086	149,115	Court of Appeals	142,947	Superior courts	135,236
North Dakota	Supreme Court	161,517	157,009	...	...	District courts	143,869
Ohio	Supreme Court	174,700	172,200	Court of Appeals	160,500	Courts of common pleas	147,600
Oklahoma	Supreme Court	155,820	154,174	Court of Appeals	146,059	District courts	139,298
Oregon	Supreme Court	150,572	154,040	Court of Appeals	150,980	Circuit courts	142,136
Pennsylvania	Supreme Court	213,748	211,027	Superior Court	199,114	Courts of common pleas	183,184
Rhode Island	Supreme Court	193,458	183,872	...	...	Superior courts	165,545
South Carolina	Supreme Court	156,234	148,794	Court of Appeals	145,074	Circuit courts	141,354
South Dakota	Supreme Court	137,270	136,893	...	...	Circuit courts	127,862
Tennessee	Supreme Court	190,128	188,952	Court of Appeals	182,664	Chancery courts	176,364
Texas	Supreme Court	170,500	168,000	Court of Appeals	158,500	District courts	149,000
Utah	Supreme Court	180,500	182,950	Court of Appeals	174,600	District courts	166,300
Vermont	Supreme Court	166,130	163,757	...	...	Superior/District/Family	155,677
Virginia	Supreme Court	210,017	197,827	Court of Appeals	181,610	Circuit courts	171,120
Washington	Supreme Court	189,374	190,415	Court of Appeals	181,263	Superior courts	172,571
West Virginia	Supreme Court	136,000	136,000	...	...	Circuit courts	126,000
Wisconsin	Supreme Court	147,403	159,297	Court of Appeals	150,280	Circuit courts	141,773
Wyoming	Supreme Court	165,000	165,000	...	...	District courts	150,000

Source: National Center for State Courts, January 6, 2019.

Note: Compensation is shown rounded to the nearest thousand, and is reported according to most recent legislation, even though laws may not yet have taken effect. There are other non-salary forms of judicial compensation that can be a significant part of a judge's compensation package. It should be noted that many of these can be important to judges or attorneys who might be interested in becoming judges or justices. These include retirement, disability, and death benefits, expense accounts, vacation, holiday, and sick leave and various forms of insurance coverage.

TABLE 5.5
Selected Data on Court Administrative Offices

State or other jurisdiction	Title	Established	Appointed by (a)	Salary
Alabama	Administrative Director of Courts	1971	CJ	$126,408
Alaska	Administrative Director	1959	CJ (b)	203,176
Arizona	Administrative Director of Courts	1960	SC	158,250
Arkansas	Director, Administrative Office of the Courts	1965	CJ (c)	120,543
California	Administrative Director of the Courts	1960	JC	288,888
Colorado	State Court Administrator	1959	SC	174,226
Connecticut	Chief Court Administrator (d)	1965	CJ	192,763
Delaware	Director, Administrative Office of the Courts	1971	CJ	137,612
Florida	State Courts Administrator	1972	SC	137,000
Georgia	Director, Administrative Office of the Courts	1973	JC	147,084
Hawaii	Administrative Director of the Courts	1959	CJ (b)	151,776
Idaho	Administrative Director of the Courts	1967	SC	137,700
Illinois	Administrative Director of the Courts	1959	SC	215,856
Indiana	Executive Director, Division of State Court Administration	1975	CJ	144,279
Iowa	Court Administrator	1971	SC	154,000
Kansas	Judicial Administrator	1965	CJ	123,038
Kentucky	Administrative Director of the Courts	1976	CJ	127,122
Louisiana	Judicial Administrator	1954	SC	158,147
Maine	Court Administrator	1975	CJ	125,632
Maryland	State Court Administrator	1955	CJ	166,633
Massachusetts	Chief Justice for Administration & Management	1978	SC	189,378
Michigan	State Court Administrator	1952	SC	166,171
Minnesota	State Court Administrator	1963	SC	188,066
Mississippi	Court Administrator	1974	SC	107,000
Missouri	State Courts Administrator	1970	SC	126,966
Montana	State Court Administrator	1975	SC	112,694
Nebraska	State Court Administrator	1972	CJ	146,029
Nevada	Director, Office of Court Administration	1971	SC	131,347
New Hampshire	Director of the Administrative Office of the Court	1980	SC	111,560
New Jersey	Administrative Director of the Courts	1948	CJ	175,534
New Mexico	Director, Administrative Office of the Courts	1959	SC	131,165
New York	Chief Administrator of the Courts	1978	CJ	210,500
North Carolina	Director, Administrative Office of the Courts	1965	CJ	143,878
North Dakota	Court Administrator	1971	CJ	141,552
Ohio	Administrative Director of the Courts	1955	SC	146,494
Oklahoma	Administrative Director of the Courts	1967	SC	138,235
Oregon	Court Administrator	1971	SC	138,468
Pennsylvania	Court Administrator	1968	SC	195,978
Rhode Island	State Court Administrator	1969	CJ	150,797
South Carolina	Director of Court Administration	1973	CJ	136,591
South Dakota	State Court Administrator	1974	SC	115,515
Tennessee	Director	1963	SC	178,908
Texas	Administrative Director of the Courts	1977	SC	171,216
Utah	Court Administrator	1973	SC	162,250
Vermont	Court Administrator	1967	SC	150,738
Virginia	Executive Secretary to the Supreme Court	1952	SC	196,370
Washington	Administrator for the Courts	1957	SC	152,736
West Virginia	Administrative Director of the Supreme Court of Appeals	1975	SC	135,000
Wisconsin	Director of State Courts	1978	SC	139,059
Wyoming	Court Coordinator	1974	SC	125,000
Dist. of Columbia	Executive Officer, Courts of D.C.	1971	(d)	208,000
American Samoa	Administrator/Comptroller	N.A	N.A.	N.A.
Guam	Administrative Director of Superior Court	N.A.	CJ	N.A.
CNMI*	Director of Courts	N.A.	N.A.	N.A.
Puerto Rico	Administrative Director of the Courts	1952	CJ	N.A.
U.S. Virgin Islands	Court/Administrative Clerk	N.A.	N.A.	N.A.

See footnotes at end of table

TABLE 5.5
Selected Data on Court Administrative Offices (continued)

Source: National Center for State Courts, January 6, 2019.
Note: Compensation shown is rounded to the nearest thousand, and is reported according to most recent legislation, even though laws may not yet have taken effect. Other information from State Court Administrator web sites.
*Commonweatlh of Northern Mariana Islands
Key:
SC–State court of last resort.
CJ–Chief justice or chief judge of court of last resort.

JC–Judicial council.
N.A.–Not available.
(a) Term of office for all court administrators is at pleasure of appointing authority.
(b) With approval of Supreme Court.
(c) With approval of Judicial Council.
(d) Joint Committee on Judicial Administration.

TABLE 5.6
Selection and Retention of Appellate Court Judges

State or other jurisdiction	Name of court	Type of court	Method of selection Unexpired term	Full term	Method of retention	Geographic basis for selection
Alabama	Supreme Court	SC	GU	PE	PE	SW
	Court of Civil Appeals	IA	GU	PE	PE	SW
	Court of Criminal Appeals	IA	GU	PE	PE	SW
Alaska	Supreme Court	SC	GN	GN	RE (a)	SW
	Court of Appeals	IA	GN	GN	RE (a)	SW
Arizona	Supreme Court	SC	GN	GN	RE	SW
	Court of Appeals	IA	GN	GN	RE	DS
Arkansas	Supreme Court	SC	GU	NP	NP	SW
	Court of Appeals	IA	GU	NP	NP	DS
California	Supreme Court	SC	GU	GU	RE	SW
	Courts of Appeal	IA	GU	GU	RE	DS
Colorado	Supreme Court	SC	GN	GN	RE	SW
	Court of Appeals	IA	GN	GN	RE	SW
Connecticut	Supreme Court	SC	GNL	GNL	GNL	SW
	Appellate Court	IA	GNL	GNL	GNL	SW
Delaware	Supreme Court	SC	GNL	GNL	GNL	SW
Florida	Supreme Court	SC	GN	GN	RE	DS and SW (b)
	District Courts of Appeal	IA	GN	GN	RE	DS
Georgia	Supreme Court	SC	GN	NP	NP	SW
	Court of Appeals	IA	GN	NP	NP	SW
Hawaii	Supreme Court	SC	GNL	GNL	JN	SW
	Intermediate Court of Appeals	IA	GNL	GNL	JN	SW
Idaho	Supreme Court	SC	GN	NP	NP	SW
	Court of Appeals	IA	GN	NP	NP	SW
Illinois	Supreme Court	SC	CS	PE	RE	DS
	Appellate Court	IA	SC	PE	RE	DS
Indiana	Supreme Court	SC	GN	GN	RE	SW
	Court of Appeals	IA	GN	GN	RE	DS
	Tax Court	IA	GN	GN	RE	SW
Iowa	Supreme Court	SC	GN	GN	RE	SW
	Court of Appeals	IA	GN	GN	RE	SW
Kansas	Supreme Court	SC	GN	GN	RE	SW
	Court of Appeals	IA	GL	GL	RE	SW
Kentucky	Supreme Court	SC	GN	NP	NP	DS
	Court of Appeals	IA	GN	NP	NP	DS
Louisiana	Supreme Court	SC	CS (c)	PE (d)	PE (d)	DS
	Courts of Appeal	IA	SC (c)	PE (d)	PE (d)	DS
Maine	Supreme Judicial Court	SC	GL	GL	GL	SW
Maryland	Court of Appeals	SC	GNL	GNL	RE	DS
	Court of Special Appeals	IA	GNL	GNL	RE	DS
Massachusetts	Supreme Judicial Court	SC	(e)	GNE (f)	(g)	SW
	Appeals Court	IA	(e)	GNE (f)	(g)	SW
Michigan	Supreme Court	SC	GU	PE (h)	PE (h)	SW
	Court of Appeals	IA	GU	PE (h)	PE (h)	DS
Minnesota	Supreme Court	SC	GU	NP	NP	SW
	Court of Appeals	IA	GU	NP	NP	SW
Mississippi	Supreme Court	SC	GU	NP	NP	DS
	Court of Appeals	IA	GU	NP	NP	DS
Missouri	Supreme Court	SC	GN	GN	RE	SW
	Court of Appeals	IA	GN	GN	RE	DS
Montana	Supreme Court	SC	GNL	NP	NP (i)	SW
Nebraska	Supreme Court	SC	GN	GN	RE	SW and DS (j)
	Court of Appeals	IA	GN	GN	RE	DS
Nevada	Supreme Court	SC	GN	NP	NP	SW
	Court of Appeals	IA	GN	NP	NP	SW
New Hampshire	Supreme Court	SC	GE	GE	(k)	SW
New Jersey	Supreme Court	SC	GL	GL	GL	SW
	Superior Court, Appellate Div.	IA	GL	GL (l)	GL (l)	SW
New Mexico	Supreme Court	SC	GN	PE	RE	SW
	Court of Appeals	IA	GN	PE	RE	SW
New York	Court of Appeals	SC	GNL	GNL	GNL	SW
	Supreme Ct., Appellate Div.	IA	GN	GN	GN	SW (m)
North Carolina	Supreme Court	SC	GU	PE	PE	SW
	Court of Appeals	IA	GU	PE	PE	SW
North Dakota	Supreme Court	SC	GN (n)	NP	NP	SW
	Temporary Court of Appeals	IA	(o)	SC (p)	(o)	SW

See footnotes at end of table

TABLE 5.6
Selection and Retention of Appellate Court Judges (continued)

State or other jurisdiction	Name of court	Type of court	Method of selection		Method of retention	Geographic basis for selection
			Unexpired term	Full term		
Ohio	Supreme Court	SC	GU	PE (q)	PE (q)	SW
	Courts of Appeals	IA	GU	PE (q)	PE (q)	DS
Oklahoma	Supreme Court	SC	GN	GN	RE	DS
	Court of Criminal Appeals	SC	GN	GN	RE	DS
	Court of Civil Appeals	IA	GN	GN	RE	DS
Oregon	Supreme Court	SC	GU	NP	NP	SW
	Court of Appeals	IA	GU	NP	NP	SW
Pennsylvania	Supreme Court	SC	GL	PE	RE	SW
	Superior Court	IA	GL	PE	RE	SW
	Commonwealth Court	IA	GL	PE	RE	SW
Rhode Island	Supreme Court	SC	GN	GN	(r)	SW
South Carolina	Supreme Court	SC	LA	LA	LA	SW
	Court of Appeals	IA	LA	LA	LA	SW
South Dakota	Supreme Court	SC	GN	GN	RE	DS and SW (s)
Tennessee	Supreme Court	SC	GL	GL	RE	SW
	Court of Appeals	SC	GL	GL	RE	SW
	Court of Criminal Appeals	IA	GL	GL	RE	SW
Texas	Supreme Court	SC	GU	PE	PE	SW
	Court of Criminal Appeals	SC	GU	PE	PE	SW
	Courts of Appeals	IA	GU	PE	PE	DS
Utah	Supreme Court	SC	GNL	GNL	RE	SW
	Court of Appeals	IA	GNL	GNL	RE	SW
Vermont	Supreme Court	SC	GNL	GNL	LA	SW
Virginia	Supreme Court	SC	GU (t)	LA	LA	SW
	Court of Appeals	IA	GU (t)	LA	LA	SW
Washington	Supreme Court	SC	GU	NP	NP	SW
	Courts of Appeals	IA	GU	NP	NP	DS
West Virginia	Supreme Court of Appeals	SC	GU (u)	NP	NP	SW
Wisconsin	Supreme Court	SC	GU	NP	NP	SW
	Court of Appeals	IA	GU	NP	NP	DS
Wyoming	Supreme Court	SC	GN	GN	RE	SW
Dist. of Columbia	Court of Appeals	SC	(v)	(t)	(t)	SW (w)
Puerto Rico	Supreme Court	SC	GL	GL	(x)	SW
	Court of Appeals	IA	GL	GL	GL	SW

See footnotes at end of table

TABLE 5.6
Selection and Retention of Appellate Court Judges (continued)

Sources: National Center for State Courts. June 2019.
Key:
SC–Court of last resort
IA–Intermediate appellate court
N/S–Not stated
N.A.–Not applicable
AP–At pleasure
CS–Court selection
DS–District
DU–Duration of service
GE–Gubernatorial appointment with approval of elected executive
  council
GL–Gubernatorial appointment with consent of the legislature
GN–Gubernatorial appointment from judicial nominating
  commission
GNE–Gubernatorial appointment from judicial nominating
  commission with approval of elected executive council
GNL–Gubernatorial appointment from judicial nominating
  commission with consent of the legislature
GU–Gubernatorial appointment
ID–Indefinite
JN–Judicial nominating commission appoints
LA–Legislative appointment
NP–Non-partisan election
PE–Partisan election
RE–Retention election
SC–Court of last resort appoints
SCJ–Chief justice/judge of the court of last resort appoints
SN–Seniority
SW–Statewide
(a) A judge must run for a retention election at the next election,
  immediately following the third year from the time of initial
  appointment.
(b) Five justices are selected by region (based on the District Courts
  of Appeal) and two justices are selected statewide.
(c) The person selected by the Supreme Court is prohibited from
  running for that judgeship; an election is held within one year to
  serve the remainder of the term.
(d) Louisiana uses a blanket primary, in which all candidates appear
  with party labels on the primary ballot. The two top vote getters
  compete in the general election.
(e) There are no expired judicial terms. A judicial term expires upon
  the death, resignation, retirement, or removal of an incumbent.
(f) The Executive (Governor's) Council is made up of nine people
  elected by geographical area and presided over by the Lieutenant
  Governor.
(g) There is no retention process. Judges serve during good
  behavior to age 70.

(h) Candidates may be nominated by political parties and are
  elected on a nonpartisan ballot.
(i) If the justice/judge is unopposed, a retention election is held.
(j) Chief Justices are selected statewide while Associate Justices are
  selected by district.
(k) There is no retention process. Judges serve during good
  behavior to age 70.
(l) All Superior Court judges, including Appellate Division judges,
  are subject to gubernatorial reappointment and consent by the
  Senate after an initial seven-year term. Among all the judges, the
  Chief Justice designates the judges of the Appellate Division.
(m) The Presiding Judge of each Appellate Division must be a
  resident of the department.
(n) The Governor may appoint from a list of names or call a special
  election at his discretion.
(o) The supreme court may provide for the assignment of active or
  retired district court judges, retired justices of the supreme court,
  and lawyers, to serve on three-judge panels.
(p) There is neither a retention process nor unexpired terms.
  Assignments are for a specified time, not to exceed one year or the
  completion of one or more cases on the docket of the supreme
  court.
(q) Party affiliation is not included on the ballot in the general
  election, but candidates are chosen through partisan primary
  nominations.
(r) There is no retention process. Judges serve during good
  behavior for a life tenure.
(s) Initial selection is by district, but retention selection is statewide.
(t) Gubernatorial appointment is for interim appointments.
(u) Appointment is effective only until the next election year; the
  appointee may run for election to any remaining portion of the
  unexpired term.
(v) Initial appointment is made by the President of the United
  States and confirmed by the Senate. Six months prior to the
  expiration of the term of office, the judge's performance is
  reviewed by the tenure commission. Those found "well qualified"
  are automatically reappointed. If a judge is found to be
  "qualified" the President may nominate the judge for an additional
  term (subject to Senate confirmation). If the President does not
  wish to reappoint the judge, the District of Columbia Nomination
  Commission compiles a new list of candidates.
(w) The geographic basis of selection is the District of Columbia.
(x) There is no retention process. Judges serve during good
  behavior to age 70.

TABLE 5.7
Selection and Retention of Trial Court Judges

State or other jurisdiction	Name of court	Type of court	Method of selection Unexpired term	Full term	Method of retention	Geographic basis for selection
Alabama	Circuit	GJ	GU (a)	PE	PE	Circuit
	District	LJ	GU (a)	PE	PE	County
	Municipal	LJ	MU	MU	RA	Municipality
	Probate	LJ	GU	PE	PE	County
Alaska	Superior	GJ	GN	GN	RE (b)	State (c)
	District	LJ	GN	GN	RE (d)	District
	Magistrate's Division	N.A.	PJ	PJ	PJ	District
Arizona	Superior	GJ	GN (e)	GN or NP (f)	NP or RE (f)	County
	Justice of the Peace	LJ	CO	PE	PE	Precinct
	Municipal	LJ	CC (g)	CC (g)	CC (g)	Municipality
Arkansas	Circuit	GJ	GU (h)	NP	NP	Circuit
	District	LJ	GU	NP	NP	District
	City	LJ	LD	LD	LD	City
California	Superior	GJ	GU	NP	NP (i)	County
Colorado	District	GJ	GN	GN	RE	District
	Denver Probate	GJ	GN	GN	RE	District
	Denver Juvenile	GJ	GN	GN	RE	District
	Water	GJ	SC (j)	SC (j)	RE	District
	County	LJ	GN	GN (k)	RE	County
	Municipal	LJ	MU	MU	RA	Municipality
Connecticut	Superior	GJ	GNL	GNL	GNL	State
	Probate	LJ	PE	PE	PE	District
Delaware	Superior	GJ	GNL	GNL	GNL	State
	Chancery	LJ	GNL	GNL	GNL	State
	Justice of the Peace	LJ	GNL (l)	GNL (l)	GU	County
	Family	LJ	GNL	GNL	GNL	County
	Common Pleas	LJ	GNL	GNL	GNL	County
	Alderman's	LJ	LD	CC	LD	Town
Florida	Circuit	GJ	GN	NP	NP	Circuit
	County	LJ	GN	NP	NP	County
Georgia	Superior	GJ	GN	NP	NP	Circuit
	Juvenile	LJ	CS (m)	CS (m)	CS (m)	County/Circuit
	Civil	LJ	GU	PE	PE	County
	State	LJ	GU	NP	NP	County
	Probate	LJ	GU	PE (n)	PE (n)	County
	Magistrate	LJ	LD	LD (o)	LD (o)	County
	Municipal/of Columbus	LJ	MA	Elected	Elected	Municipality
	County Recorder's	LJ	LD	LD	LD	County
	Municipal/City of Atlanta	LJ	MU	MU	LD	Municipality
Hawaii	Circuit	GJ	GNL	GNL	JN	State
	District	LJ	SCJ (p)	SCJ (p)	JN	Circuit
Idaho	District	GJ	GN	NP	NP	District
	Magistrate's Division	LJ	JN (q)	JN (q)	RE	County
Illinois	Circuit	GJ	SC	PE	RE	Circuit/County (r)
	Associate Division	N.A.	SC	PE	RE	Circuit/County (r)
Indiana	Superior	GJ	GU	PE (s)	PE (s)	County
	Circuit	GJ	GU	PE (t)	PE (t)	County
	Probate	GJ	GU	PE	PE	County
	County	LJ	GU	PE	PE	County
	City	LJ	GU	PE	PE	Municipality
	Town	LJ	GU	PE	PE	Municipality
	Small Claims/Marion County	LJ	GU	PE	PE	Township
Iowa	District	GJ	GN (u)	GN (u)	RE (u)	District
Kansas	District	GJ	GN and PE (v)	GN and PE (v)	RE and PE (v)	District
	Municipal	LJ	MU	MU	MU	City
Kentucky	Circuit	GJ	GN	NP	NP	Circuit
	District	LJ	GN	NP	NP	District
Louisiana	District	GJ	SC (w)	PE	PE	District
	Juvenile & Family	GJ	SC (w)	PE	PE	District
	Justice of the Peace	LJ	SC (w)	PE (x)	PE	Ward
	Mayor's	LJ	MA	LD	LD	City
	City & Parish	LJ	SC (w)	PE	PE	Ward
Maine	Superior	GJ	GL	GL	GL	State
	District	GJ	GL	GL	GL	State and District (y)
	Probate	LJ	GU	PE	PE	County
Maryland	Circuit	GJ	GNL	GNL	NP	County
	District	LJ	GNL	GNL	RA	District
	Orphan's	LJ	GU	PE (z)	PE (z)	County

See footnotes at end of table

TABLE 5.7
Selection and Retention of Trial Court Judges (continued)

State or other jurisdiction	Name of court	Type of court	Method of selection		Method of retention	Geographic basis for selection
			Unexpired term	Full term		
Massachusetts	Superior	GJ	(aa)	GNE (bb)	(cc)	State
	District	LJ	(aa)	GNE (bb)	(cc)	State
	Probate & Family	LJ	(aa)	GNE (bb)	(cc)	State
	Juvenile	LJ	(aa)	GNE (bb)	(cc)	State
	Housing	LJ	(aa)	GNE (bb)	(cc)	State
	Boston Municipal	LJ	(aa)	GNE (bb)	(cc)	State
	Land	LJ	(aa)	GNE (bb)	(cc)	State
Michigan	Circuit	GJ	GU	NP	NP	Circuit
	Claims	GJ	GU	NP	NP	Circuit
	District	LJ	GU	NP	NP	District
	Probate	LJ	GU	NP	NP	District and Circuit
	Municipal	LJ	LD	NP	NP	City
Minnesota	District	GJ	GN	NP	NP	District
Mississippi	Circuit	GJ	GU	NP	NP	District
	Chancery	LJ	GU	NP	NP	District
	County	LJ	GU	NP	NP	County
	Municipal	LJ	LD	LD	LD	Municipality
	Justice	LJ	LD	PE	PE	District in County
Missouri	Circuit	GJ	GU and GN (dd)	PE and GN (ee)	PE and RE (ff)	Circuit/County (gg)
	Municipal	LJ	LD	LD	LD	City
Montana	District	GJ	GN	NP	NP	District
	Workers' Compensation	GJ	GN	GN	RA	State
	Water	GJ	SCJ (hh)	SCJ (hh)	SCJ (ii)	State
	Justice of the Peace	LJ	CO	NP	NP	County
	Municipal	LJ	MU	NP	NP	City
	City	LJ	CC	NP	NP	City
Nebraska	District	GJ	GN	GN	RE	District
	Separate Juvenile	LJ	GN	GN	RE	District
	County	LJ	GN	GN	RE	District
	Workers' Compensation	LJ	GN	GN	RE	District
Nevada	District	GJ	GN	NP	NP	District
	Justice	LJ	CO	NP	NP	Township
	Municipal	LJ	CC	NP	NP	City
New Hampshire	Superior	GJ	GE	GE	(jj)	State
	District	LJ	GE	GE	(jj)	District
	Probate	LJ	GE	GE	(jj)	County
New Jersey	Superior	GJ	GL	GL	GL	County
	Tax	LJ	GL	GL	GL	State
	Municipal	LJ	MA or MU (kk)	MA or MU (kk)	MU	Municipality
New Mexico	District	GJ	GN	PE	RE	District
	Magistrate	LJ	GU	PE	PE	County
	Metropolitan/Bernalillo County	LJ	GN	PE	RE	County
	Municipal	LJ	MU	PE	PE	City
	Probate	LJ	CO	PE	PE	County
New York	Supreme	GJ	GL	PE	PE	District
	County	GJ	GL	PE	PE	County
	Claims	GJ	GNL	GNL	GU	State
	Surrogates'	LJ	GNL	PE	PE	County
	Family	LJ	GNL and MU (ll)	PE and MU (ll)	PE and MU (ll)	County and NYC
	District	LJ	(mm)	PE	PE	District
	City	LJ	Elected	Elected	LD	City
	NYC Civil	LJ	MA (nn)	PE	PE	City
	NYC Criminal	LJ	MA	MA	MA	City
	Town & Village Justice	LJ	LD	LD	LD	Town or Village
North Carolina	Superior	GJ	GU	PE	PE	District
	District	LJ	GU	PE	PE	District
North Dakota	District	GJ	GN	NP	NP	District
	Municipal	LJ	MA	NP	NP	City
Ohio	Common Pleas	GJ	GU	PE (oo)	PE (oo)	County
	Municipal	LJ	GU	PE (oo)	PE (oo)	County/City
	County	LJ	GU	PE (oo)	PE (oo)	County
	Claims	LJ	SCJ	SCJ	SCJ	N.A.
	Mayor's	LJ	Elected	PE	PE	City/Village
Oklahoma	District	GJ	GN (pp)	NP (pp)	NP (pp)	District
	Municipal Not of Record	LJ	MM	MM	MM	Municipality
	Municipal of Record	LJ	MU	MU	MU	Municipality
	Workers' Compensation	LJ	GN	GN	GN	State
	Tax Review	LJ	SCJ	SCJ	SCJ	District

See footnotes at end of table

TABLE 5.7
Selection and Retention of Trial Court Judges (continued)

State or other jurisdiction	Name of court	Type of court	Method of selection Unexpired term	Method of selection Full term	Method of retention	Geographic basis for selection
Oregon	Circuit	GJ	GU	NP	NP	District
	Tax	GJ	GU	NP	NP	State
	County	LJ	CO	NP	NP	County
	Justice	LJ	GU	NP	NP	County
	Municipal	LJ	CC	CC/Elected	CC/Elected	(qq)
Pennsylvania	Common Pleas	GJ	GL	PE	RE	District
	Philadelphia Municipal	LJ	GL	PE	RE	City/County
	Magisterial District Judges	LJ	GL	PE	PE	District
	Philadelphia Traffic	LJ	GL	PE	RE	City/County
Rhode Island	Superior	GJ	GN	GN	(rr)	State
	Workers' Compensation	LJ	GN	GN	(rr)	State
	District	LJ	GN	GN	(rr)	State
	Family	LJ	GN	GN	(rr)	State
	Probate	LJ	CC	CC or MA	RA	Town
	Municipal	LJ	CC	CC or MA	CC or MA	Town
	Traffic Tribunal	LJ	GN	GN	(rr)	State
South Carolina	Circuit	GJ	LA and GN (ss)(tt)	LA and GN (tt)	LA and GL (tt)	Circuit and State (tt)
	Family	LJ	LA	LA	LA	Circuit
	Magistrate	LJ	GL	GL	GL	County
	Probate	LJ	GU	PE	PE	County
	Municipal	LJ	CC	CC	CC	District
South Dakota	Circuit	GJ	GN	NP	NP	Circuit
	Magistrate	LJ	PJS	PJS	PJS	Circuit
Tennessee	Circuit	GJ	GU	PE (uu)	PE	District
	Chancery	GJ	GU	PE (uu)	PE	District
	Criminal	GJ	GU	PE (uu)	PE	District
	Probate	GJ	(vv)	PE (uu)	PE	District
	Juvenile	LJ	(vv)	PE (uu)	PE	County
	Municipal	LJ	LD	LD (uu)	LD	Municipality
	General Sessions	LJ	MU	PE (uu)	PE	County
Texas	District	GJ	GL	PE	PE	District
	Constitutional County	LJ	CO	PE	PE	County
	Probate	LJ	CO	PE	PE	County
	County at Law	LJ	CO	PE	PE	County
	Justice of the Peace	LJ	CO	PE	PE	Precinct
	Municipal	LJ	CC	LD	LD	Municipality
Utah	District	GJ	(ww)	GNL	RE	District
	Justice	LJ	MM (xx)	MM (xx)	RE and RA (yy)	County/Municipality
	Juvenile	LJ	(ww)	GNL	RE	District
Vermont	Superior (zz)	GJ	GNL	GNL	LA	State
	Judicial Bureau	LJ	PJ	PJ	AP	State
Virginia	Circuit	GJ	GU	LA	LA	Circuit
	District	LJ	CS (aaa)	LA	LA	District
Washington	Superior	GJ	GU	NP	NP	County
	District	LJ	CO	NP	NP	District
	Municipal	LJ	CC	MA/CC	MA/CC (bbb)	Municipality
West Virginia	Circuit	GJ	GU	NP	NP	Circuit
	Magistrate	LJ	PJ	NP	NP	County
	Municipal	LJ	LD	LD	LD	Municipality
	Family	LJ	GU	NP	NP	Circuit
Wisconsin	Circuit	GJ	GU	NP	NP	District
	Municipal	LJ	MU (ccc)	NP	NP	Municipality
Wyoming	District	GJ	GN	GN	RE	District
	Circuit	LJ	GN	GN	RE	Circuit
	Municipal	LJ	MA	MA	LD	Municipality
Dist. of Columbia	Superior	GJ	(ddd)	(ddd)	(ddd)	State (eee)
Puerto Rico	First Instance	GJ	GL	GL	GL	State

See footnotes at end of table

TABLE 5.7
Selection and Retention of Trial Court Judges (continued)

Sources: National Center for State Courts, June 2019.
Key:
GJ–General jurisdiction court
LJ–Limited jurisdiction court
N/S–Not stated
N.A.–Not applicable
AP–At pleasure
CA–Court administrator appointment
CC–City or town council/commission appointment
CO–County board/commission appointment
CS–Court selection
DU–Duration of service
GE–Gubernatorial appointment with approval of elected executive council
GL–Gubernatorial appointment with consent of the legislature
GN–Gubernatorial appointment from judicial nominating commission
GNE–Gubernatorial appointment from judicial nominating commission with approval of elected executive council
GNL–Gubernatorial appointment from judicial nominating commission with consent of the legislature
GU–Gubernatorial appointment
JN–Judicial nominating commission appoints
LA–Legislative appointment
LD–Locally determined
MA–Mayoral appointment
MC–Mayoral appointment with consent of city council
MM–Mayoral appointment with consent of governing municipal body
MU–Governing municipal body appointment
NP–Non-partisan election
PE–Partisan election
PJ–Presiding judge of the general jurisdiction court appoints
PJS–Presiding judge of the general jurisdiction court appoints with approval of the court of last resort
RA–Reappointment
RE–Retention election
SC–Court of last resort appoints
SCJ–Chief justice/judge of the court of last resort appoints
(a) The counties of Baldwin, Jefferson, Lauderdale, Madison, Mobile, Shelby, Talladega, and Tuscaloosa use gubernatorial appointment from the recommendations of the Judicial Nominating Commission.
(b) A judge must run for retention at the next election immediately following the third year from the time of the initial appointment.
(c) Judges are selected on a statewide basis, but run for retention on a district-wide basis.
(d) Judges must run for retention at the first general election held more than one year after appointment.
(e) Maricopa, Pima and Pinal counties use the gubernatorial appointment from the Judicial Nominating Commission process. The method for submitting names for the other counties varies.
(f) Maricopa, Pima and Pinal counties use the gubernatorial appointment from the Judicial Nominating Commission process. The other counties hold non-partisan elections.

(g) Municipal court judges are usually appointed by the city or town council except in Yuma, where judges are elected.
(h) The office can be held until December 31 following the next general election and then the judge must run in a non-partisan election for the remainder of the term.
(i) If unopposed for reelection, incumbent's name does not appear on the ballot unless a petition was filed not less than 83 days before the election date indicating that a write-in campaign will be conducted for the office. An unopposed incumbent is not declared elected until the election date. This is for the general election; different timing may apply for the primary election (see Elec. Code §8203).
(j) Judges are chosen by the Supreme Court from among District Court judges.
(k) The mayor appoints Denver County Court judges.
(l) The Magistrate Screening Commission recommends candidates.
(m) Juvenile judges are appointed by Superior Court judges in all but one county, in which juvenile judges are elected. Associate judges (formerly referees) must be a member of the state bar or law school graduates. They serve at the pleasure of the judge(s).
(n) Probate judges are selected in non-partisan elections in 66 of 159 counties.
(o) Magistrate judges are selected in nonpartisan elections in 41 of 159 counties.
(p) Selection occurs by means of Chief Justice appointment from the Judicial Nominating Commission with consent of the Senate.
(q) The Magistrate Commission consists of the administrative judge, three mayors and two electors appointed by the governor, and two attorneys (nominated by the district bar and appointed by the state bar). There is one commission in each district.
(r) There exists a unit less than county in Cook County.
(s) Non-partisan elections are used in the Superior Courts in Allen and Vanderburgh counties. Nominating commissions are used in St. Joseph County and in some courts in Lake County. In those courts that use the nominating commission process for selection; retention elections are used as the method of retention.
(t) Non-partisan elections are used in the Circuit Courts in Vanderburgh County.
(u) This applies to district judges only. Associate judges are selected by the district judges and retention is by a retention election. Magistrates are selected and retained by appointment from the County Judicial Magistrate Nominating Commission. The County Judicial Magistrate Nominating Commission consists of three members appointed by the county board and two elected by the county bar, presided over by a District Court judge.
(v) Seventeen districts use gubernatorial appointment from the Judicial Nominating Commission for selection and retention elections for retention. Fourteen districts use partisan elections for selection and retention.
(w) Depending on the amount of time remaining, selection may be by election following a Supreme Court appointment.
(x) Louisiana uses a blanket primary in which all candidates appear with party labels on the primary ballot. The top two vote getters compete in the general election.

TABLE 5.7
Selection and Retention of Trial Court Judges (continued)

(y) At least one judge who is a resident of the county in which the district lies must be appointed from each of the 13 districts.

(z) Two exceptions are Hartford and Montgomery counties where Circuit Court judges are assigned.

(aa) There are no expired judicial terms. A judicial term expires upon the death, resignation, retirement, or removal of an incumbent.

(bb) The Executive (Governor's) Council is made up of eight people elected by geographical area and presided over by the lieutenant governor.

(cc) There is no retention process. Judges serve during good behavior to age 70.

(dd) Gubernatorial appointment occurs in partisan circuits; gubernatorial appointment from Judicial Nominating Commission takes place in non-partisan circuits.

(ee) Partisan elections occur in some circuits; gubernatorial appointment from the Judicial Nominating Commission with a non-partisan election takes place in others.

(ff) Partisan elections take place in some circuits; retention elections occur in other circuits.

(gg) Associate circuit judges are selected on a county basis.

(hh) Selection occurs through Chief Justice appointment from Judicial Nominating Commission.

(ii) Other judges are designated by the District Court judges.

(jj) There is no retention process. Judges serve during good behavior to age 70.

(kk) In multi-municipality, joint, or countywide municipal courts, selection is by gubernatorial appointment with consent of the senate.

(ll) Mayoral appointment occurs in New York City.

(mm) The appointment is made by the County Chief Executive Officer with confirmation by District Board of Supervisors.

(nn) Housing judges are appointed by the Chief Administrator of the courts.

(oo) Party affiliation is not included on the ballot in the general election, but candidates are chosen through partisan primary nominations.

(pp) This applies to district and associate judges; special judges are selected by the district judges.

(qq) The geographic basis for selection is the municipality for those judges that are elected. Judges that are either appointed or are under contract may be from other cities.

(rr) There is no retention process. Judges serve during good behavior for a life tenure.

(ss) The governor may appoint a candidate if the unexpired term is less than one year.

(tt) In addition to Circuit Court judges, the Circuit Court has masters-in-equity whose jurisdiction is in matters referred to them in the Circuit Court. Masters-in-equity are selected by gubernatorial appointment from the Judicial Merit Selection Commission, retained by gubernatorial appointment with the consent of the senate, and the geographic basis for selection is the state.

(uu) Each county legislative body has the discretion to require elections to be non-partisan.

(vv) The selection method used to fill an unexpired term is established by a special legislative act.

(ww) There are no expired terms; each new judge begins a new term.

(xx) Appointment is by the local government executive with confirmation by the local government legislative body (may be either county or municipal government).

(yy) County judges are retained by retention election; municipal judges are reappointed by the city executive.

(zz) Effective 2011, the Family, District, Environmental and Probate Courts were combined into the Superior Court.

(aaa) Circuit Court judges appoint.

(bbb) Full-time municipal judges must stand for non-partisan election.

(ccc) A permanent vacancy in the office of municipal judge may be filled by temporary appointment of the municipal governing body or jointly by the governing bodies of all municipalities served by the judge.

(ddd) The Judicial Nomination Commission nominates for Presidential appointment and Senate confirmation. Not less than six months prior to the expiration of the term of office, the judge's performance is reviewed by the Commission on Judicial Disabilities and Tenure. A judge found "well qualified" is automatically reappointed for a new term of 15 years; a judge found "qualified" may be renominated by the President (and subject to Senate confirmation). A judge found "unqualified" is ineligible for reappointment or if the President does not wish to reappoint a judge, the Nomination Commission compiles a new list of candidates.

(eee) The geographic basis for selection is the District of Columbia.

TABLE 5.8
Judicial Discipline: Investigating and Adjudicating Bodies

State or other jurisdiction	Investigating body	Adjudicating body	Appeals from adjudication are filed with:	Final disciplining body	Point at which reprimands are made public
Alabama	Judicial Inquiry Committee	Court of the Judiciary	Court of Last Resort	Court of the Judiciary	Filing of the complaint with the Court of the Judiciary
Alaska	Committee on Judicial Conduct	Supreme Court	Court of Last Resort	Supreme Court	Filing of recommendation with Supreme Court
Arizona	Commission on Judicial Conduct	Commission on Judicial Conduct	Court of Last Resort	Supreme Court	Within 15 days of formal charges being brought, unless a motion for reconsideration is filed
Arkansas	Judicial Discipline and Disability Committees	Commission	Court of Last Resort	Supreme Court	At disposition of case
California	Commission on Judicial Performance	Commission on Judicial Performance	Court of Last Resort	Commission on Judicial Performance	Upon commission determination (a)
Colorado	Commission on Judicial Discipline	Commission on Judicial Discipline	No appeal	Supreme Court	Adjudication
Connecticut	Judicial Review Council	Judicial Review Council; Supreme Court (b)	Court of Last Resort	Supreme Court	Public censure is issued at between 10 and 30 days after notice to the judge, provided that if the judge appeals there is an automatic stay of disclosure
Delaware	Preliminary Committee of the Court on the Judiciary	Court on the Judiciary	No appeal	Court on the Judiciary	Upon issuance of opinion and imposition of sanction
Florida	Judicial Qualifications Commission	Judicial Qualifications Commission (b)	No appeal	Supreme Court	Filing of formal charges by Committee with Supreme Court Clerk
Georgia	Judicial Qualifications Commission	Supreme Court	No appeal	Supreme Court	Formal Hearing
Hawaii	Commission on Judicial Conduct	Commission on Judicial Conduct	No appeal	Supreme Court	Imposition of public discipline by Supreme Court
Idaho	Judicial Council	Supreme Court	Court of Last Resort	Supreme Court	Filing with the Supreme Court
Illinois	Judicial Inquiry Board	Courts Commission	No appeal	Courts Commission	Filing of decision by Courts Commission
Indiana	Commission on Judicial Qualifications	Supreme Court	Court of Last Resort	Supreme Court	After disciplinary charges are filed and case is tried or agreed resolution is accepted by Supreme Court
Iowa	Judicial Qualifications Commission	Judicial Qualifications Commission	Court of Last Resort	Supreme Court	Referral by the commission to the Supreme Court recommending formal sanction
Kansas	Commission on Judicial Qualifications	Supreme Court	Court of Last Resort	Supreme Court	Reprimand is published if approved by Supreme Court
Kentucky	Judicial Conduct Commission	Judicial Conduct Commission	Court of Last Resort	Judicial Conduct Commission	Once the judge has responded to the formal charges
Louisiana	Judiciary Commission	Supreme Court	No appeal	Supreme Court	The lodging of the record of proceedings and a recommendation by the Judiciary Commission to the Supreme Court
Maine	Committee on Judicial Responsibility and Disability	Supreme Judicial Court	No appeal	Supreme Court	Filing of report to Supreme Judicial Court
Maryland	Commission on Judicial Disabilities	Commission on Judicial Disabilities	Court of Last Resort	Court of Appeals	Unless confidential, upon filing of a response (or expiration of the time for filing a response) with the Commission
Massachusetts	Commission on Judicial Conduct	Supreme Judicial Court	No appeal	Supreme Judicial Court	Supreme Judicial Court
Michigan	Judicial Tenure Commission	Supreme Court	Court of Last Resort	Supreme Court	Filing of formal complaint by commission with Supreme Court or upon filing in the Supreme Court a consent resolution to a matter

See footnotes at end of table

TABLE 5.8
Judicial Discipline: Investigating and Adjudicating Bodies (continued)

State or other jurisdiction	Investigating body	Adjudicating body	Appeals from adjudication are filed with:	Final disciplining body	Point at which reprimands are made public
Minnesota	Board on Judicial Standards	Supreme Court	No appeal	Supreme Court	Filing of formal charges by committee with Supreme Court
Mississippi	Commission on Judicial Performance	Supreme Court	No appeal	Supreme Court	Recommendation of Commission to Supreme Court
Missouri	Commission on Retirement, Removal and Discipline	Commission on Retirement, Removal and Discipline	Court of Last Resort	Supreme Court	Filing of recommendation by Committee to Supreme Court
Montana	Judicial Standards Commission	Supreme Court	No appeal	Supreme Court	Filing of record by Committee with Supreme Court
Nebraska	Commission on Judicial Qualification	Supreme Court	No appeal	Supreme Court	Commission may issue a public reprimand
Nevada	Commission on Judicial Discipline	Commission on Judicial Discipline	Court of Last Resort	Commission on Judicial Discipline	Discretion of the Commission, upon filing of report by Committee and service upon judge
New Hampshire	Supreme Court Committee on Judicial Conduct	Supreme Court	No appeal	Supreme Court	On issuance of reprimand
New Jersey	Advisory Committee on Judicial Conduct	Supreme Court	No appeal	Supreme Court	When reprimand is filed by Supreme Court
New Mexico	Judicial Standards Commission	Supreme Court	No appeal	Supreme Court	Upon recommendation of Commission to Supreme Court
New York	Commission on Judicial Conduct	Commission on Judicial Conduct	Court of Last Resort	Commission on Judicial Conduct and Court of Appeals	After a hearing at which a judge is admonished, censured, removed or retired, and after the judge is served
North Carolina	Judicial Standards Commission	Supreme Court	No appeal	Supreme Court	Public imposition of disciplinary action by the Supreme Court
North Dakota	Commission on Judicial Conduct	Supreme Court	No appeal	Supreme Court	At formal hearing
Ohio	Office of Disciplinary Counsel	Board of Commissioners on Grievance and Discipline	Court of Last Resort	Supreme Court	Adjudication
Oklahoma	Court on the Judiciary Trial Division Council	Court on the Judiciary Trial Division; Council on Judicial Complaints	Court on the Judiciary Division; no appeal from Council on Judicial Complaints	Court on the judiciary appellate division	Filing with clerk of the appellate court
Oregon	Commission on Judicial Fitness and Disability	Supreme Court	No appeal	Supreme Court	Allegations become public when the commission issues a notice of public hearing.
Pennsylvania	Judicial Conduct Board	Court of Judicial Discipline	Court of Last Resort	Supreme Court	Once a final decision has been made
Rhode Island	Commission on Judicial Tenure and Discipline	Supreme Court	No appeal	Supreme Court	Unless private, after the commission files its recommendation with the Chief Justice
South Carolina	Commission on Judicial Conduct	Supreme Court	No appeal	Supreme Court	Adjudication
South Dakota	Judicial Qualifications Commission	Supreme Court	No appeal	Supreme Court	Filing with the Supreme Court
Tennessee	Board of Judicial Conduct	Board of Judicial Conduct	Court of Last Resort	General Assembly	Filing formal charges with Board of Judicial Conduct
Texas	State Commission on Judicial Conduct	State Commission on Judicial Conduct (d)	Court of Last Resort	Special Court of Review	When issued by the Commission
Utah	Judicial Conduct Commission	Judicial Conduct Commission (e)	Court of Last Resort	Supreme Court	10 days after filing appeal
Vermont	Judicial Conduct Board	Supreme Court	Court of Last Resort	Supreme Court	Supreme Court
Virginia	Judicial Inquiry and Review Commission	Supreme Court	Court of Last Resort	Supreme Court	Filing of formal complaint by Commission with Supreme Court
Washington	Commission on Judicial Conduct	Commission on Judicial Conduct	Supreme Court	Supreme Court	At termination of proceeding in CJC

See footnotes at end of table

TABLE 5.8
Judicial Discipline: Investigating and Adjudicating Bodies (continued)

State or other jurisdiction	Investigating body	Adjudicating body	Appeals from adjudication are filed with:	Final disciplining body	Point at which reprimands are made public
West Virginia	Judicial Investigation Commission	Judicial Hearing Board	Court of Last Resort	Supreme Court of Appeals	Upon decision by Supreme Court of Appeals
Wisconsin	Judicial Commission	Supreme Court	No appeal	Supreme Court	Filing of formal complaint with Supreme Court
Wyoming	Commission on Judicial Conduct and Ethics	Supreme Court	No appeal	Supreme Court or Special Supreme Court	Upon the recommendation of the Conduct and Ethics Commission and Order of the Supreme Court
Dist. of Columbia	Commission on Judicial Disabilities and Tenure	Commission on Judicial Disabilities and Tenure	Chief Justice of U.S. Supreme Court	Commission on Judicial Disabilities and Tenure	Public reprimands are issued with the judge's consent; orders of involuntary removal become public upon filing with the D.C. Court of Appeals
Puerto Rico	Judicial Discipline Commission	Supreme Court	No appeal	Supreme Court	Filing of formal complaint to the Judicial Discipline Commission

Source: National Center for State Courts, June 2019.
Key:
N.A.–Not applicable
(a) Public admonishments or public censures are sent to the judge describing the improper conduct and stating the findings made by the commission; these notices are made available to the press and the general public.
(b) For suspensions in excess of 1 year or removal from office, the Judicial Review Council makes a recommendation and the Supreme Court makes the decision.

(c) The Judicial Qualifications Commission investigates and makes recommendations to the Supreme Court for discipline or removal. Commission has the authority to issue sanctions, but recommendations of removal must be brought before the Supreme Court.
(d) Decision by the conduct commission cannot be implemented until reviewed and approved by the Supreme Court.

CHAPTER SIX
ELECTIONS

TABLE 6.1
State Executive Branch Officials to be Elected: 2019-2023

State or other jurisdiction	2019	2020	2021	2022	2023
Alabama	...	(a)	...	G,LG,AG,AR,A,SS,T (a)	...
Alaska	...	...	...	G,LG	...
Arizona	...	(b)	...	G,AG,SS,SP,T (b)	...
Arkansas	...	...	...	G,LG,AG,A,SS,T (c)	...
California	...	...	...	G,LG,AG,C,CI,SS,SP,T (d)	...
Colorado	...	(e)	...	G,LG,AG,SS,T (e)	...
Connecticut	...	...	...	G,LG,AG,C,SS,T	...
Delaware	...	G,LG,CI	...	AG,A,T	...
Florida	...	...	...	G,LG,AG,AR,CFO	...
Georgia	...	(f)	...	G,LG,AG,AR,CI,SS,SP (f)	...
Hawaii	...	...	...	G,LG	...
Idaho	...	...	...	G,LG,AG,C,SS,SP,T	...
Illinois	...	...	...	G,LG,AG,C,SS,T	...
Indiana	...	G,LG,AG,SP	...	A,SS,T	...
Iowa	...	...	...	G,LG,AG,AR,A,SS,T	...
Kansas	...	...	...	G,LG,AG,CI,SS,T	...
Kentucky	G,LG,AG,AR,A,SS,T	...	...	...	G,LG,AG,AR,A,SS,T
Louisiana	G,LG,AG,AR,CI,SS,T	(g)	...	(g)	G,LG,AG,AR,CI,SS,T
Maine (h)	...	...	...	G	...
Maryland	...	...	...	G,LG,AG,C	...
Massachusetts	...	...	...	G,LG,AG,A,SS,T	...
Michigan	...	(i)	...	G,LG,AG,SS (i)	...
Minnesota	...	...	...	G,LG,AG,A,SS	...
Mississippi	G,LG,AG,AR,A,CI,SS,T	...	...	...	G,LG,AG,AR,A,CI,SS,T
Missouri	...	G,LG,AG,SS,T	...	A	...
Montana	...	G,LG,AG,A,SS,SP (j)	...	(j)	...
Nebraska	...	(k)	...	G,LG,AG,A,SS,T (k)	...
Nevada	...	...	...	G,LG,AG,C,SS,T	...
New Hampshire	...	G	...	G	...
New Jersey	...	...	G, LG	...	...
New Mexico	...	(l)	...	G,LG,AG,A,SS,T (l)	...
New York	...	...	...	G,LG,AG,C	...
North Carolina	...	G,LG,AG,AR,A,CI,SS,SP,T (m)	...	...	...
North Dakota	...	G,LG,A,CI,SP,T (n)	...	AG,AR,SS (n)	...
Ohio	...	...	...	G,LG,AG,A,SS,T	...
Oklahoma	...	(p)	...	G,LG,AG,A,CI,SP,T (p)	...
Oregon	AG,SS,T	...	...	G (r)	...
Pennsylvania	...	AG,A,T	...	G,LG	...
Rhode Island	...	...	...	G,LG,AG,SS,T	...
South Carolina	...	...	...	G,LG,AG,AR,C,SS,SP,T (s)	...
South Dakota	...	(t)	...	G,LG,AG,A,SS,SP,T (t)	...
Tennessee	...	...	...	G	...
Texas	...	(u)	...	G,LG,AG,AR,C (u)	...
Utah	...	G,LG,AG,A,T	...	...	...
Vermont	...	G,LG,AG,A,SS,T	...	G,LG,AG,A,SS,T	...
Virginia	...	...	G,LG,AG	...	...
Washington	...	G,LG,AG,A,CI,SS,SP,T (q)	...	...	...
West Virginia	...	G,AG,AR,A,SS,T	...	...	...
Wisconsin	...	...	SP	G,LG,AG,SS,T	...
Wyoming	...	...	...	G,A,SS,SP,T	...
American Samoa	...	G,LG	...	...	...
Guam	...	A	...	G,LG,AG	...
CNMI*	...	...	...	G,LG	...
Puerto Rico	...	G	...	...	...
U.S. Virgin Islands	...	...	...	G,LG	...

See footnotes at end of table

TABLE 6.1

State Executive Branch Officials to be Elected: 2019-2023 (continued)

State or other jurisdiction	2019	2020	2021	2022	2023
Totals for year					
Governor	3	13	2	39	3
Lieutenant Governor	3	10	2	33	3
Attorney General	3	10	1	31	3
Agriculture	3	2	0	7	3
Auditor	2	9	0	15	2
Chief Financial Officer	0	0	0	1	0
Comptroller	0	0	0	9	0
Comm. of Insurance	2	4	0	4	2
Secretary of State	3	7	0	26	3
Supt. of Public Inst. or Comm. of Education	0	5	1	8	0
Treasurer	3	9	0	24	3

Sources: The Council of State Governments' survey of state election office websites, March 2019.

*Commonwealth of Northern Mariana Islands

Note: This table shows the executive branch officials up for election in a given year. Footnotes indicate other offices (e.g., commissioners of labor, public service, etc.) also up for election in a given year. The data contained in this table reflect information available at press time.

Key:

…–No regularly scheduled elections of state executive officials.

G–Governor

LG–Lieutenant Governor

AG–Attorney General

AR–Agriculture

A–Auditor

C–Comptroller/Controller

CFO–Chief Financial Officer

CI–Commissioner of Insurance

SS–Secretary of State

SP–Superintendent of Public Instruction or Commissioner of Education

T–Treasurer

(a) Public Service Commissioner (3)–2020–1 seat (president), 2022–2 seats (associate commissioners).

(b) Corporation Commissioner (5)–4-year term, 2020–3 seats, 2022–2 seats; State Mine Inspector–4-year term, 2022.

(c) Commissioner of State Lands–4-year term.

(d) Four (4) Board of Equalization members are elected to serve 4-year concurrent terms. The State Controller is the 5th member of the Board.

(e) University of Colorado Board of Regents (9, one elected from each of the state's congressional districts and two at-large members)–6-year term, 2020–3 districts, 2022–1 statewide, 2 districts.

(f) Commissioner of Labor–4-year term, 2022; Public Service Commissioner (5)–6-year term, 2020–2, 2022–1.

(g) Public Service Commissioner (5)–6-year term, 2020–2, 2022–2.

(h) The Maine legislature elects constitutional officers (AG,SS,T) for 2-year terms; the auditor was elected by the legislature in 2016 and serves a 4-year term.

(i) Michigan State University trustees (8)–8-year term, 2020–2; 2022–2; University of Michigan regents (8)–8-year term, 2020–2, 2022–2; Wayne State University governors (8)–8-year term, 2020–2, 2022–2; State Board of Education (8)–8-year term, 2020–2, 2022–2.

(j) Public Service Commissioner (5)–4-year term, 2020–3, 2022–2.

(k) Public Service Commissioner (5)–6-year term, 2020–1, 2022–2.

(l) Commissioner of Public Lands–4-year term, 2022; Public Education Commission (10)–4-year terms, 2020–5; 2022–5; Public Regulation Commissioner (5)–4-year terms, 2020–2, 2022–1.

(m) Commissioner of Labor–4-year term.

(n) Tax Commissioner–4-year term, 2022; Public Service Commissioner (3)–6-year term, 2020–1, 2022–1.

(p) Commissioner of Labor–4-year term, 2022; Corporation Commissioner (3)–6-year term, 2020–1, 2022–1.

(q) Commissioner of Public Lands–4-year term.

(r) Commissioner of the Bureau of Labor and Industries, 4-year term.

(s) Adjutant General–4-year term.

(t) The title is Commissioner of Schools and Public Lands, 2022; Public Utility Commissioner (3)–6-year term, 2020–1, 2022–1.

(u) Commissioner of General Land Office–4-year term, 2022; Railroad Commissioner (3)–6-year term, 2020–1, 2022–1.

TABLE 6.2
State Legislature Members to be Elected: 2019-2023

State or other jurisdiction	Total legislators		2019		2020		2021		2022		2023	
	Senate	House/ Assembly	Senate	House/ Assembly	Senate	House/ Assembly	Senate	House/ Assembly	Senate	House/ Assembly	Senate	House/ Assembly
Alabama	35	105	...	...	...	...	...	...	35	105	...	...
Alaska	20	40	...	...	10	40	...	...	10	40	...	...
Arizona	30	60	...	...	30	60	...	...	30	60	...	...
Arkansas	35	100	...	...	17	100	...	...	18	100	...	...
California	40	80	...	...	20 (a)	80	...	...	20 (b)	80	...	...
Colorado	35	65	...	...	18	65	...	...	17	65	...	...
Connecticut	36	151	...	...	36	151	...	...	36	151	...	...
Delaware	21	41	...	...	11	41	...	...	10	41	...	...
Florida	40	120	...	...	20 (a)	120	...	...	20 (b)	120	...	...
Georgia	56	180	...	...	56	180	...	...	56	180	...	...
Hawaii	25	51	...	...	13	51	...	...	12	51	...	...
Idaho	35	70	...	...	35	70	...	...	35	70	...	...
Illinois	59	118	...	...	20 (e)	118	...	...	39 (f)	118	...	...
Indiana	50	100	...	...	25	100	...	...	25	100	...	...
Iowa	50	100	...	...	25 (b)	100	...	...	25 (a)	100	...	...
Kansas	40	125	...	...	40	125	...	...	...	125	...	...
Kentucky	38	100	...	...	19 (a)	100	...	...	19 (b)	100	...	...
Louisiana	39	105	39	105	...	...	...	...	...	...	39	105
Maine	35	151 (f)	...	...	35	151	...	...	35	151	...	...
Maryland	47	141	...	...	...	...	...	...	47	141	...	...
Massachusetts	40	160	...	...	40	160	...	...	40	160	...	...
Michigan	38	110	...	...	...	110	...	...	38	110	...	...
Minnesota	67	134	...	...	67	134	...	...	...	134	...	...
Mississippi	52	122	52	122	...	...	...	...	...	...	52	122
Missouri	34	163	...	...	17 (a)	163	...	...	17 (b)	163	...	...
Montana	50	100	...	...	25	100	...	...	25	100	...	...
Nebraska	49	U	...	...	25 (a)	U	...	...	24 (b)	U	...	...
Nevada	21	42	...	...	10	42	...	...	11	42	...	...
New Hampshire	24	400	...	...	24	400	...	...	24	400	...	...
New Jersey	40	80	...	80	...	...	40	80	...	...	...	80
New Mexico	42	70	...	...	42	70	...	...	...	70	...	...
New York	63	150	...	...	63	150	...	...	63	150	...	...
North Carolina	50	120	...	...	50	120	...	...	50	120	...	...
North Dakota	47	94	...	...	23 (b)	46 (b)	...	...	24 (a)	48 (a)	...	...
Ohio	33	99	...	...	16 (b)	99	...	...	17 (a)	99	...	...
Oklahoma	48	101	...	...	24 (a)	101	...	...	24 (b)	101	...	...
Oregon	30	60	...	...	15	60	...	...	15	60	...	...
Pennsylvania	50	203	...	...	25 (a)	203	...	...	25 (b)	203	...	...
Rhode Island	38	75	...	...	38	75	...	...	38	75	...	...
South Carolina	46	124	...	...	46	124	...	...	...	124	...	...
South Dakota	35	70	...	...	35	70	...	...	35	70	...	...
Tennessee	33	99	...	...	16 (b)	99	...	...	17 (a)	99	...	...
Texas	31	150	...	...	16	150	...	...	15	150	...	...
Utah	29	75	...	...	15	75	...	...	14	75	...	...
Vermont	30	150	...	...	30	150	...	...	30	150	...	...
Virginia	40	100	40	100	...	...	...	100	...	...	40	100
Washington	49	98	...	...	25	98	...	...	24	98	...	...
West Virginia	34	100	...	...	17	100	...	...	17	100	...	...
Wisconsin	33	99	...	...	16 (b)	99	...	...	17 (a)	99	...	...
Wyoming	30	60	...	...	15 (b)	60	...	...	15 (a)	60	...	...
Dist. of Columbia	13	U	...	...	6	U	...	...	7	U	...	...
American Samoa	18 (c)	20 (c)	...	...	18 (c)	20 (c)	...	...	18 (c)	20 (c)	...	...
Guam	15	U	...	...	15	U	...	...	15	U	...	...
CNMI* (d)	9	20	...	...	3	20	...	...	6	20	...	...
Puerto Rico (e)	27	51	...	...	27	51	...	...	...	...	...	...
U.S. Virgin Islands	15	U	...	...	15	U	...	...	15	U	...	...
State Totals	1,972	5,411	131	407	1,165	4,710	40	180	1,108	4,958	131	407
Totals	2,069	5,502	131	407	1,249	4,801	40	180	1,169	4,998	131	407

See footnotes at end of table

TABLE 6.2
State Legislature Members to be Elected: 2019–2023 (continued)

Source: The Council of State Governments, March 2019.
*Commonwealth of Northern Mariana Islands
Note: This table shows the number of elections in a given year. The data presented in this table reflect information available at press time. See Chapter 3.3 table entitled, "The Legislators: Numbers, Terms, and Party Affiliations," for specific information on legislative terms.
Key:
…–No regularly scheduled elections
U–Unicameral legislature
(a) Odd-numbered Senate districts.
(b) Even-numbered Senate districts.

(c) In American Samoa, Senators are not elected by popular vote. They are selected by the county council of chiefs. House: 21 seats; 20 are elected by popular vote and one appointed, non-voting delegate from Swains Island.
(d) In 2009, voters approved a constitutional amendment (Senate Legislative Initiative 16-1) that changed future general elections from odd- to even-numbered years.
(e) Constitutionally, the Senate consists of 27 seats and the House 51 seats. However, extra at-large seats can be granted to the opposition to limit any party's control to two thirds.

TABLE 6.3
Methods of Nominating Candidates for State Offices

State or other jurisdiction	Methods of nominating candidates
Alabama	Primary election; however, the state executive committee or other governing body of any political party may choose instead to hold a state convention for the purpose of nominating candidates. Submitting a petition to run as an independent or third-party candidate or an independent nominating procedure.
Alaska	Primary election. Petition for no-party candidates.
Arizona	Candidates who are members of a recognized party are nominated by an open primary election. Candidates who are not members of a recognized political party may file petitions to appear on the general election ballot. A write-in option is also available.
Arkansas	Primary election, convention and petition.
California	Primary election or independent nomination procedure.
Colorado	Primary election, convention or by petition.
Connecticut	Convention/primary election. Major political parties hold state conventions (convening not earlier than the 68th day and closing not later than the 50th day before the date of the primary) for the purpose of endorsing candidates. If no one challenges the endorsed candidate, no primary election is held. However, if anyone (who received at least 15 percent of the delegate vote on any roll call at the convention) challenges the endorsed candidate, a primary election is held to determine the party nominee for the general election.
Delaware	Primary election for Democrats and primary election and convention for Republicans.
Florida	Primary election. Minor parties may nominate their candidate in any manner they deem proper.
Georgia	Primary election.
Hawaii	Primary election.
Idaho	Primary election and convention. New political parties hold a convention to nominate candidates to be placed on a general election ballot.
Illinois	Primary election. The primary election nominates established party candidates. New political parties and independent candidates go directly to the general election file based on a petition process.
Indiana	Primary election, convention and petition. The governor is chosen by a primary. All other state officers are chosen at a state convention, unless the candidate is an independent. Any party that obtains between 2 percent and 8 percent of the vote for secretary of state may hold a convention to select a candidate.
Iowa	Primary election, convention and petition.
Kansas	Candidates for the two major parties are nominated by primary election. Candidates for minor parties are nominated for the general election at state party conventions. Independent candidates are nominated for the general election by petition.
Kentucky	Primary election. A slate of candidates for governor and lieutenant governor that receives the highest number of its party's votes but which number is less than 40 percent of the votes cast for all slates of candidates of that party, shall be required to participate in a runoff primary with the slate of candidates of the same party receiving the second highest number of votes.
Louisiana	Candidates may qualify for any office they wish, regardless of party affiliation, by completing the qualifying document and paying the appropriate qualifying fee; or a candidate may file a nominating petition.
Maine	Primary election or non-party petition.
Maryland	Primary election, convention and petition. Unaffiliated candidates or candidates affiliated with non-recognized political parties may run for elective office by collecting the requisite number of signatures on a petition. The required number equals 1 percent of the number of registered voters eligible to vote for office. Only recognized non-principal political parties may nominate its candidate by a convention in accordance with its by laws (at this time, Maryland has four non-principal parties: Libertarian, Green, Constitution and Populist).
Massachusetts	Primary election.
Michigan	Governor, state house, state senate use primary election. Lieutenant governor runs as the running mate to gubernatorial candidate, not separately, and is selected through the convention process. Secretary of state and attorney general candidates are chosen at convention. Nominees for State Board of Education, University of Michigan Regents, Michigan State University Trustees and Wayne State University Governors are nominated by convention. Minor parties nominate candidates to all partisan offices by convention.
Minnesota	Primary election. Candidates for minor parties or independent candidates are by petition. They must have the signatures of 2,000 people who will be eligible to vote in the next general election.
Mississippi	Primary election, petition (for independent candidates), independent nominating procedures (third-party candidate).
Missouri	Primary election.
Montana	Primary election and independent nominating procedure.
Nebraska	Primary election.
Nevada	Primary election. Independent candidates are nominated by petition for the general election. Minor parties nominated by petition or by party.
New Hampshire	Primary election. Minor parties by petition.
New Jersey	Primary election. Independent candidates are nominated by petition for the general election.
New Mexico	Statewide candidates petition to go to convention and are nominated in a primary election. District and legislative candidate petition for primary ballot access.
New York	Primary election/petition.
North Carolina	Primary election. Newly recognized parties just granted access submit their first nominees by convention. All established parties use primaries.
North Dakota	Convention/primary election. Political parties hold state conventions for the purpose of endorsing candidates. Endorsed candidates are automatically placed on the primary election ballot, but other candidates may also petition their name on the ballot.
Ohio	Primary election, petition and by declaration of intent to be a write-in candidate.
Oklahoma	Primary election.
Oregon	Primary election. Minor parties hold conventions.

See footnotes at end of table

TABLE 6.3
Methods of Nominating Candidates for State Offices (continued)

State or other jurisdiction	Methods of nominating candidates
Pennsylvania	Primary election, and petition. Nomination petitions filed by major party candidates to access primary ballot. Nomination papers filed by minor party and independent candidates to access November ballot.
Rhode Island	Primary election.
South Carolina	Primary election for Republicans and Democrats; party conventions held for minor parties. Candidates can have name on ballot via petition.
South Dakota	Convention, petition and independent nominating procedure.
Tennessee	Primary election/petition.
Texas	Primary election/convention. Minor parties without ballot access nominate candidates for the general election after qualifying for ballot access by petition.
Utah	Convention, primary election and petition.
Vermont	Primary election. Major parties by primary, minor parties by convention, independents by petition.
Virginia	Primary election, convention and petition.
Washington	Primary election.
West Virginia	Primary election, convention, petition and independent nominating procedure.
Wisconsin	Primary election/petition. Candidates must file nomination papers (petitions) containing the minimum number of signatures required by law. Candidates appear on the primary ballot for the party they represent. The candidate receiving the most votes in each party primary goes on to the November election.
Wyoming	Primary election.
Dist. of Columbia	Primary election. Independent and minor party candidates file by nominating petition.
American Samoa	Individual files petition for candidacy with the chief election officer. Petition must be signed by statutorily-mandated number of qualified voters.
Guam	Individual files petition for candidacy with the chief election officer. Petition must be signed by statutorily-mandated number of qualified voters.
CNMI*	Candidates are all nominated by petition. Candidates seeking the endorsement of recognized political parties must also include in their submitted petition submission a document signed by the recognized political parties' chairperson/president and secretary attesting to such nomination. Recognized political parties may, or may not, depending on their by-laws and party rules conduct primaries separate from any state election agency participation.
Puerto Rico	Primary election and convention.
U.S. Virgin Islands	Primary election.

Source: The Council of State Governments' survey of state websites, March 2019.

Note: The nominating methods described here are for state offices; procedures may vary for local candidates. Also, independent candidates may have to petition for nomination.

*Commonwealth of Northern Mariana Islands

TABLE 6.4
Election Dates for National and State Elections (Formulas and Dates of State Elections)

State or other jurisdiction	National (a)		State (b)			Type of primary (c)
	Primary	General	Primary	Runoff	General	
Alabama	March, 1st T March 3, 2020	Nov., ★ Nov. 3, 2020	June, 1st T June 7, 2022	6th T AP July 19, 2022	Nov., ★ Nov. 8, 2022	Open
Alaska	(d)	Nov., ★ Nov. 3, 2020	Aug., 3rd T Aug. 18, 2020	…	Nov., ★ Nov. 3, 2020	(e)
Arizona	T following March 15 March 17, 2020	Nov., ★ Nov. 3, 2020	10th T Prior Aug. 25, 2020	…	Nov., ★ Nov. 3, 2020	Partially Closed
Arkansas	T 3 wks. prior to runoff May 19, 2020	Nov., ★ Nov. 3, 2020	T 3 wks. prior to runoff May 19, 2020	June, 2nd T June 9, 2020	Nov., ★ Nov. 3, 2020	Open
California	March, ★ March 3, 2020	Nov., ★ Nov. 3, 2020	March, ★ March 3, 2020	…	Nov., ★ Nov. 3, 2020	Top Two
Colorado	(d) (g) March 3, 2020	Nov., ★ Nov. 3, 2020	June, last T June 30, 2020	…	Nov., ★ Nov. 3, 2020	Partially Closed
Connecticut	April, Last T April 28, 2020	Nov., ★ Nov. 3, 2020	Aug. 2nd T Aug. 11, 2020	…	Nov., ★ Nov. 3, 2020	Closed
Delaware	April, 4th T April 28, 2020	Nov., ★ Nov. 3, 2020	Sept., 2nd T after 1st M Sept. 15, 2020	…	Nov., ★ Nov. 3, 2020	Closed
Florida	March, 3rd T March 17, 2020	Nov., ★ Nov. 3, 2020	10th T prior to General Aug. 25, 2020	…	Nov., ★ Nov. 3, 2020	Closed
Georgia	(h)	Nov., ★ Nov. 3, 2020	24th T prior to General May 19, 2020	9th T after Primary July 21, 2020	Nov., ★ Nov. 3, 2020	Open
Hawaii	(d) Rep: March 10, 2020 Dem: TBD	Nov., ★ Nov. 3, 2020	Aug. 2nd S Aug. 8, 2020	…	Nov., ★ Nov. 3, 2020	Open
Idaho	(d) Rep: March 10, 2020 Dem: TBD	Nov., ★ Nov. 3, 2020	May, 3rd T May 19, 2020	…	Nov., ★ Nov. 3, 2020	Rep: Closed (i) Dem: Partially Closed
Illinois	March, 3rd T March 17, 2020	Nov., ★ Nov. 3, 2020	March, 3rd T March 17, 2020	…	Nov., ★ Nov. 3, 2020	Partially Open
Indiana	May, ★ May 5, 2020	Nov., ★ Nov. 3, 2020	May, ★ May 5, 2020	…	Nov., ★ Nov. 3, 2020	Partially Open
Iowa	(d)	Nov., ★ Nov. 3, 2020	June, ★ June 2, 2020	…	Nov., ★ Nov. 3, 2020	Partially Open
Kansas	(d) (j)	Nov., ★ Nov. 3, 2020	Aug. 1st T Aug. 4, 2020	…	Nov., ★ Nov. 3, 2020	Closed (k)
Kentucky	May, 1st T after 3rd M May 19, 2020	Nov., ★ Nov. 3, 2020	May, 1st T after 3rd M May 21, 2019	…	Nov., ★ Nov. 5, 2019	Closed
Louisiana	March, 1st S March 7, 2020	Nov., ★ Nov. 3, 2020	Oct., 2nd to last S (l) Oct. 19, 2019	…	Nov., 4th S AP (l) Nov. 16, 2019	Top Two
Maine	(d)	Nov., ★ Nov. 3, 2020	June, 2nd T June 9, 2020	…	Nov., ★ Nov. 3, 2020	Closed (n)
Maryland	April, 4th T April 28, 2020	Nov., ★ Nov. 3, 2020	June, last T June 28, 2022	…	Nov., ★ Nov. 8, 2022	Closed (p)
Massachusetts	March, 1st T March 3, 2020	Nov., ★ Nov. 3, 2020	7th T Prior Sept. 15, 2020	…	Nov., ★ Nov. 3, 2020	Partially Closed
Michigan	March, 2nd T March 10, 2020	Nov., ★ Nov. 3, 2020	Aug., ★ Aug. 4, 2020	…	Nov., ★ Nov. 3, 2020	Open
Minnesota	(d) (r) March 3, 2020	Nov., ★ Nov. 3, 2020	Aug., 2nd T Aug. 11, 2020	…	Nov., ★ Nov. 3, 2020	Open
Mississippi	March, 2nd T March 10, 2020	Nov., ★ Nov. 3, 2020	Aug., ★ Aug. 6, 2019	3rd T AP Aug. 27, 2019	Nov., ★ Nov. 5, 2019	(s)
Missouri	March, 2nd T after 1st M March 10, 2020	Nov., ★ Nov. 3, 2020	Aug., ★ Aug. 4, 2020	…	Nov., ★ Nov. 3, 2020	Open
Montana	June, ★ June 2, 2020	Nov., ★ Nov. 3, 2020	June, ★ June 2, 2020	…	Nov., ★ Nov. 3, 2020	Open
Nebraska	May, 1st T After 2nd M May 12, 2020	Nov., ★ Nov. 3, 2020	May, 1st T After 2nd M May 12, 2020	…	Nov., ★ Nov. 3, 2020	Top Two
Nevada	(d)	Nov., ★ Nov. 3, 2020	June, 2nd T June 9, 2020	…	Nov., ★ Nov. 3, 2020	Closed
New Hampshire	(t)	Nov., ★ Nov. 3, 2020	Sept., 2nd T Sept. 8, 2020	…	Nov., ★ Nov. 3, 2020	Partially Closed (u)
New Jersey	June, ★ June 2, 2020	Nov., ★ Nov. 3, 2020	June, ★ June 4, 2019	…	Nov., ★ Nov. 5, 2019	Closed
New Mexico	June, ★ June 2, 2020	Nov., ★ Nov. 3, 2020	June, ★ June 2, 2020	…	Nov., ★ Nov. 3, 2020	Closed
New York	Feb., 1st T (aa)	Nov., ★ Nov. 3, 2020	June, 4th T June 23, 2020	…	Nov., ★ Nov. 3, 2020	Closed

See footnotes at end of table

TABLE 6.4
Election Dates for National and State Elections (Formulas and Dates of State Elections) (continued)

State or other jurisdiction	National (a)		State (b)			Type of primary (c)
	Primary	General	Primary	Runoff	General	
North Carolina	March, ★ March 3, 2020	Nov., ★ Nov. 3, 2020	March, ★ March 3, 2020	7 wks. AP April 21, 2020	Nov., ★ Nov. 3, 2020	Partially Closed
North Dakota	(d)	Nov., ★ Nov. 3, 2020	June, 2nd T June 9, 2020	…	Nov., ★ Nov. 3, 2020	Open
Ohio	March, 2nd T after 1st M March 10, 2020 (v)	Nov., ★ Nov. 3, 2020	May, ★ (v) March 10, 2020	…	Nov., ★ Nov. 3, 2020	Partially Open
Oklahoma	March, 1st T March 3, 2020	Nov., ★ Nov. 3, 2020	June, last T June 30, 2020	Aug., 4th T Aug. 25, 2020	Nov., ★ Nov. 3, 2020	Dem: Partially Closed Rep: Closed (w)
Oregon	May, 3rd T May 19, 2020	Nov., ★ Nov. 3, 2020	May, 3rd T May 19, 2020	…	Nov., ★ Nov. 3, 2020	Closed
Pennsylvania	April, 4th T April 28, 2020	Nov., ★ Nov. 3, 2020	April, 4th T April 28, 2020	…	Nov., ★ Nov. 3, 2020	Closed
Rhode Island	April, 4th T April 28, 2020	Nov., ★ Nov. 3, 2020	Sept., 2nd T after 1st M Sept. 15, 2020	…	Nov., ★ Nov. 3, 2020	Partially Open
South Carolina	(d)	Nov., ★ Nov. 3, 2020	June, 2nd T June 9, 2020	2nd T AP June 23, 2020	Nov., ★ Nov. 3, 2020	Open
South Dakota	June, ★ June 2, 2020	Nov., ★ Nov. 3, 2020	June, ★ June 2, 2020	10th T AP (x) Aug. 11, 2020	Nov., ★ Nov. 3, 2020	Rep: Closed Dem: Partially Closed
Tennessee	March, 1st T March 3, 2020	Nov., ★ Nov. 3, 2020	Aug., 1st TH Aug. 6, 2020	…	Nov., ★ Nov. 3, 2020	Open
Texas	March, 1st T March 3, 2020	Nov., ★ Nov. 3, 2020	March, 1st T March 3, 2020	May, 4th T May 26, 2020	Nov., ★ Nov. 3, 2020	Open
Utah	(y)	Nov., ★ Nov. 3, 2020	June, 4th T June 23, 2020	…	Nov., ★ Nov. 3, 2020	Rep: Closed (z) Dem: Open
Vermont	March, 1st T March 3, 2020	Nov., ★ Nov. 3, 2020	Aug., 2nd T Aug. 11, 2020	…	Nov., ★ Nov. 3, 2020	Open
Virginia	March, 1st T March 3, 2020	Nov., ★ Nov. 3, 2020	June, 2nd T June 11, 2019	…	Nov., ★ Nov. 5, 2019	Open
Washington	May, 4th T May 26, 2020	Nov., ★ Nov. 3, 2020	Aug., 1st T Aug. 4, 2020	…	Nov., ★ Nov. 3, 2020	Top Two
West Virginia	May, 2nd T May 12, 2020	Nov., ★ Nov. 3, 2020	May, 2nd T May 12, 2020	…	Nov., ★ Nov. 3, 2020	Partially Closed
Wisconsin	April, 1st T April 7, 2020	Nov., ★ Nov. 3, 2020	Aug., 2nd T Aug. 11, 2020	…	Nov., ★ Nov. 3, 2020	Open
Wyoming	(d)	Nov., ★ Nov. 3, 2020	Aug., 1st T After 3rd M Aug. 18, 2020	…	Nov., ★ Nov. 3, 2020	Closed
Dist. of Columbia	June, 2nd T (q) June 9, 2018	Nov., ★ Nov. 3, 2020	June, 2nd T (q) June 16, 2020	…	Nov., ★ Nov. 3, 2020	Closed
American Samoa	(d)	(m) …	(o) …	…	Nov., ★ Nov. 3, 2020	(o)
Guam	(d)	(m) …	Aug., last S Aug. 29, 2020	…	Nov., ★ Nov. 3, 2020	Open
CNMI*	(d)	(m) …	(o) …	…	Nov., ★ Nov. 3, 2020	(o)
Puerto Rico	Rep: (f) Dem: June 7, 2020	(m) …	N.A. March 15, 2020	…	Nov., ★ Nov. 3, 2020	Open
U.S. Virgin Islands	(d)	(m) …	Aug., 1st S Aug. 1, 2020	…	Nov., ★ Nov. 3, 2020	Closed

See footnotes at end of table

TABLE 6.4

Election Dates for National and State Elections (Formulas and Dates of State Elections) (continued)

Sources: The Council of State Governments, March 2019.
*Commonwealth of Northern Mariana Islands
Note: This table describes the basic formulas for determining when national and state elections will be held. For specific information on a particular state, the reader is advised to contact the state election administration office. All dates provided are based on the state election formula and dates are subject to change.

Key:
★–First Tuesday after first Monday.
…–No provision.
M–Monday.
T–Tuesday.
TH–Thursday.
S–Saturday.
SN–Sunday.
Prior–Prior to general election.
AP–After primary.

(a) National refers to presidential elections.

(b) State refers to election in which a state executive official or legislator is to be elected. See Table 6.1, State Executive Branch Officials to be Elected, and Table 6.2, State Legislature Members to be Elected.

(c) Open: Voters can privately select which party's ballot to vote, regardless of party affiliation.
Closed: Voters must be a registered member of the party to vote its primary ballot.
Partially Open: Voters can choose in which primary to vote but that choice is not private. In certain states, a voter's primary ballot selection may be regarded as a form of registration with the corresponding party.
Partially Closed: Unaffiliated voters may participate in any party's primary. Members of a political party are not allowed to cross over and vote in a different political party's primary.
Top Two primaries: All voters in California and Washington receive one ballot with candidates from all parties listed together. The top two finishers face each other at the general election. Louisiana has a similar election type but its primary is held in October with a runoff election in November if no candidate garners 50 percent or more of the vote. Nebraska uses a single primary ballot to elect lawmakers to its nonpartisan legislature.

(d) The dates for presidential caucuses are set by the political parties.

(e) Alaska law allows a political party to select who may participate in their party's primary. Parties may expand or limit who may participate in their Primary Election by submitting a written notice with a copy of their pre cleared by-laws to the Director of Elections no later than September 1st of the year prior to the year in which a Primary Election is to be held.

(f) The primary law allows Puerto Rico parties affiliated with U.S. national parties to select a primary date any time between the first Tuesday in March and June 15.

(g) The state parties have the option of choosing either the first Tuesday in March (March 3, 2020) date called for in the statute or moving up to the first Tuesday in February (Feb. 4, 2020).

(h) The Secretary of State has the authority to set the date of the presidential primary election. Currently held in March, the presidential primary could be held as late as June 14.

(i) In 2011, the Idaho Legislature passed HB 351, implementing a closed primary system. However, the law gives political parties the option of opening their primary elections to unaffiliated voters and members of other political parties. The party chairman must notify the Secretary of State 6 months prior to the primary if the party intends to open its primary election to those outside of the party. The Republican party currently allows only voters registered with its party to vote (closed), while the Democratic Party allows unaffiliated voters to vote in its primary (partially closed).

(j) In 2015, the Kansas legislature passed a bill (HB 2104) that repealed the statute calling for a presidential preference primary election. It replaces it with a requirement that each recognized political party select a presidential nominee in accordance with party procedures, for every presidential election beginning with the 2016 election.

(k) Unaffiliated voters may register with a party on primary day to vote in that party's primary.

(l) Louisiana has an open primary which requires all candidates, regardless of party affiliation, to appear on a single ballot. If a candidate receives over 50 percent of the vote in the primary, that candidate is elected to the office. If no candidate receives a majority vote, then a single election is held between the two candidates receiving the most votes. For national elections, the first vote is held on the first Saturday in October of even-numbered years with the general election held on the first Tuesday after the first Monday in November. For state elections, the election is held on the second to last Saturday in October with the runoff being held on the fourth Saturday after first election.

(m) Residents of U.S. territories may vote in presidential primaries, but the Electoral College system does not permit them to vote in presidential elections.

(n) Voters who have already registered but have not enrolled in a party may enroll in a party at the polls on Election Day. Any voter who wishes to change party enrollment must do so at least 15 days before the vote.

(o) American Samoa and the Northern Marianas Islands do not conduct primary elections. Instead, the law provides for a run off when none of the candidates receives more than 50% of the vote.

(p) Under Maryland law, parties may allow unaffiliated voters to cast ballots in their primaries by notifying the election board six months in advance. However, both major parties currently hold closed primaries.

(q) In 2014, the Council of the District of Columbia passed a bill (B20-0265) to move the presidential primary from the 1st Tuesday in April to the 2nd Tuesday in June.

(r) Parties must notify the Secretary of State's Office in writing prior to Dec. 1st the year preceding the date of the election of their intentions to hold a preference primary election. Unless the chairs of the two major political parties jointly propose a different date, the caucuses are held on the first Tuesday in February.

TABLE 6.4
Election Dates for National and State Elections (Formulas and Dates of State Elections) (continued)

(s) Mississippi voters do not have to register with a party, but state law requires they must intend to support the party nominee if they vote in that party's primary election. Since voter intent is difficult to dispute in court, some characterize Mississippi's system an open partisan primary.

(t) The Secretary of State selects a date for the primary, which must be 7 days or more immediately preceding the date on which any other state holds a similar election.

(u) An unaffiliated voter may choose one party's ballot, which makes them a registered member of that party. However, temporary affiliation is possible, as voters can fill out a card at the polling place to return to undeclared status after the vote is cast.

(v) In 2015, Ohio lawmakers passed a bill (HB 153) that moves the date of the primary back one week to the second Tuesday after the first Monday in March. In non-presidential election years, the primary is held on the first Tuesday after the first Monday in May. The move to a later week allows Republicans to allocate delegates in a winner-take-all fashion.

(w) In November of each odd-numbered year, recognized political parties declare whether or not they will permit Independents to vote in their primary elections during the following two calendar years. For 2016 and 2017, the Democratic Party granted permission for Independents to vote in its primaries and runoff primaries. Independents cannot vote in Republican primaries.

(x) South Dakota only holds runoffs for the offices of U.S. Senator, U.S. Representative and governor.

(y) If funded, Utah can hold a primary on either the first Tuesday of February or in conjunction with the regular primary on the fourth Tuesday in June.

(z) In November, 2015, a federal judge ruled that the state cannot force political parties to open their primaries to unaffiliated voters, invalidating a provision in a 2014 law (SB 54). This decision allows the Utah Republican Party to continue to hold closed primaries.

(aa) In the past two election presidential primary cycles, New York has chosen to move their primary to April. The 2020 date is yet to be determined.

Table 6.4 | State Election Calendar

State Primaries

2019

May 21, 2019 · Kentucky

June 4, 2019 · New Jersey

June 11, 2019 · Virginia

August 6, 2019 · Mississippi

October 19, 2019 · Louisiana

MARCH

March 3, 2020 · California, North Carolina, Texas

March 10, 2020 · Ohio

March 15, 2020 · Puerto Rico

March 17, 2020 · Illinois

APRIL

April 28, 2020 · Pennsylvania

MAY

May 5, 2020 · Indiana

May 12, 2020 · Nebraska, West Virginia

May 19, 2020 · Arkansas, Georgia, Idaho, Oregon

JUNE

June 2, 2020 · Iowa, Montana, New Mexico, South Dakota

June 9, 2020 · Maine, Nevada, North Dakota, South Carolina

June 16, 2020 · Dist. of Columbia

June 23, 2020 · New York, Utah

June 30, 2020 · Colorado, Oklahoma

AUGUST

August 1, 2020 · U.S. Virgin Islands

August 4, 2020 · Kansas, Michigan, Missouri, Washington

August 6, 2020 · Tennessee

August 8, 2020 · Hawaii

August 11, 2020 · Connecticut, Minnesota, Vermont, Wisconsin

August 18, 2020 · Alaska, Wyoming

August 25, 2020 · Arizona, Florida

August 29, 2018 · Guam

SEPTEMBER

September 8, 2020 · New Hampshire

September 15, 2020 · Delaware, Massachusetts, Rhode Island

OTHER

June 7, 2022 · Alabama

June 28, 2022 · Maryland

American Samoa and CNMI* do not conduct primary elections. Instead, the law provides for a run off when none of the candidates receives more than 50% of the vote.

The state general election in most states is **Nov. 3, 2020**

However, 4 states and one territory do not have state executive or legislative general elections in 2020.

Nov. 5, 2019 · Mississippi, Kentucky, New Jersey, Virginia

Nov. 16, 2019 · Louisiana

Nov. 8, 2022 · Alabama, Maryland

Runoff elections are held in 9 states.

August 27, 2019 · Mississippi

April 21, 2020 · North Carolina

May 26, 2020 · Texas

June 9, 2020 · Arkansas

June 23, 2020 · South Carolina

July 21, 2020 · Georgia

August 11, 2020 · South Dakota

August 25, 2020 · Oklahoma

July 19, 2022 · Alabama

TABLE 6.5
Polling Hours: General Elections

State or other jurisdiction	Polls open	Polls close	Notes on hours (a)
Alabama	7 a.m.	7 p.m.	Polling places located in the Eastern Time Zone may be open from 7 a.m. to 7 p.m. ET.
Alaska	7 a.m.	8 p.m.	
Arizona	6 a.m.	7 p.m.	
Arkansas	7:30 a.m.	7:30 p.m.	
California	7 a.m.	8 p.m.	
Colorado	7 a.m.	7 p.m.	
Connecticut	6 a.m.	8 p.m.	
Delaware	7 a.m.	8 p.m.	
Florida	7 a.m.	7 p.m.	
Georgia	7 a.m.	7 p.m.	
Hawaii	7 a.m.	6 p.m.	
Idaho	8 a.m.	8 p.m.	Clerk has the option of opening all polls at 7 a.m. Idaho is in two time zones - MT and PT.
Illinois	6 a.m.	7 p.m.	
Indiana	6 a.m.	6 p.m.	For those counties on Central time, polling places will observe these times in Central time.
Iowa	7 a.m.	9 p.m.	
Kansas	7 a.m.	7 p.m.	Counties may open the polls earlier and close them later. Several western counties are in the Mountain Time Zone.
Kentucky	6 a.m.	6 p.m.	Counties may be either in Eastern or Central Time Zones.
Louisiana	6 a.m.	8 p.m.	
Maine	Between 6 and 10 a.m.	8 p.m.	Applicable opening time depends on variables related to the size of the precinct.
Maryland	7 a.m.	8 p.m.	
Massachusetts	7 a.m.	8 p.m.	Some municipalities may open their polls as early as 5:45 a.m.
Michigan	7 a.m.	8 p.m.	Eastern Time Zone and Central Time Zone
Minnesota	7 a.m.	8 p.m.	A few polling places in small townships located outside the 11-county metropolitan area may open as late as 10 a.m.
Mississippi	7 a.m.	7 p.m.	
Missouri	6 a.m.	7 p.m.	
Montana	7 a.m.	8 p.m.	A polling place having fewer than 400 registered electors must be open from at least noon to 8 p.m. or until all registered electors in any precinct have voted, at which time that precinct in the polling place must be closed immediately.
Nebraska	7 a.m. MT/8 a.m. CT	7 p.m. MT/8 p.m. CT	
Nevada	7 a.m.	7 p.m.	
New Hampshire	No later than 11 a.m.	No earlier than 7 p.m.	Polling hours vary from town to town.
New Jersey	6 a.m.	8 p.m.	
New Mexico	7 a.m.	7 p.m.	
New York	6 a.m.	9 p.m.	
North Carolina	6:30 a.m.	7:30 p.m.	
North Dakota	Between 7 and 9 a.m.	Between 7 and 9 p.m.	Polling locations cannot open earlier than 7 a.m. and must be open by 9 a.m., with the exception of those precincts in which fewer than 75 votes were cast in the last General Election, which must open no later than noon. All polling locations must remain open until 7 p.m. and close no later than 9 p.m.
Ohio	6:30 a.m.	7:30 p.m.	
Oklahoma	7 a.m.	7 p.m.	
Oregon	7 a.m.	8 p.m.	Official dropsites open eight hours or more and until 8 p.m. for depositing cast ballots. County Clerks offices open 7 a.m.-8 p.m. for issuing and depositing ballots.
Pennsylvania	7 a.m.	8 p.m.	
Rhode Island	Between 7 and 9 a.m	8 p.m.	Polls open at 9 a.m. in special elections.
South Carolina	7 a.m.	7 p.m.	
South Dakota	7 a.m.	7 p.m.	
Tennessee	8 a.m. (may be earlier)	7 p.m. CT/8 p.m. ET	Polling places must be open a minimum of ten continuous hours, but no more than 13 hours. In any county having a population of not less than 120,000, all polling places must open by 8 a.m., but nothing prevents an earlier opening time at the discretion of the county election commission.

See footnotes at end of table

TABLE 6.5
Polling Hours: General Elections (continued)

State or other jurisdiction	Polls open	Polls close	Notes on hours (a)
Texas	7 a.m.	7 p.m.	
Utah	7 a.m.	8 p.m.	
Vermont	Between 5 and 10 a.m.	7 p.m.	The opening time for polls is set by local boards of civil authority.
Virginia	6 a.m.	7 p.m.	
Washington	NA	NA	Washington votes by mail. The ballot must be postmarked no later than Election Day; or returned to a designated ballot drop box by 8 p.m. on Election Day; or returned in person to the county elections department by 8 p.m. on Election Day.
West Virginia	6:30 a.m.	7:30 p.m.	
Wisconsin	7 a.m.	8 p.m.	
Wyoming	7 a.m.	7 p.m.	
Dist. of Columbia	7 a.m.	8 p.m.	
American Samoa	6 a.m	6 p.m.	
Guam	7 a.m.	8 p.m.	
CNMI*	7 a.m.	7 p.m.	
Puerto Rico	9 a.m.	5 p.m.	
U.S. Virgin Islands	7 a.m.	7 p.m.	

Sources: The Council of State Governments and state websites, March 2019.
*Commonwealth of Northern Mariana Islands
Note: Hours for primary, municipal and special elections may differ from those noted.

(a) In all states, voters standing in line when the polls close are allowed to vote; however, provisions for handling those voters vary across jurisdictions.

TABLE 6.6
Voter Registration Information

State or other jurisdiction	Closing date for registration before general election (Days)	Same-Day registration	Online registration	Automatic registration (a)	Residency requirements (b)	Registration in other places prohibited (c)	Provision regarding mental competency
Alabama	15	...	★		S	★	★
Alaska	30	(d)	★	★	S, D, 30	★	★
Arizona	29	...	★		S, C, 29	...	★
Arkansas	30	...	...		S, 30	★	★
California	15	★(e)	★	★	S	...	★
Colorado	22 days through voter registration drive, 8 online or by mail, Election Day in person	★	★	★	S, 22		...
Connecticut	14 by mail, 7 in person or online, Election Day	★	★	★	S, T	★	★
Delaware	24	...	★		S	★	★
Florida	29	...	★		S	...	★
Georgia	30 online, 29 in person, 28 by mail	...	★		S, C	...	★
Hawaii	29	★(g)	★		S	★	★
Idaho	25 or Election Day	★	★		S, C, 30	...	...
Illinois	28 (h)	★	★	★	S, P, 30	★	...
Indiana	29	...	★		S, P, 30	...	...
Iowa	15 by mail, 10 in person or online, Election Day	★	★		S	★	★
Kansas	21	...	★		S	★	...
Kentucky	29	...	★		S, P, 28	★	★
Louisiana	30	...	★		S, Parish, 30	★	★
Maine	21 by mail, up to Election Day in person	★	...		S, M	★	★
Maryland	21 by mail, early voting period in person	★(i)	★		S, 21	★	★
Massachusetts	20	...	★		S	...	★
Michigan	30 by mail, 21 in person	★	(j)	★	S, M, 30	★	...
Minnesota	21 or Election Day	★	★		S, 20	...	★
Mississippi	30	...	(k)		S, T, 30	★	★
Missouri	28	...	★		S	...	★
Montana	30 by mail or up to Election Day in person	★	...		S, 30	★	★
Nebraska	18 by mail or online, 11 in person	...	★		S	★	★
Nevada	31 by mail, 21 in person or online	...	★		S, C, 30; P, 10	★	★
New Hampshire	10 or Election Day	★	...		S	★	...
New Jersey	21	...	...		S, C, 30	★	★
New Mexico	28	...	(k)		S	...	★
New York	25	...	★		S, P, 30	★	★
North Carolina	25 (l)	(l)	...		S, C, 30	★	...
North Dakota	(m)	(m)	(m)		S, P, 30	(m)	...
Ohio	30 (n)	(n)	(k)		S, 30	★	★
Oklahoma	25	...	★(f)		S	...	★
Oregon	21	...	★	★	S	★	★
Pennsylvania	30	...	★		S, D, 30	★	...
Rhode Island	30	★(d)	★	★	S, T	★	★
South Carolina	30	...	★		S, C, P	★	★
South Dakota	15	...	...		S	★	★
Tennessee	30	...	★		S	★	★
Texas	30	...	...		S, C	...	★
Utah	30 by mail, 7 in person or online (o)	...	★		S, 30	★	★
Vermont	Election Day	★(p)	★	★	S, T	...	...
Virginia	22	...	★		S	★	★
Washington	29 by mail or online, 8 in person	...	★		S, 30	★	★
West Virginia	21	...	★	★	S, T, 30	★	★
Wisconsin	20 by mail or Election Day	★	★		S, P, 28	...	★
Wyoming	14 by mail or Election Day	★	...		S, P	★	★
Dist. of Columbia	30 by mail, Election Day in person	★	★	★	D, 30	★	★
American Samoa	30	...	...		D	★	...
Guam	10	...	...		Territory	★	★
CNMI*	60	...	...		Territory, 120	★	★
Puerto Rico	50	...	...		Territory (q)	...	★
U.S. Virgin Islands	30	...	...		Territory, P, 90	★	★

See footnotes at end of table

TABLE 6.6
Voter Registration Information (continued)

Source: The Council of State Governments survey of state election websites, March 2019.

*Commonwealth of Northern Mariana Islands

Key:

★–Provision exists.

...–No state provision.

(a) Eligible citizens who interact with government agencies are automatically registered to vote unless they decline.

(b) Key for residency requirements: S–State, C–County, D–District, M–Municipality, P–Precinct, T–Town. Numbers represent the number of days before an election for which one must be a resident.

(c) State provision prohibiting registration or claiming the right to vote in another state or jurisdiction.

(d) Election-day registration is available in presidential election years, but voters who do so can vote only for the offices of President and Vice President, not in state or local races.

(e) California's same-day registration will take effect on January 1 of the year following the year in which the Secretary of State certifies that the state has a statewide voter registration database that complies with the requirements of the federal Help America Vote Act of 2002.

(f) Oklahoma began the first phase of online registration in September 2018. The full online system is expected to be implemented by 2020.

(g) In 2014 Hawaii lawmakers passed legislation (HB 2590) to allow voters to register at early voting sites beginning in 2016 or at their assigned polling places on Election Day starting in 2018.

(h) Registration closes 27 days before a general election. Illinois also has a "grace period" registration that extends registration from the normal close of registration up through the 3rd day before the election. Once registered, this voter may cast a ballot during this "Grace Period" at the election authority's office or at a location specifically designated for this purpose by the election authority, or by mail, at the discretion of the election authority.

(i) A legislatively referred constitutional amendment to authorize the legislature to enact election day registration was approved by voters in November 2018.

(j) An online system allows voters to change their address for both their drivers license and voter registration at the same time. Michigan law requires that the same address be on record for both.

(k) In Mississippi, New Mexico, and Ohio, a registered voter can update an existing registration record online, but new applications must still be made on paper.

(l) In 2014, the North Carolina legislature eliminated voters' ability to register and vote on the same day at early voting locations. Registered voters may still update their name and address on their voter registration at an Early Voting site.

(m) No voter registration.

(n) In 2014, the Ohio Legislature passed a bill that eliminated the ability of voters to register during the six early voting days referred to as "Golden Week," when people could both register to vote and cast an in-person absentee ballot.

(o) Must be postmarked 30 days before an election. Voters can register in-person or online up to 7 days before the election. However, these voters will not be eligible to participate in early voting, and must vote on election day.

(p) The Vermont Legislature passed a bill (SB 29) in 2015 to allow for same-day voter registration, effective January 1, 2017.

(q) Voters must have a permanent residence in Puerto Rico to be a qualified elector.

TABLE 6.6a
Voting Information

State or other jurisdiction	Vote by mail or online (a)	Early voting allowed (b)	Voter ID required (c)	Photo ID required	Absentee voting			Provisions for felons	
					Persons eligible for absentee voting (d)	Permanent absentee status available (e)	Absentee votes signed by witness or notary (f)	Voting rights revoked	Method/process or provision for restoration (g)
Alabama	No	Yes	Yes (h)	Yes (h)	Excuse required	...	N or 2 W	★	B
Alaska	★(i)	Yes	Yes (j)	No	No excuse required	...	N or 1 W	★	C
Arizona		Yes	Yes	No	No excuse required	★	...	★	C
Arkansas		Yes	Yes	No (k)	Excuse required	...	...	★	C
California		Yes	No	No	No excuse required	★	...	★	E
Colorado	★(l)	Yes	Yes	No	N.A.	N.A.	...	★	E
Connecticut		No	No	No	Excuse required	...	...	★	E
Delaware		No	Yes	No	Excuse required	...	...	★	B
Florida		Yes	Yes	Yes	No excuse required	...	...	★	C
Georgia		Yes	Yes	Yes	No excuse required	...	...	★	C
Hawaii		Yes	Yes	No	No excuse required	★	...	★	D
Idaho	Yes (m)	Yes	Yes (n)	No excuse required	...	...	★	C
Illinois		Yes	No	No	No excuse required	...	...	★	D
Indiana	Yes (m)	Yes	Yes	Excuse required	...	...	★	D
Iowa	Yes (m)	No	No	No excuse required	...	...	★	A
Kansas		Yes	Yes	Yes	No excuse required	...	...	★	C
Kentucky	No	Yes	No	Excuse required	...	...	★	A
Louisiana		Yes	Yes	Yes	Excuse required	...	N or W	★	C
Maine	Yes (m)	No	No	No excuse required	...	...	...	N.A.
Maryland		Yes	No	No	No excuse required	...	...	★	D
Massachusetts	Yes (o)	No	No	Excuse required	...	...	★	D
Michigan	No	Yes	Yes	Excuse required	...	...	★	D
Minnesota	Yes (m)	No	No	No excuse required	★	N or W (p)	★	C
Mississippi	No	Yes	Yes	Excuse required	...	N (q)	★	B
Missouri	No	Yes	No	Excuse required	...	N (r)	★	C
Montana	Yes (m)	Yes	No	No excuse required	★	...	★	C
Nebraska		Yes	No	No	No excuse required	...	...	★	C
Nevada		Yes	No	No	No excuse required	★	...	★	B
New Hampshire	No	Yes	Yes	Excuse required	...	...	★	D
New Jersey	Yes (m)	No	No	No excuse required	★	...	★	C
New Mexico		Yes	No	No	No excuse required	...	...	★	C
New York	No	No	No	Excuse required	...	...	★	E
North Carolina		Yes	Yes	No (s)	No excuse required	...	N or 2W	★	C
North Dakota		Yes	Yes	Yes	No excuse required	...	...	★	D
Ohio	Yes (m)	Yes	No	No excuse required	...	...	★	D
Oklahoma	Yes (m)	Yes	No (t)	No excuse required	...	N (u)	★	E
Oregon	★(v)	N.A.	No	No	N.A.	N.A.	...	★	D
Pennsylvania	No	No (w)	No (w)	Excuse required	...	...	★	D
Rhode Island	No	Yes	Yes	Excuse required	...	N or 2W (x)	★	D
South Carolina	No	Yes	No (y)	Excuse required	...	W (z)	★	C
South Dakota	Yes (m)	Yes	Yes	No excuse required	...	(aa)	★	C
Tennessee		Yes	Yes	Yes	Excuse required	...	...	★	B
Texas		Yes	Yes	Yes	Excuse required	...	...	★	C
Utah		Yes	Yes	No	No excuse required	★	...	★	D
Vermont	Yes (m)	No	No	No excuse required	...	...	...	N.A.
Virginia	No	Yes	Yes	Excuse required	...	W	★	C (bb)
Washington	★(cc)	N.A.	No	No	N.A.	N.A.	...	★	C
West Virginia		Yes	No (dd)	No (dd)	Excuse required	...	...	★	C
Wisconsin	Yes (m)	Yes	Yes	No excuse required	...	W	★	C
Wyoming	Yes (m)	No	No	No excuse required	...	...	★	B
Dist. of Columbia		Yes	No	No	No excuse required	★	...	★	D
American Samoa	No	No	No	Excuse required	...	...	★	C
Guam	No	No	No	Excuse required	...	N	★	C
CNMI*	No	No	No	Excuse required	...	N	★	C
Puerto Rico	No	Yes	No	Excuse required	...	(ee)	...	N.A.
U.S. Virgin Islands	No	Yes	No	Excuse required	...	Affidavit	★	C

See footnotes at end of table

TABLE 6.6a
Voting Information (continued)

Sources: The Council of State Governments survey of state websites, March 2019.
*Commonwealth of Northern Mariana Islands
Key:
★–Provision exists.
. . .–No state provision.
N.A.–Not applicable

(a) Three states–Colorado, Oregon, and Washington–conduct elections by mail. All registered voters are automatically mailed a ballot in advance of Election Day. Alaska is the first state to allow all voters–not just those covered by the federal Uniformed and Overseas Citizens Absentee Voting Act (UOCAVA)–to submit an absentee ballot electronically. Civilian voters must apply for an electronic ballot beginning 15 days before the election.

(b) Early voting is usually done in person on the same equipment as that used on Election Day. An excuse is not required.

(c) Voter identification laws include both photo or non-photo identification requirements.

(d) Typical excuses include some or all of the following: absent on business; senior citizen; disabled persons; not absent, but prevented by employment from voting; out of state on Election Day; out of precinct on Election Day; absent for religious reasons; students; temporarily out of jurisdiction.

(e) State allows voters to be added to the permanent absentee voter list, in which an absentee ballot will be automatically sent for each election. No excuse is required. This does not include states that allow certain voters to be added to the list, including permanently disabled or ill voters, the elderly, uniformed service members and their families, or people who live outside the United States.

(f) Absentee votes must be signed by, N–Notary or W–Witness. Numbers indicated the number of signatures required.

(g) A–permanent disenfranchisement for all offenders; states that permanently disenfranchise all or some felons may allow felons to apply, on an individual basis, to the state for an exemption that will restore their voting rights.
B–restoration is dependent upon the type of conviction and/or the results of an individual petition to the state government.
C–voting rights restored after completion of sentence including prison, parole and probation.
D–voting rights restored after release from prison.
E–voting rights restored once released from prison and parole, probationers can vote.

(h) Photo identification is not required if two election officials can sign sworn statements saying they know the voter.

(i) Alaska is the first state to allow all voters–not just those covered by the federal Uniformed and Overseas Citizens Absentee Voting Act (UOCAVA)–to submit an absentee ballot electronically. Civilian voters must apply for an electronic ballot beginning 15 days before the election.

(j) An election officer may waive the identification requirement if the election officials know the identity of the voter.

(k) In October 2014, the Arkansas Supreme Court struck down a state law that requires voters to show photo identification before casting a ballot, ruling the requirement unconstitutional.

(l) While all registered voters are automatically mailed a ballot prior to the election, the state also operates in-person voting sites.

(m) Functional early voting, as the state permits in-person absentee voting, in which voters, within a certain period of time before the election, can apply in person for an absentee ballot (no excuse required) and cast a ballot in the election office.

(n) A registered voter must either present a photo ID or sign a Personal Identification Affidavit. After signing the Affidavit, the voter will be issued a ballot to be tabulated with all other ballots.

(o) Beginning in 2016, Massachusetts will have early voting only during even-year November elections. There are no early voting periods for primaries or municipal elections.

(p) Unless the witness is a notary, the witness must also be a registered Minnesota voter.

(q) Disabled voters do not need to have an absentee ballot notarized, but it must be witnessed.

(r) All absentee ballots must be notarized with the exception of the following: Missouri residents outside the U.S., including military on active duty and their immediate family members; permanently disabled voters and those voting absentee due to illness or physical disability; and caregivers.

(s) Photo identification will be required starting in 2016. However, voters who are unable to obtain an acceptable photo ID due to a reasonable impediment may still vote a provisional ballot at the polls . Examples of a reasonable impediment include but are not limited to the lack of proper documents, family obligations, transportation problems, work schedule, illness or disability, among other reasonable impediments faced by the voter. Voters must also sign a declaration describing their impediment; and provide their date of birth and last four digits of their Social Security number, or present their current voter registration card or a copy of an acceptable document bearing their name and address. (Acceptable documents include a current utility bill, bank statement, government check, paycheck, or other government- issued document.) The provisional ballot will be counted when the information on the declaration is verified and all other eligibility requirements are met.

(t) A Voter Identification Card issued by the County Election Board is the only valid proof of identity that does not include a photograph.

(u) All absentee ballots must notarized with the following exceptions: Physically incapacitated voters and voters who care for physically incapacitated persons (ballot affidavit must be witnessed by two people); voters in a nursing home; overseas voters.

(v) State conducts election by mail. All registered voters are automatically mailed a ballot in advance of Election Day.

(w) In 2012, the legislature enacted a law requiring voters to show photo identification. However, in 2014 a state judge struck down the law.

(x) All absentee ballots must be notarized or signed by two witnesses with the following exceptions: military and overseas voters.

(y) If a voter has a reasonable impediment to obtaining photo iden-tification, he or she may vote a provisional ballot after showing a non-photo voter registration card. State law defines a reasonable impediment as any valid reason, beyond a person's control, that creates an obstacle to obtaining Photo ID. Some examples include:

TABLE 6.6a
Voting Information (continued)

religious objection to being photographed; disability or illness; work schedule; lack of transportation; lack of birth certificate; family responsibilities; election within short time frame of implementation of photo ID law (January 1, 2013); and any other obstacle a person finds reasonable.

(z) All absentee ballots must be notarized or signed by one witness, with the exception of qualified voters under the Uniformed and Overseas Citizens Absentee Voters Act.

(aa) Absentee ballot applications (not absentee ballots) are required to be notarized unless a copy of the voter's photo identification is also submitted.

(bb) On Apr. 22, 2016, Virginia Gov. Terry McAuliffe signed an order restoring the vote to all felons in Virginia, regardless of their charge, who had completed their term of incarceration and their term of probation or parole. The governor's action will not apply to felons released in the future, but aides say the governor plans to issue similar orders on a monthly basis to cover people as they are released.

(cc) State conducts election by mail. All registered voters are automatically mailed a ballot in advance of Election Day. Only Pierce County offers in-person voting.

(dd) In 2016, the West Virginia Legislature approved a bill that will require voters to show some form of identification before casting a ballot. Approved forms of identification include any government-issued ID or permit, with or without a photo, including a voter registration card; any college or high school issued ID; a health insurance card; a utility bill; a bank card or bank statement; or verification of identification by another adult who has known the voter for at least 6 months, including a poll worker. It is effective January 1, 2018.

(ee) Absentee ballot applications (not absentee ballots) are required to be certified by various officials, depending on the reason for voting absentee, such as a college registrar, employer, or medical official.

TABLE 6.7
Voting Statistics for Gubernatorial Elections

State or other jurisdiction	Date of last election	Primary election Republican	Democrat	3rd Party	Independent	Total votes
Alabama	2018	591,199	283,705	0	0	874,904
Alaska	2018	71,195	39,241 (a)	0	0	110,436
Arizona	2018	655,538	505,481	2,648	0	1,163,667
Arkansas	2018	206,405	105,919	0	0	312,324
California (b)	2018	2,519,136	4,350,513	91,481	0	6,961,130
Colorado	2018	503,205	637,002	0	0	1,140,207
Connecticut	2018	142,858	212,543	0	0	355,401
Delaware	2016	30,265	(c)	0	0	30,265
Florida	2018	1,622,124	1,519,492	0	0	3,141,616
Georgia	2018	607,441	555,089	0	0	1,162,530
Hawaii	2018	31,156	242,514	454	1,138	275,262
Idaho	2018	194,536	65,882	0	0	260,418
Illinois	2018	722,162	1,324,548	0	0	2,046,710
Indiana	2016	815,699 (c)	547,375 (c)	0	0	1,363,074
Iowa	2018	94,118 (c)	178,924	1,696	1,649	276,387
Kansas	2018	317,615	156,273	0	0	473,888
Kentucky	2015	214,193	178,541	0	0	392,734
Louisiana (f)	2015	637,938	463,700	0	12,698	1,114,336
Maine	2018	94,382	125,391	0	748	220,521
Maryland	2018	157,503 (c)	391,706	0	0	549,209
Massachusetts	2018	273,011	551,470	0	0	824,481
Michigan	2018	989,525	1,131,447	6975	0	2,127,947
Minnesota	2018	289,957	582,350	0	0	872,307
Mississippi	2015	274,407	299,368	0	0	573,775
Missouri	2016	684,251	325,413	3,515 (c)	0	1,013,179
Montana	2016	145,948	122,419	0	0	268,367
Nebraska	2018	169,860	91,942	0	0	261,802
Nevada	2018	142,184 (g)	145,420 (g)	0	0	287,604
New Hampshire	2018	92,583	122,966	1110	0	216,659
New Jersey	2017	258,880	527,332	0	0	786,212
New Mexico	2018	75,162 (c)	175,898	175	0	251,235
New York	2018	(c)	1,558,352	0	0	1,558,352
North Carolina	2016	1,072,655	1,034,432	0	0	2,107,087
North Dakota	2016	114,415	17,337 (c)	1,095	0	132,847
Ohio	2018	834,967	688,788	3,031	0	1,526,786
Oklahoma	2018	452,606	395,494	3558	0	399,052
Oregon	2016	304,892	480,852	0	23,332	809,076
Pennsylvania	2018	737,312	749,812 (c)	0	0	1,487,124
Rhode Island	2018	33,087	117,875	0	0	150,962
South Carolina	2018	367,983	240,468	0	0	608,451
South Dakota	2018	102,772	(c)	0	0	102,772
Tennessee	2018	792,888	373,390	0	0	1,166,278
Texas	2018	1,549,006	1,022,558	0	0	2,571,564
Utah	2016	229,656 (m)	(i)	0	0	229,656
Vermont	2018	35,811	57,248	0	4974	98,033
Virginia	2017	365,782	542,816	0	0	908,598
Washington	2016	596,092	756,759	18,989	22,582	1,394,422
West Virginia	2016	161,127 (c)	258,350	0	0	419,477
Wisconsin	2018	455,563	538,646	0	0	994,191
Wyoming	2018	116,786	18,076	0	0	134,862
American Samoa	2016			(j)		
Guam	2018	(c)	25,699	0	0	25,699
CNMI*	2018	(k)	(k)	(k)	(k)	(k)
Puerto Rico	2016	(c)	462,973	0	0	462,973
U.S. Virgin Islands	2018	N.A.	N.A.	N.A.	N.A.	N.A.

See footnotes at end of table

TABLE 6.7
Voting Statistics for Gubernatorial Elections (continued)

State or other jurisdiction	Republican	Percent	Democrat	Percent	3rd Party	Percent	Independent and Write-In	Percent	Total votes
					General election				
Alabama	1,019,558	59.5	691,671	40.4	0	0.0	2,614	0.2	1,713,843
Alaska	145,631	51.4	125,739	44.4	5,402	1.9	6,362	2.3	283,134
Arizona	1,330,863	56.0	994,341	41.8	50,962	4.8	275	0.0	2,376,441
Arkansas	582,406	65.3	283,218	31.8	25,885	3.1	0	0.0	891,509
California (d)	4,742,825	38.1	7,721,410	61.9	0	0.0	0	0.0	12,464,235
Colorado	1,080,801	42.8	1,348,888	53.4	95,373	4.7	0	0.0	2,525,062
Connecticut	650,138 (e)	48.2	694,510 (e)	50.7	62,081	0.0	74	0.0	1,406,803
Delaware	166,852	39.2	248,404	58.3	10,528	2.5	0	0.0	425,784
Florida	4,076,186	49.6	4,043,723	49.2	47,140	3.8	53,512	0.7	8,220,561
Georgia	1,978,408	50.2	1,923,685	48.8	37,235	2.4	432	0.0	3,939,328
Hawaii	131,719	33.7	244,934	62.7	10,123	13.5	4,067	1.0	390,843
Idaho	361,661	59.8	231,081	38.2	12,338	5.8	51	0.0	605,131
Illinois	1,765,751	38.8	2,479,746	54.5	302,045	3.3	115	0.0	4,547,657
Indiana	1,397,396	51.4	1,235,503	45.4	87,025	3.2	44	0.0	2,719,968
Iowa	667,275	50.3	630,986	47.5	28,889	3.6	488	0.0	1,327,638
Kansas	453,645	43.0	506,727	48.0	20,020	4.0	75,174	7.1	1,055,566
Kentucky	511,374	52.5	426,620	43.8	0	0.0	35,698	3.7	973,692
Louisiana (f)	505,940	43.9	646,924	56.1	0	0.0	0	0.0	1,152,864
Maine	272,311	43.2	320,962	50.9	37,268	8.4	126	0.0	630,667
Maryland	855,539	57.7	608,810	41.1	16,584	1.5	1,096	0.1	1,482,029
Massachusetts	885,770	33.1	1,781,341	66.6		3.3	7,504	0.3	2,674,615
Michigan	1,859,534	43.7	2,266,193	53.3	124,826	2.2	32	0.0	4,250,585
Minnesota	1,097,705	42.4	1,393,096	53.8	95,402	2.2	1,084	0.0	2,587,287
Mississippi	476,697	66.4	231,643	32.3	9,845	0.0	0	0.0	718,185
Missouri	1,424,730	51.3	1,261,110	45.4	61,503	2.2	30,511	1.1	2,777,854
Montana	236,115	46.4	255,933	50.2	17,312	3.4	0	0.0	509,360
Nebraska	411,812	59.0	286,169	41.0	0	3.5	0	0.0	697,981
Nevada	440,320	45.3	480,007	49.4	32,607	2.7	18,865 (g)	2.9	971,799
New Hampshire	302,764	52.8	262,359	45.7	8,197	1.4	282	0.0	573,602
New Jersey	899,583	41.9	1,203,110	56.0	44,722	2.1	0	0.0	2,147,415
New Mexico	298,091	42.8	398,368	57.2	0	0.0	0	0.0	696,459
New York	2,207,602 (h)	36.2	3,635,340 (h)	59.6	254,420	4.2	0	0.0	6,097,362
North Carolina	2,298,880	48.8	2,309,157	49.0	102,977	2.2	0	0.0	4,711,014
North Dakota	259,863	76.5	65,855	19.4	13,230	3.9	653	0.2	339,601
Ohio	2,231,917	50.4	2,067,847	46.7	129,460	3.3	358	0.0	4,429,582
Oklahoma	644,579	54.3	500,973	42.2	40,833	0.0	0	0.0	1,186,385
Oregon	684,321	43.8	796,006	51.0	46,446	3.0	35,046	2.2	1,561,819
Pennsylvania	2,039,882	40.7	2,895,652	57.8	77,021	0.0	0	0.0	5,012,555
Rhode Island	139,932	37.2	198,122	52.6	14,346	21.4	24,001	6.4	376,401
South Carolina	921,342	54.0	784,182	45.9	0	1.7	2,045	0.1	1,707,569
South Dakota	172,706	51.0	161,171	47.6	4,838	0.0	0	0.0	338,715
Tennessee	1,336,106	59.6	864,863	38.6	0	3.3	42,325	1.9	2,243,294
Texas	4,656,196	55.8	3,546,615	42.5	140,632	1.8	0	0.0	8,343,443
Utah	750,828	66.7	322,462	28.7	34,687	3.1	16,936	1.5	1,124,913
Vermont	151,261	55.2	110,335	40.3	3,694	1.3	8,797	3.2	274,087
Virginia	1,175,731	45.0	1,409,175	53.9	27,987	6.5	1,389	0.1	2,614,282
Washington	1,476,346	45.6	1,760,520	54.4	0	0.0	0	0.0	3,236,866
West Virginia	301,987	42.3	350,408	49.1	61,463	8.6	0	0.0	713,858
Wisconsin	1,295,080	48.5	1,324,307	49.6	31,312	0.0	21,643	0.8	2,672,342
Wyoming	136,412	67.1	55,965	27.5	9,761	2.4	1,100	0.5	203,238
American Samoa					---------- (j) ----------				12,024
Guam	9,487	26.4	18,258	50.8	0	0.0	8,205	22.8	35,950
CNMI*	8922	62.2	0	0.0	0	0.0	5,420	37.8	14,342
Puerto Rico	614,190	38.9	660,510	41.8	39,159	4.4	266,325	16.9	1,580,184
U.S. Virgin Islands	0	0.0	9,711 (l)	39.2	0	0.0	15,811 (l)	60.8	25,522

See footnotes at end of table

TABLE 6.7
Voting Statistics for Gubernatorial Elections (continued)

Sources: The Council of State Governments' survey of state elections web sites, March 2019.

*Commonwealth of Northern Mariana Islands

Key:

N.A.–Not applicable

(a) In 2018, the Democratic Primary was known as the ADL ballot, which featured candidates from the Democratic, Libertarian and Independence Parties.

(b) California became an open primary state after passage of Proposition 14 in the June 2010 election. The top two vote-getters in primary races for congressional, state legislative and statewide offices, regardless of political party, will be in a face-off in the general election.

(c) Candidate ran unopposed.

(e) Republican vote total includes 25,388 votes from the Independent party. Democratic vote total includes 17,861 from the Working Families Party.

(f) Louisiana has an open primary which requires all candidates, regardless of party affiliation, to appear on a single ballot. If a candidate receives over 50 percent of the vote in the primary, he is elected to the office. If no candidate receives a majority vote, then a single election is held between the two candidates receiving the most votes.

(g) Nevada voters have the option to select "None of These Candidates." If the "None of These Candidates" option receives the most votes in an election, the actual candidate who receives the most votes wins the election. In the Democratic primary, the "None of

These Candidates" option received 5,069 votes. In the Republican primary, 6,136 voters selected that option. The "None of These Candidates" option received 18,865 votes in the general election.

(h) Democratic vote includes 68,713 from the Independence Party, 27,733 from the Women's Equality Party, and 114,478 from the Working Families Party. The Republican vote includes 253,624 from the Conservative Party and 27,493 from the Reform Party.

(i) Candidate nominated by convention.

(j) There are no primaries. Instead, the law provides for a run off when none of the candidates receives more than 50% of the vote. All elections and candidates are nonpartisan, but candidates do identify with specific parties. The vote total in the general election was 12,024. Incumbent Lolo Matalasi Moliga won with 7,235 votes, Faoa Aitofele Sunia was next with 4,305 and Tuika Tuika received 484 votes.

(k) There are no primaries. Instead, the law provides for a run off when none of the candidates receives more than 50% of the vote.

(l) In the general election in the U.S. Virgin Islands, a runoff was held because no candidate received more than 50% of the vote. The vote total in the runoff election was 21,635, with the Democratic candidate Albert Bryan winnning with 54.5% of the vote.

(m) Incumbent Republican Governor of Utah, Gary Herbert, lost the GOP primary convention vote to challenger Jonathan Johnson. Under the "Count My Vote" law, Herbert was still guaranteed a spot on the ballot despite losing the convention vote (forcing an official primary).

Table 6.7 | Gubernatorial Elections

Republican
PERCENT–HIGHEST

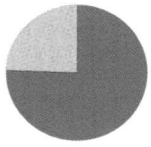  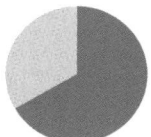 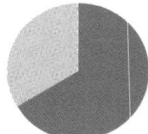 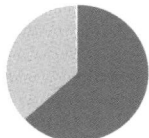

| ND · 76.5% | WY · 67.1% | UT · 66.7% | MS · 66.4% | AR · 65.3% |

Democrat
PERCENT–HIGHEST

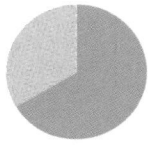 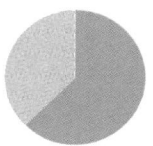   

| MA · 66.6% | HI · 62.7% | CA · 61.9% | NY · 59.6% | DE · 58.3% |

Third Party
PERCENT–HIGHEST

| RI · 21.4% | HI · 13.5% | WV · 8.6% | ME · 8.4% | VA · 6.5% |

In a gubernatorial election, NEVADA voters have the option to select "None of These Candidates."

In the most recent general election, this option received 18,865 votes.

Of the states, **KANSAS** had the **highest total percentage** of independent and write-in votes.

7.1%

TABLE 6.8
Voter Turnout for Presidential Elections By Region: 2008, 2012 and 2016 (In thousands)

State or other jurisdiction	2016 Voting age population (a)	2016 Number registered	2016 Number voting (b)	2012 Voting age population (a)	2012 Number registered	2012 Number voting (b)	2008 Voting age population (a)	2008 Number registered	2008 Number voting (b)
U.S. Total	250,056	191,316	136,665	234,564	153,161	129,140	227,719	189,391	128,628
Alabama	3,770	3,343	2,123	3,647	2,556	2,074	3,504	2,841	2,100
Alaska	3,770	514	319	523	361	300	501	496	326
Arizona	555	3,588	2,624	4,763	2,812	2,299	4,668	2,987	2,321
Arkansas	5,331	1,704	1,131	2,204	1,376	1,069	2,134	1,686	1,087
California	2,287	19,412	14,182	27,959	15,356	13,039	27,169	23,209	13,214
Colorado	4,306	3,838	2,780	3,804	2,635	2,570	3,668	3,209	2,401
Connecticut	2,822	2,358	1,645	2,757	1,760	1,558	2,682	2,210	1,645
Delaware	750	676	444	692	470	414	659	602	391
Florida	16,566	12,959	9,420	14,799	9,102	8,474	14,207	11,248	8,358
Georgia	7,828	5,638	4,115	7,196	4,767	3,898	7,013	5,266	3,924
Hawaii	1,120	750	429	1,056	547	437	997	691	454
Idaho	1,254	805	690	1,139	745	652	1,091	862	655
Illinois	9,867	671	5,536	9,701	6,425	5,242	9,653	7,790	5,578
Indiana	5,063	4,829	2,735	4,876	3,270	2,625	4,758	4,515	2,751
Iowa	2,407	2,171	1,566	2,318	1,745	1,582	2,276	2,076	1,537
Kansas	2,192	1,818	1,184	2,126	1,467	1,160	2,079	1,750	1,751
Kentucky	3,431	3,314	1,924	3,316	2,303	1,797	3,237	2,907	1,827
Louisiana	3,572	3,022	2,029	3,415	2,498	1,994	3,213	2,945	1,961
Maine	1,078	1,058	748	1,054	787	725	1,037	1,000	731
Maryland	4,671	3,963	2,781	4,421	2,888	2,707	4,259	3,429	2,632
Massachusetts	5,442	4,535	3,325	5,129	3,759	3,184	5,016	4,220	3,103
Michigan	7,745	7,514	4,799	7,540	5,620	4,731	7,624	7,471	5,044
Minnesota	4,240	3,269	2,945	4,020	3,085	2,937	3,937	3,200	2,910
Mississippi	2,268	1,879	1,209	2,212	1,794	1,286	2,150	1,873	1,290
Missouri	4,711	4,224	2,809	4,563	3,384	2,757	4,453	4,181	2,925
Montana	818	694	495	766	553	484	738	668	490
Nebraska	1,436	1,211	844	1,367	901	794	1,328	1,157	801
Nevada	2,276	1,686	1,125	2,036	1,176	1,015	1,905	1,208	968
New Hampshire	1,077	1,007	744	1,029	752	711	1,017	864	708
New Jersey	6,960	5,819	3,874	6,727	4,326	3,638	6,622	5,379	3,868
New Mexico	1,591	1,289	798	1,541	978	784	1,469	1,193	830
New York	15,558	12,493	7,721	15,053	8,887	7,117	14,884	12,031	7,675
North Carolina	7,880	6,918	4,742	7,254	5,295	4,505	6,843	6,226	4,311
North Dakota	581	(c)	344	523	383 (c)	323	496	(c)	317
Ohio	9,008	7,861	5,496	8,806	6,076	5,581	8,715	8,163	5,698
Oklahoma	2,966	2,157	1,453	2,822	1,806	1,335	2,717	2,184	1,463
Oregon	3,244	2,569	2,001	2,965	2,086	1,789	2,884	2,154	1,828
Pennsylvania	10,108	8,723	6,115	9,910	6,795	5,742	9,646	8,730	5,995
Rhode Island	849	771	464	829	552	446	824	701	470
South Carolina	3,883	3,129	2,103	3,545	2,479	1,964	3,347	2,554	1,921
South Dakota	654	544	370	611	454	364	599	508	382
Tennessee	5,165	4,110	2,508	4,850	3,210	2,459	4,685	3,978	2,600
Texas	20,672	15,101	8,969	18,280	10,749	7,994	17,281	13,575	8,077
Utah	2,145	1,558	1,131	1,893	1,138	1,017	1,828	1,433	905
Vermont	506	465	315	497	357	299	489	454	325
Virginia	6,551	5,530	3,985	6,147	4,210	3,854	5,885	5,044	3,724
Washington	5,692	4,270	3,317	5,143	3,533	3,126	4,932	3,630	3,037
West Virginia	1,453	1,277	713	1,466	982	670	1,424	1,212	713
Wisconsin	4,496	3,559	2,976	4,347	3,318	3,071	4,280	3,405	2,983
Wyoming	446	241	256	428	268	251	397	276	255
Dist. of Columbia	562	480	311	501	385	294	475	427	267

Sources: U.S. Congress, Clerk of the House, Statistics of the Presidential and Congressional Election, 2008, 2012. U.S. Census Bureau, Resident Population of Voting Age and Percent Casting Votes--States, as of July 1, 2010. U.S. Census Bureau, Table 4a: Reported Voting and Registration of the Citizen Voting-Age Population, for States: November 2012. U.S. Census Bureau, Current Population Survey, December 2008. The Council of State Governments' survey of election officials, January 2017, January 2009.

Key:
(a) Estimated population, 18 years old and over. Includes armed forces in each state, aliens, and institutional population.
(b) Number voting is number of ballots cast in presidential race.
(c) No statewide registration required.

TABLE 6.9
Statewide Initiative and Referendum

State or other jurisdiction	Changes to constitution			Changes to statutes			
	Initiative		Referendum	Initiative		Referendum	
	Direct (a)	Indirect (a)	Legislative (b)	Direct (c)	Indirect (c)	Legislative	Citizen petition (d)
Alabama	...	...	★	...	...	...	...
Alaska	...	...	★	...	★	...	★
Arizona	★	...	★	★	...	★	★
Arkansas	★	...	★	★	...	★	★
California	★	...	★	★	...	★	★
Colorado	★	...	★	★	...	★	★
Connecticut	...	...	★	...	...	...	...
Delaware	...	...	...	...	...	★	...
Florida	★	...	★	...	...	...	...
Georgia	...	...	★	...	...	...	...
Hawaii	...	...	★	...	...	...	...
Idaho	...	...	★	★	...	★	★
Illinois	★	...	★	...	...	★	...
Indiana	...	...	★	...	...	...	...
Iowa	...	...	★	...	...	...	...
Kansas	...	...	★	...	...	...	...
Kentucky	...	...	★	...	...	★	...
Louisiana	...	...	★	...	...	...	...
Maine	...	...	★	...	★	★	★
Maryland	...	...	★	...	...	★	★
Massachusetts	...	★	★	...	★	★	★
Michigan	★	...	★	...	★	★	★
Minnesota	...	...	★	...	...	...	...
Mississippi	...	★	★	...	...	...	...
Missouri	★	...	★	★	...	★	★
Montana	★	...	★	★	...	★	★
Nebraska	★	...	★	★	...	★	★
Nevada	★	...	★	...	★	★	★
New Hampshire	...	...	★	...	...	...	...
New Jersey	...	...	★	...	...	...	...
New Mexico	...	...	★	...	...	★	...
New York	...	...	★	...	...	...	...
North Carolina	...	...	★(e)	...	...	...	...
North Dakota	★	...	★	★	...	★	★
Ohio	★	...	★	...	★	★	★
Oklahoma	★	...	★	★	...	★	★
Oregon	★	...	★	★	...	★	★
Pennsylvania	...	...	★	...	...	...	...
Rhode Island	...	...	★	...	...	...	...
South Carolina	...	...	★	...	...	...	...
South Dakota	★	...	★	★	...	★	★
Tennessee	...	...	★	...	...	...	...
Texas	...	...	★	...	...	...	...
Utah	...	...	★	★	★	★	★
Vermont	...	...	★	...	...	...	...
Virginia	...	...	★	...	...	...	...
Washington	...	...	★	★	★	★	★
West Virginia	...	...	★	...	...	...	...
Wisconsin	...	...	★	...	...	...	...
Wyoming	...	...	★	...	★	...	★
American Samoa	...	...	★	...	...	...	...
CNMI*	★	★	★	★	★	★	★
Puerto Rico	...	...	★	...	...	★	...
U.S. Virgin Islands	★	...	★	...	...	★	...

See footnotes at end of table

TABLE 6.9
Statewide Initiative and Referendum (continued)

Sources: The Council of State Governments' survey of state election website, Initiative & Referendum Institute website and Ballotpedia websites, March 2019.

*Commonwealth of Northern Mariana Islands

Note: This table summarizes state provisions for initiatives and referendums. Initiatives may propose constitutional amendments or develop state legislation and may be formed either directly or indirectly. The direct initiative allows a proposed measure to be placed on the ballot after a specific number of signatures have been secured on a citizen petition. The indirect initiative must be submitted to the legislature for a decision after the required number of signatures has been secured on a petition and prior to placing the proposed measure on the ballot. Referendum refers to the process whereby a state law or constitutional amendment passed by the legislature may be referred to the voters before it goes into effect. Three forms of referendums exist: (1) citizen petition, whereby the people may petition for a referendum on legislation which has been considered by the legislature; (2) submission by the legislature (designated in table as "Legislative"), whereby the legislature may voluntarily submit laws to the voters for their approval; and (3) constitutional requirement, whereby the state constitution may require that certain questions be submitted to the voters.

Key:

★–State Provision.

...–No state provision.

(a) See "Constitutional Amendment Procedure: By Initiative," for more detail.

(b) See "Constitutional Amendment Procedure: By the Legislature," for more detail.

(c) See tables on State Initiatives, for more detail.

(d) See tables on State Referendums, for more detail.

(e) Only the legislature can make statutory changes while in session. Proposed constitutional changes must be passed by the legislature and then are submitted to the citizens to be voted on.

TABLE 6.9a
State Ballot Questions in 2018

State or other jurisdiction	Title	Type	Date	Result	Vote totals		Subject	Short description
					Yes votes	No votes		
Alabama	Amendment 1	LRCA	Nov. 6, 2018	Passed	72%	28%	Ten Commandments	Amends the state constitution to authorize the display of the Ten Commandments on public property, including public schools.
	Amendment 2	LRCA	Nov. 6, 2018	Passed	59%	41%	Abortion Policy	This amendment makes it state policy to state that no provisions of the constitution provide a right to an abortion or require funding of abortions.
	Amendment 3	LRCA	Nov. 6, 2018	Passed	60%	40%	Board of Trustees/ University of Alabama Amendment	The state constitution was amended making changes to the membership of the board of trustees of the University of Alabama.
	Amendment 4	LRCA	Nov. 6, 2018	Passed	66%	34%	Legislative Vacancies	"The state constitution was amended to establish the following: if a vacancy in the state Senate or House occurred on or after October 1 of the year before the regular election, the seat would remain vacant until the next regular election, and vacant seats could be filled without an election if only one candidate is running for the vacant seat."
Alaska	Measure 1	IndISS	Nov. 6, 2018	Failed	38%	62%	Salmon Habitat/ Protections/ Permits	The measure to establish new requirements and a new permitting process for any projects affecting bodies of water related to the activity and habitat of salmon, steelhead or other anadromous fish, and to prohibit any projects or activity determined to cause significant and unrestorable damage to such fish habitats failed.
Arizona	Proposition 125	LRCA	Nov. 6, 2018	Passed	52%	48%	Elected Officials' and Corrections Officer's Retirement Plans	This amendment to make adjustments to retirement plans based on cost-of-living adjustments, rather than permanent benefit increases, for correctional officers, probation officers, and surveillance officers and elected officials was enacted.
	Proposition 126	CICA	Nov. 6, 2018	Passed	64%	36%	Taxes on Services	This proposition prohibits the state and local governments from enacting new taxes or increasing tax rates in effect on December 31, 2018, on services performed in Arizona. Services can include personal-oriented activities, including salon services, pet grooming, amusement, and fitness activities, to financial-oriented activities including real estate transactions, banking, and investment management, to healthcare-oriented activities such as doctor visits.
	Proposition 127	CICA	Nov. 6, 2018	Failed	31%	69%	Renewable Energy	A "no" vote opposed this constitutional amendment to require electric utilities in Arizona to acquire a certain percentage of electricity from renewable resources, thereby leaving in place the state's existing renewable energy requirements of 15 percent by 2025.
	Proposition 305	CI	Nov. 6, 2018	Failed	35%	65%	Empowerment Scholarship	A "no" vote was to repeal the contested legislation, Senate Bill 1431, which would make all public school students eligible to apply for an ESA.
	Proposition 306	LRSS	Nov. 6, 2018	Passed	56%	44%	Elections	"Prohibits candidates from using their public financing accounts to give funds to political parties or tax-exempt 501(a) organizations."
Arkansas	Issue 2	LRCA	Nov. 6, 2018	Passed	79%	21%	Voter ID	Established photo identification as a constitutionally required qualification for voting,
	Issue 4	CICA	Nov. 6, 2018	Passed	54%	46%	Casino	The initiative to authorize one casino each in Crittenden, Garland, Pope, and Jefferson Counties passed.
	Issue 5	CISS	Nov. 6, 2018	Passed	68%	32%	Minimum Wage	This initiative will incrementally raise the minimum wage in Arkansas to $11 an hour by 2021.
California	Proposition 68	BI	June 5, 2018	Passed	58%	42%	Parks/ Environment/ Water	This measure authorizes $4 billion in general obligation bonds for state and local parks, environmental protection projects, water infrastructure projects, and flood protection projects.
	Proposition 69	LRCA	June 5, 2018	Passed	81%	19%	Transportation Taxes	Requires that revenue from the diesel sales tax and Transportation Improvement Fee enacted by the Road Repair and Accountability Act of 2017 (RRAA) be used for transportation-related purposes.
	Proposition 70	LRCA	June 5, 2018	Failed	37%	63%	Cap-and-Trade	The amendment to require a one-time two-thirds vote in each legislative chamber in 2024 or thereafter to pass a spending plan for revenue from the state's cap-and-trade program failed.
	Proposition 71	LRCA	June 5, 2018	Passed	78%	22%	Ballot Measures	"This amendment moves the effective date of ballot propositions, including citizen initiatives and legislative referrals, from the day after election day to the fifth day after the secretary of state certifies election results."

See footnotes at end of table

TABLE 6.9a
State Ballot Questions in 2018 (continued)

State or other jurisdiction	Title	Type	Date	Result	Vote totals		Subject	Short description
					Yes votes	No votes		
California continued	Proposition 72	LRCA	June 5, 2018	Passed	84%	16%	Environment/ Property Tax Assessments	This amendment allows the state legislature to exclude rainwater capture systems added after January 1, 2019, from property tax reassessments.
	Proposition 1	LR Bond Act	Nov. 6, 2018	Passed	56%	44%	Veterans' Housing	This measure authorizes $4 billion in general obligation bonds for housing-related programs, loans, grants, and housing loans for veterans.
	Proposition 2	LRSS	Nov. 6, 2018	Passed	63%	37%	Tax Revenue/ Homeless Housing	Ratifies existing law establishing the No Place Like Home Program, this finances permanent housing for individuals with mental illness who are homeless or at risk for chronic homelessness, as being consistent with the Mental Health Services Act approved by the electorate.
	Proposition 3	CISS	Nov. 6, 2018	Failed	49%	51%	Water Infrastructure/ Watershed Conservation	Would have authorized state general obligation bonds for various infrastructure projects.
	Proposition 4	CISS	Nov. 6, 2018	Passed	63%	37%	Children's Hospitals	"Authorized $1.5 billion in bonds for the construction, expansion, renovation, and equipping of children's hospitals in California."
	Proposition 5	CISS & CICA	Nov. 6, 2018	Failed	40%	60%	Property Tax Transfer	Would have amended Proposition 13 (1978) to change how tax assessments are transferred for homebuyers who are age 55 or older or severely disabled.
	Proposition 6	CICA	Nov. 6, 2018	Failed	43%	57%	Gas and Vehicle Taxes	The fuel tax increases and vehicle fees that were enacted in 2017, including the Road Repair and Accountability Act of 2017, were kept in place and allowing the state legislature to continue to impose, increase, or extend fuel taxes or vehicle fees through a two-thirds vote of each chamber and without voter approval.
	Proposition 7	LRSS	Nov. 6, 2018	Passed	60%	40%	Permanent Daylight Saving Time	Supports allowing the California State Legislature to (1) change the dates and times of the daylight saving time (DST) period, as consistent with federal law, by a two-thirds vote and (2) establish permanent, year-round DST in California by a two-thirds vote if federal law is changed to allow for permanent DST.
	Proposition 8	CISS	Nov. 6, 2018	Failed	40%	60%	Dialysis Clinics' Revenue	A no vote opposed requiring dialysis clinics to issue refunds to patients or patients' payers for revenue above 115 percent of the costs of direct patient care and healthcare improvements.
	Proposition 9	CISS	Nov. 6, 2018	Removed from ballot.			Split CA into 3 separate states.	The CA Supreme Court ordered Prop. 9 removed from the Nov. ballot in July of 2018 after "Significant questions have been raised regarding the proposition's validity…".
	Proposition 10	CISS	Nov. 6, 2018	Failed	41%	59%	Local Rent Control	This initiative failed, thus keeping the Costa-Hawkins Rental Housing Act and continuing to prohibit local governments from enacting rent control on certain buildings.
	Proposition 11	CISS	Nov. 6, 2018	Passed	60%	40%	Ambulance Employees Paid Breaks, Training, and Mental Health Services	Passage of this measure requires ambulance providers to require workers to remain on-call during breaks be paid at their regular rate; requires employers to provide additional training for EMTs and paramedics; and requiring employers to provide EMTs and paramedics with some paid mental health services.
	Proposition 12	CISS	Nov. 6, 2018	Passed	63%	37%	Farm Animal Confinement	This measure establishes minimum space requirements based on square feet for calves raised for veal, breeding pigs, and egg-laying hens and bans the sale of (a) veal from calves, (b) pork from breeding pigs, and (c) eggs from hens when the animals are confined to areas below minimum square-feet requirements.
Colorado	Amendment A	LRCA	Nov. 6, 2018	Passed	66%	34%	Slavery Prohibition	Removes part of the Colorado Constitution that says slavery and involuntary servitude are allowable for the punishment of a crime.
	Amendment V	LRCA	Nov. 6, 2018	Failed	36%	64%	Age Qualification for General Assembly Members	The amendment to reduce the age qualification from 25 to 21 for citizens to be members of the state House of Representatives or state Senate failed.
	Amendment W	LRCA	Nov. 6, 2018	Failed	54% (a)	46%	Judge Retention	The amendment required a 55% super majority to pass. It fell short of the required percentage. The measure would have shortened the ballot by allowing county clerks to use one judge retention question for each level of courts with individual judges listed as ballot items below the one judge retention question.

See footnotes at end of table

TABLE 6.9a
State Ballot Questions in 2018 (continued)

State or other jurisdiction	Title	Type	Date	Result	Vote totals		Subject	Short description
					Yes votes	No votes		
Colorado continued	Amendment X	LRCA	Nov. 6, 2018	Passed	61%	39%	Definition of Industrial Hemp	The amendment provides the state legislature with more flexibility in regulating the industrial hemp industry.
	Amendment Y	LRCA	Nov. 6, 2018	Passed	71%	29%	Independent Commission for Congressional Redistricting	Measure created an independent congressional redistricting commission responsible for redistricting Colorado's U.S. House districts. The commission is designed to include four members from the state's largest political party, four from the state's second largest political party, and four that are not affiliated with any political party.
	Amendment Z	LRCA	Nov. 6, 2018	Passed	71%	29%	Independent Commission for State Legislative Redistricting	The measure created a 12-member commission responsible for approving district maps for Colorado's state House of Representatives and state Senate districts.
	Proposition 109	CISS	Nov. 6, 2018	Failed	39%	61%	Transportation	Proposition would have authorized $3.5 billion in bonds with proceeds to be used exclusively for road and bridge expansion, construction, maintenance, and repair of specific statewide projects.
	Proposition 110	CISS	Nov. 6, 2018	Failed	41%	59%	Transportation/Sales Tax Increase	If passed this initiative would have authorized $6 billion in bonds to fund transportation projects, established the Transportation Revenue Anticipation Notes Citizen Oversight Committee, and raised the state sales tax rate by 0.62 percent from 2.9 percent (2018) to 3.52 percent for 20 years starting on January 1, 2019, through January 1, 2039.
	Proposition 111	CISS	Nov. 6, 2018	Passed	77%	23%	Payday Loans	This measure reduces the annual interest rate on payday loans to a yearly rate of 36 percent and eliminates all other finance charges and fees associated with payday lending.
	Proposition 112	CISS	Nov. 6, 2018	Failed	45%	55%	Distance Requirements for New Oil, Gas, and Fracking Projects	The initiative would have mandated new oil and gas development, including fracking, be a minimum distance of 2,500 feet from occupied buildings.
	Amendment 73	CISS & CICA	Nov. 6, 2018	Failed	46%	54%	Establish Income Tax Brackets	This initiative would have established a tax bracket system rather than a flat tax rate and raised taxes for individuals earning more than $150,000 per year, raised the corporate income tax rate, and created the Quality Public Education Fund.
	Amendment 74	CICA	Nov. 6, 2018	Failed	46%	54%	Decreased Property Value/ State Regulation	The initiative to require that property owners be compensated for any reduction in property value caused by state laws or regulations failed.
	Amendment 75	CICA	Nov. 6, 2018	Failed	34%	66%	Campaign Contribution Limits	If passed, this initiative would have provided that if any candidate for state office directed more than one million dollars in support of his/her own campaign, then every candidate for the same office in the same election may accept five times the amount of campaign contributions normally allowed.
Connecticut	Amendment 1	LRCA	Nov. 6, 2018	Passed	88%	12%	Transportation Revenue	Requires that all revenue placed in the state's Special Transportation Fund (STF) be used for transportation purposes, including the payment of transportation-related debts.
	Amendment 2	LRCA	Nov. 6, 2018	Passed	84%	16%	Legislative Requirements/State Properties	The amendment changes the process for passing conveyance legislation in Connecticut.
Delaware						No Ballot measures in 2018		
Florida	Amendment 1	LRCA	Nov. 6, 2018	Failed (b)	58%	42%	Homestead Exemption Increase	The amendment required a 60% super majority to pass. A simple majority vote supported exempting the portion of assessed home values between $100,000 and $125,000 from property taxes other than school taxes, bringing the maximum homestead exemption up to $75,000.
	Amendment 2	LRCA	Nov. 6, 2018	Passed	66%	34%	Nonhomestead Parcel Assessment	Passage of this amendment makes permanent the cap of 10 percent on annual nonhomestead parcel assessment increases set to expire on January 1, 2019.
	Amendment 3	CICA	Nov. 6, 2018	Passed	71%	29%	Casino Gambling	Provides voters with the "exclusive right to decide whether to authorize casino gambling in the State of Florida."

See footnotes at end of table

TABLE 6.9a
State Ballot Questions in 2018 (continued)

State or other jurisdiction	Title	Type	Date	Result	Vote totals Yes votes	Vote totals No votes	Subject	Short description
Florida continued	Amendment 4	CICA	Nov. 6, 2018	Passed	65%	35%	Voting Rights for Felons	Automatically restores the right to vote for people with prior felony convictions, except those convicted of murder or a felony sexual offense, upon completion of their sentences, including prison, parole, and probation.
	Amendment 5	LRCA	Nov. 6, 2018	Passed	66%	34%	Legislature/ Taxes/Fees	Requires a two-thirds vote of each chamber of the Florida State Legislature to enact new taxes or fees or increase existing ones.
	Amendment 6	CR	Nov. 6, 2018	Passed	62%	38%	Marsy's Law, Judicial Retirement Age, Interpretation of Laws and Rules	This amendment adds Marsy's Law to the Florida Constitution; increases judicial retirement age from 70 to 75; and prohibits state courts from deferring to an administrative agency's interpretation of a state statute or rule during a lawsuit.
	Amendment 7	CR	Nov. 6, 2018	Passed	66%	34%	Survivor Benefits/ College Fees/ State College System	This amendment requires employers to provide death benefits to the surviving spouses of first responders killed while engaged in official duties; requires a vote of the board of trustees and a vote of the board of governors to increase a college fee; and places the current structure of the state's system of higher education in the Florida Constitution.
	Amendment 9	CR	Nov. 6, 2018	Passed	69%	31%	Offshore Oil and Gas Drilling/Vaping in Workplaces	This amendment bans offshore drilling for oil and natural gas on lands beneath state waters and bans the use of vapor-generating electronic devices in indoor workplaces.
	Amendment 10	CR	Nov. 6, 2018	Passed	63%	37%	State and Local Government Structure	This amendment requires the legislature to provide for a state Department of Veterans Affairs; creates a state Office of Domestic Security and Counter-Terrorism; requires the legislature to convene a regular session on the second Tuesday of January of even-numbered years; and prohibits counties from abolishing certain local offices–sheriff, tax collector, property appraiser, supervisor of elections, and clerk of the circuit court–and requires elections for these offices.
	Amendment 11	CR	Nov. 6, 2018	Passed	62%	38%	Prohibition on Aliens' Property Ownership, Obsolete Provision and Criminal Statutes	Repeals the constitutional provision prohibiting foreign-born persons ineligible for citizenship from owning, inheriting, disposing, and possessing property; repeals an obsolete constitutional provision stating that a high-speed ground transportation system be developed in Florida; and deletes the constitutional provision that an amendment to a criminal statute does not affect the prosecution of a crime committed before the statute's amendment.
	Amendment 12	CR	Nov. 6, 2018	Passed	79%	21%	Lobbying Restrictions	Prohibits public officials from lobbying for compensation during the official's term in office and for six years after the official leaves office and prohibits public officials from using the office to obtain a disproportionate benefit.
	Amendment 13	CR	Nov. 6, 2018	Passed	69%	31%	Ban on Wagering on Dog Races	Prohibits wagering on live dog races, including greyhound races, held in Florida and banning dog races in Florida on which there is wagering.
Georgia	Amendment 1	LRCA	Nov. 6, 2018	Passed	83%	17%	Outdoor Recreation Equipment Sales Tax	Amends the state constitution to authorize the legislature to dedicate up to 80 percent of revenue from the sales and use tax on outdoor recreation equipment to the Georgia Outdoor Stewardship Trust Fund to fund land conservation.
	Amendment 2	LRCA	Nov. 6, 2018	Passed	69%	31%	Business Court	Establishes a state business court and establishes procedures and rules for judicial selection, term length, and judge qualifications for the court.
	Amendment 3	LRCA	Nov. 6, 2018	Passed	62%	38%	Forest/ Conservation and Timberland	Amends the state constitution to allow the legislature to change the formula used to calculate the tax on forest land conservation.
	Amendment 4	LRCA	Nov. 6, 2018	Passed	81%	19%	Marsy's Law	Amendment 4 provides, upon request, crime victims with specific rights. The amendment also explicitly states that the legislature is able to further define, expand, and provide for the enforcement of the rights.
	Amendment 5	LRCA	Nov. 6, 2018	Passed	71%	29%	Education/ Sales Tax	This amendment allows a school district(s) with a majority of enrolled students within a county to call for a referendum to levy a sales tax for education purposes.
	Referendum A	LRSS	Nov. 6, 2018	Passed	57%	43%	Property Tax Exemption	Provides for a homestead property tax exemption in certain municipalities.

See footnotes at end of table

TABLE 6.9a
State Ballot Questions in 2018 (continued)

State or other jurisdiction	Title	Type	Date	Result	Vote totals Yes votes	Vote totals No votes	Subject	Short description
Georgia continued	Referendum B	LRSS	Nov. 6, 2018	Passed	77%	23%	Housing Tax Exemption	This measure clarifies that an existing tax exemption for nonprofit housing for the mentally disabled can be applied to housing constructed or renovated through financing from businesses.
Hawaii	ConCon	(c)	Nov. 6, 2018	Failed	30%	70%	Constitutional Question	Opposed holding a constitutional convention to explore changes to the state constitution.
Idaho	Proposition 1	CISS	Nov. 6, 2018	Failed	46%	54%	Betting/ Instant Racing	A no vote was a vote against this measure to legalize the use of video terminals for betting on historical horse races, also known as instant racing.
	Proposition 2	CISS	Nov. 6, 2018	Passed	61%	39%	Medicaid Expansion	Passage expanded Medicaid eligibility to those under sixty-five years old whose income is 133 percent of the federal poverty level or below and who are not eligible for other state insurance coverage.
Illinois								No Ballot measures in 2018
Indiana	Public Question 1	LRCA	Nov. 6, 2018	Passed	71%	39%	Balanced Budget	Passage requires the state legislature to enact a balanced budget for each biennial budget period.
Iowa								No Ballot measures in 2018
Kansas								No Ballot measures in 2018
Kentucky	Marsy's Law Crime Victims Rights Amendment	LRCA	Nov. 6, 2018	(d)	63%	37%	Marsy's Law	The measure would have provided crime victims with specific constitutional rights. In a Kentucky Supreme Court ruling the amendment was set aside for being too vague.
Louisiana	Amendment 1	LRCA	Nov. 6, 2018	Passed	75%	25%	Felony Convictions/ Public Office	Prohibits convicted felons, unless pardoned, from seeking or holding a public office until five years after the completion of their sentences.
	Amendment 2	LRCA	Nov. 6, 2018	Passed	64%	36%	Felony Trials	This amendment requires the unanimous agreement of jurors, rather than just 10 of 12 jurors, to convict people charged with felonies.
	Amendment 3	LRCA	Nov. 6, 2018	Passed	56%	44%	State/Local Government	Amendment 3 allows political subdivisions of the state, through a written agreement, to exchange public equipment and personnel for an action or function the receiving subdivision is authorized to exercise.
	Amendment 4	LRCA	Nov. 6, 2018	Passed	56%	44%	Transportation Trust Fund	Passage ended the dedication of revenue from the Transportation Trust Fund to state police for traffic control.
	Amendment 5	LRCA	Nov. 6, 2018	Passed	72%	28%	Special Assessment for Homes in Trusts	Allows special assessments on a home in trust for a resident who is the settlor of the trust and is a disabled veteran or the surviving spouse of a person who died while performing their duties as a first responder, active duty member of the military, law enforcement officer, or fire protection officer.
	Amendment 6	LRCA	Nov. 6, 2018	Passed	58%	42%	Property Tax Increases	Requires that tax increases from reappraisals resulting in a property's value increasing more than 50 percent be phased in over the course of four years.
Maine	Question 1	CI	June 12, 2018	Passed	54%	46%	Ranked-Choice Voting	Approval of this measure had the effect of keeping Ranked-Choice Voting in place for general elections for U.S. senators and U.S. representatives. It also kept RCV in place for primary elections for U.S. senators, U.S. representatives, the governor, state senators, state representatives.
	Question 1	CISS	Nov. 6, 2018	Failed	37%	63%	Taxes for Home Care Program	Would have enacted a payroll tax and non-wage income tax to fund a program called the Universal Home Care Program.
	Question 2	LRBI	Nov. 6, 2018	Passed	55%	45%	Wastewater Infrastructure	Authorizes $30 million in bonds for wastewater infrastructure improvements
	Question 3	LRBI	Nov. 6, 2018	Passed	68%	32%	Transportation	Authorizes $106 million in bonds for transportation infrastructure projects.
	Question 4	LRBI	Nov. 6, 2018	Passed	54%	46%	University of Maine System	Authorizes $49 million in bonds for the construction and remodeling of existing and new facilities within the University of Maine System.
	Question 5	LRBI	Nov. 6, 2018	Passed	65%	35%	Community Colleges	Authorizes $15 million in bonds for improvements to instructional laboratories, information technology infrastructure, and heating/ventilating systems at Maine's community colleges.

See footnotes at end of table

TABLE 6.9a
State Ballot Questions in 2018 (continued)

State or other jurisdiction	Title	Type	Date	Result	Vote totals		Subject	Short description
					Yes votes	No votes		
Maryland	Question 1	LRCA	Nov. 6, 2018	Passed	89%	11%	Gambling Revenue/ Education	Authorizes changes to the state constitution to dedicate revenue from video lotteries to education.
	Question 2	LRCA	Nov. 6, 2018	Passed	68%	32%	Election-Day Registration	Authorizes amending the state constitution and authorizes the state legislature to enact a process for registering individuals to vote on election day.
Massachusetts	Question 1	IndISS	Nov. 6, 2018	Failed	30%	70%	Nurse & Patient Limits	Would have established patient limits for registered nurses in hospitals.
	Question 2	IndISS	Nov. 6, 2018	Passed	71%	29%	Advisory Commission/ U.S. Constitution	Establishes a 15-member citizens' commission to advocate for certain amendments to the United States Constitution regarding political spending and corporate personhood.
	Question 3	CI	Nov. 6, 2018	Passed	68%	32%	Gender Identity Anti-Discrimi- nation	This initiative upheld Senate Bill 2407, a bill that prohibits dis- crimination based on gender identity in public places–hotels, restaurants, and stores.
Michigan	Proposal 1	IndISS	Nov. 6, 2018	Passed	56%	44%	Marijuana Legalization	Legalized the recreational use and possession of marijuana for persons 21 years of age or older and enacts a tax on marijuana sales.
	Proposal 2	CICA	Nov. 6, 2018	Passed	61%	39%	Independent Redistricting Commission	Transfers power for drawing the state's congressional and legis- lative districts from the state legislature to an independent redistricting commission.
	Proposal 3	CICA	Nov. 6, 2018	Passed	67%	33%	Voting Policies/State Constitution	Adds eight voting policies to the Michigan Constitution, including straight-ticket voting, automatic voter registration, same-day voter registration, and no-excuse absentee voting.
Minnesota								No Ballot measures in 2018
Mississippi								No Ballot measures in 2018
Missouri	Proposition A	CI	Aug. 7, 2018	Failed	33%	67%	Right to Work	A "no" vote repealed Senate Bill 19, rejecting the right-to-work law mandating that no person can be required to pay dues to a labor union or join a labor union as a condition of employment.
	Amendment 1	CICA	Nov. 6, 2018	Passed	62%	38%	Lobbying, Campaign Finance, and Redistricting	Makes changes to the state lobbying laws, campaign finance limits for legislative candidates, and the legislative redistricting process.
	Amendment 2	CICA	Nov. 6, 2018	Passed	66%	34%	Medical Marijuana/ Veteran Healthcare/ Taxes	Legalized marijuana for medical purposes; taxes marijuana sales at 4 percent; and authorizes the tax revenue be spent on healthcare services for veterans.
	Amendment 3	CICA	Nov. 6, 2018	Failed	32%	68%	Medical Marijuana/ Biomedical R&D/Taxes	This amendment would have legalized marijuana for medical purposes; taxed marijuana sales at 15 percent and dedicated spending the tax revenue on a Biomedical Research and Drug Development Institute.
	Amendment 4	LRCA	Nov. 6, 2018	Passed	52%	48%	Managing and Advertising Bingo Games	Reduces the time required for a member to belong to an organi- zation and manage a bingo game for that organization from two years to six months and removes the ban on organizations advertising their bingo games.
	Proposition B	CISS	Nov. 6, 2018	Passed	62%	38%	Minimum Wage	Supports increasing the state's minimum wage each year until reaching $12 in 2023 and increases or decreases based on changes in the Consumer Price Index after 2023.
	Proposition C	CISS	Nov. 6, 2018	Failed	44%	56%	Medical Marijuana/ Veteran Healthcare/ Taxes	"Would have legalized medical marijuana; taxed marijuana sales at 2 percent; and spent the tax revenue on veterans' services, drug treatment, education, and law enforcement."
	Proposition D	LRSS	Nov. 6, 2018	Failed	46%	54%	Gas Tax Increase, Olympic Prize Tax Exemp- tion, and Traffic Reduction	A "no" vote opposed this measure to: incrementally increase the gas tax by 10 cents per gallon by June 2022, thereby leaving the rate at $0.17; exempt Olympic prizes from state taxes; and create a dedicated fund for certain road projects that reduce traffic bottle- necks that affect freight.

See footnotes at end of table

TABLE 6.9a
State Ballot Questions in 2018 (continued)

State or other jurisdiction	Title	Type	Date	Result	Vote totals Yes votes	Vote totals No votes	Subject	Short description
Montana	I-185	CISS	Nov. 6, 2018	Failed	47%	53%	Medicaid Expansion and Tobacco Taxes	The ballot initiative to extend Montana's Medicaid expansion and raise taxes on tobacco products was defeated allowing Medicaid expansion to expire on June 30, 2019.
	I-186	CISS	Nov. 6, 2018	Failed	44%	56%	Water Quality	Initiative would have established new requirements for hard rock mine permits based on standards for water quality in land restoration.
	LR-128	LRSS	Nov. 6, 2018	Passed	63%	37%	Property Tax	Renewed a six-mill tax on real estate and personal property to provide funding for the Montana University System.
	LR-129	LRSS	Nov. 6, 2018	Passed	63%	37%	Ballots/ Voting	Measure bans persons from collecting the election ballots of other people, with exceptions for certain individuals.
Nebraska	Initiative 427	CISS	Nov. 6, 2018	Passed	54%	46%	Medicaid/ Healthcare	This initiative requires the state to provide Medicaid for individuals under the age of 65 with incomes equal to or below 138 percent of the federal poverty line.
Nevada	Question 1	LRCA	Nov. 6, 2018	Passed	61%	39%	Marsy's Law	Adds specific rights of crime victims, together known as a Marsy's Law, to the Nevada Constitution.
	Question 2	LRSS	Nov. 6, 2018	Passed	56%	44%	Sales Tax Exemption/ Feminine Hygiene Products	Exempts feminine hygiene products from state and local sales taxes.
	Question 3	CICA	Nov. 6, 2018	Failed	33%	67%	Energy	Would have required electricity markets be open and competitive so all electricity customers have choices among providers.
	Question 4 (e)	CICA	Nov. 6, 2018	Passed	67%	33%	Healthcare/ Taxes	Requires the state legislature to exempt durable medical equipment, oxygen equipment, and mobility enhancing equipment prescribed by a licensed health care provider from sales and use tax.
	Question 5	CISS	Nov. 6, 2018	Passed	60%	40%	Voting	Provides for the automatic voter registration of eligible citizens when receiving services from the Nevada Department of Motor Vehicles.
	Question 6 (f)	CICA	Nov. 6, 2018	Passed	59%	41%	Energy	This initiative will require electric utilities to acquire 50 percent of their electricity from renewable resources by 2030 if it is passed again in the 2020 general election.
New Hampshire	Question 1 (g)	LRCA	Nov. 6, 2018	Passed	83%	17%	State /Local Government, Taxes	Gave taxpayers the right to take legal action against their state or local government to declare that the government spent, or has approved spending, public funds that are in violation of a law.
	Question 2 (g)	LRCA	Nov. 6, 2018	Passed	81%	19%	Government, Privacy	Establishes that individuals have a right to live free from governmental intrusion in their private or personal information.
New Jersey	Public Question 1	LRBI	Nov. 6, 2018	Passed	54%	46%	School Bond	Supports issuing $500 million in general obligation bonds for school project grants.
New Mexico	Question A	LRBI	Nov. 6, 2018	Passed	71%	29%	Senior Citizens	Authorizes $10.77 million in bonds for senior citizen facilities.
	Question B	LRBI	Nov. 6, 2018	Passed	69%	31%	Libraries	Authorizes $12.876 million in bonds for libraries.
	Question C	LRBI	Nov. 6, 2018	Passed	69%	31%	Schools	Authorizes $6.137 million in bonds to ensure all school buses have air conditioning.
	Question D	LRBI	Nov. 6, 2018	Passed	66%	34%	Schools/ Universities	Authorizes $136.230 million in bonds for institutions of higher education, special schools, and tribal schools.
	Amendment 1	LRCA	Nov. 6, 2018	Passed	58%	42%	Court System	Empowers the legislature to pass laws (1) setting the appeals process from probate courts and other inferior courts to higher courts and (2) determining which cases originating in inferior courts and tribunals fall under the appellate jurisdiction of district courts.
	Amendment 2	LRCA	Nov. 6, 2018	Passed	75%	25%	Governmental Ethics	Creates a seven-member state ethics commission charged with investigating alleged violations of ethical conduct by state officials, executive and legislative employees, candidates, lobbyists, government contractors.
New York					------- No Ballot measures in 2018 -------			
North Carolina	Income Tax Cap Amendment	LRCA	Nov. 6, 2018	Passed	57%	43%	Taxes	Lowers the maximum allowable state income tax rate from 10 percent to 7 percent.
	Judicial Selection Amendment	LRCA	Nov. 6, 2018	Failed	33%	67%	Judiciary	This amendment would have created a new process of filling judicial vacancies that occur between judicial elections for state courts. Its defeat allows the governor to continue to fill vacant seats on state courts.

See footnotes at end of table

TABLE 6.9a
State Ballot Questions in 2018 (continued)

State or other jurisdiction	Title	Type	Date	Result	Vote totals		Subject	Short description
					Yes votes	No votes		
North Carolina continued	Gubernatorial Appointments Amendment	LRCA	Nov. 6, 2018	Failed	38%	62%	Governor's Powers	Passage of this amendment would have removed the governor's power to make appointments to the Bipartisan State Board of Ethics and Elections Enforcement.
	Crime Victims Rights Amendment	LRCA	Nov. 6, 2018	Passed	62%	38%	Marsy's Law	Marsy's Law provides crime victims with specific rights.
	Right to Hunt and Fish Amendment	LRCA	Nov. 6, 2018	Passed	57%	43%	Hunting and Fishing	Creates a state constitutional right for North Carolina residents to hunt, fish, and harvest wildlife.
	Voter ID Amendment	LRCA	Nov. 6, 2018	Passed	55%	45%	Voter ID	Creates a constitutional requirement that voters present a photo ID to vote in person
North Dakota	Measure 1	CICA	Nov. 6, 2018	Passed	54%	46%	Ethics Commission	Establishes a five-member ethics commission, bans foreign political contributions, and enacts provisions related to lobbying and conflicts of interest.
	Measure 2	CICA	Nov. 6, 2018	Passed	66%	34%	Voting	Amends the North Dakota Constitution to "only a citizen" of the U.S. can vote in federal, state, and local elections.
	Measure 3	CISS	Nov. 6, 2018	Failed	40%	60%	Marijuana Legalization	The ballot initiative to legalize the recreational use of marijuana in the state of North Dakota for people 21 years of age or older and create an automatic expungement process for individuals with convictions for a controlled substance that has been legalized was defeated.
	Measure 4	CISS	Nov. 6, 2018	Passed	64%	36%	Volunteer Emergency Responders	This ballot initiative provides volunteer emergency responders in North Dakota with a special license plate and allows free entry to North Dakota state parks.
Ohio	Issue 1	LRCA	May 8, 2018	Passed	75%	25%	Congressional Redistricting Procedures Amendment	Changes the vote requirements to pass congressional redistricting maps and the standards used in congressional redistricting in Ohio.
	Issue 1	CICA	Nov. 6, 2018	Failed	37%	63%	Drug and Criminal Justice	This amendment was designed to reduce the number of people in state prisons for low-level, nonviolent crimes, such as drug possession and non-criminal probation violations.
Oklahoma	Question 788	IS	June 26, 2018	Passed	57%	43%	Medical Marijuana Legalization Initiative	A "yes" vote supported this measure to legalize the licensed cultivation, use, and possession of marijuana for medicinal purposes.
	Question 794	LRCA	Nov. 6, 2018	Passed	78%	22%	Marsy's Law	An amendment to ensure victim's rights.
	Question 798	LRCA	Nov. 6, 2018	Failed	46%	54%	Government/ Elections	The measure to amend the Oklahoma Constitution to provide for joint election of the governor and lieutenant governor was defeated, leaving the governor and lieutenant governor to each be elected with separate campaigns.
	Question 800	LRCA	Nov. 6, 2018	Failed	43%	57%	Tax Revenue	Would have amended the state constitution to establish a fund to investment 5 percent of the state's oil and gas development tax revenue and for the annual transfer of 4 percent of the fund's capital to the general fund.
	Question 801	LRCA	Nov. 6, 2018	Failed	49.6%	50.4%	Ad-Valorem Taxes	Opposed amending the state constitution to allow certain local voter-approved property taxes—known as ad valorem levies—to be used to fund school district operations as well as construction.
Oregon	Measure 101	CI	Jan. 23, 2018	Passed	62%	38%	Healthcare Insurance Premiums Tax for Medicaid Referendum	A "yes" vote supported upholding assessments/taxes on healthcare insurance and the revenue of certain hospitals to provide funding for Medicaid expansion by approving five sections of House Bill 2391. "Yes" vote approves temporary assessments on insurance companies, some hospitals, the Public Employees' Benefit Board, and managed care organizations. Assessments provide funding for health care for low-income individuals and families, and individuals with disabilities; also stabilize premiums charged by insurance companies for health insurance purchased by individuals and families. Insurance companies may not increase rates on health insurance premiums by more than 1.5 percent as a result of the assessments. Hospital assessments may not begin without approval by a federal agency.
	Measure 102	LRCA	Nov. 6, 2018	Passed	57%	43%	Affordable Housing	Amends the state constitution to allow counties, cities, and towns to use bond revenue to fund the construction of affordable housing without retaining complete ownership of the constructed housing. This is contingent upon voter approval.

See footnotes at end of table

TABLE 6.9a
State Ballot Questions in 2018 (continued)

State or other jurisdiction	Title	Type	Date	Result	Vote totals Yes votes	Vote totals No votes	Subject	Short description
Oregon continued	Measure 103	CICA	Nov. 6, 2018	Failed	43%	57%	Grocery Tax	The amendment to repeal the authority of state and local governments to enact taxes on groceries failed.
	Measure 104	CICA	Nov. 6, 2018	Failed	35%	65%	Revenue	This amendment would have applied the three-fifths supermajority vote requirement to changes to tax exemptions, credits, and deductions.
	Measure 105	CISS	Nov. 6, 2018	Failed	37%	63%	Sanctuary Laws	Keeps the state's sanctuary law which limits the cooperation of local law enforcement with federal immigration enforcement.
	Measure 106	CICA	Nov. 6, 2018	Failed	36%	64%	Abortion Funds	The ballot initiative to prohibit public funds from being spent on abortions in Oregon was defeated.
Pennsylvania					No Ballot measures in 2018			
Rhode Island	Question 1	LRBI	Nov. 6, 2018	Passed	77%	23%	Bonds for Schools	This measure authorizes $250 million in bonds over five years to fund school housing aid and the school building authority capital fund.
	Question 2	LRBI	Nov. 6, 2018	Passed	59%	41%	Higher Education	Authorized $70 million in bonds for higher education facilities.
	Question 3	LRBI	Nov. 6, 2018	Passed	79%	21%	Environment/ Infrastructure	Authorized $47.3 million in bonds for environmental, water, and recreational projects.
South Carolina	Amendment 1	LRCA	Nov. 6, 2018	Failed	40%	60%	Superinten- dent of Education	The constitutional amendment was defeated, keeping the position of state superintendent of education as an elected position instead of changing to an appointed position.
South Dakota	Amendment Y	LRCA	June 5, 2018	Passed	80%	20%	Changes to Marsy's Law Crime Victim Rights Amendment	Amendment Y made changes to the state's Marsy's Law constitutional amendment–Amendment S–approved by voters in 2016. The Marsy's Law amendment established certain rights for crime victims. Amendment Y made many of the rights guaranteed available if victims opt in, rather than requiring law enforcement and criminal justice officials to provide the rights unless victims opted out. It allowed law enforcement officials to share certain information with the public in order to assist in solving crimes or apprehending criminals. Amendment Y also contained provisions preventing any lawsuits from being filed against state or local government officials based on the Marsy's Law rights.
	Amendment W	CICA	Nov. 6, 2018	Failed	45%	65%	Lobbying, Government Accountability, and Initiative Process	The amendment would have revised campaign finance and lobbying laws, created a government accountability board, and established new laws governing the initiative and referendum process.
	Amendment X	LRCA	Nov. 6, 2018	Failed	54%	46%	Supermajority	This amendment would have required a 55 percent supermajority vote at the ballot to approve amendments to the state constitution. Its defeat leaves the requirement at a simple majority of 50 percent plus one vote.
	Amendment Z	LRCA	Nov. 6, 2018	Passed	62%	38%	Government	Amends the state constitution to require that all constitutional amendments concern only one subject.
	Measure 24	CISS	Nov. 6, 2018	Passed	56%	44%	Out-of-State Contributions to Ballot Questions	Vote was a vote in favor of banning individuals, political action committees, and other entities from outside South Dakota from making contributions to ballot question committees.
	Measure 25	CISS	Nov. 6, 2018	Failed	45%	55%	Tobacco Tax	This vote opposed increasing the tax on cigarettes from about $1.53 per pack of 20 cigarettes to $2.53 per pack of 20 cigarettes and and increasing the tax on wholesale tobacco products from 35 to 55 percent, with a portion of tobacco tax revenue dedicated to technical institutes.
Tennessee					No Ballot measures in 2018			
Texas					No Ballot measures in 2018			
Utah	Amendment A	LRCA	Nov. 6, 2018	Passed	79%	21%	Active Military Property Tax Exemption	This amendment changes the amount of time that must be served in the military under an order of active duty to receive a property tax exemption from 200 days in a calendar year (or 200 consecutive days) to 200 days in a 365-day period.
	Amendment B	LRCA	Nov. 6, 2018	Failed	28%	72%	Taxes/ Government	The measure would have amended the state constitution to allow property tax exemptions for properties leased by a local or state government entity.

See footnotes at end of table

TABLE 6.9a
State Ballot Questions in 2018 (continued)

State or other jurisdiction	Title	Type	Date	Result	Vote totals Yes votes	Vote totals No votes	Subject	Short description
Utah continued	Amendment C	LRCA	Nov. 6, 2018	Passed	63%	37%	Special Legislative Sessions	"This measure allows the state legislature to call a special session of up to ten days to deal with emergencies; it also allows a special session of the legislature to be held at a location other than the state capitol if it is not feasible due to a specified condition; and requires the governor to either (1) reduce state expenditures or (2) convene a special legislative session if the state's expenses exceed the state's revenue for a fiscal year."
	Nonbinding Opinion Question 1	CISS	Nov. 6, 2018	Failed	35%	65%	Gas Tax Increase	Measure advising the state legislature to pass a gas tax increase of 10 cents per gallon to fund local road construction and maintenance, thereby freeing up additional funding for education failed.
	Proposition 2	CISS	Nov. 6, 2018	Passed (h)	53%	47%	Medical Marijuana	Supports legalizing the medical use of marijuana for individuals with qualifying medical illnesses.
	Proposition 3	CISS	Nov. 6, 2018	Passed	53%	47%	Medicaid Expansion	This measure requires the state to do the following: Provide Medicaid for persons under the age of 65 and with incomes equal to or below 138 percent of the federal poverty line and increase the sales tax from 4.70 to 4.85 percent to finance the state's portion of the costs to expand Medicaid.
	Proposition 4	CISS	Nov. 6, 2018	Passed	50%	50%	Redistricting Commission	The measure creates a seven-member independent redistricting commission to draft and recommend to the Utah State Legislature maps for congressional and state legislative districts according to certain criteria.
Vermont					No Ballot measures in 2018			
Virginia	Question 1	LRCA	Nov. 6, 2018	Passed	71%	29%	Property Tax Exemption for Flood Abatement	Supports amending the state constitution to empower the state legislature to authorize local governments to provide a partial local property tax exemption for real estate subject to recurrent flooding that undertook improvements to prevent flooding or long-term damage from flooding.
	Question 2	LRCA	Nov. 6, 2018	Passed	84%	16%	Disabled Veteran Tax Exemption	Amends the state constitution to remove a restriction on where the surviving spouse of a disabled military veteran may have his or her principal place of residence in order to receive a property tax exemption.
Washington	Advisory Vote 19	(i)	Nov. 6, 2018	Failed	46%	54%	Oil Spill Tax	This would have repealed Senate Bill 6269, which applied a tax on crude oil and petroleum products when received through a pipeline.
	Initiative 1631	CISS	Nov. 6, 2018	Failed	43%	57%	Carbon Emissions Fee	This measure would have enacted a carbon emissions fee beginning on January 1, 2020; and used the revenue from the fee to fund various programs related to the environment.
	Initiative 1634	CISS	Nov. 6, 2018	Passed	56%	44%	Prohibit Local Taxes on Groceries	This measure prohibits local governments from enacting taxes on groceries.
	Initiative 1639	CISS	Nov. 6, 2018	Passed	59%	41%	Gun Ownership	This initiative implements restrictions on the purchase and ownership of firearms including raising the minimum age to purchase a gun to 21, adding background checks, increasing waiting periods, and enacting storage requirements.
	Initiative 940	CISS	Nov. 6, 2018	Passed	60%	40%	Police Training and Criminal Liability	This initiative creates a good faith test to determine when the use of deadly force by police is justifiable, requires police to receive de-escalation and mental health training, and requires law enforcement officers to provide first aid.
West Virginia	Amendment 1	LRCA	Nov. 6, 2018	Passed	52%	48%	Abortion	Adds language to the West Virginia Constitution stating that "nothing in this Constitution secures or protects a right to abortion or requires the funding of abortion."
	Amendment 2	LRCA	Nov. 6, 2018	Passed	72%	28%	Legislative Authority over Budgeting for State Judiciary	This amends the state constitution to authorize the legislature to reduce the budget of the state judiciary by up to 15 percent.
Wisconsin	Question 1	LRCA	Apr. 3. 2018	Failed	38%	62%	Executive Branch	Elimination of State Treasurer Amendment - A "no" vote opposed this amendment to eliminate the elected position of state treasurer.
Wyoming					No Ballot measures in 2018			
American Samoa					No Ballot measures in 2018			
Guam					No Ballot measures in 2018			
CNMI*					No Ballot measures in 2018			

See footnotes at end of table

TABLE 6.9a
State Ballot Questions in 2018 (continued)

State or other jurisdiction	Title	Type	Date	Result	Vote totals		Subject	Short description
					Yes votes	No votes		
Puerto Rico	--- No Ballot measures in 2018 ---							
U.S. Virgin Islands	--- No Ballot measures in 2018 ---							

Sources: The Council of State Governments' survey of state election sites. December 2018.

Key:
AQ–Advisory Question
BI–Bond Initiative
CI–Citizen Initiative/Referendum
CICA–Citizen Initiatated Constitutional Amendment
CISS–Citizen Initiative State Statute
CR–Commission Referred
ConCon–Constitution Convention
IndISS–Indirect Initiated State Statute
LR–Legislatively Referred
LRCA–Legislatively Referred Constitutional Amendment
LRSS–Legislatively Referred State Statute
a) This Amendment required a 55% super majority to pass. It fell short of the required percentage.
b) This Amendment required a 60% super majority to pass. It fell short of the required percentage.
c) Constitutional Convention question is automatically referred to the ballot every 10 years.

d) This amendment was ruled invalid because the entire text of the proposed constitutional amendment wasn't on the ballot, as is required by Kentucky state law. The Kentucky Supreme Court ruled that the one-sentence description to voters was inadequate.
e) In Nevada, citizen initiated constitutional amendments must be approved in two even-numbered election years. This measure was approved in 2016 and was approved again in 2018 to amend the Nevada Constitution.
f) In Nevada, citizen initiated constitutional amendments must be approved in two even-numbered election years. This measure was approved in 2018 and must be approved again in 2020 in order amend the Nevada Constitution.
g) A constitutional amendment must have a two-thirds (66.67 percent) supermajority vote of electors to be approved.
h) The Utah State Legislature may amend or make technical corrections to any initiated statute by a simple majority vote.
i) The measure was automatically referred to the ballot by Initiative 960, an initiative passed in 2007 to require an advisory vote about any law passed by the legislature that increases tax revenue.

TABLE 6.10
State Initiatives: Requesting Permission to Circulate a Petition

State or other jurisdiction	Applied to (a) Const. amdt.	Statute	Signatures required to request a petition (b) Const. amdt.	Statute	Request submitted to	Request form furnished by (c)	Restricted subject matter (d)	Individual responsible for petition Title	Summary	Financial contributions reported (e)	Deposits required (f)
Alabama	...	...	...	...	...	...	...	...	...	...	...
Alaska	...	I	...	100	LG	(p)	Y	LG	LG	Y	$100
Arizona	D	D	...	...	SS	SS	N	P, SP	P, SP	Y	N
Arkansas	D	D	...	...	AG	SP	N	AG	AG	Y	N
California	D	D	25 (g)	25 (g)	AG	...	Y	AG	AG	Y	$200
Colorado	D	D	...	...	SS	SS	N	(i)	(i)	Y	N
Connecticut	...	...	...	...	...	...	...	...	...	...	...
Delaware	...	...	...	...	...	...	...	...	...	...	...
Florida	D	...	...	...	SS	SP	N	SP	SP	Y	N (q)
Georgia	...	...	...	...	...	...	...	...	...	...	...
Hawaii	...	...	...	...	...	...	...	...	...	...	...
Idaho	...	D	...	20	SS	SP	N	AG	AG	Y	N
Illinois	D	...	...	...	...	...	Y	...	...	Y	N
Indiana	...	...	...	...	...	...	...	...	...	...	...
Iowa	...	...	...	...	...	...	...	...	...	...	...
Kansas	...	...	...	...	...	...	...	...	...	...	...
Kentucky	...	...	...	...	...	...	...	...	...	...	...
Louisiana	...	...	...	...	...	...	...	...	...	...	...
Maine	...	I	...	6 (j)	SS	SS	Y	P	SS	Y	N
Maryland	...	...	...	(k)	SS (l)	SBE	Y	...	...	Y	N
Massachusetts	I	I	10	10	AG	SS	Y	AG	AG	Y	N
Michigan	D	I	...	...	SS	...	Y	SP	SP	Y	N
Minnesota	...	...	...	...	...	...	...	...	...	...	...
Mississippi	D	...	...	...	SS	...	Y	AG	AG	Y	$500
Missouri	D	D	...	...	SS	SP	Y	SS, AG	SS, AG	Y	N
Montana	D	D	...	...	SS (o)	SP	Y	AG	AG	Y	N
Nebraska	D	D	...	...	SS	SP	Y	SP	SP	Y	N
Nevada	D	I	...	...	SS	SS	Y	P, SP	P, SP	Y	N
New Hampshire	...	...	...	...	...	...	...	...	...	...	...
New Jersey	...	...	...	...	...	...	...	...	...	...	...
New Mexico	...	...	...	...	...	...	...	...	...	...	...
New York	...	...	...	...	...	...	...	...	...	...	...
North Carolina	...	...	...	...	...	...	...	...	...	...	...
North Dakota	D	D	25	25	SS	SP	N	SS, AG	SS	Y (e)	N
Ohio	D	I	1,000	1,000	AG	(m)	Y	(m)	(m)	Y	N
Oklahoma	D	D	...	...	SS, AG	O	N	P	P	Y	N
Oregon	D	D	1,000	1,000	SS	SS	N	AG	AG	Y	N
Pennsylvania	...	...	...	...	...	...	...	...	...	...	...
Rhode Island	...	...	...	...	...	...	...	...	...	...	...
South Carolina	...	...	...	...	...	...	...	...	...	...	...
South Dakota	D	D	...	...	SS	SS	Y	AG	AG	Y	N
Tennessee	...	...	...	...	...	...	...	...	...	...	...
Texas	...	...	...	...	...	...	...	...	...	...	...
Utah	...	D, I	...	5 SP	LG	LG	N	SP	SP	Y	N
Vermont	...	...	...	...	...	...	...	...	...	...	...
Virginia	...	...	...	...	...	...	...	...	...	...	...
Washington	...	D, I	...	...	SS	SP	N	AG	AG	Y	$5
West Virginia	...	...	...	...	...	...	...	...	...	...	...
Wisconsin	...	...	...	...	...	...	...	...	...	...	...
Wyoming	...	I	...	100	SS	SS	Y	SS	SS	Y	$500
American Samoa	...	...	...	...	...	...	...	...	...	...	...
CNMI*	D	I	...	...	AG	AG	Y	SP	SP	Y	N
Puerto Rico	...	D	...	...	SBE	(n)	N	(n)	(n)	Y	$500
U.S. Virgin Islands	D	...	...	...	SBE	SBE	Y	SBE	SBE	Y	N

See footnotes at end of table

TABLE 6.10

State Initiatives: Requesting Permission to Circulate a Petition (continued)

Sources: The Council of State Governments' survey of state election website, Initiative & Referendum Institute website and Ballotpedia website, May 2019.

*Commonwealth of the Northern Mariana Islands

Key:

...–No provision

AG–Attorney General

D–Direct initiative

O–Other

I–Indirect initiative

P–Proponent

EV–Eligible voters

ST–State

LG–Lieutenant Governor

SP–Sponsor

SS–Secretary of State

Y–Yes

SBE–State Board of Elections

N–No

(a) An initiative may provide a constitutional amendment or develop a new statute, and may be formed either directly or indirectly. The direct initiative allows a proposed measure to be placed on the ballot after a specific number of signatures have been secured on a petition. The indirect initiative must first be submitted to the legislature for decision after the required number of signatures have been secured on a petition, prior to placing the proposed measure on the ballot.

(b) Prior to circulating a statewide petition, a request for permission to do so must first be submitted to a specified state officer.

(c) The form on which the request for petition is submitted may be the responsibility of the sponsor or may be furnished by the state.

(d) Restrictions may exist regarding the subject matter to which an initiative may be applied. The majority of these restrictions pertain

to the dedication of state revenues and appropriations, and laws that maintain the preservation of public peace, safety, and health. In Illinois, amendments are restricted to "structural and procedural subjects contained in" the legislative article.

(e) In some states, a list of financial contributors and the amount of their contributions must be submitted to the specified state officer with whom the petition is filed. In North Dakota, must report any contributions and/or expenditures in excess of $100. Must also report the gross total of all contributions received and gross totals of all expenditures made. Must give total cash on hand in the filer's account at the start and close of a reporting period.

(f) A deposit may be required after permission to circulate a petition has been granted. This amount is refunded when the completed petition has been filed correctly.

(g) Signatures required to seek assistance of Office of Legislative Counsel in drafting measure before filing with the Attorney General's office.

(h) The secretary of state charges a 10 cent fee per signature that must be verified for ballot consideration.

(i) Title Setting Board–secretary of state, attorney general, director of legislative legal services.

(j) The signature of six voters.

(k) Three percent of the total qualified voters from the last gubernatorial election.

(l) Secretary of state accepts and turns over to State Board of Elections.

(m) Petitioners must prepare the summary and submit it to the Ohio Attorney General, who then must certify whether the summary fully and accurately describes the proposal.

(n) Office of the Supervisor of Elections Titling Board.

(o) After submitted, the secretary of state transfers it over to the Legislative Services Division.

(p) Division of Elections.

TABLE 6.11
State Initiatives: Circulating the Petition

State or other jurisdiction	Basis for signatures (see key below) Const. amdt.	Statute	Maximum time period allowed for petition circulation (a)	Can signatures be removed from petition (b)	Completed petition filed with	Days prior to election Const. amdt.	Statute
Alabama	...	...	...	...	...	...	...
Alaska	...	10% TV from 3/4 SLD (c)	1 yr.	Y	LG	...	...
Arizona	15% VG	10% VG	2 yr.	Y	SS	4 mos.	4 mos.
Arkansas	10% VG (d)	8% VG (d)	...	N	SS	120 days	...
California	8% VG	5% VG	150 days	Y	(e)	131 days	131 days
Colorado	5% VSS	5% VSS	6 mos. (3 mos prior to election)	Y	SS	90 days	90 days
Connecticut	...	...	...	...	...	...	...
Delaware	...	...	...	...	...	...	...
Florida	8% VEP, 8% from 1/2 CD	...	2 yr.	N	SS	Feb. 1 (f)	...
Georgia	...	...	...	...	...	...	...
Hawaii	...	...	...	...	...	...	...
Idaho	...	6% EV (cc)	(g)	Y	SS	...	4 mos.
Illinois	8% VG	...	18 mos. prior to election	Y	SBE	6 mos.	...
Indiana	...	...	...	...	...	...	...
Iowa	...	...	...	...	...	...	...
Kansas	...	...	...	...	...	...	...
Kentucky	...	...	...	...	...	...	...
Louisiana	...	...	...	...	...	...	...
Maine	...	10% VG	1 yr.	...	SS	...	(h)
Maryland	...	...	...	...	...	...	...
Massachusetts	3% VG, no more than 25% from 1 county	3% VG, no more than 25% from 1 county (i) 8% VG	From 3rd Wed. in Sept. to 1st Wed. in Dec. (k)	Y (j)	SS (k)	(i)	(l)
Michigan	10% VG no more than 15% from each CD	8%VG, no more than 15% from each CD	180 days	N (m)	SS	120 days	160 days
Minnesota	...	...	...	...	(e)	...	...
Mississippi	12% VG (n)	...	1 yr.	Y	SS (e)	90 days prior to LS	...
Missouri	8% VG, 8% each from 2/3 CD	5% VG, 5% each from 2/3 CD	Approx. 18 mos.	Y	SS	6 mos.	6 mos.
Montana	10% VG and 10% in 40 of the SLD	5% VG and 5% in 34 of the SLD	(o)	Y	SS	(o)	(o)
Nebraska	10% EV	7% EV	...	Y	SS	4 mos.	4 mos.
Nevada	10% TV (p)	10% TV (p)	(q)	Y	SS	90 days	30 days prior to LS
New Hampshire	...	...	...	...	...	...	...
New Jersey	...	...	...	...	...	...	...
New Mexico	...	...	...	...	...	...	...
New York	...	...	...	...	...	...	...
North Carolina	...	...	...	...	...	...	...
North Dakota	4% resident population (r)	2% resident population (r)	1 yr.	N	SS	120 days	120 days
Ohio	10% VG, 5% each from 1/2 counties	3% VG, 1.5% each from 1/2 counties	...	Y	SS	90 days	(s)
Oklahoma	15% VG (t)	8% VG (t)	90 days	N	SS	60 days	60 days
Oregon	8% VG	6% VG	...	Y (u)	SS	4 mos.	4 mos.
Pennsylvania	...	...	...	...	...	...	...
Rhode Island	...	...	...	...	...	...	...
South Carolina	...	...	...	...	...	...	...
South Dakota	10% VG	5% VG	(v)	N	SS	...	...
Tennessee	...	...	...	...	...	...	...
Texas	...	...	...	...	...	...	...
Utah	...	10% VEP, 10% each from 26 of 29 senate districts (w)	316 days	Y	LG	...	June 1
Vermont	...	...	...	...	...	...	...
Virginia	...	...	...	...	...	...	...
Washington	...	8% VG	6 to 9 mos. (x)	N	SS	...	(y)
West Virginia	...	...	...	...	...	...	...
Wisconsin	...	...	...	...	...	...	...
Wyoming	...	15% TV, from 2/3 counties	18 mos.	Y	SS	...	120 days
American Samoa	...	...	...	...	...	...	...
CNMI*	50% (z)	20%	(aa)	Y	...	...	...
Puerto Rico	...	(bb)	...	...	...	...	...
U.S. Virgin Islands	...	10 % ED	180 days	Y	SS	...	6 mos.

See footnotes at end of table

TABLE 6.11
State Initiatives: Circulating the Petition (continued)

Sources: The Council of State Governments' survey of state election
website, Initiative & Referendum Institute website and Ballotpedia
website, May 2019.
*Commonwealth of the Northern Mariana Islands
Key:
...–No provision.
VG–Total votes cast for the position of governor in the last election.
EV–Eligible voters.
VH–Total votes cast for the office receiving the highest number of
votes in last general election.
TV–Total voters in last election.
VSS–Total votes cast for all candidates for the office of secretary of
state at the previous general election.
VEP–Total votes cast in the state as a whole on the last presidential
election.
ED–Election district.
CD–Congressional district.
SBE–State Board of Elections.
SLD–State legislative district for house.
LG–Lieutenant Governor.
SS–Secretary of State.
LS–Legislative session.
Y–Yes.
N–No.
T–Tuesday.
(a) The petition circulation period begins when petition forms have been
approved and provided to sponsors. Sponsors are those individuals
granted permission to circulate a petition, and are therefore
responsible for the validity of each signature on a given petition.
(b) Should an individual wish to remove his/her name from a petition,
a request to do so must be submitted in writing to the state officer
with whom the petition is filed.
(c) Signed by qualified voters who are equal in number to at least ten
per cent of those who voted in the preceding general election, who
are resident in at least three-fourths of the house districts of the
State, and who, in each of those house districts, are equal in number
to at least seven percent of those who voted in the preceding
general election in the house district.
(d) Distributed across at least 15 counties.
(e) County elections officials.
(f) February 1 of the general election year.
(g) Eighteen months from receipt of ballot title or April 30 of year of
election on initiative, whichever occurs first.
(h) To be placed on November ballot, petitions must be submitted to
SS by 5:00 p.m. on 50th day after convening of Legislature in 1st
regular session, or by 5:00 p.m. on 25th day in 2nd regular session.
(i) First Wednesday in December.
(j) Should an individual wish to remove his/her name from a petition,
a request to do so must be submitted in writing to the local
election official before the petition is submitted for certification of
signatures.
(k) Petitions first must be submitted to local municipal clerks for
signature certification.
(l) After legislative inaction, petitions must be filed no later than the
1st Wednesday in July, signed by not less than 1/2 of 1 percent of
the last vote cast for governor.

(m) Not after petition has been filed.
(n) the signatures must be distributed among the state's
Congressional districts. If less than the minimum in any one district,
the entire petition will be ruled invalid.
(o) There is a maximum of one year to circulate petitions and receive
certification from county election officials. The county officials must
submit each verified petition to the secretary of state by the final
filing deadline, which is the third Friday of the fourth month prior
to the election. Proponents must submit their petitions to county
officials no sooner than nine months and no later than four weeks
prior to the final filing deadline.
(p) In each "petition district" (per SB 212, effective 2009) which are
set the same as Congressional districts.
(q) Each have different deadlines and circulation periods.
Amendments: Initial filing cannot be made before Sept. 1 of the
year preceding the election year and the petition must be filed
with the county officials by the third Tuesday in June of an even-
numbered year. Statues: Initial filing cannot be made before Jan.
1 of the year preceding the next regular legislative session and the
petition must be filed with county officials by the second Tuesday in
November of an even-numbered year.
(r) Percentage of resident population of the state at the last federal
decennial census.
(s) Ten days prior to commencement of General Assembly session
for initial filing; second petition must be filed within 90 days after
General Assembly takes no action, fails to enact or passes amended
form; the petition is filed with the secretary of state.
(t) In 2012, voters approved a constitutional amendment placed on
the ballot by the legislature that changed the signature requirement
from percentage of votes cast for the office receiving the highest
number of votes in last general election to percentage of votes cast
for position of governor in the last election.
(u) Only by the chief petitioners before submitting signatures for
verification. Signatures many not be removed once the signatures
have been submitted to the Secretary of State.
(v) No more than 24 months preceding the election date specified on
the petition, however petition is submitted 12 months before the
election.
(w) Five percent in both categories for indirect.
(x) Six months for direct initiative and nine months for indirect
initiative. Signatures for direct initiatives are due at least four month
prior to the general election. Signatures for indirect initiatives are
due at least 10 days prior to the beginning of the session.
(y) Initiatives to the legislature must be turned in 10 days before the
legislature convenes. If the legislature does not act, the initiative
goes to the next General Election ballot.
(z) At least 25 percent in each senate district.
(aa) Until 120 days before the date of the election.
(bb) Ten percent district and 41 percent territorial.
(cc) Geographic distribution shall be as follows: 6% of the qualified
electors at the time of the last general election in each of at least
18 legislative districts; provided however, the total number of
signatures shall be equal to or greater than 6% of the qualified
electors in the state at the time of the last general election.

TABLE 6.12

State Initiatives: Preparing the Initiative to be Placed on the Ballot

State or other jurisdiction	Signatures verified by: (a)	Within how many days after filing	Number of days to amend/appeal a petition that is:		Penalty for falsifying petition (denotes fine, jail term)	Petition certified by: (d)
			Incomplete (b)	Not Accepted (c)		
Alabama	…	…	…	…	…	…
Alaska	Division of Elections	60 days	…	…	Class B misdemeanor	LG
Arizona	County recorder	(e)	…	…	Class 1 misdemeanor	SS
Arkansas	SS	30 days	30 days	30 days	Class A misdemeanor	SS
California	County clerk	30 days	…	…	Felony or misdemeanor (depending on severity)	SS
Colorado	SS	30 days	10 days	…	(f)	SS
Connecticut	…	…	…	…	…	…
Delaware	…	…	…	…	…	…
Florida	Supervisor of elections	N.A.	N.A.	N.A.	First degree misdemeanor	SS
Georgia	…	…	…	…	…	…
Hawaii	…	…	…	…	…	…
Idaho	County clerk	60 days	…	10 days	$5,000, 2 yrs.	SS
Illinois	SBE (g)	…	(h)	(h)	Class 3 felony	SBE
Indiana	…	…	…	…	…	…
Iowa	…	…	…	…	…	…
Kansas	…	…	…	…	…	…
Kentucky	…	…	…	…	…	…
Louisiana	…	…	…	…	…	…
Maine	Registrar of voters	…	…	…	…	SS
Maryland	…	…	…	…	…	…
Massachusetts	Local board of registrar	2 weeks	…	…	$1,000, 1 yr.	SS
Michigan	SS	Approx. 60 days	…	…	$500, 90 days	BSC
Minnesota	…	…	…	…	…	…
Mississippi	Circuit clerk	…	10 days	10 days	$1,000, 1 yr.	CC
Missouri	County clerk	63 days	…	10 days	Class A misdemeanor	SS
Montana	County election administrators	4 weeks	10 days	10 days	$500, 6 mos.	SS
Nebraska	County clerk	40 days	…	…	…	SS
Nevada	County clerk	(i)	5 days (j)	…	…	SS
New Hampshire	…	…	…	…	…	…
New Jersey	…	…	…	…	…	…
New Mexico	…	…	…	…	…	…
New York	…	…	…	…	…	…
North Carolina	…	…	…	…	…	…
North Dakota	SS	35 days	…	…	(k)	SS
Ohio	County board of elections	10 days	10 days	…	5th degree felony	SS
Oklahoma	SS	…	10 days	…	$1,000, 1 yr.	SS
Oregon	County clerk	30 days	(l)	…	(m)	SS
Pennsylvania	…	…	…	…	…	…
Rhode Island	…	…	…	…	…	…
South Carolina	…	…	…	…	…	…
South Dakota	SS	…	…	…	Class 1 misdemeanor	SBE
Tennessee	…	…	…	…	…	…
Texas	…	…	…	…	…	…
Utah	County clerk	30 days	…	14 days	Class A misdemeanor	LG
Vermont	…	…	…	…	…	…
Virginia	…	…	…	…	…	…
Washington	SS	…	5 days	5	Fine or imprisonment	SS
West Virginia	…	…	…	…	…	…
Wisconsin	…	…	…	…	…	…
Wyoming	SS	60 days	30 days	30 days	$1,000, 1 yr.	SS
American Samoa	…	…	…	…	…	…
CNMI*	Election Commission	(n)	30 days (o)	119 days	(p)	AG
Puerto Rico	Office of the Supervisor of Elections	15 days	3 days	…	…	SBE
U.S. Virgin Islands	Office of the Supervisor of Elections	15 days	7 days	…	…	Office of the Supervisor of Elections

See footnotes at end of table

TABLE 6.12

State Initiatives: Preparing the Initiative to be Placed on the Ballot (continued)

Sources: The Council of State Governments' survey of state election website, Initiative & Referendum Institute website and Ballotpedia website, May 2019.

*Commonwealth of the Northern Mariana Islands

Key:

…–No provision.

N.A.–Not Applicable.

CC–Circuit Clerk.

SS–Secretary of State.

LG–Lieutenant Governor.

BSC–Board of State Canvassers.

SBE–State Board of Elections.

(a) The validity of the signatures, as well as the correct number of required signatures must be verified before the initiative is allowed on the ballot.

(b) If an insufficient number of signatures is submitted, sponsors may amend the original petition by filing additional signatures within a given number of days after filing. If the necessary number of signatures has not been submitted by this date, the petition is declared void.

(c) In some cases, the state officer will not accept a valid petition. In such a case, sponsors may appeal this decision to the Supreme Court, where the sufficiency of the petition will be determined. If the petition is determined to be sufficient, the initiative is required to be placed on the ballot.

(d) A petition is certified for the ballot when the required number of signatures has been submitted by the filing deadline, and are determined to be valid.

(e) Removal of petition and ineligible signatures by Secretary of State's office 20 days, certification by County Recorder 15 days after receipt from secretary of State's office.

(f) Secretary conducts hearing, then turns over to the attorney general for investigation/possible criminal prosecution.

(g) State Board of Elections and County Clerks or Municipal Boards of Election Commissioners. Individual petition sheets must be from a single jurisdiction. The SBE verifies that all signatures are from a single jurisdiction and the County Clerks or Municipal Boards verify the signatures against their registration files.

(h) Amendments are not permitted. Judicial review must be sought within ten days after determination be State Board of Elections.

(i) 1. Within four days county clerk totals the number of signatures and forwards to the secretary of state. 2. The secretary of state immediately notifies county clerks if they are to proceed or not proceed with the signature verification. 3. If ordered by the secretary of state, the county clerks verify signatures within nine days (excluding weekends and holidays).

(j) In Nevada, appeal must be within 5 working days after SS determines the petition is not sufficient.

(k) Any violations discovered will be reported to the attorney general for investigation and prosecution.

(l) Additional signatures may be submitted if signatures were turned in prior to deadline for submitting signatures.

(m) Whether a penalty is assessed would be based upon what information on the petition was falsified.

(n) Within 90 days before the date of election.

(o) 30 days if submitted 150 days before the date of the election. No amendment/appeal if submitted 120 days before the date of election.

(p) Subject to statute governing fraud and perjury.

TABLE 6.13
State Initiatives: Voting on the Initiative

State or other jurisdiction	Ballot (a)		Election where initiative voted on	Effective date of approved initiative (b) Const. amdt.	Statute	Days to contest election results (c)	Can an approved initiative be:			Can a defeated initiative be refiled?
	Title by:	Summary by:					Amended?	Vetoed?	Repealed?	
Alabama	...	...	...	...	...	...	...	...	...	...
Alaska	LG	LG	GE, PR or SP	...	90 days (d)	10	Y	N	Y (e)	N
Arizona	SS, AG	SS, AG	GE	...	IM (f)	5	(g)	N	N	Y
Arkansas	AG	AG	GE	30 days	30 days	20	Y	N	Y	Y
California	AG	AG	GE	1 day (h)	1 day (h)	5 (d)	Y (i)	N	Y (i)	Y
Colorado	TB (j)	TB (j)	GE, Odd year	30 days	30 days	10	N (k)	N (k)	N (k)	...
Connecticut	...	...	...	...	...	...	...	...	...	...
Delaware	...	...	...	...	...	...	...	...	...	...
Florida	SP	SP	GE	(m)	...	10	Y (n)	N	Y (n)	Y
Georgia	...	...	...	...	...	...	...	...	...	...
Hawaii	...	...	...	...	...	...	...	...	...	...
Idaho	AG	AG	GE	...	IM	20	Y	N	Y	Y
Illinois	...	SS (o)	GE	...	...	30	(p)	...	...	Y
Indiana	...	...	...	...	...	...	...	...	...	...
Iowa	...	...	...	...	...	...	...	...	...	...
Kansas	...	...	...	...	...	...	...	...	...	...
Kentucky	...	...	...	...	...	...	...	...	...	...
Louisiana	...	...	...	...	...	...	...	...	...	...
Maine	Sponsor, SS	SS	REG or SP	...	30 days (f)	5	Y	N	Y	...
Maryland	...	...	...	...	...	...	...	...	...	...
Massachusetts	AG	AG	GE	30 days	30 days	10	Y	Y	Y	after 2 biennial elections
Michigan	BSC	BSC	GE	45 days	10 days	2 (r)	Y	N	Y	Y
Minnesota	...	...	...	...	...	...	...	...	...	...
Mississippi	AG	AG	GE	30 days	...	...	Y (s)	Y (s)	N	after 2 yrs.
Missouri	SS, AG	SS, AG	GE	30 days	IM	30 (r)	Y	N	Y	Y
Montana	AG	AG	GE	Jul. 1	Oct. 1	1 yr.	Y	N	Y	Y
Nebraska	AG	AG	GE	10 days	10 days	40	Y	N	Y	N (t)
Nevada	SS, AG	SS, AG	GE	(u)	(u)	14	(v)	(v)	(v)	Y
New Hampshire	...	...	...	...	...	...	...	...	...	...
New Jersey	...	...	...	...	...	...	...	...	...	...
New Mexico	...	...	...	...	...	...	...	...	...	...
New York	...	...	...	...	...	...	...	...	...	...
North Carolina	...	...	...	...	...	...	...	...	...	...
North Dakota	SS, AG	SS	PR or GE	30 days	30 days (w)	14	(x)	N	(x)	Y
Ohio	Ohio Ballot Board	(y)	GE	30 days	30 days	15	(z)	N	N	Y
Oklahoma	AG	P	GE or SP	IM	IM	...	Y	Y	Y	after 3 yrs. (aa)
Oregon	AG	AG	GE	30 days	30 days	40	Y	Y	Y	Y
Pennsylvania	...	...	...	...	...	...	...	...	...	...
Rhode Island	...	...	...	...	...	...	...	...	...	...
South Carolina	...	...	...	...	...	...	...	...	...	...
South Dakota	AG	AG	GE	(bb)	(bb)	...	Y	N	N	Y
Tennessee	...	...	...	...	...	...	...	...	...	...
Texas	...	...	...	...	...	...	...	...	...	...
Utah	LLS	LLS	GE	...	5 days (cc)	40	Y	N	N	after 2 yrs.
Vermont	...	...	...	...	...	...	...	...	...	...
Virginia	...	...	...	...	...	...	...	...	...	...
Washington	AG	AG	GE	...	30 days	10 days	Y (l)	...	Y (l)	Y
West Virginia	...	...	...	...	...	...	...	...	...	...
Wisconsin	...	...	...	...	...	...	...	...	...	...
Wyoming	SS	SS, AG	GE 120 days after LS	...	90 days	15 after Canvass	Y	N	after 2 yrs.	after 5 yrs.
American Samoa	...	...	...	...	...	...	...	...	...	...
CNMI*	AG	AG	GE	(q)	(q)	30	...	...	...	Y
Puerto Rico	LC	AG, LLS	GE	...	IM	...	Y	...	...	Y
U.S. Virgin Islands	Office of Supervisor of Elections	Office of Supervisor of Elections	Any election	IM	IM	7	(v)	...	(v)	Y

See footnotes at end of table

TABLE 6.13
State Initiatives: Voting on the Initiative (continued)

Sources: The Council of State Governments' survey of state election
website, Initiative & Referendum Institute website and Ballotpedia
website, May 2019.
*Commonwealth of Northern Mariana Islands
Key:
…–No provision
LG–Lieutenant Governor
SS–Secretary of State
AG–Attorney General
P–Proponent
LC–Legislative Council
LLS–Legislative Legal Services
BSC–Board of State Canvassers
SBE–State Board of Elections
PR–Primary election
GE–General election
REG–Regular election
SP–Special election
IM–Immediately
LS–Legislative session
TB–Title Board
Y–Yes
N–No
w/i–Within

(a) In some states, the ballot title and summary will differ from that
on the petition.
(b) A majority of the popular vote is required to enact a measure. In
Massachusetts and Nebraska, apart from satisfying the requisite
majority vote, the measure must receive, respectively, 30% and
35% of the total votes cast in favor. An initiative approved by the
voters may be put into effect immediately after the approving
votes have been canvassed. In California and Nebraska, the measure may specify an enacting date. In Colorado, measures take
effect from the date of proclamation by governor, but no later than
30 days after votes have been canvassed and certified by secretary
of state. In Nebraska, 10 days after completion of canvass by the
State Board of Canvassers.
(c) Individuals may contest the results of a vote on an initiative
within a certain number of days after the election including the
measure proposed.
(d) After certification of election.
(e) May not be repealed within 2 years of its effective date.
(f) Upon governor's proclamation.
(g) Initiative can be amended by three-fourths of the members of
each house of the legislature (AZ Constitution Article 4, Part 1,
Section14.
(h) Unless the measure requires otherwise.
(i) Changes must be submitted to voters unless the measure provided for legislative amendment or repeal.
(j) Ballot title: Drafted by Legislative Council of the General Assembly, then finalized by three board members called the Title Board.
Summary by: Legislative Council of the General Assembly.
(k) If it is statutory it can be changed by the legislature.

(l) No initiated statute can be amended or repealed within 2 years
without a two-thirds super majority in both chambers. Any initiated law so amended is not subject to veto referendum.
(m) It is effective the first Tuesday after the first Monday in January
following election unless specified in the amendment.
(n) Amendments or repeal must be voted on by the voters.
(o) Subject to approval of the Attorney General.
(p) Changing a constitutional amendment would require another
constitutional amendment.
(q) Effective upon approval by voters and certification of election
result by Election Commission: usually 15 days after date of election or later if there is an election contest.
(r) After election is certified.
(s) The approved initiative to amend the Constitution can be
adopted, amended or rejected by the legislature or no action can
be taken. In all cases, the initiative and alternative adopted are
placed on the next statewide general election ballot.
(t) Not on next ballot.
(u) Constitutional amendment–after passed twice by the voters it
becomes effective upon the completion of the canvass of votes by
the Supreme Court on the fourth Tuesday of November following
the election. Statute–effective on the date approved by the governor or the canvass of the vote by the Supreme Court.
(v) It cannot be amended or repealed within three years from the
date it takes effect.
(w) An initiative to repeal a statute is effective immediately following the election.
(x) A measure approved by the electors may not be amended or
repealed by the legislative assembly for seven years from its effective date, except by a two-thirds vote of the members elected to
each house; majority vote thereafter.
(y) No summary, but the Ohio Ballot Board prescribes the ballot language. Also explanations and arguments for and against the
proposal may be prepared by the petitioner and the person(s)
appointed by the governor or, if appropriate, the General Assembly. The Ohio Ballot Board must prepare any missing explanation
or argument.appointed by the governor or, if appropriate, the
General Assembly. The Ohio Ballot Board must prepare any missing explanation or argument.
(z) Initiated constitutional amendment proposed by petition cannot
be vetoed; cannot be amended or repealed except by another
constitutional amendment. Initiated statute cannot be vetoed by
the governor, but may be amended or repealed after its effective
date via legislation or another initiative.
(aa) Three year waiting period unless proponents can gather signatures equal to 25 percent of total vote cast in last governor's
election.
(bb) Upon completion of official canvass of votes.
(cc) If an indirect initiative is adopted by the legislature, it takes
effect 60 days after the adjournment of the legislative session in
which it is passed. Unless otherwise specified in the measure,
direct initiatives take effect five days after the governor proclaims
the official election results.

TABLE 6.14
State Referendums: Requesting Permission to Circulate a Citizen Petition

State or other jurisdiction	Citizen petition (a)	Signatures required to request a petition (b)	Request submitted to:	Request forms furnished by: (c)	Restricted subject matter (d)	Individual responsible for petition Title	Summary	Financial contributions reported (e)	Deposit required (f)
Alabama	...	...	...	...	...	...	...	...	...
Alaska	Y	100	LG	DV	Y	LG	LG	Y	$100
Arizona	Y	5% VG	SS	SS	Y	P	P	Y	N
Arkansas	Y	8% VG initiative; 6% referendum VG	AG	SP	N	AG	AG	Y	N
California	Y	25	AG	LC	Y	AG	AG	N	$200
Colorado	Y	At least 2 people representing issue	LS, SS	LS	Y	SP	LS	Y	N
Connecticut	...	...	...	...	...	...	...	...	...
Delaware	...	...	...	...	...	...	...	...	...
Florida	Y	8% of vote in last presidential election & 1/2 of congressional districts	SS	SS	N (g)	SP	SP	Y	N (h)
Georgia	...	...	...	...	...	...	...	...	...
Hawaii	...	...	...	...	...	...	...	...	...
Idaho	Y	20	SS	SP	N	AG	AG	Y	N
Illinois	Y	...	...	...	Y	P	...	Y, for $3,000 or more	...
Indiana	(i)	Varies	SS	SS	Y	Varies	...	...	...
Iowa	...	...	...	...	...	...	...	...	...
Kansas	...	...	...	...	...	...	...	...	...
Kentucky	...	...	.....	...	...	...	...	...	...
Louisiana	...	...	...	...	...	...	...	...	...
Maine	Y	5	SS	SS	Y	SP, SS	SS (j)	Y	...
Maryland	Y	(k)	SS	SBE	Y	SP	AG	Y	N
Massachusetts	Y	10	AG	SS	Y	AG	AG	Y	N
Michigan	Y	8% VG, initiative; 5% VG, referendum VG	SS	SS	Y	Board of State Canvassers	Board of State Canvassers	Y	N
Minnesota	...	...	...	...	...	...	...	...	...
Mississippi	Y	Any "qualified elector" may file	SS	SS	Y	AG	AG	Y	$500
Missouri	Y	...	SS	DV	Y	SS, AG	SS, AG	Y	N
Montana	Y	(l)	LS, SS, AG	SP	Y	AG	AG	Y	N
Nebraska	Y	...	SS	...	Y	SP	SP	Y	N
Nevada	Y	(r)	SS	SS	Y	P, SP	P, SP	Y	N
New Hampshire	...	...	...	...	...	...	...	...	...
New Jersey	...	...	...	...	...	...	...	...	...
New Mexico	...	...	...	...	...	...	...	...	...
New York	...	...	...	...	...	...	...	...	...
North Carolina	...	...	...	...	...	...	...	...	...
North Dakota	Y	25 "qualified voters"	SS	SP	N	SS, AG	SS	Y	N
Ohio	Y	1,000 "qualified electors"	SS, AG	PE	Y	PE	PE (m)	Y	$25
Oklahoma	Y	(n)	SS	SS	N	P	P	Y	N
Oregon	Y	4% of VG	LC, SS (o)	SS	Y	AG	AG	Y	N
Pennsylvania	...	...	...	...	...	...	...	...	...
Rhode Island	...	...	...	...	...	...	...	...	...
South Carolina	...	...	...	...	...	...	...	...	...
South Dakota	Y	5% of VG	LS	SP	Y	AG	AG	Y	N
Tennessee	...	...	...	...	...	...	...	...	...
Texas	...	...	...	...	...	...	...	...	...
Utah	Y	5 SP	LG	LG	Y (p)	SP	SP	Y	...
Vermont	...	...	...	...	...	...	...	...	...
Virginia	...	...	...	...	...	...	...	...	...
Washington	Y	8% VG, initiative; 4% VG, referendum VG	SS	SS	Y (q)	AG	AG	Y	$5
West Virginia	...	...	...	...	...	...	...	...	...
Wisconsin	...	...	...	...	...	...	...	...	...
Wyoming	Y	100	SS	SS	Y	SS	SS	Y	$500
American Samoa	...	...	...	...	...	...	...	...	...
CNMI*	Y	...	...	...	Y	SP	AG	Y	N
Puerto Rico	Y	10% district/41% territorial	Other	SBE	N	SP	Other	Y	N
U.S. Virgin Islands	...	...	L	L	N	L	L	N	N

See footnotes at end of table

TABLE 6.14

State Referendums: Requesting Permission to Circulate a Citizen Petition (continued)

Sources: The Council of State Governments' survey of state election websites, Initiative & Referendum Institute website and Ballotpedia website, April 2019.

*Commonwealth of Northern Mariana Islands

Key:

…–No provision for
EV–Eligible voters
VG–Total votes cast for the position of governor in the last election.
LG–Lieutenant Governor
LS–Legislative services
L–Legislature
SS–Secretary of State
SBE–State Board of Elections
DV–Division of Elections
AG–Attorney General
P–Proponent
PE–Petitioner
ST–State
SP–Sponsor
Y–Yes
N–No
LC–Office of Legislative Counsel

(a) Three forms of referenda exist: citizen petition, submission by the legislature, and constitutional requirement. This table outlines the steps necessary to enact a citizen's petition.

(b) Prior to circulating a statewide petition, a request for permission to do so must first be submitted to a specified state officer. Some states require such signatures to only be those of eligible voters.

(c) The form on which the request for petition is submitted may be the responsibility of the sponsor or may be furnished by the state.

(d) Restrictions may exist regarding the subject matter to which a referendum may be applied. The majority of these restrictions pertain to the dedication of state revenues and appropriations, and laws that maintain the preservation of public peace, safety and health. In Kentucky, referenda are only permitted for the establishment of soil and water and watershed conservation districts.

(e) In some states, a list of individuals who contribute financially to the referendum campaign must be submitted to the specified state officer with whom the petition is filed.

(f) A deposit may be required after permission to circulate a petition has been granted. This amount is refunded when the completed petition has been filed correctly.

(g) New fees/taxes requires 2/3 majority vote.

(h) The secretary of state charges a 10 cent fee per signature that must be verfied for ballot consideration.

(i) A referendum can only be placed on the ballot if authorized by a state law. As a result, a county or town election board cannot print any referendum on the ballot unless the legislature has already passed a law to permit the referendum. Therefore, each statute is different.

(j) Petition sponsor may submit proposed petition summary for approval to State Administrator of Elections but a formal request to circulate a petition is not required.

(k) No specific requirement to request a petition. Legislative Services receives the request and reviews it, and then the sponsor submits it to the Secretary of State and Attorney General for petition format review and legal and constitutional sufficiency review.

(l) State auditor writes the fiscal note.

(m) Petitioners must prepare the summary, and submit it to the Ohio Attorney General, who then must certify whether the summary fully and accurately describes the proposal.

(n) Five percent of legal voters based upon the total number of votes cast at the last general election for the state office receiving the highest number of votes.

(o) LC must also reasonably expect the measure to be put to a vote w/ verified # of signatures (4% for referendum of VG, stautory/const amdts different).

(p) May not challenge laws passed by two-thirds of each house of the legislature; any measure prohibiting/limiting wildlife hunting/management takes two-thirds vote in support.

(q) No bills with an emergency clause.

(r) The information required to be provided includes the name and signature of the person filing the petition, the names of up to three individuals who are authorized to withdraw or amend the petition, and the name of the Political Action Committee (PAC) formed to advocate for the passage of the petition.

TABLE 6.15
State Referendums: Circulating the Citizen Petition

State or other jurisdiction	Basis for signatures	Maximum time period allowed for petition circulation (a)	Can signatures be removed from petition (b)	Completed petition filed:	
				With	Days after legislative session
Alabama	...		...	...	...
Alaska	10% TV, from 3/4 ED	w/i 90 days of LS	Y	LG	90 days
Arizona	5% VG	24 months prior to GE	Y	SS	90 days
Arkansas	8% for initiated act; 6% for referenda VG	...	N	SS	90 days
California	5% VG	90 days; 131 days for initiatives prior to GE	Y	(c)	...
Colorado	5% of votes cast for prior SS election	6 months	Y	SS	...
Connecticut	...	...	...	...	...
Delaware	...	...	...	...	...
Florida	8% of TV in prior Presidential election	Up to 2 years (d)	.....	CES	...
Georgia	...	...	...	...	...
Hawaii	...	...	...	...	...
Idaho	6% EV	w/i 60 days after LS	Y	SS	60 days
Illinois	8% VG (e)	24 months prior to GE	Y	SBE	...
Indiana	...	...	...	...	...
Iowa	...	...	...	...	...
Kansas	...	...	...	...	...
Kentucky		...	...	...	...
Louisiana	...	...	...	...	...
Maine	10% VG	18 months	...	SS	50 days for 1st session; 25 days for 2nd session
Maryland	3 % VG	(f)	Y	SS	...
Massachusetts	1.5% VG for emergency 2% or immediate suspension	First state election 60 or more days after filing certified petition	Y (g)	SS	90 days after signed by governor
Michigan	5% VG	90 days after LS	N	SS	90 days after enactment
Minnesota	...	...	...	...	...
Mississippi	...	...	...	...	...
Missouri	5% VG, from 2/3 ED	w/i 90 days after LS	Y	SS	90 days
Montana	5% EV and 5% from 34 of 100 ED	(h)	Y	SS	6 mos.
Nebraska	5% EV	...	Y	SS	90 days
Nevada	10% EV last GE	(i)	Y	CC, SS	120 prior to next GE
New Hampshire	...	...	...	...	...
New Jersey	...	...	...	...	...
New Mexico	...	...	...	...	...
New York	...	...	...	...	...
North Carolina	...	...	...	...	...
North Dakota	2% total population	90 days	N	SS	(j)
Ohio	6% VG, 3% each from 1/2 counties	90 days	Y	SS	90 days
Oklahoma	5% VH	w/i 90 days of LS	Y	SS	90 days
Oregon	4% VG	w/i 90 days of LS	Y (k)	SS	90 days
Pennsylvania	...	...	...	...	...
Rhode Island	...	...	...	...	...
South Carolina	...	...	...	...	...
South Dakota	5% VG	24 months prior to GE	N	SS	90 days
Tennessee	...	...	...	...	...
Texas	...	...	...	...	...
Utah	10% VG	40 days after LS	Y	CC	40 days
Vermont	...	...	...	...	...
Virginia	...	...	...	...	...
Washington	4% VG	Approx. 90 days	N	SS	90 days
West Virginia	...	...	...	...	...
Wisconsin	...	...	...	...	...
Wyoming	15% TV, from 2/3 county	18 months	N	SS	90 days
American Samoa	...	...	...	...	...
CNMI*	...	Up to 120 days before election	Y	AG	...
Puerto Rico	...	...	...	...	...
U.S. Virgin Islands	No. of registered voters	180 days	...	...	...

See footnotes at end of table

TABLE 6.15
State Referendums: Circulating the Citizen Petition (continued)

Sources: The Council of State Governments' survey of state election website, Initiative & Referendum Institute website and Ballotpedia website, April 2019.

*Commonwealth of the Northern Mariana Islands

Key:

…–No provision for.

VG–Total votes cast for the position of governor in the last election.

EV–Eligible voters.

TV–Total voters in the last general election.

VH–Total votes cast for the office receiving the highest number of votes in last general election.

VSS–Total votes cast for all candidates for the office of secretary of state at the previous general election.

ED–Election district.

GE–General election.

LS–Legislative session.

LG–Lieutenant governor.

SBE–State Board of Elections.

SS–Secretary of state.

AG–Attorney General.

CC–County clerk.

CES–County election supervisor.

Y–Yes.

N–No.

w/i–Within.

(a) The petition circulation period begins when petition forms have been approved and provided to or by the sponsors. Sponsors are those individuals granted permission to circulate a petition, and are therefore responsible for the validity of each signature on a given petition.

(b) Should an individual wish to remove his/her name from a petition, a request to do so must first be submitted in writing to the state officer with whom the petition is filed.

(c) County elections office.

(d) Signatures must be verified by Feb 1 in year of election.

(e) Referenda are advisory only.

(f) No signature may be collected until the final action of the General Assembly. Session ends the second Monday in April. One third of the signatures must be submitted not later than May 31. The remaining signatures are due no later than June 30th.

(g) Should an individual wish to remove his/her name from a petition, a request to do so must first be submitted in writing to the local election official prior to the petition being submitted for certification of signatures.

(h) No specific beginning date for circulation of petitions, so there is no maximum time period. There is an ending deadline of 6 months after legislative session.

(i) Not later than the third Tuesday in May of even-numbered years.

(j) Within 90 days after the legislation is filed in the Secretary of State's office.

(k) Only by the chief petitioners before submitting signatures before verification. Signatures may not be removed once the signatures have been submitted to the secretary of state for verification.

TABLE 6.16
State Referendums: Preparing the Citizen Petition Referendum to be Placed on Ballot

State or other jurisdiction	Signatures verified by: (a)	Within how many days after filing	No. of days to amend/appeal petition that is:		Penalty for falsifying petition (denotes fine, jail term)	Petition certified by: (d)
			Incomplete (b)	Not accepted (c)		
Alabama	...	...	...	...	...	...
Alaska	Division of elections	60	10	10	Class B misdemeanor	LG
Arizona	County recorder	(e)	...	...	Class 1 misdemeanor	SS
Arkansas	SS	30	...	30	Class D felony	SS
California	County clerk	8 (f)	...	...	Felony or misdemeanor (depending on severity)	SS
Colorado	SS	(g)	15	3 months and 3 weeks before election	Fines up to $1,000 and forgery is a Class 5 felony	SS
Connecticut	...	...	...	...	...	...
Delaware	...	...	...	...	...	...
Florida	Supervisor of Elections	30	...	...	1st degree misdemeanor	SS
Georgia	...	...	...	...	...	...
Hawaii	...	...	...	...	...	...
Idaho	County clerk	...	...	...	$5,000, 2 yrs.	SS
Illinois	State Board of Elections	varies	...	...	Class 3 felony	SBE
Indiana	County clerk	...	...	...	...	...
Iowa	...	...	...	...	...	...
Kansas	...	...	...	...	...	...
Kentucky	...	...	...	...	...	...
Louisiana	...	...	...	...	...	...
Maine	Registrars of voters	30	...	...	Class E crime	SS
Maryland	Local Board of Elections	20	...	...	Misdemeanor (h)	SS, SBE
Massachusetts	Local boards of registrars	14	...	...	$1,000, 1 year	SS
Michigan	SS	Approx. 60	...	...	$500, 90 days	BSC
Minnesota	...	...	...	...	...	...
Mississippi	...	...	...	...	...	...
Missouri	County clerk	(i)	...	10	Class A misdemeanor	SS
Montana	County election administrators	28	10	10	$500, 6 mos.	SS
Nebraska	County clerk	40	...	...	Penalty up to $1,000 and 1 year in prison	SS
Nevada	County clerk	(j)	5	...	...	SS
New Hampshire	...	...	...	...	...	...
New Jersey	...	...	...	...	...	...
New Mexico	...	...	...	...	...	...
New York	...	...	...	...	...	...
North Carolina	...	...	...	...	...	...
North Dakota	SS	35	...	20	(k)	SS
Ohio	SS	no later than 105 days before election	10	...	5th degree felony	SS
Oklahoma	SS	...	10	...	$1,000, 1 year	SS, State Supreme Court
Oregon	SS, county clerk	30	...	...	(l)	SS
Pennsylvania	...	...	...	...	...	...
Rhode Island	...	...	...	...	...	...
South Carolina	...	...	...	...	...	...
South Dakota	SS	...	...	...	Class 2 misdemeanor	SS
Tennessee	...	...	...	...	...	...
Texas	...	...	...	...	...	...
Utah	County clerks	55 (m)	...	10	Class A misdemeanor	LG
Vermont	...	...	...	...	...	...
Virginia	...	...	...	...	...	...
Washington	SS	(n)	...	10	Class C felony (possible)	SS
West Virginia	...	...	...	...	...	...
Wisconsin	...	...	...	...	...	...
Wyoming	SS	60	60	60	$1,000, 1 yr.	SS
American Samoa	...	...	...	...	...	...
CNMI*	AG	...	(o)	(o)	(p)	AG
Puerto Rico	...	...	...	...	...	...
U.S. Virgin Islands	Supervisor of Elections	15	...	...	...	Supervisor of Elections

See footnotes at end of table

TABLE 6.16

State Referendums: Preparing the Citizen Petition Referendum to be Placed on Ballot (continued)

Sources: The Council of State Governments' survey of state election website, Initiative & Referendum Institute website and Ballotpedia website, April 2019.

*Commonwealth of Northern Mariana Islands

Key:

…–Not applicable.

SS–Secretary of State.

LG–Lieutenant Governor.

BSC–Board of State Canvassers.

SBE–State Board of Elections.

(a) The validity of the signatures, as well as the correct number of required signatures must be verified before the referendum is allowed on the ballot.

(b) If an insufficient number of signatures are submitted, sponsors may amend the original petition by filing additional signatures within a given number of days after filing. If the necessary number of signatures have not been submitted by this date, the petition is declared void.

(c) In some cases, the state officer will not accept a valid petition. In such cases, sponsors may appeal this decision to the Supreme Court, where the sufficiency of the petition will be determined. If the petition is determined to be sufficient, the referendum is required to be placed on the ballot.

(d) A petition is certified for the ballot when the required number of signatures have been submitted by the filing deadline, and are determined to be valid.

(e) In Arizona, the secretary of state has 20 days to count signatures and to complete random sample; the county recorder then has 15 days to verify signatures.

(f) Clerk has 8 days to report raw totals of signatures and 30 days for random sampling to verify signatures.

(g) At least 30 days for internal review process to conduct random sampling; must verify at least 90% are valid.

(h) Misdemeanor, punishable by a $10–$250 fine or 30 days–six months in jail, or both.

(i) In Missouri, must be certified as sufficient or insufficient by the 13th Tuesday prior to the general election.

(j) 1. Within four days county clerks count total number of signatures and forward to the secretary of state. 2. The secretary of state immediately notifies county clerks if they are to proceed or not proceed with the signature verification. 3. If ordered by the secretary of state, the county clerks verify signatures within nine days (excluding weekends and holidays).

(k) Any violations discovered will be reported to the attorney general for investigation and prosecution.

(l) Whether a penalty is assessed would be based upon what information on the petition was falsified.

(m) After the end of the legislative session.

(n) Not later than the third Tuesday following the primary election.

(o) Incomplete: 30 or more days if submitted 150 days before date of the election; none if submitted 120 days before date of election. Not accepted: If submitted 119 days or less before the election.

(p) Subject to statute governing fraud or perjury.

TABLE 6.17
State Referendums: Voting on the Citizen Petition Referendum

State or other jurisdiction	Ballot (a) Title by:	Summary by:	Election where referendum voted on	Effective date of approved referendum (b)	Days to contest election results (c)
Alabama	...	...	...	...	...
Alaska	LG	LG	1st statewide election 180 days after LS	30 days	10
Arizona	SS, AG	LC	GE	(d)	10
Arkansas	AG	...	GE	...	20
California	AG	AG	GE or PR	1 day	5 (e)
Colorado	..	..	...	...	...
Connecticut	...	...	...	...	...
Delaware	...	...	...	...	...
Florida	...	...	...	...	...
Georgia	...	...	...	...	...
Hawaii	...	...	...	...	...
Idaho	AG	AG	GE	30 days	20 (e)
Illinois	...	...	GE	Advisory only	30
Indiana	...	...	...	...	...
Iowa	...	...	...	...	...
Kansas	...	...	...	...	...
Kentucky	...	...	GE or SP	IM	...
Louisiana	...	...	...	...	...
Maine	...	...	GE or statewide election more than 60 days after filing	30 days	5
Maryland	SS	LSS	GE	(f)	...
Massachusetts	SS, AG	AG	GE more than 60 days after filing	30 days	10
Michigan	BSC	BSC	GE	10 days	2 (e)
Minnesota	...	...	...	...	...
Mississippi	...	...	...	...	...
Missouri	SS, AG	SS	GE	IM	30
Montana	AG	AG	GE	(g)	1 yr.
Nebraska	AG	AG	GE	...	...
Nevada	SS, AG	SS, AG	GE	Nov., 4th Tues.	14
New Hampshire	...	...	...	...	...
New Jersey	...	...	...	...	...
New Mexico	...	...	...	...	...
New York	...	...	...	...	...
North Carolina	...	...	...	...	...
North Dakota	SS, AG	SS	PR	30 days	14 (e)
Ohio	...	...	GE more than 60 days after filing.	IM	15 (h)
Oklahoma	LLS, AG	LLS	GE or SP	...	...
Oregon	AG	AG	GE (i)	30 days	40
Pennsylvania	...	...	...	...	...
Rhode Island	...	...	...	...	...
South Carolina	...	...	...	...	...
South Dakota	AG	AG	GE	July 1	...
Tennessee	...	...	...	...	...
Texas	...	...	...	...	...
Utah	LLS	LLS	GE	5 days	40
Vermont	...	...	...	...	...
Virginia	...	...	...	...	...
Washington	AG	AG	GE	30 days	10
West Virginia	...	...	...	...	...
Wisconsin	...	...	...	...	...
Wyoming	SS	SS, AG	GE more than 120 days after LS	90 days	15
American Samoa	...	...	...	...	...
CNMI*	AG	AG	GE or special election if specified	(j)	30 days
Puerto Rico	...	...	...	...	...
U.S. Virgin Islands	...	...	...	...	...

See footnotes at end of table

TABLE 6.17

State Referendums: Voting on the Citizen Petition Referendum (continued)

Sources: The Council of State Governments' survey of state election website, Initiative & Referendum Institute website and Ballotpedia website, April 2019.

*Commonwealth of the Northern Mariana Islands

Key:

…–No provision.

LG–Lieutenant Governor.

AG–Attorney General.

SS–Secretary of State.

BSC–Board of State Canvassers.

LC–Legislative Counsel.

LSS–Legislative Legal Services.

SBE–State Board of Elections.

GE–General election.

PR–Primary election.

REG–Regular election.

SP–Special election.

IM–Immediately.

LS–Legislative session.

(a) In some states, the ballot title and summary will differ from that on the petition.

(b) A majority of the popular vote is required to enact a measure in every state. In Arizona, a referendum approved by the voters becomes effective upon the governor's proclamation. In Nebraska, a referendum may be put into effect immediately after the approving votes have been canvassed by the Board of State Canvassers and upon the governor's proclamation. In Massachusetts the measure must also receive at lease 30 percent of the total ballots cast in the last election. In Oklahoma, put into effect upon certification of election results by state election board. In Utah, after proclamation by governor and date specified in petition.

(c) Individuals may contest the results of a vote on a referendum within a certain number of days after the election including this matter. In Alaska, five days to request recount with appeal to the court within five days after recount.

(d) Upon proclamation of the governor after the canvas. (AZ Const. Article 4, Part 1, Section 13).

(e) After election is certified.

(f) After the certification of election results. Depends on date Board of State Canvassers meets. They must meet within 35 days after General Election.

(g) Unless specifically provided by the legislature in an act referred by it to the people or until suspended by a petition signed by at least 15% of the qualified electors in a majority of the legislative representative districts, an act referred to the people is in effect as provided by law until it is approved or rejected at the election. An act that is rejected is repealed effective the date the result of the canvass is filed by the secretary of state under 13-27-503. An act referred to the people that was in effect at the time of the election and is approved by the people remains in effect. An act that was suspended by a petition and is approved by the people is effective the date the result of the canvass is filed by the secretary of state under 13-27-503. An act referred by the legislature that contains an effective date following the election becomes effective on that date if approved by the people. An act that provides no effective date and whose substantive provisions were delayed by the legislature pending approval at an election and that is approved is effective October 1 following the election.

(h) After election is certified or if recount conducted, 10 days after recount.

(i) Special election can be held at the request of the Legislative Assembly.

(j) Upon approval by voters and certification of election results by Election Commission, usually 15 days after date of election if no contest.

TABLE 6.18
State Recall Provisions

State or other jurisdiction	Provision for recall	Officials subject to recall	Constitutional and statutory citations for recall of state officials	Constitutional or statutory language
Alabama	No			
Alaska	Yes	All (a)	Const. Art., 11 § 8; AS § 15.45.510-710, 15.60.010, 29.26.250-350	All elected public officials in the State, except judicial officers, are subject to recall by the voters of the State or political subdivision from which elected.
Arizona	Yes	All	Const. Art. 8, § 1-6; ARS § 19-201 - 19-234	Every public officer in the state of Arizona, holding an elective office, either by election or appointment, is subject to recall from such office by the qualified electors of the electoral district from which candidates are elected to such office.
Arkansas	No			
California	Yes	All	Const. Art. 2, § 13-19; CA Election Code § 11000-11386	Recall is the power of the electors to remove an elective officer. Recall of a state officer is initiated by delivering to the Secretary of State a petition alleging reason for recall. Sufficiency of reason is not reviewable.
Colorado	Yes	All	Const. Art. 21, § 1; CRS § 1-12-101 - 1-12-122, 23-17-120.5, 31-4-501-505	Every elective public officer of the state of Colorado may be recalled from office at any time by the registered electors entitled to vote for a successor of such incumbent through the procedure and in the manner herein provided for, which procedure shall be known as the recall, and shall be in addition to and without excluding any other method of removal by law.
Connecticut	No			
Delaware	No			
Florida	No			
Georgia	Yes	All	Const. Art. 2, § 2.4; GA Code § 21-4-1 et seq.	The General Assembly is hereby authorized to provide by general law for the recall of public officials who hold elective office. The procedures, grounds, and all other matters relative to such recall shall be provided for in such law.
Hawaii	No			
Idaho	Yes	All (a)	Const. Art 6, § 6; ID Code § 34-1701 - 34-1715	Every public officer in the state of Idaho, excepting the judicial officers, is subject to recall by the legal voters of the state or of the electoral district from which he is elected. The legislature shall pass the necessary laws to carry this provision into effect.
Illinois (b)	Yes	(b)	Const. Art 3, § 7	The recall of the Governor may be proposed by a petition signed by a number of electors equal in number to at least 15% of the total votes cast for Governor in the preceding gubernatorial election, with at least 100 signatures from each of at least 25 separate counties. A petition shall have been signed by the petitioning electors not more than 150 days after an affidavit has been filed with the State Board of Elections providing notice of intent to circulate a petition to recall the Governor. The affidavit may be filed no sooner than 6 months after the beginning of the Governor's term of office. The affidavit shall have been signed by the proponent of the recall petition, at least 20 members of the House of Representatives, and at least 10 members of the Senate, with no more than half of the signatures of members of each chamber from the same established political party.
Indiana	No			
Iowa	No			
Kansas	Yes	All (a)	Const. Art. 4, § 3; KSA § 25-4301 - 25-4331	All elected public officials in the State, except judicial officers, shall be subject to recall by voters of the state or political subdivision from which elected. Procedures and grounds for recall shall be prescribed by law.
Kentucky	No			
Louisiana	Yes	All (a)	Const. Art. 10, § 26; LRS § 18:1300.1 - 18:1300.17	The legislature shall provide by general law for the recall by election of any state, district, parochial, ward, or municipal officer except judges of the courts of record. The sole issue at a recall election shall be whether the official shall be recalled. However, no recall petition may be submitted for certification to or accepted for certification by the registrar of voters or any other official if less than six months remain in the term of office.
Maine	No			
Maryland	No			
Massachusetts	No			
Michigan	Yes	All (a)	Const. Art. 2, §8; MCL § 168.951 - 168.975	Laws shall be enacted to provide for the recall of all elective officers except judges of courts of record upon petition of electors equal in number to 25 percent of the number of persons voting in the last preceding election for the office of governor in the electoral district of the officer sought to be recalled. The sufficiency of any statement of reasons or grounds procedurally required shall be a political rather than a judicial question.
Minnesota	Yes	(c)	Const. Art. 8, § 6; MS § 211C.01 et. seq.	A state officer other than a judge may be subject to recall for serious malfeasance or nonfeasance during the term of office in the performance of the duties of the office or conviction during the term of office for a serious crime.
Mississippi	No			
Missouri	No			
Montana	Yes	All	Mont. Code § 2-16-601 - 2-16-635	Every person holding a public office of the state or any of its political subdivisions, either by election or appointment , is subject to recall from such office.

See footnotes at end of table

TABLE 6.18
State Recall Provisions (continued)

State or other jurisdiction	Provision for recall	Officials subject to recall	Constitutional and statutory citations for recall of state officials	Constitutional or statutory language
Nebraska	No			
Nevada	Yes	All	Const. Art. 2, § 9; NRS § 294A.006, Chapter 306	Every public officer in the State of Nevada is subject, as herein provided, to recall from office by the registered voters of the state, or of the county, district, or municipality which he represents.
New Hampshire	No			
New Jersey	Yes	All	Const. Art. 1, § 2; NJRS § 19:27A-1 - 19:27A-18	The people reserve unto themselves the power to recall, after at least one year of service, any elected official in this State or representing this State in the United States Congress.
New Mexico	No			
New York	No			
North Carolina	No			
North Dakota	Yes	All (d)	Const. Art. 3, § 1 and 10; ND Century Code § 16.1-01-09.1	Any elected official of the state, of any county or of any legislative or county commissioner district shall be subject to recall by petition of electors equal in number to twenty-five percent of those who voted at the preceding general election for the office of governor in the state, county, or district in which the official is to be recalled.
Ohio	No			
Oklahoma	No			
Oregon	Yes	All (d)	Const. Art. 2, § 18; ORS § 249.865 - 249.880	Every public official in Oregon is subject, as herein provided, to recall by the electors of the state or of the electoral district from which the public official is elected.
Pennsylvania	No			
Rhode Island	Yes	(e)	Const. Art. 4, § 1	Recall is authorized in the case of a general officer who has been indicted or informed against for a felony, convicted of a misdemeanor, or against whom a finding of probable cause of violation of the code of ethics has been made by the ethics commission.
South Carolina	No			
South Dakota	No			
Tennessee	No			
Texas	No			
Utah	No			
Vermont	No			
Virginia	No (f)			
Washington	Yes	All (a)	Const. Art. 1, Sec. 33-34; WRC §29.82.010 - 29.82.220	Every elective public officer of the state of Washington except judges of courts of record is subject to recall and discharge by the legal voters of the state, or of the political subdivision of the state, from which he was elected whenever a petition demanding his recall, … is filed with the officer with whom a petition for nomination, or certificate for nomination, to such office must be filed under the laws of this state, and the same officer shall call a special election as provided by the general election laws of this state. and the result determined as therein provided.
West Virginia	No			
Wisconsin	Yes	All	Const. Art. 13, §12; Wisc. Stat. §9.10	The qualified electors of the state, of any congressional, judicial or legislative district or of any county may petition for the recall of any incumbent elective officer after the first year of the term for which the incumbent was elected, by filing a petition with the filing officer with whom the nomination petition is filed, demanding the recall of the incumbent.
Wyoming	No			
CNMI*	Yes	All	Const. Art. 9, § 3; 2 CMC §6502	Elected public officials are subject to recall by the voters of the Commonwealth or of the island, islands or district from which elected.
Puerto Rico	No			
U.S.V.I.	Yes	All	U.S.C., Title 48, Ch. 12, Subchapter IV, § 1593	An elected public official of the Virgin Islands may be removed from office by a recall election carried out under this subsection. The grounds for recall are any of the following: lack of fitness, incompetence, neglect of duty, or corruption.

Sources: The Council of State Governments, state constitutions and statutes, April 2019.
*Commonwealth of the Northern Mariana Islands
Note: This table refers only to officials elected to statewide office. Many local governments allow recall of elected officials.
Key:
N.A.–Not available

(a) Except judicial.
(b) Illinois allows for recall of the governor.
(c) State executive officers, legislators, and judicial officers.
(d) Except for U.S. Congress.
(e) Governor, Lieutenant Governor, Secretary of State, Treasurer, and Attorney General.
(f) Virginia permits a recall trial not a recall election. See Virginia Code §24.2-233.

TABLE 6.19
State Recall Provisions: Applicability to State Officials and Petition Circulation

State or other jurisdiction	Officers to whom recall is applicable (a)	No. of times recall can be attempted	Recall may be initiated after official has been in office	Recall may not be initiated with days remaining in term	Basis for signatures (b) (see key below)		Maximum time allowed for petition circulation (c)
					Statewide officers	Others	
Alabama	...	...	...	...	...	...	...
Alaska	All but judicial officers	...	120 days	180	25% VO	25% VO	...
Arizona	All elected officials	1 (d)	6 mos./5 days legislators	...	25% VO (e)	25% VO (e)	120 days
Arkansas	...	...	...	...	...	...	...
California	All elected officials	(f)	90 days	6 mos.	12% VO, 1% from 5 counties	20% VO	160 days
Colorado	All elected officials	(g)	6 mos	6 mos.	25% VO	25% VO	60 days
Connecticut	...	...	...	...	...	...	...
Delaware	...	...	...	...	...	...	...
Florida	...	...	...	...	...	...	...
Georgia	All state level officials, county and city elected officials	...	180 days	180	15% EV (h), 1/15 from each congressional district	30% EV (h)	(i)
Hawaii	...	...	...	...	...	...	...
Idaho	All but judicial officers	(d)	90 days	...	20% EVg	50% VO	60 days
Illinois	Governor	...	...	...	15% VO from 25 counties	20 state Rep. and 10 state Sen.	150 days
Indiana	...	...	...	...	...	...	...
Iowa	...	...	...	...	...	...	...
Kansas	All but judicial officers	1	120 days	180	40% VO	40% VO	90 days
Kentucky	...	...	...	...	...	...	...
Louisiana	All but judicial officers	(j)	1 day	6 mos.	33 1/3% EV (k)	40% EV (k)	180 days
Maine	...	...	...	...	...	...	...
Maryland	...	...	...	...	...	...	...
Massachusetts	...	...	...	...	...	...	...
Michigan	All but judicial officers	No limit	1 year	1 year	25% VG in district	25% VG in district	60 days
Minnesota	All state level officials	No limit	...	6 mos.	25% VO	25% VO	90 days
Mississippi	...	...	...	...	...	...	...
Missouri	...	...	...	...	...	...	...
Montana	All state level officers & elected officials	(l)	2 mos.	...	10% EV	(m)	3 mos.
Nebraska	...	...	...	...	...	...	...
Nevada	All but judicial officers	(d)	6 mos. (n)	...	25% VO in given	25% VO in given	90 days
New Hampshire	...	...	...	...	...	...	...
New Jersey	All elected officials	(o)	(p)	(q)	25% EV in given jurisdiction	25% EV in given jurisdiction	(r)
New Mexico	...	...	...	...	...	...	...
New York	...	...	...	...	...	...	...
North Carolina	...	...	...	...	...	...	...
North Dakota	All elected state officials	1	...	190	25% Evg	25% Evg	...
Ohio	...	...	...	...	...	...	...
Oklahoma	...	...	...	...	...	...	...
Oregon	All elected state officials	No limit	180 days (s)	...	15% (t)	15% (t)	90 days
Pennsylvania	...	...	...	...	...	...	...
Rhode Island	Gov., lt. gov., atty. gen., sec. of state, treasurer	...	6 mos.	...	15% VO	...	90 days
South Carolina	...	...	...	...	...	...	...
South Dakota	...	...	...	...	...	...	...
Tennessee	...	...	...	...	...	...	...
Texas	...	...	...	...	...	...	...
Utah	...	...	...	...	...	...	...
Vermont	...	...	...	...	...	...	...
Virginia	...	...	...	...	...	...	...
Washington	All but judges of courts of record	...	IM	180	25% VO	35% VO	(u)
West Virginia	...	...	...	...	...	...	...
Wisconsin	All elected officials	1	1 yr.	...	25% VG (v)	25% VG (v)	60 days
Wyoming	...	...	...	...	...	...	...
CNMI*	All elected officials	(w)	180 days	...	40% EV (x)	...	(y)
Puerto Rico	...	...	...	...	...	...	...
U.S. Virgin Islands	All elected officials	Unlimited	1 year	365	...	Registered electors	180 days

See footnotes at end of table

TABLE 6.19

State Recall Provisions: Applicability to State Officials and Petition Circulation (continued)

Source: The Council of State Governments, April 2019.

*Commonwealth of the Northern Mariana Islands

Key:

…–No provision.

All–All elective officials.

VO–Number of votes cast in the last election for the office or official being recalled.

EVg–Number of eligible voters in the last general election for governor.

EV–Eligible voters.

VG–Total votes cast for the position of governor in the last election.

VP–Total votes cast for position of president in last presidential election.

IM–Immediately.

(a) An elective official may be recalled by qualified voters entitled to vote for the recalled official's successor. An appointed official may be recalled by qualified voters entitled to vote for the successor(s) of the elective officer(s) authorized to appoint an individual to the position.

(b) Signature requirements for recall of those other than state elective officials are based on votes in the jurisdiction to which the said official has been elected.

(c) The petition circulation period begins when petition forms have been approved and provided to sponsors. Sponsors are those individuals granted permission to circulate a petition, and are therefore responsible for the validity of each signature on a given petition.

(d) Additional recall attempts can be made provided that the state treasury is reimbursed the cost of the previous recall attempt(s). The specific reason for recalling on one petition cannot be the basis for a second recall petition during the current term of office.

(e) 25% of the number of votes cast at the preceding general election for all candidates for the office held by the officer, even if the officer was not elected at that election, divided by the number of offices that were being filled at that election. (A.R.S.§ 19-201).

(f) Open ended.

(g) One attempt unless a second petition is circulated and valid signatures gathered are at least 50% of votes cast for all candidates in last election.

(h) Eligible voters for office at last general election to fill office.

(i) For any statewide office, 90 days. Any officer holding an office other than statewide office and for whom no less than 5,000 signatures are required for the recall petition, 45 days. Any officer is first reimbursed for all expenses of the preceding election.

(j) Unlimited. Once every 18 months.

(k) Basis for signatures 33 1/3 percent if over 1,000 eligible voters; 40 percent if under 1,000 eligible voters.

(l) No recall petition may be filed against an officer for whom a recall election has been held for a period of 2 years during his term of office unless the state or political subdivisions financing such recall election is first reimbursed for all expenses of the preceding election.

(m) 15 percent of eligible for district offices.

(n) For legislators, anytime after 10 days from the beginning of the first legislative session after their election.

(o) An elected official sought to be recalled who is not recalled as the result of a recall election shall not again be subject to recall until after having served one year of a term calculated from the date of the recall election.

(p) The recall drive may not commence before the 50th day preceding the completion of the elected official's first year of the current term.

(q) No election to recall an elected official shall be held after the date occurring six months prior to the general election or regular election for that office, as appropriate, in the final year of the officials term.

(r) The maximum time allowed for petition circulation is 320 days for a governor or U.S. Senator or 160 days for other elected officials.

(s) Unless it is a state senator or representative and then it is anytime after fifth day form the beginning of legislative session or after election of legislator.

(t) 15 percent of the total number of votes cast in the public officer's electoral district for all candidates for governor at the last election at which a candidate for governor was elected to a full term.

(u) Statewide officials 270 days; others 180 days.

(v) At least 25 percent of the vote cast for the office of governor at the last election within the same district or territory as that of the officeholder being recalled.

(w) Not more than once a year or not during the first six months in office.

(x) Grounds for recall must be stated and must be signed by 40% of voters represented by the elected official.

(y) Until 120 days before the election.

TABLE 6.20
State Recall Provisions: Petition Review, Appeal and Election

State or other jurisdiction	Signatures verified (a) by:	Days to amend/appeal a petition that is: Incomplete (b)	Not accepted (c)	Penalty for falsifying petition (denotes fines, jail time)	Days allowed for petition to be certified (d)	Days to step down after certification (e)	Voting on the recall (f) Election held	Election type	Days to contest election results (g)
Alabama	...	...	...	...	...	...	...	...	...
Alaska	Division of Elections	20	20	Class B misdemeanor	30	1	60-90 days after cert.	GE,PR,SP	10
Arizona	County recorder	...	...	Class 1 misdemeanor	70	5	(h)	(i)	5
Arkansas	...	...	...	...	...	...	...	...	...
California	County clerk/ registrar of voters	10	10	...	10	(j)	60-80 days after cert.	GE	5
Colorado	SS	...	15 (k)	...	10	5	45-75 days after cert.	SP or GE	10
Connecticut	...	...	...	...	...	...	...	...	...
Delaware	...	...	...	...	...	...	...	...	...
Florida	...	...	...	...	...	...	...	...	...
Georgia	Registrar of voters	...	...	Misdemeanor	30-45	...	30-45 days after cert.	SP	5
Hawaii	...	...	...	...	...	...	...	...	...
Idaho	County clerk	30	...	$5,000, 2 yrs.	10	5	45+ days after cert. (l)	SP , PR, GE (l)	20 (m)
Illinois	SBE	...	...	...	...	...	100 days after cert.	SP	...
Indiana	...	...	...	...	...	...	...	...	...
Iowa	...	...	...	...	...	...	...	...	...
Kansas	County clerk	...	...	Class B misdemeanor; up to $1,000, up to one year or both.	30	Next day	60-90 days after cert.	SP	5 (m)
Kentucky	...	...	...	...	...	...	...	...	...
Louisiana	Registrar of voters	(n)	(n)	...	15-20 days	(o)	(p)	SP	(q)
Maine	...	...	...	...	...	...	...	...	...
Maryland	...	...	...	...	...	...	...	...	...
Massachusetts	...	...	...	...	...	...	...	...	...
Michigan	SS, local election officials (r)	...	...	$500, 90 days	35	...	(s)	SP	2 (m)
Minnesota	SS	90	...	Felony	10	...	(t)	GE	7
Mississippi	...	...	...	...	...	...	...	...	...
Missouri	...	...	...	...	...	...	...	...	...
Montana	County election administrators	10	10	$500 or six months in county jail, or both.	(u)	5	(v)	SP or GE (dd) (v)	12 mos.
Nebraska	...	...	...	...	...	...	...	...	...
Nevada	County clerk, registrar of voters	5	...	Misdemeanor	(w)	5	(x)	SP	(y)
New Hampshire	...	...	...	...	...	...	...	...	...
New Jersey	Recall elections official	...	...	Crime of the 4th degree	10	5	(z)	SP or GE	(aa)
New Mexico	...	...	...	...	...	...	...	...	...
New York	...	...	...	...	...	...	...	...	...
North Carolina	...	...	...	...	...	...	...	...	...
North Dakota	SS	...	...	...	30	10	50-60	SP	14 (bb)
Ohio	...	...	...	...	...	...	...	...	...
Oklahoma	...	...	...	...	...	...	...	...	...
Oregon	County clerk	(cc)	...	(dd)	10	5	w/i 35 days after resignation period	SP	40
Pennsylvania	...	...	...	...	...	...	...	...	...
Rhode Island	SBE	w/i 90 days	...	Misdemeanor and/ or felony	90	...	...	SP	...
South Carolina	...	...	...	...	...	...	...	...	...
South Dakota	...	...	...	...	...	...	...	...	...
Tennessee	...	...	...	...	...	...	...	...	...
Texas	...	...	...	...	...	...	...	...	...
Utah	...	...	...	...	...	...	...	...	...
Vermont	...	...	...	...	...	...	...	...	...

See footnotes at end of table

TABLE 6.20
State Recall Provisions: Petition Review, Appeal and Election (continued)

State or other jurisdiction	Signatures verified (a) by:	Days to amend/appeal a petition that is:		Penalty for falsifying petition (denotes fines, jail time)	Days allowed for petition to be certified (d)	Days to step down after certification (e)	Voting on the recall (f)		Days to contest election results (g)
		Incomplete (b)	Not accepted (c)				Election held	Election type	
Virginia	…	…	…	…	…	…	…	…	…
Washington	SS	30	…	Class B felony or misdemeanor	not specified	…	45-60 days after cert. (ee)	SP	3
West Virginia	…	…	…	…	…	…	…	…	…
Wisconsin	SBE	…	…	Class 1 felony - $10,000, 3 yrs. prison or both.	31	10	6 weeks after cert.	GE or PR	3 (ff)
Wyoming	…	…	…	…	…	…	…	…	…
CNMI*	AG	150 days	…	Statute governs fraud or perjury.	15 days	…	(gg)	GE, SP	30
Puerto Rico	…	…	…	…	…	…	…	…	…
U.S. Virgin Islands	Office of the Supervisor of Elections	…	…	…	10	IM	…	GE	5

Sources: The Council of State Governments April 2019.
*Commonwealth of the Northern Mariana Islands
Key:
…–Not applicable.
SBE–State Board of Elections.
SS–Secretary of State.
SP–Special election.
GE–General election.
PR–Primary election.
IM–Immediate and automatic removal from office.
w/i–Within.
N.A.–Information not available.
(a) The validity of the signatures, as well as the correct number of required signatures must be verified before the recall is allowed on the ballot.
(b) If an insufficient number of signatures are submitted, sponsors may amend the original petition by filing additional signatures within a given number of days. If the necessary number of signatures have not been submitted by this date, the petition is declared void.
(c) In some cases, the state officer will not accept a valid petition. In such a case, sponsors may appeal this decision to the Supreme Court, where the sufficiency of the petition will be determined. When this is declared, the recall is required to be placed on the ballot.
(d) A petition is certified for the ballot when the required number of signatures has been submitted by the filing deadline, and are determined to be valid.
(e) The official to whom a recall is proposed has a certain number of days to step down from his position before a recall election is initiated, if he desires to do so.
(f) A majority of the popular vote is required to recall an official in each state.
(g) Individuals may contest the results of a vote on a recall within a certain number of days after the results are certified. In Alaska, an appeal to courts must be filed within five days of the recount.
(h) The election order is issued within 15 days if the officer does not resign within five days after certification.
(i) To be held on the next consolidated election date pursuant to § 16-204 that is 90 days or more after the order calling the election (A.R.S. § 19-209(A)).

(j) Prior to election being called.
(k) After determination of sufficiency.
(l) In Idaho, the dates on which elections may be conducted are the first Tuesday in February, the fourth Tuesday in May, the first Tuesday in August, or the Tuesday following the first Monday in November. In addition, an emergency election may be called upon motion of the governing board of a political subdivision. Recall elections conducted by any political subdivision shall be held on the nearest of these dates which falls more than 45 days after the clerk of the political subdivision orders that the recall election shall be held.
(m) After election is certified. In Michigan, if a petition is filed against a local officer, a recount can be requested up to 6 days after certification of recall election.
(n) The Registrar of Voters shall honor the written request of any voter who either desires to have his handwritten signature stricken from or added to the petition at any time prior to certification of the petition, or within five days after receipt of such signed petition, whichever is earlier.
(o) Election returns are certified on the fifth day after the election, and the office is immediately vacant.
(p) The local registrar of voters sends the original certified recall petition to the governor, who issues, within 15 days, a proclamation calling a special election, placing the special election on the next regularly scheduled election date.
(q) Not later than 4:30 p.m. of the 30th day after the official promulgation of the results of the election. Promulgation is on or before the 12th day after the election.
(r) Secretary of state if filed on the state level; county or local clerks if filed on county level.
(s) Under Michigan's consolidated elections, the recall election is held on the next fixed election date that falls at least 95 days after the recall petition is filed.
(t) An election will not be held in the last 6 mos. of a term after certification.
(u) County election administrators have 30 days; sponsor has three mos. to submit the petition from the date of certification.
(v) A special election is called unless the filing is within 90 days of a general election.

TABLE 6.20
State Recall Provisions: Petition Review, Appeal and Election (continued)

(w) Within four days, county clerks count signature totals and forward to the Secretary of State. The Secretary of State immediately notifies the clerks if they are to proceed with signature verification.

(x) In Nevada, a recall election is held 10-20 days after the Secretary of State completes notification of the petition sufficiency unless a complaint is filed, the clerk shall issue a call for the election which is to be held within 30 days after the issuance of the call.

(y) Five days after recount is completed or 14 days after the election if no recount is demanded.

(z) New Jersey Permanent Statutes,19:27A-13, In the case of an office which is ordinarily filled at the general election, a recall election shall be held at the next general election occurring at least 55 days following the fifth business day after service of certification, unless it was indicated in the notice of intention to recall that the recall election shall be held at a special election in

which case the recall election official shall order and fix the date for holding the recall election to be the next Tuesday occurring during the period beginning with the 55th day and ending on the 61st day following the fifth business day after service of the certification of the petition.

(aa) New Jersey Permanent Statutes, 19:27A-16.

(bb) Fourteen days after the canvas board has certified the results.

(cc) Chief petitioners may submit additional signatures if the deadline for submitting signatures has not passed.

(dd) Whether a penalty is assessed would depend on what information on the petition was falsified.

(ee) If possible to be held on a regularly scheduled election; cannot be held between the primary and general.

(ff) Business days.

(gg) The election is held at the next regular general election or at a special election set forth in the recall petition.

CHAPTER SEVEN

STATE FINANCE

TABLE 7.1
Fiscal 2017 General Fund, Actual (In millions of dollars)

State	Beginning balance	Revenues	Adjustments	Total resources	Expenditures	Adjustments	Ending balance	Rainy day fund balance
Total	$42,431	$799,009		$845,073	$808,396		$33,818	$55,389
Alabama (a)	185	8,197	50	8,432	8,166	116	150	766
Alaska (a)	0	1,354	745	2,099	4,498	764	(3,162)	4,641
Arizona	284	9,502	0	9,787	9,636	0	151	461
Arkansas (a)	0	5,349	0	5,349	5,349	0	0	123
California (a)	4,504	119,982	(132)	124,354	119,292	(640)	5,702	11,251
Colorado*(a)	513	10,276	45	10,833	10,425	(206)	614	614
Connecticut (a)	0	17,703	0	17,703	17,727	(1)	(23)	213
Delaware*(a)	568	4,013	0	4,581	4,106	0	475	221
Florida	1,892	29,945	0	31,836	30,322	0	1,515	1,384
Georgia* (a)	2,131	23,268	260	25,660	23,188	0	2,472	2,309
Hawaii	1,028	7,352	0	8,379	7,486	0	894	311
Idaho* (a)	51	3,448	27	3,526	3,262	163	101	413
Illinois* (a)	967	30,333	171	31,471	31,011	(908)	1,368	10
Indiana (a)	776	15,497	0	16,273	15,455	516	303	1,474
Iowa (a)	0	7,096	162	7,258	7,258	0	0	605
Kansas	37	6,348	0	6,385	6,277	0	109	0
Kentucky (a)	334	10,571	581	11,486	11,169	201	116	151
Louisiana (a)	(314)	9,456	155	9,297	9,149	26	123	287
Maine (a)	71	3,416	39	3,526	3,346	123	57	209
Maryland (a)	385	16,699	234	17,317	17,289	(230)	259	833
Massachusetts* (a)	1,482	41,167	617	43,267	41,202	617	1,448	1,301
Michigan (a)	604	9,872	31	10,507	9,809	75	623	710
Minnesota* (a)	3,102	21,334	0	24,436	21,103	0	3,333	1,980
Mississippi (a)	7	5,654	0	5,661	5,656	0	4	269
Missouri (a)	153	9,016	155	9,324	9,156	0	168	294
Montana (a)	257	2,142	(2)	2,396	2,365	(17)	48	0
Nebraska (a)	532	4,266	(220)	4,577	4,329	0	248	681
Nevada (a)	419	3,881	191	4,490	3,990	66	434	146
New Hampshire (a)	89	1,503	0	1,592	1,511	81	0	100
New Jersey (a)	473	33,856	874	35,203	34,416	0	787	0
New Mexico* (a)	148	6,461	78	6,687	6,130	52	505	0
New York*	8,934	66,895	0	75,829	68,080	0	7,749	1,798
North Carolina (a)	580	22,614	101	23,295	22,085	739	472	1,838
North Dakota (a)	263	1,579	828	2,669	2,503	102	65	38
Ohio (a)	1,193	34,178	0	35,371	34,814	0	557	2,034
Oklahoma (a)	0	5,706	114	5,820	5,737	0	84	93
Oregon (a)	284	9,826	(16)	10,094	9,093	0	1,000	761
Pennsylvania (a)	2	31,669	(1,269)	30,402	31,942	0	(1,539)	0
Rhode Island (a)	168	3,684	(108)	3,744	3,673	10	62	193
South Carolina* (a)	1,131	7,582	139	8,853	7,646	131	1,076	487
South Dakota (a)	14	1,541	15	1,570	1,548	14	8	157
Tennessee (a)	1,390	14,409	(217)	15,582	13,238	697	1,647	668
Texas (a)	4,278	52,285	(528)	56,035	53,683	1,469	883	10,290
Utah	165	6,321	0	6,487	6,411	0	76	508
Vermont (a)	0	1,574	0	1,574	1,540	34	0	107
Virginia (a)	1,278	19,619	0	20,898	20,115	0	783	549
Washington (a)	1,373	19,740	(673)	20,440	19,339	0	1,101	1,638
West Virginia (a)	371	4,191	98	4,660	4,248	14	398	652
Wisconsin (a)	331	15,518	680	16,528	17,099	(1,150)	579	283
Wyoming (a)	0	1,121	409	1,530	1,530	0	0	1,538

See footnotes at end of table

TABLE 7.1
Fiscal 2017 General Fund, Actual (In millions of dollars) (continued)

Source: National Association of State Budget Officers, Fall 2018.

Note: For all states, unless otherwise noted, transfers into budget stabilization funds are counted as expenditures, and transfers from budget stabilization funds are counted as revenues.

Key:

*–The ending balance includes the balance in the rainy day fund.

(a)

Alabama–Revenue adjustments include one-time BP Settlement funds of $50M. Expenditure adjustments include transfers to the ETF Budget Stabilization Fund of $59.6m and the ETF Advancement & Technology Fund of $59.4m. Designated portion of ending balance: $50,000,000 from the BP settlement was budgeted to be used for Medicaid in 2018.

Alaska–Revenues: Spring 2018 Revenue Sources Book (Total Revenue) Revenue Adjustments: SLA2017 Enacted Fiscal Summary (Lines 3–7) Expenditures: SLA2017 Enacted Fiscal Summary (Line 48) Expenditure Adjustments: SLA2017 Enacted Fiscal Summary (Line 49 and 52) Rainy Day Balance: State of Alaska Fiscal Summary FY18 and FY19 (Part 2) Number listed is EoY Balance. The rainy day fund balance listed is the anticipated end of year balance for the given fiscal year inclusive of any anticipated deposits or withdrawals. The deficits listed in the "ending balance" column are already factored into the rainy day balance.

Arkansas–Total available revenue amounts are reported as net of refunds and special dedications/payments.

California–Total revenues: reflect revenues after transfers to the rainy day fund. Revenue and expenditure adjustments to the beginning fund balance consist primarily of adjustments made to major taxes and K-12 spending. The ending balance includes the SFEU but excludes the BSA (a rainy day reserve held in a separate fund). The excluded amount is $6,713.4 million at the end of FY 2017. Adding these amounts to the FY 2017 ending balance, the projected total balance is $12,415.5 million in FY 2017. The rainy day balance is made up of the Special Fund for Economic Uncertainties and the BSA, however, withdrawals from the BSA are subject to provisions of Proposition 2, 2014. Ending balance includes a reserve for encumbrances of $1,165 million representing amounts which will be expended in the future for state obligations for which goods and services have been ordered/contracted, but have not been received by the end of the fiscal year. These amounts are shown as a reserve to the fund balance instead of a hit to the fund balance.

Colorado–The total revenue excludes income tax revenue amounts diverted to the State Education Fund per Amendment 23, which was $540 million in FY2016–17. Adjustments to revenue include money transferred from other funds to the General Fund. Adjustments to expenditures are reversions of appropriations and various accounting adjustments made by the State Controller's office each year. The FY 2016–17 adjustments to expenditures is an atypically large amount, mostly due to a large reversion of Medicaid-related dollars.

Connecticut–Expenditures Adjustments: Miscellaneous adjustments, 1,054,249.

Delaware–Ending balance includes Continuing and Encumbered Appropriations of $178.6 million.

Georgia–FY 17 beginning balance reflects general fund balances as of June 30, 2016 for Revenue Shortfall Reserve, Guaranteed Revenue Debt Common Reserve Fund, and State Revenue Collections as reported on the FY 16 Combined Balance Sheet of the Budgetary Compliance Report. Adjustments to Revenues include FY16 agency surplus returned and early remittance of FY 17 surplus from state agencies. FY 17 Actual Expenditures include $22,596,503,946 in State General fund expenditures.

Idaho–Revenue adjustments: reappropriation, $7 million; prior year reversion, $19.1 million; misc adjustments, $1 million. Expenditure adjustments: $400,000 to the Wolf Control Fund; $2,000,000 to the STEM Education Fund; $5,000,000 to the Higher Education Stabilization Fund, Community College Start-up Account; $34,500,000 to the Fire Suppression Deficiency Fund; $100,400 to Idaho Department of Water Resources Miscellaneous Revenue Fund, Priest Lake Outlet Subaccount; $2,700,000 to Broadband Infrastructure Improvement Grant Fund; $50,000,000 to the Emergency Relief Fund; $2,000,000 to the Disaster Emergency Fund; $31,836,900 to the Budget Stabilization Fund (statutory transfer); $27,464,200 to the Budget Stabilization Fund (surplus eliminator); $38,900 to the Hazardous Substance Emergency Response Fund, $342,600 to the Agriculture Pest Control Fund, $7,004,400 for prior year reappropriation.

Illinois–Total revenues include $2,438M in federal revenues. Revenue adjustments includes $171M in budgetary basis transfers adjustments (prior year transfers that cleared during the current year). Expenditures adjustments include $4,636M in transfers out, $9,331M in accounts payable at the end of the current FY, and $3,789M in accounts payable at the end of the prior fiscal year.

Indiana–Expenditure adjustments include reversions from distributions, capital, and reconciliations; transfer to the Major Moves 2020 trust fund; a transfer to the Bicentennial Capital Account; state agency and university line item capital projects; and a transfer of excess reserves for state ($235.3 million) and local ($192.6 million) roads and bridges. This one-time excess reserve transfer of $427.9 million was a move by the Governor and General Assembly to support infrastructure projects. Total revenues include forecasted General Fund revenues as well as unforecasted revenues such as HAF, QAF, dedicated fund SWCAP, and outside acts.

Iowa–Revenue adjustments include an estimated $18.2 million of residual funds transferred to the General Fund after the Reserve Funds are filled to their statutorily set maximum amounts. The ending balance of the General Fund is transferred in the current fiscal year to the Reserve Funds in the subsequent fiscal year. After the Reserve Funds are at their statutorily set maximum amounts, the remainder of the funds are transferred back to the General Fund in that subsequent fiscal year. Also included in revenue adjustments is $131.1 million transferred from the Cash Reserve Fund as authorized by the Legislature under SF 516 and $13.0 million transferred from the Economic Emergency Fund as authorized by Governor Reynolds with the issuance of an Official Proclamation to bring the General Fund into balance.

TABLE 7.1
Fiscal 2017 General Fund, Actual (In millions of dollars) (continued)

Kentucky–Revenue includes $93.4 million in Tobacco Settlement funds. Adjustment for Revenues includes $240.2 million that represents appropriation balances carried over from the prior fiscal year, and $340.6 million from fund transfers into the General Fund. The FY 2017 $115.6 million ending balance was budgeted for use in the FY 2018 enacted budget ($102.3 million for FY 2018 and $13.3 million for FY 2019).

Louisiana–Revenues adjustments–Includes $99.0 from Budget Stabilization funds, $55.8 Mid-Year Deficit action. Expenditure adjustments–Includes $6.5 in transfers to DPS License Fees. The "total revenues" amounts reported here include transfers from other state fund sources.

Maine–Revenue and Expenditure adjustments reflect Legislatively authorized transfers.

Maryland–Revenue adjustments include $29.5 million in transfers from tax credit reserves, $32.5 million in transfers from other funds, and $170 million transfer from the Revenue Stabilization Account (Rainy Day). Expenditure adjustments represent $229.9 million in reversions to the unappropriated General Fund balance.

Massachusetts–General fund is defined as all budgeted operating funds. Ending balance includes $117.4 million in reserved balances to be spent in the next fiscal year. The Commonwealth of Massachusetts credits federal reimbursements for Medicaid, as well as certain other federal reimbursements, to the General Fund. In the NASBO State Expenditure Survey, these reimbursement funds are shown as "federal funds spending" to conform to the survey definitions. Additionally, in the NASBO State Expenditure Survey, certain interfund transfers are shown as spending in "Other State Funds", but are shown in this presentation as "General Fund" spending to be consistent with the Commonwealth's accounting practices.

Michigan–Revenue totals are net of payments to local governments and balance sheet adjustments. Adjustments (Revenues): $30.6 book closing correction to prior year amount. Adjustments (Expenditures): $75 million transfer to budget stabilization fund/ rainy day fund.

Minnesota–Ending balance includes cash flow account of $350 million, budget reserve account of $1,603.443 million, and stadium reserve of $26.821 million.

Mississippi–Ending balance includes reappropriation from FY2017 to FY2018.

Missouri–Revenue adjustments include transfers from other funds into the general revenue fund.

Montana–Revenue adjustments reflect prior year revenue activity and expenditure adjustments reflect prior year expenditure activity and adjustments to fund balance as a result of the annual CAFR reconciliation.

Nebraska–Revenue adjustments are transfers from the General Fund to other funds. Among these transfers is a $202 million transfer from the General Fund to the Property Tax Credit Cash Fund for property tax relief.

Nevada–Revenue adjustments are restricted revenue, reversions, Rainy Day Fund transfers in and reserve transfers in. Expenditure adjustments are restricted transfers out.

New Hampshire–Expenditure Adjustments: $62.2 million was moved to the Education Trust Fund; $.7 million was moved to the Fish and Game Fund; $13.9 million was moved to the Highway Fund,18.7 million was moved to the Public School Infrastructure Fund and $7.0 million was moved to the Rainy Day Fund at year end. (Positive adjustments totaling $22.0 million were made for GAAP and Other also.)

New Jersey–Revenue adjustments include: Budget vs. GAAP adjustments; lapses; transfers to other funds; reservation of fund balance.

New Mexico–FY17 reflects actual amounts received from solvency legislation per LFC/DFA sweeps tracking–includes Laws 2016, Chapter 12 (HB311, $75 million fund sweeps); Laws 2016, Second Special Session, Chapter 4 (SB2, $93 million general fund sweeps and transfers), Chapter 5 (SB8, $103.2 million capital outlay sweeps), and Chapter 6 (SB9, $27.9 million PED appropriation reductions); Laws 2017, Chapter 1 (HB4, $89 million adjusted reversion date for fire protection fund and law enforcement protection fund), Chapter 2 (SB113, $55.2 million general fund sweeps), and Chapter 3 (SB114, $40.8 million school cash balances); Laws 2017, First Special Session, Chapter 1 (SB1, $82.1 million public school capital outlay swap and general fund sweeps).

North Carolina–Transfer from Rainy Day Fund for S.L. 2016-124 Disaster Recovery Act of 2016. Adjusted expenditures include transfer to the Budget Stabilization Reserve, transfer for the Medicaid Transformation Reserve, and transfer for Repair and Renovation

North Dakota–Revenue adjustments are transfers of $572.5 million from the budget stabilization fund, $155.0 million from the strategic investment and improvements fund and $100.0 million from other special fund sources, to the general fund. Expenditure adjustments include a transfer of $32.2 million to the budget stabilization fund, $2 million in misc. adjustments and $67.3 million of expenditure authority carried over to the 2015-17 biennium, obligating an equal amount of the general fund balance.

Ohio–Federal reimbursements for Medicaid expenditures funded from the General Revenue Fund (GRF) are deposited into the GRF. Federal reimbursements for Medicaid expenditures from non-GRF sources are deposited into the appropriate federal fund. Expenditures of federal funds are contained in the General Fund number to be consistent with Ohio accounting practices and with other portrayals of Ohio's general fund. This will tend to make Ohio's GRF revenue and expenditures look higher relative to most other states that don't follow this practice. FY 2017 expenditures include expenditures against prior year encumbrances as well as $310.8 million in transfers out of the GRF. The fiscal 2017 ending balance included funds to support $386.2 million in open encumbrances.

TABLE 7.1
Fiscal 2017 General Fund, Actual (In millions of dollars) (continued)

Oklahoma–Revenue adjustment for FY-2017 is the net cash flow reserve amount available for the fiscal year. FY-2017 ending balance expended in the FY-2018 budget. These numbers include collections and estimates for the two largest appropriated funds (the General Revenue Fund and the OK Education Reform Revolving Fund) which constitute the majority of the state appropriated budget.

Oregon–Revenue adjustments include: a revenue adjustment for a statutory transfer to local governments for local property tax relief.

Pennsylvania–Revenue adjustments include refunds, lapses and adjustments to beginning balances.

Rhode Island–Adjustments to revenues reflects $115.6 million to the Budget Reserve (Rainy Day) Fund,offset by reappropriation of $7.8 million from FY 2016. Expenditure adjustments reflect reappropriations to the following fiscal year (FY 2018). Reappropriations authorized by the Governor totaling $10.3 million.

South Carolina–Revenue Adjustments: Litigation Recovery Account ($139.2M). Expenditure Adjustments: Prior Yr 2% Capital Reserve ($131.0M) transferred to state agencies. Designated portion of ending balance–Capital Reserve Fund -$139.2M.

South Dakota–The beginning balance of $14.1 million and adjustment to expenditures reflects the prior year's ending balance that is transferred to the rainy day fund. Adjustments to revenue of $15.4 million is from one-time receipts. The ending balance of $7.9 million is cash that is obligated to the Budget Reserve fund the following fiscal year. This $7.9 million is not included in the total rainy day fund balance of $157.4 million.

Tennessee–Revenue adjustments: $83.9 million transfer from debt service fund unexpended appropriations; -$100.0 million transfer to Rainy Day Fund; -$147.6 million transfer to Highway Fund; -$53.7 million transfer to dedicated revenue reserves. Expenditure adjustments: $445.8 million transfer to capital outlay projects fund; $95.1 million transfer to state office buildings and support facilities fund; $3.6 million transfer to debt service fund; $1.0 million transfer to reserves for dedicated revenue appropriations; $151.5 million transfer to reserves for unexpended appropriations. Ending balance: $1,306.3 million reserve for appropriations 2017-2018; and $340.3 million unappropriated budget surplus at June 30, 2017."

Texas–Revenue adjustment of -527.7m from general fund dedicated account balances. Expenditure adjustment of $1,468.8m reserved for transfer (50/50) to the Rainy Day Fund and State Highway Fund.

Vermont–$34.3M of expenditure adjustments reflect a combination of $28.52M in contributions to reserve accounts, as well as $5.76M in transfers to other funds.

Virginia–Total Revenues includes fund transfers.

Washington–Revenue adjustments reflect the net of transfers in and out of the General Fund, as well as prior biennium recoveries and similar resource adjustments. The Total Revenues reflect total general fund revenues, before transfers in and out of the general fund (which are included as adjustments).

West Virginia–Fiscal Year 2017 Beginning balance includes $283.0 million of Reappropriations, Unappropriated Surplus Balance of $28.8 million, $0.7 million of cash balance adjustments, and FY 2016 13th month expenditures of $58.9 million. Total Revenues show the FY 2017 actual general revenue collections of $4,191.0 million. Adjustments (Revenue) are prior year redeposits of $0.4 million and special revenue expirations of $97.3 million. Total Expenditures include current year general revenue appropriatied expenditures of $3,997.1 million, surplus appropriation expenditures of $54.8 million, reappropriation expenditures of $112.5 million, $-0.2 million of cash adjustments, $24.5 million of reappropriations transferred to FY 2017 collections, and $58.9 million of 31 day prior year expenditures. Adjustment (Expenditures) represent $14.4 million which was the amount transferred to the Rainy Day Fund from 1/2 of the FY 2016 surplus. The Ending Balance is mostly the historically carried forward reappropriation from previous fiscal years (estimated amounts that will remain and be reappropriated to the next fiscal year), the estimated 13th month expenditures applicable to the current fiscal year & the any unappropriated surplus balance (estimated) from the current fiscal year.

Wisconsin–Revenue adjustments include Tribal Gaming, $27.4; Prior Year Designated Balance, $132.0; and Other Revenue, $520.1. Expenditure adjustments include Transfers to Transportation fund, $39.5; Lapses, -$1,190.7; and Compensation Reserves, $1.2

Wyoming–The State of Wyoming budgets on a biennial basis, to arrive at annual figures certain assumptions and estimates were required.

Table 7.1 | Fiscal 2017 General Fund

2017 Beginning Balances (millions)

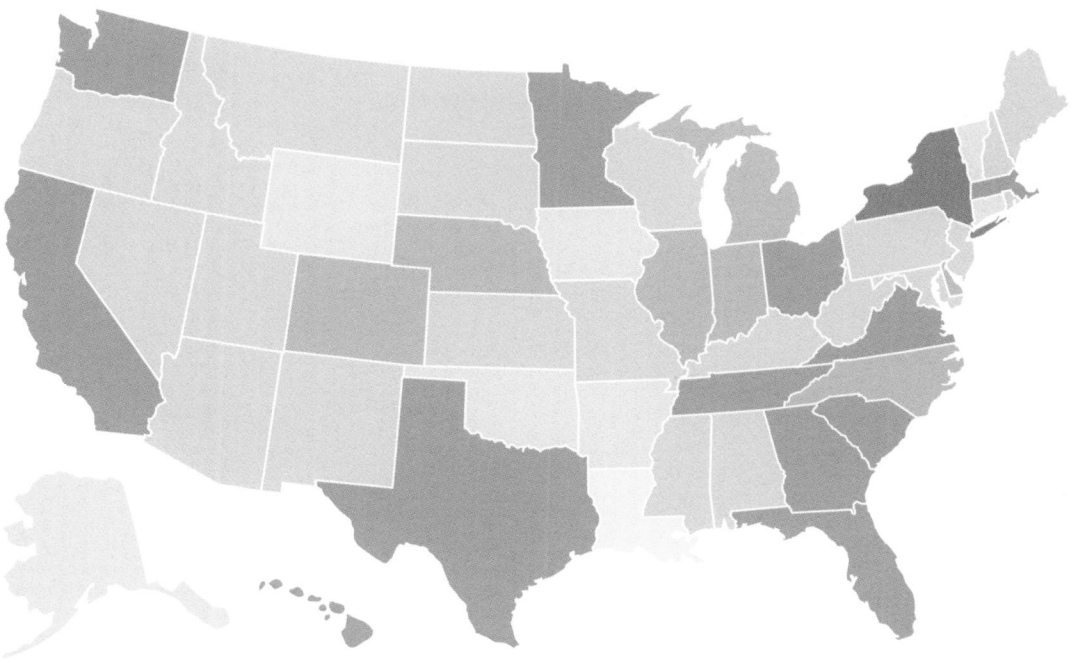

- Less than 0
- 0
- 1 to 499
- 500 to 999
- 1000 to 5000
- More than 5000

Highest Rainy Day Fund Balance Fiscal 2017 (in millions)

CALIFORNIA • $11,251
TEXAS • $10,290
ALASKA • $4,641
GEORGIA • $2,309
OHIO • $2,034

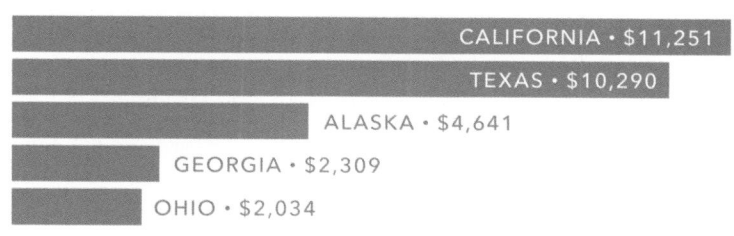

In 2017 18 states reported **REVENUES CAME IN AHEAD of** budget projections and 27 states came in **BELOW FORECAST.**

General fund revenue collections increased by 2.4% in fiscal 2017.

Table 7.1 | Fiscal 2017 General Fund *(cont.)*

2017 Ending Balances (millions)

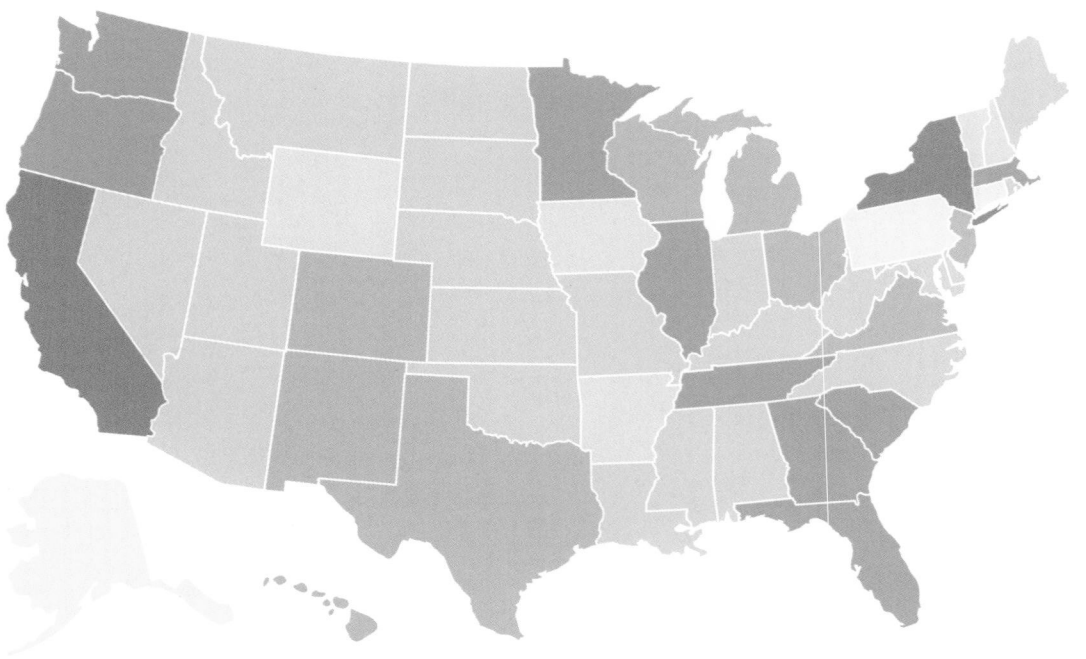

Less than 0
0
1 to 499
500 to 999
1000 to 5000
More than 5000

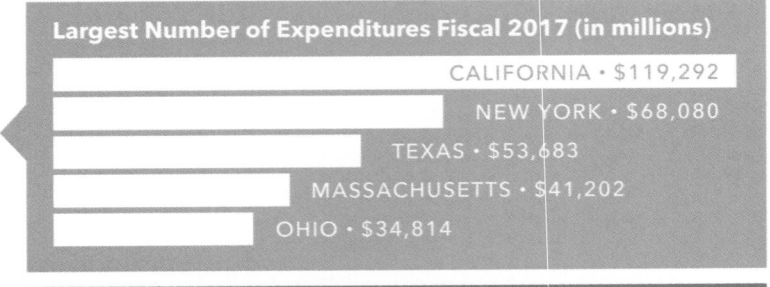

Largest Number of Expenditures Fiscal 2017 (in millions)

CALIFORNIA · $119,292
NEW YORK · $68,080
TEXAS · $53,683
MASSACHUSETTS · $41,202
OHIO · $34,814

Smallest Number of Expenditures Fiscal 2017 (in millions)

NEW HAMPSHIRE · $1,511
WYOMING · $1,530
VERMONT · $1,540
SOUTH DAKOTA · $1,548
MONTANA · $2,365

TABLE 7.2

Fiscal 2018 General Fund, Preliminary Actual (In millions of dollars)

State	Beginning balance	Revenues	Adjustments	Total resources	Expenditures	Adjustments	Ending Balance	Rainy day fund balance
Total	$37,013	$850,276		$895,857	$838,236		$43,238	$59,935
Alabama	150	8,646	0	8,796	8,393	0	403	783
Alaska (a)	0	2,337	745	3,082	4,489	820	(2,227)	2,562
Arizona	151	10,111	0	10,261	9,812	0	450	458
Arkansas (a)	0	5,495	0	5,495	5,495	0	0	127
California (a)	5,702	129,825	0	135,527	127,045	0	8,482	16,728
Colorado* (a)	614	11,723	98	12,436	11,184	(21)	1,274	1,274
Connecticut (a)	0	18,199	0	18,199	18,685	(3)	(483)	1,185
Delaware* (a)	475	4,393	0	4,868	4,118	0	750	232
Florida	1,515	31,919	0	33,434	31,989	0	1,445	1,417
Georgia (a)	2,472	24,320	144	26,935	24,207	0	2,729	N/A
Hawaii	894	7,660	0	8,554	7,804	0	750	376
Idaho (a)	101	3,732	12	3,845	3,466	140	239	394
Illinois* (a)	1,368	36,943	4,508	42,819	35,100	7,594	125	10
Indiana (a)	303	15,837	150	16,289	15,736	186	366	1,419
Iowa (a)	0	7,384	0	7,384	7,224	33	127	620
Kansas	109	7,299	0	7,407	6,645	0	763	0
Kentucky (a)	116	10,941	470	11,527	11,330	168	29	94
Louisiana (a)	123	9,588	48	9,759	9,759	0	0	321
Maine (a)	57	3,506	33	3,595	3,515	6	75	288
Maryland (a)	259	17,372	31	17,662	17,287	(211)	585	857
Massachusetts* (a)	1,448	43,909	1,134	46,491	43,077	1,134	2,280	1,793
Michigan (a)	623	9,989	0	10,611	10,185	325	101	1,008
Minnesota* (a)	3,333	21,867	0	25,200	22,695	0	2,505	1,998
Mississippi (a)	4	5,634	0	5,638	5,633	0	5	288
Missouri (a)	168	9,469	125	9,762	9,267	0	495	305
Montana (a)	48	2,406	2	2,455	2,287	(18)	186	0
Nebraska (a)	248	4,567	(12)	4,803	4,350	0	454	340
Nevada (a)	434	4,019	64	4,517	3,981	50	486	180
New Hampshire (a)	0	1,599	0	1,599	1,503	17	80	110
New Jersey (a)	787	35,234	410	36,431	35,658	0	772	0
New Mexico* (a)	505	6,809	57	7,370	6,201	57	1,112	449
New York* (a)	7,749	71,420	0	79,169	69,724	0	9,445	1,798
North Carolina (a)	472	23,565	0	24,037	22,746	295	995	1,849
North Dakota (a)	65	1,972	377	2,414	2,160	0	253	113
Ohio (a)	557	32,471	0	33,028	31,807	0	1,221	2,034
Oklahoma (a)	84	6,606	(274)	6,416	6,034	382	0	452
Oregon (a)	1,000	10,349	(34)	11,315	9,764	0	1,552	940
Pennsylvania (a)	(1,539)	34,567	(1,035)	31,993	31,948	22	22	0
Rhode Island (a)	62	3,908	(109)	3,861	3,806	10	46	199
South Carolina* (a)	1,076	8,124	21	9,221	7,895	139	1,187	509
South Dakota (a)	8	1,593	15	1,616	1,591	8	17	160
Tennessee (a)	1,647	14,321	(162)	15,806	14,485	791	530	800
Texas (a)	883	56,990	1,049	58,922	56,050	2,741	131	10,455
Utah (a)	85	7,009	0	7,094	6,739	0	355	508
Vermont (a)	0	1,641	0	1,641	1,564	77	0	133
Virginia (a)	783	19,879	0	20,662	20,450	0	212	440
Washington (a)	1,101	21,621	(320)	22,402	20,455	0	1,947	1,364
West Virginia (a)	398	4,245	4	4,648	4,232	38	378	710
Wisconsin (a)	579	16,144	608	17,332	17,139	(396)	589	320
Wyoming (a)	0	1,121	409	1,530	1,530	0	0	1,538

See footnotes at end of table

TABLE 7.2

Fiscal 2018 General Fund, Preliminary Actual (In millions of dollars) (continued)

Source: National Association of State Budget Officers, Fall 2018.
Note: For all states, unless otherwise noted, transfers into budget stabilization funds are counted as expenditures, and transfers from budget stabilization funds are counted as revenues.

Key:

*–The ending balance includes the balance in the rainy day fund.
N/A–Not available

(a)

Alaska–Revenues: Spring 2019 Revenue Sources Book (Total Revenue)
Revenue Adjustments: SLA2018 Enacted Fiscal Summary (Lines 3-7) Expenditures: SLA2018 Enacted Fiscal Summary, (line 45) Expenditure Adjustments: SLA 2018 Enacted Fiscal Summary, (line 46 and 51) Rainy Day Balance: State of Alaska Fiscal Summary FY18 and FY19 (Part 3) Number listed is EoY Balance. The rainy day fund balance listed is the anticipated end of year balance for the given fiscal year inclusive of any anticipated deposits or withdrawals. The deficits listed in the "ending balance" column are already factored into the rainy day balance.

Arkansas–Total available revenue amounts are reported as net of refunds and special dedications/payments.

California– Total revenues: reflect revenues after transfers to the rainy day fund. The ending balance includes the SFEU but excludes the BSA. The excluded amount is $9,410.4 million at the end of FY 2018. Adding these amounts to the FY 2018 ending balance, the projected total balance is $17,892.6 million in FY 2018. The rainy day balance is made up of the Special Fund for Economic Uncertainties and the BSA, however, withdrawals from the BSA are subject to provisions of Proposition 2, 2014. Ending balance includes a reserve for encumbrances of $1,165 million representing amounts which will be expended in the future for state obligations for which goods and services have been ordered/contracted, but have not been received by the end of the fiscal year. These amounts are shown as a reserve to the fund balance instead of a hit to the fund balance.

Colorado–The total revenue excludes income tax revenue amounts diverted to the State Education Fund per Amendment 23, which was $617 million in FY2017-18. Adjustments to revenue include money transferred from other funds to the General Fund. Adjustments to expenditures are reversions of appropriations and various accounting adjustments made by the State Controller's office each year.

Connecticut–BRF balance includes: $212.9 million balance from prior year, $1,471.3 million transfer due to volatility cap, $-482.9 transfer out to extinguish FY 2018 deficit, and $-16.1 million transfer out to the Retired Teachers Health Service Fund. The volatility cap which automatically transfers a portion of income tax collections above a certain threshold. Expenditures Adjustments: Miscellaneous adjustments, 3.4.

Delaware–Ending balance includes Continuing and Encumbered Appropriations of $168.9 million.

Georgia–Georgia is required by its constitution to maintain a balanced budget. The fund balances for FY 18 and 19 reflect the Governor's balanced budget report. Georgia does not project future Rainy Day fund balances but expects the reserve to continue to grow in future years.

Idaho–Revenue adjustments: $5.9 m for reappropriation; $2.6 m for prior-year reversion; $.1 m misc. adjustments; and $3.6 m from the Immunization Fund. Expenditure adjustments: $34.5 million to the Budget Stabilization Fund (statutory transfer); $2 million to the Opportunity Fund; $45.3 million to the Permanent Building Fund; $.4 million to the Wolf Control Fund; $2.5 million to the Workforce Development Training Fund; $20 million to the Fire Suppression Fund; $27.7 to the Idaho Transportation Department (prior year surplus eliminator); $1 million to the Water Management Fund; $.2 million for deficiency warrants; and $5.9 million for reappropriation.

Illinois–Total revenues increase is due primarily from the increase in income tax rates from 3.75% to 4.95% for individual and from 5.25% to 7% for corporate. Total revenues include $4,032M in base federal revenues (excludes the $1,206M referenced below). Estimated revenue adjustments include $802M in interfund borrowing and fund reallocations from other state funds, $2,500M in proceeds from the issuance of backlog borrowing bonds, and $1,206M in federal match from the paydown of prior year Medicaid liabilities. Estimated expenditures adjustments include $3,773M in transfers out, $28M in prior year adjustments, $3,721 in vouchers payable adjustments, and $128M in transfers to repay interfund borrowing.

Indiana–Revenue adjustments include a transfer to the General Fund to assist with the Integrated Tax System, a transfer from the State Tuition Reserve Account, and a transfer from the Rainy Day Fund. Expenditure adjustments include reversions from distributions, capital, and reconciliations; state agency and university line item capital projects; the cost of a 13th check for pension recipients; and transfers to the Rainy Day Fund. Total revenues include forecasted General Fund revenues as well as unforecasted revenues such as HAF, QAF, dedicated fund SWCAP, and outside acts.

Iowa–Included in expenditure adjustments are transfers from the General Fund to the State's Cash Reserve Fund ($20.0 million) and the State's Economic Emergency Fund ($13.0 million). The ending balance of the General Fund is transferred in the current year to the Reserve funds in the subsequent fiscal year. After the Reserve Funds are at their statutorily set maximum amounts, the remainder of the funds are transferred back to the General Fund in that subsequent fiscal year.

Kentucky–Revenue includes $102.6 million in Tobacco Settlement funds. Adjustments for Revenues includes $201.5 million that represents appropriation balances carried over from the prior fiscal year, and $268.9 million from fund transfers into the General Fund. Adjustment to Expenditures represents appropriation balances forwarded to the next fiscal year and budget balances to be expended in the next fiscal year. The FY 2018 $29.0 million ending balance was budgeted for use in FY 2019.

TABLE 7.2
Fiscal 2018 General Fund, Preliminary Actual (In millions of dollars) (continued)

Louisiana–Revenues adjustments–Includes $19.2 in carryforwards and $29.0 from prior year undesignated fund balance. Expenditure adjustments–None. FY18 numbers are budgeted and not actuals. The "total revenues" amounts reported here include transfers from other state fund sources.

Maine–Revenue and Expenditure adjustments reflect Legislatively authorized transfers. Dedicated portion of ending balance: Transfers funds into the Budget Stabilization Fund from unclaimed property and transfers $2M from the Budget Stabilization Fund to the General Fund, and up to $65M to a General Fund Reserve account for disallowed costs from the Centers for Medicare and Medicaid Services.

Maryland–Revenue adjustments include $21.8 million in transfers from tax credit reserves and $9.0 million in transfers from other funds. Expenditure adjustments represent $144.2 million in reversions to the unappropriated General Fund balance and $66.5 million in legislative reductions and executive branch agency mid-year reductions.

Massachusetts–General fund is defined as all budgeted operating funds; all figures are estimates as of 9/4/18. Ending balance includes $475.4 million in reserved balances to be spent in the next fiscal year. The Commonwealth of Massachusetts credits federal reimbursements for Medicaid, as well as certain other federal reimbursements, to the General Fund. In the NASBO State Expenditure Survey, these reimbursement funds are shown as "federal funds spending" to conform to the survey definitions. Additionally, in the NASBO State Expenditure Survey, certain interfund transfers are shown as spending in "Other State Funds", but are shown in this presentation as "General Fund" spending to be consistent with the Commonwealth's accounting practices.

Michigan–Revenue totals are net of payments to local governments and balance sheet adjustments. Adjustments (Expenditures): $265 million transfer to budget stabilization/rainy day fund; $35 million transfer to infrastructure fund; and $25 million transfer to Flint reserve fund for water emergency. Michigan's fiscal year is October 1 through September 30. At the time of completing this survey, Michigan was operating in FY 18.

Minnesota–Ending balance includes cash flow account of $350 million, budget reserve account of $1,608.364 million, and stadium reserve of $39.608 million.

Mississippi–Ending balance includes reappropriation from FY2018 to FY2019.

Missouri–Revenue adjustments include transfers from other funds into the general revenue fund.

Montana–Revenue adjustments reflect prior year revenue activity and expenditure adjustments reflect prior year expenditure activity and adjustments to fund balance as a result of the annual CAFR reconciliation.

Nebraska –Revenue adjustments are transfers between the General Fund and other funds. Among others, this includes a $221 million transfer from the General Fund to the Property Tax Credit Cash Fund. Also included are transfers totaling $225 million from the Cash Reserve Fund to the General Fund for budget stabilization.

Nevada–Revenue adjustments are restricted revenue, reversions, Rainy Day Fund transfers in and reserve transfers in. Expenditure adjustments are restricted transfers out.

New Hampshire–Expenditure Adjustments: As the result of standalone legislation in FY 2018, $10 million was authorized to be deposited in the revenue stabilization reserve account (Rainy Day Fund). Additionally, $6.6 million of general funds was authorized to be deposited in the Public School Infrastructure Fund at year end. Though the General Fund Ending Balance for FY 2018 is labeled as an undesignated fund balance, the legislature passed standalone legislation obligating over $ 12.7 million for pay raises; $10.0 million for infrastructure projects, and another $ 2.2 million for other initiatives in FY 2019.to be funded with these FY 2018 carry forward funds.

New Jersey–Revenue adjustments include: Estimated lapses; reservation of fund balance; transfer to other funds.

New Mexico–FY18 reflects remaining solvency transfers per Laws 2017, Chapter 1 (HB4, $10.7 million fire protection fund adjusted reversion) and Laws 2017, First Special Session, Chapter 1 (SB1, $8 million from NMFA public project revolving fund). $9 million was moved from FY18 recurring appropriations to nonrecurring appropriations to reflect DFA accounting for $7 million LEDA special and $2 million NMCD special.

New York–FY 2018 and FY 2019 annual revenue changes include an acceleration of PIT payments due in calendar year 2018 as taxpayers responded to Federal tax law changes that, starting in tax year 2018, limit the allowable aggregate itemized deduction of State and local income taxes, and local real property taxes, to a maximum of $10,000 on Federal income tax returns. DOB estimates approximately $1.9 billion was accelerated from FY 2019 to FY 2018.

North Carolina–Expenditure adjustments include funds for the R&R Reserve, $64.8M, the Capital Project Reserve $155.2, and the Medicaid Transformation Reserve, $75M.

North Dakota –Revenue adjustments are transfers of $183.0 million from the tax relief fund, $124.0 million from the strategic investment and improvements fund and $70.0 million from other special fund sources, to the general fund.

Ohio–Federal reimbursements for Medicaid expenditures funded from the General Revenue Fund (GRF) are deposited into the GRF. Federal reimbursements for Medicaid expenditures from non-GRF sources are deposited into the appropriate federal fund. Expenditures of federal funds are contained in the General Fund number to be consistent with Ohio accounting practices and with other portrayals of Ohio's general fund. This will tend to make Ohio's GRF revenue and expenditures look higher relative to most other states that don't follow this practice. FY 2018 expenditures include expenditures against prior year encumbrances as well as $80.0 million in transfers out of the GRF. The fiscal 2018 ending balance included funds to support $371.2 million in open encumbrances.

TABLE 7.2
Fiscal 2018 General Fund, Preliminary Actual (In millions of dollars) (continued)

Oklahoma–The revenue adjustment for FY-2018 is the net cash flow reserve amount available for the fiscal year. The FY-2018 expenditure adjustment amount is the amount transferred to the Constitutional Reserve Fund (Rainy Day Fund) at the end of the fiscal year. The Rainy Day Fund balance was increased by a $381.6 million deposit, but was also decreased by $23.3 million appropriated in special session, leaving the balance of $451.6 million at the end of FY-2018. These numbers include collections and estimates for the two largest appropriated funds (the General Revenue Fund and the OK Education Reform Revolving Fund) which constitute the majority of the state appropriated budget.

Oregon–Revenue adjustments include: a revenue adjustment for a statutory transfer to local governments for local property tax relief.

Pennsylvania–Revenue adjustments include refunds, lapses and adjustments to beginning balances. Expenditure adjustments include transfers to the Budget Stabilization Reserve Fund (rainy day).

Rhode Island–Adjustments to revenues reflects $119.1 million to the Budget Reserve (Rainy Day) Fund, offset by reappropriation of $10.3 million from FY 2017. Expenditure adjustments reflect reappropriations to the following fiscal year (FY 2019). Reappropriations authorized by the Governor totaling $10.1 million.

South Carolina–Revenue Adjustments: Litigation Recovery Account ($16.2M) & South Carolina Farm Aid Fund ($4.5M). Expenditure Adjustments: Prior Yr 2% Capital Reserve ($139.2M) transferred to state agencies. Designated portion of ending balance–Capital Reserve Fund–$145.4 M.

South Dakota–The beginning balance of $7.9 million and adjustment to expenditures reflects the prior year's ending balance that is transferred to the rainy day fund. Adjustments to revenue of $14.6 million is from one-time receipts. The ending balance of $16.9 million is cash that is obligated to the Budget Reserve fund the following fiscal year. This $16.9 million is not included in the total rainy day fund balance of $159.5 million.

Tennessee–Revenue adjustments: $55.5 million transfer from debt service fund unexpended appropriations; -$85.0 million transfer to Highway Fund; -$132.0 million transfer to Rainy Day Fund. Expenditure adjustments: $644.5 million transfer to capital outlay projects fund; $142.3 million transfer to state office buildings and support facilities fund; $3.5 million transfer to debt service fund; $1.0 million transfer to reserves for dedicated revenue appropriations. Ending balance: $529.8 million unappropriated budget surplus at June 30, 2018.

Texas–Revenue adjustment of $1,048.8m in general fund dedicated account balances. Expenditure adjustment of $2741.0m reserved for transfer (50/50) to the Rainy Day Fund and the State Highway Fund. Figures represent the numbers provided by the Comptroller in the revised CRE released July 2018.

Utah–Based on revenue and expenditure estimates authorized during the 2018 General Session. Since this is based on estimates, it does not include any additional balances or statutory rainy day fund deposits that will be calculated when FY 2018 is closed-out.

Vermont–The $76.9M in adjusted expenditures includes a net +$26.2M in contributions to established reserves, and +$50.7M in fund transfers. Of the $50.7M in fund transfers, $26.2M was transferred as an additional contribution to the Vermont State Teacher's Retirement System accrued liability above and beyond the Fiscal 2018 ADEC.

Virginia–Total Revenues includes fund transfers.

Washington–Revenue adjustments reflect the net of transfers in and out of the General Fund, as well as prior biennium recoveries and similar resource adjustments. A portion of the FY 2018 ending balance is programmed to be spent in FY 2019. The Total Revenues reflect total general fund revenues, before transfers in and out of the general fund (which are included as adjustments).

West Virginia–Fiscal Year 2018 Beginning balance includes $285.1 million of Reappropriations, Unappropriated Surplus Balance of $76.2 million, $1.0 million of cash balance adjustments, and FY 2017 13th month expenditures of $35.8 million. Total Revenues show the FY 2018 actual general revenue collections of $4,254.2 million. Adjustments (Revenue) are prior year redeposits of $2.6 million and special revenue expirations of $1.6 million. Total Expenditures include current year general revenue appropriatied expenditures of $4,040.1 million, surplus appropriation expenditures of $30.5 million, reappropriation expenditures of $125.7 million, $-0.3 million of cash adjustments, and $35.9 million of 31 day prior year expenditures. Adjustment (Expenditures) represent $38.0 million which was the amount transferred to the Rainy Day Fund from 1/2 of the FY 2017 surplus. The Ending Balance is mostly the historically carried forward reappropriation from previous fiscal years (estimated amounts that will remain and be reappropriated to the next fiscal year), the estimated 13th month expenditures applicable to the current fiscal year & the any unappropriated surplus balance (estimated) from the current fiscal year.

Wisconsin–Revenue adjustments include Tribal Gaming, $27.1; Prior Year Designated Balance, $52.1; and Other Revenue, $528.6. Expenditure adjustments include Transfers, $73.3; Lapses, -$469.3; and Compensation Reserves, $0.3.

Wyoming–The State of Wyoming budgets on a biennial basis, to arrive at annual figures certain assumptions and estimates were required.

TABLE 7.3
Fiscal 2019 General Fund, Enacted (In millions of dollars)

State	Beginning balance	Revenues	Adjustments	Total resources	Expenditures	Adjustments	Ending balance	Rainy day fund balance
Total	**$44,667**	**$868,401**		**$918,533**	**$874,612**		**$33,901**	**$62,376**
Alabama (a)	403	8,903	0	9,306	8,672	237	397	853
Alaska (a)	0	2,259	2,837	5,096	4,741	1,047	(692)	2,036
Arizona	204	10,421	0	10,625	10,389	0	236	463
Arkansas (a)	0	5,690	0	5,690	5,626	0	64	127
California (a)	8,482	133,332	0	141,814	138,688	0	3,127	15,930
Colorado* (a)	1,274	12,382	19	13,675	12,607	0	1,069	1,069
Connecticut (a)	0	19,009	0	19,009	18,998	0	11	1,515
Delaware* (a)	750	4,368	0	5,117	4,498	0	620	240
Florida	1,445	32,838	0	34,283	33,057	0	1,226	1,483
Georgia (a)	2,729	24,874	N/A	27,603	24,874	0	2,729	N/A
Hawaii	750	7,837	0	8,587	7,943	0	644	384
Idaho (a)	118	3,669	13	3,801	3,653	103	45	394
Illinois* (a)	125	37,420	1,100	38,645	35,323	3,183	139	10
Indiana (a)	366	16,223	130	16,720	16,199	15	507	1,355
Iowa(a)	0	7,640	93	7,733	7,362	113	258	762
Kansas (a)	763	7,003	0	7,766	7,071	48	647	0
Kentucky (a)	29	11,318	322	11,669	11,617	52	0	127
Louisiana (a)	0	9,560	0	9,560	9,560	0	0	323
Maine (a)	75	3,668	21	3,764	3,701	36	27	288
Maryland (a)	192	17,763	25	17,980	17,909	(35)	106	880
Massachusetts* (a)	2,280	44,879	1,106	48,264	44,896	1,106	2,263	2,161
Michigan (a)	101	9,926	0	10,028	10,021	0	6	1,051
Minnesota* (a)	2,505	22,934	0	25,439	23,160	0	2,279	1,991
Mississippi	5	5,656	0	5,661	5,661	0	0	314
Missouri (a)	495	9,418	152	10,065	9,745	0	320	320
Montana	186	2,476	0	2,662	2,435	0	227	46
Nebraska (a)	454	4,731	(244)	4,940	4,456	258	226	334
Nevada (a)	383	4,077	59	4,518	4,079	52	388	294
New Hampshire (a)	1	1,554	(23)	1,531	1,521	10	0	111
New Jersey (a)	772	37,127	(91)	37,808	37,043	0	764	0
New Mexico*	1,112	7,279	189	8,580	6,380	36	2,164	1,483
New York* (a)	9,445	72,660	0	82,105	76,601	0	5,504	1,798
North Carolina (a)	995	23,930	0	24,925	23,920	357	649	2,011
North Dakota (a)	253	1,664	394	2,311	2,150	96	65	209
Ohio (a)	1,221	33,708	0	34,930	34,070	0	859	2,692
Oklahoma (a)	0	7,296	0	7,296	6,997	0	298	N/A
Oregon (a)	1,552	10,096	(37)	11,611	10,162	0	1,449	1,210
Pennsylvania (a)	22	33,975	(1,274)	32,723	32,715	4	4	14
Rhode Island (a)	31	3,999	(121)	3,909	3,908	0	1	201
South Carolina* (a)	1,187	8,239	86	9,512	8,164	145	1,203	531
South Dakota (a)	17	1,642	0	1,658	1,642	17	0	176
Tennessee (a)	530	14,744	(82)	15,193	14,905	281	6	861
Texas (a)	131	56,989	188	57,308	51,445	3,189	2,675	11,851
Utah (a)	159	7,169	0	7,328	7,323	0	5	593
Vermont (a)	0	1,302	0	1,302	1,295	7	(0)	207
Virginia (a)	212	20,817	0	21,029	20,991	0	38	488
Washington (a)	1,947	21,852	(314)	23,485	22,721	0	764	1,139
West Virginia (a)	378	4,440	0	4,818	4,439	18	361	729
Wisconsin (a)	589	16,632	478	17,698	17,830	(355)	223	N/A
Wyoming (a)	0	1,014	438	1,452	1,452	0	0	1,324

See footnotes at end of table

TABLE 7.3
Fiscal 2019 General Fund, Enacted (In millions of dollars) (continued)

Source: National Association of State Budget Officers, Fall 2018.
Note: For all states, unless otherwise noted, transfers into budget
   stabilization funds are counted as expenditures, and transfers
   from budget stabilization funds are counted as revenues.
Key:
N/A–Not available
*–The ending balance includes the balance in the rainy day fund.
(a)
Alabama–Expenditure adjustments include transfers to the ETF
   Budget Stabilization Fund of $64.2M and the ETF Advancement &
   Technology Fund of $37.1M.
Alaska–Revenues: Spring 2019 Revenue Sources Book (Total
   Revenue) Revenue Adjustments: SLA2018 Enacted Fiscal
   Summary (Lines 3-7) Expenditures: SLA2018 Enacted Fiscal
   Summary, (line 45) Expenditure Adjustments: SLA 2018 Enacted
   Fiscal Summary, (line 46 and 51) Rainy Day Balance: State of
   Alaska Fiscal Summary FY18 and FY19 (Part 3) Number listed is
   EoY Balance. The rainy day fund balance listed is the anticipated
   end of year balance for the given fiscal year inclusive of any
   anticipated deposits or withdrawals. The deficits listed in the
   "ending balance" column are already factored into the rainy day
   balance.
Arkansas–Total available revenue amounts are reported as net of
   refunds and special dedications/payments. 75% of the ending
   balance is recommended to create a restricted reserve fund for
   FY19, and the remaining 25% will be transferred to the Arkansas
   Highway Transfer Fund.
California–Total revenues: reflect revenues after transfers to
   the rainy day fund. The ending balance includes the SFEU but
   excludes the BSA. The excluded amount is $13,768.4 million at
   the end of FY 2019. Adding these amounts to the FY 2019 ending
   balance, the projected total balance is $16,895.1 million in FY
   2019. The rainy day balance is made up of the Special Fund for
   Economic Uncertainties and the BSA, however, withdrawals from
   the BSA are subject to provisions of Proposition 2, 2014. Ending
   balance includes a reserve for encumbrances of $1,165 million
   representing amounts which will be expended in the future for
   state obligations for which goods and services have been ordered/
   contracted, but have not been received by the end of the fiscal
   year. These amounts are shown as a reserve to the fund balance
   instead of a hit to the fund balance.
Colorado–The total revenue excludes income tax revenue amounts
   diverted to the State Education Fund per Amendment 23, which
   was $658.6 million in FY2018-19. Adjustments to revenue
   include money transferred from other funds to the General Fund.
   Adjustments to expenditures are reversions of appropriations and
   various accounting adjustments made by the State Controller's
   office each year.
Connecticut–Budget Reserve Fund includes a net transfer of $363.1
   million due to the state's volatility cap which automatically
   transfers a portion of income tax collections above a certain
   threshold.

Delaware–Beginning balance reflects FY 2018 actual ending
   balance. FY 2019 Revenues includes DEFAC estimates as of the
   June, 2018 meeting plus enacted revenue adjustments. Ending
   balance includes Continuing and Encumbered Appropriations of
   $237.4 million.
Georgia–FY 19 beginning balance reflects general fund balances
   as of June 30, 2018 for Revenue Shortfall Reserve (Preliminary)
   as reported on the FY 18 State Funds and Funds Available from
   Beginning Fund Balance Sheet of the Report of Georgia Revenues
   and Reserves. Georgia is required by its constitution to maintain
   a balanced report. The fund balances for FY 18 and 19 reflect the
   Governor's balanced budget. Georgia does not project future
   Rainy Day fund balances, but expects the reserve to continue to
   grow in future years.
Idaho–Surplus eliminator legislation accounts for the difference
   between the FY 18 ending balance and the FY 19 beginning
   balance. The transfers were made at the beginning of FY 19.
   Revenue Adjustments: $13.1 million from the Group Insurance
   Account. Expenditure Adjustments: $32 million to the Public
   Education Stabilization Fund; $2 million to the STEM Education
   Fund; $.4 million to the Wolf Control Fund; $44.1 million to
   the Permanent Building Fund; $22 million to the Technology
   Stabilization Fund; $2.4 million to the Water Resources Revolving
   Development Fund.
Illinois–Total Revenues includes $3,785 in federal revenues.
   Revenue adjustments include $800M for interfund borrowing and
   $300M for the sale of the James R Thompson Center. Expenditure
   adjustments include $3,183M for transfers out.
Indiana–Revenue adjustments include a transfer to the General Fund
   to assist with the Integrated Tax System, a transfer from the State
   Tuition Reserve Account, and one-time revenues from the transfer of
   three gaming licenses. Expenditure adjustments include reversions
   from distributions, capital, and reconciliations; state agency and
   university line item capital projects; and the cost of a 13th check
   for pension recipients. Total revenues include forecasted General
   Fund revenues as well as unforecasted revenues such as HAF, QAF,
   dedicated fund SWCAP, and outside acts.
Iowa–Revenue adjustments include an estimated $92.6 million of
   residual funds transferred to the General Fund after the Reserve
   Funds are filled to their statutorily set maximum amounts. The
   ending balance of the General Fund is transferred in the current
   fiscal year to the Reserve Funds in the subsequent fiscal year. After
   the Reserve Funds are at their statutorily set maximum amounts,
   the remainder of the funds are transferred back to the General
   Fund in that subsequent fiscal year. Included in expenditure
   adjustments is a transfer from the General Fund to the State's Cash
   Reserve Fund of $113.1 million.
Kansas–Expenditure Adjustments equal the amount of FY 2018
   underspending that reappropriated for FY 2019 expenditure.

TABLE 7.3
Fiscal 2019 General Fund, Enacted (In millions of dollars) (continued)

Kentucky–Revenue includes $119.5 million in Tobacco Settlement funds. Adjustments for Revenues includes $18.9 million that represents appropriation balances carried over from the prior fiscal year, and $303.6 million from fund transfers into the General Fund. Adjustment to Expenditures represents appropriation balances forwarded to the next fiscal year and budget balances to be expended in the next fiscal year.

Louisiana–The "total revenues" amounts reported here include transfers from other state fund sources.

Maine–Revenue and Expenditure adjustments reflect Legislatively authorized transfers.

Maryland–Revenue adjustments include $25.2 million in transfers from tax credit reserves. Expenditure adjustments represent $35 million in reversions to the unappropriated General Fund balance. The FY 2019 Enacted starting balance does not match the FY 2018 Actual ending balance because the FY 2019 Enacted budget did not incorporate updated revenue and expenditure figures from FY 2018.

Massachusetts–General Fund is defined as all budgeted operating funds; spending represents total projected spending in fiscal 2019. Ending balance includes $64.6 million in reserved balances to be spent in the next fiscal year. The Commonwealth of Massachusetts credits federal reimbursements for Medicaid, as well as certain other federal reimbursements, to the General Fund. In the NASBO State Expenditure Survey, these reimbursement funds are shown as "federal funds spending" to conform to the survey definitions. Additionally, in the NASBO State Expenditure Survey, certain interfund transfers are shown as spending in "Other State Funds", but are shown in this presentation as "General Fund" spending to be consistent with the Commonwealth's accounting practices.

Michigan–Revenue totals are net of payments to local governments and balance sheet adjustments. Revenue totals are net of payments to local governments and balance sheet adjustments.

Minnesota–Ending balance includes cash flow account of $350 million, budget reserve account of $1,583.364 million, and stadium reserve of $57.638 million.

Missouri–Revenue adjustments include transfers from other funds into the general revenue fund.

Nebraska–Revenue adjustments are transfers between the General Fund and other funds. Among others, this includes a $221 million transfer from the General Fund to the Property Tax Credit Cash Fund, as well as a $62.0 Transfer to the Cash Reserve for Revenues in excess of the Certified Forecast for FY 2018. Also included are transfers totaling $48 million from the Cash Reserve Fund to the General Fund for budget stabilization. Expenditure adjustments include a net $258.0 million reserved for authorized reappropriations and carryover obligations from FY 2018.

Nevada–Revenue adjustments are restricted revenue, reversions, Rainy Day Fund transfers in and reserve transfers in. Expenditure adjustments are restricted transfers out.

New Hampshire–Revenue Adjustments: An increase in Liquor Revenue is expected due to expenditure reductions of $ 1.8 million with additional Liquor Revenue moving to the Governor's Commission on Alcohol Abuse totaling $3.6 million. Additional Dept. of Revenue Audit income is expected, totaling $3.1 million, as well as a reduction in Restricted Airways Toll income of $.2 million. Further, the Business Profit Tax (BPT) and Business Enterprise Taxes (BET) anticipate to be impacted by rate reductions in calendar year 2019 that will reduce budgeted tax income by $11.0 million and $9.7 million respectively. Additionally, the elimination of the Electricity Consumption tax effective January 1, 2019 will result in a $3.0 million reduction. Expenditure Adjustments: $10.0 million is anticipated to be moved to the Education Trust Fund at year end as well as $.6 million to be moved to the Rainy Day Fund.

New Jersey–Revenue adjustments include: Transfers to other funds; reservation of fund balance.

New York–FY 2018 and FY 2019 annual revenue changes include an acceleration of PIT payments due in calendar year 2018 as taxpayers responded to Federal tax law changes that, starting in tax year 2018, limit the allowable aggregate itemized deduction of State and local income taxes, and local real property taxes, to a maximum of $10,000 on Federal income tax returns. DOB estimates approximately $1.9 billion was accelerated from FY 2019 to FY 2018. FY 2019 expenditure change includes a $1.2 billion increase for the support of capital projects reflecting the timing of reimbursement from bond proceeds, planned disbursements from the Dedicated Highway and Bridge Trust Funds, and the use of extraordinary monetary settlements.

North Carolina–Expenditure adjustment includes funds transferred to Budget Stabilization Reserve (Savings Reserve), $221.5, and Medicaid Transformation Reserve, $135M.

North Dakota–Revenue adjustments are transfers of $200.0 million from interest earned on the Legacy fund, $124.0 million from the strategic investment and improvements fund and $70.0 million from other special fund sources, to the general fund. Expenditure adjustments include a potential $95.9 million transfer to the budget stabilization fund.

Ohio–Federal reimbursements for Medicaid expenditures funded from the General Revenue Fund (GRF) are deposited into the GRF. Federal reimbursements for Medicaid expenditures from non-GRF sources are deposited into the appropriate federal fund. Expenditures of federal funds are contained in the General Fund number to be consistent with Ohio accounting practices and with other portrayals of Ohio's general fund. This will tend to make Ohio's GRF revenue and expenditures look higher relative to most other states that don't follow this practice. FY 2019 expenditures include anticipated expenditures against prior year encumbrances as well as $761.2 million in expected transfers out of the GRF, including a $657.5 million transfer of FY 2018 year-end surplus revenue into the Budget Stabilization Fund. The fiscal 2019 ending balance is based on estimates; however, cash equal to open encumbrances at the end of the year will be reserved in the ending balance.

TABLE 7.3
Fiscal 2019 General Fund, Enacted (In millions of dollars) (continued)

Oklahoma–No revenue or expenditure adjustments can be calculated at this time for FY-2019. These numbers include collections and estimates for the two largest appropriated funds (the General Revenue Fund and the OK Education Reform Revolving Fund) which constitute the majority of the state appropriated budget.

Oregon–Revenue adjustments include: a revenue adjustment for a statutory transfer to local governments for local property tax relief. Because General Fund revenues for the 2017-19 biennium are anticipated to exceed projections by more than two percent, there will be a refund of personal income taxes "Kicker". This refund, which is projected at roughly $685.9 million will be returned to taxpayers as a credit on their 2019 income tax return (which will be filed in 2020).

Pennsylvania–Revenue adjustments include refunds, lapses and adjustments to beginning balances. Expenditure adjustments include transfers to the Budget Stabilization Reserve Fund (rainy day).

Rhode Island–Adjustments to revenues reflect a transfer of $120.9 million to the Budget Reserve (Rainy Day) Fund.

South Carolina–Revenue Adjustments: Litigation Recovery Account ($4M); FY2017-18 Debt Service Lapse ($16.6M); FY2017-18 Capital Reserve Fund Lapse ($0.3M) & FY2018-19 Unobligated Debt Service ($67.4M); Tax Changes (-$2.4M). Expenditure Adjustments: Prior Yr 2% Capital Reserve ($145.4M) transferred to state agencies. Designated portion of ending balance - Capital Reserve Fund - $151.6 M.

South Dakota–The beginning balance of $16.9 million and adjustment to expenditures reflects the prior year's ending balance which is transferred to the rainy day fund.

Tennessee–Revenue adjustments: $61.0 million transfer to Rainy Day Fund; $20.0 million transfer to Aeronautics Development Fund; $0.5 million transfer to Highway Fund for ORNL Signs. Expenditure adjustments: $260.4 million transfer to capital outlay projects fund. $16.3 million transfer to state office buildings and support facilities fund. $3.7 million transfer to debt service fund. $1.0 million transfer to reserves for dedicated revenue appropriations. Ending balance: $6.2 million unappropriated budget surplus at June 30, 2019.

Texas–Revenue adjustment of $187.8m in general fund dedicated account balances. Expenditure adjustment of $3,188.5m reserved for transfer to the Rainy Day Fund and the State Highway Fund. Figures represent the numbers provided by the Comptroller in the revised CRE released July 2018, Table A-1.

Utah–Includes additional revenue from tax changes enacted during the 2018 Second Special Session. See *https://le.utah. gov/interim/2018/pdf/00003644.pdf* for the revised revenue estimates.

Vermont–A net total of $7.1M in expenditure adjustments reflect the following: $76.8M in fund transfers to the General Fund, and subsequent General Fund designated reserves of $83.9M. Please note that the amount of $76.8M transferred to the General Fund is predominantly attributable to a transfer of funds from a pre-existing unrestricted special fund balance to the State's Human Services Caseload Reserve. These transfers, and subsequent reserves, account for the corresponding growth in "Rainy Day Fund Balance" of $73.9M, year-over-year. Of further note, the marked year-over-year decrease in General Fund revenue is largely attributable to the Legislature's restructuring of the Education Fund revenue sources. This restructuring resulted in a decrease of -$301.2M in the annual transfer of General Funds. In lieu of the annual transfer of General Funds to the Education Fund, 100% of Sales and Use and 25% of Meals and Rooms taxes will be deposited directly into the Education Fund. Previously, these tax revenues were deposited into the General Fund. The remaining decrease in revenue year-over-year is predominantly associated with Vermont social security tax rate changes and the restructuring of Vermont's tax laws to align with modifications to the federal tax code.

Virginia–Total Revenues includes fund transfers.

Washington–Revenue adjustments reflect the net of transfers in and out of the General Fund, as well as prior biennium recoveries and similar resource adjustments. It is currently projected that a portion of the FY 2019 ending balance will be programmed to be spent in FY 2020. The Total Revenues reflect total general fund revenues, before transfers in and out of the general fund (which are included as adjustments).

West Virginia–Total Revenue is the official estimate for FY 2019 Total General Revenue collections. Total Expenditures are FY 2019 general revenue appropriations of $4,381.9 million, FY 2019 surplus appropriations of $13.8 million, and estimated 13th month expenditures of $42.9 million. Adjustment (Expenditures) represents the $18 million transferred in August 2018 to the Rainy Day Fund from 1/2 of the FY 2018 surplus. The Ending Balance is mostly the historically carried forward reappropriation amounts that will remain and be reappropriated to the next fiscal year, the 13th month expenditures from the previous fiscal year & any unappropriated surplus balance.

Wisconsin–Revenue adjustments include Tribal Gaming, $26.1; and Other Revenue, $451.8. Expenditure adjustments include Transfers to Transportation fund, $41.6; Lapses, -$448.2; and Compensation Reserves, $52.1. The estimates are based upon the 2018 AFR closing along with revenue and expenditure estimates from the General Fund Summary in the statutes.

Wyoming–The State of Wyoming budgets on a biennial basis, to arrive at annual figures certain assumptions and estimates were required.

TABLE 7.4

Fiscal 2018 Tax Collections Compared with Projections Used in Adopting Fiscal 2018 Budgets (millions)

State	Sales Tax		Personal Income Tax		Corporate Income Tax		Gaming/Lottery Revenue		All Other Revenue	
	Original Estimate	Preliminary Actual	Original Estimate	Preliminary Actual	Original Estimate	Preliminary Actual	Original Estimate	Preliminary Actual	Original Estimate	Preliminary Actual
Total	$253,881	$259,145	$372,480	$385,933	$47,578	$47,708	$8,416	$8,794	$144,897	$150,395
Alabama	2,413	2,448	3,619	3,755	357	366	N/A	N/A	1,925	2,063
Alaska	N/A	N/A	N/A	N/A	155	145	11	11	1,666	2,181
Arizona	4,647	4,787	4,347	4,544	401	373	77	68	210	337
Arkansas (a)	2,445	2,418	3,319	3,360	475	407	63	67	455	476
California	24,470	25,384	88,821	91,971	10,894	11,246	N/A	N/A	1,695	1,224
Colorado	3,312	3,404	7,207	7,577	611	782	N/A	N/A	443	578
Connecticut (b)	4,221	4,159	9,183	10,725	933	912	607	613	3,814	1,723
Delaware	N/A	N/A	1,373	1,428	108	90	204	212	2,524	2,663
Florida	24,153	24,139	0	0	2,266	2,413	136	357	4,260	5,010
Georgia	5,849	5,946	11,455	11,644	1,043	1,004	N/A	N/A	5,367	5,726
Hawaii	3,460	3,396	2,197	2,430	83	131	N/A	N/A	1,615	1,703
Idaho	1,447	1,490	1,667	1,828	216	239	0	0	178	175
Illinois	7,970	7,810	17,250	17,725	1,882	2,017	993	991	7,804	8,400
Indiana	7,630	7,663	5,661	5,816	949	660	409	432	939	1,000
Iowa	2,981	2,942	4,743	4,747	526	565	81	85	(966)	(954)
Kansas	2,727	2,748	3,145	3,374	330	392	N/A	0	829	783
Kentucky	3,638	3,606	4,589	4,604	553	511	241	253	1,853	1,865
Louisiana	4,259	4,335	3,017	3,079	338	350	402	402	1,426	1,423
Maine	1,434	1,483	1,703	1,595	166	186	55	62	185	261
Maryland	4,727	4,646	9,406	9,508	830	820	505	535	1,701	1,864
Massachusetts	6,472	6,454	15,316	16,240	2,107	2,382	1,149	1,135	16,555	17,698
Michigan	1,362	1,425	7,192	7,300	195	79	N/A	N/A	1,004	1,184
Minnesota	5,465	5,433	11,714	11,781	1,278	1,321	65	69	3,454	3,429
Mississippi	2,295	2,340	1,841	1,827	551	572	144	136	771	816
Missouri	2,149	2,174	6,644	6,600	275	300	N/A	N/A	331	395
Montana	62	60	1,321	1,298	169	167	74	71	808	810
Nebraska	1,570	1,603	2,290	2,361	235	314	N/A	N/A	220	290
Nevada	1,200	1,189	0	0	0	0	775	711	1,941	2,118
New Hampshire	N/A	N/A	N/A	N/A	412	479	N/A	N/A	1,108	1,121
New Jersey	9,851	10,410	14,382	15,154	2,579	2,220	N/A	N/A	7,630	7,722
New Mexico	2,061	2,442	1,346	1,492	100	110	58	62	2,364	2,703
New York (c)	13,642	13,553	49,382	51,501	5,718	4,916	17	15	1,075	1,435
North Carolina	7,334	7,337	12,341	12,518	732	739	N/A	N/A	2,717	2,971
North Dakota	819	829	341	364	55	92	11	11	527	676
Ohio	10,028	10,148	7,977	8,411	1,494	1,523	N/A	N/A	12,773	12,389
Oklahoma	2,549	2,665	2,150	2,424	124	234	158	162	1,141	1,121
Oregon	N/A	N/A	8,247	8,855	510	719	N/A	N/A	597	741
Pennsylvania	10,341	10,381	13,305	13,399	3,119	2,879	123	123	7,817	7,784
Rhode Island	1,059	1,057	1,302	1,345	159	128	363	365	951	1,013
South Carolina	3,041	3,034	3,753	3,856	288	334	N/A	N/A	868	900
South Dakota	989	989	N/A	N/A	N/A	N/A	118	119	483	485
Tennessee	8,227	8,185	143	135	2,131	2,179	346	346	3,365	3,476
Texas	28,067	30,751	N/A	N/A	N/A	N/A	1,233	1,381	22,979	24,857
Utah	1,990	2,038	3,891	3,991	348	449	N/A	N/A	553	530
Vermont	258	259	795	832	87	96	N/A	N/A	444	453
Virginia	3,635	3,462	13,836	14,106	736	862	N/A	N/A	1,426	1,451
Washington	10,501	10,924	N/A	N/A	N/A	N/A	N/A	N/A	10,058	10,377
West Virginia	1,320	1,310	1,890	1,956	109	110	N/A	N/A	1,016	988
Wisconsin	5,384	5,448	8,380	8,479	951	894	N/A	N/A	1,363	1,323
Wyoming	429	442	N/A	N/A	N/A	N/A	N/A	N/A	633	637

Source: National Association of State Budget Officers, Fall 2018.

Note: Unless otherwise noted, original estimates reflect the figures used when the fiscal 2018 budget was adopted, and current estimates reflect preliminary actual tax collections.

Key:

N/A–Indicates data are not available because, in most cases, these states do not have that type of tax.

(a) Revenue amounts here are reported as "gross" (before refunds and special dedications/payments).

(b) FY18 preliminary actual General Fund revenues for Connecticut came in lower than budgeted largely due to a transfer of $1,471.3m to the Budget Reserve Fund as required under the state's new volatility cap, and a timing delay in receipt of $400m of federal funds from FY18 to FY19.

(c) Amounts reported under "Estimates Used When Fiscal 2018 Budget was Adopted Fiscal 2018" have been corrected since last reported in the Spring 2018 Fiscal Survey.

TABLE 7.5
Comparison of General Fund Revenue Collections in Fiscal 2017, Fiscal 2018, and Enacted Fiscal 2019
(In millions of dollars)

State	Sales Tax			Personal Income Tax			Corporate Income Tax		
	Fiscal 2017	Fiscal 2018	Fiscal 2019	Fiscal 2017	Fiscal 2018	Fiscal 2019	Fiscal 2017	Fiscal 2018	Fiscal 2019
Total (a)	$248,837	$258,887	$265,270	$351,629	$385,933	$392,810	$45,997	$47,708	$51,628
Alabama	2,328	2,448	2,537	3,511	3,755	3,868	382	366	387
Alaska	N/A	N/A	N/A	N/A	N/A	N/A	87	145	145
Arizona	4,506	4,787	4,956	4,131	4,544	4,582	368	373	265
Arkansas (b)	2,338	2,418	2,488	3,215	3,360	3,429	434	407	482
California	24,874	25,384	26,674	83,264	91,971	95,011	11,020	11,246	12,259
Colorado (c)	3,086	3,404	3,676	6,761	7,577	8,015	509	782	886
Connecticut	4,192	4,159	4,154	8,989	10,725	9,108	1,038	912	1,520
Delaware	N/A	N/A	N/A	1,333	1,428	1,486	121	90	93
Florida	22,947	24,139	24,137	N/A	0	0	2,366	2,413	2,320
Georgia	5,716	5,946	6,142	10,978	11,644	12,126	972	1,004	1,103
Hawaii	3,240	3,396	3,562	2,095	2,430	2,537	174	131	105
Idaho	1,382	1,490	1,545	1,651	1,828	1,759	214	239	199
Illinois	8,043	7,810	8,181	13,661	17,725	18,095	1,332	2,017	2,068
Indiana (d)	7,490	7,663	7,886	5,435	5,816	5,997	979	660	975
Iowa	2,812	2,942	3,039	4,469	4,747	4,985	550	565	649
Kansas	2,671	2,748	2,766	2,304	3,374	3,334	325	392	351
Kentucky	3,485	3,606	3,908	4,394	4,604	4,531	497	511	573
Louisiana (e)	4,284	4,335	3,919	2,960	3,079	3,413	388	350	300
Maine	1,398	1,483	1,530	1,524	1,595	1,619	175	186	204
Maryland (f)	4,539	4,646	4,751	9,019	9,508	9,874	796	820	926
Massachusetts (g)	6,211	6,454	6,720	14,684	16,240	16,632	2,197	2,382	2,339
Michigan (h)	1,457	1,425	1,433	6,594	7,300	7,040	420	79	273
Minnesota	5,405	5,433	5,745	10,931	11,781	12,436	1,205	1,321	1,343
Mississippi	2,289	2,340	2,375	1,782	1,827	1,853	564	572	531
Missouri	2,112	2,174	2,204	6,240	6,600	6,588	276	300	331
Montana	60	60	62	1,168	1,298	1,404	126	167	173
Nebraska	1,548	1,603	1,685	2,225	2,361	2,470	264	314	300
Nevada (i)	1,134	1,189	1,262	0	0	0	0	0	0
New Hampshire	N/A	N/A	N/A	N/A	N/A	N/A	401	479	418
New Jersey	9,592	10,410	11,026	13,958	15,154	15,978	2,344	2,220	3,257
New Mexico	2,062	2,442	2,652	1,381	1,492	1,557	70	110	116
New York	12,966	13,553	14,114	47,565	51,501	50,410	4,761	4,916	5,626
North Carolina	7,004	7,337	7,625	11,970	12,518	12,705	748	739	710
North Dakota	793	829	883	313	364	358	69	92	48
Ohio (j)	10,615	10,148	10,338	7,607	8,411	8,748	1,302	1,523	1,582
Oklahoma	2,292	2,665	2,764	2,122	2,424	2,542	158	234	166
Oregon	N/A	N/A	N/A	8,441	8,855	8,885	608	719	528
Pennsylvania	10,005	10,381	10,753	12,664	13,399	14,174	2,752	2,879	2,926
Rhode Island	998	1,057	1,101	1,244	1,345	1,386	119	128	118
South Carolina	2,896	3,034	3,148	3,581	3,856	3,863	270	334	314
South Dakota	951	989	1,029	N/A	N/A	N/A	N/A	N/A	N/A
Tennessee (k)	8,063	8,185	8,481	165	135	104	2,329	2,179	2,280
Texas (l)	28,797	30,751	29,506	N/A	N/A	N/A	N/A	N/A	N/A
Utah	1,857	2,038	2,102	3,609	3,991	4,128	328	449	365
Vermont (m)	245	259	N/A	756	832	847	96	96	90
Virginia	3,357	3,462	3,547	13,053	14,106	14,184	827	862	912
Washington (n)	10,133	10,924	11,418	N/A	N/A	N/A	N/A	N/A	N/A
West Virginia	1,280	1,310	1,368	1,844	1,956	2,034	116	110	142
Wisconsin	5,224	5,448	5,635	8,040	8,479	8,715	921	894	932
Wyoming	407	442	445	N/A	N/A	N/A	N/A	N/A	N/A

See footnotes at end of table

TABLE 7.5
Comparison of General Fund Revenue Collections in Fiscal 2017, Fiscal 2018, and Enacted Fiscal 2019
(In millions of dollars) (continued)

State	Gaming/Lottery Revenue			All Other Revenue		
	Fiscal 2017	Fiscal 2018	Fiscal 2019	Fiscal 2017	Fiscal 2018	Fiscal 2019
Total (a)	$8,334	$8,794	$8,878	$142,679	$150,395	$151,075
Alabama	N/A	N/A	N/A	2,027	2,063	2,093
Alaska	11	11	11	1,257	2,181	2,103
Arizona	79	68	90	419	337	529
Arkansas (b)	63	67	68	503	476	476
California	N/A	N/A	N/A	824	1,224	(612)
Colorado (c)	N/A	N/A	N/A	460	578	464
Connecticut	599	613	556	2,886	1,723	3,671
Delaware	205	212	210	2,354	2,663	2,579
Florida	139	357	299	4,492	5,010	6,082
Georgia	N/A	N/A	N/A	5,603	5,726	5,503
Hawaii	N/A	N/A	N/A	1,843	1,703	1,646
Idaho	N/A	0	N/A	201	175	166
Illinois	990	991	999	6,307	8,400	8,077
Indiana (d)	432	432	392	939	1,000	932
Iowa	78	85	86	(813)	(954)	(1,119)
Kansas	N/A	0	N/A	1,040	783	552
Kentucky	242	253	249	1,860	1,865	1,937
Louisiana (e)	410	402	402	1,385	1,423	1,409
Maine	58	62	57	299	261	258
Maryland (f)	484	535	527	1,860	1,864	1,686
Massachusetts (g)	1,188	1,135	1,182	16,332	17,698	18,005
Michigan (h)	N/A	N/A	N/A	1,401	1,184	1,181
Minnesota	64	69	67	3,728	3,429	3,439
Mississippi	133	136	140	886	816	757
Missouri	N/A	N/A	N/A	389	395	295
Montana	70	71	77	718	810	764
Nebraska	N/A	N/A	N/A	228	290	276
Nevada (i)	718	711	797	2,029	2,118	2,018
New Hampshire	N/A	N/A	N/A	1,102	1,121	1,136
New Jersey	996	N/A	N/A	7,229	7,722	7,150
New Mexico	60	62	62	2,889	2,703	2,893
New York	16	15	15	1,587	1,435	2,495
North Carolina	N/A	N/A	N/A	2,892	2,971	2,891
North Dakota	10	11	11	395	676	507
Ohio (j)	N/A	N/A	N/A	14,656	12,389	13,041
Oklahoma	152	162	158	982	1,121	1,667
Oregon	N/A	N/A	N/A	761	741	647
Pennsylvania	121	123	154	6,128	7,784	5,968
Rhode Island	363	365	392	960	1,013	1,003
South Carolina	N/A	N/A	N/A	834	900	914
South Dakota	115	119	123	475	485	489
Tennessee (k)	337	346	353	3,516	3,476	3,527
Texas (l)	1,201	1,381	1,402	22,287	24,857	26,081
Utah	N/A	N/A	N/A	527	530	575
Vermont (m)	N/A	N/A	N/A	477	453	365
Virginia	N/A	N/A	N/A	1,458	1,451	1,531
Washington (n)	N/A	N/A	N/A	8,933	10,377	10,120
West Virginia	N/A	N/A	N/A	1,036	988	998
Wisconsin	N/A	N/A	N/A	1,333	1,323	1,349
Wyoming	N/A	N/A	N/A	766	637	566

See footnotes at end of table

TABLE 7.5

Comparison of General Fund Revenue Collections in Fiscal 2017, Fiscal 2018, and Enacted Fiscal 2019
(In millions of dollars) (continued)

Source: National Association of State Budget Officers, Fall 2018.

Note: Unless otherwise noted, fiscal 2017 figures reflect actual collections, fiscal 2018 figures reflect preliminary actual collections, and fiscal 2019 figures reflect the estimates based on states' enacted budgets.

Key:

N.A.–Indicates data are not available because, in most cases, these states do not have that type of tax, or it is not part of the general fund.

(a) Totals include state collections by revenue type where amounts were provided/applicable for all three years.

(b) Revenue amounts here are reported as "gross" (before refunds and special dedications/payments).

(c) Totals include the income tax revenue amounts diverted to the State Education Fund per Amendment 23. These amounts are $540 million in FY 2016–17, $617 million in FY 2017–18, and $658.6 million in FY 2018–19.

(d) Amounts only include forecasted General Fund revenues.

(e) These revenue figures do not include fund transfers.

(f) Maryland is coupled to Federal Adjusted Gross Income. Prior to the 2018 Legislative Session, Maryland's Bureau of Revenue Estimates estimated an increase in General Fund collections of $35.5 million in FY 18 and $511.6 million in FY 19 due to the Federal Tax Cuts and Jobs Act (TCJA). Maryland set aside $200 million from the Personal Income Tax collections for education and increased the standard deduction as a result of the federal changes. The State also decoupled from the Estate credit cap that will increase revenues in FY 20.

(g) The Commonwealth of Massachusetts credits federal reimbursements for Medicaid, as well as certain other federal reimbursements, to the General Fund. In the NASBO State Expenditure Survey, these reimbursement funds are shown as "federal funds spending" to conform to the survey definitions and excluded from the revenue figures. The figures in this survey are consistent with the Commonwealth's accounting practices.

(h) Volatility in business tax revenue is largely due to timing of tax credits.

(i) Gaming Revenue forecasts are amounts estimated before tax credits are applied. There are no estimates for tax credits as they are transferrable. Actual amounts are net of tax credits.

(j) Sales and Use Tax: The fiscal year 2018 sales and use tax decline is the result of the elimination of the sales tax on Medicaid managed care companies and the adoption of a provider assessment on all managed care companies. The provider tax, unlike the sales tax, is deposited in a non-GRF dedicated purpose fund. Corporate Income Tax: Ohio doesn't have a corporate income tax and instead has a commercial activities tax (CAT). The large increase in fiscal year 2018 is the result of allocating a higher percentage of the CAT revenue to the general fund and a lower percentage to property tax replacement funds. As a biennial budget state, Ohio routinely revises revenue projections in the second year, as is the case here.

(k) Corporate income tax includes excise and franchise taxes.

(l) Figures taken from Table A-12 in revised CRE July 2018.

(m) Please note the following: All lottery proceeds benefits Vermont's Education Fund, not the General Fund; the figure of $396.6M in Sales Tax collections originally reported in the fall survey for 2018 (Enacted) is restated in this response to reflect the official portion of the revenue forecast comprised of this source; the fiscal year 2019 forecasted revenue is reflective of the structural funding changes made in the Education Fund, specifically, in lieu of the annual transfer of General Funds to the Education Fund, 100% of Sales and Use and 25% of Meals and Rooms taxes will be deposited directly into the Education Fund (previously, these tax revenues were deposited into the General Fund).

(n) Total revenues reflect total available general fund revenues, after transfers.

TABLE 7.5A
General Fund Revenue Collections Compared to Projections, Fiscal 2018 and Fiscal 2019

State	Fiscal 2018			Fiscal 2019		
	On target	Lower	Higher	On target	Lower	Higher
Total	8	2	40	14	5	19
Alabama	...	...	★	...	...	...
Alaska	...	...	★	★	...	...
Arizona	...	...	★	...	...	★
Arkansas	★	...	...	★	...	...
California	...	...	★	...	...	...
Colorado	...	...	★	...	...	★
Connecticut (a)	...	★	...	...	...	★
Delaware	...	...	★	...	...	★
Florida	...	...	★	★	...	...
Georgia	...	...	★	...	...	★
Hawaii	...	...	★	★	...	...
Idaho	...	...	★	...	★	...
Illinois	...	...	★	★	...	...
Indiana	★	...	...	★	...	...
Iowa	★	...	...	★	...	...
Kansas	...	...	★	...	...	★
Kentucky	★	...	...	★	...	...
Louisiana	...	...	★	...	...	...
Maine	...	...	★	...	★	...
Maryland	...	...	★	...	...	...
Massachusetts	...	...	★	...	...	...
Michigan	...	...	★	...	...	...
Minnesota	★	...	...	...	...	★
Mississippi	...	...	★	...	...	★
Missouri	...	...	★	...	★	...
Montana	...	★	...	★	...	...
Nebraska	...	...	★	...	...	★
Nevada	...	...	★	...	...	...
New Hampshire	...	...	★	...	...	★
New Jersey	...	...	★	★	...	...
New Mexico	...	...	★	...	...	★
New York	...	...	★	...	★	...
North Carolina	...	...	★	...	★	...
North Dakota	...	...	★	...	...	★
Ohio (b)	...	...	★	★	...	...
Oklahoma	...	...	★	...	...	★
Oregon	...	...	★	...	...	★
Pennsylvania	★	...	...	...	...	★
Rhode Island	...	...	★	★	...	...
South Carolina	...	...	★	...	...	...
South Dakota	★	...	...	...	...	★
Tennessee	...	...	★	...	...	...
Texas	...	...	★	...	...	...
Utah	...	...	★	★	...	...
Vermont	...	...	★	...	...	★
Virginia	...	...	★	...	...	...
Washington	...	...	★	...	...	★
West Virginia	...	...	★	...	...	★
Wisconsin	★	...	...	★	...	...
Wyoming	...	...	★	...	...	...

Source: National Association of State Budget Officers, Fall 2018.
Note: Fiscal 2018 reflects whether general fund revenues from all sources came in higher, lower, or on target with original projections used when the fiscal 2018 budget was adopted. Fiscal 2019 reflects whether Fiscal 2019 collections thus far have been coming in higher, lower, or on target with projections. Not all states were able to report on fiscal 2019 collections.

Key:
... – No

(a) FY18 preliminary actual General Fund revenues for Connecticut came in lower than budgeted largely due to a transfer of $1,471.3m to the Budget Reserve Fund as required under the state's new volatility cap, and a timing delay in receipt of $400m of federal funds from FY18 to FY19.

(b) Revenue collections compared to projections include state-source general revenue. If we included federal general fund revenue, fiscal 2019 would currently be lower than projected.

TABLE 7.6
Total State Expenditures: Capital Inclusive (In millions of dollars)

State	Actual fiscal 2016 General fund	Federal funds	Other state funds	Bonds	Total
Total	$768,405	$583,250	$484,758	$34,207	$1,870,620
Alabama (a)	7,921	9,738	7,875	332	25,866
Alaska	5,474	3,276	1,275	7	10,032
Arizona (b)	9,690	14,927	16,810	739	42,166
Arkansas (c)	5,170	7,416	11,392	58	24,036
California	114,465	90,690	42,100	3,644	250,899
Colorado	10,426	9,484	16,784	0	36,694
Connecticut	17,921	6,216	4,043	3,692	31,872
Delaware	3,914	2,151	3,694	477	10,236
Florida	28,813	25,254	16,598	1,654	72,319
Georgia (d)	21,019	13,896	11,519	1,099	47,533
Hawaii	6,882	2,563	3,430	961	13,836
Idaho	3,028	2,670	1,444	0	7,142
Illinois (e)	26,762	15,875	11,506	782	54,925
Indiana	15,130	12,289	3,790	0	31,209
Iowa	7,247	6,328	9,506	13	23,094
Kansas	6,115	3,637	4,958	414	15,124
Kentucky	10,230	12,182	9,247	0	31,659
Louisiana	8,697	9,256	9,200	582	27,735
Maine	3,271	2,536	2,131	101	8,039
Maryland	16,239	12,034	11,305	1,201	40,779
Massachusetts (f)	27,625	12,462	12,285	2,298	54,670
Michigan	10,095	20,871	23,030	207	54,203
Minnesota	20,152	10,484	6,218	878	37,732
Mississippi	5,672	7,884	5,835	520	19,911
Missouri	9,018	7,677	7,862	71	24,628
Montana	2,237	2,370	1,777	0	6,384
Nebraska	4,196	2,989	4,425	0	11,610
Nevada	3,602	4,158	4,558	108	12,426
New Hampshire	1,385	2,158	2,170	62	5,775
New Jersey	33,151	14,354	7,425	1,610	56,540
New Mexico	6,220	7,730	4,536	474	18,960
New York	68,042	49,476	29,441	3,748	150,707
North Carolina	21,205	14,487	10,031	218	45,941
North Dakota	3,013	1,607	2,832	7	7,459
Ohio (g)	33,591	12,493	18,876	2,490	67,450
Oklahoma	5,205	7,862	9,429	223	22,719
Oregon	8,992	10,317	17,815	142	37,266
Pennsylvania	30,128	27,073	18,636	517	76,354
Rhode Island	3,548	2,877	2,080	122	8,627
South Carolina	7,320	7,614	8,014	0	22,948
South Dakota	1,462	1,371	1,248	91	4,172
Tennessee (h)	13,256	12,567	6,080	438	32,341
Texas	53,968	36,683	17,976	1,898	110,525
Utah	6,191	3,582	3,870	0	13,643
Vermont	1,457	1,992	2,022	91	5,562
Virginia	19,672	9,838	18,477	1,102	49,089
Washington	18,171	11,807	10,742	1,059	41,779
West Virginia	4,195	4,506	7,394	77	16,172
Wisconsin	15,341	10,759	19,630	0	45,730
Wyoming (i)	1,881	784	1,437	0	4,102
Dist. Of Columbia	6,994	3,204	949	834	11,981

See footnotes at end of table

TABLE 7.6
Total State Expenditures: Capital Inclusive (In millions of dollars) (continued)

State	General fund	Federal funds	Other state funds	Bonds	Total
			Actual fiscal 2017		
Total	$792,395	$600,389	$514,917	$34,587	$1,942,288
Alabama (a)	8,295	9,885	8,005	460	26,645
Alaska	4,486	3,763	1,495	0	9,744
Arizona (b)	9,774	14,765	16,711	776	42,026
Arkansas (c)	5,267	7,875	11,925	69	25,136
California	119,291	95,337	44,249	2,340	261,217
Colorado	10,497	9,120	16,913	0	36,530
Connecticut	17,763	6,331	4,671	2,954	31,719
Delaware	4,106	2,171	4,000	398	10,675
Florida	30,267	26,320	18,127	1,667	76,381
Georgia (d)	22,597	14,266	11,836	950	49,649
Hawaii	7,486	2,571	3,927	682	14,666
Idaho	3,255	2,681	1,535	0	7,471
Illinois (e)	29,424	14,833	22,387	1,359	68,003
Indiana	15,971	12,421	3,536	0	31,928
Iowa	7,258	6,389	9,034	6	22,687
Kansas	6,277	3,759	5,144	393	15,573
Kentucky	11,075	12,354	9,373	0	32,802
Louisiana	9,118	11,159	7,841	304	28,422
Maine	3,346	2,601	2,187	114	8,248
Maryland	17,153	12,971	12,062	1,136	43,322
Massachusetts (f)	28,362	12,401	12,522	2,259	55,544
Michigan	9,882	20,291	24,137	75	54,385
Minnesota	21,103	10,406	5,318	641	37,468
Mississippi	5,645	7,819	5,786	1,124	20,374
Missouri	9,153	8,186	8,047	164	25,550
Montana	2,333	2,810	1,814	0	6,957
Nebraska	4,329	3,030	4,508	0	11,867
Nevada	3,990	4,393	5,308	223	13,914
New Hampshire	1,512	2,221	2,097	103	5,933
New Jersey	33,827	15,172	8,116	2,166	59,281
New Mexico	6,106	8,105	4,713	662	19,586
New York	68,080	52,985	31,519	4,431	157,015
North Carolina	22,143	14,778	10,707	538	48,166
North Dakota	2,600	1,616	2,574	2	6,792
Ohio (g)	34,453	12,596	18,584	2,590	68,223
Oklahoma	5,044	7,186	10,703	329	23,262
Oregon	8,954	10,189	20,759	138	40,040
Pennsylvania	31,942	29,001	18,868	513	80,324
Rhode Island	3,672	2,977	2,109	92	8,850
South Carolina	7,804	8,184	8,565	0	24,553
South Dakota	1,548	1,420	1,239	20	4,227
Tennessee (h)	14,162	12,261	6,417	0	32,840
Texas	54,070	36,255	18,260	2,505	111,090
Utah	6,274	3,809	4,140	0	14,223
Vermont	1,498	1,914	2,096	49	5,557
Virginia	20,227	10,308	18,805	962	50,302
Washington	19,357	12,270	11,741	1,316	44,684
West Virginia	4,231	4,314	8,397	77	17,019
Wisconsin	15,858	10,993	20,141	0	46,992
Wyoming (i)	1,530	927	1,969	0	4,426
Dist. Of Columbia	7,179	3,442	1,070	865	12,556

See footnotes at end of table

TABLE 7.6
Total State Expenditures: Capital Inclusive (In millions of dollars) (continued)

State	General fund	Federal funds	Estimated fiscal 2018 Other state funds	Bonds	Total
Total	$822,655	$634,802	$537,794	$37,118	$2,032,369
Alabama (a)	8,138	10,159	7,803	536	26,636
Alaska	4,535	3,985	2,535	0	11,055
Arizona (b)	9,821	15,615	17,265	642	43,343
Arkansas (c)	5,372	8,168	11,818	33	25,391
California	127,045	98,107	57,169	6,309	288,630
Colorado	11,293	9,627	16,035	0	36,955
Connecticut	18,600	6,253	4,996	2,913	32,762
Delaware	4,118	2,492	3,990	255	10,855
Florida	31,508	28,706	23,145	1,594	84,953
Georgia (d)	23,903	13,956	12,271	1,166	51,296
Hawaii	7,804	2,628	3,636	1,131	15,199
Idaho	3,465	2,683	1,783	0	7,931
Illinois (e)	35,065	18,689	16,700	481	70,935
Indiana	15,923	13,578	4,197	0	33,698
Iowa	7,258	6,389	9,034	6	22,687
Kansas	6,692	3,818	5,423	402	16,335
Kentucky	11,237	12,441	10,390	0	34,068
Louisiana	9,635	13,894	8,659	256	32,444
Maine	3,416	2,697	2,191	106	8,410
Maryland	17,131	13,053	13,530	1,455	45,169
Massachusetts (f)	28,896	13,347	13,484	2,268	57,995
Michigan	10,231	22,499	22,666	112	55,508
Minnesota	22,695	11,891	6,424	410	41,420
Mississippi	5,560	9,184	6,179	647	21,570
Missouri	9,263	8,360	8,226	189	26,038
Montana	2,242	2,863	1,847	0	6,952
Nebraska	4,350	3,101	4,690	0	12,141
Nevada	4,003	4,448	5,111	392	13,954
New Hampshire	1,526	2,289	2,234	73	6,122
New Jersey	35,324	15,937	8,135	2,000	61,396
New Mexico	6,140	8,083	4,655	501	19,379
New York	69,724	56,808	32,502	4,710	163,744
North Carolina	22,746	15,296	11,541	248	49,831
North Dakota	2,103	1,472	2,436	25	6,036
Ohio (g)	31,681	15,113	19,975	2,868	69,637
Oklahoma	5,854	7,522	8,915	378	22,669
Oregon	10,180	10,476	19,791	162	40,609
Pennsylvania	31,997	29,768	19,804	702	82,271
Rhode Island	3,832	3,231	2,398	114	9,575
South Carolina	8,040	8,592	8,428	0	25,060
South Dakota	1,591	1,406	1,445	20	4,462
Tennessee (h)	15,820	13,627	6,732	3	36,182
Texas	56,049	36,714	18,178	1,322	112,263
Utah	6,574	4,398	4,550	552	16,074
Vermont	1,587	1,926	2,098	64	5,675
Virginia	20,884	10,163	20,070	959	52,076
Washington	20,535	12,293	11,916	1,037	45,781
West Virginia	3,275	4,557	8,665	77	16,574
Wisconsin	16,464	11,575	20,160	0	48,199
Wyoming (i)	1,530	925	1,969	0	4,424
Dist. Of Columbia	N.A.	N.A.	N.A.	N.A.	N.A.

See footnotes at end of table

TABLE 7.6
Total State Expenditures: Capital Inclusive (In millions of dollars) (continued)

Source: National Association of State Budget Officers, *2018 State Expenditure Report.*

Notes: Small dollar amounts, when rounded, cause an aberration in the percentage increase. In these instances, the actual dollar amounts should be consulted to determine the exact percentage increase. "State funds" refers to general funds plus other state fund spending. State spending from bonds is excluded. "Total funds" refers to funding from all sources—general fund, federal funds, other state funds and bonds. For all states, Medicaid reflects provider taxes, fees, assessments, donations, and local funds in Other State Funds.

Key:

N.A.–Not applicable

(a) Alabama: Amounts shown in fiscal years 2016 and 2017 are based on actual expenditures during these years, regardless of the year appropriated. Fiscal 2018 amounts shown are equal to actual expenditures through 9 months (June 30, 2018) and then annualized for the year. The State of Alabama implemented a new ERP system in FY16. This affected the accuracy of some reports for the 13th Accounting period of FY15. Those issues have been resolved, but there will be some variance for FY16 reported expenditures between last year's survey and this survey. Regarding bond funds, there is a discrepancy between amounts reported in the 2016 survey and this one. When gathering expenditure data from Debt Management, it was discovered that transportation expenditures were counted by both Debt Management and Transportation. In addition, Alabama was able to sort the expenditures by category this year, which significantly decreased the "All Other" category for Bond Funds.

(b) Arizona: Bonds payments information from Approps report Lease-Purchase and Bonding Summary section.

(c) Arkansas: 2016 and 2017 amounts were modified to reflect actual final funding and were previously based on estimates.

(d) Georgia: Bond Funds reflect appropriations for the given year. An adjustment was made to FY 2016 Actual General, Federal, and Other State Funds previously reported. Expenditures reflect actual expenditures as reported in the FY 2017 Budgetary Compliance Report.

(e) Illinois: Illinois ended Fiscal Year 2016 without a fully enacted General Funds budget in place. Certain areas of the budget did not receive funding at the same levels as seen historically, including state employee health insurance, some agency operational costs, certain social service programs, and higher education.

(f) Massachusetts: Figures for FY16–FY18 are re-stated to better align with the NASBO category definitions. Certain items that were previously counted (i.e. interfund transfers, bond refundings, certain administrative items) are now excluded.

(g) Ohio: Federal reimbursements for Medicaid expenditures funded from the General Revenue Fund (GRF) are deposited into the GRF. Federal reimbursements for Medicaid expenditures from non-GRF sources are deposited into the appropriate federal fund. Expenditures of federal funds are contained in the General Fund number to be consistent with Ohio accounting practices and with other portrayals of Ohio's general fund. This amounts to $9,479.1 million in fiscal 2018. This will tend to make Ohio's GRF expenditures look higher and conversely make Ohio's federal expenditures look lower relative to most other states that don't follow this practice. Also, inherent in Ohio's budgetary accounting environment are significant overstatements of total state spending due to two phenomena. First, fiduciary fund expenditures represent the distribution of funds collected by the state on behalf of other entities. These are not operating, program, or subsidy expenditures of the state. Examples of this would be the collection and distribution of county and local permissive sales taxes or motor vehicle registration taxes. Fiduciary fund group expenditures totaled $7,445.5 million in fiscal 2018. Second, "double counting" of revenue and expenditures related to intrastate transactions overstates overall state expenditure activity. Intrastate transactions totaled $755.2 million in fiscal 2018. These accounting practices will tend to make Ohio's "All-Other" expenditures look higher, on a dollar and percentage basis, and conversely make Ohio's other categories look lower, on a percentage basis, relative to other states that don't follow similar practices.

(h) Tennessee: Tennessee collects personal income tax on income from dividends on stocks and interest on certain bonds. Tax revenue estimates do not include federal funds and other departmental revenues. However, federal funds and other departmental revenues are included in the budget as funding sources for the general fund, along with state tax revenues.

(i) Wyoming: Part of Wyoming's yearly variation in expenditure totals is due to the fact that the state budgets on a two-year cycle.

Table 7.6 | Total State Expenditures (In millions of dollars)

2016 Actual | 2017 Actual | 2018 Estimated *(in millions of dollars)*

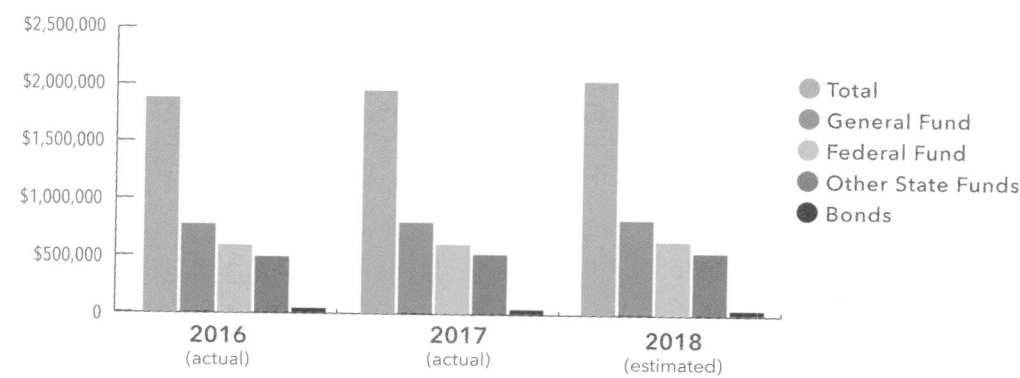

Highest and Lowest Spending by Category FY 2017 *(in millions of dollars)*

GENERAL FUND

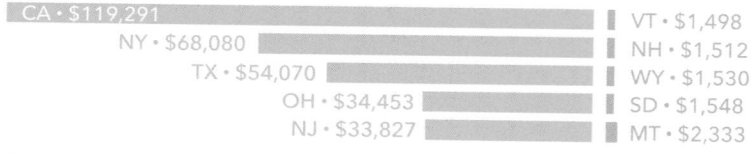

CA · $119,291	VT · $1,498
NY · $68,080	NH · $1,512
TX · $54,070	WY · $1,530
OH · $34,453	SD · $1,548
NJ · $33,827	MT · $2,333

FEDERAL FUND

CA · $95,337	WY · $927
NY · $52,985	SD · $1,420
TX · $36,255	ND · $1,616
PA · $29,001	VT · $1,914
FL · $26,320	DE · $2,171

OTHER STATE FUNDS

CA · $44,249	SD · $1,239
NY · $31,519	AK · $1,495
MI · $24,137	ID · $1,535
IL · $22,387	MT · $1,814
OR · $20,759	WY · $1,969

BONDS

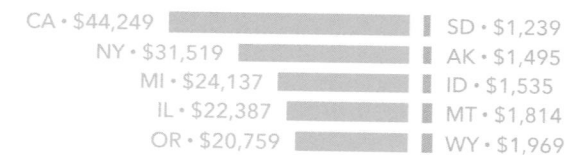

NY · $4,431		WI · $0	
CT · $2,954		CO · $0	
OH · $2,590		KY · $0	
TX · $2,505		SC · $0	
CA · $2,340		TN · $0	

CALIFORNIA HAD THE **HIGHEST TOTAL SPENDING** FY 2017

$261,217

SOUTH DAKOTA HAD THE **LOWEST TOTAL SPENDING** FY 2017

$4,227

TABLE 7.7
Elementary and Secondary Education Expenditures (In millions of dollars)

State	General fund	Federal funds	Other state funds	Bonds	Total
			Actual fiscal 2016		
Total	$272,975	$52,122	$43,230	$2,781	$371,108
Alabama (a)	4,157	1,008	189	58	5,412
Alaska	1,429	208	52	0	1,689
Arizona (b)	4,197	1,129	1,202	172	6,700
Arkansas	2,228	540	760	0	3,528
California	45,118	6,416	44	266	51,844
Colorado (c)	3,478	628	4,598	0	8,704
Connecticut	3,332	525	6	896	4,759
Delaware	1,337	200	763	102	2,402
Florida	10,639	1,774	1,141	0	13,554
Georgia (d)	8,465	2,317	583	272	11,637
Hawaii	1,680	227	62	0	1,969
Idaho	1,500	278	78	0	1,856
Illinois (e)	6,971	2,323	59	17	9,370
Indiana	7,880	1,042	149	0	9,071
Iowa	3,094	458	72	0	3,624
Kansas	3,009	474	967	0	4,450
Kentucky	4,455	839	39	0	5,333
Louisiana	3,566	1,058	695	0	5,319
Maine	1,153	201	32	0	1,386
Maryland (f)	5,925	1,036	401	314	7,676
Massachusetts (g)	5,451	1,003	806	4	7,264
Michigan (h)	98	1,661	11,952	0	13,711
Minnesota	8,507	749	50	11	9,317
Mississippi (i)	2,236	724	339	0	3,299
Missouri	3,236	978	1,465	0	5,679
Montana	788	168	55	0	1,011
Nebraska	1,248	340	60	0	1,648
Nevada	1,389	267	316	0	1,972
New Hampshire	88	181	957	5	1,231
New Jersey	12,861	837	21	0	13,719
New Mexico	2,723	414	6	214	3,357
New York	22,254	3,906	3,299	17	29,476
North Carolina	8,344	1,502	645	0	10,491
North Dakota	823	140	184	0	1,147
Ohio (j)	7,966	1,900	1,189	233	11,288
Oklahoma	1,717	690	1,097	0	3,504
Oregon	3,736	636	258	0	4,630
Pennsylvania	10,766	2,467	622	0	13,855
Rhode Island	1,065	191	33	6	1,295
South Carolina	2,688	951	739	0	4,378
South Dakota	432	164	5	0	601
Tennessee	4,467	1,078	122	0	5,667
Texas (k)	20,862	4,967	3,618	0	29,447
Utah	2,871	431	190	0	3,492
Vermont	402	125	1,246	0	1,773
Virginia	5,593	962	702	0	7,257
Washington	8,679	822	182	171	9,854
West Virginia	1,894	424	121	23	2,462
Wisconsin	6,177	763	253	0	7,193
Wyoming	1	0	806	0	807
Dist. of Columbia	1,795	258	19	318	2,390

See footnotes at end of table

TABLE 7.7
Elementary and Secondary Education Expenditures (In millions of dollars) (continued)

State	General fund	Federal funds	Actual fiscal 2017 Other state funds	Bonds	Total
Total	$282,732	$52,091	$44,264	$2,322	$381,409
Alabama (a)	4,373	1,010	193	60	5,636
Alaska	1,379	226	63	0	1,668
Arizona (b)	4,330	1,146	1,369	170	7,015
Arkansas	2,241	548	767	0	3,556
California	46,231	6,694	57	150	53,132
Colorado (c)	3,768	602	4,703	0	9,073
Connecticut	3,248	528	5	278	4,059
Delaware	1,415	195	795	133	2,538
Florida	10,939	1,722	1,319	0	13,980
Georgia (d)	9,083	2,319	388	252	12,042
Hawaii	1,709	256	55	0	2,020
Idaho	1,612	282	82	0	1,976
Illinois (e)	7,477	2,255	61	60	9,853
Indiana	8,039	1,042	157	0	9,238
Iowa	3,223	460	91	0	3,774
Kansas	3,097	489	1,014	0	4,600
Kentucky	4,974	879	42	0	5,895
Louisiana	3,575	1,163	491	0	5,229
Maine	1,193	213	29	0	1,435
Maryland (f)	5,998	1,052	498	337	7,885
Massachusetts (g)	5,535	1,010	826	18	7,389
Michigan (h)	220	1,699	12,093	0	14,012
Minnesota	8,901	775	51	2	9,729
Mississippi (i)	2,227	691	327	5	3,250
Missouri	3,297	1,013	1,505	1	5,816
Montana	819	175	47	0	1,041
Nebraska	1,268	324	54	0	1,646
Nevada	1,471	267	360	0	2,098
New Hampshire	87	190	967	12	1,256
New Jersey	13,312	920	17	0	14,249
New Mexico	2,671	414	6	244	3,335
New York	23,261	3,763	3,460	50	30,534
North Carolina	8,623	1,507	758	0	10,888
North Dakota	888	145	154	0	1,187
Ohio (j)	8,253	1,970	1,183	237	11,643
Oklahoma	1,725	674	1,041	0	3,440
Oregon	3,737	610	444	0	4,791
Pennsylvania	11,432	2,482	622	0	14,536
Rhode Island	1,113	194	32	3	1,342
South Carolina	2,978	976	907	0	4,861
South Dakota	522	168	6	0	696
Tennessee	4,715	1,124	159	0	5,998
Texas (k)	20,633	4,365	3,317	0	28,315
Utah	3,093	446	185	0	3,724
Vermont	417	129	1,269	1	1,816
Virginia	5,745	1,040	809	0	7,594
Washington	9,234	783	228	286	10,531
West Virginia	1,907	347	91	23	2,368
Wisconsin	6,744	809	276	0	7,829
Wyoming	0	0	891	0	891
Dist. of Columbia	1,909	248	19	410	2,586

See footnotes at end of table

TABLE 7.7
Elementary and Secondary Education Expenditures (In millions of dollars) (continued)

State	General fund	Federal funds	Other state funds	Bonds	Total
			Estimated fiscal 2018		
Total	$294,812	$53,645	$47,106	$3,252	$398,815
Alabama (a)	4,417	1,421	196	28	6,062
Alaska	1,389	249	58	0	1,696
Arizona (b)	4,542	1,164	1,618	170	7,494
Arkansas	2,259	543	771	0	3,573
California	49,209	6,956	108	713	56,986
Colorado (c)	4,080	595	4,804	0	9,479
Connecticut	3,084	540	5	518	4,147
Delaware	1,435	196	785	129	2,545
Florida	11,587	1,766	1,363	0	14,716
Georgia (d)	9,373	2,309	644	252	12,578
Hawaii	1,777	226	93	0	2,096
Idaho	1,713	283	96	0	2,092
Illinois (e)	8,212	2,166	61	14	10,453
Indiana	8,222	1,056	186	0	9,464
Iowa	3,254	483	96	0	3,833
Kansas	3,393	503	1,068	0	4,964
Kentucky	4,938	854	42	0	5,834
Louisiana	3,629	1,146	664	0	5,439
Maine	1,232	220	30	0	1,482
Maryland (f)	6,077	1,050	504	362	7,993
Massachusetts (g)	5,714	1,034	860	29	7,637
Michigan (h)	122	1,839	12,793	0	14,754
Minnesota	9,275	861	55	5	10,196
Mississippi (i)	2,221	835	366	5	3,427
Missouri	3,351	990	1,518	3	5,862
Montana	780	183	49	0	1,012
Nebraska	1,249	380	59	0	1,688
Nevada	1,636	286	368	0	2,290
New Hampshire	84	183	961	12	1,240
New Jersey	13,348	905	15	0	14,268
New Mexico	2,684	414	32	233	3,363
New York	24,209	3,394	3,580	111	31,294
North Carolina	8,893	1,510	731	0	11,134
North Dakota	724	126	303	0	1,153
Ohio (j)	8,402	1,848	1,204	420	11,874
Oklahoma	1,739	661	1,092	0	3,492
Oregon	4,253	639	426	0	5,318
Pennsylvania	11,858	2,613	626	0	15,097
Rhode Island	1,161	209	37	0	1,407
South Carolina	3,071	957	936	0	4,964
South Dakota	557	167	7	0	731
Tennessee	5,018	1,125	150	3	6,296
Texas (k)	21,874	5,114	3,999	0	30,987
Utah	3,298	542	284	0	4,124
Vermont	461	128	1,277	0	1,866
Virginia	6,021	1,034	791	0	7,846
Washington	10,263	788	231	222	11,504
West Virginia	1,920	351	8	23	2,302
Wisconsin	6,804	803	266	0	7,873
Wyoming	0	0	890	0	890
Dist. of Columbia	N/A	N/A	N/A	N/A	N/A

See footnotes at end of table

TABLE 7.7
Elementary and Secondary Education Expenditures (In millions of dollars) (continued)

Source: National Association of State Budget Officers, *2018 State Expenditure Report.*

Notes: Small dollar amounts, when rounded, cause an aberration in the percentage determine the exact percentage increase. "State funds" refers to general funds plus other state fund spending. State spending from bonds is excluded. "Total funds" refers to funding from all sources—general fund, federal funds, other state funds, and bonds. Medicaid reflects provider taxes, fees, assessments, donations, and local funds in Other State Funds.

Key:

N/A–Not available

(a) Alabama: Federal Funds received directly by local school systems are not reported at state budget level. Totals include capital expenditures.

(b) Arizona: Elementary expenditures included Board of Charter Schools, Schools for the Deaf and Blind, Dept. of Education, and School Facilities Board–all numbers from Appropriation Reports. Regarding early education, Arizona does pre-K programs only for children with blind/deaf disabilities.

(c) Colorado: School personnel are paid at the school district level–state costs for employer contributions to employee pensions and health benefits only reflect Colorado Dept. of Education personnel. Funds library-related programs across the state. Regarding capital expenditures, some funding for school facilities certificates of participation are included.

(d) Georgia: An adjustment was made to "Head start." The Department of Early Care and Learning uses state funds to match federal funds for the Early Head Start grant.

(e) Illinois: The reason for the change in FY16 GF/OSF is the Fund for the Advancement of Education and the Budget Stabilization Fund are now General Funds. For last year's report, the funds were treated as OSF. FY16/FY17 have been restated everywhere in this report with these two funds and the Commitment to Human Services Fund as General Funds. FY16 FF adjusted down $1M as last year incorrectly counted refunds toward the total expenditures. Payments to the Chicago Teacher's Pension Fund for normal pension cost are included in the FY18 estimate due to the fact it ran out of Illinois State Board of Education's appropriation in FY18. Historically, the appropriation has been part of the Teacher's Retirement System appropriations. Illinois Math and Science Academy is included. Non-appropriated lines are not included. Bond fund expenditures were incorrect in last year's report, these numbers now include spending from the School Construction Fund and the School Infrastructure Fund for construction projects as capital funding.

(f) Maryland: The $97 million increase in Elementary and Secondary Education Other State Funds from FY 2016 to FY 2017 is mostly due to increased Education Trust Fund revenues, generated by casino proceeds.

(g) Massachusetts: Figures for FY16–FY18 are re-stated to better align with the NASBO category definitions. Certain items that were previously counted (i.e. interfund transfers, bond refundings, certain administrative items) are now excluded.

(h) Michigan: Totals reflect K–12 education, the Michigan Department of Education (MDE), adult education, and pre-school. Employer contributions to current employees' pensions and health benefits are reported for MDE and partially included for employees of K–12 schools. State funds partially offset employer-paid retirement obligations for employees of K–12 schools. FY 18 includes a one-time payment of $200 million from restricted funds to reduce unfunded liabilities. General fund and state school aid fund resources are used interchangeably to support K–12 spending in Michigan.

(i) Mississippi: Elementary and secondary education now included in Capital Expenditures. Amounts not captured in prior years.

(j) Ohio: Employer contributions to current employees' pensions are not directly appropriated, or fully funded, by the state; however, some of the unrestricted support provided to localities for elementary and secondary education is used to help cover these costs. There are no direct appropriations for employer contributions to health benefits, though it can be assumed that some of the unrestricted support provided for elementary and secondary education is used for these costs.

(k) Texas: The figures provided for Elementary and Secondary Education have been adjusted to match the current actuals creating the difference from the previous submissions due to the timing of the report.

TABLE 7.8
Medicaid Expenditures (In millions of dollars)

State	Actual Fiscal 2016					Actual Fiscal 2017				
	General fund	Federal funds	Other state funds	Bonds	Total	General fund	Federal funds	Other state funds	Bonds	Total
Total	$272,975	$52,122	$43,230	$2,781	$371,108	$282,732	$52,091	$44,264	$2,322	$381,409
Alabama (a)	4,157	1,008	189	58	5,412	4,373	1,010	193	60	5,636
Alaska	1,429	208	52	0	1,689	1,379	226	63	0	1,668
Arizona (b)	4,197	1,129	1,202	172	6,700	4,330	1,146	1,369	170	7,015
Arkansas	2,228	540	760	0	3,528	2,241	548	767	0	3,556
California	45,118	6,416	44	266	51,844	46,231	6,694	57	150	53,132
Colorado (c)	3,478	628	4,598	0	8,704	3,768	602	4,703	0	9,073
Connecticut	3,332	525	6	896	4,759	3,248	528	5	278	4,059
Delaware	1,337	200	763	102	2,402	1,415	195	795	133	2,538
Florida	10,639	1,774	1,141	0	13,554	10,939	1,722	1,319	0	13,980
Georgia	8,465	2,317	583	272	11,637	9,083	2,319	388	252	12,042
Hawaii	1,680	227	62	0	1,969	1,709	256	55	0	2,020
Idaho	1,500	278	78	0	1,856	1,612	282	82	0	1,976
Illinois (d)	6,971	2,323	59	17	9,370	7,477	2,255	61	60	9,853
Indiana	7,880	1,042	149	0	9,071	8,039	1,042	157	0	9,238
Iowa	3,094	458	72	0	3,624	3,223	460	91	0	3,774
Kansas	3,009	474	967	0	4,450	3,097	489	1,014	0	4,600
Kentucky	4,455	839	39	0	5,333	4,974	879	42	0	5,895
Louisiana	3,566	1,058	695	0	5,319	3,575	1,163	491	0	5,229
Maine	1,153	201	32	0	1,386	1,193	213	29	0	1,435
Maryland (e)	5,925	1,036	401	314	7,676	5,998	1,052	498	337	7,885
Massachusetts	5,451	1,003	806	4	7,264	5,535	1,010	826	18	7,389
Michigan (f)	98	1,661	11,952	0	13,711	220	1,699	12,093	0	14,012
Minnesota	8,507	749	50	11	9,317	8,901	775	51	2	9,729
Mississippi (g)	2,236	724	339	0	3,299	2,227	691	327	5	3,250
Missouri	3,236	978	1,465	0	5,679	3,297	1,013	1,505	1	5,816
Montana	788	168	55	0	1,011	819	175	47	0	1,041
Nebraska	1,248	340	60	0	1,648	1,268	324	54	0	1,646
Nevada	1,389	267	316	0	1,972	1,471	267	360	0	2,098
New Hampshire	88	181	957	5	1,231	87	190	967	12	1,256
New Jersey	12,861	837	21	0	13,719	13,312	920	17	0	14,249
New Mexico	2,723	414	6	214	3,357	2,671	414	6	244	3,335
New York	22,254	3,906	3,299	17	29,476	23,261	3,763	3,460	50	30,534
North Carolina	8,344	1,502	645	0	10,491	8,623	1,507	758	0	10,888
North Dakota	823	140	184	0	1,147	888	145	154	0	1,187
Ohio (h)	7,966	1,900	1,189	233	11,288	8,253	1,970	1,183	237	11,643
Oklahoma	1,717	690	1,097	0	3,504	1,725	674	1,041	0	3,440
Oregon	3,736	636	258	0	4,630	3,737	610	444	0	4,791
Pennsylvania	10,766	2,467	622	0	13,855	11,432	2,482	622	0	14,536
Rhode Island	1,065	191	33	6	1,295	1,113	194	32	3	1,342
South Carolina	2,688	951	739	0	4,378	2,978	976	907	0	4,861
South Dakota	432	164	5	0	601	522	168	6	0	696
Tennessee	4,467	1,078	122	0	5,667	4,715	1,124	159	0	5,998
Texas (i)	20,862	4,967	3,618	0	29,447	20,633	4,365	3,317	0	28,315
Utah	2,871	431	190	0	3,492	3,093	446	185	0	3,724
Vermont	402	125	1,246	0	1,773	417	129	1,269	1	1,816
Virginia	5,593	962	702	0	7,257	5,745	1,040	809	0	7,594
Washington	8,679	822	182	171	9,854	9,234	783	228	286	10,531
West Virginia	1,894	424	121	23	2,462	1,907	347	91	23	2,368
Wisconsin	6,177	763	253	0	7,193	6,744	809	276	0	7,829
Wyoming	1	0	806	0	807	0	0	891	0	891

See footnotes at end of table

TABLE 7.8
Medicaid Expenditures (In millions of dollars) (continued)

State	Estimated Fiscal 2018				
	General fund	Federal funds	Other state funds	Bonds	Total
Total	$294,812	$53,645	$47,106	$3,252	$398,815
Alabama (a)	4,417	1,421	196	28	6,062
Alaska	1,389	249	58	0	1,696
Arizona (b)	4,542	1,164	1,618	170	7,494
Arkansas	2,259	543	771	0	3,573
California	49,209	6,956	108	713	56,986
Colorado (c)	4,080	595	4,804	0	9,479
Connecticut	3,084	540	5	518	4,147
Delaware	1,435	196	785	129	2,545
Florida	11,587	1,766	1,363	0	14,716
Georgia	9,373	2,309	644	252	12,578
Hawaii	1,777	226	93	0	2,096
Idaho	1,713	283	96	0	2,092
Illinois (d)	8,212	2,166	61	14	10,453
Indiana	8,222	1,056	186	0	9,464
Iowa	3,254	483	96	0	3,833
Kansas	3,393	503	1,068	0	4,964
Kentucky	4,938	854	42	0	5,834
Louisiana	3,629	1,146	664	0	5,439
Maine	1,232	220	30	0	1,482
Maryland (e)	6,077	1,050	504	362	7,993
Massachusetts	5,714	1,034	860	29	7,637
Michigan (f)	122	1,839	12,793	0	14,754
Minnesota	9,275	861	55	5	10,196
Mississippi (g)	2,221	835	366	5	3,427
Missouri	3,351	990	1,518	3	5,862
Montana	780	183	49	0	1,012
Nebraska	1,249	380	59	0	1,688
Nevada	1,636	286	368	0	2,290
New Hampshire	84	183	961	12	1,240
New Jersey	13,348	905	15	0	14,268
New Mexico	2,684	414	32	233	3,363
New York	24,209	3,394	3,580	111	31,294
North Carolina	8,893	1,510	731	0	11,134
North Dakota	724	126	303	0	1,153
Ohio (h)	8,402	1,848	1,204	420	11,874
Oklahoma	1,739	661	1,092	0	3,492
Oregon	4,253	639	426	0	5,318
Pennsylvania	11,858	2,613	626	0	15,097
Rhode Island	1,161	209	37	0	1,407
South Carolina	3,071	957	936	0	4,964
South Dakota	557	167	7	0	731
Tennessee	5,018	1,125	150	3	6,296
Texas (i)	21,874	5,114	3,999	0	30,987
Utah	3,298	542	284	0	4,124
Vermont	461	128	1,277	0	1,866
Virginia	6,021	1,034	791	0	7,846
Washington	10,263	788	231	222	11,504
West Virginia	1,920	351	8	23	2,302
Wisconsin	6,804	803	266	0	7,873
Wyoming	0	0	890	0	890

See footnotes at end of table

TABLE 7.8
Medicaid Expenditures (In millions of dollars) (continued)

Source: National Association of State Budget Officers, *2018 State Expenditure Report.*

Notes: States were asked to report Medicaid expenditures as follows: General funds: all general funds appropriated to the Medicaid agency and any other agency which are used for direct Medicaid matching purposes under Title XIX. Other state funds: other funds and revenue sources used as Medicaid match, such as local funds and provider taxes, fees, donations, assessments (as defined by the Centers for Medicare and Medicaid Services). Federal Funds: all federal matching funds provided pursuant to Title XIX.

(1) The states were asked to separately detail the amount of provider taxes, fees, donations, assessments and local funds reported as Other State Funds.

(2) Small dollar amounts, when rounded, cause an aberration in the percentage increase. In these instances, the actual dollar amounts should be consulted to determine the exact percentage increase.

(3) "State funds" refers to general funds plus other state fund spending. State spending from bonds is excluded.

(4) "Total funds" refers to funding from all sources–general fund, federal funds, other state funds and bonds.

(5) For all states, Medicaid reflects provider taxes, fees, assessments, donations, and local funds in Other State Funds.

Key:

(a) Other State Funds includes Medicaid provider taxes in the amounts of: $399M for FY16; $372M for FY17; and $381M for Estimated FY18.

(b) CHIP is included in "Medicaid" expenditures, all part of the Department of Health Care Policy and Financing.

(c) For fiscal 2018, Illinois borrowed approximately $6 billion to address the backlog of bills; $2.5 billion of the proceeds were deposited directly into the General Funds. A portion of the bond proceeds were used to pay prior year Medicaid bills, which generated $1.2 billion in federal match to the General Funds.

(d) Medicaid expenditure totals reflect pharmacy rebates.

(e) Figures for FY16–FY18 are re-stated to better align with the NASBO category definitions. Certain items that were previously counted (i.e. interfund transfers, bond refundings, certain administrative items) are now excluded. Medicaid figures for FY16–FY18 are re-stated to exclude federal spending for the Community Choices program; this is now categorized as All Other spending. Massachusetts credits federal reimbursements for Medicaid to the General Fund. Per the NASBO guidelines, federal reimbursements are shown as federal funds.

(f) Other State Funds used to match federal Medicaid funds include local funds of $68 million and provider revenues of $1,140 million for FY 2016, local funds of $67 million and provider revenues of $1,136 for FY 2017, and estimated local funds of $66 million and provider revenues of $1,227 for FY 2018. Public health and community and institutional care for mentally and developmentally disabled persons are partially reported in the Medicaid totals.

(g) Federal reimbursements for Medicaid expenditures funded from the General Revenue Fund (GRF) are deposited into the GRF. Federal reimbursements for Medicaid expenditures from non-GRF sources are deposited into the appropriate federal fund. Expenditures of federal funds are contained in the General Fund number to be consistent with Ohio accounting practices and with other portrayals of Ohio's general fund. This amounts to $9,479.1 million in fiscal 2018. This will tend to make Ohio's GRF expenditures look higher and conversely make Ohio's federal expenditures look lower relative to most other states that don't follow this practice.

(h) In last year's report, CHIP was included in total Medicaid expenditures. This year, CHIP has been removed from all years of the survey and is instead reflected in the "All Other" total per the instructions.

(i) Premium revenue: fiscal 2016 totals $323 million, fiscal 2017 totals $323 million, and fiscal 2018 totals $323 million. Certified Public Expenditures–Local fund from Hospitals: fiscal 2016 totals $211 million, fiscal 2017 totals $200 million, and fiscal 2018 totals $204 million. Nursing Home Tax: fiscal 2016 totals $107 million, fiscal 2017 totals $121 million, and fiscal 2018 totals $121 million. ICF/MR 6 percent Gross Receipts Tax: fiscal 2016 totals $11 million, fiscal 2017 totals $11 million, and fiscal 2018 totals $11 million. Intergovernmental Transfers: fiscal 2016 totals $100 million, fiscal 2017 totals $100 million, and fiscal 2018 totals $100 million.

(j) Medicaid figures in this survey submission reflect only programs which the non-federal share is state General Revenue. Medicaid supplemental payments (i.e. uncompensated care, delivery system reform incentive program), funded primarily through local intergovernmental transfers, are excluded from this survey.

(k) The breakdown of local funds, etc. included in Other State Funds is as follows for fiscal 2016 (in millions): provider tax $152; employee assessment $18; local match provided by schools $22; tobacco litigation settlement funds $30; other $119. The breakdown is as follows for fiscal 2017: provider tax $159; employee assessment $19; local match provided by schools $23; tobacco litigation settlement funds $30, other $131. The breakdown is as follows for estimated fiscal 2018: provider tax $164; employee assessment $20; local match provided by schools $27; tobacco litigation settlement funds $21, other $149.

TABLE 7.9
Higher Education Expenditures–Capital Inclusive (In millions of dollars)

State	Actual fiscal 2016					Actual fiscal 2017					Estimated fiscal 2018				
	General fund	Federal funds	Other state funds	Bonds	Total	General fund	Federal funds	Other state funds	Bonds	Total	General fund	Federal funds	Other state funds	Bonds	Total
Total	$75,050	$20,242	$91,869	$5,123	$192,284	$77,999	$20,149	$95,713	$4,334	$198,195	$79,911	$20,371	$99,858	$4,459	$204,599
Alabama (a)	1,493	1,175	2,634	2	5,304	1,566	1,183	2,817	0	5,566	1,597	1,055	2,816	0	5,468
Alaska	362	128	316	0	806	330	126	330	0	786	327	145	361	0	833
Arizona (b)	863	760	4,092	83	5,798	698	818	4,240	83	5,839	705	829	4,678	83	6,295
Arkansas	772	9	2,692	0	3,473	772	9	2,891	0	3,672	772	7	3,065	0	3,844
California	12,948	4,963	23	208	18,142	13,264	5,001	36	228	18,529	14,161	5,134	183	327	19,805
Colorado (c)	1,016	357	4,038	0	5,411	1,000	346	3,966	0	5,312	980	281	4,293	0	5,554
Connecticut	781	292	1,560	552	3,185	713	294	1,618	337	2,962	696	296	1,872	56	2,920
Delaware	236	51	118	16	421	241	47	115	16	419	238	51	113	5	407
Florida	3,839	90	3,088	12	7,029	4,022	98	3,324	45	7,489	4,558	109	3,197	104	7,968
Georgia	2,442	62	6,025	399	8,928	2,607	59	6,267	340	9,273	2,815	78	6,516	410	9,819
Hawaii	441	28	742	93	1,304	471	12	565	120	1,168	485	11	682	163	1,341
Idaho (d)	389	6	252	0	647	427	2	289	0	718	445	5	287	0	737
Illinois (e)	605	194	48	0	847	2,035	224	115	44	2,418	1,707	188	114	58	2,067
Indiana	1,941	1	11	0	1,953	1,936	0	10	0	1,946	1,999	2	14	0	2,015
Iowa	862	520	4,552	0	5,934	843	472	4,727	0	6,042	817	495	4,808	0	6,120
Kansas	760	318	1,603	69	2,750	759	343	1,628	74	2,804	765	348	1,704	83	2,900
Kentucky	1,207	732	4,751	0	6,690	1,145	732	5,286	0	7,163	1,147	828	6,200	0	8,175
Louisiana	655	67	1,940	155	2,817	912	59	1,566	67	2,604	1,014	81	1,725	40	2,860
Maine	284	0	8	24	316	297	0	8	6	311	301	0	7	6	314
Maryland	1,871	361	3,266	384	5,882	1,958	369	3,373	395	6,095	1,983	380	3,574	359	6,296
Massachusetts (f)	1,195	12	19	208	1,434	1,167	9	10	175	1,361	1,177	8	15	197	1,397
Michigan (g)	1,521	108	462	161	2,252	1,534	113	498	40	2,185	1,448	127	637	56	2,268
Minnesota	1,529	4	39	143	1,715	1,556	3	49	108	1,716	1,654	4	38	74	1,770
Mississippi (h)	892	211	2,693	96	3,892	841	142	2,839	97	3,919	793	164	2,924	82	3,963
Missouri	910	1	228	32	1,171	901	1	240	83	1,225	853	1	237	76	1,167
Montana	242	41	399	0	682	233	42	409	0	684	224	31	414	0	669
Nebraska	745	365	1,661	0	2,771	756	336	1,782	0	2,874	652	544	1,670	0	2,866
Nevada	531	3	315	8	857	554	3	331	9	897	605	3	327	15	950
New Hampshire	124	1	0	11	136	128	1	0	10	139	131	0	0	8	139
New Jersey	2,451	17	2,112	0	4,580	2,431	15	2,574	0	5,020	2,547	18	2,534	0	5,099
New Mexico	848	660	1,582	73	3,163	828	644	1,602	106	3,180	779	606	1,484	86	2,955
New York	2,991	334	6,672	696	10,693	2,876	318	6,745	632	10,571	2,834	347	6,995	645	10,821
North Carolina	3,798	49	2,151	0	5,998	3,957	51	2,293	41	6,342	4,060	51	2,365	99	6,575
North Dakota	523	117	635	7	1,282	443	112	651	2	1,208	418	192	781	25	1,416
Ohio (i)	2,464	22	31	209	2,726	2,540	22	38	280	2,880	2,554	21	26	296	2,897
Oklahoma (j)	803	1,024	3,840	23	5,690	653	998	3,997	23	5,671	651	954	3,930	11	5,546
Oregon	924	42	253	58	1,277	863	41	573	29	1,506	1,022	40	286	69	1,417
Pennsylvania	1,619	0	158	126	1,903	1,659	0	121	67	1,847	1,675	0	125	255	2,055
Rhode Island	181	15	886	27	1,109	198	14	877	53	1,142	221	14	948	74	1,257
South Carolina	646	115	3,765	0	4,526	690	120	4,089	0	4,899	670	126	3,986	0	4,782
South Dakota	256	68	421	90	835	235	70	450	19	774	240	70	614	14	938
Tennessee	1,660	184	2,549	194	4,587	2,014	73	2,570	0	4,657	2,314	65	2,686	0	5,065
Texas (k)	7,588	3,860	5,477	0	16,925	7,842	3,976	5,640	0	17,458	8,093	4,098	5,856	0	18,047
Utah	1,062	11	786	0	1,859	1,110	9	816	0	1,935	1,102	8	866	0	1,976
Vermont	83	0	6	4	93	85	0	6	4	95	88	0	6	7	101
Virginia	1,785	1,142	3,796	666	7,389	1,963	1,164	3,838	445	7,410	1,862	859	4,184	528	7,433
Washington	1,507	6	4,317	240	6,070	1,536	5	4,595	302	6,438	1,578	4	4,811	94	6,487
West Virginia	397	26	1,495	54	1,972	383	20	1,473	54	1,930	114	20	1,360	54	1,548
Wisconsin	1,653	1,689	3,355	0	6,697	1,700	1,652	3,411	0	6,763	1,713	1,672	3,520	0	6,905
Wyoming	355	1	7	0	363	327	1	25	0	353	327	1	24	0	352
Dist. of Columbia	72	23	55	15	165	78	21	45	10	154	N/A	N/A	N/A	N/A	N/A

See footnotes at end of table

TABLE 7.9
Higher Education Expenditures–Capital Inclusive (In millions of dollars) (continued)

Source: National Association of State Budget Officers, 2018 State Expenditure Report.

Notes:

Small dollar amounts, when rounded, cause an aberration in the percentage increase. In these instances, the actual dollar amounts should be consulted to determine the exact percentage increase.

"State funds" refers to general funds plus other state fund spending. State spending from bonds is excluded.

"Total funds" refers to funding from all sources–general fund, federal funds, other state funds, and bonds.

Key:

N/A–Not available

(a) Capital expenditures are not captured/available at state budget level. Reported Bond Funds for Higher Ed represent bond proceeds paid directly to vendors by the State's Debt Management division.

(b) Higher Ed I included Commission for Postsecondary Education, Community Colleges, Board of Regents, ASU, NAU, UA-Main, UA-Health Sciences.

(c) HED colleges and universities pay pension and health benefits out of their allotments, which include but are not limited to, state general fund appropriations (as well as tuition and other sources). Tuition and fees are paid straight to institutions by the student, or on behalf of the student, and show up as cash funds to the institution in the state budget. Only a small part of research in E&G is funded by the state; for all practical purposes it is funded by outside grants. The College Opportunity Fund (COF) provides some (stipend) funds to students who attend private colleges and universities. However, this sum is very small relative to the total expenditure; as such, it is categorized as excluded for purposes of this survey.

(d) Expenditures for the University of Idaho, College of Agriculture, Agricultural Research and Extension are now included in Higher Education expenditures.

(e) FY16/FY17 restated to include Budget Stabilization Fund/ Fund for the Advancement of Education as GF. Included Illinois Math

and Science Academy in K–12 rather than Higher Ed. There were no bonded capital expenditures in FY16, which is inconsistent with the $2m that was reported in last year's survey.

(f) Figures for FY16-FY18 are re-stated to better align with the NASBO category definitions. Higher education spending supported by non-state sources is not included. Certain items that were previously counted (i.e. interfund transfers, bond refundings, certain administrative items) are now excluded.

(g) Operating expenditures increased in the periods reported. Federal fund support reflects expenditure of TANF revenue for student financial aid. State funds are used to partially offset employer-paid retirement obligations.

(h) A correction was made to Higher Education FY2016 actual for prior year survey: a component in arriving at the total was not included, resulting in an understatement of expenditures for this category.

(i) Employer contributions to current employees' pensions and employer contributions to employee health benefits are not direct expenditures of the state; however, some of the unrestricted support provided to higher education institutions can be assumed to have been used to help cover these costs. The majority of career-technical education/vocational education is funded through appropriations made to the Ohio Department of Education for career-technical/vocational education for students starting as early as the 7th grade. Ohio provides assistance to private colleges and universities through financial aid to students with the greatest need through the Ohio College Opportunity Grant (OCOG). Students attending private colleges and universities are eligible to receive OCOG.

(j) Expenditure amounts are reported by the Oklahoma Regents for Higher Education based on budgets and campus master plan submissions. FY2017 & FY2016 have been adjusted to follow the same percentages.

(k) The figures provided for Higher Education have been adjusted to match the current actuals creating the difference from the previous submissions due to the timing of the report.

TABLE 7.10
Total Public Assistance Expenditures (In millions of dollars)

State	Actual fiscal 2016				Actual fiscal 2017				Estimated fiscal 2018			
	General fund	Federal funds	Other state funds	Total	General fund	Federal funds	Other state funds	Total	General fund	Federal funds	Other state funds	Total
Total	$8,316	$15,200	$2,469	$25,985	$8,546	$14,576	$2,319	$25,441	$8,383	$14,879	$2,361	$25,623
Alabama	0	33	0	33	0	25	0	25	0	25	0	25
Alaska	90	11	15	116	83	20	15	118	88	23	18	129
Arizona	0	224	0	224	0	222	0	222	0	220	0	220
Arizona (a)	159	322	30	511	158	297	30	485	164	296	13	473
California	3,555	4,593	2,147	10,295	3,826	4,800	2,029	10,655	3,738	4,858	2,088	10,684
Colorado	0	1,453	0	1,453	0	1,434	0	1,434	0	1,423	0	1,423
Connecticut	388	0	0	388	386	0	0	386	384	0	0	384
Delaware	21	4	1	26	21	3	2	26	20	2	2	24
Florida	141	66	0	207	137	56	0	193	126	61	0	187
Georgia (b)	0	37	0	37	0	35	0	35	0	43	0	43
Hawaii	48	19	0	67	45	25	0	70	48	10	0	58
Idaho	13	3	0	16	16	1	0	17	16	1	0	17
Illinois	125	0	0	125	93	0	0	93	100	0	0	100
Indiana	27	169	0	196	27	189	0	216	27	190	0	217
Iowa	57	24	11	92	46	30	9	85	53	26	9	88
Kansas	0	17	0	17	0	15	0	15	0	13	0	13
Kentucky	52	113	1	166	64	99	0	163	56	105	0	161
Louisiana	0	140	0	140	0	141	0	141	0	140	0	140
Maine	44	29	90	163	43	42	93	178	41	60	92	193
Maryland	57	1,220	11	1,288	64	1,100	12	1,176	59	1,196	12	1,267
Massachusetts (c)	753	0	0	753	731	2	0	733	727	1	0	728
Michigan (d)	104	66	46	216	126	60	16	202	116	70	15	201
Minnesota	191	192	0	383	175	216	0	391	175	229	0	404
Mississippi	33	909	4	946	27	842	5	874	24	1,023	5	1,052
Missouri	38	91	31	160	39	68	32	139	36	60	31	127
Montana	10	18	0	28	12	27	0	39	11	31	0	42
Nebraska	19	31	0	50	18	34	0	52	17	33	0	50
Nevada	25	19	0	44	25	17	0	42	25	20	0	45
New Hampshire	51	19	0	70	49	22	0	71	50	42	0	92
New Jersey	184	139	0	323	159	58	0	217	153	32	0	185
New Mexico	1	122	0	123	1	128	0	129	1	128	0	129
New York	1,123	2,863	0	3,986	1,130	2,300	0	3,430	1,137	2,161	0	3,298
North Carolina	60	48	61	169	58	44	58	160	58	44	58	160
North Dakota	0	2	3	5	0	2	2	4	0	0	4	4
Ohio	162	641	0	803	162	710	0	872	150	685	0	835
Oklahoma (e)	68	104	0	172	87	106	0	193	78	64	0	142
Oregon	39	93	0	132	57	63	2	122	39	89	0	128
Pennsylvania	310	656	2	968	309	652	2	963	293	655	2	950
Rhode Island (f)	31	109	0	140	30	107	0	137	31	110	0	141
South Carolina	21	56	1	78	19	62	1	82	15	58	1	74
South Dakota	9	11	0	20	9	11	0	20	9	11	0	20
Tennessee	14	52	0	66	14	43	0	57	14	99	0	113
Texas	51	9	0	60	50	8	0	58	50	6	0	56
Utah	22	68	0	90	21	82	0	103	20	78	0	98
Vermont	22	65	6	93	26	69	2	97	25	65	2	92
Virginia	39	96	0	135	40	91	0	131	39	95	0	134
Washington	48	144	0	192	51	132	0	183	71	227	0	298
West Virginia	30	88	0	118	30	85	0	115	26	70	0	96
Wisconsin	81	12	9	102	82	1	9	92	73	1	9	83
Wyoming	0	0	0	0	0	0	0	0	0	0	0	0
Dist. of Columbia	58	107	0	165	58	119	1	178	N/A	N/A	N/A	N/A

See footnotes at end of table

TABLE 7.10
Total Public Assistance Expenditures (In millions of dollars) (continued)

Source: National Association of State Budget Officers, *2018 Expenditure Report.*

Note:

This table reflects TANF and other cash assistance expenditures.

Small dollar amounts, when rounded, cause an aberration in the percentage increase. In these instances, the actual dollar amounts should be consulted to determine the exact percentage increase.

"State funds" refers to general funds plus other state fund spending. State spending from bonds is excluded.

"Total funds" refers to funding from all sources—general fund, federal funds, other state funds, and bonds.

Key:

N/A–Not available

(a) "Public Assistance" is defined as Cash Assistance, as per Department of Economic Security.

(b) TANF funds reflect only TANF funds used for cash assistance.

(c) Figures for FY16–FY18 are re-stated to better align with the NASBO category definitions. Certain items that were previously counted (i.e. interfund transfers, bond refundings, certain administrative items) are now excluded.

(d) Shifts between general fund and federal fund support for TANF public assistance expenditures reflect year-to-year adjustments based on General Fund need in other budget areas. FY 2016 federal spending for Other Cash Assistance was revised to reflect post-book closing adjustments.

(e) Amounts are reported by Oklahoma Department of Human Services.

(f) Regarding TANF, in last year's report, total reported TANF expenditures represented only those attributable to direct cash assistance. This year, all years of the survey have been adjusted to reflect the totality of TANF expenditures which, in addition to cash assistance, includes portions of the block grant used towards child care assistance, child welfare programs, and training programs run by the Department of Labor and Training, among others. In prior years, these expenditures would have shown up in either the "Other Cash Assistance" category or the "All Other" category, depending on the nature of the expenditure (ex. that portion of TANF used to child care assistance would have shown up in "Other Cash Assistance" while TANF used towards child welfare services and training programs would have shown up in "All Other"). Regarding Other Cash Assistance, in last year's report, total federal expenditures on Other Cash Assistance included the portion of the TANF block grant that is used toward child care assistance. In this year's report, these expenditures are instead reflected under TANF.

TABLE 7.11
Corrections Expenditures–Capital Inclusive (In millions of dollars)

State	Actual fiscal 2016					Actual fiscal 2017					Estimated fiscal 2018				
	General fund	Federal funds	Other state funds	Bonds	Total	General fund	Federal funds	Other state funds	Bonds	Total	General fund	Federal funds	Other state funds	Bonds	Total
Total	$51,569	$569	$4,904	$533	$57,575	$53,422	$579	$5,050	$741	$59,792	$55,773	$669	$5,153	$942	$62,537
Alabama	478	25	94	0	597	497	26	91	0	614	567	27	120	0	714
Alaska	330	7	28	0	365	323	8	36	0	367	339	9	20	0	368
Arizona	1,115	6	93	0	1,214	1,029	8	94	0	1,131	1,068	9	122	0	1,199
Arkansas	443	0	77	0	520	433	0	76	0	509	456	0	57	0	513
California	10,064	80	2,553	0	12,697	10,772	93	2,635	0	13,500	11,665	100	2,766	0	14,531
Colorado (a)	729	4	95	0	828	764	6	91	0	861	788	5	115	0	908
Connecticut	667	3	25	6	701	608	3	24	21	656	604	3	23	7	637
Delaware	290	1	5	3	299	305	0	5	4	314	320	0	5	6	331
Florida	2,553	56	111	0	2,720	2,622	59	115	0	2,796	2,730	90	140	0	2,960
Georgia (b)	1,558	13	47	44	1,662	1,678	12	86	67	1,843	1,722	8	14	89	1,833
Hawaii	241	1	13	0	255	255	1	15	0	271	259	1	13	0	273
Idaho	241	3	36	0	280	252	3	42	0	297	265	3	40	0	308
Illinois (c)	1,006	0	70	17	1,093	1,333	0	53	12	1,398	2,000	0	61	23	2,084
Indiana	744	3	49	0	796	744	3	59	0	806	755	3	56	0	814
Iowa	384	1	63	0	448	379	1	65	0	445	374	2	61	0	437
Kansas	347	8	24	4	383	347	5	20	5	377	370	4	27	5	406
Kentucky	594	13	43	0	650	626	11	45	0	682	640	9	40	0	689
Louisiana (d)	730	2	75	0	807	738	1	87	1	827	775	1	94	5	875
Maine	177	2	3	0	182	182	2	3	0	187	179	1	2	0	182
Maryland (e)	1,412	33	85	36	1,566	1,443	33	79	26	1,581	1,426	38	84	9	1,557
Massachusetts (f)	1,353	2	7	33	1,395	1,387	1	6	43	1,437	1,451	1	5	35	1,492
Michigan (g)	2,037	77	54	0	2,168	2,114	40	48	0	2,202	2,133	49	56	1	2,239
Minnesota	529	3	15	13	560	567	3	12	4	586	585	5	14	4	608
Mississippi	327	1	32	0	360	315	0	22	0	337	311	0	25	0	336
Missouri	645	2	30	0	677	654	2	30	2	688	664	2	28	9	703
Montana	199	1	14	0	214	200	1	13	0	214	199	10	16	0	225
Nebraska	312	2	27	0	341	319	1	28	0	348	318	1	33	0	352
Nevada	253	1	30	10	294	266	2	36	13	317	290	1	44	19	354
New Hampshire	107	0	5	5	117	109	0	5	28	142	115	0	5	14	134
New Jersey	1,508	7	47	0	1,562	1,535	11	48	0	1,594	1,593	11	42	0	1,646
New Mexico	297	0	30	6	333	294	0	31	9	334	297	0	34	6	337
New York (h)	2,697	25	24	238	2,984	2,646	23	33	271	2,973	2,635	28	9	348	3,020
North Carolina	1,850	81	100	0	2,031	1,965	99	141	4	2,209	2,020	106	123	7	2,256
North Dakota	100	4	11	0	115	102	4	12	0	118	101	5	1	0	107
Ohio (i)	1,819	10	68	70	1,967	1,880	7	61	77	2,025	1,940	11	60	83	2,094
Oklahoma	376	2	185	0	563	425	1	150	0	576	487	1	95	0	583
Oregon	950	15	51	3	1,019	956	15	61	38	1,070	1,024	15	32	11	1,082
Pennsylvania	2,515	17	118	0	2,650	2,677	17	119	0	2,813	2,544	17	131	0	2,692
Rhode Island	208	1	3	0	212	212	2	4	0	218	231	2	10	0	243
South Carolina	497	6	88	0	591	544	6	82	0	632	570	6	85	0	661
South Dakota	93	5	12	0	110	98	4	4	0	106	100	4	3	0	107
Tennessee	874	0	38	0	912	904	1	36	0	941	994	0	52	0	1,046
Texas	3,620	22	119	5	3,766	3,662	18	127	1	3,808	3,510	20	134	1	3,665
Utah	453	4	1	0	458	384	4	8	0	396	394	6	21	220	641
Vermont	142	1	7	0	150	148	1	7	0	156	147	1	8	0	156
Virginia	1,264	14	71	17	1,366	1,295	37	72	24	1,428	1,345	51	66	26	1,488
Washington	1,003	3	6	23	1,035	1,033	3	6	91	1,133	1,071	3	47	14	1,135
West Virginia	195	0	6	0	201	191	0	11	0	202	157	0	9	0	166
Wisconsin	1,112	2	107	0	1,221	1,086	1	109	0	1,196	1,122	0	98	0	1,220
Wyoming	131	0	9	0	140	124	0	7	0	131	123	0	7	0	130
Dist. of Columbia	222	0	18	6	246	225	0	21	2	248	N/A	N/A	N/A	N/A	N/A

See footnotes at end of table

TABLE 7.11
Corrections Expenditures–Capital Inclusive (In millions of dollars) (continued)

Source: National Association of State Budget Officers, *2018 Expenditure Report.*

Note: Small dollar amounts, when rounded, cause an aberration in the percentage increase. In these instances, the actual dollar amounts should be consulted to determine the exact percentage increase.

Key:

N/A–Not available

(a) Juvenile delinquent counseling programs are funded in the Colorado Department of Human Services, Division of Youth Corrections (DYC). Funding for the Youthful Offender System (youths convicted as adults) is in the Colorado Dept. of Corrections. Regarding institutions for the criminally insane, San Carlos services significantly mentally ill inmates, but note that the Colorado Dept of Human Services Forensics Institute serves mentally ill people including those found not guilty by reason of insanity.

(b) An adjustment was made to "Drug abuse rehabilitation programs." The state funds some services in the Corrections chapter and additional services in other chapters. An adjustment was made to "Institutions for the criminally insane." The Department of Behavioral Health and Developmental Disabilities operates forensic units that house individuals found not guilty by reason of insanity or individuals that are trying to regain competency to stand trial, but Corrections departments do not operate such institutions.

(c) FY16/FY17 restated to include Budget Stabilization Fund as GF. Department of Juvenile Justice included in Corrections.

(d) Funding is provided to local governments for housing state offenders in local jails.

(e) FY 2016 GFs revised from $1,411 to $1,412 and FY 2016 SFs revised from $90 to $85. These corrections are due to clerical errors.

(f) Figures for FY16–FY18 are re-stated to better align with the NASBO category definitions. Certain items that were previously counted (i.e. interfund transfers, bond refundings, certain administrative items) are now excluded.

(g) Totals include adult inmate and juvenile justice program expenditures.

(h) Prior years surveys included spending from the Division of Criminal Justice Services (DCJS). Based upon the provided definition of Corrections expenditures, we have determined these costs should be excluded, as such, this year's survey no longer includes DCJS spending in the reported 2016, 2017 and 2018 totals for Corrections expenditures.

(i) While employer contributions to current employees' pensions and employer contributions to employee health benefits are included in the expenditure totals, agencies do not receive specific appropriations for these purposes. As of fiscal year 2016, drug recovery services within Department of Rehabilitation and Correction (DRC) institutions are provided by the Department of Mental Health and Addiction Services. However, DRC continues to fund drug abuse rehabilitation programs in community settings through per-bed or per-diem payments to Halfway Houses and Community Based Correctional Facilities.

TABLE 7.12
Transportation Expenditures–Capital Inclusive (In millions of dollars)

State	Actual fiscal 2016					Actual fiscal 2017					Estimated fiscal 2018				
	General fund	Federal funds	Other state funds	Bonds	Total	General fund	Federal funds	Other state funds	Bonds	Total	General fund	Federal funds	Other state funds	Bonds	Total
Total	$5,707	$45,546	$86,770	$11,134	$149,157	$5,288	$44,355	$90,792	$11,792	$152,227	$5,425	$47,145	$99,148	$10,385	$162,103
Alabama	0	882	638	220	1,740	0	834	605	314	1,753	0	746	560	340	1,646
Alaska	308	1,122	201	7	1,638	275	1,216	262	0	1,753	208	1,081	302	0	1,591
Arizona	0	817	2,186	373	3,376	0	645	2,207	402	3,254	2	693	2,278	250	3,223
Arkansas	1	553	878	0	1,432	1	650	1,079	0	1,730	1	734	942	0	1,677
California	262	4,787	7,572	1,355	13,976	203	4,816	7,953	427	13,399	232	5,203	11,002	401	16,838
Colorado (a)	0	744	1,186	0	1,930	0	731	1,242	0	1,973	0	702	1,026	0	1,728
Connecticut	0	774	1,422	963	3,159	0	779	1,447	1,273	3,499	0	743	1,519	897	3,159
Delaware	0	218	585	0	803	5	217	567	129	918	5	347	584	3	939
Florida	0	2,536	5,827	379	8,742	3	2,281	6,418	398	9,100	0	2,804	7,775	275	10,854
Georgia (b)	1,270	1,641	415	186	3,512	1,612	1,438	454	115	3,619	1,927	1,593	90	110	3,720
Hawaii (c)	0	185	931	157	1,273	0	137	1,152	42	1,331	0	174	1,209	329	1,712
Idaho (d)	0	212	302	0	514	0	195	347	0	542	0	266	429	0	695
Illinois	0	108	4,732	723	5,563	0	90	4,679	770	5,539	4	75	4,714	290	5,083
Indiana	242	936	714	0	1,892	571	931	776	0	2,278	47	1,010	1,034	0	2,091
Iowa	0	537	1,347	0	1,884	0	676	1,340	0	2,016	0	563	1,231	0	1,794
Kansas	10	277	530	178	995	10	479	413	195	1,097	10	350	481	211	1,052
Kentucky	6	883	1,908	0	2,797	13	900	1,502	0	2,415	13	816	1,509	0	2,338
Louisiana	38	831	577	171	1,617	3	745	621	129	1,498	13	724	585	91	1,413
Maine	0	222	423	60	705	0	224	440	92	756	0	233	415	69	717
Maryland (e)	0	810	3,738	0	4,548	0	953	3,619	0	4,572	0	1,176	3,945	0	5,121
Massachusetts (f)	171	1,000	2,442	872	4,485	140	860	2,543	841	4,384	177	934	2,736	812	4,659
Michigan (g)	400	1,245	1,967	8	3,620	9	1,256	2,414	7	3,686	205	1,340	2,564	4	4,113
Minnesota	135	335	2,186	404	3,060	140	265	2,487	263	3,155	162	537	2,790	134	3,623
Mississippi (h)	0	547	640	91	1,278	0	566	739	122	1,427	0	595	780	91	1,466
Missouri	18	91	1,779	0	1,888	20	89	1,916	0	2,025	12	79	1,961	0	2,052
Montana	10	410	288	0	708	10	382	279	0	671	7	395	284	0	686
Nebraska	0	367	598	0	965	0	340	552	0	892	0	329	661	0	990
Nevada	0	451	283	65	799	0	369	406	180	955	0	368	567	333	1,268
New Hampshire	1	267	196	5	469	1	247	269	14	531	1	236	313	8	558
New Jersey	1,413	1,459	879	1,174	4,925	1,529	1,571	1,101	1,735	5,936	1,635	1,647	1,572	2,000	6,854
New Mexico	0	689	462	9	1,160	0	748	453	11	1,212	48	776	484	30	1,338
New York	130	1,830	6,295	1,180	9,435	107	2,095	6,748	1,559	10,509	118	1,688	6,899	1,340	10,045
North Carolina	0	1,336	3,320	131	4,787	0	1,330	3,574	431	5,335	0	1,494	4,409	110	6,013
North Dakota	544	246	1,036	0	1,826	46	303	620	0	969	18	251	403	0	672
Ohio (i)	11	1,411	1,694	340	3,456	11	1,465	1,534	338	3,348	15	1,382	1,408	391	3,196
Oklahoma	0	890	677	0	1,567	0	698	740	119	1,557	0	673	737	90	1,500
Oregon	11	47	1,602	29	1,689	11	46	2,123	20	2,200	13	39	1,720	13	1,785
Pennsylvania	2	2,278	5,801	350	8,431	2	2,108	5,800	175	8,085	2	2,500	5,999	175	8,676
Rhode Island	0	254	233	5	492	0	240	296	0	536	0	283	305	1	589
South Carolina	289	642	1,092	0	2,023	120	855	1,179	0	2,154	60	988	1,138	0	2,186
South Dakota	1	348	315	0	664	1	332	263	0	596	1	280	309	0	590
Tennessee (j)	0	859	795	0	1,654	0	874	854	0	1,728	0	996	1,080	0	2,076
Texas (k)	226	4,832	6,236	1,405	12,699	276	4,498	5,519	1,170	11,463	310	5,196	6,198	814	12,518
Utah	0	306	853	0	1,159	3	406	964	0	1,373	1	382	1,261	332	1,976
Vermont	0	284	256	1	541	0	272	266	0	538	0	311	259	0	570
Virginia	68	1,269	4,944	22	6,303	40	1,252	4,892	123	6,307	40	1,096	5,680	68	6,884
Washington	1	793	1,832	271	2,897	1	577	2,104	398	3,080	2	526	2,222	373	3,123
West Virginia	12	1,176	20	0	1,208	12	563	1,083	0	1,658	11	593	775	0	1,379
Wisconsin	97	784	1,869	0	2,750	107	752	1,909	0	2,768	120	1,139	1,963	0	3,222
Wyoming	30	25	68	0	123	6	59	42	0	107	5	59	41	0	105
Dist. of Columbia	330	132	219	204	885	317	210	250	195	972	N/A	N/A	N/A	N/A	N/A

See footnotes at end of table

TABLE 7.12
Transportation Expenditures–Capital Inclusive (In millions of dollars) (continued)

Source: National Association of State Budget Officers, 2018 Expenditure Report.

Note:

 Small dollar amounts, when rounded, cause an aberration in the percentage increase. In these instances, the actual dollar amounts should be consulted to determine the exact percentage increase.

 "State funds" refers to general funds plus other state fund spending. State spending from bonds is excluded.

 "Total funds" refers to funding from all sources–general fund, federal funds, other state funds, and bonds.

Key:

N/A–Not available

(a) Port authority operations, gasoline tax and fee collections, and motor vehicle licensing are at Dept. of Revenue. State police/highway patrol is funded at the Dept. of Public Safety. SB18-001 transferred $2.5 million to the SW Chief/Front Range Passenger Rail Fund to fund planning efforts for a Front Range Passenger Rail line in FY 2018-19.

(b) An adjustment was made to "Gasoline tax and fee collections." Gasoline tax and fee collections are "Included" in the Transportation chapter.

(c) Transportation expenditures are expenditures from Airports, Harbors, Highways, and Administration.

(d) Transportation revenue provided to local entities is not included in Transportation expenditures. Transportation Capital Expenditures include Capital Construction and Right-of-Way and Capital Facilities.

(e) Includes federal funding for transportation and New Starts funding.

(f) Figures for FY16–FY18 are re-stated to better align with the NASBO category definitions. Certain items that were previously counted (i.e. interfund transfers, bond refundings, certain administrative items) are now excluded.

(g) FY 2017 restricted fund totals reflect partial year of increased fuel and registration revenues from road funding package. FY 2018 estimate reflects full year of increase. FY 2018 general fund estimated expenditures include $175 million in accelerated funding for roads.

(h) A correction was made to Bond Funds FY2016 actual for prior year survey: Transportation included waterway (port) projects that should have been excluded, resulting in an overstatement of bond expenditures for this category.

(i) While employer contributions to current employees' pensions and employer contributions to employee health benefits are included in the expenditure totals, agencies do not receive specific appropriations for these purposes. The Ohio Department of Public Safety and the Ohio Public Utilities Commission are responsible for truck enforcement/regulatory programs. A portion of spending by the Ohio Public Works Commission to retire debt for local road and bridge projects is not included in road assistance subsidy programs for local government.

(j) Bond estimates represent bond authorizations, while actual bonds represent bond proceeds utilized.

(k) The figures provided for Transportation have been adjusted to match the current actuals creating the difference from the previous submissions due to the timing of the report.

TABLE 7.13
All Other Expenditures–Capital Inclusive (In millions of dollars)

State	Actual fiscal 2016					Actual fiscal 2017				
	General fund	Federal funds	Other state funds	Bonds	Total	General fund	Federal funds	Other state funds	Bonds	Total
Total	$204,548	$114,844	$202,054	$14,615	$536,061	$208,655	$121,662	$217,315	$15,391	$563,023
Alabama	1,071	2,222	3,081	52	6,426	1,127	2,273	3,075	86	6,561
Alaska	2,321	735	661	0	3,717	1,463	782	786	0	3,031
Arizona	1,679	3,301	8,152	111	13,243	2,032	2,924	7,671	121	12,748
Arkansas	599	915	6,477	58	8,049	605	862	6,522	69	8,058
California	22,348	16,514	21,528	1,815	62,205	23,125	17,624	20,067	1,535	62,351
Colorado (a)	2,721	916	5,746	0	9,383	2,432	937	5,873	0	9,242
Connecticut	9,141	1,018	1,030	1,275	12,464	9,025	1,110	1,577	1,045	12,757
Delaware	1,341	396	2,164	336	4,237	1,379	458	2,452	109	4,398
Florida	6,034	7,193	2,304	1,263	16,794	6,265	7,356	2,694	1,224	17,539
Georgia (b)	4,735	3,208	3,697	198	11,838	5,136	3,509	3,874	176	12,695
Hawaii	3,783	606	1,596	711	6,696	4,241	718	2,107	520	7,586
Idaho (c)	438	965	511	0	1,914	477	953	525	0	1,955
Illinois	15,358	2,543	3,977	25	21,903	16,204	2,330	13,751	473	32,758
Indiana	2,269	1,585	2,176	0	6,030	2,557	1,555	1,772	0	5,884
Iowa	1,445	1,791	2,601	13	5,850	1,447	2,109	1,987	6	5,549
Kansas	838	728	1,524	163	3,253	942	599	1,705	119	3,365
Kentucky	2,368	2,075	1,995	0	6,438	2,546	2,038	2,008	0	6,592
Louisiana	1,832	1,939	5,121	256	9,148	2,069	1,934	3,864	107	7,974
Maine	836	477	1,301	17	2,631	880	482	1,340	16	2,718
Maryland	4,151	2,543	2,765	467	9,926	4,198	2,669	3,466	378	10,711
Massachusetts (d)	12,686	2,509	7,786	1,181	24,162	13,396	2,256	7,962	1,182	24,796
Michigan (e)	3,243	5,494	6,533	38	15,308	3,161	4,997	6,952	28	15,138
Minnesota	5,126	2,676	3,207	307	11,316	5,414	2,762	2,414	264	10,854
Mississippi	1,437	1,692	1,531	333	4,993	1,558	1,758	1,197	900	5,413
Missouri	2,138	1,784	1,939	39	5,900	2,132	1,836	1,910	78	5,956
Montana	709	824	913	0	2,446	750	843	957	0	2,550
Nebraska	948	857	2,047	0	3,852	986	943	2,055	0	3,984
Nevada	874	939	3,394	25	5,232	1,081	1,016	3,933	21	6,051
New Hampshire	447	493	774	36	1,750	510	461	614	39	1,624
New Jersey	10,777	2,786	3,274	436	17,273	10,763	3,340	3,216	431	17,750
New Mexico	1,425	1,620	2,195	172	5,412	1,402	1,741	2,353	292	5,788
New York	27,295	9,292	7,834	1,617	46,038	26,350	10,814	8,737	1,919	47,820
North Carolina	3,660	2,700	2,248	87	8,695	4,025	2,725	2,249	62	9,061
North Dakota	614	368	956	0	1,938	704	361	1,129	0	2,194
Ohio (f)	4,174	2,491	13,466	1,637	21,768	4,169	2,483	13,484	1,659	21,795
Oklahoma	1,329	2,162	2,193	200	5,884	1,490	1,726	3,095	187	6,498
Oregon	2,527	3,065	14,574	52	20,218	2,278	2,349	16,435	51	21,113
Pennsylvania	6,495	5,388	8,715	41	20,639	6,924	6,466	8,844	271	22,505
Rhode Island (g)	1,010	865	916	84	2,875	1,024	888	889	36	2,837
South Carolina	2,159	1,448	1,486	0	5,093	2,350	1,550	1,469	0	5,369
South Dakota	300	290	491	1	1,082	320	308	512	1	1,141
Tennessee	2,848	3,535	1,850	244	8,477	2,982	3,445	1,958	0	8,385
Texas	9,430	265	2,233	488	12,416	9,496	3,278	3,350	1,334	17,458
Utah	1,349	1,107	1,581	0	4,037	1,228	1,127	1,674	0	4,029
Vermont	481	546	160	86	1,273	504	524	184	44	1,256
Virginia	6,373	2,038	8,962	397	17,770	6,376	2,115	9,191	369	18,051
Washington	3,714	2,743	3,919	354	10,730	3,793	2,966	4,308	239	11,306
West Virginia	1,147	182	5,352	0	6,681	1,183	185	5,301	0	6,669
Wisconsin	3,435	2,552	12,598	0	18,585	3,365	2,613	12,853	0	18,831
Wyoming	1,090	463	520	0	2,073	791	564	974	0	2,329
Dist. of Columbia	3,788	626	563	291	5,268	3,853	685	653	248	5,439

See footnotes at end of table

TABLE 7.13

All Other Expenditures–Capital Inclusive (In millions of dollars) (continued)

State	General fund	Federal funds	Other state funds	Bonds	Total
			Estimated fiscal 2018		
Total	$212,302	$128,198	$216,950	$18,069	$575,519
Alabama	856	2,101	2,842	168	5,967
Alaska	1,524	821	1,769	0	4,114
Arizona	1,680	3,118	7,379	139	12,316
Arkansas	637	854	6,683	33	8,207
California	24,565	19,095	23,970	4,868	72,498
Colorado (a)	2,466	942	4,527	0	7,935
Connecticut	9,313	1,110	1,577	1,435	13,435
Delaware	1,350	434	2,439	103	4,326
Florida	6,078	7,873	5,825	1,215	20,991
Georgia (b)	5,511	3,061	4,118	305	12,995
Hawaii	4,609	758	1,573	639	7,579
Idaho (c)	524	782	629	0	1,935
Illinois	16,595	2,874	7,783	96	27,348
Indiana	2,587	2,857	2,040	0	7,484
Iowa	1,460	1,942	2,036	6	5,444
Kansas	979	715	1,722	103	3,519
Kentucky	2,561	1,883	2,099	0	6,543
Louisiana	2,359	3,593	4,440	120	10,512
Maine	900	434	1,371	31	2,736
Maryland	3,948	2,325	4,436	725	11,434
Massachusetts (d)	13,568	2,479	8,166	1,195	25,408
Michigan (e)	3,383	6,395	4,306	51	14,135
Minnesota	5,870	2,650	3,450	191	12,161
Mississippi	1,545	2,729	1,493	469	6,236
Missouri	2,168	1,837	1,834	101	5,940
Montana	706	793	985	0	2,484
Nebraska	1,116	698	2,231	0	4,045
Nevada	765	733	3,553	25	5,076
New Hampshire	478	561	711	31	1,781
New Jersey	11,768	3,678	2,756	0	18,202
New Mexico	1,423	1,666	2,341	146	5,576
New York	25,680	12,403	9,272	2,266	49,621
North Carolina	4,061	2,826	2,826	32	9,745
North Dakota	381	134	938	0	1,453
Ohio (f)	4,137	2,547	13,920	1,678	22,282
Oklahoma	2,015	2,177	1,405	277	5,874
Oregon	2,468	2,894	16,333	70	21,765
Pennsylvania	5,888	5,487	9,267	272	20,914
Rhode Island (g)	1,076	996	1,087	39	3,198
South Carolina	2,499	1,793	1,497	0	5,789
South Dakota	326	324	508	6	1,164
Tennessee	3,783	4,124	2,021	0	9,928
Texas	9,870	245	1,680	507	12,302
Utah	1,280	1,375	1,560	0	4,215
Vermont	559	507	165	57	1,288
Virginia	6,552	2,197	9,346	336	18,431
Washington	3,558	2,916	4,082	334	10,890
West Virginia	552	301	6,083	0	6,936
Wisconsin	3,526	2,614	12,902	0	19,042
Wyoming	799	547	974	0	2,320
Dist. of Columbia	N/A	N/A	N/A	N/A	N/A

See footnotes at end of table

TABLE 7.13
All Other Expenditures–Capital Inclusive (In millions of dollars) (continued)

Source: National Association of State Budget Officers, *2018 Expenditure Report*

Note:

Small dollar amounts, when rounded, cause an aberration in the percentage increase. In these instances, the actual dollar amounts should be consulted to determine the exact percentage increase.

"State funds" refers to general funds plus other state fund spending. State spending from bonds is excluded.

"Total funds" refers to funding from all sources–general fund, federal funds, other state funds, and bonds.

Key:

N/A–Not available

(a) CHIP is included in "Medicaid" expenditures, all part of the Department of Health Care Policy and Financing.

(b) Capital expenditures for debt service are included under All Other State Expenditures.

(c) All Other Capital Expenditures includes all expenditures from the Capital Budget (Permanent Building Fund). Repairs and improvements to existing facilities, as well as the construction of new facilities, are mainly funded here. The expenditures from this budget for higher education, correction, and other facilities cannot be separated.

(d) Figures for FY16–FY18 are re-stated to better align with the NASBO category definitions. Certain items that were previously counted (i.e. interfund transfers, bond refundings, certain administrative items) are now excluded.

(e) Public health and community and institutional care for mentally and developmentally disabled persons are partially reported in the Medicaid totals.

(f) While employer contributions to current employees' pensions and employer contributions to employee health benefits are included in the expenditure totals, agencies do not receive specific appropriations for these purposes. Some expenditures in community and institutional care for the developmentally disabled are included in the Medicaid totals. Most of the expenditures of the Ohio Housing Finance Agency occur outside of the state financial system and are excluded from the housing totals.

(g) In last year's report, CHIP was included in total Medicaid expenditures. This year, CHIP has been removed from all years of the survey and is instead reflected in the "All Other" total per the instructions.

TABLE 7.14
State Tax Amnesty Programs, 1982–2019

State or other jurisdiction	Amnesty period	Legislative authorization	Major taxes covered	Accounts receivable included	Collections ($ millions) (a)	Installment arrangements permitted (b)
Alabama	1/20/84 – 4/1/84	No (c)	All	No	3.2	No
	2/1/09 – 5/15/09	Yes	Ind. Income, Corp. Income, Business, Sales & Use	N/A	8.1	N/A
	6/30/16 – 8/30/16	Yes	All	No	N/A	No
	7/1/18 – 9/30/18	Yes	All (aa)	No	N/A	No
Arizona	11/22/82 – 1/20/83	No (c)	All	No	6.0	Yes
	1/1/02 – 2/28/02	Yes	Individual Income	No	N/A	No
	9/1/03 – 10/31/03	Yes	All (t)	N/A	73.0	Yes
	5/1/09 – 6/1/09	N/A	All	N/A	32.0	N/A
	9/1/15 – 10/31/15	Yes	All	Yes	55.5	No
	9/1/16 – 10/31/16	Yes	All	Yes	N/A	Yes
Arkansas	9/1/87 – 11/30/87	Yes	All	No	1.7	Yes
	7/1/04 – 12/31/04	Yes	All	N/A	N/A	No
California	12/10/84 – 3/15/85	Yes	Individual Income	Yes	154.0	Yes
		Yes	Sales	No	43.0	Yes
	2/1/05 – 3/31/05	Yes	Income, Franchise, Sales	N/A	N/A	Yes
Colorado	9/16/85 – 11/15/85	Yes	All	No	6.4	Yes
	6/1/03 – 6/30/03	N/A	All	N/A	18.4	Yes
	10/1/11 – 11/15/11	Yes	All	No	N/A	No
Connecticut	9/1/90 – 11/30/90	Yes	All	Yes	54.0	Yes
	9/1/95 – 11/30/95	Yes	All	Yes	46.2	Yes
	9/1/02 – 12/2/02	N/A	All	N/A	109.0	N/A
	5/1/09 – 6/25/09	Yes	All	No	40.0	No
	9/16/13 – 11/15/13	Yes	All	Yes	193.5	No
	10/31/17 – 11/30/18	No	All	No	N/A	No
Delaware	9/1/09 – 10/30/09	Yes	All	Yes	N/A	Yes
Florida	1/1/87 – 6/30/87	Yes	Intangibles	No	13.0	No
	1/1/88 – 6/30/88	Yes (d)	All	No	8.4 (d)	No
	7/1/03 – 10/31/03	Yes	All	N/A	80.0	N/A
	7/1/10 – 9/30/10	Yes	All	Yes	N/A	Yes
Georgia	10/1/92 – 12/5/92	Yes	All	Yes	51.3	No
Hawaii	5/27/09 – 6/26/09	N/A	All	No	14.0	No
Idaho	5/20/83 – 8/30/83	No (c)	Individual Income	No	0.3	No
Illinois	10/1/84 – 11/30/84	Yes	All (u)	Yes	160.5	No
	10/1/03 – 11/17/03	Yes	All	N/A	532.0	N/A
	10/1/10 – 11/8/10	Yes	All	Yes	314 (y)	No
Indiana	9/15/05 – 11/15/05	Yes	All	Yes	244.0	Yes
Iowa	9/2/86 – 0/31/86	Yes	All	Yes	35.1	N/A
	9/4/07 – 10/31/07	Yes	All	Yes	N/A	N/A
Kansas	7/1/84 – 9/30/84	Yes	All	No	0.6	No
	10/1/03 – 11/30/03	Yes	All	Yes	53.7	N/A
	9/1/10 – 10/15/10	Yes	All	Yes	N/A	No
	9/1/15 – 10/15/15	Yes	All	Yes	N/A	No
Kentucky	9/15/88 – 9/30/88	Yes (c)	All	No	100.0	No
	8/1/02 – 9/30/02	Yes (c)	All	No	100.0	No
	10/1/12 – 11/30/12	Yes	All	Yes	N/A	N/A

See footnotes at end of table

TABLE 7.14
State Tax Amnesty Programs, 1982–2019 (continued)

State or other jurisdiction	Amnesty period	Legislative authorization	Major taxes covered	Accounts receivable included	Collections ($ millions) (a)	Installment arrangements permitted (b)
Louisiana	10/1/85 - 12/31/85	Yes	All	No	1.2	Yes (f)
	10/1/87 - 12/15/87	Yes	All	No	0.3	Yes (f)
	10/1/98 - 12/31/98	Yes	All	No (q)	1.3	No
	9/1/01 - 10/30/01	Yes	All	Yes	192.9	No
	9/1/09 - 10/31/09	Yes	All	N/A	303.7	N/A
	9/23/13 - 11/22/13	Yes	All	Yes	435.0	No
	10/15/14 - 11/14/14	Yes	All	Yes	N/A	Yes
	11/16/15 - 12/15/15	Yes	All	Yes		Yes
Maine	11/1/90 - 12/31/90	Yes	All	Yes	29.0	Yes
	9/1/03 - 11/30/03	Yes	All	N/A	37.6	N/A
	9/1/09 - 11/30/09	Yes	All	Yes	16.2	No
Maryland	9/1/87 - 11/2/87	Yes	All	Yes	34.6 (g)	No
	9/1/01 - 10/31/01	Yes	All	Yes	39.2	No
	9/1/09 - 10/31/09	Yes	Income, Withholding, Sales & Use	Yes	9.6	Yes
	9/1/15 - 10/30/15	Yes	All	Yes		Yes
Massachusetts	10/17/83 - 1/17/84	Yes	All	Yes	86.5	Yes (h)
	10/1/02 - 11/30/02	Yes	All	Yes	96.1	Yes
	1/1/03 - 2/28/03	Yes	All	Yes	11.2	N/A
	4/1/10 - 6/1/10	Yes	All	Yes	32.6	No
	9/2/14 - 10/31/14	Yes	All	Yes	N/A	No
	3/16/15 - 5/15/15	Yes	Corporate	Yes	18.6	No
	4/1/16 - 5/31/16	Yes	All	No	N/A	No
Michigan	5/12/86 - 6/30/86	Yes	All	Yes	109.8	No
	5/15/02 - 6/30/02	Yes	All	Yes	N/A	N/A
	5/15/11 - 6/30/11	Yes	All	Yes	76.0	No
Minnesota	8/1/84 - 10/31/84	Yes	All	Yes	12.1	No
Mississippi	9/1/86 - 11/30/86	Yes	All	No	1.0	No
	9/1/04 - 12/31/04	Yes	All	No	7.9	No
Missouri	9/1/83 - 10/31/83	No (c)	All	No	0.9	No
	8/1/02 - 10/31/02	Yes	All	Yes	76.4	N/A
	8/1/03 - 10/31/03	Yes	All	Yes	20.0	N/A
	9/1/15 - 11/30/15	Yes	All	Yes		No
Nebraska	8/1/04 - 10/31/04	Yes	All	No	7.5	No
Nevada	2/1/02 - 6/30/02	N/A	All	N/A	7.3	N/A
	7/1/08 - 10/28/08	No	Sales, Business, License	Yes	N/A	No
	7/1/10 - 10/1/10	Yes	All	Yes	N/A	No
New Hampshire	12/1/97 - 2/17/98	Yes	All	Yes	13.5	No
	12/1/01 - 2/15/02	Yes	All	Yes	13.5	N/A
	12/1/15 - 2/15/16	Yes	All	Yes	18.9	No
New Jersey	9/10/87 - 12/8/87	Yes	All	Yes	186.5	Yes
	3/15/96 - 6/1/96	Yes	All	Yes	359.0	No
	4/15/02 - 6/10/02	Yes	All	Yes	276.9	N/A
	5/4/09 - 6/15/09	Yes	All	N/A	725.0	N/A
	10/1/14 - 11/17/14	N/A	All	Yes	N/A	No
	11/15/2018 - 1/15/2019	N/A	All	N/A	N/A	N/A
New Mexico	8/15/85 - 11/13/85	Yes	All (i)	No	13.6	Yes
	8/16/99 - 11/12/99	Yes	All	Yes	45.0	Yes
	6/7/10 - 9/30/10	Yes	All	No	N/A	Yes
	11/8/2018 - 12/31/18	N/A	N/A	N/A	N/A	N/A

See footnotes at end of table

TABLE 7.14
State Tax Amnesty Programs, 1982–2019 (continued)

State or other jurisdiction	Amnesty period	Legislative authorization	Major taxes covered	Accounts receivable included	Collections ($ millions) (a)	Installment arrangements permitted (b)
New York	11/1/85 – 1/31/86	Yes	All (j)	Yes	401.3	Yes
	11/1/96 – 1/31/97	Yes	All	Yes	253.4	Yes (o)
	11/18/02 – 1/31/03	Yes	All	Yes	582.7	Yes (s)
	10/1/05 – 3/1/06	N/A	Income, Corporate	N/A	349.0	N/A
	1/15/10 – 3/15/10	Yes	All	Yes	56.5	No
New York City	10/20/03 – 1/23/04	Yes	All (v)	Yes (w)	N/A	No
North Carolina	9/1/89 – 12/1/89	Yes	All (k)	Yes	37.6	No
North Dakota	9/1/83 – 11/30/83	No (c)	All	No	0.2	Yes
	10/1/03 – 1/31/04	Yes	N/A	N/A	6.9	N/A
Ohio	10/15/01 – 1/15/02	Yes	All	No	48.5	No
	1/1/06 – 2/15/06	Yes	All	No	63.0	No
	1/1/18 – 2/15/18	Yes	All	Yes	N/A	No
Oklahoma	7/1/84 – 12/31/84	Yes	Income, Sales	Yes	13.9	No (l)
	8/15/02 – 11/15/02	N/A	All (r)	Yes	N/A	N/A
	9/15/08 – 11/14/08	Yes	All	Yes	81.0	Yes
	9/14/15 – 11/13/15	Yes	All	Yes	N/A	Yes
Oregon	10/1/09 – 11/19/09	Yes	Personal, Corporate, Inheritance	No	N/A	No
Pennsylvania	10/13/95 – 1/10/96	Yes	All	Yes	N/A	No
	4/26/10 – 6/18/10	Yes	All	Yes	261.0	No
	4/21/17 – 6/19/17	Yes	All	Yes	N/A	No
Rhode Island	10/15/86 – 1/12/87	Yes	All	No	0.7	Yes
	4/15/96 – 6/28/96	Yes	All	Yes	7.9	Yes
	7/15/06 – 9/30/06	N/A	All	Yes	6.5	Yes
	9/2/12 – 11/15/12	Yes	All	Yes	22.3	Yes
	12/1/17 – 2/15/18	Yes	All	Yes	N/A	Yes
South Carolina	9/1/85 – 11/30/85	Yes	All	Yes	7.1	Yes
	10/15/02 – 12/2/02	Yes	All	Yes	66.2	N/A
South Dakota	4/1/99 – 5/15/99	Yes	All	Yes	0.5	N/A
Texas	2/1/84 – 2/29/84	No (c)	All (m)	No	0.5	No
	3/11/04 – 3/31/04	No (c)	All (m)	No	N/A	No
	6/15/07 – 8/15/07	No (c)	All (m)	No	100	No
	6/12/12 – 8/17/12	No (c)	All (m)	No	100	No
	5/1/18 – 6/29/18	Yes	All (bb)	No	N/A	No
Vermont	5/15/90 – 6/25/90	Yes	All	Yes	1 (e)	No
	7/20/09 – 8/31/09	Yes	All	N/A	2.2	N/A
Virginia	2/1/90 – 3/31/90	Yes	All	Yes	32.2	No
	9/2/03 – 11/3/03	Yes	All	Yes	98.3	N/A
	10/7/09 – 12/5/09	Yes	All	Yes	102.1	No
Washington	2/1/11 – 4/30/11	Yes	All	Yes	346.0	No
West Virginia	10/1/86 – 12/31/86	Yes	All	Yes	15.9	Yes
	9/1/04 – 10/31/04	Yes	All	N/A	10.4	Yes
Wisconsin	9/15/85 – 11/22/85	Yes	All	Yes (n)	27.3	Yes
	6/15/98 – 8/14/98	Yes	All	Yes	30.9	N/A
Dist. of Columbia	7/1/87 – 9/30/87	Yes	All	Yes	24.3	Yes
	7/10/95 – 8/31/95	Yes	All (p)	Yes	19.5	Yes (p)
	8/2/10 – 9/30/10	Yes	All (p)	Yes	N/A	No
CNMI*	9/30/05 – 3/30/06	Yes	All	N/A	N/A	N/A

See footnotes at end of table

TABLE 7.14
State Tax Amnesty Programs, 1982–2019 (continued)

Source: The Federation of Tax Administrators, January 2019.
*Commonwealth of Northern Mariana Islands
Key:
N/A–Not available.
(a) Where applicable, figure includes local portions of certain taxes collected under the state tax amnesty program.
(b) "No" indicates requirement of full payment by the expiration of the amnesty period. "Yes" indicates allowance of full payment after the expiration of the amnesty period.
(c) Authority for amnesty derived from pre-existing statutory powers permitting the waiver of tax penalties.
(d) Does not include intangibles tax and drug taxes. Gross collections totaled $22.1 million, with $13.7 million in penalties withdrawn.
(e) Preliminary figure.
(f) Amnesty taxpayers were billed for the interest owed, with payment due within 30 days of notification.
(g) Figure includes $1.1 million for the separate program conducted by the Department of Natural Resources for the boat excise tax.
(h) The amnesty statute was construed to extend the amnesty to those who applied to the department before the end of the amnesty period, and permitted them to file overdue returns and pay back taxes and interest at a later date.
(i) The severance taxes, including the six oil and gas severance taxes, the resources excise tax, the corporate franchise tax, and the special fuels tax were not subject to amnesty.
(j) Availability of amnesty for the corporation tax, the oil company taxes, the transportation and transmissions companies tax, the gross receipts oil tax and the unincorporated business tax restricted to entities with 500 or fewer employees in the United States on the date of application. In addition, a taxpayer principally engaged in aviation, or a utility subject to the supervision of the State Department of Public Service was also ineligible.
(k) Local taxes and real property taxes were not included.
(l) Full payment of tax liability required before the end of the amnesty period to avoid civil penalties.

(m) Texas does not impose a corporate or individual income tax. In practical effect, the amnesty was limited to the sales tax and other excises.
(n) Waiver terms varied depending upon the date of tax liability was accessed.
(o) Installment arrangements were permitted if applicant demonstrated that payment would present a severe financial hardship.
(p) Does not include real property taxes. For the 1995 amnesty, all interest was waived on tax payments made before July 31, 1995. After this date, only 50% of the interest was waived.
(q) Exception for individuals who owed $500 or less.
(r) Except for property and motor fuel taxes.
(s) Multiple payments can be made so long as the required balance is paid in full no later than March 15, 2003.
(t) All taxes except property, estate and unclaimed property.
(u) Does not include the motor fuel use tax.
(v) All NYC taxes administered by the NYC Dept. of Finance are covered except for Real Estate Tax. NYC Sales & Use Tax & NYC Resident Personal Income Tax also are not covered because they are administered by the NY State Dept. of Taxation & Finance.
(w) Taxpayers under audit as of 3/10/03 are ineligible; Taxpayers with an existing installment agreement are ineligible; Taxpayers under criminal investigation are ineligible; Taxpayers party to an administrative or court proceeding must withdraw as a condition of.
(x) The Massachusetts Department of Revenue is required to hold an amnesty to end before June 30, 2010.
(y) In Illinois, the 2010 Amnesty collected a total of $717 million, $314 million for the state General Fund and the rest for local governments.
(z) In Rhode Island, the full amount must be paid by December 14, 2012.
(aa) All taxes except motor fuel, motor vehicle and property taxes.
(bb) Does not apply to local motor vehicle tax, IFTA taxes, PUC gross receipts assessments or unclaimed property payments.

TABLE 7.15A
State Excise Tax Rates (As of January 1, 2019)

State or other jurisdiction	General sales and gross receipts tax (percent)	Cigarettes (cents per pack)	Distilled spirits Excise tax rate ($ per gallon)	Sales taxes applied
Alabama	4.0	67.5 (c)	(h)	Yes
Alaska	(a)	200	12.8 (i)	N.A.
Arizona	5.6	200	3	Yes
Arkansas	6.5	115	2.5 (i)	Yes
California	7.25 (b)	287	3.3 (i)	Yes
Colorado	2.9	84	2.28	Yes
Connecticut	6.35	435	5.4 (i)	Yes
Delaware	(a)	210	4.5 (i)	N.A.
Florida	6.0	133.9 (d)	6.5 (i)	Yes
Georgia	4.0	37	3.79 (i)	Yes
Hawaii	4.0	320	5.98	Yes
Idaho	6.0	57	(h)	Yes
Illinois	6.25	198 (c)	8.55 (i)	Yes
Indiana	7.0	99.5	2.68 (i)	Yes
Iowa	6.0	136	(h)	Yes
Kansas	6.5	129	2.5 (i)	N.A.
Kentucky	6.0	110	1.92 (i)	Yes
Louisiana	4.45	108	3.03	Yes
Maine	5.5	200	(h)	Yes
Maryland	6.0	200	1.5 (i)	Yes
Massachusetts	6.25	351	4.05 (i)	N.A.
Michigan	6.0	200	(h)	Yes
Minnesota	6.875	304 (e)	5.03 (i)	N.A.
Mississippi	7.0	68	(h)	Yes
Missouri	4.225	17 (c)	2	Yes
Montana	(a)	170	(h)	N.A.
Nebraska	5.5	64	3.75	Yes
Nevada	6.85	180	3.6 (i)	Yes
New Hampshire	(a)	178	(h)	N.A.
New Jersey	6.625	270	5.5	Yes
New Mexico	5.125	166	6.06	Yes
New York	4.0	435 (c)	6.44 (i)	Yes
North Carolina	4.75	45	(h)	Yes (k)
North Dakota	5.0	44	2.5 (i)	N.A.
Ohio	5.75	160	(h)	Yes
Oklahoma	4.5	203	5.56 (i)	Yes
Oregon	(a)	133	(h)	N.A.
Pennsylvania	6.0	260	(h)	Yes
Rhode Island	7.0	425	5.40	Yes
South Carolina	6.0	57	2.72 (i)	Yes
South Dakota	4.5	153	3.93 (i)	Yes
Tennessee	7.0	62 (c)(f)	4.4 (i)	Yes
Texas	6.25	141	2.4 (i)	Yes
Utah	5.95	170	(h)	Yes
Vermont	6.0	308	(h)(i)	No
Virginia	5.3	30 (c)	(h)	Yes
Washington	6.5	302.5	14.27 (i)(j)	N.A.
West Virginia	6.0	120	(h)	Yes
Wisconsin	5.0	252	3.25 (i)	Yes
Wyoming	4.0	60	(h)	Yes
Dist. of Columbia	6.0	450 (g)	1.5 (i)	N.A.

See footnotes at end of table

TABLE 7.15A
State Excise Tax Rates (As of January 1, 2019) (continued)

Source: Compiled by The Federation of Tax Administrators from various sources, January 2019.

Key:

N.A.–Not applicable

(a) These states do not have a general sales and gross receipts tax.

(b) The tax rate may be adjusted annually according to a formula based on balances in the unappropriated general fund and the school foundation fund.

(c) Counties and cities may impose an additional tax on a pack of cigarettes: in Alabama, 1¢ to 25¢; Illinois, 10¢ to $4.18; Missouri, 4¢ to 7¢; New York City, $1.50; Tennessee, 1¢; and Virginia, 2¢ to 15¢.

(d) Florida's rate includes a surcharge of $1 per pack.

(e) In addition, Minnesota imposes an in lieu cigarette sales tax determined annually by the Department. The current rate is 58.8¢ through Dec. 31, 2019.

(f) Dealers pay an additional enforcement and administrative fee of 0.05¢ in Tennessee.

(g) In addition, District of Columbia imposes an in lieu cigarette sales tax calculated every March 31. The current rate is 44¢.

(h) In 17 states, the government directly controls the sales of distilled spirits. Revenue in these states is generated from various taxes, fees, price mark-ups, and net liquor profits.

(i) Other taxes in addition to excise taxes for the following states: Alaska, under 21%–$2.50/gallon; Arkansas, under 5%–$0.50/gallon, under 21%–$1.00/gallon; $0.20/case; 3% off–14% on-premise retail taxes; California, over 50%–6.6./gallon; Connecticut, under 7%–$2.46/gallon; Delaware, 25% or less–$3.00/gallon; Florida, under 17.259%–$2.25/gallon, over 55.780%–$9.53/gallon; Georgia, $0.83/gallon local tax; Illinois, under 20%–$1.39/gallon; $2.68/gallon in Chicago and $2.50/gallon in Cook County; Indiana, under 15%–$0.47/gallon; Kansas, 8% off–and 10% on-premise retail tax; Kentucky, under 6%–$0.25/gallon; $0.05/case and 11% wholesale tax; Maryland, 9% sales tax; Massachusetts, under 15%–$1.10/gallon, over 50% alcohol–$4.05/proof gallon; 0.57% on private club sales; Minnesota, $0.01/bottle (except miniatures) and 9% sales tax; Nevada, 5% to 14%–$0.70/gallon, 15% to 22%–$1.30/gallon; New York, under 24%–$2.54/gal.; additional $1.00/gal. in New York City; North Dakota, 7% state sales tax; Oklahoma, 13.5% on-premise; South Carolina, $5.36/case and 9% surtax; additional 5% on-premise tax; South Dakota, under 14%–$0.93/gallon; 2% wholesale tax; Tennessee, 15% on-premise; under 7%–$1.10/gallon.; Texas, 14.95% on-premise and $0.05/drink on airline sales; Vermont, 10% on-premise sales tax; Washington, $9.24/gal. on-premise, 20.5% retail sales tax, 13.7% sales tax to on-premise; Wisconsin, $0.03/gallon administrative fee; Dist. of Columbia, 9% off- and on-premise sales tax.

(j) Washington privatized liquor sales effective June 1, 2012.

(k) General sales tax applies to on-premise sales only.

TABLE 7.15B
State Motor Fuel Tax Rates (As of January 1, 2019)

State or other jurisdiction	Gasoline Excise	Gasoline Fee/Tax	Gasoline Total	Diesel fuel Excise	Diesel fuel Fee/Tax	Diesel fuel Total	Gasohol Excise	Gasohol Fee/Tax	Gasohol Total
Federal (b)	18.3	0.1	18.4	24.3	0.1	24.4	13.0	0.1	13.1
Alabama (a)	18.0		18.0	19.0		19.0	18.0		18.0
Alaska	8.0	0.95	8.95	8.0	0.95	8.95	8.0	0.95	8.95
Arizona (b)(i)	18.0	1.0	19.0	26.0	1.0	27.0	18.0	1.0	19.0
Arkansas	21.5	0.3	21.8	22.5	0.3	22.8	21.5	0.3	21.8
California (h)	41.7	6.0	47.7	36.0	31.0	67.0	41.7	6.0	47.7
Colorado	22.0		22.0	20.5		20.5	22.0		22.0
Connecticut	25.0		25.0	43.9		43.9	25.0		25.0
Delaware	23.0		23.0	22.0		22.0	23.0		23.0
Florida (i)(c)	18.1	13.925	31.425	19.1	13.8	32.3	18.1	13.925	31.425
Georgia (f)	27.5		27.5	30.8		30.8	27.5		27.5
Hawaii (a)	16.0		16.0	16.0		16.0	16.0		16.0
Idaho	32.0	1	33.0	32.0	1	33.0	32.0	1	33.0
Illinois (a)(b)(d)	19.0	1.1	20.1	21.5	1.1	22.6	19.0	1.1	20.1
Indiana (f)	29.0		29.0	48.0		48.0	29.0		29.0
Iowa	30.5		30.5	32.5		32.5	29.0		29.0
Kansas	24.0	1.03	25.03	26.0	1.03	27.03	24.0	1.03	25.03
Kentucky (d)(e)	24.6	1.4	26.0	21.6	1.4	23.0	24.6	1.4	26.0
Louisiana	20.0	0.125	20.125	20.0	0.125	20.125	20.0	0.125	20.125
Maine	30.0		30.0	31.2		31.2	30.0		30.0
Maryland (f)	35.3		35.3	36.05		36.05	35.3		35.3
Massachusetts	24.0		24.0	24.0		24.0	24.0		24.0
Michigan	26.3		26.3	26.3		26.3	26.3		26.3
Minnesota	28.5	0.1	28.6	28.5	0.1	28.6	28.5	0.1	28.6
Mississippi	18.0	0.4	18.4	18.0	0.4	18.4	18.0	0.4	18.4
Missouri	17.0	0.42	17.4	17.0	0.42	17.4	17.0	0.3	17.3
Montana	31.5		31.5	29.25		29.25	31.5		31.5
Nebraska (f)	29.6	0.9	30.5	29.6	0.3	29.9	29.6	0.9	30.5
Nevada (a)	23.0	0.805	23.805	27.0	0.75	27.75	23.0	0.805	23.805
New Hampshire	22.2	1.625	23.825	22.2	1.625	23.825	22.2	1.625	23.825
New Jersey	10.5	30.9	41.4	13.5	35.0	48.5	10.5	30.9	41.40
New Mexico	17.0	1.875	18.875	21.0	1.875	22.875	17.0	1.875	18.875
New York	8.05	17.7	25.75	8.0	15.95	23.95	8.05	17.7	25.8
North Carolina (f)	36.2	0.25	36.45	36.2	0.25	36.45	36.2	0.25	36.45
North Dakota	23.0		23.0	23.0		23.0	23.0		23.0
Ohio	28.0		28.0	28.0		28.0	28.0		28.0
Oklahoma	19.0	1.0	20.0	19.0	1.0	20.0	19.0	1.0	20.0
Oregon (a)	34.0		34.0	34.0		34.0	34.0		34.0
Pennsylvania (f)	57.6		57.6	74.1		74.1	57.6		57.6
Rhode Island (b)(j)	33.0	1	34.0	33.0	1	34.0	33.0	1	34.0
South Carolina (b)(j)	20.0	0.75	20.75	20.0	0.75	20.75	20.0	0.75	20.75
South Dakota (a)	28.0	2	30.0	28.0	2	30.0	26.6	2	28.6
Tennessee (a)(j)	25.0	1.4	26.4	24.0	1.4	25.4	25.0	1.4	26.4
Texas	20.0		20.0	20.0		20.0	20.0		20.0
Utah (e)	30.0		30.0	30.0		30.0	30.0		30.0
Vermont (f)	12.1	19.09	31.19	28.0	4.0	32.0	12.1	19.09	31.19
Virginia (a)(g)	16.2		16.2	20.2		20.2	16.2		16.2
Washington	49.4		49.4	49.4		49.4	49.4		49.4
West Virginia	20.5	15.2	35.7	20.5	15.2	35.7	20.5	15.2	35.7
Wisconsin	30.9	2.0	32.9	30.9	2.0	32.9	30.9	2.0	32.9
Wyoming	23.0	1	24.0	23.0	1	24.0	23.0	1	24.0
Dist. of Columbia	23.5		23.5	23.5		23.5	23.5		23.5

See footnotes at end of table

TABLE 7.15B
State Motor Fuel Tax Rates (As of January 1, 2019) (continued)

Source: Compiled by The Federation of Tax Administrators from various sources, January 2018.

Note: The tax rates listed are fuel excise taxes collected by distributors/suppliers/retailers in each state. Additional taxes may apply to motor carriers. Carrier taxes are coordinated by the International Fuel Tax Association.

Key:

(a) Tax rates do not include local option taxes. In AL, 1-3 cents; HI, 8.8 to 18.0 cents; IL, 5 cents in Chicago and 6 cents in Cook county (gasoline only); NV, 4.0 to 9.0 cents; OR, 1 to 5 cents; SD and TN, one cent; and VA, 2.1%.

(b) LUST tax.

(c) Local taxes for gasoline and gasohol vary from 0 cents to 6.0 cents. Includes Inspection Fee, SCETS, and Statewide Local Tax.

(d) Carriers pay an additional surcharge equal to IL–13.4 cents, KY–2% (g) 4.7% (d).

(e) Tax rate is based on the average wholesale price and is adjusted annually. The actual rates are: KY, 9%; and UT, 16.5%.

(f) Portion of the rate is adjustable based on maintenance costs, sales volume, cost of fuel to state government, or inflation.

(g) Large trucks pay an additional (d) 3.5 cents (g) 12.6 cents. Actual rates (g) 5.1%, (d) 6%.

(h) California Gasoline subject to 2.25% sales tax. Diesel subject to a 9.25% sales tax.

(i) Diesel rate specified is the fuel use tax rate on large trucks. Small vehicles are subject to 18 cent tax rate.

(j) On July 1, 2019, RI fuel excise tax will increase to 34 cents, SC tax will increase to 22 cents, and the TN tax rates will increase to 26 cents (g) and 27 cents (d).

(k)
Alaska–Refining surcharge
Arkansas–Environmental fee
California–Includes prepaid sales tax
Connecticut–Plus a 8.1% Petroleum tax (gas)
Delaware–Plus 0.9% GRT
Florida–Sales tax added to excise
Georgia–Local sales tax additional
Hawaii–Sales tax additional
Idaho–Clean water fee
Illinois–Sales tax add & env.
Indiana–Sales tax additional
Kansas–Environmental & inspection fees
Kentucky–Environmental fee
Louisiana–Inspection fee
Minnesota–Inspection fee
Mississippi–Environmental fee
Missouri–Inspection & Load fees
Nebraska–Petroleum fee
Nevada–Inspection & cleanup fee
New Hampshire–Oil discharge cleanup fee
New Jersey–Petroleum fee
New Mexico–Petroleum loading fee
New York–Petroleum Tax, Sales tax additional
North Carolina–Inspection tax
Oklahoma–Environmental fee
Pennsylvania–Oil franchise tax only
South Carolina–Inspection fee
South Dakota–Inspection fee (gasohol E10)
Tennessee–Petroleum Tax & Envir. Fee
Vermont–Cleanup Fee & Trans. Fee
West Virginia–Sales tax added to excise
Wisconsin–Petroleum inspection fee
Wyoming–License tax

TABLE 7.16A
State Sales Tax Rates and Food and Drug Exemptions (As of January 1, 2019)

State or other jurisdiction	Tax rate (percentage)	Exemptions		
		Food (a)	Prescription drugs	Nonprescription drugs
Alabama	4.0	…	★	…
Alaska	none	none	none	none
Arizona	5.6	★	★	…
Arkansas	6.5	1.5% (c)	★	…
California (b)	7.25	★	★	…
Colorado	2.9	★	★	…
Connecticut	6.35	★	★	…
Delaware	none	none	none	none
Florida	6.0	★	★	★
Georgia	4.0	★(c)	★	…
Hawaii	4.0	…	★	…
Idaho	6.0	…	★	…
Illinois	6.25	1%	1%	1%
Indiana	7.0	★	★	…
Iowa	6.0	★	★	…
Kansas	6.5	…	★	…
Kentucky	6.0	★	★	…
Louisiana	4.45	★(c)	★	…
Maine	5.5	★	★	…
Maryland	6.0	★	★	★
Massachusetts	6.25	★	★	…
Michigan	6.0	★	★	…
Minnesota	6.875	★	★	★
Mississippi	7.0	…	★	…
Missouri	4.225	1.225%	★	…
Montana	none	none	none	none
Nebraska	5.5	★	★	…
Nevada	6.85	★	★	…
New Hampshire	none	none	none	none
New Jersey	6.625	★	★	★
New Mexico	5.125	★	★	…
New York	4.0	★	★	★
North Carolina	4.75	★(c)	★	…
North Dakota	5.0	★	★	…
Ohio	5.75	★	★	…
Oklahoma	4.5	…	★	…
Oregon	none	none	none	none
Pennsylvania	6.0	★	★	★
Rhode Island	7.0	★	★	…
South Carolina	6.0	★	★	…
South Dakota	4.5	…	★	…
Tennessee	7.0	4% (c)	★	…
Texas	6.25	★	★	★
Utah	5.95 (d)	3.0% (d)	★	…
Vermont	6.0	★	★	★
Virginia	5.3 (e)	2.5% (e)	★	★
Washington	6.5	★	★	…
West Virginia	6.0	★	★	…
Wisconsin	5.0	★	★	…
Wyoming	4.0	★	★	…
Dist. of Columbia	6.0	★	★	★

Source: Compiled by FTA from various sources, January 2019.
Key:
★ –Indicates exempt from tax.
… –Indicates subject to general sales tax rate.
(a) Some states tax food, but allow a rebate or income tax credit to compensate poor households. They are: HI, ID, KS, OK, and SD.

(b) Tax rate may be adjusted annually according to a formula based on balances in the unappropriated general fund and the school foundation fund.
(c) Food sales subject to local taxes.
(d) Includes a statewide 1.25% tax levied by local governments in Utah.
(e) Includes statewide 1.0% tax levied by local governments in Virginia.

TABLE 7.16B
State Sales Tax Rates and Vendor Discounts (As of January 1, 2019)

State or other jurisdiction	State sales tax rate (percent)	Rank	Vendor discount (percent)	Max/Min
Alabama	4.0%	41	5.0%-2.0% (a)	$400/month (max)
Alaska			N/A	
Arizona	5.6	28	1 (b)	$10,000/year (max)
Arkansas	6.5	9	2.0	$1,000/month (max)
California	7.25	1	None	
Colorado	2.9	46	3.33 (c)	
Connecticut	6.35	12	None	
Delaware			N/A	
Florida	6.0	16	2.5	$30/report (max)
Georgia	4.0	41	3.0-0.5 (a)	
Hawaii	4.0	41	None	
Idaho	6.0	16	None (d)	
Illinois	6.25	13	1.75	$5/year (min)
Indiana (b)	7.0	2	0.73 (e)	
Iowa	6.0	16	None	
Kansas	6.5	9	None	
Kentucky	6.0	16	1.75-1.5 (a)	$50/month (max)
Louisiana (i)	4.5	36	84.000%	
Maine	5.5	29	None (d)	
Maryland	6.0	16	1.2-0.90 (a)	$500/return (max)
Massachusetts	6.25	13	None	
Michigan	6.0	16	0.5 (f)	$6/month (min), $15,000/month (max)
Minnesota	6.875	6	None	
Mississippi	7.0	2	2.0	$50/month (max)
Missouri	4.225	39	2.0	
Montana			N/A	
Nebraska	5.5	29	2.5	$75/month (max)
Nevada	6.85	6	0.25	
New Hampshire (k)			N/A	
New Jersey	6.625	8	None	
New Mexico	5.125	31	None	
New York	4.0	41	5.0	$200/quarter (max)
North Carolina	4.75	34	None	
North Dakota	5.0	32	1.5	$110/month (max)
Ohio	5.75	27	0.75	
Oklahoma	4.5	36	1.0	2,500/month (max)
Oregon			N/A	
Pennsylvania	6.0	16	1.0	$25/month (min)
Rhode Island	7.0	2	None	
South Carolina	6.0	16	3.0-2.0 (a)	$10,000/year (max)
South Dakota	4.5	36	1.5	$70/month (max)
Tennessee	7.0	2	None	
Texas	6.25	13	0.5 (h)	
Utah (c)	4.7	34	1.31	
Vermont	6.0	16	None (d)	
Virginia (c)	4.3	39	1.6-0.8 (j)	
Washington	6.5	9	None	
West Virginia	6.0	16	None	
Wisconsin	5.0	32	0.5	$10/period (min), $1,000 (max)
Wyoming	4.0	41	1.95-1.0 (a)	$500/month (max)
Dist. of Columbia	6.00	16	None	
U.S. Median	6.00			28 states allow vendor discounts

See footnotes at end of table

TABLE 7.16B
State Sales Tax Rates and Vendor Discounts (As of January 1, 2019) (continued)

Source: Compiled by FTA from various sources. January 2019.
Key:
N/A–Not available

(a) In some states, the vendors' discount varies by the amount paid. In AL and SC, the larger discounts apply to the first $100. In GA, the larger discount applies to the first $3,000. In KY, the larger discounts apply to the first $1,000, while MD applies the larger discount to annual collections of $6,000. In WY, the larger discount applies to the first $6,250. The lower discounts apply to the remaining collections above these amounts.

(b) In Arizona, vendor discount rate is 1.2% for electronic filers with a $12,000 annual maximum.

(c) Local option sales tax discount varies from 0% to 3.33%.

(d) Vendors are allowed to keep any excess collections prescribed under the bracket system.

(e) Utilities are not permitted to take discount. Collection allowances are 0.73% if total sales tax collected is less than $60,000; 0.53% if total taxes are between $60,000 and $600,000; 0.26% if total sales tax collected is more than $600,000.

(f) Vendor discount only applies to the first 4.0% of the tax. A 0.75% discount if paid by the 12th of the month.

(g) New Hampshire imposes a 9% tax on meals and rooms, with a vendor discount of 3%.

(h) An additional discount of 1.25% applies for early payment.

(i) Rate does not include a statewide local rate of 1.0% in VA and 1.25% in UT. In UT, a discount of 1% is applicable to local taxes.

(j) Discount varies; 1.1% (1.6% for food) of the first $62,500, 0.84% (1.2%) of the amount to $208,000, and 0.56% (0.8%) of the remainder. Applies to the state tax only. No discount allowed on electronically filed returns.

TABLE 7.17
State Individual Income Taxes (Tax rates for the tax year 2019–as of January 1, 2019)

State or other jurisdiction	Tax rate range (in percents) Low	High	Number of brackets	Income brackets Lowest	Highest	Personal exemptions Single	Married	Dependents	Standard deduction Single	Married	Federal income tax deductible
Alabama	2.0 -	5.0	3	500 (b) -	3,001 (b)	1,500	3,000	500 (e)	2,500 (y)	7,500 (y)	★
Alaska				(No state income tax)							...
Arizona (a)	2.59 -	4.54	5	10,601 (b) -	158,996 (b)	2,200	4,400	2,200	5,312	10,613	...
Arkansas (a)	0.9 -	6.9 (f)	6	4,299 -	35,100	26 (c)	52 (c)	26 (c)	2,200	4,400	...
California (a)	1.0 -	12.3 (g)	9	8,544 (b) -	572,980 (b)	184 (c)	236 (c)	367 (c)	4,401 (a)	8,802 (a)	...
Colorado	4.63		1	Flat rate		(d)	(d)	(d)	12,200 (d)	24,400 (d)	...
Connecticut	3.0 -	6.99	7	10,000 (b) -	500,000 (b)	15,000 (h)	24,000 (h)	0	(h)	(h)	...
Delaware	0.0 -	6.6	7	2,000 -	60,001	110 (c)	220 (c)	110 (c)	3,250	6,500	...
Florida				(No state income tax)							...
Georgia	1.0 -	5.75	6	750 (i) -	7,001 (i)	2,700	7,400	3,000	4,600	6,000	...
Hawaii	1.4 -	11.0	12	2,400 (b) -	200,000 (b)	1,144	2,288	1,144	2,200	4,400	...
Idaho (a)	1.125 -	6.925	7	1,504 (b) -	11,279 (b)	(d)	(d)	(d)	12,200 (d)	24,400 (d)	...
Illinois (a)	4.95		1	Flat rate		2,225	4,450	2,225	...	...	...
Indiana	3.23		1	Flat rate		1,000	2,000	2,500 (j)	...	...	...
Iowa (a)	0.33 -	8.53	9	1,598 -	71,910	40 (c)	80 (c)	40 (c)	2,080 (a)	5,120 (a)	★
Kansas	3.1 -	5.7	3	15,000 (b) -	30,000 (b)	2,250	4,500	2,250	3,000	7,500	...
Kentucky	5.0		1	Flat rate			None		2,530	2,530	...
Louisiana	2.0 -	6.0	3	12,500 (b) -	50,001 (b)	4,500 (k)	9,000 (k)	1,000	(k)	(k)	★
Maine (a)	5.8 -	7.15	3	21,450 (l) -	50,750 (l)	4,200	8,400	4,200	12,200 (d)	24,400 (d)	...
Maryland	2.0 -	5.75	8	1,000 (m) -	250,000 (m)	3,200	6,400	3,200	2,250 (z)	4,500 (z)	...
Massachusetts	5.05		1	Flat rate		4,400	8,800	1,000	...	...	...
Michigan (a)	4.25		1	Flat rate		4,050	8,100	4,050	...	...	...
Minnesota (a)	5.35 -	9.85	4	26,520 (n) -	163,890 (n)	4,150 (d)	8,300 (d)	4,150 (d)	6,500 (d)	13,000 (d)	...
Mississippi	3.0 -	5.0	3	5,000 -	10,001	6,000	12,000	1,500	2,300	4,600	...
Missouri (a)	1.5 -	5.4	9	1,053 -	8,424	(d)	(d)	(d)	12,200 (d)	24,400 (d)	★(o)
Montana (a)	1.0 -	6.9	7	3,000 -	17,900	2,440	4,800	2,400	4,580 (z)	9,160 (z)	★(o)
Nebraska (a)	2.46 -	6.84	4	3,230 (b) -	31,160 (b)	137 (c)	274 (c)	137 (c)	6,900	13,800	...
Nevada				(No state income tax)							...
New Hampshire				(State income tax of 5% on dividends and interest income only.)							...
New Jersey	1.4 -	10.75	6	20,000 (p) -	5,000,000 (p)	1,000	2,000	1,500	...	...	...
New Mexico	1.7 -	4.9	4	5,500 (q) -	16,001 (q)	(d)	(d)	(d)	12,200 (d)	24,440 (d)	...
New York (a)(aa)	4.0 -	8.82	8	8,500 (b) -	1,077,550 (b)	0	0	1,000	8,000	16,000	...
North Carolina	5.25		1	Flat rate			None		10,000	20,000	...
North Dakota (a)	1.1 -	2.90	5	39,450 (r) -	433,200 (r)	(d)	(d)	(d)	12,200 (d)	24,400 (d)	...
Ohio (a)	0.0 -	4.997	8	10,850 -	217,400	2,350 (s)	4,700 (s)	2,350 (s)	...	...	...
Oklahoma	0.5 -	5.0	6	1,000 (t) -	7,200 (t)	1,000	2,000	1,000	6,350	12,700	...
Oregon (a)	5.0 -	9.9	4	3,350 (b) -	125,000 (b)	206 (c)	412 (c)	206 (c)	2,215	4,435	★(o)
Pennsylvania	3.07		1	Flat rate			None		...	...	...
Rhode Island (a)	3.75 -	5.99	3	64,050 -	145,600	4,100	8,200	4,100	8,750 (y)	17,500 (y)	...
South Carolina (a)	0.0 -	7.0	6	3,030 -	15,160	(d)	(d)	(d)	12,200 (d)	24,400	...
South Dakota				(No state income tax)							...
Tennessee	(State income tax of 2% on dividends and interest income only (x).)					1,250	2,500	0	...	...	...
Texas				(No state income tax)							...
Utah	4.95		1	Flat rate		...	...	...	(u)	(u)	...
Vermont (a)	3.55 -	8.75	5	38,700 (v) -	195,450 (v)	4,150	8,300	4,150	6,000	12,000	...
Virginia	2.0 -	5.75	4	3,000 -	17,001	930	1,860	930	3,000	6,000	...
Washington				(No state income tax)							...
West Virginia	3.0 -	6.5	5	10,000 -	60,000	2,000	4,000	2,000	...	...	...
Wisconsin (a)	4.0 -	7.65	4	11,760 (w) -	258,950 (w)	700	1,400	700	10,860 (y)	20,110 (y)	...
Wyoming				(No state income tax)							...
Dist. of Columbia	4.0 -	8.95	5	10,000 -	1,000,000	(d)	(d)	(d)	12,200 (d)	24,400 (d)	...

See footnotes at end of table

TABLE 7.17
State Individual Income Taxes (Tax rates for the tax year 2019–as of January 1, 2019) (continued)

Source: The Federation of Tax Administrators from various sources, February 2019.

Key:

★–Provision for

…–No provision

(a) 19 states have statutory provision for automatically adjusting to the rate of inflation the dollar values of the income tax brackets, standard deductions, and/or personal exemptions. Michigan indexes the personal exemption only. Oregon does not index the income brackets for $125,000 and over.

(b) For joint returns, taxes are twice the tax on half the couple's income.

(c) The personal exemption takes the form of a tax credit instead of a deduction.

(d) These states use the personal exemption/standard deduction amounts provided in the federal Internal Revenue Code. Note, the Tax Cut and Reform Act of 2017 has eliminated personal exemptions from the IRC. CO, ID, NM, ND, SC, and DC have adopted the new exemptions and standard deduction amounts. MN conforms to a previous IRC year, while ME adopts the higher standard deduction but retains the exemption amounts.

(e) In Alabama, the per-dependent exemption is $1,000 for taxpayers with state AGI of $20,000 or less, $500 with AGI from $20,001 to $100,000, and $300 with AGI over $100,000.

(f) Arkansas has separate brackets for taxpayers with income under $75,000 and $21,000. The tax rates for lower income taxpayers are scheduled to decrease beginning in tax year 2019.

(g) California imposes an additional 1% tax on taxable income over $1 million, making the maximum rate 13.3% over $1 million.

(h) Connecticut's personal exemption incorporates a standard deduction. An additional tax credit is allowed ranging from 75% to 0% based on state adjusted gross income. Exemption amounts are phased out for higher income taxpayers until they are eliminated for households earning over $71,000.

(i) The Georgia income brackets reported are for single individuals. For married couples filing jointly, the same tax rates apply to income brackets ranging from $1,000 to $10,000.

(j) In Indiana, includes an additional exemption of $1,500 for each dependent child.

(k) The amounts reported for Louisiana are a combined personal exemption-standard deduction.

(l) The income brackets reported for Maine are for single individuals. For married couples filing jointly, the same tax rates apply to income brackets ranging from $43,700 to $103,400.

(m) The income brackets reported for Maryland are for single individuals. For married couples filing jointly, the same tax rates apply to income brackets ranging from $1,000 to $300,000.

(n) The income brackets reported for Minnesota are for single individuals. For married couples filing jointly, the same tax rates apply to income brackets ranging from $38,770 to $273,150.

(o) The deduction for federal income tax is limited to $5,000 for individuals and $10,000 for joint returns in Missouri and Montana, and to $6,500 for all filers in Oregon.

(p) The New Jersey rates reported are for single individuals. For married couples filing jointly, the tax rates also range from 1.4% to 10.75%, with 8 brackets and the same high and low income ranges.

(q) The income brackets reported for New Mexico are for single individuals. For married couples filing jointly, the same tax rates apply to income brackets ranging from $8,000 to $24,000.

(r) The income brackets reported for North Dakota are for single individuals. For married couples filing jointly, the same tax rates apply to income brackets ranging from $65,900 to $433,200.

(s) Ohio provides an additional tax credit of $20 per exemption. Exemption amounts reduced for higher income taxpayers.

(t) The income brackets reported for Oklahoma are for single persons. For married persons filing jointly, the same tax rates apply to income brackets ranging from $2,000 to $12,200.

(u) Utah provides a tax credit equal to 6% of the federal personal exemption amounts (and applicable standard deduction).

(v) Vermont's income brackets reported are for single individuals. For married taxpayers filing jointly, the same tax rates apply to income brackets ranging from $64,600 to $237,950.

(w) The Wisconsin income brackets reported are for single individuals. For married taxpayers filing jointly, the same tax rates apply income brackets ranging from $15,680 to $345,270.

(x) Tennessee Hall Tax Rate on Dividends and Interest is being phased out, 1% reduction each year.

(y) Alabama standard deduction is phased out for incomes over $23,000. Rhode Island exemptions and standard deductions phased out for incomes over $203,850; Wisconsin standard deduciton phased out for income over $15,660.

(z) Maryland standard deduction limited to 15% of AGI; Montana, 20% of AGI.

(aa) New York top tax bracket is scheduled to be repealed for tax year 2020.

TABLE 7.18
State Personal Income Taxes: Federal Starting Points (As of January 1, 2019)

State or other jurisdiction	Relation to Internal Revenue Code	Federal tax base used as starting point to calculate state taxable income
Alabama	...	...
Alaska	---No state income tax'---	
Arizona	1/1/17	Adjusted gross income
Arkansas	...	...
California	1/1/15	Adjusted gross income
Colorado	Current	Taxable income
Connecticut	Current	Adjusted gross income
Delaware	Current	Adjusted gross income
Florida	---No state income tax'---	
Georgia	2/9/18	Adjusted gross income
Hawaii	2/9/18	Adjusted gross income
Idaho	12/21/17	Taxable income
Illinois	Current	Adjusted gross income
Indiana	2/11/18	Adjusted gross income
Iowa	3/24/2018 (a)	Adjusted gross income
Kansas	Current	Adjusted gross income
Kentucky	12/31/17	Adjusted gross income
Louisiana	Current	Adjusted gross income
Maine	3/23/18	Adjusted gross income
Maryland	Current	Adjusted gross income
Massachusetts	1/1/05	Adjusted gross income
Michigan	Current (b)	Adjusted gross income
Minnesota	12/16/16	Taxable income
Mississippi	...	...
Missouri	Current	Adjusted gross income
Montana	Current	Adjusted gross income
Nebraska	Current	Adjusted gross income
Nevada	---No state income tax'---	
New Hampshire	---On interest and dividends only'---	
New Jersey	...	...
New Mexico	Current	Adjusted gross income
New York	Current	Adjusted gross income
North Carolina	2/9/18	Adjusted gross income
North Dakota	Current	Taxable income
Ohio	3/30/17	Adjusted gross income
Oklahoma	Current	Adjusted gross income
Oregon	12/31/17	Taxable income
Pennsylvania	...	...
Rhode Island	Current	Adjusted gross income
South Carolina	3/9/18	Taxable income
South Dakota	---No state income tax'---	
Tennessee	---On interest and dividends only'---	
Texas	---No state income tax'---	
Utah	Current	Adjusted gross income
Vermont	12/31/17	Taxable income
Virginia	2/9/18	Adjusted gross income
Washington	---No state income tax'---	
West Virginia	12/31/17	Adjusted gross income
Wisconsin	12/31/17	Adjusted gross income
Wyoming	---No state income tax'---	
Dist. of Columbia	Current	Adjusted gross income

Source: Compiled by the Federation of Tax Administrators from various sources. January 2019.
Note: Includes all legislation enacted through January 1, 2019. The TCJA was signed into law on December 22, 2017, and the Bipartisan Budget Act revising many expired tax breaks was sign on February 9, 2018. A conformity date before these dates would not incorporate those changes.

Key:
...–State does not employ a federal starting point.
Current–Indicates state has adopted the Internal Revenue Code as currently in effect.
Dates indicate state has adopted IRC as amended to that date.
(a) Iowa will use a conformity to Current IRC for tax years beginning in 2020.
(b) Michigan's taxpayers can choose to use either current or 1/1/2018 federal law.

TABLE 7.19

Range of State Corporate Income Tax Rates (For tax year 2019–as of January 1, 2019)

State or other jurisdiction	Tax rate (percent)	Tax brackets		Number of brackets	Financial institution tax rates (percent)(a)	Federal income tax deductible
		Lowest	Highest			
Alabama	6.5	---------- Flat Rate ----------		1	6.5	★
Alaska	0–9.4	25,000	222,000	10	0–9.4	...
Arizona	4.9 (b)	---------- Flat Rate ----------		1	4.9 (b)	...
Arkansas	1.0–6.5	3,000	100,001	6	1.0–6.5	...
California	8.84 (b)	---------- Flat Rate ----------		1	10.84 (b)	...
Colorado	4.63	---------- Flat Rate ----------		1	4.63	...
Connecticut	7.5 (c)	---------- Flat Rate ----------		1	7.5 (c)	...
Delaware	8.7	---------- Flat Rate ----------		1	8.7–1.7 (d)	...
Florida	5.5 (e)	---------- Flat Rate ----------		1	5.5 (e)	...
Georgia	5.75	---------- Flat Rate ----------		1	5.75	...
Hawaii	4.4–6.4 (f)	25,000	100,001	3	7.92 (f)	...
Idaho	6.925 (g)	---------- Flat Rate ----------		1	6.925 (g)	...
Illinois	9.5 (h)	---------- Flat Rate ----------		1	9.5 (h)	...
Indiana	5.75 (i)	---------- Flat Rate ----------		1	6.25	...
Iowa	6.0–12.0	25,000	250,001	4	5.0	★(j)
Kansas	4.0 (k)	---------- Flat Rate ----------		1	2.25 (k)	...
Kentucky	5.0	---------- Flat Rate ----------		1	(a)	...
Louisiana	4.0–8.0	25,000	200,001	5	4.0–8.0	★
Maine	3.5–8.93	350,000	3,500,000	4	1.0 (l)	...
Maryland	8.25	---------- Flat Rate ----------		1	8.25	...
Massachusetts	8.0 (m)	---------- Flat Rate ----------		1	9.0 (m)	...
Michigan	6.0	---------- Flat Rate ----------		1	(a)	...
Minnesota	9.8 (n)	---------- Flat Rate ----------		1	9.8 (n)	...
Mississippi	0–5.0	2,000	10,001	4	0–5.0	...
Missouri	6.25	---------- Flat Rate ----------		1	7.0	★(j)
Montana	6.75 (o)	---------- Flat Rate ----------		1	6.75 (o)	...
Nebraska	5.58–7.81	100,000		2	(a)	...
Nevada	---------- No corporate income tax ----------					
New Hampshire	7.7 (p)	---------- Flat Rate ----------		1	7.7 (p)	...
New Jersey	9.0 (q)	---------- Flat Rate ----------		1	9.0 (q)	...
New Mexico	4.8–5.9	500,000		2	4.8–5.9	...
New York	6.5 (r)	---------- Flat Rate ----------		1	6.5 (r)	...
North Carolina	2.5	---------- Flat Rate ----------		1	2.5	...
North Dakota	1.41–4.31 (s)	25,000	50,001	3	1.41–4.31 (s)	...
Ohio	---------- (t) ----------					(t)
Oklahoma	6.0	---------- Flat Rate ----------		1	6.0	...
Oregon	6.6–7.6 (u)	1 million		2	6.6–7.6 (u)	...
Pennsylvania	9.99	---------- Flat Rate ----------		1	(a)	...
Rhode Island	7.0 (b)	---------- Flat Rate ----------		1	9.0 (b)	...
South Carolina	5.0	---------- Flat Rate ----------		1	4.5 (v)	...
South Dakota	---------- No corporate income tax ----------				6.0–0.25 (b)	...
Tennessee	6.5	---------- Flat Rate ----------		1	6.5	...
Texas	(w)				(w)	...
Utah	4.95 (b)	---------- Flat Rate ----------		1	4.95 (b)	...
Vermont	6.0–8.5 (b)	10,000	25,000	3	(a)	...
Virginia	6.0	---------- Flat Rate ----------		1	6.0	...
Washington	---------- No corporate income tax ----------					
West Virginia	6.5	---------- Flat Rate ----------		1	6.5	...
Wisconsin	7.9	---------- Flat Rate ----------		1	7.9	...
Wyoming	---------- No corporate income tax ----------					
Dist. of Columbia	8.25 (b)	---------- Flat Rate ----------		1	8.25 (b)	...

See footnotes at end of table

TABLE 7.19

Range of State Corporate Income Tax Rates (For tax year 2019–as of January 1, 2019) (continued)

Source: Compiled by the Federation of Tax Administrators from various sources January 2019.

Key:

★–Yes

…–No

(a) Rates listed are the corporate income tax rate applied to financial institutions or excise taxes based on income. Some states have other taxes based upon the value of deposits or shares.

(b) Minimum tax is $800 in California, $250 in District of Columbia, $50 in Arizona and North Dakota (banks), $400 in Rhode Island, $200 per location in South Dakota (banks), $100 in Utah, $300 in Vermont.

(c) Connecticut's tax is the greater of the 7.5% tax on net income, a 0.31% tax on capital stock and surplus (maximum tax of $1 million), or $250 (the minimum tax).

(d) The Delaware Bank marginal rate decreases over 4 brackets ranging from $20 to $650 million in taxable income. Building and loan associations are taxed at a flat 8.7%.

(e) The Florida tax rate may be adjusted downward if certain revenue targets are met.

(f) Hawaii taxes capital gains at 4%. Financial institutions pay a franchise tax of 7.92% of taxable income (in lieu of the corporate income tax and general excise taxes).

(g) Idaho's minimum tax on a corporation is $20. The $10 Permanent Building Fund Tax must be paid by each corporation in a unitary group filing a combined return. Taxpayers with gross sales in Idaho under $100,000, and with no property or payroll in Idaho, may elect to pay 1% on such sales (instead of the tax on net income).

(h) The Illinois rate of 9.5% is the sum of a corporate income tax rate of 7.0% plus a replacement tax of 2.5%.

(i) The Indiana Corporate tax rate is scheduled to decrease to 5.5% on July 1, 2019. Bank tax rate is scheduled to decrease to 6.0% on 1/1/20.

(j) 50% of the federal income tax is deductible.

(k) In addition to the flat 4% corporate income tax, Kansas levies a 3.0% surtax on taxable income over $50,000. Banks pay a privilege tax of 2.25% of net income, plus a surtax of 2.125% (2.25% for savings and loans, trust companies, and federally chartered savings banks) on net income in excess of $25,000.

(l) The state franchise tax on financial institutions is either (1) the sum of 1% of the Maine net income of the financial institution for the taxable year, plus 8¢ per $1,000 of the institution's Maine assets as of the end of its taxable year, or (2) 39¢ per $1,000 of the institution's Maine assets as of the end of its taxable year.

(m) Business and manufacturing corporations pay an additional tax of $2.60 per $1,000 on either taxable Massachusetts tangible property or taxable net worth allocable to the state (for intangible property corporations). The minimum tax for both corporations and financial institutions is $456.

(n) In addition, Minnesota levies a 5.8% tentative minimum tax on Alternative Minimum Taxable Income.

(o) Montana levies a 7% tax on taxpayers using water's edge combination. The minimum tax per corporation is $50; the $50 minimum applies to each corporation included on a combined tax return. Taxpayers with gross sales in Montana of $100,000 or less may pay an alternative tax of 0.5% on such sales, instead of the net income tax.

(p) New Hampshire's 7.7% Business Profits Tax is imposed on both corporations and unincorporated associations with gross income over $50,000. In addition, New Hampshire levies a Business Enterprise Tax of 0.675% on the enterprise base (total compensation, interest and dividends paid) for businesses with gross receipts over $208,000 or enterprise base over $104,000, adjusted every biennium for CPI. The Business Profits Tax is scheduled to decrease to 7.5% for tax year 2021.

(q) New Jersey also imposes a 2.5% surtax on taxpayers with income over $1 million in tax year 2019; surtax is reduced to 1.5% in 2020 and 21. Small businesses with annual entire net income under $100,000 pay a tax rate of 7.5%; businesses with income under $50,000 pay 6.5%. The minimum Corporation Business Tax is based on New Jersey gross receipts. It ranges from $500 for a corporation with gross receipts less than $100,000, to $2,000 for a corporation with gross receipts of $1 million or more.

(r) New York's General business corporate rate shown. Corporations may also be subject to a capital stocks tax, which is being phased out through 2021. A minimum tax ranges from $25 to $200,000, depending on receipts ($250 minimum for banks). Certain qualified New York manufacturers pay 0%.

(s) North Dakota imposes a 3.5% surtax for filers electing to use the water's edge method to apportion income.

(t) Ohio no longer levies a tax based on income (except for a particular subset of corporations), but instead imposes a Commercial Activity Tax (CAT) equal to $150 for gross receipts sitused to Ohio of between $150,000 and $1 million, plus 0.26% of gross receipts over $1 million. Banks continue to pay a franchise tax of 1.3% of net worth. For those few corporations for whom the franchise tax on net worth or net income still applies, a litter tax also applies.

(u) Oregon's minimum tax for C corporations depends on the Oregon sales of the filing group. The minimum tax ranges from $150 for corporations with sales under $500,000, up to $100,000 for companies with sales of $100 million or above.

(v) South Carolina taxes savings and loans at a 6% rate.

(w) Texas imposes a Franchise Tax, otherwise known as margin tax, imposed on entities with more than $1,130,000 total revenues at rate of 0.75%, or 0.375% for entities primarily engaged in retail or wholesale trade, on lesser of 70% of total revenues or 100% of gross receipts after deductions for either compensation or cost of goods sold.

TABLE 7.20
State Severance Taxes: 2019

State	Title and application of tax (a)	Rate
Alabama	Iron Ore Mining Tax (c)	$.03/ton
	Forest Products Severance Tax	Varies by species and ultimate use.
	Oil and Gas Conservation & Regulation of Production Tax	1% of production from wells permitted from July 1, 1996 thru June 30, 2002 for five years from first production; 1.66% of gross proceeds from offshore production from depths greater than 8,000 feet below mean sea level; 2% of all other production.
	Oil and Gas Privilege Tax on Production	8% of gross value at point of production; 4% of gross value at point of incremental production resulting from a qualified enhanced recovery project; 4% if wells produce 25 bbl. or less oil per day or 200,000 cu. ft. or less gas per day; 6% of gross value at point of production for certain on-shore and off-shore wells. A 50% rate reduction for wells permitted by the oil and gas board on or after July 1, 1996 and before July 1, 2002 for 5 years from initial production, except for replacement wells for which the initial permit was dated before July 1, 1996; 3.65% gross proceeds from offshore production greater than 8,000 ft. below sea level.
	Coal Severance Tax	$0.335/ton (a $0.135/ton tax rate and $0.20/ton tax rate). Effective Aug. 1, 2017, the additional tax rates for coal are $0.025 per ton on underground mining and $0.05 per ton on surface mining. The additional tax will expire two years after its effective date.
	Local Solid Minerals Tax	Varies by county for sand, clay, gravel, granite, shale, and other products.
	Uniform Natural Minerals Tax	$.10/ton.
Alaska	Common Property Fisheries Assessment (b)	$0.10/lb; determined annually by the department of revenue.
	Dive Fishery Management Assessment (b)	Elective; currently 5% or 7% of value for select dive fishery species in select management regions.
	Fisheries Business Tax	Tax based on unprocessed value of fishery resources processed in or exported from the state. 1% of value for shore-based processing in developing fisheries; 3% of value for floating processing in developing fisheries or shore-based processing in established fisheries; 4.5% of value for salmon cannery processing in established fisheries; 5% of value for floating processing in established fisheries.
	Fishery Resource Landing Tax	Tax based on unprocessed value of fishery resources processed outside and first landed in the state. 1% of value for developing fisheries; 3% of value for established fisheries.
	Mining License Tax	Up to 7% of net income and royalties received in connection with mining properties and activities in Alaska. Quarry rock, sand and gravel, and marketable earth mining operations are exempt from the mining license tax. New mining operations exempt for 3-1/2 years after production begins.
	Alaska Oil Production Tax	Alaska will impose a base rate of 35 percent on oil companies' net profits in the state.
	Salmon Enhancement Tax (b)	Elective; 2% or 3% of value for salmon sold in or exported from select aquaculture regions.
	Seafood Development Tax (b)	Elective; currently 1% of value for select commercial fish species in select seafood development regions.
	Seafood Marketing Assessment (b)	Elective; currently 0.5% of value for all commercial fish species exported from, landed or processed in-state.
Arizona	Severance Tax	.025% for metalliferous mining; 0.0313% for nonmetal mining. Additional severance taxes on these and other products are levied at the city or county level. For timber, $2.13 per thousand for board fee (Ponderosa) and $1.50 per thousand board feet (other).
Arkansas	Timber Severance Tax	$0.178/ton (pine), all other $0.125/ton.
	Natural Gas Severance Tax	1.25%, 1.5%, and 5% depending on well classification.
	Oil Severance Tax	Crude oil 4% to 5% depending on production levels; additional taxes of 5 mils and $0.02 per barrel of oil produced in the state.
	Other Severance Taxes	Separate Rate for each Substance.
	Oil and Gas Conservation Assessment	Maximum 43 mills/bbl. of oil and 9 mills per MCF produced of gas.
California	Oil and Gas Production Assessment	Rate determined annually by Department of Conservation to fund agency operations; no state severance tax. The assessment rate for fiscal year 2018/19 is $0.5547977.
	Lumber Products Assessment	1% on purchases of lumber products and engineered wood products for use in California, based on the selling price of the products.
Colorado	Severance Tax	$0.803 for amount of coal produced above 300,000 tons, rate updated monthly by the department of revenue. 2.25% for metallic minerals above $19 million in gross producer income. $0.05/ton of molybdenum above 625,000 tons. Oil and gas rate varies from 2% to 5% depending on gross income brackets; up to 15 barrels per day of oil 90,000 cubic feet of gas per producing day are exempt. Oil shale is taxed based on years of operation, where 1 year = 1%, 2 years = 2%, etc. up to 4% of the gross proceeds above the threshold and after the first 180 days of production.
	Oil and Gas Conservation Levy (d)	0.07% charge on all oil, natural gas, and CO2 produced

See footnotes at end of table

TABLE 7.20
State Severance Taxes: 2019 (continued)

State	Title and application of tax (a)	Rate
Florida	Oil Production Tax	5% of gross value for small well oil, and 8% of gross value for ordinary oil production, and 12.5% for escaped oil; tiered formula for tertiary oil.
	Gas and Sulfur Production Tax	The gas base rate ($0.171) times the gas base adjustment rate each fiscal year for gas (2018–19 rate $0.219 per MCF); and the sulfur base rate ($2.43) times the sulfur base rate adjustment each fiscal year for sulfur (2018–19 rate $5.38 per ton).
	Solid Minerals Tax (e)	8% of the value of the minerals severed; heavy minerals (rate computed annually at $1.34/ton plus times the base rate adjustment currently at 2.97226). Year 2018 Tax Rate $3.98 per ton; phosphate rock (rate computed annually at a base rate of $1.80/ton).
Idaho	Mine License Tax	1% of net value of ores mined or extracted and royalties received from mining.
	Oil and Gas Production Tax	2.5% of the gross income earned for the sale of oil and gas.
Illinois	Oil and Gas Production Tax	For first 24 months, rate for oil and gas is 3% of the value. Thereafter, rate will be 6% of the value of gas and rate on oil will be based on each well's average daily production (ADP). ADP less than 25 barrels, rate is 3%; ADP of at least 25 and less than 50 barrels, rate is 4%; ADP of at least 50 and less than 100 barrels, rate is 5%; at least 100 barrels, rate is 6%.
	Timber Fee	4% of purchase price (g).
Indiana	Petroleum Severance Tax (h)	1% of value of petroleum; $0.24 per barrel for oil; and $0.03 per 1000 cu. ft. of natural gas.
Kansas	Mineral Tax (i)	8% of gross value of oil and gas, less property tax credit of 3.67%; and $1/ton of coal.
	Oil Inspection Fee/Barrel (i)	$0.015/barrel.
	Oil and Gas Conservation Tax	91.00 mills/bbl. crude oil or petroleum marketed or used each month; 12.9 mills/1,000 cu. ft. of gas sold or marketed each month.
	Mined-Land Conservation & Reclamation Tax	"The first-time fee for a mining license is $300. Licenses must be renewed annually. The annual renewal fee varies between $25 and $150 depending upon the amount of material sold or consumed in the previous year. Plus per ton fee of $.03."
Kentucky	Oil Production Tax	4.5% of market value.
	Coal Severance Tax	4.5% of gross value, less transportation expenses; $0.50/ton minimum for extraction and processing.
	Natural Resource Severance Tax	4.5% of gross value, less transportation expenses.
Louisiana	Natural Gas Severance Tax (j)	The natural gas severance tax rate effective July 1, 2018 through June 30, 2019 has been set at 12.2 cents per thousand cubic feet (MCF) measured at a base pressure of 15.025 pounds per square inch absolute and at the temperature base of 60 degrees Fahrenheit.
	Oil/Condensate Severance Tax (j)	Value on a per barrel basis (42 gallons) the rates are: full-rate, 12.5%; incapable oil rate, 6.25%; stripper oil rate, 3.125%; reclaimed oil, 3.125%; produced water full-rate, 10%; produced water incapable oil rate, 5.0%; produced water stripper oil rate, 2.5%.
	Timber Severance Tax (j)	Trees and timber: 2.25% of current stumpage value. Pulpwood: 5% of current stumpage value.
	Mineral Severance Tax (j)	Sulfur, $1.03 per long ton of 2,240 lbs; salt, $0.06 per ton of 2,000 lbs; marble, $0.20 per ton; stone, $0.03 per ton; sand, $0.06 per ton; lignite, $0.12 per ton; salt content in brine, when used in the manufacture of other products and not marketed as salt: $0.005 per ton.
	Oil Field Site Restoration Fee	$.015 per barrel of oil and condensate; $.003 for every thousand cubic feet of gas.
	Freshwater Mussel Tax	5% of revenues from the sale of whole freshwater mussels, at the point of first sale.
Maine	Mining Excise Tax	The greater of a tax on facilities and equipment or a tax on gross proceeds.
Maryland	Mine Reclamation Surcharge	$.15/ton of coal removed by open-pit, strip or deep mine methods. Of the $.15, $.06 is remitted to the county from which the coal was removed.
Michigan	Gas and Oil Severance Tax	5% (gas), 6.6% (oil) and 4% (oil from stripper wells and marginal properties) of gross cash market value of the total production. Maximum additional fee of 1% of gross cash market value on all oil and gas (2019 fee).
Minnesota	Taconite and Iron Sulfides	$2.659 per taxable ton of concentrates or pellets (rate indexed to inflation by law).
	Direct Reduced Iron (k)	$2.659 per taxable ton of concentrates plus an additional $.03 per ton for each 1% that the iron content exceeds 72%.
Mississippi	Natural Gas Severance Tax	6% of value at point of gas production; 1.3% for gas produced from a horizontally drilled well for the first 30 months from the first sale of production or until payout of the well cost is achieved, whichever comes first.
	Oil Severance Tax	6% of value at point of oil production; 3% reduced rate for wells using the enhanced oil recovery method; 1.3% for oil produced from a horizontally drilled well for the first 30 months from the first sale of production or until payout of the well cost is achieved, whichever comes first.
	Timber Severance Tax	Varies depending on type of wood and ultimate use.
	Salt Severance Tax	3% of value of entire production in state.

See footnotes at end of table

TABLE 7.20
State Severance Taxes: 2019 (continued)

State	Title and application of tax (a)	Rate
Montana	Coal Severance Tax	Varies from 3% to 15% depending on quality of coal and type of mine.
	Metal Mines License Tax (l)	Progressive rate, taxed on amounts in excess of $250,000. For concentrate shipped to smelter, mill or reduction work, 1.81%. Gold, silver or any platinum group metal shipped to refinery, 1.6%.
	Oil and Gas Conservation Tax	Maximum 0.3% on the market value of each barrel of crude petroleum oil or 10,000 cu. ft. of natural gas produced, saved and marketed or stored within or exported from the state. (m)
	Oil and Natural Gas Production Tax	Varies from 0.8% to 15.1% according to the type of well and type of production.
	Micaceous Mineral Mines License Tax	$.05/ton of concentrates mined, extracted, or produced.
	Cement and Gypsum License Tax (n)	$.22/ton of cement, $.05/ton of gypsum or gypsum products.
	Resource Indemnity Trust & Ground Water Assessment Tax	$25 plus 0.5% of gross value greater than $5,000. For talc, $25 plus 4% of gross value greater than $625. For coal, $25 plus 0.40% of gross value greater than $6,250. For vermiculite, $25 plus 2% of gross value greater than $1,250. For limestone, $25 plus 10% of gross value greater than $250. For industrial garnets, $25 plus 1% of gross value greater than $2,500.
	Electrical Energy Producers License Tax	$.0002/kilowatt-hour of electrical energy generated, manufactured or produced.
Nebraska	Oil and Gas Severance Tax	3% of value of nonstripper oil and natural gas; 2% of value of stripper oil.
	Oil and Gas Conservation Tax	0.3%.
	Uranium Tax	2% of gross value over $5 million. The value of the uranium severed subject to tax is the gross value less transportation and processing costs.
Nevada	Minerals Extraction Tax	Between 2% and 5% of net proceeds of each geographically separate extractive operation, based on ratio of net proceeds to gross proceeds of whole operation.
	Oil and Gas Conservation Tax	$50/mills/bbl. of oil and 50 mills/50,000 cu. ft. of gas.
New Hampshire	Refined Petroleum Products Tax	0.1% of fair market value.
	Excavation Tax	$.02 per cubic yard of earth excavated.
	Timber Tax	10% of stumpage value at the time of cutting. Not assessed under the general property tax but rather is taxed by municipalities.
New Mexico	Resources Excise Tax	Severance: potash .5%, molybdenum .125%, all others .75% of value. Processing: timber .375%. Potash .125%. Molybdenum .125%. All others .75%.
	Severance Tax	Copper .5%, Timber .125% of value. Pumice, gypsum, sand, gravel, clay, fluorspar and other non-metallic minerals, .125% of value. Gold, silver .20%; Lead, zinc, thorium, molybdenum, manganese, rare earth and other .125% of value.
	Oil and Gas Severance Tax	Rate varies according to type of well and production.
	Oil and Gas Emergency School Tax	3.15% of value of oil, other liquid hydrocarbons and carbon dioxide. 4% of value of natural gas.
	Natural Gas Processor's Tax	$0.116/Mmbtu tax on volume.
	Oil and Gas Ad Valorem Production Tax	Varies, based on property tax in district of production.
	Oil and Gas Conservation Tax (p)	0.19% of value.
North Carolina	Primary Forest Product Assessment Tax	$.50/1,000 board ft. for softwood sawtimber, $.40/1,000 board ft. for hardwood sawtimber, $.20/cord for softwood pulpwood, $.12/cord hardwood pulpwood.
	Extracted Energy Minerals Tax	Oil and condensates: 2% of gross price paid. Gas: 0.9% of the market value as determined in as determined in N.C. Gen. Stat. § 105-187.78.
North Dakota	Oil Gross Production Tax	5% of gross value at well.
	Gas Gross Production Tax	$0.705/MCF rate through June 30, 2019.
	Coal Severance Tax	$.375/ton plus $.02/ton. (r)
	Oil Extraction Tax	5%, adjusted between 5% and 6% whenever the average price is above or below the "trigger price" per bbl for 3 consecutive months. The "trigger price" is set by the tax commissioner each year and is $90 for 2018.
Ohio	Resource Severance Tax	$.10/bbl. of oil; $.025/1,000 cu. ft. of natural gas; $.04/ton of salt; $.02/ton of sand, gravel, limestone and dolomite; $.10/ton of coal; and $0.01/ton of clay, sandstone or conglomerate, shale, gypsum or quartzite.
Oklahoma	Oil, Gas and Mineral Gross Production Tax	0.75% levied on asphalt and metals. 7% on gross production of oil and gas after the first three years of production. During the first 3 years of production, rate of 5% of gross production. Oil Gross Production Tax is now a variable rate tax, beginning with January 1999 production, at the following rates based on the average price of Oklahoma oil: a) If the average price equals or exceeds $17/bbl, the tax shall be 7%; b) If the average price is less than $17/bbl, but is equal to or exceeds $14/bbl, the tax shall be 4%; c) If the average price is less than $14/bbl, the tax shall be 1%.
	Petroleum Excise Tax (r)	Oil and Natural gas .095%.

See footnotes at end of table

TABLE 7.20
State Severance Taxes: 2019 (continued)

State	Title and application of tax (a)	Rate
Oregon	Forest Products Harvest Tax	$4.2811/1000 board ft. harvested from public and private land.–through Dec. 31, 2019. The first 25,000 board feet of timber harvested by an owner each year is exempt.
	Oil and Gas Production Tax	6% of gross value at well.
	STF Severance Tax–Eastern Oregon Forestland Option	$4.65/1000 board ft. harvested from land under the Small Tract Forestland Option–through Dec. 31, 2019
	STF Severance Tax–Western Oregon Forestland Option	$5.98/1000 board ft. harvested from land under the Small Tract Forestland Option–through Dec. 31, 2019
Pennsylvania	Natural Gas Impact Fee	The state issues an annual fee based on the average price of gas for that year along with the number on a schedule that considers a wells years in production. Local fees and taxes determined by county.
South Carolina	Forest Renewal Tax	Softwood products: 50 cents per 1,000 board feet or 20 cents per cord. Hardwood products: 25 cents per 1,000 board feet or 7 cents per cord.
South Dakota	Precious Metals Severance Tax	$4 per ounce of gold severed plus additional tax depending on price of gold; 10% on net profits or royalties from sale of precious metals, and 8% of royalty value.
	Energy Minerals Severance Tax (s)	4.5% of taxable value of any energy minerals.
	Conservation Tax	2.4 mills of taxable value of any energy minerals.
Tennessee	Oil and Gas Severance Tax	3% of sales price.
	Coal Severance Tax (t)	$1.00/ton (effective 7/17/13).
	Mineral Tax	Up to $0.15 per ton, rate set by county legislative body.
Texas	Natural Gas Production Tax	7.5% of market value of gas. Condensate Production Tax: 4.6% of market value of gas.
	Crude Oil Production Tax	4.6% of market value or $.046/bbl.
	Cement Production Tax	$0.55 per ton or $.0275/100 lbs. or fraction of 100 pounds of taxable cement.
	Oil-Field Cleanup Regulatory Fees	5/8 of $.01/barrel; 1/15 of $.01/1000 cubic feet of gas. (f)
	Oyster Sales Fee	$1 per 300 lb. barrel of oysters taken from Texas waters.
Utah	Mining Severance Tax	2.6% of taxable value for metals or metalliferous minerals sold or otherwise disposed of.
	Oil and Gas Severance Tax	3% of value for the first $13 per barrel of oil, 5% from $13.01 and above; 3% of value for first $1.50/mcf natural gas, 5% from $1.51 and above; and 4% of taxable value of natural gas liquids.
	Oil and Gas Conservation Fee	.002% of market value at wellhead.
Virginia	Forest Products Tax	$1.15 per 1000 feet B.M. of pine lumber and 1000 board feet of pine logs. $0.475 collected per cord of pine pulpwood.
	Coal Surface Mining Reclamation Tax	Varies depending on balance of Coal Surface Mining Reclamation Fund and the type of mine.
Washington	Enhanced Food Fish Tax	0.09% to 5.62% of value (depending on species) at point of landing.
	Timber Excise Tax	5% of stumpage value for harvests on public and private lands.
West Virginia	Coal Severance Tax	Coal: State rate is greater of 5% or $.75 per ton Special state rates for coal from new low seam mines. For seams between 37" and 45" the rate is greater of 2% or $.75/ton (1.65% for state purposes and .35% for distribution to local governments). For seams less than 37" the rate is greater of 1% or $.75/ton (.65% for state purposes and .35% for distribution to local governments). For coal from gob, refuse piles, or other sources of waste coal, the rate is 2.5% (distributed to local governments). Additional tax for workers' compensation debt reduction is $.56/ton. Special reclamation taxes at $.02/clean ton.
	Natural Resource Severance Taxes	5% for sand, gravel, oil, natural gas, coalbed methane, limestone, sandstone, or other natural gas liquids
	Timber Severance Tax	1.50%
Wisconsin	Mining Net Proceeds Tax	Progressive net proceeds tax ranging from 0% to 15% is imposed on the net proceeds from mining metalliferous minerals. The tax brackets are annually adjusted for inflation based on the change in the GNP deflator.
	Oil and Gas Severance Tax	7% of market value of oil or gas at the mouth of the well.
	Forest Crop Law Severance Tax	$2.52 per acre, rate effective through 2022.
	Managed Forest Law Tax	Open land $2.04/acre; close land $10.20/acre.
Wyoming	Severance Taxes	Severance Tax is defined as an excise tax imposed on the present and continuing privilege of removing, extracting, severing or producing any mineral in this state. Except as otherwise provided by W.S. 39-14-205. The total Severance Tax on crude oil, lease condensate or natural gas shall be six percent (6%). Stripper oil is taxed at four percent (4%). Surface coal is taxed at seven percent (7%). Underground coal is taxed at three and three-fourths percent (3.75%). Trona is taxed at four percent (4%). Bentonite, sand and gravel, and all other minerals are taxed at two percent (2%). Natural Gas (6%) Uranium (4%).

See footnotes at end of table

TABLE 7.20
State Severance Taxes: 2019 (continued)

Sources: The Council of State Governments, February 2019.
Note: Severance tax collection totals may be found in the Chapter Seven table entitled "State Government Revenue, By Type of Tax."
Key:

(a) Application of tax is same as that of title unless otherwise indicated by a footnote.

(b) Tax rates and applicability for these severance taxes determined by a vote of the appropriate association within the seafood industry, by the Alaska Seafood Marketing Institute, or by the Department of Revenue. Proceeds from these elective assessments are customarily appropriated for benefit of the seafood industry.

(c) The iron ore tax was suspended as of Oct. 1, 2014 by administrative rule due to the cost of administering the collection of the tax exceeded the total amount of the tax collected.

(d) As of July 1, 2007, set at .0007 mill/$1.

(e) Clay, gravel, phosphate rock, lime, shells, stone, sand, heavy minerals and rare earths.

(f) Counties and municipalities also authorized to levy severance taxes on sand, gravel, sandstone, chert and limestone at a rate up to $.15/ton.

(g) Buyer deducts amount from payment to grower; amount forwarded to Department of Natural Resources.

(h) Petroleum, oil, gas and other hydrocarbons. Oil inspection fee rate based Department of Revenue factsheet.

(i) Coal, oil and gas, based on Department of Revenue information.

(j) Oil inspection fee rate based Department of Revenue factsheet.

(k) Coal, oil and gas, based on Department of Revenue information.

(l) Production is considered commercial when it exceeds 50,000 tons annually. There is a six-year phase-in of the tax. In years one and two, the rate is zero. In year three, it is 25% of the statutory rate and 50% and 75% in years four and five respectively. An Aggregate Materials Tax is imposed by resolution of county boards. It is not required that any county impose the tax, which is $.10/cubic yard or $.07/ton on materials produced in the county.

(m) Metals, precious and semi-precious stones and gems.

(n) The maximum rate of 0.3% is split between the Oil or Gas Conservation Tax and the Oil, Gas and Coal Natural Resource Account Fund. Currently the Oil or Gas Conservation Tax is .18% and the Oil, Gas and Coal Natural Resource Account fund tax rate is .08%.

(o) Cement and gypsum or allied products.

(p) Natural resources except oil, natural gas, liquid hydrocarbons or carbon dioxide.

(q) Oil, coal, gas, liquid hydrocarbons, geothermal energy, carbon dioxide and uranium.

(r) Rate reduced by 50 percent if burned in cogeneration facility using renewable resources as fuel to generate at least 10 percent of its energy output. Coal shipped out of state is subject to the $.02/ton tax and 30% of the $.375/ton tax. The coal may be subject to up to the $.375/ton tax at the option of the county in which the coal is mined.

(s) Asphalt and ores bearing lead, zinc, jack, gold, silver, copper or petroleum or other crude oil or other mineral oil, natural gas or casinghead gas and uranium ore.

(t) Any mineral fuel used in the production of energy, including coal, lignite, petroleum, oil, natural gas, uranium and thorium.

TABLE 7.21
State Government Tax Revenue, By State and Selected Types of Tax: 2017 (In thousands of dollars)

State	Total taxes	Sales and gross receipts	Licenses	Individual income	Corporation net income	Severance	Property taxes	Death and gift	Documentary and stock transfer	Other
United States	$942,879,767	$450,954,427	$54,953,901	$350,876,257	$44,627,601	$8,859,122	$16,495,316	$4,713,097	$8,922,512	$2,477,534
Alabama	10,418,152	5,247,294	529,607	3,624,543	520,113	54,515	395,930	0	46,150	0
Alaska	1,189,786	263,120	134,928	0	87,775	583,158	120,805	0	0	0
Arizona	13,888,611	8,539,726	505,494	3,445,650	368,136	18,377	993,615	0	17,613	0
Arkansas	9,516,281	4,701,868	384,559	2,767,767	396,989	55,815	1,137,886	198	43,255	27,944
California	155,632,088	47,940,362	10,525,972	84,196,751	10,112,520	93,928	2,681,872	1,360	0	79,323
Colorado	13,197,606	5,128,852	748,284	6,791,929	528,541	0	0	0	0	0
Connecticut	16,345,525	6,649,708	442,290	7,959,492	897,247	0	0	218,789	177,725	274
Delaware	3,588,905	556,490	1,503,083	1,180,975	246,175	0	0	2,156	98,889	1,137
Florida	40,218,365	33,339,556	2,032,331	0	2,383,783	34,148	0	644	2,427,903	0
Georgia	22,419,440	8,807,950	672,897	10,977,693	971,898	0	989,001	0	1	0
Hawaii	7,029,026	4,365,856	269,224	2,095,601	184,840	0	0	18,968	94,537	0
Idaho	4,511,208	2,245,356	383,702	1,660,248	216,641	5,261	0	0	0	0
Illinois	37,978,923	18,629,894	2,793,983	13,256,769	2,877,499	0	63,283	280,940	76,555	0
Indiana	18,051,598	10,894,428	681,547	5,435,292	1,025,498	1,011	12,251	1,571	0	0
Iowa	9,755,430	4,613,085	947,549	3,655,462	432,020	0	1,840	84,649	20,825	0
Kansas	8,173,821	4,301,565	421,080	2,327,652	386,966	52,731	683,827	0	0	0
Kentucky	11,907,759	5,649,708	500,447	4,394,185	458,650	145,122	709,772	46,345	3,530	0
Louisiana	11,104,720	7,014,497	368,318	2,949,939	291,321	410,279	70,366	0	0	0
Maine	4,232,556	2,165,142	274,760	1,534,866	175,239	0	38,643	11,718	32,188	0
Maryland	21,599,795	9,242,760	866,391	9,066,709	1,001,934	0	777,064	227,940	214,581	202,416
Massachusetts	27,518,360	8,818,347	1,112,162	14,724,277	2,196,474	0	6,598	336,633	323,869	0
Michigan	28,628,517	13,696,641	1,787,867	9,485,325	1,195,399	28,935	2,124,075	26	310,149	0
Minnesota	25,594,522	10,607,635	1,477,319	10,956,205	1,227,028	46,593	854,945	129,657	245,089	50,051
Mississippi	7,783,031	4,988,338	480,741	1,834,688	407,913	42,758	28,589	4	0	0
Missouri	12,495,505	5,403,936	590,747	6,149,468	307,443	18	31,643	0	12,191	59
Montana	2,654,444	576,214	329,874	1,177,958	125,003	167,484	274,431	0	0	3,480
Nebraska	5,103,105	2,407,514	182,791	2,228,486	264,440	3,289	123	0	16,462	0
Nevada	8,624,618	6,923,284	666,527	0	0	68,605	300,490	0	90,479	575,233
New Hampshire	2,496,719	959,384	329,719	65,467	573,653	0	405,186	0	163,310	0
New Jersey	32,325,850	13,388,614	1,550,059	13,958,119	2,109,930	0	4,761	748,630	565,736	1
New Mexico	5,776,271	3,069,641	307,671	1,338,768	91,876	886,620	81,694	1	0	0
New York	79,678,037	25,362,583	1,814,065	44,631,769	4,026,353	0	0	1,190,881	1,312,358	1,340,028
North Carolina	26,855,304	11,699,036	2,235,904	12,086,332	757,041	1,892	0	713	74,386	0
North Dakota	3,465,326	1,349,428	213,985	319,507	60,871	1,517,134	4,401	0	0	0
Ohio	30,306,468	19,573,408	2,300,778	8,377,450	8,833	45,256	0	743	0	0
Oklahoma	8,569,402	3,764,895	1,062,358	3,122,602	157,894	441,971	0	177	19,505	0
Oregon	11,914,567	1,598,677	1,067,836	8,379,225	633,046	15,293	20,065	198,363	2,062	0
Pennsylvania	37,853,091	19,629,437	2,240,809	12,063,782	2,344,344	0	43,360	931,908	577,586	21,865
Rhode Island	3,266,663	1,691,782	110,461	1,238,928	129,732	0	2,633	70,601	22,526	0
South Carolina	9,828,825	4,637,349	518,886	4,142,276	375,655	0	37,518	0	117,141	0
South Dakota	1,828,543	1,517,973	269,481	0	30,728	10,176	0	0	185	0
Tennessee	13,893,728	10,010,965	1,635,495	249,977	1,726,223	1,261	0	14,904	236,169	18,734
Texas	53,612,926	46,897,352	3,432,901	0	0	3,282,673	0	0	0	0
Utah	7,832,889	3,530,809	321,715	3,621,199	329,577	29,589	0	0	0	0
Vermont	3,127,523	1,058,569	127,049	743,630	81,395	0	1,056,635	16,670	38,857	4,718
Virginia	22,213,025	6,916,097	856,649	13,052,887	826,961	2,583	31,232	8,202	385,278	133,136
Washington	23,997,592	19,170,768	1,453,628	0	0	35,055	2,097,507	167,972	1,072,649	13
West Virginia	5,092,275	2,672,887	148,951	1,813,866	116,305	321,031	7,248	0	11,987	0
Wisconsin	18,133,496	7,972,959	1,179,054	7,792,543	959,699	10,151	132,022	1,733	70,786	14,549
Wyoming	1,649,550	762,588	161,973	0	0	446,410	274,005	1	0	4,573

Source: U.S. Census Bureau, 2017 Annual Survey of State Government Finances.

Notes:

1. Data users who create their own estimates using these data should cite only the U.S. Census Bureau as the source of the original data. Data in this table are based on information from public records and contain no confidential data. Although the data in this table come from a census of governmental units and are not subject to sampling error, the census results may contain nonsampling error. Additional information on nonsampling error, response rates, and definitions may be found within the survey methodology https://www.census.gov/programs-surveys/state/technical-documentation/methodology.html.

2. Detail may not add to total due to rounding.

TABLE 7.22
State Government Sales and Gross Receipts Tax Revenue: 2017 (In thousands of dollars)

State	Total	General sales or gross receipts	Total	Motor fuels	Insurance premiums	Public utilities	Tobacco products	Alcoholic beverages	Amusements	Pari-mutuels	Other
United States	$450,954,427	$299,777,017	$151,177,410	$45,034,425	$20,891,409	$12,383,308	$18,644,357	$6,619,789	$7,723,624	$118,408	$39,762,090
Alabama	5,247,294	2,654,883	2,592,411	588,992	339,719	688,756	188,783	217,790	0	1,226	567,145
Alaska	263,120	0	263,120	45,944	62,500	4,370	67,555	40,097	10,668	0	31,986
Arizona	8,539,726	6,566,503	1,973,223	856,495	536,820	22,325	310,706	74,126	0	129	172,622
Arkansas	4,701,868	3,384,394	1,317,474	487,517	213,212	0	228,540	55,831	60,380	2,497	269,497
California	47,940,362	35,357,699	12,582,663	4,842,749	2,422,105	728,045	852,894	370,714	0	14,743	3,351,413
Colorado	5,128,852	2,978,382	2,150,470	653,790	256,212	0	199,989	44,866	97,630	625	897,358
Connecticut	6,649,708	4,236,619	2,413,089	484,479	199,497	283,433	381,778	63,155	297,003	5,792	697,952
Delaware	556,490	0	556,490	129,487	100,144	53,798	112,349	20,577	0	63	140,072
Florida	33,339,556	25,346,166	7,993,390	2,727,802	959,339	1,972,968	1,197,666	323,393	207,144	7,800	597,278
Georgia	8,807,950	5,729,916	3,078,034	1,741,092	480,154	0	220,774	193,438	0	0	442,576
Hawaii	4,365,856	3,239,225	1,126,631	87,026	170,118	122,159	124,160	51,167	0	0	572,001
Idaho	2,245,356	1,650,498	594,858	353,548	91,985	15,752	50,883	9,468	0	637	72,585
Illinois	18,629,894	11,363,366	7,266,528	1,348,414	418,582	1,527,274	781,528	294,304	835,445	6,131	2,054,850
Indiana	10,894,428	7,556,326	3,338,102	854,529	235,171	193,613	434,351	49,403	477,977	1,866	1,091,192
Iowa	4,613,085	3,205,997	1,407,088	674,603	113,469	31,386	220,938	22,535	300,172	3,484	40,501
Kansas	4,301,565	3,209,506	1,092,059	458,008	310,420	378	138,504	137,801	313	0	46,635
Kentucky	5,649,708	3,490,639	2,159,069	701,440	153,728	58,298	243,096	146,227	174	6,643	849,463
Louisiana	7,014,497	4,215,378	2,799,119	634,883	813,975	9,110	174,001	77,107	698,306	4,659	387,078
Maine	2,165,142	1,441,867	723,275	252,870	95,943	21,944	144,243	19,266	54,400	1,479	133,130
Maryland	9,242,760	4,609,538	4,633,222	1,078,313	516,533	138,251	386,965	32,151	847,455	1,182	1,632,372
Massachusetts	8,818,347	6,240,822	2,577,525	769,442	397,519	26,727	619,437	85,397	65,744	902	612,357
Michigan	13,696,741	9,223,737	4,473,004	1,210,628	337,254	28,381	1,038,594	159,378	113,048	3,487	1,582,234
Minnesota	10,607,635	5,888,795	4,718,840	912,644	486,403	54	681,018	88,222	63,870	863	2,485,766
Mississippi	4,988,338	3,526,913	1,461,425	443,522	327,778	1,490	145,059	41,835	132,778	0	368,963
Missouri	5,403,936	3,604,570	1,799,366	720,849	432,560	0	100,391	37,863	366,839	0	140,864
Montana	576,214	0	576,214	189,561	108,383	43,505	83,606	32,926	59,819	46	58,368
Nebraska	2,407,514	1,835,037	572,477	354,234	54,350	44,297	56,954	30,911	5,780	154	25,797
Nevada	6,923,284	4,756,243	2,167,041	326,425	359,741	24,676	195,371	45,011	919,642	3	296,172
New Hampshire	959,384	0	959,384	152,086	108,013	53,427	203,102	12,678	538	633	428,907
New Jersey	13,388,614	9,591,881	3,796,733	532,878	579,642	984,612	697,577	137,757	218,650	0	645,617
New Mexico	3,069,641	2,258,767	810,874	242,627	163,453	30,633	89,703	44,916	77,959	842	160,741
New York	25,362,583	14,132,141	11,230,442	1,647,240	1,381,080	811,992	1,265,699	257,690	2,930	16,396	5,847,415
North Carolina	11,699,036	7,656,898	4,042,138	1,922,400	517,095	259	292,138	394,838	7	0	915,401
North Dakota	1,349,428	872,176	477,252	189,718	63,558	46,595	28,977	8,872	3,161	1,728	134,643
Ohio	19,573,408	13,343,149	6,230,259	1,984,392	629,684	1,147,894	1,109,777	107,060	261,950	5,525	983,977
Oklahoma	3,764,895	2,465,383	1,299,512	473,960	304,448	42,267	320,200	118,260	20,807	1,064	18,506
Oregon	1,598,677	0	1,598,677	529,658	68,481	113,022	247,406	18,796	0	1,928	619,386
Pennsylvania	19,629,437	10,509,734	9,119,703	3,143,576	808,250	1,235,942	1,401,259	386,816	1,406,354	10,381	727,125
Rhode Island	1,691,782	996,390	695,392	90,990	120,587	97,711	140,074	20,873	0	1,122	224,035
South Carolina	4,637,349	3,285,007	1,352,342	583,476	228,259	28,278	26,383	177,317	38,814	0	269,815
South Dakota	1,517,973	1,065,361	452,612	189,133	66,496	3,103	61,809	16,933	8,853	319	105,966
Tennessee	10,010,965	7,260,193	2,750,772	915,858	912,324	7,398	256,762	187,125	0	0	471,305
Texas	46,897,352	32,490,144	14,407,208	3,585,179	2,325,941	614,565	1,467,486	1,228,641	29,745	6,321	5,149,330
Utah	3,530,809	2,533,961	996,848	487,731	130,122	24,351	116,158	50,002	0	0	188,484
Vermont	1,058,569	375,870	682,699	81,020	59,895	8,589	76,686	26,028	0	0	430,481
Virginia	6,916,097	3,970,133	2,945,964	997,561	479,192	118,088	171,198	224,426	84	0	955,415
Washington	19,170,768	14,509,841	4,660,927	1,812,646	603,963	504,117	430,022	354,939	0	1,805	953,435
West Virginia	2,672,887	1,334,168	1,338,719	383,874	120,163	107,719	194,647	17,782	38,958	2,611	472,965
Wisconsin	7,972,959	5,223,935	2,749,024	1,044,996	202,387	357,757	644,478	61,203	227	131	437,845
Wyoming	762,588	588,866	173,722	114,140	24,762	3,999	22,683	1,878	0	3,191	3,069

Source: U.S. Census Bureau, 2017 Annual Survey of State Government Finances.
Notes:
1. Data users who create their own estimates using these data should cite only the U.S. Census Bureau as the source of the original data. Data in this table are based on information from public records and contain no confidential data. Although the data in this table come from a census of governmental units and are not subject to sampling error, the census results may contain nonsampling error. Additional information on nonsampling error, response rates, and definitions may be found within the survey methodology *https://www.census.gov/programs-surveys/state/technical-documentation/methodology.html.*
2. Detail may not add to total due to rounding.

TABLE 7.23
State Government License Tax Revenue: 2017 (In thousands of dollars)

State	Total license revenue	Motor vehicle operators	Occupation and business, NEC	Corporation	Motor vehicle
United States	$54,953,901	$2,579,895	$14,846,826	$5,830,604	$26,099,942
Alabama	529,607	33,730	60,763	173,265	219,393
Alaska	134,928	0	49,272	0	38,900
Arizona	505,494	31,074	170,700	41,357	215,991
Arkansas	384,559	25,521	129,289	28,106	158,446
California	10,525,972	222,241	4,999,288	74,365	4,261,054
Colorado	748,284	41,502	54,671	17,638	536,975
Connecticut	442,290	46,805	111,366	29,791	235,105
Delaware	1,503,083	6,771	120,843	1,304,919	57,982
Florida	2,032,331	164,813	180,240	238,350	1,374,140
Georgia	672,897	112,419	81,354	56,999	364,255
Hawaii	269,224	316	48,633	1,723	187,986
Idaho	383,702	11,460	78,716	2,693	187,156
Illinois	2,793,983	114,629	465,109	364,482	1,728,151
Indiana	681,547	229,689	36,207	9,488	284,202
Iowa	947,549	14,444	158,098	45,765	637,933
Kansas	421,080	32,757	95,358	19,732	224,198
Kentucky	500,447	16,827	125,994	110,072	208,389
Louisiana	368,318	13,987	104,207	125,998	83,002
Maine	274,760	11,025	109,737	10,577	109,723
Maryland	866,391	37,616	193,485	109,767	501,360
Massachusetts	1,112,162	96,905	290,524	26,645	438,855
Michigan	1,787,867	58,838	167,908	24,509	1,191,927
Minnesota	1,477,319	46,489	500,603	8,551	790,116
Mississippi	480,741	13,267	76,882	127,445	157,290
Missouri	590,747	15,888	147,569	2,678	288,210
Montana	329,874	9,007	111,462	4,594	143,624
Nebraska	182,791	10,975	36,916	6,260	110,538
Nevada	666,527	30,521	242,142	77,101	213,455
New Hampshire	329,719	8,305	104,531	63,123	102,438
New Jersey	1,550,059	58,005	516,093	234,436	667,056
New Mexico	307,671	5,374	43,208	30,013	196,303
New York	1,814,065	138,696	126,505	26,241	1,403,555
North Carolina	2,235,904	129,086	341,503	826,775	831,878
North Dakota	213,985	4,101	70,152	0	119,853
Ohio	2,300,778	87,659	901,294	263,294	840,327
Oklahoma	1,062,358	27,304	47,252	52,963	753,639
Oregon	1,067,836	38,851	367,539	37,421	539,474
Pennsylvania	2,240,809	70,067	997,941	18,752	928,512
Rhode Island	110,461	4,589	64,367	5,281	26,788
South Carolina	518,886	6,770	146,152	68,181	229,898
South Dakota	269,481	5,410	114,821	5,049	82,947
Tennessee	1,635,495	61,268	343,298	871,205	306,047
Texas	3,432,901	140,863	537,912	140,776	2,237,042
Utah	321,715	16,602	55,350	466	203,980
Vermont	127,049	8,914	25,169	3,894	76,905
Virginia	856,649	41,186	223,721	62,961	481,146
Washington	1,453,628	120,953	357,846	39,776	551,517
West Virginia	148,951	114,005	9,761	632	4,329
Wisconsin	1,179,054	40,053	465,569	22,546	496,295
Wyoming	161,973	2,318	39,506	13,949	71,657

See footnotes at end of table

TABLE 7.23

State Government License Tax Revenue: 2017 (In thousands of dollars) (continued)

State	Hunting and fishing	Public utility	Alcoholic beverages	Amusements	Other licenses
United States	$1,598,448	$1,369,494	$662,076	$542,068	$1,424,548
Alabama	24,024	14,346	4,086	0	0
Alaska	32,900	9,316	1,996	0	2,544
Arizona	35,849	0	8,921	0	1,602
Arkansas	26,912	9,157	4,787	462	1,879
California	104,176	779,990	58,202	22,212	4,444
Colorado	75,573	13,245	7,840	723	117
Connecticut	5,603	738	9,204	231	3,447
Delaware	3,249	0	2,034	312	6,973
Florida	15,166	24,526	7,005	19,181	8,910
Georgia	27,000	0	3,975	0	26,895
Hawaii	567	17,352	0	0	12,647
Idaho	42,886	54,947	1,878	260	3,706
Illinois	40,808	18,025	17,021	15,491	30,267
Indiana	18,902	0	12,582	5,782	84,695
Iowa	28,832	12,292	15,442	31,770	2,973
Kansas	30,961	4,972	2,668	7,950	2,484
Kentucky	28,532	0	6,638	277	3,718
Louisiana	30,684	6,182	0	0	4,258
Maine	16,579	0	6,698	586	9,835
Maryland	18,043	0	1,486	2,780	1,854
Massachusetts	5,482	0	3,634	14,825	235,292
Michigan	63,756	33,180	19,204	0	228,545
Minnesota	63,665	681	2,611	1,195	63,408
Mississippi	2,562	6,549	1,243	26,664	68,839
Missouri	33,083	19,937	5,304	2,178	75,900
Montana	39,240	12	3,484	7,348	11,103
Nebraska	15,861	0	715	534	992
Nevada	13,447	0	0	85,047	4,814
New Hampshire	11,233	21,540	17,263	322	964
New Jersey	13,720	7,360	4,199	47,211	1,979
New Mexico	30,779	1,438	0	556	0
New York	44,172	11,068	62,334	0	1,494
North Carolina	33,799	19,745	26,601	184	26,333
North Dakota	18,370	5	381	1,123	0
Ohio	38,186	38,590	42,978	36,094	52,356
Oklahoma	20,344	4	1,360	158,766	726
Oregon	55,759	14,577	4,706	2,858	6,651
Pennsylvania	74,991	83,718	34,222	12,672	19,934
Rhode Island	1,691	2,454	143	222	4,926
South Carolina	17,907	10,268	13,601	6,918	19,191
South Dakota	29,866	0	1,166	6,573	23,649
Tennessee	37,869	5,087	1,644	240	8,837
Texas	103,550	21,556	68,608	18,492	164,102
Utah	30,622	0	5,900	0	8,795
Vermont	7,394	0	485	26	4,262
Virginia	28,762	0	14,115	104	4,654
Washington	41,287	22,401	150,772	0	169,076
West Virginia	11,691	406	1,038	3,432	3,657
Wisconsin	67,571	83,830	1,902	467	821
Wyoming	34,543	0	0	0	0

Source: U.S. Census Bureau, 2017 Annual Survey of State Government Finances.

Notes:

1. Data users who create their own estimates using these data should cite only the U.S. Census Bureau as the source of the original data. Data in this table are based on information from public records and contain no confidentialdata. Although the data in this table come from a census of governmental units and are not subject to sampling error, the census results may contain nonsampling error. Additional information on nonsampling error, response rates, and definitions may be found within the survey methodology *https://www.census.gov/programs-surveys/state/technical-documentation/methodology.html.*

2. Detail may not add to total due to rounding.

TABLE 7.24
Summary of Financial Aggregates, By State: 2017 (In millions of dollars)

State	Revenues			
	Total	General	Utilities and liquor store	Insurance trust (a)
United States	$2,548,800	$1,970,089	$21,806	$556,905
Alabama	32,082	26,772	325	4,984
Alaska	10,562	8,345	19	2,198
Arizona	43,761	34,731	29	9,001
Arkansas	25,946	21,149	0	4,797
California	398,622	288,584	1,004	109,034
Colorado	34,759	27,870	0	6,889
Connecticut	34,641	27,798	36	6,807
Delaware	9,552	8,340	22	1,189
Florida	107,477	84,010	25	23,442
Georgia	56,852	44,066	10	12,776
Hawaii	16,136	13,452	0	2,685
Idaho	11,761	8,477	164	3,120
Illinois	87,942	67,992	0	19,950
Indiana	43,733	38,492	0	5,242
Iowa	26,798	21,134	306	5,358
Kansas	21,426	17,686	0	3,740
Kentucky	33,779	27,714	0	6,065
Louisiana	36,527	27,796	9	8,723
Maine	10,631	8,579	10	2,041
Maryland	47,557	41,021	149	6,387
Massachusetts	67,489	54,787	926	11,777
Michigan	80,390	63,999	1,082	15,309
Minnesota	53,870	41,354	104	12,412
Mississippi	24,027	18,717	350	4,960
Missouri	39,873	29,530	0	10,343
Montana	9,068	6,618	97	2,353
Nebraska	12,174	10,026	0	2,148
Nevada	22,421	15,342	43	7,036
New Hampshire	9,329	7,012	686	1,630
New Jersey	78,745	62,624	1,123	14,998
New Mexico	21,524	17,215	0	4,309
New York	217,164	164,594	7,717	44,853
North Carolina	67,494	53,199	0	14,294
North Dakota	7,921	6,648	0	1,273
Ohio	100,599	69,776	1,154	29,669
Oklahoma	27,169	21,102	621	5,445
Oregon	43,034	30,351	595	12,087
Pennsylvania	102,873	83,570	2,013	17,290
Rhode Island	9,262	7,506	25	1,731
South Carolina	34,340	26,188	1,729	6,422
South Dakota	6,106	4,400	0	1,706
Tennessee	35,415	29,406	0	6,009
Texas	163,976	128,757	0	35,219
Utah	22,643	18,700	381	3,563
Vermont	6,884	6,026	64	794
Virginia	61,398	47,186	779	13,433
Washington	63,100	47,201	0	15,898
West Virginia	16,383	13,183	96	3,105
Wisconsin	46,801	35,546	0	11,255
Wyoming	6,786	5,519	112	1,155

See footnotes at end of table

TABLE 7.24
Summary of Financial Aggregates, By State: 2017 (In millions of dollars) (continued)

State	Expenditures				Total debt outstanding at end of fiscal year	Total cash and security holdings at end of fiscal year
	Total	General	Utilities and liquor store	Insurance trust		
United States	$2,314,210	$1,984,255	$35,307	$294,649	$1,155,507	$4,684,949
Alabama	32,483	28,680	321	3,482	8,773	46,198
Alaska	11,290	9,779	144	1,368	5,922	82,984
Arizona	39,232	34,888	29	4,315	14,291	64,318
Arkansas	23,058	21,079	0	1,980	4,802	36,964
California	350,012	296,780	2,242	50,990	152,772	743,018
Colorado	34,950	29,332	15	5,603	16,981	74,412
Connecticut	31,485	26,217	515	4,753	38,756	48,293
Delaware	10,030	9,159	146	725	4,562	15,787
Florida	92,697	83,042	340	9,315	28,824	224,704
Georgia	49,540	42,924	72	6,544	13,051	103,632
Hawaii	12,681	11,192	0	1,489	9,656	24,623
Idaho	9,572	8,298	127	1,147	3,369	25,118
Illinois	85,515	70,222	0	15,293	61,821	162,757
Indiana	40,796	37,915	0	2,881	21,843	59,000
Iowa	23,252	20,409	213	2,630	6,150	45,591
Kansas	19,598	17,685	0	1,913	7,538	24,084
Kentucky	36,311	31,724	37	4,550	14,404	43,432
Louisiana	33,814	29,144	8	4,662	18,093	63,672
Maine	10,146	9,096	21	1,028	4,750	19,770
Maryland	45,314	39,693	1,254	4,367	28,027	72,752
Massachusetts	65,748	55,702	3,262	6,784	77,043	105,181
Michigan	72,118	63,187	873	8,058	33,464	105,641
Minnesota	47,309	41,304	472	5,534	16,363	85,721
Mississippi	21,632	18,598	287	2,746	7,470	34,731
Missouri	33,704	28,964	0	4,740	18,420	85,337
Montana	7,748	6,581	99	1,068	2,796	19,404
Nebraska	10,618	9,849	8	761	2,015	21,154
Nevada	16,221	13,571	44	2,606	3,249	43,753
New Hampshire	7,882	6,530	561	791	7,739	15,217
New Jersey	72,339	55,739	3,083	13,517	65,874	116,402
New Mexico	20,779	18,380	1	2,398	7,058	57,085
New York	201,211	165,472	13,207	22,532	139,235	393,074
North Carolina	55,571	49,254	152	6,165	16,310	128,898
North Dakota	7,532	6,791	81	660	2,886	29,164
Ohio	88,232	70,095	814	17,324	33,493	237,905
Oklahoma	25,252	21,342	1,057	2,852	8,457	46,663
Oregon	36,976	30,971	424	5,581	12,657	99,595
Pennsylvania	103,525	88,869	1,922	12,734	47,520	131,075
Rhode Island	8,780	7,319	173	1,289	8,932	16,621
South Carolina	33,880	28,580	1,617	3,684	15,745	45,243
South Dakota	5,265	4,693	0	572	3,528	17,051
Tennessee	33,219	30,563	1	2,654	6,127	64,259
Texas	147,926	129,694	4	18,229	50,963	374,740
Utah	20,596	18,449	275	1,872	7,453	36,228
Vermont	7,007	6,550	61	396	3,503	8,633
Virginia	53,437	47,654	774	5,009	27,826	103,445
Washington	55,159	47,718	251	7,191	33,428	112,997
West Virginia	14,686	13,029	86	1,572	7,547	23,150
Wisconsin	39,873	34,333	81	5,459	23,252	115,732
Wyoming	8,206	7,215	153	838	770	29,742

See footnotes at end of table

TABLE 7.24
Summary of Financial Aggregates, By State: 2017 (In millions of dollars) (continued)

Source: U.S. Census Bureau, 2017 Annual Survey of State Government Finances.

Notes:

1. Data users who create their own estimates using these data should cite only the U.S. Census Bureau as the source of the original data. Data in this table are based on information from public records and contain no confidential data. Although the data in this table come from a census of governmental units and are not subject to sampling error, the census results may contain nonsampling error. Additional information on nonsampling error, response rates, and definitions may be found within the survey methodology *https://www.census.gov/programs-surveys/state/technical-documentation/methodology.html*.

2. Detail may not add to total due to rounding.

Key:

(a) Within insurance trust revenue, net earnings of state-administered pension systems is a calculated statistic (the item code in the data file is X08), and thus can be positive or negative. Net earnings is the sum of earnings on investments plus gains on investments minus losses on investments. The change made in 2002 for asset valuation from book to market value in accordance with Statement 34 of the Governmental Accounting Standards Board is reflected in the calculated statistics.

TABLE 7.25

National Totals of State Government Finances for Selected Years: 2008-2017
(In thousands of dollars)

Item	2017	2016	2015	2014	2013
Revenue total	$2,548,800,396	$2,136,310,326	$2,203,229,979	$2,365,153,505	$2,216,076,231
General revenue	1,970,089,197	1,908,997,159	1,853,494,640	1,742,915,609	1,709,786,388
Taxes	942,879,767	922,855,175	911,697,759	870,437,041	847,077,345
Intergovernmental revenue	656,283,270	637,256,254	604,627,441	550,721,503	551,464,163
From Federal Government	638,676,307	621,597,499	590,480,568	535,736,745	513,478,951
Public Welfare	433,289,034	417,307,189	389,191,243	332,492,959	307,610,126
Education	83,301,859	83,018,756	82,495,588	82,981,871	84,408,057
Highways	44,545,062	44,931,663	41,748,566	43,287,751	41,431,014
Employment security administration	3,838,691	3,745,803	4,200,959	4,307,823	4,647,159
Other	73,701,661	72,594,088	72,844,212	72,666,341	70,770,258
From local government	17,606,963	15,658,755	14,146,873	14,984,758	37,985,212
Charges and miscellaneous revenue	370,926,160	348,885,730	337,169,440	321,757,065	311,244,880
Liquor stores revenue	8,200,371	8,088,520	7,732,037	7,179,065	7,480,124
Utility revenue	13,605,425	13,823,602	14,714,935	14,310,794	13,574,604
Insurance trust revenue (a)	556,905,403	205,401,045	327,288,367	600,748,037	485,235,115
Employee retirement	468,481,713	135,165,729	251,702,166	515,792,141	388,424,920
Unemployment compensation	63,448,784	46,333,152	52,281,509	62,127,840	74,232,787
Worker compensation	16,806,366	16,146,248	15,712,648	15,169,230	15,295,670
Other	8,168,540	7,755,916	7,592,044	7,658,826	7,281,738
Expenditure total	2,314,210,026	2,238,572,373	2,192,506,489	2,048,937,368	2,005,911,667
General expenditure	1,984,254,811	1,919,478,613	1,840,867,694	1,738,757,437	1,683,170,060
Education	687,903,663	677,231,512	637,315,733	613,747,859	599,151,748
Intergovernmental expenditure	372,997,261	360,117,773	345,859,861	330,140,870	324,995,548
State institutions of highereducation	253,899,794	258,132,773	232,811,232	227,411,126	232,678,490
Other education	57,414,058	55,931,789	54,436,132	51,740,480	366,473,258
Public welfare	675,534,238	638,897,229	612,553,893	544,711,480	519,178,293
Intergovernmental expenditure	60,129,920	57,049,413	52,704,375	54,781,687	55,565,254
Cash assistance, other	12,744,183	12,275,724	11,785,784	12,863,087	6,508,047
Other public welfare	637,068,389	600,825,436	576,817,660	507,740,883	484,584,008
Highways	131,698,670	126,682,211	122,472,455	119,270,200	112,174,050
Intergovernmental expenditure	20,276,398	19,675,932	20,420,805	20,992,876	18,158,521
Regular state highway facilities	118,884,747	114,763,236	111,591,023	109,242,610	104,088,029
State toll highways/facilities	12,813,923	11,918,975	10,881,432	10,027,590	8,086,021
Health and hospitals	150,427,700	144,626,375	136,661,426	135,918,963	130,680,311
Hospitals	88,630,889	80,924,025	73,917,087	71,711,969	67,433,480
Health	61,796,811	63,702,350	62,744,339	64,206,994	63,246,831
Natural resources	23,957,486	24,667,924	22,479,104	21,391,208	21,345,804
Corrections	51,233,178	51,871,719	51,725,417	50,218,902	48,407,786
Financial administration	24,882,593	24,959,910	24,050,951	23,304,855	23,136,739
Employment security administration	3,976,814	3,986,729	4,107,385	4,398,411	4,846,304
Police protection	17,242,356	16,480,160	16,108,379	15,668,996	15,106,964
Interest on general debt	43,918,062	44,623,911	44,835,071	45,479,391	46,138,932
Utility expenditure	28,593,481	27,246,160	28,826,069	26,284,373	24,661,698
Insurance trust expenditure	294,648,620	285,400,474	316,628,497	278,190,448	292,447,534
Employee retirement	248,167,257	236,985,953	267,071,846	213,328,101	203,454,835
Unemployment compensation	30,925,241	32,418,562	33,219,048	48,023,325	71,181,425
Other	15,556,122	15,995,959	16,337,603	16,839,022	17,811,274
Total expenditure by character and object	2,314,210,026	2,238,572,373	2,192,506,489	2,048,937,368	2,005,911,667
Direct expenditure	1,764,301,765	1,705,907,083	1,677,460,581	1,550,227,219	1,517,128,804
Current operation	1,243,424,366	1,198,124,432	1,144,425,741	1,063,609,670	1,020,376,950
Capital outlay	130,219,024	128,546,396	123,904,718	116,582,628	114,980,312
Assistance and subsidies	49,616,411	46,710,250	45,175,756	43,933,607	40,795,280
Interest on debt	46,393,344	47,125,531	47,325,869	47,910,866	48,528,728
Insurance benefits and repayments	294,648,620	285,400,474	316,628,497	278,190,448	292,447,534
Intergovernmental expenditure	549,908,261	532,665,290	515,045,908	498,710,149	488,782,863
Cash and security holdings at endof fiscal year	3,075,819,339	4,345,944,854	4,976,604,515	4,293,957,889	3,837,746,513

See footnotes at end of table

TABLE 7.25

National Totals of State Government Finances for Selected Years: 2008–2017

(In thousands of dollars) (continued)

Item	2012	2011	2010	2009	2008
Revenue total	$1,905,807,119	$2,266,850,424	$2,039,926,569	$1,133,446,448	$1,579,327,215
General revenue	1,629,267,996	1,658,377,770	1,567,206,839	1,493,989,614	1,509,888,971
Taxes	798,586,949	762,378,532	705,929,253	713,474,529	779,716,635
Intergovernmental revenue	533,655,081	595,028,792	575,371,668	494,782,446	441,972,830
From Federal Government	514,139,109	575,788,668	555,592,308	475,661,252	419,965,984
Public Welfare	296,964,692	332,256,781	315,808,952	280,281,988	240,299,037
Education	90,264,309	104,711,082	105,511,630	82,447,792	74,307,867
Highways	43,199,512	44,245,077	42,969,373	36,518,798	35,722,224
Employment security administration	4,771,326	5,174,051	4,888,356	4,455,882	3,952,385
Other	74,371,641	84,933,214	82,442,778	68,492,747	62,384,943
From local government	19,515,972	19,240,124	19,779,360	19,121,194	22,006,846
Charges and miscellaneous revenue	297,025,966	300,970,446	285,905,918	285,732,639	288,199,506
Liquor stores revenue	7,114,248	6,739,028	6,494,993	6,376,562	6,128,282
Utility revenue	13,626,445	14,991,180	15,121,578	16,471,341	16,521,947
Insurance trust revenue (a)	255,798,430	586,742,446	451,103,159	(383,391,069)	46,788,015
Employee retirement	152,590,817	476,654,285	353,373,854	(449,271,197)	(11,549,775)
Unemployment compensation	80,109,746	87,410,032	75,037,579	41,976,470	34,359,648
Worker compensation	15,526,364	15,032,589	15,311,140	16,618,791	18,574,527
Other	7,571,503	7,645,540	7,380,586	7,284,867	5,403,615
Expenditure total	1,981,197,761	2,005,947,956	1,943,522,632	1,832,596,801	1,739,303,201
General expenditure	1,648,195,648	1,654,428,735	1,593,693,957	1,560,046,263	1,508,097,761
Education	588,340,483	592,863,150	571,147,157	567,674,062	547,511,580
Intergovernmental expenditure	317,839,562	330,482,270	317,389,500	324,374,036	315,424,647
State institutions of highereducation	230,296,706	222,760,979	214,010,622	207,010,341	197,886,661
Other education	358,043,777	370,102,171	357,136,535	360,663,721	349,624,919
Public welfare	489,162,351	494,828,803	462,430,908	438,744,629	411,662,728
Intergovernmental expenditure	55,913,067	56,678,841	58,858,443	58,741,316	57,730,369
Cash assistance, other	6,401,260	6,582,490	6,164,123	6,290,097	5,730,497
Other public welfare	453,538,093	460,117,393	426,985,892	404,409,141	377,848,378
Highways	115,296,570	109,397,936	111,169,808	107,286,437	107,584,368
Intergovernmental expenditure	17,787,581	17,243,590	18,043,061	16,492,780	16,549,366
Regular state highway facilities	105,496,969	101,913,730	102,742,620	98,889,122	99,047,331
State toll highways/facilities	9,799,601	7,484,206	8,427,188	8,397,315	8,537,037
Health and hospitals	130,621,569	126,020,387	122,754,039	120,594,797	115,742,953
Hospitals	69,265,569	65,985,505	64,509,024	58,041,020	54,733,920
Health	61,356,000	60,034,882	58,245,015	62,553,777	61,009,033
Natural resources	22,051,093	21,989,895	21,514,767	22,605,445	22,538,841
Corrections	48,439,991	49,166,999	48,549,551	50,382,439	49,880,748
Financial administration	21,771,566	22,334,533	22,610,662	22,978,925	23,457,406
Employment security administration	5,065,317	5,214,711	5,108,615	4,520,197	4,037,994
Police protection	14,275,634	14,248,537	13,828,055	13,676,971	13,617,829
Interest on general debt	47,273,956	46,653,282	45,259,591	45,281,069	44,838,072
Utility expenditure	23,724,473	25,548,643	23,864,159	26,295,576	24,578,412
Insurance trust expenditure	303,669,929	320,563,723	320,720,833	241,080,311	201,682,378
Employee retirement	190,622,956	180,712,886	166,956,051	156,708,757	148,157,101
Unemployment compensation	95,317,830	121,384,316	134,908,383	65,974,092	35,470,883
Other	17,729,143	18,466,521	18,856,399	18,397,462	18,054,394
Total expenditure by character and object	1,981,197,761	2,005,947,956	1,943,522,632	1,832,596,801	1,739,303,201
Direct expenditure	1,499,314,531	1,509,115,520	1,457,965,445	1,341,709,410	1,260,772,627
Current operation	986,062,966	984,180,683	934,321,563	901,310,643	866,901,215
Capital outlay	119,668,339	115,570,769	118,010,630	116,989,763	112,695,425
Assistance and subsidies	40,078,288	39,762,087	37,561,512	35,005,215	32,657,676
Interest on debt	49,835,009	49,038,258	47,350,907	47,323,478	46,835,933
Insurance benefits and repayments	303,669,929	320,563,723	320,720,833	241,080,311	201,682,378
Intergovernmental expenditure	481,883,230	496,832,436	485,557,187	490,887,391	478,530,574
Cash and security holdings at endof fiscal year	3,667,671,249	3,672,783,154	3,323,047,498	3,082,511,650	3,758,006,530

See footnotes at end of table

TABLE 7.25
National Totals of State Government Finances for Selected Years: 2008–2017
(In thousands of dollars) (continued)

Source: U.S. Census Bureau, Census of Governments: Finance (years ending in '2' and '7'), and Annual Survey of State Government Finances (remaining years).

Notes:

1. Data users who create their own estimates using these data should cite only the U.S. Census Bureau as the source of the original data. Data in this table are based on information from public records and contain no confidential data. Although the data in this table come from a census of governmental units and are not subject to sampling error, the census results may contain nonsampling error. Additional information on nonsampling error, response rates, and definitions may be found within the survey methodology *https://www.census.gov/programs-surveys/state/technical-documentation/methodology.html*.

2. Detail may not add to total due to rounding.

Key:

(a) Within insurance trust revenue, net earnings of state-administered pension systems is a calculated statistic (the item code in the data file is X08), and thus can be positive or negative. Net earnings is the sum of earnings on investments plus gains on investments minus losses on investments. The change made in 2002 for asset valuation from book to market value in accordance with Statement 34 of the Governmental Accounting Standards Board is reflected in the calculated statistics.

TABLE 7.26
State General Revenue, By Source and By State: 2017 (In thousands of dollars)

State	Total general revenue (a)	Total (b)	Taxes		
				Sales and gross receipts	
			Total (b)	General	Motor fuels
United States	$1,970,089,197	$942,879,767	$450,954,427	$299,777,017	$45,034,425
Alabama	26,772,097	10,418,152	5,247,294	2,654,883	588,992
Alaska	8,345,313	1,189,786	263,120	0	45,944
Arizona	34,730,545	13,888,611	8,539,726	6,566,503	856,495
Arkansas	21,149,036	9,516,281	4,701,868	3,384,394	487,517
California	288,583,711	155,632,088	47,940,362	35,357,699	4,842,749
Colorado	27,870,020	13,197,606	5,128,852	2,978,382	653,790
Connecticut	27,797,919	16,345,525	6,649,708	4,236,619	484,479
Delaware	8,340,428	3,588,905	556,490	0	129,487
Florida	84,010,368	40,218,365	33,339,556	25,346,166	2,727,802
Georgia	44,066,051	22,419,440	8,807,950	5,729,916	1,741,092
Hawaii	13,451,636	7,029,026	4,365,856	3,239,225	87,026
Idaho	8,476,653	4,511,208	2,245,356	1,650,498	353,548
Illinois	67,992,261	37,978,923	18,629,894	11,363,366	1,348,414
Indiana	38,491,515	18,051,598	10,894,428	7,556,326	854,529
Iowa	21,134,343	9,755,430	4,613,085	3,205,997	674,603
Kansas	17,685,552	8,173,821	4,301,565	3,209,506	458,008
Kentucky	27,713,601	11,907,759	5,649,708	3,490,639	701,440
Louisiana	27,795,508	11,104,720	7,014,497	4,215,378	634,883
Maine	8,579,443	4,232,556	2,165,142	1,441,867	252,870
Maryland	41,021,463	21,599,795	9,242,760	4,609,538	1,078,313
Massachusetts	54,786,749	27,518,360	8,818,347	6,240,822	769,442
Michigan	63,998,679	28,628,517	13,696,741	9,223,737	1,210,628
Minnesota	41,353,995	25,594,522	10,607,635	5,888,795	912,644
Mississippi	18,716,811	7,783,031	4,988,338	3,526,913	443,522
Missouri	29,530,314	12,495,505	5,403,936	3,604,570	720,849
Montana	6,618,079	2,654,444	576,214	0	189,561
Nebraska	10,025,526	5,103,105	2,407,514	1,835,037	354,234
Nevada	15,342,157	8,624,618	6,923,284	4,756,243	326,425
New Hampshire	7,012,244	2,496,719	959,384	0	152,086
New Jersey	62,624,120	32,325,850	13,388,614	9,591,881	532,878
New Mexico	17,214,747	5,776,271	3,069,641	2,258,767	242,627
New York	164,594,240	79,678,037	25,362,583	14,132,141	1,647,240
North Carolina	53,199,169	26,855,304	11,699,036	7,656,898	1,922,400
North Dakota	6,648,046	3,465,326	1,349,428	872,176	189,718
Ohio	69,775,759	30,306,468	19,573,408	13,343,149	1,984,392
Oklahoma	21,102,389	8,569,402	3,764,895	2,465,383	473,960
Oregon	30,351,031	11,914,567	1,598,677	0	529,658
Pennsylvania	83,569,986	37,853,091	19,629,437	10,509,734	3,143,576
Rhode Island	7,506,405	3,266,663	1,691,782	996,390	90,990
South Carolina	26,188,283	9,828,825	4,637,349	3,285,007	583,476
South Dakota	4,400,106	1,828,543	1,517,973	1,065,361	189,133
Tennessee	29,405,724	13,893,728	10,010,965	7,260,193	915,858
Texas	128,756,803	53,612,926	46,897,352	32,490,144	3,585,179
Utah	18,699,738	7,832,889	3,530,809	2,533,961	487,731
Vermont	6,025,734	3,127,523	1,058,569	375,870	81,020
Virginia	47,186,364	22,213,025	6,916,097	3,970,133	997,561
Washington	47,201,281	23,997,592	19,170,768	14,509,841	1,812,646
West Virginia	13,182,692	5,092,275	2,672,887	1,334,168	383,874
Wisconsin	35,545,520	18,133,496	7,972,959	5,223,935	1,044,996
Wyoming	5,519,043	1,649,550	762,588	588,866	114,140

See footnotes at end of table

TABLE 7.26
State General Revenue, By Source and By State: 2017 (In thousands of dollars) (continued)

State	Taxes (con't.) Licenses Total (b)	Motor vehicle	Individual income	Corporation net income	Intergovernmental revenue	Charges and miscellaneous general revenue
United States	$54,953,901	$26,099,942	$350,876,257	$44,627,601	$656,283,270	$370,926,160
Alabama	529,607	219,393	3,624,543	520,113	9,949,247	6,404,698
Alaska	134,928	38,900	0	87,775	3,286,785	3,868,742
Arizona	505,494	215,991	3,445,650	368,136	15,247,776	5,594,158
Arkansas	384,559	158,446	2,767,767	396,989	7,916,365	3,716,390
California	10,525,972	4,261,054	84,196,751	10,112,520	93,013,830	39,937,793
Colorado	748,284	536,975	6,791,929	528,541	8,463,350	6,209,064
Connecticut	442,290	235,105	7,959,492	897,247	7,535,049	3,917,345
Delaware	1,503,083	57,982	1,180,975	246,175	2,415,919	2,335,604
Florida	2,032,331	1,374,140	0	2,383,783	27,852,122	15,939,881
Georgia	672,897	364,255	10,977,693	971,898	15,183,797	6,462,814
Hawaii	269,224	187,986	2,095,601	184,840	2,787,412	3,635,198
Idaho	383,702	187,156	1,660,248	216,641	2,622,679	1,342,766
Illinois	2,793,983	1,728,151	13,256,769	2,877,499	19,736,635	10,276,703
Indiana	681,547	284,202	5,435,292	1,025,498	14,712,679	5,727,238
Iowa	947,549	637,933	3,655,462	432,020	6,245,956	5,132,957
Kansas	421,080	224,198	2,327,652	386,966	4,160,844	5,350,887
Kentucky	500,447	208,389	4,394,185	458,650	10,829,538	4,976,304
Louisiana	368,318	83,002	2,949,939	291,321	12,636,842	4,053,946
Maine	274,760	109,723	1,534,866	175,239	3,020,597	1,326,290
Maryland	866,391	501,360	9,066,709	1,001,934	13,203,944	6,217,724
Massachusetts	1,112,162	438,855	14,724,277	2,196,474	16,331,054	10,937,335
Michigan	1,787,867	1,191,927	9,485,325	1,195,399	21,350,680	14,019,482
Minnesota	1,477,319	790,116	10,956,205	1,227,028	10,939,218	4,820,255
Mississippi	480,741	157,290	1,834,688	407,913	8,211,496	2,722,284
Missouri	590,747	288,210	6,149,468	307,443	11,322,122	5,712,687
Montana	329,874	143,624	1,177,958	125,003	3,054,845	908,790
Nebraska	182,791	110,538	2,228,486	264,440	3,179,745	1,742,676
Nevada	666,527	213,455	0	0	5,234,577	1,482,962
New Hampshire	329,719	102,438	65,467	573,653	2,720,430	1,795,095
New Jersey	1,550,059	667,056	13,958,119	2,109,930	18,615,719	11,682,551
New Mexico	307,671	196,303	1,338,768	91,876	7,226,565	4,211,911
New York	1,814,065	1,403,555	44,631,769	4,026,353	60,371,092	24,545,111
North Carolina	2,235,904	831,878	12,086,332	757,041	16,412,180	9,931,685
North Dakota	213,985	119,853	319,507	60,871	1,825,979	1,356,741
Ohio	2,300,778	840,327	8,377,450	8,833	24,305,702	15,163,589
Oklahoma	1,062,358	753,639	3,122,602	157,894	7,280,359	5,252,628
Oregon	1,067,836	539,474	8,379,225	633,046	9,988,321	8,448,143
Pennsylvania	2,240,809	928,512	12,063,782	2,344,344	29,475,131	16,241,764
Rhode Island	110,461	26,788	1,238,928	129,732	2,519,225	1,720,517
South Carolina	518,886	229,898	4,142,276	375,655	9,007,621	7,351,837
South Dakota	269,481	82,947	0	30,728	1,567,365	1,004,198
Tennessee	1,635,495	306,047	249,977	1,726,223	11,161,689	4,350,307
Texas	3,432,901	2,237,042	0	0	44,657,763	30,486,114
Utah	321,715	203,980	3,621,199	329,577	4,524,182	6,342,667
Vermont	127,049	76,905	743,630	81,395	1,991,516	906,695
Virginia	856,649	481,146	13,052,887	826,961	10,699,877	14,273,462
Washington	1,453,628	551,517	0	0	14,228,084	8,975,605
West Virginia	148,951	4,329	1,813,866	116,305	5,109,431	2,980,986
Wisconsin	1,179,054	496,295	7,792,543	959,699	9,583,175	7,828,849
Wyoming	161,973	71,657	0	0	2,566,761	1,302,732

See footnotes at end of table

TABLE 7.26
State General Revenue, By Source and By State: 2017 (In thousands of dollars) (continued)

Source: U.S. Census Bureau, 2017 Annual Survey of State Government Finances.

Notes:

1. Data users who create their own estimates using these data should cite only the U.S. Census Bureau as the source of the original data. Data in this table are based on information from public records and contain no confidential data. Although the data in this table come from a census of governmental units and are not subject to sampling error, the census results may contain nonsampling error. Additional information on nonsampling error, response rates, and definitions may be found within the survey methodology *https://www.census.gov/programs-surveys/state/technical-documentation/methodology.html*.

2. Detail may not add to total due to rounding.

Key:

(a) Total general revenue equals total taxes plus intergovernmental revenue plus charges and miscellaneous revenue.

(b) Total includes other taxes not shown separately in this table.

TABLE 7.27

State Expenditure, By Character and Object and By State: 2017 (In thousands of dollars)

State	Intergovernmental expenditures	Direct expenditures Total	Current operation	Capital outlay Total	Construction	Other
United States	$549,908,261	$1,764,301,765	$1,243,424,366	$130,219,024	$109,264,308	$20,954,716
Alabama	6,931,626	25,551,750	17,672,634	1,982,995	1,496,511	486,484
Alaska	1,829,640	9,460,820	6,557,649	1,175,802	1,027,178	148,624
Arizona	8,094,626	31,137,082	22,164,389	1,623,355	1,289,909	333,446
Arkansas	5,373,102	17,685,395	13,700,779	1,368,534	1,238,101	130,433
California	107,877,299	242,134,866	169,982,770	8,776,504	7,553,363	1,223,141
Colorado	7,604,250	27,345,585	18,708,930	1,802,663	1,485,352	317,311
Connecticut	9,190,177	22,294,905	13,315,998	2,187,546	1,904,830	282,716
Delaware	1,583,343	8,446,648	6,296,600	903,515	802,804	100,711
Florida	21,484,868	71,211,777	51,805,721	7,272,080	6,490,838	781,242
Georgia	12,325,151	37,214,641	25,548,965	3,272,796	2,748,884	523,912
Hawaii	328,020	12,352,661	9,715,969	914,929	254,400	660,529
Idaho	2,408,604	7,163,275	5,257,363	457,908	356,703	101,205
Illinois	19,192,558	66,322,693	40,462,146	5,544,884	5,151,102	393,782
Indiana	9,987,853	30,808,135	23,417,533	2,236,324	1,812,480	423,844
Iowa	5,505,683	17,746,153	12,246,043	2,043,786	1,729,735	314,051
Kansas	4,860,179	14,737,791	10,931,043	1,505,017	1,365,857	139,160
Kentucky	5,730,213	30,581,109	22,105,249	2,175,833	1,950,315	225,518
Louisiana	6,415,070	27,398,780	19,142,386	2,143,229	1,685,647	457,582
Maine	2,428,618	7,716,911	5,952,841	399,970	360,481	39,489
Maryland	9,631,764	35,681,917	25,026,384	3,329,842	2,838,344	491,498
Massachusetts	9,129,315	56,618,784	40,678,206	4,859,445	4,238,598	620,847
Michigan	21,279,004	50,838,693	37,254,365	2,529,535	2,102,618	426,917
Minnesota	13,546,867	33,762,391	24,615,533	1,847,895	1,358,712	489,183
Mississippi	4,527,299	17,104,487	12,566,720	1,077,250	953,326	123,924
Missouri	6,298,000	27,405,997	20,005,078	1,248,841	1,046,869	201,972
Montana	1,128,565	6,619,746	4,932,982	370,538	338,715	31,823
Nebraska	2,457,060	8,161,108	6,315,925	816,316	709,599	106,717
Nevada	4,772,756	11,448,513	7,313,033	896,872	803,784	93,088
New Hampshire	831,584	7,050,802	5,253,784	493,748	406,467	87,281
New Jersey	11,662,914	60,676,580	38,856,499	4,618,974	3,726,886	892,088
New Mexico	4,878,597	15,900,660	12,004,457	829,392	742,027	87,365
New York	62,034,380	139,176,893	99,198,791	9,739,145	7,638,428	2,100,717
North Carolina	13,438,382	42,132,576	29,945,538	4,170,790	3,479,300	691,490
North Dakota	1,978,549	5,553,486	3,824,129	805,462	725,802	79,660
Ohio	18,796,046	69,436,137	44,386,728	4,605,675	4,017,106	588,569
Oklahoma	4,446,655	20,805,385	14,433,262	2,509,741	2,208,509	301,232
Oregon	5,732,009	31,243,566	23,902,443	914,421	639,741	274,680
Pennsylvania	22,256,314	81,268,828	56,147,568	7,955,848	6,315,064	1,640,784
Rhode Island	1,277,277	7,503,003	5,153,303	442,114	388,842	53,272
South Carolina	6,735,297	27,145,005	19,325,690	2,338,303	2,150,982	187,321
South Dakota	863,182	4,401,985	2,998,573	587,919	530,214	57,705
Tennessee	7,882,887	25,335,862	19,566,883	1,530,839	1,300,463	230,376
Texas	30,619,865	117,306,289	83,891,069	11,054,783	9,460,211	1,594,572
Utah	3,767,592	16,828,250	12,151,372	1,739,728	1,282,203	457,525
Vermont	1,800,627	5,206,836	4,189,825	336,308	293,562	42,746
Virginia	11,927,574	41,509,374	30,985,866	3,231,529	2,627,054	604,475
Washington	12,690,612	42,468,778	29,506,720	2,943,348	2,204,363	738,985
West Virginia	2,457,100	12,229,079	9,226,052	906,260	767,857	138,403
Wisconsin	8,826,031	31,047,070	21,277,727	2,991,683	2,589,164	402,519
Wyoming	3,083,277	5,122,708	3,504,853	708,810	675,008	33,802

See footnotes at end of table

TABLE 7.27

State Expenditure, By Character and Object and By State: 2017 (In thousands of dollars) (continued)

State	Direct expenditures (con't)			
	Assistance and subsidies	Interest on debt	Insurance benefits and repayments	Exhibit: Total salaries and wages
United States	$49,616,411	$46,393,344	$294,648,620	$275,040,584
Alabama	2,024,435	389,784	3,481,902	4,922,514
Alaska	158,721	200,904	1,367,744	1,705,821
Arizona	2,499,568	534,895	4,314,875	4,090,546
Arkansas	484,283	152,101	1,979,698	3,021,356
California	5,316,416	7,069,122	50,990,054	35,729,577
Colorado	506,663	724,802	5,602,527	5,509,418
Connecticut	498,407	1,539,729	4,753,225	4,535,378
Delaware	335,566	185,956	725,011	1,424,947
Florida	1,902,844	916,442	9,314,690	9,319,466
Georgia	1,256,042	592,853	6,543,985	6,680,415
Hawaii	118,899	113,918	1,488,946	3,353,048
Idaho	159,842	141,616	1,146,546	1,470,850
Illinois	1,529,313	3,493,429	15,292,921	8,199,405
Indiana	1,382,810	890,680	2,880,788	4,578,985
Iowa	620,231	206,574	2,629,519	3,573,499
Kansas	208,775	180,129	1,912,827	2,951,778
Kentucky	1,104,855	645,169	4,550,003	4,373,700
Louisiana	636,171	814,670	4,662,324	4,049,934
Maine	167,960	168,027	1,028,113	1,069,165
Maryland	1,761,798	1,196,674	4,367,219	5,495,407
Massachusetts	1,022,829	3,273,948	6,784,356	7,084,206
Michigan	1,449,111	1,548,062	8,057,620	9,900,659
Minnesota	1,194,529	570,413	5,534,021	5,679,113
Mississippi	398,739	315,781	2,745,997	2,599,156
Missouri	639,495	772,652	4,739,931	4,027,051
Montana	139,041	108,825	1,068,360	1,149,813
Nebraska	209,343	58,245	761,279	1,579,254
Nevada	494,244	138,456	2,605,908	1,737,065
New Hampshire	193,058	318,874	791,338	1,156,326
New Jersey	1,479,192	2,204,449	13,517,466	10,181,242
New Mexico	277,563	390,966	2,398,282	2,528,205
New York	1,976,503	5,730,855	22,531,599	18,431,443
North Carolina	1,268,690	582,733	6,164,825	8,181,078
North Dakota	183,492	80,220	660,183	1,097,761
Ohio	1,803,259	1,316,926	17,323,549	8,301,530
Oklahoma	597,283	412,789	2,852,310	3,300,913
Oregon	492,836	353,289	5,580,577	4,882,807
Pennsylvania	2,929,398	1,501,902	12,734,112	10,490,084
Rhode Island	169,679	449,333	1,288,574	1,325,482
South Carolina	1,198,414	599,011	3,683,587	4,031,756
South Dakota	134,712	108,560	572,221	788,555
Tennessee	1,327,944	255,740	2,654,456	4,100,046
Texas	2,826,829	1,304,988	18,228,620	18,986,791
Utah	828,978	236,315	1,871,857	3,560,494
Vermont	183,266	101,073	396,364	959,299
Virginia	1,168,612	1,114,484	5,008,883	7,751,506
Washington	1,322,879	1,505,051	7,190,780	8,302,069
West Virginia	318,476	206,560	1,571,731	1,816,508
Wisconsin	665,198	653,454	5,459,008	4,351,591
Wyoming	49,220	21,916	837,909	703,571

See footnotes at end of table

TABLE 7.27

State Expenditure, By Character and Object and By State: 2017 (In thousands of dollars) (continued)

Source: U.S. Census Bureau, 2017 Annual Survey of State Government Finances.

Notes:

1. Data users who create their own estimates using these data should cite only the U.S. Census Bureau as the source of the original data. Data in this table are based on information from public records and contain no confidential data. Although the data in this table come from a census of governmental units and are not subject to sampling error, the census results may contain nonsampling error. Additional information on nonsampling error, response rates, and definitions may be found within the survey methodology *https://www.census.gov/programs-surveys/state/technical-documentation/methodology.html*.

2. Detail may not add to total due to rounding.

TABLE 7.28
State General Expenditure, By Function and By State: 2017 (In thousands of dollars)

State	Total general expenditures (a)	Education	Public welfare	Highways	Hospitals
United States	$1,984,254,811	$687,903,663	$675,534,238	$131,698,670	$88,630,889
Alabama	28,680,131	11,471,899	8,547,055	1,717,721	2,875,275
Alaska	9,778,966	2,524,056	2,724,651	1,164,968	28,963
Arizona	34,887,948	11,825,297	14,685,574	2,237,917	7,459
Arkansas	21,078,799	7,843,665	7,482,277	1,768,654	1,159,401
California	296,779,736	97,240,115	124,082,248	11,016,698	13,426,724
Colorado	29,332,236	12,011,319	8,465,159	2,020,138	1,024,929
Connecticut	26,217,073	11,397,615	4,261,286	1,765,957	1,458,785
Delaware	9,158,993	3,315,487	2,551,364	847,998	47,256
Florida	83,041,726	27,071,608	27,111,988	8,793,319	1,210,889
Georgia	42,923,904	18,962,098	12,475,750	3,000,618	1,360,471
Hawaii	11,191,735	3,409,731	2,984,204	327,349	619,245
Idaho	8,298,096	3,115,269	2,495,878	730,076	52,251
Illinois	70,222,330	18,520,513	23,289,719	6,889,022	1,653,877
Indiana	37,915,156	15,742,709	13,967,124	2,533,747	140,733
Iowa	20,409,385	7,282,938	6,010,233	2,321,260	1,887,069
Kansas	17,685,143	7,402,958	4,101,965	1,248,504	2,681,576
Kentucky	31,724,376	11,263,480	11,508,013	1,998,204	1,894,482
Louisiana	29,143,517	9,299,171	11,226,836	1,516,197	356,728
Maine	9,096,491	3,251,164	3,257,172	786,172	62,151
Maryland	39,692,648	12,663,513	12,929,570	2,569,027	578,878
Massachusetts	55,701,753	13,179,277	22,403,061	3,163,444	718,405
Michigan	63,187,306	25,890,299	18,791,853	3,026,871	4,385,477
Minnesota	41,303,514	16,094,986	14,507,128	2,830,689	325,095
Mississippi	18,598,310	5,540,542	6,657,719	1,181,699	1,524,943
Missouri	28,964,066	9,976,109	8,995,674	1,435,233	2,212,142
Montana	6,581,311	1,917,495	2,169,871	615,291	65,323
Nebraska	9,849,096	3,825,588	2,771,780	860,221	189,098
Nevada	13,571,159	5,150,123	3,892,730	1,029,485	269,434
New Hampshire	6,530,108	1,441,350	2,584,284	539,300	61,520
New Jersey	55,739,193	18,497,910	18,558,280	3,466,851	2,223,073
New Mexico	18,379,804	5,899,371	5,924,514	659,784	1,151,673
New York	165,472,212	45,766,742	67,311,394	5,990,770	5,325,753
North Carolina	49,253,887	21,223,986	13,031,451	4,543,569	2,179,337
North Dakota	6,791,286	2,356,127	1,287,766	989,642	27,100
Ohio	70,094,702	23,187,805	25,824,087	4,175,552	4,351,948
Oklahoma	21,342,494	8,323,116	6,747,383	2,217,476	262,911
Oregon	30,971,476	9,744,277	10,591,348	1,220,805	2,332,476
Pennsylvania	88,868,535	27,912,815	31,373,090	8,236,971	5,132,420
Rhode Island	7,319,018	2,168,254	2,770,134	327,051	66,227
South Carolina	28,580,071	10,274,900	7,811,767	2,069,964	1,871,970
South Dakota	4,692,946	1,519,557	1,154,441	682,357	23,579
Tennessee	30,562,884	10,574,305	12,447,574	1,695,353	409,713
Texas	129,693,879	55,466,634	38,496,187	10,113,473	7,134,155
Utah	18,449,015	8,444,264	3,769,434	1,266,231	1,970,170
Vermont	6,550,330	2,844,714	1,843,184	441,288	23,827
Virginia	47,653,847	16,598,849	11,120,056	4,893,904	4,954,417
Washington	47,717,753	19,541,468	12,291,087	2,985,394	4,401,811
West Virginia	13,028,758	4,285,354	4,732,909	1,166,332	149,541
Wisconsin	34,332,896	12,363,945	10,691,615	3,871,696	2,356,650
Wyoming	7,214,813	2,278,896	824,371	748,428	3,559

See footnotes at end of table

TABLE 7.28

State General Expenditure, By Function and By State: 2017 (In thousands of dollars) (continued)

State	Natural resources	Health	Corrections	Financial administration	Employment security administration	Police
United States	$23,957,486	$61,796,811	$51,233,178	$24,882,593	$3,976,814	$17,242,356
Alabama	295,316	551,627	553,944	387,248	98,753	171,607
Alaska	405,104	229,041	316,353	207,274	22,119	142,360
Arizona	306,838	583,978	1,080,923	298,242	96,683	280,662
Arkansas	283,602	245,899	420,114	432,569	93,024	125,399
California	5,747,925	7,503,590	8,528,075	3,381,701	317,598	1,907,378
Colorado	416,303	573,255	1,035,100	414,864	53,691	235,845
Connecticut	237,327	1,041,145	622,024	369,570	81,222	251,026
Delaware	113,363	410,368	324,144	225,959	17,327	148,671
Florida	1,485,972	3,957,991	2,385,256	802,151	285,476	577,197
Georgia	539,800	1,487,054	1,326,803	455,677	35,082	516,693
Hawaii	161,860	550,157	228,646	199,742	6,311	44,877
Idaho	242,630	151,848	280,588	285,040	27,005	65,099
Illinois	238,887	1,989,331	1,358,464	705,065	63,562	439,719
Indiana	380,565	571,486	708,261	330,509	35,886	267,728
Iowa	294,582	275,215	288,880	232,735	45,896	104,622
Kansas	224,912	397,821	350,931	167,693	31,195	111,385
Kentucky	396,106	500,808	666,606	395,702	133,736	274,012
Louisiana	796,006	421,737	667,656	408,965	128,135	358,733
Maine	138,331	147,214	162,568	209,668	67,344	90,368
Maryland	563,293	2,190,864	1,479,811	629,017	51,782	643,786
Massachusetts	257,190	1,484,458	954,978	613,330	197,887	922,066
Michigan	369,721	1,640,230	1,894,849	585,807	176,102	501,930
Minnesota	682,934	515,239	635,229	435,942	79,347	486,835
Mississippi	302,124	414,397	330,982	274,787	72,622	139,829
Missouri	370,717	1,988,453	827,462	211,940	9,719	235,665
Montana	284,876	206,634	212,280	175,247	46,972	39,216
Nebraska	224,856	306,760	349,865	142,111	41,897	90,473
Nevada	140,690	296,213	312,785	216,463	61,609	95,406
New Hampshire	57,885	97,799	145,827	97,210	33,732	71,944
New Jersey	474,158	1,454,264	1,380,091	693,653	158,132	715,359
New Mexico	255,992	412,096	487,467	197,890	10,539	148,580
New York	543,360	8,999,160	3,403,266	2,209,525	212,106	1,017,705
North Carolina	529,106	1,265,088	1,343,093	713,796	62,006	738,513
North Dakota	142,237	375,498	105,538	68,871	9,985	31,401
Ohio	442,609	2,459,852	1,815,411	1,302,616	167,771	390,158
Oklahoma	160,437	1,037,585	575,015	382,351	46,053	230,799
Oregon	422,795	902,075	897,609	692,471	56,778	201,595
Pennsylvania	733,442	3,428,716	2,183,012	1,346,459	103,244	1,093,448
Rhode Island	49,743	186,540	199,314	167,521	21,246	87,077
South Carolina	281,506	1,264,559	520,001	337,949	69,357	205,857
South Dakota	187,574	165,103	120,790	90,756	28,468	47,261
Tennessee	352,507	738,464	972,601	323,977	73,171	277,908
Texas	836,608	2,943,615	4,219,031	1,129,427	93,101	1,183,713
Utah	213,338	335,385	372,616	425,790	27,484	150,315
Vermont	111,555	364,778	154,553	84,255	2,144	110,600
Virginia	315,847	1,547,918	1,538,611	570,764	76,266	670,451
Washington	902,741	1,907,677	998,831	362,757	192,281	429,369
West Virginia	272,671	298,684	301,041	198,135	18,941	81,031
Wisconsin	526,931	562,177	1,069,838	165,080	97,804	51,250
Wyoming	242,614	416,965	126,045	126,322	38,223	39,435

See footnotes at end of table

TABLE 7.28
State General Expenditure, By Function and By State: 2017 (In thousands of dollars) (continued)

Source: U.S. Census Bureau, 2017 Annual Survey of State Government
Finances.
Notes:
1. Data users who create their own estimates using these data should
cite only the U.S. Census Bureau as the source of the original data.
Data in this table are based on information from public records
and contain no confidential data. Although the data in this table
come from a census of governmental units and are not subject to
sampling error, the census results may contain nonsampling error.

Additional information on nonsampling error, response rates, and
definitions may be found within the survey methodology *https://
www.census.gov/programs-surveys/state/technical-documentation/
methodology.html.*
2. Detail may not add to total due to rounding.
Key:
(a) Total includes other expenditures not shown separately in this
table.

TABLE 7.29
State Debt Outstanding at End of Fiscal Year, by State: 2017 (In thousands of dollars)

State	Total	Long-term total	Short-term total	Net long-term total (a)
United States	$1,155,507,028	$1,147,841,005	$7,666,023	$700,498,423
Alabama	8,772,871	8,715,651	57,220	7,384,295
Alaska	5,921,713	5,839,187	82,526	2,116,653
Arizona	14,291,349	14,217,606	73,743	8,576,710
Arkansas	4,801,939	4,801,939	0	2,873,834
California	152,772,292	152,772,292	0	120,423,899
Colorado	16,980,689	16,962,789	17,900	6,076,738
Connecticut	38,756,156	38,756,156	0	24,695,942
Delaware	4,561,576	4,561,576	0	3,003,885
Florida	28,823,847	28,776,077	47,770	22,892,889
Georgia	13,050,862	12,935,750	115,112	9,772,905
Hawaii	9,656,278	9,656,278	0	8,773,901
Idaho	3,369,178	3,363,457	5,721	564,830
Illinois	61,821,319	61,815,949	5,370	32,892,650
Indiana	21,842,716	21,741,627	101,089	3,995,347
Iowa	6,149,694	6,149,694	0	1,521,653
Kansas	7,538,475	7,538,475	0	4,526,329
Kentucky	14,403,514	14,375,683	27,831	8,766,749
Louisiana	18,092,508	18,087,176	5,332	10,437,250
Maine	4,750,384	4,750,384	0	1,216,507
Maryland	28,027,363	27,936,271	91,092	15,590,114
Massachusetts	77,043,165	76,993,751	49,414	44,375,948
Michigan	33,463,604	32,985,336	478,268	16,724,083
Minnesota	16,363,418	16,363,418	0	9,959,077
Mississippi	7,470,178	7,449,912	20,266	5,707,746
Missouri	18,419,751	18,368,633	51,118	4,745,594
Montana	2,795,614	2,795,026	588	135,064
Nebraska	2,014,523	2,013,585	938	567,353
Nevada	3,248,814	3,248,814	0	2,322,784
New Hampshire	7,739,447	7,739,447	0	2,998,045
New Jersey	65,874,095	65,577,943	296,152	46,922,339
New Mexico	7,057,656	7,029,849	27,807	4,118,509
New York	139,234,923	138,307,885	927,038	95,692,154
North Carolina	16,310,177	16,182,242	127,935	6,958,175
North Dakota	2,885,664	2,885,254	410	1,422,630
Ohio	33,493,235	32,770,487	722,748	13,512,426
Oklahoma	8,457,322	8,442,414	14,908	5,564,035
Oregon	12,656,643	12,653,643	3,000	8,187,092
Pennsylvania	47,519,575	47,199,314	320,261	27,543,606
Rhode Island	8,932,377	8,868,682	63,695	2,320,788
South Carolina	15,744,638	15,344,739	399,899	12,290,512
South Dakota	3,527,703	3,522,741	4,962	984,449
Tennessee	6,127,422	5,730,566	396,856	1,489,596
Texas	50,963,262	48,298,126	2,665,136	35,865,364
Utah	7,453,346	7,342,238	111,108	4,332,588
Vermont	3,502,960	3,278,290	224,670	1,071,217
Virginia	27,825,929	27,697,789	128,140	14,667,107
Washington	33,427,752	33,427,752	0	22,407,399
West Virginia	7,547,010	7,547,010	0	3,096,132
Wisconsin	23,252,381	23,252,381	0	8,305,756
Wyoming	769,721	769,721	0	107,775

Source: U.S. Census Bureau, 2017 Annual Survey of State Government Finances.

Notes:

1. Data users who create their own estimates using these data should cite only the U.S. Census Bureau as the source of the original data. Data in this table are based on information from public records and contain no confidential data. Although the data in this table come from a census of governmental units and are not subject to sampling error, the census results may contain nonsampling error. Additional information on nonsampling error, response rates, and definitions may be found within the survey methodology https://www.census.gov/programs-surveys/state/technical-documentation/methodology.html.

2. Detail may not add to total due to rounding.

Key:

(a) Long-term debt outstanding minus long-term debt offsets.

TABLE 7.30
Membership of State Public-Employee Pension Systems By State: Fiscal Year 2017

State	Membership Total	Membership Active members	Membership Inactive members	Total beneficiaries receiving periodic benefit payments
United States	18,573,702	12,922,487	5,651,215	9,181,489
Alabama (a)	252,268	224,386	27,882	140,415
Alaska	33,732	23,516	10,216	48,209
Arizona	481,101	242,987	238,114	166,974
Arkansas	170,546	136,030	34,516	90,033
California	2,188,689	1,474,731	713,958	1,102,849
Colorado	467,372	221,800	245,572	123,197
Connecticut	128,927	111,138	17,789	92,503
Delaware	48,064	43,774	4,290	28,629
Florida	627,178	520,014	107,164	405,213
Georgia	585,176	366,831	218,345	220,988
Hawaii	75,152	65,911	9,241	46,920
Idaho	83,238	70,568	12,670	45,245
Illinois	692,099	461,324	230,775	381,015
Indiana	323,305	220,970	102,335	151,185
Iowa	242,996	174,616	68,380	122,519
Kansas	212,922	159,422	53,500	104,473
Kentucky	387,186	209,212	177,974	147,350
Louisiana	294,722	189,244	105,478	169,200
Maine	61,677	51,298	10,379	44,310
Maryland	249,433	195,300	54,133	158,210
Massachusetts	296,110	214,880	81,230	151,144
Michigan (a)	280,091	249,820	30,271	317,385
Minnesota	403,347	309,171	94,176	234,646
Mississippi	219,999	153,032	66,967	104,945
Missouri	333,851	247,203	86,648	181,428
Montana	75,773	54,443	21,330	41,553
Nebraska	94,111	62,390	31,721	26,460
Nevada	122,657	105,945	16,712	64,281
New Hampshire	59,440	48,127	11,313	32,855
New Jersey	479,788	461,586	18,202	327,598
New Mexico	179,412	116,334	63,078	104,859
New York	917,123	784,982	132,141	617,075
North Carolina	701,951	488,365	213,586	293,904
North Dakota	42,545	34,276	8,269	19,784
Ohio	1,384,117	692,520	691,597	470,078
Oklahoma	178,524	145,308	33,216	113,348
Oregon	315,551	269,842	45,709	142,428
Pennsylvania	539,037	369,549	169,488	357,526
Rhode Island	52,302	39,107	13,195	28,196
South Carolina	402,677	217,832	184,845	155,551
South Dakota	58,910	40,452	18,458	27,341
Tennessee	367,606	214,500	153,106	153,918
Texas (a)	1,782,603	1,251,782	530,821	636,285
Utah	153,238	98,435	54,803	62,698
Vermont	33,152	25,950	7,202	18,690
Virginia	488,430	341,200	147,230	199,388
Washington	395,948	328,646	67,302	208,064
West Virginia	80,869	73,873	6,996	73,940
Wisconsin	424,476	257,285	167,191	197,647
Wyoming	104,281	62,580	41,701	29,037

See footnotes at end of table

TABLE 7.30

Membership of State Public-Employee Pension Systems By State: Fiscal Year 2017 (continued)

Source: U.S. Census Bureau, 2017 Annual Survey of Public Pensions: State-Administered Defined Benefit Data.

Notes:

1. Effective with the 2012 survey cycle, the Annual Survey of Public Pensions: State-Administered Defined Benefit Data revised the survey form to implement changes in asset classification. These changes apply to the categories designated as corporate stocks, corporate bonds, federal government securities, state and local government securities, and other securities. Federally-sponsored agency securities are classified under federal government securities instead of corporate bonds. Private equity, venture capital, and leverage buyouts are classified under corporate stocks instead of other securities. Due to these changes in asset classification, there are shifts in the distribution of assets from corporate bonds to federal government securities and from other securities to corporate stocks. However, since investment decisions guide the distribution of assets, we cannot calculate the exact impact that the changes in classification had on the asset distribution for 2012. As such, for the above mentioned asset categories, any data comparisons between data from 2012 to the present, and data prior to 2012 should be exercised with caution.

2. Data users who create their own estimates using these data should cite the U.S. Census Bureau as the source of the original data only. The data in this table are based on information from public records and contain no confidential data. The data in this table come from a sample of governmental units and are thus subject to both sampling and nonsampling error. Additional information on nonsampling error, response rates, and definitions may be found within the survey methodology *https://www2.census.gov/programs-surveys/aspp/ technical-documentation/methodology/2017/2017surveymethod ology.pdf?#.*

3. Detail may not add to total due to rounding.

4. Pension obligations and covered payroll for defined benefit pension systems are only collected at the state level.

Key:

(a) There are exceptions to the fiscal year rule for the state pension systems in Alabama, Michigan, and Texas. For systems in these states, the fiscal year moves beyond the June 30 cutoff. The data for the survey year 2017 covers the fiscal year ending August 31, 2017 for Texas and September 30, 2017 for Alabama and Michigan. These exceptions are made to better align the data with the Survey of State Government Finances.

Table 7.30 | Membership of State Public-Employee Pension Systems

Total Membership of State Public-Employee Pension Systems by State
(March 2017)

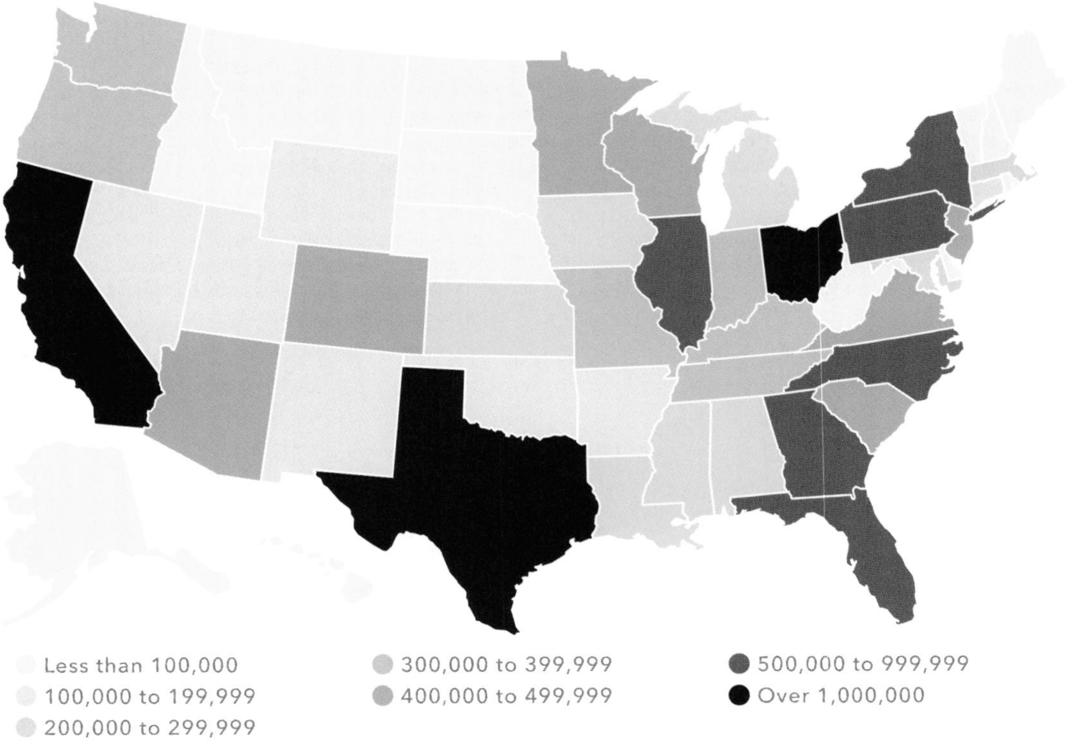

Less than 100,000
100,000 to 199,999
200,000 to 299,999
300,000 to 399,999
400,000 to 499,999
500,000 to 999,999
Over 1,000,000

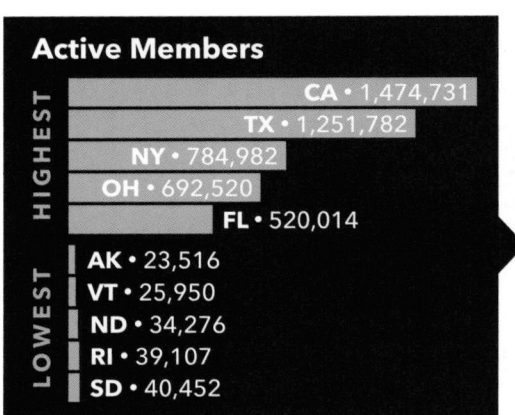

Active Members

HIGHEST
- CA • 1,474,731
- TX • 1,251,782
- NY • 784,982
- OH • 692,520
- FL • 520,014

LOWEST
- AK • 23,516
- VT • 25,950
- ND • 34,276
- RI • 39,107
- SD • 40,452

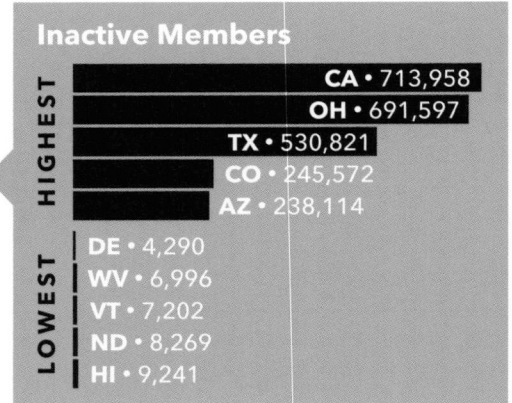

Inactive Members

HIGHEST
- CA • 713,958
- OH • 691,597
- TX • 530,821
- CO • 245,572
- AZ • 238,114

LOWEST
- DE • 4,290
- WV • 6,996
- VT • 7,202
- ND • 8,269
- HI • 9,241

TABLE 7.31
Finances of State-Administered Public-Employee Pension Systems, by State: Fiscal Year 2017*
(In thousands of dollars)

State and level of government	Total receipts	Employee contributions	Government contributions Total	From state government	From local government	Earnings on investments (b)	Total payments	Benefits	Withdrawals	Other payments
United States	$532,683,507	$47,208,653	$111,033,904	$64,204,077	$46,829,827	$374,440,950	$260,999,080	$242,003,470	$6,163,779	$12,831,832
Alabama (a)	5,699,288	723,486	1,233,930	998,048	235,882	3,741,872	3,346,950	3,202,420	103,131	41,398
Alaska	2,412,370	130,251	530,909	380,304	150,605	1,751,210	1,257,129	1,225,884	12,868	18,376
Arizona	8,823,177	1,326,179	1,900,340	424,991	1,475,349	5,596,658	4,302,145	3,766,288	287,825	248,032
Arkansas	4,685,094	250,472	841,440	331,873	509,567	3,593,182	1,941,037	1,795,814	29,471	115,751
California	98,863,050	8,576,441	21,809,970	10,869,210	10,940,761	68,476,639	40,677,487	38,133,872	537,398	2,006,218
Colorado	5,841,801	816,151	1,586,119	616,131	969,989	3,439,531	4,939,953	4,550,979	151,529	237,444
Connecticut	8,117,984	484,093	2,924,329	2,575,091	349,238	4,709,562	4,071,353	3,918,730	85,603	67,020
Delaware	1,297,795	73,835	246,279	233,504	12,775	977,681	677,310	641,830	5,278	30,202
Florida	21,967,391	710,717	2,438,659	442,631	1,996,028	18,818,015	9,460,196	8,856,514	13,482	590,200
Georgia	13,877,211	831,121	2,471,282	2,340,697	130,585	10,574,808	6,287,715	6,138,091	32,581	117,042
Hawaii	3,082,069	243,906	784,369	589,058	195,311	2,053,794	1,375,822	1,306,545	16,340	52,936
Idaho	2,635,141	240,029	368,010	100,665	267,345	2,027,102	948,444	857,368	35,329	55,747
Illinois	24,312,793	1,855,824	8,675,557	7,588,318	1,087,239	13,781,412	13,852,336	12,886,386	440,111	525,839
Indiana	4,799,948	347,818	1,868,761	1,050,547	818,214	2,583,369	2,820,437	2,507,293	69,015	244,129
Iowa	4,984,957	511,952	804,118	139,403	664,715	3,668,887	2,304,789	2,146,583	53,342	104,864
Kansas	3,864,331	452,031	1,277,264	614,592	662,672	2,135,036	1,808,286	1,652,227	70,481	85,578
Kentucky	6,581,659	651,149	2,077,896	1,558,873	519,023	3,852,614	4,218,204	3,980,989	46,841	190,374
Louisiana	9,320,679	845,818	2,541,813	1,057,086	1,484,728	5,933,048	4,671,565	4,229,979	138,268	303,318
Maine	2,228,705	186,409	380,093	328,262	51,831	1,662,203	1,037,934	909,692	23,696	104,546
Maryland	7,707,854	785,048	2,074,099	2,051,194	22,905	4,848,707	3,710,526	3,613,091	64,316	33,120
Massachusetts	11,384,625	1,700,849	2,446,047	1,602,929	843,118	7,237,729	5,586,894	5,092,549	136,546	357,799
Michigan (a)	13,885,122	1,085,736	3,788,390	3,177,916	610,474	9,010,996	7,305,621	7,197,582	37,664	70,345
Minnesota	11,512,187	1,132,939	1,350,645	269,918	1,080,726	9,028,603	4,769,041	4,600,513	65,980	102,548
Mississippi	5,227,412	572,456	1,052,147	412,672	639,475	3,602,809	2,784,311	2,544,382	113,868	126,061
Missouri	9,974,294	948,239	1,957,387	681,897	1,275,490	7,068,668	5,136,181	4,256,161	89,092	790,928
Montana	2,210,238	313,080	275,187	183,333	91,854	1,621,971	885,954	798,985	21,224	65,745
Nebraska	2,138,786	232,549	296,516	86,586	209,930	1,609,721	740,734	602,384	85,585	52,766
Nevada	5,979,117	902,020	907,635	184,400	723,235	4,169,462	2,350,569	2,264,227	30,754	55,588
New Hampshire	1,649,614	209,327	431,796	96,296	335,500	1,008,491	770,629	712,592	23,400	34,637
New Jersey	14,694,807	2,103,381	3,708,854	3,708,854	0	8,882,572	10,834,266	10,560,130	211,593	62,543
New Mexico	4,343,688	561,210	749,574	325,740	423,834	3,032,904	2,386,335	2,125,947	77,812	182,576
New York	41,216,918	458,226	6,649,907	3,547,147	3,102,760	34,108,785	19,880,518	18,417,304	362,822	1,100,392
North Carolina	13,530,180	1,329,461	1,949,778	1,469,978	479,800	10,250,941	6,490,725	5,781,700	170,374	538,651
North Dakota	942,272	126,470	202,886	81,651	121,235	612,916	379,862	354,218	14,808	10,835
Ohio	26,573,095	3,419,867	4,682,866	2,145,042	2,537,824	18,470,362	15,878,740	14,959,768	584,369	334,604
Oklahoma	5,546,546	473,970	1,267,873	693,284	574,588	3,804,703	2,480,172	2,293,726	62,248	124,199
Oregon	10,528,270	618,282	1,022,201	148,272	873,929	8,887,787	5,477,106	4,742,418	15,962	718,727
Pennsylvania	14,370,384	1,465,761	5,506,518	1,644,987	3,861,530	7,398,105	11,179,395	9,761,425	692,522	725,448
Rhode Island	1,453,795	113,414	454,000	304,419	149,581	886,381	971,566	936,037	7,501	28,029
South Carolina	6,234,122	959,028	1,380,939	604,894	776,045	3,894,155	3,755,426	3,300,921	125,664	328,842
South Dakota	1,708,452	122,145	121,908	44,670	77,238	1,464,399	578,752	517,012	24,078	37,662
Tennessee	6,694,361	317,509	1,010,855	1,008,397	2,458	5,365,997	2,469,057	2,410,601	39,944	18,512
Texas (a)	34,111,930	4,802,950	5,298,724	2,699,885	2,598,839	24,010,256	15,485,512	14,346,458	674,148	464,906
Utah	3,941,440	39,287	1,198,104	909,567	288,537	2,704,049	1,515,790	1,497,989	6,734	11,067
Vermont	733,286	98,105	159,650	143,168	16,482	475,531	343,664	317,543	8,896	17,225
Virginia	13,360,353	916,718	2,398,186	669,167	1,729,019	10,045,449	5,091,349	4,518,958	121,362	451,029
Washington	13,749,066	871,986	2,163,920	2,163,920	0	10,713,160	4,483,337	4,029,986	58,130	395,221
West Virginia	3,169,131	196,780	634,696	432,740	201,956	2,337,655	1,274,347	1,242,479	22,030	9,839
Wisconsin	9,810,110	905,694	955,407	300,548	654,860	7,949,009	5,426,630	4,951,650	39,273	435,707
Wyoming	906,609	168,485	176,068	171,318	4,749	562,056	576,981	547,251	22,461	7,269

See footnotes at end of table

TABLE 7.31
Finances of State-Administered Public-Employee Pension Systems, by State: Fiscal Year 2017*
(In thousands of dollars) (continued)

Source: 2017 Annual Survey of Public Pensions: State- and Locally-Administered Defined Benefit Data. Data users who create their own estimates using data from this report should cite the U.S. Census Bureau as the source of the original data only. The data in this table are based on information from public records and contain no confidential data. Although the data in this table come from a census of pension systems and are not subject to sampling error, the census results do contain nonsampling error. Additional information on nonsampling error, and response rates may be found at *https://www.census.gov/programs-surveys/aspp/technical-documentation/methodology/how-the-data-are-collected.html.*

*Effective with the 2012 survey cycle, the Annual Survey of Public Pensions: State-Administered Defined Benefit Data revised the survey form to implement changes in asset classification. These changes apply to the categories designated as corporate stocks, corporate bonds, federal government securities, state and local government securities, and other securities. Federally-sponsored agency securities are classified under federal government securities instead of corporate bonds. Private equity, venture capital, and leverage buyouts are classified under corporate stocks instead of other securities. Due to these changes in asset classification, there are shifts in the distribution of assets from corporate bonds to federal government securities and from other securities to corporate stocks. However, since investment decisions guide the distribution of assets, we cannot calculate the exact impact that the changes in classification had on the asset distribution for 2012. As such, for the above mentioned asset categories, any data comparisons between data from 2012 to the present, and data prior to 2012 should be exercised with caution.

Notes:
1. Pension obligations and Covered payroll for defined benefit pension systems are only collected at the state level.
2. Data users who create their own estimates using these data should cite the U.S. Census Bureau as the source of the original data only. The data in this table are based on information from public records and contain no confidential data. Although the data in this table come from a census of pension systems and are not subject to sampling error, the census results do contain nonsampling error. Additional information on nonsampling error, response rates, and definitions may be found within the survey methodology *https://www2.census.gov/programs-surveys/aspp/technical-documentation/methodology/2017/2017surveymethodology.pdf?#.*
3. Detail may not add to total due to rounding.
Key:
(a) There are exceptions to the fiscal year rule for the state pension systems in Alabama, Michigan, and Texas. For systems in these states, the fiscal year moves beyond the June 30 cutoff. The data for the survey year 2017 covers the fiscal year ending August 31, 2017 for Texas and September 30, 2017 for Alabama and Michigan. These exceptions are made to better align the data with the Survey of State Government Finances.
(b) The total of "net earnings" is a calculated statistic and thus can be positive or negative. Net earnings is the sum of earnings on investments plus gains on investments minus losses on investments. The change made in 2002 for asset valuation from book to market value in accordance with Statement 34 of the Governmental Accounting Standards Board is reflected in the calculated statistics.

TABLE 7.32
National Summary of State-Administered Defined Benefit Pension System Finances:
Fiscal Years, 2015–2017(a)

	Amount (in thousands of dollars)			Percentage distribution		
	2017	2016	2015	2017	2016	2015
Total contributions	$158,242,557	$149,657,642	$141,061,794	100.0	100.0	100.0
Employee contributions	47,208,653	43,150,277	40,455,460	29.8	28.8	28.7
Government contributions	111,033,904	106,507,365	100,606,333	70.2	71.2	71.3
State government contributions	64,204,077	59,594,514	57,386,550	40.6	39.8	40.7
Local government contributions	46,829,827	46,912,851	43,219,783	29.6	31.3	30.6
Earnings on investments (a)	374,440,950	45,411,198	125,910,359	100.0	100.0	100.0
Total Payments	260,999,080	248,284,997	236,762,496	100.0	100.0	100.0
Benefits	242,003,470	232,052,855	220,788,220	92.7	93.5	93.3
Withdrawals	6,163,779	5,080,298	5,095,571	2.4	2.0	2.2
Other payments	12,831,832	11,151,844	10,878,705	4.9	4.5	4.6
Total cash and investment holdings	3,298,801,223	3,051,596,871	3,112,089,930	100.0	100.0	100.0
Cash and short-term investments	121,772,242	114,828,590	103,936,353	3.7	3.8	3.3
Total securities	2,677,651,746	2,522,973,332	2,619,377,943	81.2	82.7	84.2
Government securities	293,651,491	234,301,397	230,654,990	8.9	7.7	7.4
Federal government	292,481,103	232,524,339	229,052,363	8.9	7.6	7.4
United States Treasury	216,799,752	149,766,700	151,999,814	6.6	4.9	4.9
Federal agency	75,681,351	82,757,639	77,052,550	2.3	2.7	2.5
State and local government	1,170,388	1,777,058	1,602,626	0.0	0.1	0.1
Nongovernmental securities	2,384,000,255	2,288,671,935	2,388,722,953	72.3	75.0	76.8
Corporate bonds	305,102,662	383,681,199	378,652,806	9.2	12.6	12.2
Corporate stocks	1,060,962,248	1,107,538,222	1,191,762,863	32.2	36.3	38.3
Mortgages	7,815,572	8,204,825	8,268,184	0.2	0.3	0.3
Funds held in trust	94,922,159	32,390,689	39,290,314	2.9	1.1	1.3
Foreign and international	708,417,090	570,655,405	605,603,064	21.5	18.7	19.5
Other nongovernmental securities	206,780,524	186,201,595	165,145,721	6.3	6.1	5.3
Other investments	499,377,235	413,794,949	388,775,634	15.1	13.6	12.5
Real property	75,952,810	118,527,861	137,170,005	2.3	3.9	4.4
Miscellaneous investments	423,424,425	295,267,088	251,605,629	12.8	9.7	8.1

Source: The 2015–2017 Annual Surveys of Public Pensions: State- and Locally-Defined Benefits Data. Data users who create their own estimates using data from this report should cite the U.S. Census Bureau as the source of the original data only. The data in this table are based on information from public records and contain no confidential data. Although the data in this table come from a census of pension systems and are not subject to sampling error, the census results do contain nonsampling error. Additional information on nonsampling error, and response rates may be found at *https://www.census.gov/programs-surveys/aspp/technical-documentation/methodology/how-the-data-are-collected.html.*

Notes:
1. Detail may not add to total due to rounding;
2. Total Receipts are the sum of earnings on investments and total contributions.

Key:
(a) Effective with the 2012 survey cycle, the Annual Survey of Public Pensions: State-Administered Defined Benefit Data revised the survey form to implement changes in asset classification. These changes apply to the categories designated as corporate stocks, corporate bonds, federal government securities, state and local government securities, and other securities. Federally-sponsored agency securities are classified under federal government securities instead of corporate bonds. Private equity, venture capital, and leverage buyouts are classified under corporate stocks instead of other securities. Due to these changes in asset classification, there are shifts in the distribution of assets from corporate bonds to federal government securities and from other securities to corporate stocks. However, since investment decisions guide the distribution of assets, we cannot calculate the exact impact that the changes in classification had on the asset distribution for 2012. As such, for the above mentioned asset categories, any data comparisons between data from 2012 to the present, and data prior to 2012 should be exercised with caution.

(b) The total of "net earnings" is a calculated statistic (the item code in the data file is X08), and thus can be positive or negative. Net earnings is the sum of earnings on investments plus gains on investments minus losses on investments. The change made in 2002 for asset valuation from book to market value in accordance with Statement 34 of the Governmental Accounting Standards Board is reflected in the calculated statistics.

CHAPTER EIGHT

STATE MANAGEMENT, ADMINISTRATION AND DEMOGRAPHICS

TABLE 8.1
Summary of State Government Employment: 1954-2017

Year (October)	Total, full-time and part-time			Full-time equivalent			Monthly payrolls (in millions of dollars)			Average monthly earnings of full-time employees		
	All	Education	Other	All	Education	Other	All	Education	Other	All	Education	Other
1954	1,149	310	839	1,024	222	802	$301	$79	$222	$294	$325	$283
1955	1,199	333	866	1,081	244	837	326	89	237	302	334	290
1956	1,268	353	915	1,136	250	886	367	109	258	321	358	309
1957 (April)	1,300	375	925	1,153	257	896	373	106	266	320	355	309
1958	1,408	406	1,002	1,259	284	975	447	123	323	355	416	333
1959	1,454	443	1,011	1,302	318	984	485	136	349	373	427	352
1960	1,527	474	1,053	1,353	332	1,021	524	168	356	386	439	365
1961	1,625	518	1,107	1,435	367	1,068	586	192	394	409	482	383
1962	1,680	555	1,126	1,478	389	1,088	635	202	433	429	518	397
1963	1,775	602	1,173	1,558	422	1,136	696	230	466	447	545	410
1964	1,873	656	1,217	1,639	460	1,179	761	258	504	464	560	427
1965	2,028	739	1,289	1,751	508	1,243	849	290	559	484	571	450
1966	2,211	866	1,344	1,864	575	1,289	975	353	622	522	614	483
1967	2,335	940	1,395	1,946	620	1,326	1,106	406	699	567	666	526
1968	2,495	1,037	1,458	2,085	694	1,391	1,257	477	780	602	687	544
1969	2,614	1,112	1,501	2,179	746	1,433	1,431	555	876	655	743	597
1970	2,755	1,182	1,573	2,302	803	1,499	1,612	630	982	700	797	605
1971	2,832	1,223	1,609	2,384	841	1,544	1,742	682	1,060	731	826	686
1972	2,957	1,267	1,690	2,487	867	1,619	1,937	747	1,190	778	871	734
1973	3,013	1,280	1,733	2,547	887	1,660	2,158	822	1,336	843	952	805
1974	3,155	1,357	1,798	2,653	929	1,725	2,410	933	1,477	906	1,023	855
1975	3,271	1,400	1,870	2,744	952	1,792	2,653	1,022	1,631	964	1,080	909
1976	3,343	1,434	1,910	2,799	973	1,827	2,894	1,112	1,782	1,031	1,163	975
1977	3,491	1,484	2,007	2,903	1,005	1,898	3,195	1,234	1,960	1,096	1,237	1,031
1978	3,539	1,508	2,032	2,966	1,016	1,950	3,483	1,333	2,150	1,167	1,311	1,102
1979	3,699	1,577	2,122	3,072	1,046	2,026	3,869	1,451	2,418	1,257	1,399	1,193
1980	3,753	1,599	2,154	3,106	1,063	2,044	4,285	1,608	2,677	1,373	1,523	1,305
1981	3,726	1,603	2,123	3,087	1,063	2,024	4,668	1,768	2,900	1,507	1,671	1,432
1982	3,747	1,616	2,131	3,083	1,051	2,032	5,028	1,874	3,154	1,625	1,789	1,551
1983	3,816	1,666	2,150	3,116	1,072	2,044	5,346	1,989	3,357	1,711	1,850	1,640
1984	3,898	1,708	2,190	3,177	1,091	2,086	5,815	2,178	3,637	1,825	1,991	1,740
1985	3,984	1,764	2,220	2,990	945	2,046	6,329	2,434	3,885	1,935	2,155	1,834
1986	4,068	1,800	2,267	3,437	1,256	2,181	6,801	2,583	4,227	2,052	2,263	1,956
1987	4,115	1,804	2,310	3,491	1,264	2,227	7,298	2,758	4,540	2,161	2,396	2,056
1988	4,236	1,854	2,381	3,606	1,309	2,297	7,842	2,929	4,914	2,260	2,490	2,158
1989	4,365	1,925	2,440	3,709	1,360	2,349	8,443	3,175	5,268	2,372	2,627	2,259
1990	4,503	1,984	2,519	3,840	1,418	2,432	9,083	3,426	5,657	2,472	2,732	2,359
1991	4,521	1,999	2,522	3,829	1,375	2,454	9,437	3,550	5,887	2,479	2,530	2,433
1992	4,595	2,050	2,545	3,856	1,384	2,472	9,828	3,774	6,054	2,562	2,607	2,521
1993	4,673	2,112	2,562	3,891	1,436	2,455	10,288	3,999	6,289	2,722	3,034	2,578
1994	4,694	2,115	2,579	3,917	1,442	2,475	10,666	4,177	6,489	2,776	3,073	2,640
1995	4,719	2,120	2,598	3,971	1,469	2,502	10,927	4,173	6,753	2,854	3,138	2,725
1996							----(a)----					
1997 (March)	4,733	2,114	2,619	3,987	1,484	2,503	11,413	4,372	7,041	2,968	3,251	2,838
1998 (March)	4,758	2,173	2,585	3,985	1,511	2,474	11,845	4,632	7,213	3,088	3,382	2,947
1999 (March)	4,818	2,229	2,588	4,034	1,541	2,493	12,564	4,957	7,608	3,236	3,544	3,087
2000 (March)	4,877	2,259	2,618	4,083	1,563	2,520	13,279	5,255	8,024	3,374	3,692	3,219
2001 (March)	4,985	2,329	2,656	4,173	1,615	2,559	14,136	5,621	8,516	3,521	3,842	3,362
2002 (March)	5,072	2,414	2,658	4,223	1,659	2,564	14,838	5,997	8,841	3,657	4,007	3,479
2003 (March)	5,043	2,413	2,630	4,191	1,656	2,534	15,116	6,154	8,962	3,751	4,115	3,566
2004 (March)	5,041	2,432	2,609	4,188	1,673	2,515	15,478	6,412	9,066	3,845	4,256	3,631
2005 (March)	5,078	2,459	2,620	4,209	1,684	2,525	16,062	6,669	9,393	3,966	4,390	3,745
2006 (March)	5,128	2,493	2,635	4,251	1,708	2,542	16,769	6,961	9,809	4,098	4,505	3,883
2007 (March)	5,200	2,538	2,663	4,307	1,740	2,566	17,789	7,419	10,370	4,276	4,670	4,063
2008 (March)	5,270	2,593	2,677	4,363	1,780	2,582	18,726	7,883	10,843	4,445	4,853	4,222
2009 (March)	5,346	2,649	2,697	4,408	1,814	2,594	19,425	8,279	11,146	4,565	5,007	4,320
2010 (March)	5,326	2,669	2,656	4,378	1,824	2,554	19,579	8,516	11,063	4,620	5,111	4,342
2011 (March)	5,314	2,704	2,609	4,359	1,847	2,512	19,972	8,813	11,159	4,735	5,233	4,446
2012 (March)	5,285	2,728	2,557	4,315	1,854	2,461	20,169	9,042	11,127	4,840	5,377	4,522
2013 (March)	5,304	2,749	2,554	4,315	1,867	2,449	20,473	9,242	11,231	4,917	5,463	4,589
2014 (March)	5,336	2,779	2,557	4,330	1,880	2,450	21,118	9,564	11,555	5,051	5,599	4,718
2015 (March)	5,353	2,794	2,559	4,342	1,890	2,452	21,591	9,766	11,826	5,159	5,708	4,824
2016 (March)	5,368	2,826	2,542	4,361	1,917	2,443	22,149	10,142	12,007	5,274	5,868	4,907
2017 (March)	5,400	2,844	2,556	4,382	1,927	2,455	22,920	10,541	12,379	5,420	6,044	5,032

See footnotes at end of table

TABLE 8.1
Summary of State Government Employment: 1954–2017 (continued)

Source: U.S. Census Bureau, Census of Governments: Employment (for the years ending in '2' and '7') and the Annual Survey of Public Employment & Payroll for remaining years. Accessed May 2019.

Note: Data users who create their own estimates using these data should cite the U.S. Census Bureau as the source of the original data only. The data in this table are based on information from public records and contain no confidential data. The data in this table for the years ending in '2' and '7' come from a census of governmental units and are subject to nonsampling error. Data for the remaining years are from a sample of governmental units, and are thus subject to both sampling and nonsampling error. Additional information on nonsampling error, response and definitions may be found within the survey technical documentation *https://www.census.gov/programs-surveys/apes/technical-documentation.html.*

Key:

(a) Due to a change in the reference period, from October to March, the October 1996 Annual Survey of Government Employment & Payroll was not conducted. This change in collection period was effective beginning with the March 1997 survey.

TABLE 8.2
Employment and Payrolls of State and Local Governments by Function: March 2017

Functions	All employees, full-time and part-time (in thousands of dollars)			March payrolls (in thousands of dollars)			Average March earnings of full-time employees
	Total	State government	Local government	Total	State government	Local government	
All functions	19,543,913	5,399,847	14,144,066	$80,276,246,286	$22,920,048,649	$57,356,197,637	5,042
Education:							
Higher education	3,281,365	2,694,538	586,827	11,707,297,941	9,902,137,143	1,805,160,798	6,063
Instructional personnel only	1,141,839	861,308	280,531	5,340,541,654	4,399,816,928	940,724,726	8,129
Elementary/Secondary schools	7,810,084	59,404	7,750,680	29,223,989,840	242,335,290	28,981,654,550	4,487
Instructional personnel only	5,324,577	44,214	5,280,363	22,900,613,813	195,283,768	22,705,330,045	4,985
Libraries	183,082	787	182,295	473,616,422	2,280,556	471,335,866	4,157
Other Education	89,631	89,631	0	396,730,249	396,730,249		4,889
Selected functions:							
Streets and Highways	504,869	214,002	290,867	2,305,426,038	1,044,043,281	1,261,382,757	4,799
Public Welfare	535,337	246,671	288,666	2,217,164,401	1,004,041,718	1,213,122,683	4,362
Hospitals	1,087,766	435,141	652,625	5,497,590,154	2,172,846,739	3,324,743,415	5,464
Police protection	985,622	103,990	881,632	5,593,113,790	645,607,018	4,947,506,772	6,160
Police Officers	729,052	65,392	663,660	4,603,361,566	476,532,002	4,126,829,564	6,579
Fire protection	441,646	0	441,646	2,310,569,167	0	2,310,569,167	6,680
Firefighters only	395,797	0	395,797	2,111,136,220	0	2,111,136,220	6,763
Natural Resources	191,388	147,224	44,164	810,995,186	633,105,523	177,889,663	4,860
Correction	719,622	448,190	271,432	3,359,323,865	2,084,090,316	1,275,233,549	4,757
Social Insurance	72,962	72,375	587	333,249,760	329,536,223	3,713,537	4,667
Financial Admin.	444,666	173,371	271,295	2,059,085,195	865,413,738	1,193,671,457	5,112
Judicial and Legal	440,094	179,610	260,484	2,286,720,188	1,013,751,701	1,272,968,487	5,537
Other Government Admin.	411,418	56,808	354,610	1,332,817,442	259,336,850	1,073,480,592	5,032
Utilities	525,359	39,209	486,150	3,038,129,334	272,838,831	2,765,290,503	6,093
State Liquor stores	13,427	13,427	0	32,870,934	32,870,934	0	3,553
Other and unallocable	1,805,575	425,469	1,380,106	7,297,556,380	2,019,082,539	5,278,473,841	4,943

Source: U.S. Census Bureau, 2017 Census of Governments: Employment.

Note: Data users who create their own estimates using these data should cite the U.S. Census Bureau as the source of the original data only. The data in this table are based on information from public records and contain no confidential data. The data in this table come from a census of governmental units and are subject to nonsampling error. Additional information on nonsampling error, response rates, and definitions may be found within the survey technical documentation *https://www.census.gov/programs-surveys/apes/technical-documentation.html.*

Note: Detail may not add to total due to rounding.

TABLE 8.3
State and Local Government Employment, By State: March 2017

State or other jurisdiction	All employees (full-time and part-time)			Full-time equivalent employment		
	Total	State	Local	Total	State	Local
United States	19,543,913	5,399,847	14,144,066	16,584,617	4,381,768	12,202,849
Alabama	319,439	112,051	207,388	281,490	90,729	190,761
Alaska	60,784	27,743	33,041	51,843	24,357	27,486
Arizona	333,628	93,321	240,307	281,188	72,850	208,338
Arkansas	191,968	72,685	119,283	168,344	62,066	106,278
California	2,249,452	533,015	1,716,437	1,861,274	424,359	1,436,915
Colorado	360,630	111,092	249,538	299,168	88,130	211,038
Connecticut	224,781	75,124	149,657	186,362	58,803	127,559
Delaware	56,747	30,604	26,143	49,757	25,872	23,885
Florida	1,006,836	211,119	795,717	890,784	179,738	711,046
Georgia	589,522	164,770	424,752	520,907	129,828	391,079
Hawaii	91,842	72,819	19,023	75,958	58,966	16,992
Idaho	108,149	31,514	76,635	84,584	24,176	60,408
Illinois	758,313	152,002	606,311	618,377	121,795	496,582
Indiana	395,579	119,270	276,309	324,678	90,341	234,337
Iowa	242,797	70,765	172,032	186,539	51,176	135,363
Kansas	245,127	66,689	178,438	201,209	53,820	147,389
Kentucky	274,945	97,718	177,227	243,100	84,042	159,058
Louisiana	291,700	86,351	205,349	259,348	73,488	185,860
Maine	87,568	26,367	61,201	69,527	20,172	49,355
Maryland	343,985	90,238	253,747	306,799	85,163	221,636
Massachusetts	391,509	122,363	269,146	328,534	98,206	230,328
Michigan	545,681	190,568	355,113	433,801	146,697	287,104
Minnesota	372,550	103,435	269,115	294,085	83,359	210,726
Mississippi	207,922	64,158	143,764	188,616	55,539	133,077
Missouri	378,893	105,707	273,186	319,206	86,498	232,708
Montana	72,730	27,312	45,418	57,296	20,870	36,426
Nebraska	145,955	36,595	109,360	121,477	31,655	89,822
Nevada	132,907	35,655	97,252	115,575	28,936	86,639
New Hampshire	88,688	26,052	62,636	71,360	18,931	52,429
New Jersey	557,514	157,781	399,733	477,619	139,048	338,571
New Mexico	141,768	54,152	87,616	123,517	45,194	78,323
New York	1,342,242	276,716	1,065,526	1,200,144	247,580	952,564
North Carolina	658,339	171,237	487,102	562,411	144,993	417,418
North Dakota	66,068	25,601	40,467	47,309	19,026	28,283
Ohio	710,876	185,019	525,857	588,784	137,560	451,224
Oklahoma	243,965	83,182	160,783	211,127	66,128	144,999
Oregon	255,217	90,226	164,991	200,962	70,153	130,809
Pennsylvania	667,578	206,384	461,194	566,129	164,285	401,844
Rhode Island	56,940	23,905	33,035	47,509	18,151	29,358
South Carolina	295,332	93,408	201,924	265,525	79,834	185,691
South Dakota	64,151	19,247	44,904	47,014	14,449	32,565
Tennessee	374,024	97,520	276,504	327,864	78,746	249,118
Texas	1,689,188	367,311	1,321,877	1,513,358	313,065	1,200,293
Utah	208,664	80,250	128,414	154,507	60,507	94,000
Vermont	51,663	17,244	34,419	40,965	14,267	26,698
Virginia	536,973	166,763	370,210	448,838	125,605	323,233
Washington	444,216	155,755	288,461	382,426	127,234	255,192
West Virginia	119,158	48,274	70,884	101,952	39,394	62,558
Wisconsin	378,116	107,368	270,748	284,715	72,899	211,816
Wyoming	60,090	15,402	44,688	50,084	13,088	36,996
Dist. of Columbia	51,204	N.A.	51,204	50,672	N.A.	50,672

Source: U.S. Census Bureau, 2017 Census of Governments: Employment.

Notes:

1. Data users who create their own estimates using these data should cite the U.S. Census Bureau as the source of the original data only. The data in this table are based on information from public records and contain no confidential data. The data in this table come from a census of governmental units and are subject to nonsampling error. Additional information on nonsampling error, response rates, and definitions may be found within the survey technical documentation *https://www.census.gov/programs-surveys/apes/technical-documentation.html*.

2. Detail may not add to total due to rounding.

Table 8.3 | State & Local Government Employment

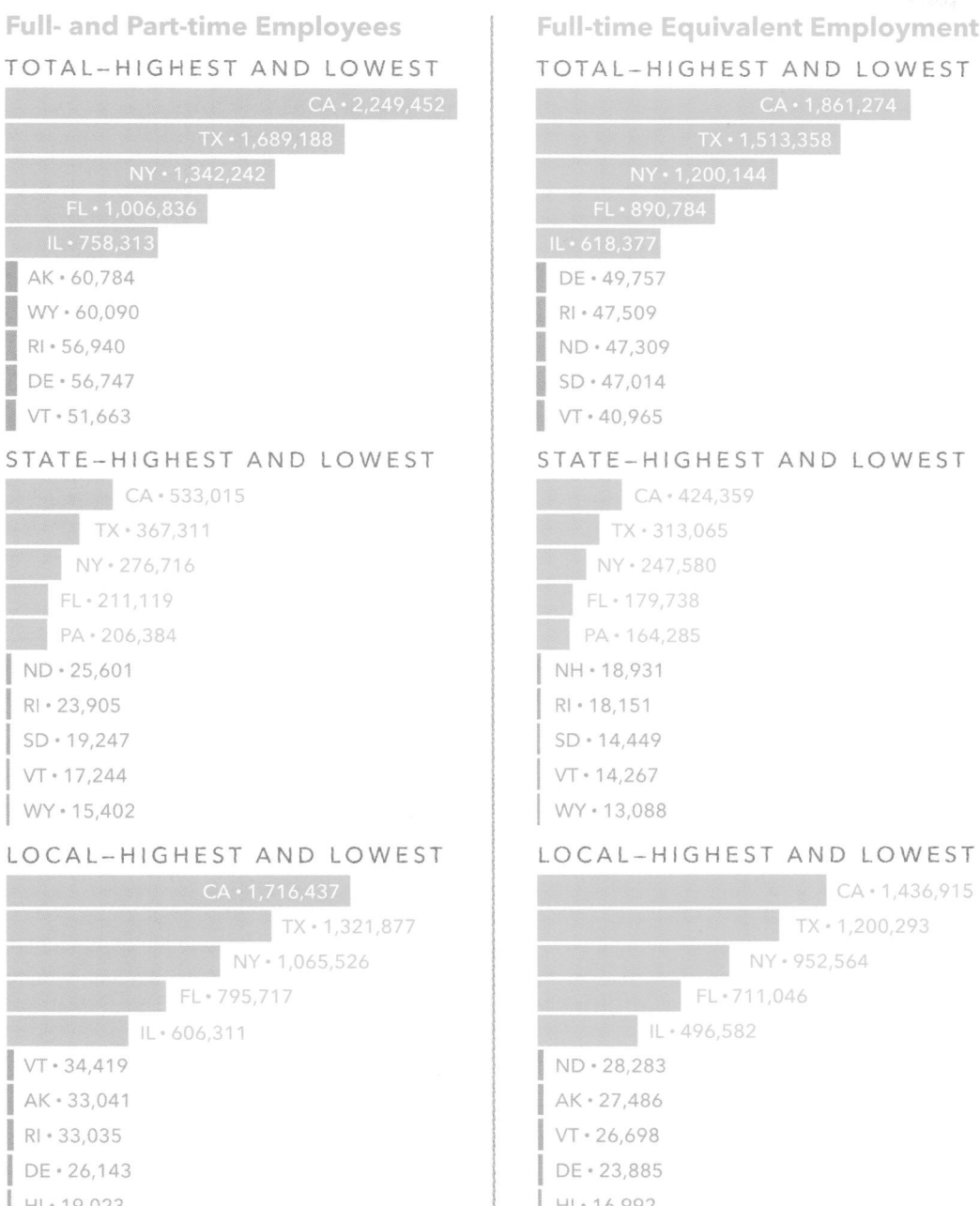

Full- and Part-time Employees

TOTAL–HIGHEST AND LOWEST

CA · 2,249,452
TX · 1,689,188
NY · 1,342,242
FL · 1,006,836
IL · 758,313
AK · 60,784
WY · 60,090
RI · 56,940
DE · 56,747
VT · 51,663

STATE–HIGHEST AND LOWEST

CA · 533,015
TX · 367,311
NY · 276,716
FL · 211,119
PA · 206,384
ND · 25,601
RI · 23,905
SD · 19,247
VT · 17,244
WY · 15,402

LOCAL–HIGHEST AND LOWEST

CA · 1,716,437
TX · 1,321,877
NY · 1,065,526
FL · 795,717
IL · 606,311
VT · 34,419
AK · 33,041
RI · 33,035
DE · 26,143
HI · 19,023

Full-time Equivalent Employment

TOTAL–HIGHEST AND LOWEST

CA · 1,861,274
TX · 1,513,358
NY · 1,200,144
FL · 890,784
IL · 618,377
DE · 49,757
RI · 47,509
ND · 47,309
SD · 47,014
VT · 40,965

STATE–HIGHEST AND LOWEST

CA · 424,359
TX · 313,065
NY · 247,580
FL · 179,738
PA · 164,285
NH · 18,931
RI · 18,151
SD · 14,449
VT · 14,267
WY · 13,088

LOCAL–HIGHEST AND LOWEST

CA · 1,436,915
TX · 1,200,293
NY · 952,564
FL · 711,046
IL · 496,582
ND · 28,283
AK · 27,486
VT · 26,698
DE · 23,885
HI · 16,992

TABLE 8.4
State and Local Government Payrolls and Average Earnings of Full-Time Employees, By State: March 2017

| State or other jurisdiction | Amount of Payroll | | | Percentage of March payroll | | Average earnings of full-time state and local government employees (dollars) | | |
	Total	State government	Local government	State government	Local government	All	State government	Local government
United States	$80,276,246,286	$22,920,048,649	$57,356,197,637	29%	71%	$5,042	$5,420	$4,910
Alabama	1,107,670,821	410,209,467	697,461,354	37%	63%	4,029	4,709	3,727
Alaska	293,307,101	142,151,749	151,155,352	48%	52%	5,851	6,026	5,693
Arizona	1,248,350,445	340,878,839	907,471,606	27%	73%	4,637	5,029	4,509
Arkansas	597,216,532	251,779,689	345,436,843	42%	58%	3,629	4,188	3,315
California	12,041,842,805	2,977,464,716	9,064,378,089	25%	75%	6,947	7,258	6,855
Colorado	1,440,232,617	459,118,172	981,114,445	32%	68%	5,117	5,836	4,874
Connecticut	1,073,698,543	377,948,174	695,750,369	35%	65%	6,026	6,692	5,730
Delaware	232,247,790	118,745,601	113,502,189	51%	49%	4,878	4,716	5,052
Florida	3,753,140,676	776,622,194	2,976,518,482	21%	79%	4,354	4,430	4,335
Georgia	2,054,914,590	556,701,241	1,498,213,349	27%	73%	4,047	4,455	3,920
Hawaii	374,318,642	279,420,700	94,897,942	75%	25%	5,048	4,862	5,644
Idaho	339,633,281	122,570,808	217,062,473	36%	64%	4,178	5,315	3,734
Illinois	3,210,078,799	683,283,763	2,526,795,036	21%	79%	5,482	5,877	5,391
Indiana	1,269,438,663	381,582,094	887,856,569	30%	70%	4,116	4,542	3,956
Iowa	868,809,883	297,791,595	571,018,288	34%	66%	5,060	6,579	4,505
Kansas	789,561,572	245,981,485	543,580,087	31%	69%	4,060	4,694	3,827
Kentucky	928,103,869	364,475,018	563,628,851	39%	61%	3,972	4,629	3,646
Louisiana	989,877,727	337,494,528	652,383,199	34%	66%	3,937	4,767	3,616
Maine	281,223,528	89,097,105	192,126,423	32%	68%	4,187	4,521	4,049
Maryland	1,660,959,685	457,950,608	1,203,009,077	28%	72%	5,668	5,451	5,754
Massachusetts	1,813,009,152	590,350,494	1,222,658,658	33%	67%	5,710	6,113	5,537
Michigan	2,099,097,221	825,054,944	1,274,042,277	39%	61%	5,155	5,953	4,763
Minnesota	1,476,880,559	473,259,378	1,003,621,181	32%	68%	5,363	6,039	5,094
Mississippi	658,166,225	216,596,303	441,569,922	33%	67%	3,526	3,997	3,333
Missouri	1,213,741,346	335,587,588	878,153,758	28%	72%	3,924	4,008	3,893
Montana	239,217,126	95,817,742	143,399,384	40%	60%	4,408	4,810	4,176
Nebraska	522,311,451	131,604,464	390,706,987	25%	75%	4,559	4,535	4,568
Nevada	589,035,054	144,755,390	444,279,664	25%	75%	5,439	5,152	5,540
New Hampshire	317,720,769	96,360,487	221,360,282	30%	70%	4,822	5,445	4,600
New Jersey	2,823,762,058	848,436,856	1,975,325,202	30%	70%	6,225	6,290	6,198
New Mexico	506,776,578	210,683,741	296,092,837	42%	58%	4,198	4,761	3,882
New York	7,092,264,046	1,535,953,566	5,556,310,480	22%	78%	6,109	6,316	6,055
North Carolina	2,357,991,745	681,756,491	1,676,235,254	29%	71%	4,312	4,855	4,127
North Dakota	212,114,190	91,480,042	120,634,148	43%	57%	4,674	4,975	4,471
Ohio	2,625,969,799	691,794,167	1,934,175,632	26%	74%	4,735	5,559	4,507
Oklahoma	775,039,210	275,076,106	499,963,104	35%	65%	3,764	4,346	3,516
Oregon	1,058,942,041	406,900,558	652,041,483	38%	62%	5,395	5,655	5,246
Pennsylvania	2,784,646,937	874,173,693	1,910,473,244	31%	69%	5,091	5,299	5,007
Rhode Island	269,168,273	110,456,856	158,711,417	41%	59%	5,846	6,142	5,658
South Carolina	1,043,492,281	335,979,627	707,512,654	32%	68%	4,025	4,347	3,891
South Dakota	184,023,342	65,712,945	118,310,397	36%	64%	4,055	4,748	3,748
Tennessee	1,273,796,413	341,670,507	932,125,906	27%	73%	4,016	4,482	3,871
Texas	6,445,748,848	1,582,232,617	4,863,516,231	25%	75%	4,356	5,206	4,147
Utah	662,639,056	296,707,807	365,931,249	45%	55%	4,628	5,159	4,266
Vermont	188,507,994	79,941,610	108,566,384	42%	58%	4,759	5,589	4,281
Virginia	2,050,972,428	645,958,864	1,405,013,564	31%	69%	4,742	5,369	4,514
Washington	2,181,704,380	691,839,114	1,489,865,266	32%	68%	6,089	5,530	6,388
West Virginia	363,455,554	151,375,663	212,079,891	42%	58%	3,604	3,890	3,425
Wisconsin	1,313,688,831	362,632,547	951,056,284	28%	72%	4,945	5,419	4,790
Wyoming	225,624,511	58,630,936	166,993,575	26%	74%	4,721	4,664	4,743
Dist. of Columbia	352,111,299	N.A.	352,111,299	N.A.	100%	7,147	N.A.	7,147

Source: U.S. Census Bureau, 2017 Census of Governments: Employment.

Notes:

1. Data users who create their own estimates using these data should cite the U.S. Census Bureau as the source of the original data only. The data in this table are based on information from public records and contain no confidential data. The data in this table come from a census of governmental units and are subject to nonsampling error. Additional information on nonsampling error, response rates, and definitions may be found within the survey technical documentation https://www.census.gov/programs-surveys/apes/technical-documentation.html.

2. Detail may not add to total due to rounding.

TABLE 8.5
State Government Employment (Full-Time Equivalent) for Selected Functions, By State: March 2017

State	All functions	Education		Selected Functions							
		Higher education (a)	Other education	Highways	Public welfare	Hospitals	Corrections	Police protection	Natural resources	Financial admin.	Judicial and legal admin.
United States	4,381,768	1,796,421	82,304	208,626	242,652	402,163	444,630	102,222	133,923	169,421	175,546
Alabama	90,729	42,936	2,997	4,302	4,232	13,447	4,288	1,283	1,941	2,322	3,002
Alaska	24,357	4,652	225	2,960	1,766	216	2,185	710	2,018	1,025	1,320
Arizona	72,850	34,804	2,735	2,468	6,123	608	9,352	1,993	1,568	2,196	2,501
Arkansas	62,066	25,988	1,321	3,670	4,216	6,573	5,780	1,214	1,886	2,254	1,578
California	424,359	170,846	4,263	18,729	4,011	48,082	58,541	11,538	16,520	26,899	6,333
Colorado	88,130	50,354	1,796	3,069	2,369	6,592	7,424	1,265	1,154	2,086	5,195
Connecticut	58,803	18,322	2,863	3,398	5,204	6,001	5,284	1,874	693	1,654	5,322
Delaware	25,872	7,829	347	1,544	1,649	1,296	2,841	1,093	459	850	1,823
Florida	179,738	66,997	2,853	6,176	9,282	4,010	23,652	4,147	7,946	6,321	19,708
Georgia	129,828	64,194	2,606	4,053	7,035	7,908	16,133	2,646	4,874	2,999	3,556
Hawaii	58,966	11,287	137	831	401	4,231	2,380	0	853	738	3,007
Idaho	24,176	8,949	391	1,323	1,811	610	2,419	520	1,958	1,303	568
Illinois	121,795	56,271	1,838	6,376	9,003	10,314	13,054	3,062	2,624	5,176	2,550
Indiana	90,341	58,960	943	3,509	6,008	1,470	6,082	1,829	2,268	1,845	1,482
Iowa	51,176	23,802	1,046	2,134	2,620	8,907	2,714	850	1,471	1,304	2,201
Kansas	53,820	23,654	617	2,600	2,959	10,685	3,265	1,062	774	1,769	2,113
Kentucky	84,042	38,272	2,047	4,362	6,957	7,210	4,109	2,049	2,392	2,302	5,560
Louisiana	73,488	24,913	2,888	4,335	5,396	10,078	5,683	1,839	3,793	2,630	1,663
Maine	20,172	6,920	271	2,105	2,174	515	1,225	549	1,117	1,270	833
Maryland	85,163	28,628	1,970	4,345	6,220	3,321	11,354	2,224	2,016	3,172	5,291
Massachusetts	98,206	31,576	1,158	2,742	7,724	5,438	11,718	2,831	1,297	3,489	9,294
Michigan	146,697	76,738	611	2,669	11,317	17,057	12,265	2,897	3,449	4,223	1,493
Minnesota	83,359	36,279	3,641	4,662	3,036	5,044	4,379	972	3,250	4,991	4,004
Mississippi	55,539	20,445	1,444	3,177	4,339	10,374	2,473	1,212	2,963	1,536	465
Missouri	86,498	30,503	1,648	5,282	6,686	10,099	11,893	2,498	2,206	2,904	4,145
Montana	20,870	7,241	377	2,072	1,843	755	1,220	502	1,579	1,022	785
Nebraska	31,655	12,613	561	1,787	2,556	3,747	2,750	744	2,182	783	780
Nevada	28,936	9,879	157	1,726	2,481	1,322	3,753	866	918	1,531	686
New Hampshire	18,931	7,065	321	1,607	1,968	572	1,032	509	367	793	856
New Jersey	139,048	35,238	2,543	5,887	8,958	13,231	8,688	3,979	1,868	5,149	12,789
New Mexico	45,194	17,543	926	2,160	1,622	7,830	3,826	629	998	1,058	3,187
New York	247,580	57,601	4,105	10,662	4,687	41,799	32,205	6,196	3,035	16,384	18,823
North Carolina	144,993	61,685	3,009	8,756	1,100	22,551	19,430	3,170	4,298	3,428	6,549
North Dakota	19,026	8,539	333	960	523	921	909	199	1,069	677	628
Ohio	137,560	74,041	2,129	6,190	2,814	14,553	13,388	2,630	2,529	6,301	2,975
Oklahoma	66,128	29,520	1,584	2,829	7,094	1,075	4,918	1,917	1,899	2,378	2,601
Oregon	70,153	25,549	869	3,679	8,364	7,536	5,318	1,501	2,868	4,118	3,086
Pennsylvania	164,285	60,887	5,268	13,098	11,151	12,018	17,945	6,679	5,698	6,713	2,985
Rhode Island	18,151	5,137	475	706	1,262	729	1,467	342	368	940	1,173
South Carolina	79,834	31,835	3,227	4,568	5,420	6,794	7,504	2,124	2,128	3,342	914
South Dakota	14,449	5,565	417	1,022	1,781	346	742	360	949	413	662
Tennessee	78,746	34,824	1,965	3,235	7,362	3,536	6,927	1,780	3,559	3,338	2,527
Texas	313,065	142,125	2,392	11,901	24,727	23,287	41,760	6,915	11,039	7,923	5,764
Utah	60,507	28,574	1,562	1,579	2,858	10,498	3,327	910	1,338	2,471	1,571
Vermont	14,267	4,811	347	1,060	1,574	239	1,083	592	635	626	660
Virginia	125,605	57,678	2,225	7,790	3,075	11,549	13,127	3,121	2,631	4,507	3,844
Washington	127,234	57,563	2,264	6,568	10,685	11,360	8,894	2,165	5,345	3,122	2,090
West Virginia	39,394	14,153	1,285	4,722	3,364	1,524	3,329	999	1,783	1,889	1,689
Wisconsin	72,899	38,748	1,086	1,528	2,293	3,606	9,402	954	2,409	2,559	2,366
Wyoming	13,088	3,888	221	1,713	552	699	1,193	282	941	698	549

Source: U.S. Census Bureau, 2017 Census of Governments: Employment.

Notes:

1. Data users who create their own estimates using these data should cite the U.S. Census Bureau as the source of the original data only. The data in this table are based on information from public records and contain no confidential data. The data in this table come from a census of governmental units and are subject to nonsampling error. Additional information on nonsampling error, response rates, and definitions may be found within the survey technical documentation *https://www.census.gov/programs-surveys/apes/technical-documentation.html.*

2. Detail may not add to total due to rounding.

Key:

(a) Includes instructional and other personnel.

TABLE 8.6
State Government Payrolls for Selected Functions, By State: March 2017 (In thousands of dollars)

| State | All functions | Education | | | Selected functions | |
		Higher education (a)	Other education (a)	Highways	Public welfare	Hospitals
United States	$22,920,048,649	$9,902,137,143	$396,730,249	$1,044,043,281	$1,004,041,718	$2,172,846,739
Alabama	410,209,467	210,682,950	11,343,633	16,183,307	14,647,854	60,758,272
Alaska	142,151,749	27,617,423	1,385,328	18,626,281	8,212,888	1,261,446
Arizona	340,878,839	185,538,619	10,449,922	11,445,373	21,210,309	2,616,929
Arkansas	251,779,689	119,497,010	5,040,450	14,061,520	13,237,933	25,522,317
California	2,977,464,716	1,166,356,176	22,886,649	152,744,222	20,100,492	439,311,479
Colorado	459,118,172	273,413,212	8,058,688	14,755,995	10,716,890	30,649,804
Connecticut	377,948,174	118,988,774	18,403,166	19,626,852	35,405,600	40,886,309
Delaware	118,745,601	43,263,662	2,080,137	5,165,622	5,464,222	4,580,237
Florida	776,622,194	374,392,428	10,196,081	28,550,304	28,035,919	13,370,408
Georgia	556,701,241	313,566,087	12,853,913	14,530,839	22,104,116	31,072,926
Hawaii	279,420,700	57,419,938	601,738	4,513,356	1,857,334	24,823,480
Idaho	122,570,808	41,313,673	2,599,443	5,704,210	7,536,370	2,177,984
Illinois	683,283,763	294,823,861	9,632,202	41,209,274	51,816,766	53,050,450
Indiana	381,582,094	263,860,941	3,751,192	13,628,094	18,157,991	5,288,399
Iowa	297,791,595	142,950,828	6,473,349	11,791,133	13,995,885	50,945,280
Kansas	245,981,485	116,497,037	2,705,965	9,391,100	10,701,311	53,291,338
Kentucky	364,475,018	186,365,512	8,815,824	15,918,617	22,573,291	34,854,989
Louisiana	337,494,528	124,456,648	12,682,306	18,466,165	19,922,620	42,754,845
Maine	89,097,105	29,950,663	1,168,358	8,681,581	8,360,897	2,364,053
Maryland	457,950,608	161,848,025	10,354,842	23,846,907	27,859,366	16,720,237
Massachusetts	590,350,494	182,497,562	7,027,712	17,474,097	44,607,021	27,508,987
Michigan	825,054,944	446,895,294	3,743,270	14,767,355	54,708,146	99,047,295
Minnesota	473,259,378	215,884,205	20,714,165	25,264,028	13,091,036	23,678,797
Mississippi	216,596,303	95,246,485	4,976,483	9,869,036	12,709,437	37,548,003
Missouri	335,587,588	144,576,251	5,731,066	18,463,440	18,951,954	36,039,186
Montana	95,817,742	32,943,354	1,738,924	10,551,645	7,472,032	2,908,464
Nebraska	131,604,464	54,134,903	2,622,553	7,410,399	8,592,578	15,058,915
Nevada	144,755,390	52,204,322	848,817	8,220,082	9,733,924	6,508,005
New Hampshire	96,360,487	39,411,140	1,532,276	7,785,399	8,722,557	2,680,795
New Jersey	848,436,856	234,305,920	15,036,418	33,037,621	51,363,884	66,652,642
New Mexico	210,683,741	91,333,217	3,953,616	8,492,964	6,022,166	36,553,940
New York	1,535,953,566	333,988,400	22,944,682	57,435,367	24,667,787	242,864,964
North Carolina	681,756,491	319,450,393	14,453,642	35,714,405	4,358,686	103,815,378
North Dakota	91,480,042	42,224,637	1,506,556	5,435,856	1,972,497	2,931,879
Ohio	691,794,167	355,463,716	11,425,084	30,880,121	16,287,178	74,678,298
Oklahoma	275,076,106	131,468,730	6,203,198	10,806,526	23,773,926	3,285,265
Oregon	406,900,558	156,675,741	4,880,175	21,385,056	36,464,183	52,686,782
Pennsylvania	874,173,693	375,238,582	23,408,411	59,118,745	45,682,040	45,085,825
Rhode Island	110,456,856	28,814,895	3,028,328	4,259,705	7,909,188	4,108,328
South Carolina	335,979,627	156,034,284	12,779,001	16,388,288	16,871,236	23,499,073
South Dakota	65,712,945	25,527,797	1,845,318	4,902,806		1,225,362
Tennessee	341,670,507	160,518,821	7,942,423	13,352,020	27,674,291	13,709,733
Texas	1,582,232,617	848,242,766	12,881,402	55,355,619	88,703,279	110,141,693
Utah	296,707,807	154,947,981	6,629,623	7,425,047	10,682,961	49,083,119
Vermont	79,941,610	27,655,244	1,848,128	5,983,624	8,288,441	1,298,285
Virginia	645,958,864	336,639,790	11,415,346	37,743,142	14,414,072	55,280,537
Washington	691,839,114		11,648,573	36,598,287	49,120,445	75,805,803
West Virginia	151,375,663	68,194,472	5,983,467	14,787,760	9,132,605	4,390,028
Wisconsin	362,632,547	195,051,132	5,261,629	8,724,505	10,384,107	16,008,848
Wyoming	58,630,936	17,097,257	1,236,777	7,569,584	2,268,266	2,461,328

See footnotes at end of table

TABLE 8.6
State Government Payrolls for Selected Functions, By State: March 2017 (In thousands of dollars) (continued)

State	Corrections	Police protection	Natural resources	Financial admin.	Judicial and legal admin.
			Selected functions, cont.		
United States	$2,084,090,316	$645,607,018	$633,105,523	$865,413,738	$1,013,751,701
Alabama	17,268,676	5,679,024	7,644,244	10,643,174	13,985,245
Alaska	13,054,640	5,025,788	11,946,370	6,741,464	8,695,406
Arizona	34,399,487	10,294,514	6,737,864	9,781,704	12,334,904
Arkansas	18,350,694	4,646,525	6,730,070	8,925,475	6,555,894
California	431,980,110	98,386,776	100,938,707	141,967,584	45,816,706
Colorado	31,647,116	7,780,568	5,875,315	11,038,985	28,884,522
Connecticut	33,997,017	14,315,171	4,387,408	11,411,890	26,402,840
Delaware	12,129,762	7,835,976	1,843,367	2,728,718	8,712,904
Florida	71,288,720	16,739,645	27,698,178	22,782,533	82,004,943
Georgia	49,615,709	12,263,544	17,963,945	12,681,586	16,740,002
Hawaii	12,586,424	0	4,206,578	3,432,794	13,717,856
Idaho	12,922,595	2,749,689	10,609,612	7,192,263	5,589,226
Illinois	74,437,381	23,274,794	12,769,917	28,076,574	23,967,702
Indiana	17,904,506	8,138,767	8,514,459	8,535,135	10,264,320
Iowa	14,475,421	5,877,763	8,350,282	7,549,431	13,044,141
Kansas	10,751,797	5,164,598	3,307,671	7,494,970	9,181,120
Kentucky	13,988,209	8,119,717	9,656,207	9,284,037	19,558,170
Louisiana	22,471,883	12,255,989	17,140,284	13,031,337	7,653,046
Maine	5,407,332	3,104,491	5,279,348	5,440,595	4,299,853
Maryland	58,510,226	14,607,614	10,980,478	15,479,611	32,342,526
Massachusetts	68,866,234	26,888,980	8,807,731	21,916,375	59,119,233
Michigan	63,727,983	15,895,376	17,558,016	25,431,196	10,848,004
Minnesota	21,753,914	5,132,168	17,109,510	32,645,493	24,269,557
Mississippi	6,891,372	4,898,115	10,184,944	5,974,547	2,568,239
Missouri	32,789,248	11,300,544	7,739,121	11,221,697	17,034,426
Montana	5,217,412	2,499,890	7,230,161	4,509,281	3,981,476
Nebraska	10,993,052	3,734,901	8,045,231	3,226,341	4,365,489
Nevada	18,296,078	5,690,925	4,486,985	6,290,702	4,995,584
New Hampshire	5,689,919	2,972,970	1,852,706	4,060,205	4,240,815
New Jersey	49,661,433	29,890,317	11,060,594	26,985,383	79,615,121
New Mexico	14,219,935	3,190,540	4,520,374	4,843,533	15,363,231
New York	192,881,838	58,241,354	17,494,243	97,993,924	145,366,774
North Carolina	71,346,341	15,152,155	17,068,554	17,599,780	33,684,393
North Dakota	4,108,040	1,324,082	4,886,733	3,252,493	3,777,455
Ohio	63,216,978	14,878,632	11,782,457	37,015,173	19,425,023
Oklahoma	16,994,900	9,934,439	6,918,848	10,340,025	12,196,492
Oregon	29,105,588	9,383,365	14,604,692	22,222,377	17,945,061
Pennsylvania	91,110,968	43,031,260	30,531,339	31,642,875	30,016,567
Rhode Island	11,596,338	2,894,651	2,260,752	5,461,967	7,386,864
South Carolina	24,215,180	8,545,704	7,371,836	12,885,607	4,930,260
South Dakota	2,953,463	1,712,450	3,908,329	2,321,435	3,471,331
Tennessee	22,225,311	8,829,122	15,756,564	15,883,873	14,866,956
Texas	138,299,381	45,322,117	50,473,533	40,399,610	33,354,722
Utah	12,796,419	4,101,411	5,432,819	12,366,788	8,431,540
Vermont	5,443,481	4,075,641	3,557,346	3,385,924	3,687,720
Virginia	46,507,712	16,728,904	13,615,465	21,247,673	19,539,144
Washington	39,788,928	12,252,077	24,881,897	17,715,680	13,340,435
West Virginia	9,474,349	4,233,735	6,116,834	5,701,514	7,740,009
Wisconsin	42,327,514	5,113,605	10,840,568	12,955,921	15,232,742
Wyoming	4,403,302	1,496,635	4,427,037	3,696,486	3,205,712

Source: U.S. Census Bureau, 2017 Census of Governments: Employment.
Notes:
1. Data users who create their own estimates using these data should cite the U.S. Census Bureau as the source of the original data only. The data in this table are based on information from public records and contain no confidential data. The data in this table come from a census of governmental units and are subject to nonsampling error. Additional information on nonsampling error, response rates, and definitions may be found within the survey technical documentation https://www.census.gov/programs-surveys/apes/technical-documentation.html.
2. Detail may not add to total due to rounding.
Key:
(a) Includes instructional and other personnel.

TABLE 8.7
State Employees: Paid Holidays**

State or other jurisdiction	Major holidays (a)	Martin Luther King's Birthday (b)	Lincoln's Birthday	President's Day (c)	Washington's Birthday (c)	Good Friday	Memorial Day (d)
Alabama	★	★(h)	…	…	★(i)	…	★
Alaska	★	★	…	★	…	…	★
Arizona	★	★	…	★	…	…	★
Arkansas	★	★(h)	…	…	★(i)	…	★
California	★	★	…	★	…	…	★
Colorado	★	★	…	★	…	…	★
Connecticut	★	★	★	…	★	★	★
Delaware	★	★	…	…	…	★	★
Florida	★	★	…	…	…	…	★
Georgia	★	★	…	…	(l)	…	★
Hawaii	★	★	…	★	…	★	★
Idaho	★	★(h)	…	★	…	…	★
Illinois	★	★	★	…	★	…	★
Indiana	★	★	(m)	…	(m)	★	★
Iowa	★	★	…	…	…	…	★
Kansas	★	★	…	…	…	…	★
Kentucky	★	★	…	…	…	★(n)	★
Louisiana	★	★	…	…	…	★	★
Maine	★	★	…	★	…	…	★
Maryland	★	★	…	★	…	…	★
Massachusetts	★	★	…	…	★	…	★
Michigan	★	★	…	★	…	…	★
Minnesota	★	★	…	★	…	…	★
Mississippi	★	★(h)	…	…	★	…	★(v)
Missouri	★	★	★	…	★	…	★
Montana	★	★	…	★	…	…	★
Nebraska	★	★	…	★	…	…	★
Nevada	★	★	…	★	…	…	★
New Hampshire	★	★(h)	…	★	…	…	★
New Jersey	★	★	…	★	…	★	★
New Mexico	★	★	…	(o)	…	…	★
New York	★	★	(j)	…	★	…	★
North Carolina	★	★	…	…	…	★	★
North Dakota	★	★	…	★	…	★	★
Ohio	★	★	…	★	…	…	★
Oklahoma	★	★	…	★	…	…	★
Oregon	★	★	…	★	…	…	★
Pennsylvania	★	★	…	★	…	…	★
Rhode Island	★	★	…	…	…	…	★
South Carolina	★	★	…	★	…	…	★
South Dakota	★	★	…	★	…	…	★
Tennessee	★	★	…	★	…	★	★
Texas	★	★	…	★	…	(r)	★
Utah	★	★	…	★	…	…	★
Vermont	★	★	…	★	…	…	★
Virginia	★	★	…	…	★	…	★
Washington	★	★	…	★	…	…	★
West Virginia	★	★	…	★	…	…	★
Wisconsin	★	★	…	…	…	…	★
Wyoming	★	★	…	★	…	…	★
Dist. of Columbia	★	★	…	…	★	…	★
American Samoa	★	★	…	★	…	★	★
Guam	★	★	…	…	…	…	★
CNMI*	★	★	…	★	…	★	★
Puerto Rico	★	★	…	★	…	★	★
U.S. Virgin Islands	★	★	…	★	…	★	★

See footnotes at end of table

TABLE 8.7
State Employees: Paid Holidays (continued)

State or other jurisdiction	Columbus Day (e)	Veteran's Day	Day after Thanksgiving	Day before or after Christmas	Day before or after New Year's	Election Day (f)	Other (g)
Alabama	★	★	(k)	(k)	...	...	★
Alaska	...	★	...	...	...	...	★
Arizona	★	★	...	...	...	...	...
Arkansas	...	★	(k)	Before	...	...	★
California	...	★	★	...	...	...	★
Colorado	★	★	...	...	...	...	★
Connecticut	★	★	...	...	...	...	...
Delaware	...	★	★	...	...	★	★
Florida	...	★	★	...	...	...	★
Georgia	★	★	(l)	(l)	...	...	★
Hawaii	...	★	...	...	...	★	★
Idaho	★	★	...	...	...	...	...
Illinois	★	★	★	...	...	★	...
Indiana	★	★	(m)	(m)	...	★	...
Iowa	...	★	★	...	...	...	★
Kansas	...	★	★	...	...	...	★
Kentucky	...	★	★	★	★	★(t)	...
Louisiana	...	★	...	...	...	★(u)	★
Maine	★	★	★	...	...	...	★
Maryland	★	★	★(aa)	...	...	★	★
Massachusetts	★	★	...	...	...	...	★
Michigan	...	★	★	Before	Before	★(z)	...
Minnesota	...	★	...	...	...	...	★
Mississippi	...	★	(k)	(k)	...	...	★
Missouri	★	★	...	...	...	...	★
Montana	★	★	...	...	...	★	...
Nebraska	★	★	...	...	...	...	★
Nevada	...	★	★(cc)	...	...	...	★
New Hampshire	...	★	★	...	...	...	★
New Jersey	★	★	...	...	...	★	...
New Mexico	★	★	(o)	...	...	(w)	...
New York	★	★	...	...	...	★	...
North Carolina	...	★	★	(x)	...	...	...
North Dakota	...	★	...	(p)	...	...	...
Ohio	★	★	...	...	...	...	...
Oklahoma	...	★	★	Before	...	...	...
Oregon	...	★	★	...	...	...	...
Pennsylvania	★	★	★	...	...	...	...
Rhode Island	★	★	...	...	...	★	★
South Carolina	...	★	★	Both	...	...	★
South Dakota	(y)	★	...	...	...	...	...
Tennessee	(q)	★	(q)	...	...	...	...
Texas	...	★	★	Both	...	...	★
Utah	★	★	...	...	...	...	★
Vermont	...	★	(dd)	...	...	...	★
Virginia	★	★	★	(ee)	...	...	★
Washington	...	★	★(aa)	...	...	...	★
West Virginia	★	★	★	(s)	(s)	★	★
Wisconsin	...	...	...	Before	Before	...	...
Wyoming	...	★	...	...	...	...	...
Dist. of Columbia	★	★	...	...	...	...	★
American Samoa	★	★	...	...	...	...	★
Guam	...	★	...	...	...	...	★
CNMI*	(ff)	★	...	...	...	...	★
Puerto Rico	★	★	...	Before	...	...	★
U.S. Virgin Islands	(gg)	★	...	(bb)	...	...	★

See footnotes at end of table

TABLE 8.7
State Employees: Paid Holidays** (continued)

**Holidays in addition to any other authorized paid personal leave granted state employees.

Source: The Council of State Governments' survey of state personnel office Web sites, 2019.

Note: In some states, the governor may proclaim additional holidays or select from a number of holidays for observance by state employees. In some states, the list of paid holidays is determined by the personnel department at the beginning of each year; as a result, the number of holidays may change from year to year. Number of paid holidays may also vary across some employee classifications. If a holiday falls on a weekend, generally employees get the day preceding or following.

*Commonwealth of Northern Mariana Islands

Key:

★–Paid holiday granted.

…–Paid holiday not granted.

(a) New Year's Day, Independence Day, Labor Day), Thanksgiving Day and Christmas Day.

(b) Third Monday in January.

(c) Generally, third Monday in February; Washington's Birthday or President's Day. In some states the holiday is called President's Day or Washington-Lincoln Day. Most frequently, this day recognizes George Washington and Abraham Lincoln.

(d) Last Monday in May in all states indicated, except Vermont where holiday is observed on May 30. Generally, states follow the federal government's observance (last Monday in May) rather than the traditional Memorial Day (May 30).

(e) Second Monday in October.

(f) General election day only, unless otherwise indicated. In Indiana, primary and general election days.

(g) Additional holidays:

Alabama–Mardi Gras Day (Baldwin and Mobile counties only)(day before Ash Wednesday), Robert E. Lee's Birthday celebrated with MLK day, Confederate Memorial Day (fourth Monday in April), Jefferson Davis' Birthday (first Monday in June).

Alaska–Seward's Day (last Monday in March), Alaska Day (October 18).

Arkansas–Employee is granted one holiday to observe his or her birthday.

California–César Chávez Day (March 31), one personal holiday (employees become eligible for a personal holiday once they have completed six months of state employment).

Colorado–State employees may have César Chávez Day (March 31) off in lieu of any other legal holiday that occurs on a weekday in the same fiscal year.

Delaware–Eligible employees are granted two floating holidays per calendar year, Return Day after 12:00 noon (second day after a general election) in Sussex County only.

Florida–Full-time employees are entitled to one personal holiday each year. Personal holidays are credited to eligible employees on July 1, and must be taken by the employee by June 30 of each year.

Georgia–Formerly known as Confederate Memorial Day, renamed to State Day in 2016 (fourth Monday in April).

Hawaii–Prince Jonah Kuhio Kalanianaole Day (March 26), King Kamehameha I Day (June 11), Statehood Day (third Friday in August).

Iowa–State employees are granted two days of paid leave each year to be added to the vacation allowance and accrued under certain provisions.

Kansas–One discretionary holiday that can be used any time during the calendar year.

Louisiana–Mardi Gras Day (Tuesday before Ash Wednesday), Inauguration Day (every four years, in Baton Rouge only).

Maine–Patriot's Day (third Monday in April).

Massachusetts–Patriot's Day (third Monday in April), Evacuation Day (March 17–Suffolk County only), Bunker Hill Day (June 17–Suffolk County only).

Minnesota–Regular and temporary employees with at least six months of employment shall receive two floating holidays each payroll year.

Mississippi–Confederate Memorial Day (last Monday in April).

Missouri–Harry Truman's Birthday (May 8).

Nebraska–Arbor Day (last Friday in April).

Nevada–Nevada Day (last Friday in October).

New Hampshire–Employees who are employed on a full-time basis are eligible for two floating holidays.

Rhode Island–Victory Day (second Monday in August).

South Carolina–Confederate Memorial Day (May 10).

Texas–The following are partial staffing holidays: Confederate Heroes Day (January 19), Texas Independence Day (March 2), San Jacinto Day (April 21), Emancipation Day in Texas (June 19) and Lyndon Baines Johnson Day (August 27). Staff offices are scheduled to be open on partial staffing holidays and optional holidays. An employee may observe optional holidays in lieu of any partial staffing holiday on which state offices are required to be open to conduct public business. Optional holidays include Cesar Chavez Day (March 31), Good Friday, Rosh Hashanah and Yom Kippur.

Utah–Pioneer Day (July 24).

Vermont–Town Meeting Day (first Tuesday in March), Bennington Battle Day (August 16).

Virginia–Lee-Jackson Day (Friday preceding the third Monday in January). State offices will close at noon on the day before Thanksgiving.

Washington–One additional paid holiday per calendar year.

West Virginia–West Virginia Day (June 20).

District of Columbia–Presidential Inauguration Day (January 20) and District of Columbia Emancipation Day (April 16).

American Samoa–American Samoa Flag Day (April 17), Manu'a Cession Day (July 16).

Guam–Guam History & Chamorro Heritage Day (March 6), Liberation Day (July 21), All Souls' Day (November 2) and Our Lady of Camarin Day (December 8).

Commonwealth of Northern Mariana Islands–Commonwealth Covenant Day (March 25), Citizenship Day (November 4) and Constitution Day (December 8).

Puerto Rico–Three Kings Day (January 6), Birthday of Eugenio Maria de Hostos (second Monday in January), Birthday of Luis Muñoz Marin (February 18), Emancipation Day (March 22), Birthday of Jose de Diego (third Monday in April), Birthday of Don Luis Munoz Rivera (third Monday in July), Constitution or Puerto Rico Day

TABLE 8.7
State Employees: Paid Holidays** (continued)

(July 25), Birthday of Dr. José Celso Barbosa (July 27), Discovery of Puerto Rico (November 19).

U.S. Virgin Islands–Three Kings Day (January 6), Holy Thursday (Thursday before Good Friday), Transfer Day (March 31), Easter Monday (Monday after Easter), Emancipation Day (July 3), Liberty Day (November 1).

(h) In Alabama, Arkansas and Mississippi, also celebrated as Robert E. Lee's Birthday. In Idaho, also celebrated as Idaho Human Rights Day. In New Hampshire, also celebrated as Civil Rights Day.

(i) In Alabama, celebrated as George Washington's and Thomas Jefferson's Birthday. In Arkansas, celebrated as George Washington's Birthday and Daisy Gatson Bates Day.

(j) The state has designated Lincoln's birthday as a floating holiday in 2019 for state employees in certain bargaining units.

(k) At the discretion of the governor.

(l) In Georgia, Robert E. Lee's Birthday is observed on the day after Thanksgiving, and Washington's Birthday is observed the day before Christmas.

(m) In Indiana, Lincoln's Birthday is observed on the day after Thanksgiving, and Washington's Birthday is observed the day before Christmas.

(n) In Kentucky, half day.

(o) In New Mexico, President's Day is observed on the day after Thanksgiving.

(p) In North Dakota, state offices close at noon on Christmas Eve when it falls on Monday through Thursday.

(q) In Tennessee, at the governor's discretion Columbus Day may be observed the day after Thanksgiving.

(r) In Texas, Good Friday is an optional holiday. An employee is entitled to observe optional holidays in lieu of any partial staffing holiday in which state offices are required to be open to conduct public business.

(s) Half day on Christmas Eve and New Year's Eve (closes at noon).

(t) Tuesday after first Monday in November of presidential election years.

(u) General Election Day is a state holiday the first Tuesday after the first Monday in November in even-numbered years.

(v) Also celebrated as Jefferson Davis' Birthday.

(w) Employees are allowed up to two hours paid administrative leave to vote.

(x) Three days when Christmas Day falls on Tuesday, Wednesday or Thursday; two days when Christmas Day falls on Friday or Monday.

(y) Celebrated as Native Americans Day.

(z) First Tuesday in November, even numbered years.

(aa) Observed as American Indian Heritage Day in Maryland and Native American Heritage Day in Washington.

(bb) Observed as Boxing Day.

(cc) Observed as Family Day.

(dd) Most state offices will be closed the day after Thanksgiving.

(ee) At the discretion of the governor. A paid holiday will be granted on the day before Christmas for 2019.

(ff) Celebrated as Commonwealth Cultural Day.

(gg) Also celebrated as V.I./P.R. Friendship Day.

TABLE 8.8
Women Governors Throughout History

Name (Party-State)	Dates served	Special circumstances
Nellie Tayloe Ross (D-WY)	1925-1927	Won special election to replace deceased husband
Miriam "Ma" Ferguson (D-TX)	1925-1927, 1933-1935	Inaugurated 15 days after Ross; elected as surrogate for husband who could not succeed himself
Lurleen Wallace (D-AL)	1967-1968	Elected as surrogate for husband who could not succeed himself
Ella Grasso (D-CT)	1975-1980	First woman elected governor in her own right; resigned for health reasons
Dixy Lee Ray (D-WA)	1977-1981	
Vesta Roy (R-NH)	1982-1983	Elected to state senate and chosen as senate president; served as governor for seven days when incumbent died
Martha Layne Collins (D-KY)	1984-1987	
Madeleine Kunin (D-VT)	1985-1991	First woman to serve three terms as governor
Kay Orr (R-NE)	1987-1991	First Republican woman governor and first woman to defeat another woman in a gubernatorial race
Rose Mofford (D-AZ)	1988-1991	Elected as secretary of state, succeeded governor who was impeached and convicted
Joan Finney (D-KS)	1991-1995	First woman to defeat an incumbent governor
Ann Richards (D-TX)	1991-1995	
Barbara Roberts (D-OR)	1991-1995	
Christine Todd Whitman (R-NJ)	1994-2001	Resigned to take presidential appointment as commissioner of the Environmental Protection Agency
Jeanne Shaheen (D-NH)	1997-2003	
Jane Dee Hull (R-AZ)	1997-2003	Elected as secretary of state, succeeded governor who resigned; later elected to a full term
Nancy Hollister (R-OH)	1998-1999	Elected lieutenant governor; served as governor for 11 days when predecessor took U.S. Senate seat and successor had not yet been sworn in
Jane Swift (R-MA)	2001-2003	Elected as lieutenant governor, succeeded governor who resigned for an ambassadorial appointment
Judy Martz (R-MT)	2001-2005	
Olene Walker (R-UT)	2003-2005	Elected as lieutenant governor, succeeded governor who resigned to take a federal appointment
Ruth Ann Minner (D-DE)	2001-2009	
Jennifer M. Granholm (D-MI)	2003-2011	
Linda Lingle (R-HI)	2003-2011	
Janet Napolitano (D-AZ)	2003-2009	First woman to succeed another woman as governor; resigned to become U. S. Secretary of Homeland Security
Kathleen Sebelius (D-KS)	2003-2009	Father was governor of Ohio; resigned to become U.S. Secretary of Health and Human Services
Kathleen Blanco (D-LA)	2004-2008	
M. Jodi Rell (R-CT)	2004-2011	Elected as lieutenant governor, succeeded governor who resigned
Christine Gregoire (D-WA)	2005-2013	
Sarah Palin (R-AK)	2007-2009	Resigned
Beverly Perdue (D-NC)	2009-2013	
Jan Brewer (R-AZ)	2009-2015	Elected as secretary of state, succeeded governor who resigned
Nikki Haley (R-SC)	2011-2017	First Asian (Indian) American woman to be elected governor; resigned to become U.S. Ambassador to the United Nations
Maggie Hassan (D-NH)	2013-2017	
Mary Fallin (R-OK)	2011-present	
Susana Martinez (R-NM)	2011-present	First Latina to be elected governor
Gina Raimondo (D-RI)	2015-present	
Kate Brown (D-OR)	2015-present	Elected as secretary of state, succeeded governor who resigned
Kay Ivey (R-AL)	2017-present	Elected as lieutenant governor, succeeded governor who resigned
Kim Reynolds (R-IA)	2017-present	Elected as lieutenant governor, succeeded governor who resigned
Laura Kelly (D-KS)	2019-present	
Michelle Lujan Grisham (D-NM)	2019-present	
Janet Mills (D-ME)	2019-present	
Kristi Noem (R-SD)	2019-present	
Gretchen Whitmer (D-MI)	2019-present	

Source: Center for American Women and Politics, Eagleton Institute
of Politics, Rutgers University.

TABLE 8.9
Women in State Legislatures: 2019

State	Senate			House			Legislature (both houses)	
	Democrats	Republicans	% Women	Democrats	Republicans	% Women	% Women	State rank (a)
Alabama	4	0	11.4	11	7	17.1	15.7	46
Alaska	1	5	30.0	6	11	42.5	38.3	7
Arizona	7	6	43.3	14	8	36.7	38.9	6
Arkansas	3	4	20.0	8	17	25.0	23.7	38
California	10	3	32.5	21	2	28.8	30.0	22
Colorado	12	1	37.1	26	8	52.3	47.0	2
Connecticut	8	1	25.0	29	23	34.4	32.6	16
Delaware	4	1	23.8	9	1	24.4	24.2	35
Florida	6	6	30.0	23	13	30.0	30.0	22
Georgia	13	2	26.8	42	15	31.7	30.5	20
Hawaii	7	0	28.0	14	3	33.3	31.6	18
Idaho	4	5	25.7	7	16	32.9	30.5	21
Illinois	18	2	33.9	36	8	37.3	36.2	11
Indiana	2	7	18.0	17	9	26.0	23.3	39
Iowa	6	5	22.0	24	10	34.0	30.0	22
Kansas	6	8	35.0	17	14	24.8	27.3	28
Kentucky	2	2	10.5	18	9	27.0	22.5	41
Louisiana	3	2	12.8	7	10	16.2	15.3	48
Maine	8	4	34.3	48	11	39.1	38.2	9
Maryland	13	2	31.9	50	7	40.4	38.3	7
Massachusetts	11	0	27.5	38	7	28.8 (b)	28.5	27
Michigan	8	3	28.9	25	17	38.2	35.8	12
Minnesota	10	6	23.9	35	13	35.8	31.8	17
Mississippi	4	5	17.3	8	7	12.3	13.8	50
Missouri	6	3	26.5	19	21	24.5	24.9	33
Montana	11	2	26.0	21	11	32.0	30.0	22
Nebraska (d)	---------Nonpartisan---------		26.5	----------Unicameral----------			28.6	26
Nevada	8	1	42.9	18	5	54.8	50.8	1
New Hampshire	7	3	41.7	109	26	33.8	34.2	14
New Jersey	9	1	25.0	21	6	33.8	30.8	19
New Mexico	6	2	19.0	24	7	44.3	34.8	13
New York	14	6	31.7	46	4	33.3	32.9	15
North Carolina	6	4	20.0	23	11	28.3	25.9	32
North Dakota	4	7	23.4	8	11	20.2	21.3	43
Ohio	4	4	24.2	19	8	27.3	26.5	30
Oklahoma	5	4	18.8	11	12	22.8	21.5	42
Oregon	7	2	30.0	22	6	46.7	41.1	3
Pennsylvania	6	6	24.1	29	22	25.1	24.9	33
Rhode Island	14	2	42.1	25	1	34.7	37.2	10
South Carolina	2	2	8.7	12	11	18.5	15.9	44
South Dakota	2	4	17.1	4	15	27.1	23.8	37
Tennessee	4	4	27.3 (d)	4	8	12.1	15.9	44
Texas	3	6	29.0	27	6	22.0	23.2	40
Utah	2	2	20.7	12	7	25.0	24.0	36
Vermont	10	2	33.3	41	13	40.7 (e)	39.4	5
Virginia	7	3	25.0	22	5	27.0	26.4	31
Washington	12	8	40.8	30	10	40.8	40.8	4
West Virginia	0	3	8.8	8	8	16.0	14.2	49
Wisconsin	6	2	24.2	18	10	28.3	27.3	28
Wyoming	1	5	20.0	4	4	13.3	15.6	47

Source: Center for American Women and Politics, Eagleton Institute of Politics, Rutgers University. Figures are as of February 2019.
Key:
(a) States share the same rank if their proportions of women legislators are exactly equal or round off to be equal (Alaska, Maryland; California, Florida, Iowa, Montana; Kansas, Wisconsin; Missouri, Pennsylvania; South Carolina, Tennessee).

(b) Massachusetts percentage includes one Independent.
(c) Nebraska has a unicameral legislature with nonpartisan elections.
(d) Tennessee percentage includes one Independent.
(e) Vermont percentage includes three Independents and four Progressives.

Table 8.9 | **Proportion of Women among State Legislators**

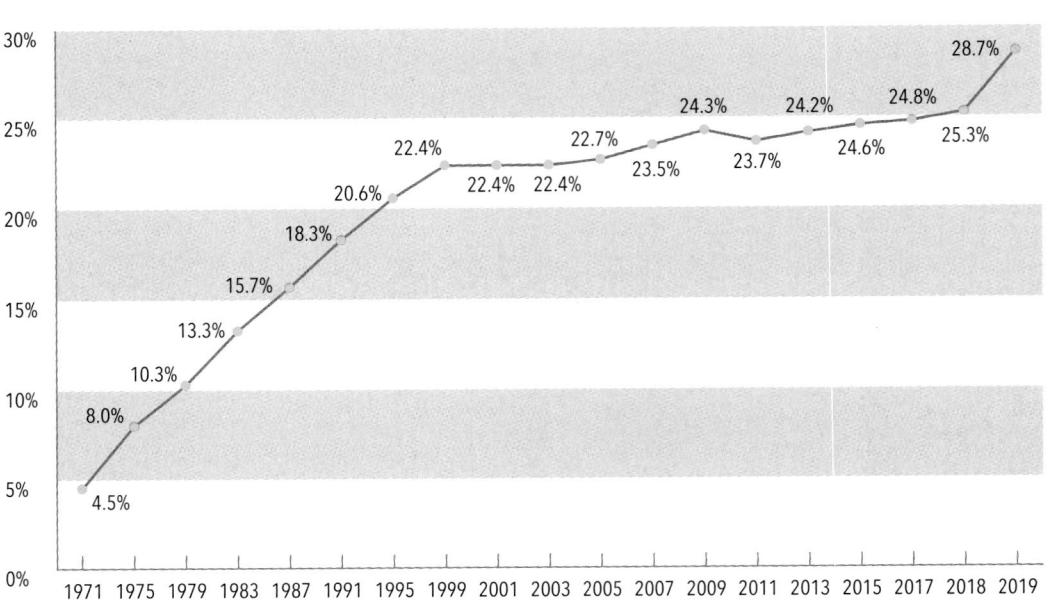

Source: Center for American Women and Politics, Eagleton Institue of Politics, Rutgers University.

TABLE 8.10
Women Statewide Elected Officials: 2019

State	Governor	Lieutenant Governor	Attorney General	Secretary of State	Treasurer
Alabama	W	★	★	★	★
Alaska	★	★	★	N.A.	N.A.
Arizona	★	N.A.	★	W	W
Arkansas	★	★	W	★	★
California	★	W	★	★	W
Colorado	★	W	★	W	★
Connecticut	★	W	★	W	★
Delaware	★	W	W	N.A.	W
Florida	★	W	W	N.A.	★
Georgia	★	★	★	★	N.A.
Hawaii	★	★	N.A.	N.A.	N.A.
Idaho	★	W	★	★	W
Illinois	★	W	★	★	★
Indiana	★	W	★	W	★
Iowa	W	★	★	★	★
Kansas	W	★	★	★	★
Kentucky	★	W	★	W	W
Louisiana	★	★	★	★	★
Maine	W	N.A.	N.A.	N.A.	N.A.
Maryland	★	★	★	N.A.	N.A.
Massachusetts	★	W	W	★	W
Michigan	W	★	W	W	N.A.
Minnesota	★	W	★	★	N.A.
Mississippi	★	★	★	★	W
Missouri	★	★	★	★	★
Montana	★	★	★	★	N.A.
Nebraska	★	★	★	★	N.A.
Nevada	★	W	★	W	★
New Hampshire	★	N.A.	N.A.	N.A.	N.A.
New Jersey	★	W	N.A.	N.A.	N.A.
New Mexico	W	★	★	W	★
New York	★	W	W	N.A.	N.A.
North Carolina	★	★	★	W	★
North Dakota	★	★	★	★	W
Ohio	★	W	★	★	★
Oklahoma	W	★	★	N.A.	★
Oregon	W	N.A.	W	★	★
Pennsylvania	★	★	★	N.A.	★
Rhode Island	W	★	★	W	★
South Carolina	★	W	★	★	★
South Dakota	W	★	★	★	★
Tennessee	★	N.A.	N.A.	N.A.	N.A.
Texas	★	★	★	N.A.	N.A.
Utah	★	★	★	N.A.	★
Vermont	★	★	★	★	W
Virginia	★	★	★	N.A.	N.A.
Washington	★	★	★	W	★
West Virginia	★	N.A.	★	★	★
Wisconsin	★	★	★	★	W
Wyoming	★	N.A.	N.A.	★	★

Source: Data for elected officials are current as of February 2019 and have been provided by the Center for American Women and Politics, Eagleton Institute of Politics, Rutgers University.

Key:
★–Denotes that this position is filled through a statewide election.
W–Denotes that this position is filled through a statewide election and is held by a woman.
N.A.–Not applicable.

Table 8.10 | Proportion of Women among Statewide Elected Officials

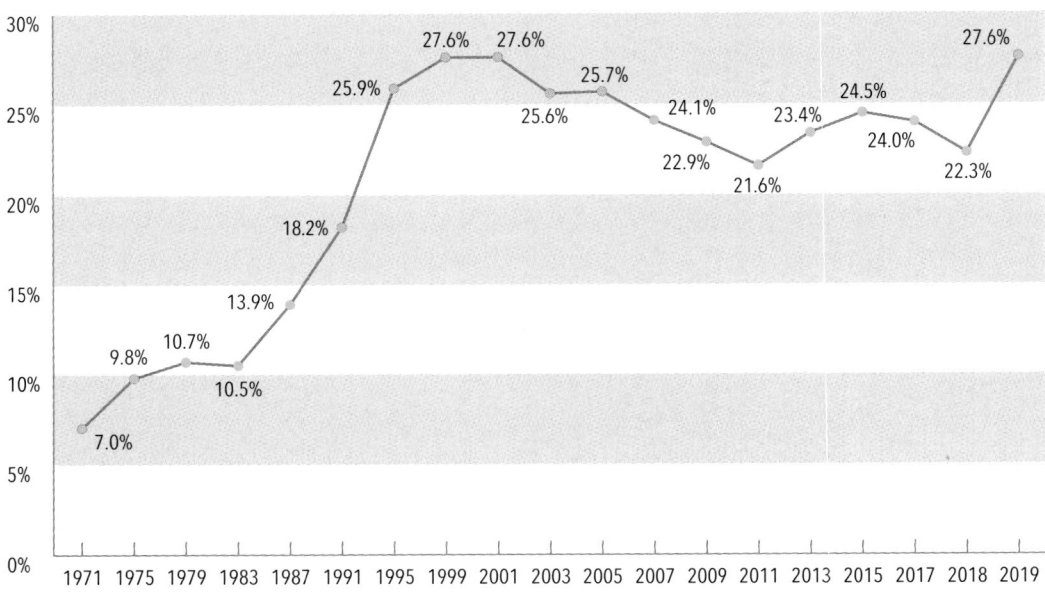

Source: Center for American Women and Politics, Eagleton Institue of Politics, Rutgers University.

CHAPTER NINE
SELECTED STATE POLICIES AND PROGRAMS

TABLE 9.1

Number of Operating Public Schools and Districts; State Enrollment, Teacher and Pupil Teacher Ratio By State or Jurisdiction: School Year 2015-16

State or jurisdiction	Number of operational schools (a)	Number of operational districts	State level Membership (b)	State level Teacher (b)	Pupil/teacher ratio
United States (c)	98,456	18,328	50,327,015	3,151,497	16.0
Alabama	1,509	180	743,789	40,766	18.2
Alaska	508	54	132,477	7,832	16.9
Arizona	2,284	692	1,109,040	47,944	23.1
Arkansas	1,088	289	492,132	35,804	13.7
California	10,303	1,163	6,226,737	263,475	23.6
Colorado	1,862	265	899,112	51,798	17.4
Connecticut	1,369	205	537,933	43,772	12.3
Delaware	223	50	134,847	8,962	15.0
Florida	4,322	76	2,792,234	182,586	15.3
Georgia	2,297	223	1,757,237	113,031	15.5
Hawaii	290	1	181,995	11,747	15.5
Idaho	744	159	292,277	15,656	18.7
Illinois	4,175	1,052	2,041,779	129,948	15.7
Indiana	1,921	418	1,046,757	57,675	18.1
Iowa	1,349	345	508,014	35,687	14.2
Kansas	1,320	317	495,884	40,035	12.4
Kentucky	1,541	186	686,598	41,902	16.4
Louisiana	1,390	179	718,711	58,469	12.3
Maine	611	267	181,613	14,857	12.2
Maryland	1,437	25	879,601	59,414	14.8
Massachusetts	1,862	408	964,026	71,969	13.4
Michigan	3,468	902	1,536,231	84,181	18.2
Minnesota	2,478	564	864,384	55,985	15.4
Mississippi	1,076	157	487,200	32,175	15.1
Missouri	2,424	567	919,234	67,635	13.6
Montana	823	490	145,319	10,412	14.0
Nebraska	1,085	284	316,014	23,308	13.6
Nevada	662	19	467,527	22,702	20.6
New Hampshire	490	299	182,425	14,770	12.4
New Jersey	2,588	694	1,408,845	114,969	12.3
New Mexico	884	158	335,694	21,722	15.5
New York	4,824	989	2,711,626	206,086	13.2
North Carolina	2,603	297	1,544,934	99,355	15.5
North Dakota	518	222	108,644	9,195	11.8
Ohio	3,619	1,103	1,716,585	101,742	16.9
Oklahoma	1,800	605	692,878	42,452	16.3
Oregon	1,242	221	576,407	29,086	19.8
Pennsylvania	3,019	784	1,717,414	120,893	14.2
Rhode Island	313	64	142,014	10,631	13.4
South Carolina	1,248	102	763,533	50,237	15.2
South Dakota	698	168	134,253	9,638	13.9
Tennessee	1,859	146	1,001,235	66,488	15.1
Texas	8,826	1,232	5,301,477	347,329	15.3
Utah	1,033	152	647,870	28,348 (d)	22.9
Vermont	314	357	87,866	8,338	10.5
Virginia	2,133	222	1,283,590	90,255	14.2
Washington	2,427	330	1,087,030	57,942	18.8
West Virginia	744	57	277,452	19,664	14.1
Wisconsin	2,255	465	867,800	58,185	14.9
Wyoming	370	60	94,717	7,653	12.4
Dist. of Columbia	228	64	84,024	6,789	12.4
Dept. of Defense (DoDEA)	173	14	74,970	N/A	N/A
Bureau of Indian Education	174	196	N/A	N/A	N/A
American Samoa	28	1	N/A	N/A	N/A
Guam	41	1	30,821	2,336	13.2
CNMI*	N/A	N/A	N/A	N/A	N/A
Puerto Rico	1,322	1	379,818	30,438	12.5
U.S. Virgin Islands	28	2	13,805	1,106	12.5

See footnotes at end of table

TABLE 9.1

Number of Operating Public Schools and Districts; State Enrollment, Teacher and Pupil Teacher Ratio By State or Jurisdiction: School Year 2015–16 (continued)

Source: U.S. Department of Education, National Center for Education Statistics, Common Core of Data (CCD), "Public Elementary/ Secondary School Universe Survey", 2015-16, Provisional Version 1a , "Local Education Agency Universe Survey", 2015-16, Provisional Version 1a, and "State Nonfiscal Survey of Public Elementary/Secondary Education", 2015-16, Provisional Version 1a.

*Commonwealth of Northern Mariana Islands

Key:

N/A–Not available.

(a) Total number of operating schools excludes schools also reported by the Bureau of Indian Education (BIE). The number of operating schools shared with the BIE include one in Arizona, one in Michigan, and eight in North Dakota.

(b) The membership and staff counts are from the state education agency (SEA) data files referenced in the source notes. Data for teachers are expressed in full-time equivalents (FTE). Counts of public school teachers and enrollment include prekindergarten through grade 13.

(c) U.S. totals include the 50 states and the District of Columbia.

(d) Utah did not report staff data in time for inclusion in this release of CCD data. The value shown here is an imputations based on the data submitted in prior years. Please see Documentation to the 2015–16 Common Core of Data (CCD) Universe Files (NCES 2017074) for a detailed description of imputations.

TABLE 9.2

Number of City, Suburban, Town, and Rural Regular Public Elementary and Secondary Schools with Membership and Percentage Distribution of Students in Membership, By State or Jurisdiction: School Year 2015-16

State or jurisdiction	Total number of schools (a)	Total number of students(b)	City Number of schools	City Percent of Students	Suburban Number of schools	Suburban Percent of Students	Town Number of schools	Town Percent of students	Rural Number of schools	Rural Percent of students
United States (c)	88,835	49,312,454	23,756	30.2	28,291	39.7	11,582	11.3	25,188	18.7
Alabama	1,315	740,713	289	23.7	232	21.9	195	14.6	599	39.7
Alaska	474	129,054	88	35.4	14	8.6	82	25.8	290	30.2
Arizona	1,910	1,090,144	895	48.6	476	31.3	243	10.3	296	9.8
Arkansas	1,052	491,390	227	28.6	120	14.2	233	23.6	472	33.6
California	8,788	6,044,665	3,592	42.7	3,592	45.8	632	5.7	972	5.8
Colorado	1,756	878,804	585	38.5	545	39.0	198	9.0	428	13.5
Connecticut	1,062	519,528	296	29.7	557	55.5	38	2.8	157	12.0
Delaware	196	124,161	36	13.3	99	52.8	31	16.7	30	17.3
Florida	3,472	2,727,105	961	25.6	1,856	58.5	217	4.4	438	11.5
Georgia	2,237	1,753,296	406	15.8	847	46.4	270	10.5	714	27.3
Hawaii	288	181,870	68	23.9	107	45.2	72	21.8	41	9.1
Idaho	635	286,447	114	23.3	119	27.8	143	23.9	258	24.8
Illinois	3,908	2,012,523	965	30.0	1,635	49.0	499	10.2	809	10.8
Indiana	1,862	1,045,085	514	30.8	394	26.9	288	14.4	664	27.9
Iowa	1,323	497,345	233	27.4	109	12.8	321	25.5	660	34.2
Kansas	1,311	488,382	249	28.3	148	17.4	321	26.3	593	28.1
Kentucky	1,221	676,793	159	16.0	224	22.1	307	25.5	531	36.5
Louisiana	1,337	714,923	367	29.5	324	29.0	231	14.2	415	27.3
Maine	581	176,396	48	12.7	66	16.6	77	17.1	390	53.6
Maryland	1,329	861,595	299	20.6	762	62.0	55	3.6	213	13.8
Massachusetts	1,793	914,148	328	17.7	1,226	72.0	39	1.4	200	8.8
Michigan	2,939	1,412,050	665	23.6	1,079	43.7	368	11.5	827	21.1
Minnesota	1,666	832,485	329	21.4	426	36.2	325	20.6	586	21.7
Mississippi	908	486,910	103	10.7	86	14.0	267	28.4	452	46.9
Missouri	2,220	913,246	378	18.5	529	34.7	388	20.3	925	26.6
Montana	817	145,240	64	25.2	11	2.0	138	36.7	604	36.1
Nebraska	1,001	316,014	211	38.8	85	14.8	190	21.0	515	25.4
Nevada	609	464,272	260	50.4	173	36.0	71	7.5	105	6.1
New Hampshire	488	181,307	49	14.8	133	36.9	71	14.1	235	34.2
New Jersey	2,374	1,337,561	232	10.4	1,884	79.7	63	2.1	195	7.8
New Mexico	834	330,429	219	34.4	83	13.6	227	27.3	305	24.7
New York	4,617	2,634,356	2,037	45.4	1,484	36.8	352	6.3	744	11.4
North Carolina	2,495	1,536,724	653	28.6	485	23.8	307	10.5	1,050	37.0
North Dakota	471	106,372	61	27.7	24	11.6	64	21.5	322	39.2
Ohio	3,479	1,708,484	751	19.1	1,288	45.3	506	13.3	934	22.3
Oklahoma	1,791	692,546	279	23.7	219	22.2	388	23.6	905	30.5
Oregon	1,207	562,870	326	34.7	254	27.0	291	23.8	336	14.5
Pennsylvania	2,921	1,692,726	569	20.8	1,344	51.3	286	9.0	722	18.8
Rhode Island	297	136,719	72	24.5	188	65.4	0	0.0	37	10.1
South Carolina	1,182	761,721	216	19.6	345	35.4	151	11.3	470	33.6
South Dakota	650	132,433	56	26.8	6	1.7	99	30.2	489	41.3
Tennessee	1,744	991,648	572	32.5	277	20.5	281	16.6	614	30.3
Texas	7,851	5,224,531	2,923	41.5	1,988	32.3	1,004	9.8	1,935	16.4
Utah	928	636,734	149	16.0	495	62.9	118	10.8	166	10.3
Vermont	298	84,355	14	7.8	17	9.4	52	27.1	215	55.7
Virginia	1,846	1,281,866	429	23.0	676	45.4	161	7.0	580	24.5
Washington	1,961	1,040,890	572	32.8	683	42.7	266	12.5	440	12.1
West Virginia	677	276,449	81	15.4	126	20.6	123	21.6	347	42.4
Wisconsin	2,145	861,518	504	29.2	445	28.1	419	19.7	777	23.0
Wyoming	358	94,717	52	25.0	6	2.0	114	44.1	186	28.9
Dist. of Columbia	212	80,914	211	100.0	0	0.0	0	0.0	0	0.0
Dept. of Defense (DoDEA)	173	74,970	22	12.5	22	11.8	11	5.5	6	3.6
Bur. of Indian Education	N/A	N/A	N/A	N/A	N/A	N/A	N/A	N/A	N/A	N/A
American Samoa	N/A	N/A	N/A	N/A	N/A	N/A	N/A	N/A	N/A	N/A
Guam	40	30,782	0	0.0	0	0.0	33	85.7	7	14.3
CNMI*	N/A	N/A	N/A	N/A	N/A	N/A	N/A	N/A	N/A	N/A
Puerto Rico	1,262	359,154	303	24.4	805	65.9	59	4.4	95	5.3
U.S. Virgin Islands	27	13,805	0	0.0	0	0.0	27	100.0	0	0.0

See footnotes at end of table

TABLE 9.2
Number of City, Suburban, Town, and Rural Regular Public Elementary and Secondary Schools with Membership and Percentage Distribution of Students in Membership, By State or Jurisdiction: School Year 2015–16 (continued)

Source: U.S. Department of Education, National Center for Education Statistics (NCES), Common Core of Data (CCD), "Public Elementary/Secondary School Universe Survey", Provisional Version 1a, and the NCES Education Demographic and Geographic Estimates (EDGE), "Public Elementary/Secondary School Universe - Geographic Data," 2015–16.

Note: Detail may not sum to total due to rounding. The locales of "city", "suburban", "town", and "rural" are a collapse of the 12 category, urban-centric locale code.

*Commonwealth of Northern Mariana Islands

Key:
N.A.–Not applicable
N/A–Not available

(a) The total number of schools is limited to regular, operational schools with membership and excludes schools also reported by the Bureau of Indian Education (BIE). The number of operating schools shared with the BIE include one in Arizona, one in Michigan, and eight in North Dakota.

(b) Total number of students is the count of students enrolled on October 1 of the reported school year.

(c) U.S. totals include the 50 states and the District of Columbia.

TABLE 9.3

Number of Operating Public Elementary and Secondary Schools, by School Type, Charter, Magnet, Title I, and Title I Schoolwide Status, and State or Jurisdiction: School Year 2015-16

State or other jurisdiction	Total number of operating schools (a)	School type							
		Regular	Special education	Vocational education	Alternative education	Charter	Magnet	Title I (b)	Title I schoolwide (b)
Reporting states (c)	98,456	89,644	2,011	1,419	5,382	6,857	3,237	68,614	53,669
Alabama	1,509	1,326	34	68	81	0	40	‡	‡
Alaska	508	478	3	3	24	28	32	358	337
Arizona	2,284	1,963	20	242	59	552	0	1,724	1,306
Arkansas	1,088	1,052	4	26	6	65	30	988	924
California	10,303	8,936	151	74	1,142	1,224	504	7,339	5,640
Colorado	1,862	1,756	6	6	94	226	28	690	539
Connecticut	1,369	1,062	168	17	122	24	85	608	270
Delaware	223	198	13	6	6	28	3	151	151
Florida	4,322	3,716	174	53	379	653	536	3,109	2,950
Georgia	2,297	2,237	19	0	41	82	80	1,630	1,548
Hawaii	290	288	1	0	1	34	N.A.	192	192
Idaho	744	635	18	14	77	54	19	576	504
Illinois	4,175	3,929	108	0	138	64	105	3,312	2,095
Indiana	1,921	1,863	22	28	8	88	30	1,510	1,219
Iowa	1,349	1,324	3	0	22	3	0	923	512
Kansas	1,320	1,315	4	0	1	10	32	1,137	873
Kentucky	1,541	1,230	8	121	182	N.A.	66	1,119	1,084
Louisiana	1,390	1,341	32	12	5	138	36	1,239	1,212
Maine	611	582	2	27	0	7	1	527	392
Maryland	1,437	1,329	37	27	44	50	97	800	704
Massachusetts	1,862	1,796	7	38	21	81	‡	1,061	596
Michigan	3,468	2,962	187	4	315	370	386	2,302	1,523
Minnesota	2,478	1,686	292	9	491	216	80	965	454
Mississippi	1,076	915	2	91	68	2	17	738	736
Missouri	2,424	2,247	53	63	61	70	29	1,887	1,569
Montana	823	817	2	0	4	N.A.	0	720	436
Nebraska	1,085	1,009	25	0	51	N.A.	N.A.	454	345
Nevada	662	610	14	0	38	47	44	349	347
New Hampshire	490	490	0	0	0	31	1	434	164
New Jersey	2,588	2,384	64	56	84	89	0	1,764	553
New Mexico	884	846	6	0	32	99	N.A.	788	767
New York	4,824	4,618	131	21	54	256	‡	3,578	2,937
North Carolina	2,603	2,498	24	7	74	158	123	2,112	1,987
North Dakota	518	474	31	13	0	N.A.	N.A.	259	109
Ohio	3,619	3,495	51	73	0	373	N/A	2,887	2,267
Oklahoma	1,800	1,791	4	0	5	45	N.A.	1,602	1,112
Oregon	1,242	1,209	1	0	32	126	N.A.	572	486
Pennsylvania	3,019	2,925	4	84	6	175	50	2,417	1,707
Rhode Island	313	297	1	10	5	29	N.A.	241	154
South Carolina	1,248	1,185	9	42	12	68	111	587	587
South Dakota	698	651	12	3	32	0	N.A.	588	329
Tennessee	1,859	1,806	16	15	22	100	126	1,575	1,516
Texas	8,826	7,872	14	0	940	702	258	7,080	6,770
Utah	1,033	935	64	6	28	117	22	321	250
Vermont	314	298	0	15	1	N.A.	2	226	200
Virginia	2,133	1,864	53	89	127	7	140	737	584
Washington	2,427	1,998	96	20	313	9	N/A	1,535	1,283
West Virginia	744	682	3	30	29	N.A.	0	350	348
Wisconsin	2,255	2,147	12	6	90	242	8	2,205	833
Wyoming	370	361	3	0	6	0	0	162	87
Dist. of Columbia	228	216	3	0	9	115	6	186	181
Dept. of Defense (DoDEA)	173	173	0	0	0	N.A.	0	N.A.	N.A.
Bur. of Indian Education	174	174	0	0	0	N.A.	0	N/A	N/A
American Samoa	28	27	0	1	0	0	N/A	N/A	N/A
Guam	41	40	0	0	1	N.A.	N.A.	0	N.A.
CNMI*	N/A	N/A	N/A	N/A	N/A	N/A	N/A	N/A	N/A
Puerto Rico	1,322	1,262	18	32	10	N.A.	N.A.	1,303	1,235
U.S. Virgin Islands	28	27	0	1	0	N.A.	1	N.A.	N.A.

See footnotes at end of table

TABLE 9.3
Number of Operating Public Elementary and Secondary Schools, by School Type, Charter, Magnet, Title I, and Title I Schoolwide Status, and State or Jurisdiction: School Year 2015–16 (continued)

Source: U.S. Department of Education, National Center for Education Statistics, Common Core of Data (CCD), "Public Elementary/Secondary School Universe Survey," 2015-16, Provisional Version 1a.
*Commonwealth of Northern Mariana Islands
Note: Every school is assigned a school type based on its instructional emphasis; numbers and types of schools may differ from those published by states. A school may also be included under the Charter, Magnet, and/or Title I statuses, which are independent of one another and of school type.

Key:
N/A–Not available
N.A.–Not applicable. Some states/jurisdictions do not have charter school authorization and some states/jurisdictions do not designate magnet schools.
‡–Reporting standards not met. Data missing for more than 80 percent of schools in the state or jurisdiction.

(a) Total number of operating schools excludes schools also reported by the Bureau of Indian Education (BIE). The number of operating schools shared with the BIE include one in Arizona, one in Michigan, and eight in North Dakota.
(b) Schools eligible for Title I schoolwide programs are also included in the count of all Title I eligible schools. A Title I eligible school is one in which the percentage of children from low-income families is at least 35 percent of children from low-income families served by the LEA as a whole. A schoolwide Title I eligible school has a percentage of low-income students that is at least 40 percent.
(c) A reporting states total is shown if data for any item in the table were not available for some, but not more than 15 percent, of all schools in the United States.

TABLE 9.4
**Percentage of High School Dropouts Among Noninstitutionalized and Institutionalized Persons
16 Through 24 Years Old (Status Dropout Rate), By Race/Ethnicity and State: 2016**

State or other jurisdiction	Total	White	Black	Hispanic	Asian	Pacific Islander	American Indian/ Alaska Native	Two or more races
United States	5.8	4.5	7.0	9.1	2.0	6.9	11.0	4.8
Alabama	6.9	6.7	6.5	12.4	‡	‡	‡	3.2 (!)
Alaska	5.6	1.9 (!)	‡	‡	‡	‡	19.0	10.1 (!)
Arizona	7.6	5.0	8.9	10.6	‡	‡	11.1	3.3 (!)
Arkansas	7.2	5.8	10.7	9.1	‡	‡	‡	8.2 (!)
California	5.3	3.0	5.7	7.7	1.6	‡	3.6 (!)	3.6
Colorado	6.4	3.5	9.0	12.5	2.5	‡	12.1 (!)	6.1
Connecticut	3.1	1.9	2.5 (!)	8.1	‡	‡	‡	‡
Delaware	7.1	3.4	10.3	18.0 (!)	‡	‡	‡	‡
Florida	6.6	5.4	7.1	8.7	2.2	‡	‡	5.2
Georgia	6.9	5.9	7.3	12.0	2.8	‡	‡	5.6
Hawaii	3.6	3.9 (!)	‡	5.0 (!)	1.2	9.0	‡	3.4 (!)
Idaho	4.1	3.6	‡	7.2 (!)	‡	‡	‡	‡
Illinois	4.8	3.2	7.4	7.5	2.1	‡	‡	5.4 (!)
Indiana	7.0	6.2	8.2	13.6	‡	‡	‡	5.0 (!)
Iowa	4.5	4.0	12.2 (!)	6.6	‡	‡	‡	‡
Kansas	5.3	4.6	5.2 (!)	10.4	‡	‡	‡	4.0 (!)
Kentucky	6.6	6.4	7.2	12.4	‡	‡	‡	‡
Louisiana	8.7	6.6	11.9	7.5	‡	‡	‡	7.0
Maine	4.1	4.2	‡	‡	‡	‡	‡	‡
Maryland	5.2	3.4	5.2	14.4	‡	‡	‡	4.8 (!)
Massachusetts	3.8	2.3	6.9	10.0	1.4 (!)	‡	‡	2.1 (!)
Michigan	6.1	5.6	9.0	7.3	1.1 (!)	‡	9.7 (!)	6.6
Minnesota	4.3	3.5	5.9 (!)	10.5	‡	‡	17.6 (!)	6.8 (!)
Mississippi	6.2	5.6	6.5	9.0 (!)	‡	‡	‡	‡
Missouri	5.8	4.8	7.9	11.9	‡	‡	‡	7.3 (!)
Montana	5.2	5.0	‡	‡	‡	‡	11.3 (!)	‡
Nebraska	5.1	3.6	12.4 (!)	13.1	‡	‡	‡	‡
Nevada	8.2	6.1	9.5	11.9	1.8 (!)	‡	‡	3.1 (!)
New Hampshire	3.9	3.5	‡	‡	‡	‡	‡	‡
New Jersey	3.7	2.1	4.9	7.3	1.4 (!)	‡	‡	2.5 (!)
New Mexico	8.2	5.4	‡	9.3	‡	‡	10.7	‡
New York	5.5	3.7	7.7	9.5	2.1	‡	‡	4.5
North Carolina	6.0	5.3	5.7	10.7	2.3 (!)	‡	11.1	5.3
North Dakota	2.7	2.2 (!)	‡	‡	‡	‡	‡	‡
Ohio	6.2	5.3	9.7	9.3	‡	‡	‡	9.1
Oklahoma	7.9	5.8	14.8	10.3	‡	‡	12.5	7.4
Oregon	5.5	5.2	‡	7.6	‡	‡	16.5 (!)	4.4 (!)
Pennsylvania	5.3	5.0	4.8	10.7	2.4 (!)	‡	‡	3.2 (!)
Rhode Island	4.1	2.6	‡	8.5	‡	‡	‡	‡
South Carolina	5.9	5.7	5.9	8.9	‡	‡	‡	6.1 (!)
South Dakota	5.1	3.1	‡	‡	‡	‡	22.0	‡
Tennessee	4.8	4.2	6.2	9.5	‡	‡	‡	‡
Texas	6.7	4.4	6.0	9.2	2.6	‡	5.3 (!)	2.1
Utah	4.7	3.7	‡	9.9	‡	‡	13.8 (!)	3.9 (!)
Vermont	4.5	4.8	‡	‡	‡	‡	‡	‡
Virginia	3.9	2.8	4.3	9.9	3.1 (!)	‡	‡	1.7 (!)
Washington	7.5	5.8	10.5	13.2	4.1	12.2 (!)	11.7	9.4
West Virginia	6.6	6.6	9.5 (!)	‡	‡	‡	‡	‡
Wisconsin	4.7	3.8	9.3	9.3	2.7 (!)	‡	‡	‡
Wyoming	5.2	5.2	‡	‡	‡	‡	‡	‡
Dist. of Columbia	3.5	‡	6.0	6.4 (!)	‡	‡	‡	‡

See footnotes at end of table

TABLE 9.4

Percentage of High School Dropouts Among Noninstitutionalized and Institutionalized Persons
16 Through 24 Years Old (Status Dropout Rate), By Race/Ethnicity and State: 2016 (continued)

Source: U.S. Department of Commerce, Census Bureau, American Community Survey (ACS), 1-year sample, 2016. (This table was prepared October 2017.)

Note: "Status" dropouts are 16- to 24-year-olds who are not enrolled in school and who have not completed a high school program, regardless of when they left school. People who have received GED credentials are counted as high school completers. Data are based on sample surveys of the entire population in the given age range residing within the United States, including both noninstitutionalized persons (e.g., those living in households, college housing, or military housing located within the United States) and institutionalized persons (e.g., those living in prisons, nursing facilities, or other healthcare facilities). Totals include other racial/ethnic groups not separately shown. Race categories exclude persons of Hispanic ethnicity.

Key:

‡–Reporting standards not met. Either there are too few cases for a reliable estimate or the coefficient of variation (CV) is 50 percent or greater.

!–Interpret data with caution. The coefficient of variation (CV) for this estimate is between 30 and 50 percent.

TABLE 9.4a
Recent High School Completers and Their Enrollment in College, By Sex and Level of Institution: 1960 Through 2016

| | Number of high school completers (a) (in thousands) | | | Percent of recent high school completers (a) enrolled in college (b) | | | | | | | | |
| | | | | Total | | | Males | | | Females | | |
Year	Total	Males	Females	Total	2-year college	4-year college or university	Total	2-year college	4-year college or university	Total	2-year college	4-year college or university
1960	1,679	756	923	45.1	N/A	N/A	54.0	N/A	N/A	37.9	N/A	N/A
1961	1,763	790	973	48.0	N/A	N/A	56.3	N/A	N/A	41.3	N/A	N/A
1962	1,838	872	966	49.0	N/A	N/A	55.0	N/A	N/A	43.5	N/A	N/A
1963	1,741	794	947	45.0	N/A	N/A	52.3	N/A	N/A	39.0	N/A	N/A
1964	2,145	997	1,148	48.3	N/A	N/A	57.2	N/A	N/A	40.7	N/A	N/A
1965	2,659	1,254	1,405	50.9	N/A	N/A	57.3	N/A	N/A	45.3	N/A	N/A
1966	2,612	1,207	1,405	50.1	N/A	N/A	58.7	N/A	N/A	42.7	N/A	N/A
1967	2,525	1,142	1,383	51.9	N/A	N/A	57.6	N/A	N/A	47.2	N/A	N/A
1968	2,606	1,184	1,422	55.4	N/A	N/A	63.2	N/A	N/A	48.9	N/A	N/A
1969	2,842	1,352	1,490	53.3	N/A	N/A	60.1	N/A	N/A	47.2	N/A	N/A
1970	2,758	1,343	1,415	51.7	N/A	N/A	55.2	N/A	N/A	48.5	N/A	N/A
1971	2,875	1,371	1,504	53.5	N/A	N/A	57.6	N/A	N/A	49.8	N/A	N/A
1972	2,964	1,423	1,542	49.2	N/A	N/A	52.7	N/A	N/A	46.0	N/A	N/A
1973	3,058	1,460	1,599	46.6	14.9	31.6	50.0	14.6	35.4	43.4	15.2	28.2
1974	3,101	1,491	1,611	47.6	15.2	32.4	49.4	16.6	32.8	45.9	13.9	32.0
1975	3,185	1,513	1,672	50.7	18.2	32.6	52.6	19.0	33.6	49.0	17.4	31.6
1976	2,986	1,451	1,535	48.8	15.6	33.3	47.2	14.5	32.7	50.3	16.6	33.8
1977	3,141	1,483	1,659	50.6	17.5	33.1	52.1	17.2	35.0	49.3	17.8	31.5
1978	3,163	1,485	1,677	50.1	17.0	33.1	51.1	15.6	35.5	49.3	18.3	31.0
1979	3,160	1,475	1,685	49.3	17.5	31.8	50.4	16.9	33.5	48.4	18.1	30.3
1980	3,088	1,498	1,589	49.3	19.4	29.9	46.7	17.1	29.7	51.8	21.6	30.2
1981	3,056	1,491	1,565	53.9	20.5	33.5	54.8	20.9	33.9	53.1	20.1	33.0
1982	3,100	1,509	1,592	50.6	19.1	31.5	49.1	17.5	31.6	52.0	20.6	31.4
1983	2,963	1,389	1,573	52.7	19.2	33.5	51.9	20.2	31.7	53.4	18.4	35.1
1984	3,012	1,429	1,584	55.2	19.4	35.8	56.0	17.7	38.4	54.5	21.0	33.5
1985	2,668	1,287	1,381	57.7	19.6	38.1	58.6	19.9	38.8	56.8	19.3	37.5
1986	2,786	1,332	1,454	53.8	19.2	34.5	55.8	21.3	34.5	51.9	17.3	34.6
1987	2,647	1,278	1,369	56.8	18.9	37.9	58.3	17.3	41.0	55.3	20.3	35.0
1988	2,673	1,334	1,339	58.9	21.9	37.1	57.1	21.3	35.8	60.7	22.4	38.3
1989	2,450	1,204	1,246	59.6	20.7	38.9	57.6	18.3	39.3	61.6	23.1	38.5
1990	2,362	1,173	1,189	60.1	20.1	40.0	58.0	19.6	38.4	62.2	20.6	41.6
1991	2,276	1,140	1,136	62.5	24.9	37.7	57.9	22.9	35.0	67.1	26.8	40.3
1992	2,397	1,216	1,180	61.9	23.0	38.9	60.0	22.1	37.8	63.8	23.9	40.0
1993	2,342	1,120	1,223	62.6	22.8	39.8	59.9	22.9	37.0	65.2	22.8	42.4
1994	2,517	1,244	1,273	61.9	21.0	40.9	60.6	23.0	37.5	63.2	19.1	44.1
1995	2,599	1,238	1,361	61.9	21.5	40.4	62.6	25.3	37.4	61.3	18.1	43.2
1996	2,660	1,297	1,363	65.0	23.1	41.9	60.1	21.5	38.5	69.7	24.6	45.1
1997	2,769	1,354	1,415	67.0	22.8	44.3	63.6	21.4	42.2	70.3	24.1	46.2
1998	2,810	1,452	1,358	65.6	24.4	41.3	62.4	24.4	38.0	69.1	24.3	44.8
1999	2,897	1,474	1,423	62.9	21.0	41.9	61.4	21.0	40.5	64.4	21.1	43.3
2000	2,756	1,251	1,505	63.3	21.4	41.9	59.9	23.1	36.8	66.2	20.0	46.2
2001	2,549	1,277	1,273	61.8	19.6	42.1	60.1	18.6	41.4	63.5	20.6	42.8
2002	2,796	1,412	1,384	65.2	21.6	43.6	62.1	20.4	41.7	68.4	22.8	45.6
2003	2,677	1,306	1,372	63.9	21.5	42.5	61.2	21.9	39.3	66.5	21.0	45.5
2004	2,752	1,327	1,425	66.7	22.4	44.2	61.4	21.8	39.6	71.5	23.1	48.5
2005	2,675	1,262	1,414	68.6	24.0	44.6	66.5	24.7	41.8	70.4	23.4	47.0
2006	2,692	1,328	1,363	66.0	24.7	41.3	65.8	24.9	40.9	66.1	24.5	41.7
2007	2,955	1,511	1,444	67.2	24.1	43.1	66.1	22.7	43.4	68.3	25.5	42.8
2008	3,151	1,640	1,511	68.6	27.7	40.9	65.9	24.9	41.0	71.6	30.6	40.9
2009	2,937	1,407	1,531	70.1	27.7	42.4	66.0	25.1	40.9	73.8	30.1	43.8
2010	3,160	1,679	1,482	68.1	26.7	41.4	62.8	28.5	34.3	74.0	24.6	49.5
2011	3,079	1,611	1,468	68.2	25.9	42.3	64.7	24.7	40.0	72.2	27.3	44.9
2012	3,203	1,622	1,581	66.2	28.8	37.5	61.3	26.9	34.4	71.3	30.7	40.6
2013	2,977	1,524	1,453	65.9	23.8	42.1	63.5	24.5	39.0	68.4	23.0	45.3
2014	2,868	1,423	1,445	68.4	24.6	43.7	64.0	21.2	42.8	72.6	28.0	44.6
2015	2,965	1,448	1,516	69.2	25.2	44.0	65.8	24.3	41.5	72.5	26.2	46.4
2016	3,137	1,517	1,620	69.8	23.7	46.0	67.5	25.3	42.2	71.9	22.3	49.6

See footnotes at end of table

TABLE 9.4a
**Recent High School Completers and Their Enrollment in College, By Sex and Level of Institution:
1960 Through 2016** (continued)

Source: American College Testing Program, unpublished tabulations, derived from statistics collected by the Census Bureau, 1960 through 1969. U.S. Department of Commerce, Census Bureau, Current Population Survey (CPS), October, 1970 through 2016. (This table was prepared July 2017.)

Note: Data are based on sample surveys of the civilian noninstitutionalized population. High school completion data in this table differ from figures appearing in other tables because of varying survey procedures and coverage. High school completers include GED recipients. Detail may not sum to totals because of rounding.

Key:
N/A–Not available.
(a) Individuals ages 16 to 24 who graduated from high school or completed a GED or other high school equivalency credential.
(b) Enrollment in college as of October of each year for individuals ages 16 to 24 who had completed high school earlier in the calendar year.

TABLE 9.5
Expenditures for Instruction in Public Elementary and Secondary Schools, by Subfunction and State or Jurisdiction: 2014–15 (In thousands of current dollars)

State or other jurisdiction	2014-15 Total	Salaries	Employee benefits	Purchased services (a)	Supplies	Tuition and other
United States	$349,453,258	$223,044,251	$88,840,559	$16,559,278	$14,060,733	$6,948,438
Alabama	3,872,177	2,486,747	964,905	144,100	257,225	19,200
Alaska	1,489,304	693,933	666,738	57,105	60,744	10,784
Arizona	4,487,506	3,040,265	916,617	297,427	199,391	33,805
Arkansas	2,701,703	1,829,292	518,679	121,267	197,297	35,168
California	39,213,957	25,433,552	8,958,204	1,959,137	2,035,673	827,392
Colorado	4,665,976	3,222,468	898,454	117,985	300,310	126,758
Connecticut	6,526,503	3,833,099	1,862,292	207,769	114,555	508,789
Delaware	1,149,485	705,383	352,172	13,330	49,110	29,490
Florida	15,420,047	9,093,724	2,711,823	2,930,569	579,077	104,853
Georgia	10,213,889	6,689,671	2,494,344	366,574	606,976	56,324
Hawaii	1,377,713	894,305	338,738	51,694	71,774	21,202
Idaho	1,198,556	820,405	288,933	43,961	43,767	1,491
Illinois	17,612,116	9,965,876	5,858,828	1,002,755	419,835	364,823
Indiana	5,735,162	3,574,920	1,859,846	101,594	190,184	8,619
Iowa	3,367,129	2,357,489	779,276	92,699	104,785	32,880
Kansas	3,077,236	2,175,821	647,283	94,674	135,740	23,719
Kentucky	3,788,481	2,597,950	995,038	59,334	121,763	14,396
Louisiana	4,488,043	2,742,976	1,331,045	135,515	225,173	53,334
Maine	1,491,376	937,483	406,804	25,823	32,386	88,881
Maryland	7,882,693	4,940,005	2,221,890	232,136	200,822	287,840
Massachusetts	10,009,583	6,415,874	2,478,063	89,398	254,192	772,055
Michigan	9,686,774	5,259,496	3,242,438	906,122	259,632	19,087
Minnesota	6,619,067	4,499,275	1,503,059	339,174	197,255	80,303
Mississippi	2,357,120	1,624,328	541,001	64,756	106,373	20,663
Missouri	5,542,173	3,826,042	1,146,422	172,822	366,253	30,634
Montana	942,042	625,968	188,777	56,859	65,515	4,923
Nebraska	2,430,511	1,588,320	574,865	128,546	118,079	20,701
Nevada	2,255,867	1,480,410	583,389	42,110	145,680	4,276
New Hampshire	1,756,353	1,060,633	472,500	47,213	36,592	139,415
New Jersey	15,639,896	9,543,271	4,256,870	601,928	478,059	759,768
New Mexico	1,890,194	1,278,415	440,845	66,080	104,541	313
New York	39,941,146	23,422,021	13,181,503	1,954,045	691,050	692,527
North Carolina	8,219,015	5,685,089	1,878,685	265,190	390,051	0
North Dakota	817,363	555,689	204,526	23,076	28,840	5,232
Ohio	11,824,870	7,488,983	2,725,876	711,778	449,802	448,431
Oklahoma	3,063,208	2,141,680	679,060	65,286	164,994	12,188
Oregon	3,480,025	2,010,753	1,128,280	122,514	178,334	40,145
Pennsylvania	15,439,796	9,105,193	4,836,293	678,116	491,423	328,771
Rhode Island	1,376,735	857,109	410,935	13,317	22,128	73,246
South Carolina	4,103,458	2,774,511	983,740	160,296	161,416	23,495
South Dakota	708,499	475,667	144,489	28,944	47,056	12,342
Tennessee	5,369,137	3,581,742	1,206,926	122,743	447,399	10,326
Texas	27,490,783	21,014,720	3,509,535	924,910	1,719,679	321,939
Utah	2,710,146	1,662,727	762,359	89,796	181,827	13,437
Vermont	1,037,584	594,644	282,120	57,925	20,459	82,435
Virginia	8,755,906	5,911,978	2,320,287	179,955	334,467	9,219
Washington	6,603,006	4,371,176	1,526,690	386,895	259,107	59,138
West Virginia	1,845,599	1,138,412	554,776	39,552	108,143	4,716
Wisconsin	5,978,996	3,812,581	1,632,340	90,694	220,874	222,507
Wyoming	898,443	578,250	241,819	32,338	42,260	3,776
Dist. of Columbia	900,908	623,929	130,180	41,453	22,667	82,679
American Samoa	30,680	20,784	4,335	940	1,005	3,616
Guam	146,165	106,308	38,700	926	230	0
CNMI*	30,646	21,544	4,447	2,872	308	1,474
Puerto Rico	1,330,000	999,279	237,820	74,461	17,972	468
U.S. Virgin Islands	94,478	63,964	25,586	2,142	2,787	0

See footnotes at end of table

TABLE 9.5

Expenditures for Instruction in Public Elementary and Secondary Schools, by Subfunction and State or Jurisdiction: 2014–15 (In thousands of current dollars) (continued)

Source: U.S. Department of Education, National Center for Education Statistics, Common Core of Data (CCD), "National Public Education Financial Survey," 2013–14 and 2014–15. (This table was prepared October 2017.)

*Commonwealth of Northern Mariana Islands

Note: Excludes expenditures for state education agencies. Detail may not sum to totals because of rounding.

Key:

(a) Includes purchased professional services of teachers or others who provide instruction for students.

TABLE 9.6

Total Expenditures for Public Elementary and Secondary Education and Other Related Programs, by Function and State or Jurisdiction: 2014-15 (In thousands of current dollars)

State or other jurisdiction	Total	Elementary/ secondary current expenditures, total	Instruction	Total	Student support (a)	Instructional staff (b)	General administration	School administration	Operation and maintenance
				Total expenditures					
				Current expenditures for elementary and secondary programs					
						Support services			
United States	$651,135,383	$575,331,825	$349,453,258	$201,692,188	$32,363,375	$26,953,637	$11,535,748	$31,792,450	$54,200,172
Alabama	7,616,860	6,806,467	3,872,177	2,449,646	408,979	289,637	183,197	422,385	644,857
Alaska	2,979,917	2,648,552	1,489,304	1,074,704	218,768	182,576	36,091	167,573	298,813
Arizona	9,672,927	8,370,884	4,487,506	3,429,604	620,897	427,327	151,555	453,075	1,028,730
Arkansas	5,482,962	4,813,321	2,701,703	1,841,202	253,504	405,500	121,203	250,517	484,217
California	75,683,277	65,953,946	39,213,957	23,820,247	3,641,156	4,025,664	637,847	4,313,320	6,779,257
Colorado	9,690,253	8,260,461	4,665,976	3,252,284	416,794	500,375	135,373	584,110	767,715
Connecticut	11,478,652	10,321,511	6,526,503	3,478,774	652,076	313,837	227,672	599,080	909,748
Delaware	2,054,363	1,860,732	1,149,485	646,552	81,052	36,203	28,598	116,983	196,623
Florida	28,033,934	25,123,548	15,420,047	8,454,101	1,098,980	1,619,748	227,364	1,389,373	2,495,767
Georgia	18,651,390	16,530,506	10,213,889	5,354,638	771,530	848,437	202,306	1,010,803	1,251,312
Hawaii	2,521,003	2,344,496	1,377,713	835,930	225,975	81,416	12,762	158,895	231,340
Idaho	2,241,635	2,015,654	1,198,556	711,215	112,319	101,749	49,087	115,641	188,743
Illinois	31,806,820	28,545,089	17,612,116	10,162,416	1,934,528	1,108,884	1,104,727	1,434,598	2,358,751
Indiana	11,452,708	9,970,350	5,735,162	3,754,660	497,924	387,180	226,029	633,437	1,149,076
Iowa	6,535,027	5,526,877	3,367,129	1,908,387	317,936	292,702	141,304	313,558	476,558
Kansas	6,341,694	5,136,532	3,077,236	1,812,005	321,454	219,512	140,983	296,473	487,495
Kentucky	7,424,343	6,583,287	3,788,481	2,376,035	313,386	365,299	157,907	385,692	593,138
Louisiana	8,971,748	7,960,448	4,488,043	3,041,507	482,232	409,862	205,076	500,736	743,309
Maine	2,680,791	2,538,313	1,491,376	941,268	169,351	136,264	83,236	135,909	257,850
Maryland	13,912,214	12,620,036	7,882,693	4,376,475	593,168	656,587	107,122	844,031	1,149,654
Massachusetts	16,586,646	15,723,617	10,009,583	5,283,798	1,141,177	714,402	245,386	678,233	1,406,337
Michigan	19,026,759	16,849,135	9,686,774	6,543,084	1,297,647	844,619	373,201	932,384	1,535,692
Minnesota	12,366,444	10,222,017	6,619,067	3,128,865	287,026	497,589	379,471	406,573	715,264
Mississippi	4,415,412	4,145,632	2,357,120	1,533,685	212,884	193,840	137,699	250,177	435,577
Missouri	10,829,315	9,390,061	5,542,173	3,404,843	426,351	425,911	335,099	549,217	955,896
Montana	1,806,322	1,601,097	942,042	585,532	106,293	60,239	52,130	87,771	160,563
Nebraska	4,348,146	3,805,871	2,430,511	1,119,073	168,602	124,010	114,879	177,476	319,475
Nevada	4,260,789	3,880,472	2,255,867	1,474,359	204,091	227,129	52,027	291,600	395,526
New Hampshire	2,937,340	2,764,233	1,756,353	938,380	209,637	86,247	96,910	153,445	235,705
New Jersey	28,107,047	25,993,208	15,639,896	9,574,610	2,661,155	839,266	529,772	1,275,869	2,586,979
New Mexico	3,854,180	3,309,622	1,890,194	1,258,330	334,466	91,761	73,674	201,469	343,060
New York	61,536,419	56,862,010	39,941,146	15,777,090	1,805,255	1,486,881	944,423	2,152,618	4,878,346
North Carolina	13,980,856	13,210,839	8,219,015	4,264,246	636,633	456,747	227,957	827,022	1,113,613
North Dakota	1,688,628	1,373,266	817,363	452,099	54,722	47,317	58,758	69,632	124,199
Ohio	23,201,835	20,231,423	11,824,870	7,734,384	1,348,398	846,987	632,309	1,159,968	1,802,842
Oklahoma	6,302,177	5,560,047	3,063,208	2,088,257	377,998	232,161	164,593	307,410	595,638
Oregon	6,820,088	5,969,321	3,480,025	2,270,157	429,146	237,083	82,210	383,243	477,279
Pennsylvania	28,546,370	25,109,991	15,439,796	8,715,690	1,359,396	844,886	768,898	1,125,163	2,398,565
Rhode Island	2,470,307	2,242,486	1,376,735	805,349	230,560	77,151	32,200	105,902	176,514
South Carolina	8,739,543	7,437,182	4,103,458	2,917,936	568,055	461,000	76,059	476,919	739,421
South Dakota	1,472,049	1,211,080	708,499	429,061	66,188	44,479	42,227	58,963	126,310
Tennessee	9,610,524	8,736,367	5,369,137	2,888,151	378,074	533,185	191,053	526,468	733,568
Texas	57,759,884	47,527,971	27,490,783	17,301,289	2,311,749	2,397,830	695,428	2,686,698	5,016,839
Utah	5,159,274	4,290,876	2,710,146	1,329,943	166,510	167,029	42,557	277,559	398,390
Vermont	1,724,283	1,638,720	1,037,584	552,644	121,758	68,629	33,264	103,576	131,039
Virginia	15,694,822	14,384,705	8,755,906	5,074,788	727,280	933,235	229,070	851,238	1,341,078
Washington	13,531,012	11,470,245	6,603,006	4,375,113	779,713	760,021	231,438	680,284	1,010,218
West Virginia	3,530,555	3,226,918	1,845,599	1,178,064	159,213	148,308	58,701	174,019	337,457
Wisconsin	11,407,269	10,054,346	5,978,996	3,700,841	494,395	521,705	284,468	504,225	942,669
Wyoming	1,929,790	1,509,532	898,443	565,486	88,272	85,163	30,762	81,886	143,998
Dist. of Columbia	2,258,775	1,668,528	900,908	705,392	78,721	90,069	139,686	109,252	129,161
American Samoa	67,466	63,693	30,680	16,188	78	6,023	780	4,394	2,797
Guam	316,501	293,713	146,165	129,513	29,227	14,663	3,300	17,902	33,808
CNMI*	68,394	65,304	30,646	26,255	6,688	5,348	3,972	3,839	3,411
Puerto Rico	3,373,394	3,247,136	1,330,000	1,508,154	330,143	271,942	122,792	140,391	383,786
U.S. Virgin Islands	160,092	158,652	94,478	54,901	13,816	5,061	6,328	8,604	6,829

See footnotes at end of table

TABLE 9.6

Total Expenditures for Public Elementary and Secondary Education and Other Related Programs, by Function and State or Jurisdiction: 2014-15 (In thousands of current dollars) (continued)

State or other jurisdiction	Total expenditures (continued)						
	Current expenditures for elementary and secondary programs (continued)						
	Support services (continued)						
	Student transportation	Other support services	Food services	Enterprise operations (c)	Current expenditures for other programs (d)	Capital outlay (e)	Interest on school debt
United States	$23,961,692	$20,885,114	$23,064,706	$1,121,673	$7,713,966	$50,610,125	$17,479,466
Alabama	348,793	151,797	484,644	0	119,901	532,055	158,438
Alaska	75,110	95,773	74,442	10,103	8,569	283,392	39,404
Arizona	366,216	381,803	452,688	1,087	78,941	985,963	237,140
Arkansas	180,402	145,858	264,826	5,590	29,843	516,484	123,315
California	1,473,279	2,949,724	2,741,143	178,599	751,167	6,416,660	2,561,504
Colorado	238,685	609,231	295,438	46,763	74,658	928,425	426,709
Connecticut	512,522	263,838	231,160	85,073	158,350	877,468	121,323
Delaware	91,322	95,771	64,696	0	52,008	119,623	22,000
Florida	973,695	649,174	1,249,401	0	566,775	1,681,662	661,949
Georgia	754,658	515,591	911,957	50,021	28,877	1,880,048	211,959
Hawaii	67,779	57,763	130,853	0	14,707	161,800	0
Idaho	93,090	50,586	105,743	140	5,400	166,757	53,825
Illinois	1,258,354	962,574	770,557	0	169,946	2,191,854	899,931
Indiana	609,809	251,205	480,528	0	155,229	1,006,597	320,532
Iowa	200,748	165,582	245,630	5,731	34,647	849,249	124,255
Kansas	211,179	134,909	247,290	0	4,506	988,606	212,049
Kentucky	391,205	169,408	402,406	16,364	75,896	579,294	185,866
Louisiana	463,999	236,294	430,226	673	44,626	855,123	111,551
Maine	127,183	31,475	105,341	328	28,487	65,528	48,464
Maryland	663,441	362,472	360,868	0	33,708	1,086,000	172,471
Massachusetts	702,807	395,456	430,236	0	65,227	568,970	228,832
Michigan	697,641	861,901	619,277	0	274,429	1,103,053	800,142
Minnesota	571,208	271,734	441,268	32,818	448,210	1,358,282	337,934
Mississippi	198,930	104,577	254,526	301	26,134	188,411	55,235
Missouri	480,483	231,886	443,044	0	232,401	887,999	318,855
Montana	76,802	41,732	71,169	2,354	10,880	173,839	20,506
Nebraska	115,170	99,461	157,910	98,376	2,075	450,868	89,332
Nevada	156,691	147,294	150,032	215	22,882	187,667	169,769
New Hampshire	122,829	33,608	69,500	0	6,434	125,488	41,185
New Jersey	1,067,007	614,564	579,948	198,754	239,236	1,253,806	620,797
New Mexico	108,548	105,353	158,836	2,262	2,927	541,463	168
New York	2,854,655	1,654,912	1,143,774	0	1,665,699	1,975,175	1,033,536
North Carolina	566,074	436,200	727,579	0	62,377	693,708	13,933
North Dakota	55,744	41,727	65,729	38,076	7,591	284,820	22,951
Ohio	977,219	966,660	670,845	1,325	430,075	1,785,331	755,007
Oklahoma	181,652	228,804	351,628	56,954	26,641	664,610	50,880
Oregon	271,383	389,812	215,786	3,352	30,335	477,494	342,940
Pennsylvania	1,269,238	949,545	849,253	105,252	602,570	1,798,799	1,035,010
Rhode Island	92,487	90,536	59,537	864	60,318	122,062	45,441
South Carolina	309,723	286,759	395,466	20,322	66,518	883,237	352,607
South Dakota	44,137	46,758	67,469	6,051	7,205	221,532	32,232
Tennessee	331,753	194,050	479,079	0	87,917	540,243	245,998
Texas	1,351,570	2,841,175	2,735,898	0	336,344	6,771,873	3,123,696
Utah	131,635	146,263	224,934	25,853	24,247	688,121	156,030
Vermont	57,106	37,273	46,877	1,615	13,970	59,389	12,204
Virginia	762,899	229,987	551,366	2,645	73,469	1,086,723	149,924
Washington	441,402	472,038	372,162	119,964	40,168	1,593,843	426,756
West Virginia	240,026	60,340	203,255	0	43,801	244,741	15,094
Wisconsin	431,632	521,747	374,399	109	315,532	868,017	169,375
Wyoming	75,506	59,899	45,052	552	6,915	410,241	3,101
Dist. of Columbia	116,268	42,235	59,038	3,190	45,200	427,737	117,311
American Samoa	826	1,291	16,825	0	1,830	1,943	0
Guam	8,987	21,627	18,036	0	0	12,834	9,954
CNMI*	1,498	1,498	8,403	0	2,273	817	0
Puerto Rico	153,083	106,018	408,983	0	73,288	52,970	0
U.S. Virgin Islands	7,244	7,018	9,125	148	1,440	0	0

See footnotes at end of table

TABLE 9.6

Total Expenditures for Public Elementary and Secondary Education and Other Related Programs, by Function and State or Jurisdiction: 2014-15 (In thousands of current dollars) (continued)

Source: U.S. Department of Education, National Center for Education Statistics, Common Core of Data (CCD), "National Public Education Financial Survey," 2014–15. (This table was prepared October 2017.)

*Commonwealth of Northern Mariana Islands

Note: Excludes expenditures for state education agencies. Detail may not sum to totals because of rounding.

Key:

(a) Includes expenditures for guidance, health, attendance, and speech pathology services.

(b) Includes expenditures for curriculum development, staff training, libraries, and media and computer centers.

(c) Includes expenditures for operations funded by sales of products or services (e.g., school bookstore or computer time). Also includes small amounts for direct program support made by state education agencies for local school districts.

(d) Includes expenditures for adult education, community colleges, private school programs funded by local and state education agencies, and community services.

(e) Includes expenditures for property and for buildings and alterations completed by school district staff or contractors.

TABLE 9.7
Total and Current Expenditures Per Pupil in Fall Enrollment in Public Elementary and Secondary Schools, By Function and State or Jurisdiction: 2014-15

State or other jurisdiction	Total (a)	Current expenditures, capital expenditures, and interest on school debt per pupil		Current expenditures					
		Total	Instruction	Total	Support services				
					Student support (b)	Instructional staff (c)	General administration	School administration	
United States	$12,796	$11,445	$6,951	$4,012	$644	$536	$229	$632	
Alabama	10,074	9,146	5,203	3,292	550	389	246	568	
Alaska	22,651	20,191	11,353	8,193	1,668	1,392	275	1,277	
Arizona	8,697	7,590	4,069	3,110	563	387	137	411	
Arkansas	11,107	9,805	5,503	3,751	516	826	247	510	
California	11,871	10,449	6,212	3,774	577	638	101	683	
Colorado	10,815	9,292	5,249	3,658	469	563	152	657	
Connecticut	20,859	19,020	12,026	6,410	1,202	578	420	1,104	
Delaware	14,938	13,882	8,576	4,823	605	270	213	873	
Florida	9,962	9,113	5,593	3,066	399	588	82	504	
Georgia	10,675	9,476	5,855	3,070	442	486	116	579	
Hawaii	13,741	12,855	7,554	4,583	1,239	446	70	871	
Idaho	7,688	6,929	4,120	2,445	386	350	169	398	
Illinois	15,443	13,935	8,598	4,961	944	541	539	700	
Indiana	10,795	9,529	5,482	3,589	476	370	216	605	
Iowa	12,864	10,938	6,663	3,777	629	579	280	621	
Kansas	12,744	10,329	6,188	3,644	646	441	284	596	
Kentucky	10,670	9,560	5,501	3,450	455	530	229	560	
Louisiana	12,454	11,106	6,261	4,243	673	572	286	699	
Maine	14,603	13,976	8,212	5,183	932	750	458	748	
Maryland	15,869	14,431	9,014	5,004	678	751	122	965	
Massachusetts	17,285	16,450	10,472	5,528	1,194	747	257	710	
Michigan	12,192	10,956	6,299	4,254	844	549	243	606	
Minnesota	13,898	11,924	7,721	3,650	335	580	443	474	
Mississippi	8,941	8,445	4,801	3,124	434	395	280	510	
Missouri	11,544	10,231	6,039	3,710	465	464	365	598	
Montana	12,422	11,078	6,518	4,051	735	417	361	607	
Nebraska	13,901	12,174	7,774	3,579	539	397	367	568	
Nevada	9,229	8,451	4,913	3,211	444	495	113	635	
New Hampshire	15,870	14,969	9,511	5,081	1,135	467	525	831	
New Jersey	19,897	18,559	11,167	6,836	1,900	599	378	911	
New Mexico	11,315	9,724	5,553	3,697	983	270	216	592	
New York	21,836	20,744	14,571	5,756	659	542	345	785	
North Carolina	8,986	8,529	5,306	2,753	411	295	147	534	
North Dakota	15,771	12,884	7,669	4,242	513	444	551	653	
Ohio	13,179	11,730	6,856	4,484	782	491	367	673	
Oklahoma	9,114	8,075	4,449	3,033	549	337	239	446	
Oregon	11,894	10,457	6,096	3,977	752	415	144	671	
Pennsylvania	16,029	14,405	8,857	5,000	780	485	441	645	
Rhode Island	16,496	15,797	9,698	5,673	1,624	543	227	746	
South Carolina	11,464	9,831	5,424	3,857	751	609	101	630	
South Dakota	11,010	9,103	5,325	3,225	498	334	317	443	
Tennessee	9,565	8,776	5,394	2,901	380	536	192	529	
Texas	10,971	9,081	5,253	3,306	442	458	133	513	
Utah	8,079	6,751	4,264	2,092	262	263	67	437	
Vermont	19,587	18,769	11,884	6,330	1,395	786	381	1,186	
Virginia	12,200	11,235	6,839	3,963	568	729	179	665	
Washington	12,565	10,684	6,150	4,075	726	708	216	634	
West Virginia	12,437	11,512	6,584	4,203	568	529	209	621	
Wisconsin	12,726	11,538	6,861	4,247	567	599	326	579	
Wyoming	20,440	16,047	9,551	6,012	938	905	327	871	
Dist. of Columbia	27,333	20,610	11,128	8,713	972	1,113	1,725	1,349	
American Samoa	N/A	N/A	N/A	N/A	N/A	N/A	N/A	N/A	
Guam	10,163	9,431	4,693	4,159	938	471	106	575	
CNMI*	N/A	N/A	N/A	N/A	N/A	N/A	N/A	N/A	
Puerto Rico	8,029	7,902	3,236	3,670	803	662	299	342	
U.S. Virgin Islands	11,141	11,141	6,634	3,855	970	355	444	604	

See footnotes at end of table

TABLE 9.7
Total and Current Expenditures Per Pupil in Fall Enrollment in Public Elementary and Secondary Schools, By Function and State or Jurisdiction: 2014-15 (continued)

State or other jurisdiction	Operation and maintenance	Student transportation	Other support services	Food services	Enterprise operations (d)	Capital outlay (e)	Interest on school debt
						Current expenditures, capital expenditures, and interest on school debt per pupil (continued)	
				Current expenditures (continued)			
	Support services (continued)						
United States	$1,078	$477	$415	$459	$22	$1,004	$348
Alabama	867	469	204	651	0	715	213
Alaska	2,278	573	730	567	77	2,160	300
Arizona	933	332	346	410	1	892	215
Arkansas	986	367	297	539	11	1,052	251
California	1,074	233	467	434	28	1,016	406
Colorado	864	268	685	332	53	1,043	480
Connecticut	1,676	944	486	426	157	1,615	224
Delaware	1,467	681	714	483	0	892	164
Florida	905	353	235	453	0	609	240
Georgia	717	433	296	523	29	1,077	122
Hawaii	1,268	372	317	717	0	886	0
Idaho	649	320	174	364	0	573	185
Illinois	1,151	614	470	376	0	1,069	439
Indiana	1,098	583	240	459	0	960	306
Iowa	943	397	328	486	11	1,680	246
Kansas	980	425	271	497	0	1,988	426
Kentucky	861	568	246	584	24	841	270
Louisiana	1,037	647	330	600	1	1,193	156
Maine	1,420	700	173	580	2	360	267
Maryland	1,315	759	414	413	0	1,241	197
Massachusetts	1,471	735	414	450	0	595	239
Michigan	999	454	560	403	0	716	520
Minnesota	834	666	317	515	38	1,580	394
Mississippi	887	405	213	518	1	383	113
Missouri	1,042	524	253	483	0	965	347
Montana	1,111	531	289	492	16	1,202	142
Nebraska	1,022	368	318	505	315	1,442	286
Nevada	861	341	321	327	0	408	370
New Hampshire	1,276	665	182	376	0	678	223
New Jersey	1,847	762	439	414	142	895	443
New Mexico	1,008	319	310	467	7	1,591	0
New York	1,780	1,041	604	417	0	715	377
North Carolina	719	365	282	470	0	448	9
North Dakota	1,165	523	391	617	357	2,671	215
Ohio	1,045	567	560	389	1	1,011	438
Oklahoma	865	264	332	511	83	965	74
Oregon	836	475	683	378	6	836	601
Pennsylvania	1,376	728	545	487	60	1,031	594
Rhode Island	1,243	652	638	419	6	379	320
South Carolina	977	409	379	523	27	1,167	466
South Dakota	949	332	351	507	45	1,665	242
Tennessee	737	333	195	481	0	542	247
Texas	959	258	543	523	0	1,293	597
Utah	627	207	230	354	41	1,082	245
Vermont	1,501	654	427	537	19	678	140
Virginia	1,047	596	180	431	2	848	117
Washington	941	411	440	347	112	1,484	397
West Virginia	1,204	856	215	725	0	871	54
Wisconsin	1,082	495	599	430	0	994	194
Wyoming	1,531	803	637	479	6	4,360	33
Dist. of Columbia	1,595	1,436	522	729	39	5,274	1,449
American Samoa	N/A	N/A	N/A	N/A	N/A	N/A	N/A
Guam	1,086	289	694	579	0	412	320
CNMI*	N/A	N/A	N/A	N/A	N/A	N/A	N/A
Puerto Rico	934	373	258	995	0	128	0
U.S. Virgin Islands	480	509	493	641	10	0	0

See footnotes at end of table

TABLE 9.7

Total and Current Expenditures Per Pupil in Fall Enrollment in Public Elementary and Secondary Schools, By Function and State or Jurisdiction: 2014-15 (continued)

Source: U.S. Department of Education, National Center for Education Statistics, Common Core of Data (CCD), "National Public Education Financial Survey," 2014-15. (This table was prepared October 2017.)

*Commonwealth of Northern Mariana Islands

Note: Excludes expenditures for state education agencies. "0" indicates none or less than $0.50. Detail may not sum to totals because of rounding.

Key:

N/A–Not available.

(a) Excludes "Other current expenditures," such as community services, private school programs, adult education, and other programs not allocable to expenditures per pupil in public schools.

(b) Includes expenditures for guidance, health, attendance, and speech pathology services.

(c) Includes expenditures for curriculum development, staff training, libraries, and media and computer centers.

(d) Includes expenditures for operations funded by sales of products or services (e.g., school bookstore or computer time).

(e) Includes expenditures for property and for buildings and alterations completed by school district staff or contractors.

TABLE 9.8
Average Undergraduate Tuition and Fees and Room and Board Rates Charged for Full-Time Students in Degree-Granting Postsecondary Institutions, by Control and Level of Institution and State or Jurisdiction: 2015-16 and 2016-17 (In current dollars)

State or other jurisdiction	In-state, 2015-16 Total	Tuition and required fees	In-state, 2016-17 Total	Tuition and required fees	Room	Board	Out-of-state tuition and required fees, 2016-17
United States	$19,204	$8,778	$19,488	$8,804	$6,017	$4,666	$24,854
Alabama	18,529	9,179	19,052	9,466	5,386	4,200	24,000
Alaska	16,719	6,880	17,370	7,210	5,830	4,330	21,431
Arizona	20,640	9,884	21,491	10,057	6,697	4,737	25,061
Arkansas	15,990	7,577	16,871	7,924	4,959	3,989	19,323
California	22,172	9,070	21,356	7,896	7,532	5,928	28,253
Colorado	20,605	9,128	20,943	9,352	5,672	5,919	28,986
Connecticut	23,380	11,110	24,174	11,726	6,715	5,733	32,836
Delaware	23,566	11,670	21,698	9,578	7,259	4,862	28,497
Florida	14,470	4,438	14,806	4,435	5,860	4,512	18,304
Georgia	17,303	7,011	17,353	7,010	6,043	4,300	21,377
Hawaii	20,121	9,263	21,016	9,712	5,756	5,547	30,929
Idaho	14,217	6,915	14,457	7,005	3,582	3,870	21,370
Illinois	24,113	13,387	24,541	13,636	5,975	4,930	28,167
Indiana	18,730	8,745	19,001	8,876	5,419	4,705	28,315
Iowa	16,748	7,879	17,604	8,361	5,236	4,007	24,912
Kansas	16,793	8,011	17,560	8,489	4,669	4,402	22,000
Kentucky	18,718	9,490	19,673	10,014	5,547	4,112	23,539
Louisiana	17,297	8,162	18,319	8,813	5,700	3,806	22,771
Maine	18,786	9,187	19,073	9,219	4,937	4,917	26,004
Maryland	20,084	8,942	20,647	9,083	6,600	4,964	22,437
Massachusetts	23,402	11,670	24,473	12,331	7,528	4,614	28,740
Michigan	21,400	11,708	21,832	11,890	4,936	5,006	36,714
Minnesota	19,275	10,701	19,727	10,883	4,772	4,072	19,088
Mississippi	16,451	7,175	16,843	7,472	5,539	3,833	19,138
Missouri	17,429	8,178	17,639	8,176	5,844	3,619	18,940
Montana	14,862	6,443	15,241	6,503	4,019	4,719	22,956
Nebraska	16,769	7,446	17,379	7,732	5,297	4,350	19,483
Nevada	15,581	5,298	17,145	5,520	5,661	5,964	20,672
New Hampshire	26,015	14,985	26,968	15,491	6,838	4,639	27,201
New Jersey	25,563	13,021	26,070	13,297	7,856	4,917	28,051
New Mexico	15,047	6,262	15,528	6,825	4,429	4,275	17,272
New York	21,505	7,647	21,750	7,709	9,099	4,942	21,454
North Carolina	16,379	6,944	16,635	7,218	5,409	4,008	23,778
North Dakota	14,864	7,208	15,388	7,376	3,205	4,806	18,288
Ohio	20,964	9,775	20,961	9,827	6,306	4,827	23,434
Oklahoma	14,689	6,680	15,754	7,219	4,579	3,957	19,174
Oregon	20,524	9,406	21,324	9,739	6,828	4,757	29,330
Pennsylvania	24,250	13,516	25,331	14,068	6,545	4,719	26,328
Rhode Island	22,722	11,321	23,135	11,386	7,352	4,397	27,815
South Carolina	21,159	11,791	21,508	12,153	5,745	3,610	29,888
South Dakota	16,124	8,273	16,054	8,301	3,724	4,029	11,845
Tennessee	17,747	8,932	18,340	9,287	4,856	4,197	24,802
Texas	17,409	8,091	17,799	8,375	4,931	4,493	23,511
Utah	13,350	6,140	13,709	6,334	3,210	4,165	19,407
Vermont	25,922	15,062	26,786	15,537	7,110	4,139	37,991
Virginia	21,900	11,669	22,567	12,126	5,907	4,534	32,250
Washington	18,687	7,782	18,053	6,903	5,886	5,264	28,128
West Virginia	16,430	6,900	17,096	7,241	5,245	4,609	20,030
Wisconsin	16,207	8,504	16,246	8,419	4,699	3,128	22,574
Wyoming	13,942	4,178	14,354	4,311	4,493	5,550	13,239
Dist. of Columbia	N.A.	5,251	N.A.	5,612	N.A.	N.A.	11,756

See footnotes at end of table

TABLE 9.8

Average Undergraduate Tuition and Fees and Room and Board Rates Charged for Full-Time Students in Degree-Granting Postsecondary Institutions, by Control and Level of Institution and State or Jurisdiction: 2015–16 and 2016–17 (In current dollars) (continued)

State or other jurisdiction	Private 4-year						Public 2-year, tuition and required fees		
	2015–16		2016–17				In-state, 2015–16	In-state, 2016–17	Out-of-state, 2016–17
	Total	Tuition and required fees	Total	Tuition and required fees	Room	Board			
United States	$39,534	$27,942	$41,468	$29,478	$6,717	$5,273	$3,038	$3,156	$7,668
Alabama	24,658	15,359	24,710	15,422	4,677	4,611	4,289	4,362	9,075
Alaska	26,388	19,956	26,132	18,876	3,623	3,632	3,340	3,820	3,820
Arizona	22,255	12,663	22,559	13,140	5,100	4,319	2,061	2,129	7,931
Arkansas	28,836	20,936	29,804	21,710	4,100	3,994	3,105	3,195	4,582
California	41,194	29,522	44,722	31,495	7,467	5,759	1,246	1,262	7,120
Colorado	33,664	22,331	34,337	22,627	6,827	4,883	3,630	3,565	10,152
Connecticut	51,587	37,679	53,198	38,975	8,110	6,113	4,039	4,189	12,528
Delaware	25,511	14,200	25,996	14,383	5,798	5,815	3,215	N.A.	N.A.
Florida	33,966	22,778	35,876	24,360	6,473	5,042	2,387	2,552	9,122
Georgia	37,471	25,754	39,118	27,220	6,618	5,279	3,181	2,895	7,958
Hawaii	27,899	15,561	28,393	15,949	5,444	6,999	2,935	3,080	8,216
Idaho	13,088	6,006	13,010	5,925	2,733	4,352	3,108	3,227	7,589
Illinois	41,344	29,638	43,382	31,298	6,986	5,097	3,692	3,749	10,748
Indiana	41,040	30,533	41,847	30,926	5,684	5,237	4,115	4,175	8,052
Iowa	34,149	25,308	35,780	26,742	4,391	4,648	4,478	4,791	6,406
Kansas	26,117	17,827	28,746	20,291	4,046	4,408	3,202	3,222	4,548
Kentucky	32,998	24,259	34,893	25,845	4,623	4,426	3,650	3,962	13,321
Louisiana	44,662	32,732	47,559	35,190	6,798	5,571	3,921	4,031	6,496
Maine	46,583	34,277	48,107	35,547	6,290	6,270	3,648	3,673	6,494
Maryland	52,020	38,352	53,775	40,209	7,767	5,798	3,810	3,983	9,170
Massachusetts	55,060	40,772	57,363	42,655	8,448	6,260	4,559	4,785	9,785
Michigan	31,058	22,067	33,498	24,058	4,543	4,897	3,181	3,423	6,474
Minnesota	38,956	29,194	40,939	30,925	5,237	4,777	5,332	5,310	6,053
Mississippi	24,048	16,450	24,698	16,949	4,036	3,713	2,642	2,830	5,176
Missouri	31,699	22,416	33,433	23,702	5,511	4,221	3,016	3,028	5,737
Montana	31,248	22,961	32,375	23,657	4,139	4,579	3,310	3,381	8,210
Nebraska	29,876	21,640	32,200	23,109	4,751	4,340	2,852	2,991	3,941
Nevada	32,293	18,818	35,053	21,423	7,295	6,335	2,805	2,910	9,555
New Hampshire	44,986	32,003	46,533	33,235	8,302	4,996	6,996	7,002	15,157
New Jersey	46,852	34,040	48,439	35,224	7,634	5,580	4,223	4,366	7,692
New Mexico	30,390	20,526	32,373	22,535	5,539	4,299	1,553	1,590	4,749
New York	50,309	36,361	51,790	37,580	8,664	5,546	4,969	5,122	8,857
North Carolina	40,546	29,307	42,312	30,701	5,993	5,618	2,391	2,470	8,481
North Dakota	20,103	13,883	20,964	14,290	2,997	3,677	4,506	4,562	9,484
Ohio	39,463	28,953	40,980	30,296	5,567	5,118	3,642	3,655	5,721
Oklahoma	32,314	23,657	33,883	24,776	4,545	4,562	3,349	3,627	8,582
Oregon	46,274	35,031	48,703	37,088	6,048	5,566	4,148	4,263	8,410
Pennsylvania	49,907	37,236	52,132	39,185	7,076	5,870	4,794	5,048	12,833
Rhode Island	51,069	37,406	52,874	38,855	8,389	5,629	4,266	4,266	11,496
South Carolina	32,114	23,167	33,748	24,523	4,660	4,564	4,219	4,418	9,730
South Dakota	29,786	22,164	30,926	23,147	3,844	3,935	5,419	5,803	5,660
Tennessee	34,516	24,948	35,929	25,985	5,625	4,319	3,940	4,048	15,540
Texas	39,623	28,878	41,979	31,009	6,125	4,845	2,016	2,099	6,100
Utah	15,238	7,571	15,212	7,445	3,901	3,865	3,569	3,690	11,728
Vermont	51,863	39,518	54,003	41,063	7,108	5,831	6,054	6,222	12,294
Virginia	30,929	21,016	32,616	22,286	5,511	4,819	4,793	4,962	11,080
Washington	45,476	34,404	46,746	35,288	6,111	5,347	3,775	3,848	6,647
West Virginia	20,193	11,721	20,898	12,206	4,250	4,442	3,825	4,009	9,241
Wisconsin	39,373	29,776	41,503	31,662	5,655	4,186	4,382	4,292	6,223
Wyoming	N.A.	18,021	N.A.	18,021	N.A.	N.A.	2,788	2,987	7,292
Dist. of Columbia	53,592	38,899	55,669	40,618	9,649	5,402	N.A.	N.A.	N.A.

See footnotes at end of table

TABLE 9.8

Average Undergraduate Tuition and Fees and Room and Board Rates Charged for Full-Time Students in Degree-Granting Postsecondary Institutions, by Control and Level of Institution and State or Jurisdiction: 2015–16 and 2016–17 (In current dollars) (continued)

Source: U.S. Department of Education, National Center for Education Statistics, Integrated Postsecondary Education Data System (IPEDS), Fall 2015 and Fall 2016, Institutional Characteristics component; and Spring 2016 and Spring 2017, Fall Enrollment component. (This table was prepared November 2017.)

Note: Data are for the entire academic year and are average charges for full-time students. In-state tuition and fees were weighted by the number of full-time-equivalent undergraduates, but were not adjusted to reflect the number of students who were state residents. Out-of-state tuition and fees were weighted by the number of first-time freshmen attending the institution in fall 2016 from out of state. Institutional room and board rates are weighted by the number of full-time students. Degree-granting institutions grant associate's or higher degrees and participate in Title IV federal financial aid programs. Some data have been revised from previously published figures. Detail may not sum to totals because of rounding.

Key:

N.A.–Not applicable

TABLE 9.9
Average Total Cost of Attendance for First-Time, Full-Time Undergraduate Students in Public Degree-Granting Postsecondary Institutions, by Level of Institution, Living Arrangement, Component of Student Costs, and State: 2014–15

	4-year institutions									
						Room and board, by living arrangement				
	Total costs					On campus		Off campus		
		Off campus						Living with family, other costs	Not living with family	
State or other jurisdictions	On campus	Living with family	Not living with family	Tuition and fees	Books and supplies	Room and board	Other costs		Room and board	Other costs
United States	$22,752	$13,920	$23,373	$8,445	$1,275	$9,760	$3,272	$4,200	$9,663	$3,990
Alabama	21,987	14,242	23,467	8,431	1,332	8,432	3,792	4,479	9,093	4,611
Alaska	18,775	10,259	22,498	5,446	1,342	9,605	2,382	3,471	12,086	3,624
Arizona	24,604	15,590	25,376	10,031	1,096	9,719	3,759	4,463	9,130	5,120
Arkansas	19,687	12,410	22,385	7,021	1,277	7,215	4,175	4,112	9,700	4,388
California	27,178	14,077	25,366	9,028	1,675	13,033	3,443	3,375	11,592	3,071
Colorado	23,691	14,794	22,671	8,543	1,393	10,693	3,062	4,858	9,770	2,966
Connecticut	25,532	14,249	25,428	10,387	1,073	11,602	2,471	2,790	10,595	3,373
Delaware	25,219	14,575	27,683	11,207	1,004	11,355	1,653	2,364	11,924	3,548
Florida	19,434	11,349	20,194	4,289	1,477	9,869	3,800	5,583	10,068	4,361
Georgia	21,004	12,051	20,519	6,085	1,376	9,480	4,063	4,590	8,464	4,594
Hawaii	23,082	11,028	23,734	7,932	1,206	12,204	1,740	1,890	12,099	2,497
Idaho	20,070	12,787	21,149	6,835	1,195	7,545	4,495	4,757	7,820	5,300
Illinois	26,988	19,825	27,609	12,824	1,135	10,091	2,938	5,866	9,522	4,128
Indiana	21,564	13,676	22,130	8,369	1,323	9,199	2,673	3,984	8,636	3,801
Iowa	19,827	11,900	19,505	7,832	1,005	8,376	2,614	3,063	7,901	2,767
Kansas	20,558	12,708	21,044	7,788	996	7,958	3,817	3,924	8,204	4,057
Kentucky	21,541	13,061	22,816	9,088	1,031	8,402	3,020	2,941	8,281	4,416
Louisiana	20,544	12,412	22,229	7,221	1,329	8,605	3,389	3,862	9,970	3,710
Maine	22,303	13,552	22,262	9,384	1,053	9,225	2,642	3,115	8,588	3,238
Maryland	23,180	14,689	24,817	8,693	1,394	10,240	2,853	4,602	11,363	3,367
Massachusetts	24,587	15,127	23,468	10,695	1,061	10,889	1,944	3,372	9,134	2,579
Michigan	22,726	15,427	23,156	10,822	1,039	8,988	1,878	3,567	8,120	3,176
Minnesota	21,887	14,276	21,914	10,379	1,045	7,957	2,505	2,852	7,602	2,889
Mississippi	21,421	13,508	20,619	6,788	1,448	8,430	4,756	5,272	7,104	5,279
Missouri	20,424	12,472	20,372	7,603	910	8,519	3,393	3,959	7,951	3,908
Montana	18,427	10,785	18,522	6,186	1,157	7,730	3,354	3,442	7,682	3,497
Nebraska	20,551	11,936	20,115	7,201	1,098	8,794	3,458	3,637	8,232	3,584
Nevada	21,197	12,152	20,870	5,543	1,197	10,359	4,098	5,412	8,945	5,185
New Hampshire	28,313	19,827	28,847	14,603	1,146	10,209	2,355	4,078	9,343	3,755
New Jersey	29,121	18,017	31,982	12,945	1,435	12,115	2,626	3,637	14,188	3,414
New Mexico	18,784	10,585	19,057	5,782	1,121	7,849	4,033	3,682	7,953	4,201
New York	22,660	12,421	26,571	7,365	1,216	11,958	2,122	3,841	13,243	4,747
North Carolina	20,001	12,125	19,826	6,466	1,169	8,694	3,672	4,490	8,545	3,646
North Dakota	18,252	11,097	18,198	6,367	1,062	6,843	3,980	3,669	6,945	3,825
Ohio	24,177	14,886	24,588	9,195	1,187	10,403	3,392	4,503	10,282	3,923
Oklahoma	18,917	11,972	19,828	6,382	1,150	7,469	3,915	4,439	7,459	4,836
Oregon	23,828	14,227	23,792	8,913	1,572	10,624	2,720	3,742	10,350	2,957
Pennsylvania	27,567	17,582	27,967	12,382	1,354	10,275	3,556	3,847	10,117	4,115
Rhode Island	24,790	14,799	25,451	10,420	1,200	11,290	1,881	3,179	10,594	3,237
South Carolina	25,420	16,378	25,472	11,259	1,316	8,637	4,207	3,802	8,859	4,037
South Dakota	21,720	13,780	20,963	7,553	1,311	7,647	5,209	4,917	7,197	4,902
Tennessee	23,299	14,715	23,087	8,501	1,577	8,608	4,613	4,638	8,210	4,799
Texas	21,154	12,728	21,783	7,807	1,105	8,717	3,525	3,816	8,954	3,916
Utah	18,578	11,027	17,722	5,601	1,322	7,061	4,594	4,104	6,452	4,347
Vermont	25,881	18,848	25,907	13,216	1,105	10,056	1,503	4,527	9,677	1,909
Virginia	25,024	15,979	25,981	10,737	1,385	9,662	3,239	3,857	10,286	3,572
Washington	24,055	13,621	23,652	9,364	1,081	10,536	3,073	3,176	10,128	3,079
West Virginia	19,089	11,390	18,111	6,209	1,159	9,160	2,562	4,022	7,380	3,363
Wisconsin	19,591	12,482	21,183	8,377	742	7,186	3,286	3,363	8,138	3,926
Wyoming	18,691	…	…	4,646	1,200	9,755	3,090	…	…	…
Dist. of Columbia	…	11,178	26,808	5,251	1,200	…	…	4,727	15,630	4,727
U.S. Service Schools	8,229	…	…	1,107	3,895	…	3,227	…	…	…

See footnotes at end of table

TABLE 9.9
Average Total Cost of Attendance for First-Time, Full-Time Undergraduate Students in Public Degree-Granting Postsecondary Institutions, by Level of Institution, Living Arrangement, Component of Student Costs, and State: 2014–15 (continued)

State or other jurisdictions	2-year institutions									
	Total costs					Room and board, by living arrangement				
		Off campus				On campus		Off campus		
									Not living with family	
	On campus	Living with family	Not living with family	Tuition and fees	Books and supplies	Room and board	Other costs	Living with family, other costs	Room and board	Other costs
United States	$13,847	$8,603	$16,371	$3,270	$1,422	$6,133	$3,022	$3,911	$7,918	$3,761
Alabama	13,074	9,366	14,704	4,080	1,523	4,723	2,748	3,763	5,398	3,703
Alaska	17,990	7,770	20,144	3,340	800	10,600	3,250	3,630	11,774	4,230
Arizona	14,432	8,677	14,629	2,052	1,337	6,629	4,415	5,288	5,985	5,254
Arkansas	12,881	8,668	16,209	2,879	1,336	4,799	3,867	4,453	7,142	4,852
California	12,690	7,193	18,581	1,242	1,729	6,611	3,108	4,222	11,477	4,133
Colorado	16,329	10,000	19,078	3,312	1,855	6,234	4,928	4,833	9,030	4,882
Connecticut	...	8,423	17,145	3,871	1,289	...	...	3,263	8,124	3,861
Delaware	...	8,700	16,575	3,530	1,600	...	...	3,570	7,875	3,570
Florida	17,334	7,281	13,355	2,381	1,154	10,020	3,779	3,746	7,146	2,673
Georgia	12,840	7,774	13,949	3,336	1,283	5,352	2,868	3,155	6,009	3,321
Hawaii	...	5,654	17,975	2,809	994	...	...	1,851	11,782	2,390
Idaho	13,438	7,389	13,742	3,020	1,000	5,464	3,954	3,369	6,215	3,506
Illinois	...	8,404	15,576	3,515	1,490	...	...	3,399	6,988	3,584
Indiana	...	8,745	15,113	4,055	1,090	...	...	3,600	5,824	4,144
Iowa	15,278	9,416	16,117	4,326	1,498	6,388	3,066	3,592	7,008	3,285
Kansas	12,670	8,014	14,228	3,113	1,095	5,502	2,959	3,805	6,306	3,713
Kentucky	...	7,495	14,470	3,645	1,000	...	...	2,850	6,975	2,850
Louisiana	17,753	8,750	17,175	3,532	1,242	9,266	3,712	3,976	8,512	3,888
Maine	15,486	9,837	16,171	3,677	1,352	7,985	2,472	4,808	6,791	4,350
Maryland	16,667	8,522	18,244	3,600	1,532	7,853	3,683	3,390	9,328	3,785
Massachusetts	...	9,464	17,220	4,363	1,262	...	...	3,839	8,169	3,426
Michigan	13,992	7,320	12,693	3,161	1,315	7,498	2,018	2,844	5,581	2,636
Minnesota	15,396	11,801	18,888	5,353	1,229	6,047	2,766	5,218	7,284	5,022
Mississippi	9,858	7,501	13,491	2,521	1,283	3,798	2,255	3,697	6,485	3,201
Missouri	12,752	9,065	14,789	2,920	1,194	5,688	2,949	4,950	6,522	4,152
Montana	13,070	8,407	15,301	3,214	1,096	5,958	2,802	4,097	7,470	3,521
Nebraska	12,818	6,947	12,885	2,800	1,440	6,224	2,354	2,707	6,259	2,386
Nevada	...	8,134	18,170	2,700	1,548	...	...	3,886	8,538	5,384
New Hampshire	20,527	14,404	26,751	6,989	1,448	8,106	3,984	5,967	12,516	5,798
New Jersey	...	9,485	17,603	4,029	1,525	...	...	3,931	8,809	3,240
New Mexico	12,238	5,856	14,895	1,506	1,040	4,018	5,674	3,311	8,718	3,632
New York	17,666	9,503	18,942	4,688	1,306	9,349	2,323	3,509	9,664	3,283
North Carolina	...	8,536	16,052	2,371	1,421	...	...	4,745	7,532	4,729
North Dakota	15,297	8,649	15,802	4,264	1,008	6,652	3,373	3,377	7,074	3,456
Ohio	15,664	7,736	13,255	3,717	1,370	7,487	3,090	2,649	5,650	2,519
Oklahoma	13,918	8,179	15,823	3,276	1,333	5,860	3,449	3,570	7,407	3,806
Oregon	15,341	8,633	16,573	4,221	1,603	7,345	2,172	2,810	7,695	3,054
Pennsylvania	16,503	9,604	14,419	4,581	1,479	8,767	1,677	3,544	5,863	2,496
Rhode Island	...	9,553	18,571	3,950	1,200	...	...	4,403	9,018	4,403
South Carolina	13,700	10,082	17,795	4,125	1,417	3,708	4,450	4,540	7,994	4,260
South Dakota	18,575	10,273	16,155	5,024	1,401	8,050	4,100	3,848	6,756	2,974
Tennessee	...	9,359	16,009	3,821	1,246	...	...	4,292	7,481	3,460
Texas	13,429	7,787	15,315	2,033	1,641	5,583	4,171	4,112	7,546	4,094
Utah	...	8,849	18,749	3,469	1,680	...	...	3,700	9,900	3,700
Vermont	...	12,718	17,968	5,886	1,000	...	...	5,832	9,370	1,712
Virginia	17,420	10,329	16,658	4,023	1,517	10,080	1,800	4,789	6,899	4,219
Washington	15,330	8,391	18,033	3,943	1,063	7,565	2,759	3,385	9,617	3,410
West Virginia	15,036	8,841	13,618	3,583	1,203	7,750	2,500	4,055	5,417	3,416
Wisconsin	15,529	10,070	16,841	4,468	1,443	5,832	3,786	4,159	7,021	3,910
Wyoming	12,410	6,533	14,349	2,701	1,248	6,054	2,407	2,583	7,703	2,697
Dist. of Columbia	...	...	...	...	...	...	...	...	...	...
U.S. Service Schools	...	...	...	...	...	...	...	...	...	...

See footnotes at end of table

TABLE 9.9

Average Total Cost of Attendance for First-Time, Full-Time Undergraduate Students in Public Degree-Granting Postsecondary Institutions, by Level of Institution, Living Arrangement, Component of Student Costs, and State: 2014–15 (continued)

Source: U.S. Department of Education, National Center for Education Statistics, Integrated Postsecondary Education Data System (IPEDS), Winter 2014–15, Student Financial Assistance component; and Fall 2014, Institutional Characteristics component. (This table was prepared October 2016.)

Note: Excludes students who previously attended another postsecondary institution or who began their studies on a part-time basis. Tuition and fees at public institutions are the lower of either in-district or in-state tuition and fees. Data illustrating the average total cost of attendance for all students are weighted by the number of students at the institution receiving Title IV aid. Detail may not sum to totals because of rounding. Some data have been revised from previously published figures.

Key:

...–Not applicable.

TABLE 9.10

Degree-Granting Postsecondary Institutions, by Control and Classification of Institution and State or Jurisdiction: 2016–17

State or other jurisdiction	Total	All public institutions	Public 4-year institutions							Public 2-year	All non-profit institutions
			Total	Research university, very high (a)	Research university, high (b)	Doctoral/ research university (c)	Master's (d)	Baccalaureate (e)	Special focus (f)		
United States	4,360	1,623	737	81	74	38	271	223	50	886	1,682
Alabama	73	39	14	1	4	0	8	1	0	25	21
Alaska	8	4	3	0	1	0	2	0	0	1	3
Arizona	80	30	10	2	1	2	2	1	2	20	12
Arkansas	52	33	11	1	0	1	6	2	1	22	16
California	436	151	46	8	2	3	18	13	2	105	148
Colorado	80	28	16	2	3	0	6	5	0	12	16
Connecticut	43	21	9	1	0	0	4	4	0	12	18
Delaware	8	3	3	1	0	0	1	1	0	0	4
Florida	208	42	39	5	2	1	4	27	0	3	73
Georgia	126	53	30	3	1	4	9	12	1	23	38
Hawaii	20	10	4	1	0	0	1	2	0	6	6
Idaho	18	8	4	0	1	2	0	1	0	4	6
Illinois	177	60	12	2	3	0	7	0	0	48	85
Indiana	78	16	15	2	2	1	7	3	0	1	41
Iowa	62	19	3	2	0	0	1	0	0	16	33
Kansas	70	33	8	2	1	0	4	0	1	25	24
Kentucky	65	24	8	2	0	0	5	1	0	16	25
Louisiana	62	33	17	1	2	2	8	1	3	16	14
Maine	31	15	8	0	1	0	1	6	0	7	13
Maryland	56	29	13	1	1	2	7	1	1	16	19
Massachusetts	120	31	15	1	3	0	7	1	3	16	81
Michigan	92	46	21	3	3	2	6	7	0	25	39
Minnesota	100	43	12	1	0	0	8	2	1	31	35
Mississippi	39	23	8	1	3	0	4	0	0	15	9
Missouri	118	27	13	1	3	0	6	3	0	14	54
Montana	23	17	6	0	2	0	1	3	0	11	5
Nebraska	41	15	7	1	0	1	4	0	1	8	19
Nevada	26	7	6	0	2	0	0	4	0	1	5
New Hampshire	25	13	6	0	1	0	2	2	1	7	12
New Jersey	73	32	13	1	2	2	8	0	0	19	29
New Mexico	42	28	9	1	1	0	4	1	2	19	3
New York	298	79	43	4	1	1	23	10	4	36	181
North Carolina	144	75	16	2	4	0	8	1	1	59	50
North Dakota	20	14	9	0	2	0	1	4	2	5	5
Ohio	195	60	35	2	7	1	1	21	3	25	71
Oklahoma	63	31	17	1	1	0	8	5	2	14	17
Oregon	57	26	9	2	1	0	4	1	1	17	24
Pennsylvania	245	62	45	3	0	1	16	23	2	17	118
Rhode Island	13	3	2	0	1	0	1	0	0	1	10
South Carolina	74	33	13	2	0	0	6	4	1	20	23
South Dakota	22	12	7	0	2	0	3	0	2	5	7
Tennessee	101	23	10	1	1	4	3	0	1	13	48
Texas	262	107	47	7	4	8	16	4	8	60	71
Utah	33	8	7	1	1	0	3	2	0	1	11
Vermont	23	6	5	0	1	0	1	3	0	1	16
Virginia	124	40	16	4	2	0	7	2	1	24	45
Washington	81	43	31	2	0	0	6	22	1	12	25
West Virginia	45	22	13	1	0	0	3	8	1	9	10
Wisconsin	74	31	15	2	0	0	9	4	0	16	30
Wyoming	10	8	1	0	1	0	0	0	0	7	2
Dist. of Columbia	19	2	2	0	0	0	1	0	1	0	12
U.S. Service Academies	5	5	5	0	0	0	0	5	0	0	N.A.
American Samoa	1	1	1	0	0	0	0	1	0	0	0
Fed. States of Micronesia	1	1	0	0	0	0	0	0	0	1	0
Guam	3	2	1	0	0	0	1	0	0	1	1
Marshall Islands	1	1	0	0	0	0	0	0	0	1	0
CNMI*	1	1	1	0	0	0	0	1	0	0	0
Palau	1	1	0	0	0	0	0	0	0	1	0
Puerto Rico	93	18	14	0	1	0	1	9	3	4	50
U.S. Virgin Islands	1	1	1	0	0	0	1	0	0	0	0

See footnotes at end of table

TABLE 9.10
Degree-Granting Postsecondary Institutions, by Control and Classification of Institution and State or Jurisdiction: 2016–17 (continued)

State or other jurisdiction	Total	Nonprofit 4-year institutions						Non-profit 2-year	For-profit institutions		
		Research university, very high (a)	Research university, high (b)	Doctoral/ research university (c)	Master's (d)	Baccalaureate (e)	Special focus (f)		Total	4-year	2-year
United States	1,581	34	30	54	412	460	591	101	1,055	514	541
Alabama	20	0	0	0	4	10	6	1	13	8	5
Alaska	2	0	0	0	1	0	1	1	1	0	1
Arizona	12	0	0	0	2	3	7	0	38	22	16
Arkansas	12	0	0	0	2	9	1	4	3	2	1
California	142	3	1	9	31	23	75	6	137	73	64
Colorado	14	0	1	0	3	3	7	2	36	19	17
Connecticut	18	1	0	1	8	4	4	0	4	4	0
Delaware	3	0	0	1	0	1	1	1	1	1	0
Florida	66	1	2	1	15	25	22	7	93	40	53
Georgia	33	1	1	1	5	17	8	5	35	13	22
Hawaii	6	0	0	0	2	3	1	0	4	3	1
Idaho	6	0	0	0	1	3	2	0	4	3	1
Illinois	82	2	2	4	19	18	37	3	32	17	15
Indiana	40	1	0	1	11	17	10	1	21	12	9
Iowa	33	0	0	0	9	15	9	0	10	8	2
Kansas	24	0	0	0	6	13	5	0	13	7	6
Kentucky	25	0	0	2	7	9	7	0	16	11	5
Louisiana	12	1	0	0	3	3	5	2	15	3	12
Maine	11	0	0	0	4	6	1	2	3	2	1
Maryland	19	1	0	0	6	4	8	0	8	3	5
Massachusetts	79	7	1	4	18	18	31	2	8	4	4
Michigan	39	0	0	1	10	13	15	0	7	4	3
Minnesota	34	0	0	2	8	11	13	1	22	20	2
Mississippi	9	0	0	0	3	4	2	0	7	1	6
Missouri	52	1	1	2	13	11	24	2	37	16	21
Montana	4	0	0	0	0	3	1	1	1	0	1
Nebraska	17	0	0	0	6	6	5	2	7	4	3
Nevada	4	0	0	0	1	0	3	1	14	6	8
New Hampshire	11	0	1	0	5	4	1	1	0	0	0
New Jersey	29	1	1	1	10	2	14	0	12	9	3
New Mexico	3	0	0	0	2	1	0	0	11	8	3
New York	170	5	5	7	36	26	91	11	38	21	17
North Carolina	49	1	1	1	10	24	12	1	19	10	9
North Dakota	5	0	0	0	1	1	3	0	1	1	0
Ohio	67	1	1	2	20	20	23	4	64	18	46
Oklahoma	14	0	1	0	6	4	3	3	15	8	7
Oregon	24	0	0	0	7	5	12	0	7	4	3
Pennsylvania	104	2	3	4	33	31	31	14	65	10	55
Rhode Island	10	1	0	0	5	1	3	0	0	0	0
South Carolina	21	0	0	0	7	13	1	2	18	8	10
South Dakota	7	0	0	0	2	2	3	0	3	3	0
Tennessee	45	1	0	3	13	11	17	3	30	12	18
Texas	64	1	3	1	18	18	23	7	84	33	51
Utah	10	0	1	0	3	3	3	1	14	13	1
Vermont	16	0	0	0	6	8	2	0	1	1	0
Virginia	40	0	0	3	6	16	15	5	39	21	18
Washington	21	0	0	1	10	4	6	4	13	9	4
West Virginia	10	0	0	0	3	4	3	0	13	3	10
Wisconsin	30	0	1	2	9	9	9	0	13	12	1
Wyoming	1	0	0	0	0	1	0	1	0	0	0
Dist. of Columbia	12	2	3	0	2	0	5	0	5	4	1
U.S. Service Academies	N.A.	N.A.	N.A.	N.A.	N.A.	N.A.	N.A.	N.A.	N.A.	N.A.	N.A.
American Samoa	0	0	0	0	0	0	0	0	0	0	0
Fed. States of Micronesia	0	0	0	0	0	0	0	0	0	0	0
Guam	1	0	0	0	0	0	1	0	0	0	0
Marshall Islands	0	0	0	0	0	0	0	0	0	0	0
CNMI*	0	0	0	0	0	0	0	0	0	0	0
Palau	0	0	0	0	0	0	0	0	0	0	0
Puerto Rico	45	0	0	3	13	12	17	5	25	15	10
U.S. Virgin Islands	0	0	0	0	0	0	0	0	0	0	0

See footnotes at end of table

TABLE 9.10

Degree-Granting Postsecondary Institutions, by Control and Classification of Institution and State or Jurisdiction: 2016–17 (continued)

Source: U.S. Department of Education, National Center for Education Statistics, Integrated Postsecondary Education Data System (IPEDS), Fall 2016, Institutional Characteristics component. (This table was prepared February 2018.)

*Commonwealth of Northern Mariana Islands

Note: Branch campuses are counted as separate institutions. Relative levels of research activity for research universities were determined by an analysis of research and development expenditures, science and engineering research staffing, and doctoral degrees conferred, by field. Further information on the research index ranking may be obtained from *http://carnegieclassifications.iu.edu/*. Degree-granting institutions grant associate's or higher degrees and participate in Title IV federal financial aid programs.

Key:

N.A.–Not applicable

(a) Research universities with a very high level of research activity.

(b) Research universities with a high level of research activity.

(c) Institutions that award at least 20 research/scholarship doctor's degrees per year, but did not have a high level of research activity.

(d) Institutions that award at least 50 master's degrees and fewer than 20 doctor's degrees per year.

(e) Institutions that primarily emphasize undergraduate education. In addition to institutions that primarily award bachelor's degrees, also includes institutions classified as 4-year in the IPEDS system, but classified as 2-year baccalaureate/associate's colleges in the Carnegie Classification system because they primarily award associate's degrees.

(f) Four-year institutions that award degrees primarily in single fields of study, such as medicine, business, fine arts, theology, and engineering.

TABLE 9.11

Average Salary of Full-Time Instructional Faculty on 9-Month Contracts in 4-Year Degree-Granting Postsecondary Institutions, by Control and Classification of Institution, Academic Rank of Faculty, and State or Jurisdiction: 2016–17 (In current dollars)

State or jurisdiction	Public doctoral (a)			Public master's (b)			Nonprofit doctoral (a)			Nonprofit master's (b)		
	Professor	Associate professor	Assistant professor	Professor	Associate professor	Assistant professor	Professor	Associate professor	Assistant professor	Professor	Associate professor	Assistant professor
United States	$128,503	$89,321	$77,687	$93,949	$76,456	$66,024	$156,716	$97,477	$82,831	$91,679	$74,060	$62,362
Alabama	125,407	87,741	72,807	82,672	69,042	60,256	99,757	73,881	39,483	66,017	56,225	48,321
Alaska	106,757	88,097	72,907	106,042	87,497	69,066	N.A.	N.A.	N.A.	60,702	53,600	44,935
Arizona	128,636	91,203	79,894	130,005	94,489	71,307	N.A.	N.A.	N.A.	61,255	77,325	70,390
Arkansas	102,728	75,954	67,971	72,981	62,365	55,377	80,727	66,801	59,288	70,023	64,211	56,454
California	151,841	102,484	89,122	102,834	86,907	77,878	166,821	105,694	90,740	106,294	85,522	71,285
Colorado	122,754	91,191	80,544	81,621	65,813	56,713	135,189	94,707	82,873	112,623	81,519	61,364
Connecticut	139,354	99,020	81,003	105,890	86,864	69,468	182,124	97,396	85,607	136,343	96,337	79,748
Delaware	142,469	99,178	85,687	N.A.	N.A.	N.A.	N.A.	N.A.	N.A.	79,631	67,988	60,703
Florida	125,717	88,918	79,832	104,309	79,872	66,986	134,523	91,891	78,086	94,052	77,853	62,854
Georgia	115,703	83,561	72,284	76,586	65,632	59,516	143,074	90,533	80,534	78,156	63,040	54,276
Hawaii	127,093	95,419	81,949	N.A.	N.A.	N.A.	N.A.	N.A.	N.A.	82,502	76,675	71,899
Idaho	94,296	75,599	65,002	87,715	72,471	68,526	N.A.	N.A.	N.A.	64,094	56,697	51,192
Illinois	122,795	85,166	81,178	96,520	75,444	65,676	175,819	101,434	90,783	84,130	71,313	61,873
Indiana	129,602	89,131	78,807	88,480	71,586	63,280	140,481	90,661	73,912	80,969	66,077	57,710
Iowa	133,798	95,052	81,450	93,593	73,248	65,430	90,993	73,654	61,009	69,710	60,249	54,850
Kansas	114,290	80,627	71,575	74,910	62,835	59,137	67,097	51,009	56,160	65,911	59,131	52,273
Kentucky	105,456	75,233	67,916	80,714	65,062	58,033	78,455	61,954	54,037	63,314	55,745	49,423
Louisiana	103,733	75,243	69,356	73,050	57,472	53,333	129,963	82,948	80,647	66,624	57,564	54,083
Maine	107,148	83,439	63,549	85,738	71,364	58,191	90,469	74,033	60,501	67,408	57,101	48,658
Maryland	135,950	97,037	81,290	93,995	76,803	69,037	134,485	96,397	96,842	87,433	74,581	61,518
Massachusetts	144,396	106,644	88,611	101,873	80,045	68,485	181,485	109,765	97,187	123,496	89,551	74,372
Michigan	134,896	93,873	80,848	94,349	81,845	70,579	103,526	83,519	73,066	78,441	66,453	60,566
Minnesota	146,844	98,052	89,299	94,593	79,135	67,790	97,239	77,280	63,358	80,941	67,345	61,442
Mississippi	101,968	76,978	69,012	69,285	60,894	52,917	83,752	68,262	57,554	78,253	61,219	59,146
Missouri	109,880	77,846	68,945	79,823	65,187	57,035	142,986	90,127	78,787	79,995	65,215	55,765
Montana	93,378	73,596	67,455	76,784	68,168	57,273	N.A.	N.A.	N.A.	61,260	49,241	53,639
Nebraska	119,791	75,236	64,840	81,998	66,202	55,539	113,826	83,452	66,968	65,013	56,709	53,418
Nevada	124,365	91,301	72,798	N.A.	N.A.	N.A.	N.A.	N.A.	N.A.	79,310	68,314	52,143
New Hampshire	129,285	101,178	82,327	95,951	79,635	65,685	189,458	121,683	102,226	95,252	70,966	63,794
New Jersey	152,700	105,365	84,482	121,452	94,579	77,994	183,047	101,564	89,129	105,493	90,772	68,693
New Mexico	104,668	75,497	70,452	77,010	65,874	57,804	N.A.	N.A.	N.A.	N.A.	N.A.	N.A.
New York	131,489	95,249	81,032	103,986	81,242	69,018	165,534	104,784	87,781	99,559	79,369	68,306
North Carolina	124,958	85,208	76,894	92,144	73,870	68,501	165,230	97,435	78,983	74,695	64,263	56,514
North Dakota	108,195	84,321	73,024	75,516	58,993	49,199	69,667	63,373	48,270	N.A.	N.A.	N.A.
Ohio	122,433	87,627	76,598	76,551	62,856	55,781	114,399	78,699	69,122	80,435	68,221	60,217
Oklahoma	110,174	79,073	71,487	80,037	66,689	56,862	110,572	77,094	77,532	68,242	62,477	53,086
Oregon	123,219	89,005	78,604	80,163	64,756	51,889	102,603	79,672	64,525	62,333	58,068	50,641
Pennsylvania	145,215	100,220	81,207	110,791	89,639	72,369	154,914	98,367	85,134	95,683	78,342	64,595
Rhode Island	119,979	87,239	82,775	81,465	71,267	60,533	176,083	115,561	95,719	115,025	87,331	75,539
South Carolina	130,745	92,457	86,150	89,774	72,640	64,444	64,591	61,417	52,243	79,550	63,400	55,377
South Dakota	95,821	78,230	70,171	89,186	72,704	69,277	N.A.	N.A.	N.A.	68,149	58,795	54,529
Tennessee	108,939	79,424	68,299	84,755	68,568	60,673	144,494	94,136	77,776	75,109	61,319	53,076
Texas	126,032	88,075	74,613	91,368	76,192	69,498	143,604	96,753	83,540	88,400	72,803	61,275
Utah	120,295	86,818	77,459	85,636	71,373	63,483	141,777	106,818	72,036	88,705	76,793	54,362
Vermont	123,337	92,839	77,850	77,603	55,240	47,230	N.A.	N.A.	N.A.	105,083	80,206	70,776
Virginia	129,329	89,856	75,703	88,710	72,915	64,428	117,659	87,562	69,106	71,404	59,753	52,949
Washington	129,100	94,140	90,158	98,969	82,607	72,096	113,360	84,245	68,903	78,671	65,026	62,648
West Virginia	97,237	76,489	67,161	68,390	61,527	53,353	58,257	56,859	47,062	60,002	55,772	45,624
Wisconsin	117,899	82,433	76,449	74,353	63,242	61,929	105,053	79,612	72,218	76,978	63,454	55,422
Wyoming	116,819	82,747	78,606	N.A.	N.A.	N.A.	N.A.	N.A.	N.A.	N.A.	N.A.	N.A.
Dist. of Columbia	151,153	118,383	99,428	105,626	76,509	64,323	160,563	104,569	86,660	114,036	80,214	69,849
U.S. Service Academies	N.A.	N.A.	N.A.	N.A.	N.A.	N.A.	N.A.	N.A.	N.A.	N.A.	N.A.	N.A.
American Samoa	N.A.	N.A.	N.A.	N.A.	N.A.	N.A.	N.A.	N.A.	N.A.	N.A.	N.A.	N.A.
Fed. States of Micronesia	N.A.	N.A.	N.A.	N.A.	N.A.	N.A.	N.A.	N.A.	N.A.	N.A.	N.A.	N.A.
Guam	N.A.	N.A.	N.A.	92,523	73,666	54,053	N.A.	N.A.	N.A.	N.A.	N.A.	N.A.
Marshall Islands	N.A.	N.A.	N.A.	N.A.	N.A.	N.A.	N.A.	N.A.	N.A.	N.A.	N.A.	N.A.
CNMI*	N.A.	N.A.	N.A.	N.A.	N.A.	N.A.	N.A.	N.A.	N.A.	N.A.	N.A.	N.A.
Palau	N.A.	N.A.	N.A.	N.A.	N.A.	N.A.	N.A.	N.A.	N.A.	N.A.	N.A.	N.A.
Puerto Rico	83,744	71,462	52,284	N.A.	N.A.	N.A.	N.A.	N.A.	50,633	14,627	N.A.	47,903
U.S. Virgin Islands	N.A.	N.A.	N.A.	85,024	71,125	57,423	N.A.	N.A.	N.A.	N.A.	N.A.	N.A.

See footnotes at end of table

TABLE 9.11

Average Salary of Full-Time Instructional Faculty on 9-Month Contracts in 4-Year Degree-Granting Postsecondary Institutions, by Control and Classification of Institution, Academic Rank of Faculty, and State or Jurisdiction: 2016–17 (In current dollars) (continued)

Source: U.S. Department of Education, National Center for Education Statistics, Integrated Postsecondary Education Data System (IPEDS), Spring 2017, Human Resources component, Salaries section. (This table was prepared November 2017.)

*Commonwealth of Northern Mariana Islands

Note: Data exclude instructional faculty at medical schools. Degree-granting institutions grant associate's or higher degrees and participate in Title IV federal financial aid programs. Data include imputations for nonrespondent institutions.

Key:

N.A.–Not applicable

(a) Institutions that awarded 20 or more doctor's degrees during the previous academic year.

(b) Institutions that awarded 20 or more master's degrees, but less than 20 doctor's degrees, during the previous academic year.

TABLE 9.12

Number and Percent of Children under 19 by Health Insurance Coverage and State: 2017 (In thousands)

State or other jurisdiction	Total	Children under 19 Insured (any coverage) Number	Percent	Uninsured Number	Percent
Alabama	1,169	1,133	96.9	36	3.1
Alaska	194	176	90.4	19	9.6
Arizona	1,729	1,596	92.3	133	7.7
Arkansas	752	718	95.6	33	4.4
California	9,567	9,267	96.9	301	3.1
Colorado	1,334	1,277	95.7	57	4.3
Connecticut	793	769	96.9	24	3.1
Delaware	218	211	96.5	8	3.5
Florida	4,450	4,126	92.7	325	7.3
Georgia	2,671	2,471	92.5	200	7.5
Hawaii	321	314	97.8	7	2.2
Idaho	472	450	95.4	22	4.6
Illinois	3,069	2,980	97.1	89	2.9
Indiana	1,670	1,565	93.7	106	6.3
Iowa	776	752	96.9	24	3.1
Kansas	755	716	94.8	39	5.2
Kentucky	1,079	1,038	96.2	41	3.8
Louisiana	1,175	1,139	96.9	36	3.1
Maine	272	258	95.1	13	4.9
Maryland	1,420	1,365	96.2	54	3.8
Massachusetts	1,479	1,457	98.5	22	1.5
Michigan	2,313	2,244	97	69	3
Minnesota	1,373	1,326	96.6	47	3.4
Mississippi	763	726	95.2	37	4.8
Missouri	1,465	1,390	94.9	75	5.1
Montana	241	227	94.2	14	5.8
Nebraska	500	474	94.9	26	5.1
Nevada	719	661	92	58	8
New Hampshire	276	270	97.7	6	2.3
New Jersey	2,094	2,015	96.3	78	3.7
New Mexico	523	496	94.9	26	5.1
New York	4,403	4,286	97.3	118	2.7
North Carolina	2,451	2,332	95.2	119	4.8
North Dakota	184	170	92.5	14	7.5
Ohio	2,759	2,634	95.5	125	4.5
Oklahoma	1,019	936	91.9	82	8.1
Oregon	928	895	96.4	33	3.6
Pennsylvania	2,835	2,710	95.6	125	4.4
Rhode Island	224	219	97.9	5	2.1
South Carolina	1,169	1,109	94.9	60	5.10
South Dakota	224	211	93.8	14	6.2
Tennessee	1,600	1,530	95.6	71	4.4
Texas	7,782	6,947	89.3	835	10.7
Utah	973	901	92.7	71	7.3
Vermont	127	125	98.4	2	1.6
Virginia	1,983	1,882	94.9	101	5.1
Washington	1,740	1,694	97.4	46	2.6
West Virginia	399	389	97.4	11	2.6
Wisconsin	1,362	1,309	96.1	53	3.9
Wyoming	146	132	90.5	14	9.5
Dist. of Columbia	134	132	98.8	2	1.2

Sources: U.S. Census Bureau, *Health Insurance Coverage in the United States: 2017*, Issued September 2018. U.S. Census Bureau, 1-Year American Community Survey.

TABLE 9.13
Number and Percent of Persons Under 65, by Health Insurance Coverage and State: 2017 (In thousands)

State or other jurisdiction	Total	Insured Number	Insured Percent	Uninsured Number	Uninsured Percent	Medicaid expansion	Difference in Uninsured: 2017 less 2013 Number	Difference in Uninsured: 2017 less 2013 Percentage pts.
Alabama	4,011	3,565	88.9	446	11.1	no	(197)	(4.2)
Alaska	635	538	84.7	97	15.3	9/1/2015	(34)	(4.8)
Arizona	5,719	5,034	88	685	12	1/1/14	(423)	(7.1)
Arkansas	2,469	2,238	90.7	231	9.3	1/1/14	(233)	(8.1)
California	33,637	30,898	91.9	2,739	8.1	1/1/14	(3,704)	(10.0)
Colorado	4,755	4,347	91.4	408	8.6	1/1/14	(315)	(6.6)
Connecticut	2,957	2,767	93.6	190	6.4	1/1/14	(139)	(3.9)
Delaware	778	728	93.6	50	6.4	1/1/14	(32)	(3.7)
Florida	16,532	13,905	84.1	2,627	15.9	no	(1,177)	(7.1)
Georgia	8,869	7,505	84.6	1,365	15.4	no	(471)	(5.4)
Hawaii	1,124	1,072	95.4	52	4.6	1/1/14	(38)	(2.9)
Idaho	1,437	1,265	88.1	171	11.9	no	(85)	(6.0)
Illinois	10,739	9,898	92.2	841	7.8	1/1/14	(759)	(5.9)
Indiana	5,581	5,050	90.5	531	9.5	2/1/2015	(367)	(5.8)
Iowa	2,602	2,458	94.5	144	5.50	1/1/14	(102)	(3.4)
Kansas	2,427	2,179	89.8	248	10.2	no	(99)	(3.5)
Kentucky	3,686	3,452	93.7	234	6.3	1/1/14	(381)	(8.9)
Louisiana	3,905	3,526	90.3	379	9.7	7/1/2016	(369)	(8.3)
Maine	1,062	955	90	107	10	TBD*	(40)	(3.1)
Maryland	5,079	4,721	93	358	7	1/1/14	(228)	(4.0)
Massachusetts	5,714	5,528	96.7	186	3.3	1/1/14	(57)	(0.9)
Michigan	8,227	7,724	93.9	502	6.1	4/1/2014	(562)	(5.8)
Minnesota	4,690	4,450	94.9	240	5.1	1/1/14	(197)	(3.8)
Mississippi	2,469	2,119	85.8	350	14.2	no	(148)	(5.0)
Missouri	5,026	4,483	89.2	544	10.8	no	(225)	(3.9)
Montana	851	765	89.8	87	10.2	1/1/2016	(77)	(8.0)
Nebraska	1,609	1,454	90.4	155	9.6	no	(52)	(3.0)
Nevada	2,508	2,181	87	327	13	1/1/14	(237)	(9.4)
New Hampshire	1,098	1,022	93.1	76	6.9	8/15/2014	(63)	(4.9)
New Jersey	7,525	6,851	91	674	9	1/1/14	(472)	(5.5)
New Mexico	1,709	1,526	89.3	183	10.7	1/1/14	(195)	(9.5)
New York	16,542	15,450	93.4	1,091	6.6	1/1/14	(957)	(5.0)
North Carolina	8,482	7,413	87.4	1,069	12.6	no	(433)	(5.0)
North Dakota	632	576	91.2	55	8.8	1/1/14	(18)	(2.8)
Ohio	9,615	8,938	93	677	7	1/1/14	(572)	(5.1)
Oklahoma	3,267	2,726	83.4	541	16.6	no	(120)	(3.5)
Oregon	3,405	3,127	91.8	278	8.2	1/1/14	(290)	(7.8)
Pennsylvania	10,405	9,723	93.4	682	6.6	1/1/2015	(530)	(4.2)
Rhode Island	874	826	94.5	48	5.5	1/1/14	(72)	(7.0)
South Carolina	4,080	3,542	86.8	538	13.2	no	(197)	(4.8)
South Dakota	716	639	89.3	77	10.7	no	(16)	(2.2)
Tennessee	5,571	4,946	88.8	625	11.2	no	(258)	(4.4)
Texas	24,467	19,713	80.6	4,755	19.4	no	(931)	(4.8)
Utah	2,746	2,468	89.9	279	10.1	no	(120)	(4.8)
Vermont	504	476	94.5	28	5.5	1/1/14	(17)	(2.7)
Virginia	7,013	6,295	89.8	718	10.2	1/1/2019	(261)	(3.5)
Washington	6,202	5,763	92.9	439	7.1	1/1/14	(514)	(7.9)
West Virginia	1,445	1,337	92.5	108	7.5	1/1/14	(146)	(7.9)
Wisconsin	4,796	4,490	93.6	306	6.4	no	(208)	(3.7)
Wyoming	481	411	85.5	70	14.5	no	(7)	(1.2)
Dist. of Columbia	602	577	95.8	26	4.2	1/1/14	(16)	(2.8)

Sources: U.S. Census Bureau, Health Insurance Coverage in the United States: 2017, Issued September 2018. U.S. Census Bureau, 2013, 2016 and 2017 1-Year American Community Survey.
*Maine voters approved a ballot initiative to expand Medicaid expansion in Nov. 2017, but Gov. LePage never submitted a state plan amendment to do so. On Jan. 3, 2019, Gov. Janet Mills signed an executive order to implement Medicaid expansion.
Key:
( )–Parentheses denote a negative number.

Table 9.13 | Adult Health Insurance Coverage, 2017

Highest Rates of Insured Adults, 18–64

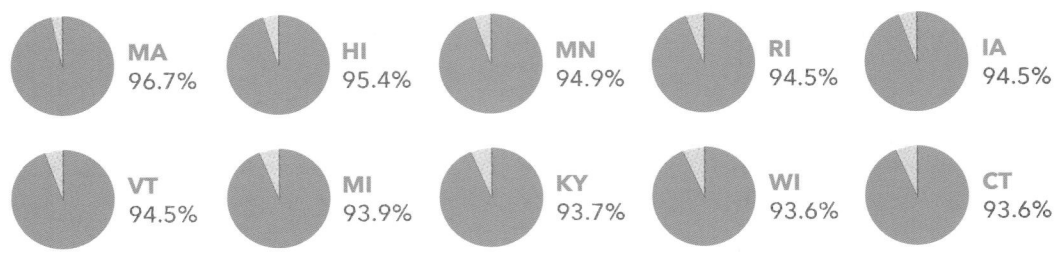

MA 96.7% HI 95.4% MN 94.9% RI 94.5% IA 94.5%

VT 94.5% MI 93.9% KY 93.7% WI 93.6% CT 93.6%

Highest Rates of Uninsured Adults, 18–64

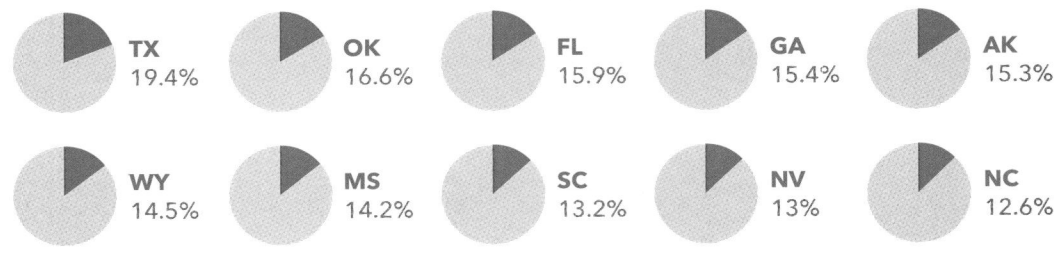

TX 19.4% OK 16.6% FL 15.9% GA 15.4% AK 15.3%

WY 14.5% MS 14.2% SC 13.2% NV 13% NC 12.6%

Highest Percent Change from 2013–2017

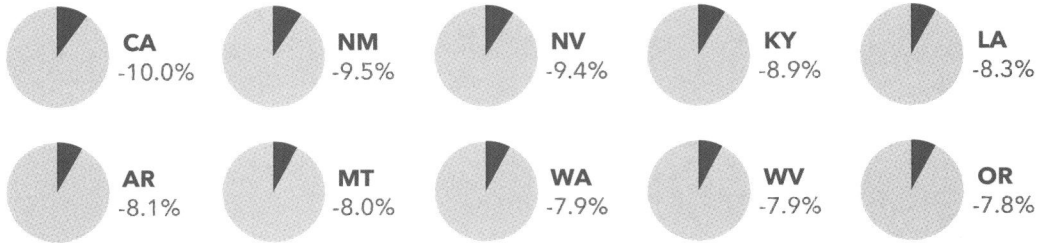

CA -10.0% NM -9.5% NV -9.4% KY -8.9% LA -8.3%

AR -8.1% MT -8.0% WA -7.9% WV -7.9% OR -7.8%

In the 14 states that had not expanded Medicaid as of January 2019, **2.5 MILLION POOR ADULTS FALL INTO A "COVERAGE GAP."**

These adults have incomes above Medicaid eligibility limits in their state but below the lower limit for marketplace premium tax credits, which begin at 100% of poverty. In non-expansion states, the median income eligibility level for parents is 43% of poverty and 0% for childless adults. **People in the coverage gap are concentrated in Southern states, with the largest number of people in the coverage gap in Texas (759,000 people, or 31%) followed by Florida (445,000, or 18%), Georgia (267,000, or 11%), and North Carolina (215,000, or 9%).**

TABLE 9.13a
School Immunization Exemptions

State	Religious exemption[1]	Philosophical exemption[2]	Only medical exemption
Alabama	Y	...	...
Alaska	Y	...	...
Arizona	Y	Y	...
Arkansas	Y	Y	
California	...	...	Y
Colorado	Y	Y	...
Connecticut	Y	...	...
Delaware	Y	...	...
Florida	Y	...	...
Georgia	Y	...	...
Hawaii	Y	...	...
Idaho	Y	Y	...
Illinois	Y	...	...
Indiana	Y	...	...
Iowa	Y	...	...
Kansas	Y	...	...
Kentucky	Y	...	...
Louisiana	Y(a)	Y	...
Maine	...	...	Y(d)
Maryland	Y	...	...
Massachusetts	Y	...	...
Michigan	Y	Y	...
Minnesota	Y(a)	Y	...
Mississippi	...	...	Y
Missouri	Y	(c)	...
Montana	Y	...	...
Nebraska	Y	...	...
Nevada	Y	...	...
New Hampshire	Y	...	...
New Jersey	Y	...	...
New Mexico	Y	...	...
New York	...	...	Y
North Carolina	Y	...	...
North Dakota	Y	Y	...
Ohio	Y	Y	...
Oklahoma	Y	Y	...
Oregon	Y	Y	...
Pennsylvania	Y	Y	...
Rhode Island	Y	...	...
South Carolina	Y	...	...
South Dakota	Y	...	...
Tennessee	Y	...	...
Texas	Y	Y	...
Utah	Y	Y	...
Vermont	Y	...	...
Virginia	Y	(b)	...
Washington	Y	Y	...
West Virginia	...	...	...
Wisconsin	Y	Y	...
Wyoming	Y	...	...

Sources: Adapted from the LexisNexis StateNet Database and the Immunization Action Coalition, May 2019, *http://www.ncsl.org/research/health/school-immunizationexemption-state-laws.aspx* and updates by The Council of State Governments, June 2019.

Notes:
1. Religious Exemption: Indicates that there is a provision in the statute that allows parents to exempt their children from vaccination if it contradicts their sincere religious beliefs.
2. Philosophical Exemption: Indicates that the statutory language does not restrict the exemption to purely religious or spiritual beliefs.

Key:
...–No provision for.
(a) The existing statute in Minnesota and Louisiana does not explicitly recognize religion as a reason for claiming an exemption, however, as a practical matter, the non-medical exemption may encompass religious beliefs.
(b) In Virginia, parents can receive a personal exemption only for the HPV vaccine.
(c) Missouri's personal belief exemption does not apply to public schools, only child care facilities.
(d) Maine enacted a measure that will ban non-medical exemptions by 2021.

Table 9.13a | School Immunization Exemptions

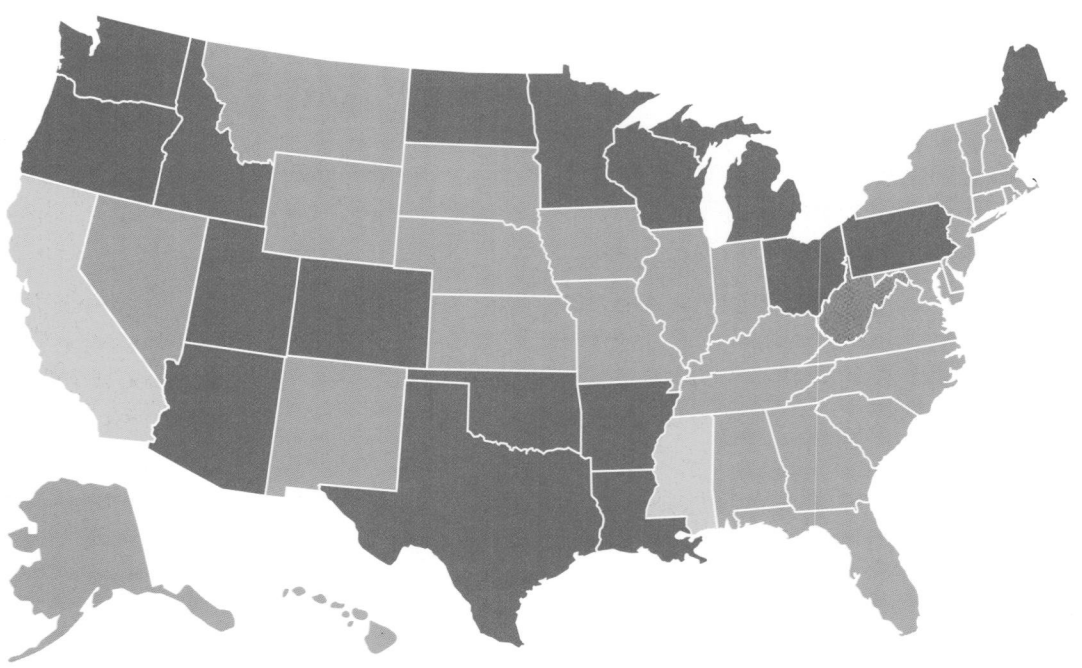

- Medical Only Exemption
- Religious Exemption
- Religious and Philosophical Exemption
- No Provision For

Religious Exemption: Indicates that there is a provision in the statute allowing parents to exempt their children from vaccination if it contradicts their sincere religious beliefs.

Philosophical Exemption: Indicates that the statutory language does not restrict the exemption to religious or spiritual beliefs.

Minnesota's and Louisiana's statutes do not explicitly recognize religion as a reason for claiming an exemption, but as a practical matter, **non-medical exemptions may encompass religious beliefs.**

IN VIRGINIA, parents can receive personal exemptions only for the HPV VACCINE.

IN MISSOURI, personal belief exemptions do not apply to public schools, but only to child care facilities.

TABLE 9.14

Revenues Used by States for State-Administered Highways: 2016* (In thousands of dollars)

State or other jurisdiction	Beginning balance total (a)	Motor-fuel taxes	Motor-vehicle and motor-carrier taxes	Road and crossing tolls	Total	Appropriations from general funds (c)	Other state imposts (d)	Miscellaneous
Total	$101,377,435	$21,786,748	$15,311,847	$12,162,871	$49,261,466	$6,208,134	$11,709,679	$12,490,951
Alabama	403,382	117,262	31,153	0	148,415	180,803	46,657	6,588
Alaska	50,000	31,392	39,831	41,174	112,397	331,708	0	65,455
Arizona	1,377,034	162,110	101,598	0	263,708	8,510	663,960	52,045
Arkansas	844,421	279,605	111,771	0	391,376	49,935	209,150	120,652
California	41,231,858	1,837,070	2,256,411	347,412	4,440,893	110,447	464,658	824,910
Colorado	976,410	294,193	519,311	149,963	963,467	252,600	0	88,089
Connecticut	1,092,527	243,824	116,075	284	360,183	63,140	196,163	53,855
Delaware	2,273,558	110,627	174,477	317,822	602,926	91,903	0	1,002,825
Florida	3,503,216	1,543,348	1,145,342	1,756,924	4,445,614	0	418,044	1,061,859
Georgia	2,258,386	1,263,667	85,609	13,582	1,362,858	475,107	0	170,666
Hawaii	376,336	61,201	129,775	0	190,976	0	0	4,746
Idaho	291,393	149,989	106,996	0	256,985	0	12,049	26,643
Illinois	3,505,969	656,130	720,310	1,269,294	2,645,734	704,912	196	142,138
Indiana	69,338	515,281	179,577	9,022	703,880	117,873	19,534	370,179
Iowa	134,237	305,412	460,841	0	766,253	58,611	35,176	4,443
Kansas	787,240	19,907	9,565	107,446	136,918	0	419,676	57,560
Kentucky	1,096,667	476,982	472,875	0	949,857	6,228	0	220,817
Louisiana	684,067	500,317	125,007	16,569	641,893	0	2,146	54,849
Maine	156,465	153,453	64,916	162,911	381,280	0	0	7,286
Maryland	1,376,400	239,984	327,693	685,001	1,252,678	108,811	216,573	188,938
Massachusetts (e)	650,734	61,330	20,842	309,675	391,847	407,635	535,205	290,765
Michigan	1,064,906	312,341	335,115	44,604	692,060	179,115	38,853	219,374
Minnesota	1,643,057	41,349	35,826	0	77,175	91,947	546,104	26,261
Mississippi	218,321	227,127	94,755	0	321,882	0	55,612	16,946
Missouri	886,151	410,452	185,455	0	595,907	2,994	393,440	15,803
Montana	53,624	101,577	106,088	0	207,665	0	7,114	45,283
Nebraska	21,931	62,702	17,107	0	79,809	49,478	0	9,160
Nevada	415,957	282,258	241,409	917	524,584	0	14,978	74,794
New Hampshire	274,186	91,704	36,198	128,400	256,302	11,505	0	64,319
New Jersey	3,452,413	156,382	357,427	1,532,889	2,046,698	80,520	612,849	633,954
New Mexico	295,563	157,989	213,523	0	371,512	37,768	26,537	18,025
New York	(233,971)	487,675	515,675	2,366,433	3,369,783	764,690	746,584	1,967,039
North Carolina	2,533,018	1,617,276	692,574	21,435	2,331,285	0	739,105	262,267
North Dakota	225,769	76,404	46,259	0	122,663	265,658	0	131
Ohio	2,380,050	696,860	323,737	290,005	1,310,602	10,891	0	408,423
Oklahoma	966,233	213,317	346,791	272,051	832,159	0	1,520,024	127,817
Oregon	3,688,176	420,891	453,531	0	874,422	61,867	12,343	38,395
Pennsylvania	4,114,155	1,830,774	572,280	949,407	3,352,461	974,005	16,967	839,509
Rhode Island	70,138	65,128	42,857	36,203	144,188	74,975	0	11,665
South Carolina	430,828	256,113	139,909	10,350	406,372	254,920	3,580	95,016
South Dakota	28,357	97,675	2,359	0	100,034	0	109,199	36,567
Tennessee	1,266,195	438,048	201,616	46	639,710	0	28,349	172,493
Texas	8,380,900	2,511,759	1,460,144	917,926	4,889,829	0	1,179,168	1,322,631
Utah	826,504	250,951	116,420	1,291	368,662	69,347	515,677	37,771
Vermont	29,619	43,964	72,963	0	116,927	43,247	1,517	17,025
Virginia	2,577,725	379,346	548,809	71,567	999,722	52,332	1,644,463	137,057
Washington	1,364,760	597,292	296,265	238,470	1,132,027	0	100,191	991,475
West Virginia	240,852	397,355	297,979	93,798	789,132	15,299	2,805	9,600
Wisconsin	918,960	460,519	307,459	0	767,978	114,646	81,801	56,593
Wyoming	35,503	77,813	48,906	0	126,719	36,780	73,232	20,229
Dist. of Columbia	67,917	623	2,436	0	3,059	47,927	0	21

See footnotes at end of table

TABLE 9.14

Revenues Used by States for State-Administered Highways: 2016* (In thousands of dollars) (continued)

	Issue of bonds		Payments from other governments			
			Federal funds			
State or other jurisdiction	For capital outlay	For debt service including refunding	Federal Hwy. Administration	Other agencies	From local government	Total receipts
Total	$15,095,095	$6,399,868	$41,191,611	$1,910,389	$3,349,439	$147,616,632
Alabama	0	0	775,145	86,094	8,174	1,251,876
Alaska	164,484	0	549,667	2,584	0	1,226,295
Arizona	0	0	860,203	14,376	939	1,863,741
Arkansas	0	0	521,303	45,887	33,410	1,371,713
California	789,931	0	4,106,430	134,814	1,018,946	11,891,029
Colorado	77,017	0	756,597	9,743	0	2,147,513
Connecticut	590,956	153,000	517,235	65,804	4,259	2,004,595
Delaware	489,444	413,857	189,935	1,401	0	2,792,291
Florida	1,763,553	613,420	2,356,242	29,933	296,137	10,984,802
Georgia	127,007	0	1,271,639	226,312	17,495	3,651,084
Hawaii	0	0	199,914	2,251	0	397,887
Idaho	34,373	182,170	271,742	4,485	9,966	798,413
Illinois	1,173,266	0	1,520,783	50,926	3,771	6,241,726
Indiana	0	0	993,079	320	45,063	2,249,928
Iowa	0	0	421,521	92,846	0	1,378,850
Kansas	0	0	390,389	8,800	23,618	1,036,961
Kentucky	601,024	0	751,980	6,150	0	2,536,056
Louisiana	128,307	0	812,721	8,349	42,027	1,690,292
Maine	0	0	229,607	4,755	123,080	746,008
Maryland	359,916	0	543,040	1,995	120,872	2,792,823
Massachusetts (e)	684,681	0	522,773	7,772	0	2,840,678
Michigan	52,649	762,195	858,268	1,839	20,309	2,824,662
Minnesota	358,300	50,800	707,932	20,644	489,223	2,368,386
Mississippi	180,000	0	489,358	4,242	53,436	1,121,476
Missouri	0	0	827,843	21,970	2,655	1,860,612
Montana	25,796	0	424,661	7,814	2,875	721,208
Nebraska	0	0	330,665	8,041	354,598	831,751
Nevada	358,464	0	444,425	1,750	21,702	1,440,697
New Hampshire	2,826	0	146,371	36,592	678	518,593
New Jersey	218,199	838,416	938,651	117,731	0	5,487,018
New Mexico	0	0	378,694	13,736	0	846,272
New York	1,788,149	392,945	1,803,966	230,619	21,822	11,085,597
North Carolina	0	0	1,004,509	42,191	15,880	4,395,237
North Dakota	0	0	230,395	6,730	27,868	653,445
Ohio	275,799	0	1,417,384	0	72,950	3,496,049
Oklahoma	0	0	686,662	15,443	37,179	3,219,284
Oregon	45,332	0	427,593	44,950	0	1,504,902
Pennsylvania	1,585,247	812,865	1,807,812	51,723	11,364	9,451,953
Rhode Island	201,819	0	223,158	5,256	0	661,061
South Carolina	0	0	602,444	3,911	38,475	1,404,718
South Dakota	0	0	274,512	5,537	5,221	531,070
Tennessee	0	0	810,576	42,955	38,823	1,732,906
Texas	1,353,339	2,089,105	3,738,905	125,686	0	14,698,663
Utah	0	0	294,972	45,297	20,184	1,351,910
Vermont	2,600	0	226,868	15,689	1,839	425,712
Virginia	303,740	91,095	1,151,426	48,266	102,616	4,530,717
Washington	604,943	0	991,220	21,704	163,458	4,005,018
West Virginia	0	0	420,299	57,972	1,403	1,296,510
Wisconsin	753,123	0	742,686	72,138	97,124	2,686,089
Wyoming	0	0	218,948	30,719	0	506,627
Dist. of Columbia	811	0	0	8,463	3,647	0

See footnotes at end of table

TABLE 9.14
Revenues Used by States for State-Administered Highways: 2016* (In thousands of dollars) (continued)

Source: U.S. Department of Transportation, Federal Highway Administration, *Highway Statistics, 2016,* (June 2018).

*This summarizes receipts and disbursements for State-administered roads and bridges. Amounts shown reflect activities of State highway departments, State park boards, other State agencies, and quasi-State toll facilities. Includes direct work on local roads under State control, and State highway debt service transactions. This table is compiled from reports of State authorities.

Key:
(a) Any differences between beginning balances and the closing balances on last year's table are the result of accounting adjustments, inclusion of funds not previously reported, etc.
(b) Amounts shown represent only those highway-user revenues that were expended on State-administered roads.
(c) Amounts shown represent gross general fund appropriations for highways reduced by the amount of highway-user revenues placed in the State General Fund.
(d) Includes sales and use taxes, severance taxes, and other State taxes. Amounts shown represent data reported for 2010 and 2011.
(e) Amounts shown represent data reported for 2011.

TABLE 9.15
State Disbursements for Highways: 2016* (In thousands of dollars)

State or other jurisdiction	Capital outlay State administered highways (a)	Local roads and streets	Total	Maintenance and service total State administered highways (a)	Local roads and streets	Total	Administration, research and planning	Highway law enforcement and safety
Total	$71,752,847	$6,247,004	$77,999,851	$23,359,255	$811,804	$24,171,059	$9,169,317	$9,535,550
Alabama	777,419	385,146	1,162,565	30,633	0	30,633	214,615	231,181
Alaska	899,986	0	899,986	221,032	0	221,032	100,529	44,633
Arizona	1,054,975	29,175	1,084,150	147,934	0	147,934	253,127	170,496
Arkansas	927,320	0	927,320	220,336	72,187	292,523	142,885	86,525
California	2,212,144	207,316	2,419,460	1,391,995	147,909	1,539,904	623,529	2,122,467
Colorado	1,130,916	149,884	1,280,800	363,083	0	363,083	133,714	173,275
Connecticut	1,039,596	0	1,039,596	174,570	0	174,570	375,577	20,243
Delaware	449,479	0	449,479	445,961	0	445,961	302,443	97,715
Florida	6,099,136	142,033	6,241,169	1,022,865	0	1,022,865	344,169	369,158
Georgia	1,303,783	171,618	1,475,401	343,254	971	344,225	521,436	266,087
Hawaii	194,446	0	194,446	59,426	0	59,426	18,700	8,746
Idaho	299,863	70,967	370,830	97,399	0	97,399	30,230	48,364
Illinois	4,220,642	67,385	4,288,027	750,060	9,616	759,676	172,616	88,327
Indiana	1,355,349	0	1,355,349	703,307	85,412	788,719	102,703	12,414
Iowa	928,893	0	928,893	208,480	0	208,480	64,412	136,585
Kansas	780,185	113,697	893,882	131,488	0	131,488	68,089	93,576
Kentucky	1,657,291	269,500	1,926,791	467,006	55,480	522,486	35,020	107,783
Louisiana	1,088,686	4,952	1,093,638	405,258	4,101	409,359	48,357	13,230
Maine	423,579	50,570	474,149	219,923	200,902	420,825	61,423	31,098
Maryland	1,411,409	44,793	1,456,202	476,926	0	476,926	115,770	184,157
Massachusetts (b)	1,064,039	281,767	1,345,806	286,495	0	286,495	274,098	203,205
Michigan	1,018,096	1,088,044	2,106,140	334,003	0	334,003	141,574	232,384
Minnesota	1,403,704	0	1,403,704	412,789	0	412,789	157,713	146,910
Mississippi	725,208	122,551	847,759	82,369	0	82,369	75,804	24,111
Missouri	759,083	137,812	896,895	476,822	0	476,822	72,380	246,313
Montana	445,024	0	445,024	126,282	0	126,282	54,558	67,680
Nebraska	572,870	318,051	890,921	226,212	134,384	360,596	114,085	76,642
Nevada	600,834	0	600,834	129,275	0	129,275	172,078	100,996
New Hampshire	239,972	9,364	249,336	154,826	0	154,826	45,366	41,080
New Jersey	2,631,624	9,090	2,640,714	743,425	0	743,425	172,045	390,476
New Mexico	392,440	0	392,440	14,396	0	14,396	290,461	16,065
New York	4,288,149	484,377	4,772,526	1,517,616	0	1,517,616	485,059	489,652
North Carolina	2,676,904	0	2,676,904	932,297	0	932,297	265,451	171,896
North Dakota	549,947	46,277	596,224	28,619	0	28,619	26,695	32,440
Ohio	2,665,280	421,881	3,087,161	477,420	0	477,420	163,623	312,703
Oklahoma	1,450,103	182,654	1,632,757	1,032,441	0	1,032,441	282,320	195,076
Oregon	544,865	92,725	637,590	229,118	10,124	239,242	133,821	74,950
Pennsylvania	4,658,248	208,794	4,867,042	1,526,224	0	1,526,224	500,340	787,017
Rhode Island	270,486	3,562	274,048	114,550	1,420	115,970	53,273	27,551
South Carolina	741,114	0	741,114	276,198	76,948	353,146	119,105	0
South Dakota	326,422	63,455	389,877	85,135	0	85,135	67,373	36,188
Tennessee	1,016,158	49,753	1,065,911	308,041	0	308,041	181,779	33,395
Texas	7,175,281	283,469	7,458,750	2,264,782	0	2,264,782	368,713	684,585
Utah	456,922	0	456,922	397,410	0	397,410	94,706	82,380
Vermont	183,444	76,657	260,101	110,690	103	110,793	59,580	70,383
Virginia	2,014,981	0	2,014,981	1,747,168	0	1,747,168	402,217	221,394
Washington	1,930,114	257,824	2,187,938	700,937	0	700,937	245,361	300,197
West Virginia	830,046	0	830,046	353,215	0	353,215	97,531	41,744
Wisconsin	1,553,075	132,264	1,685,339	256,391	0	256,391	233,233	79,907
Wyoming	313,317	-	313,317	108,443	0	108,443	50,803	42,175
Dist. of Columbia	0	269,597	269,597	24,730	12,247	36,977	38,828	0

See footnotes at end of table

TABLE 9.15

State Disbursements for Highways: 2016* (In thousands of dollars) (continued)

State or other jurisdiction	Interest	Bond retirement			Grants-in-aid to local governments	Total disbursements	Balances end of year		
		Current revenues or sinking funds	Refunding bonds				Reserves for current highway work	Reserves for debt service	Total
Total	$8,378,889	$9,129,877	$8,216,563	$16,071,737	$162,672,843	$109,586,946	$228,991	$109,815,937
Alabama	39,188	29,830	0	239,949	1,947,961	332,392	0	332,392
Alaska	4,769	5,346	0	778	1,277,073	0	0	0
Arizona	121,802	183,130	0	613,352	2,573,991	1,312,634	0	1,312,634
Arkansas	43,478	42,680	0	0	1,535,411	834,520	26,670	861,190
California	449,452	67,451	0	4,397,864	11,620,127	46,257,596	0	46,257,596
Colorado	22,517	298,522	0	703,341	2,975,252	1,001,896	0	1,001,896
Connecticut	223,037	256,845	152,775	82,787	2,325,430	854,479	0	854,479
Delaware	114,432	160,326	413,857	0	1,984,213	3,001,134	80,502	3,081,636
Florida	623,513	562,547	1,644,075	423,886	11,231,382	3,822,555	0	3,822,555
Georgia	97,143	284,316	63,638	170,934	3,223,180	3,030,066	0	3,030,066
Hawaii	41,851	15,881	0	62,671	401,721	435,173	0	435,173
Idaho	45,236	29,100	182,170	161,787	965,116	357,444	0	357,444
Illinois	312,313	828,357	0	457,529	6,906,845	3,375,380	0	3,375,380
Indiana	45,619	54,800	0	324,514	2,684,118	45,074	0	45,074
Iowa	0	0	0	842,789	2,181,159	174,717	0	174,717
Kansas	112,566	119,850	0	153,631	1,573,082	518,447	0	518,447
Kentucky	153,147	117,240	369,580	0	3,232,047	729,657	0	729,657
Louisiana	146,428	48,543	45,627	59,649	1,864,831	578,230	0	578,230
Maine	30,663	34,000	0	0	1,052,158	142,472	0	142,472
Maryland	221,827	419,619	0	177,304	3,051,805	1,327,136	12,379	1,339,515
Massachusetts (b)	349,534	295,437	0	168,447	2,923,022	1,018,604	0	1,018,604
Michigan	131,755	141,990	762,195	33,000	3,883,041	1,127,571	0	1,127,571
Minnesota	76,795	131,535	50,800	984,541	3,364,787	1,631,197	0	1,631,197
Mississippi	42,559	39,390	0	96,722	1,208,714	352,981	0	352,981
Missouri	111,767	168,470	0	275,495	2,248,142	911,928	0	911,928
Montana	5,077	12,270	24,040	27,969	762,900	39,901	0	39,901
Nebraska	0	0	0	327,626	1,769,870	(41,336	0	(41,336
Nevada	22,928	45,600	146,045	0	1,217,756	638,898	0	638,898
New Hampshire	32,434	39,848	0	46,416	609,306	239,253	0	239,253
New Jersey	1,325,530	660,550	343,686	147,017	6,423,443	2,672,095	0	2,672,095
New Mexico	65,595	68,640	0	37,027	884,624	294,238	0	294,238
New York	535,524	1,323,751	392,945	409,154	9,926,227	1,830,247	0	1,830,247
North Carolina	115,416	114,193	0	147,729	4,423,886	2,652,098	0	2,652,098
North Dakota	1,151	4,165	0	111,017	800,311	239,701	0	239,701
Ohio	98,920	260,730	0	1,128,490	5,529,047	1,897,423	0	1,897,423
Oklahoma	79,767	95,325	0	0	3,317,686	1,051,957	0	1,051,957
Oregon	152,514	88,859	45,189	0	1,372,165	3,925,228	0	3,925,228
Pennsylvania	604,561	440,407	838,630	366,011	9,930,232	4,122,993	87,688	4,210,681
Rhode Island	23,888	114,851	0	1,815	611,396	126,600	0	126,600
South Carolina	19,995	48,247	0	159,490	1,441,097	630,887	0	630,887
South Dakota	0	0	0	0	578,573	44,309	0	44,309
Tennessee	0	0	0	309,376	1,898,502	1,459,728	0	1,459,728
Texas	1,152,859	300,625	2,349,248	525,648	15,105,210	8,783,470	0	8,783,470
Utah	85,361	265,720	0	29,969	1,412,468	795,915	0	795,915
Vermont	2,505	3,061	2,600	26,659	535,682	23,068	0	23,068
Virginia	168,324	201,970	91,095	913,515	5,760,659	2,239,546	21,752	2,261,298
Washington	435	349,544	179,410	443,140	4,406,962	1,687,887	0	1,687,887
West Virginia	19,028	63,264	0	7,806	1,412,634	132,534	0	132,534
Wisconsin	305,686	254,449	118,958	474,893	3,408,856	831,119	0	831,119
Wyoming	0	0	0	0	514,738	27,392	0	27,392
Dist. of Columbia	0	38,603	0	0	384,005	68,512	0	68,512

Source: U.S. Department of Transportation, Federal Highway Administration, *Highway Statistics, 2016* (June 2018).

*This table shows the disbursements by States for highways. This table is compiled from reports of State authorities.

Key:

(a) Includes expenditures for local roads and streets under State control. Most local roads are under State control in Delaware, North Carolina, Virginia, and West Virginia.

(b) Amounts shown represent data reported for 2013.

TABLE 9.16
Public Road Length Miles by Ownership: 2016

State or other jurisdiction	State highway agency	County	Rural Town, township, municipal (a)	Other jurisdiction (b)	Federal agency (c)	Total
Grand Total	611,699	1,576,416	558,382	51,286	133,372	2,931,154
U.S. Total	610,674	1,576,416	556,325	51,286	133,349	2,928,050
Alabama	8,285	59,093	6,345	149	819	74,691
Alaska	4,941	2,316	1,489	2,312	1,653	12,710
Arizona	5,530	13,571	2,456	4,047	14,081	39,686
Arkansas	14,087	64,613	4,637	0	2,148	85,485
California	10,259	56,858	1,030	864	7,002	76,013
Colorado	7,535	51,286	2,100	832	6,505	68,258
Connecticut	1,170	0	4,232	266	21	5,689
Delaware	2,829	0	52	41	72	2,994
Florida	5,645	26,399	2,582	80	1,733	36,440
Georgia	12,499	58,236	4,074	87	1,081	75,978
Hawaii	483	1,023	0	47	113	1,666
Idaho	4,589	16,021	1,588	14,807	8,180	45,185
Illinois	10,429	13,838	71,301	416	217	96,201
Indiana	8,295	53,981	2,836	519	774	66,406
Iowa	7,830	88,298	5,466	435	114	102,144
Kansas	9,480	112,050	5,229	173	887	127,819
Kentucky	24,526	37,193	1,874	491	794	64,877
Louisiana	12,961	27,967	2,209	15	649	43,801
Maine	7,245	369	11,421	229	160	19,424
Maryland	2,659	9,637	365	107	755	13,523
Massachusetts	589	0	5,650	247	21	6,507
Michigan	6,858	72,706	2,827	79	1,683	84,153
Minnesota	10,197	43,458	58,725	1,711	2,579	116,670
Mississippi	9,487	50,528	3,184	79	792	64,070
Missouri	30,756	69,910	5,481	95	1,183	107,426
Montana	10,502	42,606	1,188	4,232	10,874	69,402
Nebraska	9,457	60,456	17,046	114	160	87,233
Nevada	4,659	24,212	140	14	3,274	32,299
New Hampshire	3,185	0	7,742	18	148	11,093
New Jersey	356	1,590	3,070	565	174	5,755
New Mexico	11,026	37,144	1,531	154	10,897	60,752
New York	9,617	15,542	37,660	625	350	63,794
North Carolina	59,268	0	2,367	1,018	2,878	65,530
North Dakota	7,170	10,489	65,307	19	1,546	84,531
Ohio	13,554	25,213	35,570	989	186	75,511
Oklahoma	10,851	75,373	7,607	980	13	94,824
Oregon	6,426	29,108	1,254	1,376	20,428	58,592
Pennsylvania	28,159	33	42,208	1,436	741	72,577
Rhode Island	374	0	949	16	25	1,365
South Carolina	29,781	24,088	610	194	1,589	56,262
South Dakota	7,497	34,944	32,867	1,417	2,428	79,155
Tennessee	10,022	49,132	3,625	384	1,172	64,335
Texas	64,729	127,691	10,759	6	2,037	205,222
Utah	4,700	23,295	2,157	522	4,368	35,043
Vermont	2,371	0	10,226	0	157	12,754
Virginia	46,005	62	441	19	2,105	48,632
Washington	5,523	32,836	1,396	8,334	8,207	56,295
West Virginia	30,423	0	601	239	834	32,098
Wisconsin	9,591	19,071	62,143	0	861	91,666
Wyoming	6,264	14,179	705	488	3,878	25,513
Dist. of Columbia	0	0	0	0	0	0
Puerto Rico (d)	1,024	0	2,057	0	22	3,104

See footnotes at end of table

TABLE 9.16
Public Road Length Miles by Ownership: 2016 (continued)

State or other jurisdiction	State highway agency	County	Urban Town, township, municipal (a)	Other jurisdiction (b)	Federal agency (c)	Total	Total rural and urban
Grand Total	173,346	248,060	789,391	6,434	8,372	1,225,603	4,156,799
U.S. Total	169,788	248,060	779,382	6,434	8,365	1,212,029	4,140,108
Alabama	2,644	3,078	20,880	0	683	27,285	101,975
Alaska	688	1,734	327	25	44	2,818	15,528
Arizona	1,250	4,308	20,178	376	238	26,349	66,035
Arkansas	2,344	1,396	12,897	0	493	17,131	102,616
California	4,833	19,191	79,701	156	907	104,787	180,800
Colorado	1,511	4,753	14,240	20	45	20,570	88,828
Connecticut	2,549	0	13,163	72	57	15,842	21,531
Delaware	2,583	0	763	37	50	3,433	6,427
Florida	6,461	44,009	35,360	7	459	86,296	122,736
Georgia	5,412	29,132	15,931	31	1,751	52,257	128,235
Hawaii	460	2,303	0	22	17	2,803	4,469
Idaho	403	427	4,342	968	17	6,157	51,342
Illinois	5,487	2,650	41,117	409	29	49,692	145,892
Indiana	2,321	11,092	16,601	79	117	30,210	96,616
Iowa	1,054	1,642	9,689	184	25	12,594	114,741
Kansas	812	2,084	11,262	66	3	14,227	142,047
Kentucky	3,124	2,859	8,844	78	159	15,064	79,942
Louisiana	3,716	4,753	9,124	10	7	17,610	61,411
Maine	1,107	0	2,296	67	4	3,474	22,898
Maryland	2,492	11,874	3,960	187	112	18,624	32,147
Massachusetts	2,401	0	27,238	378	83	30,100	36,632
Michigan	2,810	16,763	18,372	16	0	37,962	122,115
Minnesota	1,556	2,899	17,616	52	1	22,125	138,794
Mississippi	1,401	2,731	8,752	14	60	12,957	77,027
Missouri	3,100	3,667	17,526	30	59	24,382	131,807
Montana	514	0	3,694	0	0	4,208	73,610
Nebraska	486	765	6,426	7	71	7,755	94,988
Nevada	744	4,994	4,476	45	24	10,283	42,582
New Hampshire	714	0	4,261	88	0	5,064	16,157
New Jersey	1,976	5,057	25,702	447	134	33,316	39,071
New Mexico	968	3,615	3,770	0	6	8,359	69,111
New York	5,424	4,642	38,537	776	326	49,706	113,499
North Carolina	20,369	0	20,427	22	173	40,991	106,522
North Dakota	244	23	2,599	0	0	2,866	87,397
Ohio	5,675	4,123	37,432	147	86	47,463	122,974
Oklahoma	1,403	2,695	13,945	121	0	18,164	112,988
Oregon	1,229	3,721	9,856	101	30	14,937	73,529
Pennsylvania	11,578	374	35,355	486	75	47,869	120,446
Rhode Island	724	0	3,817	78	69	4,688	6,052
South Carolina	11,559	5,209	3,033	1	3	19,805	76,067
South Dakota	258	286	2,598	259	2	3,402	82,557
Tennessee	3,866	8,678	18,822	15	20	31,402	95,737
Texas	15,755	19,270	72,444	365	600	108,434	313,656
Utah	1,181	953	9,583	0	9	11,726	46,769
Vermont	259	0	1,234	0	7	1,499	14,253
Virginia	12,816	1,678	11,252	20	697	26,463	75,096
Washington	1,549	6,390	15,633	92	433	24,097	80,392
West Virginia	3,985	0	2,645	42	0	6,672	38,770
Wisconsin	2,148	1,698	19,867	0	78	23,791	115,458
Wyoming	469	545	1,794	5	0	2,813	28,326
Dist. of Columbia	1,374	0	0	33	102	1,509	1,509
Puerto Rico (d)	3,558	0	10,009	0	7	13,574	16,691

Source: U.S. Department of Transportation, Federal Highway Administration, *Highway Statistics*, 2016,(September 18, 2017).
Note: Detail may not add to totals due to rounding. This table was compiled from reports of state authorities.
(a) Prior to 1999, municipal was included with other jurisdictions.

(b) Includes State park, State toll, other State agency, other local agency and other roadways not identified by ownership.
(c) Roadways in Federal parks, forests, and reservations that are not part of the State and local highway systems.
(d) 2009 data.

TABLE 9.16a
National Highway System Travel 2016–Annual Vehicle Miles by Functional System*
(In millions of miles)

State or other jurisdiction	Total rural and urban miles	Rural							
		Interstate	Other freeways and expressways	Other principal arterial	Minor arterial	Major collector	Minor collector	Local	Total rural
Grand Total	1,749,457	247,178	34,318	183,586	3,933	841	3	5	469,864
U.S. Total	1,742,067	246,716	34,318	183,522	3,933	841	3	5	469,338
Alabama	30,638	6,333	0	5,400	35	4	0	0	11,772
Alaska	3,056	896	0	326	34	11	0	0	1,267
Arizona	31,280	6,550	30	3,245	18	30	0	0	9,874
Arkansas	17,633	3,995	275	3,677	5	5	0	0	7,958
California	222,370	15,316	4,884	9,680	112	92	0	0	30,085
Colorado	33,047	4,683	248	4,153	0	1	0	0	9,085
Connecticut	19,055	470	296	422	0	0	0	0	1,187
Delaware	5,755	0	601	861	20	0	0	0	1,482
Florida	109,145	10,256	2,040	7,971	15	6	0	0	20,289
Georgia	60,424	7,710	0	6,181	838	86	0	0	14,816
Hawaii	5,066	0	0	329	2	0	0	0	331
Idaho	8,652	2,604	351	1,993	0	0	0	0	4,948
Illinois	59,579	8,951	173	3,304	228	2	0	0	12,659
Indiana	31,989	7,694	684	3,584	214	86	0	0	12,262
Iowa	18,503	5,021	0	6,175	1	1	0	0	11,198
Kansas	15,621	3,664	1,308	3,193	0	0	0	0	8,166
Kentucky	25,758	8,039	1,862	3,470	10	8	0	0	13,390
Louisiana	27,948	5,931	208	2,904	164	23	0	0	9,230
Maine	6,107	2,056	0	1,813	30	0	0	0	3,899
Maryland	37,254	2,128	509	1,962	22	0	0	0	4,621
Massachusetts	36,923	1,029	187	321	28	0	0	0	1,566
Michigan	53,617	5,268	2,492	4,168	9	5	0	0	11,941
Minnesota	28,827	3,904	231	6,830	0	0	0	0	10,965
Mississippi	19,590	4,466	0	5,148	69	25	0	0	9,708
Missouri	40,490	7,026	4,435	3,583	21	4	0	0	15,069
Montana	6,812	2,566	0	2,547	0	0	0	0	5,113
Nebraska	11,117	2,956	943	2,307	75	0	0	0	6,281
Nevada	13,092	2,245	0	1,571	9	0	0	0	3,824
New Hampshire	7,241	1,091	147	1,048	186	0	0	0	2,472
New Jersey	47,549	1,229	494	707	0	0	0	0	2,431
New Mexico	13,900	4,503	0	3,000	30	0	1	0	7,533
New York	67,524	5,890	798	3,740	13	1	0	0	10,443
North Carolina	54,193	6,011	2,591	5,592	831	232	0	1	15,258
North Dakota	5,237	1,594	0	2,213	0	1	0	0	3,807
Ohio	60,195	8,762	1,868	4,238	101	23	0	0	14,991
Oklahoma	23,608	5,383	0	5,164	2	13	0	0	10,563
Oregon	20,800	3,921	0	4,189	0	1	0	1	8,111
Pennsylvania	55,465	10,376	2,047	4,042	14	11	0	0	16,490
Rhode Island	5,579	311	66	227	0	0	0	0	603
South Carolina	29,515	8,179	265	4,338	1	0	0	0	12,782
South Dakota	5,137	2,015	427	1,523	5	0	0	0	3,971
Tennessee	42,837	8,142	136	4,493	27	2	0	0	12,800
Texas	162,395	18,142	0	20,392	208	50	0	0	38,791
Utah	19,567	3,267	81	1,831	371	77	1	0	5,628
Vermont	2,953	1,235	5	707	0	0	0	0	1,946
Virginia	51,461	9,302	608	6,240	28	15	0	1	16,194
Washington	36,651	4,781	1,832	2,281	29	9	0	0	8,932
West Virginia	10,469	2,338	0	2,290	0	0	0	0	4,629
Wisconsin	33,283	6,012	1,196	6,599	128	17	0	0	13,952
Wyoming	5,285	2,472	0	1,551	3	0	0	0	4,025
Dist. Of Columbia	1,877	0	0	0	0	0	0	0	0
Puerto Rico (a)	7,390	462	0	64	0	0	0	0	526

See footnotes at end of table.

TABLE 9.16a
National Highway System Travel 2016–Annual Vehicle Miles by Functional System*
(In millions of miles) (continued)

State or other jurisdiction	Interstate	Other freeways and expressways	Other principal arterial	Minor arterial	Major collector	Minor collector	Local	Total urban
Grand Total	563,421	249,243	453,349	11,784	1,411	107	278	1,279,594
U.S. Total	558,388	248,291	452,480	11,774	1,411	107	278	1,272,729
Alabama	8,988	548	9,114	188	17	0	11	18,865
Alaska	768	0	971	45	4	0	0	1,789
Arizona	7,572	7,796	5,877	144	17	0	0	21,406
Arkansas	5,400	965	3,212	83	12	0	3	9,676
California	74,066	62,102	55,552	366	132	68	0	192,286
Colorado	9,375	5,405	9,111	60	11	0	0	23,962
Connecticut	9,886	4,174	3,803	3	0	0	0	17,867
Delaware	1,432	646	2,144	52	0	0	0	4,273
Florida	29,799	14,805	42,898	1,266	74	6	7	88,856
Georgia	24,351	3,581	16,904	663	84	0	25	45,608
Hawaii	2,059	488	2,073	12	4	0	98	4,735
Idaho	1,619	158	1,907	19	2	0	0	3,704
Illinois	24,853	1,200	19,254	1,364	236	5	10	46,921
Indiana	11,428	1,127	6,291	814	64	1	3	19,727
Iowa	3,137	0	4,112	54	1	0	1	7,305
Kansas	4,158	1,955	1,329	12	2	0	0	7,455
Kentucky	6,652	885	4,790	28	10	1	2	12,368
Louisiana	9,739	784	7,873	289	21	2	10	18,719
Maine	1,228	144	779	41	16	0	0	2,208
Maryland	15,456	6,702	10,195	241	34	1	5	32,633
Massachusetts	16,772	6,468	10,980	1,069	67	0	0	35,358
Michigan	17,640	6,347	17,654	31	4	0	0	41,676
Minnesota	9,086	4,370	4,365	16	6	0	17	17,861
Mississippi	4,203	482	5,123	74	0	0	1	9,882
Missouri	14,268	5,342	5,785	21	4	0	1	25,421
Montana	625	0	1,075	0	0	0	0	1,699
Nebraska	1,563	1,048	1,959	244	20	1	0	4,836
Nevada	4,307	1,726	3,176	53	0	5	0	9,268
New Hampshire	1,958	1,378	1,347	80	4	0	2	4,769
New Jersey	15,090	13,293	16,375	325	34	0	1	45,118
New Mexico	2,654	104	3,491	83	25	10	0	6,366
New York	20,743	16,690	19,278	311	45	0	14	57,081
North Carolina	19,239	5,745	12,906	970	44	5	25	38,935
North Dakota	519	0	911	0	0	0	0	1,430
Ohio	24,871	6,329	12,842	1,068	83	0	11	45,204
Oklahoma	5,701	3,177	4,139	11	17	0	0	13,045
Oregon	5,653	1,435	5,455	123	17	0	5	12,688
Pennsylvania	15,644	7,108	15,997	182	45	0	0	38,976
Rhode Island	1,895	1,222	1,858	0	1	0	0	4,976
South Carolina	7,673	774	8,209	72	5	0	0	16,733
South Dakota	736	67	363	1	0	0	0	1,166
Tennessee	14,747	2,397	12,675	188	28	0	0	30,036
Texas	50,831	33,860	38,318	480	115	0	0	123,604
Utah	7,982	424	5,265	231	17	0	20	13,938
Vermont	566	39	384	11	6	0	0	1,007
Virginia	16,988	5,317	12,679	250	29	2	3	35,267
Washington	12,104	5,893	9,609	77	34	0	3	27,719
West Virginia	3,470	76	2,291	3	0	0	0	5,840
Wisconsin	7,936	3,320	8,002	53	19	0	0	19,330
Wyoming	488	12	759	0	0	0	0	1,259
Dist. Of Columbia	474	382	1,020	0	0	0	0	1,877
Puerto Rico (a)	5,033	952	869	10	0	0	0	6,864

Source: U.S. Department of Transportation, Federal Highway Administration, *Highway Statistics, 2016,* (September 2017).
*Travel for all systems are FHWA estimates based on State provided HPMS data.

Key:
(a) Excludes 788 miles of Federal agency owned roads.

TABLE 9.17
Licensed Drivers, By State, 2005-2016*

State or other jurisdiction	2005	2006	2007	2008	2009	2010
U.S. Totals	200,548,972	202,810,438	205,741,845	208,320,601	209,618,386	210,114,939
Alabama	3,637,414	3,665,180	3,691,762	3,753,550	3,782,284	3,805,751
Alaska	486,582	489,024	495,249	503,162	507,759	515,239
Arizona	3,943,180	4,032,643	4,153,739	4,315,579	4,403,390	4,443,647
Arkansas	2,024,466	2,034,975	2,046,039	2,055,189	2,065,065	2,077,806
California	22,895,965	23,021,279	23,467,452	23,697,667	23,680,643	23,753,441
Colorado	3,341,275	3,341,275	3,502,709	3,605,682	3,704,561	3,779,273
Connecticut	2,740,270	2,805,124	2,848,602	2,883,324	2,916,143	2,934,576
Delaware	610,406	619,877	624,472	651,877	699,745	695,036
Florida	13,373,700	13,988,630	14,138,846	14,033,844	14,005,066	13,949,726
Georgia	5,939,513	5,906,834	6,134,298	6,257,484	6,315,035	6,507,888
Hawaii	856,163	867,375	862,903	884,767	889,918	909,407
Idaho	978,450	1,008,016	1,027,502	1,038,314	1,055,269	1,069,542
Illinois	7,870,872	8,071,253	8,190,023	8,260,940	8,301,118	8,373,969
Indiana	4,246,189	4,246,189	4,308,845	5,550,469	5,550,469	5,550,469
Iowa	2,033,417	2,040,873	2,093,649	1,989,663	2,145,333	2,166,759
Kansas	1,974,238	2,003,112	2,018,219	2,021,905	2,045,426	2,033,092
Kentucky	2,860,729	2,896,460	2,933,266	2,932,659	2,939,423	2,950,191
Louisiana	3,083,516	3,014,191	3,033,966	2,998,162	3,086,004	3,133,631
Maine	1,003,972	1,005,160	1,009,780	1,006,057	1,013,533	1,019,738
Maryland	3,709,594	3,694,290	3,737,847	3,786,650	3,904,685	3,918,305
Massachusetts	4,612,829	4,711,735	4,699,301	4,674,058	4,629,636	4,592,500
Michigan	7,105,272	7,112,992	7,058,955	7,118,378	7,082,820	7,083,107
Minnesota	3,083,757	3,086,610	3,149,109	3,190,183	3,245,441	3,281,463
Mississippi	1,965,464	1,929,636	1,926,969	1,935,764	1,930,603	1,928,487
Missouri	4,135,394	4,139,632	4,161,957	4,196,682	4,217,910	4,246,249
Montana	715,512	723,976	735,753	738,982	737,964	743,611
Nebraska	1,320,617	1,327,916	1,330,698	1,346,406	1,349,295	1,351,516
Nevada	1,596,353	1,626,021	1,661,588	1,678,550	1,690,431	1,691,318
New Hampshire	998,214	1,027,582	1,026,546	1,031,158	1,034,329	1,037,083
New Jersey	5,870,720	5,834,227	5,782,155	5,782,155	5,923,538	5,952,583
New Mexico	1,304,721	1,338,246	1,365,249	1,365,249	1,377,983	1,405,926
New York	11,071,911	11,146,367	11,369,280	11,284,545	11,329,488	11,285,830
North Carolina	6,227,817	6,315,667	6,383,542	6,457,000	6,504,269	6,536,601
North Dakota	466,701	468,711	470,731	473,019	476,561	483,097
Ohio	7,707,842	7,739,410	7,975,774	7,962,266	7,937,498	7,963,372
Oklahoma	2,234,114	2,264,151	2,283,178	2,301,848	2,320,985	2,348,718
Oregon	2,692,948	2,767,291	2,827,188	2,856,085	2,841,972	2,769,734
Pennsylvania	8,460,530	8,526,204	8,600,691	8,646,273	8,687,206	8,737,162
Rhode Island	746,465	741,921	743,793	748,351	746,032	747,875
South Carolina	2,987,593	3,067,747	3,126,890	3,185,408	3,268,498	3,337,247
South Dakota	566,255	582,517	588,546	597,326	602,165	602,275
Tennessee	4,351,868	4,387,883	4,425,881	4,450,644	4,476,539	4,418,210
Texas	14,659,390	14,906,701	15,184,123	15,374,063	15,374,063	15,157,650
Utah	1,599,514	1,619,085	1,651,790	1,687,306	1,720,015	1,659,835
Vermont	563,162	532,041	534,495	541,990	506,977	513,481
Virginia	5,178,156	5,210,685	5,259,512	5,301,182	5,347,745	5,402,347
Washington	4,681,927	4,790,864	4,879,705	4,953,872	5,026,521	5,106,367
West Virginia	1,327,569	1,335,303	1,358,529	1,360,926	1,328,992	1,206,026
Wisconsin	3,993,348	4,049,450	4,066,273	4,075,764	4,105,142	4,133,377
Wyoming	382,735	390,538	398,283	404,489	410,813	419,466
Dist. of Col.	330,363	357,569	396,193	373,735	376,086	384,940

See footnotes at end of table

TABLE 9.17
Licensed Drivers, By State, 2005-2016* (continued)

State or other jurisdiction	2011	2012	2013	2014	2015	2016
U.S. Totals	211,874,649	211,814,830	212,159,728	214,092,472	217,628,863	221,222,087
Alabama	3,798,552	3,827,522	3,859,403	3,881,542	3,907,038	3,943,082
Alaska	521,280	526,371	528,873	531,744	533,227	534,585
Arizona	4,592,398	4,697,579	4,791,450	4,881,801	4,978,762	5,082,305
Arkansas	1,956,091	2,199,164	2,097,201	2,111,873	2,119,578	2,391,103
California	23,856,600	24,200,997	24,390,236	24,813,346	25,532,920	26,199,436
Colorado	3,669,816	3,807,673	3,837,488	3,883,362	3,974,521	4,066,580
Connecticut	2,986,267	2,485,708	2,534,090	2,542,588	2,566,673	2,611,007
Delaware	716,109	720,290	723,657	732,349	742,524	756,328
Florida	13,882,423	13,896,581	13,670,441	13,898,347	14,262,715	14,675,160
Georgia	6,505,690	6,581,534	6,607,016	6,650,434	6,906,191	6,975,900
Hawaii	911,660	915,033	915,033	902,639	909,797	931,703
Idaho	1,083,992	1,092,977	1,111,485	1,128,497	1,135,009	1,160,922
Illinois	8,373,969	8,235,745	8,261,582	8,373,565	8,462,193	8,514,644
Indiana	6,569,665	5,375,973	4,500,403	4,448,099	4,467,848	4,553,259
Iowa	2,191,715	2,217,304	2,143,665	2,227,950	2,224,130	2,245,640
Kansas	2,025,581	2,018,029	2,017,759	2,021,271	2,028,657	2,030,025
Kentucky	2,959,881	2,985,234	3,019,283	3,004,919	3,021,266	3,031,447
Louisiana	3,186,227	2,923,744	3,278,143	3,312,630	3,357,091	3,395,095
Maine	1,014,826	1,008,190	1,011,385	1,018,918	1,019,879	1,021,332
Maryland	3,856,604	4,102,154	4,140,105	4,142,997	4,185,752	4,264,875
Massachusetts	4,683,323	4,733,936	4,765,586	4,765,586	5,040,662	5,040,662
Michigan	7,059,509	7,018,713	6,986,587	7,046,433	7,104,484	7,074,674
Minnesota	3,306,139	3,321,760	3,330,725	3,357,468	3,351,430	3,377,910
Mississippi	1,926,603	1,957,980	1,968,907	1,977,679	1,988,396	2,018,862
Missouri	4,277,037	4,288,488	4,280,438	4,295,224	4,213,302	4,249,579
Montana	752,483	757,812	766,716	768,703	781,427	797,145
Nebraska	1,356,377	1,363,596	1,374,529	1,383,693	1,394,301	1,404,479
Nevada	1,700,829	1,728,060	1,756,095	1,796,443	1,835,511	1,872,376
New Hampshire	1,056,889	1,064,604	1,061,433	1,071,963	1,074,766	1,096,234
New Jersey	5,977,458	6,039,623	6,081,386	6,152,634	6,179,318	6,238,436
New Mexico	1,418,641	1,430,475	1,456,500	1,444,857	1,467,782	1,521,785
New York	11,210,783	11,248,617	11,210,783	11,318,198	11,689,839	11,947,568
North Carolina	6,569,341	6,677,693	6,822,902	7,025,333	7,160,621	7,267,042
North Dakota	490,146	502,807	513,838	527,541	545,027	555,935
Ohio	7,982,149	8,006,183	8,030,421	7,915,907	7,923,439	7,974,951
Oklahoma	2,370,643	2,400,358	2,418,307	2,451,972	2,621,733	2,498,178
Oregon	2,773,956	2,769,757	2,773,373	2,785,446	2,808,548	2,855,746
Pennsylvania	8,796,774	8,842,587	8,896,590	8,915,641	8,942,967	8,996,815
Rhode Island	749,706	749,706	749,232	748,337	745,470	753,143
South Carolina	3,408,318	3,455,931	3,536,404	3,617,535	3,683,824	3,746,681
South Dakota	603,258	606,779	603,643	609,908	655,707	622,663
Tennessee	4,543,759	4,573,871	4,605,100	4,613,166	4,621,401	5,197,904
Texas	15,122,518	15,252,192	15,447,273	15,648,733	15,879,876	15,879,876
Utah	1,747,487	1,788,822	1,661,219	1,425,703	1,913,564	1,960,366
Vermont	521,666	529,501	543,057	545,312	548,799	553,670
Virginia	5,467,045	5,538,480	5,602,765	5,769,063	5,820,209	5,912,048
Washington	5,178,789	5,227,889	5,301,630	5,401,139	5,516,134	5,635,715
West Virginia	1,198,837	1,241,586	1,177,136	1,171,907	1,167,346	1,159,348
Wisconsin	4,147,470	4,056,649	4,171,427	4,188,194	4,194,759	4,206,770
Wyoming	421,928	421,580	421,473	423,987	422,450	421,098
Dist. of Col.	395,442	400,993	405,555	419,896	455,602	489,831

Source: U.S. Department of Transportation, *Highway Statistics,* various years, Table DL-1C.

*The data in this table were obtained chiefly from State authorities. Where data are not available, estimates were made by the Federal Highway Administration. Total licensed drivers represents the total of male and female drivers.

TABLE 9.18
Licensed Total Drivers, by Age 2016*

State or other jurisdiction	19 and under	20-24	25-29	30-34	35-39	40-44	45-49	50-54
U.S. Totals	8,821,455	17,718,332	19,755,328	19,494,719	18,690,308	17,830,080	19,255,964	20,162,725
Alabama	218,838	327,633	344,923	314,454	304,705	293,645	317,944	330,367
Alaska (a)	20,313	44,909	58,759	58,752	51,286	42,782	43,824	45,981
Arizona	171,744	382,303	445,318	468,191	465,333	452,107	463,321	461,224
Arkansas	117,979	204,062	205,515	192,639	188,488	175,338	183,454	194,080
California	871,659	2,336,483	2,653,048	2,608,790	2,414,107	2,262,230	2,368,335	2,391,224
Colorado (a)	156,660	311,295	395,989	398,245	370,229	337,043	351,726	347,465
Connecticut	113,607	200,901	223,137	212,366	202,710	198,393	236,984	259,304
Delaware	36,387	59,485	67,126	63,979	58,639	54,198	61,252	66,622
Florida	470,557	1,047,981	1,202,968	1,169,368	1,127,851	1,127,423	1,260,909	1,354,702
Georgia	296,820	579,622	620,832	602,245	602,195	610,752	657,206	661,264
Hawaii	23,485	62,479	71,619	84,337	82,569	78,088	82,716	86,248
Idaho	66,694	99,636	99,276	99,617	99,275	89,887	91,723	95,138
Illinois (a)	410,301	687,787	745,596	748,587	742,745	694,631	738,868	760,044
Indiana	192,773	382,095	402,835	382,890	375,589	362,968	388,432	414,229
Iowa	139,220	188,643	191,283	187,930	179,510	161,269	175,207	193,205
Kansas	144,750	170,944	174,824	173,588	164,179	147,199	153,882	166,017
Kentucky	75,426	234,606	252,973	252,158	257,988	252,825	270,174	288,717
Louisiana	145,071	253,649	290,109	313,961	299,479	268,102	281,341	298,686
Maine	34,748	67,983	78,196	76,620	74,181	72,254	86,110	96,521
Maryland	130,949	309,487	395,553	414,137	387,344	357,125	392,523	416,318
Massachusetts (b)	175,586	407,948	476,181	448,254	402,325	398,810	449,744	487,517
Michigan	312,714	579,909	601,042	552,131	539,180	521,231	599,608	638,696
Minnesota	168,068	230,057	244,008	264,989	270,203	246,304	283,965	312,952
Mississippi	109,798	166,789	164,222	157,259	161,504	156,542	167,806	177,773
Missouri	200,783	338,899	370,284	364,191	346,848	318,105	344,478	379,892
Montana	35,132	58,441	70,123	67,459	63,666	55,773	58,782	66,599
Nebraska	74,617	118,780	130,450	127,976	118,774	103,353	106,306	114,866
Nevada	55,852	139,910	165,073	171,730	167,740	162,183	171,036	169,335
New Hampshire	45,954	84,480	90,956	84,755	78,150	79,806	96,853	109,791
New Jersey	237,103	518,001	528,790	505,988	502,564	505,473	569,804	614,002
New Mexico	55,809	115,848	135,447	141,706	135,742	122,381	122,430	131,465
New York	316,454	839,747	1,047,316	1,026,730	984,384	949,564	1,070,758	1,153,965
North Carolina	223,000	586,177	667,868	637,738	611,041	613,058	663,784	666,162
North Dakota	32,773	52,271	59,321	54,401	45,284	39,105	40,126	45,987
Ohio	345,449	624,399	638,336	627,126	619,185	608,011	682,680	731,378
Oklahoma	149,763	219,670	221,984	218,156	197,405	181,250	186,948	203,501
Oregon	101,516	202,254	240,646	254,511	247,367	222,148	232,602	229,168
Pennsylvania	296,895	668,551	742,600	724,404	686,693	666,805	772,580	840,563
Rhode Island	22,719	58,347	66,748	62,728	58,589	54,658	64,783	71,936
South Carolina	215,843	290,665	328,380	310,438	294,424	285,933	305,503	322,416
South Dakota	35,007	49,217	52,626	52,797	50,759	43,121	44,511	50,115
Tennessee	280,797	429,217	447,145	424,338	412,764	406,127	438,240	459,429
Texas	653,365	1,422,874	1,515,946	1,490,985	1,436,130	1,394,164	1,439,318	1,449,481
Utah	133,215	202,667	204,814	202,717	204,957	169,760	148,209	139,315
Vermont	18,875	36,918	46,442	48,063	44,012	39,883	44,840	49,916
Virginia	206,274	448,710	524,209	525,967	504,784	487,753	533,876	566,615
Washington	211,501	437,214	529,022	561,899	530,578	479,069	488,687	483,566
West Virginia	55,153	66,023	77,310	76,566	84,131	87,415	97,343	101,115
Wisconsin	190,637	324,857	351,148	357,037	331,470	313,980	352,854	400,906
Wyoming	22,079	33,233	36,939	38,021	35,628	30,634	31,213	33,264
Dist. of Columbia	743	14,276	60,073	90,805	75,625	49,422	40,366	33,683

See footnotes at end of table

TABLE 9.18
Licensed Total Drivers, by Age 2016* (continued)

State or other jurisdiction	55–59	60–64	65–69	70–74	75–79	80–84	85 and over	Total
U.S. Totals	20,323,220	18,115,884	15,468,076	10,680,982	7,174,386	4,615,188	3,887,777	221,994,424
Alabama	339,786	313,427	275,808	208,039	147,997	104,470	101,046	3,943,082
Alaska (a)	49,235	44,987	33,045	20,366	9,476	5,604	5,266	534,585
Arizona	458,453	414,504	332,656	239,781	159,896	97,772	69,702	5,082,305
Arkansas	198,165	183,061	165,814	130,367	95,340	66,622	90,179	2,391,103
California	2,308,313	1,985,371	1,618,249	1,031,043	648,641	398,880	303,063	26,199,436
Colorado (a)	367,320	331,916	273,567	165,571	108,998	73,589	76,967	4,066,580
Connecticut	255,892	214,705	174,939	124,292	81,687	57,049	55,041	2,611,007
Delaware	66,764	60,539	57,138	41,774	28,289	18,543	15,593	756,328
Florida	1,348,423	1,223,728	1,127,941	897,309	612,084	392,178	311,738	14,675,160
Georgia	620,452	537,852	464,769	308,984	201,704	123,391	87,812	6,975,900
Hawaii	88,320	85,629	75,427	52,176	28,581	16,807	13,222	931,703
Idaho	101,785	96,072	85,083	58,455	39,032	23,211	16,038	1,160,922
Illinois (a)	782,922	695,724	572,958	404,823	264,530	125,450	139,678	8,514,644
Indiana	424,836	378,315	319,143	215,762	149,623	93,116	70,653	4,553,259
Iowa	206,553	189,107	159,624	105,465	76,857	51,834	39,933	2,245,640
Kansas	181,761	169,535	139,969	95,019	65,251	44,785	38,322	2,030,025
Kentucky	290,922	261,944	228,630	151,876	104,339	63,640	45,229	3,031,447
Louisiana	305,710	275,304	232,608	157,105	112,019	76,186	85,765	3,395,095
Maine	104,835	98,540	87,690	60,433	38,892	25,337	18,992	1,021,332
Maryland	398,271	335,537	277,987	186,497	121,273	77,759	64,115	4,264,875
Massachusetts (b)	468,138	404,851	341,546	230,542	150,924	104,665	93,631	5,040,662
Michigan	675,461	621,715	521,500	369,650	246,857	159,651	135,329	7,074,674
Minnesota	340,393	303,224	250,926	177,379	124,190	84,081	77,171	3,377,910
Mississippi	184,898	169,235	148,360	101,684	72,853	45,719	34,420	2,018,862
Missouri	400,019	355,209	306,212	214,800	147,939	94,090	67,830	4,249,579
Montana	76,603	75,710	66,227	44,575	29,015	17,883	11,157	797,145
Nebraska	123,805	113,923	96,102	66,265	46,096	33,131	30,035	1,404,479
Nevada	163,977	150,385	138,829	98,115	62,386	34,649	21,176	1,872,376
New Hampshire	112,856	96,533	82,120	54,678	35,436	23,860	20,006	1,096,234
New Jersey	599,463	503,714	418,577	291,279	192,614	131,903	119,161	6,238,436
New Mexico	140,150	131,774	118,797	79,819	46,493	27,299	16,625	1,521,785
New York	1,131,109	985,192	843,786	583,717	405,330	292,087	317,429	11,947,568
North Carolina	650,103	571,851	517,811	360,459	234,929	149,632	113,429	7,267,042
North Dakota	49,288	43,934	32,872	22,280	16,273	11,998	10,022	555,935
Ohio	780,463	701,710	603,042	395,372	283,960	186,139	147,701	7,974,951
Oklahoma	216,509	200,012	175,788	127,361	91,450	60,914	47,467	2,498,178
Oregon	251,420	256,237	232,517	164,663	104,595	63,105	52,997	2,855,746
Pennsylvania	884,961	800,835	683,078	463,681	331,872	231,455	201,842	8,996,815
Rhode Island	74,731	67,013	55,528	39,854	24,289	16,032	15,188	753,143
South Carolina	321,498	303,712	289,457	204,521	130,549	81,446	61,896	3,746,681
South Dakota	57,208	55,087	48,076	33,557	22,568	15,190	12,824	622,663
Tennessee	453,724	410,238	367,345	258,663	180,612	120,242	109,023	5,197,904
Texas	1,441,772	1,251,741	1,032,226	697,100	461,602	287,185	188,493	16,162,382
Utah	141,882	127,406	104,616	71,920	49,627	33,023	26,238	1,960,366
Vermont	53,348	49,807	43,176	29,415	27,377	13,421	8,177	553,670
Virginia	550,154	476,266	408,555	278,851	185,139	117,187	97,708	5,912,048
Washington	491,767	452,337	385,441	253,602	157,711	96,834	76,487	5,635,715
West Virginia	112,046	114,103	107,073	73,952	51,587	32,208	23,323	1,159,348
Wisconsin	406,543	359,490	292,253	198,470	140,186	98,281	88,658	4,206,770
Wyoming	39,541	38,906	31,416	21,390	14,031	8,533	6,270	421,098
Dist. of Columbia	30,672	27,937	21,779	18,231	11,387	7,122	7,710	489,831

Source: U.S. Department of Transportation Federal Highway Administration, Highway Statistics, various years, Table DL-1C. September 2017.

Note: Includes restricted drivers and graduated driver licenses.

Key:
(a) Age and/or sex distribution estimates by FHWA using Census population figures for that State and age group.
(b) State did not provide current data. Table displays 2015 data.

TABLE 9.19
Licensed Drivers by Sex and Ratio to Population–2016*

State or other jurisdiction	Male drivers	Percent male drivers of total	Female drivers	Percent female drivers of total	Total drivers	Ratio–licensed drivers/ private and commercial motor vehicles registered
U.S. Total	109,587,219	49.4	112,124,699	51	221,711,918	0.84
Alabama	1,913,487	48.5	2,029,595	51	3,943,082	0.74
Alaska (b)	252,875	47.3	281,710	53	534,585	0.69
Arizona	2,552,249	50.2	2,530,056	50	5,082,305	0.89
Arkansas	1,158,338	48.4	1,232,765	52	2,391,103	0.86
California	13,331,944	50.9	12,867,492	49	26,199,436	0.88
Colorado (b)	2,086,189	51.3	1,980,391	49	4,066,580	0.80
Connecticut	1,291,397	49.5	1,319,610	51	2,611,007	0.92
Delaware	367,808	48.6	388,520	51	756,328	0.76
Florida	7,206,475	49.1	7,468,685	51	14,675,160	0.90
Georgia	3,327,867	47.7	3,648,033	52	6,975,900	0.86
Hawaii	481,461	51.7	450,242	48	931,703	0.77
Idaho	583,602	50.3	577,320	50	1,160,922	0.63
Illinois (b)	4,200,790	49.34	4,313,854	51	8,514,644	0.84
Indiana	2,237,101	49.1	2,316,158	51	4,553,259	0.74
Iowa	1,111,840	49.5	1,133,800	50	2,245,640	0.62
Kansas	1,004,834	49.5	1,025,191	51	2,030,025	0.77
Kentucky	1,492,573	49.2	1,538,874	51	3,031,447	0.73
Louisiana	1,632,808	48.1	1,762,287	52	3,395,095	0.89
Maine	504,674	49.4	516,658	51	1,021,332	0.94
Maryland	2,103,981	49.3	2,160,894	51	4,264,875	1.04
Massachusetts (c)	2,473,050	49.1	2,567,612	51	5,040,662	1.01
Michigan	3,464,410	49.0	3,610,264	51	7,074,674	0.86
Minnesota	1,697,475	50.3	1,680,435	50	3,377,910	0.64
Mississippi	957,284	47.4	1,061,578	53	2,018,862	0.98
Missouri	2,066,910	48.6	2,182,669	51	4,249,579	0.75
Montana	405,029	50.8	392,116	49	797,145	0.45
Nebraska	704,348	50.2	700,131	50	1,404,479	0.74
Nevada	956,291	51.1	916,085	49	1,872,376	0.79
New Hampshire	549,729	50.2	546,505	50	1,096,234	0.84
New Jersey	3,066,313	49.2	3,172,123	51	6,238,436	1.06
New Mexico	758,190	49.8	763,595	50	1,521,785	0.85
New York	5,814,353	48.7	6,133,215	51	11,947,568	1.08
North Carolina	3,515,543	48.4	3,751,499	52	7,267,042	0.89
North Dakota	288,618	51.9	267,317	48	555,935	0.64
Ohio	3,866,323	48.5	4,108,628	52	7,974,951	0.75
Oklahoma	1,154,923	46.2	1,343,255	54	2,498,178	0.67
Oregon	1,406,168	49.2	1,449,578	51	2,855,746	0.77
Pennsylvania	4,461,263	49.6	4,535,552	50	8,996,815	0.85
Rhode Island	368,146	48.9	384,997	51	753,143	0.88
South Carolina	1,799,712	48.0	1,946,969	52	3,746,681	0.91
South Dakota	314,356	50.5	308,307	50	622,663	0.51
Tennessee	2,683,909	51.6	2,513,995	48	5,197,904	0.94
Texas	7,824,635	49.3	8,055,241	51	15,879,876	0.74
Utah	988,484	50.4	971,882	50	1,960,366	0.86
Vermont	275,292	49.7	278,378	50	553,670	0.92
Virginia	2,846,993	48.2	3,065,055	52	5,912,048	0.83
Washington	2,908,119	51.6	2,727,596	48	5,635,715	0.82
West Virginia	574,199	49.5	585,149	50	1,159,348	0.70
Wisconsin	2,098,274	49.9	2,108,496	50	4,206,770	0.77
Wyoming	214,785	51.0	206,313	49	421,098	0.50
Dist. of Columbia	241,802	49.4	248,029	51	489,831	1.62

See footnotes at end of table

TABLE 9.19
Licensed Drivers by Sex and Ratio to Population–2016* (continued)

State or other jurisdiction	Population (a)				Drivers	
		Driving age (16 and over)				
	Total resident	Male	Female	Total	Per 1,000 total resident population	Per 1,000 driving age population
U.S. Total	323,127,513	116,502,331	122,231,724	238,734,055	686	929
Alabama	4,863,300	1,862,731	2,033,606	3,896,337	811	1,012
Alaska (b)	741,894	302,472	272,432	574,904	721	930
Arizona	6,931,071	2,706,102	2,779,736	5,485,838	733	926
Arkansas	2,988,248	1,148,262	1,215,626	2,363,888	800	1,012
California	39,250,017	15,378,392	15,811,628	31,190,020	668	840
Colorado (b)	5,540,545	2,211,819	2,207,221	4,419,040	734	920
Connecticut	3,576,452	1,409,891	1,509,885	2,919,776	730	894
Delaware	952,065	369,049	402,404	771,453	794	980
Florida	20,612,439	8,200,700	8,749,239	16,949,939	712	866
Georgia	10,310,371	3,889,622	4,199,268	8,088,890	677	862
Hawaii	1,428,557	575,568	576,619	1,152,187	652	809
Idaho	1,683,140	645,248	650,014	1,295,262	690	896
Illinois (b)	12,801,539	4,973,453	5,245,319	10,218,772	665	833
Indiana	6,633,053	2,557,592	2,684,104	5,241,696	686	869
Iowa	3,134,693	1,227,404	1,259,188	2,486,592	716	903
Kansas	2,907,289	2,272,404	2,272,404	4,544,808	698	447
Kentucky	4,436,974	1,728,719	1,813,875	3,542,594	683	856
Louisiana	4,681,666	1,785,544	1,907,555	3,693,099	725	919
Maine	1,331,479	538,121	570,553	1,108,674	767	921
Maryland	6,016,447	2,306,124	2,516,466	4,822,590	709	884
Massachusetts (c)	6,811,779	2,688,163	2,914,133	5,602,296	740	900
Michigan	9,928,300	3,900,957	4,104,099	8,005,056	713	884
Minnesota	5,519,952	2,162,790	2,212,345	4,375,135	612	772
Mississippi	2,988,726	1,123,917	1,227,419	2,351,336	675	859
Missouri	6,093,000	2,364,551	2,501,669	4,866,220	697	873
Montana	1,042,520	421,152	418,958	840,110	765	949
Nebraska	1,907,116	734,392	750,361	1,484,753	736	946
Nevada	2,940,058	1,166,322	1,171,830	2,338,152	637	801
New Hampshire	1,334,795	544,866	562,536	1,107,402	821	990
New Jersey	8,944,469	3,476,185	3,720,808	7,196,993	697	867
New Mexico	2,081,015	809,169	837,421	1,646,590	731	924
New York	19,745,289	7,699,982	8,351,526	16,051,508	605	744
North Carolina	10,146,788	3,896,650	4,217,131	8,113,781	716	896
North Dakota	757,952	307,492	291,456	598,948	733	928
Ohio	11,614,373	4,515,078	4,797,181	9,312,259	687	856
Oklahoma	3,923,561	1,506,744	1,561,122	3,067,866	637	814
Oregon	4,093,465	1,633,718	1,690,773	3,324,491	698	859
Pennsylvania	12,784,227	5,057,124	5,372,990	10,430,114	704	863
Rhode Island	1,056,426	419,557	454,243	873,800	713	862
South Carolina	4,961,119	1,913,729	2,075,344	3,989,073	755	939
South Dakota	865,454	338,429	336,246	674,675	719	923
Tennessee	6,651,194	2,565,245	2,757,358	5,322,603	781	977
Texas	27,862,596	9,116,438	9,521,795	18,638,233	570	852
Utah	3,051,217	1,113,127	1,114,630	2,227,757	642	880
Vermont	624,594	255,087	266,036	521,123	886	1,062
Virginia	8,411,808	3,290,937	3,463,319	6,754,256	703	875
Washington	7,288,000	2,901,736	2,937,958	5,839,694	773	965
West Virginia	1,831,102	736,272	763,695	1,499,967	633	773
Wisconsin	5,778,708	2,292,297	2,350,197	4,642,494	728	906
Wyoming	585,501	235,117	226,243	461,360	719	913
Dist. of Columbia	681,170	267,681	303,051	570,732	719	858

Source: Bureau of the Census and U.S. Department of Transportation Federal Highway Administration, *Federal Highway Statistics,* December 2017.
Note: Includes restricted drivers and graduated driver licenses.

Key:
(a) Source: Bureau of the Census.
(b) Age and/or sex segregation estimated by FHWA.
(c) Current data was not provided. Table shows 2015 data.

TABLE 9.20

Sentenced Prisoners Under the Jurisdiction of State or Federal Correctional Authorities, by Sex: December 31, 2016 and 2017

State or other jurisdiction	December 31, 2016 population			December 31, 2017 population			Percent change, 2016–2017		
	Total	Male	Female	Total	Male	Female	Total	Male	Female
U.S. total (a)	1,459,948	1,354,109	105,839	1,439,808	1,334,775	105,033	(1.4)	(1.4)	(0.8)
Federal (b)	171,482	160,090	11,392	166,203	154,931	11,272	(3.1)	(3.2)	(1.1)
State (a)	1,288,466	1,194,019	94,447	1,273,605	1,179,844	93,761	(1.2)	(1.2)	(0.7)
Alabama	27,799	25,593	2,206	23,724	21,968	1,756	(14.7)	(14.2)	(20.4)
Alaska (c)	2,089	1,982	107	1,905	1,828	77	(8.8)	(7.8)	(28.0)
Arizona	40,849	37,131	3,718	40,263	36,543	3,720	(1.4)	(1.6)	0.1
Arkansas	17,476	16,111	1,365	18,028	16,617	1,411	3.2	3.1	3.4
California (d)	129,080	123,261	5,819	129,920	124,127	5,793	0.7	0.7	(0.4)
Colorado	19,862	17,963	1,899	19,824	17,925	1,899	(0.2)	(0.2)	0.0
Connecticut (c)	10,365	9,804	561	9,626	9,142	484	(7.1)	(6.8)	(13.7)
Delaware (c)	4,090	3,889	201	4,066	3,882	184	(0.6)	(0.2)	(8.5)
Florida	99,974	93,111	6,863	98,504	91,779	6,725	(1.5)	(1.4)	(2.0)
Georgia	53,064	49,324	3,740	53,094	49,315	3,779	0.1	0.0	1.0
Hawaii (c)	3,629	3,271	358	3,425	3,154	271	(5.6)	(3.6)	(24.3)
Idaho	7,376	6,416	960	7,752	6,761	991	5.1	5.4	3.2
Illinois	43,657	41,044	2,613	41,427	39,148	2,279	(5.1)	(4.6)	(12.8)
Indiana	25,530	23,325	2,205	26,001	23,587	2,414	1.8	1.1	9.5
Iowa	8,998	8,181	817	8,999	8,197	802	0.0	0.2	(1.8)
Kansas	9,628	8,831	797	9,687	8,846	841	0.6	0.2	5.5
Kentucky	23,018	20,077	2,941	23,539	20,518	3,021	2.3	2.2	2.7
Louisiana	35,646	33,665	1,981	33,706	31,749	1,957	(5.4)	(5.7)	(1.2)
Maine	1,828	1,675	153	1,795	1,643	152	(1.8)	(1.9)	(0.7)
Maryland	19,821	19,010	811	19,232	18,399	833	(3.0)	(3.2)	2.7
Massachusetts	8,494	8,140	354	8,286	7,976	310	(2.4)	(2.0)	(12.4)
Michigan	41,122	38,880	2,242	39,666	37,515	2,151	(3.5)	(3.5)	(4.1)
Minnesota	10,592	9,818	774	10,708	9,974	734	1.1	1.6	(5.2)
Mississippi	18,666	17,397	1,269	18,471	17,184	1,287	(1.0)	(1.2)	1.4
Missouri	32,461	29,124	3,337	32,592	29,197	3,395	0.4	0.3	1.7
Montana	3,814	3,405	409	3,698	3,282	416	(3.0)	(3.6)	1.7
Nebraska	5,235	4,825	410	5,257	4,837	420	0.4	0.2	2.4
Nevada	13,637	12,403	1,234	13,671	12,405	1,266	0.2	0.0	2.6
New Hampshire	2,818	2,591	227	2,750	2,524	226	(2.4)	(2.6)	(0.4)
New Jersey	19,786	18,952	834	19,585	18,811	774	(1.0)	(0.7)	(7.2)
New Mexico (e)	6,972	6,276	696	7,189	6,422	767	N.C.	N.C.	N.C.
New York	50,620	48,356	2,264	49,360	47,103	2,257	(2.5)	(2.6)	(0.3)
North Carolina	34,596	32,085	2,511	35,283	32,649	2,634	2.0	1.8	4.9
North Dakota (e)(f)	1,779	1,568	211	1,711	1,514	197	N.C.	N.C.	N.C.
Ohio	52,175	47,581	4,594	51,478	47,052	4,426	(1.3)	(1.1)	(3.7)
Oklahoma	29,531	26,145	3,386	27,729	24,615	3,114	(6.1)	(5.9)	(8.0)
Oregon	15,150	13,846	1,304	15,200	13,877	1,323	0.3	0.2	1.5
Pennsylvania	49,000	46,188	2,812	48,074	45,281	2,793	(1.9)	(2.0)	(0.7)
Rhode Island (c)	2,030	1,962	68	1,808	139	69	(10.9)	(11.4)	1.5
South Carolina	20,371	18,981	1,390	19,541	18,233	1,308	(4.1)	(3.9)	(5.9)
South Dakota	3,820	3,323	497	3,959	3,424	535	3.6	3.0	7.6
Tennessee	28,203	25,481	2,722	28,980	25,969	3,011	2.8	1.9	10.6
Texas	157,903	144,928	12,975	157,584	144,750	12,834	(0.2)	(0.1)	(1.1)
Utah	6,171	5,765	406	6,437	5,945	492	4.3	3.1	21.2
Vermont (c)	1,229	1,146	83	1,126	1,021	105	(8.4)	(10.9)	26.5
Virginia	37,813	34,704	3,109	37,158	34,004	3,154	(1.7)	(2.0)	1.4
Washington	19,019	17,377	1,642	19,540	17,811	1,729	2.7	2.5	5.3
West Virginia	7,162	6,286	876	7,092	6,274	818	(1.0)	(0.2)	(6.6)
Wisconsin	22,144	20,734	1,410	22,682	21,147	1,535	2.4	2.0	8.9
Wyoming	2,374	2,088	286	2,473	2,181	292	4.2	4.5	2.1

See footnotes at end of table

TABLE 9.20
**Sentenced Prisoners Under the Jurisdiction of State or Federal Correctional Authorities, by Sex:
December 31, 2016 and 2017** (continued)

Source: Bureau of Justice Statistics, National Prisoner Statistics (NPS), 2016–2017. *Prisoners in 2017* NCJ 252156.

Note: Jurisdiction refers to the legal authority of state or federal correctional officials over a prisoner, regardless of where the prisoner is held. Counts are based on prisoners with sentences of more than 1 year.

Key:

N.C.–Not calculated

(a) Total and state estimates for 2016 include imputed counts for North Dakota, which did not submit 2016 NPS data. Total and state estimates for 2017 include imputed counts for New Mexico and North Dakota, which did not submit 2017 NPS data.

(b) Includes prisoners held in nonsecure, privately operated community corrections facilities and juveniles held in contract facilities.

(c) Prisons and jails form one integrated system. Data include total jail and prison populations.

(d) State submitted updated 2016 sentenced population counts.

(e) State did not submit 2017 NPS data. Counts were imputed for 2017 and should not be compared to 2016 counts.

(f) State did not submit 2016 NPS data. Counts were imputed for 2016 and should not be compared to 2017 counts.

TABLE 9.21
Admissions and Releases of Sentenced Prisoners Under Jurisdiction of State or Federal Correctional Authorities, 2016 and 2017

State or other jurisdiction	Admissions (a)					Releases (b)				
	2016 Total	2017 Total	Percent change, 2016-2017	2017 New court commitments	2017 Post-custody supervision violations (c)	2016 total	2017 total	Percent change, 2016-2017	2017 Unconditional (d)(e)	2017 Conditional (e)(f)
U.S. total (g)	606,000	606,571	0.1	418,579	174,210	626,019	622,377	(0.6)	160,596	446,785
Federal (e)	44,682	44,708	0.1	40,180	4,527	52,035	49,461	(4.9)	48,457	318
State (g)	561,318	561,863	0.1	378,399	169,683	573,984	573,916	(0.2)	112,139	446,467
Alabama	10,749	12,170	13.2	8,045	1,624	12,711	13,624	7.2	3,130	8,808
Alaska (h)	1,804	1,580	(12.4)	1,446	134	2,159	1,941	(10.1)	460	1,476
Arizona	13,663	13,423	(1.8)	10,787	2,557	13,857	14,075	1.6	2,332	11,610
Arkansas	9,911	8,971	(9.5)	4,623	4,348	10,370	8,443	(18.6)	752	7,610
California (i)	35,730	37,077	3.8	32,396	4,644	34,528	36,203	4.9	98	35,576
Colorado	8,707	9,638	10.7	6,038	3,600	8,934	9,669	8.2	1,116	8,419
Connecticut (h)	4,747	4,401	(7.3)	3,658	606	5,618	5,169	(8.0)	2,451	2,707
Delaware (h)(j)	3,096	2,897	(6.4)	2,237	646	4,041	2,736	(32.3)	310	2,272
Florida (k)	29,038	28,189	(2.9)	27,423	85	31,166	30,467	(2.2)	18,703	11,313
Georgia	17,585	16,699	(5.0)	14,567	2,124	15,053	15,210	1.0	6,713	8,320
Hawaii (h)	1,538	1,528	(0.7)	876	652	1,666	1,834	10.1	345	781
Idaho	5,766	5,747	(0.3)	1,671	4,076	5,479	5,395	(1.5)	400	4,926
Illinois	25,661	24,468	(4.6)	16,401	8,062	28,615	26,850	(6.2)	3,982	22,763
Indiana	12,600	12,249	(2.8)	9,240	2,888	14,561	11,708	(19.6)	910	10,730
Iowa	5,541	5,619	1.4	3,790	1,773	5,305	5,632	6.2	1,182	4,378
Kansas	6,442	6,453	0.2	3,865	1,276	6,394	6,406	0.2	1,690	4,685
Kentucky	20,111	21,239	5.6	12,366	8,605	18,552	20,555	10.8	4,572	15,371
Louisiana	15,877	16,337	2.9	10,662	5,674	16,308	17,868	9.6	1,142	16,584
Maine	657	960	46.1	455	505	647	684	5.7	320	354
Maryland (l)	8,843	8,243	N.C.	5,823	2,415	9,459	8,850	N.C.	2,871	5,919
Massachusetts	2,059	2,141	4.0	1,909	223	2,458	2,309	(6.1)	1,745	533
Michigan	12,573	12,013	(4.5)	6,670	2,720	14,081	13,470	(4.3)	557	10,486
Minnesota	8,027	8,195	2.1	4,804	3,391	8,254	8,092	(2.0)	956	7,125
Mississippi	7,510	7,553	0.6	5,488	2,049	7,080	7,748	9.4	444	6,963
Missouri	18,426	18,551	0.7	9,816	8,729	18,410	18,431	0.1	1,528	16,779
Montana	2,666	2,644	(0.8)	1,961	683	2,546	2,770	8.8	261	2,492
Nebraska	2,310	2,436	5.5	1,979	445	2,366	2,387	0.9	654	1,710
Nevada (m)	6,059	5,862	(3.3)	4,990	794	5,778	6,548	13.3	2,401	4,100
New Hampshire	1,538	1,338	(13.0)	668	670	1,601	1,409	(12.0)	82	1,320
New Jersey	8,837	8,611	(2.6)	6,189	2,422	9,685	8,959	(7.5)	5,072	3,683
New Mexico (n)	3,615	3,848	N.C.	2,461	1,387	3,631	3,631	N.C.	989	2,626
New York	21,081	20,421	(3.1)	12,594	7,727	22,047	21,667	(1.7)	2,330	19,042
North Carolina	16,009	18,242	13.9	13,873	4,366	16,677	17,244	3.4	2,685	14,463
North Dakota (o)	1,590	1,570	N.C.	904	665	1,583	1627	N.C.	216	1407
Ohio (p)	22,792	21,602	(5.2)	16,554	4,401	22,850	22,299	(2.4)	889	13,246
Oklahoma	8,778	10,228	16.5	7,658	2,570	10,404	9,682	(6.9)	2,973	6,623
Oregon (q)	5,020	5566	N.C.	3707	1717	4,712	5428	N.C.	35	5185
Pennsylvania	20,326	19,297	(5.1)	9,116	9,128	20,418	19,673	(3.6)	3,151	16,321
Rhode Island (h)	767	572	(25.4)	482	90	939	875	(6.8)	610	257
South Carolina	6,688	6,017	(10.0)	4,922	1,087	6,709	6,847	2.1	2,239	4,494
South Dakota	2,891	3,896	34.8	1,507	499	2,832	3,859	36.3	311	2,467
Tennessee	12,898	11,541	(10.5)	6,877	4,664	13,508	13,307	(1.5)	5,080	8,136
Texas	77,385	76,877	(0.7)	47,697	27,474	76,733	77,196	0.6	9,977	64,519
Utah	3,293	4,047	22.9	1,814	2,233	3,611	3,781	4.7	674	3,085
Vermont (h)(o)	1,715	1,737	1.3	607	1,130	1,733	1,795	3.6	284	1,504
Virginia (r)	12,163	12,163	0.0	12,030	133	12,648	12,698	0.4	1,054	11,537
Washington (p)	25,055	25,483	1.7	7,385	18,089	24,940	25,658	2.9	2,217	23,393
West Virginia	3,584	3,590	0.2	1,991	1372	3,543	3,652	3.1	849	2,275
Wisconsin	6,600	6,865	4.0	4,557	2,282	5,743	5,592	(2.6)	212	5,324
Wyoming	997	1,069	7.2	820	249	1,041	963	(7.5)	185	770

See footnotes at end of table

TABLE 9.21

Admissions and Releases of Sentenced Prisoners Under Jurisdiction of State or Federal Correctional Authorities, 2016 and 2017 (continued)

Source: Bureau of Justice Statistics, National Prisoner Statistics (NPS), 2016–2017. *Prisoners in 2017* NCJ 252156.

Note: Jurisdiction refers to the legal authority of state or federal correctional officials over a prisoner, regardless of where the prisoner is held. Counts cover January 1 through December 31 for each year and are based on prisoners admitted to or released from state or federal correctional authorities with a sentence of more than one year.

Key:

N.C.–Not calculated

(a) Excludes transfers, escapes, and those absent without leave. Includes other conditional release violators, returns from appeal or bond, and other admissions.

(b) Excludes transfers, escapes, and those absent without leave. Includes deaths, releases to appeal or bond, and other releases.

(c) Includes all conditional release violators returned to prison from post-custody community supervision, including parole and probation, for either violations of conditions of release or new crimes.

(d) Includes expirations of sentence, commutations, and other unconditional releases.

(e) Includes prisoners held in nonsecure, privately operated community corrections facilities and juveniles held in contract facilities. The Federal Bureau of Prisons reports prison releases as unconditional even though prisoners may serve post-custody community supervision. The 318 conditional releases are persons who were sentenced before the 1984 Sentencing Reform Act that eliminated federal parole.

(f) Includes releases to probation, supervised mandatory releases, and other unspecified conditional releases.

(g) U.S. total and state estimates for 2016 include imputed counts for North Dakota and Oregon, which did not submit 2016 NPS data on admissions and releases. U.S. total and state estimates for 2017 include imputed counts for New Mexico and North Dakota, which did not submit 2017 NPS data on admissions and releases.

(h) Prisons and jails form one integrated system. Data include total jail and prison populations.

(i) California reported that 16,887 prisoners were released as transfers in 2016. These prisoners were released from state jurisdiction to post-custody supervision by county authorities. BJS counted these as conditional releases.

(j) Releases include offenders who received a combined sentence of prison and probation of more than one year.

(k) Florida does not report technical violation prison admissions. All admissions represent new sentences, with the 85 supervision violation admissions representing persons who committed new crimes while on post-custody community supervision.

(l) Due to implementation concerns with a new information system, Maryland's counts of admissions and releases for 2017 are estimates and should not be compared to earlier years.

(m) Admissions include local jail inmates admitted to the Nevada Department of Corrections due to medical, behavioral, protective, or local staffing issues and persons ordered by judges to serve six months or less in prison prior to actual sentencing for felonies.

(n) State did not submit 2017 NPS data on admissions or releases. Total and detailed types of admissions and releases were imputed from counts reported in 2016 and included in U.S. and state totals. All admissions and releases were included in the reported 2016 data, regardless of sentence length. Estimates of admissions and releases in 2017 are not comparable to previous years' data.

(o) State did not submit 2016 or 2017 NPS data on admissions or releases. Total and detailed types of admissions and releases were imputed and included in U.S. and state totals.

(p) Includes all admissions and releases from state prison, regardless of sentence length.

(q) State did not submit 2016 NPS data on admissions or releases. Total and detailed types of admissions and releases were imputed and included in U.S. and state totals. Estimates of admissions and releases in 2016 are not comparable to reported 2017 data.

(r) Admission and release counts are preliminary estimates for fiscal year 2017. Counts for 2016 have been updated.

TABLE 9.22
Prison Facility Capacity, Custody Population, and Percent Capacity, December 31, 2017

State or other jurisdiction	Type of capacity measure			Custody population	Custody population as a percent of:	
	Rated capacity	Operational capacity	Design capacity		Lowest capacity	Highest capacity
Federal (a)	135,792	N/A	N/A	155,006	114.1	114.1
Alabama (b)	N/A	25,784	12,852	21,570	167.8	83.7
Alaska (c)	4,838	N/A	4664	4,378	93.9	90.5
Arizona (d)	38,098	44,003	38,098	41,964	110.1	95.4
Arkansas	16,505	16,544	15,721	15,879	101.0	96.0
California	N/A	121,426	89,763	118,058	131.5	97.2
Colorado	N/A	14,706	13,125	15,900	121.1	108.1
Connecticut	N.R.	N.R.	N.R.	13,649	N.R.	N.R.
Delaware (b)	5,514	5,566	4,092	6,140	150.0	110.3
Florida	N/A	88,384	N/A	84,929	96.1	96.1
Georgia (d)	59,481	53,861	N/A	53,514	99.4	90.0
Hawaii (e)	N/A	3,527	3,527	3,536	100.3	100.3
Idaho (d)	N/A	7,615	N/A	7,637	100.3	100.3
Illinois (f)	54,543	54,543	N/A	41,065	75.3	75.3
Indiana (g)	N/A	28,866	N/A	25,773	89.3	89.3
Iowa	7,200	7,200	7,200	8,290	115.1	115.1
Kansas	10,435	10,435	10,435	9,701	9.0	93.0
Kentucky	11,971	11,971	12,226	12,008	100.3	98.2
Louisiana	17,956	16,344	N/A	15,152	92.7	84.4
Maine	2,421	2,602	2,602	2,354	97.2	90.5
Maryland (h)	N/A	21,256	N/A	19,919	93.7	93.7
Massachusetts	N/A	10,208	7,492	8,859	118.2	86.8
Michigan	42,044	41,039	N/A	39,666	96.7	94.3
Minnesota	N/A	9,504	N/A	9,547	100.5	100.5
Mississippi (i)	N/A	17,909	N/A	15,559	86.9	86.9
Missouri (b)	N/A	32,536	N/A	32,564	100.1	100.1
Montana	N/A	1,689	N/A	1,769	104.7	104.7
Nebraska (b)	N/A	4,094	3,375	5,198	154.0	127.0
Nevada	14,092	11886	N/A	132,436	111.4	94.0
New Hampshire	2,760	2,760	1,810	2,533	139.9	91.8
New Jersey	16,590	17,439	23,337	16,597	100.0	71.1
New Mexico (j)	N/A	7,055	7,055	4,048	57.4	57.4
New York	51,409	51,603	50,892	49,514	97.3	96.0
North Carolina	N/A	38,159	32,684	36,663	112.2	96.1
North Dakota (j)	N/A	1,353	1,353	1,335	98.7	98.7
Ohio	N.R.	N.R.	N.R.	44,257	N.R.	N.R.
Oklahoma	17,730	19,809	17,730	19,931	112.4	100.6
Oregon	14,712	15,612	14,712	14,660	99.6	93.9
Pennsylvania (d)	48,644	48,644	48,644	47,236	97.1	97.1
Rhode Island	3,989	3,774	3,975	2,683	71.1	67.3
South Carolina	N/A	21,404	N/A	19,409	90.7	90.7
South Dakota (b)(d)	N/A	4,444	N/A	3,890	87.5	87.5
Tennessee	16,006	15,488	N/A	14,391	92.9	89.9
Texas (b)	157,528	151,431	157,528	137,926	91.1	87.6
Utah	N/A	6,771	7,127	4,982	73.6	69.9
Vermont	1,602	1,602	1,668	1,333	83.2	79.9
Virginia	N/A	29,306	N/A	29,836	101.8	101.8
Washington	N/A	16,775	N/A	17,674	105.4	105.4
West Virginia	5,922	5,976	5,922	5,922	100.0	99.1
Wisconsin	N/A	23,056	17,031	23,513	138.1	102.0
Wyoming	2,298	2,298	2,417	2,182	95.0	90.3

See footnotes at end of table

TABLE 9.22
Prison Facility Capacity, Custody Population, and Percent Capacity, December 31, 2017 (continued)

Source: Bureau of Justice Statistics, National Prisoner Statistics (NPS), 2016–2017. *Prisoners in 2017* NCJ 252156.

Note: Excludes inmates held in local jails, other states, or private facilities, unless otherwise stated. Rated capacity is the number of inmates or beds a facility can hold set by a rating official; operational capacity is the number of inmates a facility can hold based on staffing and services; and design capacity is the number of inmates a facility can hold set by the architect or planner. Lowest capacity represents the minimum capacity estimate submitted by the jurisdiction, while highest capacity represents the maximum capacity estimate. When a jurisdiction could provide only a single capacity estimate, it was used as both lowest and highest capacity.

Key:

N/A–Not available. Specific type of capacity is not measured by state.

N.R.–Not reported.

(a) Due to differences in the dates when data were extracted, the federal custody count reported for the calculation of capacity differs slightly from the year-end custody count reported in the NPS. It includes prisoners of all sentence lengths.

(b) State defines capacity differently than BJS.

(c) Alaska's capacity excludes non-traditional confinement such as halfway houses or electronic monitoring.

(d) Private facilities included in capacity and custody counts.

(e) Hawaii's custody count excludes 248 offenders who were relocated out-of-state while an in-state facility was being repaired.

(f) Illinois's rated capacity is under revision, and these numbers are the ceiling operational capacity. Numbers are not comparable to prior reports.

(g) Indiana's capacity includes facilities owned by the state but staffed with employees of a private correctional company.

(h) Maryland's capacity may include some pre-trial detainees excluded from the custody count.

(i) Local facilities included in Mississippi's capacity and custody counts.

(j) State did not submit 2017 NPS custody or capacity. Custody count was imputed, and capacities were assumed to have not changed from the most recent year the state submitted NPS data.

TABLE 9.23
Adults on Probation, 2016

State or other jurisdiction	Probation population				Change during 2016		Number on probation per 100,000 adult residents, 12/31/2016 (a)
		2016					
	1/1/2016 (a)	Entries	Exits	12/31/2016 (a)	Number	Percent	
U.S. total	3,725,638	1,574,587	1,928,687	3,673,120	-52,518	-1.4	1,466
Federal	18,320	8,240	9,155	17,284	-1,036	-5.7	7
State	3,707,318	1,566,347	1,919,532	3,655,836	-51,482	-1.4	1,459
Alabama	51,694	14,477	13,994	52,177	483	0.9	1,382
Alaska	6,513	6,942	6,834	6,621	108	1.7	1,193
Arizona	76,005	24,136	22,768	77,373	1,368	1.8	1,447
Arkansas	29,003	11,328	9,450	30,881	1,878	6.5	1,347
California (b)	238,911	138,876	136,166	239,735	824	1	791
Colorado	78,810	55,501	53,701	80,740	1,930	2.4	1,870
Connecticut	42,064	21,483	20,920	41,311	-753	-1.8	1,461
Delaware	15,646	12,463	12,714	15,395	-251	-1.6	2,049
Florida	221,446	128,167	136,484	214,066	-7,380	-3.3	1,288
Georgia (c)	410,964	..	..	..	..	..	..
Hawaii	20,912	4,400	4,796	20,516	-396	-1.9	1,828
Idaho	32,898	12,480	12,969	32,409	-489	-1.5	2,578
Illinois	122,125	42,970	51,106	113,989	-8,136	-6.7	1,154
Indiana	111,709	77,640	81,047	108,302	-3,407	-3	2,135
Iowa	29,819	15,502	16,067	29,254	-565	-1.9	1,213
Kansas	16,588	21,493	21,427	16,654	66	0.4	758
Kentucky	52,266	17,125	17,834	48,457	-3,809	-7.3	1,411
Louisiana	40,959	12,875	13,660	40,174	-785	-1.9	1,124
Maine	6,702	3,290	3,307	6,817	115	1.7	632
Maryland	76,505	33,494	37,470	72,529	-3,976	-5.2	1,550
Massachusetts	64,934	65,772	68,917	61,789	-3,145	-4.8	1,133
Michigan	175,189	..	..	..	..	..	..
Minnesota	98,165	47,266	48,579	96,852	-1,313	-1.3	2,280
Mississippi	36,333	9,753	17,019	29,067	-7,266	-20	1,280
Missouri	44,762	25,127	26,090	43,799	-963	-2.2	928
Montana	8,818	4,444	4,143	9,132	314	3.6	1,115
Nebraska	12,626	9,951	12,425	13,489	863	6.8	937
Nevada	13,724	5,724	5,414	13,724	0	--	601
New Hampshire	3,861	2,508	2,430	3,939	78	2	366
New Jersey	136,137	32,456	28,004	140,589	4,452	3.3	2,015
New Mexico	13,778	6,288	13,615	12,714	-1,064	-7.7	798
New York	101,789	26,494	30,355	97,928	-3,861	-3.8	628
North Carolina	85,634	48,995	52,163	82,466	-3,168	-3.7	1,044
North Dakota	6,343	4,591	4,593	6,341	-2	--	1,090
Ohio	236,375	122,295	123,450	236,754	379	0.2	2,624
Oklahoma	31,281	13,004	10,723	33,562	2,281	7.3	1,129
Oregon	35,938	28,028	27,308	36,658	720	2	1,127
Pennsylvania	183,868	94,091	97,467	180,492	-3,376	-1.8	1,783
Rhode Island	23,920	..	..	22,781	-1,139	-4.8	2,680
South Carolina	33,652	13,483	14,501	32,634	-1,018	-3	839
South Dakota	6,959	3,311	3,660	6,610	-349	-5	1,009
Tennessee	62,829	23,703	23,431	62,609	-220	-0.4	1,209
Texas	378,514	144,055	148,284	374,285	-4,229	-1.1	1,805
Utah	12,164	5,616	5,551	12,229	65	0.5	568
Vermont	5,164	..	..	4,904	-260	-5	969
Virginia	55,472	33,897	37,532	60,821	5,349	9.6	927
Washington	93,953	37,969	37,108	89,317	-4,636	-4.9	1,565
West Virginia	7,008	..	1,539	6,523	-485	-6.9	448
Wisconsin (d)	46,183	..	6,351	44,489	-1,694	-3.7	988
Wyoming	5,113	2,564	2,758	4,666	-194	-4	1,046
Dist. of Columbia	5,546	4,576	4,284	5,838	292	5.3	1,034

See footnotes at end of table

TABLE 9.23
Adults on Probation, 2016 (continued)

Source: Bureau of Justice Statistics, Annual Probation Survey and Annual Parole Survey, 2016.

Note: Data quality may vary across jurisdictions for counts of entries and exits; therefore, the population on December, 31, 2016, does not equal the population on January 1, 2016, plus entries, minus exits. Counts may not be actual as reporting agencies may provide estimates on some or all detailed data. January 1, 2015, plus entries, minus exits. Counts may not be actual as reporting agencies may provide estimates on some or all detailed data.

Key:

-- Less than 0.05%.

.. Not known.

(a) Rates were computed using the estimated U.S. adult resident population in each jurisdiction on January 1, 2017.

(b) January 1, 2016, reflects a reporting change resulting in a decrease of 24,650 from the population reported for December 31, 2015.

(c) January 1, 2016, reflects a reporting change resulting in a decrease of 21,271 from the population reported for December 31, 2015.

TABLE 9.24
Adults on Parole, 2016

State or other jurisdiction	Parole population						Number on parole on 12/31/16 per100,000 adult residents (a)
	1/1/2016	2016			Change during 2016		
		Entries (a)	Exits (a)	12/31/2016	Number	Percent	
U.S. total	870,657	422,975	428,022	874,777	4,120	0.5	349
Federal	114,746	45,469	48,108	114,385	-361	-0.3	46
State	755,911	377,506	379,914	760,392	4,481	0.6	303
Alabama	8,150	2,515	2,103	8,562	412	5.1	227
Alaska	2,100	717	1,005	1,812	-288	-13.7	326
Arizona	7,379	11,481	11,360	7,500	121	1.6	140
Arkansas	22,910	10,868	9,902	23,792	882	3.8	1,038
California (b)	86,053	26,007	23,212	93,598	7,545	8.8	309
Colorado	9,953	7,657	7,424	10,186	233	2.3	236
Connecticut	2,939	2,591	2,151	3,379	440	15	119
Delaware	425	129	167	387	-38	-8.9	52
Florida	4,611	6,110	6,155	4,566	-45	-1	27
Georgia	24,413	9,434	11,461	22,386	-2,027	-8.3	285
Hawaii	1,479	629	822	1,367	-112	-7.6	122
Idaho	4,875	3,055	2,876	5,054	179	3.7	402
Illinois	29,629	23,889	25,083	29,428	-201	-0.7	298
Indiana	9,420	7,056	8,091	8,385	-1,035	-11	165
Iowa	5,901	3,810	3,660	6,051	150	2.5	251
Kansas	4,331	4,465	3,966	4,830	499	11.5	220
Kentucky	16,536	10,757	11,910	15,383	-1,153	-7	448
Louisiana	31,187	15,888	16,168	30,907	-280	-0.9	864
Maine	21	1	1	21	0	..	2
Maryland	10,887	4,295	4,877	10,305	-582	-5.3	220
Massachusetts	1,995	2,111	2,255	1,851	-144	-7.2	34
Michigan	..	..	..	..	..	..	216
Minnesota	6,810	7,129	6,864	7,075	265	3.9	167
Mississippi	8,424	6,597	6,376	8,645	221	2.6	381
Missouri	17,657	13,255	13,120	17,792	135	0.8	377
Montana	1,092	533	551	1,074	-18	-1.6	131
Nebraska	1,050	1,537	1,499	1,088	38	3.6	76
Nevada	5,507	3,635	3,881	5,261	-246	-4.5	230
New Hampshire	2,451	1,461	1,476	2,436	-15	-0.6	226
New Jersey	15,180	5,539	5,591	15,128	-52	-0.3	217
New Mexico	2,763	2,384	2,367	2,780	17	0.6	175
New York	44,562	20,443	20,579	44,426	-136	-0.3	285
North Carolina	11,744	13,647	12,388	12,726	982	8.4	161
North Dakota	634	1,545	1,375	804	170	26.8	138
Ohio	18,284	8,085	6,735	19,634	1,350	7.4	218
Oklahoma	2,116	383	604	1,895	-221	-10.4	64
Oregon	24,077	9,561	8,927	24,711	634	2.6	760
Pennsylvania	112,351	61,179	62,443	111,087	-1,264	-1.1	1,097
Rhode Island	441	239	220	460	19	4.3	54
South Carolina	4,963	2,460	3,076	4,347	-616	-12.4	112
South Dakota	2,673	1,788	1,774	2,687	14	0.5	410
Tennessee	13,063	3,353	4,324	12,092	-971	-7.4	234
Texas	111,892	35,398	36,003	111,287	-605	-0.5	537
Utah	3,502	2,640	2,435	3,707	205	5.9	172
Vermont	1,083	..	..	935	-148	-13.7	185
Virginia	1,576	711	601	1,650	74	4.7	25
Washington	11,131	5,782	5,591	11,322	191	1.7	198
West Virginia	3,123	2,113	1,686	3,550	427	13.7	244
Wisconsin (c)	20,241	..	1,450	20,401	160	0.8	453
Wyoming	783	691	632	842	59	7.5	189
Dist. of Columbia	4,548	1,330	1,853	4,025	-523	-11.5	713

See footnotes at end of table

TABLE 9.24
Adults on Parole, 2016 (continued)

Source: Bureau of Justice Statistics, Annual Parole Survey, 2016. Probation and Parole in the United States, 2016 NCJ 250230, December 2016.

Note: Data quality may vary across jurisdictions for counts of entries and exits; therefore, the population on December, 31, 2016, does not equal the population on January 1, 2016, plus entries, minus exits. Counts may not be actual as reporting agencies may provide estimates on some or all detailed data.

Key:

-- Less than 0.05%.

.. Not known.

(a) Rates were computed using the estimated U.S. adult resident population in each jurisdiction on January 1, 2017.

(b) Includes Post-Release Community Supervision and Mandatory Supervision parolees: 44,687 parolees on January 1, 2016; and 27,093 entries, 22,343 exits, and 49,437 parolees on December 31, 2016.

(c) Exits reported were deaths and absconders.

TABLE 9.25
Adults Under Community Supervision, 2016

State or jurisdiction	Community supervision population, January 1, 2015 (a)	Entries	Exits	Community supervision population, 12/31/2015/(a)	Change, 2015		Number under community supervision per 100,000 adult residents, December 31, 2015 (b)
					Number	Percent	
U.S. total	4,723,100	2,244,000	2,307,800	4,650,900	-72,200	-1.5	1,868
Federal	128,400	58,600	55,600	132,800	4,400	3.4	53
State	4,594,700	2,185,400	2,252,300	4,518,100	-76,600	-1.7	1,814
Alabama	60,900	20,500	16,900	64,600	3,700	6	1,714
Alaska	..	..	..	..	..	..	..
Arizona	80,700	38,100	35,500	83,300	2,600	3.2	1,589
Arkansas	49,200	20,800	18,800	51,500	2,200	4.5	2,256
California	372,800	182,500	192,700	349,600	-23,200	-6.2	1,158
Colorado	89,100	62,000	62,900	89,200	100	0.1	2,102
Connecticut	45,600	25,000	23,700	45,300	-400	-0.8	1,598
Delaware	16,300	12,800	13,100	16,100	-300	-1.7	2,155
Florida	232,100	155,100	161,600	225,400	-6,700	-2.9	1,381
Georgia	502,200	267,700	324,100	451,800	-50,300	-10	5,823
Hawaii	22,500	5,700	6,000	22,500	0	-0.1	1,996
Idaho	37,700	15,600	15,500	37,800	100	0.2	3,071
Illinois	151,800	..	..	151,300	-600	-0.4	1,526
Indiana	126,100	83,600	87,200	122,500	-3,600	-2.8	2,423
Iowa	35,400	18,000	17,700	35,600	200	0.7	1,481
Kansas	20,400	25,200	24,700	20,900	500	2.6	951
Kentucky	70,700	37,800	37,800	70,600	0	-0.1	2,063
Louisiana	70,600	29,800	28,400	71,900	1,300	1.8	2,014
Maine	6,600	3,300	3,200	6,700	100	2.2	626
Maryland	91,100	42,900	46,600	87,400	-3,700	-4	1,870
Massachusetts	70,200	68,800	72,100	66,900	-3,300	-4.7	1,232
Michigan	192,700	104,500	104,600	193,900	1,200	0.6	2,507
Minnesota	103,700	55,200	53,800	105,100	1,400	1.3	2,489
Mississippi	44,300	17,800	17,300	44,800	500	1.1	1,972
Missouri	65,600	37,800	40,800	62,600	-3,000	-4.6	1,329
Montana	9,800	4,400	4,600	9,700	-100	-0.6	1,198
Nebraska	13,700	10,500	10,500	13,700	0	-0.1	955
Nevada	18,000	9,700	8,400	19,200	1,300	7.1	858
New Hampshire	6,300	4,100	4,100	6,300	0	0.1	590
New Jersey	152,000	33,200	33,900	151,300	-700	-0.5	2,167
New Mexico	17,600	8,200	7,900	16,800	-900	-4.9	1,054
New York	150,300	45,800	50,600	145,600	-4,800	-3.2	931
North Carolina	99,300	63,700	64,400	97,400	-1,900	-1.9	1,249
North Dakota	6,200	5,600	4,900	6,900	700	11.8	1,179
Ohio	258,400	131,200	129,700	262,000	3,600	1.4	2,908
Oklahoma	31,100	13,000	10,700	33,400	2,300	7.3	1,126
Oregon	..	..	..	..	..	..	..
Pennsylvania	281,400	177,700	162,800	296,200	14,900	5.3	2,923
Rhode Island	24,000	300	200	24,400	400	1.6	2,873
South Carolina	39,600	16,100	17,200	38,500	-1,000	-2.6	1,006
South Dakota	9,300	5,200	4,700	9,800	500	5.6	1,505
Tennessee	77,800	26,400	28,800	75,400	-2,400	-3.1	1,470
Texas	496,900	182,600	191,300	488,800	-8,000	-1.6	2,390
Utah	15,100	7,900	7,300	15,700	600	3.8	746
Vermont	6,300	..	..	6,300	0	--	1,236
Virginia	56,700	29,900	29,600	57,000	400	0.6	873
Washington	105,000	44,900	38,900	104,700	-300	-0.2	1,870
West Virginia	9,900	2,000	2,600	10,100	200	2.1	692
Wisconsin (c)	65,900	..	200	65,600	-300	-0.5	1,462
Wyoming	5,700	3,000	2,800	5,900	200	4	1,323
Dist. of Columbia	11,100	5,700	7,100	9,900	-1,100	-10.3	1,776

See footnotes at end of table

TABLE 9.25
Adults Under Community Supervision, 2016 (continued)

Source: Bureau of Justice Statistics, Annual Probation Survey and Annual Parole Survey, 2016.

Note: Counts are rounded to the nearest 100. Detail may not sum to total due to rounding. Data quality may vary across jurisdictions for counts of entries and exits; therefore, the population on December 31, 2016, does not equal the population on January 1, 2016, plus entries, minus exits.

Key:

-- Less than 0.05%.

.. Not known.

(a) The January 1, 2016, population excludes 9,375 offenders and the December 31, 2016, population excludes 10,822 offenders under community supervision who were on both probation and parole.

(b) Rates were computed using the estimated U.S. adult resident population in each jurisdiction on January 1, 2017.

(c) Exits reported were deaths and absconders.

TABLE 9.26
Capital Punishment

State or other jurisdiction	Capital offenses by state	Prisoners under sentence of death	Capital punishment abolished	Method of execution
Alabama	Intentional murder with 18 aggravating factors (Ala. Stat. Ann. 13A-5-40(a)(1)-(18)).	182		Electrocution or lethal injection
Alaska	...	...	1957	...
Arizona	First-degree murder, including pre-meditated murder and felony murder, accompanied by at least 1 of 14 aggravating factors (A.R.S. § 13-703(F)).	121		Lethal gas or lethal injection (a)
Arkansas	Capital murder (Ark. Code Ann. 5-10-101) with a finding of at least 1 of 10 aggravating circumstances; treason.	32		Lethal injection or electrocution (b)
California	First-degree murder with special circumstances; sabotage; train wrecking causing death; treason; perjury causing execution of an innocent person; fatal assault by a prisoner serving a life sentence.	740		Lethal injection
Colorado	First-degree murder with at least 1 of 17 aggravating factors; first-degree kidnapping resulting in death; treason.	3		Lethal injection
Connecticut	... (c)	0	2012	...
Delaware	... (d)	(d)	2016	...
Florida (e)	First-degree murder; felony murder; capital drug trafficking; capital sexual battery.	354		Electrocution or lethal injection
Georgia	Murder with aggravating circumstances; kidnapping with bodily injury or ransom when the victim dies; aircraft hijacking; treason.	56		Lethal injection
Hawaii	...	...	1957	...
Idaho	First-degree murder with aggravating factors; first-degree kidnapping; perjury resulting in death.	9		Lethal injection
Illinois	... (f)	0	2011	...
Indiana	Murder with 17 aggravating circumstances (IC 35-50-2-9).	11		Lethal injection or electrocution
Iowa	...	...	1965	...
Kansas	Capital murder with 8 aggravating circumstances (KSA 21-3439, KSA 21-4625, KSA 21-4636).	10		Lethal injection
Kentucky	Capital murder with presence of at least one statutory aggravating circumstance; capital kidnapping (KRS 532.025).	31		Electrocution or lethal injection (g)
Louisiana (e)	First-degree murder; treason (La. R.S. 14:30 and 14:113).	70		Lethal injection
Maine	...	...	1887	...
Maryland	... (h)	...	2013	(h)
Massachusetts	...	...	1984	...
Michigan	...	...	1846	...
Minnesota	...	...	1911	...
Mississippi	Capital murder (Miss Code Ann. § 97-3-19(2)); aircraft piracy (Miss Code Ann. § 97-25-55(1)).	46		Lethal injection
Missouri	First-degree murder (565.020 RSMO 2000).	25		Lethal injection or lethal gas
Montana (e)	Capital murder with 1 of 9 aggravating circumstances (Mont. Code Ann. § 46-18-303); aggravated kidnapping; felony murder; capital sexual intercourse without consent (Mont. Code Ann. § 45-5-503).	2		Lethal injection
Nebraska	(s)	12		...
Nevada	First-degree murder with at least 1 of 15 aggravating circumstances (NRS 200.030, 200.033, 200.035).	76		Lethal injection
New Hampshire	... (i)	1	2019	(i)
New Jersey	... (j)	...	2007	...
New Mexico	... (k)	2	2009	Lethal injection (k)
New York	(l) First-degree murder with 1 of 13 aggravating factors (NY Penal Law §125.27).	0	2007	Lethal injection
North Carolina	First-degree murder with the finding of at least 1 of 11 statutory aggravating circumstances. (NCGS §14-17).	143		Lethal injection
North Dakota	...	...	1973	...
Ohio	Aggravated murder with at least 1 of 10 aggravating circumstances (O.R.C. secs. 2903.01, 2929.02, and 2929.04).	142		Lethal injection
Oklahoma (e)	First-degree murder in conjunction with a finding of at least 1 of 8 statutorily-defined aggravating circumstances.	48		Electrocution, lethal injection or firing squad (m)
Oregon	(n) Aggravated murder (ORS 163.095-150).	33		Lethal injection
Pennsylvania	First-degree murder with 18 aggravating circumstances.	158		Lethal injection
Rhode Island	...	...	1984	...
South Carolina (e)	Murder with 1 of 12 aggravating circumstances (§ 16-3-20(C)(a)).	39		Electrocution or lethal injection
South Dakota	First-degree murder with 1 of 10 aggravating circumstances.	3		Lethal injection
Tennessee	First-degree murder (Tenn. Code Ann. § 39-13-202) with 1 of 16 aggravating circumstances (Tenn. Code Ann. § 39-13-204).	61		Lethal injection or electrocution (o)
Texas (e)	Criminal homicide with 1 of 9 aggravating circumstances (TX Penal Code § 19.03).	228		Lethal injection
Utah	Aggravated murder (76-5-202, Utah Code Annotated).	9		Lethal injection or firing squad (p)
Vermont	...	...	1964	...
Virginia	First-degree murder with 1 of 15 aggravating circumstances (VA Code § 18.2-31).	3		Electrocution or lethal injection
Washington	(t)	8	2018	(t)
West Virginia	...	...	1965	...

See footnotes at end of table

TABLE 9.26
Capital Punishment (continued)

State or other jurisdiction	Capital offenses by state	Prisoners under sentence of death	Capital punishment abolished	Method of execution
Wisconsin	...	...	1853	...
Wyoming	First-degree murder; murder during the commission of sexual assault, sexual abuse of a minor, arson, robbery, burglary, escape, resisting arrest, kidnapping, or abuse of a minor under 16 (W.S.A. § 6-2-101 (a)).	1		Lethal injection or lethal gas (q)
Dist. of Columbia	...	...	1981	...
American Samoa	First-degree murder (ASC §46.3513). (p)	0		Hanging (r)
Guam	...	...		...
CNMI*	...	...		...
Puerto Rico	...	...		...
U.S. Virgin Islands	...	...		...

Sources: The Council of State Governments' survey March, 2019; U.S. Department of Justice, Office of Justice programs, Bureau of Justice Statistics, Capital Punishment, 2015–Statistical Tables, December 2015. The Death Penalty Information Center, 2019.
*Commonwealth of Northern Mariana Islands
Notes:
1. The United States Supreme Court ruling in *Roper v. Simmons*, 543 U.S. 551 (2005) declared unconstitutional the imposition of the death penalty on persons under the age of 18.
2. The United States Supreme Court ruling in *Atkins v. Virginia*, 536 U.S. 304 (2002) declared unconstitutional the imposition of the death penalty on mentally handicapped persons.
3. The method of execution of Federal prisoners is lethal injection, pursuant to 28 CFR, Part 26. For offenses under the Violent Crime Control and Law Enforcement Act of 1994, the execution method is that of the State in which the conviction took place (18 U.S.C. 3596).
Key:
...–No capital punishment statute.
(a) Arizona authorizes lethal injection for persons sentenced after November 15, 1992; inmates sentenced before that date may select lethal injection or gas.
(b) Arkansas authorizes lethal injection for those whose offense occurred on or after July 4, 1983; inmates whose offense occurred before that date may select lethal injection or electrocution.
(c) On April 25, 2012, Connecticut Governor Dannel Malloy signed into law a bill (SB 280) repealing the state's death penalty. The repeal law did not affect the status of the 11 prisoners then on death row. The Connecticut Supreme Court subsequently ruled in August 2015 that the death penalty violated the state constitution. The Court reaffirmed that holding in May 2016 and reiterated that the state's remaining death row prisoners must be resentenced to life without possibility of parole.
(d) The Delaware Supreme Court declared the state's death-penalty statute unconstitutional in 2016. The state's 13 former death-row prisoners have been resentenced to life without parole.
(e) The United States Supreme Court struck a portion of the Louisiana capital statute on June 25, 2008 (*Kennedy v. Louisiana*, U.S. 128 S.Ct. 2641). The statute (La. Rev. Stat. Ann. § 14:42(D)(2)) allowing execution as a punishment for the rape of a minor when no murder had been committed had been ruled constitutionally permissible by the Louisiana Supreme Court. The U.S. Supreme Court found that since no national consensus existed for application of the death penalty in cases of rape where no murder had been committed, such laws constitute cruel and unusual punishment under the Eighth

and Fourteenth Amendments. The ruling affects laws passed in Florida, Oklahoma, South Carolina, Texas, and Montana.
(f) Governor Pat Quinn signed a bill (SB 3539) on March 9, 2011 that abolishes the death penalty effective July 1, 2011. He commuted all death sentences to life without parole.
(g) Kentucky authorizes lethal injection for persons sentenced on or after March 31, 1998; inmates sentenced before that date may select lethal injection or electrocution.
(h) On May 2, 2013, Governor Martin O'Malley signed into law a bill (SB 276) that abolishes the death penalty for future crimes. Gov. O'Malley announced on December 31, 2014, that he would commute the sentences of the four remaining death-row inmates to life in prison without the possibility of parole.
(i) The N.H. Legislature abolished the death penalty when they voted to override Gov. Sununu's veto of the legislation on May 30, 2019. The state has only one person on death row and last carried out an execution in 1939. It is not known what the disposition of his sentence will be at press time.
(j) New Jersey repealed its death penalty statute in 2007.
(k) Governor Bill Richardson signed a bill in March of 2009 abolishing the death penalty. The law is not retroactive and leaves two inmates on death row.
(l) The New York Court of Appeals has held in 2004 that a portion of New York's death penalty sentencing statute (CPL 400.27) was unconstitutional (*People v. Taylor*, 9 N.Y.3d 129 (2007)). As a result, no defendants can be sentenced to death until the legislature corrects the errors in this statute. Efforts to restore the statute have been voted down. By 2007, all seven of those sentenced to death under the state law had their sentences overturned. New York has had an effective moratorium on capital punishment since then.
(m) Oklahoma authorizes electrocution if lethal injection is held to be unconstitutional, and firing squad if both lethal injection and electrocution are held to be unconstitutional.
(n) In November 2011, Governor John Kitzhaber placed a moratorium on all executions in Oregon. An amended bill to narrow the circumstances in which the death penalty may be imposed in Oregon has passed the state senate. On May 21, 2019 the Oregon Senate passed SB 1013, which would limit the state's use of capital punishment to three aggravating circumstances. The bill would allow prosecutors to pursue the death penalty for only three crimes: acts of terrorism in which at least two people are killed, the murder of a child younger than age 14, and murder committed in prison by a person already incarcerated for a previous murder conviction. Under Oregon's current law, 12 aggravating factors can make a murder death-eligible.

TABLE 9.26
Capital Punishment (continued)

(o) Tennessee authorizes lethal injection for those whose capital offense occurred after December 31, 1998; those who committed the offense before that date may select electrocution by written waiver.

(p) Authorizes firing squad if lethal injection is held unconstitutional. Inmates who selected execution by firing squad prior to May 3, 2004, may still be entitled to execution by that method.

(q) Wyoming authorizes lethal gas if lethal injection is ever held to be unconstitutional.

(r) The last execution was in the 1920s.

(s) In a referendum on the November 8, 2016 ballot 60 percent of Nebraska voters elect to keep the death penalty and lethal injection as state law. On January 26, 2017 Gov. Ricketts signs new, flexible execution protocol, allowing acquisition of necessary drugs to resume. As of November 9, 2017 the state is prepared to use a four-drug protocol, signaling a new death warrant could be issued in 2018. Legal challenges are underway.

(t) On October 11, 2018, the Washington Supreme Court declared the state's death penalty statute unconstitutional, saying that it was applied in an arbitrary and racially discriminatory manner.

CHAPTER TEN
STATE PAGES

TABLE 10.1

Official Names of States and Jurisdictions, Capitals, Zip Codes and Central Switchboards

State or other jurisdiction	Name of state capitol (a)	Capital	Zip code	Area code	Central switchboard (b)
Alabama, State of	State House	Montgomery	36130	334	242-7100
Alaska, State of	State Capitol	Juneau	99801	907	465-2111
Arizona, State of	State Capitol	Phoenix	85007	602	542-4331
Arkansas, State of	State Capitol	Little Rock	72201	501	682-2345
California, State of	State Capitol	Sacramento	95814	916	445-2841
Colorado, State of	State Capitol	Denver	80203	303	866-2471
Connecticut, State of	State Capitol	Hartford	06106	860	566-4840
Delaware, State of	Legislative Hall	Dover	19903	302	744-4101
Florida, State of	The Capitol	Tallahassee	32399	850	717-9337
Georgia, State of	State Capitol	Atlanta	30334	404	656-1776
Hawaii, State of	State Capitol	Honolulu	96813	808	586-2121
Idaho, State of	State Capitol	Boise	83720	208	334-2100
Illinois, State of	State House	Springfield	62706	217	782-0244
Indiana, State of	Statehouse	Indianapolis	46204	317	232-4567
Iowa, State of	State Capitol	Des Moines	50319	515	281-5211
Kansas, State of	The Capitol	Topeka	66612	785	296-3232
Kentucky, Commonwealth of	State Capitol	Frankfort	40601	502	564-2611
Louisiana, State of	State Capitol	Baton Rouge	70804	225	342-7015
Maine, State of	State House	Augusta	04333	207	287-3531
Maryland, State of	State House	Annapolis	21401	410	974-3901
Massachusetts, Commonwealth of	State House	Boston	02133	617	725-4005
Michigan, State of	State Capitol	Lansing	48909	517	373-3400
Minnesota, State of	State Capitol	St. Paul	55155	651	201-3400
Mississippi, State of	State Capitol	Jackson	39215	601	359-3150
Missouri, State of	State Capitol	Jefferson City	65101	573	751-0290
Montana, State of	State Capitol	Helena	59620	406	444-3111
Nebraska, State of	State Capitol	Lincoln	68509	402	471-2244
Nevada, State of	State Capitol	Carson City	89701	775	684-5670
New Hampshire, State of	State House	Concord	03301	603	271-2121
New Jersey, State of	State House	Trenton	08625	609	292-6000
New Mexico, State of	State Capitol	Santa Fe	87501	505	476-2200
New York, State of	State Capitol	Albany	12224	518	474-8390
North Carolina, State of	State Capitol	Raleigh	27601	919	733-5811
North Dakota, State of	State Capitol	Bismarck	58505	701	328-2200
Ohio, State of	Statehouse	Columbus	43215	614	466-3555
Oklahoma, State of	State Capitol	Oklahoma City	73105	405	521-2342
Oregon, State of	State Capitol	Salem	97301	503	378-4582
Pennsylvania, Commonwealth of	The Capitol	Harrisburg	17120	717	787-2500
Rhode Island and Providence Plantations, State of	State House	Providence	02903	401	222-2080
South Carolina, State of	State House	Columbia	29201	803	734-2100
South Dakota, State of	State Capitol	Pierre	57501	605	773-3212
Tennessee, State of	State Capitol	Nashville	37243	615	741-2001
Texas, State of	State Capitol	Austin	78711	512	463-2000
Utah, State of	State Capitol	Salt Lake City	84114	801	538-1000
Vermont, State of	State House	Montpelier	05609	802	828-3333
Virginia, Commonwealth of	State Capitol	Richmond	23219	804	786-2211
Washington, State of	Legislative Building	Olympia	98504	360	902-4111
West Virginia, State of	State Capitol	Charleston	25305	304	558-2000
Wisconsin, State of	State Capitol	Madison	53702	608	266-1212
Wyoming, State of	State Capitol	Cheyenne	82002	307	777-7434
Dist. of Columbia	John A. Wilson Building	...	20004	202	727-6300
American Samoa, Territory of	Maota Fono Complex	Pago Pago	96799	684	633-4116
Guam, Territory of	Congress Building	Hagatna	96910	671	472-8931
No. Mariana Islands, Commonwealth of	Capital Hill	Saipan	96950	670	664-2280
Puerto Rico, Commonwealth of	The Capitol	San Juan	00902	787	721-7000
U.S. Virgin Islands, Territory of	Legislature Building	Charlotte Amalie, St. Thomas	00802	340	774-0001

Key:
(a) In some instances the name is not official.
(b) Numbers generally come from an executive branch office, such
as the office of the governor.

TABLE 10.2
Historical Data on the States

State or other jurisdiction	Source of state lands	Date organized as territory	Date admitted to Union	Chronological order of admission to Union
Alabama	Mississippi Territory, 1798 (a)	March 3, 1817	Dec. 14, 1819	22
Alaska	Purchased from Russia, 1867	Aug. 24, 1912	Jan. 3, 1959	49
Arizona	Ceded by Mexico, 1848 (b)	Feb. 24, 1863	Feb. 14, 1912	48
Arkansas	Louisiana Purchase, 1803	March 2, 1819	June 15, 1836	25
California	Ceded by Mexico, 1848	(c)	Sept. 9, 1850	31
Colorado	Louisiana Purchase, 1803 (d)	Feb. 28, 1861	Aug. 1, 1876	38
Connecticut	Fundamental Orders, Jan. 14, 1638; Royal charter, April 23, 1662	(e)	Jan. 9, 1788 (f)	5
Delaware	Swedish charter, 1638; English charter, 1638	(e)	Dec. 7, 1787 (f)	1
Florida	Ceded by Spain, 1819	March 30, 1822	March 3, 1845	27
Georgia	Charter, 1732, from George II to Trustees for Establishing the Colony of Georgia	(e)	Jan. 2, 1788 (f)	4
Hawaii	Annexed, 1898	June 14, 1900	Aug. 21, 1959	50
Idaho	Treaty with Britain, 1846	March 4, 1863	July 3, 1890	43
Illinois	Northwest Territory, 1787	Feb. 3, 1809	Dec. 3, 1818	21
Indiana	Northwest Territory, 1787	May 7, 1800	Dec. 11, 1816	19
Iowa	Louisiana Purchase, 1803	June 12, 1838	Dec. 28, 1846	29
Kansas	Louisiana Purchase, 1803 (d)	May 30, 1854	Jan. 29, 1861	34
Kentucky	Part of Virginia until admitted as state	(c)	June 1, 1792	15
Louisiana	Louisiana Purchase, 1803 (g)	March 26, 1804	April 30, 1812	18
Maine	Part of Massachusetts until admitted as state	(c)	March 15, 1820	23
Maryland	Charter, 1632, from Charles I to Calvert	(e)	April 28, 1788 (f)	7
Massachusetts	Charter to Massachusetts Bay Company, 1629	(e)	Feb. 6, 1788 (f)	6
Michigan	Northwest Territory, 1787	Jan. 11, 1805	Jan. 26, 1837	26
Minnesota	Northwest Territory, 1787 (h)	March 3, 1849	May 11, 1858	32
Mississippi	Mississippi Territory (i)	April 7, 1798	Dec. 10, 1817	20
Missouri	Louisiana Purchase, 1803	June 4, 1812	Aug. 10, 1821	24
Montana	Louisiana Purchase, 1803 (j)	May 26, 1864	Nov. 8, 1889	41
Nebraska	Louisiana Purchase, 1803	May 30, 1854	March 1, 1867	37
Nevada	Ceded by Mexico, 1848	March 2, 1861	Oct. 31, 1864	36
New Hampshire	Grants from Council for New England, 1622 and 1629; made Royal province, 1679	(e)	June 21, 1788 (f)	9
New Jersey	Dutch settlement, 1618; English charter, 1664	(e)	Dec. 18, 1787 (f)	3
New Mexico	Ceded by Mexico, 1848 (b)	Sept. 9, 1850	Jan. 6, 1912	47
New York	Dutch settlement, 1623; English control, 1664	(e)	July 26, 1788 (f)	11
North Carolina	Charter, 1663, from Charles II	(e)	Nov. 21, 1789 (f)	12
North Dakota	Louisiana Purchase, 1803 (k)	March 2, 1861	Nov. 2, 1889	39
Ohio	Northwest Territory, 1787	May 7, 1800	March 1, 1803	17
Oklahoma	Louisiana Purchase, 1803	May 2, 1890	Nov. 16, 1907	46
Oregon	Settlement and treaty with Britain, 1846	Aug. 14, 1848	Feb. 14, 1859	33
Pennsylvania	Grant from Charles II to William Penn, 1681	(e)	Dec. 12, 1787 (f)	2
Rhode Island	Charter, 1663, from Charles II	(e)	May 29, 1790 (f)	13
South Carolina	Charter, 1663, from Charles II	(e)	May 23, 1788 (f)	8
South Dakota	Louisiana Purchase, 1803	March 2, 1861	Nov. 2, 1889	40
Tennessee	Part of North Carolina until land ceded to U.S. in 1789	June 8, 1790 (l)	June 1, 1796	16
Texas	Republic of Texas, 1845	(c)	Dec. 29, 1845	28
Utah	Ceded by Mexico, 1848	Sept. 9, 1850	Jan. 4, 1896	45
Vermont	From lands of New Hampshire and New York	(c)	March 4, 1791	14
Virginia	Charter, 1609, from James I to London Company	(e)	June 25, 1788 (f)	10
Washington	Oregon Territory, 1848	March 2, 1853	Nov. 11, 1889	42
West Virginia	Part of Virginia until admitted as state	(c)	June 20, 1863	35
Wisconsin	Northwest Territory, 1787	April 20, 1836	May 29, 1848	30
Wyoming	Louisiana Purchase, 1803 (d)(j)	July 25, 1868	July 10, 1890	44
Dist. of Columbia	Maryland (m)	…	…	…
American Samoa	---------------------------------- Became a territory, 1900 ----------------------------------			
Guam	Ceded by Spain, 1898	Aug. 1, 1950	…	…
CNMI*	…	March 24, 1976	…	…
Puerto Rico	Ceded by Spain, 1898	…	July 25, 1952 (n)	…
U.S. Virgin Islands	--------------------------- Purchased from Denmark, March 31, 1917 ---------------------------			

See footnotes at end of table

TABLE 10.2
Historical Data on the States (continued)

Source: The Cuncil of State Governments
Key:
*Commonwealth of Northern Mariana Islands

(a) By the Treaty of Paris, 1783, England gave up claim to the 13 original Colonies, and to all land within an area extending along the present Canadian to the Lake of the Woods, down the Mississippi River to the 31st parallel, east to the Chattahoochee, down that river to the mouth of the Flint, border east to the source of the St. Mary's down that river to the ocean. The major part of Alabama was acquired by the Treaty of Paris, and the lower portion from Spain in 1813.
(b) Portion of land obtained by Gadsden Purchase, 1853.
(c) No territorial status before admission to Union.
(d) Portion of land ceded by Mexico, 1848.
(f) Date of ratification of U.S. Constitution.

(g) West Feliciana District (Baton Rouge) acquired from Spain, 1810; added to Louisiana, 1812.
(h) Portion of land obtained by Louisiana Purchase, 1803.
(i) See footnote (a). The lower portion of Mississippi also was acquired from Spain in 1813.
(j) Portion of land obtained from Oregon Territory, 1848.
(k) The northern portion of the Red River Valley was acquired by treaty with Great Britain in 1818.
(l) Date Southwest Territory (identical boundary as Tennessee's) was created.
(m) Area was originally 100 square miles, taken from Virginia and Maryland. Virginia's portion south of the Potomac was given back to that state in 1846. Site chosen in 1790, city incorporated 1802.
(n) On this date, Puerto Rico became a self-governing commonwealth by compact approved by the U.S. Congress and the voters of Puerto Rico as provided in U.S. Public Law 600 of 1950.

TABLE 10.3
State Statistics

State or other jurisdiction	Land area		Population (a)		Percentage change 2017 to 2018	Density per square mile	Rank in nation
	In square miles (2010)	Rank in nation	Size	Rank in nation			
Alabama	50,645	28	4,887,871	24	0.3	96.5	27
Alaska	570,641	1	737,438	48	(0.3)	1.3	50
Arizona	113,594	6	7,171,646	14	1.7	63.1	33
Arkansas	52,035	27	3,013,825	33	0.4	57.9	34
California	155,779	3	39,557,045	1	0.4	253.9	11
Colorado	103,642	8	5,695,564	21	1.4	55.0	37
Connecticut	4,842	48	3,572,665	29	0.0	737.8	4
Delaware	1,949	49	967,171	45	1.1	496.4	6
Florida	53,625	26	21,299,325	3	1.5	397.2	8
Georgia	57,513	21	10,519,475	8	1.0	182.9	17
Hawaii	6,423	47	1,420,491	40	(0.3)	221.2	13
Idaho	82,643	11	1,754,208	39	2.1	21.2	44
Illinois	55,519	24	12,741,080	6	(0.4)	229.5	12
Indiana	35,826	38	6,691,878	17	0.5	186.8	16
Iowa	55,857	23	3,156,145	31	0.4	56.5	36
Kansas	81,759	13	2,911,505	35	0.0	35.6	41
Kentucky	39,486	37	4,468,402	26	0.3	113.2	23
Louisiana	43,204	33	4,659,978	25	(0.2)	107.9	25
Maine	30,843	39	1,338,404	42	0.3	43.4	39
Maryland	9,707	42	6,042,718	19	0.3	622.5	5
Massachusetts	7,800	45	6,902,149	15	0.6	884.9	3
Michigan	56,539	22	9,995,915	10	0.2	176.8	18
Minnesota	79,627	14	5,611,179	22	0.8	70.5	30
Mississippi	46,923	31	2,986,530	34	(0.1)	63.6	32
Missouri	68,742	18	6,126,452	18	0.3	89.1	28
Montana	145,546	4	1,062,305	43	0.9	7.3	48
Nebraska	76,824	15	1,929,268	37	0.6	25.1	43
Nevada	109,781	7	3,034,392	32	2.1	27.6	42
New Hampshire	8,953	44	1,356,458	41	0.5	151.5	21
New Jersey	7,354	46	8,908,520	11	0.2	1,211.3	1
New Mexico	121,298	5	2,095,428	36	0.1	17.3	45
New York	47,126	30	19,542,209	4	(0.2)	414.7	7
North Carolina	48,618	29	10,383,620	9	1.1	213.6	15
North Dakota	69,001	17	760,077	47	0.6	11.0	47
Ohio	40,861	35	11,689,442	7	0.2	286.1	10
Oklahoma	68,595	19	3,943,079	28	0.3	57.5	35
Oregon	95,988	10	4,190,713	27	1.1	43.7	38
Pennsylvania	44,743	32	12,807,060	5	0.1	286.2	9
Rhode Island	1,034	50	1,057,315	44	0.1	1,022.7	2
South Carolina	30,061	40	5,084,127	23	1.3	169.1	19
South Dakota	75,811	16	882,235	46	1.0	11.6	46
Tennessee	41,235	34	6,770,010	16	0.9	164.2	20
Texas	261,232	2	28,701,845	2	1.3	109.9	24
Utah	82,170	12	3,161,105	30	1.9	38.5	40
Vermont	9,217	43	626,299	49	0.3	68.0	31
Virginia	39,490	36	8,517,685	12	0.6	215.7	14
Washington	66,456	20	7,535,591	13	1.5	113.4	22
West Virginia	24,038	41	1,805,832	38	(0.6)	75.1	29
Wisconsin	54,158	25	5,813,568	20	0.4	107.3	26
Wyoming	97,093	9	577,737	50	(0.2)	6.0	49
Dist. of Columbia	61	N.A.	702,455	N.A.	1.0	11,515.7	N.A.
American Samoa (b)	76	N.A.	55,519	N.A.	(3.1) (c)	730.5	N.A.
Guam (b)	210	N.A.	159,358	N.A.	2.9 (c)	758.8	N.A.
CNMI* (b)	182	N.A.	53,833	N.A.	(22.2) (c)	295.8	N.A.
Puerto Rico	3,424	N.A.	3,195,153	N.A.	(3.9)	933.2	N.A.
U.S. Virgin Islands (b)	134	N.A.	106,405	N.A.	(2.0) (c)	794.1	N.A.

See footnotes at end of table

TABLE 10.3
State Statistics (continued)

State or other jurisdiction	Number of Representatives in Congress	Capital	Population (j)	Rank in state	Largest city	Population (j)
Alabama	7	Montgomery	199,518	2	Birmingham	210,710
Alaska	1	Juneau	32,094	2	Anchorage	294,356
Arizona	9	Phoenix	1,626,078	1	Phoenix	1,626,078
Arkansas	4	Little Rock	198,606	1	Little Rock	198,606
California	53	Sacramento	501,901	6	Los Angeles	3,999,759
Colorado	7	Denver	704,621	1	Denver	704,621
Connecticut	5	Hartford	123,400	4	Bridgeport	146,579
Delaware	1	Dover	37,538	2	Wilmington	71,106
Florida	27	Tallahassee	191,049	7	Jacksonville	892,062
Georgia	14	Atlanta	486,290	1	Atlanta	486,290
Hawaii	2	Honolulu	350,395	1	Honolulu	350,395
Idaho	2	Boise	226,570	1	Boise	226,570
Illinois	18	Springfield	114,868	6	Chicago	2,716,450
Indiana	9	Indianapolis	863,002	1	Indianapolis	863,002
Iowa	4	Des Moines	217,521	1	Des Moines	217,521
Kansas	4	Topeka	126,587	5	Wichita	390,591
Kentucky	6	Frankfort	27,621	13	Louisville (e)	621,349
Louisiana	6	Baton Rouge	225,374	2	New Orleans	393,292
Maine	2	Augusta	18,594	10	Portland	66,882
Maryland	8	Annapolis	39,321	7	Baltimore	611,648
Massachusetts	9	Boston	685,094	1	Boston	685,094
Michigan	14	Lansing	116,986	6	Detroit	673,104
Minnesota	8	St. Paul	306,621	2	Minneapolis	422,331
Mississippi	4	Jackson	166,965	1	Jackson	166,965
Missouri	8	Jefferson City	42,895	15	Kansas City	488,943
Montana	1	Helena	31,429	6	Billings	109,642
Nebraska	3	Lincoln	284,736	2	Omaha	466,893
Nevada	4	Carson City	54,745	6	Las Vegas	641,676
New Hampshire	2	Concord	43,019	3	Manchester	111,196
New Jersey	12	Trenton	84,964	6	Newark	285,154
New Mexico	3	Santa Fe	83,776	4	Albuquerque	558,545
New York	27	Albany	98,251	6	New York City	8,622,698
North Carolina	13	Raleigh	464,758	2	Charlotte	859,035
North Dakota	1	Bismarck	72,865	2	Fargo	122,359
Ohio	16	Columbus	879,170	1	Columbus	879,170
Oklahoma	5	Oklahoma City	643,648	1	Oklahoma City	643,648
Oregon	5	Salem	169,798	2	Portland	647,805
Pennsylvania	18	Harrisburg	49,192	10	Philadelphia (f)	1,580,863
Rhode Island	2	Providence	180,393	1	Providence	180,393
South Carolina	7	Columbia	133,114	2	Charleston	134,875
South Dakota	1	Pierre	14,004	7	Sioux Falls	176,888
Tennessee	9	Nashville (g)	667,560	1	Nashville (g)	667,560
Texas	36	Austin	950,715	4	Houston	2,312,717
Utah	4	Salt Lake City	200,544	1	Salt Lake City	200,544
Vermont	1	Montpelier	7,484	6	Burlington	42,239
Virginia	11	Richmond	227,032	4	Virginia Beach	450,435
Washington	10	Olympia	51,609	24	Seattle	724,745
West Virginia	3	Charleston	47,929	1	Charleston	47,929
Wisconsin	8	Madison	255,214	2	Milwaukee	595,351
Wyoming	1	Cheyenne	63,624	1	Cheyenne	63,624
Dist. of Columbia	1 (h)	N.A.	N.A.	N.A.	N.A.	702,455
American Samoa (b)	1 (h)	Pago Pago	3,656 (b)	3	Tafuna	9,756 (b)
Guam (b)	1 (h)	Hagatna (d)	1,051 (b)	13	Dededo (d)	44943 (b)
CNMI* (b)	1 (h)	Saipan (d)	48,220 (b)	1	Saipan (d)	48,220 (b)
Puerto Rico	1 (i)	San Juan	337,288	1	San Juan	337,288
U.S. Virgin Islands (b)	1 (h)	Charlotte Amalie, St. Thomas	18,481 (b)	1	Charlotte Amalie, St. Thomas	18,481 (b)

See footnotes at end of table

TABLE 10.3
State Statistics (continued)

Source: U.S. Census Bureau, information available as of December 2018.

*Commonwealth of Northern Mariana Islands

Key:

N.A.–Not applicable

N/A–Not Available

(a) July 1, 2018 Census Bureau estimates.

(b) 2010 Census Bureau counts.

(c) Population change calculations are from 2000-2010.

(d) Municipality.

(e) This city is part of a consolidated city-county government and is coextensive with Jefferson County.

(f) Philadelphia County and Philadelphia city are coextensive.

(g) This city is part of a consolidated city-county government and is coextensive with Davidson County.

(h) Represented by one non-voting House Delegate.

(i) Represented by one non-voting House Resident Commissioner.

(j) July 1, 2017 Census Bureau estimates (released May 2018).

TABLE 10.4
Personal Income, Population, and Per Capita Personal Income, by State and Region, 2017-2018

State or other jurisdiction	Personal income (millions of dollars)				Population (Thousands of persons) 2018ᵖ (a)	Per capita personal income (dollars)		
	2017	2018ᵖ	Percent change 2017-18	Rank of percent change 2017-18		2018ᵖ	Rank in U.S. 2018ᵖ	Percent of U.S. 2018ᵖ
United States	$16,820,250	$17,572,929	5	N.A	327,167	$53,712	N.A	100
Alabama	198,916	206,924	4	30	4,888	42,334	46	79
Alaska	42,301	44,015	4	26	737	59,687	10	111
Arizona	296,649	313,040	6	5	7,172	43,650	42	81
Arkansas	123,313	128,286	4	28	3,014	42,566	45	79
California	2,364,129	2,475,727	5	14	39,557	62,586	6	117
Colorado	306,411	323,767	6	4	5,696	56,846	13	106
Connecticut	257,714	266,382	3	42	3,573	74,561	1	139
Delaware	47,782	49,760	4	24	967	51,449	21	96
Florida	1,000,624	1,052,550	5	8	21,299	49,417	26	92
Georgia	460,403	481,213	5	17	10,519	45,745	39	85
Hawaii	75,355	77,509	3	50	1,420	54,565	16	102
Idaho	71,813	75,703	5	6	1,754	43,155	43	80
Illinois	693,914	725,394	5	16	12,741	56,933	12	106
Indiana	301,008	312,151	4	39	6,692	46,646	35	87
Iowa	148,043	154,091	4	25	3,156	48,823	28	91
Kansas	141,459	146,028	3	46	2,912	50,155	23	93
Kentucky	180,827	186,685	3	44	4,468	41,779	47	78
Louisiana	204,517	212,223	4	38	4,660	45,542	40	85
Maine	62,060	64,566	4	27	1,338	48,241	30	90
Maryland	368,258	380,172	3	45	6,043	62,914	5	117
Massachusetts	463,931	483,657	4	22	6,902	70,073	2	131
Michigan	460,270	475,626	3	43	9,996	47,582	32	89
Minnesota	303,141	316,327	4	20	5,611	56,374	14	105
Mississippi	109,324	113,469	4	37	2,987	37,994	50	71
Missouri	274,976	285,704	4	33	6,126	46,635	36	87
Montana	47,677	50,055	5	9	1,062	47,120	34	88
Nebraska	97,557	100,534	3	49	1,929	52,110	20	97
Nevada	138,386	146,333	6	3	3,034	48,225	31	90
New Hampshire	80,122	83,293	4	31	1,356	61,405	7	114
New Jersey	581,199	602,297	4	40	8,909	67,609	4	126
New Mexico	83,127	86,328	4	36	2,095	41,198	48	77
New York	1,281,082	1,341,914	5	13	19,542	68,667	3	128
North Carolina	454,307	475,927	5	12	10,384	45,834	38	85
North Dakota	39,484	41,277	5	15	760	54,306	18	101
Ohio	544,828	563,926	4	41	11,689	48,242	29	90
Oklahoma	174,435	181,886	4	21	3,943	46,128	37	86
Oregon	199,422	209,148	5	10	4,191	49,908	25	93
Pennsylvania	682,534	708,862	4	35	12,807	55,349	15	103
Rhode Island	55,934	57,648	3	48	1,057	54,523	17	102
South Carolina	209,180	217,276	4	34	5,084	42,736	44	80
South Dakota	42,455	44,236	4	23	882	50,141	24	93
Tennessee	305,691	319,401	5	19	6,770	47,179	33	88
Texas	1,340,568	1,411,021	5	7	28,702	49,161	27	92
Utah	134,804	143,324	6	2	3,161	45,340	41	84
Vermont	32,570	33,569	3	47	626	53,598	19	100
Virginia	466,743	485,098	4	32	8,518	56,952	11	106
Washington	428,765	458,017	7	1	7,536	60,781	8	113
West Virginia	69,873	73,278	5	11	1,806	40,578	49	76
Wisconsin	283,636	295,073	4	29	5,814	50,756	22	95
Wyoming	33,221	34,719	5	18	578	60,095	9	112
Dist. of Columbia	55,510	57,518	4	N.A	702	81,882	N.A.	152

Source: U.S. Bureau of Economic Analysis
Key:
N.A.–Not applicable
p–Preliminary
(a) Census Bureau midyear population estimates available as of
    December 2018.

Table 10.4 | Personal Income

2018 Personal Income Per Capita by State

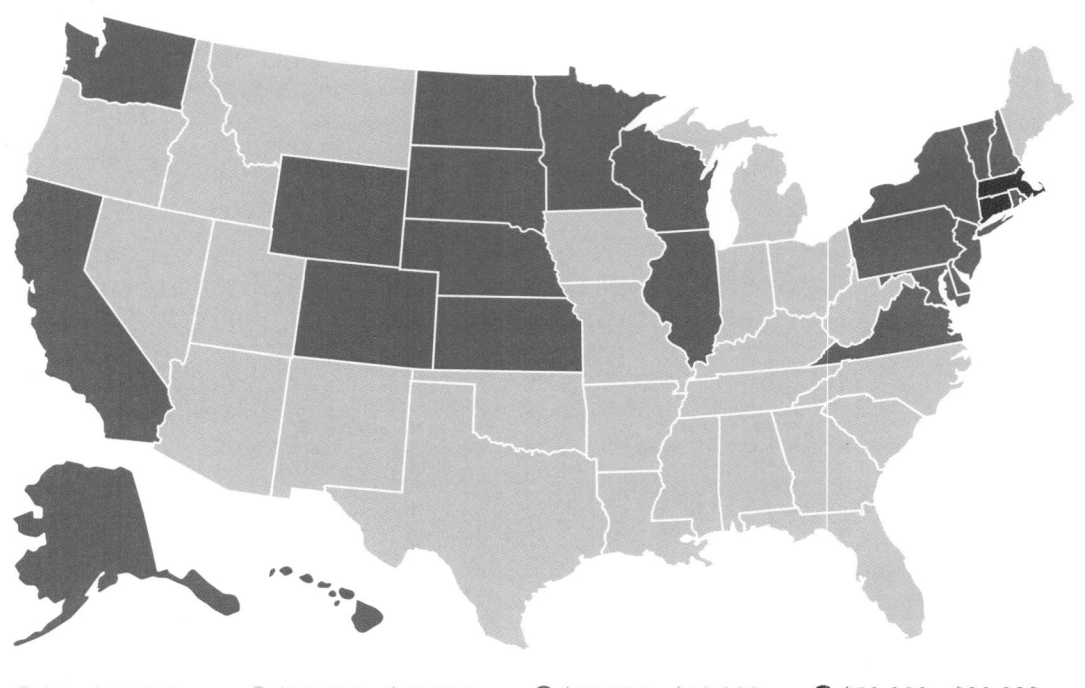

● $0 – $29,999 ● $30,000 – $49,999 ● $50,000 – $69,999 ● $70,000 – $90,000

Rank of Percent Change

1. WASHINGTON	18. WYOMING	35. PENNSYLVANIA
2. UTAH	19. TENNESSEE	36. NEW MEXICO
3. NEVADA	20. MINNESOTA	37. MISSISSIPPI
4. COLORADO	21. OKLAHOMA	38. LOUISIANA
5. ARIZONA	22. MASSACHUSETTS	39. INDIANA
6. IDAHO	23. SOUTH DAKOTA	40. NEW JERSEY
7. TEXAS	24. DELAWARE	41. OHIO
8. FLORIDA	25. IOWA	42. CONNECTICUT
9. MONTANA	26. ALASKA	43. MICHIGAN
10. OREGON	27. MAINE	44. KENTUCKY
11. WEST VIRGINIA	28. ARKANSAS	45. MARYLAND
12. NORTH CAROLINA	29. WISCONSIN	46. KANSAS
13. NEW YORK	30. ALABAMA	47. VERMONT
14. CALIFORNIA	31. NEW HAMPSHIRE	48. RHODE ISLAND
15. NORTH DAKOTA	32. VIRGINA	49. NEBRASKA
16. ILLINOIS	33. MISSOURI	50. HAWAII
17. GEORGIA	34. SOUTH CAROLINA	

Percentage Change

HIGHEST

#1 Washington
#2 Utah
#3 Colorado
#4 Nevada
#5 Arizona

LOWEST

#1 Hawaii
#2 Nebraska
#3 Rhode Island
#4 Vermont
#5 Kansas

TABLE 10.5

Earnings Growth by Industry, State and Region, 2017-2018 (In millions of dollars)

State or other jurisdiction	Total earnings	Farm	Earnings by industry				Manufacturing	
			Forestry, fishing, and related activities	Mining, quarrying, and oil and gas extraction	Utilities	Construction	Durable goods	Nondurable goods
United States	$529,817	$2,419	$1,310	$15,110	$3,530	$51,924	$33,166	$10,858
Alabama	5,403	549	22	102	91	549	545	219
Alaska	910	(3)	4	96	23	172	1	0
Arizona	12,034	(130)	39	323	52	1,742	860	231
Arkansas	3,082	911	16	60	35	8	169	250
California	80,984	(2,154)	500	204	129	8,511	4,807	40
Colorado	12,308	(51)	(1)	1,442	77	1,718	184	227
Connecticut	3,881	(16)	1	19	26	260	474	222
Delaware	1,176	80	(D)	(D)	(7)	86	32	117
Florida	31,977	(106)	(20)	46	128	4,717	1,278	328
Georgia	14,860	703	27	79	77	2,326	1,084	299
Hawaii	1,317	5	(2)	2	29	83	1	17
Idaho	2,550	(192)	12	3	22	427	121	136
Illinois	19,888	(47)	1	37	94	863	1,645	506
Indiana	7,194	174	14	30	106	493	1,357	85
Iowa	4,048	502	18	15	14	433	650	403
Kansas	3,159	(659)	21	195	21	244	412	167
Kentucky	3,254	(7)	17	93	42	142	66	296
Louisiana	5,298	65	19	485	69	899	202	384
Maine	1,521	(25)	23	1	(5)	198	59	38
Maryland	7,234	23	(3)	5	67	253	217	107
Massachusetts	15,244	(17)	(14)	34	33	1,647	(125)	326
Michigan	10,549	(52)	0	51	107	985	1,644	379
Minnesota	8,956	661	7	41	94	581	618	161
Mississippi	2,859	917	43	33	19	116	76	161
Missouri	7,592	296	13	32	28	334	737	329
Montana	1,321	265	5	119	(3)	161	21	47
Nebraska	1,823	(430)	(1)	15	157	215	133	251
Nevada	5,429	(22)	1	72	19	846	598	83
New Hampshire	1,962	(13)	2	2	9	159	303	19
New Jersey	12,627	(70)	11	210	315	667	955	259
New Mexico	2,217	(106)	12	543	15	315	8	10
New York	44,229	(338)	12	642	200	2,699	552	152
North Carolina	14,796	331	10	19	209	1,810	947	402
North Dakota	1,408	193	(1)	496	23	(19)	101	15
Ohio	13,442	130	19	275	104	393	1,660	630
Oklahoma	6,035	(161)	15	1,680	(23)	494	1,127	143
Oregon	7,013	12	131	11	59	1,108	990	100
Pennsylvania	18,677	(205)	37	188	190	1,535	1,310	582
Rhode Island	704	(3)	(D)	(D)	14	(D)	94	(49)
South Carolina	4,405	145	11	9	(103)	49	433	251
South Dakota	1,176	148	6	8	11	116	123	81
Tennessee	10,619	267	19	46	16	845	572	(216)
Texas	56,220	923	66	6,621	442	5,961	3,322	1,194
Utah	6,798	30	10	136	44	858	348	173
Vermont	598	(62)	2	2	7	49	65	8
Virginia	12,482	25	17	51	216	866	592	452
Washington	23,417	(138)	140	46	101	2,245	815	271
West Virginia	3,075	27	1	198	22	1,582	108	9
Wisconsin	7,594	5	18	54	18	831	817	567
Wyoming	894	38	(D)	225	23	105	(D)	(D)
Dist. of Columbia	3,583	0	0	1	75	(D)	(D)	(D)

See footnotes at end of table

TABLE 10.5

Earnings Growth by Industry, State and Region, 2017-2018 (In millions of dollars) (continued)

State or other jurisdiction	Earnings by industry								
	Wholesale trade	Retail trade	Transportation and warehousing	Information	Finance and insurance	Real estate and rental and leasing	Professional, scientific, and technical services	Management of companies and enterprises	Administrative and waste management services
United States	$9,796	$23,718	$30,461	$27,182	$30,052	$10,105	$84,513	$19,385	$27,990
Alabama	207	233	283	33	302	34	801	(72)	259
Alaska	21	22	111	(24)	9	10	22	(1)	5
Arizona	469	530	897	437	1,198	325	1,097	(342)	966
Arkansas	75	71	243	(190)	230	38	257	(40)	209
California	(2,485)	3,119	5,108	11,487	2,303	1,438	18,618	5,736	3,158
Colorado	429	441	584	428	571	284	2,245	(158)	573
Connecticut	(9)	217	293	220	(153)	149	591	128	311
Delaware	23	36	38	(41)	174	14	158	(46)	151
Florida	1,437	2,094	1,694	335	2,435	639	4,728	561	2,414
Georgia	(540)	641	967	21	870	431	1,713	1,340	873
Hawaii	(22)	124	44	66	24	30	120	39	105
Idaho	133	109	137	(1)	156	38	288	149	195
Illinois	312	347	1,758	402	2,761	511	3,960	(45)	1,297
Indiana	532	120	695	(168)	510	188	744	184	407
Iowa	160	80	274	41	328	29	243	100	178
Kansas	180	82	333	32	93	69	307	173	309
Kentucky	134	140	348	(63)	91	38	408	178	234
Louisiana	168	69	286	31	194	115	610	(131)	380
Maine	48	99	0	16	100	23	269	107	62
Maryland	145	276	417	141	542	77	1,816	348	307
Massachusetts	132	645	456	550	1,617	235	5,058	1,420	666
Michigan	463	513	692	86	505	258	1,208	74	694
Minnesota	(29)	417	386	14	1,180	84	1,048	567	6
Mississippi	43	87	218	(28)	82	15	152	87	75
Missouri	557	195	271	412	649	97	921	623	326
Montana	33	69	56	13	67	26	96	1	58
Nebraska	50	52	333	11	246	33	196	(220)	134
Nevada	98	269	341	147	246	101	444	483	405
New Hampshire	108	144	66	79	15	39	274	(53)	131
New Jersey	287	462	852	345	1,087	317	1,824	369	857
New Mexico	30	89	180	(18)	91	29	299	23	98
New York	446	1,588	1,095	3,999	(761)	852	5,568	679	3,452
North Carolina	156	598	719	434	1,624	279	2,668	274	515
North Dakota	84	4	115	9	72	24	83	22	31
Ohio	631	229	1,336	56	1,259	146	1,481	458	756
Oklahoma	131	199	145	(8)	183	73	445	31	321
Oregon	85	332	310	235	195	159	522	246	304
Pennsylvania	(59)	642	1,330	1,349	1,497	385	2,177	939	781
Rhode Island	19	107	55	0	(241)	18	145	(154)	112
South Carolina	43	325	288	54	295	121	713	187	237
South Dakota	60	38	42	5	65	11	94	37	23
Tennessee	229	677	720	226	942	190	1,491	954	383
Texas	3,070	2,598	3,638	552	3,248	1,252	8,326	2,399	2,719
Utah	208	502	337	294	605	110	1,155	94	169
Vermont	30	40	21	(10)	4	13	97	(1)	44
Virginia	165	382	425	80	1,109	158	2,997	575	1,061
Washington	731	3,222	967	4,799	682	392	3,329	238	609
West Virginia	13	37	45	(7)	74	37	276	85	140
Wisconsin	536	356	366	88	462	101	769	630	387
Wyoming	29	17	115	(5)	31	25	84	0	37
Dist. of Columbia	(2)	40	30	216	185	42	1,578	110	64

See footnotes at end of table

TABLE 10.5
Earnings Growth by Industry, State and Region, 2017-2018 (In millions of dollars) (continued)

State or other jurisdiction	Educational services	Health care and social assistance	Arts, entertainment, and recreation	Accommodation and food services	Other services (except public administration)	Federal, civilian	Military	State and local
							Government	
United States	$6,070	$56,039	$7,202	$18,802	$17,234	$5,559	$3,149	$34,245
Alabama	(3)	504	49	150	231	86	64	166
Alaska	3	214	10	43	16	37	78	41
Arizona	153	1,499	255	511	409	93	53	368
Arkansas	55	355	16	73	143	20	1	75
California	1,047	9,443	1,324	3,410	1,147	323	(107)	3,876
Colorado	137	862	271	542	436	(7)	168	907
Connecticut	87	463	38	127	227	48	21	136
Delaware	5	170	(41)	97	33	13	13	53
Florida	216	3,548	620	1,752	1,274	495	268	1,099
Georgia	242	1,711	45	473	486	130	259	605
Hawaii	8	253	5	166	92	76	104	(52)
Idaho	20	325	34	109	89	52	14	175
Illinois	190	1,951	299	684	647	142	202	1,370
Indiana	10	811	81	233	308	70	11	200
Iowa	(4)	264	29	70	134	13	10	62
Kansas	23	446	37	74	147	65	48	339
Kentucky	46	494	53	138	182	16	151	14
Louisiana	46	490	73	179	242	74	57	292
Maine	3	213	21	87	63	66	8	46
Maryland	317	919	10	244	335	189	146	333
Massachusetts	781	(94)	272	370	529	53	33	638
Michigan	14	1,307	(43)	407	562	101	17	579
Minnesota	114	1,363	207	187	208	40	16	985
Mississippi	16	315	14	62	71	59	46	181
Missouri	19	857	76	254	262	155	47	101
Montana	4	131	27	53	55	44	14	(42)
Nebraska	(4)	450	6	56	84	42	27	(12)
Nevada	59	565	166	159	176	56	57	61
New Hampshire	48	278	40	92	102	40	(4)	81
New Jersey	91	1,912	352	713	407	18	29	358
New Mexico	3	190	25	96	100	35	53	92
New York	489	6,591	896	1,275	1,164	111	128	12,738
North Carolina	443	1,367	161	442	556	145	(314)	1,003
North Dakota	17	69	27	19	13	10	28	(26)
Ohio	67	1,703	255	396	481	208	53	714
Oklahoma	23	386	62	163	173	118	106	207
Oregon	17	688	90	406	317	92	9	594
Pennsylvania	347	3,314	214	419	787	194	25	699
Rhode Island	37	103	(6)	63	32	37	10	115
South Carolina	40	461	41	198	218	88	79	223
South Dakota	(4)	141	8	32	51	23	16	41
Tennessee	32	1,198	224	564	465	114	28	635
Texas	328	3,225	291	1,746	1,784	630	467	1,418
Utah	107	389	47	193	264	185	30	512
Vermont	(4)	123	8	19	40	27	5	71
Virginia	85	977	51	341	421	507	335	596
Washington	85	1,660	135	477	485	263	173	1,691
West Virginia	0	275	13	34	62	16	(10)	38
Wisconsin	113	931	246	170	288	69	16	(241)
Wyoming	0	63	7	63	29	19	15	(61)
Dist. of Columbia	104	165	60	171	412	57	47	150

Source: U.S. Bureau of Economic Analysis.
Key:
N.A.–Not applicable.
(D) Data are suppressed to avoid disclosure of confidential information.

INDEX

–A–

–B–

–C–

—G—

–J–

judges
 appellate courts, 199–201
 chief justices, 189–190, 191
 compensation, 196
 conduct, 207–209
 general trial courts, 192–193
  judges, number of, 192–193, 202–206
  judges, qualifications, 194–195
  retention, 199–201
  selection, 199–201
   geographical basis, 199–201
  terms, 192–193, 202–206
 judges, number of, 192–193
 judicial compensation, 189–190, 196
 judicial discipline, 207–209
 last resort, 189–190, 191
 qualifications, 194–195
 retention, 199–201
 selection, 189–190, 191, 199–201
 terms, 192–193, 199–201
judicial administration offices, 197–198
judicial discipline, 207–209
justices on courts of last resort,
 chief justices, 189–190, 191

–K–

–L–

last resort (courts), 189–190, 191
leaders
 house/assembly
  compensation, 55–56
  methods of selecting, 43–46
 senate
  compensation, 53–54
  methods of selecting, 39–42
legal provisions (legislative sessions), 28–31
legislative bodies, 27
legislative duties (secretaries of state), 150–151, 152–153
legislative sessions, 28–31

legislators
 compensation, 48–49
  method of setting, 47
 election of, 215–216
 number of, 32–33
 parties, 32–33
 qualifications, 36–38
 retirement, 57–61
 staff, 80–82
 terms, 32–33
 term limits, 32–33
 turnover, 35
 women, 381–382
legislatures
 administrative regulations,
  powers, 94–97
  procedures, 91–93
  review of, 94–97
  rules reviewed, 91–93
  structure, 91–93
  time limits, 91–93
 appropriations process
  bills, 72–73
  budgets, 72–73
  budget documents, 72–73
 bills
  carryover, 62–64, 91–93
  enactments, 76–77
  introductions, 76–77
  limits on introducing, 65–67
  pre-filing, 62–64
  reference, 62–64
  time limits, 65–67
  veto, 68–71
 chamber control, 35
 changes in, 35
 elections, 215–216
 enacting legislation
  effective date, 68–71
  veto, 68–71
  veto override, 68–71
 fiscal notes
  content, 74–75
  distribution, 74–75
 legislation, sunset, 98–101
 legislative bodies, 27
 legislative powers, 94–97
 legislative review, 94–97
 legislative seats, 32–35, 215–216
 legislative staff, 80–82

–Q–

–R–

–S–

—T—

–U–

–V–

–W–

–X-Y-Z–